Ph
04.02.08

FOURTH EDITION

INTRODUCTION TO COMMUNICATION RESEARCH

JOHN C. REINARD

California State University, Fullerton

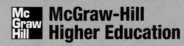 **McGraw-Hill**
Higher Education

Boston   Burr Ridge, IL   Dubuque, IA   New York   San Francisco   St. Louis
Bangkok   Bogotá   Caracas   Kuala Lumpur   Lisbon   London   Madrid   Mexico City
Milan   Montreal   New Delhi   Santiago   Seoul   Singapore   Sydney   Taipei   Toronto

Mc Graw Hill McGraw-Hill Higher Education

Published by McGraw-Hill, an imprint of The McGraw-Hill Companies, Inc., 1221 Avenue of the Americas, New York, NY 10020. Copyright © 2008. All rights reserved. No part of this publication may be reproduced or distributed in any form or by any means, or stored in a database or retrieval system, without the prior written consent of The McGraw-Hill Companies, Inc., including, but not limited to, in any network or other electronic storage or transmission, or broadcast for distance learning.

This book is printed on acid-free paper.

1 2 3 4 5 6 7 8 9 0 DOC/DOC 0 9 8 7

ISBN: 978-0-07-286295-9
MHID: 0-07-286295-5

Editor in Chief: *Emily Barrosse*
Publisher: *Frank Mortimer*
Sponsoring Editor: *Suzanne S. Earth*
Marketing Manager: *Leslie Oberhuber*
Developmental Editor: *Craig Leonard*
Editorial Assistant: *Erika Lake*
Project Manager: *Carey Eisner*
Manuscript Editor: *Jan McDearmon*
Design Manager: *Andrei Pasternak*
Cover Designer: *Andrei Pasternak*
Art Editor: *Ayelet Arbel*
Photo Research: *Natalia Peschiera*
Production Supervisor: *Tandra Jorgensen*
Composition: *10/12 Bembo by Laserwords Private Limited*
Printing: *45# New Era Matte Plus, R. R. Donnelley & Sons, Inc.*

Cover: *Wetzel and Company*

Library of Congress Cataloging-in-Publication Data

Reinard, John C.
    Introduction to communication research / John Reinard. — 4th ed.
        p. cm.
    ISBN-13: 978-0-07-286295-9
    ISBN-10: 0-07-286295-5
    1. Communication—Research—Methodology. I. Title.
P91.3.R38 2007
302.207'2—dc22

                                                              2007009628

The Internet addresses listed in the text were accurate at the time of publication. The inclusion of a Web site does not indicate an endorsement by the authors or McGraw-Hill, and McGraw-Hill does not guarantee the accuracy of the information presented at these sites.

www.mhhe.com

CONTENTS

PART 2
Understanding Rudiments of Research Reasoning   71

CHAPTER 3
Conceptualizations in Communication Research   72

CHAPTER 4
Measurement in Communication Research   113

CHAPTER 5
Composing the Communication Argument: The Reasoning and the Evidence   149

PART 3
Design of Research   201

CHAPTER 6
Conducting Textual Analyses   202

CHAPTER 7
Qualitative Methods: Ethnography, Participant Observation, and Fieldwork   242

CHAPTER 8
Content Analysis of Communication   301

CHAPTER 11
Sampling   427

PART 4
Statistical Analysis of Data   455

CHAPTER 12
Descriptive Statistics   456

CHAPTER 15
Meta–Analysis 548

PREFACE

In the preface to the first edition of this book, I wrote:

> Research is not library work.
> Nor is it statistics.
> Nor is it field observation.
> Research is an argument. In particular, communication research is a process by which we answer questions and try to draw conclusions from information gathered about message-related behavior.

Somewhat surprisingly to me, these words have been repeated on panels of scholarly conventions, reprinted in newsletters of professional organizations, and (judging by the e-mail I have received) drilled into the consciousness of thousands of otherwise unsuspecting students. This fourth edition of *Introduction to Communication Research* is premised on the view that *sound research is sound argument* that appeals to high-quality research evidence. The major task in learning research methods involves developing skills that help us sift through the "information" that is available so that we can make reasoned claims based on data.

In the years since the first edition of this work was published, a curious division in "research" has emerged. On one hand, there are large and growing bodies of sound research evidence relevant to important claims that researchers and world citizens make. On the other hand, there are large bodies of pseudo-information that distract from drawing conclusions based on solid information and reasoning. Communication research has not avoided this rift in information. Hence, a major challenge for modern students is to acquire ways to distinguish between credible research information and pseudo-research claims. By viewing research as a form of argument, students can learn how to separate valuable information from widely available imposters. The craft of research is merciless on shoddy thinking and readily exposes invalid reasoning and insufficient examination of evidence for conclusions. Indeed, with the growth in the availability of resources on the Internet (containing information, mostly, rather than wisdom), this concern for sound reasoning in research has become more important than ever. The major task in learning research methods involves developing skills to help us sift through the available "information morass" so that we can make reasoned claims based on data. Solid research has *topoi* or lines of argument for different sorts of claims to be made legitimately. Students need to know how to evaluate these *topoi* and how to construct them. Naturally, this approach develops skills that are helpful in life generally. Thus, studying research methods according to the approach of this book provides a way to improve critical thinking skills. This concern is shared by many fields in modern colleges and universities, and it is central in the study of communication research methods.

The purpose of this introductory book is to provide information on the tools of scholarship (such as literature review writing, statistical analysis of data, and completing fieldwork) to help students learn ways to find and assess high-quality evidence. This book attempts to train students to gather research evidence, to develop research arguments, and to think critically about them. In short, this book is designed to teach students how to "do scholarship," make reasoned cases, and offer research conclusions.

This edition benefits from the feedback received from teachers and students along with much experimentation with these instructional materials over the years. This book has been praised for its student-friendly approach, and both teachers and students have paid the author the compliment of recommending ways to refine the work's structure and coverage of concepts. The extensive materials available on the book's Web site (www.mhhe.com/reinard4) have made it possible to learn and study key concepts at the student's own pace. Furthermore, moving guides to writing and citation style to the Web site has provided students the freedom to learn these rudimentary matters according to their individual needs.

Those familiar with the third edition will note that this edition is a major revision that involves a great deal more than updating examples, though such updating also has taken place.

- ♦ A new chapter on meta-analysis appears. This method of conducting quantitative assessment of literature is in widespread use in communication and the social sciences. Modern students cannot ignore meta-analyses. Yet, surprisingly, this book currently is the only volume on communication research methods to include a full presentation of this important tool.

- ♦ Material on qualitative methods has been expanded. Separate chapters appear on "Conducting Textual Analyses," and "Qualitative Methods: Ethnography, Participant Observation, and Fieldwork."

- ♦ A separate chapter is presented for textual analysis in the form of "Content Analysis of Communication." New materials on the steps in interaction and relational analyses now are featured. The discussion of content analysis has been enhanced to describe different approaches to developing category systems and applications to vital communication questions.

- ♦ The chapter on "Using Communication Research Sources" has been moved to a detailed Appendix G. Thus, instructors who wish students to study such materials directly still have the choice, but those who prefer to emphasize their own approaches may act in an unimpeded way.

- ♦ The chapter on "Measurement in Communication Research" now appears at an early location in the book. With this treatment, students can study the conceptual foundations of communication research and see links to measurement of variables before immersing themselves in the specific methods of different research approaches. Though the approach of this chapter is quantitative, the emphasis on sound measurement of variables is an appropriate extension of the materials on operational definitions of concepts found in the preceding chapter.

- ♦ The Appendixes on using SPSS and Excel XP have been updated to reflect the most recent versions of these tools at the time of the writing of this edition.

- ♦ The treatment of ethics has been enhanced. Along with consideration of the National Communication Association Credo and the analysis of major codes of ethics, extended treatments with examples are provided for informed consent forms and procedures for the ethical conduct of quantitative and qualitative research. In addition, each chapter includes a discussion under the title "A Question of Ethics. . . . " These discussions consider issues ranging from the respect of human participants in research, use of deception, and maintaining confidentiality, to the problems of conducting ethical research in cyberspace.

- Profiles of communication researchers and professionals using communication research are included. Not only do these profiles put a personal face on communication research, but they can inspire students to think about engaging in the exciting world of communication scholarship for themselves.

- Definitions of key terms are boxed in the margin of the page on which the term first appears.

- A timeline on the inside front cover shows the process of communication research is included for qualitative and quantitative research. Rather than attempt to provide all the details involved in the process, this material permits students to see the "big picture" of how the materials in the book are linked to their level of needs.

- Materials on qualitative research are enhanced. Expanded material appears on the practical applications of such approaches as grounded theory, qualitative interview studies, and triangulation strategies. Since there has been a dramatic growth in work on these methods, the forms of such tools identified also have reflected this diversity.

- Though at one time the Internet was a new information medium for which students needed special instruction, modern students enter colleges and universities with an understanding of how to use browsers and access the Internet. Hence, this basic material has been removed. Yet, guides to valuable electronic resources available through the Internet remain in Appendix G and on the book's Web site. A frequently updated list of links to valuable communication research sources is provided on the *COMFILE* hyperlink on this book's Web site. This resource permits students to use the Internet efficiently to find sources of communication-related resources that they can access at the click of a mouse button.

The fourth edition of *Introduction to Communication Research* is not just a book, but a *package* that includes other resources and modules. For instructors, an extensive *Instructor's Manual* is available including exercises, visual aids, lecture supplements, and full sets of discussion questions that may animate classroom exchanges. For students, a *Web site* contains extensive materials to help students succeed in their research classes. The Web site includes the following resources:

- A handbook on writing and usage, including samples of papers for key assignments (especially for students exposed to writing scholarly work, this guide is remarkably helpful in providing details on grammar and usage that seem to be covered incompletely in typical high school instruction)

- A guide to APA style

- A guide to writing and usage

- Data files in both SPSS and Excel XP formats to permit students to complete applied assignments and projects

- Interactive study guide quizzes for each chapter that provide immediate feedback to the students

- Detailed outlines of the chapters

- Links to other electronic sites relevant to the chapter content
- Applied assignment study sheets to provide students with opportunities to develop skills in analyzing and composing research

Many things that teachers and students have found praiseworthy about this book remain. Most fundamentally, this book is designed to meet student needs, not to impress professors. This book is written for—and to—students who are taking their first course in research methods, typically on the sophomore or junior levels. To help students efficiently study and review content from this book, each chapter

- starts with an outline of all major topics;
- begins with an orienting paragraph to describe the thrust of the chapter;
- ends with a list of *Terms for Review* when studying the chapter;
- includes margin notes to point out important concepts covered in the text;
- highlights key terms in boldface the first time they appear;
- relies on tables when they may reduce otherwise extended text discussions;
- features a concluding summary that is an actual and detailed chapter synopsis (which students will find very helpful when reviewing for examinations);
- contains provocative *Just for the Sake of Argument* review questions designed to stimulate thought and concern over issues raised in the chapter;
- includes a set of *Activities to Probe Further,* which consists of hands-on projects and instructor-tested exercises;
- features a "Checklist to Evaluate . . . " at the ends of chapters that introduce different methods of communication research. Such questions help students to assess the merits of different sorts of research approaches.

In addition, a glossary is included to help students define critical terms swiftly.

By the end of the academic term, students should know how to do a few things.

- Students should know how to present and evaluate a research argument. Since most classes that follow the research methods course require research-based writing by students, they need to know how to complete the process of drawing conclusions and making arguments from credible research literature.
- Students should know how to deal with the brass tacks of research: how to isolate a problem statement; how to distinguish independent and dependent variables; how to identify the suitability of qualitative and quantitative research methods to answer specific research questions; how to criticize and evaluate definitions; what theories are and why they are important; how to use the library and documentary resources available in both hard copy and electronic form; how to apply methods of sound research and standards to evaluate and propose worthwhile studies; how to compose scholarly arguments; how to collect data and execute rudimentary but logical quantitative and qualitative designs; and how to analyze simple data.

To avoid overwhelming students with detailed elements of each methodological twist in communication research, this textbook spends time teaching the "survival skills" that students need to know, supplemented with clearly identified enrichment information labeled as "Special Discussions." These discussions range from such things as ways of knowing to the confidence interval/statistical significance debate.

This book deliberately uses research examples from the broad range of communication studies. Since communication research courses serve students from several communication areas—including speech communication, journalism, telecommunications, public relations, and speech and hearing science—examples from all these areas are chosen in discussions of content.

This textbook is divided into four parts that correspond to the major units successfully taught in introductory communication research methods courses. The first part introduces the field of communication as a research area. Students are guided through Chapters 1 and 2, which introduce communication research as a distinct form and then review the issues involved in composing communication research problems, using hypotheses, and isolating types of variables.

The second part of the textbook deals with "Understanding Rudiments of Research Reasoning." This section begins with Chapter 3, concerning conceptualizations in communication research including use of theory and definitions. Chapter 4 describes measurement in communication so that students understand the transition from conceptualization to operationalization in research. Chapter 5 emphasizes a point of view for this book by addressing methods to compose communication research arguments, including understanding the anatomy of a research article, mechanics of writing different forms of scholarly and classroom reports, evaluating the logic of the research argument, and ways to evaluate research and evidence.

The third section of the book emphasizes the "Design of Research" for both qualitative and quantitative studies. The primary task in this section lies in presenting essential materials that students need to know most, without ignoring other unique applications that have invigorated the field. Chapters 6 and 7 are dedicated to conducting textual analyses of messages and undertaking qualitative studies using participant observation, ethnographic, grounded theory, and historical methods. Chapter 8 is an expanded treatment of content analysis featuring new examples and extended applications. Chapters 9 and 10 concern designing descriptive empirical research (including questionnaire and interview studies) and conducting experimental studies. Chapter 11 involves sampling in communication research. In each case, examples across the broad realm of communication studies are covered.

The fourth part of the book concerns the statistical analysis of data. The individual chapters involve traditional topics of such an introductory treatment. Chapter 12 addresses beginning descriptive and correlational statistics. Chapter 13 introduces the logic of statistical hypothesis testing and applies it to the case of comparisons between two means.

Chapter 14 extends significance testing to cases that go beyond two means, including analysis of variance and chi-square tests. Chapter 15 presents meta-analysis with an emphasis on comparisons of effect sizes that are so common in modern communication studies. Both the method and the ways to deal with its unique challenges are presented on an introductory level. In fact, the entire final section of *Introduction to Communication Research* presents "survival guide" information in plain language. Though some "Special Discussions" introduce some advanced statistics that students may read, there is no effort to provide introductory students with detailed training in them.

Many people helped me develop this work. My sincere thanks must go to my own teachers of research methods. These teachers included not only those who provided instruction in empirical methods, but those who directed my studies in rhetorical theory, argumentation, and qualitative methods. My students of introductory research methods courses for more than a score of years deserve thanks since this book and Web site reflect the product of experimenting with them to find ways to teach this course most effectively. I am very grateful to the scholars and teachers who reviewed drafts of this work and provided invaluable advice and support for the direction of this project. These individuals offered invaluable insights in preparing this fourth edition, in addition to those who have provided expert criticism and advice on previous versions—Ron Warren of the University of Alaska, Richard Olsen of the University of North Carolina, James Katz of Rutgers, Mary Lee Hummert of the University of Kansas, Robert Brown of Salem State College, James A. Danowski of the University of Illinois at Chicago, Diane Furno-Lamude of the University of New Mexico, Len Shyles of Villanova University, B. Scott Titsworth of Ohio University, Samuel P. Wallace of the University of Dayton, Sharmila Pixy Ferris of William Patterson College, Susan Holton of Bridgewater State College, Rebecca Lind of the University of Illinois at Chicago, John D. Bee of Ashland University, Judith Dallinger of Western Illinois University, Lyle Flint of Ball State University, William J. Schenck-Hamlin of Kansas State University, and Judy R. Sims of Georgia Highlands College. I wish to thank the staff at McGraw-Hill. In particular, I must offer special appreciation to Sponsoring Editor Suzanne Earth for her vision for a comprehensive book to meet the needs of all beginning students. In addition, I wish to thank Developmental Editor Craig Leonard and Production Editor Carey Eisner for their extraordinary patience and help in shepherding this project to completion and offering their wise counsel to create this fourth edition. Copyeditor Jan McDearmon did a masterful job of fine-tuning the presentation of topics and removing prolix and turgid writing. In the early stages of this project, Developmental Editor Jennie Katsaros provided both her support and great suggestions for items to add in this edition. Finally, I wish to thank my family. Without their willingness to permit my dedication of many hours, it would not have been possible to complete this volume.

PART 1

Introduction to the Field

The Role of Research in Communication

If politics is the art of the possible, research is surely the art of the soluble.

—SIR PETER MEDAWAR

CHAPTER OUTLINE

What Is Research in Communication?

Research

Communication Research

The Challenges of Communication Research

The Challenge of Breadth and Focus

The Multiple Methods Challenge

The Scholarly Rigor Challenge

The Personal Challenge, or What Do I Need to Do to Study Communication Research Methods Successfully?

The Ethical Challenge

The Structure of the Field Challenge

BEFORE WE GET STARTED . . .

Welcome to communication research! Though you may be skeptical, "doing" communication scholarship is an exciting and very enjoyable personal experience. Rather than just accepting what others tell you, you will learn how scholars (a term that includes you now) draw conclusions in our field. You will see how research should look so that you can evaluate the stuff that often gets passed off to us. Along the way, you will learn how to improve your thinking, your scholarly writing, and your ability to evaluate research arguments. Getting there can be challenging, but it is well worth the trip. This book does not assume that you have any background in research methods—just an interest. To get started, you need to know why you are here and what communication research is. This chapter is designed to get you moving in the right direction.

WHAT IS RESEARCH IN COMMUNICATION?

A field defines itself by its **research.** Research determines what content is taught in courses, the social contribution the field makes, and the sort of publicity an area gets.

Research "a process of asking a question (or related series of questions) and then initiating a systematic process to obtain valid answers to that question" (Meltzoff, 1998, p. 13).

Research

Research questions are not ordinary ones, such as Have you seen my keys? or Want to see a movie? Instead, research questions deal with issues requiring reference to data[1] and information, such as Did Patrick Henry deliver the "Give Me Liberty or Give Me Death!" speech that is reprinted in all those anthologies?[2] Do women self-disclose private information more often than men do?[3] and Do people who arrive "fashionably late" to parties receive higher credibility ratings than people who arrive on time?[4] Research is not an "ivory tower" activity by a few elect scholars. It is a very practical effort to get answers for questions. Research usually requires examining past inquiry into the issue. We often rely on reports found in libraries to learn about related work and to avoid repeating past mistakes. Regardless of sources of information, all research involves gathering information that goes beyond personal feelings or hunches alone. We search for some light on the facts of matters when we do research.

Sometimes people distinguish between two types of research. In **basic research,** researchers hope to make useful contributions though no immediate economic payoff

basic research distinguished from applied research

Basic research research completed to learn about relationships among variables, regardless of any immediate commercial product or service.

---

[1]Let's get something straight right now. The word "data" is plural. Thus, we have to say "data *are*" and "data *were,*" not "data *is*" and "data *was.*" A single piece of data is called a datum, but people do not use that word very often. Instead, they refer to a datum as "a piece of data," a usage that sounds natural to most people.

[2]He didn't. Though Henry said "Give me liberty or give me death," the text of the often reprinted "speech" was written by his biographer, William Wirt.

[3]They do.

[4]We don't know.

is imminent. Most things we call "pure" scientific research fall into this category. In fact, controversial rocket scientist Wernher von Braun explained the role of this sort of inquiry with the expression, "Basic research is when I'm doing what I don't know I'm doing." On the other hand, when communication researchers survey employee attitudes as part of a consulting contract, the work is considered **applied research.** Even so, trying to separate basic and applied research causes problems. Regardless of whether pure or applied research is involved, the methods of inquiry *are identical.* Furthermore, last year's basic research may be today's source of new products. Work that started to find out how to store information in digital form now is the basis for patents on satellite transmission of television signals. Though the terms have their place, for our purposes, it is enough to know that good research can be basic or applied.

> **Applied research** study completed to develop a product or solve an immediate practical problem.

Communication Research

Sometimes students have difficulty separating communication research from work in psychology, sociology, or literature. They figure that since "meanings are in people" (Berlo, 1960, p. 175), any study of people is communication research. Straightening out this exaggerated view has taken a little work. In 1995, a group of over 100 scholars met at the Summer Conference on Defining the Field of Communication sponsored by the Association for Communication Administration. The result of that conference was the unanimous adoption of the definition of **communication** that appears at the left. This definition not only has been promoted by the National Communication Association but also has been adopted by the U.S. Department of Education and the National Center for Education Statistics. Communication research focuses on message-related behavior as a specialty. The scope of our research area is now clear. Other fields may study personality traits, trends in society, medicine, or the beauty of poetry. Yet, communication research is a specialty that studies message-related behavior.

> **Communication** "The field of communication focuses on how people use messages to generate meanings within and across various contexts, cultures, channels and media. The field promotes the effective and ethical practice of human communication" (Daley et al., 1995).

> *messages are composed of*

> **Verbal cues** words people use in communication.

> **Nonverbal cues** communication elements beyond the words themselves.

> **Message** the set of verbal and nonverbal cues communicators exchange.

You may have been asked by relatives or acquaintances what your major is. When you have told them "communication," you might have received puzzled expressions in response. Unless you explained things, they may have thought you were learning to install telephones. Next time you might tell them that you are training to be a "message specialist" or "message scientist." You may also explain that your concentration in communication prepares you in a specific area of communication. To be clear, you need to explain that communication is composed of **messages,** which, in turn, are composed of **verbal** and **nonverbal cues.** When doing so, it is helpful not to confuse "verbal" cues with "spoken" cues (as in the phrase "verbal agreement"). Yet, spoken cues are called "oral cues" (from the orifice or mouth). Though verbal cues deal with the words we exchange, nonverbal cues involve such diverse elements as variations in voice, facial expressions, gestures, movement, touch, timing, physical closeness, and even media treatments. Taken together, these verbal and nonverbal cues provide plenty for us to study.

SPECIAL DISCUSSION 1-1

NORMS IN THE "CULTURE" OF RESEARCHERS

It is possible to overstate the matter, but there is a set of norms—almost a culture—that distinguishes most people who do research. In his book *Foundations of Behavioral Research,* Fred Kerlinger describes four characteristics. Two of them are shared by nearly all researchers:

> Organized skepticism: Researchers are responsible for verifying the results on which they base their work. [Researchers do not accept claims blindly. They question research claims and offer criticism for each other.]
> Communality: Researchers are willing to share knowledge freely and contribute to public knowledge. (Kerlinger, 1986, p. 9)

In other respects, there are differences in the norms accepted by different groups of researchers. Em Griffin (2000, p. 9) draws a convenient distinction between "scientists" who try to do objective studies and "interpretive" researchers who are concerned with discovering subjective meanings. These researchers differ on many issues.

Behavioral Researchers (Scientists)	Interpretive Researchers in Communication
"*Universalism:* Scientific laws are the same everywhere. A scientific law states a relation between phenomena that is invariable under the same conditions" (Kerlinger, 1986, p. 9).	Discovering lawlike behaviors may not always be possible, and searching for the unique is at least as valuable.
"*Disinterestedness:* Researchers must ban ulterior motives and be relatively free from bias. Any known or possible biases must not be admitted" (Kerlinger, 1986, p. 9). It should be noted that the word "disinterested" does not mean "uninterested"—it means that one is impartial because one does not have a financial or personal stake in the outcome. If a researcher receives grants from sponsors who specify the results they wish the researcher to find, the researcher loses the "disinterest" that separates research from ordinary pandering.	Personal biases need not be put aside, but integrated into the project as part of the process of discovery.

(Continued)

SPECIAL DISCUSSION 1-1 (Continued)

Epistemalogy (ways of knowing): Reality is "waiting to be discovered through the five senses" (Griffin, 2000, p. 10).

"Truth is largely subjective; meaning is highly interpretive. . . . We can never entirely separate the knower from the known" (Griffin, 2000, p. 10).

"*Communality:* Individual researchers pool their findings and build a collective body of knowledge about how the world operates" (Griffin, 2000, p. 10).

"A text may have multiple meanings" (Griffin, 2000, p. 10). Success occurs when scholars "convince others to share their interpretation" (Griffin, 2000, p. 10).

THE CHALLENGES OF COMMUNICATION RESEARCH

communication covers a wide scope of topics

Communication covers a broad set of topics, and no single research method is embraced by the field. To study communication—even its specialties of journalism and speech and hearing science—we must have very broad knowledge. This breadth will challenge you and invite you to enter the field to make contributions.

The Challenge of Breadth and Focus

The number of communication applications can seem enormous, but there really is a rational order to it. Over the years, the U.S. Department of Education's National Center for Education Statistics has refined its list of the professional areas in many fields. The most recent effort has identified a core of specialties in communication studies in which people are working and conducting research. The list of communication specialties used by the NCES is shown in Table 1.1. The left column shows the official taxonomy with an emphasis on the career areas of scholars. In the column to the right you will see definitions of the sorts of research issues that are addressed in each of these professional program areas. As you can tell, each area is broad enough to promote many interesting studies.

the NCES taxonomy of communication studies

The Multiple Methods Challenge

communication uses both qualitative and quantitative methods

In studying literature, qualitative methods most often are used. In history, the historical method is employed. In psychology, the experiment holds a prominent position. Yet, communication researchers use all these methods to answer questions. Thus, modern students are exposed to many methods. Though single studies may use multiple

TABLE 1.1   APPLICATIONS IN THE COMMUNICATION PROFESSION

NATIONAL CENTER FOR EDUCATION STATISTICS
CLASSIFICATION OF INSTRUCTIONAL PROGRAMS (CIP 2000)

Classification Category	Definition
09. Communication, Journalism, and Related Programs	"Instructional programs that focus on how messages in various media are produced, used, and interpreted within and across different contexts, channels, and cultures, and that prepare individuals to apply communication knowledge and skills professionally" (2002a, ¶ 1).
01 Communication and Media Studies	
01 Communication Studies/Speech Communication and Rhetoric	"A program that focuses on the scientific, humanistic, and critical study of human communication in a variety of formats, media, and contexts. Includes instruction in the theory and practice of interpersonal, group, organizational, professional, and intercultural communication; speaking and listening; verbal and nonverbal interaction; rhetorical theory and criticism; performance studies; argumentation and persuasion; technologically mediated communication; popular culture; and various contextual applications" (2002a, ¶ 6).
02 Mass Communication/ Media Studies	"A program that focuses on the analysis and criticism of media institutions and media texts, how people experience and understand media content, and the roles of media in producing and transforming culture. Includes instruction in communications regulation, law, and policy; media history; media aesthetics, interpretation, and criticism; the social and cultural effects of mass media; cultural studies; the economics of media industries; visual and media literacy; and the psychology and behavioral aspects of media messages, interpretation, and utilization" (2002a, ¶ 7).
04 Journalism	
01 Journalism	"A program that focuses on the theory and practice of gathering, processing, and delivering news and that prepares individuals to be professional print journalists, news editors, and news managers. Includes instruction in news writing and editing; reporting; photojournalism; layout and graphic design; journalism law and policy; professional standards and ethics; research methods; and journalism history and criticism" (2002a, ¶ 12).
02 Broadcast Journalism	"A program that focuses on the methods and techniques for reporting, producing, and delivering news and news programs via radio, television, and video/film media; and that prepares individuals to be professional broadcast journalists, editors, producers, directors, and managers. Includes instruction in the principles of broadcast technology; broadcast reporting;

(Continued)

TABLE 1.1 (Continued)	
Classification Category	**Definition**
	on- and off-camera and microphone procedures and techniques; program, sound, and video/film editing; program design and production; media law and policy; and professional standards and ethics" (2002a, ¶ 13).
04 Photojournalism	"A program that focuses on the use of still and motion photography in journalism and prepares individuals to function as news photographers and photographic editors. Includes instruction in photography, journalism, studio procedures and techniques, camera and equipment operation and technique, news editing, print and film editing, news scene composition, subject surveillance, media law and policy, news team field operations, and professional standards and ethics" (2002a, ¶ 15).
07 Radio, Television, and Digital Communication	
01 Radio and Television	"A program that focuses on the theories, methods, and techniques used to plan, produce, and distribute audio and video programs and messages, and that prepares individuals to function as staff, producers, directors, and managers of radio and television shows and media organizations. Includes instruction in media aesthetics; planning, scheduling, and production; writing and editing; performing and directing; personnel and facilities management; marketing and distribution; media regulations, law, and policy; and principles of broadcast technology" (2002a, ¶ 23).
02 Digital Communication and Media/ Multimedia	"A program that focuses on the development, use, and regulation of new electronic communication technologies using computer applications and that prepares individuals to function as developers and managers of digital communications media. Includes instruction in the principles of computers and telecommunications technologies and processes; design and development of digital communications; marketing and distribution; digital communications regulation, law, and policy; the study of human interaction with, and use of, digital media; and emerging trends and issues" (2002a, ¶ 29)
09 Public Relations, Advertising, and Applied Communication	
01 Organizational Communication, General	"A program that focuses on general communication processes and dynamics within organizations. Includes instruction in the development and maintenance of interpersonal group relations within organizations;

(Continued)

TABLE 1.1 (Continued)	
Classification Category	**Definition**
	decision-making and conflict management; the use of symbols to create and maintain organizational images, missions, and values; power and politics within organizations; human interaction with computer technology; and how communications socializes and supports employees and team members" (2002a, ¶ 34).
02 Public Relations/ Image Management	"A program that focuses on the theories and methods for managing the media image of a business, organization, or individual and the communication process with stakeholders, constituencies, audiences, and the general public; and that prepares individuals to function as public relations assistants, technicians, and managers. Includes instruction in public relations theory; related principles of advertising, marketing, and journalism; message/image design; image management; special event management; media relations; community relations; public affairs; and internal communications" (2002a, ¶ 35).
03 Advertising	"A program that focuses on the creation, execution, transmission, and evaluation of commercial messages in various media intended to promote and sell products, services, and brands; and that prepares individuals to function as advertising assistants, technicians, and managers. Includes instruction in advertising theory, marketing strategy, advertising design and production methods, campaign methods and techniques, media management, related principles of business management, and applicable technical and equipment skills" (2002a, ¶ 36).
04 Political Communication	"A program that focuses on human and media communication in the political process and that prepares individuals to function as members of political and public affairs organizations, political campaign staffs, and related government and media entities. Includes instruction in media effects, political speaking and debating, political advertising and marketing, image management, political journalism, opinion polling, and aspects of print and broadcast media related to the production and distribution of media messages in political settings" (2002a, ¶ 41).
05 Health Communication	"A program that focuses on how people, individually and collectively, understand and accommodate to health and illness and the role of communication and media in shaping professional health care messages and public acceptance of these messages. Includes instruction in the development and use of health-related and care-related messages and media; the goals and strategies of health care promotion; *(Continued)*

TABLE 1.1 (Continued)	
Classification Category	**Definition**
	relationships, roles, situations, and social structures in the context of health maintenance and promotion; and applications to disease prevention, health advocacy, and communications concerning treatments" (2002a, ¶ 42).
10 Publishing	"A program that focuses on the process of managing the creation, publication, and distribution of print and electronic books and other text products and prepares individuals to manage the editorial, technical, and business aspects of publishing operations. Includes instruction in product planning and design, editing, author relations, business and copyright law, publishing industry operations, contracting and purchasing, product marketing, electronic publishing and commerce, history of publishing, and professional standards and ethics" (2002a, ¶ 49).
23. English Language and Literature/Letters 10 Speech and Rhetorical Studies 01 Speech and Rhetorical Studies	"A program that focuses on human interpersonal communication from the scientific/behavioral and humanistic perspectives. Includes instruction in the theory and physiology of speech, the history of discourse, the structure and analysis of argument and types of public speech, the social role of speech, oral interpretation of literature, interpersonal interactions, and the relation of speech to nonverbal and other forms of message exchanges" (2002b, ¶ 21).
51. Health Professions and Related Clinical Sciences	"Instructional programs that prepare individuals to practice as licensed professionals and assistants in the health care professions and focus on the study of related clinical sciences" (2002d, ¶ 1).
02 Communication Disorders Sciences and Services 01 Communication Disorders, General	"A program that focuses on the general study of the application of biomedical, psychological, and physical principles to the study of the genesis, development, and treatment of speech, language, hearing, and cognitive communication problems caused by disease, injury, or disability. Includes instruction in language science, hearing science, speech and voice science, biology of communication, behavioral linguistics, psychology, and applications to the development of diagnostic and rehabilitative strategies and technologies" (2002d, ¶ 11).
	(Continued)

TABLE 1.1 (Continued)

Classification Category	Definition
02 Audiology/ Audiologist and Hearing Sciences	"A program that focuses on the scientific study of hearing processes and hearing loss, and that prepares individuals to diagnose hearing loss and impairments and advise patients on means to use their remaining hearing and select and fit hearing aids and other devices. Includes instruction in acoustics, anatomy and physiology of hearing, hearing measurement, auditory pathology, middle and inner ear analysis, rehabilitation therapies and assistive technologies, and pediatric and other special applications" (2002d, ¶ 15).
03 Speech-Language Pathology/ Pathologist	"A program that prepares individuals to evaluate the speaking, language interpretation, and related physiological and cognitive capabilities of children and/or adults and develop treatment and rehabilitative solutions in consultation with clinicians and educators. Includes instruction in the anatomy and physiology of speech and hearing; biomechanics of swallowing and vocal articulation; communications disorders; psychology of auditory function and cognitive communication; language assessment and diagnostic techniques; and rehabilitative and management therapies" (2002d, ¶ 16).
04 Audiology/ Audiologist and Speech-Language Pathology/ Pathologist	"An integrated or coordinated program that prepares individuals as audiologists and speech-language pathologists. Includes instruction in a variety of communication disorder studies, audiology, speech pathology, language acquisition, and the design and implementation of comprehensive therapeutic and rehabilitative solutions to communications problems" (2002d, ¶ 17).
16. Foreign Languages, Literatures, and Linguistics 16 American Sign Language	"Instructional programs that focus on foreign languages and literatures, the humanistic and scientific study of linguistics, and the provision of professional interpretation and translation services" (2002c, ¶ 2).
03 Language Interpretation and Translation	"A program that prepares individuals to function as simultaneous interpreters of American Sign Language (ASL) and other sign language systems employed to assist the hearing impaired, both one-way and two-way. Includes instruction in American Sign Language (ASL), alternative sign languages, finger spelling, vocabulary and expressive nuances, oral and physical translation skills, cross-cultural communications, slang and colloquialisms, and technical interpretation" (2002c ¶ 194).

NOTE: All quotations are from publications of the National Center for Education Statistics.

methods, for the most part, a piece of research tends to rely on qualitative *or* quantitative methods.[5]

Qualitative Methods

At one time (and even in previous editions of this book) qualitative methods were defined as avoiding numerical information. Though quantitative studies certainly can be distinguished by their use of numerical information, any simple view can be strained at times. As can be seen from Table 1.2, on one hand, many qualitative studies that criticize speeches use public opinion survey data to help identify the effects of significant messages. On the other hand, some quantitative content analyses examine detailed message qualities and rely on theories drawn from traditions in qualitative research. Furthermore, the distinction has sometimes seemed to imply that qualitative research is an "ugly stepsister" or is inferior in the research craft. After many years of wrangling, the U.S. National Science Foundation held the NSF Workshop on Scientific Foundations of Qualitative Research to consider how to define sound qualitative social science research and how to guide researchers to propose worthwhile qualitative studies (Ragin, Nagel, & White, 2004). The report of this undertaking began by emphasizing that qualitative and quantitative studies have a great deal in common. There are elements of qualitative research thinking in much quantitative research and vice versa. The NSF report explained:

the NSF distinction of qualitative methods

> A qualitative/quantitative divide permeates much of social science, but this should be seen as a continuum rather than as a dichotomy. At one end of this continuum is textbook quantitative research. . . . At the opposite end of this continuum is social research that eschews notions of populations, cases, and variables altogether and rejects the possibility of hypothesis testing. . . . In between these two extremes are many different research strategies including many hybrid and combined strategies. (Ragin, Nagel, & White, 2004, p. 9)

In quantitative studies, researchers try to find interesting variables that describe and explain the cases of communication. Yet, researchers completing qualitative studies often view making "comparisons across cases [as involving] . . . difficult compromises because these features may be seen as obstacles to the conduct of good research" (Ragin, Nagel, & White, 2004, p. 10). Figure 1.1 on page 14 illustrates the orientations taken by different sorts of researchers. The definition of **qualitative research** found at the left "posits a trade-off between in-depth, intensive knowledge based on the study of small Ns on the one hand, and extensive, cross-case

Qualitative research
"involves in-depth, case-oriented study of a relatively small number of cases, including the single-case study. Qualitative research seeks detailed knowledge of specific cases, often with the goal of finding out 'how' things happen (or happened). Qualitative researchers' primary goal is to 'make the facts understandable,' and often place less emphasis on deriving inferences or predictions from cross-case patterns" (Ragin, Nagel, & White, 2004, p. 10).

---

[5]Reasonable people differ on the classification of some of these types of studies. Many scholars like to distinguish rhetorical/critical studies from the sorts of qualitative studies often done by field researchers. Though that view has justification, the *introduction* to different methods provided in this book represents a mainstream view that you are likely to find others using.

TABLE 1.2 TYPES OF QUALITATIVE STUDIES

Description	Examples
Historical-critical methods: research designed to describe a period, person, or phenomenon for the purpose of interpreting or evaluating communication and its effects	◆ Studying whether Lincoln's Gettysburg Address really met with negative reaction at the time it was delivered ◆ Studying the actual impact on Americans from Orson Welles's 1938 "War of the Worlds" broadcast. ◆ Studying dominant methods of treating stuttering since 1900 *Criticism:* ◆ Assessing use of argument by George W. Bush in his presidential debates ◆ Assessing whether newspaper reports gave politically balanced accounts of U.S. entry into Iraq, in 2003 ◆ Assessing the ethical use of surgery in the treatment of speech-handicapped patients in the nineteenth century
Qualitative observational studies: methods designed to use predominantly attribute-type data to interpret contemporaneous communication interactions	
Case studies and interpretive studies: intensive inquiries about single events, people, or social units (interpretive studies attempt to look for themes or stories that are helpful to *interpret* or understand the case)*	◆ Investigating the practice of a successful speech therapist to pick up some pointers ◆ Studying the communication inside a newspaper that is in the process of being sold
Ethnography and participant observation studies: inquiries in which the researcher takes the role of an active agent in the situation under study (sometimes may be used to gather quantitative data)	◆ Studying the process of news writing for a television station by joining the writing staff to report events from the inside ◆ Investigating the development of public strategy for a political campaign by joining a campaign as an active worker who makes observations from within the organization
Ethnomethodology: originally developed by anthropologists to study societies of humans, an approach (rather than a rigorous method) in which researchers find an ethnic group, live within it, and attempt to develop insight into the culture; emphasis is on ordinary behavior, which participants take for granted, to	◆ Investigating how people react to television by living with an isolated group of people without television and watching their reactions in the days and weeks that follow introduction of televisions ◆ Inquiring into the specialized language of street gang members by moving around with a gang during an extended time period

(Continued)

TABLE 1.2   (Continued)

Description	Examples
find hidden meanings and unwritten rules people use to make sense of their world	
Discourse/conversational analysis: a method of examining utterances people exchange—for the purpose of discovering the rules and strategies people use to structure, sequence, and take turns in speaking—to learn how people manage their interactions with others	♦ Studying the structure of interpersonal arguments among husbands and wives ♦ Examining judge and attorney communication by looking at the structure of their abbreviated exchanges in court ♦ Inquiring into children's speech development by identifying language competency levels among six-year-old and eight-year-old schoolchildren
Creative studies: use of the method of performance or demonstration to explore an aesthetic or creative experience	♦ Examining the problems of communicating Renaissance poetry to modern audiences by undertaking special performances in oral interpretation to contemporary student audiences ♦ Examining whether a public relations campaign using multimedia news releases is perceived as a suitable way to transmit information by designing such a campaign directly

*Though located elsewhere in this book according to common use, it should be remembered that case studies (intensive inquiries about single events, people, or social units) also may be completed using quantitative methods. Furthermore, these case studies may involve surveys of relationships among existing variables or inquiries regarding experimental manipulations of variables.

"eschews notions of populations, cases, and variables altogether and rejects the possibility of hypothesis testing . . . . conventional theory is highly suspect, and the distinction between researcher and research subject vanishes" (Ragin, Nagel, & White, 2004, p. 9); emphasis on explaining the case	"concepts of cases, analyzable case aspects, and the possibility of cross-case analysis" (Ragin, Nagel, & White, 2004, p. 10).	"sharply defined and delineated populations, cases, and variables, and well-specified theories and hypotheses" (Ragin, Nagel, & White, 2004, p. 9); emphasis on explaining variables across cases
Qualitative research ————	**Hybrid research** ————	**Quantitative research**

FIGURE 1.1

knowledge based on the study of large *N*s on the other hand" (Ragin, Nagel, & White, 2004, p. 10).[6]

Most qualitative research in our field tends to *describe* or *interpret* communication exchanges. These studies try to describe the human condition by using general views of social action. They may critique communication by relying on standards from a body of existing theory. Researchers who use qualitative methods often try to interpret the meanings to be found in communication exchanges. They may look at individual examples of communication research, rather than searching for patterns that run across individuals. Our language is very broad here, but the differences in emphasis will become pronounced as we continue.

approach of most qualitative research methods: description and interpretation

Quantitative Methods

Some research data are in numbers. In basic terms, "it is the job of the quantitative researcher to employ statistical tools that will summarize trends and test hypotheses that describe samples and predict the likelihood of event occurrences" (Bashi, 2004, p. 40). These sorts of studies reduce the raw research information to quantities that may be analyzed using statistical analyses.[7] As Table 1.3 shows, **quantitative research** has two major branches: surveys (of all varieties, including content analysis) and experiments.

Quantitative research inquiries in which observations are expressed predominantly in numerical terms.

Why would researchers in their right minds want to represent the world of communication as a bunch of numbers? Surely there must be something going on other than a love of numbers by some people. Though the types of data distinguish these

---

[6]This approach to defining qualitative methods as primarily concerned with the case and quantitative methods as primarily concerned with explanatory variables across cases is similar to a distinction often made between research seeking *idiographic* or *nomothetic* explanations, a topic that is covered in Chapter 6. Though applied mostly to efforts to find causal relationships (see Schutt, 2006, pp. 172–174), the general approach of the National Science Foundation associates qualitative research most with idiographic scholarship that is designed to develop a full understanding of "a particular event or individual [English & English, 1958, p. 347]," and qualitative research most with nomothetic scholarship, which attempts to find explanations and laws that apply to many instances.

[7]According to David Collier, Jason Seawright, and Henry E. Brady (2004), there are at least four ways researchers distinguish between quantitative and qualitative research. First, if the data are measured on the nominal level (see Chapter 4), or sometimes on the ordinal level (according to some scholars), the research is considered qualitative. Yet, quantitative research has been known to involve statistical analysis of data measured on the nominal level. Second, quantitative research usually involves larger sample sizes than qualitative research. Nonetheless, some qualitative studies, such as fantasy theme analysis or movement studies, often examine very large numbers of messages. Third, "In contrast to much qualitative research, quantitative analysis employs formal tests grounded in statistical theory. Statistical tests provide explicit, carefully formulated criteria for descriptive and causal analysis; a characteristic strength of quantitative research" (pp. 74–75). Fourth, sometimes called "thick vs. thin analysis" of individual cases, qualitative research tends to rely "on detailed knowledge of cases vs. more limited knowledge of cases. Detailed knowledge associated with thick analysis is likewise a major source of leverage in research; a characteristic strength of qualitative analysis" (p. 75).

TABLE 1.3 TYPES OF QUANTITATIVE STUDIES	
Description	**Examples**
Survey methods: techniques that involve carefully recorded observations that provide quantitative descriptions of relationships among variables	
Opinion surveys: assessments of reports from individuals about topics of interest	♦ Analyzing surveys regarding which candidate people think won a political debate ♦ Examining whether the public believes that speech correction therapy should receive increased funding in the public schools ♦ Assessing surveys of the favorite television programs
Descriptive or observational surveys: direct observations of behavior by use of some measurement (the researcher does not manipulate or change any variables)	♦ Discovering what sorts of things small-group communicators say predict their becoming group leaders ♦ Identifying the relationship between the number of newspapers a person reads on a regular basis and the amount of fear of society the person reports
Content analysis: "a systematic, quantitative study of verbally communicated material (articles, speeches, films) by determining the frequency of specific ideas, concepts, or terms" (*Longman Dictionary of Psychology and Psychiatry,* 1984, p. 176; used through courtesy of Walter Glanze Word Books)	♦ Studying the amount of violence on children's television programs ♦ Inquiring into the amount of newspaper space dedicated to stories about the women's movement ♦ Analyzing the types of speech defects shown by children in samples of spontaneous speech
Experimental methods: a method of studying the effect of variables in situations where all other influences are held constant. Variables are manipulated or introduced by experimenters to see what effect they may have.	♦ Studying the impact of the use of evidence by exposing one group to a speech with evidence and another group to a speech without evidence ♦ Studying the effect of color in advertising by exposing one group to an ad with color printing and another group to an ad without color printing

approach of qualitative research methods: description and interpretation

methods from qualitative tools, the research issues probed also tend to be different. Quantitative research tends to be *explanatory,* especially when experiments are involved, or it attempts to use precise statistical models to achieve comprehensive understandings of human communication (as in survey studies and polls of public opinion). These methods often try to explain communication behavior by looking at processes that allow researchers to *predict* future behavior, frequently using models of causal processes. Thus, quantitative research usually attempts to answer questions about people. Hence, any statistical tools are means to ends—not ends in themselves. If researchers wish to have precise explanations that characterize processes, or if they wish to develop methods to study communication behavior, quantitative research methods are invited. Of course, as the timeline on the inside front cover shows, the research question guides selection of methods, not the other way around. It is improper to decide that you want to be either a quantitative or qualitative researcher. You have to choose methods to suit research questions.

some research skills are important regardless of the methods used

You and Forms of Research Methods

All research methods require the same basic skills to frame a question, look in the library and on the Internet, and reason to conclusions from data. This book will start by helping you with these common tasks. The first section introduces the field as a research area, methods for isolating the research problem (a surprisingly difficult task, as it turns out!), and developing different forms of hypotheses. The second part, "Understanding Rudiments of Research Reasoning," deals with using theory and definitions in research, measurement concerns, and writing logical research arguments that evaluate research evidence and reasoning. Appendix G supplements this presentation by including information about library and Internet research strategies. As you can see, the first two parts of the book consider topics all researchers must know, regardless of the particular methods they eventually select to analyze data.

The third part examines the "Design of Research," focusing first on qualitative methods and then moving to approaches in quantitative research. This discussion starts with a survey of textual and critical analysis studies, followed by other qualitative approaches including ethnography and participant observation approaches. A review of content analysis (a method that often is considered qualitative research) in its various forms is included as a transition to chapters on quantitative methods. Chapters dedicated to descriptive empirical survey research, experimental design, and sampling issues round out this section. Since this book is an introductory treatment, it is limited to matters that reasonably can be learned in a one-term course, given the major interests of current communication students. Other methods—such as conversation analysis, detailed rhetorical analysis, and causal modeling—are defined but not covered in depth. Completing such research requires first studying underlying theoretic material properly covered in other classes. Hence, after taking advanced coursework in linguistics, you may demonstrate your skill by completing a conversational analysis. After taking advanced coursework in rhetorical theory, you can count on completing rhetorical criticisms. After completing work in path modeling, you may be expected to construct and test a causal model of communication activity. Each of these methods presumes advanced study that you must complete elsewhere. This choice is not a judgment about the value of one method over another (no single method is best for all research questions) but reflects a practical decision to make your learning reasonable.

advanced studies of applied methods require coursework beyond the scope of the introduction-to-research class

The final part of this book addresses statistical analysis of data and introduces some fundamentals of these methods, including a popular tool to review literature known as "meta-analysis." The common theme throughout this book is that research is an argument in which scholars (including you) are supposed to employ their best thinking and available evidence. Both the merit of the data and worth of research reasoning must be evaluated. Therefore, research requires us to train our minds and our abilities to express ourselves—as well as to be familiar with tools for inquiry.

The Scholarly Rigor Challenge

scholarly rigor:

Research must meet standards of excellence. In particular, we must conduct our research with the recognition of some key challenges (after Tuckman, 1999, pp. 12–13):

1. systematic

researchers may profit from serendipity

Serendipity finding something valuable while looking for something else.

1. *Research is systematic.* Productive research follows steps that carry out some sort of design. Researchers ask questions and implicitly agree in advance to search for answers by examining pertinent information. Researchers often profit from unexpected results that emerge. The effect is called **serendipity.** It seems that systematic researchers stand the best chance of grasping the importance of unexpected findings.

2. sound argument

Arguments claims advanced on the basis of reasoning from evidence.

2. *Research is a sound argument.* Though students sometimes are surprised to learn it, research actually is a process of advancing arguments. But this statement does not mean that researchers are just trying to "win over" others with clever appeals. Though in everyday life people can be persuasive by the force of their styles or personalities, research arguments reason from research data and information to draw conclusions. Thus, **arguments** in this context are defined as claims advanced on the basis of reasoning from evidence. Sound reasoning is vital for effective research. Flippant or sloppy thinking is not valued. Thus, logic and the methods to evaluate arguments are valuable tools to judge research.

3. data driven

3. *Research is data driven.* Issues that ask us to investigate things that cannot be tested in this life (e.g., does God exist?) are not matters that we can settle by our research methods. Furthermore, researchers are supposed to be willing to change their minds in light of new data. If data cannot be collected, or if we are unwilling to alter our opinions, the issue is not suitable for research.

4. a reductive process

4. *Research is a reductive process.* Qualitative and quantitative researchers use concepts to help "reduce the confusion of particular events and objects" (Tuckman, 1999, p. 13) into understandable general terms. Researchers do not just present data and information. They translate "reality to an abstract or conceptual state in an attempt to understand" (p. 13).

5. capable of replication

5. *Research is capable of replication.* By attempting to replicate or reproduce the research of scholars, we can tell if research findings are generally true or accidental. If research methods are so vaguely described that it is impossible to repeat the procedures in a study, the worth of the entire research project is questioned.

Regardless of whether replications actually are completed, the ability to replicate studies is essential for any piece of sound research.

In addition to these five scholarly challenges, a sixth may be added.

6. *Research is partial.* There is always more that could be said about a topic. Research findings are partial because we may discover new relationships involving other variables that make us modify or qualify the conclusions we have found. Thus, communication researchers do not claim to have discovered "The Truth" for all time. Instead, they advance tentative—but meaningful—insights for communication phenomena.

6. partial

RESEARCHERS IN THE FIELD: JAMES C. McCROSKEY

James C. McCroskey is the most published scholar in the communication field. Since his first article appeared in 1957, he has published over 200 articles and book chapters, and over 30 books and revisions. He has received top academic honors from the National Communication Association, the Eastern Communication Association, the World Communication Association, and the International Communication Association. He has been editor in chief for *Human Communication Research, Communication Education, Communication Research Reports,* and *Journal of Intercultural Communication.* He is Scholar in Residence at the University of Alabama and chaired the Department of Communication Studies at West Virginia University from 1972 to 1997.

♦ *What drew you into our field?*
Like most people in communication who are of my generation (the Depression babies), I began my career in speech, debate, and argumentation. I taught speech and coached debate for three years in high schools in South Dakota, and three years in college (at the University of Hawaii and Old Dominion University) before beginning my doctoral program at Pennsylvania State University. There was no field called communication in those days. Oddly, however, my first published article (written in 1957 during my first year of high school teaching) was an opinion piece arguing that speech activities should focus more on communication and less on performance behaviors. I had no idea that people who held that view were only a tiny minority of the speech field at that time, but would become the majority by the time I was in midcareer.

♦ *You have been the field's most published scholar for decades. Was this productivity something you planned early in your career?*
One of my mentors, Dr. Donald W. Klopf, was my supervisor while I was teaching and coaching at the University of Hawaii. He pushed me to go on to doctoral school, and once he got me to agree to that, he told me if I ever wanted to amount to anything in higher education, I had to get some publications—preferably before starting on my doctoral program. We published some articles together (and two books later on). When I got to Penn State, my first mentor was Robert T. Oliver—who was at that time one of the all-time leaders in publishing in the field. We talked about scholarship many times, and I observed his behavior

(writing seven days a week, always being in the office even though he was the Department Chair and didn't need to be). Looking back, I realize that I modeled his behaviors—which led to my productivity.

Over the years, I learned that I am what is called a "high achiever," which is a trait that probably has a strong genetic base. However, I am not an "upwardly mobile" person, which also is a trait that probably has a strong genetic base. I enjoy the work I do, and think that it is worth doing. But I have never been interested in "moving up the ladder" to be a dean or other administrator.

♦ *In general, what have you hoped that your research would accomplish?*
I wanted to advance scientific understanding of the human communication process. When I entered the field there was only a handful of people doing quantitative research. Now there are hundreds, many of whom are my former students.

♦ *What part of your research undertakings have made you most proud?*
This question is very much like asking parents which of their children they like best! I love all my kids!

Yet, four of my research "kids" stand out to me. First, my early research on the role of evidence in persuasion led to my career-long study of ethos (mostly the source credibility aspect, but also attraction and homophily elements). As Aristotle had suggested centuries ago, we learned that messages are always interpreted by the source of those messages. My research has made a contribution toward understanding this phenomenon. Second, my work with communication apprehension has made a major impact on the way teachers and researchers respond to people who are quiet and/or fearful about communication. This work led to a whole program of research on communication traits, which has been very helpful in gaining a better understanding of the variability in the ways humans communicate. I think many people would point to this work as my most important contribution. Third, the program of research that my colleagues and I have pursued related to communication in instruction may have been my most significant one. By researching such instructional communication variables as nonverbal immediacy, power strategies, clarity, assertiveness, and responsiveness, we have been able to explain (with a high degree of accuracy) what it is about teacher behavior that has a major impact on student learning, particularly affective learning—an area that has been underresearched in the field of education. Fourth, though only time will tell, the research paradigm that Michael Beatty and I launched may turn out to be the most important thing either he or I have done. This "communibiology" paradigm is now being advanced by numerous researchers and theorists and may prove to be the approach that will make the most important contribution to understanding human communication behavior.

♦ *What one or two things do you think students should know to deal successfully with communication research either as consumers or as researchers?*
First, it is rare that a single study ever makes a major contribution to the advancement of knowledge. To accomplish that goal requires an ongoing program of research—many studies, and the contributions of more than a single researcher. Second, theory is the product of research and never should be seen as a necessary prerequisite of research in a new area. Often, a simple question ("I wonder what would happen if . . . ") gets a researcher on the right path toward meaningful research. Theory should be used to explain research findings.

The Personal Challenge, or What Do I Need to Do to Study Communication Research Methods Successfully?

Researchers hardly ever tell you how much fun they have making new discoveries. In fact, they might be a little embarrassed to tell you about the rush they get from completing successful research projects. But for all the excitement that research provides (and it can be an addicting pleasure), it can also be demanding. As you begin to look at research methods, it might help to know that students who do well in research methods classes tend to satisfy certain needs:

1. *The need to think in an orderly way.* Though learning research methods will help improve your critical thinking abilities, orderly thinking also is a key to success. Researchers quickly find that half-considered ideas are exposed as weak. We must train our minds to separate the relevant from the irrelevant, the observable from the unobservable, and the complete from the incomplete.

   1. orderly thinking

2. *The need to write clearly.* Research includes communicating the effort to others. To succeed, you must write crisply and clearly. Writing research and scholarship is not the same as writing a typical essay, short story, or letter. Research writing is very precise, structured, and to the point. Effective writing does not mean writing beautiful prose, but using crystal clear language, grammar, and support. While we are on the subject, we might as well get something else straight: first drafts are not acceptable in scholarship. Everybody's first draft of a paper is lousy. Despite what you may have been told in high school, you must revise, edit, and polish research to put it in proper form. You may be familiar with the writing of William Faulkner. After having been awarded the Nobel Prize for literature, a reporter asked him what it felt like to be recognized as one of the world's greatest writers. He responded, "I am not one of the world's greatest writers, but I am among the world's top two or three greatest *re*writers." Faulkner had to revise his work, and so do the rest of us. Taking a course in research should help you improve your writing abilities.

   2. clear writing

3. *The need to set aside personal prejudices in light of data.* In research and scholarship, we must be willing to let the data decide our conclusions, even if we do not like them very much. When Galileo first observed moons around planets other than Earth, many Church fathers refused to look through his telescope. Church doctrine had decided that such a thing was impossible, and no data were allowed to contradict it. Galileo was persecuted for letting data—not prejudice—guide his conclusions. Though the world now respects Galileo's position, many people are unwilling to let data decide matters. They have a difficult time studying research methods since research methods place priority on the data, not on prior beliefs.

   3. set aside prejudice

4. *The need to stay organized and follow instructions.* Research requires carefully following protocols and methods. Thus, it is important for scholars—even those studying research methods for the first time—to follow directions and stay organized. Students must fight the urge to leave out steps, take shortcuts, or ignore instructions. There is much that is creative in research, but we must harness that creativity by being organized and following instructions in detail. Researchers know that details matter.

   4. stay organized and follow instructions

*5. know reasons to study re-
search methods*

5. *The need to know the reason for studying research methods.* Students sometimes take a required class in research methods, but they may not know why. Yet, most successful students take time to learn the reasons for studying this subject (and all others, for that matter). Why study communication research methods? Among the most potent reasons are:

- ◆ To learn to think rigorously and critically, especially about research evidence that is advanced in a variety of popular and scholarly outlets
- ◆ To learn how to find answers to questions about communication
- ◆ To acquire survival skills to help read and use the field's literature
- ◆ To learn how to sort through past research for answers to research questions

Any of these reasons justifies studying research methods. Your personal goals for approaching this subject can be a great resource for you.

The Ethical Challenge

Research is not amoral. Indeed, over 2,400 years ago, Aristotle, the intellectual father of our field, explained that "rhetoric [communication studies, as it was called at the time] is a branch of ethics."[8] Thus, ethics is not just something "tacked on" to communication studies. Each choice made in communication and communication research is both a practical and an ethical move. Conducting research is bound up in the ethical standards our society has accepted. Research is judged not only by the rigor of procedures and the results obtained but by the ethics of the researchers. The Archbishop of York challenged British scientists to consider the ethical consequences of their research by urging them to ask "What applications will be made of my research?" before they undertake their studies.

professional codes of conduct

Many organizations have developed formal codes of conduct to guide practitioners and researchers. The most well known of these guides is the Code of Conduct for the American Psychological Association. Others exist in our field as well. The National Communication Association's Credo for Ethical Communication expresses the ethical values of the communication community (see Table 1.4). The American Association for Public Opinion Research developed a Code of Conduct for researchers involved primarily in public survey research. Similarly, the American Forensic Association has a detailed code of conduct to guide debate and contest speaking activities. Regulations of the U.S. Office of Education, the Department of Health and Human Services, and some federal laws protect the rights of individuals who participate in our research. At modern colleges and universities, independent research boards first must evaluate research proposals to evaluate the ethical choices proposed by researchers. Even if one is not a

---

[8]Aristotle defined rhetoric as "the faculty for discovering in the particular case what are the available means of persuasion." The term "persuasion" can be traced back to *suasori* acts, which refer to giving advice. When we give advice, we suggest to others what would be "good" for them to do or believe. The study of the good is called "ethics." Hence, from the early beginnings, communication studies has been part of the study of ethics.

TABLE 1.4   NCA CREDO FOR COMMUNICATION ETHICS

Questions of right and wrong arise whenever people communicate. Ethical communication is fundamental to responsible thinking, decision making, and the development of relationships and communities within and across contexts, cultures, channels, and media. Moreover, ethical communication enhances human worth and dignity by fostering truthfulness, fairness, responsibility, personal integrity, and respect for self and others. We believe that unethical communication threatens the quality of all communication and consequently the well-being of individuals and the society in which we live. Therefore we, the members of the National Communication Association, endorse and are committed to practicing the following principles of ethical communication:

We advocate truthfulness, accuracy, honesty, and reason as essential to the integrity of communication.

We endorse freedom of expression, diversity of perspective, and tolerance of dissent to achieve the informed and responsible decision making fundamental to a civil society.

We strive to understand and respect other communicators before evaluating and responding to their messages.

We promote access to communication resources and opportunities as necessary to fulfill human potential and contribute to the well-being of families, communities, and society.

We promote communication climates of caring and mutual understanding that respect the unique needs and characteristics of individual communicators.

We condemn communication that degrades individuals and humanity through distortion, intimidation, coercion, and violence and through the expression of intolerance and hatred.

We are committed to the courageous expression of personal convictions in pursuit of fairness and justice.

We advocate sharing information, opinions, and feelings when facing significant choices while also respecting privacy and confidentiality.

We believe that unethical communication threatens the quality of all communication and consequently the well-being of individuals and the society in which we live.

We accept responsibility for the short- and long-term consequences for our own communication and expect the same of others.

psychologist, the ethical standards adopted by the American Psychological Association have become a model to guide many such decisions. Table 1.5 compares the major provisions of the American Psychological Association's Ethical Principles of Psychologists and Code of Conduct and a draft version of the National Communication Association's "Code of Professional Responsibilities for the Communication Scholar/Teacher" under consideration by that organization. Though there are some different emphases, many of the similarities are striking. Awareness of these requirements may put you in a good position to understand the ethical standards that have been embraced by our field and social science research generally. Furthermore, when you propose research of your own, it would make sense to obey these standards. Clear breaches of ethical standards are treated harshly in the field. Violations can—and have—resulted in termination of employment and virtual expulsion from the field. Ignorance of such codes is not considered an excuse. Reasonable adults are supposed to think about the likely consequences of their conduct before they act. In addition to this list, this book includes a number of "Special Discussions" dedicated to ethical issues (listed under the heading "A Question of Ethics").

TABLE 1.5   COMPARATIVE CODES OF ETHICS FOR RESEARCH IN COMMUNICATION

Ethics Issue	Selections from American Psychological Association Ethical Principles of Psychologists and Code of Conduct (2002)* (www.apa.org/ethics)	Selections from Draft of National Communication Association "Code of Professional Responsibilities for the Communication Scholar/Teacher" (www.natcom.org/nca/Template2.asp?bid=509)
	8 *Research and Publication*	Responsibility to others entails honesty and openness. Thus, ...
Institutional Approval	8.01 When institutional approval is required, psychologists provide accurate information about their research proposals and obtain approval prior to conducting the research. They conduct the research in accordance with the approved research protocol.	◆ Professional responsibility requires that communication researchers know and comply with the legal and institutional guidelines covering their work.
Informed Consent	8.02 (a) When obtaining informed consent . . . psychologists inform participants about (1) the purpose of the research, expected duration, and procedures; (2) their right to decline to participate and to withdraw from the research once participation has begun; (3) the foreseeable consequences of declining or withdrawing; (4) reasonably foreseeable factors that may be expected to influence their willingness to participate such as potential risks, discomfort, or adverse effects; (5) any prospective research benefits; (6) limits of confidentiality; (7) incentives for participation; and (8) whom to contact for questions about the research and research participants' rights. They provide opportunity for the prospective participants to ask questions and receive answers. (b) Psychologists conducting intervention research involving the use of experimental treatments clarify to participants at the outset of the research (1) the experimental nature of	◆ Obtain informed consent to conduct the research, where appropriate to do so.

(Continued)

the treatment; (2) the services that will or will not be available to the control group(s) if appropriate; (3) the means by which assignment to treatment and control groups will be made; (4) available treatment alternatives if an individual does not wish to participate in the research or wishes to withdraw once a study has begun; and (5) compensation for or monetary costs of participating including, if appropriate, whether reimbursement from the participant or a third-party payor will be sought.

Informed Consent for Recording Voices and Images

8.03 Psychologists obtain informed consent from research participants prior to recording their voices or images for data collection unless (1) the research consists solely of naturalistic observations in public places, and it is not anticipated that the recording will be used in a manner that could cause personal identification or harm, or (2) the research design includes deception, and consent for the use of the recording is obtained during debriefing.

Client/Patient, Student, and Subordinate Research Participants

8.04 (a) When psychologists conduct research with clients/patients, students, or subordinates as participants, psychologists take steps to protect the prospective participants from adverse consequences of declining or withdrawing from participation.

(b) When research participation is a course requirement or an opportunity for extra credit, the prospective participant is given the choice of equitable alternative activities.

Dispensing with Informed Consent for Research

8.05 Psychologists may dispense with informed consent only (1) where research would not reasonably be assumed to create distress or harm and involves (a) the study of normal educational practices, curricula, or classroom management methods conducted in educational settings; (b) only anonymous questionnaires, naturalistic observations, or archival research for which disclosure of responses would not

26

TABLE 1.5 (Continued)

Ethics Issue	Selections from American Psychological Association Ethical Principles of Psychologists and Code of Conduct (2002)* (www.apa.org/ethics)	Selections from Draft of National Communication Association "Code of Professional Responsibilities for the Communication Scholar/Teacher" (www.natcom.org/nca/Template2 .asp?bid=509)
	place participants at risk of criminal or civil liability or damage their financial standing, employability, or reputation, and confidentiality is protected; or (c) the study of factors related to job or organization effectiveness conducted in organizational settings for which there is no risk to participants' employability, and confidentiality is protected or (2) where otherwise permitted by law or federal or institutional regulations.	
Offering Inducements for Research Participation	8.06 (a) Psychologists make reasonable efforts to avoid offering excessive or inappropriate financial or other inducements for research participation when such inducements are likely to coerce participation. (b) When offering professional services as an inducement for research participation, psychologists clarify the nature of the services, as well as the risks, obligations, and limitations.	
Deception in Research	8.07 (a) Psychologists do not conduct a study involving deception unless they have determined that the use of deceptive techniques is justified by the study's significant prospective scientific, educational, or applied value and that effective nondeceptive alternative procedures are not feasible. (b) Psychologists do not deceive prospective participants about research that is reasonably expected to cause physical pain or severe emotional distress.	◆ Avoid deception as part of the research process, unless the use of deception has been approved in advance by an appropriate review body.

(c) Psychologists explain any deception that is an integral feature of the design and conduct of an experiment to participants as early as is feasible, preferably at the conclusion of their participation, but no later than at the conclusion of the data collection, and permit participants to withdraw their data.

Debriefing

8.08 (a) Psychologists provide a prompt opportunity for participants to obtain appropriate information about the nature, results, and conclusions of the research, and they take reasonable steps to correct any misconceptions that participants may have of which the psychologists are aware.

(b) If scientific or humane values justify delaying or withholding this information, psychologists take reasonable measures to reduce the risk of harm.

(c) When psychologists become aware that research procedures have harmed a participant, they take reasonable steps to minimize the harm.

Reporting Research Results

8.10 (a) Psychologists do not fabricate data.

(b) If psychologists discover significant errors in their published data, they take reasonable steps to correct such errors in a correction, retraction, erratum, or other appropriate publication means.

- Do not falsify data or publish misleading interpretations of events or of results.
- Authors have an obligation to submit their work to professional conventions or to scholarly journals according to the guidelines set forth by the publication or convention call for papers.
- Provide adequate citations when available and relevant in research reports to support theoretical claims and to justify research procedures.
- Disclose results of the research, regardless of whether those results support the researcher's expectations or hypotheses.

(Continued)

TABLE 1.5 (Continued)		
Ethics Issue	**Selections from American Psychological Association Ethical Principles of Psychologists and Code of Conduct (2002)*** (www.apa.org/ethics)	**Selections from Draft of National Communication Association "Code of Professional Responsibilities for the Communication Scholar/Teacher"** (www.natcom.org/nca/Template2 .asp?bid=509)
Plagiarism	8.11 Psychologists do not present portions of another's work or data as their own, even if the other work or data source is cited occasionally.	• They do not use the work of others as their own, plagiarizing others' ideas or language or appropriating the work of others for which one serves as a reviewer.
Publication Credit	8.12 (a) Psychologists take responsibility and credit, including authorship credit, only for work they have actually performed or to which they have substantially contributed. (b) Principal authorship and other publication credits accurately reflect the relative scientific or professional contributions of the individuals involved, regardless of their relative status. Mere possession of an institutional position, such as department chair, does not justify authorship credit. Minor contributions to the research or to the writing for publications are acknowledged appropriately, such as in footnotes or in an introductory statement. (c) Except under exceptional circumstances, a student is listed as principal author on any multiple-authored article that is substantially based on the student's doctoral dissertation. Faculty advisors discuss publication credit with students as early as feasible and throughout the research and publication process as appropriate.	• Communication researchers share credit appropriately and recognize the contributions of others to the finished work. They also decide through mutual consultation whether authors should be added or deleted from the finished product.
Duplicate Publication of Data	8.13 Psychologists do not publish, as original data, data that have been previously published. This does not preclude republishing data when they are accompanied by proper acknowledgment.	• Authors also have an obligation to submit their work to only one scholarly journal (after review, authors may then decide whether to revise, if that is an option, or to

send the specific work to another journal). In addition, authors have a responsibility to send a paper to only one programming unit of a convention or conference.

◆ If portions of the submitted work have been presented or published previously, the author has an obligation to note that fact, and the editor or planner has an obligation to take this disclosure into account in deciding whether to accept the present version of the work.

Sharing Research Data for Verification	8.14 (a) After research results are published, psychologists do not withhold the data on which their conclusions are based from other competent professionals who seek to verify the substantive claims through reanalysis and who intend to use such data only for that purpose, provided that the confidentiality of the participants can be protected and unless legal rights concerning proprietary data preclude their release. This does not preclude psychologists from requiring that such individuals or groups be responsible for costs associated with the provision of such information. (b) Psychologists who request data from other psychologists to verify the substantive claims through reanalysis may use shared data only for the declared purpose. Requesting psychologists obtain prior written agreement for all other uses of the data.
Reviewers	8.15 Psychologists who review material submitted for presentation, publication, grant, or research proposal review respect the confidentiality of and the proprietary rights in such information of those who submitted it.
Sponsorship	◆ Report all financial support for the research and any financial relationship that the researcher has with the persons or entities

(Continued)

TABLE 1.5 (Continued)

Ethics Issue	Selections from American Psychological Association Ethical Principles of Psychologists and Code of Conduct (2002)* (www.apa.org/ethics)	Selections from Draft of National Communication Association "Code of Professional Responsibilities for the Communication Scholar/Teacher" (www.natcom.org/nca/Template2.asp?bid=509)
		being researched, so that readers may judge the potential influence of financial support on the research results.
Research Argument		◆ Accurately reveal assumptions made in advancing specific interpretations of historical events.
		◆ Criticism of another's language, ideas, or logic is a legitimate part of scholarly research, but communication researchers avoid *ad hominem* attacks. Avoiding personal attack does not mean that critics or reviewers refrain from commenting directly and honestly on the work of others, however.
Social Responsibility		◆ Communication researchers who work with human subjects honor their commitments to their subjects. Those who work with communities honor their commitments to the communities they research.
Equality of Opportunity or Access		◆ Authors have an obligation to communicate in a manner that makes their work accessible to the community for which it is intended.

Creative Scholarship	◆ Creative scholars have an obligation to submit their work to professional outlets according to the guidelines set forth by those inviting an exhibit or soliciting submissions through an open call.
	◆ Creative scholars have an obligation to acknowledge properly those who contributed to the creation of a piece of work or project.
	◆ If earlier versions of the submitted work have been shown previously, the creative scholar has an obligation to note that fact, and the exhibitor may take this disclosure into account in deciding whether to accept the present version of the work.
	◆ Creative scholars have an obligation to communicate in a manner that makes their work accessible to the community for which it is intended.
Confidentiality	◆ Researchers and those engaged in creative activity should uphold the confidentiality and autonomy of participants as set forth in informed consent documents sanctioned by an institution's "use of human subjects" protocols.

*Section 8.09 on treatment of animals is excluded given the rarity of communication studies dealing with animals.

The Structure of the Field Challenge

People in communication, speech and hearing science, journalism, and telecommunications work in a field that is structured across many departmental lines. Similarly, communication research has been promoted by many organizations whose members often cross the barriers created by the organization of different schools. It is helpful to know how the diverse and major organizations in our field showcase our research.

National Communication Association (www.natcom.org)[9]

Founded in November 1914, the National Communication Association was the first organization to sponsor research publications.[10] Originally called the National Association of Academic Teachers of Public Speaking, it changed its name to the Speech Association of America until 1970, when the organization adopted the Speech Communication Association (SCA) as its title. In March 1997 the current name was adopted, reflecting the breadth of the field. In addition to promoting research and employment networking at its annual convention, this organization publishes several journals that report research:

- ◆ *Quarterly Journal of Speech* (founded 1915) Call # PN 4071.Q3.[11] The oldest journal in the field, it deals with general speech communication focusing heavily on communication and rhetorical theory and criticism.
- ◆ *Communication Monographs* (founded 1934) PN 4077.S61. Originally designed to publish lengthy research pieces, it is now dedicated to communication theory with emphasis on quantitative studies.
- ◆ *Communication Education* (founded 1952—formerly *Speech Teacher*) PN 4071.S741. In the 1980s, this journal was divided into two publications: *Communication Education* and *Communication Teacher* (previously called *Speech Communication Teacher*). The latter publication is an online journal with an annual print version available to subscribers.
- ◆ *Text and Performance Quarterly* (founded 1981)—called *Literature in Performance* until 1989) PN 2.T49. Dedicated to oral interpretation of literature and aesthetics in communication.
- ◆ *Critical Studies in Media Communication* (founded 1984—formerly *Critical Studies in Mass Communication*) P 87.C74. Study and analysis of mass media with an emphasis on scholarship taking critical and cultural studies approaches.

---

[9]These Web addresses change from time to time, and you should examine the website for this book or for the author for updates.

[10]The Eastern Communication Association was founded before the National Communication Association, but it did not begin publishing a research journal until 1953.

[11]For these journals the Library of Congress call numbers are provided, so that you may conveniently find these periodicals in your local library. Newsletter call numbers are not included. Some minor variation in call numbers may occur as local operations make their own clerical lists and as new volumes of multivolume series are acquired.

- *Journal of Applied Communication Research* (founded 1973, NCA sponsorship began in 1991) HM 258.J67. Research on applied topics in field settings.
- *The Review of Communication* (founded 2001—online journal restructured in 2004). Focuses on analyses of books in the field, and includes critical essays dealing with multiple publications with unifying topics.
- *Communication and Critical/Cultural Studies* (founded 2004). Online journal directed primarily to critical assessment of international issues related to communication in the exercise of power dealing with such subjects as class, race, ethnicity, and gender issues.

Two additional yearbooks are also published by the NCA, the *International and Intercultural Communication Annual* (HM 258I.58) and the *Free Speech Yearbook* (P 87.F853).

International Communication Association (www.icahdq.org)

Founded in 1949 as the National Society for the Study of Communication, the organization changed its name to the International Communication Association in the mid-1960s. The ICA encourages participation from all branches of communication (except speech and hearing science), drawing especially strong links between those studying mass communication and those studying interpersonal communication. Every three years the annual convention is held outside the United States. Its major journals are:

- *Journal of Communication* (founded 1951; from 1974 through 1991 ICA turned over editorship to the Annenberg School for Communication at the University of Pennsylvania) P 90.J6. Designed to promote the broad study of communication, it is oriented primarily toward studies of mass media, television, and popular culture.
- *Human Communication Research* (founded 1974) P 91.3 H85. A premier outlet for research in communication theory with emphasis on quantitative studies.
- *Communication Theory* (founded 1991) P 87.C59737. Dedicated to essays on theoretic and metatheoretic developments in communication.
- *Journal of Computer-Mediated Communication* (founded 1995—prior to 2004, published electronically by the USC Annenberg School for Communication). Presents mostly reviews, social science, and quantitative research related to computer-mediated communication over the Internet and by use of wireless technologies.

ICA also sponsors the *Communication Yearbook* (P 87.C5974) particularly dedicated to showcasing literature reviews of critical areas. The Political Communication Division of ICA collaborates with its sister division in the American Political Science Association to produce another journal:

- *Political Communication* (founded 1984—previously called *Political Communication and Persuasion*) JF1525.P8 P64. Features interdisciplinary work on communication in political settings.

SPECIAL DISCUSSION 1-2

CLASSICAL ROOTS OF THE COMMUNICATION FIELD

Communication is one of the world's oldest academic studies. The first book on communication was written in Egypt sometime around 2675 B.C.E. by Ptah Hotep, the governor of Memphis and Grand Vizier (Prime Minister). Upon his retirement he wrote a book of advice called *Precepts,* and it served as a textbook on communication for many centuries. Yet, widespread communication studies did not really begin until around 500 B.C.E., when the city-state of Athens instituted a democratic system and people found that they had to speak for themselves to exercise their rights. Athenian freemen were expected to participate in the popular assembly (if they gave consistently bad advice, they could be banished outright) and on juries (ranging in size from a low of 51 to a high of 1,501 members—though most were near 501). People needed communication skills, and they were eager to find teachers to help them. The first groundswell of teachers to make their way to Athens were called *sophists.* Today that term means a person who uses clever but fallacious arguments. In ancient times, however, sophists (from the Greek word *sophos* meaning wisdom) were teachers who traveled around instructing people wherever there was a market. These teachers gave very practical instruction that was useful to common folk who direly needed to improve their skills.

Sometime around 470 B.C.E. a Sicilian named Corax (generally believed to be the earliest of these teachers) "invented" the study of communication (called *rhetoric*). At the very least, he wrote the first detailed work on the art of effective public speaking, *Rhetorike Techne,* including details on organization and uses of arguments from probability. Other sophists included Protagoras (called the father of debate), Theodorus of Byzantium (who studied figures of speech such as puns), and Prodicus of Ceos (an early expert in the study of words, or *philology*).

Surely the greatest contributor to communication studies in the classical age was Aristotle (384–322 B.C.E.). He made the first attempt to develop a complete rhetoric that was philosophically compelling. In his book *Rhetoric,* he defined our study as "the faculty of discovering in the particular case what are the available means of persuasion." Thus, rhetoric was not a *practice* but a *field of study*—an advance that still gives us intellectual integrity as a distinct field. Though Aristotle did not write about all "canons of rhetoric," he became associated strongly with them because he discussed many of them in detail. These canons were five major categories that may be studied to help understand communication: *invention* (types and sources of ideas), *arrangement* (organization of ideas), *style* (use of words), *delivery* (use of voice and gesture), and *memory* (ability to recall passages and examples for utterance). When European universities were founded during the Middle Ages, three primary subjects were studied: logic, rhetoric, and grammar. Remnants of this tradition can be seen today in the communication student's wearing a silver tassel at graduation ceremonies to symbolize study of "oratory" in the silver age.

The study of speech and hearing science also had its roots in ancient times. Plutarch, the Greek biographer, recounted that Demosthenes had a monotonous voice and stammered when he spoke. Under the guidance of an actor named Satyrus (the oldest known speech therapist?) Demosthenes improved his diction by practicing a number of drills including speaking with pebbles in his mouth. Though the deaf were routinely put to death in ancient Rome and Greece, during the Middle Ages, speech and hearing science was pursued as a sacred duty. In the seventh century, when Bishop John of Beverly was successful in teaching a deaf-mute to speak, the Roman Catholic Church promptly declared it a miracle and made him a saint. Later, developing a code of charitable deeds, the Church promoted compassion for handicapped people in general, but it also unknowingly declared speech and hearing science not a profession but an act of charity.

Journalism and mass communication professions also began in the classical period. At the order of Julius Caesar, the world's first "newspaper," *Acta Diurna* (*Daily Events*), was published in Rome during the first century B.C.E. In reality, the newspapers were little more than hand-duplicated bulletins that were posted in the Forum, but large numbers of people made a daily routine of reading them. It would not be until the seventh and eighth centuries that the world's first printed newspapers would appear in Beijing. The method of printing employed wood blocks, which was a time-consuming process since blocks were prepared individually for each issue and then discarded. Since reporting the news was controlled by the government, only a very limited form of journalism appears to have been practiced. Though a form of movable-type printing was invented in China at least as far back as the eleventh century, it was rapidly abandoned since Chinese has no alphabet and over 40,000 characters. When movable mitered type was developed in Europe in the fifteenth century, widespread and rapid dissemination of the news became possible and journalism emerged as a recognized profession.

American Speech-Language-Hearing Association (www.asha.org)

Though once part of the Speech Communication Association, the American Academy of Speech Correction was founded in 1926. The organization changed its name four times after 1926, settling on its current name in 1979. ASLHA is best known for its certification programs for practitioners of speech correction and speech and hearing science. It also promotes research and scholarship by its publications:

- *Journal of Speech, Language, and Hearing Research* (originally founded as the *Journal of Speech and Hearing Research* in 1958) RC 423.J86. In 1990, the *Journal of Speech and Hearing Disorders* (founded in 1936 as the *Journal of Speech Disorders* until the name change in 1948) merged with the *Journal of Speech and Hearing Research* in 1990. Published six times a year, this publication features research and theoretic essays across the realm of speech and hearing science.

- *ASHA Leader Online* (online version of *ASHA,* founded 1959) www.asha.org/about/publications/leader-online/. Print version of *ASHA:* RC 423.A2. Focuses on professional speech and hearing research issues and the administration of the organization.

- *Language, Speech and Hearing Services in Schools* (founded 1970) RC 423.A1 L25. Attention paid to issues of interest to speech and hearing specialists with emphasis on speech-handicapped children.

- *American Journal of Speech-Language Pathology* (founded 1991) RC 423.A1 A43. Focuses on clinical practice issues for therapists.

- *American Journal of Audiology* (founded 1991) RC 1.A416. Clinical issues in audiology and hearing disorders. Now available online (journals.asha.org/aja), the journal is published twice a year.

From time to time, the association also publishes a *Monograph* series (HD 929.H65 C45x) and *ASHA Reports* (W 1.AS151) containing proceedings from annual meetings.

Association for Education in Journalism and Mass Communication (www.aejmc.org)

This organization is the largest national professional organization in mass communication. Founded as the American Association of Teachers of Journalism in 1912, it adopted its current name in 1982. In addition to its annual meetings that showcase research, the organization sponsors these journals:

- *Journalism & Mass Communication Quarterly* (founded 1924) PN 4700.J7. Originally called *Journalism Bulletin,* then *Journalism Quarterly,* it features predominantly nonquantitative studies of journalism.

- *Journalism & Mass Communication Educator* (founded 1945) PN 4700.J6. Originally called *Journalism Educator,* it focuses on educational issues and essays related to instruction.

- *Journalism & Communication Monographs* (founded 1966) PN 4722.J6. Previously called *Journalism Monographs* and *Journalism & Mass Communication Monographs,* this publication includes extended studies in mass communication issues and theory.

- *Mass Communication Review* (founded 1973) P 87.M28. Studies on the influence of mass communication on society.

Many divisions also publish journals that have nearly achieved equivalent status of publications sponsored by the organization as a whole. Prominent among these journals are the *International Communication Bulletin* (PN 4700.I32), the *Journal of Public Relations Research* (HM 263.J65), the *Newspaper Research Journal* (PN 4700.N525), *Communication Law and Policy* (KF 2750.C66), the *Journal of Communication Inquiry* (P 87.J62), and the *Journal of Mass Media Ethics* (BJ 1725.E84x).

Broadcast Education Association (www.beaweb.org)

Called the Association of Professional Broadcast Education for many years, this organization held its first annual convention in 1954 and focuses its attention exclusively on electronic media and its effects. This group publishes these journals:

- *Journal of Broadcasting & Electronic Media* (founded 1956) PN 1991.J61. Originally called the *Journal of Broadcasting,* this publication features essays and research on broadcasting with emphasis on showcasing quantitative research and applied commentaries.

- *Feedback* (founded 1959) PN 1990.83 F38. Includes essays and news on broadcast education.

American Forensic Association (www.americanforensics.org)

Founded in 1949 by a group of debate coaches and teachers of competitive forensics, the American Forensic Association (AFA) is dedicated to issues surrounding competitive forensics. Through 1963, the AFA published the *Register,* a quarterly newsletter that included some research. The *Journal of the American Forensic Association* began in 1964 and is now called *Argumentation and Advocacy* (PN 4171.A51), reflecting the expansion in content beyond the traditional arenas of competitive forensics. The organization sponsors national forensic events and promotes research through a program of competitively awarded grants.

American Communication Association (www.americancomm.org)

The American Communication Association was founded in 1993 to promote communication studies in North America. This organization was one of the first to embrace the Internet to promote its efforts. Membership in this organization is free. It hosts an annual research conference, and since 1998 it has published the *American Communication Journal,* an electronic journal produced three times annually (www.acjournal.org). The ACA sponsors electronic discussion groups, collects directories of communication research available online, and offers accrediting services.

Special Interest Organizations

The number of organizations with specialized concerns in communication has blossomed in recent years. Some have their own publications and conferences, whereas others meet with other professional organizations. Though a complete listing would be inappropriate here, some of the most prominent of these groups are:

- ◆ *Business communication:* Association for Business Communication (www.businesscommunication.org) publishes *Business Communication Quarterly* (founded 1969) HF 5718.B941 and the *Journal of Business Communication* (founded 1938) HF 5718.J6.
- ◆ *Forensics and argumentation:* Cross Examination Debate Association (cedadebate.org) (publishes journal, *Contemporary Argumentation and Debate,* founded as an annual in 1980); Delta Sigma Rho-Tau Kappa Alpha (www.mnsu.edu/spcomm/dsr-tka/dsr-tka.htm) (publishes journal *Speaker and Gavel,* PN 4177.S65, founded 1964); Pi Kappa Delta and Phi Rho Phi (www.phirhopi.org) honor societies all publish their own journals; International Forensic Association (www.idebate.org) (publishes *iDEBATE* magazine, founded in 2000); National Federation of State High School Associations (www.nfhs.org) (publishes *Forensic Quarterly,* founded 1950, PN 4177.F6); National Forensic Association (www.bethel.edu/Majors/Communication/nfa.html) (publishes *National Forensic Journal,* founded 1977, PN 4177.N38); National Forensic League (www.nflonline.org/Main/HomePage) (publishes a magazine, *The Rostrum,* founded 1918); National Association of Urban Debate Leagues (www.naudl.org); National Parliamentary Debate Association

(cas.bethel.edu/dept/comm/npda) (publishes annual *Journal of the National Parliamentary Debate Association,* founded 1992); International Society for the Study of Argumentation (cf.hum.uva.nl/issa), associated with the University of Amsterdam in the Netherlands.

♦ *General semantics:* The Institute of General Semantics (formerly the International Society for General Semantics) (www.generalsemantics.org) (publishes *ETC: A Review of General Semantics,* founded 1943, B 840.E851; and the *General Semantics Bulletin,* the yearbook of the Institute published since 1950.

♦ *Intercultural and international communication:* International Society for Intercultural Education Training and Research (www.sietarinternational.org) (publishes *International Journal of Intercultural Relations,* founded 1977, GN 496.I15); International Association for Intercultural Communication Studies (www.trinity.edu/org/ics) (publishes journal *Intercultural Communication Studies* twice a year, founded 1991); International Association for Languages and Intercultural Communication (www.ialic.arts.gla.ac.uk) (publishes *Journal for Language and Intercultural Communication,* founded 2001); Nordic Network for Intercultural Communication (www.ling.gu.se/projekt/nic) publishes *Journal of Intercultural Communication* (founded 1999); Japan Center for Intercultural Communications (home.jcic.or.jp/index-e.html) (founded 1953, sponsors conferences); Pacific and Asian Communication Association (www.ku.edu/npac2) (publishes journal, *Human Communication,* founded 1996); Prologos, Finnish Speech Communication Association (www.cc.jyu/prologos) (publishes *Prologos Newsletter*); World Communication Association (facstaff.uww.edu/wca) (publishes journal, *World Communication,* founded 1972, P 87A.C58).

♦ *Journalism and telecommunications:* Alpha Epsilon Rho and Sigma Delta Chi (websites located at www.nbs-aerho.org/aerho.shtml and spj.org/sdx_main.asp respectively) (honor societies); American Journalism Historians Association (www.berry.edu/ajha) (publishes *American Journalism,* founded 1983, PN 4700.A48); Newspaper Association of America, formerly the American Newspaper Publishers Association (www.naa.org) (publishes *PRESSTIME* magazine, *Fusio,* and *Labor & Employment Law Letter*); National Broadcasting Society (www.nbs-aerho.org) (publishes newsletter *Signals Online*); Society of Professional Journalists (spj.org) (publishes *Quill,* founded 1903, PN 4700.Q5); International Television Association (www.itva.org) (emphasis on visual communication from film to Web design); National Association of Broadcasters (nab.org).

♦ *Media use in education:* Association for Educational Communications and Technology (www.aect.org) (publishes *Educational Technology Research and Development,* founded 1953, LB 1028.35 E38; *Interpersonal Computing and Technology Journal,* founded 1993).

♦ *Public relations:* Public Relations Society of America (www.prsa.org) (publishes *Public Relations Journal,* HM 263.A1 P83, founded 1945); Center for Media & Democracy (www.prwatch.org) (publishes *PRWatch* and investigative reports on the public relations industry); Institute for Public Relations (www.instituteforpr.com)

(formerly, the Foundation for Public Relations Research and Education) (publishes *Public Relations Review,* HM 263.P767, founded 1975; and the *Public Relations Quarterly,* founded 1937, HM 263.P76).

♦ *Rhetorical studies:* American Society for the History of Rhetoric (www.ashr.org); Kenneth Burke Society (www.home.duq.edu/~thames/kennethburke/Default.htm) (publishes *Kenneth Burke Society Newsletter*); Rhetoric Society of America (www.rhetoricsociety.org) (publishes *Rhetoric Society Quarterly,* founded 1971, PN 171.4.R46); International Society for the History of Rhetoric (ishr.cua.edu) (publishes *Rhetorica*).

♦ *Speech and hearing science:* American Academy of Audiology (www.audiology.com) (publishes *Journal of the American Academy of Audiology,* founded 1990, RF 286.A92; and *Audiology Today,* founded 1989, RF 286.J68x); International Clinical Phonetics and Linguistics Association (www.ucs.louisiana.edu/%7Emjb0372/ICPLA.html) (publishes *Clinical Linguistics & Phonetics,* founded 1987, RC423.A1 C57; *Journal of Multilingual Communication Disorders,* founded 2003); International Phonetic Association (www.arts.gla.ac.uk/IPA/ipa.html) (holds annual International Congress; publishes the *Journal of the International Phonetic Association,* founded 1886, P 215.I6; and *foNETiks,* a monthly electronic newsletter [www.jiscmail.ac.uk/lists/fonetiks.html]); International Society of Phonetic Sciences (www.isphs.org) (publishes *The Phonetician,* newsletter, founded 1962).

♦ *Women and gender issues in communication:* The Organization for Research on Women and Communication (www.orwac.org) (publishes journal, *Women's Studies in Communication,* founded 1977, P 96.S48 W66); Association for Women in Communications (www.womcom.org) (founded 1909, previously Women in Communications Inc.; publishes newsletter, *The Matrix*); Organization for the Study of Communication, Language, and Gender (www.osclg.org) (publishes *Women & Language,* founded 1978).

♦ *Other applied communication areas:* Association of Communication Administrators (www.natcom.org/aca) (publishes *Journal of the Association for Communication Administration,* founded 1972); Commission on American Parliamentary Practice (faculty.ssu.edu/~capp) (publishes a newsletter, *CAPP News*); International Listening Association (www.listen.org) (publishes *International Journal of Listening,* founded 1987, and a newsletter, *Listening Post*); Lambda Pi Eta (national communication honor society) (www.natcom.org/nca/Template2.asp?bid=21); Religious Speech Communication Association (www.americanrhetoric.com/rca) (publishes *Journal of Communication and Religion,* founded 1977, BV 4319.R46).

Regional and Local Organizations

Every region and nearly every state has at least one organization representing the interests of that area and publishing at least one journal. Become familiar with the organization that is dominant in your area. It will greatly enhance your study of research methods. Your instructor can give you information about joining your regional organization. All these organizations have student membership rates and agreements with other regional associations to give complimentary copies of their publications to sustaining members of the other associations. These regional organizations often change the names of the journals they publish. Table 1.6 indicates the various name changes. Such information may be helpful when you start reading research and wonder why all those old copies of journals are missing (in reality, the journals simply changed names).

It is beyond the scope of this book to list all the state and local organizations in the field. Ask your instructor about them since many—such as the California Speech Communication Association, the Arizona Communication Association, the New York State Speech Communication Association, and the Tennessee Speech Communication Association—regularly publish research of more than local interest. Many schools and departments also publish their own outlets for scholarship. For

TABLE 1.6 REGIONAL RESEARCH JOURNAL NAMES

Regional Association	Original Title	Revised Title
Eastern Communication Association	*Today's Speech* (founded 1953) PN 4071.T6	*Communication Quarterly* PN 4071.T61
	Communication Research Reports (founded 1984) P 87.C65	
	Qualitative Research Reports in Communication (founded 1999) PN 4071.Q29	
Central States Communication Association	*Central States Speech Journal* (founded 1949) PN 4001.C4	*Communication Studies* PN 4001.C4
Southern States Communication Association	*Southern Speech Bulletin* (founded 1935) PN 4001.S68	*Southern Speech* PN 4071.S651
	Southern Speech	*Southern Speech Communication Journal* PN 4071.S651
	Southern Speech Communication Journal	*Southern Communication Journal* PN 4071.S651
Western States Communication Association	*Western Speech* (founded 1937) PN 4071.W45	*Western Speech Communication* PN 4071.W451
	Western Speech Communication	*Western Journal of Speech Communication* PN 4071.W4511
	Western Journal of Speech Communication	*Western States Communication Journal* PN 4071.W4511
	Communication Reports (founded 1988) PN 4700.C64	

example, the *Columbia Journalism Review* (PN 4700.C72) was established in 1962 by the Columbia University School of Journalism, the University of Iowa Center for Communication Study began publishing the *Journal of Communication Inquiry* (P 87.J62) in 1974, and Washburn University started the *Journal of Radio Studies* (PN 1991.3 U6 J65) in 1992. The trend toward numbers of school-sponsored publications seems to be growing, not diminishing.

Organizations Outside the United States

Interest in communication studies has been blossoming outside the United States. Furthermore, the growth has been worldwide. Thus, students of today must think internationally when they consider research questions. Such groups as the following represent the tip of the iceberg in a very exciting development in our field: the Association for Chinese Communication Studies (www.uni.edu/comstudy/ACCS/home.html) (which publishes the *ACCS Newsletter*); the Association for Rhetoric and Communication in Southern Africa (web.uct.ac.za/depts/rhetoricafrika), which hosts a biennial symposium and publishes a newsletter; the Canadian Communication Association (www.acc-cca.ca); the Center for Global Communications (Japan) (www.glocom.ac.jp/top/index.e.html); the Chinese Communication Association (bettercommunication.edu/cca.html); the Chinese Communication Society, based in Taiwan (ccs.nccu.edu.tw), which publishes the *Chinese Communication Society Magazine* yearly; the European Communication Association; International Speech Communication Association (formerly the European Speech Communication Association) (www.isca-speech.org/index.html) (publishes *Speech Communication,* founded 1961); Communication Association of Japan (www.japonet.com/caj/annually) (publishes *Human Communication Studies,* founded 1973, and *Speech Communication Education* [previously called *Speech Education*], founded 1972); European Institute for Communication and Culture (www.euricom.si); European Institute for the Media (www.eim.org) (founded 1983 in cooperation with the European Cultural Foundation in Amsterdam and subsequently moved to Düsseldorf); European Institute for Communication and Culture (www.euricom.si) (based in Slovenia; publishes *Javnost—The Public,* the Journal of the European Institute for Communication and Culture, founded 1994); Asian Media Information and Communication Centre (www.amic-web.org/index.php) (founded 1971 with support of the government of Singapore and the Friedrich Ebert Foundation from the Federal Republic of Germany; publishes *Asian Journal of Communication,* founded 1990, P92.A7 A74; *Media Asia,* founded 1974, P 92.A7 M43; and *Asian Mass Communication Bulletin,* founded 1971); Canadian Women in Communication (www.cwc-afc.com) (hosts conferences and publishes newsletter); the European Institute for Media Research Projects; the International Telecommunication Society (www.itsworld.org) (which publishes *Information Economics and Policy*); the Nordic Information Center for Mass Communication Research (www.nordicom.gu.se/eng.php?portal=about&main=) (which publishes the *Nordicom Review of Nordic Research on Media & Communication*).

   With the rise of the Internet, "electronic journals" (such as the *Electronic Journal of Communication* [www.cios.org/www/ejcmain.htm], *Effective Communication* [www.hodu.com], *Communications News* [www.comnews.com], and *Computer-Mediated*

Communication Magazine [www.december.com/cmc/mag/index.htm]) have emerged as very real research publication options. Newly formed organizations have been able to use this "information superhighway" to create new journals and promote their research interests. So, we should expect growth in the lists of research sources available to help us answer questions. Fortunately, because of the Internet, we should be able to get at such information sources rapidly and inexpensively.

SUMMARY

Research is the systematic effort to secure answers to questions. Research questions deal with issues requiring reference to data and information. Research regularly invites examining past inquiry into the issue. Basic research is completed to learn about relationships among variables, regardless of any immediate commercial product or service. Applied research is completed to develop a product or solve an immediately practical problem. Yet, regardless of whether pure or applied research is involved, the methods of inquiry are identical. In 1995, the special Conference on Defining the Field of Communication explained, "The field of communication focuses on how people use messages to generate meanings within and across various contexts, cultures, channels and media. The field promotes the effective and ethical practice of human communication." Thus, communication research is a specialty that studies message-related behavior. A message is the set of verbal and nonverbal cues communicators exchange. Verbal cues are the words people use in communication (as opposed to oral cues, which are spoken). Nonverbal cues are communication elements beyond the words themselves.

There are many challenges in communication studies. First, the challenge of breadth and focus involves the large number of communication applications. Second, the multiple methods challenge means that communication researchers use both qualitative and quantitative methods. As distinguished by a report of the National Science Foundation, qualitative research "involves in-depth, case-oriented study of a relatively small number of cases, including the single-case study. Qualitative research seeks detailed knowledge of specific cases, often with the goal of finding out 'how' things happen (or happened). Qualitative researchers' primary goal is to 'make the facts understandable,' and often place less emphasis on deriving inferences or predictions from cross-case patterns." Most qualitative research in our field tends to *describe or interpret* communication exchanges. Quantitative research methods are inquiries in which observations are expressed predominantly in numerical terms. Quantitative research tends to be *explanatory,* especially when experiments are involved, or it attempts to use precise statistical models to get comprehensive understandings of human communication (as in survey studies and polls of public opinion). These methods often try to explain communication behavior by looking at processes that allow researchers to *predict* future behavior, frequently using models of causal processes. Thus, quantitative research usually attempts to answer questions about *many* people.

Third, the scholarly rigor challenge means that research involves recognition of six key conditions: research is systematic (though unexpected results often emerge—the effect is called serendipity and refers to researchers' finding something of value while looking for something else); research is a sound argument (arguments in this context are claims advanced on the basis of reasoning from evidence); research is a reductive process; research is capable of replication; research is partial; research is data driven. Fourth, the personal challenge means that successful students of research tend to meet the need to think in an orderly way, write clearly, set aside personal prejudices in light of data, stay organized and follow instructions, and recognize reasons to study communication research methods (to learn to think rigorously and critically, to learn how to find answers to questions about communication, to acquire survival skills to help read and use the field's literature, and to learn how to sort through research for an answer). Fifth, the ethical challenge means that researchers must recognize the central role of ethics in communication research and they must abide by formal codes of conduct. Sixth, the structure of the field challenge involves recognizing that communication research is promoted by many organizations whose members often cross the barriers created by organizational frameworks at different schools.

TERMS FOR REVIEW

research

basic research

applied research

communication

message

verbal cues

nonverbal cues

qualitative research

historical-critical methods

qualitative observational studies

case studies and interpretive studies

idiographic

homothetic

ethnography and participant observation studies

ethnomethodology

discourse/conversational analysis

creative studies

quantitative research

survey methods

descriptive or observational surveys

content analysis

opinion surveys

experimental methods

serendipity

arguments

JUST FOR THE SAKE OF ARGUMENT: A REVIEW

Look at the following questions and prepare your own answers to them. Be careful. They are more complicated than they appear at first. Rather than try to come up with simple answers, ask yourself what sorts of issues and controversies are raised by them.

1. What are the differences between basic and applied research?

2. How is communication research distinct from studies in psychology, sociology, or English?

3. What is the difference between qualitative and quantitative research methods?

4. Why is it necessary to be both a clear thinker and a clear writer to be successful in research methods?

5. What prejudices have prevented research findings from being widely shared with people?

6. Can't research be viewed as "amoral"—neither good nor bad, but just a set of tools?

ACTIVITIES TO PROBE FURTHER

Go to the website and look for the Student Study Materials for Chapter 1.

1. Take the study quiz and print out your answers. (*Word of caution:* These questions are tricky and require some of your best thinking. Do not give a simple answer until you have thought out your response.)

2. Look at the COMFILE website at http://commfaculty.fullerton.edu/jreinard/ internet.htm. Identify the websites for the national and (as relevant) the regional organizations that guide work in your specialty, and contact them to find out the latest news and membership arrangements.

3. Find an electronic source in your field that you have never read and review it. Be prepared to share your reactions in a class discussion and perhaps on a study sheet or journal.

4. Look in popular newsmagazines and newspapers. Are there any stories that deal with the issues that could be the object of communication research? What does this information tell you about the practicality of communication research?

CHAPTER 2

Communication Research Problems and Hypotheses

The one real object of education is to leave a man in the condition of continually asking questions.

—Bishop Creighton

CHAPTER OUTLINE

BEFORE WE GET STARTED . . .

Students who study research methods for the first time tend to think that the hardest part of inquiry is carrying out a study. In fact, one of the hardest parts is finding the right question to ask and the right hypothesis to advance. Accordingly, this chapter will explain problem statements, hypotheses, and steps to guide you in developing them.

QUALITIES OF RESEARCH PROBLEMS

problem statements
1. set limits on relevant information

2. structure inquiry

Problems (also known as research problem questions) questions we expect to answer through research.

Selecting and wording purpose statements are vital parts of the research craft. Inexperienced researchers sometimes do not recognize how important problem statements are—until they have gotten in over their heads. There are two reasons problem statements must be identified before completing studies. First, they set limits on relevant information. They allow researchers to know what information to examine and what information to set aside.

Second, clear purposes structure inquiry. Problem statements invite certain methods and techniques. This fact is the basic reason that researchers must state the **problem** before launching a study. Consider, for instance:

♦ In a study of graduate students' perceptions of academic advisors, Wrench and Punyanunt (2004, p. 228) phrased the problem question as, "What is the relationship of an advisee's perception of her or his advisor's nonverbal immediacy, credibility, and communication competence with an advisee's perception of her or his cognitive learning?" Since this question involved describing a phenomenon for the purpose of predicting or explaining relationships among variables, the descriptive empirical method of research (a form of quantitative research) was invited.

♦ An inquiry into studying threatening conversations female employees may face was completed by Irizarry (2004, p. 15) seeking "to describe the nature of face-threatening interactions women professionals similarly experience when entering their respective fields of expertise." Since this problem involved describing a phenomenon for the purpose of describing and interpreting individual communication encounters, the qualitative approach known as the interpretive approach was invited.

♦ An investigation of antidrug persuasive messages by Harrington and her associates (2003, p. 22) proposed the question, "Does the cognition value of an anti-marijuana message influence an individual's attitude, behavioral intention, and behavior toward marijuana?" Since the problem asked about the effects of a variable in a setting where the chief variables were controlled by the researchers, the experimental quantitative method was invited.

♦ A study examining the usefulness of two methods of rhetorical visual analysis developed by Sonja Foss ("message formulation from images" and "evaluation of images") was advanced by Mullen and Fisher (2004, p. 185) to answer several problem questions, including "Does the elaborated method [combining Foss's two methods] explain the nature of the image better than the two techniques do separately?" Since the research question asked about ways to interpret and evaluate individual messages, the qualitative method known as rhetorical criticism (a form of historical-critical research) was invited.

Our research questions guide us to the methods that are relevant to a proper answer. Of course, problem statements may be revised—usually involving fine-tuning language or adding qualifiers—after some inquiry into the topic. Yet, a working problem statement should be constructed to get the process rolling.

Useful Problem Statements

It is important to pose problem statements that are possible to answer. Thus, there are two prerequisites for useful problem statements.

Problem Statements Must Be within the Researcher's Capabilities

Let's be honest about it: many questions you care about cannot be answered by you now—or ever. Some questions cannot be answered unless you have the money or special skills that may not yet be yours. You may want to learn if the disintegration of the former Soviet Union led to increases in the number of "underground press" publications in the independent states. But if you do not speak Russian, you probably cannot complete such a study. Furthermore, you may not have a way to get access to formal collections of underground publications. Fundamentally, you must choose problem statements that are "do-able" given your resources and abilities.

questions must be within the researcher's competence

Problem Statements Must Be Narrow but Not Trivial

Perhaps the biggest difficulty with problem statements is that some are either too broad to answer or so limited as to be insignificant. Students often are assigned the task of composing problem statements to investigate at a later time. Without thinking, some students propose such problems as the causes of stuttering, the rise of public relations as a profession, ways to increase communication among spouses, or the speaking habits of American preachers. Writing a term paper or research article on these matters is unrealistic. Conversely, a subject can be narrowed to the point where its answer is trivial. Newspaper headlines include accounts of studies that seem to ask trivial questions:

questions must be narrow but nontrivial

> "Study Finds Better Nursing Equals Better Care"—Reuters (May 30, 2002) [So, bad nursing means bad care? I'm confused.]
>
> "Very Heavy Pot Use Clouds Mental Function: Study"—Reuters Health (May 30, 2002) [We tried to study it a couple of years ago, but we forgot.]
>
> "Study: Most Wild Chimps Are Southpaws" *USA Today* (August 15, 2005) [It helps to know the direction they are hurling their feces.]

"Caffeine May Be Keeping Kids Awake at Night"—Reuters Health (*Pediatrics*, January 2003) [At least they're sleeping during classes.]

"To Psychopathic Murderers, Violence Is Not So Bad"—Reuters Health (May 28, 2003). [Let's not rush to any conclusions.]

Good research questions must avoid the extremes of triviality and excessive breadth.

Sometimes problem statements are so isolated that communication researchers forget that they are supposed to be studying communication. One student-scholar asked, "What is the relationship between sex of employees and rates of promotion?" Unfortunately, there is no communication variable here. As obvious as it might sound at first, it is important that communication research problem questions ask about message-related behavior.

Criteria for Sound Problem Statements

Proper phrasing of problems is required to make them useful. We will consider some criteria for worthwhile research problems.[1]

1. unambiguous statements, usually in question form

1. *Problem statements must be stated unambiguously, usually as questions.* These problem statements have been found in published research articles:

   ♦ Do student perceptions of communication with professors differ based on whether the student has a learning disability or physical disability? (Frymier & Wanzer, 2003, p. 178)

   ♦ Will attention, prominence, and valence emerge as major factors of the media salience of issues in *New York Times* news content during the 2000 presidential election? (Kiousis, 2004, p. 77)

   ♦ Do domestic product advertisements rely on traditional values more heavily than advertisements for imported products? (Zhang & Harwood, 2004, p. 160)

   Sometimes research problem questions are stated as "purpose statements" or study "objectives." For instance, such problems as these have been posed:

   ♦ The purpose of this study is to compare the role of two aspects of social interaction to the quality of marital relationships: the frequency of casual interaction between marital partners versus the quality of social interaction as exhibited by partners' reliance on universal rules of social interaction. (Kline & Stafford, 2004, p. 11)

   ♦ The primary purpose of the present study was to assess whether people who stutter believe that stuttering has a negative impact on employment

---

[1]Some scholars believe that quantitative and qualitative methods are selected by researchers because they like the philosophical assumptions that underlie them. Then, this reasoning goes, researchers select problem questions that are compatible with the methods. The position taken here, however, is that research questions should guide selection of methods, not the other way around. After a coherent problem question is advanced, the most appropriate method may be chosen. Nevertheless, *hypotheses* most often are differentiated by whether they guide qualitative or quantitative studies, and such a recognition will be accepted here.

SPECIAL DISCUSSION 2-1

WHERE DO WE DISCOVER RESEARCH QUESTIONS?

At first, finding solid research questions may sound like a very sterile process. But scholars select problem questions that they care about very deeply. They often have sources that you might check to develop your own research questions. Ronald Schutt lists four places to look for interesting research problem questions (2006):

"Your own experience" (p. 54). If you have gone through a romantic breakup that caused you pain, you might ask about the things that were said in the breakup that were most hurtful. Such research might even help you find ways to deal with this situation in the future.

"Research literature" (p. 54). Research articles often include suggestions for future research. Some of these ideas may stimulate your thinking to explore interesting research avenues.

"Social theory" (p. 55). The exploration and testing of fascinating theories, such as Berger's uncertainty reduction theory or Ting-Toomey's face-saving theory may stimulate a host of useful research questions.

"Pragmatic sources" (p. 55). Sometimes you may be hired to do research or you may volunteer to help a group explore its communication issues. In these cases, research questions may come out of a formal request for proposals or a practical problem of immediate interest.

---

opportunities and job performance. A secondary purpose, if findings indicate that people who stutter *do* perceive that stuttering impacts employability and job performance, was to assess whether factors such as age, gender, ethnicity, and stuttering severity significantly impact these beliefs. (Klein & Hood, 2004, p. 257)

Sometimes problems have "subproblems" that narrow the issues further. In some articles, the research problem is phrased as a purpose statement. In other research pieces, the problem statement is placed near the end of the literature review as a summary claim to be tested. A problem statement may or may not be followed by a question mark.

2. *Except for simple exploratory studies, problem statements must include at least two variables.* Researchers try to relate one **variable** to another. The term "variable" has a very special meaning in research. Variables have more than one value or level, unlike constants, which are restricted to only one value or level. This statement sounds as though it is restricted to quantitative studies, but it is not. The following question has clear variables in it: Has the use of threat appeals declined in American preaching from 1900 to 2005? To answer this question, we might survey manuscripts of preachers of each time period to identify the frequency of such appeals at each time frame. The use of threat appeals is a variable. It is capable of taking on two values: either preachers use them in sermons or they do not (100 percent or 0 percent use). Of course, the number of such threats is an obvious variable. The time frame, 1900 to 2005, is also a variable. The opposite

2. must include two variables

Variable a characteristic to which numbers may be assigned.

Constant a characteristic to which only one number may be assigned.

of a variable is a **constant.** Many research questions ask about relationships between some variables while holding others constant. Look at this problem statement: What is the relationship between communication apprehension and grades in public speaking among freshman college students? The class level of the college students is held constant, since it is restricted only to freshman college students. You might sometimes hear researchers talk about the need to have control in their studies. What they mean is that they want to take variables that can be nuisances and make them into constants. Some problem statements involve such low-level questions that only one variable is involved, such as:

- What proportion of daily newspapers do people read?
- Which medium of advertising is most popular among small businesses?
- How many women chair communication departments in America?

Though in the early stages of research such questions may be useful to characterize a process or field, they elicit rather low levels of information. Of course, researchers often combine such problem questions to include follow-up research questions that take standard form. For instance, Orbe and Groscurth (2004) posed these two problem questions about first-generation college (FGC) students:

RQ$_1$: What co-cultural communication orientations and practices do FGC students enact in their interactions with others?

RQ$_2$: What, if any, differences exist in how they communicate in and between different contexts (e.g., campus and home)? (p. 42)

The first problem question included only one variable (co-cultural communication orientations and practices), and the second research problem question included two variables (adding differences in context as a second variable).

3. problems must be testable

3. *Problem statements must be testable.* A testable problem must be capable of yielding more than one answer. Yet, sometimes researchers ask questions that can have only one answer. Look at these examples from the work of pupils and some established scholars:

Example	Deficiency
How can politicians sell themselves to the public?	The example asks about a logical possibility: what *can* politicians do? Future options are nearly endless, and there is no way to find an appeal that is *not possible* in the future.
Is there a pattern to the ways people watch television?	The example is answerable only by saying "yes." Anything forms a pattern, even if the regularity is random. The question answers itself by its own construction.
Do charismatic leaders increase group productivity?	This example cannot be answered because notions of "charismatic leaders" and "productivity" may be so broad that they cannot be pinned down. The problem is not in testable language.

4. *Problem statements must not advance personal value judgments.* Research can reveal whether computerized therapy reduces stuttering in children. But it cannot tell if computerized therapy *should* be used for stutterers. That choice requires moving beyond research and evaluating pragmatic choices. Research questions, therefore, may not substitute value judgments for appeals to facts, as in the following attempts: Is public speaking training *better* at reducing communication apprehension than counseling therapy? *Should* trials be videotaped? Is it a *bad* idea for newspapers to use unnamed sources for news reports?

4. problems make no personal value judgments

   In qualitative studies employing rhetorical criticism some research questions might seem to deal with value judgments, but a close look reveals that they are just as rigorous as any problem questions in so-called clearly "scientific" research. For instance, in Chapter 1 the following examples were used for rhetorical criticism topics in qualitative studies:

rhetorical criticism studies do not just make personal value judgments

- Evaluating use of argument by George W. Bush in his presidential debates

- Evaluating whether newspaper reports gave politically balanced accounts of U.S. entry into Iraq, in 2003

- Evaluating the ethical use of surgery in the treatment of speech-handicapped patients in the nineteenth century

Though these topics (and specific problem questions derived from them) clearly ask for assessments based on systems and standards, you will notice that they do not invite researchers to make personal recommendations. Each of these examples invites a study to apply a standard of assessment (such as tests of arguments listed in argumentation textbooks, isolation of positive and negative phrases identified in books on language, or standards of ethics [e.g., the categorical imperative, the golden mean, or situation ethics] clearly described in texts on the subject). In each case, the scholar takes the applicable standards, applies them to examples of communication, and asks what conclusions *must* be drawn, *regardless* of the critic's personal value judgments about the way things ought to be in the future. It makes no difference if the researcher likes the results of the assessment. Using the chosen standards, the researcher must accept the results obtained. As you can see, applying standards of assessment involves great attention to detail and places strong checks on interference from personal value judgments.

criticism applies standards to draw conclusions virtually regardless of the researcher's value judgments about the way things ought to be

5. *Problem statements must be clear grammatical statements.* In the fever of enthusiasm, some scholars may compose incomplete or ungrammatical problem statements that are inevitably unclear. By expressing problem statements with great clarity, it is possible to promote thoughtful research that gets the job done efficiently. Using nonstandard grammar can also cause misunderstandings. A student turned in this problem statement: "Does humor make a speech more persuasive?" In standard English one cannot say *more* without following it with a *than*. Anything less than this form is a sentence fragment. *More* than what? one might ask. More than nothing? More than it once was? More than messages using other types of appeals? Indeed, all comparative forms (such as higher, lower, less, and fewer) require *than* to complete the sentence. It is wise to use standard grammar if problem statements are to be capable of standing on their own and guiding research.

5. must be grammatical

SPECIAL DISCUSSION 2-2

A QUESTION OF ETHICS: PLANNING THE ETHICAL RESEARCH QUESTION

Conducting ethical communication research starts with a concern for problem questions and hypotheses that are meaningful. Not only is it wasteful to ask insignificant questions but, if human beings are involved in the research, asking unimportant questions raises an ethical difficulty. As far back as 1975, Paul D. Reynolds reviewed ethical research guidelines advanced by 24 professional organizations and found that four required that studies involving human participants should ask important intellectual questions to be ethical. Another two organizations required that involving human participants was not ethical when there was another way to resolve the intellectual question. The researcher has "three sets of responsibilities: to science—to do research that indeed extends knowledge or deepens understanding; to society—as in the case of determining how the results of research are used or publicized; to students, apprentices, or trainees—to contribute to their education in regard to ethical issues in the conduct of research" (p. 565). Hence, developing a meaningful research problem question has an important ethical dimension.

Even so, how do researchers develop research questions that meet these ethical requirements? Joan Sieber (2000) suggested that careful planning for the research to examine the implications of research questions and hypotheses should be undertaken.

> Research planning often begins with an inchoate but beneficent goal—to create useful knowledge about a specified topic via scientific means. The researcher then chooses tools for crafting a sound research approach. Flexibility and tolerance of ambiguity are important attributes at this stage of planning. The ethical problems inherent in a research plan—and possible solutions to those problems—may be obscure and subject to multiple interpretations. The realities of human nature and society often present the researcher with practical constraints and frustrating ambiguities. Researchers who are inflexibly wedded to a particular research design may be severely handicapped in designing a research plan that is scientifically and ethically sound. (p. 13)

Examining the implications of the research question for ethical challenges includes several elements, such as considering whether the research problem carries

- *potential negative risks for participants in the study*. In addition to physical risks in some studies, there may be psychological risks ("boredom, depression, altered self-concept, increased anxiety, or loss of confidence in others" [p. 15]), social risks (damage to or loss of relationships), economic risk ("loss of opportunity for a job interview or opportunity to earn money" [p. 15]), or legal risk ("being arrested or having one's data subpoenaed" [p. 15]).

- *the potential for disrespecting or harming persons*. Some research may "involve significant psychological costs to research participants, such as guilt, shame, fear, or embarrassment, to which the researcher may not be sensitive" (p. 16).

In contrast to these risks, potential benefits should be balanced when considering the ethical integrity of asking a research problem question, including

---

- *potential benefits for participants,* such as "referral to local services, providing relevant related information such as an annotated bibliography, money, food . . . " (p. 17).

- *potential benefits for communities,* such as clearly defining "problems to be solved, developing new methods and approaches to solving problems, creating an opportunity for favorable media attention, and discovering an opportunity to continue the research relationship" (p. 17).

- *potential benefits to research participants,* such as providing student participants some "insight into the research process, depending on the quality of the post-study debriefing that describes the research and explains how . . . research is conducted" (p. 17).

Another concern in examining problem questions involves checking to see that they do not propose unthinkable studies. For instance, one student proposed this research question to the author of this book: "What is the effect of child abuse on the individual's subsequent communication competence?" To complete such a study would require an unthinkable experiment involving making groups of children victims of child abuse. Such a research question would be unethical since it would invite repugnant choices by researchers.

Researchers also are responsible for the ethical dimensions of their hypotheses. Sieber explained that unethical conduct often occurs when researchers fail to consider alternative hypotheses.

An instructive example of scientists who failed to do this occurred during the 1920s. Distinguished scientists (psychologists and geneticists among them) speculated that Jewish, Russian, Italian, and Polish immigrants were mentally incompetent and would introduce a criminal element into American society. Intelligence tests administered in English to non-native speakers "proved" the theory about mental incompetence, and IQ tests to persons in prison "proved" that low-IQ persons were criminals (reports in Doris, 1982). Clearly, the investigators failed to consider the alternative hypothesis that it was skill in English as a second language rather than immigrant status that produced the correlational differences. (2000, p. 17)

Constructing Problem Statements

Once a meaningful problem issue has been found, composing a problem statement can be handled with relative ease. The following format can be used to construct worthwhile problem statements. The format involves filling in blanks in the following question:

> What is the relationship between ____ and ____ ?

format for phrasing problem questions

By substituting variables of interest, many research questions can be composed. Of course, this format is just a starting point since statements may require great modification to put them in their final form. Some problems involve more than two variables. Even so, all problems ask about relationships between variables, and useful problems may be found as clear formal statements. Pupils sometimes advance first drafts of problem statements that are sentence fragments (little more than topic titles). Yet, useful problems can be developed by thoughtful revisions as in these examples:

First Draft Example	Revised Example
(from a student of mass communication) "The image of girls in children's programming"	"What is the relationship between the frequency of girls as characters in children's programming and their portrayal in submissive or dominant roles?"
(from a student of interpersonal communication) "Self-disclosure and relationship development"	"What is the relationship between the amount of self-disclosure among romantic partners and their level of communication satisfaction?"
(from a student of speech and hearing science) "Aphasia and therapy"	"What is the relationship between the use of group or individual therapy for aphasic patients and their use of correct initiation and response to questions?"

problems should exclude interpretation of results

Sometimes problem statements are overwritten. Difficulties emerge when problem statements include motives or explanations of observations. This submission is an example of such an overwritten statement: "In an effort to avoid potential charges of sexual harassment, do male managers avoid socially oriented interpersonal communication episodes with female employees?" The introductory phrase is not a meaningful part of the problem statement, but a possible *interpretation* of results. Eventually the question became, "Do male managers in complex organizations report fewer socially oriented interpersonal communication episodes with female employees than with male employees?"

Now that we have noticed that problem statements play a vital role in research, it is obvious that each area in our field makes great use of them. Table 2.1 shows examples of the sorts of research questions we might probe. Both qualitative and quantitative research efforts require full problem statements to guide efforts. You might wish to look at the list of sample questions to see if any stimulate your interest or give you some ideas of directions you may wish to take on your own.

USING HYPOTHESES

Hypothesis "an expectation about events based on generalizations of the assumed relationship between variables" (Tuckman, 1999, p. 74).

Working hypothesis a tentative hypothesis assumed for the purposes of initiating research and subject to change as research progresses.

Whereas problem statements ask about relationships that might be found, **hypotheses** give direct declarative answers to the problem. Here is an analogy that might explain how research is completed (after Auer, 1959, pp. 72–73). Suppose you were a detective solving a murder mystery. Before you answered the question "Who killed Mr. Body?" with a formal hypothesis, you might explore several tentative **working hypotheses:** Colonel Mustard did it in the ballroom with the candlestick; Mrs. White did it with the revolver in the kitchen; Professor Plum did it with the rope in the library. Each working hypothesis could be tested against available information. Then you could eliminate each working hypothesis until one reasonable explanation emerged. You might finally

TABLE 2.1   EXAMPLES OF PROBLEM STATEMENTS IN COMMUNICATION RESEARCH

Qualitative Research	Quantitative Research
COMMUNICATION STUDIES	
In what ways have studies of the use of facial expressions changed from 1600 through 2005?	What is the relationship between the use of facial displays of interest and interpersonal attraction?
What methods of speech preparation were used in the Lincoln–Douglas debates?	What is the impact of heckling of a speaker on audience sympathy for the speaker?
What communication training areas were most prominent for the founders of the American Society for Training and Development?	Do managers who use responsive listening behaviors with subordinates report greater communication satisfaction than other managers?
SPEECH AND HEARING SCIENCE	
What were the major sources of influence on the development of the modern phonetic alphabet?	What is the relationship between the use of visualization therapy and traditional drills on reduction of stuttering in adults?
What events led to the founding of the American Speech-Language-Hearing Association's certification processes for educational institutions?	Do speech-handicapped schoolchildren report lower self-esteem than other children?
What trends in the role for speech therapists in the treatment of brain-injured patients have taken place from 1925 through 2005?	What is the relationship between timing of therapy for aphasic patients and their levels of phonological skill following therapy?
MASS COMMUNICATION	
What changes in public funding have contributed significantly to the rise of the educational use of television?	What is the relationship between the use of satellite television in developing nations and changes in literacy rates?
What major justifications have been used by the Federal Communications Commission to deny license renewals to radio and television stations?	What is the relationship between the amount of television watched by adults and the level of anxiety about personal safety?
What is the relationship between the establishment of ethics codes for public relations professionals and the rise of public relations as an academic discipline?	Do saturation advertising campaigns on television significantly increase product name recognition more than saturation campaigns using newspaper advertising?
SPECIAL APPLICATION AREAS	
What phases were important to the development of communication education in the western region of the United States from 1880 through 1940?	What is the relationship between the use of videotaped speeches in public speaking classes and perceptions of speaker delivery?
What was the role of oral interpretation of literature in the practice of elocution of Dr. James Rush?	What is the relationship between the size of oral interpretation programs in U.S. universities and the number of ethnic minority students involved in the activity?
What conditions in education led to the development and spread of tournament debating in America?	What is the relationship between the sex composition of debate teams and their win/loss records?

SPECIAL DISCUSSION 2-3

WHAT RESEARCH QUESTIONS ARE NOT

Though we may find some useful standards for research questions, it also is a good idea to know what are *not* useful research questions. These pseudo-research questions may trick us into spending our time on them when, in fact, they may not be worth our time.

1. Questions asking for obvious yes or no answers (after Leedy, 1989, p. 49). It is not worthwhile to ask, "Do communication classes affect the skills of students?" Any stimulus has some kind of effect—even if it is an insignificant one. The answer may be trivial, such as "Yes, the classes affect students very little."

2. Questions asking about applying a statistical tool (after Leedy, 1989, p. 48). These questions confuse the method of answering the question with the research questions themselves. Problem questions should ask for relationships, not statistical methods.

3. Questions proposing personal learning goals (after Leedy, 1989, pp. 47–48). In fact, personal references have no role in productive research questions. The following example is inappropriate: "The purpose of this study is to learn ways advertisers sell products." Purpose statements do not "learn" anything. The research question should get to the point and ask about relationships.

4. Questions that already have been competently studied (after Auer, 1959, p. 64). If the question already has been answered effectively, there is little reason to repeat the research.

5. Questions that cannot really be solved (after Auer, 1959, pp. 66–67). Whether because of the lack of resource materials or because the question deals with broad, philosophical issues that cannot be resolved, such questions are not suitable for research.

---

conclude that Mr. Green did it in the bedroom with the knife. This hypothesis could be used as a formal criminal charge against the defendant, Mr. Green.

hypotheses are more than "educated guesses"

You may have heard that a hypothesis is an "educated guess." Unfortunately, most people using that definition place emphasis on the word "guess" rather than the word "educated." In fact, a hypothesis takes a general expectation—perhaps from a fully developed theory—and predicts what would be expected in the research project's new application. Furthermore, a hypothesis must have some kind of rationale provided for it. There is a lot more education than guesswork in hypotheses.

hypotheses often are working tools of theory

Some experts claim that hypotheses are the working tools of theory. They recognize that theorists apply their theories by developing hypotheses based on them (Giere, 1979, pp. 69–70). Though many hypotheses are based directly on applications of formal theories, some are not. Sometimes informal thinking is used to develop initial hypotheses.[2]

---

[2]There is controversy regarding whether all hypotheses must be applications of theories. Schutt (2006) submits that a hypothesis "is a specific expectation deduced from the more general theory" (p. 71). Ray and Ravizza (1988) state that hypotheses are "developed in relation to an explicit or implicit theory" (p. 370). Similarly, the authors of the *Longman Dictionary of Psychology* (1984) believe that all hypotheses are "based on theory" (p. 361). Yet, others think that hypotheses sometimes come from very casual speculation (Mason & Bramble, 1989, p. 72). The second view seems most typical of the facts, and it is endorsed here.

Using Hypotheses to Test Explanations

Although a formal presentation of the role of logic in using hypotheses to test theories is beyond the scope of this book, a few basics can be shared. Hypotheses allow us to contrast one theory against another by reasoning with tools of formal logic. A theory is an explanation of how concepts or constructs are related to each other. A hypothesis relates the theory to specific observations of variables. So, if a hypothesis derived from a theory is rejected, then the theory from which it derives also is rejected. Technically, when using the logic of formal deductive reasoning, it does not work the other way around. We do not use hypotheses to "prove" that a theory is "true"—we use hypotheses to find out if the theory has or has not survived one additional test. So, when we say that research is sound and logical argument, we *do not* mean that researchers are in the business of *proving* their favorite theories. If you hear people say that they are trying to "prove" a theory, you know they got the concept a trifle confused.

hypotheses let researchers examine and disprove unsound theories

Reasoning from hypotheses often involves comparing different theoretic expectations and eliminating options. Arthur Stinchcombe (1968, p. 22) explained:

> The basic logical process of science is the elimination of alternative theories (both those we know and those we do not) by investigating as many of the empirical consequences of each theory as is practical, always trying for the greatest possible variety in the implications tested.

Since hypotheses allow us to eliminate alternative explanations, Stinchcombe suggested the desirability of pitting the predictions of one theory against another in "crucial experiments." Though there is some difficulty in doing so, the idea that we make progress by eliminating unacceptable theories by testing hypotheses remains central in our studies.

hypotheses used to eliminate alternative theories

A Note on Hypothesis in Qualitative Studies

Researchers in qualitative studies often omit hypotheses since, more often than not, at the beginning of their efforts, the researchers may not have enough past research and theorizing to permit making statements of what they expect to find. Yet, sometimes qualitative studies will produce a list of statements that resemble hypotheses. For instance, these hypothesis-like statements have appeared in critical and qualitative studies.

♦ In a historical study of the way that nuclear weapons production has been criticized, Kinsella (2004) wrote, "I argue that nuclear discourse and nuclear institutions reached an apex of hegemonic power during the Cold War era, and have faced a growing set of challenges since the mid-1980s" (p. 9).

♦ In an examination of discourse involved in narratives or stories used by people when making requests, Goldschmidt (2004) "hypothesized," "The present study seeks to determine if identity construction, in the form of favor narratives, functions to support the favor askers' interpretation of themselves (Bell, 2002) . . . as 'good people' while trying to gain favor compliance" (p. 29).

RESEARCHERS IN THE FIELD:
LINDA L. PUTNAM

Linda L. Putnam is among the field's most prominent scholars of organizational communication and conflict communication. She is the George T. and Gladys H. Abell Professor of Communication at Texas A&M University. She has edited or authored nine books, 48 articles and reviews, 50 book chapters, and 96 papers presented at professional meetings. She has won major awards for her research productivity from the National Communication Association and the International Communication Association, the latter group for which she also served as president. She received her Ph.D. from the University of Minnesota in speech communication with a minor in management and psychology, after which she served on the faculty at Purdue University. From 1996 to 2003 she served as the director of the Program on Conflict and Dispute Resolution for the Bush School of Government and Public Service, Institute for Science, Technology, and Public Policy at Texas A&M University.

♦ *Most students in our discipline started with other academic majors. What drew you into our field?*
I took several courses in communication [at Hardin-Simmons University in Texas]—oral interpretation and public speaking—and enjoyed them so very much that I decided to do a double major in speech communication and English. Both subjects entailed analyses of messages, meanings, and symbols, and both appealed to my love of ideas. Eventually, I gravitated into communication through my interest in what makes interactions with people work effectively. I was also drawn into the field through my interest in audiences and public communication issues.

♦ *Your work in organizational communication has been a significant influence in communication studies. What encouraged you to specialize in organizational communication?*
After I finished my M.A. work in rhetoric at the University of Wisconsin, I took an interest in interpersonal and small group communication. My work in these two areas led me to organizational communication, particularly studies of negotiation and conflict. My primary interest as a doctoral student was small group communication, and my Ph.D. dissertation was on this topic. However, I had a minor in management and industrial relations, and I took a number of classes in organizational communication. When I was hired at Purdue in 1977, they asked me to teach courses in both small group and organizational communication. My teaching in organizational communication led me to emphasize this area for my primary domain of research.

♦ *You've been honored for your research and conceptual writing. What kind of balance have you tried to strike between theoretic work and data-based work?*
I really enjoy thinking broadly about the concepts that I am investigating. My interest in theory was driven more by searching for alternative ways of thinking about phenomena rather than by a love of philosophical issues. Hence, I strike a balance in these two areas by moving back and forth between empirical research, syntheses of research studies, critiques of work, and conceptual development. The different types of work infuse each other. I have found that my

interest in concepts and theoretical perspectives sharpens my data-based studies and vice versa.

♦ *What personal qualities do you have that you think have contributed to your achievements as a communication scholar?*

The personal qualities that help me as a communication scholar are analytical thinking, curiosity about social situations, and puzzle-solving abilities. Since I was in college, I have enjoyed analyzing social problems, retrospective thinking about situations, and sensitivity to communication nuances. I really love training students to analyze their own interactions and reflect back on how to do them differently. I often use my own experiences as a template to think about communication issues and problems. I also like to address social problems and find ways of improving on them. I also think that being a scholar entails autonomy—working alone at times, writing and thinking independently, and enjoying the solitude of crafting ideas. Perseverance and independence, then, are also qualities that help productivity as a communication scholar.

♦ *What do you think is the most exciting future direction for the field's research?*

One of the most exciting directions our field is currently taking is to forge interdisciplinary lines and to pursue academic areas that address health, environmental, organizational, and public problems. Our field is now a major player with medical sociology in addressing health communication problems. In like manner, we are now viewed as a player in focusing on organizations and communities of practice. Our field's role in applying for and receiving major grants from national organizations and foundations is indicative of these new directions.

♦ *What part of your research undertakings have made you most proud?*

I am probably most proud of my early work on the interpretive approaches to organizational communication and the effect that this work has had on opening the field to cultural, critical, and feminist studies. I am also proud of the work that I have done on discourse and organizations and the way it has interfaced with management and organizational behavior scholars who are learning from communication scholars about our field.

♦ *What one or two lessons have you learned along the way that could help the beginning student have a successful career in the field's research?*

One of the first lessons is to have a passion for what you do. If a scholar is not internally driven and excited about research, then he or she will have trouble finishing the project. The passion drives the desire and the perseverance that is necessary to return time and time again to a project.

A second lesson is that a scholar needs to broaden his or her horizons with interdisciplinary work and bigger projects. The academic world is so overloaded with potentially relevant information for various studies that scholars are often tempted to draw very narrow boundaries around their expertise. Although this practice often makes a scholar comfortable with his or her specialty, it stifles creativity, growth, and academic development. One way to get new ideas, to push the envelope, and to think about bigger problems is to expand one's horizons and think about an area of expertise from alternative perspectives. For example, if you have always done interviews and participant observation research, it is valuable to think what a project would look like with surveys or experimental designs. If you always viewed organizational communication from the perspective of individual members, it is wise to think about it from a systems perspective. Often the merger of two disparate arenas or paradoxical ways of thinking is the source of creative energy.

♦ *What advice would you give students who might be interested in becoming communication researchers?*
The major advice would be to become well-rounded in various areas of communication and to take a wide array of courses that provide a broad foundation for the specialty area that interests you. It helps for scholars to think about what makes communication studies different as a discipline and what contributions we can make to knowledge in particular areas of our field.

♦ In a conversational analysis study examining what happens when communicators repeat words for emphasis, Stivers (2004) explored a working hypothesis that stated, "This study argues that multiple sayings are not simply upgrades of the single term. In fact, at times the interactional work being done by the repeating of the item may be at odds with the work being done by the single item" (p. 261).

In many qualitative studies working hypotheses are suggestions that might be used to probe the area of inquiry, but they are not the highly detailed hypotheses often found in quantitative studies. Such working hypotheses as "Lincoln relied on deductive arguments more than Douglas in the first debate of 1858" or simply "the U.S. President relied on evidence of doubtful veracity during speeches attempting to justify the U.S.-Iraq war" are examples of such statements. Sometimes scholars may announce these tentative probes when describing their explorations, but sometimes these working hypotheses are implied.

Requirements of Hypotheses

hypothesis requirements:

To have worthwhile research hypotheses, scholars must meet several obligations, including the following:

1. state relationship between variables

1. *Hypotheses must state relationships between variables.* Hypotheses make statements or predictions. They are not simple statements of definitions. It is not a hypothesis to state, "Intercultural communicators speak with different cultural influences." Similarly, the statement "Intercultural communicators speak differently" is not a hypothesis. "Speak differently" is not a variable. What does it mean? Speaking rapidly? Speaking with an accent? Speaking with great reserve? We do not know.

Sometimes hypotheses appear that really are just circular predictions about one variable. For instance, one student submitted this hypothesis: "Stutterers will exhibit greater disfluencies than nonstutterers." Though different words are used, the hypothesis actually had only one variable. Stutterers are identified because of their disfluencies. To predict that they have such disfluencies is circular—actually a definition. One hypothesis took the form "The more media literacy instruction students receive, the more instructional information students will report knowing about media literacy." In other words, the more information you hear, the more information you hear. Such matters really are what researchers call "manipulation checks," not substantive research hypotheses. It is questionable whether this hypothesis really has more than one meaningful variable. Such hypotheses do not advance our understanding very much.

2. *Hypotheses must be consistent with what is known in the literature.* Hypotheses often are derived directly from theories. Hence, hypotheses should be rooted in past knowledge. If past research has shown that the amount of television violence has been increasing, it would not be consistent to advance a hypothesis predicting that the amount of violence in prime-time television has been decreasing.

2. consistent with literature

3. *Hypotheses must be testable.* Though powerful, research methods are limited to observations that can be made in this life. Consider this "wannabe" hypothesis: "Public speaking instruction improves self-confidence better than oral interpretation instruction." This hypothesis asks the researcher to make a personal value judgment. One could advance a testable hypothesis by stating the issue this way: "Public speaking instruction increases self-confidence more than oral interpretation instruction." Research questions must deal with matters that can be resolved by examining information. Of course, hypotheses can deal with evaluations people make. Researchers frequently study attitudes and values. But in these cases, the hypotheses still are matters that can be tested by gathering specific information.

3. testable—hypotheses may deal with attitudes and values

4. *Hypotheses must be clear, grammatical, and unambiguous declarative sentences.* Since a hypothesis answers a research question, we expect it to be a crisp declarative statement. Declarative statements are sentences that make claims, rather than ask questions, give commands, or express wishes. Even so, you might be surprised at the number of beginning research students who compose hypotheses that are not full declarative sentences. Table 2.2 provides a sample of such hypotheses submitted to the author by students. In addition to the examples, you can see a brief statement of the flaw in the hypothesis. In some research fields, hypotheses are stated as descriptions, not predictions. Yet, in communication studies it is common to encounter hypotheses that are phrased as predictions. Though disproving a prediction with current data is complicated logically, this phrasing is common enough that communication students should not puzzle over the matter very much.

4. clear, grammatical, and unambiguous declarative sentences

Constructing Sound Hypotheses

After—and *only* after—you have asked a worthwhile problem question, you can begin to think about methods that might be most appropriate to help answer it. Indeed, by the time you construct hypotheses, it is a good idea to have a rough

TABLE 2.2   HYPOTHESIS PHRASING DIFFICULTIES

Submitted Hypotheses	Comment
Stuttering rate and age of onset.	This hypothesis is not even a sentence!
A journalism student earns more money after graduation than their peers.	This statement is an insult to grammar. "*A* journalism student" is predicted to differ from "*their* peers." Singular or plural pronouns are required for grammatical construction.
People who own computers have lower communication satisfaction with their wives.	The construction has two flaws. (1) Language is vague, though some specific meaning must be intended. "People who own computers" could be male or female, single or married. But this writer has assumed that people who own computers are husbands. (2) The sentence is a fragment. In English, one cannot use the word "lower" without the word "than" appearing in the sentence somewhere else. As stated, the sentence leaves us hanging. It states that computer owners have "lower communication satisfaction with their wives" than what? than whom? We do not know because the sentence is not complete.
Communication teachers who grade on the curve increase difficulties for students.	The hypothesis is ambiguous. "Difficulties" could mean almost anything. Specific observable difficulties must be identified instead of the current vagueness (by the way, this definition's assertion of causes and effects commits the researcher to complete an experiment—we can hope the researcher meant to do so).
Communicators in Latino families differ from communicators in Anglo families.	The ambiguity of this hypothesis makes it unacceptable and untestable. "Differ" is not a variable. Thus, this hypothesis does not have two variables put into relationship. Furthermore, the form of the difference is hopelessly vague.
Because women have been stereotyped, they are not credible television news broadcasters.	This double-barreled statement does not ask about a relationship, but asks us to *explain* a relationship when it is found to exist. One would not test the hypothesis by finding that women newscasters in the major television markets *are not* perceived as lowly credible sources. Neither would it test the hypothesis if women newscasters *were* perceived as lowly credible sources (only the reasons for such a relationship are asked).

format of hypotheses predicting differences

notion of the research methods you wish to use. Sometimes researchers will compare two or more groups to look for differences (as in typical experiments and some surveys). Sometimes researchers look for associations and simple relationships. Thus, since hypotheses are potential answers to research questions, they should be stated in words that are related to the methods that will be later employed.[3]

researchers should think ahead to study methods when phrasing hypotheses

Two formats can help you compose and develop worthy hypotheses. The first is used to predict that a difference will be observed between groups and has the following form:

---

[3]When writing research proposals many researchers find it helpful to pose a research question, outline a study method to answer the research question, and then return to complete their literature reviews and compose formal hypotheses. Of course, they often find they must revise their first thoughts in light of their reading, but that's no big deal.

> Subjects {or people or characteristics} who are
>> high in {or low in, characterized as, exposed to, etc.}
>>> (*insert favorite input variable of interest*)
> will have higher {or more, or greater, or less}
>> (*insert favorite output variable of interest*)
>>> than others {or others who are high in, or low in, or not characterized
>>> as, not exposed to, etc.}
>>>> (*insert favorite input variable of interest*).

This format is found in such hypotheses as the following:

> Subjects who are low in self-esteem will have more attitude change in re-
> sponse to a persuasive message than others who are high in self-esteem.

A second way to phrase hypotheses involves statements of simple relationships and has the following common pattern.

format for predicting simple relationships

> There will be a direct {or positive, or negative, or inverse, or curvilinear} relationship
>> between (*insert favorite first variable of interest*)
>>> and (*insert favorite second variable of interest*).

> or

> As (*insert favorite first variable of interest*)
>> increases {or decreases, etc.}
>>> the (*insert favorite second variable of interest*)
>>>> decreases {or increases, etc.}.

Such a hypothesis could be phrased as follows:

> As the amount of eye contact used by speakers increases, the credibility ratings of
> the speakers increase.

One also could phrase this statement in a slightly different form:

> There will be a direct relationship between the amount of eye contact used by
> speakers and their credibility ratings.

Though you probably will need to revise your final wording somewhat, these patterns are simple ways for you to begin constructing your own hypotheses.

Types of Hypotheses in Quantitative Studies

In quantitative research, we often subdivide hypotheses into two forms: material hypotheses and null hypotheses. Sometimes called the *research hypothesis* or just *the hypothesis,* the material hypothesis states what the researcher predicts will be found by gathering data. There are two forms of research hypotheses to consider.

distinguishing material hypotheses

Nondirectional material hypotheses hypotheses that state simply that there will be some kind of relationship between variables (sometimes called "two-tailed" hypotheses because of the way statistics are used to test them).

Nondirectional material hypotheses express the presence of a relationship without identifying the shape or trend of that relationship. Because the statistical tools that often are used to examine such hypotheses permit using two sides of their distributions, these tests sometimes are called "two-tailed" hypotheses. Suppose, for example, that we wished to compare the amount of television watched by children from Protestant and Catholic homes. A nondirectional hypothesis would predict the existence of a difference, but would not specify *which* children were above the average of television viewing. This nondirectional hypothesis can be abbreviated by using the Greek letter mu (μ) to represent the population average of each group. We could use μ_1 to represent the average amount of TV viewing by children in Protestant homes and μ_2 for the average TV viewing by children in Catholic homes. The nondirectional research hypothesis would appear as

$$H_1: \mu_1 \neq \mu_2$$

Directional material hypotheses hypotheses that state the form of predicted differences.

Directional material hypotheses are the working tools of quantitative researchers since they speculate about the shape or trend of relationships. Suppose a researcher suspected that Protestant children watched more television than Catholic children. The directional hypothesis would appear as

$$H_1: \mu_1 > \mu_2$$

The symbol > means "greater than" and the symbol < means "less than."[4] This hypothesis predicts the direction of the differences.

Null hypotheses statistical hypotheses that state that there is no relationship between variables.

As the name suggests—null, nil, *nada*—**null hypotheses** state that, just for the sake of argument, there is no relationship between variables. Using the same abbreviations as previously employed, the null hypothesis would be represented as

$$H_0: \mu_1 = \mu_2$$

When dealing with directional hypotheses, researchers often expand the null hypothesis to include all results that would oppose the material hypothesis. Thus, if the research hypothesis is $H_1: \mu_1 > \mu_2$, the null hypothesis might be expanded to state $H_1: \mu_1 \leq \mu_2$.

null hypotheses used as a statistical hypothesis

What good is such a hypothesis for researchers? Null hypotheses are used in quantitative research as statistical hypotheses. Researchers try to find data that reject null hypotheses. In a nutshell, here is the logic behind it. Testing our material hypothesis requires that we present a case for it. But any data we find could be dismissed by our opponents as atypical. They may say, "You haven't found a *relationship* with your samples; in fact, if you kept sampling, you could find that there are no differences at all." So, we reason the other way around. We pretend—just for the sake of argument—that the null hypothesis is true. Then we ask if data we have gathered are so inconsistent with the world of the null hypothesis that it is improbable that the data could be found if the null hypothesis were true. Thus, researchers support research hypotheses by rejecting the opposing null hypotheses as improbable.

one argues for material hypotheses by rejecting null hypotheses

---

[4]In English grammar, of course, one can say "less than" only when the things identified *cannot* be counted. If things can be put in numerical terms, one grammatically is required to say "fewer than." Thus, the signs at the supermarket *should* say "Use the Express Lane if you have 10 or *fewer* items"—but they rarely do. Yet, we still say "less than" when translating the term <, recognizing that it is not English.

So, by a process of elimination we can conclude that the research hypothesis is tenable. This language may seem a bit strange because of all the negative words we have to use. But the situation is much like the presumption of innocence we have in our court system (Erickson & Nosanchuck, 1977, pp. 145–49). We start with a null hypothesis that the defendant is not guilty. Then the prosecution tries to show that facts make it unlikely that the defendant has acted like someone who is not guilty. People are not found innocent—there is no way to get positive evidence to show that evil acts have not occurred. Instead, a defendant is found either "guilty" or "not guilty" of the specific charges. As you can see, we use null hypotheses all the time. Technically, we are not allowed to say that a null hypothesis is "accepted." You can think it, but don't say it or write it. We cannot logically accept a statement without evidence, but the null hypothesis claims that there is no evidence of anything to begin with. So, if we do not reject the null hypothesis, we can only say that we "failed to reject the null hypothesis." Similarly, we never can claim to "prove" or "confirm" a research hypothesis. A future study might destroy our research hypothesis. The strongest statements we are allowed to make are that research hypotheses are "supported" or "found tenable." The hypothesis actually only survived one more test—so these claims are fairly strong ones to make. If you read an article where the researcher oversteps these bounds, you know that the article has at least one flaw and may contain other mistakes as well.

null hypothesis like the presumption of innocence in criminal trials

cannot "accept" a null, but can "fail to reject"

IDENTIFYING VARIABLES IN HYPOTHESES AND PROBLEMS

Hypotheses put variables into relationship with each other. They identify the roles of variables and their functions in research. Identifying the forms of variables is most often found in quantitative research where hypotheses are most likely to appear, but sometimes (though rarely) the distinction is even discussed in studies employing other methods.

Isolating Variables in Hypotheses

When looking at hypotheses, it is important to identify the chief variables involved. Yet, students sometimes confuse the number of *variables* in the hypothesis with the *levels* of a variable. For instance, how many variables are there in this hypothesis?

distinguishing variables from levels of variables

H_1: People with high self-esteem read newspapers more often than people with low self-esteem.

If you think that there are two variables, self-esteem and amount of newspaper reading, you are correct. Some look at this example and see three variables: high self-esteem, low self-esteem, and amount of newspaper reading. But high and low self-esteem are merely *levels* or degrees of the same variable, self-esteem. It is important not to confuse levels of a variable with a completely new variable. How many variables are in this hypothesis?

H_1: Women are persuasive sources.

distinguishing variables from constants

Assuming that persuasiveness is measured on a standard attitude scale, there is no second variable in the hypothesis. Sampling only women holds *constant* the potential variable of sex. We suspect that the author really wanted to know if women and men differed in their persuasiveness. But the author did not say so. It is as important to spot the difference between a constant (a control) and a true variable in a hypothesis as it is to resist confusing levels of variables for variables themselves.

Hypotheses use variables to make predictions. Some variables are used to start predictions and others are predicted effects. Examining hypotheses lets us identify the role of variables. There are two major variable types, independent and dependent.

Independent Variables

Independent variables
variables that predict outcomes (dependent variables) posited in hypotheses.

Independent variables predict influences on other variables. These variables are easy to remember. The *in*dependent variables are the same as *in*put variables. These independent variables are starting points for making predictions.

Sometimes researchers refer to **moderator variables** that shape the independent variable's influences on other variables. In reality, moderator variables are just additional independent variables that help predict the effects of chief independent variables. For instance, look at the following hypothesis:

Moderator variables
variables that mediate the independent variable's prediction of the dependent variable.

H_1: Female communication students who study research methods pursue graduate studies more than male communication students who study research methods and female communication students who do not study research methods.

The independent variable in this study is whether one takes research methods courses. A moderator variable has been added: student sex. Moderator variables permit subtle relationships to be explored.

Dependent Variables

Dependent variables
variables whose values or activities are presumed to be conditioned on the independent variable in the hypothesis.

A **dependent variable** is the consequent, the *predicted* variable, and/or the *output* variable of a hypothesis. If the hypothesis is tenable, changes will be seen in the dependent variable. Thus, in our research hypothesis, the dependent variable is the degree to which students pursue graduate studies.

It is important to identify independent (input) and dependent (output) variables by looking at a hypothesis. Yet, many students may have some initial difficulty with this skill. It may be useful to have some examples to work with as we develop our skills. Table 2.3 shows some hypotheses along with identification of independent and dependent variables. You should cover the right side of the table to see if you can identify the independent and dependent variables accurately. After time you will find it easy to identify these two forms of variables.

TABLE 2.3 HYPOTHESES AND VARIABLE IDENTIFICATION	
Hypothesis	**Variable Identification**
H: Anglo speakers will stand a further distance away from receivers than will Asian speakers.	*independent variable:* national background of speaker *dependent variable:* distance from receivers
H: Stuttering children will report higher levels of anxiety than nonstuttering children.	*independent variable:* stuttering level of children *dependent variable:* anxiety
H: The voting behavior of lowly educated people exposed to negative political campaign advertisements will be affected more than will the voting behavior of highly educated people exposed to positive political campaign advertisements.	*independent variables:* (1) type of political campaign advertisement and (2) level of voter intelligence (NOTE: depending on the rationale, level of voting behavior could be identified as a moderator variable) *dependent variable:* voting behavior
H: Regardless of level of ego-involvement, newspaper readers with sophisticated listening skills will have greater critical thinking ability than newspaper readers with unsophisticated listening skills.	*independent variables:* sophistication and level of listening skills *dependent variable:* critical thinking ability (ego-involvement is a constant, not a variable)
H: National politicians will use more metaphorical language and more examples of ambiguity than will local politicians.	*independent variable:* type of politician (national or local) *dependent variables:* amount of metaphorical language and number of examples of ambiguity
H: Students who are high in communication apprehension will show greatest improvement in communication competence when presented with teachers using nondirective styles in comparison with highly communication apprehensive students exposed to teachers using directive styles.	*independent variable:* type of style used by teachers *dependent variable:* communication competence (high communication apprehension is a constant, not a variable)
H: Computer-literate people will initiate fewer conversations than will computer-illiterate people.	*independent variable:* level of computer literacy *dependent variable:* amount of initiation of conversations

SUMMARY

Problems we investigate are the questions for which we expect to find answers through research. There are two reasons that problem statements must be specified in advance of completing studies. First, problem statements set limits on relevant information. Second, clear purposes structure inquiry. Research questions invite certain methods and techniques. Useful problem statements must satisfy two prerequisites: (1) research questions must be within the researcher's capabilities; (2) research questions must be narrow but not trivial. Criteria for phrasing worthwhile research problems include five requirements: First, problem statements must be stated unambiguously, usually as questions. Second, except for simple exploratory studies, problem statements must include at least two variables. A variable is a characteristic to which numbers may be assigned. The opposite of a variable is a "constant." A constant is a characteristic to which only one number may be assigned. To control variables, researchers take variables that can be nuisances and make constants out of them. Third, problem statements must be testable. Fourth, problem statements must not advance value judgments. Fifth, problem statements must be clear grammatical statements.

A hypothesis is "an expectation about events based on generalizations of the assumed relationship between variables." Though sometimes called an "educated guess," a hypothesis takes a general expectation—perhaps from a fully developed theory—and predicts what would be expected in the research project's new application. Furthermore, a hypothesis must have a rationale provided for it. Hypotheses are the working tools of theory. Hypotheses allow us to contrast one theory against another by reasoning with tools of formal logic. Researchers test hypotheses by gathering data to see if valid forms of logical reasoning are supported. Hypotheses may compare different theoretic expectations to eliminate options. Pitting one theory's prediction against another is called conducting "crucial experiments." Researchers in qualitative studies usually omit hypotheses since the questions they ask usually are in areas where there is inadequate past research and theorizing to permit them to make specific statements of what they expect to find, even if their research efforts were designed to discover bases for predictions. Yet, sometimes qualitative studies make hypothesis-like statements or use working hypotheses, which are general suggestions that might be used to probe the area of inquiry.

Worthwhile research hypotheses must (1) state relationships between variables, (2) be consistent with what is known in the literature, (3) be testable, and (4) be clear, grammatical, and unambiguous, usually in the form of a declarative sentence. There are two generic ways to phrase hypotheses. The first predicts that a difference will be observed. A second way to phrase hypotheses involves statements of simple relationships. In quantitative research, we often subdivide hypotheses into two forms. First, the material hypothesis states what the researcher wishes to support by gathering data. There are two forms of research hypotheses to consider: (1) Nondirectional material hypotheses simply state that there will be *some kind* of relationship between variables (they sometimes are called "two-tailed" hypotheses because of the way statistics are used to test them); (2) directional material hypotheses state the form of the differences. Second, the null hypothesis states that there is no relationship between variables. The null hypothesis is used in quantitative research as a statistical hypothesis and actually is the hypothesis that a researcher tries to get data to reject. Quantitative researchers start with assuming the truth of the null hypothesis (just for the sake of argument) and then ask if data that have been gathered are inconsistent with the world of the null hypothesis. If it is improbable that our data could be found if the null hypothesis were true, we conclude that it is unreasonable to continue presuming that the null hypothesis is true.

Hypotheses put variables into relationship with each other and identify their roles and functions in research. There are two major forms of variables. Independent variables are variables that predict the outcome (dependent variable) posited in the hypothesis. Moderator variables mediate the independent variable's prediction of the dependent variable. Dependent variables are variables whose values or activities are presumed to be conditioned upon (variables that are consequent to) the independent variable in the hypothesis.

TERMS FOR REVIEW

problems	**hypothesis**
variable	**working hypothesis**
constant	**nondirectional material hypotheses**

directional material hypotheses   **moderator variables**

null hypotheses   **dependent variables**

independent variables

JUST FOR THE SAKE OF ARGUMENT: A REVIEW

Look at the following questions and prepare your own answers. Make sure you understand the issues and controversies that are found beneath them.

1. What requirements should be satisfied by all useful problem statements? What are the differences between criteria for useful problem questions and criteria for constructing problem questions? What kinds of decisions would these concerns raise for you as a researcher?

2. What is the difference between a variable and a constant? Why is this distinction important to researchers?

3. In what ways is a hypothesis an educated guess? In what ways do people misinterpret this term?

4. Are most research advances made by getting results to show that a hypothesis is true, or by getting results to show that a hypothesis is false? What kinds of justifiable claims can be made if a researcher finds that data support a hypothesis?

5. What is the difference between moderator and independent variables? What impact do they have on the wording of hypotheses and the interpretation of results?

6. Why do we have to use null hypotheses in research?

7. Some research articles do not include either hypotheses or problem statements. Does this fact give you clues about the quality of the work? When might problem questions be unnecessary to guide research?

ACTIVITIES TO PROBE FURTHER

1. Go to the indicated website and look for the Student Study Materials for Chapter 2.
   a. Take the study quiz and print out your answers. (Remember, do not give an answer until you have thought out your response.)
   b. For this chapter look in the section on communication research. Look at the list of variables for STUDY 1. Compose three problem questions that you could study if you were examining this research area.
   c. If you were to identify a hypothesis that might answer one research question in step (b), how would you state it?
   d. Look at the hypothesis that you have identified in step (c). Is it directional or nondirectional? Does this fact tell you anything about the level of sophistication in this application area?

2. Review some letters to the editor of the local newspaper. What implications for communication problems are suggested by such letters? Compose one communication research problem question for each letter you select for examination.

3. Find a research article in your field of interest. Read the last six or so paragraphs. What suggestions for future research did you find? After you have listed them, identify a hypothesis that you would find to be a suitable response.

PART 2

Understanding Rudiments of Research Reasoning

Conceptualizations in Communication Research

There is nothing so practical as a good theory.

—Kurt Lewin

CHAPTER OUTLINE

BEFORE WE GET STARTED . . .

Research is guided by the conceptualizations scholars use. Theories play a central role in scholarship and give us ways to organize bodies of knowledge. Indeed, a purpose of research is to develop theoretic explanations for things. Yet, using concepts requires defining them so that they can be studied. Thus, this chapter explains what theories are, the forms of coherent definitions, and standards you can use to evaluate them.

DEVELOPING THEORETIC CONCEPTUALIZATIONS IN COMMUNICATION

importance of theory

Research attempts to find relationships and explain them. Theories are used to help us understand these relationships. Whether we are aware of it or not, most significant claims we make rely on theory-oriented statements. Moreover, formal and informal theories are sources of research hypotheses. In fact, theory construction is a purpose of all research, scholarship, and science. Some have made this goal central to research. Look at these typical statements about theory in research:

- The purpose of basic communication research is to increase our knowledge about communication phenomena by testing, refining, and elaborating theory. (Frey, Botan, & Kreps, 2000, p. 32)
- The basic aim of science is theory. (Kerlinger, 1986, p. 8)
- We found the fundamental aim of science to be the development of explanatory conceptualizations, called *theories.* (Mason & Bramble, 1989, p. 29)
- A researcher's aim . . . is *to generate theoretical explanations for observed patterns of human communication.* (M. J. Smith, 1988, p. 10)
- We do science to determine how theories should be modified to better describe and explain the process under investigation. (Hayes, 2005, p. 4)

In general, research is a means to an end, not an end in itself. A major goal of research is to develop theory and explanations. Thus, we should consider whether communication is scientific enough to have true theories, the anatomy of theories, and the roles communication theories have for us.

Is Communication "Scientific" Enough to Have Theories?

To decide whether communication can be approached as a science (or social science), it makes sense to define "science" and remove some myths about it. Then we can ask if communication is a science (though you may have a good idea about the position taken here).

Prerequisites for Science

Defining science once was a relatively uncontroversial matter. Yet, in the United States in recent years renewed challenges to teaching evolution in the public schools have sparked disagreement about the meaning of science and what should "count" as a science. The word "science" comes from the Latin word *scientia,* which means "knowledge." Thus, science is some systematic way to obtain knowledge or "know" things. Table 3.1 shows some of the ways "science" has been defined by various state governments in the United States.

meanings of science:

There are three prominent ways in which science is identified.[1] First, some explain that science is as much an attitude as anything else. As far back as 1954 Stuart Chase described science as "a label for our attempts to find out how the universe works by the means of careful observations rather than armchair speculation" (p. 110). In fact, rather

1. science as an attitude

---

[1]This discussion will not consider another option frequently heard by laypeople in which "theory" is considered to be some impractical idea or something that is not factually sound. The expression that someone's opinion is "just a theory" has no particular value in research circles. Contrariwise, to say that gravity is "just a theory" justifiably strikes most people as a little silly. This discussion is an attempt to develop useful definitions, rather than to present a list of common and frequently unhelpful usage.

TABLE 3.1   SOME OFFICIAL DEFINITIONS OF SCIENCE

Not content to rely on scholars, many states in the United States have adopted working definitions of science to guide their instructional priorities and identify what topics may be required in science classes. In addition to those already listed, the following is a list of some choices made by different states.

♦ "Science is both a body of knowledge and a set of processes for advancing that knowledge. More specifically, science is mankind's interconnected, internally consistent, growing body of knowledge about natural and man-made objects and phenomena of the past, present, and future; a body of knowledge that is based on repeatable experimentation with, or observation of, these natural and man-made objects and phenomena, that is organized and extended using logic and mathematics, and that is validated by the testing of hypotheses" (New Mexico Public Education Department, 2005, ¶ 10).

♦ "Science is not merely a collection of facts and theories but a process, a way of thinking about and investigating the world in which we live. This standard addresses those skills that are used by scientists as they discover and explain the physical universe—skills that are an essential and ongoing part of learning science" (New Jersey Department of Education, 2004, p. E5).

♦ "Science is an inquiry process used to investigate natural phenomena, resulting in the formation of theories verified by direct observations. These theories are challengeable and changeable. Data used to support or contradict them must be reproducible. Although science as a body of knowledge is ever changing, the processes of science are constant. In scientific inquiry, a problem is identified, pertinent data is [*sic.*] gathered, hypothesis is formulated, experiments are performed, the results are interpreted, and conclusions are drawn" (Montana Office of Public Instruction, 2002, p. 1).

♦ "Science is a way of thinking and a system of knowledge that uses reason, observation, experimentation, and imagination. The goal of science is to describe, explain, and predict natural phenomena and processes. Science shares some characteristics with other forms of scholarly inquiry, but it is unique in several important ways. Science attempts to meet the criteria of testability, objectivity, and consistency. Scientific information is continuously open to review and modification; science is not a static body of knowledge" (Louisiana Department of Education, 1997, p. 11).

♦ "Science is a way of knowing about the world that is characterized by empirical criteria, logical argument and skeptical review" (Minnesota Academic Standards Committee, Minnesota Department of Education, p. 8).

"To be valid, scientific knowledge must meet certain criteria including that it: be consistent with experimental, observational and inferential evidence about nature; follow rules of logic and reporting both methods and procedures; and, be falsifiable and open to criticism" (Minnesota Academic Standards Committee, Minnesota Department of Education, 2003, p. 16).

or any inquiry practicing sound thinking and reasoning

than describing aspects of science, the Illinois State Board of Education explained, "Science is a creative endeavor of the human mind. It offers a special perspective of the natural world in terms of understanding and interaction" (2005, p. 2). This approach explains that science is, in essence, the practice of sound thinking. Though this view has some appeal, it includes many matters that are not sciences, provided they involve sound thinking about the natural world. Such studies as logic or even music could fit this definition.

A second way to identify science is to claim that it is a body of knowledge organized around the fields of the natural (and sometimes the social) sciences. Though not ultimately accepting this view as the sole definition, the 2061 Project of the American Academy for the Advancement of Science explained,

2. knowledge organized around science departments

> Organizationally, science can be thought of as the collection of all of the different scientific fields, or content disciplines. From anthropology through zoology, there are dozens of such disciplines. They differ from one another in many ways, including history, phenomena studied, techniques and language used, and kinds of outcomes desired. With respect to purpose and philosophy, however, all are equally scientific and together make up the same scientific endeavor. (Rutherford & Ahlgren, 1994, p. 10)

This view holds that science is what people in science departments do. In a commentary rejecting this sort of distinction, Horace and Ava English in their classic *Comprehensive Dictionary of Psychological and Psychoanalytical Terms* (1958) argued:

> This usage, while common, arbitrarily excludes most investigations and systematizations of knowledge in the psychological and social disciplines. Such a division is not warranted either by historical development or by the contemporary state of affairs, and it gives to science in English a narrower connotation than that of related expression in other European languages. (pp. 479–480)

It would seem that science—though often considered a body of knowledge—cannot really be understood as a collection of organizational units under the title natural and social sciences.

A third view is that science is a body of knowledge that is distinctive because of the methods used to answer research questions. It is the use of the scientific method that makes something a science. The North Dakota Department of Public Instruction (2002) noted clearly that science is "(1) a process which attempts to understand the order in nature and which uses that knowledge to make predictions about what might happen in nature; (2) knowledge resulting from scientific investigations" (p. 59). This definition tells us that a field becomes a science when it uses the scientific method. After time, as well, each field concentrates on some key concepts of its own to study. In our field, we have focused on such concepts as communication apprehension, speech and hearing disorders, and broadcast of messages through television and radio. Using the scientific method makes a field a science even before a great deal of information exists on it. For instance, we could ask when chemistry became a science instead of a magician's bag of illusions. Chemistry certainly is a science now. Yet, how many chemistry studies had to be completed before we recognized chemistry as a science worthy of the name? The question sounds a bit silly. The reason is that chemistry—as with all fields that qualify as sciences—became a **science** when the scientific method was used in research. The method to gather information defines a field as a science, not simply the results of applying the method.

3. science is inquiry that applies the scientific method

Science a way of testing statements by systematic application of the scientific method[2]

---

[2]This statement is not a circular definition. The term "scientific method" has been defined here by the distinctive steps of the approach. There has been no reference back to science in the definition of scientific method. It also should be noticed that the definition does not use the term defined since the term "scientific method" is a single term that cannot be broken down into smaller units of "scientific" and "method" without also dissolving the meaning it has been given here.

SPECIAL DISCUSSION 3-1

A LITTLE EPISTEMOLOGY: MAKING KNOWLEDGE CLAIMS IN RESEARCH

Scholarship and research are not the only ways to answer questions and draw conclusions. In fact, sometimes reasonable actions are based on nonresearch methods. The most well known nonscholarly methods include (after Peirce, 1955, especially chapter 2):

♦ The method of *tenacity,* in which we claim to know something because we have always known it (the method of tenacity may be correct most of the time, but it is misguided when facts change and decisions need to be revised).

♦ The method of *authority,* in which a claim is accepted because authority figures have accepted it (though this method leads people to correct conclusions most of the time, under some conditions, it may be flawed).

♦ The *a priori* (Latin for "from the earlier part") *method,* which claims knowledge before having any experience with it (thus, we believe *a priori* that "all men are created equal" without needing to gather data on the matter: this method usually leads to timeless conclusions that are beyond research).

♦ The method of *trial and error,* which claims knowledge by making repeated trials to eliminate unacceptable answers (eventually, persistent failures disprove so many alternatives that an answer will emerge—though trial and error provides very sure knowledge, "learning through experience" is a very slow and inefficient way to develop claims about things we know).

Research, on the other hand, makes claims by using the tools of scholarship and science, which involve two processes: making observations of things and using the tools of reasoning to evaluate different explanations of observations. Using the scientific approach to guide development of claims involves application of the scientific method. Though the scientific method has been described by different scholars as including various numbers of steps, at minimum, the scientific method involves collecting data and establishing "a functional relationship among these data" (Bachrach, 1981, p. 4). Some others list as many as seven steps (Jones, 1973). The steps are not necessarily followed in order. In fact, most researchers find that they cycle back from one step to another. In practice:

> Few scientists actually follow the orderly steps of what is known as the "scientific method." Instead, they may omit, move, or augment one or more of these steps. Scientists' explanations about what happens in the world come partly from what they observe and partly from what they infer; sometimes scientists have different explanations for the same set of observations. Scientists also use their imaginations to consider possible causes or outcomes: A number of scientific discoveries have been based on a scientist's idea, which was then tested for validity. (Louisiana Department of Education, 1997, p. 11)

The important thing is that the scientific method forces scholars to stay close to the facts of a matter. We will suggest four steps to the scientific method:[*]

1. Observing facts either casually or formally leading to developing a fundamental research question;

2. Developing a working hypothesis or theoretical solution to guide the research (though researchers may revise their ideas and develop formal explanations);

3. Testing expectations against information;

4. Establishing a conclusion or functional relationship based on deciding whether the working hypothesis or theoretic solution is supported.

In fact, any time researchers check expectations against information, they are applying the scientific method. Indeed, both quantitative and qualitative research can be completed by using the scientific method.

*This listing is based on those provided by Auer (1959, p. 25), which in turn were based on the writing of John Dewey (1910).

Is Communication a Science?

Since science has been defined as the use of the scientific method to gather information, we might ask if communication can be considered a science. It all depends on the method a researcher chooses to use. If a communication scholar relies on nonresearch methods of knowing about communication—tenacity, authority, *a priori* belief, or trial and error—then the scholar is not "doing science." If communication scholars rely on the method of aesthetics or art to explore communication (as is often done in oral interpretation of literature studies), then the inquiries would not be defined as "science." On the other hand, if the scholar uses the research methods to know things about communication, then communication is a science. All communication research states problems, sets criteria for permissible interpretation, and makes careful observations of communication transactions. Thus, using research methods in communication makes communication a scientific study area.

communication is a science if the scientific method is used to study it

To say that communication is a science if the methods of science are used to study it, however, should not be misinterpreted. We are only talking about the *study* of communication, not the *practice* of communication by artists and practitioners. The study of communication is a science if one chooses to use the scientific method to inquire into it. The practice of communication remains an art to be performed and refined.

yet the practice of communication is an art

Communication Research and Pseudoscience

Though communication research includes the use of the scientific method among several approaches, a form of thinking known as **pseudoscience** has emerged over the years. Though one often associates pseudoscience with interest in the occult and new-age thinking, there also are instances that have been introduced in communication studies.

communication confronted by pseudoscience

Pseudoscience "fake science" in which the self-correcting nature of science is absent and scientific claims are made without serious regard for competent use of the scientific method (Carey, 1998, pp. 125–130).

Examples of Pseudoscience. There are more examples of pseudoscience in communication than one might think at first. The author once encountered a debate

examples of pseudoscience   coach who used debaters' astrological signs to "aid" in predicting winners of intercollegiate contests. There are other examples of pseudoscience that have attempted to enlist some of the language of scientific research in communication and the social sciences.

- ◆ *Personology*. At the 1986 Western States Communication Association Convention, speech scholars were, well, speechless when trial consultant Bruce L. Vaughan explained that his approximately 90% success rate was due to his application of the science of "personology" (Vaughan, 1986b). This practice involves selecting favorable jurors based on "face-reading," which examines such things as the shapes of noses, droopy eyelids, and contours of ear lobes. Vaughan published a book promoting personology (Vaughan, 1986a) and defended his work based on studies by Robert L. Whiteside and William Burtis, who claimed to have completed research dealing with 1,200 people. Unfortunately, none of this research has been published in professional journals and it remains largely unavailable to outside researchers.[3]

  Though not properly considered pseudoscience, some communication-trained jury consultants have taken pieces of research in nonverbal communication and extrapolated them into areas beyond the confines of the communication research itself. Starr (1979) adapted general nonverbal work to suggest assessing juror dispositions by (among other things) body type, manner of walking to the jury box, and the distance prospective jurors stand from each other during breaks. Such approaches have been controversial. Although they praised scientific jury selection as a form of "community or courtroom research involving systematic attention to the problem of bias," Rieke and Stutman (1990, p. 78) also accused many commercial research firms of passing off "canards of nonverbal behavior as proprietary wisdom" (p. 79) and compared many jury consultants with astrologers relying on "stereotypical signs, ranging from particular nonverbal behaviors to the dress or cosmetics worn by prospective jurors" (p. 79). Making unqualified translations from one area of research to another is troubling at best (Reinard, 1986), and Rieke and Stutman (1990) declared, "Evidence for generalizing from juror idiosyncrasies does not exist, and claims based on this evidence are generally without foundation" (p. 79).

- ◆ *Facilitated communication*. In communication disorders, a method called "facilitated communication" emerged during the early 1990s. In this method, people (most often children with cerebral palsy, brain damage, or severe autism) who were unable to speak or use sign language communicate

---

[3]A request by the author for a copy of the key research reports produced a friendly response and receipt of a report other than the one requested. In this alternative report, surveys were summarized indicating that people were generally satisfied with the assessments they received based on the body parts examination. Data about the validity of different face-reading aspects (e.g., whether, as claimed, a hooked nose really indicates an individual's preoccupation with money), however, do not seem to be available.

through a facilitator who places her hand over that of the patient's hand, arm, or wrist, which is placed on a board or keyboard with letters, words, or pictures. The patient is allegedly able to guide the facilitator's hand to a letter, word, or picture, spelling out words or expressing complete thoughts. Through their facilitators, previously mute patients recite poems, carry on high-level intellectual conversations, or simply express their feelings or beliefs (Carroll, 2003, p. 134).

Controlled research has found that this method actually only taps into the facilitator's mind, not the patient's. One widely broadcast test "shows facilitators allegedly describing what their clients were viewing, when it was clear their clients' heads were tilted so far back they couldn't have been viewing anything but the ceiling. When facilitators could not see an object that their client could see (a solid screen blocked each from seeing what the other was seeing) they routinely typed out the wrong answer" (Carroll, 2003, p. 135). The American Psychological Association Council of Representatives includes in its Policy Manual the warning that facilitated communication is "a controversial and unproved communicative procedure with no scientifically demonstrated support for its efficacy" (American Psychological Association Council of Representatives, 1994, ¶ 22).

♦ *Neurolinguistic programming.* Variously defined by different proponents ranging from its founders Richard Bandler and John Grinder (1979) to Anthony Robbins, the basic notion of neurolinguistic programming (NLP) is that ways of thinking affect many behaviors of individuals in ways that usually are not controlled. For students of communication, the most interesting aspects of this approach have been a "map" of eye movements people use when thinking in different ways (Bandler & Grinder, 1979, p. 24). Another product of neurolinguistic programming has been the promotion of "mirroring," in which adapting communicators attempt to match their own nonverbal behaviors with those of target individuals. Unfortunately, the map of eye movements (despite some early promising explorations) is grounded mostly in intuition and unsupported by actual scientific research. Other research on mirroring has found that people tend to respond negatively to the method. LaFrance and Ickes (1981) observed that mimicking the posture of another person actually reduced rapport. In fact, most tests of neurolinguistic programming have found the method to be ineffective (Singer & Lalich, 1996, chap. 8; Heap, 1989). Though some promoters of NLP have argued mightily for their industry, scholars on the subject have identified neurolinguistic programming as typical of pseudoscience (Carroll, 2003, pp. 252–257; Drenth, 2003).

neurolinguistic programming as pseudoscience

> The 1988 US National Committee (a board of 14 prepared scientific experts) report found that "Individually, and as a group, these studies fail to provide an empirical base of support for NLP assumptions . . . or NLP effectiveness. The committee cannot recommend the employment of such an unvalidated technique" (Druckman & Swets, 1988, [pp. 138–149]). In addition, Edgar Johnson, technical director of the Army Research Institute heading the NLP focused

Project Jedi stated that "Lots of data shows that NLP doesn't work" (Squires, 1988). NLP has failed to yield convincing evidence for the NLP model, and failed to provide evidence for its effectiveness (Heap 1989). (Neuro-linguistic programming, 2005, ¶ 59)

subliminal persuasion as pseudoscience

♦ *Subliminal persuasion.* Messages that are undetectable to conscious perception have been suspected of having potent influences. Though subliminal *perception* research has fairly well established that people can perceive things without remembering them and that people can perceive things of which they are not conscious. Yet, in subliminal persuasion, messages are assumed to have great powers to influence behavior and learning. In the 1950s, an advertising man named James Vicary got the bandwagon going by reporting that he increased popcorn sales by 58% and Coke sales by 18% when he used a machine to flash "Drink Coca-Cola" and "Hungry—Eat Popcorn" for one-third of a millisecond at five-second intervals during showings of the film *Picnic* at a movie theater in Fort Lee, New Jersey. In 1957 Norman Cousins promoted the idea in an article called "Smudging the Subconscious," and the subliminal advertising and persuasion business was off and running. The only problem was that the story of a six-week-long experiment at a movie theater was fake. In 1958, when challenged, Vicary could not produce either the data or the effects he claimed (Subliminal ad . . . , 1958). In 1962 he admitted that he had made up the story in an effort to revive his struggling advertising agency (Danzig, 1962). After years of challenges, when the study finally was replicated under the supervision of an independent firm, there was no impact observed on the purchase of either Coke or popcorn (Weir, 1984).

Though research on subliminal *perception* has produced interesting results, subliminal *persuasion* and behavior change have been claimed rather than proven. At present, companies sell DVDs, CDs, videotapes, and audiotapes claiming to use subliminal communication "to improve everything from self esteem to memory, to employee and customer relations, to sexual responsiveness, and—perhaps most controversial—to overcoming the effects of family and sexual abuse (Natale 1988)" (Pratkanis, 1992, ¶ 22).

One problem involves identifying what is truly "subliminal." In studies using film or tape, exposures range from 1 to 125 milliseconds in length. Not surprisingly, the really short exposures suffer in comparison of their effects with others. To determine if the exposure is subliminal, most studies just ask people if they identified any subliminal material (which, of course, primes them to respond to some special treatments). On the other hand, to be sure, a researcher could use an objective standard whereby individuals are tested to ensure that their identification of stimulus materials from a group of options is no greater than would be expected by chance. In Greenwald's (1992) review of literature on unconscious cognition, he joined others (Lewicki, Hill, & Czyzewska, 1992) in concluding that researchers who use an objective standard for subliminal perception have not found consistent effects on cognition. Even a fairly recent study by Cooper and Cooper (2002) failed to use the objective approach to examine perceptions of thirst following a subliminal message inserted into a TV show. A second problem with such subliminal persuasion studies is that they frequently do not relate to the issue of influence at all. One critic warned of the strategy used by purveyors of subliminal tape programs:

> Tape company representatives are likely to provide you with a rather lengthy list of "studies" demonstrating their claims. Don't be fooled. The studies on these lists fall into two camps—those done by the tape companies and for which full write-ups are often not available, and those that have titles that sound as if they apply to subliminal influence, but really don't. For example, one company lists many subliminal perception studies to support its claims. It is a leap of faith to see how a lexical priming study provides evidence that a subliminal self-help tape will cure insomnia or help overcome the trauma of being raped. Sadly, the trick of claiming that something that has nothing to do with subliminal influence really does prove the effectiveness of subliminal influence goes back to the turn of the century. (Pratkanis, 1992, ¶ 24)

When controlled and double-blind studies are completed, claims made that tapes with subliminal messages enhanced self-esteem or memory wound up being unfounded (Greenwald, Spangenberg, Pratkanis, & Eskenazi, 1991). Subliminal influence to lose weight and enhance self-esteem similarly was worthless (Bower, 1990). Any improvement effects were in the imaginations of tape users and the result of the placebo effect. A review of more than 200 articles and papers on the subject (Pratkanis & Greenwald, 1988) caused researchers to conclude that there was no clear evidence that people are influenced by truly subliminal messages under controlled circumstances. Despite heavy marketing of subliminal products, persuasion through subliminal means remains more myth than reality. Listing subliminal persuasion as a form of pseudoscience, Terence Hines (1990) explained that "years of research has resulted in the demonstration of some very limited effects of subliminal stimulation and no support for its efficaciousness in behavior modification" (p. 312; see also Moore, 1982, 1988).

Characteristics of Pseudoscience. As has been seen, pseudosciences call upon the language of science to advance themselves. But though they talk the science talk, they are unable to walk the science walk. Though pseudoscientific approaches may attempt to use some scientific lingo, there actually is a set of characteristics of pseudoscience that tends to distinguish it from actual scientific inquiry. Barry L. Beyerstein made a study of these elements for the Centre for Curriculum and Professional Development in Victoria, British Columbia. He observed six major factors that characterize pseudosciences:

six characteristics of pseudosciences

- ♦ *Isolation.* "A major strength of science is that its various branches are interrelated and mutually supportive. . . . Not so with pseudosciences. Pseudosciences are typically isolated from mainstream research organizations and from workers in relevant academic fields. . . . Rarely do pseudoscientists submit their findings and theoretical work to the appropriate refereed academic journals. Instead, their work is likely to appear in the popular press or in proprietary journals belonging to their own organizations" (Beyerstein, 1996, pp. 27–28).

- ◆ *Non-falsifiability.* "Any explanation for which there is no set of data that could possibly refute it is really no explanation at all. . . . Many of these [pseudoscience theories] are non-falsifiable, in principle, because they are not stated in a testable way, or they are so vague that there is no evidence which could not be accommodated by *ad hoc* tinkering with the theory's postulates" (p. 30).

- ◆ *Misuse of data.* "Pseudoscientists frequently distort or misuse reliable scientific data (phrenologists carried the quite defensible notion of cerebral localization of function to absurd lengths, and 'scientific creationists' are fond of mangling the second law of thermodynamics for their own polemical purposes). . . . It is common among advocates of bogus science to start with a position that opponents will readily concede. They then proceed, almost imperceptibly, to add increasingly contentious and unsupported arguments until the shred of truth with which they began can no longer support the edifice that has been constructed upon it" (p. 30).

- ◆ *Failure to be cumulative and self-correcting.* "Their core concepts, methods, and explanations rarely, if ever, change because of new empirical findings or the application of new technological or theoretical advances. . . . Instead of breaking new ground, pseudosciences tend to rely on the exegesis of 'sacred texts' which devotees soon learn not to question or modify. Likewise, oldness is venerated for its own sake, the assumption being that if it has survived so long, the field must be sound" (pp. 30–31).

- ◆ *Special pleading.* "Pseudoscientists often venerate their long heritage and still plead for special treatment because they are engaged in new explorations that should entitle them to more time in which to 'iron out the bugs.' . . . Most pseudosciences have been around long enough to have outlived the period of grace that should be granted to proto-sciences in their formative 'Pre-paradigmatic' stages" (p. 31).

- ◆ *Purveyance of uplifting, congenial beliefs.* "Pseudosciences invite us to buy into the desirable, but unobtainable dream of abundance, health, and happiness for all. They add to their appeal when they assert that all this can be had in return for minimal effort or sacrifice" (p. 32).

Anatomy of Theories

"theory" often misinterpreted

We had better get rid of a common misconception. Theories are not just wild ideas people have. When somebody tells us that he or she "has a theory" about something, it usually is just a bold, unsupported claim. Theories worthy of the name must meet certain obligations and standards. Theories allow us to organize and—if we do it right—understand communication phenomena. Kenneth Hoover (1979) explained this role for theory:

SPECIAL DISCUSSION 3-2

THE ASSUMPTIONS OF THE SCIENTIFIC STUDY OF COMMUNICATION

Though the scientific approach to the study of communication has naturally been a source of great insight, it also rests upon some fascinating assumptions. In fact, these assumptions are ones that often separate thoughtful nonscientists from scientists in the field. In 1985 (the year of Halley's Comet), a committee of the American Academy for the Advancement of Science met to draft priorities for information about science that modern students should know. Since they hoped that these priorities would make a difference in the level of general science knowledge within a generation, they called themselves the 2061 Project (to commemorate the next year Halley's Comet visits Earth). As part of their authoritative report compiled for the committee by F. James Rutherford and Andrew Ahlgren (1994), these professional scientists listed a worldview assumed in scientific research.

- **The World Is Understandable**
  Science presumes that the things and events in the universe occur in consistent patterns that are comprehensible through careful, systematic study. Scientists believe that through the use of the intellect, and with the aid of instruments that extend the senses, people can discover patterns in all nature. Science also assumes that the universe is, as its name implies, a vast single system in which the basic rules are everywhere the same. (p. 2)

- **Scientific Ideas Are Subject to Change**
  Change in knowledge is inevitable because new observations may challenge prevailing theories. . . . Scientists assume that even if there is no way to secure complete and absolute truth, increasingly accurate approximations can be made to account for the world and how it works. (pp. 2–3)

- **Scientific Knowledge Is Durable**
  Although scientists reject the notion of attaining absolute truth and accept some uncertainty as part of nature, most scientific knowledge is durable. The modification of ideas, rather than their outright rejection, is the norm in science, as powerful constructs tend to survive and grow more precise and to become widely accepted. . . . Continuity and stability are as characteristic of science as change is, and confidence is as prevalent as tentativeness. (p. 3)

- **Science Cannot Provide Complete Answers to All Questions**
  There are many matters that cannot usefully be examined in a scientific way. There are, for instance, beliefs that—by their very nature—cannot be proved or disproved (such as the existence of supernatural powers and beings, or the true purposes of life). . . . Nor do scientists have the means to settle issues concerning good and evil, although they can sometimes contribute to the discussion of such issues by identifying the likely consequences of particular actions, which may be helpful in weighing alternatives. (p. 3)

Despite the fact that the natural sciences study physical nature and the social sciences study human nature, when it comes to methods of inquiry "scientific disciplines are alike in their reliance on evidence, the use of hypotheses and theories, the kinds of logic used, and much more" (p. 3). In particular,

(Continued)

SPECIAL DISCUSSION 3-2 (Continued)

♦ **Science Demands Evidence**

Scientists concentrate on getting accurate data. Such evidence is obtained by observations and measurements taken in situations that range from natural settings (such as a forest) to completely contrived ones (such as the laboratory). (p. 4)

♦ **Science Is a Blend of Logic and Imagination**

Although all sorts of imagination and thought may be used in coming up with hypotheses and theories, sooner or later scientific arguments must conform to the principles of logical reasoning—that is, to testing the validity of arguments by applying certain criteria of inference, demonstration, and common sense. . . . (p. 5)

♦ **Science Explains and Predicts**

The essence of science is validation by observation. But it is not enough for scientific theories to fit only the observations that are already known. Theories should also fit additional observations that were not used in formulating the theories in the first place; that is, theories should have predictive power. Demonstrating the predictive power of a theory does not necessarily require the prediction of events in the future. The predictions may be about evidence from the past that has not yet been found or studied. A theory about the origins of human beings, for example, can be tested by new discoveries of humanlike fossil remains. (p. 6)

♦ **Scientists Try to Identify and Avoid Bias**

Bias attributable to the investigator, the sample, the method, or the instrument may not be completely avoidable in every instance, but scientists want to know the possible sources of bias and how bias is likely to influence evidence. (p. 7)

♦ **Science Is Not Authoritarian**

No scientist, however famous or highly placed, is empowered to decide for other scientists what is true, for none are believed by other scientists to have special access to the truth. There are no preestablished conclusions that scientists must reach on the basis of their investigations. (p. 7)

Science rests its claim to authority upon its firm basis in something called "reality." We occasionally described science as, simply, reality testing. Since everybody thinks they [*sic*] know what reality is, science acquires a fundamental appeal. Yet the necessary partner of realism in science is that wholly imaginary phenomenon, theory. Without the many roles that theory plays, there would be no science (and, some would argue, there would be no understandable "reality" either). (p. 37)

Theory "a body of interrelated principles that explain or predict" (*Longman Dictionary of Psychology,* 1984, p. 744).

It would help if we understood what a theory truly is and what its elements are. Contrary to one popular usage, theories are not just wild ideas that people have. Instead, a **theory** is a logical system that organizes and explains the facts. Though theories often are modified as they develop and reflect research, they still are composed of elements that have a fairly fixed form. Theories help answer research questions. Furthermore, their development and modification are objectives of research.

SPECIAL DISCUSSION 3-3

MODELS, LAWS, RULES, AND METATHEORIES

Theory construction has developed a language of its own. Though these terms often are mixed together, they actually are different things.

- *Model.* Though a model (such as a communication model) often is just a picture used to explain a concept, a model actually is an expression that not only states relationships but displays them. All mathematic statements (e.g., $E = mc^2$) and physical prototypes are models since they display relationships.

- *Law.* "A verbal statement, supported by such ample evidence as not to be open to doubt unless much further evidence is obtained, of the way events of a certain class consistently and uniformly occur" (English & English, 1958, p. 288). Of course, all laws have limits (e.g., the laws of falling bodies apply to objects in a vacuum) and communication laws often hit their boundaries very rapidly.

- *Rule.* "A theory that explains a pattern of effects by referring to human intentions, reasons, or goals" (M. J. Smith, 1988, p. 354). Rules express patterns of expected activity, though changing intentions, reasons, or goals may make people occasionally appear inconsistent (people break rules on occasion, but the rules are a regularity nonetheless).

- *Metatheories.* Ways we think about theories are called "metatheories" to indicate notions "beyond the theories" themselves. These matters influence issues to explore, definitions, and designs in research. Some prominent metatheories include positivist/atomist views, phenomenology, general systems theory, and constructivism.

Components of Theory

elements of a theory

Suppose a theory ran over you in the street. What kind of description could you give? To provide details, you need to know its characteristics and features. All theories must have three characteristics: an abstract calculus, theoretic constructs, and rules of correspondence (after Deutsch & Krauss, 1965, pp. 6–8).

An **abstract calculus** states relationships in a theory. The word "calculus" refers to any deductive system. So, what is a deductive system? A deductive system is a logical method in which conclusions are drawn from premises. The logical form called the "conditional syllogism" often is used by researchers. For example:

1. Abstract calculus the logical structure of relationships in a theory.

Major premise: If p, then q

Minor premise: p

Conclusion: (therefore,) q

The relationships in the theory are its abstract calculus. This example states that as one event occurs another event also should occur. The exact form of the relationships defines the nature of the theory. For instance, suppose we had a little theory with a principle stating that as a speaker's physical attractiveness increases, the speaker's persuasiveness also increases. The theory has a major premise:

> If a speaker's physical attractiveness increases, then the speaker's persuasiveness will increase.

To test the soundness of the theory, we could gather data to see if we could complete the rest of the argument. We might plan an experiment that has a persuasive message given by an attractive source (and, for control purposes, an unattractive source as well). If the theory has any merit, the results of the experiment should be reflected in facts that are consistent with the logical conclusion that must follow from the premises. For instance:

- *Major premise:* If a speaker's physical attractiveness increases, then the speaker's persuasiveness will increase.
- *Minor premise:* (An experiment is completed in which) a speaker's physical attractiveness increases.
- *Conclusion:* (Therefore, the experimental results must show that) the speaker's persuasiveness increases.

If the facts do not support the conclusion that must follow logically, then no valid argument can be made for the theory.

The abstract calculus is just the relationship expressed in the statement "if p, then q." The statement that as one increases, the other does, too, is the statement of relationship, regardless of the terms involved in the relationship. But to have a theory, we do need some specific terms.

2. Constructs "generalizations about observables according to some common property" (Deutsch & Krauss, 1965, p. 7).

Theoretic **constructs** are the terms that we substitute into the abstract calculus of a theory. Constructs are general terms that group many instances of activity together into meaningful units. But constructs are the generalizations, not the events themselves. For instance, self-esteem is a construct. So is source credibility. So is newspaper sensationalism. But nobody has ever seen your self-esteem. Nobody has ever seen your source credibility. Nobody can see your newspaper's sensationalism. These terms are used to describe a collection of variables that have been found. Though nobody has seen your self-esteem, there are behaviors—variables—that people have seen about you. People could say that you have been observed (1) stating that you trust your own opinions, (2) setting high goals for yourself, and (3) stating that you believe you are competent in many ways. But people don't talk that way. Instead, these variables in your activity may be summarized by the useful general term, "self-esteem." So, constructs are summary descriptions about collections of specific variables.

In the little theory we have been considering, two constructs have been identified: physical attractiveness and persuasiveness. These key terms cannot be seen. Instead, there are collections of variables that share attractiveness in common (such as measurable evaluations of personal appearance, style of dress, and ratings of personal beauty), and there are collections of variables that share persuasiveness as a common feature (such as variables of measurable attitude change, reported behavioral intentions to perform future activities, and changes in reported value systems). These key terms—constructs—are the matters related by the abstract calculus of a theory.

Even though constructs are general terms, it is possible to get full definitions for them by selecting related specific variables that we can see or measure. You sometimes may hear of things called "**hypothetical constructs,**" or concepts. These terms refer to constructs for which we cannot make related observations. Such things as "cognitive consistency," "motivational inertia," and "individual needs" are examples of matters that have been axioms employed in some very interesting theories. They cannot be seen, but they can often be useful as starting assumptions to get us thinking in interesting ways.

Hypothetical constructs also known as concepts; constructs for which direct observations cannot be made.

Rules of correspondence show how well the theory can be applied to the world around us. We occasionally hear people say that something "looks good in theory" but won't work in practice. But if a theory will not work in practice, it is a bad theory. It is a contradiction in terms to say that a theory will not work in practice. All theories must have sound rules of correspondence.

3. Rules of correspondence the degree to which a theory's constructs and abstract calculus can be applied to actual experience.

The three components of a theory are like a three-legged stool. If any one of the legs is knocked away, the entire structure falls. Similarly, if any element of theory is missing, one does not have a theory that can stand. In the theory on source physical attractiveness that we have been examining, rules of correspondence are fairly strong. Studies have linked physical attractiveness to influence in a number of settings. For instance, requests from attractive sources are more likely to be accepted than requests from unattractive sources (Greitemeyer, 2005). Endorsement messages from attractive sources are more influential on corporate credibility (Lafferty & Goldsmith, 2004) and in stimulating purchasing behaviors (Pornpitakpan, 2003) than endorsement messages from unattractive sources. There are applications of this theory in several different areas. MacCoun (1990) found that juries were more likely to be lenient for attractive defendants than for unattractive ones, regardless of their jury deliberations. In job performance reviews, attractive employees were rated as higher performers than were unattractive employees (DeGroot & Motowidlo, 1999). Of course, in some cases, one must wait for rules of correspondence to catch up to the theory.

all elements required for theory to exist

Requirements of Theory

Some strange things may masquerade as theories. It is important to recognize them so that we are not misled. Fortunately, there are two requirements that help separate true theories from counterfeits.

1. The requirement of **falsification** holds that any theory must be testable in such specific terms that evidence that could refute the theory is clearly identified.[4] In the late seventeenth century, Johann Becher and Georg Stahl put forward a theory that a hypothetical substance they called "phlogiston" could

Falsification the requirement that any theory must deal with statements that could be falsified by data and information if the theory were untrue.

---

[4]Sir Karl Popper wrote in detail on the importance of falsification in scientific research (1968a, 1968b, 1972). He takes the view that the ability of a theory to be falsified if it is untrue distinguishes scientific propositions from nonscientific propositions. He does not believe that only scientific propositions are meaningful, but he is most concerned that we not be misled by people who claim to advance scientific "theories" that really are counterfeit theories.

explain combustion. This substance had to be present to cause a fire, but was completely combusted (leaving no trace) by fire. So, if you rubbed two sticks together and got a fire, you knew phlogiston had been present, even though you could not prove it now. If you could not start a fire by rubbing sticks together, then there simply was no phlogiston in the sticks (you could look and you wouldn't find any). The problem, of course, is that the theory of combustion was incapable of falsification. Today we know that phlogiston does not exist, but in those days there was no acceptable evidence that ever could disprove the phlogiston theory. Phlogiston, then, was not actually a theory. Today, similar problems abound and articles of faith sometimes are advanced as scientific theory. Sometimes students say that they hope to prove a theory true. In reality, they are attempting to falsify alternative theories. We must recognize the difference if we are to avoid wasting our time.

Tentativeness the requirement that scholars recognize that a theory's answers are provisional.

2. The requirement of **tentativeness** emphasizes that theories can only describe part of the reality that exists. Other theories may emerge at a later time that provide improved explanations. We do not mean that existing theories are proven wrong by new ones. Instead, relationships are redefined by new theories. Sometimes existing theories are shown to be special cases of the new theory's applications. Using theories means that a researcher's explanations are not the only ones that will be found. Thus, conclusions should be developed with a certain amount of tentativeness.

Functions of Theory

Theories can operate for four interrelated purposes. These purposes can serve as a sort of hierarchy of theory, and they all play an important role in scholarship.

1. Description the lowest level of theorizing in which behavior is characterized into different forms.

1. **Description** consists of reports of essential features of phenomena. For instance, for years it was accepted that communicators in small groups tended to advance ideas, suggestions, and proposals, but then they would "spiral back" and repeat the same sorts of things before moving forward (Scheidel & Crowell, 1964). Nearly forty years later, other researchers (Pavitt & Johnson, 2001, 2002) found that the actual type of spiraling was dominated by comments dealing with elaboration of previous ideas and information giving. Continual descriptive studies continue to refine underlying theory of idea development in group communication (Pavitt, Philipp, & Johnson, 2004). Such work can challenge ways people think about basic concepts.

2. Explanation taking an event and treating it as an instance of a larger system of things (after Homans, 1961, p. 10).

2. **Explanation** involves giving reasons for relationships. Logical explanations occur when a behavior is shown to be a logical application of theory. The uses and gratifications theory, for instance, has been used to explain the reasons people use the Internet as a mass media source (Ruggiero, 2000).

3. Prediction descriptions of what can be expected in subsequent tests to be made.

3. **Prediction** describes expectations that indicate relationships in advance of making observations. Prediction sometimes is considered a separate step for theories, but as one writer put it:

> Predicting events that will occur in the future and explaining events that have occurred in the past are, except for a difference in temporal perspective, essentially the same activity as long as scientific statements are abstract. (Reynolds, 1971, p. 5)

In fact, predicting is one useful way to explain things. For instance, Berger and Calabrese (1975) developed a theory of initial interactions people have with each other. The theory submits that we communicate in ways that help us reduce our uncertainty when we meet new people. One specific prediction in this theory has received a lot of attention: "High levels of uncertainty cause increases in information seeking behavior" (p. 103). This statement has guided researchers' expectations in scores of studies. Moreover, it allows ordinary folks a way to predict what might happen when they meet new people as well.

prediction may be one means for explanation

4. **Control** involves using theories to provide information to influence our own personal environment. Thus, control really is the degree to which we can find useful additional applications for the explanations of a theory. Certainly, if people know what is expected to occur in the future, that information might be used to affect the environment.

4. Control the power to direct things.

Applications of Theory

The ways researchers use theories reflect their preferences. Developing theories involves setting priorities and making some choices.

Data First versus Theory First Inquiry

In general, there are two approaches to theory and inquiry. Sometimes called the "inductive approach" to research, the **data first inquiry** initially gathers information and follows with attempts to develop theoretic explanations. Rather than becoming locked into a formal theory, one gathers information on an open canvas of observation. Researchers doing exploratory work often employ this approach. In addition, scholars who study samples of naturally occurring conversations tend to use this approach (they often try to gather samples of conversation to develop theories rather than test existing theories). The second approach is just the opposite: we develop theoretic thinking and then gather data to test it (particularly its limits). **Theory first inquiry** is sometimes called the "deductive approach." Table 3.2 shows the advantages and disadvantages typically claimed for each approach. As you can see, some of the advantages argued for the data-to-theory method involve the flexibility of the approach. Similarly, most of the advantages of the theory-to-data method deal with the rigor and logic it provides.

Data first inquiry sometimes called the inductive approach to research, a method of inquiry that starts with gathering information and follows by developing theoretic explanations.

Theory first inquiry sometimes called the deductive approach to research, a method of inquiry that develops theory and then gathers data to test it (particularly its limits).

Scholars often engage in hot controversy about the desirability of each approach. For all the division drawn between them, however, the two approaches share many elements in common. People who write about research methods, however, are not surprised in the least. For some time, these writers (Babbie, 2003, pp. 56–57; Schutt, 2006, pp. 69–71; Punch, 2005, p. 16) have reminded scholars that in research, theory and data collection interact as part of a cycle. Whether theory or data come first (or neither)

both approaches share much in common

TABLE 3.2   THEORY FIRST VERSUS DATA FIRST RESEARCH

	Theory First	Data First
Advantages	1. "Theories may develop from any source and are not limited to phenomena that can be observed with current measuring instruments" (M. J. Smith, 1988, p. 13). 2. One may be free to take advantage of serendipity since unexpected findings are readily identified. 3. Promotes efficient research since key variables of interest are identified early.	1. One does not enter research with predetermined expectations. 2. One may be free to follow the unexpected directions. 3. One stays close to data and avoids tendencies toward reification (the fallacy of thinking that abstract concepts are concrete things).
Disadvantages	1. Researchers may force theoretic explanations on information even if it is inappropriate to do so. 2. Theories may become articles of faith to their followers, even after the theories have outlived their usefulness. 3. Theories are difficult to construct and require exhaustive thinking beyond the energies of most scholars.	1. "Explanations are limited to phenomena that can be observed with current measuring instruments" (M. J. Smith, 1988, p. 13). 2. Does not test alternative theoretic explanations, but develops suggestions for theory. 3. Promotes inefficient research since key variables of interest are not identified early.

depends upon where one wishes to enter the research process. Figure 3.1 illustrates this cycle. When first developing theories, researchers make informal notes about activities they find interesting. Such often unstructured data collection may take the form of descriptive research that leads to thinking about concepts and relationships (often called empirical generalizations). Thus, to develop theories, some sort of data collection (though we may not want to call it formal research) enriches the effort.

theory and data form a research cycle

data first researchers use theories or little hypotheses to select variables for study

Similarly, it is hard to imagine how researchers could select variables to study unless they had some hunches that stimulated them to look at some activities instead of others. Arthur Bachrach (1981) described how these little undeveloped (or unstated) theoretic orientations appear: "I think all investigators make these on-the-spot hypotheses. Some call them hunches: I choose to call them *hypothesitos,* which is semi-Spanish for 'little hypotheses'" (p. 70). Thus, it really may be impossible to have "theory free" research. These thoughts may evolve into tentative theories for testing by reference to some kind of data. The cycle may repeat many times with great difficulty in finding a true starting point. There may always be some idea behind selecting concepts and variables for study. But some researchers prefer not to work from fully developed theoretic statements at the beginning of their inquiries. As can be seen, theory development *both* follows and precedes researchers' observations. This position cannot be understated. In the nineteenth century, philosopher Auguste Comte explained in the introduction to his book *Positive Philosophy* (p. 1):

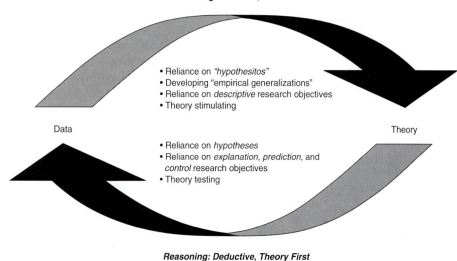

Reasoning: Inductive, Data First

- Reliance on *"hypothesitos"*
- Developing "empirical generalizations"
- Reliance on *descriptive* research objectives
- Theory stimulating

Data

Theory

- Reliance on *hypotheses*
- Reliance on *explanation, prediction,* and *control* research objectives
- Theory testing

Reasoning: Deductive, Theory First

FIGURE 3.1   THE CYCLE OF RESEARCH, THEORY, AND DATA

All good intellects have repeated, since Bacon's time, that there can be no real knowledge but that which is based on observed facts. This is incontestable, in our present advanced stage; but if we look back to the primitive stage of human knowledge, we shall see that it must have been otherwise then. If it is true that every theory must be based upon observed fact, it is equally true that facts can not be observed without the guidance of some theory. Without such guidance, our facts would be desultory and fruitless; we would not retain them; for the most part we could not even perceive them. (Adler & Van Doren, 1977, p. 1120)

Thus, it is clear that theory and data go hand in hand in the research craft.

Normative, Ethical, and Rhetorical Theories

Predictive theories are not the only sorts of theories we have in communication. We often hear about such things as "rhetorical theory," "information theory," or "argumentation theory." Such theories are known as normative or ethical theories. In communication studies, you are likely to see references to both predictive and normative theories. Furthermore, these two categories have promoted very different sorts of research efforts.

Normative and prescriptive theories deal with matters of preferred ways of acting or communicating. The area of normative theory comes from work in what sometimes is called **normative science,** which involves research completed for the purpose of finding ways to improve things. Though they are called normative theories, you should not think that they are just a bunch of value judgments made by eggheads. Instead, these theories explore activities that try to explain correct patterns of behavior. For instance, the theories of logic, ethics, and mental health are examples

Normative and prescriptive theories theories whose principles involve defining the qualities that make communication meaningful or desirable.

Normative science "a discipline that systematically studies man's attempts to determine what is correct, valuable, good, or beautiful" (English & English, 1958, p. 349).

of normative theories (Chaplin, 1985, p. 307) because they involve explanations of behavior that, when applied by other people, have the potential to improve our ability to reason and to adapt to each other. Because these behaviors seem to invite theorists to give advice based on their theories, they are called normative theories.

Ethical theory and rhetorical theory have gone hand in hand. The rhetorical theories developed by Aristotle, Cicero, Campbell, Whately, and Perelman are examples. Though these theories contain some statements that make predictions (such as Aristotle's proposition that "*ethos* is the most potent of all means to persuasion"), most statements are meant to organize principles of communication that describe appropriate and effective communication. Rather than predict relationships alone, these theories try to define how communication may be suitable and worthy. Ethical theories posit standards of what are considered to be good actions of people. As applied to communication, ethical theories are used to explain whether communicators (called rhetors) use suitable and worthy methods to influence others.

> **Ethical and rhetorical theories** principles that describe good and effective communication, respectively.

SPECIAL DISCUSSION 3-4

THEORETIC APPROACHES TO THE STUDY OF COMMUNICATION

Communication research methods are influenced by the communication metatheories that are used. In a broad sense there are at least three major ways to approach the research: the objectivist view, the subjectivist view, and the critical realist perspective. Though much could be (and has been) written on the subject, a brief sketch of these different perspectives is included here.

- The *objectivist view* takes the perspective that research is designed to discover the systematic or lawlike patterns that exist in the world of experience. It views reality as something that can be revealed by attempting to use methods that try to separate the researcher from the actual data. This approach is most commonly associated with a general philosophy called *positivism*. In this view, researchers are advised to use methods similar to those of the natural sciences to develop statements that depict an observable reality. In the version known as "logical positivism"★ concepts that cannot be observed are dismissed as metaphysical (things beyond the world of experience) statements. In the form known as "logical atomism" statements beyond what can be observed are acceptable if they can be shown to be composed of other statements that deal with matters that can be observed. The most common form, "logical empiricism," takes the view that concepts that cannot be observed directly are acceptable matters for theorizing if they stimulate other statements that can be tested by looking at observable phenomena.

- The *subjectivist view* takes the perspective that research and the researcher cannot be separated and that (in the extreme statement) the reality of research data does not exist apart from the influences brought to bear upon it by the researcher. As a result, subjectivist researchers take the view that all research is value-laden, a fact that researchers should admit and embrace, rather than trying to control its influences. In the extreme form, some take the view that reality does not exist at all, but is a "social construction." In its most extreme form, this viewpoint is a "solipsism" in which people believe that there is no reality except that which they personally encounter. This viewpoint "reached its culmination with

---

★There are no logical positivists today. The movement officially ended in 1936 when the "Vienna Circle" was dissolved.

Derrida's claim 'there is nothing beyond the text' and the belief that there is no extradiscursive dimension to social reality" (McAnulla, 2005a, p. 6). Many researchers find that the best way to delve into such studies is to take the hermeneutic approach. "Literally, the study of interpretation," the term *hermeneutics* "was originally associated with biblical studies, but a philosophical tendency has been developed" emphasizing the importance of understanding "beyond mere external description. . . . Gadamer has emphasized the way interpretation develops gradually by an interplay between the interpreter and the subject-matter, denying both that there is a single objectively correct interpretation and that we can never get beyond our own initial interpretation" (Bothamley, 1993, p. 281). In an extension, the form known as "Interpretivism asserts that reality, as well as our knowledge therefore, are social products and hence incapable of being understood independent of the social actors (including the researchers) that construct and make sense of that reality" (Orlikowski & Baroudi, 1991, p. 13).

♦ The *critical realist view* holds that although an objective reality exists, understanding it involves recognizing that there are two faces of reality. Modern critical realism began with the work of Roy Bhaskar in the late twentieth century. (Reviews of critical realism may be found in the works of Collier [1994] and Archer et al. [1998].) At the same time he was refuting the excesses spawned by objectivist/positivist and subjectivist/hermeneutic viewpoints, Bhaskar explored two dimensions of what we call reality. First, there is an *intransitive* dimension that is the actual structure of events.★ Second, there is a *transitive* dimension that consists of our understanding of reality. Because human knowledge was incomplete and never completely accurate, the view developed in some circles of interpretivist researchers that there may not be any such thing as reality at all. Bhaskar argues that during the 20th century the *epistemic fallacy* took root. The epistemic fallacy refers to the idea that statements about *being* can be reduced to or analysed in terms of statements about *knowledge*.

♦ With this understanding in mind, critical realists consider the causes of human behavior to involve partly individual choice *and* partly pressures from the systems in which individuals live and operate. For the individual, critical realists accept that, all other things being equal, intentional behavior is a free choice by humans (Bhaskar, 1998, p. 96).

♦ Critical realists also reject confusing causality with activities that are somehow preordained. Objectivists are chided for neglecting that "Causal agents are integrated things which, at least in the social world, can never be reduced to simple atomistic considerations (or effects) of their past formation, present composition or future behaviour. And the systems in which such agents act can never, from this standpoint of the action (or indeed any other), be closed" (Bhaskar, 1986, p. 218). Similarly, interpretivists are criticized for thinking that autonomy and free will mean the absence of causal processes in human activity. In the first place, there are predictable patterns in the actions of people. In the second place, when people behave in predictable or habitual ways, they alter their societies. "The environment that controls human decision making is *itself* made by human decisions" (Lane, 2001, p. 113). In turn, these societies influence individuals by preventing some behaviors, promoting others, and often limiting choices of acceptable conduct. Thus, for critical realists, agency and cause are real elements of what might be called "ubiquity determinism" in which it is held that every event has a real cause (Bhaskar, 1978, p. 70).

★Bhaskar (1998) argues that making knowledge claims as substitutes for reality (with such assertions as that reality is a social construction) is problematic. He observes, "Notice, that as human activity is in general necessary for constant conjunctions, if one identifies causal laws with them then one is logically committed to the absurdity that human beings, in their experimental activity, cause even change in the laws of nature!" (p. 9).

(Continued)

SPECIAL DISCUSSION 3-4 (Continued)

♦ Despite similarities, critical realists recognize that social behavior is studied differently than other subjects:

> If what distinguishes human action from the rest of the natural order is that it is caused by states of mind, and such states . . . are real, then one can formulate, as a presupposition of investigation in the domain of the human sciences, a principle of psychic ubiquity determining: viz. that for every action (or belief) there is a set of real reasons, constituting its rationale, which explains it. (Bhaskar, 1998, p. 96)

♦ The major shift is that social realists have promoted the use of triangulation of research using both empirical research methods and humanist approaches. Critical realists believe that human behavior is so complex that relying on one form of research alone is likely to oversimplify answers to important questions.

♦ Though there have been some attacks on critical realism from followers of the interpretivist approach (e.g., King, 1999b), many objections have turned out to be instances of the epistemic fallacy (Archer, 2000). Furthermore, the development of international organizations and scholarly journals dedicated to the study of critical realism has promoted this view as a significant force in metatheory underlying research methods.

♦ One way to summarize the different metatheoretic perspectives covered here is by reference to the chart below. Derived in part from the summary made by Gudykunst and Nishida (1989) of some work completed by Burrell and Morgan (1979) and others, this chart also includes a summary of some aspects of the critical realism approach.

	Objectivist Approach	Subjectivist Approach	Critical Realist Approach
Goals	Development of theories that explain and predict	Development of theories that describe and interpret	Development of theories that describe, interpret, explain, predict, and control
Assumptions Ontology (sense of existence or being)	"There is a 'real' world external to the individual; things exist even if they are not perceived and labeled" (Gudykunst & Nishida, 1989).	"There is no 'real' world external to individuals; 'names,' 'concepts,' and 'labels' are artificial and used to construct reality" (Gudykunst & Nishida, 1989).	There are two dimensions to reality: the intransitive dimension is the actual structure of events; the transitive dimension is the understanding we have of reality.
Human Nature	"*Determinism:* Communication is 'determined' by the situation,	"*Volunteerism:* Communicators are completely 'autonomous' and have 'free will'"	Determinism is possible only in closed systems (unlike social systems that are open since the number of people entering the system is always growing

	environment in which it occurs or by individuals' traits" (Gudykunst & Nishida, 1989).	(Gudykunst & Nishida, 1989).	and changing); because communicators (agents of action) make choices and fall into habitual patterns, there can be predictable causal processes at work.
Epistemology	*Positivism* (including logical positivism, logical atomism, and logical empiricism); a search for regularities	"*Antipositivism:* Communication can be understood only from the perspective of the individuals communicating; no search for underlying regularities" (Gudykunst & Nishida, 1989).	*Critical realism:* Though reality consists of an intransitive dimension (the actual structure of events) and a transitive dimension (our understanding of reality), the latter is subject to imperfections and is affected by the perspectives of individuals; the *epistemic fallacy* is committed "when statements about *being* can be reduced to or analyzed in terms of statements about *knowledge* [of reality]" (McAnulla, 2005a, p. 5).
Prominent Research Approach	Surveys and experiments	Rhetorical criticism (e.g., critical theory, fantasy theme analysis, feminist theory)	Triangulation using different methods: "In many cases, the most effective approach will involve the application of two or more methodological techniques, followed by the 'triangulation of research findings'" (Pratschke, 2003, p. 15).
Aspects Valued in Theory	Testability of theory (particularly falsifiability of false theories); parsimony of theories, coherence of theories, usefulness of theories	"Probing the relativism of the world" (West & Turner, 2007, p. 55)	Development of theory by approaching intransitive elements of phenomena in theory that attempts to be coherent, useful, parsimonious, and realistically testable, and recognizing the tentativeness that comes with recognizing that understanding can be only relatively approximated
Preferred Research Approach	*Nomothetic:* attempting "to generalize about many like cases" (West & Turner, 2007, p. 55)	*Idiographic:* attempting "to illuminate the individual case" (West & Turner, 2007, p. 55)	Triangulation of qualitative and quantitative methods encouraged, involving both nomothetic and idiographic approaches
Position of the Researcher	"Separate" (West & Turner, 2007, p. 55)	"Involved" (West & Turner, 2007, p. 55)	Recognition of the role of the researcher as an element in the transitive dimension of reality and engaging in efforts to identify the intransitive dimension of reality

(Continued)

SPECIAL DISCUSSION 3-4 (Continued)

| Axiological Elements | "Values should have no role in the practice of researchers" (Miller, 2005, p. 30) | "Goes beyond the argument that we cannot expunge values from the research process to contend that we should not separate values from scholarship" (Miller, 2005, p. 31) | Though there is a reality complete with lawlike behaviors and rules of conduct, our theorizing, the very selecting of variables to study, and research approaches reflect values of the researcher; thus, use of multiple methods reflecting different axiological starting points makes the most sense to approach answers to questions about underlying relationships |

SPECIAL DISCUSSION 3-5

A QUESTION OF ETHICS: SPONSORSHIP OF PET THEORIES

Many communication research projects could not be done without a sponsor's funding. Researchers naturally have to seek financial support for some of the work they wish to do. There is no problem—unless one of the following difficulties occurs.

First, some sponsors may be interested only in research that advances their own limited pet theories. As a result, sometimes other critical viewpoints do not get a fair hearing. Christopher Simpson's history of mass communication research, *Science of Coercion: Communication Research and Psychological Warfare 1945–1960* (1994), describes the link between early communication studies and government-sponsored psychological warfare during the cold war with the former Soviet Union. He noted:

> Leading mass communication researchers were not "bought off" in some simplistic sense during the 1950s; they instead internalized and reflected the values of the agencies they had been hired to assist for reasons that seemed to them to be proper, even noble. (p. 94)

Most of the research was designed to help the U.S. government influence citizens of both the United States and other nations as part of a means of social control. Such sponsorship led to the dominance of some scholars in research publication, preference for some theories and variables in publications, and prominence of sponsored pet theories, such as the "two-step model" of communication, which were the basis for largely counterproductive propaganda programs in

> Guatemala, Nicaragua, El Salvador, the Philippines, Turkey, Indonesia, and more recently Panama and the Soviet Union . . . [leaving them] today, both materially and spiritually, less democratic, less free, and often living in worse health and greater terror than before this purportedly benign form of intervention began. (Simpson, 1994, p. 116)

By the late 1950s, even labels for variables changed to match official desires. Studies of propaganda were published without ever using the clear term. Instead, only studies that used such antiseptic words as "social influence" and "attitude change" were tolerated.

Second, an ethical problem emerges when the sponsor is unwilling to be identified as the funding source. Such concealment of support has often been followed by the sponsor's claim to have found "independent evidence" to support that sponsor's positions. In 1954, to avoid charges of violating international law and United Nations' conventions by carrying out psychological warfare during peacetime, the United States Central Intelligence Agency filtered research funds to mass communication researchers through the Voice of America and an unnamed government agency (American Association for Public Opinion Research, 1954–1955; Simpson, 1994, p. 88). Such failure to identify sources of funding is generally considered an ethical breach.

Third, researchers face an ethical difficulty when the sponsor indicates the study results that are desired. A scholar who agrees to complete such research gives up a willingness to be guided by the data, rather than prejudice. Yet, it is surprising how many times sponsors issue "rewards" for researchers who can "prove" the existence of parapsychology phenomena, the existence of the soul as a physical element, or support for assertions that cigarettes are not harmful.

RESEARCHERS IN THE FIELD: CHARLES R. BERGER

Charles R. Berger is one of the most influential theorists and scholars in the field. He is a professor of communication at the University of California at Davis and has served as president of the International Communication Association and has edited both *Human Communication Research* and *Communication Research*. He was not always a communication studies major, earning an undergraduate degree in psychology from Pennsylvania State University. He has authored or coauthored 39 articles, 36 book chapters, two books, and three edited books. His seminal work in developing and studying the "uncertainty reduction theory" earned him honors and a central role as one of the field's most important thinkers in interpersonal communication. Even so, his research has included explorations of intercultural communication, cognitive processes in message production, and studies of ways individuals estimate personal risks in response to news stories about threatening phenomena.

♦ *What drew you into our field?*
  I was accepted to the psychology graduate program at UCLA but decided not to attend; by so doing, I became eligible for the military draft. I entered the Army and spent one year studying Korean at the Army Language School (now Defense Language Institute) in Monterey, California. Then I spent 14 months in Seoul, Korea, as a translator in an electronic intelligence unit. Just before going to Korea I met a person who had completed an M.A. in communication at Stanford. The area sounded a lot more like the one I wanted to study than did psychology. So I applied for graduate school in communication. Two weeks

after returning from Korea and being discharged from the Army, I was in East Lansing, Michigan, to begin the program at Michigan State University [where he received his M.A. and Ph.D.].

♦ *You are a very active researcher. Yet, some of the greatest praise you have received has been in the area of theory development, especially for uncertainty reduction theory. What kind of balance have you tried to maintain between theory and research? Is the distinction ever helpful?*

Because of the way the communication discipline has grown, its main problem is that it has been slow to develop a unique body of theory about communication. Too much early communication research was based on theories developed in other disciplines such as sociology and social psychology. Knowing how to practice research methods well is very important, but having a body of theory that uniquely defines the discipline is even more important. Data without theory are like children without parents; their life expectancy is short.

♦ *Your personal background is eclectic. You had an undergraduate major in psychology and your writing shows your broad interest in research fields that go beyond communication research literature. Do you think this broad personal background has contributed to your achievements as a communication scholar?*

If one hopes to develop theory, one has to think broadly and divergently, always alert for alternative explanations. Formal education tends to stress analytical thinking, which is of course highly useful, but theory development requires divergent thinking and the ability to synthesize apparently disparate concepts.

♦ *What one or two things do you think students should know to deal successfully with communication research either as a consumer or as a researcher?*

As consumers of research, students should understand that there are flaws in any single piece of research, and even if one grants the validity of a study's findings, there are usually alternative explanations for them that the author has not yet considered. As researchers, students should recognize that researchers need to take intellectual risks. Many times theories are only partially correct, and sometimes they are just plain wrong. Yet, one has to learn how to risk being wrong and try to advance an explanation or a set of alternative explanations.

♦ *What do you think is the most exciting future direction for the field's research?*

New communication technologies are driving a considerable amount of research; however, quite a bit of this work is not driven by theory. One cannot simply build a productive research program that is based on studying the effects of a series of technological innovations.

♦ *Is there any advice you would give students who might be interested in becoming communication researchers?*

Becoming a good researcher is not merely a matter of mastering research techniques and methods. Methodological sophistication in the absence of a focus on theory and explanation will not lead to the development of a useful body of knowledge about the workings of communication.

DEVELOPING DEFINITIONS FOR CONCEPTS

Theories provide relationships among concepts, but if a concept cannot be defined, it cannot be studied. Thus, early in the research process terms must be defined to identify variables clearly. Careful definitions determine if research can be understandable and coherent.

Not only do definitions give us a shorthand for research, but definitions may be taken as premises for research. They also may suggest ways to complete studies and the sorts of information that might be collected. Thus, the definitions a researcher selects can be premises for later decisions. For instance, the concept of source credibility has been the object of several definitions. One view defined credibility as "*image* of a source in any communication situation" (Mortensen, 1972, p. 147 [italics added]). Adopting this definition, a host of researchers identified handfuls of credibility factors, ranging from source competence to source tallness (the latter found in a clever study by McCroskey and Young, 1981). On the other hand, an alternative definition of source credibility explained it as "the *attitude* toward a source of communication held at a given time by a receiver" (McCroskey, 1972, p. 63 [italics added]). When researchers have adopted this definition, only the attitude factors of source credibility (character and competence) have been studied. In very real ways, a scholar's choices of definitions are premises for subsequent research selections.

definitions as premises for research

You probably have thought that definitions were things found in *Webster's* or *Random House* dictionaries. But these dictionaries were developed to provide spellings and accounts of the ways people have used words, not technical meanings for terms. In scholarship, we mean something very precise when we use the term "definition." One way or another, **definitions** tell us what concepts and variables really mean by isolating their essential qualities. These definition statements are not shown to be "true" in a strict sense because they are not tested against data. But we test the degree to which definitions are truly useful, reasonable, and applicable in research. To grasp the use of definitions, it is helpful to look at two forms: conceptual and operational definitions.

Definitions statements asserting that one term may be substituted for another.

Using Conceptual Definitions

A **conceptual** (or constitutive) **definition** uses other words to define a word. Most of the time what we call "dictionary definitions" are conceptual definitions. For instance, "salience" may be defined as the "prominence" of something. This type of definition gives us a feeling for a term by relating it to other terms.

Conceptual (or constitutive) definition a definition that relies on other concepts to describe a term.

Levels of Conceptual Definition: Daily, Poetic, and Scholarly

People define things on three general levels: daily, poetic, and scholarly.[5] Much difficulty people sometimes have in understanding research is the result

conceptual definitions

---

[5]This discussion benefits from the writing and headings developed by Arthur J. Bachrach (1981, pp. 80–84). Though Bachrach calls the third type of definition "the scientific definition," here it is called a "scholarly definition," reflecting the breadth of research methods.

of confusing these three types of definitions. Thus, we should distinguish among them.

Daily definitions involve common meanings of terms. Consider a term used extensively in intercultural communication studies: "culture." A daily definition of this word might be the customs, arts, and crafts of people in a society. This definition is almost general knowledge and can be useful when we talk to each other. Yet, for research purposes, it may not be detailed enough to serve as a premise for study.

Poetic definitions include a certain amount of exaggerated language. We sometimes hear of "poetic license," or exaggerations. These exaggerations are examples of poetic definitions. A poetic definition of "culture" might be "the civilizing tradition that elevates and invigorates society." The definition cannot be taken literally because it makes a poetic judgment of the term. We understand that poetic definitions are not to be taken as highly specific statements. Yet, we sometimes can confuse poetic definitions with other sorts of definitions.

Scholarly definitions provide precise explanations for advanced audiences. Intercultural communication is a major part of our field. "Culture" has been defined in this manner as "a community of meanings and a shared body of local knowledge" (Gonzales, Houston, & Chen, 2004, p. 5). In turn, this shared body of knowledge includes such things as customs, systems of beliefs, arts, crafts, traditions, acceptable social relationships, and ways objects are used in material life (after Hall & Jefferson, 1975, p. 10). This definition certainly is technical. But it is useful to researchers because it identifies elements to be examined (and perhaps measured) when studying culture.

Daily definitions
statements generally adopted by members of a society.

Poetic definitions
statements that involve figurative interpretations of objects.

Scholarly definitions
highly specific statements that have technical meanings for a group of scholars.

The Problem of Clarity

One difficulty scholars have in being clear involves some sorry compromises researchers often make involving interchanging definitions, using circular definitions, and assuming "mutual understanding."

interchanging nonscholarly definitions with scholarly definitions is dangerous

Inappropriateness of Interchanging Definitions. It is dangerous to use daily, poetic, and scholarly definitions interchangeably. Yet, many times researchers do just that. Psychologist Arthur Bachrach (1981) explained that

> a major error is the transference of a daily definition (or, less likely, a poetic one) to scientific usage. . . . It might also be observed at this point that the transfer of scientific communication to the daily or poetic realm would be equally inappropriate. (p. 81)

In research, we must rely on scientific definitions rather than daily definitions. This point cannot be emphasized too much. Scholarly definitions are required in scientific and scholarly communication. Unfortunately, one usually does *not* find scholarly definitions in dictionaries of the English language, and you should *not* use these sources (e.g., *Webster's Dictionary, Random House Dictionary, Oxford Dictionary,* etc.) for the scholarly definitions you are required to identify in academic papers that you write. To summarize research accurately, we must know when scholarly definitions are used and when research is based on very different definitional premises.

The Problem of Circularity. Circularity involves substituting repetition for explanation. One must attempt to avoid circularity that often comes with many daily definitions. Rather than explain concepts, most daily definitions refer us to other concepts that, after definition, often send us back to the term we started with! For instance, returning to a previous example, a daily definition of "culture" might be the "society" of a group of people. So, what is the society of a group of people? Answer: It is their culture. You have probably seen the flag of the Olympic games in which five circles intersect. Circular definitions are "Olympic flag statements." One term moves us to another term, which then cycles back to give us the first term again. We must avoid permitting daily definitions to be used where scholarly definitions are required. It is not acceptable to say that speeches are dull since they are boring, that speakers are credible since they are respected, or that audiences are attentive since they are alert. These statements merely state equivalently that speeches are boring since they are dull, that speakers are respected since they are credible, and that audiences are alert since they are attentive. Each statement uses Olympic flag circular definitions that refer us back to our original terms. Technically, circular definitions are flawed because they are illogical. They commit the fallacy of begging the question in which the conclusion of an argument is used as a premise for the argument. Thus, using circular definitions is unreasonable for researchers. Useful definitions must not be circular.

> **Circularity** definitions that simply repeat things.
>
> *circular definitions are to be avoided*
>
> *circular definitions are illogical*

Assuming Mutual Understanding. Researchers sometimes mistakenly assume that "everybody knows" what they mean, even though there is no useful scholarly definition. Former U.S. Supreme Court Justice Potter Stewart asserted that although he could not define obscenity, "I know it when I see it." Such assumption of common understanding is dangerous in research. If we cannot define what we mean, we probably cannot make important statements about it. Furthermore, as philosopher Willard Quine (1946) commented: "The less a science has advanced the more its terminology tends to rest upon an uncritical assumption of mutual understanding" (p. 84). Using daily definitions often boils down to our assuming that "everyone knows" what we mean, even though scholarly definitions are not available. The problem, of course, is that everybody does not really know what we mean precisely. If communication is to be recognized as a mature area of inquiry, it is vital that the assumption of common understanding *not* be made in research.

> *relying on assumption of common understanding is dangerous*

Sources of Conceptual Definitions

To find definitions you will need to go to the library and find how scholars have defined terms. Definitions can be found in many different places. Kevin M. Carragee and Wim Roefs (2004) explored competing definitions for the concept of media "frames" (elements that promote political power of some groups over others) in an article called "The Neglect of Power in Recent Framing Research." Sometimes research articles have titles indicating that they contain definitional discussions. For instance, conceptual discussions were found in articles with titles such as "Reconciliation—A Rhetorical Concept/ion" (Doxtader, 2003) and "Polysemy: Multiple Meanings in Rhetorical Criticism" (Ceccarelli, 1998). Similarly phrased titles can reveal when articles deal with conceptual and definitional issues. Yet, most articles do *not* provide detailed discussions of definitions. There are three additional locations where you can find useful definitional treatments:

- *Handbooks and collected essays.* Many conceptual essays regularly appear in handbooks and annual reviews.

- *Textbooks.* Many textbooks you have used in your classes define their terms and explain their choices by reviewing competing definitions (if you have sold your books, shame on you!—you will need to visit the library to renew acquaintances with them).

- *Specialized dictionaries.* Surely the quickest way to find definitions is by searching specialized dictionaries, such as *Longman Dictionary of Psychology and Psychiatry: A Walter D. Glanze Book; The Communication Handbook: A Dictionary* by Joseph A. Devito; *The Broadcast Communications Dictionary,* edited by L. Diamant; *Terminology of Communication Disorders: Speech, Language, and Hearing* by Nicolosi, Harryman, and Kresheck; *Diagnostic and Statistical Manual of Mental Disorders* published by the American Psychiatric Association (includes all speech and hearing disorders); *Dictionary of Mass Communication & Media Research: A Guide for Students, Scholars, and Professionals* by Demers; *The Dictionary of Media Studies; The Nonverbal Dictionary of Gestures, Signs & Body Language Cues* by Givens; *Dictionary of Media and Communication Studies* by Watson and Hill; *Dictionary of Marketing Communications* by Govoni; *Webster's New World Dictionary of Media and Communications; Dictionary of Media Literacy* by Silverblatt and Eliceiri; *Dictionary of Marketing Terms* by Bennett; *Dictionary of Marketing Terms* by Imber and Toffler; *The Practical Media Dictionary* by Orlebar; *Communication, Cultural and Media Studies: The Key Concepts* by Hartley; *Dictionary of Communication Disorders* by Morris; *Historical Dictionary of Political Communication in the United States* by Stempel and Gifford; *A Dictionary of Quotations about Communication* by Nowlan and Nowlan; *Encyclopedic Dictionary of Semiotics, Media, and Communications* by Danesi; *Communications Standard Dictionary* by Weik; *Longman Dictionary of Mass Media & Communication* by Connors; *Dictionary of Broadcast Communications* by Diamant; *Terminology of Communication Disorders: Speech-Language-Hearing* by Nicolosi, Harryman, and Kresheck; and *Encyclopedia of Communication and Information* edited by Schement. Some of these dictionaries provide only one definition for each concept, reflecting the "best" choice in the opinion of the editors. Thus, you will need to examine several sources.

Criticism of Conceptual Definitions

In research literature you will find more than one meaning for the central core of a concept. These meanings may have very different implications for ways you may study the concept. So, it is important to evaluate the meaning of these definitions in some detail. Sound conceptual definitions are found by sifting competing alternatives. This sifting requires relying on standards to judge whether definitions are useful and reasonable. Five of the most useful of these guidelines are (after Auer, 1959, p. 70):

1. *Conceptual definitions must include all situations or instances properly included in the term defined.* Conceptual definitions cannot leave out examples of the concept

that might be found. The term "propaganda" often has received attention by communication researchers. Elspeth Tilley (2005) attempted to refine previous definitions of the concept with the following statement: "Propaganda is understood in this study as communication that uses a specific set of rhetorical devices and cognitive heuristics to make claims or assertions, and to generalize (often unstated) broader assumptions from those claims without providing evidence" (p. 70). In turn, the devices were derived from work by another scholar (Black, 2001) who defined propaganda differently and explained that the method included rhetorical devices of "closure: 'simplified, pat answers (usually relayed by "authoritative sources");' 'a world in which the good guys and the bad guys are readily identifiable;' and 'simplistic and direct connection between causes and effects' [Black, 2001, p. 129]" (Tilley, 2005, p. 71). Of course, this revised definition excludes many examples of propaganda, provided that they include evidence. Thus, most political party platforms, which regularly include statistical evidence, would not be considered propaganda—even though these party platforms are usually considered archetypes of propaganda.

2. *Conceptual definitions must exclude situations or instances that are not properly included in the term defined.* Definitions must have limits. After all, if something is defined as everything, it is uniquely nothing. Some definitions are so broad that the constructs are left terribly confused. For instance, Joseph DeVito defined self-disclosure as "communication about yourself to another person" (2007, p. 65) including information about values, behaviors, beliefs, or desires. This definition makes nearly anything a person says to another "self-disclosure" as long as a person uses "I" or "me" in the phrasing of the message. For instance, this definition would consider it "self-disclosure" if a person gave a persuasive speech in which the speech purpose was phrased as "I believe the United States should adopt a comprehensive program of national health insurance." As long as a speaker states "I" or "me" in the message, sales presentations, mass-mailed advertising, and insincere exchanges all would be considered "self-disclosure." But the literature of the field usually describes self-disclosure as a "risky" process in which one person "reveals" potentially damaging information that the other person would not know otherwise. Since too much is included in DeVito's definition, it has doubtful value.

3. *Conceptual definitions must not use the term defined.* It is not very helpful to define a "fear appeal" as "an appeal that arouses fear." The term is used to define itself! This sort of definition creates big logical difficulties. Consider the paradox created by using the term defined as part of the definition. In developing his theory of types, Bertrand Russell showed the following square (Bachrach, 1981, p. 83):

> Every statement
> in this square
> is false.

The situation is a paradox. If the statement in the square is true, then it has declared itself to be false. If the statement in the square is false, then it must be

2. must exclude situations or instances not properly included

3. must not include the term defined

true. It turns into an intellectual mess. In our field such statements occasionally are found in only slightly more subtle forms. At a recent convention one scholar presented a paper advocating that researchers adopt a postmodern view of their research. Correctly or incorrectly, this person explained that a starting point for this view was accepting the statement that "there are no true statements." If the statement is true, then it is not true. But if it is false, it must be true. In one form or another, when a term defined is included in the definition, the potential for this sort of pointless paradox is very great.

4. must be more precise than the term defined

4. *Conceptual definitions must be more precise than the term defined.* Definitions try to get specific with terms. Accepting definitions that are broader (and more vague) than the original term defeats the entire process of trying to define terms precisely. Eric Eisenberg and H. L. Goodall (2004) defined organizational communication as "interaction required to direct a group toward a set of common goals" (p. 4). The new terms were even broader than the original concept. Rather than limit the concept to message-related behavior in organizations, the authors used even less precise language than the term with which they started. Their definition would include small classroom discussion groups as well as changes in policies for commissions paid to salespeople from the payroll department as examples of "organizational communication." Perhaps these comments would be unfair if their definition of "communication" were more precise than the term defined. Yet, they defined communication as "the moment-to-moment working out of the tension between individual creativity and organizational constraint" (p. 30). Unfortunately, this definition also used terms ("creativity" and "organizational constraint") that seemed even less concrete than the term with which they started. Furthermore, even though the definitions were supposed to define "communication" of some sort, neither of them was limited to message-related behavior at all, making them much less precise than "communication" itself. Indeed, in the Freudian view of things, all behavior is tension reduction. With such a substitution, the definition used by these authors actually reduced to the statement that communication is "the moment-to-moment behavior involving individual creativity and organizational constraint." Such a definition could apply to almost anything in an organization, and certainly not communication in particular.

5. must exclude loaded language

5. *Conceptual definitions must exclude loaded language.* Definitions should avoid making value judgments. The extra emotional language means the definition is not strictly equivalent to the term defined. Definitions should stick to specifics. For example, "democratic group leadership" could be defined as "exercise of direction that respects the individual while promoting the greatest good for the greatest number." We can hope so, of course, but it does not actually *characterize* democratic leadership. Definitions must avoid loaded language to be reasonable.

Operational definition
a description of what is to be observed by specifying what researchers must do to make observations.

Using Operational Definitions

An **operational definition** describes what is to be observed by specifying what researchers must do to make observations. Operational definitions do not, however, give you a "feeling" for the concept. Instead, this type of definition tells you the steps that must be followed to make an observation. They usually take the form of descriptions of research methods to isolate or measure variables or specific examples of types of observations. An operational definition is like a recipe. The recipe tells you steps to follow in preparing food, but it does not tell you conceptually how the dish tastes. Similarly, a restaurant guide could describe the appearance and taste of meals, but operational definitions for them may be the steps taken by the chef to create the dish.

Researchers know the importance of having both conceptual and operational definitions. They make it possible to shuttle back and forth between two worlds: the conceptual and the empirical. As you might imagine, there probably is only a small number of reasonable conceptual definitions for a concept. But there can be many potential operational definitions from which the researcher may select. For instance, one might define communication competence as "the ability to interact well with others" (Spitzberg, 1988, p. 68) or "the extent to which judgments about the observed communicator match conceptions of the 'ideal' " (Pavitt, 1990, p. 9). These definitions describe communicator competence by relating it to other concepts. Operational definitions, on the other hand, identify observations by describing the methods to make an observation. For instance, one could state that communicator competence is operationally defined as one's score on Wiemann's communicative competence scale (1977) or any other numerous measures that are widely available. Thus, the uses of conceptual and operational definitions go hand in hand in isolating research for further study.

though there are few reasonable conceptual definitions, there may be many potential operational definitions

An Attempt at Precision of Definition

After one has reasonable conceptual definitions, researchers who want to get specific must use operational definitions. Although operational definitions sometimes are used in the absence of conceptual definitions, doing so is a mistake. When used in combination with conceptual definitions, however, operational definitions help us get specific. The more specific we can be, the more precise our research evidence will be. Operational definitions take conceptual definitions and describe the methods that would be used to make direct observations of instances and examples of the variables. In research dealing with the effects of speakers' use of notes on attitude change, operational definitions of "attitude change" would include descriptions of attitude scales to be used. Since operational definitions are attempts to get specific, the desire for precision requires their use.

operational definitions promote precision

After identifying the problem statement, it should be possible to restate it with operational definitions substituted for the variable names. For instance, look at the problem statements in Table 3.3 and the translations into operational terms. In each case operational definitions were used for each variable. Restated, each problem may be specifically isolated. By doing so, the link between the general understanding provided by conceptual definitions and that provided by the operational definitions can be seen.

definitions for terms in the problem statement

Operational definitions are not entire definitions of concepts by themselves. Thus, we ordinarily expect researchers to cover *both* conceptual and operational matters. Researchers should use operationalizations that are consistent with their

operational definitions must be used with conceptual definitions

TABLE 3.3   OPERATIONAL DEFINITIONS AND PROBLEM RESTATEMENTS

A Qualitative Study Example

Problem: What dialectical tensions are experienced by community theatre group members as they communicate to produce a group performance? (Kramer, 2004, p. 314)

Variable	Operational Definition
Dialectical tensions	Dialectical tension categories (commitment to group vs. commitment to other life activities; ordered activities vs. emergent activities; inclusion vs. exclusion; acceptable behaviors vs. unacceptable behaviors)
Communication to produce a group performance	Communication among members of the Midwest Community Theatre during more than 120 hours of auditions, rehearsals, and performances.
Restatement:	What categories of dialectical tension (commitment to group vs. commitment to other life activities; ordered activities vs. emergent activities; inclusion vs. exclusion; acceptable behaviors vs. unacceptable behaviors) are experienced by the Midwest Community Theatre during more than 120 hours of auditions, rehearsals, and performances?

A Quantitative Study Example

Problem: Did people's media role expectations predict their assessment of media performance? (Lambe, Kaplan, Cai, & Signorielli, 2004, p. 302)

Variable	Operational Definition
Media role expectations	Scores on five five-point scales to measure the perceived importance of media roles (in providing information, explaining the significance of what was happening, strengthening national solidarity, reducing tension, and promoting a sense of comfort and well-being)
Assessments of media performance	Scores on four five-point scales evaluating the credibility of media performance in reporting U.S. military action in Afghanistan following the 2001 terrorist attack on America
Restatement:	Did people's scores on five five-point scales measuring the importance of media roles (in providing information, explaining the significance of what was happening, strengthening national solidarity, reducing tension, and promoting a sense of comfort and well-being) predict their scores on four five-point scales evaluating the credibility of media performance in reporting U.S. military action in Afghanistan following the 2001 terrorist attack on America?

conceptual definitions. But without stating conceptual definitions first, it may be very difficult to tell if operational definitions make sense. If the researcher provides references to sources where conceptual definitions may be found, there may be little harm since we can look at the original if we wish. None of this discussion means that researchers actually remember to define their terms in research articles. Regrettably, the facts are quite the contrary, depending on the publication and its editor. But we expect operational definitions to be fitting exemplifications of the concepts or variables defined.

Forms of Operational Definitions

Operational definitions can be of three forms. Furthermore, these types may be used in combination in a single study.

1. **Manipulated independent variables** are introduced and controlled by researchers. In a classic study, for instance, a researcher looked at the effects of source credibility on student audiences at Northwestern University (Haiman, 1949). The independent variable, source credibility, was manipulated by having speeches advocating national health insurance introduced as having come from different sources: Thomas Parran, then Surgeon General of the United States; a Northwestern University sophomore; and Eugene Dennis, then Secretary of the American Communist Party. This manipulated independent variable was effective in showing that credible speakers are most persuasive.

   > **Manipulated independent variables** sometimes called "stimulus variables" because researchers introduce and control them in experiments.

2. **Measured/assigned variables** involve variables or characteristics that can be identified, though it would be impossible (or unthinkable) to manipulate them. If one wanted to learn if women were more persuasible than men, it would be impossible to manipulate sex of the receiver (get serious!), but we could identify men and women and *assign* their persuasibility ratings to distinct categories for analysis. To know if highly dogmatic people talk more in small group discussions than lowly dogmatic people, researchers might *measure* the degree of dogmatism using established scales.

   > **Measured/assigned variables** variables not introduced or controlled by the researcher, but carefully observed and/or measured.

3. **Direct classification** of variables relies on simple descriptions. For instance, Wendy Geiger, Jon Bruning, and Jake Harwood (2001) completed a survey examining differences between the "young," "middle aged," or "older" audiences in their discussion of different sorts of television programs with their acquaintances. To operationally define these terms, these researchers used the method of direct assignment and identified "young" viewers as ages 18 to 34, "middle aged" viewers as 35–54, and "older" viewers as over 54. They concluded, "Older adults were most likely to discuss highbrow (e.g., PBS) and news programs, whereas younger adults were more likely to discuss niche programming (i.e., soap operas, animation, science fiction)" (p. 49).

   > **Direct classification variables** operational definitions that rely on simple identification or classification of observable characteristics of information.

Standards for Operational Definitions

Operational definitions are examined in detail when measurements are involved. Direct tests of the consistency and accuracy of measures are part of the process of describing measurement tools. Yet, operational definitions are expected to meet some minimum standards. Herbert Feigl (1945) established criteria for sound operational definitions that give useful guidance.

> *standards for evaluating operational definitions*

1. *Empirically based and definite.* The word "empirical" means observable (though many people think that it refers to scientific information). For operational definitions to make sense, they must be specific and they must be related to something that can be identified through observation.

2. *Logically consistent.* If operational definitions are inconsistent with conceptual definitions, then the operationalizations may be irrelevant to the concept under investigation. One study included a variable known as "ethnic identity" of African Americans. Yet, the operational definition consisted only of terms that African Americans preferred as the label for their race. One might question how racial labels relate to one's total sense of ethnic identity. In sum, operational definitions must have clear relationships with conceptual definitions.

Intersubjectivity the degree to which different researchers with essentially different beliefs draw essentially the same interpretations of the meaning of observations.

3. *Intersubjective.* Certainly different people have different views, but they also share some common interpretations. This area of shared agreement on meaning is what we mean by **intersubjectivity.** A useful operational definition should be one that different scholars could identify as related to the concept at hand. Therapists have different favorite definitions for the concept of stuttering. But when presented with the same set of patients most therapists still show strong agreement when identifying the behaviors that distinguish stuttering from nonstuttering patients. Indeed, their consistent use of the same sort of operational definitions across studies is one (though fallible) index of the degree of intersubjectivity for the operational definition.

4. *Technically possible.* A good operational definition should be capable of being put into direct application in research. If an operational definition requires technologies that are not yet available or that are not morally or tactically possible, the operationalization's usefulness is cast into doubt. For instance, if we wanted to study the impact of persuasive messages on the electrical resistivity of the left hemisphere of the brain, it might not be possible to do such research in the absence of technology (and surgery) that is not available.

5. *Repeatable.* Operational definitions must be capable of repeated use by different researchers. Sometimes therapists claim that they can tell operationally whether a patient is responding positively to therapy by looking at the patient's "general demeanor." If the therapist is asked how he or she is able to draw conclusions from that vague operationalization, the therapist may respond that it is based on his or her own experience. Such a defense of an operational definition—even if true—means that a scholar is using a vague method that probably cannot be employed by others. But if others cannot duplicate a scholar's methods, the operationalizations fail to meet the standard of **repeatability.**

Repeatability the ability of operational definitions and methods to be used by different researchers.

6. *Suggestive of constructs.* Operational definitions are examples of conceptual definitions put into direct observation and experience. But operational definitions also can point researchers toward new concepts. To advance theory, operational definitions should stimulate attention to other concepts. Thus, the ability of operational definitions to suggest other constructs can be helpful to advance comprehensive theory building by scholars.

SUMMARY

Theory construction is a purpose of all research, scholarship, and science. A science is a particular body of knowledge—for example, physics, physiology, psychology—distinguished by the special set of operations employed in gathering empirical facts and by a distinctive set of constructs employed in interpreting the data. Thus, we can define science as a way of testing statements by systematic application of the scientific method. Since all communication research states problems, sets criteria for permissible interpretation, and makes careful observations of communication transactions, using these methods makes the study of communication a scientific study area, though the practice of communication may remain an art.

Despite the use of scientific thinking in much communication research, pseudoscience ("fake science," in which the self-correcting nature of science is absent and scientific claims are made without serious regard for competent use of the scientific method) sometimes has emerged. Examples of pseudoscience in communication have included personology (a form of "face-reading"), "facilitated communication" (in which disabled people unable to use sign language communicate through a facilitator who places her hand over that of the patient's hand, arm, or wrist as the patient uses a keyboard or chart of letters or symbols), neurolinguistic programming (the most popular aspects of which have included using a map to read subtle movements of the eyes, and mirroring body postures), and subliminal persuasion (not to be confused with subliminal perception or subliminal cognition) (transmitting messages that are consciously undetectable to create substantial effects on overt behavior). Pseudoscience is characterized by isolation from mainstream research organizations, workers in relevant academic fields, and publication in refereed academic journals; non-falsifiability of theories; misuse of data; failure to be cumulative and self-correcting; special pleading that the pseudosciences have not been given enough time to be tested scientifically; and purveying uplifting, congenial beliefs that advantages to followers can be obtained in return for minimal effort or sacrifice.

A theory is a body of interrelated principles that explain or predict. Theories have three components: (1) an abstract calculus, which is the logical structure of relationships; (2) theoretic constructs or generalizations about observables according to some common property ("hypothetical constructs" or concepts refer to constructs for which we cannot make observations directly); and (3) rules of correspondence, which show how well the theory's constructs and abstract calculus can be applied to actual experience. Two requirements help separate theories from counterfeits: (1) the requirement of falsification holds that any theory must deal with statements that could be falsified by data and information if the theories were untrue, and (2) the requirement of tentativeness demands that scholars recognize that a theory's answers are provisional. Theories can operate for four interrelated functions: (1) description in which behavior is characterized into different forms, (2) explanation that takes an event and treats it as an instance of a larger system of things, (3) prediction that describes what can be expected in the future (prediction also is a way to explain things), and (4) control, which is the power to direct things.

There are two approaches to theory and inquiry. Sometimes called the "inductive approach" to research, the "data first" method involves gathering information and then developing theoretic explanations. The second approach, "theory first," develops theoretic thinking and then gathers data to apply and test it. In actual practice, research is a cycle from data to theory and back with no identifiable starting point. Theory development *both* follows and precedes researchers' observations. Normative and prescriptive theories are those whose principles involve defining the qualities that make communication meaningful or desirable. The area of normative theory comes from work in what sometimes is called "normative science," which is a discipline that systematically studies humanity's attempts to determine what is correct, valuable, good, or beautiful. Ethical and rhetorical theories consist of principles that describe good and effective communication, respectively.

If a concept cannot be defined, it cannot be studied. Not only do definitions give us a short-hand for research, but they may be taken as premises for research, may suggest ways to complete studies, and may invite some sorts of information for collection. Definitions are statements asserting that one term may be substituted for another. There are two forms of definitions: conceptual and operational. A conceptual (or constitutive) definition relies on other concepts to describe a term. There are three general levels people use to define things: daily definitions (statements generally adopted by members of a society), poetic definitions (statements that involve figurative interpretations of objects), and scholarly definitions (highly specific statements that have technical meanings for a group of scholars). One difficulty scholars have in being clear involves some sorry compromises researchers often make: interchanging daily, poetic, and scholarly definitions; using circular definitions; and assuming "mutual understanding." Conceptual definitions can be found in many different places including some articles, handbooks and collected essays, textbooks, and specialized dictionaries. To criticize conceptual definitions one may apply the following guidelines: (1) conceptual definitions must include all situations or instances properly included in the term defined, (2) conceptual definitions must exclude situations or instances that are not properly included in the term defined, (3) conceptual definitions must not use the term defined, (4) conceptual definitions must be more precise than the term defined, and (5) conceptual definitions must exclude loaded language.

An operational definition describes what is to be observed by specifying what researchers must do to make observations. Researchers know the importance of having both conceptual and operational definitions since they make it possible to shuttle back and forth between two worlds: the conceptual and the empirical. Though there probably is only a small number of reasonable conceptual definitions for a concept, there can be many potential operational definitions from which the researcher may select. Operational definitions are not entire definitions by themselves. Thus, we require researchers to cover *both* conceptual and operational matters since without stating conceptual definitions first, it may be very difficult to tell if operational definitions make sense. Operational definitions can be of three forms: (1) manipulated independent variables (sometimes called "stimulus variables" because researchers introduce and control them in experiments); (2) measured/assigned variables (not introduced or controlled by the researcher, but carefully observed and/or measured); (3) direct classification variables (operationally defining concepts by simple identification or classification of observable characteristics of information). Operational definitions are required to be (1) empirically based and definite, (2) logically consistent, (3) intersubjective (the degree to which different researchers with essentially different beliefs draw essentially the same interpretations of the meaning of observations), (4) technically possible, (5) repeatable, and (6) suggestive of constructs.

TERMS FOR REVIEW

science	metatheories
pseudoscience	tenacity
theory	authority
model	trial and error
law	abstract calculus
rule	constructs

hypothetical constructs

rules of correspondence

falsification

tentativeness

description

explanation

prediction

control

data first inquiry

theory first inquiry

normative and prescriptive theories

normative science

ethical and rhetorical theories

objectivist view

positivism

subjectivist view

hermeneutics

critical realism

epistemic fallacy

determinism

nomothetic research

idiographic research

definitions

conceptual definition

daily definitions

poetic definitions

scholarly definitions

circularity

operational definition

manipulated independent variables

measured/assigned variables

direct classification variables

intersubjectivity

repeatability

JUST FOR THE SAKE OF ARGUMENT: A REVIEW

Look at the following questions and prepare your own answers to them. Be sure to identify any underlying issues and controversies they raise.

1. What is meant by a science? What are the elements that must be present in the scientific method? What elements commonly considered a part of the scientific method are not defining characteristics of it?

2. A quotation at the beginning of this chapter states that there is nothing so practical as a good theory. In what way is such a claim true or not true?

3. Doesn't the requirement of falsification for theories mean that all theories eventually are proved untrue? How may new theories redefine old ones? Can you think of any examples of this phenomenon?

4. Which option is preferable, theory first research or data first research? At the very least, what advantages typically are claimed for each approach?

5. What's wrong with using daily, poetic, and scholarly definitions interchangeably? What is wrong with using sources such as *Webster's Dictionary* for a term paper that includes a definition of a variable? Is there ever an exception to this rule? What are useful sources for scholarly definitions?

6. Suppose a conceptual definition does not really exist for a concept. What elements should go into developing a new definition?

7. What are the differences between conceptual and operational definitions? To what extent should operational definitions be independent of conceptual definitions?

ACTIVITIES TO PROBE FURTHER

Go to this book's website and look for the Student Study Materials for Chapter 3.

1. Take the study quiz and print out your answers. (Make sure you think over your answer before offering it.)

2. On the website for Chapter 3, go to the section on "Sources of Theories." This section includes hyperlinks to Web pages that deal with theories in communication, the social sciences, and related fields. Search three of them, and answer the following questions for each of these sources.
   a. To what extent did this source really review theories or theoretical orientations as described in the chapter? What side issues were raised?
   b. What seemed to be the motives behind this source for the website? What were the sponsors really trying to achieve?
   c. If you wanted to find information about this theoretic approach, how useful would this site be to you? What alternatives should you search?

3. Metatheories often guide the choices that researchers make in their variables and their methods. Look up three sources (from either traditional or electronic sources) about any of these metatheories: constructivism, logical positivism, logical empiricism, logical atomism, phenomenology, critical realism.
   a. What sorts of studies are done by scholars who follow each tradition? What do they seem to have in common?
   b. What kinds of theories do they tend to produce? What theoretic functions are most commonly served (description, explanation, prediction, or control)?

4. Look at a newspaper for the next two days and see if there are any stories that suggest communication problems that people have. Answer the following questions about one of these stories.

   a. What is the source for this story?
   b. What is the communication problem identified by the story?
   c. What major sources for the communication problem could you find?
   d. If the problem were solved, what empirical or tangible evidence of this fact could you get?
   e. Given the sources listed in question (c), what underlying constructs are suggested here? Make an initial effort to define these constructs.
   f. Using a simple calculus in the form of "if p, then q," insert your answers to question (e) and try to make a relational or predictive statement with these constructs.
   g. What initial evaluation would you offer for this "theory"? How could you establish its rules of correspondence?

CHAPTER 4

Measurement in Communication Research

When you cannot measure, your knowledge is meager and unsatisfactory.

—Lord Kelvin

CHAPTER OUTLINE

The Role of Sound Measurement in Communication Research

Measurement as a Foundation for Research

Levels of Measurement

Characteristics of Operational Definitions and Measures

The Requirement of Reliability

The Requirement of Validity

Reliability and Validity in Qualitative Research

Popular Approaches and Tools in Communication Studies

Using Existing Measures

Composing Measures

Popular Methods for Measurement

BEFORE WE GET STARTED . . .

Though in qualitative research, measurement is not usually an important matter, in quantitative research it is a vital matter. In such inquiry it is understood that if you can't measure variables of interest, it is difficult to investigate communication.

Researchers are expected to describe the measurements they use and to provide evidence that they are good ones. In this chapter we will describe how variables are measured, how evidence of good measurement is provided, and popular tools you find in communication studies.

THE ROLE OF SOUND MEASUREMENT IN COMMUNICATION RESEARCH

reasons measurement issues have practical importance for researchers

The ways researchers identify and measure variables are important factors in determining the integrity of research. Measurement is not an "ivory tower" study. Accurate measurement is vital to sound research for several reasons. First, you may have heard of the expression "Garbage In, Garbage Out," or "GIGO" for short. This concept reminds us that our conclusions are only as good as our data. If researchers have sound and accurate data, they can draw meaningful conclusions. Poor measurement and isolation of variables produces studies from which only weak claims can be drawn. Second, the types of measures a researcher employs determine the statistical tools that may be used to examine the data. On Table 14.1 is a list of statistical tests that are selected largely by knowing how many groups we wish to compare and the level of measurement of the dependent variable. Third, we cannot claim to be interested in relationships between variables unless it is possible to identify those variables in actual operation. Moreover, this concern is shared to some extent by all researchers.

Some traits we wish to measure are inherently elusive. Consider cheerfulness. We've all known people whose cheerfulness is contagious. But how can we measure this trait in order to study it? We could ask a series of questions on how subjects interact with others in various types of contexts, how they view adversity, etc. Or we might observe subjects and rate them for cheerfulness in their interactions with others (Do they smile? Is the tone of their voices upbeat? etc.)[.] While these procedures may tap aspects of cheerfulness, it should be clear that they will fail to capture the *full essence* of the trait. It illustrates the old principle that often the whole is greater than the sum of its parts—but, in this case, the situation is even worse because we usually can sample only some of the parts.

The problem of elusiveness, at first glance, seems to plague those with a quantitative orientation more than those with a qualitative orientation since quantitative researchers seek to reduce a construct such as cheerfulness to numerical scores. Qualitative researchers tend to measure in ways (such as unstructured interviews) that yield words to describe the extent to which traits are present. Yet, unless qualitative researchers refer to specific behaviors and events in their reports, they will fail to describe results in enough detail so that readers can picture the meanings that have been attached to the constructs.

Thus, listing events, quoting subjects, and describing specific interactions, while less artificial than numerical scores, can also miss the essence of a trait—such as the feeling you get when you are with a genuinely cheerful person. (Patten, 1997, p. 51)

Measurement as a Foundation for Research

Another reason researchers cannot live with poor measurement is that less-than-accurate measurement works against researchers—it never works in their favor. The reason for this fact is that imperfect measurement introduces additional variation or background noise into a study in addition to variation that already exists in samples. Thus, relationships that truly exist in the data may get lost in the background "noise." This problem is called **attenuation** of results and means that the observed effect sizes are reduced as measurement reliability is inhibited. The lack of adequate measurement of variables, then, creates a bias against the researcher's finding relationships (even if they really exist).

measurement error creates attenuation of results

Attenuation a reduction in the size of observed effects because of measurement imperfections.

Levels of Measurement

Measurement involves assigning numbers to variables according to some system. Even in qualitative studies, variables are classified and identified on some level of measurement, though there does not tend to be much formal discussion of the matter in most of these studies. It is important to understand that there are many ways numbers can be assigned to different kinds of variables. We should understand these measurement "levels" and the ways that they build upon each other.

Measurement assigning numbers to variables according to some system.

♦ *Nominal level measurement.* The term "nominal" comes from the Latin word *nomen,* which means "name." Hence, in **nominal level measurement** a number is used to identify or "name" a category. Numbers on football jerseys are examples of nominal level measurement since the numbers are used just to name the players. Studies that compare men to women, stutterers to nonstutterers, speeches with evidence to speeches without evidence, newspapers to television broadcasts all use the nominal level of measurement. One could assign numbers to each category (such as calling men "category 1" and women "category 2"), but the numbers are only labels for the categories. There is no measure of the *degree* to which a variable is present. Nominal level measurement is often called the lowest level of measurement because it uses numbers to identify categories. You might suppose that nominal level measurement is of limited use to researchers. But you should avoid this judgment. Nominal level measurement is used to identify attributes of variables we study. Hence, nominal level measurement is used whenever we are interested in qualitative variables. In qualitative research most variables are identified (or not) on this nominal level of measurement. Other sorts of research also use nominal level measurement of variables. For instance, experiments take nominal categories (an experimental group versus a control group) and check for effects on an output variable.

Nominal level measurement use of numbers as simple identifications of variables.

Ordinal level measurement measurement involving rank order on some variable.

Interval level measurement assignment of numbers to items as a matter of degree such that "intervals between numbers are equal in size" (Cozby, 1989, p. 149).

Ratio level measurement assignment of numbers to items such that "any adjoining values are the same distance apart and in which there is a true zero point" (Vogt, 2005, p. 264).

♦ **Ordinal level measurement** uses rank order to determine differences. Thus, if you were ranking a speech competition, you could rank the best speaker as "number 1," the second best as "number 2," the third best as "number 3," and so forth. But this method would not tell you *how much* difference exists among speakers. For that information you must add a rating scale.

♦ **Interval level measurement** identifies values that indicate measured *amounts* or degrees. This level of measurement permits researchers to use meaningful arithmetic, including addition and subtraction. Most exams you have taken fall into this category. Most rating scales tend to be interval data as well.

♦ **Ratio level measurement** extends interval measurement to include an "absolute zero." An absolute zero means that a score of 0 indicates that the property measured is completely absent. For instance, if we measured your income, we would have ratio level measurement since 0 would mean that you had no money at all. Suppose you got up one morning and the outdoor temperature happened to be 0 degrees Fahrenheit. Would that number mean there is "no temperature" outside? Of course not—even though it might feel like it. The Fahrenheit scale is an interval scale, not a ratio level scale. But 0 on the Kelvin scale *is* the complete absence of heat, since 0 Kelvin is the theoretic point at which thermal motion of atoms of molecules ceases—the point at which there would be no heat. When we measure the number of newspaper column inches dedicated to news stories about the Internet, we are using ratio level measurement. Many behaviors can be counted on the ratio scale, including such things as a therapist's counting the number of dysfluencies by a client during a five-minute period, the number of phone calls made yesterday, the number of hours you watched TV last week, and the number of Internet hosts per domain name. In each case, the complete absence of the property would be indicated by a score of zero. This level of measurement permits researchers to use meaningful arithmetic, including multiplication and, most critically, division. This latter quality permits researchers to compute meaningful ratios among measures, consistent with the name used for this measurement level.

distinction between categorical data and continuous data

Categorical data data taking the form of identification of attributes or levels of a variable.

Continuous variables data taking the form of numbers indicating matters of degree on some variable.

levels arranged from lowest to highest

The distinction among nominal, ordinal, interval, and ratio measurement is useful in a couple of ways. In the first place, the distinction can help us understand the difference between categorical and continuous data. **Categorical data** are composed of qualitative varieties or kinds of variables. Such variables as sex, academic major, and whether or not a person is a veteran are all categorical variables. Categorical variables are discrete variables and, as such, are on the nominal level of measurement. **Continuous variables** are expressed numerically to indicate matters of degree. Thus, continuous variables are measured on the ordinal, interval, or ratio level. In the second place, these levels of measurement arrange themselves from lowest to highest. Nominal level measurement includes only categories to which numbers are assigned. Hence, it is measurement at the lowest level. As we move through ordinal and interval levels, we acquire additional information and it makes sense to describe them as increasingly higher and higher levels of measurement. In such a way, each level more or less builds on the unit before it by adding precision. Reaching ratio level measurement means that the highest form of measurement has been achieved since starting points and ending points are clearly identified.

It is worth noting that interval and ratio levels of measurement allow us to use standard arithmetic to examine data. Some writers have been suspicious that most popular measurement tools actually use scales with equal intervals (Stevens, 1951). Other researchers, however, have studied the impact of violating assumptions of pure intervals, and they found the alleged difficulties to be trivial on eventual statistical analyses of data (e.g., Baker, Hardyck, & Petrinovich, 1966). At least, we can follow the lead of scholars who have decided to call most of our popular tools **"quasi-interval" measures** (Hopkins & Glass, 1978, p. 13) because they act enough like interval measures to permit using statistical tools designed for them.

many measures are "quasi-interval"

Quasi-interval measures though perhaps not strictly measured on the interval or ratio level, data that share enough qualities of interval data to permit the use of interval level statistical tools.

It should be mentioned that measurement levels depend on the tools that we may have available. For instance, a speaker's voice pitch could be identified in simple nominal categories (speakers with high-pitched voices, speakers with low-pitched voices), or voice pitch could be measured by using an oscilloscope to identify ratio level cycles. In many studies researchers often start with interval level variables, and then group them down into nominal level categories. For instance, groups of highly intelligent and lowly intelligent people might be created out of a sample that originally measured everybody's IQ on an interval scale. Thus, measurement levels are often determined by the methods researchers choose. These conditions lead to some choices for researchers:

researchers often collapse variables down into lower levels of measurement

> At what level should we measure? First, some variables are inherently nominal in nature. For example, when we need to know subjects' gender or state of residence, nominal data is [*sic*] the natural choice. Second, many novice researchers overuse the ordinal scale. For instance, if we want to measure reading ability, it usually would be much better to use a carefully constructed standardized test (which measures at the interval level) than having teachers rank order students in terms of their reading ability. Remember, measuring at the interval level gives you more information because it tells you by *how much* students differ. Also, as you will learn when we explore statistics, you can do more interesting and powerful types of analyses when you measure at the interval rather than the ordinal level. Thus, when planning instruments for a research project, if you are thinking in terms of having subjects ranked (for ordinal measurement), you would be well advised to consider whether there is an alternative at the interval level. (Patten, 1997, pp. 96–97)

CHARACTERISTICS OF OPERATIONAL DEFINITIONS AND MEASURES

Once researchers have chosen variables to study, they select operational definitions for them. To determine if wise selections have been made, two interrelated characteristics are argued for the operational definitions: reliability and validity. Though in a broad sense these concerns influence all researchers, the rest of this chapter emphasizes applications predominantly to quantitative research.

SPECIAL DISCUSSION 4-1

THE FALLACY OF MISPLACED PRECISION

Researchers know that the results of a study can only be as good as the data. But some researchers may claim precision that goes beyond the data. Sometimes labeled *false precision* (Kaplan, 1964, p. 204), the basic idea is that researchers claim more precision in analyzing data than was present in the original data.

Here is how it works. Suppose a researcher collects data from 500 people to find out how they feel about this statement: "Third party candidates should not be elected U.S. President." Subjects may give their reactions on 5-point scales ranging from "strongly disagree" (scored as 1) to "strongly agree" (scored as 5). The researcher might report an average response in absurd detail, such as 4.26667. But, in reality, this precision is bogus since the original rating system was only a 1 to 5 scale. Carrying out general data to incredibly precise points is meaningless. It is a false precision because the numbers researchers compute cannot be better than the data themselves.

So, what should researchers do? One school of thought holds that researchers should round back to the level of precision in the original data. But this method may introduce great rounding error when other statistics are computed from the data. A second method advises carrying out computations no more than two digits beyond the level of precision in the original measures. In our example, we would be permitted to carry out our computations no more than two decimal places. Thus, we might report an average of 4.27. Researchers are warned to avoid the temptation to commit the *fallacy of misplaced precision*.

The Requirement of Reliability

As a standard requirement in scholarly journals, empirical researchers are expected to produce evidence showing that their measures are reliable.

Defining Reliability

Reliability the internal consistency of a measure.

A consistent measure tends to produce the same measurements over time. Thus, **reliability** really is a test of the stability of a measure. Suppose you had a bathroom scale and it was very unstable, perhaps because it was not on a flat surface when you used it. Even if you kept your same weight, sometimes you might "weigh" one thing and other times you would "weigh" something very different. So, how much do you weigh? With an unstable scale, you would not know. The measures we use in communication research often involve questionnaires and rating sheets, rather than mechanical devices such as scales. But the same lesson applies here: if a measure is unstable, it cannot produce an accurate report of the data.

ways unreliability is introduced

Unreliability can be introduced many ways. Items on a measure might be inconsistent with each other because they are vague, confusing, or simply irrelevant to common concepts. But individuals who take the test can also introduce sources of unreliability. Bruce Tuckman explained (1999):

Among the factors which contribute to the unreliability of a test are (1) familiarity with the particular test form (such as a multiple choice question), (2) fatigue, (3) emotional strain, (4) physical conditions of the room in which the test is given, (5) health of the test taker, (6) fluctuations of human memory, (7) amount of practice or experience by the test taker of the specific skill being measured, and (8) specific knowledge that has been gained outside of the experience being evaluated by the test. A test which is overly sensitive to these unpredictable (and often uncontrollable) sources of error is not a reliable test. Test unreliability creates *instrumentation bias,* a source of internal invalidity in an experiment. (p. 198)

For the most part, standardized tests—such as IQ tests, personality tests, and placement tests sold by commercial testing firms—have been examined for reliability. The tests are often accompanied by reports and manuals that describe how such reliability has been established. Though there is controversy about the accuracy or validity of some of these measures, at least there has been enough evidence of reliability to encourage researchers to use them.

Assessing Reliability

Researchers can determine a measure's reliability several ways. Despite differences, all these methods are comparable. The methods really differ in how the data are collected, rather than in the sorts of information they provide. All these methods take information about the consistency of a measure with itself and compute a **reliability coefficient.** This coefficient actually is a correlation, which measures the amount of association or coincidence of things. Without getting into the details here, let us just say that a reliability coefficient can range from 0 (no reliability) to 1 (perfect reliability). But you will not see many coefficients of 0 or 1. Instead, you will see numbers with decimal points, such as .82, .91, or .77. A measure with *really* good consistency should have reliability of .9 or higher. A good measure may have reliability in the .80 to .89 range. A fair measure should have reliability of at least .7. As a matter of publication policy, the American Psychological Association has decided that tests with coefficients below .6 should not be analyzed in studies.

> **Reliability coefficient** a correlation of the internal consistency of a measure.

> *reliability coefficients interpreted*

> *methods to assess reliability*

> **Test-retest reliability** giving the measure twice and reporting consistency between scores.

♦ **Test-retest reliability** involves repeated application of the same measure. If a measure is consistent, then people should have pretty much the same scores each time. Of course, people can change from one testing time to another. But a reliable test should give tolerably consistent results from one occasion to the next. An audiometer used in speech and hearing science might be tested one week against standard pitches. The next week the process might be repeated. If the observed pitch drifted, this degree of unreliability might be noted and an adjustment made in the machine. Test-retest reliability is time-consuming since two data collections are involved. But this method is often useful when measures contain single items or when test items combine matters that are largely independent of others on the same measure. For instance, Ritchie and Fitzpatrick (1990) developed the Revised Family Communication Patterns Instrument and found test-retest correlations ranging from .64 to .82 for the subscales that composed the scale.

**Alternate forms relia-
bility** constructing different forms of the same test
from a common pool of
measurement items, giv-
ing them to a group of
people, and determining
the degree of consistency
between them.

Split-half reliability
computing measurement
reliability by dividing a
test into two parts, scoring them separately, and
checking the consistency
between the two scores.

Item to total reliability
computing measurement
reliability by correlation of
items with the total test.

Intercoder reliability
determining the consis-
tency of different raters
who respond to the same
events by using some sort
of check sheet.

- ◆ **Alternate forms reliability** (or parallel forms technique) uses different versions of the same test to assess reliability. You may remember taking standard achievement tests in high school or before attending college. You may have noticed that the tests had different forms (such as Form A, Form B, and Form C) so that people sitting next to each other did not have the same test. Professional test designers often combine alternate forms reliability with other reliability methods.

- ◆ **Split-half reliability** takes two halves of a test and checks their inconsistency. Research such as Wheeless, Frymier, and Thompson's (1992) examination of the 16-item Communication Satisfaction Scale found very high reliability by use of split-half reliability methods. You might suppose that researchers with a 40-item true-false test create halves by scoring the first 20 items as one test and the second 20 items as the second test. But they don't. People may become fatigued near the end of a test and score worse than they did on the first part. So, researchers may create halves by scoring the even numbered items as one test and scoring all the odd numbered items as the other test. Hence, sometimes this method is called "odd-even reliability."[1]

- ◆ **Item to total reliability** examines the intercorrelation of items to a total. Here is the idea. If you take an exam and answer the first test question correctly, then you would expect to get a higher overall test score than somebody who got the first answer wrong. There should be a high correspondence or correlation between your score on a test *item* and your score on the *total* test. Using this method, researchers drop unreliable items and keep the remaining test (often recomputing reliability). Under what circumstances could your score on a test item correlate 0 with the total (that's exactly zero—no rounding)? There are only two ways such a thing is possible: either everybody passed the item or everybody failed it. In either case, your score on that item would give no information about whether you did well or poorly on the test as a whole. Sometimes a test item is related inversely with the total test score. This condition means that if you pass an item, you are likely to get a lower score on the rest of the test than did someone who failed the item. These sorts of test items must be measuring something completely apart from the rest of the test. Therefore, researchers automatically delete them from their final measures.

- ◆ **Intercoder reliability** takes a slightly different approach. Sometimes people will look at behavior and categorize it by using some sort of check sheet. The basic question becomes, Do different people rate things the same way? If researchers complete a content analysis of communication, any check sheet categories used by researchers can be examined for reliability. We may look at the way the two (or more) researchers (also called "raters") complete the same

---

[1]Researchers do not actually compute simple correlations between the two forms of the test. The reason is that long tests tend to have higher reliability than short tests. Since split-half reliability relates to shorter tests than the original measure, researchers apply the Spearman-Brown prophecy formula when computing reliability. For split-half reliability, the formula becomes $r_{sb} = \frac{2r_{xy}}{1 + r_{xy}}$, in which r_{xy} is the raw correlation between the two halves of the measure. These matters of correlations are covered in Chapter 12.

RESEARCHERS IN THE FIELD: STELLA TING-TOOMEY

Dr. Stella Ting-Toomey is an international authority in the area of intercultural communication. Born in Hong Kong, she is a professor of human communication studies at California State University, Fullerton. She is the developer of face-negotiation theory, a central theory in intercultural communication. She has authored or coauthored five books and more than 20 articles, and edited eight additional books and annuals of professional organizations. Her scholarship and service has earned her eight major awards from national scholarly organizations. She is known as a person who is quick with a compliment, loyal to friends, and modest about her own significant achievements.

♦ *Your personal story is one of a successful immigrant to the United States. How did you make the decision to study in America?*

It's a funny story. Three American universities accepted my undergraduate applications from Hong Kong in the spring of 1972—one in Hawaii, one in Ohio, and one in Iowa. Since I had no clue how one university differed from another, I wrote the names of the universities on three pieces of paper and asked my then nine-year-old brother, Victor, to close his eyes and pick one. He picked Iowa. I decided that fate called me to the University of Iowa. I packed. I came. I have lived in the United States ever since—first as an international student and later as a U.S. immigrant.

I spent approximately five years in Iowa City—doing my undergraduate and master's degree work there. My undergraduate work was in broadcasting and television production. At the time, I intended to pursue my master's degree in mass communication theory with the intent to return to work in Hong Kong. There were no bachelor's or master's degrees offered in mass communication at the two major universities in Hong Kong in the early 1970s.

♦ *What drew you away from mass communication to our field?*

I still have a strong interest in mass communication studies. Yet, as I moved upward in my education I was fascinated with human communication behavior across cultures. Because of my own culture shock experiences in Iowa and my Asian traditional upbringing, I was very fascinated by cultural differences and by similarities between Asian and Western cultures in general. My doctoral degree was in speech communication at the University of Washington, and my dissertation was in the area of marital conflict negotiation. After intensive readings of hundreds of studies in the area of conflict negotiation across contexts, I also realized that many speech communication concepts reflected one cultural worldview—the U.S. cultural worldview.

♦ *In general, what have you hoped that your research would accomplish?*

I've had several research goals or "visions." First, I wanted to do work that would expand the theorizing boundaries of the intercultural and interpersonal communication fields by including more international/global perspectives. So much of the intercultural communication research dealt only with issues Americans confront when communicating with people from other countries. I wanted the challenges faced by the rest of the world not to be ignored. Second, I wanted to include more U.S. ethnic diversity "voices" and perspectives in the study of intercultural/interpersonal communication. Third, I wanted my research to connect intercultural theorizing with practical applications, especially in the area of intercultural conflict competence.

♦ *What personal qualities do you have that you think have contributed to your achievements as a communication scholar?*
This is an embarrassing question to answer, but I'll try. I think my personal assets as a communication scholar are that I have a creative and curious mind-set to move beyond existing theorizing or research boundaries. I also have the discipline to focus my energy and get the work done. Most important, I put in the time to complete just plain hard work—thinking, reading, imagining, and writing. Definitely, a love for playing with ideas, a mindful attention to both the "small" and "big" pictures of a story (and noticing their connections), and willingness to write and re-draft papers 20 times on the same topic have been a very real help. Living an "uncluttered" simple life would also help.

I also tend to do quite a bit of collaborative work with coauthors and graduate students—they also keep my thinking fresh. Teaching different classes and encountering curious undergraduate and graduate students who ask thoughtful questions also helps tremendously.

♦ *What are some things you think students should know to deal successfully with communication research either as a consumer or as a researcher?*
First, learn to ask some good research questions concerning human communication. Ask yourself the following reflective questions also: "Why is this an important human communication research question?" "What could be gained by answering this question?" "Am I willing to devote the next five months or the next five years in pursuing answers to this question?" Second, develop a sustained passion for one or two communication themes for which you want to find answers. Third, read everything you can about this particular research theme or topic—read everything you can about this theme and read across disciplinary boundaries. Read widely—from academic journals and texts to everyday magazines. Read all the classical theories and research the contemporary standpoints and controversies about this particular topic. Fourth, continue to ask good questions and do not be satisfied by the status quo of existing research. Start fine-tuning your research questions and start drafting out your ideas for a research project. Fifth, take the plunge and start writing. Learn to develop a love for writing—because for the most part, writing and re-drafting is part of playing with and fine-tuning ideas inside your head. Learn to enjoy solitude in writing. Learn to write well.

♦ *You obviously are very passionate about the kinds of training modern students should have. What advice would you give students who might be interested in becoming communication researchers?*
Develop these two qualities: creativity and discipline. The creativity to imagine and play with ideas and the discipline to translate your ideas into a well-designed research project are both vital. You will also need these two qualities to sustain you from the start of a project to the completion of a project. Furthermore, take

some risks and do what you want to do—but do not try to squeeze in everything in one research project. Take one piece of the big research puzzle and zoom in on this precious piece and do an exquisite, thorough job. Love what you're doing— research is indeed exhilarating and discovery a new journey.

♦ *What do you think is the most exciting future direction for the field's research?*
The development of communication theories that are both practical and sophisticated is exciting. It wasn't always that way. The attention that is being paid in every communication specialty to including intercultural and diversity issues in its theorizing and researching efforts is a solid move in the right direction.

In the area of intercultural communication, the struggle between intercultural ethical relativism issues and intercultural ethical universalism issues (but not pseudo-imposed universal ethics) should be on top of everyone's research or scholarly agenda. In our shrinking world, I think conflict competence research and peace-building efforts from ecological, culturally sensitive perspectives (i.e., connecting macro-, meso-, exo-, and micro-level analyses) also have significant domestic and global implications.

♦ *Those future directions are certainly important. What part of your specific work has made you most proud?*
I've been most proud of the systematic development and testing of the face-negotiation theory since 1988. I have been encouraged by the collaborative work that includes international colleagues and graduate students. It is one thing to have one's friends pay compliments, but researchers and writers I respect— and many of whom I have never met—have acknowledged and included this theory in their research and theorizing, not only within the human communication discipline but across different academic disciplines. This theory is now regularly incorporated into some of my own and others' textbook writings, and face-negotiation theory is a part of many intercultural conflict training and consulting programs. The extent to which this theory has been embraced by scholars around the world has been very gratifying.

check sheets to rate the same communication. The more ratings are the same between raters, the more reliable the check sheet is. Though one could use some applications of correlation to get the job done, scholars have made things easy for us by developing shortcut formulas that give us intercoder reliability. Though there are several forms that have been used, prudent researchers tend to rely on either Cohen's *kappa* (Cohen, 1960), which compensates for the number of times rating categories are used, or Scott's *pi* (Scott, 1955), which also compensates for the rates of agreement that would be expected by chance alone. Table 4.1A illustrates the use of Scott's *pi* in a typical example. Though this example involves a case of two coders, the formula can be extended to any number of coders (see Fleiss, 1971). This method permits researchers to identify how reliably content analysis check sheets are used to code communication. Cohen's *kappa* involves some cumbersome computation, and we will not include an example for this introductory treatment. A good review of these different methods is found in Fleiss (1981).

Cohen's kappa *and Scott's* pi *for reliability of content analysis categories*

TABLE 4.1   STATISTICAL RELIABILITY FORMULAS

A. INTERCODER RELIABILITY FOR CONTENT ANALYSIS OR DIAGNOSTIC CATEGORIES: (SCOTT'S *pi*)

Formula:

$$pi = \frac{\text{proportion observed agreement} - \text{proportion expected agreement}}{1 - \text{proportion expected agreement}}$$

where:

$$\text{proportion observed agreement} = \frac{(\text{number of raters}) \star (\text{number of same ratings made})}{\text{total number of ratings by all raters}}$$

proportion expected agreement = sum of the squared proportions in each category

EXAMPLE: Coders rated the proportion of violence in children's TV programs observed during a two-week period. They reported the proportion of agreement among themselves at .80 (leave in the decimal point). The violence was categorized into five categories:

threatening violence	.40
punching others	.10
slapping	.30
using weapons	.10
off-screen violence	.10

$$pi = \frac{\text{proportion observed agreement} - \text{proportion expected agreement}}{1 - \text{proportion expected agreement}}$$

$$= \frac{.80 - (.40^2 + .10^2 + .30^2 + .10^2 + .10^2)}{1 - (.40^2 + .10^2 + .30^2 + .10^2 + .10^2)}$$

$$= \frac{.80 - (.28)}{1 - (.28)}$$

$$= \frac{.52}{.72}$$

$$pi = .72$$

B. K-R 20: USED WHEN A TEST DEALS WITH "CORRECT" AND "INCORRECT" ANSWERS

Formula:

$$\text{K-R 20} = \frac{k}{k-1} \star \left(1 - \frac{\text{sum of P} \star \text{Q of each test item}}{s^2 \text{ of the total test score}}\right)$$

where:

k = the number of items on the test
P = the proportion (keep the decimal point in) of people who answered the item correctly
Q = the proportion (keep the decimal point in) of people who answered the item incorrectly
s^2 = the variance (a measure of variability [see chapter 12])

(Continued)

TABLE 4.1 (Continued)

EXAMPLE: A measure of retention of information in radio ads was assessed by use of a five-item true-false test. The first item was answered correctly (P) by 70% of the people, the second item was passed by 65%, the third item was passed by 50%, the fourth item was passed by 60%, and the last item was passed by 80%. The variance of the total test was 2.4.

$$= \frac{k}{k-1} \star \left(1 - \frac{\text{sum of P} \star \text{Q of each test item}}{s^2 \text{ of the total test score}}\right)$$

$$= \frac{5}{5-1} \star \left(1 - \frac{(.7 \star .3) + (.65 \star .35) + (.50 \star .50) + (.60 \star .40) + (.80 \star .20)}{2.4}\right)$$

$$= 1.25 \star \left(1 - \frac{(.21) + (.23) + (.25) + (.24) + (.16)}{2.4}\right)$$

$$= 1.25 \star \left(1 - \frac{1.09}{2.4}\right)$$

$$= 1.25 \star (1 - .45)$$

$$= 1.25 \star (.55)$$

K-R 20 = .69

C. COEFFICIENT ALPHA: USED WHEN A TEST DOES NOT HAVE "CORRECT" AND "INCORRECT" ANSWERS

Formula:

$$\alpha = \frac{k}{k-1} \star \left(1 - \frac{\text{sum of } s^2 \text{ of each test item}}{s^2 \text{ of the total test score}}\right)$$

where:

k = the number of items on the test
s^2 = the variance (a measure of variability [see chapter 12])

EXAMPLE: A measure of speech fluency rating scale containing five seven-point scales. The variance for the first scale item was 3.2, the variance for the second item was 3, the variance for the third item was 3.8, the variance for the fourth item was 2.5, and the variance for the fifth item was 3.4. The variance of the total test was 38.

$$\alpha = \frac{k}{k-1} \star \left(1 - \frac{\text{sum of } s^2 \text{ of each test item}}{s^2 \text{ of the total test score}}\right)$$

$$= \frac{5}{5-1} \star \left(1 - \frac{3.2 + 3 + 3.8 + 2.5 + 3.4}{38}\right)$$

$$= 1.25 \star \left(1 - \frac{15.9}{38}\right)$$

$$= 1.25 \star (1 - .42)$$

$$= 1.25 \star (.58)$$

$$\alpha = .73$$

K-R 20 Kuder-Richardson formula 20 for reliability, used when researchers want to determine the reliability of a measure that has items that are scored as "correct" or "incorrect" answers.

♦ *Statistical shortcuts* are not really different forms of reliability. They simply are ways to get reliability coefficients rapidly, especially when major computer programs are used. It should be remembered, however, that these different tools are mathematically equivalent and can be interpreted similarly. There are two options that are most often used. As Table 4.1B shows, one tool is called **K-R 20,** which is shorthand for Kuder-Richardson formula 20 for reliability. This method is used when researchers want to determine the reliability of a measure that has items that are scored as "correct" or "incorrect" answers. Most exams that you have taken in classes as well as tests of comprehension and skills use this sort of method for reliability. But suppose we measure perceptions or ratings that people may have—such as attitudes, self-esteem, ratings of speech intelligibility, or ratings of newspaper sensationalism. Under these conditions there is no "correct" answer. But the consistency with which people react to the items on the measure may be tapped by using **Cronbach's coefficient alpha**[2] (α) (Cronbach, 1970, pp. 160–161), as illustrated in Table 4.1C.

Cronbach's coefficient alpha a formula for reliability, used when researchers want to determine the reliability of a measure that has no "correct" answer.

An interesting fact about measurement is that the longer a test is, the more reliable it becomes. With increasing test length, variation from item to item tends to balance out. A mathematic proof of this relationship is called the Spearman-Brown prophecy formula. Thus, major statistical formulae for reliability tend to be "corrected" for test length so that comparisons of different measures can be made regardless of their length.

The Requirement of Validity

In our discussion of reliability, we mentioned a troublesome bathroom scale. Suppose, instead, we had a reliable scale (because we placed it on a level surface when we used it). It would give us consistent results. So far, so good. But suppose that the bathroom scale were adjusted incorrectly so that it weighed everything 10 pounds under its true weight. We might want to keep this flattering scale, of course, but its biases would make it impossible to obtain an accurate weight. This scale would have reliability, but it would not produce a valid measure of our weight. Another example might illustrate the relationship between reliability and validity. Imagine that you had a stairway in your home. If the stairway were not firm and stable, you would not get to your destination because the stairs would become shaky when you tried to stand on them. That's an example

---

[2]Cronbach developed a "shortcut" formula called coefficient alpha$_k$ for tests that have correct and incorrect answers—or items on the nominal scale. In fact, as Cronbach explained (p. 161), this formula is the same as K-R 20. Similarly, Kuder and Richardson developed a formula called K-R 21, which is equivalent to Cronbach's coefficient alpha. Yet, researchers usually report coefficient alpha for measures that don't have "correct" answers and reserve K-R 20 for tests that feature correct and incorrect answers. Mathematically, when Cronbach's coefficient alpha is used with categorical data, the results are equivalent to K-R 20.

of an unreliable stairway. When a measure is unreliable, it is unstable, and you can't use it to get where you want to go. Instead, suppose the stairway is sturdy. It would be reliable, and you could use it the same way every time you walked on it. But if the carpenters built it to lead to the roof, rather than to the upstairs rooms, it could not get you where you want to go. This stairway is not a valid path to the upstairs rooms because it is pointed in the wrong direction. That's the notion of reliability and validity in a nutshell: reliability means the measure is stable; validity means the stable test truly measures what we intended (it's pointed in the right direction).

Defining Validity

Validity or "test validity" represents the degree to which a measure actually measures what is claimed. Reliability is determined by looking at the *internal* consistency of a measure. But looking at internal consistency will not reveal if a measure is "pointed in the right direction." To assess validity, researchers need to find some *external* evidence to allow them to believe that they are measuring what they intended. Thus, we say that validity is the consistency of a measure with some outside criterion or standard by which to judge the test.

Validity (properly "test validity') the consistency of a measure with a criterion; the degree to which a measure actually measures what is claimed.

Reliability versus Validity

As you can tell, it is possible to have a reliable test without having a valid one (you can have a stable stairway that does not go where you intended). But you cannot have a valid measure without its first being reliable. Thus, validity presumes reliability. Hence, if a person has a valid test, that person is telling us that the measure also is reliable.

validity presumes reliability

Assessing Validity

methods to assess validity based on its face and content

There are four major ways to determine validity, though researchers usually combine some of them to argue for their measures. Each of the major methods is discussed below.

- ◆ **Face validity** involves researchers' arguing that a measure seems sound looking at the content of the measurement. Sometimes arguments about content can be quite reasonable. Furthermore, this method has been the most common approach taken by researchers to argue the validity of their measures. It is limited, however, by the absence of additional direct evidence and, of course, by the reasoning powers of the researcher.

- ◆ **Expert jury validity** involves experts' reviewing the measure. Researchers sometimes report the number of positive assessments received from the experts. Most often, experts give advice to help the researcher make improvements. Thus, expert juries frequently are consulted to help develop measures. As a method of validation, the expert jury method boils down to face validity that involves additional people.

Face validity a method of test validity that involves researchers' looking at the content of the measurement items and advancing an argument that, on its face, the measure seems to identify what it claims.

Expert jury validity a method of test validity that involves having a group of experts in the subject matter examine the measurement device and judge its merit.

Criterion validity
methods including concurrent and predictive validity that assess a measure's worth by examining its relation to some outside criterion.

Concurrent validity
a method of test validity that involves correlating a new measure with a previously validated measure of the same construct.

Predictive validity (also called "known group" validity) a method of test validity that examines the degree to which scores on a measure predict membership in a known group in which the construct must exist.

Construct validity
a method of test validity that involves correlating the new measure with at least two other measures, one of which is a valid measure of a construct that is known conceptually to be directly related to the new measure, and another one of which should be a valid measure of a construct that is known conceptually to be inversely related to the construct of interest.

♦ **Criterion validity** is a category of methods that check a measure with external criteria. There are two forms of this method.

1. **Concurrent validity** correlates a new measure with a previously validated measure of the same thing. This method is commonly used when a traditional research area is extended with updated measures. For example, as part of her work on the measure of teacher affinity-seeking, Danielle Dolin (1995) validated her new measure by concurrent validity with a previously validated measure of student affect for the teacher.

2. **Predictive validity** is also called "known group" validity. It compares scores on a new measure with a previously validated one. Thus, if you were developing a measure of one's tendency to self-disclose private information about oneself, you might find a group of people and see if this test predicts whether self-disclosure actually occurs. Rubin and Shenker (1978) used this technique to show that their self-disclosure scale successfully predicted whether self-disclosure was actually received by college students' roommates. If you developed an instrument to measure successful sales communication, you might find a group of successful salespeople and a group of not-so-successful salespeople. After administering the test to both groups, you could see if it distinguished between the two known groups. If so, then a claim of predictive validity could be made.

♦ **Construct validity** studies are among the most impressive works in communication research. Construct validation requires that a new measure be administered to subjects along with at least two other measures. One of these measures should be a valid measure of a construct that is known conceptually to be directly related to the new measure (that is, as scores on the new measure increase, scores on the related construct should also increase). For instance,

> if a physiological measure of heartbeat is supposed to be indicative of communication anxiety, then it would be reasonable to expect people in high stress communication situations to have more rapid heartbeats (higher measured communication anxiety) than would be expected of people in low stress communication settings. (Emmert, 1989, p. 114)

Another of these measures should be a valid measure of a construct known conceptually to be inversely related to the new measure (that is, as scores on the new measure *increase,* scores on the related construct should *decrease*). Some researchers add a third variable known to be unrelated to the construct measured by the new instrument. Yet, most construct validation studies exclude this final comparison. If the new measure is valid, it should produce significant findings in the correct directions. Obviously, the conceptual bases for the measures must be very well understood and the theoretic foundations clear. Such studies are not easy, and they are major inquiries in and of themselves. One influential effort was completed by James McCroskey (1978)[3] to validate

---

[3]This study actually relied on information from other published and unpublished works to make its case. Furthermore, a section of personality correlates is excluded from this description.

the "Personal Report of Communication Apprehension" (also known as the PRCA). Since communication apprehension is one's "fear or anxiety associated with either real or anticipated (oral) communication with another person or persons" (McCroskey, 1977, p. 78), he isolated a valid measure of "verbal reticence," which was known to have a direct relationship to communication apprehension. He also found valid measures of three constructs that were known to have theoretically inverse relationships with communication apprehension: extroversion, self-esteem, and self-acceptance. When all the measures were administered, the patterns were as predicted. Though it does not always work out so well for researchers, construct validation was completed for the PRCA and it has become a very popular research tool.

Reliability and Validity in Qualitative Research

Reliability and validity issues also influence researchers who attempt to draw conclusions from studies using qualitative research methods. Though in quantitative research, reliability and validity are examined numerically with statistical tools, in qualitative research, reliability and validity are terms that have somewhat different meanings. Whereas reliability in quantitative studies involves exploring whether different individuals use instruments with consistency when looking at the same things, in most qualitative research, the researcher *is* the instrument.

in qualitative studies, reliability involves the consistency of the researcher as the chief research instrument

Some qualitative researchers dismiss issues of reliability and validity because they believe they are tied up with philosophical assumptions about reality that they are not willing to accept. But other qualitative researchers have observed that reliability and validity involve questions about the researcher as interpreter. Of course, these fundamental concerns emerge any time *any* sort of research is involved. Two sociologists specializing in qualitative research explained:

a form of reliability is a concern in qualitative research

> In qualitative sociology, the key reliability question is: would any qualitative sociologist examining the texts or images that constitute the data develop (roughly) the same analytic description? From a quantitative standpoint, the answer would be no, because qualitative analysis is interpretive, with members' meanings examined through a particular analytic lens and located in a specific interaction bounded by time and space. However, if you are a qualitative sociologist, the answer might be yes or it might be no. (Warren & Karner, 2005, p. 217)

Hence, it seems that the issue of reliability and validity cannot be entirely divorced from qualitative research.

Yet, what does the concept of reliability mean in qualitative research? Certainly, the notion does not refer to consistency of questionnaires and survey forms. But the notion can mean the steadiness of sound interpretations. As part of their discussion of all forms of validity (including experimental validity), two qualitative researchers suggested that "to demonstrate what may be taken as a

reliability is a concern for dependability

methods to assure dependability

Dependability in qualitative research, the counterpart of measurement reliability in which efforts are made to assure stability in identifications and interpretations.

Overlap methods in qualitative research, an approach to assure dependability by use of multiple methods to triangulate a dependable set of interpretations of communication phenomena.

Stepwise replication in qualitative research, an approach to assure dependability by involving at least two researchers in comparisons of fieldwork experiences at different times.

methods to assure trustworthiness

Dependability audits in qualitative research, an approach to assure dependability by having experts evaluate procedures and interpretations.

validity is a concern for trustworthiness in qualitative research

a case of dependability and trustworthiness issues: Margaret Mead and Samoa

substitute criterion for reliability—*dependability*—the naturalist seeks means for taking into account both factors of instability and factors of phenomenal or design induced change" (Lincoln & Guba, 1985, p. 299). Thus, qualitative researchers are expected to show that their accounts are dependable interpretations. To assure such **dependability** exists, researchers may use these approaches (Lincoln & Guba, 1985, pp. 316–318):

- ♦ **overlap methods** in which multiple methods are used to triangulate or converge on a set of dependable interpretations;
- ♦ **stepwise replication,** which requires that at least two qualitative researchers who conduct fieldwork separately compare their interpretations at different times (sometimes daily or at critical points where previous qualitative research plans need to be reconsidered); and
- ♦ **dependability audits** in which experts are called in to examine the process and the interpretations involved in the qualitative research.

What does the concept of validity mean in qualitative research? For scholars of qualitative work, the question of validity is transformed into a question about the trustworthiness of the data and the findings. "The basic issue in relation to trustworthiness is simple: How can an inquirer persuade his or her audiences (including self) that the findings of an inquiry are worth paying attention to, worth taking account of?" (Lincoln & Guba, 1985, p. 291). So, how do qualitative researchers demonstrate the trustworthiness or validity of their work? Four activities are suggested to increase the chances that credible findings will be produced by the qualitative research (Lincoln & Guba, 1985, pp. 304–315):

- ♦ extended participation in the field experience;
- ♦ persistent observation so that key phenomena are not likely to be overlooked;
- ♦ **negative case analysis,** which requires researchers to draw conclusions only after accounting for any negative cases that disprove the general relationship;
- ♦ **referential adequacy,** which includes recording qualitative interviews and observations, and carefully keeping records of actual encounters under analysis; and
- ♦ member checks in which the researcher checks with some members of the group studied to assess whether the concepts, reconstructions, categories, and interpretations are accurate and make sense.

Of course, just because such checks on the trustworthiness of qualitative data and interpretations may be undertaken does not mean that they usually are. In fact, the opposite is the case more often than not.

A controversial case in point will show the difficulty of dealing with such dependability and trustworthiness issues in interpreting what is seen in a qualitative study. In 1928, Margaret Mead spent nine months in Samoa living with an American couple in a naval dispensary. She conducted over 61 interviews with Samoan teenage girls and made fieldnotes of her observations. She concluded that expectations of virginity (called the *taupou* system) were restricted only to Samoan girls of the highest social class. Typical Samoan teenage girls had frequent premarital sexual encounters and seemed to experience much less difficulty than girls from Western societies in making transitions into adulthood and married life. Mead took this information as proof that behavior is influenced more by "nurture" than by "nature." Mead's work was commercially published and became a "best seller," making her one of the most famous anthropologists of the twentieth century. Derek Freeman, an Australian anthropologist, lived in Samoa for four years and found that his ethnographic studies could not replicate Mead's conclusions. After an exchange of letters with Mead (in which she was generally dismissive of his concerns), he wrote a critical book, *Margaret Mead and Samoa: The Making and Unmaking of an Anthropological Myth* (1983). He concluded that the typical Samoan girls of all classes did, in fact, follow the expected virginity of the *taupou* system. He could not find support for Mead's major claims of superior adult adjustment following a promiscuity during adolescence. In some of the most startling work, he contacted some of Mead's interview participants who explained that they had not actually engaged in casual sexual relations before marriage. They explained that they had hoaxed Mead by mischievous joking about sexual exploits. In 1999, Freeman reported an additional interview with another of Mead's informants who admitted engaging in "recreational lying" (using a dry sense of humor to tell entertaining "whoppers") about casual sex in Samoa. Freeman concluded that Mead had preconceptions about what she would find, was naïve about the practical joking of Samoans, and tended to ignore inconvenient facts. He also argued that her major conclusions were even inconsistent with her own fieldnotes. As a result, her major conclusions were not credible—nor could they be replicated in his own work. Until his death in 2001, Freeman was personally attacked and villified by a cadre of anthropologists who nearly worshipped Mead. The trustworthiness of Mead's interpretations remains uncertain because there were no checks to show the dependability of observations she made. The validity or trustworthiness of Mead's reports and interpretations also have been doubted, and none of the approaches listed for checking these matters was satisfactorily completed. For any of the misstatements that may be involved in criticism of her work, Mead's interpretations remain in the realm of the controversial.

Negative case analysis in qualitative research, an approach to assure trustworthiness by accounting for negative or contrary cases that seem to disagree or disprove the researcher's interpretations.

Referential adequacy in qualitative research, an approach to assure trustworthiness by maintaining referential materials such as recordings and documentary materials to ground the credibility of research interpretations.

POPULAR APPROACHES AND TOOLS IN COMMUNICATION STUDIES

There are two options when measuring a construct: find preexisting measures or develop your own. We will consider each of these approaches and will emphasize the popular formats that you may use.

Using Existing Measures

sources of measures in communication

Many important variables have been the object of considerable attention. Measures of source credibility (McCroskey, 1966), communication anxiety (McCroskey, 1982), and social distance (Bogardus, 1933) are found in this chapter. Additional measures of test-taking behavior are found in Chapter 9 on Table 9.5. For other tools, however, you might wish to check the following:

♦ *Communication Research Measures: A Sourcebook* (Rubin, Palmgreen, & Sypher, 2004): 61 measures for major variables researched in the field

♦ *A Handbook for the Study of Human Communication: Methods and Instruments for Observing, Measuring, and Assessing Communication Processes* (Tardy, 1988a): discussions of measurement issues for 15 construct areas in the field

♦ *Measurement of Communication Behavior* (Emmert & Barker, 1989): chapters dealing with data analysis approaches, general scaling techniques, and measurement applications

♦ *Measures of Personality and Social Psychological Attitudes* (Robinson, Shaver, & Wrightsman, 1991): 70 measures ranging from test-taking behavior to anxiety

♦ *Mental Measurements Yearbook* (www.silverplatter/catalog/mmyb.htm): over 2,000 commercially available measurements dating from 1989 reviewed by the Buros Institute of Mental Measurements (the Institute will answer a sample request for free; many libraries pay for the full service through the Silverplatter database)

Yet, these sources can only scratch the surface. To find additional measures you can look at research articles to find the tools that have been developed to measure variables of interest to you.

selecting measures depends on

Of course, finding measures is one thing, but deciding whether they should be selected is quite another. You should examine these tools to see if they meet your needs.

1. suitability to sample

First, you should ask if the measure is suited to the type of sample you are thinking of using. If the measure is designed for adults and your sample will involve children, a search should be completed for child-suitable measures. Second, the evidence for relia-

2. reliability and validity

bility and validity should be examined. Naturally, those measures that are most worthy should have some support for their claims of reliability and validity. Third, the length of

3. length

a measure should be examined. Measures that strike respondents as too long may be difficult to use. Though length should not replace concern for validity, the fact is that a long measure may create problems with respondent fatigue and willingness to

4. format

participate. Fourth, the format of the measure should be considered. Ideally, instructions should be a small part of a set of measures. If researchers use different measures employing the same formats, the number of different sets of instructions may be minimized.

Composing Measures

Surely for beginning students it is most comforting to find measures whose properties are already believed to be known. But sometimes researchers need to create new measures. The task is not as difficult as some students might suppose, and there is no reason that you should shrink from it.

SPECIAL DISCUSSION 4-2

USE OF SELF-REPORT MEASURES

Much communication research relies on reports and evaluations of people who were participants in communication. The problem is that such reports may or may not be valid. Thus, researchers have to be careful with self-report measures. There are two sorts of self-report measures that have raised concern: personal evaluations by participants and recall of past communication exchanges by participants.

Concerns With Direct Account Reports

Sometimes people cannot give accurate reports of their reactions to communication. They may not know what they are being asked, they may not know how they feel about issues, or they may feel pressure to answer so that they look good. One researcher (Sypher, 1980) called such research "illusory research" since analyzing such data is far removed from the variables the researcher originally wished to study. With such tools as semantic differential scales, for instance, "measures may be tapping semantic similarity rather than actual communication behavior" (p. 80).

Many times people make reports that exaggerate the frequency with which they do socially desirable things. For instance, public opinion surveys of church attendance in the United States are quite high with over 40% of Americans reporting that they attend church service regularly. Yet, one study (Hadaway et al., 1993) found that actual observed attendance at churches was much lower. In one county, 33% of the Protestants said they went to church, though only 20% really attended. Among Roman Catholics, 51% reported going to church, whereas only 28% actually went.

To ensure valid measurement with self-report data, researchers often add "control checks." As a form of predictive validity, one may determine whether self-reports accurately reflect what people really do. For instance, Duncan and Lieberson (1959) examined self-reports of social distance among different ethnic groups in Chicago. To check on the validity of the self-reports, they examined the relationship between social distance scores and the degree to which the members of different ethnic groups physically segregated themselves from each other. They found a high correlation between these variables. By using such validity checks, limitations on self-report validity claims may be made.

Concerns With "Recall" Studies

Some studies ask subjects to recall recent communication encounters and to report what occurred and their feelings about them. Naturally, these studies introduce another limitation on results—the ability of subjects to recall accurately what occurred. In most network analysis studies, people were asked to write the names of people with whom they had communicated. Unfortunately, the ability to recall names accurately led to significant doubts about the data to be analyzed. In fact, network analyses were strongly criticized in a collection of studies in the 1970s that compared self-report data with observer reports (Bernard & Killworth, 1977; Bernard, Killworth, & Sailer, 1982; Killworth & Bernard, 1979a, 1979b). To control such problems, researchers often include "control checks" on their data. For instance, Trapp and Hoff (1985) asked people to recall arguments in which they had been involved. They found that people reported that the arguments were rarely resolved, though pauses occurred in the exchanges. To control for subject recall problems, they attempted to get independent reports from at least two different witnesses or participants to the communication event.

SPECIAL DISCUSSION 4-3

A QUESTION OF ETHICS: QUALITY MEASUREMENT AS AN ETHICAL PRIORITY

Though one might wonder about it, the quality of measurement is an ethical matter. The American Psychological Association Ethical Principles of Psychologists and Code of Conduct includes Section 9.02b and 9.02c, which addresses issues in measurement and test construction. Individual researchers who measure variables in research for clinical practice may be subject to sanctions if they violate the standard:

(b) Psychologists use assessment instruments whose validity and reliability have been established for use with members of the population tested. When such validity or reliability has not been established, psychologists describe the strengths and limitations of test results and interpretation.

(c) Psychologists use assessment methods that are appropriate to an individual's language preference and competence, unless the use of an alternative language is relevant to the assessment issues.

This standard has been taken to mean that the researcher must be competent and knowledgeable in test construction.

A related issue is the problem of test bias.

Test bias may refer to systematic errors in test scoring. The term is more frequently associated with test fairness and refers to assessment norms applied to persons from different populations that fail to establish measurement equivalence: the degree to which reliability and validity coefficients associated with a measure are similar across populations. (Fisher, 2003, p. 197)

Using measures that are biased can lead to misleading interpretations of test scores and, if action is taken on them, to over- and underidentification of clients for special attention.

When researchers develop tests, they are under ethical obligations to

♦ identify the populations for which the measure is appropriate;

♦ provide guides to interpreting the meaning of reported scores, both for researchers and in reports that may be made to research participants;

♦ revise the measures against new data and research insights that may be forthcoming;

♦ specify the purpose of the measure; and

♦ guard against use of the measurement tools by unqualified people (Fisher, 2003, pp. 198–202).

Though researchers in communication studies may not believe that these guidelines for psychology necessarily apply to them, they may not have a reason to be completely unbound by such standards. The APA ethical standards are so widely distributed and so commonly described in scholarly work that social scientists in all applied fields have taken them as presumptive ethical standards that apply to all.

The lessons for you are clear. In the first place, when evaluating others' research and when designing your own research, you should use measurement tools for which you have evidence of reliability, validity, language appropriateness, and suitability for the population of interest. You should not *assume* anything about these matters. Since these issues may be tested, you should insist on seeing new evidence of test reliability and validity. In the second place, for newly developed measurement tools, you should provide full reports of information about the adequacy of the measures. For both new and previously developed instruments, anything less than these contributions may be considered ethical breaches.

To measure a variable, it is important to begin with a conceptual definition. Then, you may examine parts of the definition to see if there are elements that should be included in the measure. For instance, suppose you wanted a measure of the audience's general perceptions of a speaker's understandability. You might look up some definitions of the word "understandability," such as this one: "1. to come to know the meaning or import of; apprehend. 2. to comprehend the nature or character of. 3. to have comprehension or mastery of . . . " (*Funk & Wagnalls Standard Desk Dictionary,* 1983, vol. 2, p. 740; used with permission). This definition reveals that understandability may include several interrelated perceptions: a general perception of the degree to which the speaker is understandable, whether the speaker's meaning is clear, and whether the speaker's message is comprehensible. Following a search for definitions, you might read what writers in the field say are traits of understandable speakers. Reading relevant book chapters and articles might add characteristics to your list. For instance, you might find that authors of public speaking books recommend that speakers stay organized if they wish to be understandable.

steps to develop new measures:

1. examine conceptual definitions and search scholarly discussions

As a second step, you should decide on a format such as one of those covered in the rest of this chapter. Then the questions, statements, or word pairs may be inserted into the larger study with the minimum of difficulty. In our example of understandability, we might find that other measures we planned to use involved scales bounded by bipolar adjectives. Thus, we might wish to use the same format, rather than introducing a different format to present to respondents. The items then could be composed.

2. decide on format

As a third step, you could present the new instrument to a small group of people (often fewer than a dozen) from the population in which you plan to conduct the final study. Though many researchers leave out this step, they are taking their chances. It is particularly helpful for beginning researchers to get such feedback. Suppose people were asked to evaluate "The Speaker You Just Heard" based on the following criteria: understandable–confusing, clear–unclear, comprehensible–incomprehensible, and organized–disorganized. Phrases that are confusing might be changed, and advice for improving the measure could be accepted.

3. secure feedback from small sample

Finally, you would attempt to get evidence of reliability and validity of the measure. Some researchers like to complete a little pilot study to get data on the adequacy of their measures before they complete a full study. Other researchers prefer

4. examine reliability and validity

to gather data in the study and check for reliability and validity before they actually examine how the data answer the research question. If they find that a particular item on a measure is unreliable, they simply discard it and score the measure with the remaining scale items. Regardless of their approach, the researchers select methods already described in this chapter as ways to argue for the reliability and validity of their measures.

Popular Methods for Measurement

Some major measurement techniques have been popular in our field. Two categories include measures that express judgments of some kind, and measures that identify achievement or behaviors.

Methods to Measure Judgments

Communication researchers often ask people to report their attitudes, rate some behavior, or evaluate some message quality. These assessments can be measured in many ways, but the most popular tools in communication have been Thurstone scales, Likert scales, Guttman scales, and semantic differential-type scales.

Thurstone equal appearing interval scales scales composed of statements for which agreement with any individual item is assigned a predetermined point value.

Thurstone Equal Appearing Interval Scales. Named for their creator, L. L. Thurstone, these scales are actually called **equal appearing interval scales.** If you wanted to use Thurstone scales to rate the bias in newspaper coverage of political campaigns, you might use statements such as "Newspapers are very biased," "Newspapers do not tell the truth," and "Newspapers have a hard time being impartial." Respondents are asked to identify the statements with which they agree. Then, unbeknownst to the subjects, you would determine a total score by adding up the point values for each of the statements with which subjects agreed. How do we get the point values? That's the time-consuming part. The researcher typically puts together a list of 50 to 100 statements (on cards) and then asks a group of people (from the same population that will later use the scales) to sort the cards on a scale ranging from 1 to 11 indicating how extreme the statements are. For instance, the statement "Newspapers are very biased" is more extreme than the statement "Newspapers have a hard time being impartial." So, these statements would be placed at different locations on the scale. After the raters finish, the researcher identifies statements that had consistent ratings. Then these statements are given an average score based on their ratings. In using the scales in a study, the researcher simply tallies the total points of the statements with which each person agreed. Table 4.2 shows such a scale.

applications, advantages, and limitations

The method is quite sound and continues to be used in many studies in communication. Researchers who study effects of stress in communication often use a rating scale of stressful life events that is a Thurstone scale of events (Reinard & Boster, 1978). Subjects receive a total stress score by adding up the points associated with the events that they report happening to them in the recent past. Yet, the method can often be tedious, time-consuming, and expensive. The scales also must be done anew every time the topic of evaluation is changed.

TABLE 4.2   EXAMPLES OF RATING SCALES

Thurstone Scales

Place a check mark in the blank next to each statement with which you agree.

_____ 1. This class in research methods is more challenging than other courses I am taking this term.   (9.8)
_____ 2. This class in research methods teaches me valuable information.   (10.1)
_____ 3. This class in research methods is what I expected.   (6.0)
_____ 4. This class in research methods is interesting.   (8.9)

NOTE: Numbers in parentheses indicate the point value for each statement. The scale is scored by adding the points for all items for which the respondent indicates agreement.

Semantic Differential-Type Scales

Rate the concept "The President" according to the way you perceive it or feel about it by placing an X on each of the seven-point scales to indicate your evaluation.

The President

reliable ___:___:___:___:___:___:___	unreliable★
uninformed ___:___:___:___:___:___:___	informed
unqualified ___:___:___:___:___:___:___	qualified
intelligent ___:___:___:___:___:___:___	unintelligent★
valuable ___:___:___:___:___:___:___	worthless★
inexpert ___:___:___:___:___:___:___	expert
dishonest ___:___:___:___:___:___:___	honest
unfriendly ___:___:___:___:___:___:___	friendly
pleasant ___:___:___:___:___:___:___	unpleasant★
selfish ___:___:___:___:___:___:___	unselfish
awful ___:___:___:___:___:___:___	nice
virtuous ___:___:___:___:___:___:___	sinful★

NOTE: Items followed by asterisks (★) indicate reverse scoring. Scores on the first six items are added to produce a "competence" score. The remaining items are added to produce a "character" score.

SOURCE: McCroskey, J. C. (1966). Scales for the measurement of ethos. *Speech Monographs, 33,* 72. Copyright 1966. Reproduced by permission of James C. McCroskey and the National Communication Association, www.natcom.org.

Guttman Scale

Consider a person who is Chinese and circle the number next to each of the situations listed below in which you would accept a person from this group.

1. as a visitor to my country

2. to citizenship in my country

3. to employment in my occupation

4. to my street as a neighbor

5. to my club as a personal friend

6. to close kinship by marriage

NOTE: This scale is an adapted version of the Bogardus Social Distance scale (Bogardus, 1933). The number of items circled is the individual's score.

(Continued)

TABLE 4.2 (Continued)

Likert Scale

PERSONAL REPORT OF COMMUNICATION APPREHENSION (PRCA-24)

Directions: This instrument is composed of 24 statements concerning your feelings about communication with other people. Please indicate in the space provided the degree to which each statement applies to you by marking whether you (1) Strongly Agree, (2) Agree, (3) Are Undecided, (4) Disagree, or (5) Strongly Disagree with each statement. There are no right or wrong answers. Many of the statements are similar to other statements. Do not be concerned about this. Work quickly, just record your first impression.

_____ 1. I dislike participating in group discussions.

_____ 2. Generally, I am comfortable while participating in group discussions.

_____ 3. I am tense and nervous while participating in group discussions.

_____ 4. I like to get involved in group discussions.

_____ 5. Engaging in a group discussion with new people makes me tense and nervous.

_____ 6. I am calm and relaxed while participating in group discussions.

_____ 7. Generally, I am nervous when I have to participate in a meeting.

_____ 8. Usually I am calm and relaxed while participating in meetings.

_____ 9. I am very calm and relaxed when I am called upon to express an opinion at a meeting.

_____ 10. I am afraid to express myself at meetings.

_____ 11. Communicating at meetings usually makes me uncomfortable.

_____ 12. I am very relaxed when answering questions at a meeting.

_____ 13. While participating in a conversation with a new acquaintance, I feel very nervous.

_____ 14. I have no fear of speaking up in conversations.

_____ 15. Ordinarily I am very tense and nervous in conversations.

_____ 16. Ordinarily I am very calm and relaxed in conversations.

_____ 17. While conversing with a new acquaintance, I feel very relaxed.

_____ 18. I'm afraid to speak up in conversations.

_____ 19. I have no fear of giving a speech.

_____ 20. Certain parts of my body feel very tense and rigid while giving a speech.

_____ 21. I feel relaxed while giving a speech.

_____ 22. My thoughts become confused and jumbled when I am giving a speech.

_____ 23. I face the prospect of giving a speech with confidence.

_____ 24. While giving a speech I get so nervous, I forget facts I really know.

SCORING

Group = 18 − (1) + (2) − (3) + (4) − (5) + (6)

Meeting = 18 − (7) + (8) + (9) − (10) − (11) + (12)

Dyadic = 18 − (13) + (14) − (15) + (16) + (17) − (18)

Public = 18 + (19) − (20) + (21) − (22) + (23) − (24)

Overall CA = Group + Meeting + Dyadic + Public

NOTE: This instrument is copyrighted by James C. McCroskey. Appropriate citation is: James C. McCroskey. *An Introduction to Rhetorical Communication,* 4th ed. (Englewood Cliffs, NJ: Prentice-Hall, 1982). The instrument may be reprinted and used for research and instructional purposes without additional authorization of the copyright holder. Uses for which there is expectation of profit, including publication or instruction outside the normal college or school environment, are prohibited without written permission of James C. McCroskey.

Likert Scales.[4] The technique presents statements that reflect clear positions on an issue and then asks subjects to indicate their responses on five-point scales: strongly agree, agree, neither agree nor disagree, disagree, strongly disagree. A few researchers use four-point scales, leaving out the middle position entirely. Occasionally, researchers have added scale positions to create seven-, nine-, or eleven-point scales, but the basic system is not defined by the number of points used. Instead, items that have high reliability with each other are combined by adding the ratings that respondents give. Unlike Thurstone scales, which assign a value for each item with which a person agrees, **Likert scales** simply gauge the degree to which there is agreement or disagreement with statements representing a common issue.

> **Likert scales** scales composed of statements that reflect clear positions on an issue, for which subjects indicate their agreement (on) typically five-point scales.

You have filled out Likert scales on teacher evaluation forms and, very probably, on some surveys you have completed in your classes. Yet, the format you have seen may look a little different from the example found on Table 4.2. The format often includes a layout with the response categories along one side following the statements, as shown below.

applications, advantages, and limitations

Directions: Circle one answer for each question.

	Strongly Agree	Agree	Neither Agree nor Disagree	Disagree	Strongly Disagree
I think communication research is exciting	1	2	3	4	5

These scales are very popular because they are relatively easy to develop. In fact, that ease has sometimes led researchers to use them even when more precise alternatives are available.[5] Yet, a total score sometimes hides specific details of the response from a person. Moreover, if researchers change their topics, the items on the Likert scale may have to be composed all over again.

To create an index out of some Likert scales, the researcher begins by assigning a number to each scale position for each item. For instance, a teacher humor assessment instrument was developed by Wrench and Richmond (2004). Some of the items from this index are shown on the next page, along with the responses from one study participant.

---

[4]Likert scales are named after Likert, who pronounced the name "lick-ert," not "Like-ert." You may test the matter yourself, by calling Likert and Associates and listening to the way they answer the telephone.

[5]For instance, Barnett, Hamlin, and Danowski (1981) noted that many researchers used "crude" four- or five-point rating scales when, in fact, they might have used true ratio level scales. Their suggestion was that researchers avoid using Likert scales when they are unnecessary. To measure such a thing as the amount of communication from the boss that employees report receiving at work, Barnett and associates argued that the method of "fractionation scales" that include an absolute zero could be used. For instance, they suggested using such a response format as this:

How much information do you get from your boss?	0	50	100	150
	None	Average	Twice Average	Three Times Average...

Participants report numbers to indicate their ratings.

	Strongly Agree	Agree	Neither Agree nor Disagree	Disagree	Strongly Disagree
1. My teacher regularly communicates with others using humor	1	②	3	4	5
2. People usually laugh when my teacher makes a humorous remark	①	2	3	4	5
3. My teacher is not funny or humorous	1	2	3	④	5
4. Being humorous is a natural communication orientation for my teacher	1	②	3	4	5

To score these scales into this person's score for the entire index, you add the scores from each of the individual scale items, after making adjustments. For instance, you probably notice that the statements are phrased positively—except for statement 3. So, to make sure that the scales make sense, item 3 must be "reverse coded." You could change the value of 1 to 5, 2 to 4, 4 to 2, and 5 to 1. But an easy way is simply to subtract the score from statement 3 from the number 6 (1 more than the number of scale points). Using this latter approach, the researcher would add: $2 + 1 + (6 - 4) + 2 = 7$. The lower the score, the greater the teacher's use of humor.

Guttman Scalogram. Developed by Louis Guttman, this scale involves a series of statements dealing with one topic and arranged according to their level of intensity. Surely the most popular **Guttman scalogram** has been the Bogardus "Social Distance" scale (see Table 4.2), which has often been featured in studies of racial and ethnic prejudice. The more prejudiced a person is, the reasoning goes, the fewer circumstances this person would find acceptable. Because the statements are arranged on a single continuum, if we know the number of statements with which a person agreed, we probably also know which statements the person accepted. For instance, if a respondent rates it acceptable for a person to have employment in one's profession, that respondent also probably would find it acceptable for the target person to be a citizen in the country and to visit the country. Thus, the number of statements with which a person agrees also lets us know *which* particular statements they probably were.

The Guttman scale is scored by counting the number of statements with which a respondent agrees. In our example, the fewer items circled, the more "socially distant" the respondent is from others. Of course, some people may not follow a set pattern in their responses. Thus, Guttman developed a criterion called the "coefficient of reproducibility" to assess the reliability of these "scalograms." To compute a coefficient of reproducibility, the researcher places the statements in order, ranging from the most frequently agreed-to items in a sample through the least frequently agreed-to items. Then, the researcher looks at each subject's total scores to count the proportion of the time that the respondent answered as

Guttman scalogram a scale involving a series of statements dealing with one topic and arranged according to their level of intensity.

scoring Guttman scales

use of the coefficient of reproducibility

expected. That is, if people agreed with three statements, they should have answered the three most frequently accepted statements. Any time an answer appears outside the predicted pattern, an exception is noted. Guttman recommended that consistent responses be observed at least 90% of the time, or a coefficient of reproducibility of .90.[6]

This scaling method is highly useful when there is a clear continuum of responses that people could make on some issue. Yet, the stringent requirements for such a scale may make it challenging to come up with new Guttman scales. Furthermore, they are specific to topics and must be developed from scratch each time a new topic is investigated. Thus, you should not be surprised to learn that such scales are not used as much as they once were.

applications, advantages, and limitations

Semantic Differential-Type Scales. In 1957, Charles Osgood, George Suci, and Percy Tannenbaum wrote *The Measurement of Meaning* in which they reported research to discover how people assign meaning to words. To help them along the way, they developed a type of scale that involved using pairs of "bipolar" adjectives (often separated by seven points, sometimes six, sometimes five) that could be used by people to indicate their reactions (see Table 4.2). Since they were studying semantics (the study of the relationship between words and their meanings), they called their scale the "Semantic Differential." The method became popular among researchers who were *not* studying semantics. Thus, these applications to other subjects resulted in their being called **semantic differential-type scales.**

Semantic differential-type scales scales (often seven-point intervals) bounded by pairs of bipolar adjectives.

This scale method has become the most popular measurement approach in communication studies. An object of evaluation is presented to people who indicate their responses by checking or circling scale positions. A total score is obtained by assigning values from 1 to 7 to each item (though scales have been known to range from five to nine points) and simply adding up items on the same dimension. Actual numbers are not displayed on the scales that study participants use. But afterward, when the data are entered into some spreadsheet or data editor for subsequent data analysis, each scale position is assigned a number, such as shown here:

$$\underline{1} : \underline{2} : \underline{3} : \underline{4} : \underline{5} : \underline{6} : \underline{7}$$

To identify a study participant's score using an index composed of a set of semantic differential-type scales, you add the numerical values for the scale positions that have been checked. For instance, to measure the competence dimension of source credibility using McCroskey's scales to measure ethos (shown on Table 4.2), the researcher might be faced with a set of responses from a study participant as shown on the next page:

---

[6]The coefficient of reproducibility is computed by counting the number of "errors" and dividing by the total number of responses. Then this proportion is subtracted from 1.0. Originally Guttman (1944) stated that a coefficient of .90 was required for an acceptable scale. At a later time, Guttman permitted the scale to be used if the coefficient of reproducibility were .80 or higher (since one imperfection created two potential errors to count—one for the "incorrectly" used scale and one for the scale that "incorrectly" should have been used but was not). But the requirement of .9 has remained as the most typical standard.

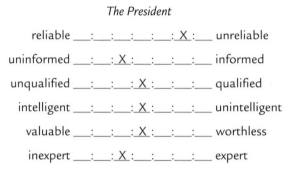

The President

reliable	__:__:__:__:_X_:__	unreliable
uninformed	__:__:_X_:__:__:__	informed
unqualified	__:__:__:_X_:__:__:__	qualified
intelligent	__:__:__:_X_:__:__:__	unintelligent
valuable	__:__:__:_X_:__:__:__	worthless
inexpert	__:__:_X_:__:__:__:__	expert

Since three of the scales (reliable/unreliable; intelligent/unintelligent; valuable/worthless) have the negative pole (the lowest score) on the right of the continuum, they would erroneously be assigned the highest scores unless they were "reverse coded." Reverse coding would be accomplished easily if you just subtracted the observed scale values from the number 8 (1 more than the number of scale points). Thus, the researcher would add: $(8 - 6) + 3 + 4 + (8 - 4) + (8 - 4) + 3 = 20$. The greater the score (possible range of 6 to 42 points), the higher are the ratings of the President's competence.

applications, advantages, and limitations

This method is very convenient to use and, unlike other tools, can be employed almost regardless of the topic under evaluation. For instance, the same scales can be used to assess credibility of any source. Researchers don't need to construct new scales to evaluate each different source. Yet, the responses on each dimension give only a composite reaction, rather than information about the contours of responses. For instance, suppose a person received a score of 16 on four semantic differential-type scales. The person might have "flip-flopped" from one extreme positive position to an extreme negative position and back again. Or, the response might have emerged if the person neither agreed nor disagreed on all items. A simple total may miss such differences in response patterns. Overall, however, the method seems to have gained popularity because of its great versatility.

Methods for Measurement of Achievement

Researchers often obtain data on achievement or knowledge of some content. The formats to measure such information provide a repertoire that researchers can use. On one level, achievement or knowledge of content can be tested by such methods as true-false or multiple-choice tests. Sometimes researchers give respondents questions that request them to choose between two alternatives. Called the "forced choice format," the researcher gives subjects two statements, one of which they must choose. This method is useful to help identify how individuals make choices, but sometimes the choices are difficult for respondents to complete accurately (Hale, Boster, & Mongeau, 1991).

A variation of sorts is the paired comparison method. In this format, subjects receive alternatives with all possible combinations given two at a time. This method is invaluable for ranking alternatives that may seem to have a great overlap in quality. If you were asked to rank a list of 10 newspapers for general credibility, it might be difficult to rate them all at once. Instead, you could be given two newspapers and asked to choose which of the two is more credible. Then all other combinations would follow, a pair at a time. The final ranking could be found by counting the number of times each paper was preferred.

SPECIAL DISCUSSION 4-4

CATEGORIES OF MEASUREMENT IN COMMUNICATION

Communication research has tended to focus on a fairly consistent set of measurement categories. Though originally doing their thinking from the perspective of educational research, two scholars of research methods (Isaac & Michael, 1981, especially p. 149) identified six different dimensions of measures that also apply to communication studies:

1. Cognitive assessments that focus on things that people know or believe; cognitive measures deal with two major things:

   ♦ Aptitude measures (e.g., college entrance exams and intelligence tests)
   ♦ Achievement (such as midterm exam scores, and even such items as grade point averages)

2. Affective assessments that deal with sentiments and feelings people have toward things; such measures include tools to identify:

   ♦ Preferences (such as job interest inventories)
   ♦ Attitudes (such as evaluations of political candidates)
   ♦ Socioemotional characteristics (such as scales to measure optimism or satisfaction with life)

3. Perceptual-motor assessments that deal with one's aptitude to perform specific tasks, including skills involving manual activity (such as measures of typing skill)

4. Personality assessments that isolate elements of an individual's character (such as self-esteem or locus of control)

5. Behavior assessments, which are observation techniques to identify the activities of people (such as by use of Bales Interaction Process Analysis or the Riley Articulation and Language Test)

6. Demographic assessments that identify environmental or physical conditions (such as socioeconomic status or sex of employees)

CHECKLIST TO EVALUATE MEASUREMENT

For quantitative studies:

_____ Is there evidence of measurement reliability (with clear descriptions of the methods used for reliability assessment)?

_____ How sound are the arguments for measurement validity (are methods to establish validity clearly presented)?

_____ Is reliability established *before* claims of validity are made?

_____ If previously developed measures are employed, is new evidence of reliability and validity presented?

_____ Were sound methods used for any construction of new measures?

_____ Was the scoring method of measures properly described and appropriate?

For qualitative studies:

_____ Is evidence of dependability of identification and interpretations presented (with clear arguments and descriptions of methods used to claim dependability)?

_____ Is evidence of trustworthiness of data and findings provided (with clear arguments and descriptions of methods used to claim trustworthiness)?

Are any self-reports from study participants critically evaluated to check accuracy and recall (regardless of whether these matters are central to the research question)?

SUMMARY

Accurate measurement is vital to sound research for many reasons; for example, (1) research conclusions are only as good as the data, (2) the types of measures a researcher employs determine the statistical tools that may be used to examine the data, and (3) one cannot claim to be interested in relationships between variables unless it is possible to identify those variables in actual operation. Measurement imperfections introduce additional variation or background noise into a study in addition to variation that already exists in samples. This problem is called attenuation of results, which means that there is a reduction of the size of observed effects because of errors in measurement. There are four measurement levels for data: (1) nominal level measurement uses numbers as simple identification of variables; (2) ordinal level measurement uses rank order to determine differences; (3) interval level measurement identifies items as a matter of degree (the intervals between the numbers are equal in size); and (4) ratio level measurement extends interval measurement to include an "absolute zero" (in which a score of zero indicates that the property measured is completely absent). The distinction among nominal, ordinal, interval, and ratio measurement is useful since (1) the distinction can help us understand the difference between categorical data (measures that identify attributes or levels of a variable: they are discrete variables and, as such, are on the nominal level of measurement) and continuous data (measures expressed numerically to indicate matters of degree: thus, continuous variables are measured on the ordinal, interval, or ratio level); (2) these levels of measurement arrange themselves from lowest to highest (in such a way, each level more or less builds on the unit before it by adding precision). Some writers have been suspicious that most popular measurement tools actually use scales with equal intervals. Other researchers, however, have studied the impact of violating assumptions of pure intervals, and they found the alleged difficulties to be trivial on eventual statistical analyses. Measurement levels depend on the tools that one may have available, and researchers often start at one level of measurement for a variable and then move to lower levels of measurement for design purposes. Thus, measurement levels are often determined by the methods researchers choose.

Reliability is the internal consistency of a measure. There are several ways researchers can determine a measure's reliability. All these methods take information about the consistency of a measure with itself and compute a reliability coefficient, which is a correlation that measures the amount of association or coincidence of things. Test-retest reliability involves giving the measure twice and reporting consistency between scores (this method is time-consuming but is often useful when measures contain single items or when test items combine matters that are largely independent of others on the same measure). Alternate forms reliability (or parallel forms technique) involves constructing different forms of the same test from a common pool of measurement items and correlating scores that sample groups receive on both. Split-half reliability divides a test into two parts, scores them separately, and checks the consistency between the two scores for a sample group (sometimes this method employs odd-even reliability). Item to total reliability computes the correlation of items with the total test. Intercoder reliability examines the degree to which different raters consistently categorize things by using some sort of check sheet (in content analysis of communication, prudent researchers tend to rely on either Cohen's *kappa,* which compensates for the number of times rating categories are used, or Scott's *pi,* which also compensates for the rates of agreement that would be expected by chance alone). Statistical shortcuts are ways to get reliability coefficients rapidly using such methods as K-R 20 (used when researchers want to determine the reliability of a measure that has items that are scored as "correct" or "incorrect") or coefficient alpha (when correct answers are not identified).

Validity is the consistency of a measure with a criterion. In plain terms, validity is the degree to which a measure actually measures what is claimed. Though it is possible to have a reliable test without having a valid one, one cannot have a valid measure without its first being reliable. Thus, validity presumes reliability. There are four major ways to determine validity. Face validity involves researchers' looking at the content of the measurement items and advancing an argument that, on its face, the measure seems to identify what it claimed. Expert jury validity involves having a group of experts in the subject matter examine the measurement and judge its merit. Criterion validity assesses a measure's worth by examining its relation to some outside criterion, such as (a) concurrent validity, which correlates a new measure with a previously validated measure of the same thing, and (b) predictive validity, which is the degree to which a measure predicts known groups in which the construct must exist. Construct validation requires that a new measure be administered to subjects along with at least two other measures, one of which is known to be directly related to the concept, and one of which is known to be inversely related to the concept (if the new measure is valid, it should produce significant findings in the correct directions).

Reliability and validity issues also influence researchers who attempt to draw conclusions from studies using qualitative research methods. In most qualitative research, the researcher *is* the instrument. Hence, many qualitative researchers have observed that reliability and validity involve questions about the researcher as interpreter. In qualitative research, a substitute criterion for reliability is dependability, which is "the effort to account for both factors of instability and factors of phenomenal or design induced change" (Lincoln & Guba, 1985, p. 299). To assure such dependability, researchers may use "overlap methods" (in which multiple methods are used to triangulate a dependable set of interpretations of communication phenomena); "stepwise replication" (in which at least two qualitative researchers compare their interpretations at different times); and "dependability audits" (in which experts examine the process and the interpretations involved in the qualitative research). In qualitative research, the question of validity is transformed into a question about the trustworthiness of the data and the findings. To assure trustworthiness or validity of their work, researchers may use extended participation in field experiences; persistent observations so that key phenomena are not likely to be overlooked; negative case analysis (drawing conclusions only after accounting for any negative cases that disprove the general relationship); referential adequacy (recording qualitative interviews and observations, and carefully keeping records of actual encounters under analysis);

and member checks involving comparisons with members of the group studied). Some cases, such as Margaret Mead's interpretations of the behaviors of adolescent girls in Samoa, are archetypes of qualitative studies that have been criticized for a failure to be both dependable and trustworthy.

Communication researchers often ask people to report their attitudes or rate some behavior. There are two options when measuring a construct: find preexisting measures or create new measures. To find measures for important communication variables, you may look in this book and in ancillary sources, including measurement handbooks and research articles. To select a measure you should ask if (1) the measure is suited to the type of sample you are thinking of using, (2) there is evidence for reliability and validity, (3) the measure has appropriate length, and (4) the measure has an appropriate format. To create new measures, researchers should (1) analyze parts of conceptual definitions and scholarly discussions for the variable to isolate elements to measure, (2) decide on a format for the measure, (3) secure feedback from a small sample, and (4) examine reliability and validity of the new measure. The most popular measurement tools in communication have been the Thurstone equal appearing interval scales (which have assigned point values for each of the statements with which subjects agree); the Likert scales (which consist of statements for which subjects indicate their agreement or disagreement, typically on five-point scales); the Guttman scalograms (which involve a series of statements dealing with one topic and arranged according to their level of intensity); and the semantic differential-type scales (most often featuring seven-point scales bounded by bipolar adjectives). Researchers often obtain data on achievement or knowledge of some content by using such formats as true-false or multiple-choice tests. Sometimes researchers give respondents "forced choice format" items that request them to choose between two alternatives. A variation is the paired comparison method in which subjects receive alternatives in all possible combinations taken two at a time.

TERMS FOR REVIEW

attenuation	split-half reliability
measurement	item to total reliability
nominal level measurement	intercoder reliability
ordinal level measurement	KR-20
interval level measurement	Cronbach's coefficient alpha
ratio level measurement	validity
categorical data	face validity
continuous variables	expert jury validity
quasi-interval measures	criterion validity
reliability	concurrent validity
false precision	predictive validity
fallacy of misplaced precision	construct validity
reliability coefficient	dependability
test-retest reliability	overlap methods
alternate forms (parallel forms) reliability	stepwise replication

dependability audits

negative case analysis

referential adequacy

Thurstone equal appearing interval scales

Likert scales

Guttman scalogram

semantic differential-type scales

JUST FOR THE SAKE OF ARGUMENT: A REVIEW

Look at the following questions and prepare your own answers to them. Look for the assumptions that underlie them.

1. What is the difference between interval and ratio level measurement? When would identification of the two levels be important?

2. If a test is valid, is it necessary to report separate information on reliability? What elements of measurement adequacy must be presented for a thorough analysis?

3. If measures of reliability are correlations that show the consistency of a measure with itself, what does a correlation coefficient of validity show?

4. What is the chief alleged advantage of semantic differential-type scales over Likert scales? What are the disadvantages associated with the use of these scales?

5. What are the differences among the different methods to determine test reliability? What are the mathematic differences in computation and in terms of comparing different reliability techniques?

6. How do projective tests differ from other standardized methods?

7. Which is the superior approach: using measurement tools that already have been developed, or using tools developed by the researcher? What are the advantages and disadvantages of each approach?

ACTIVITIES TO PROBE FURTHER

Go to the website for this book and look for the Student Study Materials for Chapter 4.

1. Take the study quiz and print out your answers. (Make sure to review these text materials before you answer the questions so that you avoid giving answers that are your first impressions.)

2. Go to the website for the National Communication Association, and look up the questionnaire used in a national survey completed by Roper Starch on communication attitudes and views (www.natcom.org/research/Roper/how_americans_communicate.htm).★ Are there any examples of variables measured on the nominal level? Are there any examples of variables measured on the ordinal level? Are there any examples of variables measured on the interval level? Are there any examples of variables measured on the ratio level? As with any good survey, many items appear to ask about the same ideas from different approaches. How would you determine the reliability of measures composed of multiple items?

★If this measure is no longer on the NCA website, please check the website for this chapter for a copy.

3. Look at the activity titled "Operational Definitions from Research Articles" on the website for this chapter of the book. After completing this assignment, answer these questions.
   a. Where are operational definitions of variables most often found in research?
   b. How easy would it be to replicate the study, given the description of operationalizations that you found?
   c. How would you rate the evidence for measurement reliability and validity?

4. Computer assignment: This assignment involves assessing whether the semantic differential-type attitude scales were reliable for this pilot study of the effects of the use of *non sequitur* fallacies on receivers' attitudes.

   a. Turn to this book's website for Chapter 4, and then go to "Measurement of an Attitude."
      (1) For this task, complete the following steps:
         (a) Read the summary of the study and identify the hypotheses under investigation. Notice how the dependent variable, attitude change, is to be measured. Identify both the level of measurement and the specific composition of the measure.
         (b) Determine coefficient alpha for this measure by using one of the computer programs described here. Print out your answer.
         (c) Describe how you would compose a composite measure of attitude that includes only the reliable scale items.
      (2) This exercise will use major computer data analysis tools: SPSS for Windows or Excel.* If you are unfamiliar with these programs, you may wish to look at the brief introductions found in Appendixes E and F. Fortunately, each program comes bundled with a useful tutorial that can guide you easily through the program.
      (3) If you wish to complete this data analysis using SPSS, download the file "ATTITUDE.SAV". If you wish to complete this data analysis using Excel, download the file "ATTITUDE.XLS".

   b. Determine the reliability of the attitude measure, which is composed of four semantic differential-type scales (wise–foolish, good–bad, positive–negative, beneficial–harmful). Determine coefficient alpha, and compose the attitude scales. Under some circumstances we would subject these data to factor analyses to determine their underlying structure before using coefficient alpha. But because these scales have been widely used in research on attitudes, we will skip that exploratory step here (as largely unnecessary). The website will guide you through the same steps here to help you get comfortable with the tools.

---

*Excel and Windows are registered trademarks of Microsoft Corporation.

Composing the Communication Argument: The Reasoning and the Evidence

Science is simply common sense at its best—that is, rigidly accurate in observation, and merciless to fallacy in logic.

—THOMAS HUXLEY

CHAPTER OUTLINE

BEFORE WE GET STARTED . . .

Research is not like most other writing. Research is a form of argument. Thus, research is not expository or informative writing, even though much information is shared in communication research. Students new to the craft may be surprised that the research argument is presented in very terse writing. To be successful scholars, we need to know how the research argument is mapped out and composed. Furthermore, we need to understand how tests of good reasoning and logic apply directly to our field's inquiry. This chapter will show you where different kinds of arguments appear in research, the evidence used, and how to test arguments found in research studies.

CONSTRUCTION OF THE ARTICLES YOU WILL READ AND REVIEW

Arguments claims advanced on the basis of reasoning from evidence.

In this book we have defined an **argument** as a process of advancing conclusions based on reasons and evidence. Since researchers draw conclusions from evidence (some very well, some poorly), they are engaged in advancing arguments that can be tested by standards of reasoning and evidence. Yet, this statement does not mean that researchers are successful at haggling. Research and scholarly argument are different from other social interactions and arguments. Research is argument that makes appeals to the standards of sound scholarship. R. Michael Bokeno (1987) examined the use of argument in science and concluded that it is an oversimplification to say that research is just an exercise in persuasion. Instead, science requires arguments to be based on the methods of science without appealing to the prejudices or biases of the masses. In fact, good research virtually requires that you understand how to construct and evaluate sound arguments. It makes sense to look at the reasoning patterns and evidence types that researchers and scholars legitimately can use in their reports and writing.

You may have wondered why research articles look the way they do.[1] This section will help you understand how articles are designed so that you can use them comfortably. As an aid you will find a brief article that shows how these sections typically are handled.

construction of research articles

Title

Let's be blunt about it. Research articles have boring titles. They could have catchy, poetic titles, but indexing services might misplace them if titles did not reveal the content. Such titles as "The Effects of Source Credibility of Women on Attitude Change" may not have verve and punch, but you know what is studied.

specific titles aid accurate indexing

Abstract

Many journals include abstracts. The abstract is a courtesy summary for the reader, not part of the article itself. If you write a paper, you probably should quote from the article itself and not from the abstract. Abstracts can help you decide whether you want to read the entire article. For your own term papers, you probably do not need to include an abstract, but it is required for work that is published or presented at professional meetings.

abstract is courtesy summary to the reader

Introduction and Context of the Problem Argument

In introductions to articles and research papers the author must show why the topic is relevant to the field and indicate the article's approach. Authors mention the field's name frequently in their introductions to let both editors and readers know that the article is central to the field, rather than peripheral to it. Studying the relationship between age and self-esteem may be interesting, but it is not a communication question since no message-related behavior is involved. Strange as it may seem, the introduction to a research paper is an argument. Researchers must prove that the topic they have selected is relevant to the field under discussion. Most introductions end with a preview of the paper itself. This preview is a contract of sorts between the writer and the reader: if the paper moves in other directions, the work is not logically related to its purposes (a fallacy logicians call *non sequitur* when conclusions are "not in sequence" with premises). Thus, a failure to deliver on what is promised for the article may be not only disappointing but illogical as well.

introductions prove that the topic is relevant to the field

the preview commits the researcher to present certain information to draw conclusions

Some articles cannot be understood without some background. Thus, authors may extend introductory remarks to place the topic into perspective. Researchers often include definitions of terms unless there is controversy about them and full

context of the problem

---

[1]In our presentation, most of the description applies to quantitative reports. For types of qualitative research, sensible adjustments must be made to any standard format.

discussion must be presented elsewhere. In addition, any conditions that make the issue timely to society are covered as part of the context.

Justification

Researchers are expected to make an argument in which they prove that the research study they report needed to be completed. This justification for new research does not have to be proven by showing that the world would come to an end without it. Instead, researchers need to present a case to prove that the research is *invited*. Though the specific lines of reasoning may differ, this justification is usually argued from a combination of quoting authoritative sources, referring to past research, and arguing directly for the need for this work. Three major reasons tend to be used:

ways to justify new research:

1. filling a gap in knowledge

♦ *Filling a gap in knowledge.* One or more variables of interest may have been examined separately, but there may be a void in the area researchers want to probe. Finding a gap in knowledge is a good way to argue that new research would be wise. Thus, scholars review literature to find "holes" that invite new work.

2. solving practical problems

♦ *Solving practical problems.* Sometimes there is an immediate need to help overcome a tangible problem. In such efforts, literature from popular sources—such as controversial books, newspaper articles, and magazines—may be referenced. Research foundations or government agencies may identify practical issues that they wish to be addressed. Sometimes practical problems involve measurement difficulties. For many years it was difficult to study communication apprehension (of which stage fright is only one particular form) since valid measures were unavailable. James McCroskey (1978) used this problem to justify studies to validate a new measure, called the Personal Report of Communication Apprehension.

3. extending and improving on past research

♦ *Extending and improving on past research.* Research articles frequently end with suggestions for future inquiry. Though most follow-up work tends to be completed by the same researcher who made the initial suggestions, the recommendations are clear calls for additional research. Sometimes inquiry is invited because past methods have been flawed and improvements are needed.

Statement of the Problem

importance of stating the problem

Among the most important parts of research articles is the problem statement. Some researchers place it in the introduction. Some place it near the end of a brief literature review. Some research skips it altogether, a choice that usually is a hallmark of unfocused study.[2] The problem statement tends to be stated early in

---

[2]You need to drop the idea that research must be good if it is published. Some poor work sometimes gets published despite weaknesses. Perfect research probably has not been completed in our field—although some have come very close. It is all right, therefore, for you to criticize portions of research articles for deficiencies that exist. You are not attacking the person writing the article when you do so, and you are not pretending to be superior to those authors when you evaluate research according to standards found in this book.

research articles because it helps readers understand the new research contributions and the author's goals. Sometimes problem statements are hidden as "purpose statements." Thus, when you read "The purpose of this research was to discover the extent of the use of 'devil terms' in the speeches of Senator Joseph McCarthy," you should recognize that it is equivalent to a problem statement that asks "What was the extent of the use of 'devil terms' in the speeches of Senator Joseph McCarthy?" When reading articles you should look for these problem statements—wherever they are hiding—to include them in your notes.

problems often appear as purpose statements

Review of Literature Argument

Though not always formally labeled, every research article contains a literature review. The review of literature extends the context of the problem by providing additional discussion, definitions, and notes on methods. Three basic questions should be answered in this section:

review of literature elements

♦ What do we already know or do?

♦ How does the new research question relate to what we already know or do?

♦ Why select this particular method of investigation?

Researchers often end literature reviews with statements of the status of the subject. Lists of chief conclusions and priorities for future studies often appear. Such summaries can be very helpful when researchers have reviewed a fairly large body of research and thinking.

Rationale for Hypotheses

Immediately before statements of any hypotheses, you should expect to find a paragraph or two in which the rationale for hypotheses is provided. If our thinking about the related literature is correct, then the hypotheses are what we expect to see. If an article does not include hypotheses, it probably has a detailed problem statement. Though some authors fail to give a specific rationale for hypotheses, experienced researchers usually show links between the literature and hypotheses. Bruce Tuckman explained (1999, p. 331):

isolating hypotheses

> Hypotheses may be justified on two grounds—logical and empirical arguments. Logical justification requires a researcher to develop arguments based on concepts or theories related to the hypotheses; empirical justification requires reference to other research. A research report's introduction must provide justification for each hypothesis to assure the reader of its reasonableness and soundness. (Justification is especially critical in a proposal for a study that requires approval.)

justifications of hypotheses

The hypotheses are often set off in reduced type with symbols such as H_1, H_2, H_3 to indicate different hypotheses. If a hypothesis is not clearly identified, the article just plain doesn't have one.

BOX 5.1   SAMPLE ARTICLE

Title and key
words ————————— **Organizational Newcomers: Temporary and Regular
Employees, Same-Sex and Mixed-Sex Superior-Subordinate
Dyads, Supervisor Influence Techniques, Subordinates,
Communication Satisfaction, and Leader-Member Exchange**

Authors
and affiliations ————— KEVIN G. LAMUDE   DONNA SIMMONS
California State University, San Bernardino   *California State University, San Bernardino*

JOSEPH SCUDDER   PATRICIA TORRES
Northern Illinois University   *Wells Fargo Home Mortgage*

This study examined the relationship between newly hired employees' characteristics (i.e., temporary vs. regular employee, superior-subordinate gender-dyad combinations), supervisors' initial tactics of influence, subordinate communication satisfaction, and quality of leader-member exchange. Results from 148 (71 temporary) new hires indicated (a) employee characteristics were not significantly related to the leader-member exchange, (b) supervisors' initial use of prosocial influence tactics was significantly and positively related to the quality of leader-member exchange, and (c) subordinates' satisfaction with communication was significantly and positively related to the quality of leader-member exchange.

Context of the
problem ——————————— The Leader-Member Exchange (LMX) theory (Graen & Scandura, 1987) posits that supervisors develop dyadic relationships among employees characterized by varying quality levels ranging from a highly interactive, interpersonally supportive relationship ("the in-group"), to a less attractive, very formal relationship (the "out-group"). A considerable amount of research has shown that the relationships developed in these LMX dyads are characterized by many positive and negative employee experiences, such as higher or lower levels of job autonomy, flexibility, decision-making authority, job satisfaction, performance, turnover, and better or less desired assignments (Liden & Graen, 1980; Graen, Liden, & Hoel, 1982, Scandura, Graen, & Novak, 1986; Sherony & Green, 2002). While the outcomes associated with the LMX relationship are well documented, much less attention concerns newly hired organizational members and LMX. In this connection, researchers (Dienesch & Liden, 1986;

Gap in knowledge
indicated ————————

Kevin G. Lamude (Ph.D., University of Utah, 1989) is a Professor in the Department of Communication Studies at California State University, San Bernardino, 5500 University Parkway, San Bernardino, CA 92407. **Joseph Scudder** (Ph.D., Indiana University, 1985) is Associate Professor and Assistant Chair of the Department of Communication Studies at Northern Illinois University. **Donna Simmons** (Ph.D., Ohio University, 2000) is Assistant Professor in the Department of Communication Studies at California State University, San Bernardino. **Patricia Torres** (M.A., California State University, San Bernardino, 2001) is Human Resource Regional Staffing Coordinator with Wells Fargo Home Mortgage. The authors are grateful to the editor of *CRR*, John Sherblom, and the reviewers for their thoughtful review of our article. This paper was presented to the organizational communication interest group at the 2003 annual conference of the International Communication Association in San Diego, CA.

COMMUNICATION RESEARCH REPORTS, Volume 21, Number 1, pages 60–67. Copyright 2004. Reproduced by permission of Eastern Communication Association, www.ecasite.org.

Major, Kozlowski, Chao, & Gardner, 1995) argue that subordinate characteristics, supervisor interaction, and interaction outcomes may be related to LMX, and may help determine the quality of relationship that a newly hired subordinate develops with his/her supervisor. Thus, the purpose of the present study is to examine the influence of (a) differences between newly hired temporary and permanent employees, (b) gender-linked differences and similarities in supervisor-subordinate dyads, (c) supervisor perceived use of influence tactics with newly hired subordinates, and (d) subordinates' satisfaction with communication on LMX.

Research problem
————— statement

Differences of Newly Hired Temporary and Regular Employees in Leader-Member Exchange

Research has shown that quality level associations developed in LMX dyads form rather quickly and early in the superior-subordinate relationship (Varma & Stroh, 2001). Yet, to date, little research concerns newly hired employees and LMX. Perhaps one of the largest increases in new hires in the last decade are members of the contingency population known as temporary employees (temps). Research indicates people perform temporary work to (a) enjoy the flexibility of work hours; (b) to explore career options; and (c) to eventually be hired on a permanent basis (Polivka & Nardone, 1989). In the present study, temps refers to permanent temporary employees (members motivated to be temporary to eventually obtain a permanent position). Previous studies indicate temporary employees take a more passive approach to communication with their managers and coworkers than newly hired regular employees (Sias, Krammer, & Jenkins, 1997; Rogers, 1995). In contrast, Smith (1998) reported permanent temporary employees actively seek information (knowledge and skill development, mentoring) and provide unsolicited information (circulate résumés) to managers to affect their outcome. These competing explanations suggest the following research question:

Justification for
advancing a problem
question: conflicting
————— predictions

R1: Do *newly hired* permanent *temporary employees and newly hired* permanent regular employees differ in their perceptions of LMX they report receiving?

Differences of Same-Sex and Mixed-Sex Superior-Subordinate Dyads in Leader-Member Exchange

Previous research indicated subordinates with same-sex supervisors develop higher quality LMXs than subordinates with opposite-sex supervisors (Wayne, Liden, & Sparrowe, 1994). Similarly, Tsui and O'Reilly (1989) found subordinates in mixed-sex superior-subordinate dyads were less liked and related less to subordinate out-group status than subordinates in same-sex superior-subordinate dyads. This suggests the following hypothesis:

Justification for a
————— hypothesis

H1: Newly hired employees in same-sex superior-subordinate dyads will report higher levels of LMX than newly hired employees in mixed-sex superior-subordinate dyads.

Differences of Initial Supervisor Use of Tactics of Influence and Leader-Member Exchange

Influencing subordinates is one of the most important determinants of supervisor effectiveness and figures prominently in the coordination of work units, subordinate motivation, and control of the decision-making process (Kipnis, Schmidt, Swaffjh-Smith, & Wilkinson, 1984). Superior-subordinate researchers have indicated prosocial and antisocial communication techniques can enhance or detract from the overall effectiveness of supervisor use of influence (Lamude & Scudder, 1993; Richmond, Davis, Saylor, & McCroskey, 1984; Richmond,

(Continued)

McCroskey, & Davis, 1986). Dienesch and Liden (1986) suggest these controlling tactics may impact the quality of LMX. For instance, prosocial tactics involving the use of rewards, rationality, flattery, and friendliness should not only foster subordinate compliance but also increase LMX potential. In contrast, antisocial tactics involving direct assertive requests, higher authority and sanctions should tend to damage the superior-subordinate relationship and thus reduce exchanges. Despite Dienesch and Liden's (1986) appeal for research on influence tactics, few studies have examined these relationships. Existing research indicated use of prosocial techniques such as flattery, friendliness, and less use of antisocial tactics such as assertive requests are positively associated with LMX. However, these studies have focused only on several influence tactics (Dockery & Steiner, 1990) or employed unpublished measures (Schriesheim, Castro, & Yammarino, 2000). This makes it difficult to assess the use of unmeasured tactics and combinations of tactics, as well as generalize findings.

In sum, a great deal of tactics of influence research suggests more use of prosocial techniques and less use of antisocial techniques lead to positive outcomes. LMX commentary and research indicate supervisor use of prosocial tactics of influence may be related to LMX, and may help determine the quality of the relationship that a newly hired subordinate develops with his or her supervisor. Thus, the following hypotheses were tested:

H2: Supervisors' perceived use of prosocial influence tactics with newly hired subordinates will be positively related to LMX.

H3: Supervisors' perceived use of antisocial influence tactics with newly hired subordinates will be negatively related to LMX.

Subordinates' Communication Satisfaction and Leader–Member Exchange

Satisfaction with communication is the pleasure one feels after successful and fulfilling experiences in interpersonal communication (Hecht, 1978). Previous research indicated that as the quality of the relationship becomes more intimate, satisfaction with the communication interaction generally increases (Hecht & Marston, 1987). Other researchers have reported a relationship between subordinates' satisfaction with immediate supervisors' communication and variables linked to LMX, such as supportiveness (Daniels, Spiker, & Papa, 1997) and receptivity (Wheeless, Wheeless, & Howard, 1984). Given that communication satisfaction has been demonstrated to be positively associated with relationship closeness and increased communication interactions we would anticipate newly hired employees in LMX relationships with their supervisors may be very well satisfied with their communication. Thus, we propose:

H4: Subordinates' perceived satisfaction with communication will be positively related to LMX.

The Method of Study Argument

methods described in enough detail for replication

The method section of a study describes what the researchers did in enough detail so that others could repeat or replicate it. For critical or qualitative studies—such as evaluating the speeches of Susan B. Anthony or engaging in extended naturalistic studies of police—the method section tends to be *very* brief. Often, no formal section labeled "Method" appears, though many qualitative or historical-critical studies include justifications for critical standards or analysis tools. For quantitative studies, the methods may be explained in detail, complete with subheadings. We will consider these elements next.

in qualitative study, presentation of methods differs

RESEARCHERS IN THE FIELD: DAVID ZAREFSKY

A champion high school debater, David Zarefsky subsequently attended Northwestern University as an undergraduate student and earned three degrees there. Then he joined the faculty there and became a respected professor in the Department of Communication. Northwestern knew a great talent when it saw it. He has specialized in research into argumentation and public address. In fact, his articles and books on the speaking of Abraham Lincoln and the Lincoln-Douglas debates are among the most important produced by the field. He has received two awards from the National Communication Association for his books *Lincoln, Douglas, and Slavery: In the Crucible of Public Debate* and *President Johnson's War on Poverty: Rhetoric and History.* His textbook, *Public Speaking: Strategies for Success,* is coming out in its sixth edition. He has authored two other books, edited three volumes, and published over 50 scholarly articles and reviews. He also served as editor of *Argumentation and Advocacy* (then called the *Journal of the American Forensic Association*).

♦ *You have written that early on you were greatly influenced by professors in departments of English, Communication Studies, Political Science, and History. What kind of broad preparation would you recommend for students who might be preparing for communication scholarship?*
I think the best preparation is a broad liberal arts curriculum including especially work in literary studies, history, and social sciences. Coursework in communication ought also to be broad in scope and, especially for undergraduate students, should sample different areas of the field. In my own case, it was my participation in high school debate and speech competitions that made me aware of the existence of the field and drew me to it.

♦ *You have had an enviable career as a scholar. In addition to your publication of studies of argumentation and rhetoric, you have received awards from NCA for two books you have written related to the speaking career of Abraham Lincoln and President Johnson's war on poverty. What part of your research undertakings has made you most proud?*
Thank you for the compliment. I think that my work on Lincoln is probably the best research and writing I have done (so far), and I guess I am most proud of the fact that it has developed into something of a research program, that it has sustained my interest, and that I've been able to make it interesting and meaningful to others.

♦ *Very early in your career you were actively involved in promoting scholarship through professional organizations How important is it for a student approaching the field's research to get involved in professional organizations?*
One can certainly approach the field's research without it, but I think that to have a career in the field without becoming involved in professional organizations is irresponsible. The scholarly and pedagogical activities of this or any discipline are not self-sustaining. Investment in the field by those who have benefited from it is necessary to preserve and build upon its strength for the future.

♦ *What do you think is the most exciting future direction for the field's research?*
For me personally, I'm excited by the reinvigoration of historical studies in public address that are much more sophisticated than they used to be. For the field in general, it's gratifying to see the embrace of both the innovative and the traditional, and the development of a strong interdisciplinary core, while also establishing strong interdisciplinary links.

> ♦ *What personal qualities do you have that you think have contributed to your achievements as a communication scholar?*
> It's hard for me to say. I guess I'd mention that I am well organized, that I am fairly sensitive to language and to the relation between messages and audiences, that I write clearly, and that I have a pretty strong work ethic.
>
> ♦ *What one or two things do you think students should know to deal successfully with communication research either as consumers or as researchers?*
> First, it helps to realize that the organization of the discipline is messy because communication is involved in virtually every human activity; it is not something that can be easily sorted out. Second, the most important steps in research are to formulate interesting and important questions and to figure out what methods are appropriate to answer those questions.
>
> ♦ *Is there any advice you would give students who might be interested in becoming communication researchers?*
> If you have a *passion* for understanding communication in any of its numerous dimensions, go for it. If not, consider doing something else.

Data or Documentary Sample

content analysis samples are documents

samples in empirical studies

Regardless of the type of research, some actual conversation, discourse, documents, or sample data are used. Researchers explain the characteristics of such materials, where they came from, and how they were selected. For content analysis of mass media communication, the materials in the sample are documents, including oral and video records. The accuracy of the records must be explained, as well as any omissions of materials. For empirical or experimental work, samples of people (often called "participants") are typically gathered. In addition to reporting the number of subjects, sample characteristics (e.g., age, sex), and sources (e.g., college students, adults in field settings, volunteers), any methods for random sampling should be detailed (since this method requires extra steps).

Operational Definitions of Variables

Operational definition
isolating a concept by specifying the steps researchers follow to make observations of the variables.

operational definition distinguished

Conceptual definitions—such as those found in specialized dictionaries—give you an idea of the meaning of a term. An **operational definition** isolates a concept by specifying what researchers must do to make observations or measurements of the variables. Operational definitions are nothing like dictionary definitions. These descriptions include (1) manipulations of tasks completed to make observations, (2) special measures used for key variables, or (3) methods for assignment of subjects to different conditions based on some common characteristics. Articles are also expected to provide information on the accuracy and reliability of their operational techniques. Reports of measurement reliability have been routinely demanded in most professional journals since the early 1980s. Thus, justifications—not just descriptions—for the choices made to make observations are a major part of the discussion of measures used.

SPECIAL DISCUSSION 5-1

ANATOMY OF ARTICLES THAT PRESENT NEW THEORIES

Some articles present research and some present theories and conceptual discussions of things. Just as articles that present research have a fairly well-known organizational pattern shared in common, articles that advance new theories also have some common (though different) features.

The first part of each of these theory articles begins with a review of the context of the problem. Theories of attitude change review work on predicting attitude change, argumentation theories review different ways to describe arguments, and theories on the effects of violence on television review the status of theory on violence. The conclusion of the context of the problem is a statement of the desirability of isolating a different theoretic perspective. Sometimes articles attempt to "trash" past efforts, but this strategy is not highly regarded by scholars. Showing a meaningful new contribution is enough of a justification for the new orientation.

The second major section of the theory article is expected to define all terms clearly and concisely. The discussion of definitions is detailed and filled with justifications. Since definitions are based on key assumptions, new theories are expected to state them explicitly.

The third section includes statements of key propositions (in predictive theories) and implications of definitions (in the case of definitional theories). These statements include defining the roles of key concepts.

Fourth, the theory article is expected to present information on the usefulness of applying the theory. Any advantages in interpreting research and explaining phenomena should be reviews. In addition, any limitations are advanced. Finally, the implications for future work with the theory are expected to be listed and explained as part of a call to future research.

Procedures

Researchers describe how the study was completed—step by step. The best studies are written so clearly that you could understand what it was like to be a participant. Information on instructions, debriefing, and protection of subjects should be shared.

procedures identified

Methods for Analysis of Data

Though qualitative studies rely on theoretic orientations to interpret data, empirical and experimental studies employ statistical tools. Specific names—such as "t tests" or "analysis of variance"—are mentioned with little explanation, since they are recognized by scholars who have taken a course such as the one you probably are completing now. If statistics are not so widely understood, the author may explain them. Box 5.2 shows this section from a research article.

in quantitative studies, data analysis refers to statistics

Results

The results section of an article does not explain the meaning of study findings. The results are simply that—presentations of findings—without comment on their substantive importance. The results section often includes tables and sometimes graphs to report analyses. Since the results section is technical, researchers are expected to provide enough detail to help readers understand what was found. This section tends to be brief.

results section does not interpret findings

BOX 5.2   SAMPLE ARTICLE, PART 2

Method divided into
sections ———————   # Method

Sample ———————   **Participants and Setting.** The sample consisted of 148 subordinates (71 temporary) of middle managers from two financial organizations located in a western state. All the temporary employees reported they were motivated to be part of the temporary work force to obtain a permanent position in their organization eventually. All respondents began employment less than two months prior to the data collection. Supervisor-to-subordinate gender-dyad combinations included male/male ($n = 37$), female/female ($n = 57$), male/female ($n = 32$), female/male ($n = 24$). All participants held non-management positions and performed similar duties. Other demographic information was not available. Data were collected by self-administered surveys distributed and completed on-site during normal working hours by two of the researchers.

Materials and
measures ———————   **Measures.** *Leader-member exchange.* Leader-member exchange was measured using a five-item scale (Graen, Liden, & Hoel, 1982). Respondents were asked to make a choice among four item-specific response options for each question regarding their relationships with supervisors (scored so that 1 = low LMX and 4 = high LMX). The questions asked

Chapter 4 explains
this concept ———————   about a variety of topics, including the newcomer's confidence in the supervisor, the supervisor's advocacy of the newcomer, and the degree of mutual understanding between the newcomer and the supervisor. In this study, a coefficient alpha of .82 was obtained ($M = 2.51$, $SD = .93$).

Influence tactics. Supervisor influence techniques was measured using the Behavior Alteration Techniques (BAT) instrument generated by Richmond, McCroskey, and Davis (1986). Participants were directed to reflect on a manager-to-subordinate influence situation in the last 10 days in which they had actually been involved and to assess "how likely your immediate supervisor would be to use each of the 22 message-based techniques to influence you in that situation." Participants were instructed to respond to the twenty-two items using a Likert-type scale, ranging from 1 = never to 5 = constantly. In this study, a coefficient alpha of .92 was obtained ($M = 2.34$, $SD = 1.22$).

For the purposes of this study, two categories were used: prosocial and antisocial (see Punyanunt, 2000). Prosocial techniques are: Immediate reward from behavior, Deferred reward, Reward from supervisor, Reward from others, Self-esteem, Superior/Subordinate relationship positive, Personal subordinate responsibility, Responsibility to others, Normative Rules, Altruism, Peer Modeling, Supervisor Modeling, Expertise, and Supervisor Feedback. Antisocial techniques are: Punishment from behavior, Punishment from supervisor, Punishment from others, Guilt, Supervisor/Subordinate Relationship: Negative, Legitimate-Higher Authority, Legitimate-Supervisor Authority, and Debt.

Communication satisfaction. Subordinates' satisfaction with communication was measured on a 14-item measure developed by Wheeless, Wheeless, & Howard (1984) for application to superior-subordinate relationships in organizational settings. The items describe communication experiences typically perceived as satisfying. This measure has been described as reliable and valid (Downs, 1990; Lamude, Daniels, & Graham, 1988). In this study, a coefficient alpha of .94 was obtained ($M = 3.13$, $SD = 1.35$).

Results

To answer the research question, a Student t test for mean differences was performed. Results ($t = .22$, $p = .06$) indicated that the temporary employees' perceptions of leader-member exchanges ($M = 2.48$, $SD = .87$) did not differ significantly from regular employees' perceptions ($M = 2.43$, $SD = 1.12$).

Comparisons of mean differences by looking at statistical significance of differences between means (see Chapter 14)

To answer hypothesis one, a one-way analysis of variance (ANOVA) was used to determine differences between same-sex and cross-sex superior-subordinate dyads as a function of LMX. Results indicated no significant differences among groups ($F(3,144) = .246$; $p > .05$). Mean scores and (SDs) for supervisor-to-subordinate gender combinations were 2.64 (1.01) for male/male, 2.45 (.88) for female/female, 2.50 (.92) for male/female, and 2.47 (.99) for female/male.

See Chapter 14 for information about ANOVA

Pearson correlations (see Table 1) were calculated to answer hypotheses two through four. Hypothesis two expected that there would be a positive relationship between supervisor use of prosocial influence techniques and LMX.

Interpreting results by looking at correlations

Results found eleven prosocial techniques were positive and significant ($p < .001$). The highest correlations were Immediate Reward ($r = .78$), Self-Esteem ($r = .68$), Superior-Subordinate Relationship (positive) ($r = .66$), and Supervisor Reward ($r = .64$).

TABLE 1   MEANS, STANDARD DEVIATIONS, AND CORRELATIONS BETWEEN BEHAVIOR ALTERATION TECHNIQUES AND LEADER-MEMBER EXCHANGE

Behavior Alteration Technique	M	SD	r*
1. Immediate Reward	.9	1.4	.78
2. Deferred Reward	2.2	1.3	.37
3. Supervisor Reward	2.4	1.2	.64
4. Others Reward	2.0	1.2	.39
5. Self-esteem	2.6	1.3	.68
6. Superior-Subordinate Relationship (+)	2.7	1.4	.66
7. Altruism	2.0	1.1	.39
8. Peer Modeling	1.7	.8	.27
9. Superior Modeling	2.4	1.2	.10
10. Behavior Punishment	2.0	1.1	−.44
11. Supervisor Punishment	2.2	1.3	−.55
12. Others Punishment	1.9	1.2	−.33
13. Guilt	1.8	.9	−.32
14. Superior-Subordinate Relationship (−)	2.7	1.4	−.59
15. Legitimate Authority	2.8	1.3	−.71
16. Supervisor Authority	2.7	1.3	−.82
17. Personal Responsibility	2.8	1.4	−.49
18. Debt	2.0	1.2	−.43
19. Others Responsibility	2.1	1.1	.23
20. Normative Rules	2.2	1.1	.03
21. Expertise	2.7	1.4	.31
22. Supervisor Feedback	2.6	1.2	.29

*$p < .001$

(Continued)

Hypothesis three predicted that there would be a negative relationship between supervisor use of antisocial influence techniques and LMX. Results found nine antisocial techniques were negative and significant ($p < .001$). The highest correlations were Supervisor Authority ($r = -.82$) and Legitimate Authority ($r = -.71$).

Hypothesis four looked at the relationship between subordinate communication satisfaction and LMX. Supporting hypothesis four, there was a significant and positive relationship ($r = .45$, $p < .001$).

Discussion

This investigation had as its goal the examination of newly hired subordinates' characteristics, their supervisors' influence techniques, and subordinates' communication satisfaction with their supervisor and the relationships between these variables and LMX. The results of the study produced two significant results.

First, consistent with previous research, findings from hypotheses two and three show that superiors tend to use prosocial influence techniques more often than antisocial influence techniques in attempting to influence their subordinates. Moreover, correlations between prosocial influence techniques and LMX were positive. In contrast, correlations between antisocial techniques and LMX were negative. These findings suggest superiors' perceived initial use of prosocial influence techniques are more likely to enhance LMX development than superiors' use of antisocial influence techniques. Thus, this study confirmed previous findings with abbreviated measures that superiors' influence techniques were significantly related to LMX. However, in the present study, not only did we find significant influence techniques associated with referent, reward, and coercive power bases, but also influence techniques associated with expert and position power bases were significantly related to LMX. An area of future research is the investigation of upward-influence and influence resistance tactics in the development of LMX.

Limitations suggested for study interpretations ⎯⎯⎯⎯

Second, the results indicated that subordinate communication satisfaction is positively related to LMX. This finding is not surprising, given that researchers have established a relationship between subordinates' satisfaction with immediate supervisors' communication and variables linked to LMX. An area for future study is the investigation of newcomer communication satisfaction/dissatisfaction with superior-subordinate interactions over time in the development of LMX. Such research would help determine the relative importance of subordinate communication satisfaction/dissatisfaction in determining the development of "in-group" and "out-group" working relationships.

Results indicated demographic characteristics, specifically subordinate job classification and biological sex combinations of superior-subordinate dyads, were not significantly related to LMX. Specifically, correlation results indicate newly hired "permanent" temporary and regular employees did not significantly differ on their perceptions of LMX. The findings also suggest that respondents' perceptions of biological sex combinations did not significantly differ in the quality of the LMX relationship. However, the high moderate mean LMX scores of both demographic characteristics suggests newly hired subordinates in this study assessed themselves as being more likely to have in-group relationships with their supervisors. A plausible explanation for these findings may be because of the short nature of the interactions. Perceptions of gender and job-classification differences would more likely follow rather than precede the formation of "in-group" and "out-group" relationships.

Finally, we used the previous 5-item measure of leader-member exchange to increase the likelihood of a reliable assessment and to ensure that our study would yield data comparable with those of previous research. We recognize that this rating scale may have limitations so replication of these findings is desirable.

References

Daniels, T. D., Spiker, B. K., & Papa, M. J. (1997). *Perspectives on organizational communication* (4th ed.). Madison, WI: Brown & Benchmark.

Dienesch, R. M., & Liden, R. C. (1986). Leader-member exchange model of leadership: A critique and further development. *Academy of Management Review, 11,* 618–634.

Dockery, T. M., & Steiner, D. D. (1990). The role of the initial interaction in leader-member exchange. *Group & Organizational Studies, 15,* 395–413.

Downs, T. M. (1990). Predictors of communication satisfaction during performance appraisal interviews. *Management Communication Quarterly, 3,* 334–354.

Graen, G., Liden, R., & Hoel, W. (1982). Role of leadership in the employee withdrawal process. *Journal of Applied Psychology, 67,* 686–872.

Graen, U., & Scandura, T. A. (1987). Toward a psychology of dyadic organizing. In L. L. Cummings & B. M. Staw (Eds.), *Research in Organizational Behavior, 9,* 175–208. Greenwich, CT: JAJ Press.

Hecht, M. L. (1978). The conceptualization and measurement of interpersonal communication satisfaction. *Human Communication Research, 4,* 253–264.

Hecht, M. L., & Marston, P. J. (1987). Communication satisfaction and the temporal development of conversations. *Communication Research Reports, 4,* 60–65.

Kipnis, D., Schmidt, S. M., Swaffin-Smith, C., & Wilkinson, I. (1984). Patterns of managerial influences: Shotgun managers, technicians, and bystanders. *Organizational Dynamics, 12,* 58–67.

Lamude, K. G., Daniels, T. D., & Graham, E. E. (1988). The paradoxical influence of sex on communication rules coordination and communication satisfaction in superior-subordinate communication. *Western Journal of Speech Communication, 52,* 122–134.

Lamude, K. G., & Scudder, J. (1993). Compliance-gaining techniques of Type-A managers. *The Journal of Business Communication, 30,* 65–81.

Liden, R. C., & Graen, G. (1980). Generalizability of the vertical linkage model of leadership. *Academy of Management Journal, 23,* 451–465.

Major, D. A., Kozlowski, W. J., Chao, G. T., & Gardner, P. D. (1995). A longitudinal investigation of newcomer expectations, early socialization outcomes, and the moderating effects of role development factors. *Journal of Applied Psychology, 80,* 418–431.

Polivka, A. E., & Nardone, T. (1989, December). On the definition of "contingent work." *Monthly Labor Review, 112,* 9–16.

Punyanunt, N. M. (2000). The effects of humor on perceptions of compliance-gaining in the college classroom. *Communication Research Reports, 17,* 30–38.

Richmond, V. P., Davis, L. M., Saylor, K., & McCroskey, J. C. (1984). Power strategies in organizations: Communication techniques and messages. *Human Communication Research, 11,* 85–108.

Richmond, V. P., McCroskey, J. C., & Davis, L. M. (1986). The relationship of supervisor use of power and affinity-seeking strategies with subordinate satisfaction. *Communication Quarterly, 34,* 178–193.

Rogers, J. K. (1995). Just a temp: Experience and structure of alienation in temporary clerical employment. *Work and Occupations, 22,* 137–166.

Scandura, T. A., Graen, G. B., & Novak, M. A. (1986). When managers decide not to decide automatically: An investigation of leader-member exchange and decision influence. *Journal of Applied Psychology, 71,* 579–584.

Schriesheim, C. A., Castro, S. L., & Yammarino, F. J. (2000). Investigating contingencies: An examination of the impact of span of supervision and upward controllingness on leader-member exchange using traditional and multivariate within- and between-entities analysis. *Journal of Applied Psychology, 85,* 659–677.

Sherony, K. M., & Green, S. G. (2002). Coworker exchange: relationships between coworkers, leader-member exchange, and work attitudes. *Journal of Applied Psychology, 87,* 542–548.

Sias, P. M., Kramer, M. W., & Jenkins, E. (1997). A comparison of the communication behaviors of temporary employees and new hires. *Communication Research, 24,* 731–754.

Smith, V. (1998). The fractured world of the temporary worker: *Social Problems, 45,* 411–430.

——This study uses APA citation form and placed all references at the end, rather than as footnotes

(Continued)

Tsui, A. S., & O'Reilly, C. A. (1989). Beyond simple demographic effects: The importance of relational demography in superior-subordinate dyads. *Academy of Management Journal, 32,* 402–423.

Varma, A., & Stroh, L. K. (2001). Different perspectives on selection for international assignments: The impact of LMX and gender. *Cross Cultural Management, 8,* 85–97.

Wayne, S. J., Liden, R. C., & Sparrowe, R. T. (1994). Developing leader-member exchanges: The influence of gender and ingratiation. *American Behavioral Scientist, 37,* 697–714.

Wheeless, L. R., Wheeless, V. E., & Howard, R. D. (1984). The relationships of communication with supervisor and decision-participation to employee job satisfaction. *Communication Quarterly, 32,* 222–232.

The Discussion Argument

discussion interprets results

Though short articles may combine the results and discussion sections (as in our example), most authors write a separate discussion section. The discussion section is the researcher's chance to argue about the meaning of results. Though researchers are given freedom to draw conclusions, the rules of sound reasoning must be obeyed, and the arguments must appeal to research evidence (and not go far beyond them). Structurally, the discussion section usually interprets hypothesized and unexpected results, describes the significance of the study, mentions study limitations (problems that may be overcome in future research), and advances implications for future inquiry. Since the literature review raised invitations to new research, the discussion of results should respond to *each* issue raised early in the paper. Otherwise, the research would not have been a fitting response to research invitations. Box 5.2 shows how such a commentary is included in the discussion.

Conclusion

conclusion is a summary

The conclusion usually is a statement of one or two paragraphs in which the researcher summarizes what was done in the study. The conclusion is not a stirring call to future inquiry: it simply tells what was accomplished.

References

references using the APA format

The final part of a research article is a list of references. To understand the *detail* of citation methods, it is a good idea to read the materials in this book's website section dedicated to the "APA Citation Form" page and the APA *Publication Manual.*

WRITING SCHOLARSHIP

demands of effective writing

There is no way around it. Research involves crisp and clear writing. You may expect to develop your own writing skills as a result of studying research methods. You might have to write only short papers in the class you are taking, but you certainly will be expected to *write well.* Though developing good writing skills is, and should be, a lifelong undertaking, you can take some immediate steps to improve your writing. This section provides some advice about planning and structuring your scholarly writing.

Using Past Research to Develop Arguments

After inventing the calculus, Newton was asked how he developed his great break-through. Giving credit to past thinkers, he replied, "If I see farther than others, it is because I stand on the shoulders of giants." Though all researchers owe a debt to the work done previously by others, it is surprising how many students new to the subject of research methods fail to check past research to build arguments. In fact, all research is rooted in the past. Hence, researchers often find that there are several ways they can develop their own research arguments by examining past research.

past research is the basis for making arguments for new research

♦ *To find arguments to prove that the subject matter of the research question is relevant to the field,* you may look at past research. To be taken seriously in any discipline, a topic or problem question must be directly related to that discipline. You can make such an argument for the relevance of a topic by looking at past research and observing that at least one of the concepts or variables in your research problem question has been considered a valuable topic for past research.

topics for argument found in research reports

♦ *To find arguments to prove that the concepts and variables in the research question can be defined coherently,* you may look at past research and see what solutions to conceptual matters others have found in the past

♦ *To find arguments to prove that the concepts and variables in the research question can be studied coherently and that any variables may be measured soundly,* you may look at past research. In fact, making arguments for choices of approaches and measurements often can be completed only by looking at past similar research.

♦ *To find arguments to prove that the concepts and variables in the research question are important,* you must look at past research. By showing that other researchers have found some benefit in looking at one or more of the concepts or variables in the problem question, you can argue with evidence that your research question is meaningful. In addition, this part of your argument may be used to justify advancing any study hypotheses to follow.

♦ *To find arguments to prove that there is a gap in our knowledge about the concepts and variables in the research question,* you must look at past research. If a study has already been done, researchers probably wish to extend on it, rather than re-visit captured territory. Even so-called replication studies usually add some additional variables or settings to the research mix. To show a gap in knowledge requires you to complete a serious review of the actual research found in journals, handbooks, and annuals. Then, after proving that past researchers appear to have looked *separately* at the variables and concepts in your research question, you can explain how past researchers have not yet put those concepts or variables *together* in a single study. Thus, you may show that a gap remains in our knowledge to justify asking the new research question.

When you write a paper for a class, the assignment you are given will have some directions and guidelines regarding the sorts of topics you must cover. In each of these areas, you will find that you are expected to make arguments—not just present information—about the probable state of affairs on your topic. In these efforts, looking at past research will be vital.

Purposeful Inquiry

research argument requires that conclusions be drawn and then supported by past literature, rather than reports of background research

Success in making an argument for research requires looking for relevant evidence. In this electronic information age, you can find information rather easily. Nevertheless, students often approach research as "background" information, rather than as evidence to use in making arguments. But, of course, you probably cannot write an argumentative paper by starting with source information and then attempting to draw conclusions on the fly. Instead, you have to know what conclusion (claim) you are trying to argue. Then research can be found to test it. What happens if you find that your thinking is mistaken and your argument is moving in the wrong direction? No problem—you change the argument to reflect new findings. But not everything will need to be changed.

use of a research argument planning outline

Obviously, you have to start with the claims and then search for information that bear upon them. The easiest way is to start with a full outline (in pencil because you will have to make changes as you find the unexpected along the way). Then you may create an efficient research argument planning outline—a very efficient way to help you complete your research. Because we recommend this method so strongly, we will tell you how to use a research argument planning outline. Figure 5.1 shows a research outline to plan library work for a paper on the status of a topic. Here's how to put one together:

FIGURE 5.1   RESEARCH PLANNING OUTLINE

Paper Outline	Research Items	Sources to Check
Credibility of Newspaper Sources		
I. Definitions		
A. Source Credibility →	Definition of Source Credibility →	Handbooks of Communication, Mass Communication
	(check other terms: ethos, prestige) →	Books: persuasion Dictionaries: Longman of Psych and Mass Communication
B. Kinds of Source Credibility →	Dimensions of credibility (check measurement methods) →	Articles: Abstracts: Psychological Abstracts, Journalism Abstracts, CIOS
II. Credibility Research in Newspapers		
A. Impact of Newspaper Credibility →	Studies of credibility by readers (not TV or radio studies) →	Unpublished work, Resources in Education
B. Levels of Credibility of Different Newspapers →	Surveys of credibility ratings of readership pool →	Unpublished work, Resources in Education, Internet search

♦ Divide a large piece of paper into three columns (you may wish to turn your paper sideways to have enough room).

♦ Title the first column "Paper Outline," title the second column "Research Items," and title the third column "Sources to Check."

♦ In the column labeled "Paper Outline," put together a very rough outline of the paper or assignment you plan to write (these things give you a reason to visit the library). At the beginning of your work, you cannot know every detail of the paper's argument, of course, but you know the instructions you were given by your teacher. These topics are points on which you are expected to take positions and draw some (at least tentative) conclusions. On your research argument planning outline, you should dedicate at least one main point (typically numbered with Roman numerals) to each broad topic you were assigned to cover. In Figure 5.1 the student was told to write a paper about the credibility of newspaper sources, making sure to define terms and to summarize research on the topic. So, a main point has been dedicated to each issue. Make sure to leave plenty of space so that new items can be added if necessary.

♦ In the column labeled "Research Items," list the information you need to get so that you can write each section of the paper.

♦ In the column labeled "Sources to Check," list library sources to review. The sources are identified in Appendix G. In particular, Table G.1 identifies the best categories of information sources for different sorts of information you may need (definitions, ways concepts and variables have been measured, general summary statements about the subject, classic research studies in the field, research showing what methods to use, and research regarding what mistakes to avoid). Then, this table lists major sources that may be used to find information (complete with call numbers used in most research libraries).

This approach permits you to identify the claims you wish to argue, the evidence to be used, and lines of reasoning to establish points of view. Thus, you are given a chance to evaluate your reasoning before committing yourself to the lines of argument.

Identifying Vital Information

When searching for information to construct a research argument, students often make one of two mistakes. On one hand, student-researchers may gather too much information that they cannot really use to help construct an argument. For instance, securing information about the sampling deficiencies of some studies that relied on student participants may not be helpful if the new problem question raises no such contrast of different sorts of samples. The information gathered, though true, may not be helpful to make a vital argument. Eventually, the argument will have to be dropped. On the other hand (and most commonly), student-researchers may gather too little information to permit constructing meaningful arguments. Some guidance seems invited in preparing arguments that appeal to research information.

mistake of examining too much or too little literature to make an argument

Vital research information can be obtained from examination of the research argument planning outline. Support for each main point and subpoint can be obvious places to look. Yet, there are some sorts of information that, when found, should be saved

find vital arguments by looking at the research argument planning outline; information that must be included from the literature

under any set of circumstances. As Appendix G identified, any information dealing with the following matters should be retained by the student-researcher—even when the student-researcher may be in the process of looking for something else at the time:

- ◆ definitions of key concepts and variables;
- ◆ ways concepts and variables have been measured and studied;
- ◆ summary statements and quotations that people (especially textbook writers) seem to make about the subject;
- ◆ classic research studies on a subject (the studies that all the textbooks seem to reference);
- ◆ research that shows what methods to use; and
- ◆ research that shows what mistakes to avoid.

These matters are certainly items that will be useful in making vital arguments that appeal to research.

limiting scope of research sought

Setting limits on the scope of your research is critical before you look for resources. If you have an exhaustive literature review for which a month's preparation time is provided, you may set limits very broadly. If you have only a week to complete a review of chief definitions, you may need to limit your examination to key books, specialized dictionaries, and "think piece" articles. The vital information, therefore, may depend greatly on the time pressures you face and the goals of the assignment you have been given.

The Truth about Writing Research

mistakes of
1. reviewing past research one at a time

Some students new to the craft of arguing for research related to problem questions make two basic mistakes. Do not be among them. First, they figure that the best way to appeal to past research in making arguments is by reviewing the sequence of the search process itself. Since researchers often find research studies one at a time, they figure that they should present summaries or little "book reports" for each study, one at a time. This approach is misguided because it fails to "group" studies to make arguments and common criticisms about similar arguments. Rather than critique every piece of research, the student-researcher needs to use arguments to justify the choices made for the researcher's own conclusions, and (in the case of proposals) they need to use past research as a foundation for justifying the new choices made for future research. Certainly, criticism of past work has a role to play in the process, but criticism does not mean that a researcher engages in venomous attacks of past work or tries to show that past research reeks with failure. Instead, criticism usually involves noting a gap that remains as a result of researchers' stopping too soon to answer a new research question. It also is criticism to note that particularly excellent methods and approaches have been used in past research (especially if the student-researcher intends to use similar methods and approaches in future inquiries).

2. writing the literature review before deciding on methods recommended for future studies

A second mistake student-researchers make is writing a literature review before deciding on study methods. Though this approach might not seem to be a mistake at first glance, a little thought reveals its flaw. When writing work that eventually involves making suggestions or proposals for future research, the researcher is expected to include information in a literature review that justifies the choices made in the methods section. In quantitative research, these choices typically involve the use of materials, samples, measures, study designs, and controls. In qualitative research, these choices typically involve selecting a basic approach (such as ethnography, participant observation, or qualitative interviews), underlying orientations (such as feminist perspectives, rhetorical standards, or postmodern viewpoints), and targets of investigation (such as conversation, narratives, or documents).

Here is the problem. You cannot justify these research choices unless you first know what choices you plan to suggest in future research. Hence, you cannot write a literature review until you know what methods and approaches you plan. Even though people *read* a literature review before looking at the methods section of a proposal, a paper cannot be *written* in that order. You have to know what conclusion (claim) you are trying to argue. Then, research-based reasoning may be advanced to support it or attempt to redeem it. So, how do you compose an argument that suggests future research directions or actually proposes new research? You must start by outlining the methods to be used. This outline must be complete with a listing of all variables and concepts, any methods of measurement to be used, and all methods and orienting approaches to be used. Then, and only then, can the literature be reviewed in a coherent way. Thus, in addition to proving that the proposed study should be completed, the literature may be used to justify the methods that are to be used in any future inquiry. This process may be used by writing that makes a point to include discussion of

important to outline the methods section before completing the literature review

- ◆ the appropriate definition of the concept;
- ◆ sound ways to measure or identify the variables or concepts (including explanations and justifications for the proposed methods to investigate this concept, based on fruitful past work in related inquiries);
- ◆ review of how research shows the importance of the variable or concept; and
- ◆ identification of the gap in knowledge, desire to extend on past research, or intention to solve a practical problem.

What happens if you encounter research literature that makes you realize that your initial thinking is mistaken and that your argument is moving in the wrong direction? No problem. Working from an outline, you may change the argument to reflect new findings and new choices. But you probably will be pleased how sound your initial thinking is and how few changes you actually will have to make.

Writing and Style Mechanics

Effective research argument presumes that clear and acceptable writing will be used.

The flow of a paper can get lost unless you use some helpful aids. The most obvious way to enhance understanding is to use headings to highlight your main points. Like it or not, your instructors often grade your papers while facing frequent interruptions. In all but your shortest projects, headings and subheadings can help keep main ideas in the instructor's mind despite distractions (we are talking about "defensive writing" here). You should start with a major heading for each main point on your outline (the introduction and conclusion are *not* main points) and add subheadings as the discussion gets involved or lengthy.

desirability of using subdivisions

Style the choice and use of words.

meaning of style

Writing style does not mean a special sense of fashion or personal flair. **Style** involves matters of appropriate language usage. Indeed, many books that discuss good writing use the word "style" in their titles (such as *The Elements of Style* by William Strunk and E. B. White [1979]). By consulting such books, you may make rapid progress by looking at ways to make your writing clear and precise.

Internal organizers phrases that preview, summarize, and provide transitions between main points.

Clear writing is led by very organized thoughts. In addition to outlining, other elements can promote clear writing. Making active use of **internal organizers** to make clear the flow of ideas can underscore your content. It is helpful to preview all the subpoints before you cover any of them. A summary of each subpoint provided at subsection endings emphasizes the order of ideas in the paper. Using summaries and previews increases chances for your ideas to be understood.

ambiguity shunned in scholarly writing

It is important to avoid ambiguity in scholarly writing. You should use terms that are direct, and, whenever possible, you should rely on language that is understandable to the greatest number of intelligent people. Einstein expressed this concern best: "Ideas should be stated as simply as possible, but no simpler." You should not avoid topics that are technical—quite the contrary! But your writing should use only those specialized terms that are essential. Furthermore, you should define every major term you use. Clear writing often can be enhanced by employing paragraph structures that have obvious topic sentences. If you use active summaries, previews, and internal organizers, avoid ambiguity, and rely on standard paragraph structures, your writing will be clear and understandable.

use summaries, previews, and topic sentences

WRITING CLASSROOM REPORTS

Communication students are often asked to write papers that refer to research. Though your instructors will give you specific details for each assignment, you should observe some general formats. This section describes the obligations you routinely should expect to satisfy. It covers three types of papers: the definitional criticism paper, the literature review (or explication) paper, and the research prospectus (or proposal).

Strategies for a Definitional Criticism Paper

A definitional paper takes a concept of interest to you—such as propaganda, stuttering, or comparative advertising—and considers issues that involve the proper definition of the concept. You do not just choose your favorite definition. Instead, these papers contrast different approaches to understand definitional questions.

Organizing a Definitional Review Paper

format and design of the definitional criticism paper

The definitional paper usually begins with an introduction that mentions the topic area and justifies it as a part of the study of communication. The introduction actively refers to the field and cites communication sources (and other related subjects) to show that the concept is important enough to investigate. Any context needed to understand the topic often is included in the introduction, rather than as a completely separate discussion. Depending on the paper's length, the introduction ends by previewing the rest of the paper's main points.

SPECIAL DISCUSSION 5-2

A QUESTION OF ETHICS: COMPLETE REPORTING AND ATTRIBUTION OF SOURCES

Research is a social act since it engages the minds of at least two people. Yet, it is also an ethical act reflecting the choices of the researcher to provide full and honest reporting and to give credit where credit is due. Both active researchers and students writing classroom reports share two categories of obligations (among others): full reporting and avoiding inadvertent plagiarism.

Full Reporting

Research quality is reflected in completeness and accuracy in reporting of such work. Scholars are obligated to communicate their research. So, when researchers decline to report research details—sometimes claiming that it is "proprietary" or secret research—others have a reason to suspect that there is an ethical problem. In addition, if a researcher declines to present his or her research—sometimes claiming that professional journals are unwilling to consider new thinking—there may be an ethical breach.

If a student writes a classroom paper and finds that some research exists that conflicts with his or her own viewpoints on the subject, it is important to include the information. Unfortunately, even in formal research reports, there have been occasions when scholars have not fully reported what they have found. Furthermore, in formal research, reports are expected to be so complete that their lessons can be learned by others. Russell Schutt (2006, p. 511) lists the following elements that should be reported:

- ◆ *Provide an honest accounting of how the research was carried out and where the initial research design had to be changed. . . .*
- ◆ *Maintain a full record of the research project so that questions can be answered if they arise. . . .*
- ◆ *Avoid "lying with statistics" or using graphs to mislead. . . .*
- ◆ *Acknowledge the sponsors of the research.* This is important, in part, so that others can consider whether this sponsorship may have tempted you to bias your results in some way.
- ◆ *Thank staff who made major contributions. . . .*
- ◆ *Be sure that the order of authorship for co-authored reports is discussed in advance and reflects agreed-upon principles.*

Of course, reports need not describe irrelevant things that occurred during the research, but all important information should be included. Schutt warns:

> You do not need to report every twist and turn in the conceptualization of the research problem or the conduct of the research. But be suspicious of those reports that don't seem to admit to the possibility of any room for improvement. Social science is an ongoing enterprise in which one research report makes its most valuable contribution by laying the groundwork for another, more sophisticated research project. Highlight important findings in the research report, but also use the research report to point out what are likely to be the most productive directions for future researchers. (Schutt, 2006, p. 512)

(Continued)

SPECIAL DISCUSSION 5-2 (Continued)

Avoiding Inadvertent Plagiarism

Plagiarism is cheating. It takes others' ideas and benefits from them without giving credit where credit is clearly due. Specifically, plagiarism refers to "the false assumption of authorship: the wrongful act of taking the product of another person's mind, and presenting it as one's own" (Lindey, 1952, p. 2). Most students realize that it is plagiarism to copy others' words or material from the Internet without giving credit. But it is also plagiarism to express another person's *ideas* without giving credit. And claiming not to know that ideas came from somewhere else is not considered an acceptable excuse.

A writer who fails to give appropriate acknowledgment when repeating another's wording or particularly apt term, paraphrasing another's argument, or presenting another's line of thinking is guilty of plagiarism. "You may certainly use another person's words and thoughts in your research paper, but the borrowed material must not appear to be your creation" (Gibaldi, 1999, p. 31). Penalties for using uncredited sources are severe and may include academic punishment, failing grades, or expulsion. There is an obvious way to avoid plagiarism: document everything, except your unique interpretations and comments regarding research literature. The *MLA Handbook* . . . explains (Gibaldi, 1999, p. 33):

> Of course, common sense as well as ethics should determine what you document. For example, you rarely need to give sources for familiar proverbs ("You can't judge a book by its cover"), well-known quotations ("We shall overcome"), or common knowledge ("George Washington was the first President of the United States").

Yet, if you make a statement you think is common knowledge, think again. What is "common knowledge" to you may not be common knowledge to other people. So, if there is any possible doubt, it makes sense to back up what you say with source materials—otherwise, omit the uncredited material.

The bulk of a definitional paper compares and contrasts different schools of thought for the concept of interest. The writer does not try to explain the variable's role in everyday life but considers the proper way to define the term. Schools of thought are distinguished by different details or key starting points. Each school of *evaluating definitions* thought is usually introduced with a typical quotation expressing that point of view. Then, comments are made to point out any weaknesses in the definition. Though Chapter 3 provided you with standards for definitions to satisfy, for now you should know that criticisms are made by applying specific criteria, not by giving your personal feelings about the authors or their implied values. You should also examine problems that exist in finding useful operational definitions (measurement or methods to observe the concept in action) for your concept of interest.

After discussing each definitional school of thought and its limitations, you will need to offer some sort of conclusion. Is one definition clearly superior to the others? Are all the definitions acceptable but apply to different situations? Do you have an alternative definition that is superior to the others? If so, are you prepared to show how your new definition meets all the standards expected of good definitions? Any of these conclusions is acceptable, but you must choose an approach and defend it.

Isolating and Categorizing Schools of Thought

Students sometimes doubt their ability to identify different schools of thought. The task, however, is quite simple. You simply look for definitions of the concept and then you categorize them. Most of the time definitions are found in specialized dictionaries, encyclopedias, or books. Once you have found books that might contain such definitions, seek your term in the indexes. If you find it, jot down the definition on a bibliographic note card. In specialized dictionaries, more than one definition may be provided. Do not assume that the first definition is preferred. By protocol, dictionary authors list definitions in a general chronological order, though archaic definitions are usually placed at the end of the list. Make sure to identify any critiques of definitions, since you may use these comments to help complete your own paper. *sources for definitional schools of thought*

The easiest way to identify different schools of thought is to sort bibliographic cards containing definitions. Take the cards that seem to say the same thing and put them in one stack. Those definitions that add an element or that seem to move in a unique direction can be placed in a different stack. You soon will see that you have identified the major schools of thought on an issue. To write the paper, you will need to consider each school of thought. Sometimes students who are new to research ask instructors how many sources are to be included in such a paper. Though instructors sometimes set limits for novice researchers, the question really cannot be answered. All conflicting schools of thought must be included—involving only a few sources or perhaps dozens. *methods to identify different schools of thought*

Strategies for the Literature Review

Perhaps the most common papers you will write during your academic career will be literature reviews. These papers attempt to tell the reader what is known about a subject and the current state of knowledge about the matter.

Organizing a Literature Review

The literature review generally has seven sections: *review sections:*

1. An introduction that justifies the study of the topic in the field and previews the rest of the paper (it is typical to indicate how the topic is related to the field and to cite sources to support one's selection of the variables of interest). *1. justify subject as communication*

2. The context of the problem (a section that usually but not always is included), which isolates the role of the concepts in communication studies by such methods as quoting authoritative sources, referring to past research that invites new work, or arguing directly for a need for this work. *2. context of the problem*

3. The background definitions of terms (not as extended as in a definitional paper), which assess *major* conceptual and operational definitions, including *problems* that researchers have faced when measuring or observing the concept or variable (general expository listings of operational definitions are not very interesting in a literature review paper—your attention should focus on operational problems that limit conclusions that researchers have drawn). *3. background definitions of terms*

4. review of relevant theory

4. The relevant theory reviewed to explain how and why the variable or concept functions in communication (theories should be stated in enough detail to show their ability to explain the role of your variable or concept in the communication process, but you need not complete a full review of the theory).

5. survey of literature

5. The research survey, which is usually the longest part of the study. Based on limits set on your review, you may complete either an exhaustive or exemplary literature review:

Exhaustive literature reviews research surveys that include all material related to the subject.

- ◆ **Exhaustive literature reviews** attempt to cover everything related to the subject.

Exemplary literature reviews surveys of only the most important contributions to the literature.

- ◆ **Exemplary literature reviews** attempt to cover only the most important contributions.

Published articles tend to use exemplary reviews because of space limits, and you probably will be asked to complete exemplary literature reviews in your classes (but do not let yourself off the hook—you must review research extensively before completing any sort of review).

6. research opportunities or heuristic merit described

6. A list of the opportunities for future research that suggest the heuristic merit of research (the term "heuristic" comes from the Greek word that means "to invent"; the **heuristic merit** of research, hence, is its ability to lead scholars to new thinking explanations, or research avenues).

7. conclusion

7. A conclusion that summarizes main points and states a bottom-line conclusion.

Heuristic merit the ability of a theory or research effort to stimulate scholars to discover new inventions, ideas, applications, or research directions.

Selecting a Summary Organization

using a summary organization

The literature review makes arguments for which the research studies serve as evidence. Studies are arranged to create a logical discussion of research findings. Instructors frequently complain that students write literature reviews that are nothing more than paragraphs summarizing a string of articles. This method is to be avoided. Begin by deciding what summary arguments you can make about different parts of the literature. Then, reference articles as evidence for those arguments. The most prominent summary patterns are found in Table 5.1, though they often are combined.

chronological method most popular

You should select a literature summary pattern with care. If there is not much known about a research subject, you may wish to rely on the known-to-unknown format. Though we don't recommend your using it, the most frequently employed literature review strategy is probably the chronological method (remember: we are discussing *summary* patterns, not library *search* strategies). Even so, many students also find the topical and the known-to-unknown patterns very useful. The extensiveness of research and the question investigated should guide selection of the method. Remember, the review must stick to scholarly research completed on the subject. Personal applications are not relevant and should not be included.

Explication a literature review that makes an issue clear and comprehensive.

You may be requested to write a general **explication** of a topic. The assignment requires you to complete a literature review that comprehensively reviews both conceptual issues and research findings on a subject. Make sure to cover all points

TABLE 5.1 REVIEW SUMMARY STRATEGIES	
NOTE: Experience suggests that you will find the first patterns listed most useful for those situations in which there seems to be little research directly related to your specific research question.	
Summary Strategy	**Description**
Known to unknown	Reviews literature by considering what (little) is known separately about each variable in the research review question and then announces what remains to be learned.
Deductive	Reviews literature by considering what is known in general categories, followed by increasingly specific categories that are related to the topic (e.g., starting with studies of communication climate, followed by related studies on communication climate in high-tech organizations, followed by perceptions of communication climate of women in high-tech organizations).
Problem-solution	A problem and its cause are suggested followed by a research suggestion that might solve the problem (e.g., the problem of identifying highly communication apprehensive students in the elementary schools has resulted in many children going without help in developing this social skill; thus, a research solution in the form of a quick rating scale to be completed by teachers following interviews with students is proposed as a solution).
Chronological	Studies are summarized in their order of publication from the oldest study through the most recent one. Since this organizational pattern almost invites "mini–book reports" of literature, students should be very cautious about selecting this method.
Inductive	Study findings in a given area are summarized by producing general propositions (laws or rules) that are demonstrated by each sub-collection of them (studies are grouped largely by their findings, rather than their input variables).
Topical	Studies are summarized by reference to content categories into which the studies fall (e.g., studies related to effects of mass media sources, public figure sources communicating directly, and interpersonal sources on formation of voter opinion are covered in three different categories).

listed in this brief description of literature reviews to be certain that you have addressed all the important issues.

explication paper indicated

Strategies for the Research Prospectus

Of all the papers you may write, the research prospectus may be the most demanding since it includes the components of definitional and literature review papers along with new suggestions for research. A **research prospectus** lays out a proposal for future research. Though a prospectus may be composed by undergraduate students, it is a routine form of paper for graduate students. All the details are set out so that the study could be executed immediately after the proposal's acceptance.

Research prospectus
a complete proposal for a research activity to be completed at a future date.

Standard Steps

first five steps of the research prospectus unchanged

The first five portions of a research prospectus are identical to those described for other papers. Only the remaining steps diverge.

1. The paper begins with an introduction showing the relevance of the topic to communication and overviewing the parts of the prospectus.

2. The context and the problem statement may be separated into different categories depending on the flow of the paper.

3. The significance of the problem area is frequently indicated before methods are described, though some prefer it to be placed as part of the discussion section of the paper. This discussion shows why the area posed by the research question is meaningful and important, rather than peripheral and trivial.

4. A full statement of definition of terms is included. Concerns for both conceptual and operational definitions are a part of this discussion. The review is meant to justify later choices for identifying or measuring variables.

5. The literature review argues for variables chosen, sets up hypotheses, and presents evidence to support methods proposed.

unique steps:

The following steps are unique to the prospectus:

♦ *rationale and hypotheses*

6. The rationale and hypotheses are stated. These expectations are stated with a brief justification for each. It is *not* a rationale to say "based on the literature review, the following hypothesis was advanced. . . ." Explanations of the links are required.

♦ *methods described*

7. The method to collect data is described. Quantitative researchers describe and justify proposed sample methods, measures, materials for study, procedures, design, and additional control steps. In the full prospectus, complete instruments, including questionnaires and coding forms, are attached.

♦ *analysis methods*

8. The proposed methods of analysis (including statistical tools) are explained and justified.

♦ *conclusions drawn if hypotheses were or were not supported*

9. A final section suggests conclusions that would be drawn if the hypotheses were supported and what would be concluded if the hypotheses were not supported. This section previews the discussion that would emerge if the study were completed. Some subdivide this section into discussions on study limitations, suggestions for future research, and potential importance of the research. Yet, these subdivisions are matters of preference by researchers.

additional elements

If a proposal is submitted to some group for evaluation, such as the submission of research for funding, a timetable, budget, and proposed method of presenting and publishing results are also included along with the researcher's own professional credentials.

In much qualitative research, the proposal is a bit different from the traditional quantitative proposal described here. Insofar as possible, the first five elements on the previously identified "standard steps" list are much the same in both types of research (though the reference to "operational definitions" in step 4 and explanations of formal "hypotheses" as found in step 5 are not typical of most qualitative studies).

Afterward, there can be substantial divergence. Chapter 1 of this book explained that according to the National Science Foundation's report of the *Workshop on Scientific Foundations of Qualitative Research,*

> Qualitative research involves in-depth, case oriented study of a relatively small number of cases, including the single-case study. Qualitative research seeks detailed knowledge of specific cases, often with the goal of finding out "how" things happen (or happened). Qualitative researchers' primary goal is to "make the facts understandable," and often place less emphasis on deriving inferences or predictions from cross-case patterns. (Ragin, Nagel, & White, 2004, p. 10)

This emphasis on cases, rather than variables, indicates that the method cannot always be identified in as much detail as is the case in quantitative research. The reason is not sloppiness at all. Yet, in most qualitative work, the emphasis is placed on interpreting the meaning of cases and the interpretations often produce changes in the categories that researchers use. The National Science Foundation report explained:

> In much qualitative research, by contrast, data collection and data analysis are not sharply differentiated. Researchers analyze data as they collect them and often decide what data to collect next based on what they have learned. Thus, in qualitative research it is often a challenge to specify a structured data collection and analysis plan in advance, though the logic of data collection and analysis can be presented in a proposal. In this respect, qualitative research is a lot like prospecting for precious stones or minerals. Where to look next often depends on what was just uncovered. (Ragin, Nagel, & White, 2004, p. 12)

Nevertheless, many standard steps found in most proposals are often found in qualitative studies. Qualitative sociologist Susan S. Silbey (2004, p. 122) explained that although some order may change, qualitative research designs include

- a description of the conceptual topic and aspect of social relations to be studied;
- a review of what is already known about this and the ways in which that knowledge was produced;
- what is not known and needs to be explored;
- identification of the population or setting about which the researcher will draw conclusions or develop hypotheses (theories) (e.g. who will be observed, interviewed, differentiated by status? gender? organizational location?);
- justification of the focus on these population(s) and setting(s) as likely to be generative for what needs to be explored further from what is already known;
- what forms of data will be collected (e.g. observations, interviews, documents);
- how the data will be put into a form appropriate for manipulation and analysis (e.g. through notes in computer files, visual images, transcribed tape recordings);

- how these data sets will be analyzed and synthesized (e.g. by conceptual coding, by textual or narrative structure); and

- how the results will be reported.

Mistakes Often Found in the Prospectus

mistakes found in writing the prospectus

Research writing requires attention to detail. Naturally, students often make some mistakes in their initial efforts. Some of the most frequent errors (translation: your instructor has seen them and does not like them) are the following:

- Selecting a problem that is too vast or too vague to investigate meaningfully (Borg, 1963, p. 38)

- Relying too heavily on secondary sources for literature reviews (Borg, 1963, p. 67)

- Concentrating on research findings when reading research articles, thus overlooking valuable information on methods, measures, and so forth (Borg, 1963, p. 67)

- Failing to provide information on validity and reliability of research instruments to be used

- Reciting facts without synthesizing or integrating these facts into meaningful generalizations (Borg, 1963, p. 233)

- Excessively using secondary sources of information—frequently found in studies not dealing with recent events (Borg, 1963, p. 233)

- Failing to specify detailed plans for analysis of data

- Describing procedures incompletely

- Assuming the results of causal comparative or correlational research to be proof for a cause and effect relationship (Borg, 1963, p. 286)

CHECKING ON THE RESEARCH ARGUMENT

The quality of reasoning to conclusions depends on a combination of both the evidence and the logic of the argument made. In this discussion, we will consider each of these major issues.

Checking on the Quality of Research Evidence

Evidence information used to support claims.

In research, **evidence** is the information that scholars use in their research arguments. Though you can group such research evidence, there appear to be two general categories: factual information, including statistics, and opinions offered to interpret facts.

SPECIAL DISCUSSION 5-3

THE SPECIAL FALLACIES OF RESEARCH

Though flaws of research reasoning are extensions of the study of fallacies generally, there are also some fallacies that are unique to researchers. They are ones that, if identified, may place a research effort into some doubt since they are mistakes in reasoning.

The ecological fallacy (Schutt, 2006, p. 179) is committed when a researcher uses data from groups of people to draw conclusions about individuals. For instance, researchers might observe that the smallest number of newspapers are sold on college campuses with the youngest mean age. A problem is created when a researcher then concludes that the youngest students are uninformed since they do not buy newspapers.

The Delphi fallacy (Giere, 1979, pp. 137–138) is the use of vague predictions as research claims. The fallacy takes its name from the Oracle of Delphi, which made such vague predictions that they were certain to come true. Once King Croesus asked the Oracle if he should wage war on Persia. The Oracle responded, "If you wage war on Persia a mighty empire will be destroyed." So, Croesus waged war and an empire was destroyed—his own. The problem with vague predictions in research is that if they cannot be shown untrue, they are not really testable.

The Jeane Dixon fallacy (Giere, 1979, pp. 139–141) involves making multiple predictions and claiming partial support. "Psychic" Jeane Dixon became famous when she claimed to have predicted the assassination of President John F. Kennedy (she actually only predicted that Kennedy would die in office). Making thousands of predictions each year, she publicizes her few correct calls. But if you make enough predictions, some are likely to happen by dumb luck. This research flaw occurs when scholars advance many hypotheses to support a theory, find most of them disproved, but claim "partial support" because of the few remaining successes. There is a story,

> perhaps apocryphal, about a group of confidence men. . . . They contacted a lot of people (for purposes of example, say 1,000,000), told them that they had developed a new economic model that accurately predicts stock-market fluctuations, and mentioned one or two stocks which would shortly go up. . . . In fact, they had . . . made about fifty different predictions to fifty groups of 20,000. In some cases, the stock mentioned did go up. . . . After three or four series of predictions a few thousand people had had outstanding financial advice and many were lured to sign up and pay handsomely for future advice. (Alcock, 1981, p. 96)

The patchwork quilt fallacy (Giere, 1979, pp. 141–145) involves making no predictions but offering explanations after the fact. The fallacy gets its name from a quilt composed of random pieces of cloth, forming a pattern. Yet, in research, we expect justifications for selecting evidence. Erich Von Daniken wrote a book titled *Chariots of the Gods?* in which he argued that remarkable advances in architecture and recurrent legends existed between the new and old worlds. He argued that these facts resulted from the Earth's visitation by beings from other worlds. When dissimilarities existed, he simply ignored them. Thus, we actually have no way to test whether Von Daniken is correct or incorrect. Moreover, the pieces of his patchwork quilt were not justified as uniquely relevant to his explanation.

(Continued)

SPECIAL DISCUSSION 5-3 (Continued)

The ad hoc rescue (Giere, 1979, pp. 145–147) involves claiming support for a theory despite failed predictions. A large religious group that sells newsletters door-to-door predicted the end of the world for six dates in the twentieth century. Each time the world did not end, they added additional explanations including computation errors and imprecise biblical references. In the last few years they began denying ever making any predictions at all, though a written record exists to the contrary. Religious beliefs are personal matters, of course. But in research, the *ad hoc* rescue occurs when a failed theory is followed by an effort to rescue it with random excuses. In scholarship, the false prophecy of a failed theory is enough to make people reject the entire research argument.

Fallacies in the Name of Science

Philosopher Stephen Carey (1998, chapter 5) noted that failures to follow scientific method rudiments lead to a host of general flaws, including these:

♦ Fallacies involving initial observations: anecdotal evidence (basing a general claim on a few anecdotal reports), omitting facts (creating an air of mystery by leaving out facts that might account for the mystery), distorting the facts (altering facts to create the impression of mystery).

♦ Fallacies involving rival explanations: fallacious argument by elimination (claiming support for one's own position by attacking opposing explanations) and fallacious inference to a causal link (claiming causation without using methods to permit making causal claims).

♦ Fallacies in proposing and testing explanations: exploiting analogies and similarities (drawing false analogies to well-accepted notions to claim support for the new unsupported approach); proposing unfalsifiable claims (making predictions that could not be falsified even if the claims were untrue); eliciting ad hoc rescues (advancing auxiliary assumptions that cannot be verified as a way of saving an explanation or extraordinary claim).

Factual evidence descriptions and characterizations of things used to support arguments.

Reports accounts of what took place whether by participants or by outside observers.

Primary sources reports provided by individuals who have firsthand experience with the events reported.

Secondary sources reports provided by individuals who do not have firsthand experience with the events reported.

Factual Information

Solid research appeals to facts, rather than to authority or personalities. **Factual evidence** deals with literal characterizations of things from the past (as in historical research) or things from the present (as in new samples gathered in experimental research, qualitative field observations, or descriptive research). The two major categories of factual information are reports and statistics.

Reports deal with information about events. In qualitative as well as quantitative research, reports are actively used. Researchers can gather these reports themselves, or they can use reports that others have previously gathered. Reports may be subdivided into two groups. **Primary sources** involve directly witnessed events. On the other hand, **secondary sources** are beyond directly witnessed events. Thus, primary sources provide evidence "straight from the horse's mouth." Secondary sources provide information that is a step removed from direct observation. Diaries and news accounts written by eyewitnesses to speeches are considered examples of primary evidence. Most history books, however, are secondary sources since their authors were usually not eyewitnesses to all the events described. As you might suspect, we usually have greater confidence in research reports from primary sources than from secondary sources. There are exceptions, of course, and scholars (including you) must always test the credibility of reports.

We ask questions that test the credibility of reports to determine whether evidence offers compelling support for a researcher's claims. If the evidence and reasoning are strong, then we may be eager to accept research claims. If the evidence is weak, there may be little reason to accept the statements advanced by researchers. The major tests of reports are listed on Table 5.2.

Statistical reports in common usage are just collections of numerical information. But a precise understanding of the meaning of statistics is essential for everyone. **Statistics** deal with numbers in samples. When researchers gather facts, they may wish to summarize their findings with numbers. If these numbers are based on samples, we call them statistics.

> **Statistics** quantitative reports based on observations in a sample (contrasted with the study of quantitative information).

To read communication research, you will have to deal with statistics. Political polls, surveys of needs for speech therapy, and trends in the use of cable television involve statistics that are used by all sorts of researchers in communication (not just experimental researchers). If every single event in a population were included in the study (difficult to pull off, unless the population is very narrowly defined), the numbers would be called

---

TABLE 5.2   QUESTIONS TO TEST THE CREDIBILITY OF REPORTS

1. *Can the reports be corroborated?* Reports are often made even though they are not consistent with other established facts. For instance, you may have heard the oft-repeated statement that Lincoln's Gettysburg Address was not received positively by the immediate audience. Such a claim (along with the baloney that it was dashed out on the back of an envelope) is not true, no matter how often it is repeated. The *New York Tribune* reported that the speech was interrupted by applause five times and received "long continued applause" at its conclusion (Sandburg, 1954, p. 445). Though some partisan newspapers used the occasion to continue attacks on Lincoln, the Gettysburg Address was received very positively by the immediate audience.

2. *Are primary sources used?* Secondary sources may get stories wrong. You may have heard that in the 1960 presidential debates between John Kennedy and Richard Nixon, polls supposedly showed that people who watched television thought that Kennedy won though people who listened on the radio thought Nixon won. It is frequently repeated by secondary sources and has become political folklore (e.g., Germond & Witcover, 1989, p. 54). Yet, David Vancil and Sue Pendell (1987) found that primary sources told a different story. In fact, credible polls distinguishing between TV viewers and radio listeners could not be found, though anecdotes and nonscientific samples were reported. Even so, you are likely to hear this misinformation repeated—but always from secondary sources.

3. *Is the reporter reliable?* Researchers may have to rely on reporters who lack the special skills or education required to grasp what they witness. Sometimes reporters cannot report competently because of factors beyond their control. For instance, scholars studying the debates in the British House of Commons often have been frustrated since reporters did not always take accurate shorthand notes of important debates. Indeed, G. Jack Gravlee (1981) found that in some of the most significant debates conducted in the House of Commons, incomplete notes taken by reporters without shorthand skills made it nearly impossible to be confident about the reports of actual speeches presented. In contemporary times, the use of audio and video recordings finally has improved the matter.

Parameter numbers computed from a population.

parameters.[3] The numbers that people deal with can cause difficulty if we are not careful. Hence, it makes sense to ask some simple questions to test their proper use. At another point in this book, the forms of statistics are mentioned in increasing detail. Though some of the tests on Table 5.3 discuss related statistical concepts covered in Chapters 4 and 12, the tests will be described only in simple terms here.

Opinions

Opinions interpretations of the meaning of collections of facts.

Expert opinions opinions from people who have special knowledge or training in the field of inquiry (in contrast with lay opinions, which come from people without expertise in the subject under discussion).

Though scholars work with the facts, they often use opinion statements as evidence in their research arguments. **Opinions** interpret facts. Such opinions can be used to help researchers make sense of the facts that they have reviewed. Researchers use opinions, regardless of whether they complete qualitative or quantitative research. Though opinions often come from laypeople, in research, we seek opinions only from people who are experts in the field of inquiry (sometimes called **expert opinions**). You may see quotations from experts who have summarized a body of literature in the field or offered a judgment about the importance of an area of study. These statements are examples of expert opinions if they are derived from scholars who have special training and ability. Researchers can ask key questions to determine when opinions deserve respect and when they may be discounted. These questions (see Table 5.4 on page 185) can be applied to opinion information regardless of the location of the opinion in a research article or paper.

Checking on the Adequacy of Research Reasoning

arguments are found in each location of a research effort

research arguments must meet standards

Research arguments are found in each major section of a research piece. These arguments function a bit differently in each section, and it helps to understand the sorts of arguments that people make in each section before considering ways to evaluate them. For instance, though an article's study method section may look like a simple report of tools that the researcher has selected, it is much more than a simple description. The researcher is expected to make a "good faith" effort to prove that the methods are appropriate. Similarly, the discussion of results of any study provides the researcher with a forum to make broad general interpretations. But there are limits to the sorts of conclusions that can be drawn. Scholars cannot make statements that go beyond the information analyzed in the study, and they must use sound reasoning since the methods and actual information examined in the study are the premises for these conclusions. Thus, the forms of reasoning used to draw conclusions can be evaluated by using the tools of logic, in which the relationships between argument premises and conclusions can be evaluated. In similar ways, all sections of research pieces advance arguments in each section.

---

[3]Don't confuse the word "parameter" with a boundary or limit. The word for a boundary is "perimeter"—close in spelling, but miles away in meaning. Speaking metaphorically, parameters can refer to defining characteristics of a population. Boundaries could be one of many parameters researchers look at (not very often, though), but most parameters are not boundaries. Got it? Don't say parameter when you mean boundary or perimeter. They do not mean the same thing at all.

TABLE 5.3   QUESTIONS TO TEST THE CREDIBILITY OF STATISTICS

1. *Are the statistics recent?* Statistics are only as good as the time period they cover. In 1986 *Newsweek* magazine took some statistical evidence of the time and concluded that "a single 40-year old woman had a better chance of being killed by a terrorist than getting married." On the cover of the June 5, 2006 issue of the magazine, *Newsweek* admitted that it had been wrong. *Newsweek* recanted the statistics, acknowledging that the evidence for the so-called "marriage-crunch" was fundamentally incorrect (*Newsweek,* 2006, cover).

2. *Was the sampling properly completed?* As the name suggests, samples do not include every person or event in the population. Instead, events are left out when samples are drawn. But since screwy samples probably can be found to prove any foolish thing, researchers are supposed to draw samples that represent the populations. The most famous example of a misleading sample is the *Literary Digest* presidential poll of 1936. The magazine collected over 2 million responses—the largest public opinion survey ever. The *Literary Digest* predicted that Alf Landon of Kansas would win. In reality, Landon was crushed in a landslide election for Roosevelt. Obviously, the sampling was not properly completed (see Wheeler, 1977, pp. 82–86). In the first place, magazine subscribers—not a representative group—were asked to mail postcards to the magazine to indicate their presidential preferences. In the second place, people who purchased new automobiles in the middle of the Great Depression—another unrepresentative group—were surveyed. In the third place, people with listed telephone numbers were contacted—but in the 1930s telephones were not the essential utility that they are today. In the fourth place, people were permitted to send in additional postcards during the survey. But the individual's previous "ballot" was not replaced with the new one. In the latter part of the campaign, when Republican voters turned against Landon in large numbers, the survey made the shift impossible to detect. The magazine went out of business early in 1937. Research statistics must be based on sound sampling to be worthwhile.

3. *Were the measures accurate?* Statistics are only as good as the data measured. One study evaluated the social interaction and communication of mental patients taken on a camping trip by the staff of a mental hospital (Tuttle, Terry, & Shinedling, 1977). Patients' interactions were recorded, and their interaction patterns were evaluated at the beginning of the trip on Monday and on the following Friday. The staff members used Bales' Interaction Process Analysis forms (without training) and assessed all the patients. They noticed that at the end of the week, the patients' quantity and variety of communication increased. The problem probably has occurred to you. Though the raters were unfamiliar with the rating scale at the beginning of the week (and surely missed examples of communication), by the end of the week, their experience had improved their ability to identify and rate communication on the scales. Thus, the responses on the instrument were not reliable from the pretest to the posttest. If the researchers had trained raters before the camping trip, this problem might have been avoided. Yet, the differences may have had less to do with the effects of the camping trip than the unreliable use of the measure.

4. *Were the methods appropriate?* Some public relations research has been criticized for using inappropriate procedures. For instance, in one mass media blitz, Coke and Pepsi compared taste tests (Coke-Pepsi Slugfest, 1976). Pepsi asked people to give their preferences between cola drinks from containers marked Q (Coke) or M (Pepsi). Pepsi "won." The procedures were doubtful since the labeling may have produced the reaction, not the quality of the drinks. Coca-Cola repeated the study placing Coke in *both* the M and Q containers. People still favored the M container soda. Thus, the original Pepsi preference should be treated with suspicion. Reasonable conclusions require statistics from studies in which the procedures and methods are appropriate.

(Continued)

TABLE 5.3   (Continued)

5. *Were the statistics misleadingly presented?* Sometimes statistics can suggest things that they cannot really support. There are different ways this problem might emerge. On one hand, there might be simple errors in analysis. For instance, Nicotera and Rancer (1994) explored whether men and women differ in their self-perceptions and stereotyping of aggressive communication behavior. Because they used the incorrect statistics, they reported differences between men and women related to one of their research questions. Following feedback from some alert readers, a subsequent correction (Errata Note, 1995) was published in which the error was noted and readers were advised to revise some of the study conclusions for themselves. On the other hand, reports of data might be misleading. For instance, a graph produced by the consulting firm of BoozAllen & Hamilton appeared to predict a steady decline in ratings for TV network news broadcasts from 1970 through 1996 (Fearless Predictions, 1999, p. 110). But the average TV ratings from two years (1996–1997) were compared with the average for each of the preceding *five*-year periods. If the time line had been consistent, the "trend" would have shown a steeper decline for ABC and a steeper increase for CBS and NBC broadcasts (Kovach, 1999, p. 21).

Inductive reasoning a process of reasoning "by which we infer that what we know to be true in a particular case or cases, will be true in all cases which resemble the former in certain assignable respects. In other words, Induction is the process by which we conclude that what is true of certain individuals is true of the whole class, or that what is true at certain times will be true in similar circumstances at all times" (Mill, 1872/1959, p. 188).

Argument from definition method of reasoning in which people submit that things do or do not belong in a certain class.

We should remind ourselves that researchers do not just attempt to get others to believe their claims. Researchers want such belief to be based on sound information that any researcher could verify as relevant to their conclusions. So, what types of claims do researchers make? Table 5.5 on page 186 includes a list of the lines of argument that appear in each major section of a typical research article (though many articles also have other formats). In addition, Table 5.5 shows the types of reasoning that scholars employ in advancing their claims. It should be noted that this table reflects the author's personal view of dominant patterns and not what must—or should—happen in all research.

In general, there are two forms of reasoning researchers can use: inductive reasoning and deductive reasoning. Each of these should be mentioned in turn.

Checking Inductive Research Reasoning

Inductive reasoning, as shown in the definition at the left of this page, deals with general inferences we make on the basis of examples of instances. Hence, we start with incomplete information on an issue and try to draw some (tentative) conclusions. It might help to mention some major species of inductive arguments identified on Table 5.5.

- ◆ **Argument from definition.** Many times the arguments used in conclusions of articles really are just applications of definitions, though they may *sound* like explanations of facts (Reinard, 1991, p. 333; see also Ray & Zavos, 1966, pp. 89–93). For instance, Halualani (2004) led a group of researchers in a two-and-a-half-year study of multicultural interaction among students at one American university. Although the students claimed to value multiculturalism, they seemed to avoid interactions with people of different intercultural groupings. Among the possibilities to explain results, the authors stated that "the contradictory attitude between declarations of diversity and limited intercultural interaction suggests that ethnic and racial fragmentation and enclave formation have been taking hold and framing insular community spaces of university students, even in culturally heterogeneous

TABLE 5.4   QUESTIONS TO TEST THE CREDIBILITY OF OPINIONS

1. *Is the opinion maker's source competent?* Among other things, a trustworthy opinion is the result of competent examination of the facts by knowledgeable people. Often things that amaze laypeople disappear when examined by an expert. For instance, in the 1970s an Israeli man named Uri Geller claimed to have supernatural powers. He claimed that his mind had the power to start watches, bend keys, guess the images others were thinking, and make things appear and disappear. For many years, his manager, Yasha Katz, expressed the opinion that Geller's activities were the results of actual psychic powers. Geller amazed many people including a host of celebrities and members of the public. When others trained in spotting magic tricks examined Geller's actions, however, each of his feats was revealed as a magic trick or sleight of hand (Randi, 1981; Marks & Kammann, 1981). Even Geller's manager eventually confessed to participating in Geller's magic tricks (in Carroll, 2003, pp. 153–155; Randi, 1981, pp. 125–126). Thus, we probably should learn a lesson. Opinions from sources who have special competence deserve respect, whereas opinions from the inexpert can be misleading.

2. *Is the opinion maker biased so much that the opinion is unreliable?* Everyone is entitled to his or her opinion (and most are *welcome* to them!). But a source who has very strong biases may not have reliable opinions. Consider these examples of clearly biased opinions found by comedian Jay Leno (1991) in U.S. newspapers:

   Headline: "Attorneys don't want ban on lawyer-client sex"

   [Leno's comment: "Now there's a shock."] (p. 10)

   Headline: "MGM bounces checks, but says finances OK"

   [Leno's comment: "Yeah, right, tell it to my landlord."] (p. 39)

   Headline: "Ten Commandments declared obsolete by 'News King' Turner: TV mogul issues his own 10 rules"

   [Leno's comment: "I guess if you've broken them all, they *are* obsolete."] (p. 16)

   Obviously, such opinions are difficult to swallow, and the biases of the sources give one reason to question them.

3. *Is the opinion consistent?* Contradictory or internally inconsistent opinion statements should be criticized by readers of research since they are not compelling interpretations of the facts. For instance, many books in communication (Thill & Bovee, 1991, pp. 57–59) and decision making (Levine, 1988, pp. 82–85) recommend brainstorming as a deliberation tool that is allegedly superior to individual problem solving. Brainstorming involves gathering a group of people together to have a free-flowing oral sharing of ideas under strict time limits and set rules. Yet, studies since 1964 have failed to support the superiority of decisions made by brainstorming. In fact, direct research indicates that brainstorming can lead people to generate fewer alternatives than if they were left alone (Lamm & Trommsdorf, 1973), and the method may be very inefficient (Graham & Dillon, 1974). The body of research has impressively shown that the "conventional wisdom" has been horribly overstated (Jablin, Seibold, & Sorenson, 1977; Mongeau, 1993). Thus, the consistency of claims with the facts they interpret is a vital part of assessing the worth of such opinions.

regions . . . " (p. 283). Cultural enclaves are typically defined as distinct cultural units within another cultural territory. So, the reason students rarely interact with people outside their own cultural groups is that they are in enclaves, which means that they rarely interact with people outside their own cultural groups. The definition offers a label for the condition, but not really an explanation.

TABLE 5.5 LOCATIONS OF RESEARCH ARGUMENTS

Section of Research Report	Line of Argument to Prove	Typical Type of Dominant Reasoning
The review of literature argument	Why current study is invited (filling a gap in knowledge, solving a practical problem, or extending past research)	Reasoning from specific examples of past research
	What future methods should be used (including a justification for the selection of methods or measures eventually used in a study)	Argument by example and generalization Applications of theories related to the variables Deductive reasoning: categorical, disjunctive, or conditional syllogism (depending on study type)
	What mistakes to avoid	Argument by example and generalization
	Why a given research area is legitimate	Argument by example and generalization or argument by analogy
	Reasons for any hypotheses to be advanced	Argument by analogy
The method of study argument	Why examples of communication behavior selected in the study are relevant and representative	Argument by example and generalization
	How methods of assessing and evaluating communication are sound responses to research questions	Argument by example and generalization and argument by analogy Conditional syllogism in hypothesis testing studies
	Why tools of analysis are responsive to the data	Argument by example and argument by analogy
Discussion	How the study answered the problem questions and tested hypotheses	In experiments and surveys: argument from example and generalization In hypothesis testing studies: conditional syllogism In experiments or long-term historical studies: causal argument
	That there are meaningful implications of the research findings	Argument from definition Argument by analogy
	The theoretic importance of the research findings	Argument by analogy Deductive reasoning: categorical, disjunctive, or conditional syllogism (depending on study)
	That there are limitations on study findings and invitations to future inquiry	Argument by example and by analogy

Consider these two statements that have stimulated researchers to argue actively with each other:

Argumentative communication among people may be transacted nonverbally (Willard, 1981; Burleson, 1980). [A definition of communication is the use of both nonverbal and verbal cues—to say that "argumentative verbal and nonverbal cues may be transacted nonverbally" is actually a definition.]

All-news radio stations succeed because their programming is monotonous (Woal, 1987). [One definition of monotonous is "repetitive"—to say that "all-news radio stations are repetitive," that is, they repeat the news, is a definition.]

Though these statements may seem to be research matters that deal with facts, they really are controversies about the proper meanings of words. No data one could collect could prove or disprove the statements. In fact, the statements are assertions of definitions. As you can tell, this method of arguing is one of the most frequent approaches taken by researchers. When reading research, therefore, we must be vigilant to see if an article really draws conclusions about the facts or about applications of special definitions.

♦ **Argument from example and generalization.** Relying on specific instances to make a claim is common in research. This method may be considered a form of pure inductive reasoning. As such, you find that most conclusions drawn in surveys and carefully controlled experiments are arguments by example and generalization. Even studies that analyze past speeches draw conclusions from specific communication instances. For example, as part of their proof for their claim that "President Reagan lied when he suggested the invasion [of Grenada] was undertaken primarily to rescue imperiled American citizens" (p. 105), Ralph Dowling and Gabrielle Ginder (1995) presented at least five examples of claims for which he lacked evidence, at least two examples of fabricating evidence, and a host of examples of misrepresenting or misinterpreting evidence. In fact, this reasoning method is among the most popular forms of drawing conclusions in research.

Argument from example and generalization a method of reasoning taking some particular cases and arguing that what is true of instances is generally true in the population of events.

♦ **Argument from analogy.** Though examples are in the same category of events as the conclusions researchers attempt to draw, analogies provide lessons by comparing similar, but different cases. There are two forms of analogies. As the definition at the right of this page shows, **literal analogies** usually search past history to try to find similar cases or events. Yet, **figurative analogies** try to make comparisons to things "made up" for the purposes of the comparison.

Researchers argue from analogies when they claim that because past research has found a pattern of results, a new study might produce similar results, despite some admitted differences from past inquiry. Researchers also use many analogies in their interpretations of results, especially when they try to draw similarities between their research and theories that have been developed by others. Sometimes these claims are strained, and sometimes they seem to be well founded. In her analysis of "participatory television" programs such as *Big Brother* and *Pop Idol,* van Zoonen (2004) explored "whether there is any relevance in these zeniths of audience activity for understanding and advancing

Argument from analogy a method of reasoning that compares "two things known to be alike in one or more features and . . . suggests that they will be alike in other features as well" (McDonald, 1980, p. 164).

Literal analogy an analogy that compares something to an event or object that really exists.

Figurative analogy an analogy that compares something to a hypothetical situation.

distinguishing literal and
figurative analogies

political activity and involvement" (p. 39). She drew an analogy between fan communities in entertainment and in politics. She explained that they were structurally similar because they both stimulated community involvement through some performance; great amounts of discussion, participation, imagination of alternatives, and implementation; and emotional involvements linked to rationality. She concluded that television entertainment programs could be viewed as helpful to political involvement. Researchers can also expose poorly constructed analogies. In response to a frequently repeated analogy alleging that press freedom may be relatively unfettered in the Beijing Olympic Games since the press were largely left free during the 1988 Olympic Games in Seoul, Wasserstrom (2002) issued a warning: based on both China's constitution and its political structure, the world press could not assume that widespread press freedom would be allowed.

Causal argument
reasoning that "a given factor is responsible for producing certain other results" (Reinard, 1991, p. 197).

♦ **Causal argument.** Cause-and-effect reasoning appears in most historical and experimental studies, just as it should be. Yet, causal arguments are often made in the conclusion and discussion sections of survey and descriptive studies—where they usually are *not* appropriate. Though experimental research and long-term historical studies use methods to permit making cause-and-effect statements, descriptive research does not. Language using cause-and-effect claims often creeps into interpretations of survey research anyway. For instance, Lippert, Titsworth, and Hunt (2005) surveyed a number of communication variables that they believed might distinguish regular-admission college students from probationary students (the latter called "at risk"). In the discussion of results, these researchers struggled to resist tendencies to insert cause-and-effect language. At one point they explained, "On the individual level, communication characteristics such as communication apprehension and verbal aggression may predispose some students to have more or less academic success" (p. 14). Elsewhere, the authors assumed that the first variable listed was the cause of the second variable listed (surveys, of course, could only show associations or degrees of coincidence): "The implication of this finding is that male at-risk students may be at an academic disadvantage *because* they have higher levels of CA whereas female at-risk students may be at a disadvantage *because* they have lower levels of CA" (p. 16, italics inserted). Of course, it could be that communication apprehension is a *result* of living a life "at risk" of academic failure. The authors were careful to use words such as "may" to cover themselves, but the causal claims that "may" be found were not completely eliminated by this strategy.

Checking Deductive Research Reasoning

Deductive reasoning a form of reasoning in which a valid conclusion necessarily follows from premises.

You might have heard someone say that **deductive reasoning** is "reasoning from general to specific" and inductive reasoning is "reasoning from specific to general." But some deductive arguments seem to move from one generalization to another generalization. Others seem to move from one set of specifics to other specifics. In everyday use of this form of reasoning, a general principle is often applied to a related case. This method is deductive since it starts with a general rule and then states that what is true of the larger class is true of a specific event in the class.

Deductive reasoning involves using syllogisms. A **syllogism** contains premises and a conclusion statement. They are formal logical arguments and can be tested by rules developed by logicians. You do not have to study much formal logic to appreciate how people use syllogisms in research. An article with a strong theoretic rationale uses deductive reasoning. So do articles that appeal to some general principle to explain their research findings. Researchers use three major forms of syllogisms.

> **Syllogism** a formal logical system in which the premises lead to a conclusion.

♦ The **categorical syllogism:** A categorical statement is an "allness" statement about things. Hence, the following example illustrates this reasoning:[4]

Major premise: All men are mortal.

Minor premise: Socrates is a man.

Conclusion: (Therefore) Socrates is mortal.

The terms all have names to help in applying rules. The biggest term of all, "things that are mortal," is called the major term. The smallest or most specific term, "Socrates," is called the minor term. The remaining term between the major and minor terms, "men," is (appropriately) called the middle term. Violations of proper structure make the reasoning "invalid" because the conclusion cannot follow logically from the premises. This method is the chief tool in the literature review and the discussion section argument.

> **Categorical syllogism** a syllogism composed of categorical or "allness" statements (in everyday practice, a syllogism whose major premise makes a categorical statement, regardless of whether minor premises are related particulars or other categorical statements).

♦ The **disjunctive syllogism:** These syllogisms are found in research arguments in which scholars try to compare the predictions of conflicting theories or expectations. For instance, there is a body of research on the impact of violent programming on television viewers. Two conflicting theories have been developed (see Huesmann, 1982). One theory called *arousal* predicts that watching TV violence stimulates people (especially children) to other acts of violence. A second theory called *catharsis* holds that watching TV violence reduces tendencies to engage in violence. The rationale for the studies focused on an obvious disjunctive syllogism:

> **Disjunctive syllogism** a form of syllogism whose major premise makes an "either–or" statement.

MP: Either the arousal theory is supported by research or the catharsis theory is supported by research.

mp: [for example] The catharsis theory is not supported by the research.

  C: (Therefore) the arousal theory is supported by research.

By the way, this syllogism has been the basis of major literature reviews (e.g., Milavsky, Kessler, Stipp, & Rubens, 1982), leading to the general conclusion that its reasoning is materially true and structurally valid.

---

[4]Technically, this example is not a categorical syllogism since the minor premise and conclusion deal with related particulars, not categories. Nevertheless, both by tradition and as a matter of convenience, the example shown here is employed as a quick way to introduce the concept. In addition, the major premise could be stated negatively as in "No researchers are sinful," which is equivalent to "Researchers are not sinful."

Conditional syllogism
a form of syllogism whose
major premise makes a
conditional or "if-then"
statement.

*used in the logic of hypothesis
testing*

◆ The **conditional syllogism:** When people speak of the logic of hypothesis testing, they are not kidding. The conditional syllogism is the logic that is used in the hypothesis, methods, and discussion of results sections of research articles that test hypotheses. In essence, when a researcher states a hypothesis, the major premise of the conditional syllogism is being composed. All hypotheses boil down to "if-then" statements, such as "If stutterers are given delayed speech feedback, then the amount of stuttering will decrease." The major premise of a conditional syllogism is simply a hypothesis. The methods section of a research article is designed to describe the materials and procedures that are used to complete the minor premise. The minor premise of these syllogisms must either affirm the "if" part of the hypothesis or deny the "then" part of the hypothesis. The conclusion is simply a statement of the results that must occur if the hypothesis can reach a valid conclusion. The material for the conclusion describes the eventual findings that relate to the hypothesis. If the hypothesis, the methods, and the results all match up, then a logical argument for the hypothesis can be made. If there is an error, then the hypothesis cannot be supported. The form of the conditional syllogism typically used in research is as follows:

MP: If stutterers are given delayed speech feedback, then the amount of stuttering will decrease.
mp: Stutterers in a study were given delayed speech feedback.
C: (Therefore) the amount of stuttering will decrease.

Each section of a research article serves as support for the premises and conclusions. If the truth of the premises and conclusions is accompanied by valid reasoning, then the hypothesis is supported.

Checking Soundness of Research Reasoning

A well-reasoned piece of research is most likely to earn respect and make a meaningful contribution to the field. Fortunately, it is possible to test these lines of reasoning by asking reasonable questions. For the inductive arguments presented in this chapter—example and generalization, analogy, and causal argument—appropriate tests may be completed by asking the questions found on Table 5.6. Combined with an effort to avoid the fallacies of thought unique to research reasoning, these tests enable scholars at any level to avoid reasoning difficulties.

Table 5.7 on page 192 shows the *major* tests used to assess the validity of syllogisms. As you can see, if the premises are true and the reasoning is valid, the conclusions are guaranteed to be true. Obviously, we expect good arguments to pass these formal tests and be based on sound evidence so that we can be sure that the premises are true. You may use them to evaluate the merit of the reasoning researchers use in literature review arguments and conclusions. Of course, you may examine your own work to make sure that it is free of such trouble.

TABLE 5.6   STANDARDS FOR EVALUATING THE WARRANTS

We can test whether these argument forms are acceptable by asking the critical questions listed for each type below. If the answer to any of these questions is unsatisfactory, the conclusions drawn from the reasoning type can be limited accordingly.

Argument from Definition

1. Is the definition truly equivalent to the term defined?
2. Is there sound evidence for the appropriateness of "word meanings or usage" (Ray & Zavos, 1966, p. 93)?
3. If the reason for a conclusion is a definition, are conclusions properly limited to the meaning of terms in the research setting (after Ray & Zavos, 1966, p. 93)?

Argument from Example and Generalization

1. Are the examples typical and representative?
2. Are enough examples cited?
3. Are the examples relevant to the conclusions drawn?

Argument from Analogy

1. Are the cases similar in many, rather than a few, essential respects?
2. Are there so many dissimilarities that comparison is not reasonable?
3. Since literal analogies are preferred as proof, were literal analogies relied on instead of figurative analogies?

Causal Arguments

1. Is there a direct and potent relationship between the cause and effect?
2. Can other causes actually explain the effects instead?
3. Can something else prevent the effect from occurring?
4. Is the cause capable of producing the effect all by itself (or must it be accompanied by other forces to produce the effect)? (*Note:* This distinction between types of causes involves what are called necessary and sufficient causes or conditions. A *necessary condition* is one of several contributors required to produce the effect. A *sufficient condition* is capable of producing the effect all by itself. People often say that a cause is "necessary but not sufficient" when they mean that more than one contributor to the effect must exist to produce the effect.)

CHECKLIST TO EVALUATE COMPOSITION OF THE RESEARCH ARGUMENT

_____ Does the article or paper begin by demonstrating that the topic of the work is relevant to the field of study?

_____ Is enough context of the problem provided to permit understanding the research argument?

TABLE 5.7   RULES FOR THE SYLLOGISM

Rules	Example of Forbidden Reasoning
The Categorical Syllogism	
1. The syllogism must have a middle term that is distributed (used in an "allness" statement) at least once.	MP: Many credible speakers are persuasive. mp: Attractive speakers are credible. C: Therefore, attractive speakers are persuasive.
2. No term may be distributed in the conclusion if it is not distributed in a premise.	MP: Stutterers have high communication anxiety. mp: Teenage boys have high communication anxiety. C: Therefore, teenage boys are stutterers. (This flaw is called an illicit conversion.)
3. A negative conclusion can occur only when one of the premises is negative.	MP: All freshman speakers are anxious. mp: Tom is a freshman. C: Therefore, Tom is not anxious.
4. Both premises cannot be negative.	MP: No newspapers report lies. mp: The *New Republic* is not a newspaper. C: Therefore, (?)
5. A syllogism must have three terms, each used twice.	MP: All war is hell. mp: Bosnia is in civil turbulence. C: Therefore, (?)
The Conditional Syllogism	
1. The minor premise must not deny the antecedent.	MP: If speakers are men, they will be credible. mp: Speakers are not men. C: Therefore, (?)
2. The minor premise must not affirm the consequent.	MP: If speakers are men, they will be credible. mp: Speakers are credible. C: Therefore, (?)
The Disjunctive Syllogism	
1. The major premise must include all alternatives.	MP: People write essays either in favor or against their personal beliefs. mp: People write essays irrelevant to their personal beliefs. C: Therefore, (?)
2. The minor premise must deny or affirm a term in the major premise.	MP: People write essays either in favor or against their personal beliefs. mp: People write essays neither in favor nor against their personal beliefs. C: Therefore, (?)
3. The alternatives must be mutually exclusive of each other.	MP: People write essays either in favor or against their personal beliefs. mp: People write essays in favor and against their personal beliefs. C: Therefore, (?)

_____ If the work proposes new research, is a sound argument presented to show why the work should be completed?

_____ Is the purpose of the work or the research problem question clearly and acceptably stated?

_____ Is past research appropriately used to make arguments relevant to the current work?

_____ Is the review of literature complete in

- ◆ defining terms?
- ◆ arguing to conclusions about what is known?
- ◆ arguing why new research is relevant?
- ◆ justifying methods to be used in future work?

_____ Is a rationale provided for each hypothesis that may appear?

_____ Are study methods described in enough detail to permit replication?

_____ Are sources of samples of documents, conversation, discourse, or sample data described completely?

_____ Are any measures and materials described (with information on measurement adequacy when appropriate)?

_____ Are study procedures and/or design completely described?

_____ Are methods for analyzing data or making interpretations described and justified?

_____ Are results completely presented?

_____ Does the discussion argument show sound reasoning? In particular, does the discussion

- ◆ avoid making interpretations beyond the actual scope of the research?
- ◆ interpret all relevant materials including answering research questions and consideration of hypotheses?
- ◆ (even if combined with suggestions for future research) are appropriate limitations on study conclusions made?

_____ Is the paper clearly written?

_____ Were all sources clearly identified and full attribution made?

For a literature review:

_____ Does the review meet its goals as an exemplary or exhaustive literature review?

_____ Does the review's summary organization promote understanding the research arguments?

_____ Is the literature review complete with arguments dedicated to

- ◆ justifying the subject as relevant to the field?
- ◆ providing adequate context to the problem?

◆ providing background definitions of terms?

◆ reviewing insights from relevant theory?

◆ (according to goals set) surveying all relevant literature?

◆ suggesting the heuristic merit of research on the subject?

For a research prospectus or proposal for a quantitative study:

_____ In addition to the standard steps for a literature review,

◆ is there a rationale for any hypotheses?

◆ is the method to collect data sound and adequately described?

◆ are any methods of analysis of information or data described and justified?

◆ are major interpretations explained for supporting or failing to support the research hypothesis?

For a research prospectus or proposal for a qualitative study:

_____ Is there a clear description of the conceptual topic and aspect of social relations to be studied?

_____ Is there a review of what is already known and the ways in which such knowledge was produced?

_____ Does the research identify what is not known and needs to be explored?

_____ Is the population or setting about which the researcher will draw conclusions or develop hypotheses (theories) clearly identified (including who will be observed, interviewed, differentiated by status, gender, or organizational location)?

_____ Does the researcher justify focusing on the populations and settings as likely to be generative for what needs to be explored further?

_____ Does the researcher indicate what forms of data will be collected (e.g., observations, interviews, documents) and why they are most suitable?

_____ Is information provided about the ways data will be put into a form appropriate for manipulation and analysis (e.g., through notes in computer files, visual images, transcribed tape recordings)?

_____ Is a justification provided for how the data, conversations, or texts will be analyzed and synthesized (e.g., by conceptual coding, by textual or narrative structure)?

_____ Is all evidence used to draw conclusions and to make research arguments sound?

◆ Did any reports satisfy tests for this type of evidence?

◆ Did any statistics satisfy tests for this type of evidence?

◆ Did any opinions satisfy tests for this type of evidence?

_____ Is all reasoning from data and events (inductive reasoning) sound?

◆ Did any arguments from definition satisfy tests for this type of reasoning?

◆ Did any arguments from example and generalization satisfy tests for this type of reasoning?

◆ Did any arguments from analogy satisfy tests for this type of reasoning?

◆ Did any causal arguments satisfy tests for this type of reasoning?

_____ Is all reasoning from general statements to events or categories (deductive reasoning) valid?

◆ Did any arguments in the form of categorical syllogisms (often expressed without stating one of the premises) use valid logic?

◆ Did any arguments in the form of conditional syllogisms use valid logic?

◆ Did any arguments in the form of disjunctive syllogisms use valid logic?

SUMMARY

Research is a form of argument because it is a process of advancing conclusions using reasons and evidence. But research argument must be based on the methods of science without appealing to the prejudices or biases of the masses.

Research articles are organized in very specific ways. The titles of research articles are descriptive to aid in their indexing. The abstract summarizes an article as a courtesy for the reader. The introduction and context of the problem show why the general topic is relevant to the field. As part of the context discussion, scholars are expected to advance clear definitions and to argue that research is invited. Three reasons are used: new research would fill a gap in knowledge, new research would solve a practical problem, new research would extend or improve on past research. The statement of the problem is included, though sometimes hidden as a "purpose statement." Though formats differ for quantitative and qualitative studies, the review of literature extends the context of the problem by answering three basic questions: What do we already know or do? How does the new research question relate to what we already know or do? Why select this particular method of investigation?

The rationale for each hypothesis immediately precedes the statement of the hypothesis. The methods section describes what the researchers did in enough detail so that others could repeat or replicate the study. For qualitative studies, often no formal section labeled "Method" appears. For quantitative studies, the methods may be explained in detail under the headings of (1) data or documentary sample; (2) operational definitions of variables (conceptual definitions give you an idea of the meaning of a term; operational definitions isolate a concept by specifying the steps researchers follow to make observations of the variables); (3) procedures that describe how the study was completed; and (4) methods for analysis of data (qualitative studies rely on theoretic orientations to interpret data; empirical and experimental studies employ statistical tools). The results section in a quantitative study simply presents findings. The discussion interprets results and explains their meaning. The conclusion summarizes what was accomplished. References identify source materials used and tend to follow the APA format.

Scholarship must be written clearly. Five aspects of this activity are involved. First, you must know how to use past research since past study is the basis for new research. Researchers can develop their own research arguments by examining past research (1) to find arguments to prove that the subject matter of the research question is relevant to the field; (2) to find arguments to prove that the concepts and variables in the research question can be defined coherently; (3) to find arguments to prove that the concepts and variables in the research question can be studied coherently and that any variables may be measured soundly; (4) to find arguments to prove that the concepts and variables in the research question are important; and (5) to find arguments to prove that there is a gap in our knowledge about the concepts and variables in the research question. Second, you must complete purposeful inquiry, which means that you must make arguments by looking for relevant evidence. Yet, to do so, you must first know what conclusion (claim) you are trying to argue. Then, research can be found to test it. A recommended way to organize claims and evidence is to use the research argument planning outline. Third, you must identify vital information. Novice student-researchers often make the mistake of gathering too much information or too little information that they can use to help construct an argument. Vital arguments to make may be found on the research argument planning outline. Then support may be sought for each main point and subpoint. In addition, information should be retained dealing with definitions of key concepts and variables; ways concepts and variables have been measured and studied; summary statements and quotations about the subject; classic research studies on a subject; research that shows what methods to use; and research that shows what mistakes to avoid. Setting limits on the scope of your research is critical before you look for resources. Fourth, the truth about writing research is that you should avoid the temptation to make arguments from past research by reviewing the sequence of the search process and presenting little "book reports" for each study, one at a time (studies should be "grouped" to make arguments and common criticisms). The researcher needs to use arguments to justify the choices made for the researcher's own conclusions and as a foundation for justifying the new choices. You should also avoid the mistake of writing a literature review before deciding on study methods. Since you cannot justify these research choices unless you first know what choices you plan, you cannot write a literature review until you know what methods and approaches you intend. Thus, in addition to proving that the proposed study is relevant to the field of study, the literature may be used to justify the methods that are to be used in any future inquiry. This writing process includes discussion of the appropriate conceptual definition of the concept; sound ways to measure or identify the variables or concepts (including explanations and justifications for the proposed methods); how research shows the importance of the variable or concept; and identification of the gap in knowledge, desire to extend on past research, or intention to solve a practical problem. Fifth, writing and style mechanics need to be observed. Using proper formats and subdivisions and paying attention to effective style (choice and use of words) can help you achieve clarity. You can make your writing clear by using internal organizers (phrases that preview, summarize, and transition between main points), avoiding ambiguity, relying on standard paragraph structures, and defining every term you use.

Writing classroom reports may involve three major forms. The definitional paper takes a concept of interest and considers issues that involve the proper definition of the concept. In addition to structuring the definitional paper, the paper involves following steps to isolate each key school of thought (usually through a process of sorting definitions into categories). The literature review paper attempts to tell the reader what is known about a subject and the current status of the knowledge about the matter. The literature review generally has seven sections: (1) an introduction, which justifies the study of the topic in the field; (2) the context of the problem; (3) background definitions of terms; (4) the review of relevant theory to explain the variable or concept; (5) the survey of the research (completed either as an exhaustive literature review that includes all material related to the subject or as an exemplary literature review that surveys only the most important contributions); (6) a list of opportunities for future research, suggesting the "heuristic" merit of research (its ability to lead scholars to new inventions, ideas, explanations, or research avenues); and (7) a summary of main points. In addition, the literature review follows clear strategies to summarize research. An explication assignment requires you to complete a literature review that makes an issue clear and comprehensive. The research prospectus is a complete proposal for a research activity to be completed in the future. The first five steps of a research prospectus are identical with those steps described for other papers. The remaining steps include statement of the rationale and hypotheses, description of methods to collect data, justification of proposed methods of analysis, and conclusions that would be drawn if the hypotheses were supported or not supported. If a proposal is submitted to some group for evaluation, such as the submission of research for funding, a timetable, budget, and proposed method of presenting and publishing results are also included along with the researcher's own professional credentials. In much qualitative research, the proposal is a bit different. Though the first five elements of the previously identified "standard steps" may share much in common, there can be substantial divergence afterward. Since qualitative research places emphasis on cases, rather than on variables, data collection and data analysis may not always be "sharply differentiated. Researchers analyze data as they collect them and often decide what data to collect next based on what they have learned. Where to look next often depends on what was just uncovered" (Ragin, Nagel, & White, 2004, p. 12). Yet, standard steps in qualitative research proposals include "a description of the conceptual topic and aspect of social relations to be studied; a review of what is already known about this and the ways in which that knowledge was produced; what is not known and needs to be explored; identification of the population or setting about which the researcher will draw conclusions or develop hypotheses (theories); justification of the focus on these population(s) and setting(s) as likely to be generative for what needs to be explored further from what is already known; what forms of data will be collected (e.g. observations, interviews, documents); how the data will be put into a form appropriate for manipulation and analysis (e.g. through notes in computer files, visual images, transcribed tape recordings); how these data sets will be analyzed and synthesized (e.g. by conceptual coding, by textual or narrative structure); and how the results will be reported" (Silbey, 2004, p. 122). In addition to effective writing of the prospectus, students need to avoid making critical errors in composing the prospectus.

Scholars reason from evidence (information scholars use to support claims) to advance their conclusions. Two categories of research evidence are used: factual information, including statistics, and opinions offered to interpret facts. Factual information consists of descriptions and characterizations of things. The two forms of factual information are reports and statistics. A report is an account of what took place whether by a participant or by an outside observer. Primary sources of reports provide information obtained from individuals who have firsthand experience with the events reported, whereas secondary sources are from individuals who do not have firsthand experience. Statistics are quantitative reports based on observations in a sample. If every single event in a population were included in the study, the numbers that describe the population would be called parameters. Opinions are interpretations of facts. Expert opinions come from people who are experts in the field of inquiry.

Research arguments are found in each major section of a research piece. Scholars argue for researcher claims, which are statements advanced for the adherence of others. The starting points for research arguments are called grounds, or statements made about things that say support is available to provide a reason for a claim. Most of these grounds are past evidence or theory. The reasonings for such claims are called warrants, or general statements that justify using the grounds as a basis for the claim.

There are two general forms of research reasoning that scholars can use: inductive and deductive. Inductive reasoning is the process by which we conclude that what is true of certain individuals is true of a class, what is true of part is true of the whole class, or what is true at certain times will be true in similar circumstances at all times. There are several sorts of inductive arguments, including (1) the ubiquitous argument from definition (in which people submit that things do or do not belong in a certain class); (2) the argument from example and generalization (which takes some particular cases and argues that what is true of instances is generally true in the population of events); (3) the argument from analogy (which is often used in sections of the study dedicated to the rationale and to the conclusion); and (4) the causal argument (which reasons that a given factor is responsible for producing certain other results). An analogy compares two things known to be alike in one or more features and suggests that they will be alike in other features as well (a literal analogy compares something to an event or object that really exists, whereas a figurative analogy compares something to a hypothetical situation).

Deductive reasoning involves inference in which a valid conclusion necessarily follows from premises. It includes some use of a syllogism (a set of two premises that result in a conclusion). The categorical syllogism starts with a categorical statement and is a chief tool in the literature review and the discussion section arguments. The disjunctive syllogism has an "either–or" statement in the major premise and is found in research arguments that try to compare the predictions of conflicting theories or expectations. The conditional syllogism has an "if–then" statement in the major premise and is used in the hypothesis, methods, and discussion of results sections of research articles. The major premise of a conditional syllogism is simply a hypothesis.

TERMS FOR REVIEW

arguments

operational definition

style

internal organizers

exhaustive literature reviews

exemplary literature reviews

heuristic merit

explication

research prospectus

evidence

factual evidence

reports

primary sources

secondary sources

statistics

parameters

opinions

expert opinions

inductive reasoning

argument from definition

argument from example and
generalization

argument from analogy

literal analogy

figurative analogy

causal argument

deductive reasoning

syllogism

categorical syllogism

disjunctive syllogism

conditional syllogism

JUST FOR THE SAKE OF ARGUMENT: A REVIEW

Look at the following questions and prepare your own answers to them. Make sure to consider any assumptions that may lie beneath them.

1. What types of reasons are advanced to justify problems posed in research articles? In particular, what lines of argument are advanced in the "introduction" or "context of the problem" sections of the literature review?

2. What is expected in any literature review regardless of whether the research examined is qualitative or quantitative?

3. What are the chief differences between operational and conceptual definitions?

4. What kind of explanations are expected in the results section of an article? How may the study findings be explained fully?

5. Why are internal organizers so important in writing? Don't they run the risk of boring readers? When is this deliberate repetition a realistic problem?

6. What are the differences between the major types of literature reviews? Which types are expected of undergraduates? Of graduate students? Of professors?

7. When in doubt, shouldn't students use the chronological pattern to summarize literature? Since this format is the simplest to understand, shouldn't students start with it and then develop their skills with other methods at a later time?

8. Many studies that test hypotheses announce their hypotheses with general phrases such as "Based on this literature, the following hypotheses were advanced." Why is this approach so much of a problem? What kinds of statements are researchers supposed to make when advancing hypotheses?

9. Is there ever a time when preference is given to opinion information as opposed to factual information?

10. Why are primary sources of reports preferred to secondary sources? How fallible are eyewitness reports? How can researchers be sure of the actual reliability of sources?

11. Do we test reports by asking if the reporter has biases? What is the role of identifying biases in crediting or discrediting reports?

12. When is lay opinion (as opposed to expert opinion) considered acceptable as an information source?

13. What sorts of arguments are advanced in the literature review? What is the impact of any failure to present any of these arguments?

14. Is a knowledge of logic really essential to master research methods?

15. When is it appropriate for researchers to assert that they have found a cause-and-effect relationship?

ACTIVITIES TO PROBE FURTHER

Go to the website for this book, and look for the Student Study Materials for Chapter 5.

1. Take the study quiz and print out your answers. (Avoid giving answers that are your first impressions only. To review the materials, take a look at the page on "Dissecting the Research Argument.")

2. Look at the activity titled "Urban Folklore and Fits of Fancy." These "debunked" stories deal with reports that are materially untrue. Take your "favorite" from the list, and answer the following questions:
   a. What flaws in evidence did believers of this story make?
   b. What flaws in reasoning did believers of this story make?
   Now, look for two additional urban legends that are on the Internet.
   c. Make a copy of the Web page in which each urban legend is discussed.

    d. Answer these questions about the legends:
       (1) What may be the motivations for spreading these urban legends?
       (2) What do these legends have in common (e.g., type of target, underlying values, moral to be derived from it)?
       (3) Using the tests of evidence found in this chapter, what question(s)—if asked—might have prevented the spread of the rumors?

3. On the same Web page, go to the APA Style Exercise. Complete the exercise by placing the citation materials in proper APA form for references. Print out your responses.

4. Alan Sokal, a professor of physics at New York University, tried an experiment to test the limits of credulity in cultural studies, a field with a distinctly postmodern epistemological bent. He wrote a scholarly sounding article on a preposterous topic and wondered if his parody would be found out. The article was called "Transgressing the Boundaries: Toward a Transformative Hermeneutics of Quantum Gravity" and was accepted for publication in the Spring/Summer 1996 issue (vols. 46/47) of *Social Text*. Go to Sokal's website (www.physics.nyu.edu/faculty/sokal) and scroll down the page to the heading "Papers by Alan Sokal on the 'Social Text Affair.'" Look at the article and the responses by the editorial board of *Social Text*.
    a. What questions of reasoning or evidence should have been asked to expose the parody?
    b. What was the response from the *Social Text* editorial staff?
    Did this response surprise you?

5. Explore the Web. Look up the source "Pitfalls of Data Analysis (or How to Avoid Lies and Damned Lies)," which deals with questions to ask about potential flaws in the use of statistics in research reasoning: www.vims.edu/~david/pitfalls/pitfalls.htm. Which problems do you believe are most frequent among research pieces? Which problems can be easily overcome by asking the questions listed in this chapter for evaluating statistical information?

Conducting Textual Analyses

The interest in life does not lie in what people do, nor even in their relations to each other, but largely the power to communicate with a third party.

—VIRGINIA WOOLF

CHAPTER OUTLINE

Analysis of Message Qualities

Critical Studies of Texts

Applications of Textual Analysis

BEFORE WE GET STARTED . . .

Many studies examine the content and flow of messages directly. These methods for analyzing message qualities are popular in communication studies. This chapter introduces qualitative work in the form of critical interpretations of texts. It is not intended to teach you how to be a rhetorical critic, conversation analyst, or discourse analyst. Rather, this chapter is designed to give you information so that you may read such studies, and so that you may understand the elements that are typically expected in such work. To develop these skills requires coursework specifically dedicated to advanced studies in theory areas that use these methods.

ANALYSIS OF MESSAGE QUALITIES

Much communication research analyzes message structures. Researchers use this approach when they want to focus on message qualities that are unique, rather than generic. They often distinguish nomothetic from idiographic research. **Nomothetic research** is designed to find general lawlike patterns that apply to many instances. **Idiographic research** focuses on individual instances. Though messages can be analysed in nomothetic research, these methods can also be used for intensive idiographic studies of a single communication event, such as a presidential debate or a discussion between a particular pair of communicators. We will consider three general categories of communication analysis: criticism; formal content analysis of messages, especially of public and mass media communication; and interactional and relational analyses of conversations.

Nomothetic research scholarship designed to find general laws that apply to many instances.

Idiographic research scholarship designed to develop a full understanding of "a particular event or individual" (English & English, 1958, p. 347).

What Are the Data in Textual Analysis?

What are the data in textual analysis? The "data" of such analyses are the examples and instances drawn from the message text. Of course, we should understand that the word **text** means only that we are dealing with actual communication. We do not mean that the text originally must be (or could be) written down, entirely or in part. Thus, texts might include a television show, a political debate, or even (under some circumstances) an influential movie. There are many types of message treatments, and these elements may be examined as part of the text for analysis. Of course, after researchers have determined a text for analysis, they must spend time determining authorship and textual authenticity before proceeding.

To find such data for textual analyses, scholars may search many sources. They may look at collections of speeches found in standard textbooks and anthologies. Many newspapers publish transcripts of important speeches in the news. The *New York Times* regularly prints texts of speeches and reports, which are available online

texts as data

Texts what are believed to be the actual messages or words of a communicator.

sources of texts

at www.nytimes.com (at the time of this writing, the service is free, though readers must register). Furthermore, the presidential White House website (www .whitehouse.gov) provides copies of speeches from the president and vice president (and occasionally from their spouses as well). The U.S. Congress broadcasts texts through C-SPAN, and the website (www.c-span.org) provides texts and video of speeches and testimony of congressional and political interest. Internet sources, such as "Douglass Archives of American Public Address" (douglassarchives.org), provides transcripts as well as audio and video files of many speeches. Nontraditional texts have their own resources, such as "Footage.Net: Searchable Library of Film Clips and Photos for a Past Century" (www.footage.net), which contains film and still photography materials. The number of sources for such electronic materials is growing weekly, and their addresses change from time to time. Thus, you would be wise to check "Comfile" (commfaculty.fullerton.edu/jreinard/internet.htm) regularly for the latest sources of texts.

When Do We Complete Textual Criticism?

As always, the problem question determines the research method that should be selected. Both qualitative criticism of texts and quantitative forms of content analysis are procedures selected by the researcher after the problem question is composed.

characteristics of problem questions that invite use of qualitative/critical methods

Researchers are invited to use qualitative/critical methods of analysis when their research problem questions ask about the following:

♦ Characteristics of the message that contributed to its level of effectiveness (such as, What is the relationship between Ronald Reagan's use of humor and the level of building identification with the American audience?)

RESEARCHERS IN THE FIELD: KARLYN KOHRS CAMPBELL

When people speak of a significant rhetorical critic, the name of Karlyn Kohrs Campbell quickly enters the conversation. She is an internationally renowned expert in rhetorical theory and criticism, political communication, women's communication, and social movement rhetoric. She has published scholarship in every major journal that showcases the theory and practice of rhetorical criticism. Her book *Critiques of Contemporary Rhetoric* became a modern classic in the instruction of students in rhetorical criticism. Her work exploring the contributions of women speakers in her two-volume study, *Man Cannot Speak for Her,* is a turning point in the serious criticism of the rhetoric of the women's movement. Not surprising, this work won accolades and the prestigious Winans-Wichelns Award sponsored by the National Communication Association. She is the author of eight books and has been the editor of the *Quarterly Journal of Speech.* She also has received every major National Communication Association–sponsored award for a scholar in rhetorical studies. She was married to the late Paul Campbell, and together they established an endowment to award outstanding book-length scholarship in rhetorical theory.

♦ *What drew you into our field?*

I took a speech course in high school from an excellent teacher who had majored in speech at St. Catherine's in St. Paul. She encouraged me to do extemporaneous speaking in contests, and then to begin debating, which I did as a junior and senior. I started debating as a first-year student at Macalester College and by my sophomore year I was fortunate enough to go to the National Debate Tournament national tournament at West Point. At that time in the 1950s, young women had limited options, and I assumed I would become a high school teacher. So, I followed a course that involved lots of English literature, speech and drama, and education to gain a high school teaching certificate. I received a scholarship that enabled—and forced—me to finish an M.A. in communication studies at the University of Minnesota in one year.

I was poor, so poor I couldn't pay for my own health care. So, I went on the job market and encountered pervasive sex discrimination, although there were literally hundreds of jobs for which I was qualified. It was a rude awakening. I took the only job I was offered at the State University of New York at Brockport, then 1,700 students, most of them phys. ed. majors, just as the school was becoming a liberal arts rather than a normal school.* Because of my experience on the job market, I stayed there for four years, at the end of which I bought a one-way ticket to Europe, arranged to study in Salzburg and then at the University for Foreign Students in Perugia, Italy, after which I went to Palermo, Sicily, and taught students of all backgrounds and levels of competence at the British College. In the course of that experience, I decided I wanted to go back to the USA and I wanted to work for a Ph.D., which I did. I worked through a network to obtain a job at Cal State Los Angeles, which is where I met my husband. Because I shared an office with the program director of KPFK, Pacifica Radio, who overheard my working with students, I was invited to deliver the editorial segment of the news once a week as a critique of some piece of public discourse. Edited and revised, those became *Critiques of Contemporary Rhetoric,* which, I believe, was the first rhetorical criticism textbook published in the USA.

♦ *Though you have focused your research on rhetorical theory and criticism, your applications are diverse. You especially have been prominent in influencing thought in political rhetoric and social movements, especially in women's communication. What drew you to focus your attention on these areas?*

I was lucky enough to live through the second wave [of the women's movement], which had a lot of relevance to my life, as I've said previously. I was also lucky enough first to be in LA where lots of movement material was available. In 1971, Paul and I moved to New York City where even more of that material was available in print and on radio. At SUNY Binghamton [State University of New York at Binghamton], where I was then teaching, I taught a course on the rhetoric of the contemporary movement, and I wrote the "Oxymoron" essay during that time.† In 1974, Paul and I moved to the University of Kansas, Lawrence, and Wil Linkugel invited me to team-teach a course on women's rhetoric with him—he'd do the first wave and I'd do the second. Well, the rest is history. I fell in love with

---

*"Normal" schools were mostly land grant colleges established primarily for the purpose of training teachers.

†Referring to the highly esteemed article, "The Rhetoric of Women's Liberation: An Oxymoron," published in the February 1973 issue of the *Quarterly Journal of Speech.*

the women of the first wave, and I decided to devote my energies to making sure that everyone came to know what great speakers and thinkers they were.

I've also published several essays on African American rhetoric. That really began at Cal State Los Angeles, because I was at an institution that was really diverse, majority nonwhite, and in the midst of protest about the Vietnam War and the intense conflicts over the counterculture and Black Power in the civil rights movement. When Martin Luther King, Jr., was murdered, I felt responsible, responsible in the sense of never again putting civil rights on the back burner. I organized my basic public speaking classes around civil rights issues (all speeches had to deal with issues of ethnicity/civil rights, and all students read the Kerner Report on the so-called riots). Paul and I volunteered in a program in Watts aimed at improving employment skills—writing résumés, preparing for interviews, handling on-the-job conflict. I did one of my KPFK editorials on the rhetoric of Black Power (revised and published in *Critiques*), wrote an article published in *Central States*,* and at Kansas was the principal investigator on a grant funded by the Kansas Endowment for the Humanities to preserve materials from and do oral histories with members of the Kansas Association of Colored Women's Clubs and Links.

I honestly don't remember what sparked the interest in genre, but when I was appointed to the NCA research board, each member was expected to foster a project, and I chose form and genre. After I'd moved to Kansas, I made the culminating part of that a conference on form and genre. Kathleen Hall Jamieson [see profile in Chapter 8] volunteered to become part of that, and I urged her to become a partner. The result was the book we coedited out of papers from that conference. As we talked about the issues, we decided that a very powerful test of the usefulness of a generic approach would be presidential inaugurals, so each of us went to work analyzing all of them. We got together, compared notes, and wrote an essay that we presented first at a conference at Temple (and published in the proceedings), and that led us on to ascendant vice presidential speeches, which led us to farewells, and pretty soon it was clear that this was a book about the interaction between an institution—the presidency—and its public discourse, and the result was *Deeds*.†

I also spent a sabbatical studying media because I'd heard an awful lot of not very insightful public statements about media by rhetorical scholars, and I didn't want to be in that position. This, of course, was a big interest of Jamieson's, and the result of our joint interest was *Interplay,* which is now in its sixth edition!‡

♦ *You have received every major honor in the field for your rhetorical studies and scholarship. But rather than simply receiving awards, you and your late husband, Paul Newell Campbell, established the very generous Kohrs-Campbell Prize in Rhetorical Criticism awarded by the Michigan State University Press to recognize outstanding book-length research in rhetorical theory. What led you to give back so much to the field?*
From the very beginning of my career, it has been my dearest wish to make my field better. As rhetoricians, we have an incredible history; Greco-Roman rhetorical

---

*"The Rhetoric of Radical Black Nationalism: A Case Study in Self-Conscious Criticism" was the lead article in the Fall 1971 issue of the *Central States Speech Journal,* now called *Communication Studies.*

†Referring to Karlyn Kohrs Campbell and Kathleen Hall Jamieson's 1990 book, *Deeds Done in Words: Presidential Rhetoric and the Genres of Governance* (University of Chicago Press).

‡Referring to Kathleen Hall Jamieson and Karlyn Kohrs Campbell, *Interplay of Influence: Mass Media and Their Publics in News, Advertising, Politics,* sixth edition, published by Wadsworth in 2005.

works were the foundation of the Renaissance and the basis for European education. I hated it that rhetoric had fallen into disrepute, and I wanted to produce texts that I hoped would make the field better. I hoped that *The Rhetorical Act*[*] would encourage teachers to do more in basic public speaking classes, for example, and I thought of *Critiques* as a way to stimulate the teaching of rhetorical criticism to undergrads. The field is much stronger than when I entered it, but Paul and I saw giving money for a prize as a way to stimulate the best scholars to do work in rhetoric. Of course, some of them do it anyway, such as Garry Wills [who wrote a] Pulitzer Prize–winning book on Lincoln's Gettysburg Address, but I'd like to see lots more of that.

♦ *What part of your research undertakings have made you most proud?*
Well, it took me ten years to do the research and write *Man Cannot Speak for Her,* so I think I am proudest of that. I'm also proud of other publications on women's discourse and on the two volumes of *Women Public Speakers in the United States,*[†] which I hope will continue to be a foundation for subsequent research and publication.

♦ *Judging by numbers alone, the communication field has been particularly attractive to women, who now make up the majority of students. Yet, in your 2001 Carroll Arnold Lecture to the National Communication Association you explained that traditional contributions to male rhetorical theorists, "interesting as their works may be, are late, late comers. For centuries, women (and other oppressed groups) have been writing about and practicing an alternative rhetoric." Are you making a call to a new research agenda for the young women who now are the majority of communication students?*
I don't know how to answer that directly. Sage is going to publish a handbook on *Gender and Communication* edited by Bonnie J. Dow and Julia Wood. I edited the section on Gender and Rhetoric, and coauthored with my brilliant advisee Zornitsa Keremidchieva an essay on Gender and Public Address that speaks to this. There's also an essay in it by Nathan Stormer on contemporary rhetorical theory that explores these issues. I hope young women will read those and think hard about the ideas in them. We still have a lot to do.

♦ *What one or two lessons have you learned along the way that could make the novice research student have a successful career in the field's research?*
It has to be your passion, or you'll never succeed. It takes long hours to do research, endless hours to write and edit and polish, and you have to want it a lot, you have to feel real joy in doing it, or it's drudgery. You need to find projects that engage you deeply, projects you are eager to pursue and topics on which you have a deep desire to say something important and original.

♦ *What personal qualities do you have that you think have contributed to your achievements as a communication scholar?*
I love my work, and work and play are closely linked in my world. I find teaching invigorating, and issues that arose in class have often stimulated me in a new direction and given me a special insight. I have always been curious, I have read a lot in all kinds of areas, novels, biography, history, as well as materials in the field. I love the world of ideas, in all forms, with a special love for theatre and other forms of drama.

---

[*]Referring to *The Rhetorical Act*, which was published in its third edition by Wadsworth in 1996.
[†]Referring to *Women Public Speakers in the United States, 1800–1925: A Bio-Critical Sourcebook* and *Women Public Speakers in the United States, 1925–1993: A Bio-Critical Sourcebook* (both published by Greenwood Press in 1993 and 1994, respectively).

- Reasons for the impact of the message (such as asking whether advertisements promoting active consumer purchasing following the 9/11 attacks on America were successful because corporations "suggested that enacting consumption was a central mode of enacting citizenship and patriotism" [Dickinson, 2005, p. 273]).

- Whether the message measures up to standards of excellence (such as, Does the widespread information about breast cancer meet Aristotelian standards in the categories of ethos, logos, and pathos?) (after Matelski, 2001).

- Testing the usefulness of explanations from rhetorical theory (such as when Stroud [2005] examined the *Bhagavad Gita* as a persuasive text and found that its influence could be explained as a form of "invitational rhetoric" as developed in the theorizing of Foss and Griffin [1995] much more than it could be explained from the traditional "masculine persuasion" view).

- Examining meanings as revealed through rhetorical visions held by groups (such as when Perry and Roesch used fantasy theme analysis to answer the question "What religious meanings did the life of Fred Rogers and his long-running children's television program, *Mister Rogers' Neighborhood,* have for his audience?" [2004, p. 204]).

Thus, if the researcher asks questions about the theoretically important elements of a message, questions about the social impact of the message, or "questions for which only evaluations will make fitting answers" (Carter & Fife, 1961, pp. 85–86), the method of textual criticism is invited.

characteristics of problem questions that invite use of conversation or discourse analysis

To decide if discourse or conversational analysis forms are appropriate procedures for your study, you also need to look at your problem question. Above all else, problem questions ask about characteristics of messages that could be categorized and counted (such as, What is the relationship between the amount of news coverage given to third-party candidates on the three commercial television networks?). Research questions also invite conversation or discourse analyses when they deal with the following:

- The "description and explication of the competencies that ordinary speakers use and rely on in participating in intelligible, socially organized interaction. At its most basic, this objective is one of describing the procedures by which conversationalists produce their own behavior and understand and deal with the behavior of others" (ten Have, 1990, p. 24).*

- Examinations of influences of technology and external forces on communication. For example, in a study comparing computer-mediated software for distance meetings (eventually recommending CU-SeeMe software), Dingley (2002) used conversational analysis "to evaluate the content of real-life meetings to ascertain whether an example of this software facilitated task focused conversations that led to productive outcomes " (p. 1).†

---

*After drawing a distinction, the researcher announced the use of discourse analysis methods to answer this research question.

†After drawing a distinction, the researcher announced the use of conversational analysis methods.

- ♦ Comparisons of strategic uses of conversational elements to achieve certain effects. For example, in a study of the ways that toddlers (under $2\frac{1}{2}$ years of age) monitor the behavior of their daycare providers before engaging in mischief against other toddlers, Kidwell and Zimmerman (2006) explored the problem of whether "Even very young children have an understanding of how appearances matter for whether or not caregivers intervene in their sanctionable acts and, further, . . . [whether] they are attentive in highly nuanced ways to the attentional focus of caregiver during these movements" (p. 6).[*]

- ♦ Comparisons of conversations in specific settings to general communication encounters. For instance, a study of methods of using signals to regulate turn taking in exchanges occurring in chatrooms asked the question "Are non-moderated chatrooms closer to casual conversation than moderated chatrooms, where there may be a perception of censorship, and attempts to steer the talk?" (Neuage, 2004, p. 6.0.3)[†]

- ♦ Examinations of new interventions on the discourse activities of groups of people. For instance, Katzmarek (2001) studied the impact of new study groups composed of secondary school literature and language arts teachers for research purposes "of understanding how and why these teachers talk about their practices and, in doing so, [how] they construct teacher knowledge" (p. 1) (particularly using the thinking devices often employed in discourse analyses).[‡]

In all these instances, the messages are analyzed to provide keys to understanding significant issues in communication studies. Furthermore, the methods employ the evidence from texts as the foundation for their inferences.

CRITICAL STUDIES OF TEXTS

Our field often discovers new insights and theories through criticizing speeches, written messages, and communication movements. Though **rhetoric** involves the study of the means of persuasion, **rhetorical criticism** deals with application of these standards to help assess messages. By studying texts of speeches and other examples of messages, you can understand social and historical movements, form explanations for effective communication practices, and discover excellent communication practices.

To engage in a process of critical analysis of texts, students new to research often assume that it is wise to plunge into the speech, the report, or the text and begin applying judgments. Certainly, use of assessment tools will come. But critics must first look at matters that are primarily *external* to the content of messages. These matters are often called elements of **extrinsic criticism.** They involve two elements: examination of textual authenticity and determination of authorship.

Rhetoric according to Aristotle, "the faculty of discovering in the particular case what are the available means of persuasion."

Rhetorical criticism the use of standards of excellence to interpret and evaluate communication.

Extrinsic criticism in rhetorical criticism, evaluation of aspects beyond the text of a message, focusing predominately on assessing textual authenticity, authorship, settings, and message effects.

---

[*]After drawing a distinction, the researcher announced the use of conversational analysis methods.

[†]After drawing a distinction, the researcher announced the use of conversational analysis methods.

[‡]After drawing a distinction, the researcher announced the use of discourse analysis methods to answer this research question.

Textual Authenticity

Any analysis is pointless without working with the actual texts and any critical comments may be seriously flawed. Sometimes television commentators accuse speakers of taking positions that—examination of the texts themselves—are not accurately reported. This approach actually is an example of the logical fallacy known as attacking a **"straw man."** For instance, in debates about the United States' policy in the Iraq war, Representative John Murtha proposed redeploying American troops to locations outside, but near to Iraq. Fox News commentator Sean Hannity called Murtha a coward for his policy of "surrender" to the enemy and "cutting and running." Murtha's supporters did not need to justify Murtha's position—they only needed to point out that the attacks were based on proposals Murtha never made. For critics as well, advancing research arguments based on the wrong texts can be a problem. Researchers may find themselves evaluating messages that were not actually heard.

Straw man fallacy
attacking of a person for a position that was not actually taken by the person.

There are several ways that such texts may become flawed or "corrupted."

sources of corruption:

1. use of advance copies

♦ Speakers, especially presidents and significant public speakers, may deviate from advance copies that are distributed before a message is delivered. President Franklin Roosevelt was notorious for adding parts to his speeches after distributing advance copies—after a time members of the press learned that they needed to listen to him before writing their stories. Most of today's so-called "instant analyses" of presidential speeches are based on advance copies that may not be the same words that speakers actually say.

2. reporters let biases interfere with accurate recording

♦ People who are supposed to record the messages may let their biases or expectations interfere with reporting accurately what was said by communicators. In the eighteenth century, Samuel Johnson regularly wrote reports of the speeches that took place in the House of Commons on behalf of various London newspapers. Unfortunately, since the House of Commons met in the evening, attending the debates often interfered with the dinner parties at which Johnson was a desired guest. So, Johnson frequently filed stories without hearing the speeches themselves. He appeared not to be very bothered by the matter because he admitted that he always "let the Whig dogs have their day."

3. use of memorial editions

♦ Memorial editions of messages may revise works to improve on the original texts. For instance, most people know that Winston Churchill never said "blood, sweat, and tears," but some memorial versions of his speeches have promoted the phrase as his. On July 20, 1969, when he stepped on the moon, Neil Armstrong made one of the most misquoted statements of all time. He said, "That's one small step for a man, one giant leap for mankind." Yet, many reporters listening at the time who heard background static left out the word "a," "thus ruining the contrast he had made between one man ("a" man) and all mankind ("man"). Newspapers and wire services soon reported Armstrong's correction, but the faulty version continues to circulate" (Boller & George, 1989, p. 5). The problem was compounded when NASA brochures, official films, and tapes were edited to reflect the inaccurate phrasing.

4. editing for readability

♦ Efforts to improve readability may cause editors and reporters to improve on the original text. For instance, in the first 1984 presidential debate, Ronald

Reagan became ungrammatical and incoherent after Walter Mondale challenged his honesty in denying his desire to cut Medicare. Yet, in their "word for word" transcript of the debate, the *New York Times* revised the text so that most of the incoherencies were deleted. Readers, therefore, did not get the actual text of the debate. Granted, the original text was often unreadable, but the effort to improve on the original corrupted the actual text to which people were exposed. Table 6.1 shows both the actual words spoken and the errors that were created by the *New York Times* editing process.

TABLE 6.1 DIFFERENT TRANSCRIPTS OF THE 1984 REAGAN–MONDALE DEBATE

This selection is quoted from the *New York Times* of October 8, 1984. Differences in the transcription found in the actual audiotape are indicated in italics. "Uhs" and "ums" are not included in either transcription although Reagan's remarks featured them extensively. After Reagan had answered, "There you go again . . . " in response to a question about raising taxes during his presidency:

Right?

MONDALE: Now, Mr. President, you said, "There you go again." Right. Remember the last time you said that?

REAGAN: Um hmm

MONDALE: You said it when President Carter said that you were going to cut Medicare. And you said, "Oh, no, there you go again, Mr. President." And what did you do right after the election? You went out and tried to cut $20 billion out of Medicare. And so when you say, "There you go again," people remember this, you know. And people will remember that you signed the biggest tax increase in the history of the United States. And what are you going to do? You've got a $260 billion deficit. You *wish*
can't wash it away. . . .

REAGAN: Yes. With regard to Medicare, no. But it's time for us to say that Medicare is in pretty much the same condition that Social Security was, and something is going to have to be done in the next several years to make it fiscally sound. And, no, I never proposed any $20 billion should come out of Medicare. I have proposed that the program—we must treat with that particular problem. And maybe part of that problem is *that*
because during the four years of the Carter-Mondale administration, medical costs in this country went up 87 percent.

MODERATOR: . . . all, er . . . [laughter]

REAGAN: (comment unintelligible) . . .

QUESTION: . . . The Census Bureau just a month ago reported that there are more people living
people living under than
under poverty now—a million more people—   than you took office. . . . What
head
relief can you offer to the working poor, to the minorities and to the women heads of
?
households who have borne the brunt of these economic programs.

(Continued)

TABLE 6.1 (Continued)	

Well,

REAGAN: Some of those facts and figures just don't stand up. Yes, there has been an increase in poverty, but it is a lower rate of increase than it was in the preceding years before we got here. It has begun to decline, but it is still going up. . . . We have found also in our studies that in this increase in poverty it all had to do with their private earnings.
had   on all
It has nothing to do with the transfer payments from government, by way   of
the, well,
many programs. . . . We're spending a third more on   all the programs of
—*we have*—
human service. We have   more people receiving food stamps than were ever receiving them before. . . . Some time ago, Mr. Mondale said something about education
the
and college students and help of that kind—half, one out of two of full time college students in the United States are receiving some form of federal aid, but there again, we
people . . . . under
found people that there were under the previous administration—families that had no limit to income were still eligible for low-interest college loans.

5. permitting author revisions

♦ Permitting sources to revise their remarks often introduces errors. Speakers may improve on their arguments and phrasing. The *Congressional Record* is notorious for permitting revisions of materials. A related situation occurs when sources supply texts after the message is presented (the texts appearing in the magazine *Vital Speeches of the Day* are supplied by this method).

dealing with textual authenticity

To deal with corruption and find a way to approach the actual text, the critic has several methods that might be used. They are not equally effective, of course. Among the most popular tools are the following:

1. comparison with the original

♦ Comparing the available text to the original, if the original is available. Of course, there may be more than one version claimed to be the original. So, other methods must be found.

2. comparison with recordings

♦ Comparisons may be made of the available version against recordings, if a recording is available. As identified in Appendix G, records for many speeches are available for a long time. In fact, the Vincent Voice Library includes speeches of presidents going back to Cleveland and Hayes. Regrettably, there are no recordings of Lincoln. Yet, sometimes audio or video recordings can be used to verify textual authenticity and correct mistakes in available versions. For the example in Table 6.1, the author used an audio recording to identify errors in the available transcript from the *New York Times*. When there is no original text and when recordings are not available, critics often attempt to recreate their work by using a third option, conjectural emendation.

◆ Conjectural emendation based on comparisons of all texts may be used. This sort of work is serious research that requires dedication and time. In this case, critics examine all versions of existing texts to identify points of agreement indicating where statements are accepted by all (or nearly all) versions. Where they agree, one may be comfortable with the account. Where differences are found, critics make note of the disagreement in extended notes called **conjectural emendation,** in which they suggest which alternative seems most likely. This work is not guessing. Instead, the conjectural emendation should use materials from historical context, experience with the author, and other evidence to make an argument.

3. conjectural emendation

> One should be careful about accepting agreeing texts as authentic just because they agree. Sometimes different versions agree because a "fix" is in the works (such as the common fiction that Richard III murdered his way to the throne of England—the evidence points more to Henry Tudor VII [the first Tudor King of England] than to Richard III, but the subsequent authors on the subject wrote under the aegis of the Tudors [see Tey, 1951; after Rogers-Millar & Millar, 1979]).

Conjectural emendation when attempting to assess textual authenticity, a method in which researchers with different available versions of texts make arguments to explain which of the competing textual alternatives is most reasonable and, thus, should be accepted.

Of these alternatives, obviously the first two are most desired. But researchers should not be afraid to offer sound interpretations of the most likely versions of the texts, provided they have evidence to support their reasoning. In the absence of a clear answer, serious qualifications need to be added to the conclusion and discussion sections for the pieces of rhetorical criticism.

Authorship

To offer meaningful analysis of a message one should be sure to know the actual author of the message. One might wonder why identifying "ghost writers" and other authors may be so important. After all, a speaker is responsible for the words he or she speaks, regardless of who composed them. But knowing authorship is essential. The issue is fundamental: if you want to evaluate whether the communicator chose wisely from the methods available, you need to identify the author who is responsible so that you can know what universe of methods was available.

necessity of determining authorship to make critical statements

In an age of ghostwriting as a profession, it is difficult to tell who the true author of a work is. Yet, there are two general pathways to find clues to authorship of message texts.

◆ *External reports.* Sometimes external documents will reveal the true author of a text. For instance, most people have read the stirring conclusion to the "Give Me Liberty or Give Me Death" speech of Patrick Henry. Most people do not know that the speech we have was not written by Patrick Henry. He did issue a press release in which he announced the famous phrase, but the text of that speech is not Henry's. His biographer, William Wirt, identified himself as the author of the text that we have in anthologies to this day. Wirt said that he based it on his interpretations, but he made it clear that the speech was his construction, not Henry's. No other version of the speech ever has been found (Mallory, 1943).

1. using external reports to asses authorship

SPECIAL DISCUSSION 6-1

AUTHORSHIP FOR FAMOUS STATEMENTS

Many statements that people know to be associated with certain sources are not really attributable to them. For instance, you probably have encountered these statements associated with each of the sources listed.

1. "Anybody who hates children and dogs can't be all bad."—W. C. Fields
2. "Go west, young man."—Horace Greeley
3. "To the victors belong the spoils."—Andrew Jackson
4. "That government is best which governs least."—Thomas Jefferson
5. "There are three kinds of lies: lies, damned lies, and statistics."—Mark Twain
6. "Everybody talks about the weather, but nobody does anything about it."—Mark Twain

In fact, none of the people associated with the statements said them. Other people did. The answers are found below.

6. The expression was invented by Charles Dudley Warner in an editorial appearing in the *Hartford Courant*, August 24, 1897.

5. Benjamin Disraeli said it (Twain, 1959 ed., p. 149).

4. The quotation is the first line of Henry David Thoreau's essay on civil disobedience. Yet, he put it in quotation marks as if it were an old saying.

3. New York Senator William L. Marcy said it in January 1832 when responding to Henry Clay, who had attacked Jackson for nominating Martin Van Buren to be ambassador to Great Britain (Drummond, 1951).

2. John Basone Soule wrote this statement in the 1851 *Terre Haute Express* and Greeley reprinted it in the *New York Tribune*, with full credit given to Soule (Richardson, 1945, p. 39).

1. Leo Rosten made this statement when introducing Fields at a dinner (Burnham, 1975, p. 123).

---

2. using comparisons with other communication

♦ *Comparisons with other communication.* Comparing messages of different individuals may produce clues to authorship. Though the method rarely settles the issue for all time, it often can identify when different authors were involved. For instance, historian Allan Nevins's classic investigation of the texts of the Federalist Papers (a series of persuasive messages intended to influence the states to ratify the new United States Constitution of 1789) revealed shifts in style suggesting at least three different authors. On the basis of a short list of likely contributors whose identities were hidden to avoid additional controversy, Nevins compared the styles of various messages in the Federalist Papers with other written work completed by possible authors. Comparisons of style strongly suggested that some of the essays were written by Alexander Hamilton and some by John Jay, even though James Madison was the official author (Nevins, 1938, pp. 155–156).

In full **criticism,** however, the critic identifies standards of excellence (which, in turn, can be argued as relevant or irrelevant) for application. To the extent that a message meets the standards, it is evaluated positively. The further away from the standard the message is, the harsher is the negative evaluation. Sometimes we use the term **impressionistic criticism** to refer to the personal impressions of reviewers, such as those who "review" movies for newspapers and magazines. Yet, scholarly criticism is not a matter of personal opinion: it is a direct application of standards. We can evaluate a critic's argument since the standards are known in advance and we can double-check descriptions of data.

In essence, therefore, all criticism involves three steps. First, standards of excellence are presented. Second, the messages are described and applied to the standards. Third, the degree to which the messages meet or fall short of the standards is described. Thus, researchers make critical statements that point out how far an actual message is from the ideal. Scholars rely on systems of categories that list matters to examine so that they may determine what is good or bad, right or wrong, sound or unsound in communication.

> **Criticism** message evaluation in which standards of excellence are announced and the degree of conformity of the message to the standards determines the evaluation made.

> **Impressionistic criticism** statements of opinion (or personal impression) made by reviewers.

> *the three steps of criticism*

Neo-Aristotelian Criticism

When Aristotle developed his discussion of rhetorical communication about 2,400 years ago, he employed categories that came to be known as the canons of rhetoric. Over time, when people used the canons to organize their criticism, their work was called **neo-Aristotelian criticism** ("neo" is a word form that means "new"). Hence, neo-Aristotelian criticism really is a new use of Aristotelian standards. Aristotle was not the only major writer who used the canons of rhetoric. Among others, the Romans Cicero and Quintilian also used them. Yet, each of these authorities offered very different advice. Technically, we should reserve the term "neo-Aristotelian criticism" for situations in which Aristotle's standards are used, "neo-Ciceronian" when Cicero's standards are referenced, and "neo-Quintilianic" when Quintilian's standards are employed. When selecting a standard, critics are expected to identify sources used to develop criteria for evaluation. Thus, critics must prepare by reading a lot. If they wish to do neo-Aristotelian criticism, they must read what relevant discussions Aristotle made in at least seven books ranging from *Ethics* to *Rhetoric*. For contemporary theorists there may be fewer books to read, but there is a fair amount of background work required before one is ready to complete serious criticism. Thus, this chapter gives you a working vocabulary and set of expectations for evaluating textual analyses. You should plan to take additional coursework to develop a firm foundation for using any of these forms of rhetorical criticism—and participating in this exciting branch of communication research.

When applying the canons of rhetoric in neo-Aristotelian criticism, these major issues are covered:

> **Neo-Aristotelian criticism** criticism using Aristotelian standards and involving the canons of rhetoric.

> *use of canons not unique to Aristotle*

> *critics using the canons must find a standard*

+ **Invention** consists of two sets of appeals or proofs. Nonartistic proofs are composed of materials not created by the speaker though used as proof in messages (such as testimony, contracts, documents, and the like). Artistic

> **Invention** the canon of rhetoric concerning the types and sources of ideas.

proofs are composed of elements that the speaker may demonstrate through the speech. These artistic proofs are divided into three categories of appeals. The first category is *ethos,* sometimes called "ethical appeal." **Ethos** is actually the speaker's credibility and includes the methods the speaker uses to build and use credibility in a speech. The second category is *pathos,* also known as "pathetic appeals." **Pathos** is the use of emotional or pathetic appeals by a speaker. Both the sources of the appeal and the audience emotions are considered by the critic. The third category is **logos,** which most critics treat as logical appeals, including the evidence and reasoning used by a speaker, though *logos* is a Greek word that has no direct translation into English (in context, this term means the rational idea behind things *and* the symbolic expression of those ideas through words).[1]

♦ **Arrangement** deals with message organization. In this category, critics assess the structure of the introduction, body, conclusion, previews, transitions, and organizing patterns.

♦ **Style** concerns the choice and use of words (although we sometimes see commercials claiming that using a particular brand of cologne will give a person "style," this meaning is not the classical sense of the term). The critic looks at the suitable vocabulary of the speaker, the tone of the words used, and the clarity of expression.

♦ **Delivery** involves the use of nonverbal cues by communicators when presenting messages. Major nonverbal categories of voice, movement, and eye contact are examined to find clues to effective communication.

At one time a fifth canon, memory, was included in a list of "Five Canons of Rhetoric." **Memory** was the speaker's ability to memorize materials for subsequent use. Though communicators often train their memories to avoid using notes, memory rarely is examined by critics. Hence, memory is sometimes called the "lost canon" (Hoogestraat, 1960).

Neo-Aristotelian critics constantly ask whether speakers made good choices of persuasive appeals from the means that were available to them. The method can often be extended to movements or campaigns that involve more than one speech. Table 6.2 shows basic questions that guide completing neo-Aristotelian criticism. The neo-Aristotelian method has been employed successfully in much research, including now-classic studies of Lincoln's speaking at Cooper Union in 1860 (Mohrmann & Leff, 1974); the analysis of Richard Nixon's November 3, 1969, address defending his Vietnam policy (Hill, 1972); and the speeches of Woodrow Wilson (Craig, 1952). Another study found that ethos, pathos, and logos proofs could be used to evaluate breast cancer websites, which were disappointingly weak in logos

---

[1]These three categories have occasionally been called the "Three Musketeers of Rhetoric" because of the reference to the main characters in the novel by Alexandre Dumas. As a rather dry joke, Dumas named his three Musketeers Athos, Porthos (ethos, pathos, get it?), and Aramis.

TABLE 6.2 CRITICISM STARTING QUESTIONS FOR NEO-ARISTOTELIAN CRITICISM

I. *Invention*

   A. *Ethos:*

      1. Is the speaker intelligent?

      2. Does the speaker reveal good character?

      3. Is the speaker a person of goodwill?

      4. Is the speaker telling the whole truth?

      5. Is the speaker credible?

      6. Does the speaker's reputation enhance the speech?

   B. *Pathos:*

      1. Does the speaker establish identification with the audience?

      2. What types of appeal are used?

      3. Are appeals specific and concrete?

      4. Does the speaker stimulate attention and interest?

   C. *Logos:*

      1. Does the speaker proceed from assumptions and hypotheses that are fair and reasonable?

      2. Is the speaker's analysis of the subject complete and clear?

      3. What types of argument are used?

      4. Does the speaker's reasoning meet appropriate tests of validity?

      5. Are the supporting materials sufficient?

      6. Are data sufficiently documented?

      7. Does the speaker substitute emotional appeals for evidence and argument?

II. *Arrangement*

   A. Is the thesis or central idea clear?

   B. Is the subject partitioned according to a clearly definable pattern?

   C. Are materials coordinated and subordinated correctly?

   D. Are the divisions and subdivisions of the subject complete and clear?

   E. Are there clear transitions that develop relationships among ideas?

III. *Style*

   A. Is the language clear?

   B. Is the language appropriate to the speaker, audience, and occasion?

   C. Is the language vivid?

   D. Is the language direct?

   E. Is the language forceful?

(Continued)

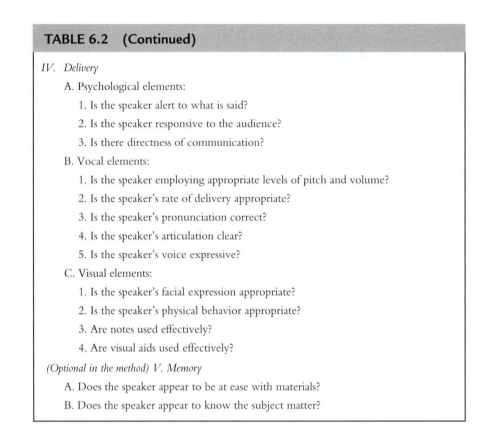

TABLE 6.2 (Continued)

IV. *Delivery*

    A. Psychological elements:

        1. Is the speaker alert to what is said?

        2. Is the speaker responsive to the audience?

        3. Is there directness of communication?

    B. Vocal elements:

        1. Is the speaker employing appropriate levels of pitch and volume?

        2. Is the speaker's rate of delivery appropriate?

        3. Is the speaker's pronunciation correct?

        4. Is the speaker's articulation clear?

        5. Is the speaker's voice expressive?

    C. Visual elements:

        1. Is the speaker's facial expression appropriate?

        2. Is the speaker's physical behavior appropriate?

        3. Are notes used effectively?

        4. Are visual aids used effectively?

(Optional in the method) V. Memory

    A. Does the speaker appear to be at ease with materials?

    B. Does the speaker appear to know the subject matter?

Question checklist adapted from William E. Lewis and Ron R. Tabor. *Guidelines: Rhetorical Criticism.* Norwalk, CA: Cerritos College, 1966, pp. 3–5.

(Matelski, 2001). The method may be difficult to apply to messages relying chiefly on extralogical strategies. The strategy of a speaker who chants at an audience is difficult to capture within the categories of this approach. Despite its limits, however, this method is a useful way to organize criticism of messages.

Burke's Dramatistic Criticism

foundations of the Burkean approach

Identification the uniting of people by the use of ideas, images, and attitudes.

Many critics have benefited from the thinking of Kenneth Burke (1945/1969, 1950/1969), a poet, essayist, and critic. Burke's communication notions start with the idea that people are essentially the same, with the same drives and motives. But they have grown apart from each other by society's artificial boundaries. Thus, the job of communication is to help bring people together. The key concept in this system is identification. By creating a sense of **identification,** communication creates a sense of "oneness" between speakers and audiences. If you identify with another person, you accept that person's words because they almost seem to be your own thoughts. Thus, Burke explained, "Wherever there is persuasion, there is rhetoric. And wherever there is 'meaning' there is 'persuasion'" (1950/1969, p. 172).

SPECIAL DISCUSSION 6-2

A QUESTION OF ETHICS: DISCLOSING BIAS AND PERFORMING CRITICISM

In rhetorical criticism, there would not seem to be many ethical problems to face. Since documents are used, problems with the ethical use of human participants may not be issues. But there may be more to the story than such an appearance suggests. Two concerns involve use of documents that are presumed to be private and the substitution of personal political musings for rhetorical criticism of messages.

In a fascinating and insightful examination of the Vietnam Veterans' Memorial in Washington, D.C., Cheree Carlson and John Hocking observed that the Memorial had become a place where large numbers of messages, birthday cards, teddy bears, and remembrances regularly were left. They examined over 2,000 items including nearly 1,000 written messages. Many items were moving private messages addressed to the dead, whose names appeared on the monument. Each evening, the National Park Service collected these items and stored them (they still do). When Carlson and Hocking's article was published in 1988, it received the Western States Communication Association's award for outstanding article published that year. It also received criticism on ethical grounds. At a presentation the author attended, Carlson was surprised by the reaction from many that the messages to the dead were not public documents. In fact, one observed that the Vietnam Veterans' Memorial had become nearly comparable to the Wailing Wall, a remnant of the great temple built in Jerusalem by King Solomon (where the cracks in the wall are filled with messages to God sent by the faithful—as far as is known, no one collects these writings and it is often presumed that the wind blows these messages heavenward). For people to read such private messages would incur the wrath of nearly all members of one of the world's great faiths. Similarly, the argument went, it was a violation of a sacred trust to read the personal messages of those who were still alive, who had addressed messages to others, and from whom the authors had not received permission. Since *some* artifacts and messages left at the Memorial were published in an oversized book (Lopes, 1987), Carlson and Hocking could argue that they had not violated any confidences. Yet, of course, the thousands of messages they examined in detail were not likely to have been made part of the public domain by publication of the "coffee-table book." The issue of permission to use documents remains a matter of concern. Researchers using documentary materials still face the issue of assuming consent and guarding against inadvertent ethical lapses.

A second ethical issue facing those engaging in rhetorical criticism is the very approach that they take. Should they attempt to evaluate messages against standards, or should they use texts points of departure for promoting their personal political opinions? The idea that there can be a completely objective application of rhetorical theory to texts is not at issue here. But if different critics apply the same standards to the same speeches, one should expect that they all would give credit where credit is due and (on the other side) let the critical chips fall where they may. The process may not be objective, but rhetorical methods can be used to draw "intersubjective" conclusions.

Dana Cloud, however, has asserted a very different view. Responding to an article written by Jim Kuypers, she submitted (Cloud, 2001, ¶ 3):

(Continued)

SPECIAL DISCUSSION 6-2 (Continued)

The most significant difference between conscious political critique and what Jim Kuypers (2000) calls "independent criticism" [criticism that evaluates messages rather than taking the message as a starting point for making a general political argument] is that criticism that shuns overt politics is either ignorant of or masking its own investments in the status quo. Despite Kuypers' claim to the contrary, "independent criticism" is quite often the affirmation of the status quo disguised as neutrality. Affirmation bears the privilege of invisibility; it possesses the luxury of never appearing "heavy-handed" (Black's [2000] charge against Marxist critics). Nonetheless, affirmation is an act of advocacy. Even when criticism claims to be descriptive of social reality rather than offering normative correctives to unethical or malign rhetorical practices, the retreat into description is profoundly ideological.

The author once attended a convention program in which one scholar, who will remain nameless, was scheduled to address the use of logical positivism in modern communication research. Instead, he made a presentation expressing his views in opposition to (then) President Reagan's proposed "Strategic Defense Initiative" (I felt tricked—when I wanted to learn about the Strategic Defense Initiative, I knew other sources and places that could provide superior information). Certainly, there often are occasions when researchers should—and must—combine discussions of political positions they hold with criticism of messages. But when a researcher *fails to identify* that the purpose of a piece of criticism is primarily to advance a personal political argument, there may be room for concern over the absence of full disclosure.

What should be done? For some, the view is that nothing should be done. For others, it seems that three things are required in the ethical report of criticism. First, the author should identify his or her biases and preferences. Craig Smith explains that "with the ensuing fragmentation and ennui, I believe we are in danger of failing to communicate with one another in meaningful ways. Some advance an ideological agenda while doing criticism. My good friend Philip Wander makes no secret about his Marxist reading of matters" (2000, ¶ 5). Regrettably, not every writer is so forthcoming in identifying his or her own viewpoint. Second, critics should make sure to include and to consider any contrary examples and interpretations before drawing global conclusions that support their own political preferences. According to Smith:

> Others indulge in local narratives no matter how atypical they are. Thomas Benson, whom I admire very much, wandered off the academic reservation and into impressionism when he recounted his experiences in a political campaign. He did not identify the candidate, nor the staff, nor many of his sources. His experience was completely different from the one I had when I managed a senatorial campaign during the same time period. Neither of us had enough data to do a scholarly take; we could do biography or journalism, but that is not good criticism. (¶ 6)

Third, critics should ask themselves if communication research journals are the appropriate locations for expressions of primarily personal political opinions. Though a controversial position, Smith suggests that

> when we write criticism in our journals, we ought to confine ourselves to solid argumentation inclusive of valid arguments built on sufficient and high quality evidence

produced from close readings and masterings of context. If we do not, we shall soon find that we will be unable to talk to one another in our journals, that our research will lack credibility, and we will fall into disrepute among those outside our field who monitor disciplinary integrity. For those who wish to issue subjective criticism, passionate ideological critiques, or impressionism, I respectfully suggest that they take it to other outlets designed to facilitate such discourse. (¶ 18)

You have heard Shakespeare's words, "All the world's a stage. And all the men and women merely players." Taking that notion very seriously, Burke called his system the dramatistic pentad and asked critics to look at communication as they would examine a play. He views communication as including five (that's where the word "pentad" comes in) categories:

the dramatistic pentad:

♦ The **act** is the message actually exchanged. The message document is examined. The critic is expected to provide evidence of its textual authenticity and complete accuracy.

Act in Burke's dramatistic pentad, the symbolic action (the speech, for instance).

♦ The **scene** includes the entire situation in which the message is exchanged, including the effects of the message on the audience. But the general condition of society is also a matter that influences the ability of the speech to create a sense of identification.

Scene in Burke's dramatistic pentad, the setting in which the act takes place.

♦ The **agent** is the person responsible for the communication. The individual's history is searched to determine why he or she said the sorts of things that were contained in the message. Thus, this category requires critics to complete biographical criticism and verify authorship for the act.

Agent in Burke's dramatistic pentad, the actor or rhetor who performs the act.

The first three elements of the pentad are matters that critics might be concerned about regardless of the critical method they use. The remaining elements are unique to the Burkean system.

♦ **Agency** involves ways communicators achieve identification. Sometimes these linguistic strategies are arguments. Sometimes they are appeals to common interest. Sometimes they are subtle uses of language such as irony or satire. The critic explains the strategies used to achieve identification by communicators. Usually speakers rely on a small number of such strategies (or "agencies") in a single message. For instance, in 1965 at a rally in Montgomery, Alabama, a young man named Stokely Carmichael (later Kwame Toure) grabbed a microphone and began to shout "Black power!" over and over. Soon some members of the audience began to join in. Before long, the entire crowd was chanting in unison "Black power, black power, black power." After the chanting, Carmichael was cheered loudly and his calls for action were received enthusiastically by the crowd. This strategy of chanting was not an argument, but the language created a sense of oneness between the audience and the speaker. The Burkean concept of agency requires critics to identify this strategy and explain how it helped the speaker and audience

Agency in Burke's dramatistic pentad, the symbolic and linguistic strategies used to secure identification.

achieve identification with each other. Researchers do not just look at the categories of identification strategies. Instead, they weigh the proportions that each was used. By looking at the ratios, the attempt is made to explain which appeals were dominant and which were effective or ineffective.

♦ The **purpose** of the message is vital to assess the worth of a message. A message's impact can be evaluated by determining whether the speaker's intentions are satisfied. But the intention of a speaker is also checked to see if the purposes are clear, relevant, and socially responsible.

Taken together, the dramatistic pentad provides a way to organize communication and to explain how people influence each other.

The flexibility of Burke's approach has been attractive to many scholars because they are not obligated to use traditional methods that focus on formal arguments and systems of appeals. In fact, McGee has asserted with a little exaggeration, "Kenneth Burke is now more important than Aristotle is" (2001, ¶ 5). The method has been used to analyze scores of key messages including the defense strategy of Clarence Darrow in the *New York v. Gitlow* case (Sanbonmatsu, 1971), the rhetoric of the frontier women's suffrage movement in the United States (Burkholder, 1989), the confrontation of churches and their opponents in the sanctuary movement (Nelson & Flannery, 1990), the rhetoric of the 1992 presidential campaign (Stuckey & Antczak, 1994), and the rhetoric of the political correctness debate in U.S. colleges (Bello, 1996). People who use the Burkean system focus heavily on the language used by communicators. Though this attention can lead to valuable insights, the method has its limitations. First, the way a message is judged is largely based on its effects: if identification is promoted, the message is judged effective. There is no artistic standard beyond the "bottom line." Second, the method may occasionally be difficult to apply systematically since it is not really a fixed system. Burke's added interest in developing notions of redemptive rhetoric and his suggestion that there might be a sixth element to the pentad called "attitude" indicate that the system is so fluid it could prove occasionally difficult for scholars to pin down. Even so, the Burkean approach has aroused a great deal of respect and use among critics in communication.

Fisher's Narrative Paradigm

One of the most influential alternative views was developed by Walter R. Fisher in his **"narrative paradigm."** In his book, *Human Communication as Narration: Toward a Philosophy of Reason, Value, and Action,* Fisher explained that people have a natural need to tell stories to each other. He believes that "all forms of human communication need to be seen fundamentally as stories" (Fisher, 1987, p. xi). Through exchanging stories, people develop understandings of each other. People "experience and comprehend life as a series of ongoing narratives, as conflict, characters, beginnings, middles, and ends" (Fisher, 1987, p. 24). In fact, he defined humanity as *homo narrans,* or "man, the narrator" (or storyteller).

Thus, when people communicate, they are telling stories to each other. Fisher defines **narrative** very broadly. Sometimes the stories are about one's own life, and sometimes they are about others' lives. To persuade others, people share examples, analogies, and lines of argument that show a general picture of what is desired. Even abstract statistical discussions are simply ways to summarize the human experience and tell stories. Moreover, the very act of speaking may be taken as part of the performance of one's own life story.

To influence each other, people often attempt to exchange good reasons that have a foundation in their common history, biography, culture, and character. In fact, our understanding of the world is really a reflection of the stories we have accepted. Of course, not all experiences and stories are as compelling as others. Hence, Fisher suggested some standards by which critics can evaluate the stories people use for "narrative rationality."

- First, Fisher believes that good stories, as with good reasons, have strong probability.
- Second, Fisher asks critics to evaluate the **"narrative fidelity"** of messages.

Since most communication makes use of storytelling, the method has created considerable interest. It has been applied to scores of communication encounters extending from controversies over nuclear weaponry (Fisher, 1984) to evaluations of the ethics of advertising techniques (Bush & Bush, 1994). Critics who employ the narrative paradigm tend to select storytelling examples in the messages they analyze and then apply the two standards listed for narrative rationality.

Naturally, the approach has invited some critical response of its own. First, some believe that the definition of narrative is so broad that it includes virtually anything people say (Rowland, 1987). The definition is a trick definition, they say, because it includes more than strict storytelling. Thus, claiming that everything is narrative means that stating that all communication is storytelling is actually saying only that all communication consists of "symbolic actions—words and/or deed—that have sequence and meaning for those who live, create, or interpret them"—an acceptable definition of communication that need not involve storytelling at all. Second, if the definition is really intended to be specific to storytelling behavior, then the narrative paradigm may not apply to all communication. Rowland (1989) used the narrative paradigm to analyze three books of very different types. He found that it applied effectively to one, somewhat to a science fiction book, and not at all to a technical book loaded with statistics. He concluded that the narrative paradigm applied to much, but not all, communication.

Fantasy Theme Analysis

Fantasy theme analysis is an application of symbolic convergence theory. Rather than evaluating whether a piece of communication is good or bad, sound or unsound, or worthy or unworthy, fantasy theme analysis attempts to find out how groups of people must view the world, given the sorts of things that they say and find persuasive (Cragan & Shields, 1981). Symbolic convergence theory makes an

---

Sidebar notes:

Narrative in Fisher's narrative paradigm, "symbolic actions—words and/or deed—that have significance and meaning for those who live, create, or interpret them" (Fisher, 1987, p. 58).

standards of narrative rationality:

1. probability

2. narrative fidelity

Narrative fidelity in Fisher's narrative paradigm, the consistency of new accounts with other stories people have heard.

criticisms of the narrative paradigm

fantasy theme analysis applies symbolic convergence theory

Fantasy theme analysis a method of analyzing collections of communication to determine underlying "world views" that people hold, judging by the messages that they use.

assumes language reveals world views of groups of people

assumption that the language used by groups of people reveals and even reinforces "world views" of people. These worldviews contribute to the creation of a "social reality" (Bormann, 1972; Bormann, Cragan, & Shields, 2001). Getting at these views of social reality can be accomplished by amassing and sifting communication because members of a group or movement use communication that dramatizes their point of view. Bormann, Knutson, and Musolf explain, "Dramatizing comments are rich in imaginative language and consist of the following: puns, word play, double entendres, figures of speech, analogies, anecdotes, allegories, parables, fables, jokes, gags, jests, quips, stories, tales, yarns, legends, and narratives" (1997, p. 225). When the same dramatizing comments are shared and repeated, researchers common patterns reveal underlying images of the way the world is.

Rhetorical vision "a representation of the collective consciousness of the participants in the interaction and is a product of the community's fantasies" (Alemán, 2005, p. 9).

These images are **rhetorical visions** of the way the world is organized. Though the term **fantasy** is used in these discussions, the word does not necessarily refer to something that is fanciful but untrue (some "fantasies" have a factual basis). One person begins to share a message or story about a person or situation. Then, other people respond by telling their stories on the same topic. Eventually, the group shares a dominant image of the way the world is or ought to be. This chain of contributions leads to some dominant views for the group, which eventually converge with a dominant fantasy theme.

Fantasy "a story about people, real or fictitious, in a dramatic situation or setting other than the here-and-now communication of the group" (Bormann, 1993, p. 365).

"Participants construct shared rhetorical visions as they repeat shared fantasy themes, or fantasy types. The rhetorical vision, best identified as the overarching analogy that holds the fantasies together, then, constitutes the community's social reality" (Alemán, 2005, p. 9). Since these rhetorical visions are sustained by fantasies that are arranged into themes, they are believed to guide the social realities communities of people construct for themselves. The method does not attempt to judge the quality of messages, although most scholars comment on it in passing. Thus, fantasy theme analysis draws conclusions that deal with the structure of society more than they draw conclusions that are directly about communication. The method uses communication to find clues about the ways that groups or communities of people think about the world.

rhetorical visions create a group's social reality

conclusions drawn about structure of society using communication materials

The process of fantasy theme analysis involves making arguments about the meaning of collections of common themes in messages and how these matters may signal underlying worldviews. This reasoning requires some careful thinking since this form of reasoning is an example of argument from signs, which may be particularly fallible if any contrary signs can be found or if any examples exist contrary to the conclusions drawn by the researchers. So, the process of making arguments is done carefully in fantasy theme analysis. Though they certainly overlap, there are three general steps that are followed when conducting a fantasy theme analysis.

method requires careful reasoning from sign and may be fallible if there are contrary examples

step 1: collect samples

First, researchers collect samples of all sorts of communication from groups of people who speak out on an issue. The actual messages can take rather nontraditional forms. For instance, speeches and bumper stickers can be collected and analyzed together. In addition, folk/protest songs, leaflets, and e-mail messages may be counted among valued examples of messages that signal fantasy themes and rhetorical visions. The number of messages can be quite large. In their analysis of the rhetorical visions of people who responded to the death of Fred Rogers (the host of *Mr. Rogers' Neighborhood*), Stephen Perry and Amanda Roesch (2004) collected 1,200 individual tributes that appeared on the PBS website dedicated to *Mr. Rogers' Neighborhood*. The message "thread" quickly reflected chains of themes. Such large samples are typical in fantasy theme analysis. For instance, Alemán (2005) sampled 560 posts in the "Meeting New People" discussion board sponsored by SeniorNet, a service dedicated to the interests of senior citizens.

Second, researchers sift the messages to find recurring phrases, themes, or strategies. They look for expressions that different communicators use. They look for common themes used in different messages. This sifting often takes the form of sorting messages according to common phrases, arguments, or types of dramatic imagery used. Somewhat contrary to expectations, Margaret Duffy (2003) found that messages of Internet websites for hate groups tended to reflect language typical of the American value system—freedom, fairness, hard work—even though these groups actually promoted positions that were contrary to these basic values. Duffy was forced to conclude that the rhetorical vision promoted by these websites was typical of mainstream America, thus suggesting the potential impact of the websites' appeal. *step 2: sift messages*

Third, the researcher attempts to label the fundamental fantasy themes that indicate the "rhetorical visions" held by the collective mind of the group of people who use them. The researcher asks how people must view the world given the common patterns they use. In the study of SeniorNet, Melissa Alemán (2005) first identified three major fantasies—"the knight in shining armor, searching for a bargain, and fishing for men" (p. 5)—in the communication of the seniors using the website. Then she argued that these fantasies reflect an underlying rhetorical vision that "a good man is hard to find," particularly among the elderly. *step 3: label fantasy themes to identify rhetorical visions*

There are advantages to using fantasy theme analyses. First, the method is particularly useful for the analysis of groups and social movements. Fantasy theme analyses have been completed on many different social groups, including the rise of the original interdenominational Christian Church (Disciples of Christ) (Hensley, 1975). Second, it "gives the critic the ability to look at a message from within the group and see it from their perspective aside from any other existing views. Using this method adds a new perspective to the message as it holds great value for the rhetorical community" (Drumheller, 2005, p. 53). Third, the method has been adapted to help interpret data in many different fields and with data in different forms. For instance, Kristina Drumheller gathered data from "Millennials" (the generation born after 1982) in focus groups in reaction to viewing the film *Dogma*. She found that fantasy theme analysis was helpful to uncover the religious information-gathering needs beneath the actual comments shared in the focus group. *advantages of fantasy theme analysis*

Yet, the method is not without limitations. First, fantasy theme analysis does not really draw conclusions about the quality of communication in particular messages. Instead, the method attempts to explore how different communities of people must view the world, given the messages they use. So, the approach uses communication data to help draw essentially sociological conclusions. Second, the method cannot be applied to small numbers of cases or to single messages. So, the tool cannot really help reveal characteristics of excellence in messages in general. Nor can it reveal characteristics of excellence in particular. Third, most fantasy theme analysts attempt to abstract fantasy themes, but they do not search for negative cases that would cause them to reject the conclusions they wish to draw. *disadvantages of fantasy theme analysis*

The Never Ending Development of Critical Methods

development of new methods

The way scholars actually do criticism is not restricted to the two formal systems described here. Scholars are always developing additional methods and models. A few examples might give you an idea.

Starting in the late 1970s some critics started examining communication by using the **mythic perspective.** Though most of us define myth as an untrue story, those who use the mythic perspective do not view it that way. They prefer to define myth as something like "a story about a particular incident which is put forward as containing or suggesting some general truth" (Sykes, 1970, p. 17). These stories are the legends and folklore that we take as part of a culture. Critics look at these stories to explain how some appeals are more influential than others. Applications have been made to the broad news coverage of the Patty Hearst kidnapping of the mid-1970s (Mechling, 1979), mass media treatment of the "New Frontier" rhetoric of President John F. Kennedy (Rushing, 1986), the structure of Hitler's *Mein Kampf* (McGuire, 1977), and use of the "myth of white superiority" in the film *Mississippi Burning* (Brinson, 1995). Though there is controversy about whether myths should be restricted to stories that are believed to be true, the use of myth has become a popular way to look at some communication.

> **Mythic perspective** an approach to criticism that attempts to identify the underlying stories to which speakers appeal (a myth is defined as "a story about a particular incident which is put forward as containing or suggesting some general truth" [Sykes, 1970, p. 17]).

comparisons with religious models

Comparisons of speeches with religious models, such as the Sermon on the Mount, have been popular in the literature of speech criticism. For instance, Malinda Snow (1985) examined Martin Luther King's letter from the Birmingham Jail and found that its structure was consistent with the most complex epistles of St. Paul. Since these religious images are prominent in Western cultures, it is not surprising that such comparisons can be made.

creative analogies

Sometimes a creative analogy can be used to explain communication that defies traditional understanding. For instance, Larry S. Richardson (1970), a musician and communication scholar, examined the unusual speaking of Stokely Carmichael by comparing it with the interaction between an audience and a jazz musician who is improvising on a theme. Carmichael's deliberate repetition and frequent movement from one idea to the next without transition was explained by the same sort of dynamic that leads a jazz musician to repeat successful "hot licks" and to shift quickly to another motif when the audience begins to lose interest. By looking for creative analogies, critics can explore interesting new ways to investigate communication.

Sometimes there are comparisons made with other forms of performance. For instance, Selby (2005) looked at the civil rights rhetoric of Dr. Ralph David Abernathy, a contemporary of Martin Luther King Jr. who led the Southern Christian Leadership Conference after King's death. During his speeches, though Anglos often were mentioned as sources of oppression of people of color, Abernathy did not arouse a sense of dread or fear among his audience. Selby incorporated the notion of "burlesque," a form of comedy in which the targets of jokes are exaggerated caricatures, to explain how Arbernathy led his audiences to scoff at Anglo opponents of civil rights. By doing so, people of color were willing to stay active in the movement and felt a reduced sense of threat from White opponents. Similarly, Anker looked at the immediate television news coverage of the 9/11 attacks on the United

States as a melodrama as portrayed on television broadcasts. "Melodrama is traditionally defined as a dramatic story line of villainy, victimization, and retribution, in which characters' emotional states are hyperbolized and externalized through grandiose facial expression, vivid bodily gestures, and stirring musical accompaniment; music is the '*melos*' of the melodrama (Brooks, 1995; Elsaesser, 1972; Singer, 2000)" (Anker, 2005, p. 23). To add dramatic flourishes, news programs included stirring music and signboards announcing the next "act" to follow in the broadcast.

One of the most exciting directions in rhetorical criticism has been the combination of rhetorical analysis with other methods. Consistent with the critical realism perspective that encourages multiple methods, rhetorical criticism often has enriched other work. For instance, Todd Frobish (2000) combined case study with rhetorical criticism methods to explore the ways in which the Scientology website attempted to build ethos following fundamental attacks on its credibility. Similarly, focus group results were combined with methods drawn from rhetorical criticism in Drumheller's (2005) analysis of the ways that members of the millennial generation use entertainment films to get information about religious issues.

Creative methods of criticism do more than evaluate messages. They also help develop new theories. For instance, as a result of her analysis of President Bush's speaking about the Persian Gulf war, Kathleen M. German (1995) both described the importance of "directive language" in Bush's rhetoric and promoted a descriptive theory of this method. Furthermore, applying new approaches may reveal insights that can help people improve their own communication effectiveness.

creative methods may help develop new theory

RESEARCHERS IN THE FIELD: MARTIN MEDHURST

Marty Medhurst is Distinguished Professor of Rhetoric and Communication at Baylor University in Waco, Texas. He probably is best known for his pioneering work in presidential rhetoric and for his founding and editing of *Rhetoric & Public Affairs,* an interdisciplinary journal that focuses on political communication. Before joining Baylor University, he served on the faculties of communication studies programs at the University of California, Davis, and at Texas A&M University. He has authored or edited 10 books and more than 60 articles and book chapters. In addition to publishing in communication journals, his work has been showcased in such diverse publications as the *Journal of Church and State* and the *Journal of Communication and Religion.* His opinions are widely sought, and he serves as a series editor for Michigan State University Press, Texas A&M University Press, and Baylor University Press.

◆ *What drew you into our field?*
I became a "speech" major in the middle of my freshman year in college. At that time, I was especially interested in the media, particularly in radio. I remained a "speech communication" major throughout my undergraduate years

and worked as the Sports Director of the college radio station, doing play-by-play and color commentary in a wide range of sports. I didn't really discover rhetoric or political communication until I did my M.A. work. It was during those years that I made the switch from media to rhetorical studies, with an emphasis on both political and civil-religious discourse.

◆ *You are known as an expert in political communication, but you have been involved in many areas of specialization. How did you come to focus on the applied areas you have chosen?*
Well, I have "specialized" in at least three or four areas of the field. My first love was media, particularly radio. My dissertation was in civil-religious rhetoric, as are a number of my articles. Much of my early work as a young assistant professor was in media criticism, particularly film and other visual forms. And my more recent work has been in political communication, especially presidential rhetoric. The thing that drew me to all of these areas was a deep, personal interest in the subject matter.

◆ *You've presented your research widely, including fairly recently at the Clinton Presidential Library. In general, what have you hoped that making your research especially visible would accomplish?*
I like to share my ideas with a wide audience. In addition to colleagues in communication, I often attend political science and history conferences, and I publish in a wide range of interdisciplinary journals. I also present my ideas to as many different kinds of audiences as I can, including public presentations at presidential libraries, church groups, student clubs, junior statesman seminars and the like. I'll talk to whomever is willing to listen.

◆ *What part of your research undertakings have made you most proud?*
I'm proud of all of my research. I suspect that the most important may be my books and articles about the Cold War in general, and about Dwight D. Eisenhower in particular.

◆ *Are there directions in the field's research that you find particularly exciting?*
There are many exciting things happening in the various areas of communication studies. For my little part of the world, I am especially impressed by two things: (1) the movement toward writing scholarly books as well as articles and (2) the use of archival and other kinds of primary sources.

◆ *What personal qualities do you think have contributed to your achievements as a communication scholar?*
It's always difficult to evaluate one's self. I guess I'd say I have a good work ethic, a sort of inquisitiveness or curiosity about the world, a talent for writing and making arguments, and the good fortune of having had first-rate teachers and colleagues throughout my career.

◆ *What one or two things do you think students should know to deal successfully with communication research either as a consumer or as a researcher?*
As a consumer, students need to realize that professors are not infallible—they may be wrong. So a healthy dose of skepticism is warranted. As researchers, students need to have a real interest in and commitment to their subject matter.

◆ *Is there any advice you would give students who might be interested in becoming communication researchers?*
It's a wonderful life, if that is what you're called to be. But teaching and research really are callings in that not everyone is cut out to be a teacher or researcher. Find what you love and pursue it.

APPLICATIONS OF TEXTUAL ANALYSIS

There are many ways textual analysis may be completed in communication studies. Two of the most popular have focused detailed attention on the nature of the message. Known as conversational and discourse analyses, these methods are usually distinguished conceptually, as they are here. In practice, however, there is often quite a bit of overlap in what they accomplish as they attempt to reach their primary objectives. Conversational and discourse analyses feature categories suggested from naturally occurring conversations. These approaches do not produce numerical information. These two textual analysis tools will be introduced here.

Conversational Analysis

In **conversational analysis,** researchers sample conversations (typically from the field, though some laboratory settings also have been objects of conversational analysis). Historical, literary, and mass media conversations have sometimes been examined. Conversational analysis actually can be traced back to the work of Harvey Sacks, who answered phones on an emergency psychiatric line. When reviewing transcripts of emergency calls, he noticed that people seemed to be following unwritten rules of human action about appropriate ways to introduce themselves, explain a problem, or sound concerned (Antaki, 2004a, ¶ 4). He was struck by the fact that the recordings he had were very high-quality data to be used to discover rules of human interaction through talk. Many other theorists made up examples to illustrate what they believed were critical behaviors. Instead, Sacks began by looking at the actions of communicators. He was particularly interested in the ways that people used words to create meaning and control action. Sacks reported being puzzled over an encounter in which a caller to the emergency line did not reveal his name. Most of the time, when the call-taker answered the phone by giving his or her name, the caller responded by giving a name in reply. Here is the exchange that Sacks found curious (Sacks, 1992, pp. 7–8):

> 1 A: This is Mr. Smith. May I help you?
>
> 2 B: I can't hear you.
>
> 3 A: This is Mr. Smith.
>
> 4 B: Smith?
>
> 5 A: Yes. Can I help you?
>
> 6 B: I don't know hhh I hope you can.

Sacks found that the caller's failure to give his name was revealing. Sacks suggested that there was an implied rule that "if what precedes your turn is an introductory greeting then you must respond in the same way" (Antaki, 2004a, ¶ 12). To permit an exception, without a person's sounding "strange or rude . . . he must be using another rule, something like: 'not-hearing is an acceptable reason to be excused the demands of the previous turn'" (Antaki, 2004a, ¶ 13–14). In short, Sacks identified

Conversational analysis textual analysis that attempts to identify "turns" taken by people during exchanges.

original work attempted to identify rules of conversation from transcripts of messages

that there were regularities—rules, if you will—that seemed to underlie communication exchanges. When people follow the unwritten rules, the conversation seems to flow without anyone noticing. Philosophically, conversational analysis is most often associated with ethnomethodology (see Chapter 7), which concerns itself with matters that people take for granted, rather than unusual behavior. Hence, conversational analysts find it valuable to look for unwritten rules that make communication flow without anyone's noticing. Even so, the violations of the rules indicate the need to discover an exception—or another rule. For conversational analysts, there are normative rules that are expected to be observed. If these rules are not followed, the conversation may suffer *interactional* difficulties (such as when the communicator is unintelligible), or *implicational* difficulties (such as when the speaker's words imply something not contained in the words alone).

assumptions of conversational analysis

Three assumptions underlie the use of conversational analysis (Gubrium & Holstein, 2000, p. 492):

1. Interaction is sequentially organized, and talk can be analyzed in terms of the process of social interaction rather than in terms of motives or societal status.

2. Talk, as a process of social interaction, is contextually oriented—it is both shaped by interaction and creates the social context of that interaction.

3. These processes are involved in all social interactions, so no interactive details are irrelevant to understanding it.

Conversational analysis, then, attempts to identify "turns" taken by people during the exchange. The **utterance** is the chief message unit of analysis. Both nonverbal and verbal cues are coded from transcriptions of the conversation, complete with symbols to indicate vocal inflections and pauses. Eventually, researchers attempt to extract rules for conversational structures.

Utterance in conversational analysis, what a person actually says in conversation.

Two major concepts in conversational analysis relate to ways that people take turns in conversations. An **adjacency pair** is a conversation unit that conversational analysts examine to explore turn-taking behavior. For instance, one expects that a person gives an answer in response to a previous question (see Levinson, 1983, pp. 303–304). Among the most predictable pairs are question/answer pairs, greeting/reciprocated greeting pairs, and summons/acknowledgment pairs, though there are scores of such adjacency pairs (and more discovered all the time). When a response does not seem to fit in the adjacency pair, researchers may use the concept of a **dispreferred response.** Such responses tend to be avoided in typical conversation and create tense responses. For instance, when denying a request, in a typical exchange,

Adjacency pair in conversational analysis, a pair of utterances in which the latter element is supposed to be related to the previous element.

Dispreferred response in conversational analysis, a response not consistent with the first part of a common adjacency pair.

> the rejection is (it is empirically found) marked by hesitation and hedging and an account of why the preferred response wasn't given. The mark is so powerful that it alone will suffice as a rejection:
>
> A: "Why don't you come to our party on Sunday?"
>
> *(pause)*
>
> B: "Well . . . "

And A knows that B is declining the invitation.

Imagine what would happen if you gave the dispreferred reply without marking it:

A: "Why don't you come to our party on Sunday?"

B: "No"

That would look strange and rude. You would infer something about what B was saying (e.g. that they were sulking). The informativeness of such deviation shows us that the substance of the dispreferred SPP (e.g. that it is a rejection) and its markers (e.g. a pause, a hedge) normally go together. (Antaki, 2004b, ¶ 16–20)

Another important aspect of conversational analysis is the study of **sequences,** which consist of at least two adjacency pairs. The placement of an utterance in a sequence can greatly affect the actions of others and can influence the entire interpretation. Eventually, the study of sequences leads researchers to study the turn-taking behavior of people in active conversation.

Sequence in conversational analysis, "a sequence is a unit of conversation that consists of two or more adjacent and functionally related turns" (LinguaLinks Library, 2004, ¶ 1).

Though the language that may be used in conversational analysis may become increasingly complex and may require some immersion in the study of linguistics to understand fully, the procedures for completing such an analysis are relatively straightforward. After posing a question dealing with turn-taking behavior in one form or another, the researchers complete the following steps:

steps in conversational analysis

1. *Obtain materials for analysis.* This process involves conducting interviews, recording actual people in conversations, or finding archival materials that already exist. After identifying them and verifying their sources and authenticity, the researcher prepares a transcription.

2. *Prepare the transcription.* Though many researchers code visual nonverbal cues, most work is completed on written transcripts that can be abstracted and shared with others. In such coding, all the pauses, vocal inflections, and variations in voice are included. The result is a collection of materials that may be noted in some detail for review by any interested researchers. A portion of the coding system that is most commonly used is found on Table 6.3. This system was developed by Gail Jefferson and, not surprising, is most often called the "Jefferson system." It is the most popular notation system for conversational analysis, though others are in use.

3. *Complete the analysis.* This step involves examining the transcript to look for underlying rules that seem to guide the choice of turn taking. The structure, sequence, and content of the turn-taking exchanges all are examined. At each point in the analysis, the researcher looks for rules that would explain the sequence of utterances. For example, Amy Paugh (2005) examined the role of conversation about work within families and noted that dinnertime conversation was a chance for children to get socialized into the world of work. She observed one conversation (pp. 69–70):

> Children's requests for more information can also prompt parents to make comparisons between children's lives and the world of adult work.

TABLE 6.3   COMMON TRANSCRIPTION METHOD FOR CONVERSATIONAL ANALYSIS

`(.)`	Just noticeable pause
`(.3), (2.6)`	Examples of timed pauses
`↑word,↓word`	Onset of noticeable pitch rise or fall *(can be difficult to use reliably)*
`Word [word`	Square brackets aligned across adjacent lines denote the start of overlapping talk. Some transcribers also use "]" brackets to show where the overlap stops
`.hh, hh`	In-breath (note the preceding fullstop) and out-breath respectively
`Gh`	A guttural sound
`wo(h)rd`	(h) is a try at showing that the word has "laughter" bubbling within it
`wor-`	A dash shows a sharp cut-off
`wo:rd`	Colons show that the speaker has stretched the preceding sound
`(words)`	A guess at what might have been said if unclear
`( )`	Unclear talk. Some transcribers like to represent each syllable of unclear talk with a dash
`[[`	When placed around names, simultaneous utterances
`[`	Overlapping utterances
`A: word=` `B: =word`	The equals sign shows that there is no discernible pause between two speakers' turns or, if put between two sounds within a single speaker's turn, shows that they run together
`Word, WORD`	Underlined sounds are louder, capitals louder still
`°word°`	Material between "degree signs" is quiet
`>word word<` `<word word>`	Inward arrows show faster speech, outward slower
`→`	Analyst's signal of a significant line
`((sobbing))`	Transcriber's go at representing something hard, or impossible, to write phonetically
`Do`	Dot used as a subscript indicates a hard sound, such as a strongly dentalized "t"
`XX xx`	Audience applause with caps indicating loud applause; string of Xs indicated length of applause episode

Sources: Antaki (2002) and Transcript notation (1999).

For example, in the Schultz family, Chuck (6 years) questions his father about his social relationships at work after the father told about a recent business trip to Pennsylvania:

1 **Chuck: Daddy do you know lots of people there?**

2 Father: In - where? In Pennsylvania?

3 (0.6)

4 **Chuck: [Yeah whe- where you work?**

5 Father: [Where - where I'm going to -

6 Father: Oh where I work? <u>Yes</u> I know a lot of people there.

7 **Chuck: (It's) - almost everyone?**

8 Father: Oh yeah - well - i:t's: - think of it kind of like your school.

9 **Chuck: Oh::! You mean class?**

10 Father: Okay? Now - in this way - in this way - (I mean) you know
    just about everybody in your:: - <u>class</u> right?

11 **Chuck: Uh huh - (I know   )**

12 Father: That's like the group that I work with. I - I know everybody
    that I <u>work</u> with fairly well - bu:t? *(using hands to suggest sur-*
    rounding group) - there are a lot of other people in the company
    - who are like - other people in the <u>school</u> - Okay - and I
    know some of them? But there are a lot that I <u>don't</u> know.

13 **Chuck: (I know like) I know [(John and Bobby) -**

14 Mother: [But

15 **Chuck: He's in (my) class.**

16 Father: [Hm hmm.

17 Mother: [Hm hmm?

18 Mother: *(one nod yes, then shaking head no slightly)* But you don't
    know all John's friends.

19 Father: Yeah and there are a lot of [people in the=

20 **Chuck: [Right**

21 Father: =school that you don't know - right?

22 **Chuck: Hm hmm.**

Chuck's father does not simply say "yes" about knowing a lot of people
at work, nor does he change the topic. He offers a detailed analogy,
which, although not directly about what he does for a living, nevertheless gives Chuck a sense of how social relations are organized at work,
and may help him to relate his life now—being in school—to a possible
future as a working adult. The mother also contributes, indicating the
willingness of both parents to explain about work when questioned.
Such background information is rarely otherwise provided in work narratives, despite the presence of children at the dinner table.

Since conversational analysis borrows much of its intellectual tradition from ethnomethodology, the researcher places attention on taken-for-granted rules of turn
taking and attempts to find the unstated sources of regularities in ordinary exchanges. Transcripts are the raw data of analysis, and the conversational analyst
stays close to actual interactions to derive theoretic conclusions. Theory advanced

conversational analysis focuses
on taken-for-granted regularities

prior to conversation analysis traditionally has not been given great attention. Yet, new research has attempted to link theory and conversation analysis together.

4. *Interpret turn taking.* The conversational analyst interprets the meaning of the conversation by attempting to abstract the unstated rules of conversation behavior and to show the existence of these rules by the citation of exemplars from the conversational analysis text. This process is not supposed to be a simple repeat of the conversation, but the identification of underlying principles of conversation. Regrettably, conversational analysts simply repeat the obvious conversational exchanges in slightly more abstract terms. For explanation, of course, the functional relationships between the underlying turns must be reported and explained. When contradictory patterns are found, the researcher either adds a new rule to qualify the previous one or reconsiders the original rule.

claims drawn from conversational analysis

Anita Pomerantz (1990) explained the sorts of claims drawn from conversational analysis. The first form asserts that

interactants are "doing" particular social actions, identities, and/or roles. For example, we may assert an utterance is "agreeing," "rejecting an invitation," "fishing for information," "being an expert," "being a teacher," etc. A second type of claim is when we offer analyses of methods that interactants use in accomplishing particular actions, roles, or identities. The third type of claim is when we propose how methods work: their sequential features and interactional consequences.

As can be seen, solid conversational analysis is considerably more than simply restating the exchanges that go on.

Discourse Analysis

Discourse analysis Considerations of naturally occurring messages to examine "sequential and hierarchical organization, system and structure" using methods that are fairly "standard in phonology and linguistics" (Stubbs, 1981, p. 107).

Though conversational analysis attempts to explore the structure and the sequencing of turn-taking exchanges, **discourse analysis** examines naturally occurring messages for the purpose of determining "how talk and texts are used to perform actions" (Potter, 2003, p. 73). Though in many ways conversational analysis and discourse analysis use methods that overlap, the practice of discourse analysis usually features four elements that move to distinguish the approach (Potter, 2003, pp. 84–85):

characteristic elements of discourse analysis research methods

1. *Search for a Pattern:* We should look through our corpus to see how regular this pattern is. If such a pattern is not common, then our speculation will start to look weak. . . .

2. *Consider Next Turns:* [In] discourse work, the sequential organization of interaction [suggested in working hypotheses] is a powerful resource for understanding what is going on. As conversation analysts have shown, speakers' utterances display an understanding of the earlier utterance. . . .

3. *Focus on Distant Cases:* These might be ones in which very different question constructions were used; or where surprising turns appeared. Such cases are rich analytically. . . .

4. *Focus on Other Kinds of Material:* [Consider] an infinite set of alternative materials that we might use for comparison.

Ultimately, the accumulation of research from different discourse analyses lets researchers make a case for the coherence of results (Potter, 2003, p. 86). In such a way, the evaluation of such contributions often depends on the general consistency of results. Focusing, as it does, on the structure or organization of discourse among people, the chief emphasis is on the functions that conversations and discourse forms perform for communicators. These studies tend to get very specific in identifying rules that guide using language and symbols. For instance, Labov and Fanshel (1977) examined the discourse between psychotherapists and patients. Among other things, they found that the exchanges were distinguished by the use of indirect requests as substitutes for direct statements. Blommaert, Bock, and K. McCormick, (2006) looked at the interrogation methods used to present testimony at South Africa's Truth and Reconciliation Commission hearings, which revealed abuse of the Black African majority in South Africa. Relying on transcripts from the hearings, the authors noted the deliberate effort to use these historic exchanges to create public transcripts that might protect the weak against the powerful. Discourse analysis techniques have also been usefully applied in studies of language uses: in "letters to the editor" written by people of different nationalities immediately following the 9/11 attacks on America (Hogan, 2006); in high school Chinese immigrant students' communication with each other during group activities (Liang, 2006); and in medical investigation inquiries into a Marseilles hospital (Rouveyrol, Maury-Rouan, Vion, & Noël-Jorand, 2005). Such work illustrates how discourse analysis attempts to discover the structures that underlie messages people use.

coherence of results argued by accumulated studies

applications of discourse analysis

Naturally, there are limitations in using these methods. First, conversational and discourse analyses draw conclusions from examples, though the examples may not be typical and may not show what occurs in communication generally. Furthermore, it is hard to disconfirm falsely asserted rules by using examples (Cappella, 1990). Second, methods for interpreting the conversation/discourse may be so personal that it may be difficult to replicate many such analyses. Third, much research from this tradition has produced such microscopic information about communication that conclusions often seem to be simple relabeling rather than explanations.

limitations of conversational and discourse analysis

CHECKLIST TO EVALUATE TEXTUAL ANALYSES

_____ Does the research question involve examining texts for the purpose of providing criticism, or identification of conversational rules, or isolation of worldviews of groups of people?

When conducting criticism:

_____ Did the research problem question deal with questions that ask about characteristics of the message that contributed to its effectiveness, reasons for the impact of the messages, or whether the message measures up to standards of excellence?

_____ Were steps taken to assure textual authenticity?

_____ Were steps taken to determine authorship?

_____ Was evidence presented to reveal anything about the effects of the message(s)?

_____ Was the choice of critical standards justified?

_____ Were all categories of analysis included?

When using fantasy theme analysis:

_____ Did the research question deal with images of reality accepted by groups of people, rather than the evaluation of individual messages?

_____ Were appropriate principles referenced from symbolic convergence theory?

_____ Were the examples of repeated dramatizing comment sufficient to prove the existence of rhetorical visions?

_____ How strong was the evidence that the group shared the rhetorical vision?

_____ Were the labels for fantasies compatible by exemplars?

_____ Were there any contrary examples that seemed to disprove the identification of fallacies and rhetorical visions?

When using conversational or discourse analysis:

_____ Did research problem questions deal with description and explication of the competencies that ordinary speakers use and rely on during participation in intelligible, socially organized interaction?

_____ Are message transcripts accurately identified?

_____ Were all steps of conversational or discourse analysis completed?

SUMMARY

Researchers sometimes focus on message qualities that are unique, rather than generic. Thus, researchers distinguish nomothetic research (designed to find general laws that apply to many instances) from idiographic research (designed to develop a full understanding of a particular event or individual). The "data" in textual analyses and content analysis are the examples and instances drawn from the message text (text means only that we are dealing with what we believe are the actual messages or words of a communicator). Even mass mediated examples and their message treatments are elements of the text that may be examined. To find such data for textual analyses, scholars may search many sources ranging from textbooks and anthologies, to newspapers, to government sources, to online sources that often provide audio and video materials to supplement written texts.

Researchers complete textual criticism when their research problem questions ask about characteristics of the message that contributed to its level of effectiveness, reasons for the impact of the message, or whether the message measures up to standards of excellence. Conversation and discourse analyses are invited by research problem statements dealing with "description and explication of the competencies that ordinary speakers use and rely on in participating in intelligible, socially organized interaction" (ten Have, 1990, p. 24). Such issues include examinations of influences of technology and external forces on communication; comparisons of strategic uses of conversation elements to achieve effects; comparisons of conversation in a specific setting to general communication encounters; and examinations of the new interventions on the discourse activities of groups of people.

Before engaging in a process of critical analysis of texts, one must examine matters of extrinsic criticism. Extrinsic criticism in rhetorical criticism involves evaluation of aspects beyond the text of a message, focusing predominately on assessing textual authenticity, authorship, settings, and message effects. It is necessary to assure textual authenticity to avoid criticizing a speaker for making statements that were not, in fact, made (called the straw man fallacy, which is attacking of a person for a position that was not actually taken by the person). Texts may be flawed or "corrupted" by the speaker's deviation from advance copies that are distributed before a message is delivered; recorders' biases or expectations that interfere with reporting accurately what was said; memorial editions of messages that may revise works; efforts to improve readability; and permitting sources to revise their remarks. To deal with textual corruption questions, researchers may compare the available text to the original, if the original is available; compare the available version against recordings, if recordings are available; or use conjectural emendation (a method in which researchers with different available versions of texts make arguments to explain which of the competing textual alternatives is most reasonable and, thus, should be accepted). Assessing authorship of a text is important because if you want to evaluate whether the communicator chose wisely from the methods available, you need to identify the author who is responsible so that you can know what universe of methods was available. Two methods have been used to find clues to authorship: external reports composed of external documents that reveal the true author of a text, and comparing messages of different individuals to produce clues to authorship.

Rhetorical criticism uses standards to interpret and evaluate communication (rhetoric is the study of the available means of persuasion). Impressionistic criticism refers to opinion (or personal impressions) made by reviewers. Criticism involves (1) presenting standards of excellence, (2) contrasting the messages against the standards, and (3) explaining the degree to which the messages meet or fall short of the standards (critical statements tell how far an actual message is from the ideal). Neo-Aristotelian criticism relies on the canons of rhetoric: invention—the types and sources of ideas—consists of nonartistic proofs that are composed of materials not created by the speaker (such as testimony, contracts, documents, and the like), and artistic proofs that the speaker may demonstrate through a speech. These artistic proofs include *ethos* (ethical appeal or the speaker's credibility), *pathos* (pathetic appeals or the use of emotion), and *logos* (logical appeals); arrangement (message organization); style (choice and use of words); and delivery (use of nonverbal cues). Though helpful to examine significant speeches, the method strains when applied to messages that rely chiefly on extralogical strategies. Burke's dramatistic criticism method places the concept of identification (uniting people by the use of ideas, images, and attitudes shared in common) central to the system. The dramatistic pentad examines the act (the symbols actually exchanged), scene (the setting for the act), agent (the actor or rhetor), agency (symbolic and linguistic strategies used to secure identification), and purpose (intention of the rhetor). Though the approach is flexible, messages are judged largely by their effects and the method may occasionally be difficult to replicate. Fisher's narrative paradigm holds that "all forms of human communication need to be seen fundamentally as stories." These narrations may be defined as symbolic actions—words and/or deed—that have significance and meaning for those who live, create, or interpret them.

To influence each other, people most often attempt to exchange good reasons that have a foundation in their common history, biography, culture, and character. To evaluate the stories people use, their narrative rationality is evaluated by looking at the probability associated with the stories and the narrative fidelity of messages (the consistency of new accounts with other stories people have heard). Despite its wide application, the narrative paradigm has been criticized for its broad definition of narrative and its apparent inability to be applied to all forms of communication if a narrow definition of narrative is used. Fantasy theme analysis is an application of symbolic convergence theory. Rather than evaluating a piece of communication per se, fantasy theme analysis attempts to find out how groups of people must view the world, given the sorts of things that they say and find persuasive. Symbolic convergence theory assumes that the language used by groups of people reveals and even reinforces "world views" of people. Identifying these views of social reality can be accomplished by amassing communication of a group and looking for dramatizing comments that, when shared and repeated, may reveal an underlying image of the way the world is. These images are "rhetorical visions" of the way the world is organized. The term "fantasy" used in these discussions involves a dominant image of the way the world is or ought to be. The method requires careful reasoning from signs, which may be particularly fallible if any contrary signs can be found. To complete a fantasy theme analysis, researchers (1) collect samples of all sorts of communication from groups of people; (2) sift the messages to find recurring phrases, themes, or strategies; and (3) attempt to label the fundamental fantasy themes that indicate the "rhetorical visions" held by the collective mind of the group of people who use them. Advantages to fantasy theme analysis include that it is particularly useful for the analysis of groups and social movements; it gives the critic the ability to look at a message from within the group and see it from their perspective; and the method may be adapted to interpret data in many different fields and with data in different forms. Limitations of fantasy theme analysis include that it does not really draw conclusions about the quality of communication in particular messages; it cannot be applied to single messages or small numbers of cases; and most fantasy theme analysts attempt to abstract fantasy themes, but they do not search for negative cases that would cause them to reject the conclusions they wish to draw. Other critical methods are constantly being developed, including systems based on the "mythic perspective," comparisons with religious models, and use of creative analogies.

Two applications of textual analysis include conversational analysis and discourse analysis. Conversational analysis is a form of textual analysis that attempts to identify "turns" taken by people during exchanges. The method looks at actual conversations and tries to identify unstated and taken-for-granted rules that underlie the exchanges. Conversational analysis assumes that interaction is sequentially organized, and talk can be analyzed in terms of the process of social interaction; talk, as a process of social interaction, is contextually oriented; and these processes are involved in all social interactions—so no interactive details are irrelevant to understanding it. Conversational analysis attempts to identify "turns" taken by people during the exchange. The utterance is what a person actually says in conversation. An adjacency pair is a pair of utterances in which the latter element is supposed to be related to the previous element. A response not consistent with the first part of a common adjacency pair is called a dispreferred response. A sequence is a unit of conversation that consists of two or more adjacent and functionally related turns. The steps in conversational analysis include (1) obtaining materials for analysis; (2) preparing the transcription using an extended coding system; (3) completing the analysis by looking for underlying rules that seem to guide the choice of turn taking (structure, sequence, and content); (4) and interpreting the turn taking by identifying the meaning of the conversation in terms of the unstated rules of conversation behavior. Claims drawn from conversational analysis involve assertions that interactants are "doing" particular social actions, identities, and/or roles; analyses of methods that interactants use in accomplishing particular actions, roles, or identities; and claims about how methods work, including their sequential features and interactional consequences. Discourse analysis attempts to look at naturally occurring messages to examine their sequential and hierarchical organization, system, and structure using methods that are fairly standard in phonology and linguistics. Though in many ways conversational analysis and discourse analysis use methods that overlap, the practice of discourse analysis usually features four elements: (1) search for a pattern in discourse; (2) consideration of the next turns; (3) focus directed to distant cases; and (4) focus directed to other kinds of material. Focusing, as it does, on the structure or organization of discourse among people, the chief emphasis is on the functions that conversations and discourse forms perform for communicators. These studies tend to get very specific in identifying ways that guide using language and symbols. Limitations exist with the use of conversational and discourse analyses. First, these methods draw conclusions from examples, though the examples may not be typical and may not show what occurs in communication generally. Second, methods for interpreting the conversation/discourse may be so personal that it may be difficult to replicate many such analyses. Third, much research from this tradition has produced such microscopic information about communication that conclusions often seem to be simple relabeling.

TERMS FOR REVIEW

nomothetic research	identification
idiographic research	act
texts	scene
rhetoric	agent
rhetorical criticism	agency
extrinsic criticism	purpose
straw man fallacy	narrative paradigm
conjectural emendation	narrative
criticism	narrative fidelity
impressionistic criticism	fantasy theme analysis
neo-Aristotelian criticism	rhetorical vision
invention	fantasy
ethos	mythic perspective
pathos	conversational analysis
logos	utterance
arrangement	adjacency pair
style	dispreferred response
delivery	sequence
memory	discourse analysis

JUST FOR THE SAKE OF ARGUMENT: A REVIEW

Look at the following questions and prepare your own answers to them. Make sure to consider any assumptions that may lie beneath them.

1. What is the difference between nomothetic and idiographic research? Why do qualitative and quantitative research methods seem to divide into these two approaches to explanation?

2. What is the difference between a review (such as a movie review) and criticism? Which is preferable to help you make a decision in the short term? Which is preferable to help you make a decision in the long term?

3. What are the major differences among neo-Aristotelian, Burkean, and narrative paradigm criticism? What kinds of questions can you answer with each that cannot be answered by the other?

4. Do mythic criticism and fantasy theme analysis focus on messages that are essentially untrue? What is a myth and a fantasy? Why does the use of these terms differ from everyday life and scholarship? Should they?

5. What has been the impact of ghostwriters on the overall quality of public speech in the nation? How has the rise of speechwriters made the task of speech criticism increasingly difficult for scholars?

6. In what ways are conversational and discourse analysis similar? In what ways are they different? When is each one invited for researchers?

ACTIVITIES TO PROBE FURTHER

Go to the website for this book, and look for the Student Study Materials for Chapter 6.

1. Take the study quiz and print out your answers. (Avoid giving answers that are your first impressions. Make sure to review these text materials before you answer the questions, not as an introduction to them.)

2. Turn to the website chapter section titled "Traditional Criticism Checklist."
   a. Take any recent speech and obtain a photocopy of it. Attach it to your final project.
   b. Apply the check sheet to analyze this speech in a very brief report that you will turn in to your instructor. Do not just answer the questions. Write an essay-style response in each of the categories of the check sheet.
   c. Sometimes it is easy to get evidence of the impact of a speech. Most of the time, however, this task is not so easy. Robert Cathcart stated that in the absence of other evidence, the best indication of the impact of the speech is the degree of audience adaptation revealed in it. What impact do you believe this speech had? Include a paragraph in your paper in which you indicate your conclusion and the evidence upon which you base it.

3. Consider the differences between a review as opposed to criticism. Take a movie you have seen and do the following:
   a. Write a paragraph in which you give your review of it.
   b. Write a paragraph in which you give a partial critique of it.

4. Look up each of these websites:
   a. Vincent Voice Library (www.lib.msu.edu/vincent/presidents/index.htm).
      (1) Go to the link for "U.S. Presidents of the 20th Century." The oldest instance is an Edison cylinder recording of Benjamin Harrison in 1888. Listen to this one.
      (2) Listen to (at least) two others.
   b. History Channel Speech Archives (www.history.com/media.do?action=listing&sort By=1&sortorder=A&topic=GREAT%20SPEECHES). Their listing is for fairly recent speeches, when compared with the Vincent Voice Library. Listen to (at least) two speakers.
   c. For each speaker, answer these questions:
      (1) Did the voices seem to match your expectations for the way the speakers would sound? Why or why not (for each speaker)?
      (2) What do you suppose would have been the audience reaction to the speakers' words?
      (3) If you had only the written text of the message, how might your interpretation have changed?
5. Go to the American Rhetoric website (www.americanrhetoric.com/top100speechesall .html) where they have a list of the 100 greatest American speeches.
   a. Listen to or watch one of the top ten speeches and answer these questions:
      Which of these speeches do you think is most likely to have been ghostwritten?

      _____

      Which of these speeches do you think was the most fitting response to the occasion?

      _____

      Which of these speeches do you think featured the best use of language?

      _____

      Which of these speeches do you think featured the best use of argument?

      _____

   b. Are there any speakers in the top 50 whom you did not recognize? If so, who are they?

      _____

      Look up information about one of these speakers and prepare a one-page summary of this person's contribution to the nation.

      Listen to a speech by this person and write a paper of no more than three pages in which you evaluate it using the general categories employed by those using neo-Aristotelian criticism (use the guidelines found on Table 6.2).

CHAPTER 7

Qualitative Methods: Ethnography, Participant Observation, and Fieldwork

The way to do research is to attack the facts at the point of greatest astonishment.

—CELIA GREEN

CHAPTER OUTLINE

BEFORE WE GET STARTED . . .

Communication researchers often become active participants in the research setting. They may join Alcoholics Anonymous to learn of the informal communication that reinforces the famous 12-step program, they may work in a car dealership to study special methods of influence, or they may live with the Tasaday "stone age" people of the Philippines to learn how legends are communicated. They "get their hands dirty" by gathering data in the natural environment rather than relying on formal questionnaires or experiments. This type of active inquiry is the subject of this chapter.

THE ROLE OF ETHNOGRAPHY, PARTICIPANT OBSERVATION, AND FIELDWORK STUDIES

Ethnographic observation studies are based on a desire to focus on communication behavior that is not affected by the research process. The researcher explores communication by engaging in the natural environment. Many terms are used to describe this form of research, including fieldwork, participant observation, naturalistic study, and, of course, ethnography and qualitative research. In **fieldwork,** the fieldworker ventures into the worlds of others in order to learn firsthand about how they live, how they talk and behave, and what captivates and distresses them" (Emerson, 1983, p. 1). For our purposes, fieldwork and naturalistic studies are interchangeable terms. **Naturalistic studies** involve inquiries in the natural environment. **Participant observation** is the most well known form of fieldwork. In this chapter we will not equate naturalistic studies with qualitative research. Some fieldwork may yield quantitative data, though most of it does not. Thus, naturalistic/fieldwork designs are used to gather information, regardless of whether it is qualitative or quantitative. This chapter's applications focus on naturalistic fieldwork with special emphasis on participant observation.

As ethnographic research has become increasingly popular,[1] the language of the method has become very encompassing. In a traditional sense, ethnography emphasized the *ethno* part of its name. In fact, the word "ethnography" is a combination of two terms that literally means "portrait of a people." It was originally developed in anthropology as a method to describe people of different cultures (Hancock, 2002, p. 4). Spradley (1979) defined it as "the work of describing a culture. The essential core of this activity aims to understand another way of life and from the native point

Fieldwork "the study of people acting in the natural course of their daily lives" (Emerson, 1983, p. 1).

Naturalistic studies nonexperimental inquiries completed as subjects are involved in the natural course of their lives.

Participant observation fieldwork in which researchers study groups by gaining membership or close relationships with them (see Wax, 1968, p. 238).

"ethnography" means "portrait of a people," a view that points to cultural studies

---

[1]At the author's university, a very successful debate team completed its own ethnographic research into the plight of migrant farmworkers and reported much of this original ethnographic work as evidence in competitive national tournaments.

of view" (p. 3). Over the years, the concept of a culture has grown so much that nearly any interesting group of people can be studied from a cultural perspective. Thus, the concept of ethnography has grown to encompass a broad range of research. Two specialists in qualitative methods, Carol Warren and Tracy Karner, defined ethnography in just such a broad sense (2005, pp. 1–2):

> Field research or ethnography (sometimes called participant observation) involves present-time face-to-face interaction in a setting, which can be anything from a bus stop to a casino to a small town. The field researcher enters and spends a certain amount of time interacting and observing the setting—more time in a larger and more complete setting such as the small town, less time in a smaller and less complex setting such as the bus stop (the casino is in the middle; one might get there at least once a week for a few months). The fieldworker takes extensive fieldnotes . . . as soon as possible after she leaves the field; these fieldnotes, then, become the basis of ethnographic analysis.

Ethnography research in which the investigator participates, overtly or covertly, in people's lives for an extended period of time, collecting whatever data are available to describe behavior.

As used in this book, **ethnography** involves an extended participation with groups of people being studied. One day's service as a potential juror waiting for possible assignment to a trial would not be considered ethnography, though it might be considered a limited participant observation study. Ethnography is a broad term that includes a great deal, including much participant observation research (though participant observation work need not occur over very long time periods).

A couple of things should be mentioned before we get further into this discussion. First, researchers often use different words to identify the same thing. This "terminological jungle" (Lofland & Lofland, 1995, p. 6) means that some labels used by one scholar may not be used by others, even though their methods are surprisingly identical. Hence, our discussion hits the high points for you using the mainstream view of forms that are dominant in participant observation qualitative research. Second, there is no more need to decide that you are going to be an ethnographic qualitative researcher than there is a need to decide that you are going to be a quantitative researcher. The research problem question should determine what methods are used. If your research problem question involves a matter that might invite both approaches, there is nothing to keep you from using both quantitative and qualitative tools and then "triangulating" study results.

Ethnography has been used quite a bit in communication and educational studies. For instance, by working (for free during the study) at a harness racetrack for seven months, James Helmer (1993) found that the stories people told each other helped them draw distinctions between different sorts of people in the horse-racing world. Stories drew strong distinctions between (1) track administrators, who were characterized as bureaucrats, and horsemen and horsewomen, who were identified as sporting people; (2) "chemists," who doped horses, and honest horsemen and horsewomen, who practiced fair play; and (3) men, whose orders were followed, and women, whose opinions were not seriously considered. Michael Kramer (2005) applied ethnography to a temporary group composed of people who participated in a marathon race to raise money for a nonprofit diabetes organization. He found that the members used internal and external communication to support individuals' efforts to contribute to the group's effort. Margit Bock (2004) used ethnography to explore communication practices in a "digital divide" confronting an isolated Austrian rural area. She found that society seemed to be fragmenting into a group of people who have access to mass media and technology and another group that cannot participate in technology's innovations. Another ethnography explored how a televised miniseries broadcast in Macambira (an isolated region in the backlands of northeast Brazil) "intensified the perceived gap between the local patriarchal culture and the urban reality constructed in the television text" (La Pastina, 2004, p. 162). John Youngblood and J. Emmett Winn (2004) looked at the African American Pentecostal Genuine Deliverance Holiness Church located in the Southern part of the United States. They found that the communication codes used in this church promoted messages that membership in the church promotes spirituality and serves as a correction to racist communication from the nearby community.

Interestingly enough, ethnography has been combined with other methods to complete sound research. For instance, one group of researchers (Morales-Lopez, Prego-Vazquez, & Dominguez-Seco, 2005) combined qualitative interviews, ethnography of communication, and critical discourse analysis in their study of the confusion created when a city privatized the Water Department without training company employees in communication with the public. The effort to triangulate findings from different research traditions has promoted our understanding of communication encounters and also permitted researchers to explore the stability of research findings.

The Purposes of Ethnography and Participant Observation Methods

Participant observation methods are characterized by the attempt to use nonintrusive ways to gather information.[2] Rather than asking individuals to complete questionnaires reporting about themselves, as they might in a survey, participant observation researchers join with groups of people to observe them from within the group. Scholars who use naturalist methods look at such things as how people say good-bye at airports, the stories people tell each other at work, and ways newscasters choose

---

[2]Some writers like to emphasize three qualities that must exist in naturalistic settings. Kraut and Johnston (1979) explain that naturalistic research involves unobtrusive ways of gathering information, of natural events, in a natural setting, stimulated by naturally occurring events. Yet, some so-called naturalistic studies have actually employed "unnatural" settings and artificial stimuli (e.g., Byrne, Ervin, & Lamberth, 1970). Thus, for purposes of accuracy, we will limit naturalistic studies to situations in which, at minimum, natural behavior is studied through unobtrusive means.

stories to cover. Though researchers who complete laboratory experiments try to get some distance from the subjects in the research, participant observation researchers try to get "up close and personal" with the people they study, short of passing out questionnaires or conducting structured interviews.

purposes:
1. *when questionnaires are inappropriate*

Ethnographic and fieldwork studies have three major purposes. First, they try to answer questions in settings where use of questionnaires and direct reports would be inappropriate or impractical. In studies of health communication, for example, it is often not possible for a nurse to conduct research by asking several hundred patients detailed questions about the "bedside manner" of physicians. Yet, a nurse might watch patients who try to explain their medical problems to apparently uninterested physicians. Patterns may be identified in conversations between patients and doctors. Such naturalistic studies may explore questions where tight survey or experimental methods are impossible.

2. *when the setting is so new that hypotheses are undeveloped*

Second, ethnography or fieldwork is often undertaken when a setting has been so unexplored that formal hypotheses may not have been developed. Though this invitation to research is not unique to ethnography, it is true that by immersing yourself in the field setting you might be able to acquire insight that cannot be gained as well in other ways. By looking for unexpected events, researchers can develop intriguing hypotheses to be explored in other inquiries.

3. *when developing analytic inductions*

Third, these studies are completed by researchers who wish to develop grounded theory. Through a process of **analytic induction,** researchers start with some very tentative hypotheses that they apply in fieldwork. If these hypotheses are inadequate, they may be abandoned or reformulated. Eventually, a theory may emerge. Though further distinctions sometimes are drawn, many researchers use analytic induction to help draw important conclusions. An interesting case in point was Laura Ellingson's (2003) study of the communication that occurs "backstage" at a regional cancer treatment center. By making fieldnotes when the individual members of the geriatric oncology team were not involved in teamwork or team meetings, Ellingson analyzed comments and developed "seven inductively derived categories [to] describe the communication involved in backstage teamwork in the clinic: informal impression and information sharing; checking clinic progress; relationship building; space management; training students; handling interruptions; and formal reporting" (2003, p. 93).

Analytic induction "An approach in qualitative research that develops theory by examining a small number of cases. Theory then leads to formulation of a [very tentative] hypothesis, which is tested through the study of more cases. This usually leads to refinement or reformulation of the hypothesis, which is then tested with further cases until the researcher judges that the inquiry can be concluded" (Vogt, 2005, p. 10).

Surely, the chief difference between ethnographic and participant observation work on one hand, and other studies is the method of gathering data. This approach still argues from information to conclusions. The data are empirical (empirical means "observable," not statistical) and can be examined by others. Hence, solid participant observation fieldwork is at least as demanding as any other research.

Suitability of Ethnography and Participant Observation Methods to Research Questions

research questions involve naturally arising behavior not consistently produced in laboratories

Fieldwork and ethnographic methods are invited when a researcher is interested in naturally arising behavior that has not always been shown to have regularities that can be produced in the laboratory. There are several specific guidelines for the selection of this approach to answer research questions. First, if the research problem deals with fields in which naturally occurring communication phenomena exist, the method certainly is invited. Second, the method is suitable for such things as "campus demonstrations, courtroom proceedings, labor negotiations, public hearings, or similar events taking place within a relatively limited area and time" (Babbie, 2003, p. 283).

1. explicitly asks about naturally occurring phenomena

2. the phenomena are within a limited area and time

The objects of such inquiry may range from communication practices to behaviors within specific subcultures. It bears remembering that the form of the research question may invite qualitative work in general. "Qualitative research is concerned with finding the answers to questions which begin with: why? how? in what way? Quantitative research, on the other hand, is more concerned with questions about: how much? how many? how often? to what extent?" (Hancock, 2002, p. 2). In turn, exploring such research questions gives rise to such fundamental concerns as

research questions deal with issues of "why?" "how?" and "in what way?" not "how much?" "how many?" "how often?" "to what extent?"

why people behave the way they do,

how opinions and attitudes are formed,

how people are affected by the events that go on around them, and

how and why cultures have developed in the way they have.

Despite the broad leeway permitted when identifying a "people" or a culture on whom to focus, the researcher needs to realize that ethnographies are not about a sole person, but they are about groups of people who share something in common.

ethnography is not about a sole person, but about people who have something in common

Ethnographers often find it useful to draw a distinction between two approaches to interpreting qualitative research data. The **emic approach** focuses attention on interpreting the study's obtained information from the perspective of a member of the group or culture being studied. When applied to an ethnography in health communication, the implications for the researcher's preparation and research procedures are important matters.

Emic approach "Culturally relative approaches . . . that stress participants' understanding of their own culture. Derived, by an indirect route, from the linguistic term phon*emic*" (Vogt, 2005, p. 105).

> The results are expressed as though they were being expressed by the subjects themselves, often using local language and terminology to describe phenomena. For example, a researcher may explore behaviour which we traditionally in the westernised medical world would describe as mental illness. However, within the population under study, the behaviour may not be characterised as illness but as something else—as evidence that the individual is "blessed" or "gifted" in some way. Ethnographic research can be problematic when researchers are not sufficiently familiar with the social mores of the people being studied or with their language. (Hancock, 2002, p. 5)

In contrast, the **etic approach** to research is that of the outsider who views the situation with some distance that may place perspective on what is observed. Since the *etic* perspective is that of an outside observer, the ethnographer is usually encouraged to avoid potential misinterpretations by returning "to the field to check

Etic approach "Methods of study . . . stressing material—rather than cultural—explanations for social and cultural phenomena. Derived, by an indirect route, from the linguistic term phon*etic*"(Vogt, 2005, p. 109).

his interpretations with informants thereby validating the data before presenting the findings" (Hancock, 2002, p. 5).

By recording conversations and exchanges, researchers can gain special insights. As three scholars of the subject explained:

> Field-workers and participant observers become engaged in the conversations, actions, and lives of the people they study. And unlike the standardized questions and procedures used by experimenters and survey researchers, the questions and actions of a field-worker may vary from one person and setting to the next. Instead of approaching each respondent with the same list of questions, a field-worker engages in conversations and observations that may last several hours or continue for several days, weeks, or months. The conversations move in directions that cannot be anticipated, so the researcher's questions cannot be duplicated from one person to the next. To the extent that the researcher participates in the lives of the people under study, each day will provide new opportunities as a result of the previous day's activities.
>
> How can field research be systematic if the procedures vary so from one person or day to the next? The systematization occurs not by having uniform procedures but by recording faithfully what is seen and heard. (Judd, Smith, & Kidder, 1991, p. 299)

FORMS OF ETHNOGRAPHY AND PARTICIPANT OBSERVATION STUDIES

The role and the approach of the researcher can be very different among participant observers and ethnographers. In fact, to do such inquiry, you must decide what position to take, the advantages of different levels of participation, and the wisdom of taking an ethnographic approach.

The Position of the Observer

Researchers can observe communication at a distance, or they can attempt to become involved in the communication activities themselves. The sort of involvement scholars have affects their ability to acquire highly subjective information that otherwise might be lost. Yet, the level of participation the researcher has with groups studied also can affect the researcher's objectivity and the degree to which conclusions drawn may be free from undue bias. There are two general ways to enter the field.

Full participant observation a role in ethnography or participant observation research characterized by the investigator's gathering data while taking part in the activities of a group—and while concealing his or her research identity.

Full Participation Observation

Full participant observation research involves the investigator's covert gathering of data. In short, people are studied and they do not know it. A researcher might join an organization and follow its activities as an insider, just as Alfred (1976) did in his study of a group of Satanists. He or she might record conversations with others in the organization. Rather than just observe a political campaign, newspaper staff, or activities in a speech clinic, the researcher might work within them. The reports might suggest interesting interpretations since the full participant may gain intimate information as opportunity invites.

Full participation observation is not easy. In a famous participant observation case study, Leon Festinger, Henry W. Rieken, and Stanley Schachter (1956) studied a woman they called Mrs. Keech who had predicted the end of the world by a mighty flood. After reading about Mrs. Keech in a newspaper, Festinger's group joined her followers to see what would happen when the world did not, in fact, come to an end. Mrs. Keech claimed to have been receiving messages from *case study of a full participant* a group called the Omnipotent Guardians from the planet Clarion. They had sent *observation inquiry* her messages through a combination of telepathy, automatic writing, and crystal ball gazing to indicate that at midnight on a particular December evening the world would be destroyed, killing all humanity except for Mrs. Keech's group. They were to be rescued by flying saucers sent from Clarion to Mrs. Keech's home. During the weeks before the "end of the world," several of the group members quit their jobs and spent their savings in preparation for the end. Messages continued to arrive daily to Mrs. Keech. At meetings Festinger and his associates frequently would excuse themselves and write down their notes while in the bathroom. At one meeting, the members were asked to look into a crystal ball and report any new pieces of information. One member of Festinger's group was forced to participate, even though he was hesitant to take a vocal role in meetings. After he remained silent for a time, Mrs. Keech demanded that he report what he saw. Choosing a single-word response, he truthfully announced, "Nothing." Mrs. Keech reacted theatrically, "That's not nothing. That's the void." On the final evening, members of the group waited for midnight. During the evening other instructions arrived. Cultists were told to remove their shoelaces and belt buckles since these items were unsafe aboard flying saucers. When midnight passed without any end of the world in sight—and without any flying saucers visible—members of the group began questioning whether they had misunderstood the instructions. Mrs. Keech began to cry and whimpered that none of the group believed in her. A few of the group comforted her and reasserted their belief in her. Some members reread past messages, and many others sat silently with stony expressions on their faces. Finally in the wee hours of the morning, Mrs. Keech returned to the group with a new "automatically written" message from the Omnipotent Guardians. Because of the faith of the group, the Earth had been spared. The cult members were exuberant and during the weeks that followed actually attempted to secure additional converts. One can find both insight and some entertainment in such a participant observation study. To Festinger's group of scholars, the experience permitted them to provide a field study examination (in the form of a case study) of the theory of cognitive dissonance that they were trying to develop at the time—a theory that became a major force in communication and social psychology.

SPECIAL DISCUSSION 7-1

OBSERVATIONAL STUDIES

Researchers who look at naturally occurring communication, but avoid direct involvement with the phenomena, are engaged in observational studies. In such work, one may take the view of a complete observer or unobtrusive measurer.

A *complete observer* has no contact with the individuals he or she is observing. Research of this form typically occurs when scholars go to field settings, such as airports or bus stations, and watch behaviors of interest from a distance. Behavior may be recorded by photographs or by taking detailed notes. For instance, one scholar watched overweight students in a college cafeteria (Krantz, 1979). Heavy people selected the least food when they planned to carry on conversations with others during lunch.

Unobtrusive measurement uses artifacts that do not influence the behavior being studied. These unobtrusive methods include accretions and erosions, though some lists of these methods include other techniques (see Webb et al., 1981, who include archival information, private records, simple observations, and contrived observations).

Accretions are deposits of material left by some action. Sometimes layers are placed down naturally, but communicators may often deposit remnants of their own. Much work on accretion resembles archaeology. Two researchers examined the graffiti left on the walls of a juvenile corrections facility in New England (Klofas & Cutshall, 1985). The language and kinds of remarks revealed that the young people in the facilities had been socialized into a unique "incarceratory culture" in which the outside world and authority were viewed as objects to manipulate and where ordinary trust was viewed very suspiciously. Thus, by looking at deposits, some interesting clues may be found. One area of study that examines such artifacts is called *urban archaeology*. These studies survey objects created by humans that are the "leftovers" of communication activity. Searching trash cans in a neighborhood to find evidence of the rate of alcoholism is an example of the sort of work that often passes for such inquiry. Of course, such artifacts can be sketchy or misleading (one might have many liquor bottles in a trash can because of a recently held party for a large number of people, or someone might have run out of room and deposited liquor bottles in a neighbor's trash cans). Thus, researchers usually try to find several signs before interpreting results.

Erosions consist of the wear or use of objects. One of the most popularly cited erosion studies involved inquiry into attention paid to different exhibits at the Chicago Museum of Science and Industry.

> The vinyl tiles around the exhibit containing live, hatching chicks had to be replaced every six weeks or so; tiles in other areas of the museum went for years without replacement. A comparative study of the rate of the replacement around the various museum exhibits could give a rough ordering of the popularity of the exhibits. (Webb et al., 1981, p. 7)

Though such data could have more than one explanation, there was reason to believe that the chick exhibit had attracted a larger amount of traffic (and attention) than many others. By finding examples of such erosions, it is possible to gather interesting circumstantial evidence related to key questions.

Unobtrusive methods may be used in many sorts of studies. For example, an experimental study in the laboratory *could* use erosion measures (such as the amount of scratch paper used in a discussion as an indicator of the amount of thoughtful activity used in the group). Yet, unobtrusive methods are most often associated with naturalistic research.

Though the ability to get involved in groups that otherwise would not welcome a researcher permits gathering data, the method creates ethical difficulties. The invasion of others' privacy is an obvious objection that may not have a satisfactory defense. In addition, concealing the researcher's identity has been charged with introducing "false and hypocritical interpersonal relationships between the actual participants and the participant observers" (Fox, 1969, p. 513).

ethical problems with the full participant approach

Participant as Observer

Most participant observation research follows the **participant as observer** method in which the group to be studied is made aware of the researcher's role. Upon agreeing to permit the researcher's participation, other group members typically become resources who explain and help interpret that group's actions. In one such study, Martin S. Weinberg (1965) visited three nudist camps to study nonverbal behavior of participants. In each case, he first identified himself as a researcher and requested permission to attend the camps as a nudist during the summer months. Inside the camps Weinberg also identified himself as a researcher to the nudists. He reported that the nudists seemed uninfluenced by his presence, and they were willing to discuss matters with him. He had two potential hypotheses to guide his work, each one of which was opposite of the other. Perhaps people in nudist camps might be as unrestrained in their language and gestures as in their clothing. Or, perhaps since displays of the body are obvious, nudists might compensate by increased restraint in their language and gestures. He found strong support for his second hypothesis. He noticed that "verbal modesty" was common: there were few dirty jokes told, and sexual innuendo in conversation was frowned upon. Staring and body contact were discouraged. Similarly, use of alcohol was strictly forbidden. When Weinberg later interviewed 101 nudists in the Chicago area, he found that they were harsh in their judgments of others who violated their very strict norms. Furthermore, nudists lived a lifestyle in which nudity and sexuality were largely unrelated matters. As this example illustrates, the participant as observer does not hide his or her identity (or much of anything else). Instead, the observer identifies himself or herself, becomes an active participant, and develops increased appreciation for the actions and communication of the group.

Participant as observer a role in ethnography or participant observation research characterized by the investigator's gathering data while taking part in the activities of a group—and after making his or her research identity known to the group.

One might suppose that announcing one's identity as a researcher would be sufficient to remove ethical dilemmas, but it does not always work that way. Taking the participant-as-observer role, Van Maanen (1982) worked with police officers and was witness to some incidents of "police burglaries, drug dealings, payoffs, planting of evidence, and so on" (p. 273) and on one occasion was involved in a patrol that filed a false police report as coached by a supervising sergeant. Yet, under questioning from the Internal Investigation Division, he failed to reveal the coaching incident as part of honoring the unofficial "no ratting" code (p. 274). Thus, ethical issues can arise in any research and are not to be handled flippantly.

Sometimes it is difficult to tell what role the researcher assumes. For instance, Mark West and John Gastil (2004) used participant observation methods as part of their study of the experiences and planning for the protests of the World

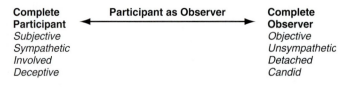

FIGURE 7.1   CONTINUUM OF FIELDWORKER ROLES

From *Strategies for Social Research*, first edition by Smith, 1991. Reprinted with permission of Wadsworth, a division of Thomson Learning, www.thomsonrights.com.

Trade Organization meeting in Seattle and Prague in 1999 and 2000, respectively. Mark West participated in these demonstrations, which included considerable destruction of property and many violent encounters. Yet, there is no evidence in the published report whether West identified himself as a researcher to anyone (or at least to the nearby demonstrators who would otherwise assume that he could be counted among those who would provide direct aid to them). The point is not whether West may have greatly influenced crowds numbering in the scores of thousands to take action they would not have taken otherwise. Instead, the question is whether the report of the communication study included an identification of the researcher's role in the participant observation phase of the study.

Balancing Involvement

The two approaches involve some trade-offs. Figure 7.1 shows the relationship between the researcher's approach and the types of claims drawn (after H. Smith, 1991, p. 332). When the researcher tends toward complete participation, interpretations become subjective, the researcher shares sympathy and concern for the communicators studied, plays an active role in the communication to be studied, and usually goes into the research setting in disguise to get close to the data. On the other hand, researchers who tend toward complete observational research—such as watching people in an airport, often without their knowing that they are being studied—are objective, unsympathetic, detached, and usually candid about the sorts of research completed. Since the fieldwork of the participant observer tends to emphasize the involvement in the setting, his or her work may be tipped more toward one side of the continuum than the other. Participant observers must weigh the advantages and disadvantages of each approach to balance some of the benefits of one position against the costs that go with the levels of involvement.

Ethnography and Ethnomethodology

The word **ethnomethodology** is sometimes used as though it were interchangeable with ethnography, when, in fact, it is a distinct specialty. The "new ethnography" (Berg, 2007, pp. 173–174) attempts to impose a rational scheme onto essentially practical activities (practical reasoning). When it works properly, we can find patterns to explain the implicit rules or guidelines that people use to make sense

Ethnomethodology
(also called the "new ethnography," originally developed by anthropologists to study societies of humans) an approach (rather than a rigorous method) in which researchers find an ethnic group, live within it, and attempt to develop insight into the culture; emphasis is placed on the mundane and ordinary activities of everyday life, concentrating on the methods used by people to report their commonsense practical actions to others in acceptable rational terms.

of exchanges with each other. Although ethnomethodology occasionally has been criticized for being "almost willfully obscure" (McNeill, 1990, p. 94), it has grown in popularity among students of communication since it focuses on how people use messages to perceive the world as they do.

The reason you might want to take an ethnomethodological approach is part philosophical and part practical. On the philosophical level, it seems only fair to look at the activities of ordinary people, including "the everyday, 'seen but unnoticed' ways in which members of society, social scientists included, constituted the facts of society as part of their ordinary activities" (ten Have, 2002, p. 1). By looking at the things that people assume, rather than what they find novel and remarkable, researchers believe that they can gain improved understanding of communication transactions among people of a common culture or group. On the practical level, this desire to look at ordinary taken-for-granted communication meant that using ethnomethodology would require naturalistic and essentially qualitative research methods, such as ethnography (at least up to a point). Paul ten Have explained:

> An essential part of the ethnomethodological program is the effort to study members' practices as such, rather than some sociological work-up of their products, as in survey research tables or archived documents. This is not an easy matter, as the constitutive aspects of those practices are, for members (again including sociologists) "essentially uninteresting," and therefore hard to get in focus. Working with tapes and transcripts can be seen, then, as not just a practical way of getting detailed data, but also as a solution to the problem of "the invisibility of common sense procedures." (2002, pp. 1–2)

The belief in the importance of communication that is perceived as mundane has encouraged researchers to investigate the unstated presumptions underlying communication in groups and even thought processes among members of groups.

THE FLUID PROCESS OF ETHNOGRAPHY AND PARTICIPANT OBSERVATION RESEARCH

As with other research approaches, participant observation studies follow some fairly consistent methods. Furthermore, they have some limitations of which researchers must be aware.

A Philosophic Foundation

Whaddaya want, realism or control? Though one should strive for both, the fact is that a tension exists between the two in research. There is difficulty in the practice of any research when it comes to maximizing

SPECIAL DISCUSSION 7-2

OTHER QUALITATIVE-NATURALISTIC METHODS

Though the typical naturalistic methods used in communication are common enough, other tools sometimes appear. Some of the most frequently heard methods are the following:

- "A 'life-history' or 'life story' is the autobiography of a person which has been obtained through interview and guided conversation" (McNeill, 1990, p. 85). The terms "biographical study" and "oral history" are often used as synonyms for the *life history study*. This method does not result in composing an autobiography, but it uses life histories (usually witnesses to major communication events) to gather information on significant times or events. Such studies are useful since collecting many of them allows one to reconstruct a sense of a time period and the practice of communication across time.

- *Time-budgeting studies* are inquiries in which "the researcher asks the subjects of the research to keep a detailed diary over a given period" (McNeill, 1990, p. 88). Time-budgeting studies are often used in organizational communication and communication education to help determine whether professionals are using their time in ways that are most constructive and expected given their job descriptions. The maps constructed by time-budgeting studies can help identify areas of dominant focus and areas where readjustments might be advised.

- *Community studies* "involve a researcher or a team of researchers in studying a whole community of people, usually in a small town or village, or possibly part of a larger town" (McNeill, 1990, p. 90). Unlike ordinary ethnographic research, many methods are used, including such tools as direct observation, use of informants, and informal and formal interviews with individuals.

- *Case studies* are intensive inquiries about single events, people, or social units. When employed in interpretive studies, efforts are made to look for themes or stories that are helpful to interpret or understand the case. Dougherty and Smythe (2004) completed a case study at a university where a wealthy donor had sexually harassed a female graduate student and held her close to him, all the while keeping a light-hearted banter. He made a pass at a female senior faculty member by suggestively commenting on her appearance and initiating unwanted hand-holding. While conducting a conversation about a possible research opportunity at his company, he moved his chair so close to a female junior faculty member that for a time their knees touched, and he moved his hand slowly in the space between their noses while suggesting that most of his executives were women and that he got along very well with them. Dougherty and Smythe found that humor seemed to be used as a coping device. Before long, the anger and indignation across the department had eased into a comfortable return to normal roles. Somewhat in contrast to the literature on sexual harassment, these authors found that the men of the academic department were active in promoting a community to support the women. Women victims, both before and after the harassment episodes, reported a preference for using "social politeness" comments to fend off unwanted advances. Such a study may both stimulate theorizing and lead to some research using other methods.

A variation of this form is the *negative case study,* in which the researcher attempts to obtain a case that has the potential to negate a generally accepted view. For instance, in the field of stuttering, for nearly two decades it was believed that stuttering was caused by the labeling of the child, usually by a nervous parent. Among other things, this notion was based on the often-repeated observation that among Hopi and Navajo, there were no stutterers and no words for stuttering. Lemert (1953) refuted this belief by completing a negative case study in which he found a group of Native Americans who stuttered, even though their language had no word for the malady. By doing this negative case study, Lemert showed that a widely promoted hypothesis was, in fact, a myth.

simultaneously both external validity (representativeness of real world contexts) and internal validity (precision and control). Although it is misleading to make an absolute distinction between "naturalistic" and "scientific" research, it is clear that experimental research usually requires a degree of artificial manipulation of control of the key variables, whereas qualitative research typically seeks to maximize the ecological validity of the data by gathering it in real-world contexts. (Camic, Rhodes, & Yardley, 2003, p. 8)

ethnography in qualitative and quantitative research

As may be remembered from Chapter 1, qualitative studies typically attempt to examine details of cases, and quantitative methods typically attempt to examine variables across numbers of cases. In that chapter, qualitative research was defined as

in-depth, case-oriented study of a relatively small number of cases, including the single-case study. Qualitative research seeks detailed knowledge of specific cases, often with the goal of finding out "how" things happen (or happened). Qualitative researchers' primary goal is to "make the facts understandable," and often place less emphasis on deriving inferences or predictions from cross-case patterns. (Ragin, Nagel, & White, 2004, p. 10)

The emphasis of naturalistic observations free from questionnaires and experimentation is particularly strong in ethnographic research. In this kind of inquiry, groups of people who already share things in common are not the objects of further generalization. Instead, the elements that give meaning to their distinctive communities are to be the primary focus of attention.

All this discussion may seem very general, but here is the question to which it is leading: What are these common groupings that make a people distinctive? There is more than one reasonable way to approach the matter. For instance, anthropologists may look for clear cultural boundaries. Sociologists may look for groupings including very transient groups, such as the people who may visit a website or chatroom. Health communication specialists may apply ethnographic work to various clinics or medical teams.

the search for groups may be based on several things including:

Researchers who study from the perspective of the ethnography of communication do so usually with reference to a special sub-disciplinary interest, such as Intercultural or Cultural Communication, Interpersonal Communication, Organizational Communication or by positioning the work as within a framework of Language as Social Interaction. However one is labeled or describes one's work, the commitments are shared. That is, **communication should be examined as a social and cultural practice and recognition should be given to the ways that the participants themselves describe and use communication.** (Milburn, 2006b, ¶ 4; bold in original)

communication, which serves as a social and cultural practice identifying a group

While ethnographers in other fields (and many in Communication Studies) have taken a traditional approach to ethnography, another perspective known as the "ethnography of communication" has emerged as a major—and some would say—dominant force in ethnographic studies. As far back as 1962, Dell Hymes, a scholar of anthropology and sociolinguistics who served as a professor of folklore, linguistics, sociology, and education at the University of Pennsylvania, suggested looking at the way people use talk in what he called the "ethnography of speaking." By the 1970s many had included communication forms other than speech in variations on this system and the approach became known as the "ethnography of communication."

Hymes' ethnography of communication

Speech community "a set of people with a common language, or who share a repertoire of varieties (accents, styles, even languages in multilingualism); people who live together and interact through language; people with shared social attributes (young people, lawyers, women); people in the same social system. The term is most relevant to small well-defined, stable communities" (Bothamley, 1993, p. 499).

Since the terms "communication" and "community" have the same root, it made sense to Hymes that "the starting point is the ethnographic analysis of the communication conduct of a community" (1974, p. 9). The **speech community** consists of the people who have a common system of speech to bind them together. Members of these speech communities not only have common language elements, but they also have common rules about the ways they should and should not speak (Hymes, 1972, p. 54). This process means that people in a speech community share common meanings for many, if not most, of the signs they use. In this approach, "for instance, users of a particular website may be considered a speech community if they share particular rules for speaking online" (Milburn, 2006d, ¶ 5).

This notion of community led Hymes to identify five additional units that use communication to emphasize different aspects of the culture at work. By looking at these notions, the serious ethnographer of communication actually uses communication and message exchange behavior to identify important aspects of culture and the influence of groups on people. Following are the five additional units:

units using communication to emphasize aspects of culture

♦ The **speech situation** is an occasion that influences whether people actively communicate with each other. Such situations include seeing a movie in a theater (where people do not talk) and taking an airplane trip (where people regularly talk to each other).

Speech situation "situations associated with (or marked by the absence of) speech (Hymes)" (Malcolm, 2001, ¶ 71).

♦ The **speech event** is the communication encounter involving the active encounter with messages. For instance, going to a college class would be a speech situation and the professor's lecture would be the speech event.

◆ The **communicative act** is the specific components or details of the speech event. As an example, during a professor's lecture, there could be a communicative act consisting of responding to a student's question, or presenting a case study to illustrate the lecture's content.

◆ The **communicative style** is one's typical use of verbal and nonverbal language, especially when engaged in communication with specific groups of people. Communicative style may reflect whether people use slang during interactions with others in their peer groups, or whether there are typical patterns of assertiveness or responsiveness communicated while speaking.

◆ The **ways of speaking** include following a group's unwritten rules of communication conduct. For instance, these unstated rules may include such things as saying "Excuse me" when accidentally bumping another or responding to someone who says "Hello" by saying "Fine. How are you?" (out of a sense of politeness, whether or not you really feel fine).

This approach is based on the presumption that communication not only is a *tool* of culture, but is a key to help discover cultural meanings. Hymes' approach provides a communications based philosophical foundation that has greatly influenced communication scholars (e.g., Milburn, 2000). By starting with a decision to look at the fundamental units listed above, the ethnographer can get down to the specific interpretations that arise from a sound ethnography. In the next section, we will return to Hymes' approach to consider how to analyze communication in field settings.

Steps in Conducting the Study

Ethnographic studies are completed by steps that often overlap and cycle back and forth. The entire method has a fluid quality about it, though a protocol has established some clear phases in the research.

Selecting a Position for the Researcher

Once upon a time, there was an assumption that researchers could ignore their own opinions and complete relatively dispassionate research. Their own positions were often assumed to be something that they could "rise above" if they tried hard enough. Among qualitative researchers and ethnographers, the reasons for selecting certain cultures and groups always reflected a personal stance, whether this stance was identified or not. Yet, the type of data one collects, about what one chooses to make fieldnotes, and the type of interpretation vary greatly. Hence, contemporary communication researchers using ethnographic methods are urged to identify their **research positions** early—both for themselves and for the benefit of the eventual consumers of their research.

Though there could be combinations, and though there may be other positions, three major positions for qualitative researchers were identified by Michelle Fine (1994, p. 17).

Speech event "the basic unit for the analysis of verbal interaction in speech communities; it covers stretches of utterances and focuses on the exchange between speakers; (Gumperz)" (Malcolm, 2001, ¶ 67).

Communicative act utterances examined "in terms of what they do and how we use them in conversation" (Malcolm, 2001, ¶ 70).

Communicative style "linguistic difference according to the formality of the interaction" (Malcolm, 2001, ¶ 30).

Ways of speaking "rule-governed patterns of communicative behaviour within a speech community (Hymes)" (Malcolm, 2001, ¶ 72).

steps:

1. selecting a position for the researcher

Research positions the stances that researchers take on the objectives for research (ventriloquizing others' interests, giving voice to silenced groups, engaging direct activism).

major positions for the researcher

1. The *ventriloquist stance* that merely transmits information in an effort toward neutrality and is absent of a political or rhetorical stance. The position of the ethnographer aims to be invisible, that is, the "self" strives to be nonexistent in the text.

2. The *positionality of voices* is where the subjects themselves are the focus, and their voices carry forward indigenous meaning and experiences that are in opposition to dominant discourses and practices. The position of the ethnographer is vaguely present but not addressed.

3. The *activism stance* in which the ethnographer takes a clear position in intervening on hegemonic practices and serves as an advocate in exposing the material effects to marginalized locations while offering alternatives.

ventriloquist stance

giving voice to groups studied

Each of these positions has a legitimate role to play. The ventriloquist position—despite the negative connotation that might be created by the language used by Fine—is an effort to provide direct reports and to meet the research goal of simple description. This approach is consistent with the efforts made in the Chicago school of fieldwork study in the early part of the twentieth century. These researchers endeavored to provide replicable, scientifically oriented reports where the researchers tried (at least) to keep strict control over their feelings and expectations of the field.

The position in which the researcher attempts to give voice to a group of people is noteworthy for its commitment to groups that do not otherwise have people to speak out for them. The researcher is on a quest to secure a fair hearing for meaning perspectives that are not understood or valued by society's dominant powers. This position would lead researchers to investigate matters that would help make their views known to a third party. When John Nance wrote *The Gentle Tasaday* (1974), about a stone-age people discovered in the Philippine rain forest, he used translations of their experiences, and even accounts of their speech, to communicate to the outside world that this tribe had significance and a legitimate desire to live their lives according to their own culture. By giving a voice to this group, Nance was instrumental in efforts to protect the Tasaday mountain region from development and casual tourism.

the activism stance

The activism stance invites the researcher to gather information to help make a case for a change in the treatment of marginalized groups. Rather than letting the voices of the cultural group studied speak for themselves, the researcher gathers information designed to make a political case, often involving attempts to change the society in which the studied people live. Such participants are change agents, rather than scholars interested in developing theory and understanding of communication alone.

Postcritical ethnography
a research position in which researchers include a critique of the ways in which their own experiences studying groups of people in an ethnographic project may contribute to domination of the groups under study.

Though actually a combination of the positionalities of giving voice to the marginalized and engaging in out-and-out activism, Noblit, Flores, and Murillo (2004) added another position to the mix, **postcritical ethnography.** This approach requires researchers to critique their own position in regard to the research subject and include explicit study of "how their own acts of studying and representing people and situations are acts of domination even as critical ethnographers reveal themselves in what they study" (p. 3). There is little doubt that when outsiders study people, they may have any number of unintended influences. In this respect, however, postcritical ethnography takes the position that the researcher should check for subtle signs of domination and control. For instance, a researcher who announces that he or she will use information to help local people resist unfair labor practices is assuming the position of a superior to the people, a person who must step in to save the local people from failing to act in their own best interests. Not only is such an attitude a little presumptuous, it also places the researcher from another society in a position of dominance. The research effort may then become another tool to reinforce the image of cultural superiority of the researcher's group over that under study.

Selecting Settings and Cases

2. selecting settings and cases

Researchers often choose research settings and fields that appeal to their personal interests. Thus, in the case of participant observation studies, one researcher may focus on observing people at airports, another may attempt to spy on private conversations, and still another might try to have long visits with subjects. In the case of ethnographies, researchers may decide to spend extended time periods interacting with migrant farmworkers, residents of safe houses for battered women, or parents of stuttering children receiving therapy in speech clinics. There is some disagreement about whether it is more desirable to study unusual and exotic settings or to stick to the ordinary and mundane. Those who urge study of exotic practices believe that looking at unusual activities may reveal things that challenge conventional wisdom. Those who want researchers to emphasize ordinary behavior hold that regularities in communication can be identified most efficiently by looking at typical rather than aberrant behaviors.

controversy over study of exotic or ordinary behavior

Getting into the Setting

3. getting into the setting

Participant observers must take time to define their levels of activity. A passive observer may have difficulty getting a group's permission to observe key behavior. Yet, a researcher who does not reveal his or her own purposes to the individuals under study may face some dangers. In classic field research, Laud Humphreys (1970) studied the practice of casual homosexual sexual encounters. Without identifying himself as a researcher, and without choosing to participate, Humphreys agreed to serve as a "lookout" at a public restroom where men had brief homosexual affairs. He was presumed to be a voyeur or "watch queen." He found that many of the men were married and led otherwise heterosexual lives. Yet, such research proved dangerous. Humphreys was arrested once and was beaten up by a gang of kids another time.

The ethical difficulties of concealing one's identity can be great. One research team (Berg, Ksander, Loughlin, & Johnson, 1983) studied a group of teenagers' criminal activities. Along the way, they acquired information about plans for car robberies, burglaries, assaults, shoplifting, and drug deals. These clearly illegal and violent activities were never reported to police, nor were victims warned. Did the researchers owe society or the victims anything? They apparently did not think so—nor was their own property stolen, nor were they assaulted. The authors possessed a Federal Certificate of Confidentiality, which guaranteed that researchers would not have their records subpoenaed, and which required that confidential materials not be revealed. The ethics involved in learning more than one wishes to know constitutes a major challenge in much, but not all, naturalistic study.

ethical challenges in research

RESEARCHERS IN THE FIELD: MELBOURNE S. CUMMINGS

Melbourne S. Cummings teaches courses in rhetoric, public address, intercultural communication, and nonverbal communication at the Department of Communication and Culture at Howard University, a program for which she served as the chair during a period of great growth and development of a reputation for scholarly excellence in the field. She received a bachelor's degree from Southern University, and a master's degree from North Carolina Central University before attending the University of California, Los Angeles, where she earned her doctorate in speech after beginning graduate studies in English. Though her many publications can be found in communication journals, she has welcomed opportunities to work across disciplines and to publish in many fields, especially those dealing with popular culture, African American studies, and education. Among her most respected pieces of scholarship have been qualitative and historical/critical studies with an emphasis on African American rhetoric, such as "The Changing Image of the Black Family on Television" and "Developing Strategies That Promote Early Identification and Recruitment of Persons of Color to Speech Communication." She has participated in the Fulbright-Hays Fellowship program, which sponsored her studies in East Africa. When she received the 2002 NCA Mentor Award, her students and supporters emphasized her role as an inspirational teacher and model for others. In the book, *Black Pioneers in Communication Research,* she is listed as one of the 11 most influential African American scholars in the field's history.

♦ *You weren't always a scholar in communication studies. What drew you to the field of communication?*
Actually what drew me to the field of communication was a newly published book, *Rhetoric of Black Revolution,* by then Arthur L. Smith, a young assistant professor in the Department of Speech at UCLA, where I was a Ph.D. student in the Department of English. I had taught English for three years (one year in high school and two in college). I wanted to study Black literature, both African and African American, which I was doing, but was told that I had to follow the departmental program of study, which did not provide for a major concentration in African and African American literature. Smith's book intrigued me. So, I went to see him. We talked for hours. I transferred to speech. Eventually, I was graduated with the honor of being Molefi Asante's first Ph.D. student.

♦ *You have received some of the National Communication Association's most coveted awards for scholarship and service. Recently you were named as one of eleven most significant Black Pioneers in Communication Research in a book of the same name. What is it about your scholarly work that you think has made you most proud?*
I think that I am most proud of my dissertation on Bishop Henry McNeil Turner, for it was my first extended research project in Black communication. My advisor, Molefi Asante (Smith, at that time), had so intrigued me with his groundbreaking research, that I wanted to follow in his footsteps. When he gave

me his approval of the work that I had done, even though it was done using a traditional method, I felt that I had arrived and that I had something to offer.

♦ *When you received the NCA Mentor Award, over ten thousand dollars were raised in your name to support students initiating their careers in communication research, scholarship, and teaching. You are probably as well known for your teaching and mentoring as you are for your scholarship. What kind of a balance have you tried to maintain between teaching and mentoring on one hand, and conducting active research on the other hand?*

Actually, I don't think I maintained a balance. The scales always tipped to the side of mentoring students. I published because that's a part of effective mentoring: students must see that you do what you say they must do. Additionally, if as a teacher, I spark an interest in a subject, or if students come to me with an interest in a subject, I have to know something about it as well as be willing to learn about it in order that I may be of benefit to my students. For example, this generation of students has been affected by the hip-hop culture and rap. I am not particularly fascinated by rap, but I am by the culture. For my students to be able to study it and make an impact as scholars, there must be someone who can assist them in their pursuits. There must also be someone with a scholarly reputation in the field to legitimize hip-hop. I teach at Howard University, the only HBCU (Historically Black College or University) that is on par with predominantly white research-extensive institutions. It is my responsibility, and that of my colleagues, to publish in the area of the communication of rap and the culture of hip-hop. So, if there is a balance that I have struck, it is for my students and any other young Black person in the field of communication and culture.

♦ *In addition to your scholarship, you have been in the forefront of encouraging involvement in the field by people of color. Your founding leadership of the Black Caucus of the National Communication Association established a group that grew from a relatively small number to over 400 members now. How would you evaluate the progress that has been/is being made by our field?*

I think there has been tremendous progress in the field of African American communication. When I was a student, all I had to research were speeches by Black leaders and accounts of them and their impact from the fields of history and political science. There were few speech anthologies with accompanying commentary emerging, but now we have full-blown theories and methods for analyses and studies. I am so proud of our new researchers like Ronald Jackson for the strides they have made, the ground that they are breaking, and the books and articles that they are writing. At our national and regional conferences, I honestly sit back and bask in what I see and hear from our young people. What brilliance! What courage! What creativity! What commitment! What professionalism!!

♦ *A lot a researchers talk about immersing themselves in the extended field of their inquiries, but your actions have been exceptional in this regard. You had a Fulbright-Hays Fellowship to study in East Africa, and you have lived in more than a dozen African nations over the years. How have these extended experiences influenced your research?*

I have been blessed to be able to travel, experience, and learn about the cultures of our people. It has allowed me to know that we really cannot make assessments and judgments about others if we don't understand the cultures from which they've come. It makes me know how very much our world is dependent on the research and teaching of our field, and that realization gives me a responsibility to young people that I do not take lightly.

♦ *Your commitment to communication scholarship is well documented. In addition to completing an impressive body of work specializing in African American communication, you were a founding associate editor of the* Howard Journal of Communication. *You have seen some excellent and some weak research over the years. Is there any advice you would give students who might be interested in becoming communication researchers?*

I always advise my students and others to "go for it." Of course, it is necessary for them to learn all they can about the process. I encourage them to apply for graduate school and try to decide on their area(s) of interest as early in their first year of study as possible. This allows them to immerse themselves in their discipline, in their research interests, and in the methodologies that would most appropriately support their research interests.

♦ *What one or two lessons have you learned along the way that could make the novice research student have a successful career in the field's research?*

I would suggest that students choose their fields of research according to their interests, even their passions. One is more likely to be successful in a field where she or he is most passionate. I think, also, that the novice researcher should find a person with whom she or he shares research interests, even across disciplines, and do collaborative research. Cross-disciplinary research is fascinating. We find more information about our area of interest when we look at it from various perspectives.

4. selecting types of behaviors to monitor

Sampling within the Case: Selecting the Types of Behaviors to Monitor.

Based on their knowledge and theoretic interests, researchers gather data that they believe will be most meaningful. Though some researchers keep their early observations relatively unstructured, all seem to give attention to information about the physical setting, relationships among people, information that is overheard, and locating guides who can help explain the new surroundings (Berg, 2007, p. 185–186). Researchers usually begin by noting nearly everything that they can identify as a potentially useful piece of information. Most, however, choose behaviors to track based on a combination of personal interest and the level of talk they notice other participants giving the concepts. When examining behavior, many participant observers ask themselves the following questions to isolate and describe key behavior (Nachmias & Nachmias, 1996, p. 294, after Lofland & Lofland, 1995):

1. What type of behavior is it?
2. What is its structure?
3. How frequent is it?

4. What are its causes?

5. What are its processes?

6. What are its consequences?

7. What are people's strategies?

By a combination of direct observation and asking questions, meaningful communication processes and variables can be identified.

In the previous section of this chapter we introduced Dell Hymes' "ethnography of communication" approach. As you may recall, Hymes' major contribution was identification of the types of groups to be examined. The essential unit is the "speech community," which is essentially a group of people "who live together and interact through language; people with shared social attributes (young people, lawyers, women); people in the same social system" (Bothamley, 1993, p. 499). The units that use communication to emphasize different aspects of the culture at work include the speech situation, the speech event, the communicative act, communicative style, and ways of speaking. After choosing the focus of ethnographic attention, Hymes provided a useful system to organize an ethnographic inquiry so that the unit could be analyzed. *Hymes' ethnography of communication system used*

The categories for analysis of different speech events may be organized according to the memory device formed by the word "S-P-E-A-K-I-N-G." These categories identify the elements that ethnographers should cover to complete a thorough analysis of the communication unit the researcher has chosen. *elements of the model summarized by a memory device based on the word "speaking"*

As an illustration of this approach, Claudia Angelelli's (2000) article, "Interpretation as a Communicative Event: A Look Through Hymes' Lenses," was an interesting case in point. She looked at two major types of translation. "Community translation" services are provided when a person must communicate with another person who speaks a different language. Such applications take place in government agencies, hospitals, courts, and the like. In such a setting, one person speaks and the translator immediately translates the message into another language, and back and forth through the exchange. In one example, a translator was provided for a Spanish-speaking man who was attempting to learn the procedures for avoiding delays in registering his car. The officer for the Office of Car Registration attempted to explain the forms that would have to be completed. "Conference translation" services are provided before large meetings, such as international press conferences, United Nations General Assembly meetings, and international conferences. In these formal settings, the translators dedicated to translating one language sit in booths removed from the speakers and listeners (who receive translations through electronic ear pieces). As a case for analysis, Angelelli examined a press conference in which the CEO of a large corporation announced the new models of automobiles. Table 7.1 shows the general application of this work. As you can see, Hymes' model was very helpful in organizing the observations in this fieldwork inquiry. In reality, Angelelli had many other translation examples that she could draw upon for her analyses. In general, Hymes' system worked well to organize qualitative observations. One difficulty, however, involved identifying the role of the translator. Certainly, the *application of "SPEAKING" in communication research*

TABLE 7.1 ANALYSIS USING HYMES' S.P.E.A.K.I.N.G. SYSTEM		
	Angelelli's Study of Interpreters (2000, pp. 586–589)	
Hymes' S.P.E.A.K.I.N.G. Components (1974, pp. 53–62)	Community Interpreting	Conference Interpreting
S. **(Situation)** the time and place of a speech act and, in general, the physical circumstances	*Setting:* the time and place of a speech act and, in general, the physical circumstances	Interpreter located at the Office of Car Registration (OCR), sitting between the officer and client	Interpreter located in the conference room, between speaker and audience (but separated from them) in simultaneous mode in a booth
	Scene: the cultural definition of an occasion; the "psychological setting"	Speakers and listeners do not share it, as they do not belong to the same *speech community*. Therefore, it might be more accessible or evident for the interpreter as she/he explores it not so much as an outsider does but as a "discovering" party. The situation allows for clarification.	Speaker generally shares it with listener since both belong to the same *speech community*. It might not be as accessible or evident to the interpreter. There is little possibility to "explore and discover." The situation does not always allow for clarification.
P. **(Participants)** including the people present and the roles they play, including "speaker or sender; addressor; hearer, or receiver, or audience; addressee"	*Participants:* may include the following: speaker, or sender; addressor; hearer, or receiver, or audience; addressee	*Speaker or sender:* the roles are interchangeable. As it is a dialogic mode (Wadensjo, 1998), the speaker becomes the listener and the listener becomes the speaker. *Addressor:* if we stretch Hymes' definition, we could say that the interpreter becomes the spokesperson of both speakers in the language into which she/he is interpreting. *Hearer, or receiver, or audience:* the interaction between speaker and listener is constant. The interpreter considers the speakers' and listeners' native language code to convert the message as she/he also acknowledges different linguistic varieties and registers. It is always	*Speaker or sender:* the conference interpreter normally follows one speaker at a time in a monologic form (Wadensjo, 1998). *Addressor:* if we stretch Hymes' definition, we could say that the interpreter becomes the spokesperson of the speaker in the language into which she/he is interpreting. *Hearer, or receiver, or audience:* in a conference setting, the audience is silent except for the period of questions and answers. The interaction between speaker and audience is therefore limited. The interpreter considers the audience's
			(Continued)

TABLE 7.1 (Continued)

		possible to negotiate meaning. *Addressee:* the interpreter identifies the addressees in each exchange; she/he is able to see how the message and event may be anticipated at its destination. (Is the officer going to be surprised by a tone? Is the driver going to feel intimidated by the tone?)	native language code to convert the message (even when different linguistic varieties cannot generally be acknowledged or negotiated). There is no dialogue between the interpreter and the audience at this marketing conference except for the Q&A period. *Addressee:* when the interpreter identifies the addressees, she/he is able to see how the message and event may be anticipated at its destination. (Are the sellers expecting this new marketing campaign?)
E. **(Ends)** or the purposes including outcomes ("the expected outcome of a speech event as recognized by the speech community") and goals ("the intentions of participants and the strategies they define")	*Purposes-outcomes:* the expected outcome of a speech event as recognized by the speech community	The interpreter cannot do the job if she/he does not understand what is the particular outcome of the communicative event. (Is it a decision to renew a license, an intention to extend a deadline to pay registration?) There is room for negotiation.	The interpreter will benefit if she/he understands what is the particular outcome of the communicative event. (Is it a decision on a new model, a legal ruling about some sales?) There is almost no room for negotiation.
	Purposes-goals: the intentions of participants and the strategies they define	The interpreter will focus more on the participants' intentions, on their goals within the outcome. (Who is making the decision about the renewal? Who will the decision affect and how is that party accommodating to the making of that decision?) As there is interaction, the interpreter has the opportunity to clarify.	The interpreter will focus more on the participants' intentions, on their goals within the outcome. (Who is making the decision about the new model? Who will the decision affect and how is that party accommodating to the making of that decision?)
A. **(Acts)** speech acts including message form	*Message form:* how something is said by members in a	The community interpreter by virtue of being a	"The more a way of speaking has become shared

(Continued)

TABLE 7.1   (Continued)

("how something is said by members in a given speech community and according to the descriptive characteristics") and message content ("topic and change of topic")	given speech community and according to the descriptive characteristics . . .	community member could be familiar with how members of that community speak. She/he may or may not be familiar with how OCR officers speak to community members who do not work there (depending if she/he ever went through the same experience herself/himself). In this sense, she/he has an advantage over the "temporary guest" at least for being familiar with one of the parties.	and meaningful within a group the more likely that crucial clues will be efficient" ([Hymes, 1974,] p. 55). It would be reasonable to say then that the interpreter should be aware of the competence that speakers of the automobile marketing community have and share in order to be able to go beyond the content of an explicit statement. But, is this possible? Can a "temporary guest" of a *speech community* achieve this [status]? How much time does a "temporary guest" have to spend within that community in order to grasp the *ways of speaking* of this *speech community*?
	Message content: topic and change of topic	The interpreter can follow a topic and a change of topic by carefully following the meaning of what is being said. Since the parties do not necessarily share the same communicative competence, negotiation on the part of the interpreter may be necessary. The situation allows negotiation.	Members of the automobile marketing group know what is being said and when what is being said has changed. Their communicative competence within the group allows them to manage maintenance and change of topic. Apparently, the message content is more concrete than the message form and therefore might be more accessible to a "temporary guest." The interpreter can follow a topic and a change of topic by carefully following the meaning of what is being said.
K. **(Key)** including the "tone, manner, or spirit	*Key:* tone, manner, or spirit of a speech act (e.g.	The interpreter will focus on the tone, manner, or	The interpreter will focus on the tone,

(Continued)

TABLE 7.1   (Continued)

of a speech act (e.g. seriousness, sarcasm, etc.)"	seriousness, sarcasm, etc.)	spirit of each of the interlocutors.	manner, or spirit of the speaker.
I. **(Instrumentality)** including the channels ("the medium of speech transmission [e.g. oral, written, visual, etc.]") and forms of speech ("the different languages, dialects, varieties, and registers used in a speech event/act; may be joined with channels as means or agencies or speaking")	*Channels:* the medium of speech transmission (e.g. oral, written, telegraphic, etc.) *Forms of speech:* the different languages, dialects, varieties, and registers used in a speech event/act; may be joined with *channels* as means or agencies of speaking	The interpreter has only one input and that is the oral channel. The interpreter needs to be aware of different registers, varieties, etc. used by both the speaker and the listener. The situation allows for negotiation and clarification.	The interpreter may have more than one input since the oral channel may be complemented by visual or written modes projected on a screen. The interpreter needs to be aware of different registers, varieties, etc. used by the speaker. There is no room for negotiation or clarification.
N. **(Norms)** rules of interaction ("rules of governing speaking") and norms of interpretation: ("the belief system of a community and how that interacts with the frame of reference for under-standing utterances")	*Norms of interaction:* rules governing speaking	The interpreter will see a wide variety of interactions during this event. Often, the OCR officer and the non-English speaker (NES) do not share the same sense of appropriateness of ways of speaking. For example, if the NES is from Argentina, overlapping will be the rule during a conversation, while the officer may expect turn-taking.	The interpreter will not see many interactions during this conference, except for the period of questions and answers. Generally, speaker and audience share the same sense of appropriateness of asking and answering questions in public.
	Norms of interpretation: the belief system of a com-munity and how that interacts with the frame of references for understanding utterances	Generally, the interpreter will have a two-way focus on interpretation of utterances. He will be concerned about how to portray the speaker in a way that is acceptable to the listener and vice versa. If the driver is a Korean, she/he will probably not look the officer in the eyes;	Generally, the interpreter will have a one-way focus on interpretation of utterances. He will be concerned about how to portray the speaker in a way that is acceptable to the interaction of the target audience (again, the exception being the period of questions and *(Continued)*

TABLE 7.1   (Continued)

		if the officer is not familiar with Korean culture, he will probably be suspicious. The interpreter will need to be on the watch!	answers when it will be a two-way concern).
G. **(Genres)** including the "categories of speech (e.g. poem, myth, tale, proverb, riddle, curse, prayer, oration, lecture, etc.); though often coincidental with speech event, genres must be treated as analytically independent"	*Genres:* categories of speech (e.g. poem, myth, tale, proverb, riddle, curse, prayer, oration, lecture, etc.); though often coincidental with speech events, genres must be treated as analytically independent.	The interpreter will benefit from recognizing the genre of the speech that does not always coincide with the event. For example, the officer may lecture the community member about a certain occurrence but certainly the event is not a lecture.	The interpreter will benefit from recognizing the genre of the speech that does not always coincide with the event. For example, the marketing expert may be giving part of a sermon to imitate a priest's advice to use the new model Laville [not the actual name], but he will most definitely not be preaching.

translator was not a simple "channel" in the communication process, but a spokesperson for the people whose messages were translated. Hymes' original thinking did not directly consider this role. After applying this approach, Angelelli observed that the system revealed something very important: conference translation techniques were inadequate for community translation. She concluded that when translators attempt to use conference translation techniques in community translation tasks,

> [t]his blind transfer does not allow a full understanding of the complexities involved in community interpreting. Hymes' taxonomy of speaking is used to compare and analyze two interpreting events, one occurring in a community setting and the other in a conference one. The analysis suggests that there are more differences than similarities between the two settings. (p. 580)

By application of Hymes' system to her qualitative data, Angelelli was able to identify priorities for training community translators and to suggest the helpfulness of the Hymes approach for other qualitative research.

5. keeping records and observations

Keeping Records and Observations

While attempting not to distract participants from their ordinary actions, researchers maintain records of the things they have recalled and observed. These pieces of information are the hard data to be analyzed later. Often the setting requires that they keep records "on the run." Researchers try to record words and phrases they hear, the sequences of events, and their impressions. Though some researchers seem to invest a small lifetime into making observations, others set time limits on their entry into a setting. They frequently leave the setting and attempt to give themselves some room to "clear their minds" and organize their thoughts. The quality of a participant observation study is only as good as the records kept by researchers. Hence, the following questions are often raised to decide whether reports are sound ones (after Lofland & Lofland, 1984, p. 51):

Question:	Evaluation of Answer:
1. Is the report firsthand?	Hearsay may be very inaccurate.
2. Where was the observer?	The observer should be in a position to see or hear what is described.
3. Did the participant have a reason to give false or biased information?	Information from biased sources is unreliable. Participants who cannot tell the truth cannot give solid information to draw conclusions.
4. Is the report internally consistent?	Equivocal information prevents drawing clear conclusions.
5. Can the report be validated by other independent reports?	Reliance on isolated reports from participants may be unreliable.

Fieldnotes. It cannot be overstated that the quality of the fieldnotes kept by the qualitative researcher can make or break an ethnography. With camcorders, digital cameras, and audio recording devices so readily available, many researchers have begun to rely on them to the near exclusion of written fieldnotes. Yet—and this matter is a big exception—the use of fieldnotes cannot be avoided in qualitative work. Solid ethnography and participant observation research requires that some effort to be systematic is employed in the process of taking and managing fieldnotes.

importance of fieldnotes in ethnography

To accomplish the task of keeping solid fieldnotes, researchers have to develop some competence. Thus, if more than one person is involved in the process of observation, it will be necessary for some sort of training to occur. In her preparation for ethnographic research into the condition of impoverished women and children under the welfare system, Burton (2004) found it necessary to have her team of ethnographers trained in a workshop at her university, prior to proposing her own training.

training may be required

> Each ethnographer is being provided with a variety of documentary support that further explains the research themes and methods. These include a "structured discovery" document that sets forth the primary and secondary goals of the ethnography and a "fieldnotes procedures" document that explains basic protocols to follow in writing and coding fieldnotes. The "buckets" or core coding categories included in the latter document represent the core theoretical questions being addressed in the ethnography, and will remind ethnographers of the major themes to be explored through participant observation and interviews. (pp. 64–65)

Though the details of what is to be observed cannot be specified in advance, there are some things that are known to be important when the research begins (without some direction, the researcher may simply be overwhelmed). Burton called these elements "buckets" or "core coding categories." Not every researcher may include such detailed guidance, but obvious directions for attention should be made objects of training.

requirements for fieldnotes content   Crafting the fieldnote is a little bit of an art, but there are some things that must be part of any set of fieldnotes (Hall, 2005, ¶¶ 5–9). Most qualitative researchers jot things down (words and phrases that were overheard) in notebooks or on note cards while they are in the field and then prepare a formal set of fieldnotes as soon afterward as they can. In addition to such material, researchers make a point of including descriptions of things that occurred, whether or not they relate directly to the research question. Any analysis that reveals what the field researcher has learned is to be included so that the big picture can emerge. Questions often arise in this step about both the research problem and the additional information that may be needed to address it. Barbara Hall suggests concentrating on such questions as these: "What themes can you begin to identify regarding your guiding question? What questions do you have to help focus your observation on subsequent visits? Can you begin to draw preliminary connections or potential conclusions based on what you learned?" (2005, ¶ 6). Finally, of course, researchers are encouraged to reflect personally on their own feelings about the field experiences. Since ethnographers embrace the ways in which researchers use perceptions and feelings to enlighten the process, it is important for them to reveal something of their own along the way.

organization of usable fieldnotes   To be usable, the fieldnotes must be organized to include information that can help explore the research question (and lead to new ones). Taking one's jottings, descriptions, analytical thoughts, and feelings, and making them usable requires organizing the material. Usable fieldnotes tend to have sections dedicated to the following items (Chiseri-Strater & Sunstein, 1997, p. 73):

- Date, time, and place of observation (including start and stop times)
- Specific facts, numbers, details of what happens at the site
- Sensory impressions: sights, sounds, textures, smells, tastes
- Personal responses to the fact of recording fieldnotes
- Specific words, phrases, summaries of conversations, and insider language
- Questions about people or behaviors at the site for future investigation
- Page numbers to help keep observations in order

Since the fieldnotes are pieces of the raw material for the research, scholars must make sure that they are orderly and usable.

importance of writing fieldnotes immediately after leaving the fieldsite   Above all, it is vital for researchers to write their fieldnotes **"as soon as possible after leaving the fieldsite,** immediately if possible. Even though we may not think so when we are participating and observing, we are all very likely to forget important details unless we write them down very quickly" (Hall, 2005, ¶ 2, emphasis in original). Many field researchers find that it is important to set aside times to complete the fieldnotes (many do fieldwork in the day and write fieldnotes at night, or vice versa).

Qualitative Interviews. The material in Chapter 9 shows the ways that information may be gathered by both interviews and questionnaires. These sorts of measures produce data that are typical of the kind used in quantitative studies. Even so, interviews are described that may be open-ended or highly structured. Many of the techniques for phrasing and organizing questions may be used in qualitative studies as well. Yet, the qualitative interview is a form that carries the unstructured interview to a new level. In particular terms, the **qualitative interview** attempts to obtain detailed information that reveals the reasons behind what is actually being said.[3] In many ways, the interview appears much more like a conversation than a formal interview.

> **Qualitative interview**
> an unstructured interview method aimed toward discussing topics in depth.

As a tool of ethnography, though it is sometimes used as its own research method, the qualitative interview may be used to answer research questions that require delving into matters of intimacy, privacy, or even aberrant behavior. In her examination of families coping with the tragedy that is Alzheimer's disease, Denise Polk (2005) used qualitative interviews to gather basic information that eventually was used for her interpretive analysis. Over a six-month period, she engaged in interviews with caregivers who had a blood-related relative with Alzheimer's disease. Following an hour-long interview designed mostly to build rapport, she decided whom to contact for extended interviews over time. Open-ended interview questions and probes were prepared for subsequent interviews. Five monthly telephone interviews were scheduled for caregivers. To maintain rapport, the interviewer began each exchange with a reference to something that had gone before, such as the prompt "You mentioned that you planned to take your wife to a picnic. Tell me about that experience" (p. 263). Eventually, Polk had transcripts of 102 single-spaced pages. By analyzing their accounts of communication associated with the caregiving process, she found that caregivers were most preoccupied about three things. First, caregivers shared confidence in their abilities to tell when the person with Alzheimer's disease experienced actual pleasure and displeasure. Second, caregivers avoided blaming the disease entirely for the behavior of the person with Alzheimer's disease. Third, caregivers "reported increased patience when they believed that AD [Alzheimer's disease] caused a loss of functioning" (Polk, 2005, p. 265). Fourth, caregivers reported using humor as a coping mechanism. Fifth, caregivers reported using efforts to gather additional knowledge and to use ordinary distractions (such as coloring or playing BINGO) to relieve their own tensions. The author believed that the study had revealed an important relationship between uncertainty and ambiguity.

example of a qualitative interview study

A qualitative interview is an unstructured interview, which means that although researchers interact with respondents by asking for details, such as explanations and clarifications, researchers do not guide the respondents to any type of response on

qualitative interviews do not guide respondents to particular variables

---

[3]Though writers distinguish between "qualitative," "depth," and "creative" interviews, for this introductory treatment, details of these contrasts will not be addressed.

particular variables. Naturally, the process can be time-consuming since it involves using indirect methods in ways that are similar to nondirective therapy. The entire process is a combination of an attitude and a set of question strategies.

qualitative interviewers adopt an attitude of responsive listening

The researcher must adopt the attitude of a willingness to listen responsively. Not only do qualitative interviewers ask the right questions, but they actively show that they are paying attention. Such behavior as using facial expressions that show concern, nodding one's head, and giving the respondent active eye contact are nonverbal signs that attention is being paid and that the interviewee has a willing listener. Such behavior can reinforce the ability of the interviewee to open up and respond with candor. On a verbal level, asking for additional explanations and information often is all it takes to communicate a desire to listen. Naturally, communicating a desire to listen is something that cannot be faked over a long time period, and some people are better at showing this people-orientation than others. Yet, "when you do want to listen and respond empathically, you must shift the focus to your partner and try to understand the message from his or her perspective" (Beebe, Beebe, & Ivy, 2004, p. 120). The process starts with a desire to understand the other's feelings. "You attempt to decenter—consider what someone may be thinking—by first projecting how you might feel, followed by appropriate questions and paraphrases to confirm the accuracy of your assumptions" (p. 120). This attitude means that qualitative interviewers have to be willing to be empathic people as a precondition for their work.

qualitative interviewers use strategic questions

qualitative interviewers try to make the interviewee look interesting

A set of question and response strategies also guides researchers. Since a qualitative interview strongly resembles a conversation between friends, the questions often appear to reveal something from the experience of the interviewer. The researcher may have a general outline of the issues that should be discussed, but the manner of phrasing those questions is not set in concrete. Though in conversation, all members of the exchange want to be interesting, when it comes to the qualitative interview, the interviewer's "desire to appear interesting is counterproductive. The interviewer needs to make the other person seem interesting, by being interested—and is listening more than talking" (Babbie, 2003, p. 302). Frequently, however, questions appear to provide reactions from interviewers, such as "I was really interested in what you said about the way the doctor told you about your father's illness. What made it stand out for you?" or "I like the way you said that. Did anything else make you concerned about your father's hospital care?" In each case, the seemingly personal comments are designed to encourage others to speak. There are several sorts of questions that researchers ask in qualitative interviews. Patton (1990) identified five types of questions:

types of interview questions

- ♦ experience/behavior questions (e.g., What do you do to cope with the stress of caring for a father with Alzheimer's disease?);
- ♦ opinion/belief questions (e.g., What do you think of treating Alzheimer's patients in hospitals?);
- ♦ feeling questions (e.g., How did you feel when you first heard that your father had Alzheimer's disease?);
- ♦ knowledge questions (e.g., Have you studied much about Alzheimer's disease?);

- ◆ sensory questions (e.g., I am sensing some hesitance in your answer. Do you find this topic especially troubling?);

- ◆ demographic questions (e.g., How long has your father been diagnosed with Alzheimer's disease?).

To encourage the interviewee to continue the conversation and offer information, **paraphrasing** may be very helpful. Paraphrasing may be introduced by such phrases as "Here's what I understand you to mean. . . ." "So, the point you seem to be making is . . ." "You seem to be saying . . ." and "Are you saying . . . ?" (Beebe, Beebe, & Ivy, 2004, p. 121). After such comments, the researcher may summarize the interviewee's message. If it is an accurate paraphrase, the conversation may continue. If it is not accurate, it may be corrected and the interviewer has avoided making a misinterpretation. Other sorts of comments can also influence people to share additional information, including such methods as these:

> **Paraphrasing** in interviews, summarizing the interviewee's message in one's own words, usually to check understanding.

> *comments to stimulate additional information sharing*

- ◆ *Repetition as a question:* stating the previous comment in question form (e.g., Interviewee: I suspected my father was ill. Interviewer: You suspected he was ill? Interviewee: Yes, he was always forgetting things, like where he left the car keys.)

- ◆ *Request:* directly soliciting information (Interviewer: Tell me more.)

- ◆ *Acquiring meaning:* requests for definitions (e.g., Interviewee: My father went off on me. Interviewer: What do you mean when you say he "went off on you"? Interviewee: He shouted at me.)

- ◆ *Repetition of a key word or phrase:* implicit requests for explanations created by emphasizing something that was previously said (e.g., Interviewee: I was afraid that my father might become violent. Interviewer: Violent. Interviewee: You know, he is a big guy and I was worried that a slap from him would knock me to the floor.)

- ◆ *Asking for an example:* requesting details or instances (e.g., Interviewee: In our family, my father liked to be in charge. Interviewer: Could you give me an example?)

- ◆ *Encouraging comments:* statements that suggest how interesting the conversation is (e.g., "I like the way you said that." "That's really interesting.")

Of this partial list, there is no statement asserting "I understand." Of course, qualitative interviewers may use such a comment to validate the interviewee's participation, but it is not included here to emphasize a point. In the qualitative interview, the researcher needs to acquire information. To do so, it is helpful to appear to be a "socially acceptable incompetent" who is friendly, but who "does not understand. She or he is 'ignorant' and needs to be 'taught.' This role of watcher and asker of questions is the quintessential *student* role" (Lofland & Lofland, 1995, p. 56). In the qualitative interview, the informal nature of things cannot hide the fact that the process is designed to gather information relevant to a research question.

> *qualitative interviewers assume the role of the "socially acceptable incompetent"*

Interpretive Analysis of Data

> *6. interpretive analysis*

The results of participant observation studies involve descriptions of communication settings. Scholars often rely on references to transcendent perspectives (such as phenomenology or symbolic interactionism) to explain their results. Other times they may look at the language of communicators to find the underlying structures or "grammars." Researchers may look at the so-called surface devices that people use to express themselves. Or they may search for evidence of "deep structures" that underlie language use. In reality, there is no real limit on the imagination of researchers in finding creative ways to assess their results.

One of the most popular methods has been the development of the "interpretive approach" (Denzin, 1983). This method identifies communicators' interactions to determine such things as the situations in which people find themselves, the structures within which they work, and the practical features of their world. Researchers frequently listen to the stories people tell and their use of language. Laura Dorsey (2003) participated in an interpretive analysis of the stories, conversation, and language of a group of African American women who revealed their life experiences through active communication with one another. Since the group was led by an African American woman, it permitted the discussions to be particularly frank. Dorsey was joined by another researcher (who was not a participant in the group discussion), and together they examined the language and themes communicated by the women. The researchers found that the communication by the women gravitated around the themes of issues of inclusion and exclusion and an expressed desire for increased connection and relationships with African American men. By looking at the language and stories of communicators, you can interpret the function of messages to structure reality in specific social settings.

As another matter, the conclusions reached by ethnographers often can be evaluated by their contribution to explaining things that were not previously known. Regrettably—and this matter is a fault of researchers, not the method—many conclusions of ethnographies make little new contribution. "What ethnographers always find [is]: that people act collaboratively and that what outsiders think of as the product of individual personality is in fact the result of social interaction" (Katz, 1997, pp. 400–401). To offer interpretations that are meaningful and worthy of the time and expense of ethnographic work, the conclusions should be stated directly and deal with insights that were not previously understood.

Exiting the Field Setting

Though it may seem obvious, participant observers need to set a time at which they exit the setting (at least as researchers). Yet, many participant observation researchers develop personal attachments to other participants and have a difficult time leaving the research setting. Moreover, if researchers "go native" and never leave the setting, they may lose their ability to make scholarly contributions. Participant observation researchers are usually expected to make arrangements in advance to terminate the research process. Researchers who end the experience unexpectedly and abruptly may create additional troubles. Participants may feel used and irritated. If the researcher wishes to renew contact at another time, he or she might find the participants to be reluctant. Thus, the timing and manner of exiting the research setting should be scheduled at the time the research is begun. Though many fieldworkers ignore this part of the project, they soon learn how important it is.

SPECIAL DISCUSSION 7-3

A QUESTION OF ETHICS: ETHICAL PREDICAMENTS IN QUALITATIVE RESEARCH

Since qualitative researchers do not specifically rely on experimental methods, many have assumed that the ethical treatment of study participants is not really an issue. In fact, these matters can become increasingly subtle and challenging. Two experts on qualitative methods explained (Edwards & Mauthner, 2002, p. 13):

> The issue of informed consent has been subject to fierce debate among qualitative social researchers generally: in particular the ethics of carrying out covert research (see reviews in Hornsby-Smith, 1993; Lee, 1993; May 1993; Wise, 1987) and the nature and time frame of consent (David et al., 2001; Denzin, 1997; Morrow & Richards, 1996). The time frame involved in assessing the benefits or harm of social research has also been an issue in discussion (for example, Wise, 1987).

Thus, qualitative researchers dedicate a serious amount of time to assuring ethical choices are made in the research. In addition to the role of the researcher as an overt or covert observer (a matter covered elsewhere in this chapter), at least three other ethical issues remain troublesome: whether efforts at informed consent are credible, developing insincere rapport with participants in the field, and dealing with emotional consequences of research on the researchers and their associates.

The Credibility of Informed Consent in Qualitative Research

If the researcher requests permission to enter a field setting, the consent requires that the study participants—the people observed—know what they are getting into. Researchers in the social sciences, regardless of whether they use qualitative or quantitative methods, are obligated to live "by a code of ethics dictating that no harm should be done to research participants, that participation in research is voluntary, that participants must be informed about the research they are participating in, and that their privacy and confidentiality be maintained" (Martin & Butler, 2001, p. 284). This general set of ethical guides usually requires that qualitative researchers, ethnographers, and fieldworkers assure confidentiality and voluntariness and, when possible, secure informed consent. Yet, qualitative researchers may have particular difficulty assuring informed consent and voluntariness in their work. The reason is that details of qualitative research often emerge during the process of doing a study. Hence, it is not always possible to let study participants know what they are "in for." Their voluntariness and the informed consent may not be very meaningful in the absence of full disclosure from the researchers.

One troublesome ethical dilemma involved Linda Nutt's qualitative study of "how foster carers make sense of their everyday lives in relation to their own families and to the 'extra' children for whom they care" (Bell & Nutt, 2002, p. 75). Though she was a social worker, she conducted qualitative interviews with foster care providers who were not on her client list. She assured confidentiality of information and explained what could be expected during the process of conducting the interviews.

> As she was leaving the home of a new carer following the research interview Linda Nutt noticed an unambiguously sexually explicit picture in the hallway. For most

(Continued)

SPECIAL DISCUSSION 7-3 (Continued)

researchers this would not be an issue: art is a matter of personal taste. But Linda Nutt wasn't just a researcher [*sic*] she was also a practitioner. Frequently when children are placed in foster homes little is known about their life experience [*sic*] so new carers are instructed to assume that all children have been sexually abused unless specifically told otherwise. It is thus always considered essential not to give fostered children messages that could be interpreted as in any way sexual. . . . confidentiality is an absolute for researchers but cannot always be for practitioners. There is a statutory responsibility to disregard confidentiality where children are at risk." (Bell & Nutt, 2002, p. 79)

She eventually decided to report the foster carer to the National Foster Care Association and to renege on her promise of confidentiality. Clearly, the process of the observation was more than the foster carer was told it could be. Fieldwork is often touted as dynamic and exciting, but its changing qualities also mean that the researcher may find out things that make living up to promises very difficult.

Developing Insincere Rapport with Participants in the Field

In much qualitative research, the researcher must enter the research setting and quickly establish rapport with study participants. Some feminist scholars claim that women studying women often gain a sense of rapport that is emotionally supportive, egalitarian, and reciprocal. In contrast, many research methods books take the view that rapport is instrumental (designed to get information from the other person), hierarchical (controlled by the researcher), and nonreciprocal (getting information from the research participants, but not from the researcher) (Duncombe & Jessop, 2002, p. 108). When nearly unlimited time is available to the researchers, there is a lot to be said for this position. Yet, Jean Duncombe and Julie Jessop (2002) note that with single qualitative interviews (often provided by paid interviewers operating with a number of interviews to complete within a certain time period), there may not be much opportunity to develop a true sense of rapport and friendship. They observe that researchers (including some outstanding feminist scholars) engage in an ethically questionable activity they call "faking friendship."

> Rapport is tantamount to trust, and trust is the foundation for acquiring the fullest, most accurate disclosure a respondent is able to make. . . . In an effective interview, both researcher and respondent feel good, rewarded, and satisfied by the process and the outcomes. The warm and caring researcher is on the way to achieving such effectiveness. (Glesne & Peshkin, 1992, pp. 79, 87)

Of course, the rapport appears to be one-sided. The interviewer wants the rapport to create a sense of trust that will enable the participant to reveal useful information. The purpose is to get information from the participant that will be relevant to the research project. The perceived friendship will be terminated quickly, and the information sharing is one-way only.

The ethical bind created by faked friendships is threefold. First, the participant is led to expect a certain amount of dialogue that is typical at the beginning of a new friendship. Yet, short-term qualitative interviewers terminate the friendship as soon as the interview is over. Such feelings of rejection engendered so shortly after the beginning of a new friendship can create very real feelings of rejection and self-doubt. Second, to build rapport based on the use of a few techniques, such as keeping "eye contact, speaking in a friendly tone, never challenge, and avoid inappropriate expressions of surprise or disapproval; and practice the art of the encouraging by 'non-directive "um"'" (Duncombe & Jessop, 2002, p. 110) means that the study participant is manipulated to reveal information. "If interviewees are persuaded to participate in the interview by the researcher's show of empathy and the rapport achieved in conversation, how far can they be said to have given their 'informed consent' to make the disclosures that emerge during the interview?" (Duncombe & Jessop, 2002, p. 111). The techniques used to build rapport help the qualitative researcher control the agenda and "manage the consent" of the study participant. In fact, by "doing rapport 'too effectively' interviewers run the risk of breaching the interviewees' 'right *not* to know' their own innermost thoughts" (Duncombe & Jessop, 2002, p. 112). A third problem is that the methods of doing rapport for short-term effects may lead the researcher to agree or even reinforce offensive statements made by respondents. "Listening to views, nodding or saying simple 'ums' or 'I see' to views you strongly disagree with" (Luff, 1999, p. 698) could make the researcher feel like a hypocrite. Strategic friendliness may, in fact, seem to be taken as social support for views that by other standards should not be treated with so little critical attention.

Emotional Consequences for Researchers

Though such organizations as Institutional Review Boards are concerned with the possible negative impact of the research on study participants, they generally do not care much if researchers place themselves at risk. After all, the free choice was theirs from the beginning. They need not take chances if they do not wish. Yet, researchers may not work alone. Qualitative researchers with financial support for their projects often hire students or outside staff to help them with project details, such as preparing transcripts of fieldnotes or interviews. This sort of problem is an ethical challenge that is rarely addressed, despite its great effects.

  Kathleen Gilbert (1987/1988; also Gilbert & Smart, 1992) examined interviews with couples who had lost babies during pregnancy or whose babies had died in infancy. Among other things, she was concerned with the ways that husbands and wives communicated with each other during their process of grieving. Gilbert hired a number of young women (aged 18 to 21) to transcribe the qualitative interviews into written form. Gilbert told the transcribers to speak with her if they found the interviews too upsetting. Most of her students soon became listless, "lackadaisical . . . , often making errors in their typing and missing deadlines" (Gilbert 2001, p. 151). Gilbert soon learned that reviewing the interviews shocked and horrified the research assistants. One assistant reported that the material was "really upsetting" and described her feelings with phrases including "'made me angry,' 'felt like crying,' and 'wanted to hit someone'" (Gilbert, 2001, p. 151). Some reported feelings of guilt over not being able to help the grief-stricken parents. Yet others reported "thinking about the [parents] . . . and their babies, even dreaming about them at unpredictable times" (Gilbert, 2001, p. 152). To avoid the twin problems of overinvolvement and underinvolvement by research staff members, Gilbert suggested extending protection of study participants to staff members as well, obtaining help for those needing additional assistance, and holding regular meetings to monitor stress levels. Not all qualitative research involves such risk to staff members, but it is interesting to note that so far, formal protections in social science ethics codes focus on the risks to study participants and fairly well ignore risks to research staff members.

limitations:

1. *time-consuming and expensive*

2. *unknown measurement properties*

Limitations of the Approach

Though participant observation methods have many benefits, there are limits on the approach.[4] First, these methods are very time-consuming and expensive. The amount of labor and required finances make them impractical for many research outings.

Second, and perhaps most obvious, is the fact that such work tends to rest on measurement whose properties are unknown. Since researchers rarely have the privilege of using standardized research tools, inquiries may suffer from measurement deficiencies. Certainly, there are scholars (e.g., Altheide & Johnson, 1998) who believe that measurement issues are largely irrelevant to qualitative research such as ethnography. Yet, Anne Lacey and Donna Luff explain, "Reliability and validity are important issues in all research including qualitative research. Demonstrating that your qualitative data analysis is rigorous is especially important given a common criticism (from those less favourable to qualitative research) that qualitative results are anecdotal" (2001, p. 22; see additional support from Kuzel & Engel, 2001; Mays & Pope, 2000). Though in qualitative research the concept of reliability has been replaced with "dependability" and the concept of validity has been replaced with the concern for "trustworthiness," the concern for demonstrating these matters remains more of a desire than a reality. Indeed, the *Journal of Communication* website (www.icahdq.org/membership/publications.html#joc) lists this advice about trustworthiness for qualitative researchers: "Qualitative research should articulate the standards employed to assure the quality and verification of the interpretation presented (e.g., member-checking, negative case analysis)" (¶ 17). The tools of member checking and negative case analysis are recommended to examine the tenability of trustworthiness of qualitative studies. Though some researchers disagree with this concern for trustworthiness, it remains the case that research based on measures that are not trustworthy may not be stable.

3. *overidentification with a group leading to researcher bias*

Third, the participant observers can become overidentified with a group. By becoming an active participant, a researcher may develop biases and sympathies that color the fairness and accuracy of reports or interpretations. A researcher may begin subconsciously to report what he or she expected or what may put the studied group in the best light. Moreover, though they may try to avoid influencing the group, the behavior of participant observers might alter actions seen in the natural setting. The prudent researcher must be careful of such tendencies. You should know that some scholars believe that such notions as "researcher bias" come from a set of assumptions that are not really relevant to ethnography. Perhaps. But you should expect to see these questions asked when such research is presented.

4. *cannot reach comprehensive conclusions alone*

Fourth, naturalistic studies cannot reach comprehensive conclusions without combining many different sorts of data. There is a tendency to draw fascinating conclusions from sketchy evidence. Yet, in participant observation work, conclusions probably cannot be argued successfully unless many different sorts of information are available.

---

[4]The first three limits are drawn from the discussion by Berg (1989, pp. 83–84).

Fifth, though it may not be much of a limitation for the many talented students reading this book, including you, ethnographic research requires talent to complete successfully. Many details of an ethnographic study must be addressed on the fly. Facing the many unexpected problems requires using one's gifts to make a project succeed. Qualitative research "is not, however, an easy option or the route to a quick answer. As Dingwall et al. [1998] conclude, 'qualitative research requires real skill, a combination of thought and practice and not a little patience'" (Mays & Pope, 2000, p. 52).

5. requires particular talent

QUALITATIVE RESEARCH IN ACTION

Qualitative research extends beyond ethnographic and participant observation research. In fact, qualitative research methods are a sort of growth industry in communication research methods. Some of the most popular methods have been grounded theory approaches, use of focus groups, and autoethnography. Each of these approaches will be considered in turn.

Grounded Theory

Despite the name, grounded theory is not a specific theory. Instead, **grounded theory** is a way of organizing research to lead to the development of theory. It is "grounded" in repeated returning to the field to generate and examine the tenability of different explanations. Grounded theory goes back to work completed by sociologists Barney Glaser and Anselm Strauss while they were examining the process of dying in hospitals, particularly in the teaching hospital at the University of California, San Francisco, where they also were on the faculty. Their work in developing the grounded theory research method was originally explained in the 1967 book *The Discovery of Grounded Theory*. In this volume, they identified the objective of grounded theory as finding "a core category, at a high level of abstraction but grounded in the data, which accounts for what is central in the data" (Punch, 2005, p. 205).

grounded theory is a method, not a theory

> **Grounded theory** a set of explanations that has immediate relevance to a specific field setting under investigation. Participant observers attempt to discover categories to describe their observations after they have entered the field. Then, researchers make additional observations to refine and modify these categories and potentially develop theory.

The Stages of Grounded Theory

The general process of grounded theory may be introduced to give you an idea of the way this approach is used in qualitative research.[5]

grounded theory stages

---

[5]Grounded theory is linked to qualitative research methods. Yet, though it was developed to study social behavior using qualitative data, the method itself is a general approach to gathering evidence to examine related statements. Grounded theory "is equally applicable to quantitative data, especially in Glaser's view" (Punch, 2005, p. 157). In fact, many examples in *The Discovery of Grounded Theory* deal with quantitative data.

1. *state the problem and find a location to study it*

Stage 1:[6] Instead of starting with a theoretic framework, begin with a general subject or research problem and identify a location where it could be studied. Then, with a clear desire to "avoid theoretical preconceptions [and] ignoring the literature in that area (at first)" (Dey, 1999, p. 4), the researchers rely on field observations (using various tactical methods including interviews, documentary analysis, and participant observation) to find categories that show uniformity in the data. The actual record-keeping of such observations is called **coding.**

Coding in grounded theory, "the process of deciding how to conceptually divide up raw qualitative data" (Lacey & Luff, 2001, p. 34).

> Sections of text transcripts, for example, may be marked by the researcher in various ways (underlining in a coloured pen, given a numerical reference, or bracketed with a textual code in the margin). These sections contain data which the researcher is interested in exploring and analysing further. In the early stages of analysis, most if not all sections of the text will be marked and given different "codes" depending on their content. As the analysis progresses these codes will be refined or combined to form themes or categories of issues. (Lacey & Luff, 2001, p. 34)

Open coding in grounded theory, "initial familiarisation with the data" (Lacey & Luff, 2001, p. 7) with no initial categories.

In this initial stage of theory-free exploration, this process is known as **open coding** because no initial categories exist to guide researchers. In communication research, the examination of message-related behavior is key. Hence, when looking at ways people attempt to finding meaning, a rich set of information could be "coded" or observed. In this process, Strauss (1987, p. 30) gave four guidelines for open coding: (1) ask the data a specific and consistent set of questions; (2) analyze the data minutely; (3) frequently interrupt the coding to write a theoretic note called a **memo;** and (4) never assume the analytic relevance of any traditional variables such as age, sex, or socioeconomic status.

gaidelines for open coding

When this initial sifting of the open coding is completed, patterns may emerge that suggest explanations and even directions for theory. This inductive thinking pattern, however, involves creative thinking about the meaning of many separate pieces of information.

Memo in grounded theory, a note the researcher makes about the meaning of a category or property, or about possible relationships among categories.

> In the process of emergence, the research[ers] had to rely on their own "theoretical sensitivity" to generate relevant categories from the data. The researchers had to be able to think theoretically—to glean insights from the evidence, to conceptualize their data, and then to analyze relationships between concepts. (Dey, 1999, p. 4)

Theoretical sensitivity the ability "to see the research situation and its associated data in new ways, and to explore the data's potential for developing theory" (Strauss & Corbin, 1990, p. 44).

Theoretical sensitivity is a loose concept that involves a process of thinking creatively to derive concepts and explanations. There is little in the way of a method involved in this "theoretical sensitivity" and, hence, the system depends on a certain amount of innate talent by the researcher.

2. *develop initial categories and use theoretically based sampling*

Stage 2: After developing an initial set of categories and some theoretical ideas, theoretically informed data sampling could be used.

> Theoretical sampling is the process of data collection for generating theory whereby the analyst jointly collects, codes and analyzes his data and decides

---

[6]Though we call them stages or steps, you should know that their order is routinely altered in actual research.

what data to collect next and where to find them, in order to develop his theory as it emerges. This process of data collection is controlled by the emerging theory. . . . (Glaser & Strauss, 1967, p. 45)

Unlike scientific research where the analysis of data follows the data collection, this approach makes sampling choices based on previous analyses. The new sampling looks to new sites where there would be interesting comparisons to be made. Instead of sampling for the purpose of getting a "representative" set of observations from a population, researchers look for new samples that would show increased variation or even negative cases to observe.

Stage 3: After the field observations are made and the coding system is used, the researchers can cycle back and forth to enter the field and check the new revision against the new data—after which, they can revise the work and enter another field setting again, and so on. Glaser and Strauss suggested that this **constant comparative method** is essential in the process of developing grounded theory. It is helpful to understand that the researchers are *not* attempting to find cases or field sites that simply support the emerging theory's revision. Since the theorizing is already based on an observation, these researchers attempt to find settings where the emerging theory is challenged. Searching for field sites with large variability and showing contrasts with previously used field sites is designed to promote finding such examples, which may lead to increasingly sophisticated theoretic explanations. One tool of this process is the search for exceptional or "negative cases" that seem to contradict the categories in the emerging theory. Rather than avoid such negative cases, the researchers attempt to identify them so that further theoretic refinements may be made.

Researchers do not just appreciate the new field observations they have made. Instead, they use these matters to revise and improve their emerging theories. This process involves elaborating on relationships and categories of the emerging theory. **Elaboration** in this sense indicates that the details for the category get reexamined. In the presence of generally or partially disconfirming cases, elaboration involves including additional properties of a category and reconsidering it.

The grounded theory process is illustrated in Figure 7.2. In this figure, the use of theoretically based sampling leads to finding cases that do not support the categories in grounded theory. Identifying these "inconsistent" cases is the primary task of analysis in most grounded theory research. After identifying these inconsistent cases, an opportunity is taken to elaborate and revise the categories in the grounded theory model. Researchers in this tradition find that most of their time is spent on the cycle from field site observations three through N (the number of field site observations completed before the work is finished) to analysis that still shows inconsistent or negative cases, back to the revision or elaboration of categories using the coding systems, and then to a new field site observation.

Stage 4: After the observation of inconsistent or negative cases begins to wane, the process of grounded theory produces a set of vital categories and a grounded theory emerges. This stage of the work occurs when the alternatives have been systematically rejected and a tenable survivor remains through a process of reasoning by residues. At this point, returning to the field has reached a level of **theoretical saturation,** where the field data produce only trivial amounts of new information

3. repeated checks against data; then theory revisions

Constant comparative method in grounded theory, "concepts or categories emerging from one stage of the data analysis are compared with concepts emerging from the next. The researcher looks for relationships between these concepts and categories, by constantly comparing them, to form the basis of the emerging theory" (Lacey & Luff, 2001. p. 7).

Elaboration in grounded theory, "elaboration involves developing and examining its variation systematically" (Punch, 2005, p. 214).

revisions occur through elaboration

4. after inconsistent cases cease being found, a theory is advanced

Theoretical saturation in grounded theory, the point at which "no new significant categories or concepts are emerging" (Lacey & Luff, 2001. p. 7) from the process of constant comparison despite a reasonable search.

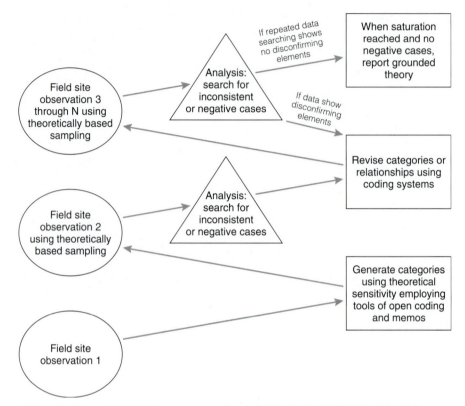

FIGURE 7.2   THE FLOW OF GROUNDED THEORY RESEARCH

about the chief categories and concepts. The researchers may cease coding those categories and advance the grounded theory. Of course, the researcher must have made a thorough search of fields where inconsistent or negative cases might be found. It is not possible to claim theoretical saturation if one simply avoids looking for the contrary cases.

steps taken to assure credibility of qualitative studies

Researchers of this tradition also take steps to assure that their methods are rigorous. Some basic techniques used to assure the credibility of qualitative data (and described in Chapter 4) are routine matters for ground theory studies. Such techniques as extended participation in the field experience, persistent observation, negative case analysis, referential adequacy, member checks, and dependability audits (Lincoln & Guba, 1985, pp. 304–315) are typical of grounded theory studies.

applications of grounded theory

Grounded theory studies have been popular in communication. Standard applications of this method have been frequent enough. For instance, Tamara Afifi and Stacia Keith (2004) developed a model of family resiliency to nondeath losses to the family structure. Based on a string of qualitative interviews with 81 stepfamily members, they refined a theoretic framework and found that family members' communicative responses to the loss of the nuclear family, a single-parent bond, or a noncustodial parent-child bond could be explained by levels of open "communication among family members, and the contextual factors surrounding divorce and re-marriage" (p. 65).

Yet, the most common application of grounded theory in communication has been in using open coding strategies to derive themes to open-ended comments in interviews. Many communication researchers have found this part of grounded theory to be most valuable. For instance, Myers and Bryant (2004) took inspiration from the open coding method of grounded theory to content-analyze the themes college students used to indicate their views of how teachers communicated classroom credibility. They explained:

> Using the constant comparative approach, each example was compared to prior data for its similarity or difference. Each time an example was perceived as different from a previous example, a new category was added. This was an iterative process, as categories were added, combined, and revised in an emergent manner until the set of categories did not require further modification with additional data cases." (p, 24)

Julia Wood (2004) used a similar method to construct themes from interviews with 22 men who had been violent toward women with whom they lived. She explored the research question "How do men account for their own intimate partner violence and how [do] their accounts draw upon understandings of manhood" (p. 555). She used open coding methods to derive three categories of themes: justifications (such as. "she provoked me;" "she took it"), dissociations (such as "my violence was limited, and abusers don't limit their abuse"), and remorse ("I regret I abused her"). She looked for divergences from these themes and explained them by the different codes of manhood that were common among those in prison. Mazur and Hubbard (2004) also used open coding to derive 12 strategies of communication responses adolescents used to avoid revealing information to their parents.

Limitations of Grounded Theory

For all its usefulness, grounded theory has been the object of some criticism. In the first place, the notion that one can set aside all theory and make an initial set of observations of raw phenomena is generally considered to be naïve. Without at least some implicit theories that can be used to guide early analyses, it is difficult to understand how researchers would even know what behavior to select for examination. In the second place, an advantage of grounded theory—that it strives for verification—may, in fact, be inconsistent with the goals of much qualitative research in a postmodern world (Glaser, 1992, esp. pp. 29–30). In the third place, the reiterative effort to identify categories so that they include all possible examples of behavior to be coded strikes some as searching for a general set of terms that then may be forced on data, rather than helping to explain it. There currently is a small war under way among people who take different looks at grounded theory and who wonder about its future (Dey, 1999, pp. 14–23). Finally, it should be mentioned that many researchers who claim to use grounded theory stop after developing categories. Though there may be some justification for this approach when completing forms of content analysis, this premature halting means that the strength of grounded

Limitations of grounded theory:

1. implicit theories always present during initial theory-free field observations

2. verification may be inconsistent with qualitative methods

3. the reiterative process may force categories on data

4. researchers often stop after initial categorization

theory in constant comparison may be lost. Though this criticism is of researchers and not the method, it remains disappointing that the fullness of this method is not used as regularly as we might wish.

The Focus Group Survey

focus group purposes

In a **focus group** a carefully selected collection of people is interviewed together in a session led by a moderator or facilitator. By asking key questions, the moderator finds the sentiments of the group and the reasons for their views. Unlike many group discussions, focus groups feature controlled group discussion in which infor- mation is gathered to meet the researcher's needs. There are four general purposes of focus groups (Wimmer & Dominick, 1997, p. 97):

> to gather preliminary information for a research project,
>
> to help develop questionnaire items for survey research,
>
> to understand reasons behind a particular phenomenon, or
>
> to test preliminary ideas or plans.

This method can be very helpful in both field and applied settings, and the most prominent uses have been in mass media, advertising, political campaigns, and com- munication and the law. In fact, any time researchers are interested in knowing *why* people feel as they do, rather than the proportions that feel a certain way, focus groups may be appropriate. This distinctive purpose is very important:

> If quantification is important, it is wise to supplement the focus group with other research tools that permit more specific questions to be addressed to a more rep- resentative sample. Many people unfamiliar with focus group research incorrectly assume that the method will answer questions of "how many" or "how much." In fact, focus group research is intended to gather qualitative data to answer ques- tions such as "why" and "how." (Wimmer & Dominick, 1997, p. 98)

*background of the focus group
method*

application of focus groups

The method of focus group interviews was developed during World War II when efforts were made to assess the effectiveness of morale-boosting radio pro- grams (Libresco, 1983; Merton, 1987, p. 552). After the war most work with focus groups was completed by advertising and marketing researchers (Hayes & Tathum, 1989). Yet, in recent years focus groups have become popular in other research fields including family studies (Scantlin & Jordan, 2006), health communication (Burke et al., 2006), speech and hearing science (Markham & Dean, 2006), cultural studies of mass media (Park, Gabbadon, & Chernin, 2006), and organizational com- munication (Pepper & Larson, 2006).

The Focus Group Method

steps for focus groups:

Focus group studies usually involve five general steps (after Wimmer & Dominick, 1997, pp. 99–100, 455–456).

1. assembling groups

1. *Assembling the groups.* Focus groups are not random samples of individuals, though focus groups may be randomly assigned to different conditions where

they may be exposed to different messages. Focus group participants are screened to obtain a particular sample of interest. For instance, researchers might want to sample only people over 45 years old to react to a commercial. Others might wish to create a "shadow jury" composed of people who have the same backgrounds, ages, occupations, and religions as actual jurors in a court trial. In such cases as these, collecting samples is based on careful screening of individuals often by use of a series of questions to make sure that the participants are "qualified" to be in a study.

There is some controversy about the ideal size for a focus group. Some (Morgan, 1998, p. 72) recommend between 6 and 10 participants. Others recommend as many as 12 (Lengua et al., 1992, p. 163). Regardless of the size, the groups are composed of people who are targeted because they possess characteristics of interest to the researchers. Sometimes researchers use only one focus group, but most of the time at least two focus groups are obtained. The participants are typically paid for their time, and most of the time, participants are requested to sign forms in which they promise to keep the focus group discussions confidential.

size ranges from 6 to 12

more than one group typically used

2. *Preparing study mechanics.* The physical surroundings of the focus group are fairly standard. Group participants may be recruited (often by a field service that specializes in securing focus group members) in shopping malls, by telephone, or even by referrals. Once they agree, they may be asked to attend a focus group session, sometimes immediately but often some days later. The session may be at special facilities or perhaps at a conference room in a hotel or motel. In some settings, observers watch the group from behind a one-way mirror. On other occasions, observers may listen to the discussion from another room. The focus group exchanges are recorded on audio- or videotape. A variation of the traditional focus group involves what is called the **telefocus session,** which is completed by teleconferencing methods of one sort or another.

2. preparing study mechanics

Telefocus sessions forms of focus groups in which discussion sessions are completed by teleconferencing methods typically involving telephones or linked computers with visual transmission capabilities.

3. *Preparing focus group session materials and questions.* Experienced focus group leaders prepare a "moderator's guide" that describes the events to occur during the session, their order, and the questions that are to be asked (though the moderator is invited to ask additional unscripted follow-up questions). Many focus group facilitators like to have the participants complete a questionnaire before the formal focus group begins. This step makes sure that the participants are thinking about the topic before the discussion begins. This step may also ask respondents to take a stand on particular issues. By doing so, respondents may be increasingly willing to speak up even if their opinions are in the minority. A set of questions, usually of the open-ended format, are designed to get information from group participants. For instance, in a shadow jury, participants may be asked to watch the trial each day and then indicate what evidence they found most memorable, which lawyers they liked or disliked (and why), and things they did not understand. They might be asked to watch a "rough draft" of an opening statement so that they might give their reactions to it. Regardless of the application, initial questions to be asked of the focus group are prepared in advance.

3. preparing session materials and questions

a presession questionnaire may increase willingness to speak

4. conducting the session

4. *Conducting the session.* The moderator usually introduces the broad topic to the group, and the participants are often presented with some type of stimulus message to get the discussion going. Focus group members may be shown a TV commercial, or they might listen to a radio version of a political campaign message. Then members are asked to begin considering questions related to the topic. The group members are encouraged to respond to others in the group and to link new ideas to others they have heard.

questions not restricted to moderator's guide

Facilitators are not restricted to the questions that are prepared as part of the moderator's guide. Instead, the facilitator is free to explore comments and issues raised by group members. Of course, this exploration requires as much art as preparation on the part of the moderator. Yet, by asking follow-up questions and tracing new ideas, the moderator helps the group complete a thorough analysis of the topic.

challenges to deal with people

Sometimes moderators have to deal with different sorts of group members, including the following (Wimmer & Dominick, 1997, p. 460):

shy people who must be encouraged to speak up;

know-it-all people who must be prevented from dominating the group;

over-talkers who must be encouraged to be brief;

obnoxious people who must be cut off and perhaps removed from the group.

A skillful facilitator is vital in dealing with such different people. Above all else, the moderator must help the members of the focus group work well together despite any differences they may bring with them.

single or multiple meetings

Sometimes focus group deliberations can be completed in one meeting, such as the focus groups collected at shopping malls to react to products and services. Many times, however, focus groups involve many meetings over a period of weeks. Thus, the pacing of sessions becomes an issue of interest. Rather than hold a few lengthy sessions, most moderators prefer to host many short sessions.

5. analyzing data and reporting

5. *Analyzing data and preparing a summary report.* The moderator or research team is responsible for documenting the results of the focus group. The report given to the sponsor may be brief or lengthy depending on the agreement that is made. In most cases, the facilitator draws conclusions about the trends observed in the group, paying particular attention to the reasons group members had for their opinions. In some cases, the report consists of a detailed content analysis of the comments made by the group members. When an outside sponsor is involved, the sponsor is permitted to take possession of any recordings of the focus groups.

Focus Group Advantages

advantages:

Focus groups have become popular not just in marketing and the law but in general social science research as well. The reasons for this popularity are not hard to understand.

First, focus groups are very flexible. The ability to ask additional questions beyond those in the moderator's guide makes the method helpful to probe unexpected issues. Rather than restricting the moderator, focus groups often are designed to give the facilitator the freedom to move into areas that were uncharted by the original researchers.

1. flexible

Second, focus groups are very helpful in pilot studies. By giving a focus group copies of survey forms or questionnaires, it is possible to get feedback regarding areas of possible misunderstanding. Researchers can often avoid research disasters by using focus groups to catch mistakes before they actually happen. In addition, when an area has not yet been explored, focus groups appear to be useful ways to discover what variables and settings are most worth identifying and studying (Morgan, 1998, pp. 13–14).

2. useful in pilot studies

Third, many focus groups promote frank and honest sharing of ideas that might not occur in other settings. Not only does probing for reasons behind answers promote insight, but people are often willing to "open up" when they are in groups. They may be stimulated by comments from other group members to share their frank opinions in ways that would be lost in other interviews or questionnaires. Unfortunately, research has also revealed that group interviews produce fewer original ideas than individual interviews (Fern, 1983).

3. may promote honest idea sharing

but fewer original ideas

Focus Group Disadvantages

For all their benefits, focus groups have some drawbacks. In each case, however, the drawbacks limit their applications, rather than negate the method as a whole.

disadvantages:

First, one cannot generalize results from one focus group to an entire population. Since the people in focus groups are not selected at random, it may be that results gathered from this setting are not shared to the same degree in the population as a whole. In addition, since every group is not asked the same exact questions (though a set of starting questions is held in common), the sessions themselves are not identical. This limitation aside, however, focus groups are not undertaken for purposes of generalizing samples to entire populations. They are completed to help make improvements in future research and to discover the reasons behind opinions people have. Thus, researchers who wish to generalize results of focus groups must complete additional survey research as well.

1. cannot generalize to population

Second, the focus group is only as good as the ability of the moderator. An unskilled moderator may act in ways that bias the group. Especially in lengthy focus groups, the moderator may unintentionally reveal his or her own biases on the topic. By the tone of questions or the use of strategic nonverbal cues, the facilitator may encourage some kinds of responses and inhibit others. In addition, the moderator must be capable of controlling members who might attempt to dominate the group. Unless the moderator is in control of the group, the group may not be productive.

2. only as good as the moderator

Third, as a result of group discussion, many sets of reasons and comments tend to become more and more extreme. In one study (Sussman et al., 1991), focus group responses were compared to questionnaire responses. Those deliberating in focus

3. reasons may become increasingly extreme

groups became more extreme and less moderate as a result of their deliberations. Thus, the effect of additional group participation may lead to extreme shifts of opinion that may mislead researchers about true feelings.

Autoethnography

uses of autoethnographies

criticisms of autoethnography

If ethnography is research in which the investigator participates, overtly or covertly, in other people's lives for an extended period of time, **autoethnography,** the researcher *is* the same person supplying information. By writing themselves into their own research, autoethnographers implicitly reject the idea that *any* researcher can be a silent third party to observations that are made. The voice of the researcher is always present in making research choices, they reason (Charmaz & Mitchell, 1997). Hence, why hide this voice when reporting research?

Such autoethnographies have been useful to explain intriguing events and communication challenges. For example, Kathy Miller (2002) reported an autoethnography in which she described her experience attempting to continue her teaching and research at Texas A&M after a sports-related bonfire accident had led to the loss of student life. Kathy Krone (2005) listed this work as an exemplar of organizational communication research and praised it by asking rhetorically before introducing it, "What could be more relevant to explore than the experience and expression of emotion during the aftermath of a major tragedy?" (p. 98). In another work, Olson (2004) wrote an autoethnography of her participation in a violently abusive relationship. She explained how her self-concept was ravaged during the entrapment phrase of the relationship, though eventually "an autonomous, self-confident sense of self emerged from the shackles of an enmeshed identity" (p. 1). Tracey Patton (2004) completed an autoethnography (combined with a "narrative analysis") in which she described her disappointment in going to a largely Euro-American college and experiencing what she concluded was proof of "the interdependence of sexist and racist ideologies that persist in university classrooms in the guise of civility." She argued that "inferential sexism and racism are endemic to U.S. higher education and classrooms and are as dangerous as overt forms of sexism and racism because they are harder to identify, and more naturalized and acceptable" (p. 60). In a curious example of life imitating methodology, Nicholas Holt (2003) published an autoethnography in the *International Journal of Qualitative Methods* describing how difficult it was to publish an autoethnography. Tierney (1998) asserted that when done properly, "autoethnography confronts dominant forms of representation and power in an attempt to reclaim, through self-reflective response, representational spaces that have marginalized those of us at the borders" (p. 66).

Autoethnography has been the object of some stout criticism, and some claim that it is "at the boundaries of disciplinary practices" (Sparkes, 2000, p. 21). Coffey (1999) warned that unless they are very careful autoethnographers are "in danger of gross self-indulgence" (p. 132). Since the story of the events is completely in the hands of the storyteller, there is no test against competing claims of knowledge (see criticism by Denzin & Lincoln, 2000; Sparkes, 2000). This fact has not gone unnoticed among critics, one of whom remarked:

> The academic is invited to present a self-referential anecdote or "story," with little regard to such considerations as craft, rigor, verifiability, or other widely accepted criteria. Freed from these constraints, a variety of personal stories may be presented, but no story may claim greater value or credence than any other. This practice sidesteps the assessment of competing claims of knowledge, moral authority, and legitimacy, thorny issues that form the very substance of the academic endeavor and human existence. Consequently, the new scholar not only reduces her or his scope of inquiry but also, in support of not "privileging" any particular reading, can scarcely refute an assertion such as *Mein Kampf* provides as valid a call to arms as The Declaration of Independence, The Communist Manifesto, or a shopping list. (Taft-Kaufman, 2000, ¶ 5)

Researchers sometimes have difficulty when the autoethnographer fails to identify his or her own biases and orientations before getting into the work. "Rather than being invited to function in an active, critical manner, listeners/readers are asked to take on the implied audience roles of non-directive therapist, voyeur, or disciple. All lead to passive acceptance of the assumptions, values, and relevance of the discourse" (Taft-Kaufman, 2000, ¶ 7). To some extent, the concern comes down to the fact that measurement validity (so near and dear to many other social scientists) is not particularly critical to many autoethnographers, so long as they believe their reported perceptions are trustworthy. As an alternative, a research team led by Morse (2002) suggested that after-the-fact "evaluation checks on reliability and validity should be replaced with relevant descriptions as part of a set of "constructive" techniques. "For example, describing investigator responsiveness during the research process would be a constructive approach to validity, as opposed to the inclusion of evaluative checks to establish the trustworthiness of completed research (e.g., an external audit). Both viewpoints question the application of 'traditional criteria' (i.e., post-hoc evaluative measures based largely on the parallel perspective) to judge contemporary qualitative investigations" (Holt, 2003, p. 8).

Despite some occasional criticism, however, the use of autoethnography has been growing in popularity. To be considered as serious research, autoethnography should meet several criteria. These matters are particularly important for autoethnographers since there is reason to believe that typical standards used to evaluate qualitative research may not be suitable for this type of research (Garratt & Hodkinson, 1999). Some thinking has gone into developing such criteria. First, the autoethnography should include accounts that link at least two cultures or groups (Dyer, 2006b, ¶ 7). Autoethnography is not a "what I did on my summer vacation" essay. Instead, it attempts to identify meanings constructed among members of cultures or subcultures. Second, the autoethnographer "does not adopt the 'objective outsider' convention of writing common to traditional ethnography. [It] entails the incorporation of elements of one's own life experience when writing about others through biography or ethnography" (Reed-Danahay, 1997, ¶ 6). Third, autoethnography should not confuse itself with autobiography, in which the focus is on the individual person, rather than on the

autoethnography requirements:

1. *should link at least two cultures or groups*

2. *not written as an "objective outsider"*

3. *not autobiography*

cultural grouping. If researchers wish to analyze their positions within their cultures, the task demands autobiography. Yet, if researchers wish to understand "their society and issues surrounding them" (Dyer, 2006a, ¶ 3), ethnographic tools would seem invited. Fourth, since the raw materials for autoethnography are personally derived, a sound autoethnography should include examples of dialog, descriptions of emotions and feelings, and culture-based stories that are affected by such elements as social structures and common histories (Ellis & Bochner, 2000). A set of five additional evaluation factors was suggested by Richardson (2000, pp. 15–16):

4. should include examples

autoethnography also should have

5. a substantive contribution

Fifth, substantive contribution—how well the autoethnography promotes understanding of social interaction;

6. aesthetic merit

Sixth, aesthetic merit—how lively, interesting, and aesthetically pleasing the autoethnography is;

7. reflexivity

Seventh, reflexivity—what led the researcher to complete the autoethnography and deal with subjectivity as a "producer and product of the text";

8. impact

Eighth, impact—the effect of the autoethnography on readers (emotionally and intellectually) and the heuristic merit of the work for other researchers;

9. expression of reality

Ninth, expression of reality—use of dramatic recall, vivid language, typical metaphors to create a sense of lived experience for the reader of the autoethnography.

With such tools available, the modern researcher using autoethnography can attempt to assess the merits of the work with some clear understanding going into the research effort.

CHECKLIST TO EVALUATE QUALITATIVE RESEARCH, ETHNOGRAPHIES, AND PARTICIPANT OBSERVATION STUDIES

_____ Is the qualitative study done under circumstances where use of questionnaires and direct reports would be inappropriate or impractical?

_____ Does the qualitative study examine a setting that has been so unexplored that formal hypotheses may not have been developed?

_____ Does the research question involve questions of how and why?

_____ Are the philosophical foundations of the research approach identified (e.g., phenomenology, hermeneutics)?

_____ Are the assumptions of the qualitative research approach (including assumptions about the nature of knowledge and reality) explained?

_____ Is the research approach justified?

_____ Is the researcher qualified by training or experience to conduct such a qualitative study?

_____ Are steps taken to assure the "quality and verification of the interpretation presented (e.g., by member-checking, negative case analysis)" (www.icahdq.org/membership/publications.html#joc, ¶ 17)?

When considering the qualitative data,

_____ are issues of validity (confirmability) addressed?

_____ are issues of reliability (trustworthiness) addressed?

_____ are issues of generalizability (transferability) addressed?

_____ Are limitations on the study listed and conclusions clearly qualified accordingly?

_____ What procedures are followed to protect the rights of study participants or informants (e.g., informed consent, human participants' approval, and debriefing)?

Ethnography and Participant Observation Work

Is the situation suited to ethnography because

_____ the research question deals with fields in which naturally occurring communication phenomena exist?

_____ the research question deals with phenomena that occur within a relatively short time frame?

_____ Does the researcher identify an appropriate research position (e.g., ventriloquizing others' interests, giving voice to silenced groups, engaging in direct activism, or advancing postcritical ethnography) for the study?

_____ If claimed to be ethnography, is it really ethnography or some form of participant observation research?

_____ Is an emic or etic approach used? If etic, is it justified?

_____ Does the study involve full participant observation or participant as observer? (If full participant, what steps are taken to deal with associated ethical issues?)

_____ What steps are taken to get permission to enter the field site?

_____ Is there an explanation for the method used to gain entry into the research setting?

_____ Does the researcher explain the type of relationship that she or he has with the study participants (e.g., unobtrusive observer, participant observer)?

_____ Is there a justification for the ways study participants and groups are selected for study?

_____ Are the types of data to be collected clearly described (such as fieldnotes from memory, audio- or videotapes)?

_____ Are fieldnotes written as soon as possible after leaving the field site?

_____ If interviews were used, are their formats described and sample questions included?

_____ Are analytic inductions derived to reformulate working hypotheses?

If ethnomethodology is employed:

_____ Does the researcher actually capture examples of the mundane and ordinary in participants' lives?

_____ Does the researcher have evidence that the examples interpreted show people's reports of their commonsense practical actions to others in acceptable, rational terms?

If Dell Hymes' "ethnography of communication" approach is used:

_____ Is the speech community clearly defined?

_____ Is the speech situation clearly identified?

_____ Is the communicative act completely identified?

_____ Is the communicative style identified?

_____ Are the ways of speaking clearly identified and underlying rules explained?

_____ Are all elements of the S.P.E.A.K.I.N.G. model covered? (If not, is a justification provided for the selection of some, but not all, of the elements?)

_____ What did the researcher do to avoid becoming overidentified with the group studied?

If qualitative interviews are used:

_____ Does the researcher take steps to demonstrate an attitude of a willingness to listen responsively?

_____ Does the researcher effectively use strategic questions and responses to encourage the interviewee to continue the conversation?

_____ Does the researcher use paraphrasing effectively to check on understanding?

Grounded Theory

_____ Is the method applied to a problem question that involves "identifying a core category which accounts for what is central in the data" (Punch, 2005, p. 205)?

_____ Does the researcher begin with (as much as possible) a theory-free observation of locations where the critical phenomena could be studied?

_____ Are details of coding provided (including an explanation of open coding procedures)?

_____ Is there evidence that the researcher had "theoretical sensitivity"?

_____ Are theoretically informed data sampling methods used to secure as many varieties of cases and contrasting cases as possible?

_____ Are the categories elaborated to produce revised category descriptions?

_____ Are frequent "constant comparisons" made by cycling through elaboration and field site observations?

_____ Does the research actually complete the grounded theory process, rather than stopping after the initial categorization stage?

_____ Is theoretical saturation achieved as repeated returning to the field produces few new significant categories?

_____ Does the research complete a thorough examination of field sites before making claims of theoretical saturation?

Focus Groups

_____ Is a competent leader in charge of the groups?

_____ Is the purpose limited to gathering preliminary information for a research project, developing questionnaire items for survey research, understanding reasons behind a particular phenomenon or relationship, or to test preliminary ideas?

_____ Is the size of the focus group manageable (typically 6 to 12 people)?

_____ Is the focus group communication recorded accurately?

_____ Are details of the group interview session organized in advance?

_____ Does the researcher make the mistake of generalizing results from a focus group to an entire population?

Autoethnography

_____ Is the study actual autoethnography or is it autobiography? (If the former, did the researcher take time to link work to more than one group?)

_____ Does the autoethnography confront dominant forms of representation and power?

_____ Does the autoethnographer identify his or her own biases and orientations before getting into the work?

_____ Are examples included of dialog, descriptions of emotions and feelings, and culturally based stories that are affected by such elements as social structures and common histories?

_____ Does the report make a substantive contribution?

_____ Does the report have aesthetic merit?

_____ Does the report have an impact on readers?

_____ Was the autoethnography a vivid expression of reality?

SUMMARY

Ethnographic and participant observation studies are based on a desire to examine communication behavior that is not affected by the research process. Fieldwork is the study of people acting in the natural courses of their daily lives. Participant observers study groups by gaining membership or close relationships with them. Naturalistic studies are nonexperimental inquiries completed as subjects are involved in the natural course of their lives. It may be noted that (1) researchers often use different words to identify the same thing, and (2) there is no need to decide on a preference for methods (since your research problem question will invite appropriate methods and researchers may use different tools to "triangulate" study results).

Ethnographic and fieldwork studies have three major purposes: (1) answering questions in settings where use of questionnaires and direct reports would be inappropriate or impractical, (2) examining a setting that has been so unexplored that formal hypotheses may not have been developed, and (3) developing grounded theory and analytic inductions. Such research still argues from empirical facts to conclusions. Ethnography is research in which the investigator participates, overtly or covertly, in people's lives for an extended period of time, collecting whatever data are available to describe behavior. Ethnography is a broad term that includes a great deal, including most participant observation research (though participant observation work need not occur over very long time periods). Analytic induction "develops theory by examining a small number of cases. Theory then leads to formulation of a [very tentative] hypothesis, which is tested through the study of more cases. This usually leads to refinement or reformulation of the hypothesis, which is then tested with further cases until the researcher judges that the inquiry can be concluded" (Vogt, 2005, p. 10).

Ethnography and participant observation methods are most often invited for research questions that deal with (1) fields in which naturally occurring communication phenomena exist and (2) phenomena that occur within a relatively short time frame. Qualitative methods are also invited when the research question concerns the "why? how? and the answers to questions which begin with: why? how? in what way?" (Hancock, 2002, p. 2). In qualitative work, the emic approach involves "culturally relative approaches . . . that stress participants' understanding of their own culture. Derived, by an indirect route, from the linguistic term phon*emic*" (Vogt, 2005, p. 105). In contrast, the etic approach involves "methods of study . . . stressing material—rather than cultural—explanations for social and cultural phenomena. Derived, by an indirect route, from the linguistic term phon*etic*" (Vogt, 2005, p. 109).

One can enter the field in two ways. Full participant observation research is characterized by the investigator's gathering data while taking part in the activities of a group—and while concealing his or her research identity. The method creates obvious ethical difficulties. The researcher may not satisfactorily be able to defend others' privacy. In addition, concealing the researcher's identity can lead to potentially harmful interpersonal relationships. Most participant observation research follows the participant as observer method in which the group to be studied is made aware of the researcher's role. The different approaches involve some trade-offs. As the researcher tends toward becoming a complete participant, interpretations become subjective, the researcher shares sympathy and concern for the communicators studied, the researcher plays an active role in the communication studied, and the researcher usually goes into the research setting in disguise. Ethnomethodology, or the "new ethnography," is the study of the mundane and ordinary activities of everyday life, concentrating on the methods used by people to report their commonsense practical actions to others in acceptable, rational terms.

Philosophically, in qualitative inquiry, groups of people who already share things in common are not to be generalized further. Instead, the elements that give meaning to their distinctive communities are to be the primary focus of attention. Researchers search for an answer to the question, What are these common groupings that make a people distinctive? To explore these matters, Dell Hymes developed his "ethnography of communication." "The starting point is the ethnographic analysis of the communication conduct of a community" (Hymes, 1974, p. 9). The speech community consists of the people who have a common system of speech to bind them together. Five additional units involve communication to emphasize different aspects of the culture at work. These five additional units include (1) the speech situation ("associated with [or marked by the absence of] speech [Hymes]" [Malcolm, 2001, ¶ 71]); (2) the speech event ("the basic unit for the analysis of verbal interaction in speech communities; it covers stretches of utterances and focuses on the exchange between speakers; . . . [Gumperz]" [Malcolm, 2001, ¶ 67]); (3) the communicative act ("the minimal term of the speech event [Hymes] utterances considered in terms of what they do and how we use them in conversation" [Malcolm, 2001, ¶ 70]); (4) communicative style ("linguistic difference according to the formality of the interaction [which depends on such factors as the social occasion, the social, age and other differences of the participants, the emotional involvement, etc.]" [Malcolm, 2001, ¶ 30]); and (5) ways of speaking ("rule-governed patterns of communicative behaviour within a speech community [Hymes]" [Malcolm, 2001, ¶ 72]).

The steps of participant observation include (1) selecting a position for the researcher (research positions are the stances that researchers take to the objectives for research: ventriloquizing others' interests, giving voice to silenced groups, engaging direct activism, or postcritical ethnography [a research position in which researchers include a critique of the ways in which their own experiences studying groups of people in an ethnographic project may contribute to domination of the groups under study]), (2) selecting settings and cases, (3) getting into the setting, (4) sampling within the case by selecting the types of behaviors to monitor, (5) keeping records and observations, (6) interpretive analysis of data, and (7) exiting the field setting.

After the researcher chooses the focus of ethnographic attention, Hymes' system to organize an ethnography may be used. It is based on a memory device formed by the word "S-P-E-A-K-I-N-G." S designates situation, which includes both the scene and the setting. P refers to the participants involved. E refers to the ends or goals of communication. A refers to the speech acts, including both form and content. K focuses on the key or tone of speech. I refers to the instrumentality or channels through which communication flows can be examined. N consists of the norms of communication or the rules guiding talk and its interpretation. G deals with cultural or traditional speech genres, such as proverbs, apologies, prayers, small talk, or problem talk. Fieldnotes are vital to keeping sound records for ethnographies. Fieldnotes must include basic information, and they also must be organized to include information that can help explore the research question (and lead to new ones). Fieldnotes should be written as soon as possible after leaving the field site. Qualitative interviews often are used to gather information for ethnographies. A qualitative interview is an unstructured interview method aimed toward discussing topics in depth. In qualitative research the researcher must adopt the attitude of a willingness to listen responsively. The researcher uses strategic questions including experience/behavior questions, opinion/belief questions, feeling questions, knowledge questions, sensory questions, and demographic questions. To encourage the interviewee to continue the conversation and offer information, paraphrasing (summarizing the interviewee's message in one's own words, usually to check understanding) may be very helpful. Other comments to promote additional information sharing include repetition as a question, request, acquiring meaning, repetition of a key word or phrase, asking for an example, and using an encouraging comment. Limitations in the use of the approach include the following: (1) these methods are very time-consuming and expensive, (2) such work tends to rest on measurement with unknown properties, (3) researchers can become overidentified with a group and develop biases and sympathies that color the fairness and accuracy of reports or interpretations, and (4) such studies cannot reach comprehensive conclusions alone.

Qualitative research extends beyond ethnographic and participant observation research. Grounded theory is a set of explanations that has immediate relevance to a specific field setting under investigation. Participant observers attempt to discover categories to describe their observations after they have entered the field. Then researchers make additional observations to refine and modify these categories and potentially develop theory. The objective of grounded theory "is to find a core category, at a high level of abstraction but grounded in the data, which accounts for what is central in the data" (Punch, 2005, p. 205). The first stage of grounded theory is beginning with a general subject or research problem and identifying a location where it could be studied. The actual record-keeping of such observations is called coding ("the process of deciding how to conceptually divide up raw qualitative data" [Lacey & Luff, 2001, p. 34]). This stage involves "initial familiarisation with the data" (Lacey & Luff, 2001, p. 7) with no initial categories. Memos are notes researchers make about the meaning of a category or property, or about possible relationships among categories. To permit categories to emerge, researchers rely on their own "theoretical sensitivity" (the ability "to see the research situation and its associated data in new ways, and to explore the data's potential for developing theory" [Strauss & Corbin, 1990, p. 44]) to generate relevant categories from the data. The second stage of grounded theory involves taking an initial set of categories and some theoretical ideas and conducting theoretically informed data sampling. Researchers look for new samples that would show increased variation or even negative cases to observe. In the third stage in grounded theory, after the field observations are made and the coding system is used, the researchers cycle back and forth to enter the field and check the new revision against the new data—after which, they can revise the work and enter another field setting. This approach is a constant comparative method ("concepts or categories emerging from one stage of the data analysis are compared with concepts emerging from the next. The researcher looks for relationships between these concepts and categories, by constantly comparing them, to form the basis of the emerging theory" [Lacey & Luff, 2001, p. 7]) in which researchers attempt to find settings where the emerging theory is challenged. Revision of theories entails elaboration, which "involves developing and examining its variation systematically" (Punch, 2005, p. 214). The fourth stage occurs after the observation of inconsistent or negative cases begins to wane, and the process of grounded theory produces a set of vital categories and a grounded theory emerges. At this point, returning to the field has reached a level of theoretical saturation (the point at which "no new significant categories or concepts are emerging" [Lacey & Luff, 2001, p. 7] from the process of constant comparison despite a reasonable search). Grounded theory is limited because (1) the notion that one can set aside all theory and make an initial set of observations of raw phenomena is generally considered to be naïve; (2) grounded theory's concern for verification may be inconsistent with the goals of much qualitative research in a postmodern world; (3) the reiterative effort to identify categories so that they include all possible examples of behavior to be coded strikes some as searching for a general set of terms that then may be forced on data; and (4) many researchers who claim to use grounded theory stop after developing categories.

A focus group is an interview style designed for small groups. To be specific, focus group interviews are either guided or unguided discussions addressing a particular topic of interest or relevance to the group and the researcher. There are four general purposes of focus groups: (1) to gather preliminary information for a research project; (2) to help develop questionnaire items for survey research; (3) to understand reasons behind a particular phenomenon; and (4) to test preliminary ideas or plans. Focus group studies usually involve five general steps: (1) assembling the groups (participants—usually 6 to 12 people—are screened to obtain a particular sample of interest); (2) preparing study mechanics including settings and recording devices (a variation is called the telefocus session in which focus group sessions are completed by teleconferencing methods over the telephone); (3) preparing focus group session materials and questions, including a "moderator's guide" that describes the events to occur during the session, their order, and the questions that are to be asked (participants often complete a questionnaire before the formal focus group begins to assure that participants are thinking about the topic and to stimulate respondents to speak up even if their opinions are in the minority); (4) conducting the session, including introducing the topic, presenting some type of stimulus message, answering questions related to the topic, and responding to others in the group (the moderator is free to explore comments and issues raised by members of the group and also must deal with problem people in the group); and (5) analyzing data and preparing a summary report that may be a facilitator's summary or a detailed content analysis of the comments made by the group members. Focus groups have three primary advantages: (1) focus groups are very flexible and give the facilitator the freedom to move into areas that were uncharted by the original researchers; (2) they are very helpful in pilot studies; and (3) they promote frank and honest sharing of ideas that might not occur in other settings. Focus groups have three disadvantages: (1) one cannot generalize results from one focus group to an entire population; (2) focus groups are only as good as the ability of the moderator; and (3) as a result of group discussion, many sets of reasons and comments tend to become more and more extreme.

Autoethnography is a combination of "autobiography, the story of one's own life, with ethnography, the study of a particular social group" (Dyer, 2006b, ¶ 1). By writing themselves into their own research as significant figures, autoethnographers implicitly reject the idea that *any* researcher can be a silent third party to observations that are made. When done properly, "autoethnography confronts dominant forms of representation and power in an attempt to reclaim, through self-reflective response, representational spaces that have marginalized those of us at the borders" (Tierney, 1998, p. 66). Autoethnography has been criticized for being at the fringe of research, for risking self-indulgence, and for avoiding any test against competing claims of knowledge. Researchers sometimes have difficulty when the autoethnographer fails to identify his or her own biases and orientations before getting into the work. Though after-the-fact evaluation checks on credibility of reports have been attempted, some researchers recommend "constructive" techniques (such as describing investigator responsiveness during the research process). Criteria for serious autoethnography include the following: (1) the autoethnography should include accounts that link at least two cultures or groups; (2) the autoethnographer "does not adopt the 'objective outsider' convention of writing common to traditional ethnography" (Reed-Danahay, 1997, ¶ 6); (3) the autoethnography should not confuse itself with autobiography, in which the focus is on the individual person, rather than on the cultural grouping; (4) the autoethnography should include examples of dialog, descriptions of emotions and feelings, and culture-based stories that are affected by such elements as social structures and common histories; (5) the work should make a substantive contribution; (6) it should have aesthetic merit; (7) it should feature reflexivity explanations (e.g., what led the researcher to complete the autoethnography and deal with subjectivity as a "producer and product of the text"); (8) it should have impact on readers; and (9) it should be a vivid expression of reality.

TERMS FOR REVIEW

fieldwork

naturalistic studies

participant observation

ethnography

analytic induction

emic approach

etic approach

full participant observation

accretions

urban archaeology

erosions

participant as observer

ethnomethodology

life history study

time-budgeting studies

community studies

case studies

negative case study

speech community

speech situation

speech event

communicative act

communicative style

ways of speaking

research positions

ventriloquist stance

positionality of voices

activism stance

postcritical ethnography

qualitative interview

paraphrasing

grounded theory

coding

open coding

memo

theoretical sensitivity

constant comparative method

elaboration

theoretical saturation

focus group

telefocus sessions

autoethnography

JUST FOR THE SAKE OF ARGUMENT: A REVIEW

Look at the following questions and prepare your own answers to them. Consider seriously the assumptions that underlie these questions.

1. Why would you want to do participant observation studies? Some people join a group, take a vacation abroad, or have a unique experience that they use as the basis for their studies. Is this approach wise or not?

2. What is the difference between full participant observation studies and participant as observer studies?

3. In another chapter in this book, we contrasted theory first and data first research. What is the relationship between these two notions and the concepts of participant observation work pursuing grounded theory and the use of analytic induction?

4. Researchers often attempt to achieve some level of objectivity. Yet, scholars note that efforts at scientific work still contain implicit values and choices. Thus, values are involved

in any research efforts. How is objectivity handled by participant observation researchers? What efforts are made to deal with inevitable biases?

5. What is the difference between unobtrusive measurement and direct measurement methods? Are all unobtrusive methods unintentional? How could they be misleading indicators of variables?

6. What is the difference between simple participant observation research and ethnography? How is ethnomethodology distinguished from ethnography?

7. Of all the steps involved in completing participant observation studies, which one probably is most difficult? Why is this element most troublesome for researchers? What can researchers do about it?

ACTIVITIES TO PROBE FURTHER

1. Go to the website for this book and find the Student Study Materials for Chapter 7. Take the study quiz and print out your answers. (Avoid giving your first impressions. Many questions can be tricky.)

2. Do a mini–ethnographic study of how your family watches television. Make sure to include this information:
   a. Who the people are
   b. How long the observations were taken
   c. How you decided to select behaviors to monitor
   d. How you kept records of observations
   e. How you would offer an interpretive analysis of data

   Write a brief report (two or three pages) in which you describe this study and include a discussion of problems you had with the method of ethnography. How would you deal with this matter if you were an independent field researcher instead of a permanent member of your family?

3. Suppose you got word that the staff of a nearby restaurant treats minority students rudely. What kind of qualitative study design would you recommend? Make sure you start with a problem question that invites the use of such a qualitative design. Answer these questions:
   a. How would you get into the setting?
   b. How would you sample within the case?
   c. How would you keep records of observations?
   d. How would you interpret your data?
   e. How would you exit the field setting (and how long would you be in the setting)?
   f. How well could you answer this research question? What future studies would help you in any "triangulation" of studies?

4. There are entire courses dedicated to studying communication by use of ethnography, participant observations, and qualitative fieldwork methods. Search on the Internet for such courses or course units. Use the keywords "ethnography" and "communication." You will find such class unit sources as "Reading the Ethnography of Communication" (www.utexas.edu/courses/maxwell/teach/384/read.htm). You also will find commercial sites such as the Innovare Corporation (www.innovare-inc.com/srv_ethnography.htm),

Content Analysis of Communication

If anything characterizes the cultural life in America, it is an insistence on preventing failures of communication.

—RICHARD DEAN ROSEN

BEFORE WE GET STARTED . . .

Since the early study of mass communication, content analyses have been popular tools. They remain a staple of communication research in many settings. Whether dealing with interpersonal communication exchanges, speech therapy screenings, assessments of television violence rates, the accuracy of messages broadcast about the 9/11 attacks on America, or examinations of the sorts of messages functional groups use when dealing with conflict, content analysis is a method of choice.

There are several forms of content analysis, and this chapter will attempt to introduce you to some of the most popular ones, including interactional analysis and relational analysis.

ANALYSIS OF MESSAGE QUALITIES: WHEN DO WE COMPLETE CONTENT ANALYSIS?

Content analysis "any of several research techniques used to describe and systematically analyze the content of written, spoken, or pictorial communication—such as books, newspapers, television programs, or interview transcripts" (Vogt, 2005, p. 59).

Content analysis can be considered qualitative research because it deals with qualities of messages and because it can be applied to interpret individual cases in an intensive manner. Though typical content analyses provide numbers to help summarize findings, the information itself deals with matters that the researcher has decided to track. These matters may include broad themes, recurring phrases, semantics, or concepts. Thus, the methods may be used by those practicing grounded theory (see Chapter 7) to help develop categories for analysis of communication phenomena. Furthermore, the entire process may be viewed as consistent with the interpretive approach to the analysis of texts. As a respected proponent of qualitative methods explained:

despite use of numbers, content analysis may be a tool of qualitative research

> Content analysis can be effective in qualitative analyses— . . . "counts" of textual elements merely provide a means for identifying, organizing, indexing, and retrieving data. Analysis of the data, once organized according to certain content elements, should involve consideration of the literal words in the text being analyzed, including the manner in which these words are offered. . . . From this perspective, content analysis is not a reductionistic, positivistic approach. Rather, it is a passport to listening to the words of the text and understanding better the perspective(s) of the producer of these words. (Berg, 2007, pp. 307–308)

Thus, it seems that the method may be used by those with questions that invite a qualitative or a quantitative approach. Of course, combining content analysis with other approaches may be one of the most exciting directions it has taken in recent years.

content analysis is an efficient way to sift through large amounts of content

Why would anyone want to do a content analysis? As the timetable on the inside front cover shows, some research questions clearly invite it. In addition, the method lets researchers move very efficiently through a lot of information and data. In its book on content analysis, *Content Analysis: A Methodology for Structuring and Analyzing Written Material* (1996),[1] the United States General Accounting Office claimed that the ability to sift a large amount of data was perhaps the greatest advantage of this tool. A pioneer of the method, Klaus Krippendorff, made much the same argument—that content analysis uses "techniques to infer from symbolic data what would be either

---

[1]This book is available for free from the General Accounting Office.

too costly, no longer possible, or too obtrusive by the use of other techniques" (1980, p. 51). More than anything else, then, content analysis permits researchers to simplify a large amount of message detail and information.

To decide if any of the many forms of content analysis is an appropriate procedure for your study, you also need to look at your problem question. Above all else, content analysis tools are invited when the problem question asks about characteristics of messages that could be categorized and counted (such as, What is the relationship between the amount of news coverage given to third party candidates on the three commercial television networks?). As an indication of the versatility of content analysis, research questions also invite content analysis and interactional/relational analysis when they deal with:

characteristics of problem questions that invite use of content analysis and interactional/relational analysis

- ◆ Comparison patterns of messages, message flow, or dominance from different sources (such as, What is the relationship between the balance of coverage of controversial news stories and prestige or mass appeal newspapers?) (after Lacy, Fico, & Simon, 1991)

- ◆ Comparisons of message content with real life (such as, What is the relationship between the amount of violence portrayed during prime-time television and the actual amount of violence in society?) (Wimmer & Dominick, 1997, p. 166)

- ◆ Contrasting the image of specific groups of people in society (such as, What is the relationship between the race of TV characters in entertainment programs and the types of occupations they are portrayed as having?)

- ◆ Changing uses of messages by different people or groups (such as, What is the relationship between the amount of messages of relational dominance and the amount of control in the interaction?)

- ◆ Applications of standard evaluation systems to actual messages[2] (such as, What is the relationship between the propaganda techniques categories and the varieties of appeals used in the Australian terror kit information package?) (after Tilley, 2005)

- ◆ Comparisons of communication patterns across cultures (such as Frith, Shaw, & Cheng's study [2005] in which they stated, "The purpose of this research is to compare the portrayals of beauty in women's fashion and beauty magazine advertisements from Asia and the U.S. to help understand how beauty is constructed across cultures" [p. 57][3])

- ◆ Studies challenging assumptions of fairness, equality, and diversity (such as, "[in communication journals] What is (a) the proportion of editors from countries other than the U.S., (b) the national diversity score and the proportion of authors from (c) the U.S. and (d) English-speaking countries?" [Lauf, 2005, p. 142][4])

---

[2]The first time the author studied content analysis by reading a whole book on the subject was in a course in rhetorical criticism—just thought you'd like to know.

[3]They found that Asian ads focused mostly on cosmetics (indicating an orientation to the face) and U.S. ads focused mostly on clothing (indicating an orientation to the body). In addition, Caucasian models were most frequently used in both Asian and U.S. ads.

[4]So-called young journals are more international than noninternational journals. Most of the field's journals were dominated by U.S. and English-language publications.

In all these instances, the messages are analyzed to provide keys to understanding significant issues in communication studies. Furthermore, the methods employ the evidence from texts as the foundation for their inferences.

FUNCTIONS OF CONTENT ANALYSIS

There is more than one function served by content analysis. The uses of content analysis differ greatly from one research question to another. Yet, what really makes a difference is the sort of goal that researchers have for their work. The bottom line is that content analysis has emerged as a highly versatile tool that may be used to promote both description and explanation.

of the research goals of description, explanation, prediction, and control, content analysis functions for description and explanation

Though the broad scope of research includes the possibility of description, explanation, prediction, and control, content analysis is most suited to the first two of these elements (Hocking, Stacks, & McDermott, 2003, p. 172). In describing aspects of communication phenomena, researchers naturally look for elements of individual instances or of general patterns across cases. In the sorts of qualitative research described in Chapter 7, the use of ethnography, focus group interviews, and the like may be used to get a sense of the nature of the messages and their meaningfulness to people. Content analysis often takes the form of describing communication phenomena so that other sorts of analyses may follow.

content analysis functioning for description may assist other research methods and generate new suggestions for research

As a case in point, rhetorical scholars have been interested in the role that religious themes have played in political speech. Rhetorical critic Roderick Hart (1977) recognized the link between presidential imagery and religion, explaining that when "an American president is inaugurated, he is also ordained" (p. 9). Communication scholars Kurt Ritter and David Henry examined Ronald Reagan's public speaking career and observed that a "union between the scared and the secular . . . defined Reagan's public discourse" (1992, p. 4). Based on news reports, prominent links between politics and fundamentalist religious groups are believed to be growing in frequency and prominence. For critics interested in such rhetoric, it would be helpful to know the answers to such questions as, What is the extent of religious language in presidential speeches? Has there been an increase in religious appeals in the speeches of presidents? and What topics—religious or secular—actually were discussed most by presidents during public speeches? Such information would be very helpful to critics, indeed. In response to such an interest, Coe and Domke (2006) completed a content analysis of the State of the Union and inaugural addresses of presidents starting with Franklin Roosevelt and extending through President Bush's 2005 inaugural speech. In fact, they found that presidents Reagan, both Bushes, and Clinton used nearly twice as many "God references" as the previous panoply of presidents (with Reagan and George W. Bush leading the way with the greatest amount of religious language). By looking to content analysis methods, the communication phenomenon may be described and other work in the field may be promoted.

Explanation can be advanced by content analyses that attempt to relate communication phenomena to larger issues. Sometimes content analysts can measure another variable of interest and to discover interesting cues. For instance, the use of websites for political candidates is now routine and a regular way to keep in touch with supporters, to promote positive images, and to post responses to attacks. Using a 28-attribute coding sheet to measure the visual imagery used on websites maintained by Gore and Bush during the 2000 campaign, Verser and Wicks (2006) explained why different websites seemed to produce different effects. Comparing the nature and extent of photographs used, "the most frequent [sic] occurring theme observed from the data collected was that the Al Gore photographs presented a candidate who appeared actively interacting with ordinary American citizens, dressing casually, and appearing in places like schools, restaurants, and kitchens. . . . By contrast, Bush's images seemed to convey a dignified leader . . . " (p. 194). Because the measurement of details of message content was possible, researchers were able to show the influence of explanatory variables and to provide direct tests of them.

content analysis functioning for explanation may
1. rely on explanatory variables that can be measured

Sometimes content analyses provide explanations by completing separate work over time. For instance, the studies completed on the extent of television violence over the years by George Gerbner at the University of Pennsylvania Annenberg School for Communication were startling in showing nearly steady rises in the amount of violence directed toward children (e.g., Gerbner et al., 1980). In a three-year comparative content analysis, the National Television Violence Survey (Wilson et al., 1997, 1998) was able to explain how the amount and content of violence had changed. By 1998, 61% of television shows had violence and only 4% of them included an antiviolence theme. Not only had the amount of violence grown somewhat, but only 25% of the time was violence immediately punished or condemned. Indeed, 40% of the time, even "bad" characters went unpunished for their violence. The explanation of the particularly cynical treatment of violence led the surgeon general to list television violence as a national problem confronting parents and policy makers alike. By linking violence to another variable—the passage of time, the situation was disturbing because it showed that television violence brought in viewers and was being emulated across the medium. By identifying the content of the violence across time, researchers were able to explain the violence as part of a rise of cynical treatment of violence in a steadily coarsening society.

2. complete content analyses over time

Because content analysis can help researchers deal with these two functions—explanation and prediction—one should not be surprised to see content analysis combined with other methods. By doing so, researchers may "triangulate" research findings and enrich work that is completed by fundamentally different methods. Such an effort was successfully completed by Scott Myers and Leah Bryant (2004), who combined content analysis with a grounded theory approach to the study of college students' unstructured accounts of ways that their teachers showed credibility. After using content analysis, the authors followed up by including use of the "constant comparative approach" recommended in grounded theory. This willingness to cross from one approach to another would seem particularly invited for modern scholars who put research questions above dedication to a particular research methodology.

content analysis may be used in combination with other methods to triangulate findings

RESEARCHERS IN THE FIELD: KATHLEEN HALL JAMIESON

Kathleen Hall Jamieson is one of the most visible and respected communication scholars in the world. She is a regular interviewee on such television programs as *NOW* and *The News Hour* (PBS), and her books have been best sellers. She is the Elizabeth Ware Packard Professor of Communication at the Annenberg School for Communication and director of the Annenberg Public Policy Center at the University of Pennsylvania. She has authored, coauthored, or edited 13 books, including *Dirty Politics: Deception, Distraction and Democracy; Everything You Think You Know About Politics . . . and Why You're Wrong; Packaging the Presidency* (which received the National Communication Association's Golden Anniversary Book Award) and *Eloquence in an Electronic Age: The Transformation of Political Speechmaking* (which received the National Communication Association's Winans-Wichelns Book Award). Her scholarship and service has earned her eight major awards from national scholarly organizations.

♦ *What drew you into our field?*

At Marquette University, which I attended as an undergraduate, debate was administered through the Speech Department. I attended Marquette on a debate scholarship. My intent as an undergrad was to go to law school upon graduation. My advisor suggested a Ph.D. in communication instead. I applied both to law schools and to the University of Wisconsin's Communication Arts department. Ed Black's criticism book [*Rhetorical Criticism: A Study in Method*] was published during my senior year. I based part of my senior thesis on it. After visiting law schools, I realized that I would be much happier in graduate seminars than the law school classes I'd attended. I accepted the fellowship offered by the University of Wisconsin with the hope that I would be able to study with Black. It was a good decision.

♦ *Why did you decide to specialize in political communication?*

As a grad student, I thought of myself as a rhetorical critic. "Political communication" sounded to me a lot like "deliberative rhetoric." My dissertation studied the conflict over the papal birth control encyclical. The presidency—like the papacy—is a long-lived institution whose rhetorical characteristics are shaped in part by the past.

My husband, Bob, and I were married after I finished my M.A. He took a job at the Navy Department in Washington, D.C. There were not many jobs for him in other places in the United States, so I looked for jobs in the D.C. area. A position opened at the University of Maryland in political communication. I argued that because I had a strong background in rhetorical theory and criticism I was qualified for the job. The Speech Department at the University of Maryland was under pressure to hire women. I was hired and had to make good on my promise that I could teach political communication.

♦ *How did you become such a widely sought figure on radio and television? Was this aspect of your career part of your personal plan for professional growth?*

It never occurred to me. I first appeared on TV as a staff member of the House Committee on Aging in 1978 speaking about a report I had written on Age

Stereotyping and Television. The next time I showed up on PBS was when an enterprising reporter did a literature search and found that I had written about papal rhetoric. So, I appeared again when Pope Paul VI died. Then my book *Packaging the Presidency* was published. It was favorably reviewed in the *New York Times* and *Washington Post*. We were living in the D.C. area. I was a low-cost interviewee at a time at which the networks were under assault for putting very few women on air and in print.

♦ *What personal qualities do you have that you think have contributed to your achievements as a communication scholar?*
I don't think personal qualities have much to do with it. I have had great teachers and terrific students.

♦ *What part of your research undertakings have made you most proud?*
Creating FactCheck.org with my colleague Joe Cappella [FactCheck.org is regularly used by mass media sources as a primary authority on accuracy of claims made in political communication and advertising]. Creating and testing the structure for broadcast ad watches has been very satisfying.

♦ *What do you think students should know to use and create communication research?*
There are many ways of knowing. Find brilliant co-authors whose methodological and statistical dispositions complement your own.

♦ *What do you think is the most exciting future direction for the field's research?*
Strong training in both qualitative and quantitative methods is becoming more and more commonplace. There is an increasing number of graduates who are fluent in both approaches.

♦ *Is there any advice you would give students who might be interested in becoming communication researchers?*
Go for it!

PERFORMING CONTENT ANALYSIS

Content analyses are useful to monitor the content of mass media communication. The information can be highly revealing, as were the famous studies showing an increase in violence in children's cartoons at a time when violence in other television programs did not increase (Gerbner, 1971), the emphasis on the "cult of femininity" (not feminism) in women's magazines (Ferguson, 1983), the generally evil portrayal of businesspeople in television entertainment programs (Therberge, 1981; Thomas & LeShay, 1992), and the sexiness of women's business clothing in media presentations (White, 1995). Content analyses can be useful to characterize communication and make intriguing comparisons, such as the type of language used in closing statements at the Nuremberg Trial (Schmid & Fiedler, 1996). Content analysis has been used to assess organizational behavior. For instance, Zeldes and Fico (2005) examined whether increased efforts to hire women and ethnic minorities into broadcast newsrooms had resulted in any changes in the news coverage of the 2000 U.S. presidential campaign.

uses of content analysis:
1. characterize communication

They found that although female and ethnic minority reporters still tended to feature predominantly white male noncandidate sources, their reporting did make increased use of women and ethnic minority sources. These reporters also tended to feature more experts and ordinary people as on-camera sources than did white broadcast news reporters.

2. study nontraditional settings

Though once used almost exclusively by scholars in mass media studies, content analysis methods are now used in many other settings. In studies of organizational communication, comments by employees may be assessed by using content analysis methods. Sometimes speech therapists content-analyze the conversation of aphasic clients to find clues to the type of injury the patient has. An interesting twist has been the use of content analysis of newspapers to gauge trends in society (Naisbitt & Aburdene, 1990).

Steps in Content Analysis

content analysis steps:

Some fairly standard elements should be included in any sound content analysis. Though many content analyses can be completed by a computer, others involve work done by hand. Should you decide to complete content analysis studies of your own, you will want to check for the availability of such computer programs to aid you. We will consider the basic steps along with an example.

1. define communication population to be studied

First, define and limit the communication population to be studied. The communication domain must be isolated so that it is consistent with the problem question raised by the researcher. Furthermore, the population to be sampled should be defined narrowly enough to permit gathering manageable types of information. For studies on the rise of the number of sexual references in rock music lyrics, it is important to decide which types of rock are to be included (rap, heavy metal, light rock) and which sources are to be used to select such lyrical material (lists from *Billboard* and local top 40 lists have notoriously different listings). The communication population to be studied must be carefully defined and distinguished from others. Suppose the problem statement asked what the relationship was between the time a television news report about the 9/11 attack was broadcast and the accuracy of the report (Reinard et al., 2002). A hypothesis was advanced: "There will be a significant inverse correlation between the time a televised report is broadcast and the inaccuracy of the story" (pp. 9–10). Thus, the earlier a story was reported, the more likely it was to be inaccurate.

2. select coding units

Coding units in content analysis, categories used to count the communication forms in the examples chosen.

Second, select coding units and classification systems for study. **Coding units** are the exact categories we use. In the example of looking at the inaccuracy of stories broadcast on television on September 11, 2001, the researchers needed a set of categories for inaccurate news stories. Two major matters had to be recorded, the time of the television broadcasts and the content type and accuracy. For television stations and news sources, the time period was recorded in half-hour intervals beginning with the half hour in which the first September 11, 2001, attack (8:45 a.m. EDT) took place. For the content type and accuracy of the news story, the unit of analysis was the report, not the extended story filed by the reporter. Hence, a given story could—and many did—contain multiple reports and claims of fact that could be examined. The report categories included the following table:

Type of Report	Definition	Example(s)
Accurate reports	reports of events that actually occurred	
Questionable reports	reports asserting claims that were inaccurate, untrue, or very doubtful	At 10:40 a.m., CBS affiliate WUSA reported that "there has been another hijacking. A 737—unknown what airline—has been hijacked. CBS has been reporting that plane is now circling Dulles International Airport." In reality, there were no 737s involved in any of the attacks. At that time no new hijackings had occurred (the crash of the last hijacked plane was at 10 a.m. in Somerset County, Pennsylvania). No hijacked plane was circling at Dulles International Airport. Two military jets, however, flew in the D.C. area and the airport, unnerving nearby residents.
Reports providing opinions and analysis	assertions that interpret or explain the significance or meaning of events, rather than reporting of information	Sandy Berger appeared several times on CBS during the 9/11 broadcast day to offer expert interpretations, such as: "We may have to reach deep [*sic*] into a far away place in a very robust way to deal with this problem. We may have to do this over a sustained period of time. And those actions themselves will have their own consequences. So, it . . . it . . . there is no silver bullet literally or figuratively here [?] that is going to deal with the kind of unspeakable evil that we've seen today, the escalation in a massive way both in terms of capability and malevolent intent we've seen today. What we need now is buckle down, serious, concerted effort that's going to have to be long-range" (8:14 p.m.; periods indicate interruptions, not ellipses). —Frequent advice to viewers to avoid blaming Islam for the attacks also were coded in this category.
Caution-urging reports	claims made about the importance of exercising prudence in interpreting	At 10:02 a.m., warned, "I want to emphasize again—not to be redundant—but this is a day in which rumors are going to spread like mildew in damp basements." At 2:30 p.m., during an *(Continued)*

	initial reports	interview referencing previous crises, Dan Rather told Rand Corporation analyst Brian Jenkins, "On other occasions, there has been a lot of conclusion jumping, and a lot of conclusion jumping has been wrong."
Rumor-mongering reports	transmission of speculation not based in facts reported, transmission of reports identified as unverified, or reports identified as likely rumors	At 11:04 a.m., Peter Jennings noted that no information was available about the ways that hijackers managed to get control of aircraft. Nevertheless, he made up a scenario or two, which he shared with the audience: "Pilot either force to fly? [sic] Very hard to believe and, of course, we'll never know, unless they find the black boxes from these aircraft or somebody on board that aircraft killed or got rid of the pilot and went to the controls and flew the plane into the building themselves [sic]." At 11:21 a.m., after Tony Dorsey of NBC affiliate station WRC announced that "no one seems to be telling us exactly why all of this is happening [evacuating Ronald Reagan Airport in Washington, D.C.]," he shared an unconfirmed rumor that since the Pentagon had been attacked, "They [?] suspect that Reagan National could as well be [the object of an attack]."
Repeated reports	the number of times the same story was repeated during each time frame	

Though many researchers find it helpful to include a category labeled "other" to catch any other items to be coded, it was not necessary to do so because the level of analysis was the report, rather than the sentence, the story, or the wry comment. If researchers use an "other" category, they should realize that this category is not one element, but a number of categories. Regardless of the categories chosen, the classifications should

♦ be "exhaustive" and cover all the possibilities (to make sure, categories sometimes will include an "other" division, but the number of items that fall into that category should be fairly small);

♦ be mutually exclusive (that is, an event should not fall into more than one category); and

♦ include a coding rule for placing items in categories (criteria should be established in advance to decide what must occur for an item to be coded at all).

In formal content analysis, categories are established before collecting data. In reality, many content analysis categories are created by revising previous coding sheets on the fly. Researchers may find that unexpected categories should be separated from the rest or that the "other" category is inadequate. Especially when researchers are exploring a communication area for the first time, it is common for coding units to be changed after the study analysis is begun and the content analysis begun again. Since the message data are always available to the researcher, the analysis may begin again without difficulty (except for lost time, of course).

Many different units of analysis might be coded, of course. In the example on the relationship between the accuracy of 9/11 news stories and the time of their broadcasting on television, the unit of analysis included the number of reports of information within each half-hour time period. To determine when a report was questionable, three types of sources were used.

variations in coding systems

♦ Many questionable reports were corrected or withdrawn by the same television broadcasters. For instance, at 10:26 a.m. the news anchor at CBS affiliate WUSA reported that a car bomb had exploded outside the State Department. Within a minute, at 10:27 a.m., Frank Herzog, a field reporter, announced that he could verify, "Nothing is happening there now [at the State Department]. It looks all quiet. But I am getting reports from park police that another plane was hijacked out of Pittsburgh" (it actually had departed out of Newark and crashed near Pittsburgh). At 10:54 the same broadcast reported from an eyewitness that the plane crashing into the Pentagon was a small commuter plane. In each case, half an hour later the errors in all these reports were "corrected" by CBS reporters.

♦ Other news sources were used to identify questionable reports. At 11:27 a.m., a CBS reporter in Washington, D.C., began to spread the erroneous report that the jet crashing in Pennsylvania was aiming its terror for Camp David: "The thinking is among law enforcement, only a theory or speculation, they were targeting Camp David." By 3:31 p.m., as reported by a WUSA broadcaster, the account became, "One of the reports we're getting is that the plane that went down in Pennsylvania reportedly was targeting Camp David." Finally, on September 13, authoritative reports from other sources were published that the targets were the White House and Air Force One, not Camp David (Rosenthal, 2001). In addition, authoritative timelines prepared by news organizations were used to verify reports, especially those timelines of *The Television Archive* (http://tvnews3.televisionarchive.org/tvarchive/html/chronology.html), *Fox News* (www.foxnews.com/story/0,2933,34513,00.html), *CNN* (www.cnn.com/2001/US/09/11/chronology.attack/index.html), and *AirDisaster* (www.airdisaster.com/special/special-0911.shtml).

♦ Dedicated sources of information about urban legends and hoaxes were reviewed. These "hoax busters" included the *Urban Legends Reference Pages: Rumors of War* (www.snopes2.com/rumors/survivor.htm), the *About Urban Legends and Folklore* site (http://urbanlegends.about.com/library/weekly/aa091101aa.htm), *HoaxWatch* sponsored by the Committee for the Scientific Investigation of Claims of the Paranormal (www.csicop.org/hoaxwatch), and *SkepticWeb.com* (www.skepticweb.com/sections.php?op=viewarticle&artid=3). These sources had sections devoted to debunking errors in reports related to the 9/11 attacks (such as the myths of the attack survivors who "surfed" down 82 floors to safety when the World Trade Center collapsed and the alleged notices sent to Jewish workers in the World Trade Center).

A clearly false report was coded as 1, indicating one example of that form. Yet, sometimes things were said that proved to be incorrect though they were accurately reported. For instance, estimates of the number of dead in the attack were uncertain. Yet, rather than give high or low estimates, some officials announced exact numbers without qualifications. When such statements were accurately reported, but subsequently proved to be false, a score of .5 was added to the tally in this category. There are other ways that things could be coded of course. If they wanted, the researchers could have coded the amount of time male or female experts were interviewed. Other approaches could have been used. For instance, individual news reports could be evaluated on a seven-point rating scale ranging from -3 (certainly false) to $+3$ (certainly true). The use of such rating systems is quite common. For instance, Deborah Coker and Judee Burgoon (1987) composed and tested a content analysis check sheet that can be used to examine nonverbal communication used by people in conversations. This rating sheet is found on Table 8.1. It is a versatile tool that may be completed by observers of conversations following some initial training. As you can see, the format calls for different dimensions to be scored by adding individual items. Furthermore, the degrees to which the nonverbal cues were perceived to function in different ways are tapped by this format. They could have rated the number of words spoken in each questionable story. In short, researchers have great freedom in selecting many different things that can be enumerated or counted. When examining newspapers, researchers often identify the number of column inches dedicated to a topic. Sometimes they attempt to identify themes, which are recurring similar assertions made by communicators (after Budd, Thorp, & Donohew, 1967, p. 34). For instance, Brown (1961) used content analysis to study the use of anti–Roman Catholic themes developed to oppose the presidential candidacy of John F. Kennedy. He found 18 major themes in anti-Kennedy campaign materials mailed to voters, including such outrageous assertions as the claim that Roman Catholics are assassins of presidents (supported by observing that "Lincoln, Garfield, and McKinley were assassinated by Roman Catholics"). In their analysis of Internet messages sent to NBC Nightly News, Newhagen, Cordes, and Levy (1995) coded the types of messages in many categories including the type of audience targeted by the e-mail (macro-scopic messages written in the style of public pronouncements, mezzo-scopic messages written in the style of messages to a small group of respondents, micro-scopic messages written in the style of messages to single individual respondents). Krippendorff (1980) observed that content analysts have examined five kinds of units to study: (1) a physical unit (such as number of articles, inches of space, or number of pages); (2) a syntactic unit (such as number of words, phrases, or sentences); (3) a referential unit (such as presence or absence of objects); (4) a propositional unit (such as statements or argument units); and (5) a thematic unit (such as repeating patterns of ideas or treatments). In the above example, the problem question could be answered best by simply tallying the number of times male and female characters in commercials were portrayed as having different occupations.

TABLE 8.1　RATINGS OF NONVERBAL ENCODING

Immediacy

Orientation/Gaze			
	Body orientation	direct ___:___:___:___:___:___:___ indirect	
	Face orientation	direct ___:___:___:___:___:___:___ indirect	
	Gaze	appropriate ___:___:___:___:___:___:___ inappropriate	
Body Lean (proxemics)		forward ___:___:___:___:___:___:___ backward	
Positive Reinforcers			
	Nodding	frequent ___:___:___:___:___:___:___ none	
	Smiling	frequent ___:___:___:___:___:___:___ none	
	Smiling	appropriate ___:___:___:___:___:___:___ inappropriate	
Gesturing			
	Gestures	animated ___:___:___:___:___:___:___ impassive	
	Illustrators	frequent ___:___:___:___:___:___:___ none	

Expressiveness

Facial Animation		
	Facial expression	pleasant ___:___:___:___:___:___:___ unpleasant
	Facial animation	animated ___:___:___:___:___:___:___ impassive
	Smiling	frequent ___:___:___:___:___:___:___ none
	Smiling	appropriate ___:___:___:___:___:___:___ inappropriate
	Concern	concerned ___:___:___:___:___:___:___ indifferent
Vocal Expressiveness		
	Loud	loud ___:___:___:___:___:___:___ soft
	Loudness	appropriate ___:___:___:___:___:___:___ inappropriate
	Rate	fast ___:___:___:___:___:___:___ slow
	Tempo	varied ___:___:___:___:___:___:___ no variation
	Pitch	appropriate ___:___:___:___:___:___:___ inappropriate
	Pitch	varied ___:___:___:___:___:___:___ monotone
	Expression	expressive ___:___:___:___:___:___:___ inexpressive
	Relaxed laughter	frequent ___:___:___:___:___:___:___ none

Interaction Management

Fluency		
	Fluent	fluent ___:___:___:___:___:___:___ nonfluent
	Nervous vocalizations	frequent ___:___:___:___:___:___:___ none
Silence/Latencies		
	Silences	frequent ___:___:___:___:___:___:___ none
	Latencies	appropriate ___:___:___:___:___:___:___ inappropriate
Coordinated Body Movement		
	Movements	coordinated ___:___:___:___:___:___:___ uncoordinated
Coordinated Speech		
	Speech	coordinated ___:___:___:___:___:___:___ uncoordinated

Altercentrism

Kinesic/Proxemic		
	Involved	involved ___:___:___:___:___:___:___ uninvolved

(Continued)

TABLE 8.1   (Continued)

Attentiveness		
Interested	interested ___:___:___:___:___:___:___	bored
Interested	attentive ___:___:___:___:___:___:___	inattentive
Focused	focused ___:___:___:___:___:___:___	distracted
Alert	alert ___:___:___:___:___:___:___	unalert
Vocal Warmth/Interest		
Warmth	warm ___:___:___:___:___:___:___	cold
Interested	interested ___:___:___:___:___:___:___	bored
Involved	involved ___:___:___:___:___:___:___	apathetic
Pleasant	pleasant ___:___:___:___:___:___:___	unpleasant
Friendliness	friendly ___:___:___:___:___:___:___	unfriendly
Appealing	appealing ___:___:___:___:___:___:___	unappealing

Social Anxiety

Composure		
Cool	cool ___:___:___:___:___:___:___	bothered
Calm	calm ___:___:___:___:___:___:___	anxious
Still	still ___:___:___:___:___:___:___	restless
Composed	composed ___:___:___:___:___:___:___	uncomposed
Postural Relaxation		
Slumped	slumped ___:___:___:___:___:___:___	erect
Relaxed	relaxed ___:___:___:___:___:___:___	tense
Loose	loose ___:___:___:___:___:___:___	rigid
Self-Adaptors		
Self-Adaptors	frequent ___:___:___:___:___:___:___	none
Object-Adaptors		
Object-Adaptors	frequent ___:___:___:___:___:___:___	none
Random Movement		
Trunk/limb movement	frequent ___:___:___:___:___:___:___	none
Rocking/twisting	frequent ___:___:___:___:___:___:___	none
Head movement	frequent ___:___:___:___:___:___:___	none
Vocal Relaxation		
Rhythm	rhythmic ___:___:___:___:___:___:___	jerky
Clear	clear ___:___:___:___:___:___:___	unclear
Resonant	resonant ___:___:___:___:___:___:___	flat
Relaxed	relaxed ___:___:___:___:___:___:___	tense
Calm	calm ___:___:___:___:___:___:___	anxious
Composed	composed ___:___:___:___:___:___:___	uncomposed
Vocal Attentiveness		
Focused	focused ___:___:___:___:___:___:___	distracted
Attentive	attentive ___:___:___:___:___:___:___	inattentive
Alert	alert ___:___:___:___:___:___:___	unalert
Pitch		
Pitch	low/deep ___:___:___:___:___:___:___	high

Source: Copyright 1987. From "The Nature of Conversational Involvement and Nonverbal Encoding Patterns" by D. A. Coker and J. K. Burgoon. Reproduced by permission of International Communication Association, www.icahdq.org.

SPECIAL DISCUSSION 8-1

CONTENT ANALYSIS OF LATENT AND MANIFEST MEANINGS

Ever since content analyses became serious studies in the early 1950s, there has been a decision researchers have been forced to make: should they examine manifest content or latent content? Whether the variables identified by content analysis categories are the actual variables of interest or whether they are indicators of underlying concepts of interest determines what interpretations researchers make of their findings. When looking at research problem questions and hypotheses, researchers have to make these same sorts of decisions today.

Manifest content consists of the expression of communication elements that are immediately visible. This approach is the tradition started by Berelson (1952) and by Krippendorf (1980) as content analysis was in its developing stages. The basic coding units in content analysis category systems are manifest variables. For instance, a researcher might be interested in the types of occupations held by male and female characters in television commercials, as was the case in a classic study completed in 1972 (Dominick & Rauch, 1972). By using a set of occupational categories modified from the U.S. Department of Labor's *Occupational Outlook Handbook,* the researchers identified occupation categories, for which counts could be taken. They observed that the majority of female portrayals were of housewives and nearly half of male characters were husbands or fathers, professional athletes, celebrities, construction workers, or airline pilots. The overt information is what the researchers were interested in examining. Such content analyses tend to have high reliability because the overt measures are what the researcher wishes to know. Though researchers typically offer comments to interpret the results, the actual interpretations are usually limited to the realm of observable materials and their possible applications and usefulness to stimulate future research.

Latent content deals with the underlying meaning to which sets of manifest indicators point. Thus, the researchers take observable material (actually manifest variables) and seek interpretations about the collective meaning of the collection of indicator variables. The measured variables are not studied for their own sake, but for the underlying concept or construct to which they point. For instance, researchers may be interested in examining the degree of "civic attachment," which is a "perception of being closely linked to the community and its well-being" (Schmierbach, Boyle, & McLeod, 2005, p. 324), contained in newspaper and magazine editorials and commentaries. The terms "community involvement" may never be used, but the researchers could examine indicators or manifest variables that suggest the presence of "community involvement." Categories could be organized to identify the number of times mentions are made of positive values toward government, positive references toward voting, positive references toward participation in political activity, and positive references toward engaging in political discussion. The word counts and observable results are taken as indicators of something greater than themselves. The researcher attempts to "read between the lines" to interpret the manifest variables as indicators of the underlying construct. Latent variables, such as efforts to communicate a sense of "community involvement," cannot be measured very easily, and reliability often remains an open question in many cases. So, the use of many manifest indicators that point in a common

(Continued)

SPECIAL DISCUSSION 8-1 (Continued)

underlying direction may be meaningful. To get at these matters, researchers often rely on interpretations that take several manifest variables and offer an assessment about some underlying meaning. Sometimes researchers try to handle such matters directly by identifying themes that underlie several sets of information in the data. Of course, researchers often combine looking at both manifest and latent variables to conduct their content analyses. Under these circumstances, researchers may benefit from the best of thinking at an object level and thinking at an increasingly abstract level.

3. sample messages

Third, *sample messages* from the population of events. The sampling must be large enough to permit meaningful conclusions to be drawn. Furthermore, the samples are taken so that the communication can be claimed as representative of the larger population. Content analysts usually take pains to explain how they gathered their samples and when the sampled communication actually occurred. Sometimes it is not possible to obtain every event in a sampling frame. So, researchers may select a reduced number of events.

sampling methods

In content analysis there is no one "best" sampling method. You can choose from several options (Budd, Thorp, & Donohew, 1967, pp. 21–23):

- ♦ Random—in which every instance in the population has an equal chance of selection
- ♦ Stratification—in which strata are identified (such as geographic region, type of radio station format, type of ad) and a sample (usually random) within each strata is proportionately selected
- ♦ Interval—in which a sample is drawn by selecting instances of communication at specific units (such as coding every third commercial during prime time for a month)
- ♦ Cluster—in which groups of messages appear in a cluster that already exists (such as the cluster of articles from a single newspaper)
- ♦ Multistage—in which instances are selected sequentially (such as selecting commercials from one month, selecting one week from that month, selecting three hours from the days of the week, and so on).

Researchers are expected to sample events so that the conclusions drawn can be representative of such communication. Sampling may be a significant issue. In one survey of content analyses completed during a 25-year period ending in 1996, Riffe and Freitag (1997) found that 9.7% of content analyses used convenience samples, 22.2% used some form of random sampling, and 68.1% used "purposive sampling" in which a particular event or issue was identified and only content related to the particular case was included. Though for statistical purposes, random or stratified random sampling would be advised whenever possible, it is easier said than done. Sampling coverage of stories in newspapers and on local television may be particularly difficult. Simply making a selection of newspapers at random from standard statistical metropolitan areas may not be helpful. After all, the size of the newspaper readerships or television station viewing audiences may vary in vast ways. Some form of stratified random sampling would seem invited. For this reason, Long and her colleagues explored an alternative strategy. The researchers began by selecting a number of "Designated Marketing Areas" (DMAs) provided by the *Broadcasting/Cable Yearbook*. Some recommend selecting a number at random. Other sources recommend sampling a number from the four "strata," which correspond to each quartile of marketing area sizes.

application of stratified random sampling for content analysis of newspapers and local television

For newspapers within each DMA, a two-stage process is recommended:

1. Rank order the newspapers by readership size and include the largest newspaper in the DMA.

2. Rank order the remaining newspapers and select one newspaper at random in the area above the median and one newspaper at random below the median.

For local television stations (where viewership information may be very difficult for researchers to obtain), simply identify all network-affiliated stations within each selected DMA and take a random sample from this listing.

When these methods were examined over a two-year period extending from 2002 to 2003, the method was found to yield a very high degree of sampling representativeness in regard to distinguishing strata, making meaningful distinctions within each stratum, and adequately representing geographic distributions.

In our content analysis example, broadcasts from September 11, 2001, were analyzed for five networks: ABC, CBS, CNN, NBC, and PBS (the latter of which was the extended *News Hour* reports airing from 6:00 p.m. to 9:00 p.m. EDT). Broadcast samples were obtained in a purposive sample by analyzing 53 hours of recordings maintained by *The Television Archive* (http://tvnews1.televisionarchive.org/prog). Time periods for sample data collection for TV stations were the half-hour broadcasts from 8:30 a.m. through 9:00 p.m. (all times were eastern daylight time). Thus, 25 half-hour time periods from the major network sources must be considered. This sampling would have to be considered a nearly exhaustive survey, except for the fact that the Fox News system was excluded. The choice was made as a practical matter since Fox News would not make its broadcasts available and transcripts were only available for purchase. Since the authors did not have additional research funds at the time the research was completed, Fox News was not included in the final sample. The commercial broadcasts on these sources actually were drawn from affiliated stations in the Washington, D.C., area. In particular, the ABC data were drawn from the broadcasts of WJLA, CBS data were gathered from the broadcasts of WUSA, and NBC broadcasts were tracked by examining WRC television.

Fourth, code message content to produce numbers that can be tallied and reported. Whether general themes or specific measures, frequencies are tallied. Sometimes the process can be computerized (such as content analysis of readability of textbooks). But most of the time researchers rely on other people to help. In many cases, it is a good idea to have the data recorded by coders who are not aware of the researcher's hypotheses. Regardless of the individuals involved, the messages are presented to the coders (in some written, audio, or visual form), who then record their observations on tally sheets.

4. code message treatment or content

Researchers are expected to show that the categories are used consistently and in meaningful ways (along with statistics to show the degree of consistency or **reliability** in using the categories). It is important to describe the methods used to train content analysts since incompetent coding of communication can result in meaningless data. If several coders are involved, their degree of agreement is sometimes called "intercoder reliability." If consistency is not very high (if coders disagree with each other too often), the inconsistency should be noted and the unreliably coded data should not be included as part of the data set finally analyzed. In the example of televised broadcasts of the 9/11 attacks, two coders (one of whom was the lead author and the other of whom was *not* the same rater involved in the reliability assessment of written messages) completed content analyses of three half-hour broadcasts across two networks (the 9:00–9:30 a.m. ABC broadcast, the 9:00–9:30 a.m. CBS broadcast, and the 10:00 to 10:30 a.m. CBS broadcast). The content analyses were compared and revealed a Scott's *pi* coefficient of .751 (see Chapter 4). Though these reliabilities were not exceptionally high, this fact was ameliorated somewhat by recognizing that they were not inflated estimates and that they were generally in the acceptable range for this variety of initial research with a new measurement tool. Another approach might involve the comparison of coding consistency of multiple raters who code all the data for the entire study. If practical, it would yield high-quality evidence of the reliability of a measure.

Validity test validity is the consistency of a measure with a criterion.

Validity usually is a question of whether the measures really identify the variables alleged. Arguments typically are made by looking at matters of face validity or content validity. In the case of the study of 9/11 television broadcasts, the consistency of the definitions with a sampling of coded examples was taken as an argument for face validity. Sometimes, however, validity issues involve whether the revealed data actually include measures of what is claimed. The issues are reduced to whether the data are valid representations of reported variables. For instance, in the study of 9/11 broadcasts, a close examination of network coverage, the USA (Voice of America) network was originally included in the sample. But this source was excluded when its atypical qualities became obvious. First, USA did not have its own news-reporting operation and at 9:58 a.m. the network began broadcasting the Bloomberg service, which specializes in financial news. Second, the lack of experience in reporting general news seemed to result in great confusion. Bloomberg broadcast many more inaccurate reports than the other television sources coded in this study. For instance, at the 10 a.m. half-hour slot, Bloomberg provided 26 reports, of which 5 were plainly false. These items included the following dramatic assertions: "Tens of thousands of people are dead"; "A hotel near the White House is on fire"; "A third explosion has been made at the World Trade Center"; "There has been an explosion on Capitol Hill"; and "There has been an explosion on the Virginia side of the mall." Thus, this reporting clearly reflected a sampling "outlier" that did not reveal the mainstream reporting activity found in other television sources. Though a case could be made for including these broadcasts, the fact that they were so aberrant suggests that the information was not a valid reflection of reporting by trained *news* reporters (as opposed to financial news reporters).

5. analyze data

Fifth, analyze the data, most often by reporting simple descriptive statistics. Sometimes, however, advanced statistical tests might be applied to the data to spot key patterns and underlying factors of interest. It is typical for content analysts to report tables of results, such as the one for our study in Figure 8.1. As can be seen here, the

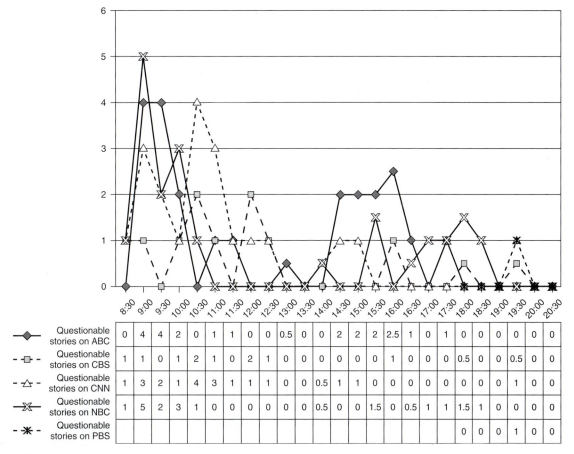

	8:30	9:00	9:30	10:00	10:30	11:00	11:30	12:00	12:30	13:00	13:30	14:00	14:30	15:00	15:30	16:00	16:30	17:00	17:30	18:00	18:30	19:00	19:30	20:00	20:30
Questionable stories on ABC	0	4	4	2	0	1	1	0	0	0.5	0	0	2	2	2	2.5	1	0	1	0	0	0	0	0	0
Questionable stories on CBS	1	1	0	1	2	1	0	2	1	0	0	0	0	0	0	1	0	0	0	0.5	0	0	0.5	0	0
Questionable stories on CNN	1	3	2	1	4	3	1	1	1	0	0	0.5	1	1	0	0	0	0	0	0	0	0	1	0	0
Questionable stories on NBC	1	5	2	3	1	0	0	0	0	0	0	0.5	0	0	1.5	0	0.5	1	1	1.5	1	0	0	0	0
Questionable stories on PBS																				0	0	0	1	0	0

FIGURE 8.1   QUESTIONABLE STORIES

number of questionable news stories was minimal in the first half-hour period (as television personalities tried to overcome their shock and begin presenting reports). Then, the number of questionable news stories jumped to 13 at the 9:00 a.m. period before beginning a general decline throughout the afternoon and evening. Since the research examined whether stories presented early would have an increased probability of reporting questionable material, an inverse correlation would be expected between the time of day and the number of questionable reports. As Chapter 12 explains, a correlation expresses the association between variables and can take a possible range of −1 to +1. Negative signs before correlations do not suggest subtraction from correlations—negative signs indicate an inverse relationship (that as one variable increases the other decreases). In this case, after PBS broadcasts were deleted (since they broadcast only between 6:00 p.m. and 9:00 p.m., the correlation between time of broadcast and the frequency of questionable reports was −.482 (with CNN reporting the highest inverse correlation). Thus, the results of both means and correlations showed support for the expected relationship. Of secondary interest was whether networks differed in their reporting of questionable materials. In fact, no "statistically significant" difference was found among the network broadcasts across the entire day. The simple descriptive statistics tell much of the story in these data. To explore the exact nature of the relationship, other statistics were used. In particular, it appeared that an increase in the number of questionable reports dramatically shifted upward (from 3 questionable reports to 13) at 9 a.m. and then started a steady decline—a curvilinear trend. Trends analysis (see Chapter 14) is a tool that allows researchers to explore whether data show any kind of nonlinear relationship. In this case, a "statistically significant" trend showing an inverted-U shape was found—consistent with the curvilinear trend suggested above.[5]

6. interpret results

    Sixth, interpret results to illuminate the research question. Many content analyses are also completed to help evaluate whether communication patterns are as they should be. Yet, describing results can be troublesome. Roger Wimmer and Joseph Dominick (1997) warned about one aspect of this problem:

> Researchers are often faced with a "fully/only" dilemma. Suppose, for example, that a content analysis of children's television programs reveals that 30% of the commercials in these programs were for snacks and candy. What is the researcher to conclude? Is this a high or low amount? Should the researcher report, "*Fully* 30% of the commercials fell into this category," or should he or she present this same percentage in a different light: "*Only* 30% of the commercials fell into this category"? The point is that the investigator needs some benchmark for comparison. Thirty percent may indeed be a high figure when compared to commercials for other products or those shown during adult programs. (p. 126)

Thus, as with other types of research, interpreting results is a vital but challenging process.

    To help analyze such results, researchers often make comparisons with other variables. When taken as a percentage of the total (not including admonitions to be cautious and repeats of the same report), the percentage of questionable reports among total 9/11 stories averaged 3.9% in each half-hour period. Yet, the time frame that featured the greatest percentage of questionable reports was between 8:30 a.m. and noon. During this time, 7.9% of the reports were in the questionable category. In other words, from 8:30 to noon, nearly one report of every 12 reports proved to be untrustworthy. From 9 a.m. to 10 a.m., the proportion of questionable or false reports to the total was 11.7, which approached one out of every eight reports. During this time period, CBS made only one questionable report. When CBS was excluded from the data set, the number of questionable or false reports reported by ABC, CNN, and NBC averaged 13.6%, or nearly one questionable report out of every seven.

---

[5]Though some may see another peak of questionable stories from 2:30 p.m. through 4:00 p.m. (especially since ABC increased questionable reports during this time period), statistical analyses did not show that this difference was beyond what would be expected to occur by chance. A related question was whether networks differed in their reporting of questionable news stories. Excluding PBS from the mix (since it did not begin broadcasting analysis of the attack until late in the day), the networks did not differ in their accuracy.

Limitations of the Approach

Naturally, there are some limits on content analysis methods. Some questions can be answered by content analyses and some questions cannot. Though these methods are useful in describing major communication trends, they are restricted to descriptions. Thus, the first limitation is that content analyses do not permit one to draw cause-and-effect conclusions (see Wimmer & Dominick, 1997, p. 115). One may describe the number of anti-Iraqi references in newspapers, but content analysis does not reveal the impact of those references on people. Of course some content analysts make causal statements anyway. But you should recognize that such conclusions are examples of drawing conclusions from irrelevant evidence—hasty generalizations, at best.

limitations:
1. cannot draw cause-effect conclusions

A second limitation involves the difficulty in finding representative examples of communication (see Berg, 2007, p. 328). Searching through newspapers and watching videotapes of television programs may sound simple, but it can be very tedious. There is some controversy about whether using audio or visual records as opposed to transcripts is preferable. On one hand, transcripts frequently have errors in them (often in efforts to make the written materials easy to read). Yet, using audio or visual records also may introduce errors unless the researcher is very careful about coding material accurately. Thus, researchers need to balance these concerns. Sometimes researchers select convenient examples and, hence, miss important matters. Unfortunately, it is not easy to tell if researchers have made these mistakes just by reading their articles. Scholars can be very clever in vaguely describing the exhaustiveness of their searches. In other situations, such as content analysis of the notes left at the Vietnam War Memorial, access to such materials might be difficult or ethically controversial to obtain. Thus, access to important communication examples may be difficult on occasion.

2. difficult finding representative samples

A third limitation is that the results of one content analysis cannot be generally applied to others that use different categories (see Wimmer & Dominick, 1997, p. 115). The systems that have been used by scholars to study violence on television, for instance, have been very different: some include threats as violence, some include only overt violent acts, some include good-natured roughhousing, some include contact sports, some include psychological violence, some include references to off-screen violence, some include slapstick comedy as violence. Comparing different analyses may be very troublesome since similar units may not be used. In general, one must be prudent when trying to generalize results from one content analysis to another.

3. cannot generalize to other categories of content analysis

APPLICATIONS OF CONTENT ANALYSIS

Scholars of interpersonal communication often look at examples of messages people have exchanged to see if they can discover something about the nature of the relationship between the people. The messages give clues regarding who is in charge and who is controlling the exchange. In a general sense, **interactional and relational analyses** apply content analysis to interpersonal communication. These methods apply categories to conversations and discussions to find out how people affect and control each other.

Interactional and relational analyses forms of content analysis designed to describe the continuing oral communication between people.

SPECIAL DISCUSSION 8-2

A QUESTION OF ETHICS: USING INTERNET SOURCES FOR CONTENT ANALYSIS

Using Internet resources has become popular. Markham (1998) has recommended what she calls a "virtual ethnography" on the Internet. Susan Herring (1996) observed that linguistic analyses on the Internet raise some serious ethical concerns. Work viewing the Internet as a culture with its own language use has not avoided ethical issues (Miller & Arnold, 2001; Senft, 2002). On the surface, use of these sources would not seem to create many ethical difficulties from a research point of view. After all, these sources would seem to be public communication sites where issues of confidentiality, anonymity, and deception would not be significant issues. Yet, when examining such matters as communication in chat rooms (as completed by Neuage [2004]), researchers must consider that real people are interacting and their rights must be respected.

Among the concerns has been the desire to observe assurances of anonymity and informed consent. A failure by the researcher to recognize the

> dichotomy between offline and online identity may lead to <u>un</u>ethical conse-
> quences: if we ignore the multiple ways in which embodied persons are con-
> nected with and emotionally invested in their online identities as part of their
> existential choices and projects—we run the risk of ignoring the very real harms
> that can follow when information about online identities is revealed, say, in a
> research report that fails to anonymize the pseudonyms used in a chatroom by
> specific persons. The limits of a metaphysical distinction are clear when we
> consider the history of legal protection of personal data for instance in Germany
> and the problems faced by such a legislation when related (!) to digitized data
> collected by different private and/or political bodies with different purposes. . . .
> It is also clear that after the events of September 11 the US will face serious
> conflicts when applying methods of digital surveillance that may interfere, for
> better or for worse, in the bodily and digital life projects of people.
> (Capurro & Pingel, 2001, ¶¶ 13–14)

Even when people make up names to enter chat rooms, their names reflect some effort to represent aspects of themselves that they consider safe to reveal. Unless names (ficti-tious or not) are changed in reports and unless records are kept under strict security, the rights of these individuals may be jeopardized. Such information may be used in ways that are not in the best interests of the individuals.

Not everyone agrees that researchers should take the time to let other chat room members know that they are being studied. Bassett and O'Riordan (2001, ¶ 4) submit that the Internet is fundamentally different from places where people congregate and might be observed. It is a site, not a special space where people congregate. Further-more, they submit that the Internet is a publication venue, not a private sphere. As such, they submit that the Internet—even in chat rooms—is best viewed as a set of published texts, not a collection of individuals who are gathered together.

Despite the unsettled status of these debates, gathering data on the Internet, such as is often done in modern content analyses, has made many scholars wonder what should be done to "be on the safe side" of offering protections. Chris Mann and Fiona Steward

(2000) suggested that ethical practices of collecting information from the Internet should feature the following imperatives:

Personal data should be collected for one specific legitimate purpose (p. 40);

People should have access to the data collected about themselves (41);

Existence of data banks should be publicly known (p. 42);

Personal data should be reasonably guarded against risk such as unauthorized access, modification or disclosure (p. 42);

Data should be collected in a context of free speech (p. 44);

Personal data are not to be communicated externally without the consent of the subject who supplied the data (p. 45).

Though such concerns seem to relate mostly to collecting information through interviews or some similar method, many of these ethical priorities also seem to apply to observations of communication in such arenas as Internet chat rooms.

Interaction Analysis

Interaction analysis focuses on ways of tracking individual acts of communicators. Scholars studying interpersonal and small-group communication have often looked at such communication examples. One of the most popular early forms was Robert Bales' interaction process analysis (1948; see Figure 8.2). The method involves recording a group as it deliberates and listening to each statement a person makes. Those statements, in turn, are counted in each of the categories listed on the figure. Bales himself moved to an increasingly complicated system called SYMLOG (see Bales & Cohen, 1979), and researchers in communication have also been interested in developing uses of the SYMLOG system (e.g., Cegala, Wall, & Rippey, 1987). Yet, the notion of interaction analysis can be demonstrated by looking at Bales' initial approach. Bales was able to explain that successful groups of people need to balance the task dimension of their work with the social-emotional dimension. The chart in Figure 8.2 allows us to identify the sorts of activities that take place from one phase of group decision making to another.

> **Interaction analysis** studies that focus on ways of tracking individual acts of communicators.

To interpret the meaning of different patterns of results, Bales urged attention to the information contained in the structure of interaction forms. The method emphasizes five different categories describing group actions that are promoted by individual statements made by group members:

> *interpreting Bales' analysis categories by looking at underlying patterns*

- ◆ Orientation (indicated by use of categories 6 and 7)
- ◆ Evaluation (indicated by use of categories 5 and 8)
- ◆ Control (indicated by use of categories 4 and 9)
- ◆ Positive reactions (indicated by use of categories 1, 2 and 3)
- ◆ Negative reactions (indicated by use of categories 10, 11, and 12)

To obtain useful information, researchers examine whether there are patterns of action and interaction that seem to form a logical pattern and that seem to promote

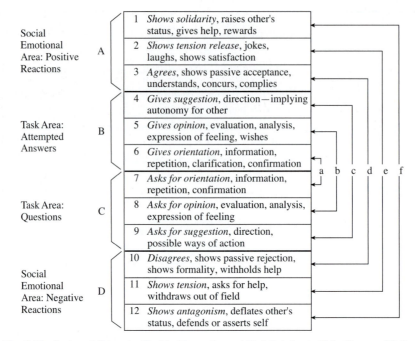

Chart I. The System of Categories Used in Observation and Their Relation to Major Frames of Reference.

Key:

a. Problems of orientation   c. Problems of control   e. Problems of tension-management
b. Problems of evaluation   d. Problems of decision   f. Problems of integration

FIGURE 8.2 BALES' INTERACTION PROCESS ANALYSIS CATEGORIES

Adapted from Robert Freed Bales. "A Set of Categories for the Analysis of Small Group Interaction." *American Sociological Review,* 15 (1948): p. 59. Courtesy of American Sociological Association.

sound group efforts. The check sheet invites the researcher to interpret results by looking at

♦ the frequency of the acts in each category;

♦ a matrix of categories showing who gave particular comments to whom, dominance of categories for each person, and comparisons against total interaction contributions; and

♦ a ratio of instrumental acts to socioemotional acts, indicating the relative balance between attention to socioemotional and task matters.

Though distributions may be examined at one time, there also can be comparisons of different patterns of interaction over time and during different phases of group decision making.

study of acts and double interacts

B. Aubrey Fisher and his associates contributed a variation of the interaction process analysis approach (Fisher & Drexel, 1983). They urged that the interaction between people, especially people taken two at a time (called dyads), be studied by looking at what were called "interacts" and "double interacts." The researcher looks at one person's conversation and the reaction of another—an interact. The researcher also looks at the first person's response to the other's reaction—the double interact. Though the concept was originally associated with management theorist Karl Weick (esp. 1969, p. 46), Fisher's work extended this method to discover how people develop a sense of belongingness in groups and how leaders emerge in groups (Fisher, Glover, & Ellis, 1977; Fisher & Hawes, 1971) as well as how people conduct themselves during formal interviews (Hawes, 1972). Taken as a whole, the method of interaction analysis has taken researchers in some interesting directions.

Bales' work stimulated work in both interactional analysis and relational control studies. In fact, authors cited in this chapter gave direct acknowledgment to Bales' work when advancing their own contributions. For instance, Gouran, Hirokawa, Julian, and Leatham (1993) reported that their functional approach to decision making and problem solving in groups was strongly influenced by Bales' (1950b) work. Yet, there are some difficulties with Bales' interaction process analysis when applied to details of communication. It

> does not allow the researcher to account for the task-relevancy of a particular communicative behavior. For example, according to Bales' system, a group member who (1) asks the group for ideas regarding the solution of the group problem, and (2) asks the group where they should go for dinner after the meeting, would, in either case, have to be "credited" with producing a question "asking for opinion." To the extent, however, that the former question is more likely to facilitate effective decision-making or problem-solving than the latter, it seems rather obvious that unless the researchers distinguished between those two types of questions "asking for opinion," it is not surprising that none of the three investigations found a consistent relationship between the total number of questions "asking for opinion" and overall decision-making or problem-solving effectiveness. The same problem would hold true for any of the other 11 categories which comprise Bales' analysis system. (Hirokawa, 1982, p. 135)

To improve on the matter, Randy Hirokawa and his various associates developed a coding system to identify functional group activity as part of his work on what became known as functional group theory. In this system, rather than coding each statement made by group members, the **functional utterance** is used.[6] This flexible notion of an utterance means that such a contribution is the uninterrupted functional contribution of one person and may include more than one contribution in a single turn.

Table 8.2 shows how the coding may work. Three-digit codes are assigned to each functional utterance made by each person. The top portion of the table shows the first digit of the code that would be assigned. The numbers, ranging from 1 to 4, reveal the functional categories or contributions to the group task: establishing operating procedures; analyzing and understanding the problem; generating feasible alternative solutions; and evaluating alternatives. The actual types of behaviors (many resembling items from Bales' system) are coded as the second and third digits of the coding system. Table 8.2 provides both these category codes and the working definitions

Bales' IPA is the basis for much other work

limitations of Bales' system

Hirokawa's functional group theory extends on Bales' work

Functional utterance in functional group theory, "an uninterrupted utterance of a single group member which appears to perform a specific function within the group interaction process" (Hirokawa, 1982, p. 139).

functional theory relies on "functional utterance" as analysis units

---

[6]A functional utterance is similar to the "speech act" identified as the unit of analysis in Fisher's (1970) theory of decision emergence.

TABLE 8.2   FUNCTION-ORIENTED INTERACTION ANALYSIS SYSTEM

Functional Categories Served by the Utterance
(first digit of code)

1 = Establish Operating Procedures: decide "what needs to be done to solve the problem and, more importantly, how they should go about doing it" (p. 137).	2 = Analysis of the Problem: steps that involve the group's effort to "(a) identify the nature of the problem, (b) determine the extent of the problem, (c) identify the possible causes of the problem, and (d) identify the symptoms of the problem" (p. 137).	3 = Generation of Solutions: steps to "consider as many feasible alternatives as possible before deciding on a final decision or solution" (p. 137).	4 = Evaluation of Solutions: efforts by the group to use care to "evaluate all alternative solutions, making certain that all important implications and consequences of accepting such a solution have been considered, and the one finally selected meets the criteria for a 'good' solution" (p. 137).

Behavioral Categories
(second and third digits of code)

Assertions

01 = Introduction: "Any statement which introduces a fact, opinion, belief, idea, or judgment into the group discussion" (p. 138).

02 = Restatement: "Any statement which repeats an earlier statement of fact, opinion, belief, or judgment in the same or similar terms" (p. 138).

03 = Development: "Any statement which seeks to develop or expand upon an earlier statement of fact, opinion, belief, or judgment; or to make that earlier statement more understandable through elaboration, example, illustration, or explanation" (p. 138).

04 = Substantiation: "Any statement which attempts to provide proof, support, or evidence which establishes the correctness, truth, or validity of an earlier statement of fact, opinion, belief, or judgment" (p. 138).

05 = Modification: "Any statement which reflects an attempt to alter or change an idea presented earlier in the discussion" (p. 138).

06 = Agreement: "Any statement which reflects direct agreement, approval, or consent with a fact, idea, opinion, or judgment under consideration by the group" (p. 138).

07 = Disagreement: "Any statement which reflects direct disapproval or disagreement with a fact, idea, opinion, or judgment under consideration by the group" (p. 138).

08 = Summarization/ synthesis: "Any statement which reflects an attempt to summarize, bring together, narrow, or add emphasis to elements (e.g., facts, ideas, etc.) previously introduced, substantiated, developed, or modified in previous lines of discussion" (p. 138).

(Continued)

TABLE 8.2 (Continued)

Requests

09 = Asks for ideas:	"Any question which seeks facts, ideas, opinions, beliefs, or judgments from some member(s) of the group" (p. 138).
10 = Asks for approval:	"Any question which seeks consent or approval from group members regarding a specific fact, idea, opinion, belief, or judgment previously brought before the group" (p. 138).
11 = Asks for clarification:	"Any question which seeks to have a particular statement of fact, idea, opinion, belief, or judgment made more understandable or precise" (p. 138).
12 = Asks for summary/ synthesis:	"Any question which seeks to have some member(s) bring together, narrow, or add emphasis to facts, ideas, opinions, or judgments introduced in earlier portions of the discussion" (pp. 138–139).

Examples of Coding Functional Utterances★	**Coding**
Ron: OK, does everyone know what the problem is?	211
Group: Yeah ... yeah ...	No Code
Jack: I think they should, you know, like put those speed bumps on the road ...	301
Dave: Yeah ... that's a thought ...	306
Ron: Yeah, but wouldn't that kinda' wreck the cars? I mean ...	409
Jan: Yeah, I think they would really, you know, wreck the bottoms of the cars, the shocks and stuff like that ...	401
Ron: Plus, you know, I really don't think they'd slow guys down ... I mean if you speed ...	401
Jack: [Are you nuts, man?] ...	307
[Try going over one of them things at 40 miles an hour ... I bet you won't speed on that street again ... scares the pants off 'ya ...]	304
Jan: Don't you think we should, you know, go back and think about this problem some more ...	201
Jack: What for? We already know the problem, control speeding ...	207
Ron: Now wait, Jan has a point ... Don't you think we need to know why people speed? ...	203
Jan: Right, like if they speed 'cause they're drunk we might propose one thing, but if they speed for fun, we might try something else ...	203
Jack: What does the paper say? ...	211
Dave: Doesn't say anything ... just that speeding is a problem ... doesn't tell us why people ...	201
Jack: I don't think the cops know ...	201
Jan: [It would depend on when the accident occurred, wouldn't it?]	201
[I mean if it occurred like at 3:00 in the morning, it could be caused by drinking ...]	203
	(Continued)

TABLE 8.2	(Continued)	
Jack:	[But that doesn't mean the guy was speeding] . . .	207
	[He could have fell asleep] . . .	201
Ron:	[Couldn't we, like, try to find a solution that isn't tied to a specific cause] . . .	101
	[I mean, something that would work regardless of the cause of speeding?]	103
Jan:	Yeah, right, ok . . .	106

★First six comments from Hirokawa, 1982, p. 139; others from page 140.
Source: Hirokawa (1982).

used for each category. Armed with this coding sheet, researchers find examples of exchanges of messages in group behavior and code them, similar to the example in Table 8.2. Then, interpretations can be made about the communication health of different groups and their functional (or dysfunctional) behavior. Such an extension of the pioneering work of Bales has led to stimulating theorizing in the field of group communication.

Relational Control Analysis

relational control analysis studies that track message sequences to determine the relative patterns of position and control in the relationship.

using the categories for relational coding

A dominant force in interpersonal communication research since the 1970s (Berger, 2005, p. 416), **relational control analysis** processes combine tools of interactional analysis and a certain amount of detective work to explore who is in a dominant or submissive role in a conversation (Mark, 1971; Millar & Rogers, 1976, 1987; Rogers & Millar, 1988). Rogers and Farace (1975) developed a set of methods to categorize who is "in charge" in personal exchanges. Thus, researchers check communication to see who seems to be in control of interpersonal exchanges. This method records people in conversations, usually in groups of two, but sometimes in increased numbers (DeStephen, 1983; Ellis, 1979). Table 8.3 shows how the system works. At the top of the table, the "interactors," or people involved in a two-person conversation, are identified as Speaker A and Speaker B. The researcher assigns codes to each message beginning with a "1" or "2" to indicate who made an *utterance* that is to be coded. The second part of the table provides the "control codes." The second digit in the assigned code involves the grammatical format of the utterance made by the speaker (an assertion, a question, an effort to talk over the other person, a noncomplete response, and other unclassifiable statements). The response from the other person is indicated by items in the "response mode" category, which includes the categories of offering support, disagreeing (nonsupport), extending on previous comments, offering instructions, issuing an order, offering a disconfirming response, changing the topic, initiating or terminating another's comments, and other unclassifiable responses. After looking at the combinations of initial comments and responses, the fun begins.

TABLE 8.3   RELATIONAL CODING

| *Interactors:* (first digit of code) | 1 – Speaker A 2 – Speaker B |

CONTROL CODES
Grammatical Format of the Message:
(second digit of code)

Response Mode: (third digit of code)	1 = Assertion: "any completed referential statement, either declarative or imperative in form" (p. 229)	2 = Question: "any speech which takes an interrogative grammatical form" (p. 229)	3 = Talk-over: "an interruptive manner of entering an ongoing utterance by the other actor" (p. 229)	4 = Noncomplete: "any utterance that is initiated but not expressed in a completed format" (p. 229)	5 = Other: "utterances that are unclassifiable as to their form" (p. 229)
1 = **Support:** "giving and seeking of agreement, assistance, acceptance, and approval" (p. 229)	↓	↑	↓	↓	↓
2 = **Nonsupport:** "disagreement, rejection, demands, and challenges" (p. 229)	↑	↑	↑	↑	↑
3 = **Extension:** "a message that continues the flow or theme of the preceding message. Included under this category is a noncommittal response to a question" (p. 229)	→	↓	↑	→	→
4 = **Answer:** "a response to a question which has substance and/or commitment" (p. 229)	↑	↑	↑	↑	↑
5 = **Instruction:** a statement making a suggestion and an "evaluative statement which is often accompanied with qualifications and clarification" (p. 229)	↑	↑	↑	↑	↑

(Continued)

TABLE 8.3   (Continued)

6 = Order: "an unqualified command with little or no explanation" (p. 229)	↑	↑	↑	↑	↑
7 = Disconfirmation: "a message exchange in which one interactor requests a response and the other interactor ignores the request" (p. 229)	↑	↑	↑	↑	↑
8 = Topic Change: "an exchange in which the second message has no theme in common with the first message, but also that no re-sponse commonality was requested by the first message" (p. 230)	↑	↑	↑	↑	↑
9 = Initiation-termination: "a message that either begins, or attempts to end, an interaction" (p. 230)	↑	↑	↑	→	↑
0 = other	→	↓	↓	→	→

Interpretations of second- and third-digit code combinations	Type of Control Indicated:	Designated Symbol:
12, 14, 15, 16, 17, 18, 19	one-up	↑
11	one-down	↓
13, 10	one-across	→
22, 24, 25, 26, 27, 28, 29	one-up	↑
21, 23, 20	one-down	↓
32, 33, 34, 35, 36, 37, 38	one-up	↑
31, 30	one-down	↓
42, 44, 45, 46, 47, 48	one-up	↑
41	one-down	↓
43, 49, 40	one-across	→
52, 54, 55, 56, 57, 58, 59	one-up	↑
51	one-down	↓
53, 50	one-across	→

Note: Page references to definitions are from Rogers and Farace (1975).

The numerical notation reveals what is being said and how another person responds. But to understand who is gaining or losing control, it is vital to translate these relationships into relational control codes. The second part of Table 8.3 includes these codes.

types of control code patterns

♦ If a pair of message exchanges suggests that a person is moving toward gaining control of the exchange, the message is identified as "one-up" (symbolized ↑) for the individual initiating the conversation turn.

♦ If a pair of message exchanges suggests that a person is giving control to the respondent or "accepting control of the other" (Rogers & Farace, 1975, p. 230), the message is identified as "one-down" (symbolized ↓) for the individual initiating the conversation turn.

♦ If a pair of message exchanges suggests that a person is moving toward "neutralizing control, which has a leveling effect "(Rogers & Farace, 1975, p. 230), the message is identified as "one-across" (symbolized →) for the individual initiating the conversation turn.

The combinations of grammatical forms and response modes create such patterns and are illustrated in the second part of Table 8.3. As can be seen in the third part of this table:

interpreting relational codes

> Code categories representing message forms and response modes that are viewed as control maneuvers toward *one-up* are: nonsupport responses (including questions demanding an answer), answers with substance, instructions, orders, disconfirmations, topic changes, complete statements of initiation, and all talk-overs except supportive talk-overs and those with unclassifiable response modes.
>
> The one-down code categories are: all support responses, including questions that seek supportive responses, noncomplete phrases that seek others to take control, supportive talk-overs, and questions that continue the dialogue (extension) or have uncodable responses (other).
>
> Neutralizing, or control-leveling categories, are viewed as carrying an interaction along with a minimized effort at controlling the relationship. Code categories that are seen as one-across maneuvers are assertions of extension, utterances with uncodable response modes, noncomplete phrases, and "other" (unclassifiable message forms) that are extensions. This includes questions (i.e., the "empty" answer response). Also included in the one-across category are noncompletes that initiate or terminate and that have unclear response modes (i.e., have third digit codes of "other"), and finally, utterances with both uncodable form and response modes (i.e., "other-other"). (Rogers & Farace, 1975, p. 230)

These control codes are clever ways to look at messages and identify who is in control during a particular exchange.

Relational control analysis, however, really takes off when researchers take time to explore sequences and to identify "transaction codes" across a series of exchanges. Much like examining an "interact" in interactional analysis, transaction codes consider a statement and the type of response that follows it as a pair of statements that

transaction codes for relational control

relational control analysis

show the structure of the relational control at work. For instance, the following example shows what happens when there is an effort to include the transaction codes (Rogers & Farace, 1975, p. 232):

categories of relational control

	Message Code	Control Code	Transaction Code
Wife: We don't do anything together anymore.	119	↑	↑↓
Husband: What do you mean?	223	↓	↓↑
Wife: Well, as a family we don't do very much.	114	↑	↑→
Husband: Oh, I don't know.	213	→	→↓
Wife: Don't you feel I do the major portion of disciplining the children?	121	↓	↓↑
Husband: The time we're together you don't.	214	↑	↑↑
Wife: Well, just for the record, I have to disagree.	112	↑	↑↑
Husband: Well, just for the record, you're wrong.	212	↑	↑↑
Wife: Well then, we completely disagree.	119	↑	↑↑

As can be seen, researchers can identify several forms of relationships among people who struggle for control:

different forms of control relationships

♦ Symmetrical forms involve interactants making the same kinds of contributions. Though in our example above, the symmetry involves conflict, it is not always so. Sluzki and Beavin (1965, p. 326) include these forms:

referential statement / referential statement

agreeing / agreeing

giving instructions / countering with instructions

Different kinds of symmetry can produce very different challenges in resolving relational control issues. For instance, when both relational partners are trying to be one-up (↑↑), the conversation shows *competitive symmetry,* which indicates an assertive conflict. When both partners are trying to be one-down (↓↓), the conversation shows *submissive symmetry* in which each attempts to defer to the other, often in a chain of avoidance communication, When both partners are trying to be one-across (→→), the exchange may be called *neutralized symmetry.*

♦ Complementary forms involve interactants making virtually the opposite kinds of contributions to the relational control issue. The complementary patterns may include these forms (Sluzki & Beavin, 1965, p. 326):

giving / taking instruction

asking / answering

asserting / agreeing

In each of these matters, there is a maximum difference between the contributions of interactants. The patterns may take the form of one-down/one-up ($\downarrow\uparrow$) or one-up/one-down ($\uparrow\downarrow$). These forms illustrate a maximum differentiation between the types of contributions that are made.

◆ Transitory forms include a one-across contribution ($\rightarrow$) at some location. The paired messages represent "neutralized" comments that the researchers identify among the participants.

Based on the contributions made by the interactional school of communication theory, symmetrical forms—despite any unpleasant conflict that might be seen—stress "equality and the minimization of difference, while complementary interaction is based on the maximization of difference" (Watzlawick, Beavin, & Jackson, 1967, p. 69). In a complementary relationship, one partner's exercise of control over the other is accepted (at least for the moment) and dominance is immediately identifiable.

SPECIAL DISCUSSION 8-3

CONTENT ANALYSIS IN COMMUNICATION POLICY AND REGULATION

In many nations, including the United States, regulation of material that may be directed at children has aroused a special interest. Though regulating televised material directed to adults has not received much support, children are a different class of people altogether. In recent years, content analysis has persuasively revealed how the avowed policies of protecting children have not always been satisfied. As such, the tool has moved from the domain of academics and scholars to communication policy makers whose actions may influence parents and children alike. Two cases in point are the regulations dealing with the V-chip and broadcast of alcohol-related advertisements.

Content analysis has revealed the impact of communication regulation policies. In the United States, the Telecommunications Act of 1996 required broadcasters to implement a V-chip rating system to protect children from exposure to inappropriate violent and sexual material. Signorielli (2005) used content analysis and discovered how poorly operated television's age-based ratings (*TV-G, TV-PG, TV-14,* and *TV-MA*) and content-based ratings (*V, S, L,* and *D*) actually were. Among prime-time programs, 20% were broadcast without age-based ratings, and 40% had no content-based ratings. Most disturbingly, large numbers of programs that were broadcast without content-based ratings featured violence and sexual content. The author suggested the 1996 Telecommunications Act provisions were not being implemented by broadcasters and the federal government had done precious little to make broadcast corporations comply.

(Continued)

SPECIAL DISCUSSION 8-3 (Continued)

In the realm of alcohol advertising, content analysis has revealed subtle ways that advertisers have attempted to "get around" regulations. In the United States, underage drinking is a significant national problem. Most young people begin drinking alcohol at age 13 (Flewelling, Praschell, & Ringwalt, 2004), and over half of 18- to 21-year-old youths are regular drinkers who tend to drink heavily (Johnson, O'Malley, & Bachman, 2002). As an alternative to stave off government regulation, the Beer Institute, the Distilled Spirits Council of the United States, and the Wine Institute agreed to self-regulate through a set of codes for the use of advertising. The self-regulations include many prohibitions on showing people actually drinking, prohibitions on showing situations where people drink to excess, and prohibitions on showing situations where drinkers are engaged in risky behavior where a high sense of alertness is required (such as driving or engaging in extreme sports). Lara Zwarun (2005) content-analyzed alcohol advertising in 70 televised football and basketball games from 1994 to 1997 and from 1999 to 2002 to test how well the self-regulation was working. As a result of the content analysis, the researchers observed that in each category, advertisements frequently implied the forbidden activity, even if not directly showing it. For instance, though no one was seen drinking a beer, many were seen with half-filled glasses of beer. Though no drunken partiers were shown, a Foster's beer advertisement depicted a "designated driver" wheeling a group of passed-out revelers across the Australian outback. Similarly, though no individuals were shown engaging in risky behaviors while drinking (with the possible exception of standing on the side of a toilet bowl or racing through a supermarket with an adult sprawled across the shopping cart), many commercials imply risky behavior while drinking. One ad showed two men holding open beers while they held their skis over their shoulders. Others showed motorcycling, snowboarding, and mountain climbing with quick editing to images of people holding beers. Another showed a man holding a six-pack of beer jump off a cliff into a lake where he swam some distance underwater as part of an extreme sports exhibition. In each case, it seemed that the advertisers played a game of seeing how much they could stretch their own codes before actually breaking them. By use of content analysis, these researchers found that advertisers designed messages that *communicated* recent alcohol drinking, drunkenness, and risky behaviors. But since arguably they could claim they did not show these things, advertisers could claim to abide by their own self-regulation. Is anybody swallowing that?

Using Interaction and Relational Control Analyses

steps in interaction and relational control studies:

Using these methods involves deciding on a coding system to use, training people to code messages, gathering samples of communication, coding message content, and analyzing and interpreting message content.

First, Decide on a Coding System

1. deciding on a coding system

Researchers have several choices when selecting the coding system. For interaction analyses, the classification systems developed by Bales might be contrasted with modifications developed by others. For instance, some researchers wish to focus attention on the impact of interaction in different time units (e.g., Amidon & Hough, 1967; Hawes, 1972). These researchers rely on methods that code the behavior at specific time intervals (such as 10-second intervals in the Hawes study). Other researchers have decided to look at each "speech act" during an interaction. For researchers of relational control, the coding systems can be fairly complicated. A popular check sheet was developed by Rogers and Farace (1975). Others have modified this form to improve validity. In their criticism of the coding methods, Joseph Folger and Marshall Scott Poole (1982) suggested that coding should be checked with individual communicators' reports of whether *they* believe their own messages indicate "one-up," "one-down," or "one-across" relationships. This method is recommended to ensure "representational validity." Researchers following this advice add an interview with communicators as part of their research. Whether such a step is necessary is controversial, but the use of alternative approaches must be explained and justified.

Second, Train People to Code Communication Examples

Researchers do not do this sort of research alone. They work with other people to make sure that there is some consistency in using the categories. Thus, raters must be trained so that they know how to use coding check sheets and charts. Regardless of whether interaction analysis or relational analysis is involved, researchers are expected to explain how the training was completed. Furthermore, researchers are expected to reveal how consistently different people rated the same communication behavior.

2. training coders

Third, Sample Communication Transactions

Though we can attempt to get very scientific in such sampling, the reality of the matter is that sampling of conversations or a group discussion tends to involve a lot of compromises. A researcher must get permission to record deliberations of a group. Securing signed consent forms is typically required. Sometimes researchers ask people to come to a specially prepared room to carry on a discussion. Sometimes people are sampled in a naturally occurring environment. Researchers report the number of conversations sampled, the number of people involved, their ages, their sex, the length of the conversations, and the topics discussed. These days, researchers are expected to interview participants after the project, explain any purposes of the research, and ask for feedback. Any information from these "debriefing" sessions is made part of the final research report. The best analyses are those for which the researcher can provide some argument for the representativeness of the samples drawn.

3. gathering samples

Fourth, Code the Message Content

Researchers find that they must spend most of their time listening to tapes (or reading transcripts) and coding messages by using the rating sheets or check sheets that have been chosen. Some analyses are simple tallies of the numbers of statements that fall into each category. Most relational control research has used this sort of method. Other times researchers can look at combinations of sequences of messages. In one outing, researchers found that marital satisfaction was most highly associated with the frequency of "one across" messages between husbands and wives (Vanlear & Zeitlow, 1990). Work in interactional analysis has occasionally been fairly subtle. For instance,

4. coding message content

in a piece of classic research in small-group communication, Scheidel and Crowell (1964) adapted Bales' interaction process analysis by adding a few specific categories and completed what they called "contiguity analysis." Contiguity analysis asks what sort of message *follows* immediately after another message type. They observed that the first reaction to a statement was another person's *repeating* the same sort of statement. Instead of group members responding to another's "asking for information" by "giving information" (which would seem logical), someone else in the group first repeated the request for information in different words. Groups seemed to do everything twice before making progress! Scheidel and Crowell suggested that group interactions might be described as a spiral in which forward progress is anchored in a backward spiral. (Put another way, groups take two steps forward and one step backward.) Coding the message content and relationship can be as simple or as sophisticated as the imagination of the researcher.

RESEARCHERS IN THE FIELD: JUDEE K. BURGOON

Judee Burgoon is a professor of communication, family studies and human development, and director of human communication research for the Center for the Management of Information at the University of Arizona. She is a scholar who has promoted student activity at a remarkable level. Her publications show names of (then) students of hers who have gone on to become some of the most active scholars in the field. She has authored or coauthored seven books and monographs and over 240 articles, chapters, and reviews. Her specialties have been in the areas of nonverbal and relational communication, deception detection, interpersonal relationships, and the impact of new communication technologies. Her development of the expectancy violations theory has influenced a generation of scholars and changed the way teachers learn to adapt to their students. Furthermore, her work in the public and private sector has been extensive, ranging form a long association with Gannett to work for the United States Department of Defense, the Department of Homeland Security, and various intelligence agencies (for which she has studied human deception, nonverbal communication, and detection technologies). She has also edited *Communication Monographs*. Among her many honors are the National Communication Association's Golden Anniversary Monographs Award, the Charles H. Woolbert Research Award for Scholarship of Lasting Impact, and the International Communication Association's B. Aubrey Fisher Mentorship Award. In 1999, she was awarded the National Communication Association's Distinguished Scholar Award, its highest award for a lifetime of scholarly achievement.

◆ *What drew you into our field ?*
   I first became enamored with communication when I took a speech course in ninth grade [at J. B. Young Jr. High in Davenport, Iowa] and became part of a "voice chorus" that did oral interpretations of all kinds of literary materials in unison. Next came debate, which I loved. I was a debater throughout high school [Central High School in Davenport] and college [graduated with a

bachelor's degree *summa cum laude* from Iowa State University, received a master's degree from Illinois State University, and earned a doctorate from West Virginia University] and became a director of forensics and a debate coach for my first postdoctorate faculty position [at the University of Florida].[*] But I also got exposed to social science research along the way—especially research in nonverbal communication—and that eventually eclipsed debate as my first love.

♦ *Your work on Expectancy Violations Theory is one of the most influential contributions to communication theory. It continues to fascinate researchers and has undergone refinements in light of new research insights. Did you think that this theory would have such a great impact?*

No, I never would have predicted it. Although in retrospect, the concepts of expectancies, violations, and communicator valence have been such powerful explanatory variables in the history of human relationships that it should not surprise us that putting these variables together in a model might have staying power.

♦ *You've been widely honored for your research. In general, what have you hoped that making your research especially visible would accomplish?*

Rather than answer about visibility, I think the question for me is, What have I hoped to accomplish with the research itself? I wanted to do many things along the way, but among them, trying to shed light on some of the most fundamental aspects of human behavior such as how people use communication to define their interpersonal relationships, how communication can be used on the one hand to build trust and rapport and how on the other hand it can be used to manipulate and deceive. I have hoped that my research would not just be tucked away on some dusty library shelves but would lead to better relationships, interventions, training, or tool development. I guess that's why I was drawn to this "practical" discipline in the first place—like so many of us, there is real gratification coupling knowledge generation with knowledge application.

♦ *You have been a champion of research that examines vital issues in extended contexts, including newspaper usage, health communication, and homeland security. Has this extensive work been something you planned early in your career?*

No, I doubt that anyone could have imagined getting involved in such diverse areas. My research path has been influenced by the opportunities that opened up for me along the way.

♦ *What personal qualities do you have that you think have contributed to your achievements as a communication scholar?*

I suppose an inquisitive and restless mind, persistence (or some might call it obstinacy), and genuine pleasure in working with others on research problems.

---

[*]Before beginning her master's degree studies, Judee taught and directed debate and drama and taught English and speech at Boone High School in Boone, Iowa.

The Last Step in Interactional and Relational Analysis Is Interpretation

5. analyzing and interpreting message content

Researchers try to develop theoretic explanations for their findings. Interactional and relational analyses do not tell whether the communication is "good" or "bad," but describe how people use messages. Relationships with other variables can be drawn, but explaining *why* those patterns exist requires researchers to develop ideas and suggest models. Most often researchers explain how current theories are supported or challenged by their work. Yet, some studies lead researchers to suggest new directions for theories.

Limitations of the Approach

limitations:
1. may not be useful to assess perception or interpretation of others

2. cannot yield cause-effect statements

The interaction and relational analysis approach has two limitations that focus on the validity of the information measured. First, the methods may not be useful if the researcher's theoretical or explanatory basis is the perception or shared interpretation of individuals. Rather, these procedures are most appropriate when individual motivations are considered less important than other bases for understanding or explaining human behavior (Tardy, 1988b, pp. 292–293). Such a limitation may make these methods impossible for attempts to answer many mainstream research questions. Second, since the method takes actual communication and observes relationships with other variables, it cannot be used to draw conclusions about cause-and-effect relationships. Variables related to interaction or relational categories can be assessed, but the method does not allow determining which came first. Third, though some may have tried, interactional analyses really offer only descriptions of phenomena. Thus, "a critical approach demands more than an interactional analysis of language acts" (Billig, 2006, p. 17). Those wishing to make critical statements must step outside these systems.

CHECKLIST TO EVALUATE CONTENT ANALYSIS FORMS

_____ Does the problem question invite content analysis by asking about the amount or the frequency of occurrence of communication qualities?

_____ Does the research question involve matters that invite description or explanation, rather than prediction or control?

Using content analysis generally:

_____ Is the communication to be examined accurately characterized by the researcher?

_____ Is the communication population to be studied carefully defined and limited?

_____ Are the coding units appropriately chosen?

_____ Are the coding units exhaustive?

_____ Are the coding units mutually exclusive?

_____ Are the coding units accompanied by clear coding rules?

_____ Is an "other" category included (if not, is a rationale provided for its omission)?

_____ Is the communication sampling appropriate?

_____ Is the sample sufficiently large to represent the population of interest?

_____ Is the method of sampling clearly identified and justified?

_____ Were the coders appropriately trained?

_____ Is there evidence of reliability in coding?

_____ Is there an argument made for the validity of the coding of categories?

_____ Are the data appropriately analyzed with clear descriptive statistics and other relevant accounts of the data?

_____ Are the results appropriately interpreted?

_____ Are claims of cause and effect avoided?

_____ Is the casual use of the "fully/only" comparison avoided?

_____ Do the researchers avoid generalizing to other categories of content analysis?

Using interactional analyses (in addition to the elements required for content analysis in general):

_____ Is an appropriate coding sheet used (e.g., Bales, Hirokawa) and justified?

_____ Are sample codings of "utterances" and "functional utterances" completed with examples provided in the report?

_____ Is the choice to examine the "act," "interact," or "double interact" form justified?

_____ Are analyses completed to identify not just raw frequencies but underlying interaction and functional dimensions of communication?

Using relational control analyses (in addition to the elements required for content analysis in general):

_____ Did the research problem question deal with issues of control, dominance, or submission?

_____ Are sample codings of relational control exchanges completed with examples provided in the report?

_____ Are reports of transaction codes included?

_____ Are analyses completed to identify not just raw frequencies but underlying patterns of control and dominance in interpersonal relationships?

_____ Were the types of transaction forms identified (symmetrical, complementary, transitory) and interpreted?

_____ Did interpretations of results avoid consideration of criticism or issues of shared interpretations of participants?

SUMMARY

Content analysis is "any of several research techniques used to describe and systematically analyze the content of written, spoken, or pictorial communication—such as books, newspapers, television programs, or interview transcripts" (Vogt, 2005, p. 59). This effort can be considered quantitative research since it deals with counts of message characteristics. This effort can be considered qualitative research since it deals with qualities of messages and because it can be applied to interpret individual cases in an intensive manner (usually by looking at such things as broad themes, recurring phrases, semantics, or concepts). Thus, the entire approach can be considered consistent with grounded theory and the interpretive approach to the analysis of texts. The method lets researchers move very efficiently through a lot of information and data. To select any of the many forms of content analysis as an appropriate procedure for a study, one determines that the problem question asks about characteristics of messages that could be categorized and counted. Research questions also invite content analysis and interactional/relational analyses when they deal with comparison patterns of messages, message flow, or dominance from different sources; comparisons of message content with real life; the image of specific groups of people in society; changing uses of messages by different people or groups; applications of standard evaluation systems to actual messages; comparisons of communication patterns across cultures; and assessing matters that may challenge assumptions of fairness, equality, and diversity.

Completing content analysis serves several functions. Of the research goals of description, explanation, prediction, and control, content analysis is most suited to description and explanation. Content analysts often find that this method is most useful for looking at individual instances or general patterns across cases. Content analysis may be combined with approaches such as ethnography, focus group interviews, and criticism. Sometimes content analyses provide explanations by completing separate work over time. Content analysis is a systematic method designed to analyze the content and treatment of communication. Content analysis steps include (1) defining and limiting the communication population to be studied, (2) selecting coding units and classification systems (coding units are the categories used to count the communication forms), (3) sampling messages, (4) coding message content (including determining consistency of coders and providing adequate training), (5) analyzing data (usually by reporting simple descriptive statistics), and (6) interpreting results. Limitations of the method are (1) inability to draw cause-and-effect conclusions, (2) difficulties in finding representative communication examples, and (3) generalizing from one content analysis to another.

Interactional and relational analyses are forms of content analysis designed to describe the continuous oral communication between people. Interaction analysis focuses on ways of tracking individual acts of communicators. A variation of direct coding approaches (such as Bales' interaction process analysis) is the examination of "interacts" (one person's conversation and the reaction of another) and "double interacts" (which add the first person's response to the other's reaction). This approach stimulated progress developing Hirokawa's functional group theory coding sheet. Relational control analysis tracks message sequences to determine the relative patterns of position and control in the relationship. Statements made in these conversations are coded into categories called "one-up" (in which somebody is dominant over another because he or she asserts one's "definitional rights"), "one-down" (in which a person submits to the opinions or definitional rights of another), and "one-across" (message extensions that extend discussion without increasing assertions or accepting others' statements). Using these methods involves (1) deciding on a coding system to use, (2) training people to code messages, (3) gathering samples of communication, (4) coding message content, and (5) analyzing and interpreting message content. These methods are limited by the fact that they may not be useful if the researcher's theoretical or explanatory basis is the perception or shared interpretation of individuals, the methods cannot be used to draw conclusions about cause-and-effect relationships, and they do not permit making criticism comments.

TERMS FOR REVIEW

content analysis

coding units

latent content

manifest content

reliability

validity

interactional and relational analyses

interaction analysis

functional utterance

relational control analysis

JUST FOR THE SAKE OF ARGUMENT: A REVIEW

Look at the following questions and prepare your own answers to them. Make sure to consider any assumptions that may lie beneath them.

1. In which ways is content analysis a qualitative method and in which ways is it a quantitative method?

2. Can we draw cause-and-effect relationships from content analysis methods?

3. When are interactional analyses invited in preference to relational analysis?

4. What methodological problems do content analysts have that other researchers examining texts do not have?

5. How does the method of content analysis differ from any survey method using check sheets and questionnaires?

6. Sometimes content analysis forms are revised while the project is under way. To what extent is this practice "rigging" a study to produce desired results?

7. Content analysis is often used to identify major trends in society. Based on what you read in this chapter, are there any trends that seem to be identified based on work that is studied?

ACTIVITIES TO PROBE FURTHER

Go to the website for this book, and look for the Student Study Materials for Chapter 8.

1. Take the study quiz and print out your answers. (Avoid giving answers that are your first impressions. Make sure to review these text materials before you answer the questions, not as an introduction to them.)

2. In your class, you will notice that students often ask the instructor for information, definitions, and explanations. Though most of the time the answers are useful, sometimes they are not helpful. Watch for an encounter a student has with an instructor during class and take notes.

Write out the exchange (or as much as you remember of it):
Speaker A: _____
Speaker B: _____
Speaker A: _____
Speaker B: _____
Speaker A: _____
Speaker B: _____

a. If you were using interaction analysis, what would be the nature of the act and interact? In particular, did the exchange involve efforts at the following (check the number of times that each applied)?
_____ Orientation
_____ Evaluation
_____ Control
_____ Positive reactions
_____ Negative reactions

b. If you were using relational control analysis, who was in the dominant position? How many utterances of the following nature were included?
_____ One-up
_____ One-down
_____ One-across

c. Which of these methods was most useful to help you understand the exchange? Why?

3. Suppose you wished to construct a coding sheet to evaluate the number of sexually suggestive messages used in network-televised situation comedy programs. What would be the content categories you would use? (*Hint*: Rather than describe highly specific types of language and comments, rely on categories, such as sexually themed joking, references to past sexual activities, etc.).

a. List this set of categories in Column A.

Column A	Column B
_____	_____
_____	_____
_____	_____
_____	_____
_____	_____
_____	_____

b. Provide working definitions that you would use to train coders in Column B.
c. Include an "Other" category.

4. After composing the check sheet in item 3, choose two television situation comedies, one of which you believe has a lot of sexually suggestive messages and one that you think does not include a lot of sexually suggestive messages.
Situation comedy with expected high amounts of sexually suggestive messages:

_____

Situation comedy with expected low amounts of sexually suggestive messages:

_____

After applying the check sheet to one viewing of each of these programs, did you find a great or small difference in the actual amount of sexually suggestive messages?_____

Were there any noticeable differences in categories used by the comedies? (Provide report of amounts.)

	Frequency of message type in:	
	Comedy A	**Comedy B**
Type of message _____	_____	_____
Type of message _____	_____	_____
Type of message _____	_____	_____
Type of message _____	_____	_____
Type of message _____	_____	_____
Type of message _____	_____	_____
Other	_____	_____

What do these facts tell you about your expected differences?

5. Join the content analysis listserv for a month, and see what sorts of issues and controversies are faced by researchers using this method (listproc@listproc.gsu.edu, CONTENT, and Internet mailing list for those interested in the study of content analysis). To subscribe to CONTENT, send an e-mail stating "subscribe CONTENT <insert your name here>" to the above address.

    a. What issues in content analysis methodology were addressed?

    b. What controversies about the usefulness of the approach were considered?

6. For the next six days, complete a content analysis. Take two news broadcasts from each of the major television networks, and watch them for two nights each. Take the following rating scale, and tally the number of times mention was made of news stories involving Japan, Canada, Africa, or Europe. Use the following rating scale.

    Which locations received significantly greater and less coverage than the average? Which networks gave more coverage to some locations than to others? Was there any evidence of a network-by-location bias?

Number of Times Stories Mentioned About:

	Japan	Canada	Africa	Europe	Latin America
ABC Broadcast	_____				
CBS Broadcast	_____				
NBC Broadcast	_____				

CHAPTER 9

Design of Descriptive Empirical Research in Communication

A science is any discipline in which the fool of this generation can go beyond the point reached by the genius of the last generation.

—MAX GLUCKMAN

CHAPTER OUTLINE

BEFORE WE GET STARTED . . .

Descriptive empirical research in communication tends to rely on quantitative methods, though qualitative analysis of interview data is quite common. The tools discussed in this chapter involve collecting survey information and summarizing data, most often in numbers. Hence, this chapter deals with the very basic issue of how descriptive survey research is completed. It will introduce you to the forms of such research and give you some details about survey research.

INVITATIONS TO EMPIRICAL RESEARCH IN COMMUNICATION

The study of communication often relies on empirical research. Taking the **empirical** approach applies to all communication research that tests statements against observable data. **Descriptive empirical research** involves gathering fresh data to survey a matter. In fact, some use the term "survey research" as a substitute for the category of inquiry described in this chapter. Empirical descriptive research is most invited when problem questions ask about current descriptions of things and explore explanations that characterize things as they are now. J. Jeffrey Auer explained that such questions may have three emphases (1959, p. 147):

1. *Ascertaining norms:* Where are we? What is?

2. *Establishing goals:* Where should we be? What is best?

3. *Developing methods:* How do we advance from norm to goal? What is best to do?

Surveys, content analyses, and observational (including network analysis) studies can help researchers understand what is occurring. Surveying attitudes and opinions can show sentiments about directions to move. Scholars who attempt to develop new research methods and measurement tools can promote other studies to help solve practical problems.

Some questions ask about cause-and-effect relationships between variables. Although historical research can answer such questions if we have enough time, the

Empirical refers to those things that are observable.

Descriptive empirical research survey research in which contemporaneous data are gathered to answer research questions dealing with ascertaining norms, establishing goals, or developing methods.

questions asked in attempts to describe

experiments show causal relationships

Experiment a type of study using experimental methods in which researchers examine the effects of variables manipulated by the researcher in situations where all other influences are held constant. Variables are manipulated or introduced by experimenters for the purpose of establishing causal relationships.

Survey a study that uses questionnaires or interviews to discover descriptive characteristics of phenomena.

surveys are used in all branches of communication

only way to get contemporaneous evidence of cause-and-effect relationships is through experimentation. An **experiment** introduces a variable and determines its effects while controlling all other variables. Achieving such control is difficult, but if successful, experiments provide direct, immediate evidence of cause-and-effect relationships. This chapter focuses attention on nonexperimental methods, and the next chapter explores experimental research.

SURVEY RESEARCH

The term "survey" means the process of looking at something in its entirety. It scrutinizes the complete scope of something. As a type of empirical study, a **survey** relies on questionnaires and interviews. We often think of surveys as polls, questionnaire studies, and interviews in which large groups of people are asked their views. Yet, relatively small groups of people such as employees of a company or a plant can be surveyed. Their responses may be used to identify employee sentiment. Or their responses could form the basis of a network analysis. Furthermore, researchers could survey the language used in communication research literature to detect hidden relationships, and even some potential biases.

Surveys are used across communication studies. In fact, students often find that after graduation they are asked to construct questionnaires in their jobs. Professionals also use this method actively. In health communication, Morgan and Miller (2002) used mail surveys of 798 adults from two organizations to find out what factors were associated with signing an organ donor card or indicating a willingness to be an organ donor. The variables most associated with donating an organ were knowledge about organ donation, altruism perceptions of social norms about the desirability of donating an organ, and attitudes toward organ donation in general. Another survey of the perceptions that school-age children have of stutters was revealing (Franck, Jackson, Pimentel, & Greenwood, 2003). The researchers were particularly harsh in their views of stutterers, especially in perceptions of intelligence and desirable personality traits. In some rare survey work completed on the subject of respect for the elderly among young Americans, McCann, Dailey, Giles, and Ota (2005) found that there was a curious paradox. If young people stereotyped the elderly as benevolent and personally vital (in short, as sweet old "characters"), they tended to report less avoidance of communication with the elderly. On the other hand, if they believed that the elderly should be treated with great respect (consistent with many biblical suggestions), they tended to avoid communication with them. As you can see, survey research can add intriguing information to our store of knowledge. The three general forms of survey studies are questionnaire studies, interview studies, and network analysis.

THE QUESTIONNAIRE SURVEY

Completing a questionnaire study involves the six steps described below. At each point along the way, researchers explain and justify their choices.

SPECIAL DISCUSSION 9-1

FORMS OF DESCRIPTIVE STUDIES

Though surveys are the dominant form of descriptive studies, there are other forms of such studies (after Auer, 1959, chapter 6).

Studies of Behavior: Facts and Opinions

These studies are designed to determine the current status of conditions or attitudes. In addition to surveys by questionnaires and interviews, researchers may make direct observations of communicators. Sometimes the observation can rely on special technologies, such as special screening rooms equipped with "wiggle-meters" (which measure how attentive people are by tracking how often they shift weight [wiggle] during a broadcast).

Studies of Status and Development

Intensive detailed study of individual cases and events often reveals information that can be used to develop other hypotheses or to answer practical questions. This form of research includes what are sometimes called case studies or genetic studies (inquiries into the "growth and development among individuals and groups" [Auer, 1959, pp. 151–152]). These studies are usually long-term inquiries that trace the genesis and change of a group of people throughout a life cycle.

Methodological Studies

These studies deal with the development and validation of new tools and measuring instruments. Some studies examine the integrity of different research approaches generally, such as Burgoon, Hall, and Pfau's (1991) check on the validity of persuasion studies that employ only one persuasive message topic (they found no major statistical or logical difficulty when different studies had provided replications across topics). Another type of methodological study develops research instruments, such as Wrench and Richmond's (2004) assessment of the psychometric properties and the validation of the "Humor Assessment" Scale.

Selecting Questions and Providing Instructions

Questionnaires solicit written responses. Questionnaires ask people to report their understanding of things, often including their own behavior. Though beginning students are often nervous about developing their own questionnaire items, with experience—and often with a model of similar questions to guide you—the task can be made fairly simple.

In general, there are three ways to develop survey items, as Chapter 4 indicated. First, you may find standard forms in resource works and handbooks. Second, you may select measurement forms that have been used in research articles you read. Yet, you may find that researchers have not bothered to report details of ways to measure your specific variables of interest (good for you, since it means

Questionnaires survey forms in which individuals respond to items they have read.

three ways to develop survey items

RESEARCHERS IN THE FIELD: HOWARD GILES

Howard Giles is one of the top specialists in language, intercultural communication, intergenerational communication, and intergroup communication. He has written over 40 articles and four books and edited six others, including the *New Handbook of Language and Social Psychology* (2001). He is a professor of communication studies at the University of California at Santa Barbara with affiliated appointments with the Departments of Psychology and Linguistics. He has edited the journal *Human Communication Research* and was a founding coeditor for both the *Journal of Language and Social Psychology* and the *Journal of Asian Pacific Communication*. This sort of background might sound like the experience of a cloistered academic, but Howard Giles is also very involved in his community. He has been active in the work of the Center on Police Practices and Community, and he is dedicated to promoting community policing and effective law enforcement–civilian interactions. He is a reserve police officer in Santa Barbara and has clocked more than 3,000 hours of actual law enforcement work. His colleagues praise him as much for his sense of humor as for the integrity of his research. As an example of this droll humor, in this interview he peppered his comments with humorous interjections and used witty names, referring to psychology scholars as "psychos" and communication researchers as "commies."

♦ *You have been one of the most prolific and respected scholars in intercultural communication for some time. What moved you to this specialty in the field?*
I was born and studied high school in Wales. Twenty-six percent of Welshpeople speak the native language and I studied it during the last two years of high school—one studies three topics in the last two years of British high school. Getting a very, very good grade in this subject was essential, not only to get to my college of choice but to *any* one. A very small percentage of high school students actually went to university in those days (and still it's way smaller than in the USA). My Welsh teacher at the time received an honorary master's degree from the University of Wales for his contributions to Welsh life and the teaching of the language. He was an inspirer and a great teacher. With us, he was finishing his teaching career, which had spanned some 40 years. Never had he given lower than a B grade in all those years—and a B grade in the UK is much different than from the States. More than that, a number of the texts (viz., poetry and literature) we were to study were actually written by his "old boys." I remember his telling us that it was wonderful to end his career with us as, by all prior standards, we could be his very best!! Woof, what a commendation!

The others got As with distinction and I was his first and last failure! You can imagine my misery and embarrassment, not only as I might not qualify for college but for my beloved mentor. I was lucky to make college at all. Once I was there, I thought I'd devote myself to understanding why it was I was a miserable failure at learning another language (my own!) and why people in general find it difficult. I also saw it even in those days as a social identity and communication issue. By researching this ultimately, I thought I could pay Mr. Elvet Thomas back in some way. Actually, we did remain in good and happy contact for many a year and I ended up being one of the only monolingual scholars (!) studying bi- and even multilingualism—what nerve, eh?

♦ *What drew you into our field?*
I had been working in social psychology since graduate days. However, language and communication studies were at the periphery rather than the mainstream of this discipline. This was fine, although it was constantly "hard work" making oneself relevant and salient to "psychos." It was actually delightful to spend probably more time with sociolinguists and communication scholars. I joined the International Communication Association and we convened the first few International Conferences on Language and Social Psychology at Bristol, England in 1979, 1983, and 1987. At these conferences I met with and collaborated with what I called "commies" as opposed to "psychos." In 1987, I spent a semester at the University of Wisconsin at the Department of Communication Arts and Sciences and I became intrigued with rhetorical studies for the first time. Then, I moved to UC Santa Barbara for 6 to 9 months; they had *just* started up their new [doctoral] program in communication. We made more friends at UCSB than we had at Bristol. I never really thought of myself as a prototypical Brit and now in Santa Barbara I found myself at the center of things, rather than in the mainstream of the field. Hence, I was very attracted to the great scholars at UCSB, its paradisical location!, and to the very interdisciplinarity that constituted communication.

♦ *Research in the field obviously is a personal matter in your life. What personal qualities do you have that you think have contributed to your great success as a communication scholar?*
Hmmm . . . I'm not so sure about "personal" qualities *per se*—but relational ones have been critical. I have been fortunate enough to work with great minds and wonderful *fun* people—these include both extant scholars as well as driven undergraduates and graduate students. This teamwork, sparking off each other to the point you don't know who contributed what, has been really energizing. To return to your question (and knowing you'll still push me), I think, although I was also "lousy" at English too, I am a frustrated writer. I really enjoy this process, as it is only during the process of communicating what you did in a study do you really come to appreciate what it is all about, where it came from, what you actually did and why, and what it could lead to. I think also it's important to build a life that is not one-dimensional, such that when the inevitable rejections come your way (or similar) your whole world doesn't come down crashing. In the last ten years or so, I have trained to become and eventually selected to be a Reserve Police Officer in the local Police Department. This experience has allowed me to see many facets of communication the vast majority of people in my city have never seen . . . the underbelly if you like of paradisical Santa Barbara. It has really invigorated my academics and also allowed me to pursue another realm of intercultural relations—police-civilian encounters.

♦ *Have you had a goal you wanted your research to accomplish?*
I'm not so sure I ever had wild or even concrete ambitions in the way this question is crafted. I just wanted to knuckle down, enjoy the privilege of being a member of the academy and the freedoms and excitements that it engenders, and get on with it. I suppose in retrospect I hoped that my communication accommodation theory might have an impact, and I get a very real warm glow whenever I see someone cite it and use it—and especially by those in another discipline.

♦ *What one or two things do you think students should know to deal successfully with communication research?*

As a consumer, they need to get as many diverse experiences of research as possible. Ideally, you should work with different professors (with whom you can have a meaningful social relationship and who are excited by research) from different methodologies and, especially, varying ideologies. That way you can appreciate a wide range of empirical research and not be ignorantly dismissive of certain brands of work because of stereotypes and misconceptions ungrounded in personal practice. As a researcher, you obviously need these diverse experiences, too. However, it is not for everyone and has its peaks and troughs that need to be appreciated for what they are. It is almost impossible now even to be "up" with one's own speciality. You can never go home and feel you've done it all . . . there is always something else you can read and think about. You can never do enough. To live with this—let alone doing it for decades—takes some planning and foresight. So discuss this with those in research—those still excited after many years, those branching out, and/or even those disillusioned. That way you might decide, "No I don't want this other than a nice hobby. I'd prefer to teach mainly and/or consult."

♦ *What do you think is the most exciting future direction for the field's research?*

Oooo this is a broad question. My own biases necessarily have to come into being here. Our field in general is too youth-centered (e.g., in respondents, constructs so derived). We need a field that is more lifespan oriented and one that can appeal to people of all ages, even those close to end of life. In tandem, we need a communication field that understands and appreciates that we don't interact with everybody as an individual—often (probably most of the time) we deal with each other (for good and for bad) as members of a social category. In other words, there are great prospects on the horizon for a truly *intergoup* communication as we belong to and/or identify with so many social categories. Then, there is exciting research in health, and new technology, and one could go on, and on, and on, and . . .

♦ *What part of your research undertakings have made you most proud?*

Perhaps above all, the friends I have made and students I have known. At another level, and besides its being cited, would be talking to people about matters of communication that intrigue, irritate, or baffle them and giving them answers that make them sit up, take notice, and change their own and others' communication practices.

♦ *Is there any advice you would give students who might be interested in becoming communication researchers?*

Advice given me was useful: When trying to advance the field, don't stomp on the heads of those before you. Settle down nicely and appreciatively on their shoulders. In like fashion, a number of my own mentors (when reviewing scholarship, or judging people) always tried to see the good in them. There is a tendency for junior scholars to flex their muscles and only go for the jugular; if we listened to this all the time (and much of it is incisive and on the money) we'd never publish anything. My mother-in-law also said in like mind, "if you can't say good about someone, shut up!" There are enormous personal and social benefits to such an orientation that are important in any occupational quest, research or not.

that you are thinking creatively). So, you need to pursue another pathway. The third option involves developing your own measures by (a) reading on the subject, (b) composing a rough draft of items based on your reading of statements on the issue, (c) putting them into a suitable format, such as those found in this chapter (and Chapter 4), and (d) evaluating them against the standards discussed in this chapter (and Chapter 4, too). Even though it may sound daunting, do not be afraid to compose your own questions, statements, and measures—you can always get help in revising and fine-tuning them (that's one of the things your instructor gets paid for, isn't it?).

Researchers face several tactical challenges when phrasing questions and preparing survey forms. People must cooperate in completing questionnaires. Moreover, respondents must report the way they honestly perceive things. This reporting can be difficult since respondents sometimes do not know how they perceive things. Other times, respondents may feel pressure to react in ways they believe the researcher wants. Naturally, these matters are not to be taken lightly. Thus, researchers usually try to use methods that avoid contaminating data.

Challenges when phrasing questions:

1. respondent awareness

2. reactions to researcher desires

In general, preparing questionnaires and interview schedules requires researchers to observe three criteria (Tuckman, 1999, p. 237):

criteria for questions

1. To what extent might a question influence respondents to show themselves in a good light?

2. To what extent might a question influence respondents to be unduly helpful by attempting to anticipate what researchers want to hear or find out?

3. To what extent might a question be asking for information about respondents that they are not certain, and perhaps not likely, to know about themselves?

There are several options for designing survey items. Table 9.1 shows the sorts of questionnaire forms that communication researchers typically use.

Researchers must also decide on a format for their questions. Alternatives include the following:

format for questions

♦ *Direct or indirect questions* (Tuckman, 1999, p. 238). Though direct questions ask for obvious reports, indirect questions ask respondents to react in ways that imply information. Instead of asking whether people enjoy programs on public television, a researcher might ask subjects to describe the quality of programs on public television. Speech and hearing therapists may ask clients to describe their communication problems, rather than asking them to identify the disorder they believe they have. Though it usually requires more indirect questions than direct questions to obtain information, these questions can often yield honest responses when topics involve sensitive matters or issues people may try to answer in ways that put them in the best light.

♦ *Specific or general questions.* Specific questions focus on individual activities, whereas general questions ask about global evaluations. In organizational communication, employees are often asked about their satisfaction with the physical work environment. They may be asked specific questions regarding how satisfied they are with the temperature of the work environment, the

TABLE 9.1   TYPES OF QUESTIONS

Type and Description	Example	Useful When
Open-Ended Questions: questions to which people respond in their own words	12. What fringe benefits offered by this company are most important to you? _____ _____ _____	1. Respondents may not have information on the topic 2. Respondents are motivated to communicate and spend time in the project
Closed-Ended Questions: questions to which people respond in fixed categories of answers	12. The fringe benefits at this company are: (check one) [ ] superior [ ] excellent [ ] good [ ] fair [ ] poor	1. Possible answers are limited in number 2. Respondents are known to possess information on the topic 3. Terms are commonly understood by respondents
Paired-Comparison Questions: questions that ask respondents to make a judgment between alternatives taken two at a time	12. If you had to choose between the following two options, which one would you prefer in your career? [ ] enjoyable work [ ] high income 13. If you had to choose between the following two options, which one would you prefer in your professional career? [ ] good people to work with [ ] high income	1. Items to be rated are very close in desirability, and simple ranking is difficult 2. Options are fairly limited in number 3. It is practical to contrast all options against each other
Contingency Questions: (also called "filter questions") questions, the answers to which, direct respondents to other items	12. Have you given a speech in the last three months? [ ] Yes (If yes, please go to question 13) [ ] No (If no, please go to question 20)	1. Situations in which responses from only certain subjects are desired 2. Questions apply only to some sorts of people
Ranking Questions: closed-ended questions that ask respondents to rank a set of options	12. Which sources of news do you rely on most? (rank your first choice number 1, your second choice number 2, and so forth until you have ranked all five sources) ___ television ___ newspapers ___ radio ___ magazines ___ friends	1. A small number of items is to be ranked 2. All categories to be ranked are applicable to all subjects 3. When priority information is desired, rather than information about degree of differences in evaluations

(Continued)

TABLE 9.1 (Continued)

Inventory Questions: closed-ended questions that ask respondents to list all responses that apply to them	12. How did you hear about the speech and hearing clinic services? (check all that apply) [ ] newspapers [ ] school officials [ ] health professionals [ ] friends [ ] radio [ ] television [ ] yellow pages listing	1. Respondents differ in their backgrounds in items on the inventory 2. Categories are fairly well known 3. Categories are not mutually exclusive of others
Matrix questions: closed-ended questions that ask respondents to use the same categories to supply information	For each of the following statements, circle SA if you strongly agree with the statement, A if you agree with the statement, N if you neither agree nor disagree with the statement, D if you disagree with the statement, and DS if you disagree strongly with the statement. 12. Management is competent SA A N D DS 13. Management is inept SA A N D DS 14. Management is trustworthy SA A N D DS 15. Management is honest SA A N D DS	1. Standard methods such as Likert scaling are invited 2. Many reliable statements are known to measure the domain of interest 3. Items can reasonably be added together to create a logical scale
Multiple-Choice Questions: closed-ended questions that ask respondents to select a category response from a range of possible responses	12. How long have you been a major in your current field? [ ] 0–1 semesters [ ] 2–3 semesters [ ] 3–4 semesters [ ] 5–6 semesters [ ] over 6 semesters	1. It is desirable to group responses into meaningful underlying units 2. Exclusive categories can be found

cleanliness of the workplace, and the ease of operating equipment. General questions may ask about their overall view of the work environment, for example, "How satisfied are you with the company's physical work environment?" Though specific questions are used extensively by researchers to get precise information, in some cases individuals may grow unusually "cautious or guarded and give less-than-honest answers. Nonspecific questions may lead circuitously to the desired information but with less alarm by the respondent" (Tuckman, 1999, p. 238).

◆ *Questions versus statements* (Tuckman, 1999, p. 239). Some questionnaire items ask questions. Others make statements and ask subjects to indicate how much they agree or disagree with them. Both methods are useful. Yet, researchers typically select one mode or the other to minimize the number of different instructions that respondents must follow.

Of course, researchers often combine forms on a single questionnaire. Thus, questionnaires may include a broad repertoire of response modes.

Phrasing questionnaire items is a major challenge. Through tricky phrasing, a researcher can "rig" a survey to produce results that he or she wants. Thus, one must carefully look at survey items to make sure that they are worded appropriately. Table 9.4 on page 366 lists generally accepted requirements for wording items. These requirements are standards that you may use to double-check questionnaires you compose or read. The actual composition of new survey items requires the researchers to get their acts together. In particular, they must decide what kind of information they really wish. Then, the actual drafting of materials can be completed. Pearson Education's "Survey Tool Kit" suggests that a draft of survey items may be completed if the researchers follow some commonsense rules:

Use consistent scales.

All rating scales should mimic the first one used. It can confuse respondents if you change from, for example, a five-point to a seven-point scale. Keep the scales going the same way. In other words, if "5" is high on the first scale, don't make "1" high on the next. Use similar wording for the anchors. Finally, group questions under the same scale. If you need to change scales, wait until you reach a new section of the questionnaire.

Use consistent wording.

The use of similar phrases for the text of the survey can unify your questionnaire. For example, questions can be set up with a lead phrase which is a phrase that can be used to lead off each question. For example:

How satisfied are you that our staff is:

Responsive to your service requests . . .

Knowledgeable about products . . .

Knowledgeable about your business . . .

(How to ask the questions . . . , 1995–2006, ¶¶ 6–7 © Pearson Education, Inc.)

In the next stages of composition, researchers need to consider survey items that can be used most efficiently by participants. Completing a pilot study is probably the best way to assure that new items created by the researcher can be used in meaningful ways by study participants. Yet, sometimes researchers have to go without a pilot test. Instead, they may collect data, hope that things go well, and then check for reliable use of scales afterward. Even so, there are some phrasings of items and instructions that researchers may use to increase the chances that items will be used.

Developing Instructions and Securing Informed Consent

Telling people to complete a questionnaire or to participate in an interview is not acceptable in modern research. Instead, researchers are required to secure informed consent, to provide instructions about completing materials, and to present debriefing.

Securing Informed Consent

All study participants must be treated with respect and given every opportunity to engage in voluntary choice. A way to deal with this matter is to secure informed consent. In such a manner, participants in a study are informed about the study and given the choice to participate or not. The authority on the subject remains the American Psychological Association's Ethical Principles of Psychologists and Code of Conduct (2002). Though communication studies is a different field from psychology, these standards have been incorporated into the decisions made by most researchers and they are the presumptive standards.

To give instructions and convey information necessary to secure voluntary and informed consent, section 8.02 of the APA Code specifies the following: *requirements for informed consent*

> When obtaining informed consent as required in Standard 3.10, Informed Consent, psychologists inform participants about (1) the purpose of the research, expected durations, and procedures; (2) their right to decline to participate and to withdraw from the research once participation has begun; (3) the foreseeable consequences of decline or withdrawing; (4) reasonably foreseeable factors that may be expected to influence their willingness to participate such as potential risks, discomfort, or adverse effects; (5) any prospective research benefits; (6) limits of confidentiality; (7) incentives for participation; and (8) whom to contact for questions about the research and research participants' rights. They provide opportunity for the prospective participants to ask questions and receive answers.

For anonymous surveys where the identities of the study participants is not likely to be revealed, it is possible communicating this information to the study participants is all that is necessary. Other studies may require obtaining signed consent forms from participants. The APA Code (section 8.05) explains that researchers may dispense with informed consent only

> (1) where research would not reasonably be assumed to create distress or harm and involves (a) study of normal education practices, curricula, or classroom management methods conducted in education settings; (b) only anonymous questionnaires, naturalistic observations or archival research for which disclosure of responses would not place participants at risk of criminal or civil liability or damage their financial standing, employability, or reputation, and confidentiality is protected; or (c) the study of factors related to job or organization effectiveness conducted in organization settings in which there is no risk to participants' employability, and confidentiality is protected, or (2) where otherwise permitted by law or federal or institutional regulations.

The example on Table 9.2 illustrates how such an anonymous survey may appear, complete with its informed consent form.

TABLE 9.2   SAMPLE INFORMATIVE CONSENT STATEMENT AND QUESTIONNAIRE

SENSE OF COMMUNITY QUESTIONNAIRE

The following questionnaire is designed to gather information to help us understand the sense of community students have toward California State University, Fullerton. To have a sense of community, students should feel a sense of belonging to and membership in the social group. Though many factors may account for this sense of community, it is especially important to know the nature of the students' communication within and outside the campus community.

The questionnaire should only take about ten minutes to complete. Your responses are completely anonymous; in other words, only grouped results will be reported and no one will know how you answer the items in the questionnaire. Your participation in this study is completely voluntary. By returning the completed questionnaire, you are giving your consent to participate in the study. You have the option to skip any question that makes you feel uncomfortable. If your discomfort is such that you wish to discuss it with personal counselors, you may call the Counseling Center at California State University, Fullerton, at (xxx) xxx-xxxx or (xxx) xxx-xxxx.

If you have any questions or are interested in the outcomes of this study, please contact Dr. Rich Wiseman at (xxx) xxx-xxxx.

Thank you in advance for participating in this study. Your answers are important to us!

Dr. Rich Wiseman
Human Communication Studies Department
California State University, Fullerton

Part I. Sense of Community

The first part of this questionnaire is concerned with your sense of community here at California State University, Fullerton. For each of the items below, circle the number which best reflects your degree of agreement with that item. Please use the following scale: **1 = Strongly Disagree, 2 = Disagree, 3 = Agree, and 4 = Strongly Agree.**

	SD	D	A	SA
1. I can recognize a number of people at CSUF.	1	2	3	4
2. I care what my classmates think of my actions at CSUF.	1	2	3	4
3. I think CSUF is a good place to learn.	1	2	3	4
4. It is very important to me to be a student at CSUF.	1	2	3	4
5. I feel comfortable at CSUF.	1	2	3	4
6. I have no influence over what this campus is like.	1	2	3	4
7. My classmates and I have very different goals at CSUF.	1	2	3	4
8. People at CSUF generally do **not** socialize with each other.	1	2	3	4
9. Very few of my classmates know me at CSUF.	1	2	3	4
10. If there is a problem at CSUF, students can get it solved.	1	2	3	4
11. I think CSUF is a good place to socialize.	1	2	3	4
12. After graduation, I will be proud of my connections with CSUF.	1	2	3	4

(Continued)

TABLE 9.2   (Continued)

Part II. Communication Activities

This section is concerned with the types and degrees of activities with which you may be involved. Some of the items focus on activities that occur on-campus, though others focus on some of your off-campus activities. For each item, indicate the degree to which you engage in the activity referred to in the item. Please use the following scale: **1 = Never, 2 = Rarely, 3 = Sometimes, and 4 = Often.**

	N	R	S	O
1. I talk with students who are in my classes at CSUF.	1	2	3	4
2. I read the student newspaper (that is, the <u>Daily Titan</u>).	1	2	3	4
3. I participate in student clubs at CSUF.	1	2	3	4
4. I attend special events and social programs at CSUF (plays, concerts).	1	2	3	4
5. I use the "My CSUF" computer portal located on the CSUF web page.	1	2	3	4
6. I participate in sorority/fraternity functions.	1	2	3	4
7. I participate in CSUF sports (either competitive or intramural).	1	2	3	4
8. I use the computer terminals located at CSUF (for example, library).	1	2	3	4
9. I engage in extracurricular activities (for example, music, debate).	1	2	3	4
10. I talk with my teachers outside the classroom.	1	2	3	4
11. I frequently talk with my non-student friends.	1	2	3	4
12. I regularly talk with members of my immediate family (parents, sibs).	1	2	3	4
13. I often use e-mail at home to communicate with friends.	1	2	3	4
14. I participate in student government (ASI, committees) at CSUF.	1	2	3	4
15. I belong to campus religious clubs.	1	2	3	4
16. I work with fellow students in study groups for my classes at CSUF.	1	2	3	4
17. I go and visit with my teachers during their office hours.	1	2	3	4
18. I use some of the student services provided at CSUF (advisement).	1	2	3	4
19. I eat at CSUF's Food Court, Pub, or Carls.	1	2	3	4
20. I sometimes remain on-campus even though my daily classes are over.	1	2	3	4

Part III. Problems and Benefits of CSUF

This section focuses on your perceptions of the problems and benefits of our campus. For each of the following characteristics, please indicate your degree of agreement. Please use the following scale: **1 = Strongly Disagree, 2 = Disagree, 3 = Agree, and 4 = Strongly Agree.**

	SD	D	A	SA
1. Parking is a problem at CSUF.	1	2	3	4
2. CSUF is conveniently located for me.	1	2	3	4
3. CSUF is providing me a good education.	1	2	3	4
4. CSUF is a safe place (that is, not physically threatening, low crime).	1	2	3	4

(Continued)

TABLE 9.2	**(Continued)**					

5. The cost of tuition is very high at CSUF.		1	2	3	4
6. There are many recreational activities at CSUF.		1	2	3	4
7. CSUF faculty are good teachers.		1	2	3	4

Part IV. Social and Personal Characteristics

Finally, for us to make conclusions about other students similar to yourself, we need to know a little about you. In most cases, just circle the answer that corresponds to you.

Are you? (circle one) **Male**   or   **Female**

Class Level? (circle one) **Frosh   Soph   Junior   Senior   Grad**

Are you a transfer student or did you begin CSUF as a freshman? (circle one) **Transfer   Freshman**

Are you employed? (circle one) **Yes   No**   If yes, how many hours a week do you usually work? _____

How many units a semester do you usually take? _____

What is your major? _____

What is your cultural/ethnic group? _____

Is there anything else you would like to tell us about your opinion about CSUF and how we might improve this campus?

Thank you very much for your assistance!

Used with courtesy of Richard Wiseman. (telephone number redacted)

Sometimes researchers wish to complete surveys that deal with children or teenagers. In such circumstances, the individuals studied are not of an age that permits them to make such a decision for themselves. Hence, one of the parents of these minors must be contacted to secure informed consent on behalf of their children. Unfortunately, this two-step process often creates a problem. If parents do not give their permission, their children must be excluded from research. Yet, in research completed in public schools, about "20 to 30 percent of parents typically fail to return the consent forms" (Berg, 2007, p. 68). Such a fact means that it may be difficult to obtain representative samples from entire classes of students.

Sometimes researchers wish to survey and record overt behavior, such as the voices of people interviewed. Sometimes they wish to take pictures of people at various times for the purpose of making observations of overt behavior. There are ethical demands created by surveying such data. The American Psychological Association's Ethical Principles of Psychologists and Code of Conduct (2002) states in section 8.03 that researchers must

> obtain informed consent from research participants prior to recording their voices or images for data collection unless (1) the research consists solely of naturalistic observations in public places, and it is not anticipated that the recording will be used in a manner that could cause personal identification or

harm, or (2) the research design includes deception, and consent for the use of the recording is obtained during debriefing. . . .

Thus, regardless of the material that is reviewed, securing informed consent remains a vital matter.

Providing Instructions about Completing Materials

Questionnaire instructions are designed to enlist involvement of respondents and to explain how they are to answer questions. The instructions must be clear and should explain to people how they are to complete the questionnaire. As a matter of routine, many researchers find it useful to provide a category where the respondent can indicate "no response" or "not applicable." This strategy is useful since researchers can separate incomplete responses from thoughtful refusals to respond. Table 9.3 shows some typical instruction methods for some major response formats. Although instructions usually take a fairly standard form, experienced researchers learn the wisdom of running a pilot study on the instructions and survey items. Such a study helps find problems and prevent confusion before completing a full inquiry.

use of questionnaire instructions

Researchers also notice that if they introduce different sorts of questions, it is helpful to make sure that instructions for such materials are understandable to the people who eventually will complete such surveys. In particular, researchers often ask people to rank items and to provide assessments of the percentage contributions. But this sort of work is more suitable for some groups of study participants than for others. Thus, it is important to consider how comfortable the potential study participants may be with different instructions. For instance, one might wonder which of the following two instructions it might be easiest for respondents to follow:

> Please indicate the percentage of importance for each attribute. (Must total 100%)
>
> Please place a check mark next to the three attributes that are most important to you.
>
> (after How to ask the questions . . . , 1995–2006, ¶ 14 © Pearson Education, Inc.)

Obviously, there are great differences among the instructions that may be used for different sorts of respondents.

It is helpful for researchers to consider the wording of instructions. It is helpful to indicate the specific methods to complete a survey form. If individuals are to circle letters, underline numbers, or fill in circles, the instructions should state it explicitly. As a general approach, you should make instructions "as easy as possible for your respondents by using phrases such as 'Mark all that apply' and 'Mark only one.' Avoid asking them to calculate anything, such as percentages, and try to avoid the use of skip patterns" (How to ask the questions . . . , 1995–2006, p. 10). As a rule of composing items, the presence of the word "if" in a set of instructions usually indicates that a contingency question is being used (see Table 9.1). In such circumstances, researchers should probably number their items and just make a point of directing participants to different parts of the survey form.

TABLE 9.3   SAMPLE INSTRUCTIONS

Example 1:

Please help us by rating a number of behaviors related to your communication on the job. Using the scales provided, please indicate your degree of performing each behavior on the job and your confidence in your ability to perform the behavior. Just circle the number that best reflects your response to each item. If the statement does not apply to you, circle NA.

	MY PERFORMANCE OF THIS SKILL ON MY JOB						MY CONFIDENCE IN MY ABILITY TO PERFORM THIS BEHAVIOR SUCCESSFULLY					
	Very Rarely				Very Regularly		Very Low				Very High	
Encouraging others to communicate problems before they turn into major issues	1	2	3	4	5	NA	1	2	3	4	5	NA
Using communication patterns that promote a supportive climate	1	2	3	4	5	NA	1	2	3	4	5	NA

Example 2:

Please use the scales below to indicate you evaluation of the underlined term. For each scale, place a check mark on the position that best reflects your feelings. If you believe that a term applies extremely to the concept, check the positions closest to the adjective as in the following example:

        bad   _X_ : ____ : ____ : ____ : ____ : ____ : ____ good
    or bad   ____ : ____ : ____ : ____ : ____ : ____ : _X_ good

If you believe that the term applies quite a bit to the concept, check the positions indicated as follows:

        bad   ____ : _X_ : ____ : ____ : ____ : ____ : ____ good
    or bad   ____ : ____ : ____ : ____ : ____ : _X_ : ____ good

If you believe that the term applies slightly to the concept, check the positions indicated as follows:

        bad   ____ : ____ : _X_ : ____ : ____ : ____ : ____ good
    or bad   ____ : ____ : ____ : ____ : _X_ : ____ : ____ good

If you are undecided or if you believe the scale does not apply to the concept, check the central position. Check only one position for each scale. Please work quickly. We are most interested in your first impressions.

Management of This TV Station

        positive : ____ : ____ : ____ : ____ : ____ : ____ negative
        unfair   : ____ : ____ : ____ : ____ : ____ : ____ fair
        friendly : ____ : ____ : ____ : ____ : ____ : ____ unfriendly

(Continued)

TABLE 9.3 (Continued)

Example 3:

Please look at the items below. Place a check mark next to all statements that apply to you. If a suggestion box program were adopted at this speech clinic,

____ I would be willing to participate if cash awards were given for outstanding suggestions.

____ I would be willing to participate if noncash awards were given for outstanding suggestions.

____ I would be willing to participate if additional vacation time were awarded for outstanding suggestions.

____ I would be willing to participate if no awards were given for outstanding suggestions.

Providing Debriefing

Following nearly any study, researchers usually provide debriefing. If there is any deception involved in a study, the debriefing may be extensive including information about the steps that may be completed to provide assistance to distressed study respondents. Yet, for anonymous surveys dealing with ordinary opinions, the debriefing may be rather direct. Even with oral debriefing, it is important to provide some sort of written statement that conveys useful information. The debriefing should include

recommended debriefing information

- information (if not previously revealed on the informed consent form) about the purpose of the study, including the general nature of the research question;

- information about an address where participants can get copies of the research report (either a physical address or a website);

- a contact person who may answer any questions about the project; and

- additional thanks for participating in the study.

Afterward, an opportunity for questions often is included.

Formatting

The actual composition of the survey tends to be fairly direct. Most survey forms begin with a brief statement of introduction to announce the survey, request participation, assure confidentiality (if appropriate), and indicate how to return the survey form. A letter of introduction is included with mailed survey forms, though sometimes such letters are used in other settings as well.

format issues: introduction

The meat of the survey form usually includes the questions or statements to which respondents must react. In practice, most questionnaires place demographic

order of questions

grouping of items

questions (sex, age, academic major, etc.) first. Yet, some argue that demographics should be placed last to avoid boring people with dull background questions at the outset (Babbie, 2003, pp. 254–255). Of course, if you have any contingency question items that guide respondents to questions depending on the information supplied to demographic questions, you are pretty much obligated to place the personal background questions first. Next, questions that rely on the same sort of response mode are grouped together, preceded by instructions for completing the items. Some researchers recommend that questions dealing with the same issue be grouped together. Particularly, when an area of concern requires participants to concentrate on a common subject, it makes sense to group the items that deal with the same general topic. Yet, this advice bears some qualification. If individuals are asked to respond to dimensions of the same construct (such as different dimensions of source credibility), it may make sense to mix up the items from different dimensions. For instance, when using McCroskey's popular scales for the measurement of ethos found on Table 4.2 in Chapter 4, the respondent looks at a source as an object of evaluation, and then completes a set of scales. The scales to measure source competence include uninformed/informed, unqualified/qualified, and unintelligent/intelligent. Scales to measure source character include dishonest/honest, selfish/unselfish, and sinful/virtuous. Though they all deal with evaluating a source, there is no need to group them according to their underlying dimensions. In fact, most researchers (after including some polarity rotation of the adjective pairs) would arrange the scales in some sort of random order such as this:

```
unintelligent___:___:___:___:___:___:___intelligent
   dishonest___:___:___:___:___:___:___honest
    virtuous___:___:___:___:___:___:___sinful
  unqualified___:___:___:___:___:___:___qualified
  uninformed___:___:___:___:___:___:___informed
   unselfish___:___:___:___:___:___:___selfish
```

When the very subjects of assessment or evaluation change, however, it makes sense to group items according to the common subject. Yet this ordering can sometimes create bias in response. People may try to respond in ways that are consistent with early statements on the survey. For instance, suppose subjects are asked to evaluate the quality of teaching in communication classes. At a later point in the survey they may be asked to state what they believe are the most important needs at their school. It is quite likely that they will mention the quality of teaching—perhaps more than they would have otherwise. There is no simple way around this difficulty.

> The safest solution is sensitivity to the problem. Although you cannot avoid the effect of item order, try to estimate what the effect will be so you can interpret results meaningfully. If the order of items seems an especially important issue in a given study, you might construct more than one version of the questionnaire containing the different possible ordering of items. You would then be able to determine its effects. At the very least, you should pretest your questionnaire in the different forms. (Babbie, 2003, p. 254)

Though similar classes of questions may be grouped together, it does not follow that all the items within each category should be grouped together. For instance, if you wished to evaluate the credibility of management at a company, you might group all these ratings together. But since there are at least two dimensions of credibility, character and competence, it makes some sense to mix the order of such credibility items within the same section of the survey form.

There is a question about how many scale positions should be included. This question actually involves two issues: Is there a best number for the scale positions that should be available? and Should researchers include "neutral" points on their research?

- *The number of scale positions that should be used* remains controversial. Scales ranging from at least 3 to 11 points have been used effectively. Weems (2004) found that measurement reliability was enhanced as scale points were increased from three to seven points. In addition, as the number of scale positions increased, seemingly overreliance on the middle position decreased. In fact, in one study contrasting four- to seven-point scales, researchers found reliability of Likert scales did not increase after five points (McDonald, 2004). Study participants preferred five-point scales primarily because they believed that such scales seemed to cover all the relevant options, because they were easy to use, and because most respondents simply preferred to have a midpoint available to them. Taking a different approach, researchers who started with a ten-point scale found that teachers could show the same level of measurement reliability with four-point scales used to assess self-efficacy for writing (Smith et al., 2003).

- *Whether to include a midpoint scale position* remains hotly debated. On one level, the meaning of the midpoint needs to be identified. If survey participants use the midpoint to indicate that they firmly refuse to take sides (as in the case of a person who refuses to take a position on the existence of reincarnation since a decision either way would require drawing a conclusion in the absence of evidence), including a midpoint position would be meaningful. Not surprisingly, researchers have often produced results that seemed to argue for including a midpoint position as a way to enhance measurement reliability (Courtenay & Weidemann, 1985; Madden & Klopfer, 1978; Ryan, 1980; Warland & Sample, 1973). In contrast, some researchers have noted that in many samples of study participants, the midpoint position seems to be "overused," a fact that reduces observed scale reliability (Weems & Onwuegbuzie, 2001). If respondents using midpoint scale positions are apathetic (don't care, and don't know how they feel), including a midpoint may just be a convenient place for them to avoid seriously responding altogether. If so, they may not be in the population of respondents with judgments that were to be sampled in the survey. Some research has tried to find out what people mean by the midpoint position. Among 200 Dutch youths under 24 years old, the midpoint responses most often indicated "undecided" (Raaijmakers et al., 2000). In an effort to define the matter, Armstrong (1987) placed the words "neutral" or "undecided" above the midpoint position of a five-point Likert scale, but the markers did not change the seeming overuse of the middle scale position. Based on independent survey research, Barsalou (1983) concluded that the midpoint seems to be used to indicate ambivalent

scale items can be placed in random order

controversy about number of scale points

different numbers of scale points have been successfully used

especially those ranging from 4 to 7 points

meaning of midpoint open to many interpretations

midpoint often overused by those who are apathetic

or irrelevant responses. Kaplan (1972) argued that current measurement scales need to be replaced with new approaches since current scaling tools cannot distinguish between "neutral" and "ambivalent" people.

including a "don't know" position increases reliability and reduces overuse of the midpoint

Some detective work has suggested that the midpoint position too often is being used to indicate a lack of opinion. In a contrast of semantic differential-type scales and Likert scales, Gannon and Ostrom (1996, study 4) asked survey respondents to rate the relevance of the statements. They found evidence that on a seven-point semantic differential-type scale, the midpoint means "neither." Yet, for Likert scales, respondents tend to use the midpoint to indicate "irrelevance" of the item. When another scale position marked "Don't know" was added to the list of scale responses (permitting the response to be treated as a piece of missing data), reliability increased and inflated use of the midpoint position ceased (Harter, 1997).

many who use the midpoint are disposed to disagree with a statement

In a contrast of sorts, many people seem to use the midpoint as a "polite" way to avoid expressing their disagreement with a statement. Most telling, Weems (2004) found that when survey forms without midpoint positions were used, previously "neutral" respondents overwhelmingly chose the "disagreement" sides of the Likert scales. Similar results were found by Harter (1997) and by Gilljam and Granberg (1993), who claimed that many midpoint responses are "false negatives." Thus, it seems that the middle position is often used by those disposed toward negative responses.

recommended: 4 to 7 points and a midpoint (unless an argument can be made that a "neutral" response is not sensible)

So, how many scale positions should be included and should a midpoint be identified? Legitimate arguments may be found for different points of view. Even so, it seems that scales ranging from 4 to 7 points are most advisable. In addition, if there is a sound reason for believing that no "neutral" response is sensible, scales without a midpoint might be considered. If there is no such reason, including a midpoint response is a sensible course of action to assure covering all the logical possibilities that respondents might wish to have included as options. In the examples found in this chapter, both approaches are illustrated. Likert scales without midpoints are found on Table 9.2. Elsewhere, on Table 9.3, scales with midpoint positions are included.

placement of demographic items in questionnaires: usually at the end

One formatting issue that sometimes gets attention is whether demographic items—such as participant sex, class level, cultural/ethnic group[1]—should be placed first or last. An argument can be made for both positions. Yet, researchers generally find that placing demographic information at the end of the questionnaire can be best. The reason is that most survey participants may be fresh at the beginning of the survey, but a little fatigued at the end. If material that does not call for much concentration is placed at the end, the fatigue effects many be minimized. On the other hand, many researchers prefer to ask a question about the age

---

[1] A word to the wise may be in order. When asking individuals to identify their sex, you will receive silly written comments (such as "Always," "Yes!" or "As often as I can"). Since the word seems to make some respondents act strangely, you might wish to use the following format:

I am (check one) ___male ___female

of the study participant on the first page of a survey form. Since in most places people under 18 years old cannot given informed consent, anyone who is under 18 may be instructed to stop and not complete the rest of the survey. As we shall see, however, in interview studies, it makes sense for demographic information to be asked first, during a period when nonthreatening information can be gathered and rapport can be established.

Determining the appropriate length for a survey form is a constant struggle for researchers. In general, brief surveys are preferred to lengthy ones. But sometimes researchers may be stuck with long questionnaires. If you use standard measures of some personality traits, you may have to include many questions. In addition, when developing measures of your own, you may wish to use at least three scale items for each concept. It is difficult to determine the reliability of a single question or item. Hence, if you use three items to measure a concept (such as Example 2 on Table 9.3), you have some insurance. If one of the items proves unacceptable, you will still have two items left to complete analyses. If you use only a single item, however, and it proves unacceptable, you might wind up with a fistful of air.

length of questionnaires

use of at least three items to measure a concept

You should be careful about using very lengthy questionnaires and avoid the temptation to "throw in" scales to measure other unrelated matters. If you use a lengthy survey, it is a good idea to prepare several questionnaire forms that put the scale groups in different orders to control for subject fatigue. For self-administered questionnaires, a combination of research and experience led Ronald Czaja and Johnny Blair (1996, p. 90) to suggest:

guidelines for questionnaire length

- ♦ Limit instruments to six to eight pages.
- ♦ Precode response categories by assigning a number to each possible answer for the respondent to circle.
- ♦ Space the categories so that it is easy to circle one response without touching an adjoining one. . . .
- ♦ Provide simple instructions of no more than two sentences describing how to answer questions—for example, "Please circle the number of your answer unless otherwise instructed."
- ♦ Use a different typeface for questions, response categories, and transitions or section headings.
- ♦ Whenever possible, use arrows to indicate "skip" instructions.

These guidelines would require you to have the fewest number of questionnaire items you can tolerate. For most researchers, this requirement means that we must "prune" our items to eliminate the unnecessary ones. Subject to any requirements for a minimum number of items to measure a common dimension, Czaja and Blair suggest that you look at each item on the questionnaire. If you cannot show that a question measures a variable in the problem question or related variable, it should be deleted. If the item survives these tests, we should ask if the respondents will understand the question, have information required to answer it, and would be willing to answer it. If the item fails any of these tests, you should delete the item.

standards to help prune items from a questionnaire

TABLE 9.4   PROBLEMS IN WORDING QUESTIONS

Difficulty	Example	Comment and Suggestions
Double-barreled questions	Do you favor expanded bus and fixed rail mass transit systems?	If you want only one option, you must answer *no* to this question. Instead, two questions should be used, one for each alternative.
Loaded language	Do you favor reduced military expenditures in light of the reduced world threat from the former Soviet Union?	The justification for the position is advanced along with the question itself. Questions should leave out the arguments for one side or another.
Improper grammar	Do you know any one of U.S. taxpayers who are willing to pay for increases in public higher education?	Some questionnaire respondents will detect the incorrect grammar and will be distracted from the content. The question should read, "Do you know any one of U.S. taxpayers who *is* . . . ?"
Incompleteness	Do you believe that more money should be spent on public higher education?	More than what? Technically, this wording is a fragment, rather than a complete interrogative sentence.
Vagueness	What do you think of your local cable TV company?	Such a question makes it impossible to get at specific, interpretable information. Researchers should ask questions to gather information they wish to have.
Ambiguous terms	Do you believe that women get their due at your company?	The term "get their due" is subject to many different interpretations. If the researcher wants specific information, unambiguous language must be used.
Lengthy items	When engaged in special project teams, do members of management rely on responsive listening techniques prior to giving reactions to suggestions made by subordinates?	Questions should be asked as briefly as possible, but no briefer.
Complex questions	Should serious communication students be required to take a foreign language?	If one disagrees with requiring communication students to take a foreign language, the question still would be answered "yes." The question only asks about "serious" students—an extra weasel word that restricts the question to a small group.
Averaging or reconstructive questions	In the average week, how many hours of television news do you watch?	It may be difficult for a person to come up with an average. Instead, one should ask about a limited time period, such as a week.
Leading questions	Do you agree with most Americans who believe that the quality of public argument is poor?	Such a question creates pressure to go along with the wishes of the questioner. Such prompts as "wouldn't you agree with me that . . . " similarly are dangerous examples of leading questions.

(Continued)

TABLE 9.4	**(Continued)**	
Abbreviations	"Should the city council approve the construction of an interactive CATV system?" (Wimmer & Dominick, 1983, p. 113)	Abbreviations and acronyms may not be universally understood. It is best to preface this question with a brief explanation of the meaning of the abbreviated term.
Imprecise questions	Does your cable TV company leave something to be desired?	Such imprecise language guarantees useless data. Whether a person is satisfied or dissatisfied with a local cable TV company, the answer would be yes since there is *always* something more that one could desire.
Misspelling	Should children with cleft palates increase there time spent on drills?	Questionnaires are communication encounters. Misspellings show contempt for readers who notice them.
Awkward construction	How many students do you have broken down by sex?	Drinking is more of a problem with us.
Items with only one logical answer	Can television programs promote acquisition of language skills among immigrants?	Anything is possible in the future. Thus, questions that ask if something "can" or "might" occur have only one logical answer.
Presumptive questions	How severe is your child's stuttering?	Assuming information in a question makes it impossible to answer fairly. This example is much like the famous "wife beating" question. One might ask a man, "Have you stopped beating your wife?" If he answers yes or no, you got him cornered.
Elevated vocabulary	Is the personal life of a presidential candidate germane to your choice of a candidate?	Simple words should be used where possible. Surprisingly, many people do not know that germane means relevant. Though one should not "dummy down" to respondents, simple language should be used as much as possible.
Imprecise agents of action	Should we adopt a guaranteed income to replace welfare?	Who is "we"? Items should specify the active agency, as in the question, "Should the federal government adopt a guaranteed income to replace welfare?"
False bipolar	Do you like coffee with or without caffeine?	Such a question misleads since it assumes that the respondent likes coffee at all.

Determining Reliability and Validity

Researchers must evaluate questionnaires to determine whether they are valid measures of the concepts under question. **Validity** involves the degree to which a measure actually measures what is claimed. To show that a set of questions is valid, we first must show that it is stable. This requirement, called **reliability,** deals with the consistency of a measure with itself. In Chapter 4 you found specific methods to determine validity and reliability.

In addition to formal methods to establish validity, researchers often include other controls in their surveys. Sometimes they try to detect when people are not responding consistently or accurately. Three types of controls are check questions,

Validity in measurement, test validity is the consistency of a measure with a criterion; the degree to which a measure actually measures what is claimed

Reliability the internal consistency of a measure.

additional controls

test-taking measures, and alternating polarity of items. A **check question** involves
making the same statement twice but with the second phrased opposite the first
phrasing, at different locations in the questionnaire. For example:

The physical working conditions are good.	SA	A	N	D	DS
The physical working conditions are poor.	SA	A	N	D	DS

If people pay attention, they should answer the items consistently. If they answer in
very different ways, then they are not really alert when completing the survey. Check
questions help identify people who are not responding consistently so that they can be
discarded from the final sample. Because, as we shall see, many study participants have
difficulty with negatively phrased items, especially in using the "strong disagreement"
scale position in Likert scales, some care must be shown. Some scholars believe that the
check question should be a simple repetition of the previous questions, though at another location in the survey form. Yet, this method may not detect inconsistency of
responses. The view taken here is that for the purpose of check questions, a negatively
phrased item will be acceptable because the researcher will discard a survey form only if
opposite responses occur, regardless of their intensity. If a person indicates "Strong
Agreement" with the statement "The physical working conditions are good," an inconsistent response will be identified only if that survey participant "Disagrees" or
"Strongly Disagrees" with the check statement "The physical working conditions are
poor." The failure to use the extreme response scale positions would not affect the interpretations. A second control method is the use of measures of test-taking behavior.
Scales have been developed to reveal whether an individual is responding in unrealistic
ways to survey items. Table 9.5 shows some of these popular measures. A survey researcher can sprinkle these types of measures throughout a questionnaire. Then, scoring
these subscales will reveal biases among respondents.

A third method of control is the use of **polarity rotation** of items. This process
means that researchers using bipolar adjectives in semantic differential scales should avoid
placing all positive adjectives on the same side of measurement items. Researchers are
often concerned about **response set,** which is a tendency for subjects to follow predictable patterns of responding to test items. If a person gets in the habit of responding
positively to items on a survey form, he or she may not be attentive to the content. Furthermore, at one time research reported (probably apocryphal) that when right-handed
people got tired, they tended to check positions toward the right sides of questionnaires,
whereas when left-handed people got tired, they tended to check positions toward the
left sides of questionnaires. To control this matter, many researchers suggest that the
poles of the measurement items should be reversed from time to time. In this way, survey participants can be encouraged to slow down and consider seriously the content of
the scale materials. With semantic differential-type scales, it is a simple matter to rotate
the poles of the items so that all the positively oriented adjectives do not appear on the
right or the left side of the scales. For instance, instead of using the scales arranged here:

Good___:___:___:___:___:___:___Bad
Positive___:___:___:___:___:___:___Negative
Wise___:___:___:___:___:___:___Foolish
Beneficial___:___:___:___:___:___:___Harmful

TABLE 9.5   MEASURES OF TEST-TAKING BEHAVIOR

Type and Description	Example	Comment
Social Desirability Scale A measure of the degree to which people attempt to describe themselves in ways that they think are acceptable, desirable, or approved by others (Crowne & Marlowe, 1960)	Circle T if the statement is true for you and circle F if the statement is false for you. T F** It is sometimes hard for me to go on with my work if I am not encouraged. T F* I have never intensely disliked anyone. T F** On occasion I have had doubts about my ability to succeed in life. *Credit for socially desirable response scored if person answers true. **Credit for socially desirable response scored if person answers false.	◆ The scale consists of 33 items, but researchers sometimes choose a subset, such as the examples provided here, to identify any responses that indicate answering in socially desirable ways. ◆ If people score high on these items (the mean for nondepressed people is approximately 14 [Tanaka-Matsumi & Kameoka, 1986]), they are answering in ways to put themselves in the best light, rather than giving candid reactions. Many researchers delete such respondents from their final samples, and others prefer to study this effect directly. ◆ Some researchers view this scale as measuring a general tendency to seek approval (Strickland, 1977) or, at least, to avoid disapproval (Millham & Jacobson, 1978).
MMPI Lie (L) Scale A scale to identify respondents who are attempting to avoid being candid and honest in their responses (not a general personality disposition toward dishonesty) (Meehl & Hathaway, 1946)	Circle T if the statement is true for you and circle F if the statement is false for you.* T F At times I feel like swearing. T F I get angry sometimes. T F Sometimes when I am not feeling well I am cross. *Any answer of "false" is scored as a lie.	◆ The scale consists of 15 items interspersed in the Minnesota Multiphasic Personality Inventory (the most popular general personality test in the world). ◆ Scoring high on these items (mean = 4.2 for males and 4.8 for females [Swenson, Pearson, & Osbourne, 1973]) often requires a minimum score of eight. Such respondents can be deleted from the sample. ◆ Some believe that the lie scale can be faked by testwise respondents (Dahlstrom, Welsh, & Dahlstrom, 1972).
Infrequency Index A measure of the inconsistency of response, indicative of a person giving random responses (Jackson, 1973)	Circle T if the statement is true for you and circle F if the statement is false for you. T F* Sometimes I get hungry or thirsty.	◆ The full scale includes 20 items systematically dispersed through the Jackson Personality Inventory. ◆ For each item there is only one correct answer. Thus, individuals

(Continued)

TABLE 9.5 (Continued)

T F** I make all my own
     clothes and shoes.

T F* I can run a mile in
     under three minutes.

*Credit for infrequency
response if a person answers
false.

**Credit for infrequency if a
person answers true.

who respond incorrectly are not
responding consistently to items on
the research instrument.

♦ Though the infrequency index
is useful to identify those who are
answering questions in random
ways, attentive respondents are
sometimes surprised at being asked
such stupid questions.

you might reverse the polarity of one of the scales, such as:

Good___:___:___:___:___:___:___Bad
Positive___:___:___:___:___:___:___Negative
Foolish___:___:___:___:___:___:___Wise
Beneficial___:___:___:___:___:___:___Harmful

You would not want to form a pattern (such as having the positive term on the left
of the scale every other item). The idea is to break up habits of responding to encourage fresh reactions.

*polarity rotation of statements
involves negative phrasing,
which is not advised*

    When measures involve *statements* to which survey participants must indicate
degrees of agreement or disagreement, however, there is some controversy about
what to do. On one hand, it seems to make sense to include some negatively
worded items to avoid response set among participants. Previous editions of this
book made that recommendation. Yet, the direction of the evidence suggests that
people often have so much difficulty with negatively phrased statements that it may

*many people have difficulty
responding to negatively
phrased statements*

be best to avoid them.[2] There are some reasons for this recommendation. Some
people tend to have a difficult time affirming negative statements. For instance, a
researcher might design a study in which respondents are given the statement "Foreign language classes should not be required of all Communication Studies majors."
In everyday conversation a person who opposed a foreign language requirement
probably would answer with something such as, "No, I think foreign language
classes should not be required." But to indicate the same attitude on a five-point
scale ranging from "Strongly Disagree" to "Strongly Agree," the person would
have to indicate "Agree" or "Disagree" responses, similar to saying "Yes, I think
foreign language classes should not be required." Language itself can be a complicated matter. Though in some studies the negatively worded items seemed to examine
the same variables as their positively worded alternatives (Bergstrom & Lunz, 1998),

---

[2]This statement does not apply to "check questions," which may include a negatively worded item to
verify the validity of responses. In those cases, one does not "score" the check question as part of the
measure of interest. Instead, the question is used simply to determine if the survey form should be discarded from the rest of the sample.

others argue that negatively worded items are not always equivalent to their positively worded counterparts (Chang, 1995; Woo, 2000).

As a matter of measurement, there are some challenges that negatively worded items may create. In particular:

- Negatively worded statements often reduce the reliability of the measure (see Chapter 4 for information about measurement reliability), especially for some sorts of survey participants. Including negatively worded items may decrease measurement reliability in evaluations people report (Barnette, 2000; Johanson & Osborn, 2000; Weems & Onwuegbuzie, 2001), and in rating scales teachers use to assess student hyperactivity (Sandoval & Lambert, 1978). Using double negatives (e.g., "I do not dislike myself") greatly damaged measurement validity. Yet, not all researchers have found these effects (Ory, 1982; Barnette, 1999). When dichotomous response methods were used, one study observed that very specific negative items improved reliability (Williams et al., 2001). Another study found that including negatively worded items enhanced measurement validity, but not measurement reliability (Schriesheim & Hill, 1981).

  negatively phrased statements can reduce reliability

- Some people, including senior citizens (Eggers, 2000; Lawton et al., 2001) and preadolescent children regardless of their reading ability (Marsh, 1984) also have a difficult time responding consistently to negatively worded statements. Students have particular trouble with negative items if they have negative perceptions about their academic ability, have a low sense of perfectionism, or lack a cooperative learning orientation (Weems et al., 2003).

  some groups of people are particularly affected by negative phrasing

- When negatively worded statements are included, people may avoid using the full range of scale positions. In contrast to our previous discussion, many people may tend to avoid using the "Strongly Disagree" position to disagree with a negatively phrased item, even when the disagreement actually comes closest to representing their true reactions to statements. For instance, when given the statement "I am not happy with the amount of communication I have with my boyfriend," a person who is happy would have to disagree with being "not happy." For many people, the process of negating a negative statement causes them to resist expressing any strong opinions. Hence, the "Strongly Disagree" position rarely gets used. This very tendency has been found generally (Weems et al., 2003) and among college students (Follman et al., 1974) and middle school children (Benson & Hocevar, 1985) in particular.

  negative phrasing reduces use of all scale positions

- As a technical matter, some of the statistics researchers like to use can be adversely affected by use of negative items. When measures use both positively and negatively worded scale items, the results of a method called "factor analysis" may be troubled (Campbell & Grissom, 1979; Deemer & Minke, 1999; Eggers, 2000; Johanson & Osborn, 2000). It is common enough for positively worded items to appear on one factor and negatively worded items to appear on another, even though such findings are statistical artifacts, not meaningful matters (Anderson et al., 1979; McInerney et al., 1994; Magazine et al., 1996).

  ability to use some statistics can be adversely affected

Sampling Subjects

samples are drawn to be representative

Researchers carefully select groups of respondents by defining the universe they wish to sample. After identifying important population characteristics, researchers must define the sampling units. They decide whether to sample reports, actual behavior, or examples of communication. In each case, they try to secure a sample that is representative of the population. Often this requirement means that a random sample is drawn, but other times researchers must use a nonrandom sample. Regardless of the methods they use, researchers are expected to describe and justify their sampling methods and their choice of a sample size.

Administering the Questionnaire

administering the questionnaire

In questionnaire studies, people are given survey instruments along with instructions and left to provide their answers in writing. In experimental studies, the questionnaires may be accompanied by some sort of variable the researcher introduces, but in typical survey research, the respondent is pretty much left alone. Questionnaires can be administered through the mail, by fax, e-mail, or even in classrooms. In each case, the researcher is guided by the limits of subject willingness and the expense of such methods. People do not participate in survey research just because they are

response rates

asked. Some people will not participate—for any number of reasons. Researchers face sampling biases when people choose not to respond to a survey. For mailed questionnaires, one popular guideline is that "a response rate of at least 50 percent is *adequate* for analysis and reporting. A response rate of at least 60 percent is *good*. And a response rate of 70 percent is *very good*" (Babbie, 1999, p. 240). Though these guidelines are just suggestions, they highlight the sorts of choices that researchers often make and possible ways to evaluate their efforts. After collecting questionnaires, it is typical for researchers to explain—in person or in writing—what the study was about and to offer additional feedback to subjects who wish it. This "debriefing" is not just a nicety: it is required in all ethical research.

sound questionnaire studies include a section for participants to write open-ended comments in reaction to the survey materials

One thing that survey researchers know is that securing detailed feedback from participants is very helpful to researchers for understanding the results of a study. So, solid research includes gathering comments and opinions about the study from those involved as survey participants. Sometimes this process is completed by holding an active oral debriefing and keeping careful fieldnotes of the comments made. Yet, most of the time, wise researchers using questionnaires add a section at the end of the questionnaire in which they invite study participants to make comments about the study, and their reactions to it. These comments can be very revealing. If the participants write generally hostile comments, the researcher knows that the study results may reflect that sort of antagonistic climate. If the comments show interest in the topic of the research, the researcher may have reason to be comfortable with the sample. Once, the author of this book conducted a survey in which a sample of students produced very unusual responses. Open-ended comments revealed that many took a similar tone to one who complained, "I'm too busy to think about this sort of [#%&@!#] stuff. What kind of moron passes out questionnaires the week before final exams?" That person had a good point and the author has not made a similar mistake again. Without asking for open-ended responses, however, the researcher may remain unaware of any trouble.

Analyzing and Interpreting Results

Survey research establishes information about relationships, but not about causal relationships (we need experiments or long-term historical studies to make those sorts of claims). In particular, researchers use statistical tools to analyze the data. They can use simple descriptive statistics to show averages and spread of data. They can also use additional statistics to measure associations and to identify significant relationships.

surveys cannot establish causal relationships directly

Regardless of the extent of statistical analyses, questionnaire studies—and interview survey studies for that matter—interpret results to reveal answers to problem statements that focus on descriptions of current affairs and relationships. In each case, the emphasis is on describing patterns, rather than asserting cause-and-effect relations.

THE INTERVIEW SURVEY

Though questionnaires can be handy, researchers sometimes find interview methods most useful for a couple of reasons. First, though it is easy for many people to ignore a cold questionnaire, it may be difficult for them to ignore a live person who asks questions. Of course, the interviewer may arouse some suspicions, but it is part of the job to involve respondents in the task. Second, the interviewer may record information (such as a respondent's manner and nonverbal actions) that might be lost with the questionnaire method. Of course, there is some art involved in completing interview studies. Thus, when you read studies that use the interview method, you can imagine the give-and-take involved in the interviews and the sorts of pressures the researcher and respondent felt.

reasons for interview studies:

1. reducing refusal rate

2. record information missed in questionnaires

Selecting Questions

First and foremost, interviews are ways for researchers to get answers to questions. The same question formats used in questionnaires may be employed in interviews. Indeed, most major polling organizations use formats that make their interviews sound like oral questionnaires. These interviews are called **structured interviews** since they restrict themselves to set questions. In contrast, **unstructured interviews** permit respondents to move beyond highly detailed questions. Furthermore, unstructured interviews allow interviewers to participate in extended exploration and follow up on new matters introduced by the respondent. Given their tendency to yield interpretive information, unstructured interviews are among the favorite approaches of many qualitative researchers.

Structured interviews interviews that use specific lists of questions.

Unstructured interviews interviews that permit respondents to indicate their reactions to general issues without guidance from highly detailed questions.

Interviewers sometimes use special strategies to organize their questions. Unlike questionnaires that may place demographic questions at the end of the survey, interviewers usually place these items first to help respondents get comfortable with the interview process. Table 9.6 shows these strategies along with examples and explanations

strategies for organizing questions

TABLE 9.6 MAJOR INTERVIEW QUESTION STRATEGIES		
TYPE AND DESCRIPTION	**EXAMPLE**	**COMMENT**
I. Strategies for Initial Questioning		
		This question format is useful when:
A. Funnel Questions: a strategy that starts with an open-ended question and follows up with increasingly narrow questions	Q: How do you feel about the newspapers in your city?	♦ Respondents must be screened to determine whether a question area applies to them.
	Q: How would you rate coverage of business news by the newspapers in your city?	♦ Respondents may need to think about the general issue before answering thoughtfully.
	Q: How would you rate coverage of the stock market by the newspapers in your city?	♦ Respondents "know the topic, feel free to talk about it, and want to express their feelings . . . open questions are easier to answer, pose less threat to interviewees, and get interviewees talking" (Cash & Stewart, 1988, p. 75).
		This question format is useful when:
B. Inverted Funnel Questions: a strategy that starts with a very specific question and expands by asking increasingly general questions	Q: What is your favorite TV show?	♦ The larger issue is so broad that vague answers might be given if the final question were asked at first.
	Q: Do you like other shows that have the same format?	♦ Respondents need specific referents to answer logically.
	Q: What types of TV shows do you like?	♦ Respondents need encouragement to talk.
II. Strategies for Follow-up Questioning		
		This question is useful when the interviewer:
A. Mirror Questions: questions repeating previous responses to gain additional information	Q: What types of news programs do you watch on television?	♦ Does not understand what the respondent means or simply wants to double-check.
	A: Nontabloid shows.	♦ Wishes to get further explanation without making judgmental statements.
	Q: Nontabloid shows?	*(Continued)*

TABLE 9.6 (Continued)		
		This question is useful when:
B. Probing Questions: questions that directly ask for elaboration and explanation	Q: Why did you seek speech therapy for your son? A: He was having problems with other kids at school.	♦ Specific areas require definition.
	Q: In what way? Could you explain that?	♦ It is important to elicit examples.
		This question is useful when:
C. Climate Questions: questions asking respondents to explain how they feel about the interview	Q: You seem to become uncomfortable when I ask about the reasons you wanted speech therapy for your son. Is there some problem with talking about this matter?	♦ The respondent is acting in ways that indicate an unwillingness to be candid. ♦ The interviewer senses difficulty in completing the interview with the subject.

of applications. Good advice on the phrasing of interview questions has been around for some time. As far back as 1940, the Gallup organization, which runs the Gallup polls, advanced these six recommendations for interviewers (Gallup & Rae, 1940, p. 101):

1. The question should be brief and to the point. Long conditional or dependent clauses tend to confuse people.

2. The words and phrases should be simple and in common day-to-day use among all groups in the community.

3. The question should not include words which have strong emotional content.

4. The question must avoid all possible bias or suggestion in favor of or against a particular point of view.

5. The question should include all the important alternatives which may emerge on a given issue.

6. When the individual is being asked to choose between different alternatives, this choice of alternatives must be given as early in the interview as possible.

The order of the questions can make a difference in person-to-person interviews. We previously noted that most demographic information should be obtained at the end of a questionnaire survey. For interviews, the placement of most such questions is just the opposite. After making contact with a person, introducing oneself, and obtaining informed consent, experienced interviewers usually begin the interview with a series of questions that deal with ordinary information that would be known publicly about a person. Thus, demographic questions dealing with sex, age, education levels, occupation, and the like would be asked before getting into the significant

placement of demographic items in interviews: usually at the beginning

SPECIAL DISCUSSION 9-2

A QUESTION OF ETHICS: CONFIDENTIALITY AND ANONYMITY

Asking people questions and watching their communication behavior frequently means probing into their lives. Even if they consent to it, ethical questions about privacy are raised unless care is taken to ensure anonymity where possible and confidentiality generally.

Anonymity is the "protection of research participants by separating specific identities from the information given" (Frankfort-Nachmias & Nachmias, 1996, p. 585). Most research data can be collected without requiring subjects to identify themselves. Such responses can remain nameless, and neither researchers nor any others can identify whose responses are involved. Unfortunately, in much research (especially ethnographic research) the names of people are known and anonymity is impossible. At least researchers can guarantee a high degree of confidentiality.

Confidentiality is the "protection of the identity of research participants" (Frankfort-Nachmias & Nachmias, 1996, p. 587). Though researchers may know the identities of the people they interview or ask to complete questionnaires, the requirement of confidentiality requires that they not reveal those identities to others outside the research team. If confidentiality cannot be maintained, it must be communicated to participants before they participate in the study. To help ensure confidentiality, researchers may (after Riecken & Boruch, 1979, pp. 258–259) delete all names and identifiers from data revealed about individuals, report only broad categories of responses, use macroaggregation (constructing "average persons" from the data), and add errors to the original data to detour others from identifying participants.

content of the interview. Hence the formatting of the interview items would begin with background and demographic information. The interview participant may use the time to get comfortable with the interviewer's voice, manner, and appearance. Then key issues for the research may be completed.

Training and Controlling Behavior of Interviewers

training interviewers as a necessity

Interview data can be strongly affected by the interviewer. Thus, if several people conduct interviews, researchers must train them to avoid actions that might bias results. Interviewers are trained to use the same introductions, the same answers to respondent questions, and the same manner of asking questions. Typically, the trainer instructs interviewers on ways to provide common instructions and ways to deal with typical problems that they might face in the field.

selection of interviewers can bias results

Sometimes the very selection of interviewers can bias results. For instance, in a classic study following the Watts riots of August 1965, H. Edward Ransford completed some survey work in the area (1968). When Ransford and other white interviewers conducted door-to-door surveys in south-central Los Angeles, results indicated great sadness about the riots among the predominantly African American community. Yet, when Ransford hired African American interviewers, he found very different results. Respondents told African American interviewers that they

thought the riots were proud symbols of anger and perhaps even inevitable. Furthermore, the African American interviewers found that the likelihood of a person's participation in the riots was linked to isolation from whites and a deep sense of
powerlessness. In contrast, the McCone Commission, which investigated the riots on
behalf of the City of Los Angeles, employed white interviewers to complete its work.
That commission concluded that the riot was an aberration and was regretted in the
African American community. Its major recommendations included hiring increased
numbers of African American police officers and installing two-way radios in ambu-
lances. Obviously, the interviewers can make a difference in the data collected.

Part of the training involves the use of **"scripts,"** which are, more or less, the
"lines" to be spoken during the interview process. But there can be something more
to it than memorizing a part and acting it out each time an interview occurs. Sometimes the script can be very fluid and leave room for improvisation. If this discussion
sounds like a description of a theatrical event, there is more in common than might
be imagined by students new to the research craft. There are several sorts of interviews and interview schedules that might be used by researchers.

For a structured interview, the script might look a great deal like the instructions for
studies using questionnaires, since much of the same information will be obtained. As
an example, consider the script from the *Field Interviewer Manual* prepared for the U.S.
Public Health Service's *2001 National Household Survey on Drug Abuse* (2000, § 4.8):

> ### Identify SR [screening respondent]
>
> Line: 015 30 Gordon Street
>
> Hello, my name is Pat Smith. . . . We are in your neighborhood conducting a
> nationwide study sponsored by the U.S. Public Health Service. You should
> have received a letter explaining the study.
>
> [HAND R(respondent) COPY OF LETTER IF NEEDED]
>
> First, just let me verify: do you live here?
>
> IF NOT OBVIOUS: and are you 18 or older?
>
> IF NO TO EITHER, ASK FOR AN ADULT RESIDENT AND BEGIN
> AGAIN.
>
> ○ SR AVAILABLE (Continue)
>
> ○ SR NOT AVAILABLE (Go to ROC) (Record of Call form)

Following the introduction, the interviewer was instructed to read the informed
consent form to the respondent and then to give the respondent a copy of it. It
stated, in part:

> We are interviewing approximately 70,000 people across the Nation. You
> have been selected to participate based on scientific sampling procedures. The
> answers you give to our questions will represent 3,100 other Americans simi-
> lar to you. Your participation is voluntary, but we cannot substitute anyone if
> you decide not to participate.
>
> This study collects information on tobacco, alcohol, and drug use; knowl-
> edge and attitudes about drugs; as well as mental health and other health related

Scripts in interview
studies, the instructions
given to the interviewers
regarding what they will
say to respondents and
how they will answer
questions and probe for
further information.

scripts for structured interviews

issues. The interview takes about 1 hour. You cannot be identified as the source of any information you provide in the interview because no personal information is attached to your responses. . . .

It is important to get the most accurate information possible and we hope that protecting your privacy will encourage you to provide careful answers. While some of the questions may be sensitive, your honest responses will be of great value. The answers you provide to the questions will only be used for research and analysis and cannot be used for any other purpose. You are free to withdraw from this survey at any time or to refuse to answer any question.

We would like to conduct this interview in as private an area as possible. Can we find a reasonably private spot to complete the interview?

If it's all right with you, let's get started. (2000, § 7.6.1)

As you can see, the process of covering all the bases of ethical research is extensive in interview studies. Furthermore, it may become increasingly time-consuming to answer research questions with this technique. Even so, when the research question invites it, there can be little doubt about the value of this method.

scripts adapted for unstructured interviews

In a relatively unstructured interview, many of the same protocols must be followed. For instance, researchers must identify themselves and obtain informed consent. But the details of the interview may not be apparent until the work is well under way. Scripts of unstructured interviews will include identifying only a few main issues or questions that may start a conversation along a certain path. Yet, unstructured interviews secure most of their information through the use of follow-up or probing questions. As a result, the depth of understanding provided can be great, but it requires a very skilled and talented interviewer to make the system work. Furthermore, with unstructured interviews, less and less of the work can be done before the interview actually begins.

Determining Reliability and Validity

interviewers look for additional clues of reliable and valid responses

In structured interviews, the methods to determine reliability and validity are identical with those for questionnaires. Interviewers are also expected to make notes on the nature of the interview so that responses can be put in context. If a respondent seems distracted, the interviewer is expected to provide such a report on the interview form. If a respondent indicates difficulty in understanding questions, such information should be recorded. Check questions frequently are added to interviews to make sure that consistent responses are received. Thus, signs of reliability may be found from several different sources.

When an interview goes properly, validity claims are often quite strong. Since interviews permit use of follow-up questions, researchers can often tell whether the respondents are reacting to the questions as the researcher intended. In fact, interpreting items may be quite clear. The interviewer attempts to figure out what the subject is "driving at" in addition to getting simple answers to questions. Thus, validity claims are a natural counterpart of sound interview methods.

Sampling Subjects

As with questionnaire studies, interviewees should be selected to represent the population. Interviewers must isolate populations, decide on methods to sample events, and select an appropriate number. To secure a useful sample, individuals must be contacted to get their permission to be interviewed. Thus, interviewers must take time to promote participation before the sample can be taken. Face-to-face interviews may have a higher completion rate than questionnaires since most people have difficulty refusing to talk to another person. For interview studies, response rates in the neighborhood of 70 percent or more are quite common (McNeill, 1990, p. 40). Thus, collecting a sample may be as involving for interviews as it is for questionnaire methods. Sometimes researchers—especially those interested in qualitative research approaches to communication—use interviews to secure information about very limited populations. For instance, they may employ interviews of only a handful of Japanese Americans who were placed in internment camps during World War II. Such interviews might reveal perceptions of U.S. government communication from unique perspectives that other samples could not provide. Thus, whether engaging in quantitative or qualitative research, the sampling methods are objects of very serious attention.

sampling in interviews

Analyzing and Interpreting Results

Interview studies typically employ statistical tools to analyze results, but interviews need not always be analyzed with such methods. Since some information—such as unstructured answers, comments, and explanations made by respondents—may be qualitative data. Sometimes content analyses or interpretive guides are employed. Regardless of the methods, however, the researcher tries to interpret results to illuminate relationships posed in the research problem question.

interpretation

Unlike many questionnaire studies, interviews can produce interpretations for the reasons behind answers. By reporting on the results of follow-up questions and funnel question patterns, interviewers often gain insight to explain previously unknown reasons. Of course, the interviewer may report what he or she expects to see rather than the facts of the matter. But interviews can also yield information that might otherwise "fall between the cracks" of formal questions. Interviews permit the use of follow-up questions that may allow the researcher to develop a detailed understanding of what is being said. The use of **probes** allows the interviewer to get information beyond the surface. This feature of interviews often makes it particularly inviting for scholars, but it has to be handled with care. The follow-up questions should attempt to gather information to prevent misunderstandings and to clarify matters. The probes should not be the effort of an interviewer to influence the respondent to take different positions. Instead, probes should be designed to make sure questions are understood and to assure that answers are complete. The *Field Interviewer Manual* prepared for the U.S. Public Health Service's *2001 National Household Survey on Drug Abuse* gave quite a bit of advice about the use of such probes (2000, § 8.2.3). Above all other concerns, interviewers are advised to make sure that probes are as neutral a set of words as possible. Table 9.7 provides both some guidelines and some examples of strategic probing.

interviews can probe for reasons behind the answers

Probe in interviews, the use of scripted or spontaneous follow-up questions designed to help interviewers secure additional detail, elaboration, or clarification.

purpose of probes:

promote understanding and completeness

TABLE 9.7 PROBES

Rules for Probing

1. Repeat the *question* if the respondent misunderstood or misinterpreted the question.

After hearing the question the second time, the respondent may understand what is being asked. This is usually the best and most straightforward method of probing. . . .

2. Repeat the *answer* if the response is too vague to answer the question.

For example, if you ask the respondent for his/her current marital status and he/she answers, "I'm on the loose," an effective probe is, "On the loose?"

3. *Pause* to indicate to the respondent that you need more or better information. . . .

4. Use *neutral questions or statements* to encourage a respondent to elaborate on an inadequate response.

Examples of neutral probes are "What do you mean?" . . . "Tell me what you have in mind" or "Tell me more about . . . ."

5. Use *clarification probes* when the response is unclear, ambiguous, or contradictory.

Be careful not to appear to challenge the respondent when clarifying a statement and always use a *neutral* probe. Examples of clarification probes are "Can you give me an example?" or "Could you be more specific?"

Examples of Acceptable Probes

Repeating All or Part of the Question

- "Let me read the question again." Repeat the full question with emphasis.
- "Let me read the question again just to be sure we are focusing on the same time period." Repeat the full question with emphasis.
- Repeat the answer choices with emphasis.
- Wait 10–15 seconds. If no answer is given, repeat the full question.

Requesting a Clarification

- "For this question, I need an answer of either 'yes' or 'no'." -or- "Is that a 'yes' or a 'no'?"
- "Can you give me a specific number of (hours/days/weeks/etc.)?"
- "Would you say 9 or 10?"

Reassurances

- "To the best of your knowledge . . . "
- "Remember that we will not tell anyone what you say."
- "Remember, there are no right or wrong answers."

(Continued)

TABLE 9.7   (Continued)
♦ "Take your time."
♦ "I have to ask all of the questions in order."
♦ "We're interested in your own interpretation of the question."
♦ "We just want to know what you think."
♦ "Whatever [WORD] means to you."
Repeating an Earlier Question
♦ "Let me read you an earlier question."

Source: *2001 National Household Survey on Drug Abuse: Field Interviewer Manual* (2000, § 8.2.3).

Interviewers often complete an evaluation sheet in which they describe the non-verbal cues exhibited by the respondent. In addition, any characteristics of giving answers or expressing positive or negative feelings about the interview process are included. Some researchers include a special form for this purpose, but others encourage interviewers to make unstructured reports of what they have seen.

It should be emphasized that research using interviews is not somehow superior to questionnaire research. In many ways, questionnaires provide controls on investigator behavior that interviews do not. Whether a particular study should use questionnaires or interviews must be decided by considering the purpose of the research and the degree of maturity of the research area.

NETWORK ANALYSIS

Network analyses are most often used in studies of organizational communication, though, as we shall see, studies in many other application areas have grown in popularity. We will consider the traditional use of network analyses and the exciting applications of network analysis beyond these boundaries.

Network analysis attempts to examine the links that exist among elements of communication systems. Sometimes those elements are people in interpersonal networks, but sometimes they can be ideas and language, psychological organizations, groups, and nations.

Traditional Network Analysis

Traditionally, network analysis has served as a tool to study organizational and group structures among people. This application of **network analysis** obtains individuals' reports of their communication activities with others for the purpose of observing

Network analysis
1. traditionally, a method that obtains individuals' reports of their communication activities with others for the purpose of observing and describing the flow of information in a particular organizational system; 2. in its most general sense, "a set of research procedures for identifying structures in social systems based on the relations among the system's components rather than the attributes of individual cases" (Barnett, 1998, p. 154).

SPECIAL DISCUSSION 9-3

CREDIBILITY OF QUESTIONNAIRE AND INTERVIEW DATA

Some researchers question whether we can trust information from questionnaires and interviews (Nisbett & Wilson, 1977a, 1977b; Wilson & Nisbett, 1978). There are two general concerns. First, they doubt that respondents are aware enough to give useful reactions. Sometimes people may not know how they feel about topics. Though there have been responses to such attacks (e.g., White, 1980), there is little doubt that it is not sensible to ask people questions that they cannot answer. Researchers have tried to deal with these matters by including questions that test whether respondents are responding accurately and with awareness. Martin Orne (1970) recommended that accuracy of respondent reports should be checked by the use of "sacrifice groups." These groups are interrupted during the interview or questionnaire process to see if they really understand what is meant by specific questions. Since these respondents have been distracted somewhat, they are "sacrificed" and their responses are used only to validate the survey question content.

A second problem involves subjects' *recall* of information. Researchers often ask people to remember such things as an argument with a parent or a recent conversation with a friend (e.g., Motley & Reeder, 1995). But people often recall things inaccurately. Researchers have sometimes dealt with the difficulty by asking more than one person to describe the same event—such as a conversation—and obtaining a common description. Another method involves using carefully designed *funnel questions,* which start very broadly and then move to increasingly specific details. This method appears to enhance the accuracy of recalled information from respondents (Adair & Spinner, 1981). Sometimes simply instructing the respondents to respond honestly and accurately can enhance accuracy (Bowers, 1967).

and describing the flow of information in a particular organizational system. In a network, some people are "in the loop" of information and others are "out of the loop." Network analysis identifies such patterns so that the situation might be described and improved. Network analysis often results in a detailed chart showing the actual flow of messages. Though it is called "traditional" here, you should not think that it is "old fashioned" or passé. Indeed, most of the network analysis work is involved in just such applications.

The Traditional Approach of Network Analysis

purposes:

In the traditional application of network analysis, researchers identify people with whom others are in contact. In these applications, there are three general purposes that may be achieved.

1. to construct a map of the interaction

♦ First, network analysis is used to construct a map of the interaction among people in an organization. Whereas business scholars ask, "Who has the power in the organization?" communication scholars using network analysis ask,

---

SPECIAL DISCUSSION 9-4

SECONDARY DATA ANALYSIS

At one time, students had to design and execute their own survey research studies—or not do any survey work at all. Things have changed. There are large-scale surveys that supply data for others who have questions of interest. Though most surveys are not dedicated to research in communication, some applications are of relevance to our field.

The General Social Survey (webapp.icpsr.umich.edu/GSS/) is a series of omnibus surveys (surveys of many topics potentially useful to people in the social sciences) that originally were completed each year starting in 1972. In 1992 it changed to a biennial schedule of surveys composed of 153 to over 750 questions, though nearly a third of them are repeated items. The survey solicits suggestions for questions and makes the data available to subscribers. Your university or local research library probably subscribes to the service in your behalf. The files are widely available in SPSS and raw data formats.

The Roper Center for Public Opinion Research (www.ropercenter.uconn.edu/) is a database depository for the national polling data of the Roper Organization. The materials are available on subscription (already purchased by many schools) or from the marketing section of Lexis/Nexis.

The International Social Survey Program (www.issp.org/homepage.htm) is an international group, based in the United Kingdom, that attempts to coordinate international social science survey efforts. Data sets include such topics as public attitudes toward government, social support systems, and racial and gender bias.

"Who has the information?" Granted, information is a major source of power, but communication scholars focus primary attention on the nature of the message and information flow.

♦ Second, network analysis may help diagnose problems in communication flow. Often there are failures (we hesitate to call them communication breakdowns because that term is technically contradictory) in the flow of messages, and people who are supposed to get information do not. By finding the roadblocks, researchers can identify these sources of difficulty so that action can be taken. In one factory in the Midwest where the author completed an applied project, changes in company procedures on sick leave and lateness policy were communicated to employees in writing on a bulletin board located outside the break room (a room with vending machines and a microwave oven). Since many employees did not read very well, checking the written messages was a chore for them—a chore they usually ignored during their short breaks. The block in the flow of information was identified, and the plant manager adopted a system to make important announcements orally to the incoming shift, rather than relying on the bulletin board alone.

2. to diagnose problems in communication flow

3. to identify roles played by different group members

◆ Third, network analysis may identify the roles played by different group members. Informal methods of communication exist in organizations. Network analyses can help identify these "grapevines." Sometimes small groups or cliques talk almost exclusively with each other. Yet, some people serve as bridges or "liaisons" between these groups, keeping up communication between them. With a knowledge of such informal communication channels, organizations may look at ways to spread critical information and methods for spotting problems before they turn into major crunches.

Thus, if researchers have problem questions that ask about the flow of information in a particular organizational system, or if the question involves the roles played by different individuals in a social structure, network analysis may provide a useful means to get answers.

The Method of Network Analysis

choosing categories may be challenging

Network analysis involves gathering data to construct a communication map or diagram. Choosing important categories may be a challenge for researchers. Networks are not "things" that can be touched. They are patterns of communication. Thus, networks are abstract notions that people "construct" to organize information about the structure of communication. Peter Monge explained:

> All communication networks are constructed out of two elements: a set of communicators and one or more relations among the communicators. The relations define the nature of the connections among the communicators. Many forms of relations can be used to study societal networks. For example, a kinship relationship could be "is the partner of," "is the sister of," or "is married to." An authority relationship could be of the form "reports to" or "supervises"; a resource relation might be "shares workers with" (Monge & Miller, 1985). Communication networks are constructed out of communication relations, which describe the nature of information flow among people. Typical communication relations are "shares information with," "talks to," "receives reports from," and "discusses new ideas with." (Monge, 1987, p. 243)

steps:

1. select communication variables

Finding the structure of communication flow traditionally requires carrying out four steps. First, network analysts select communication variables of interest consistent with the problem question that guides all inquiry. Such elements are often the frequency people communicate with each other, the importance (or perceived importance) of the information, the direction of the communication flow, and types of communication exchanged.

2. secure individual reports

Second, the researcher secures individual reports from all members of the group or **nodes.** Questionnaires are often constructed for group members to identify their communication with others. But sometimes actual uses of messages can be traced (such as numbers of telephone calls placed to a given location, or numbers of memos sent *to* a person as a ratio of the number of memos sent *from* a person). Thus, network analyses may use observational or self-report data.

> **Nodes** in network analysis, the members of the network that report data.

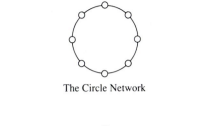

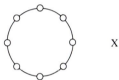

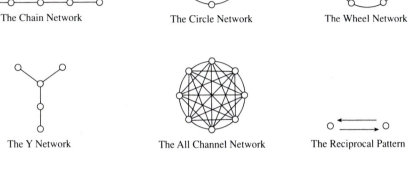

The Chain Network   The Circle Network   The Wheel Network

The Y Network   The All Channel Network   The Reciprocal Pattern

Liaison Between Wheel Networks   All Channel and Isolate   X

FIGURE 9.1

Third, researchers construct network maps to track information flow. As Figure 9.1 shows, some general patterns may emerge. Each pattern has some predictable communication effects. For instance, the chain pattern tends to be efficient when direct orders are to be given along a strict command structure, but the overall member satisfaction can be low since often only a limited picture of the entire project is possible for most group members. On the other hand, the all channel pattern permits individuals to coordinate their activities with others, but if there is a struggle for leadership or power within the group, or if any network members are hostile to any others, the all channel model may not be particularly useful. Of course, network analyses can be very complicated, even when there are relatively few members of the network. For instance, Russo and Koester (2005) completed a network analysis of the members of an online class in genetics. In addition to looking at ordinary patterns (for instance, identifying Magdelena as an isolate), they were interested to see if there were any relationships between network location on one hand, and learning on the other. They used network analysis to produce a diagram found in Figure 9.2. They found that centrality in a network (indicated by the number of messages sent outward) and prestige (indicated by the messages coming into the node) were strongly and positively related to the grades a student received. As you can tell, doing this sort of work by hand is not feasible.

Developing the network patterns can be complex since the flow of information among many people can become nested and quite involved. To help in the task,

3. construct network map

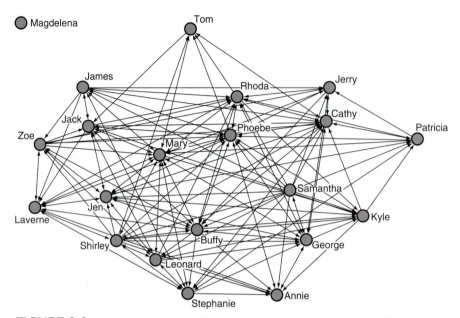

FIGURE 9.2   3D Image representation of prestige and centrality in the online class. In-bound arrows represent prestige; outbound arrows represent centrality.

From: Russo, T. C., & Koester, J. (2005). Brief report: Prestige, centrality, and learning: A social network analysis of an online class. *Communication Education, 54*, p. 258. Copyright 2005. Reproduced by permission of the National Communication Association, www.natcom.org.

computer programs have been developed, the most popular of which has been NEGOPY. Had it not been for the availability of the NEGOPY program, much of the flurry of network analysis research during the 30 years beginning with a first serious study in 1968 would not have been possible (Susskind et al., 2005). In the case of the study completed by Russo and Koesten, the "3D Mage" feature of the UCInet 6.0 program (Borgatti, Everett, & Freeman, 2002) was used.

network patterns: reciprocal, liaison, and isolate

    The reciprocal, liaison, and isolate patterns are interesting. A reciprocal pattern is one in which individuals share a nearly identical network pattern among themselves. People who are personally close or who have similar sorts of positions that include a lot of teamwork are examples of such a pattern. The liaison person (partial or complete) links people of different networks. In Figure 9.1 the liaison between two groups (identified by the X) is performed by one person who—officially or unofficially—is a member of both groups. The isolate is an individual who is not actively involved in any established communication network (or, in the case of an "attached isolate," has only one link with others). This person usually is bypassed and occasionally may not even be aware that he or she is an isolate in the eyes of others. These individuals are out of the communication flow and, thus, may not hold potential for making productive contributions until their involvement levels are altered. These patterns may be interpreted and the description used to help make improvements.

A final step in traditional network analysis involves interpreting results by comparing the network with a desired standard, such as an organizational chart. Checking whether people who *should* be communicating with each other really *are* allows evaluation of the flow of information. By contrasting the network against the organizational chart, the logic of the organization's structure can be verified—or questioned. By finding that people who are not expected to communicate actively with each other actually are involved in extensive conversation, it is possible to identify informal channels. These channels may be nurtured and attempts to explain them explored.

comparing the network with a desired standard

Network Analysis beyond the Traditional

Traditional network analysis focused on who was talking to whom, but network analysis has not stopped there. The units in networks do not have to be people in an organization. To understand what is going on, it would be helpful to look at different network analysis applications.[3]

Semantic Networks

Semantics is the study of the relationship between words and their meanings. **Semantic networks** look at patterns of words in a message. This sort of effort involves comparing word-pair links—the degree to which one word occurs with another. This method combines content analysis with network analysis methods to determine semantic networks that underlie communication activities. Alexander and Danowski (1990) used this technique to analyze the actors mentioned in Cicero's works. They were able to identify those who were recurring favorites in Cicero's comments. In another inquiry, Myra Doerfel and Stacey L. Connaughton (2005) looked at words that were frequently paired by candidates (such as "peace" with "honor") in presidential debates. They found that they could predict who would win elections by identifying which candidates most often used terms located near the center of the network. Doerfel and Barnett (1999) attempted to determine if the variables studied in research papers (as indicated by the paper titles) presented at the 1991 International Communication Association Convention showed differences from the research interests expected by the organization's structure. They found that although ICA had 13 divisions, the papers really organized themselves according to whether they employed scientific or humanistic methods, examined interpersonal or mediated communication, and were applied or theoretical papers. Other research has used semantic network

Semantic network an application of network analysis to examine the relationships among words in a message.

---

[3]Some writers study "cognitive networks" as a distinct form for network analysis. Yet, most of these network analyses seem to be creative efforts to develop theories of cognitive behavior, rather than communication issues. Since our concern is message-related behavior here, we will not cover such applications (no offense, we just have limits).

analysis to explore organizational cultures (Freeman & Barnett, 1994; Jang & Barnett, 1995), managers' perceptions of strategies to enhance participation (Stohl, 1993), and the impact of computer-mediated communication (Danowski, 1982).

Networks among Groups

network analyses completed with groups as nodes

The structure of an organization—formal or informal—may be defined by the interrelationships among the groups that compose it. A study of the relationships among groups in a professional organization was completed by Barnett and Danowski (1992). Because individuals in one division could have co-membership with others, one might expect great diversity. In fact, by looking at the secondary memberships people held, these researchers were able to find network groupings or cliques. Though there were slight differences in results according to the analysis methods used, two cliques typically emerged: a humanities clique (in contrast to a scientific clique) and a mass media clique (as opposed to the interpersonal communication clique). Interestingly, mass communication and intercultural communication divisions seemed to be liaison groups that brought together people from divisions with other research interests.

Networks among Organizations

network analysis completed with organizations as nodes

Instead of looking at the flow of communication within an organization, one may take organizations themselves as the nodes of interest. Websites maintained by commercial organizations providing search engines (such as Google and Yahoo) have been evaluated to determine their structural density and centrality (Sohn & Jee, 2005). Since a Web page can be designed to feature fewer outgoing than incoming links, some sites, such as Yahoo, appear to use this approach to maintain a central position in their networks, regardless of the information they may be providing. In other work, Chon, Choi, Barnett, Danowski, and Joo (2003) used network analysis to check on the sources of mergers among mass media firms. Following up on a 1998 study by Danowski and Choi (1998), which found shifting sources of mass media control, lists available from the *Journal of Mergers & Acquisitions* were examined to explore the convergence of companies in the communications industry (including telephony, broadcasting, data processing services, publishing, and motion pictures). Unlike the 1998 study, which found that the leadership for acquisitions changed from time to time, the 2003 study found that telephone companies "played the most central role in the transformation of the information industries. As well, cable and Internet industries noticeably transformed their industrial relations over this time period" (Chon et al., 2003, p. 142). Before 1996 the biggest consolidations occurred in publishing (Danowski & Choi, 1998, p. 137). After 1996, the greatest consolidations occurred among telephone companies that supplied cable and Internet services. In addition, consolidation was most active among cable and Internet companies (Chon et al., 2003, p. 142).

Networks among Nations

The patterns of communication around the world can produce useful insights to nation-building and the progress of technologies. Rather than use individuals, or groups of individuals, or even their message language as units of analysis, researchers may use nations. Some researchers have found that using nations as nodes has permitted them to identify sources of change in the world. Danowski, Barnett, and Friedland (1986) looked at telephone call frequencies among nations (nodes). Though one network continued to be found, the number of elements continued to grow (Barnett, Jacobson, Choi, & Sun-Miller, 1996). Barnett and Choi (1995) found that the amount of participation in the international telephone system was predicted by whether the nations spoke any of four dominant languages (English, French, Spanish, or German) and not (surprisingly) by the relative proximity to other countries. One line of research indicated that in a world economy, when organizations within a nation cooperated to obtain increased information and adequate resources, their persuasive effect on society could be very great. Doerfel and Taylor (2004) found this fact particularly important in the development of the Croatian Civil Society Movement. Barnett and Salisbury (1996) observed that since 1980, the Asian industrialized countries and Eastern Europe were moving from the periphery of the network toward the center. Of course the political implications of these networks had not been spared attention. It is strongly suspected that the international telephone network actually holds the potential to promote democracy—or at least discussion with Western democracies—in many parts of the world where government control of its people has been very strong (Sun & Barnett, 1994). By completing network analyses of nations, one may find interesting explanations of changes in the international community. One network analysis led researchers to conclude that interdependence through communication may reduce international conflict (Barnett & Kim, 2005).

network analysis may use nations as nodes

Limitations of Network Analysis

Though most often used in studies of organizations and bureaucracies, network analyses have looked at communication within families, job networking groups, social groups, and links among people of different organizations. Even so, there are two major limitations to network studies. First, they emphasize structural information rather than content information. Though we can identify who is talking with whom, it is difficult to know the content of the information. People could be socializing or working on common projects. We may not know. Some researchers attempt to get additional information about dominant sorts of information exchanged, but structure of communication flow is emphasized in network analyses. Second, network analysis allows researchers to identify relationships among communicators, but the technique does not permit researchers to make claims about the reasons for the relationships. We cannot know for sure why a person was bypassed in the network, though the network may show that bypassing has occurred. We cannot identify why someone became a liaison between groups. But one can identify relationships to be explored with other research methods.

limitations:

1. emphasis on structural information rather than content

2. reasons for the relationships not known

CHECKLIST TO EVALUATE SURVEYS

_____ Does the research question involve ascertaining norms, establishing goals, or developing methods?

_____ Does the research question avoid asking about cause-and-effect relationships?

_____ Was informed consent to the survey obtained from a person in authority?

_____ Did informed consent forms/instructions explain the purpose of the research, expected duration, procedures, rights to decline, consequences of declining, research benefits, limits of confidentiality, incentive for participants, whom to contact for questions about the study and about participants' rights?

_____ Were steps taken to check on the validity of responses to survey items?

_____ Was a representative sample drawn?

_____ Were data appropriately and completely analyzed?

_____ Was (if possible) anonymity maintained?

_____ Was confidentiality of respondents and survey data maintained?

Questionnaire Studies

_____ Are items phrased to avoid influencing respondents to show themselves in a good light?

_____ Are items phrased to avoid influencing respondents to anticipate what researchers want to hear or find out?

_____ Are items within the survey participant's memory and awareness?

_____ Were survey instructions clear and complete?

_____ Was the length of the questionnaire appropriate?

_____ Was there a rationale for the number of items used and the decision about whether to include a midpoint?

_____ Were problems in question wording avoided?

_____ Did the research avoid negatively phrased statements?

_____ Was evidence of the reliability and validity of the questionnaire measures provided?

_____ Did the sequencing of items minimize fatigue effects?

Interview Studies

_____ Was there a rationale for using interviews, rather than questionnaires?

_____ Was the decision to use structured or unstructured interviews made on a sound basis, given the availability of measures and ways to obtain relevant information?

_____ Were interviewers thoroughly trained?

_____ Were interview scripts appropriate to the setting?

_____ Was evidence of the reliability and validity of the structured interview items obtained?

_____ What efforts were made to obtain full field reports to permit interpreting the meaning of interview data?

_____ Were any interview probes appropriate without biasing responses from study participants?

Network Analysis

_____ Is network analysis used to answer questions dealing with maps of critical interaction elements, dealing with diagnoses of problems in communication flow, or dealing with roles played by different group members in the networks?

_____ Were appropriate communication variables chosen for the research question?

_____ Were complete reports obtained from individual members or network nodes?

_____ Was a comprehensive map constructed?

_____ Were network patterns correctly and completely identified?

_____ Was the map compared to an appropriate standard for interpretation purposes?

_____ Did the researcher resist the tendency to interpret reasons behind network patterns based on the network map alone?

SUMMARY

The term *empirical* actually means "observable." Descriptive empirical research involves gathering data to test statements. It is most invited when problem questions ask about current descriptions of things and explore explanations that characterize things as they are now. Surveys cannot answer questions about cause-and-effect relationships, though experiments can (an experiment introduces a variable and determines its effects while controlling all other variables). A survey is an empirical study that uses questionnaires or interviews to discover descriptive characteristics of phenomena.

Questionnaires are survey forms in which individuals respond to items they have read. There are six steps in completing a questionnaire survey: (1) selecting questions and instructions (including developing instructions and securing informed consent, facing tactical issues in phrasing questions, preparing survey forms, and preparing debriefing materials; (2) formatting questionnaires to promote response (including deciding on the number of scale points and whether to include a midpoint); (3) determining reliability (the consistency of a measure) and validity (the degree to which a measure actually measures what is claimed), including other controls such as check questions that ask the same question twice (once phrased positively and once phrased negatively) at different locations, measures of test-taking behavior, and polarity rotation of items (avoiding negatively phrased items while attempting to avoid response set, or the tendency for subjects to follow predictable patterns of responding to test items); (4) sampling; (5) administering the questionnaire; (6) analyzing and interpreting results.

Interview methods are used to increase willingness to participate and to gather information that might be lost in the questionnaire method. The steps of interview studies include (1) selecting questions (structured interviews use specific lists of questions; unstructured interviews permit respondents to indicate their reactions to general issues without guidance from highly detailed questions); (2) training and controlling behavior of interviewers; (3) determining reliability and validity; (4) sampling subjects; and (5) analyzing and interpreting results.

In its most general application, network analysis is a set of research procedures for identifying structures in social systems based on the relations among the system's components rather than the attributes of individual cases. Traditional network analysis served as a tool to study organizational and group structures among people. This application of network analysis obtains individuals' reports of their communication activities with others for the purpose of observing and describing the flow of information in a particular organizational system. There are three general purposes for traditional network analyses: (1) to construct a map of the interaction among people in an organization, (2) to diagnose problems in communication flow, and (3) to identify the roles played by different group members. Informal channels of communication exist in organizations. Network analyses involve four steps: (1) selecting communication variables consistent with the problem question, (2) securing individual reports from members of the group, (3) constructing network maps and tracking information flow, and (4) interpreting results by comparing the network with a desired standard, such as an organizational chart. Beyond the traditional applications of network analysis, researchers examine networks among social units, called "nodes," that can be people, departments, organizations, nations, or message elements such as words. Semantic networks (semantics is the study of the relationship between words and their meanings) are examinations of the relationships among words in a message. This method combines content analysis with network analysis methods to determine semantic networks that underlie communication activities. Networks among groups may be studied to examine the structure of an organization, formal or informal. Networks among organizations may be studied as an alternative to the flow of communication within an organization. Networks among nations may be examined to explain changes in the international community. There are two major limitations to network studies: (1) they emphasize structural information rather than content information; and (2) they allow researchers to identify relationships among communicators, but not the reasons for the relationships.

TERMS FOR REVIEW

empirical	structured interviews
descriptive empirical research	unstructured interviews
experiment	anonymity
survey	confidentiality
questionnaires	scripts
validity	probe
reliability	funnel questions
check question	network analysis
polarity rotation	nodes
response set	semantic network

JUST FOR THE SAKE OF ARGUMENT: A REVIEW

Look at the following questions and prepare your own answers to them. Look for the assumptions that underlie them.

1. When is descriptive research invited and not invited? What kinds of problem questions invite the use of these methods? When are these methods not appropriate?

2. What is the difference between a survey and survey research? What are the similarities and differences between questionnaire and interview studies?

3. When are questions to be preferred over statements in survey inventories? When are open-ended questions invited?

4. How can researchers be sure that the responses they receive in interviews and questionnaires are honest and accurate? What test-taking measures can help, and what are their purposes?

5. Why would one use an interview study, rather than a questionnaire study?

6. What values can network analyses have? In what ways are they quantitative studies and in what ways are they qualitative studies?

ACTIVITIES TO PROBE FURTHER

Go to the website for this book and look for the Student Study Materials for Chapter 9.

1. Take the study quiz and print out your answers. (Make sure to review these text materials before you answer the questions so that you avoid giving answers that are your first impressions.)

2. Go to the website for a commercial designer of questionnaires, SurveyZ! This site includes survey forms developed by others. Go to the list of survey instruments listed on www.surveyz.com/showLibrary.do. Click on the link to "Demographics/Psychographics Surveys" and take a look at the questionnaires presented for the Life Attitude Survey, the Leisure Time Activities Survey, and Maslow's Higher Order Life Values Survey.

   a. How would you rate the instructions for completing these surveys?
   b. Why are open-ended questions so rarely used? What does this fact tell you about the type of information desired by the questionnaire designers?
   c. How would you evaluate the surveys for their control on the validity of responses and checks on test taking?

3. Go to the Web page for this chapter. Click on the hyperlink "Survey Studies." Now that you see a list of survey research studies in the field, choose one that you think sounds the most interesting. Meet with some other students (no more than six in the group), and prepare a very brief oral report with a one-page handout that you can give to the rest of the class. Make sure to address the following matters.

   a. Citation of the article
   b. The purpose of the research (use a direct quotation of the research problem question to the extent possible)
   c. Methods used (interview or questionnaire or some other tool?)
   d. Soundness of the items used in the survey instrument
   e. Revisions you would have made if this survey had been one of your own
   f. Chief findings of the study

4. Look at these questionnaire items. In each case, there is at least one thing wrong. Describe the problem, and then revise the example so that it is free of the problem.

   a. EXAMPLE 1 (from a set of instructions—assume that this statement is the entire set of instructions for a set of scales to follow):

       Indicate your degree of agreement with the following statements.

   b. EXAMPLE 2 (from a survey of employee satisfaction; assume that sound instructions have been presented):

Discipline is handled in a fair and equal manner	SA	A	N	D	DS

   c. EXAMPLE 3 (from a survey of employee satisfaction; assume that sound instructions have been presented):

Discipline is handled in a fair manner	SA	A	N	D	DS
Discipline is handled equally for employees	SA	A	N	D	DS
Discipline is handled professionally	SA	A	N	D	DS
Discipline is handled tactfully	SA	A	N	D	DS

   d. EXAMPLE 4: (from a measure of comprehension and recall):

Fifteen people were executed in the United States last year	SA	A	N
	D	DS	

   e. EXAMPLE 5 (from a measure of message comprehension):

Fifteen people were executed in the United States in 1993	SA	A	N	D	DS
Capital punishment is a bad idea	SA	A	N	D	DS

   f. EXAMPLE 6 (from a measure of teacher effectiveness):

The teacher made students feel ignominiously	SA	A	N	D	DS
Was the teacher prepared?	SA	A	N	D	DS

CHAPTER 10

Design of Experimental Research in Communication

Experiment is the consummation of the marriage of reason and experience, and although it is not in itself the life of the mind, it is the most passionate and fruitful expression of our intellectual life and loves.

—ABRAHAM KAPLAN

CHAPTER OUTLINE

BEFORE WE GET STARTED . . .

Though descriptive empirical studies can reveal many relationships, some questions require experiments to answer. This chapter defines experiments, explains how they are designed, and discusses sources of invalidity and strategies to deal with special problems. It also explains the sorts of "hidden codes" and research abbreviations that experimenters use to examine hypotheses.

THE NOTION OF AN EXPERIMENT

Most people think that an experiment is just another name for a carefully completed study. But experiments involve much more than being careful. It is helpful to understand the logic of an experiment, the concept of control, and the sorts of research questions that are suitable for experimental research.

Experiment a study of the effects of variables manipulated by the researcher in situations where all other influences are held constant. Variables are manipulated or introduced by experimenters for the purpose of establishing causal relationships.

An **experiment** is more than a carefully completed study. As the definition at the left shows, it involves an attempt to introduce variables, holding everything else constant, in an effort to establish cause-and-effect relationships. It might help to break that definition down into its parts. First, experiments study "the effects of variables manipulated by the researcher." Unlike surveys, experimenters introduce variables (called "manipulating variables") that were not present to begin with. Then, they can assess the impact of these variables. Survey studies just try to identify associations among variables, but experiments add experimental variables to the existing setting to see what effects might be found. The second part of the definition states that "all other variables are held constant." This requirement is the hard part. Most of the topics covered in this chapter involve ways to exercise experimental control. The third part of this definition states that we complete experiments "for the purpose of establishing causal relationships." Though the method of history can permit researchers to draw long-term cause-and-effect relationships, only experiments can provide immediate evidence. If we can control other sources of variation and introduce one new experimental variable, then any effects must have been caused by the experimental variable.

Even though some are completed in the laboratory, experiments are not "ivory tower" studies. In light of the U.S. War on Terror, a communication researcher was struck by the angry rhetoric that was so widespread in popular mass media publications and broadcasts. He could have completed a rhetorical analysis, but Nabi (2002) chose to explore some immediate causal relationships. In particular, he wondered if people were most influenced by fear or anger. He suspected that angry messages would be more effective than fear-inducing messages in persuading people to support antiterrorist legislation. In a laboratory experiment, Nabi gave one group of students some newspaper articles expressing fear about terrorism. The other group read newspaper articles that communicated an angry tone. The author found that the angry messages were most persuasive. Though completed in the laboratory, the practical significance of this research is undoubted.

As mentioned, exercising control is not easy. When introducing variables, a careless researcher might manipulate other variables by accident. For instance, in a study on the impact of evidence on persuasion, researchers may manipulate message length or language as well. Thus, the evidence manipulation may be mixed up with other sources of variation. This situation is called **confounding** and makes it impossible to identify the exact source of variation. Such confounding may mislead researchers. A hypothesis may deal with only one experimental variable, but the actual experiment might involve a complex of uncontrolled and confounding independent variables. Confounding hides another variable in the hypothesis and makes the inference impossible.

Confounding mixing (or confusing) variation from one source with variation from another source so that it is impossible to know whether effects are due to the impact of either variable separately or some combination of them.

Questions and Hypotheses in Experimental Designs

Experiments are designed to answer research questions that deal with cause-and-effect relationships. But there is a slight catch. The causes must be matters that can be manipulated by the researcher. Thus, you cannot complete an experiment to show that being a woman causes a person to be more persuaded by a fear appeal than does being a man. One cannot reasonably manipulate sex of subjects—we have to take people pretty much as they are. You can conclude that the sex of the receiver is *related* to the persuasiveness of fear appeals, but there is no way to say that the sex of the receiver *caused* the effect (as opposed to influences from self-esteem or levels of submissiveness). On the other hand, it is possible to find out if messages that use internal organizers (previews and summaries) cause more attitude change than messages that omit them. Messages can be prepared by the experimenter with and without internal organizers and then presented to randomly selected audiences. Thus, experiments are limited to dealing with causal relationships stemming from *experimental independent variables*.

experimental designs permit drawing causal claims about variables that can be manipulated

experimental independent variables

Hypotheses in experiments are phrased to explore such causal relationships. Here are some hypotheses from experimental studies, with explanations of variables added where appropriate:

experimental hypotheses probe causal relationships

♦ $H_{1,2}$: Men will like male HPC helpers [college students who attempted to use high person-centered (HPC) comforting messages to comfort distressed same-sex friends] less than (a) they like female HPC helpers or (b) women like either male or female HPC helpers. (Burleson, Holmstrom, & Gilstrap, 2005, p. 473)

♦ We hypothesized that news information about genetic susceptibility to smoking addiction would affect efficacy to quit smoking and the intention to obtain a genetic test for smoking addiction through a cognitive mediator. That mediator is the inference (measured as a likelihood) that the recipient of the genetic information is at risk for a genetic addiction to smoking. (Cappella, Lerman, Romantan, & Baruh, 2005, p. 481)

♦ H_{1b}: When individuals support the cause advocated by activists [whose civil liberties the government is trying to restrict], those who encounter a group story frame [a news story that explains that the activist targeted by the government is a group of people] will be more expressive [engaging in such activities as speaking about the issue with friends, writing letters to newspapers, or attending public meetings on the topic] than those who encounter an individual story frame [a news story that explains that the activist targeted by the government is a single person]. (Boyle, Schmierbach, Armstrong, Cho, McCluskey, McLeod, & Shah, 2006, p, 276)

SPECIAL DISCUSSION 10-1

A QUESTION OF ETHICS: DECEPTION IN RESEARCH DESIGNS

Deception in an experiment occurs when "the research participants have been either: (1) uninformed that an experiment was being conducted or (2) intentionally misled about the nature of the study in which they are participating" (Greenberg & Folger, 1988, p. 40). Despite heated debate about the issue among scholars, most research in psychology before 1983 involved some deception (Adair, Dushenko, & Lindsay, 1985), and it still is routine in many fields. Deception may occur in three major ways.

1. *Concealing the true purpose of the experiment.* Though researchers are not expected to reveal their research hypotheses to subjects in experiments, it does not follow that researchers have a right to lie to subjects. Indeed, a respect for others requires that researchers follow the same standards as the rest of society—standards that view lying as wrong (Warwick, 1975; Goldstein, 1981). Kelman (1967) sadly observed that in some experimental settings "the usual criteria for ethical interpersonal conduct become irrelevant" (p. 5). Yet, even Kelman admitted that sometimes deceiving subjects could be justified to secure scientific knowledge (see also Baron, 1981). Most researchers can avoid this form of deception by telling subjects what the study is about in very broad language—without revealing the independent and dependent variables. Instead of saying "This project is a study examining the amount of evidence used in speeches on attitude change," you could say "This project is a study of the ways people respond to different sorts of persuasive messages."

2. *Concealing the purpose of the participants' own actions.* This problem is created when subjects are told that their behavior is designed for one purpose when, in fact, it is not. For instance, Festinger and Carlsmith (1959) completed a classic study in which "subjects expressed their attitudes about an experimental task under the pretext of informing a waiting participant about the task they just completed" (Greenberg & Folger, 1988, p. 42). Such behavior raises a problem regarding deception.

3. *Concealing experiences that researchers have planned for subjects.* This form of deception occurs when the researchers keep the subjects ignorant of the things that will happen to them in the course of the experiment.

The second and third sources of deception are not easily handled. Aside from the ethics of lying to subjects, there is also a matter of informed consent. If subjects do not know the true reasons they are asked to perform behavior or if subjects do not know what researchers have planned for them, they cannot really give their informed consent to participate. Without knowing what is in store for them, they do not really have a free choice about whether to participate in the research.

Granted, most subjects do not view experimental deception as a problem (Clark & Word, 1974; Ring, Wallston, & Corey, 1970), but the ethical issues raised do not disappear just because no one complains. One suggested alternative involves asking subjects to role-play their behavior. Instead of telling a person that he or she is writing an essay to be used by representatives of the U.S. State Department for a pamphlet they are preparing (Elms & Janis, 1965), subjects may be asked to write essays "as if " they were to be used in such a setting. Though this role-playing strategy avoids many ethical difficulties (Bok, 1974; Darroch & Steiner, 1970; Kelman, 1967), the ability to generalize such results remains controversial (see Freedman, 1969; Ginsburg, 1979).

In each case, the hypotheses suggested cause-and-effect relationships that were manipulated successfully in experimental research.[1]

The Concept of Control

The effort to improve **control** increases the ability of researchers to make clear statements that experimental variables are responsible for observed effects. To make sure that all elements in an experiment are controlled except for the new variables introduced by the experimenter, several major approaches are used: elimination, holding constant, matching, blocking, randomization, and statistical control (after Kerlinger, 1986, pp. 287–289).

- ◆ *Elimination and removal.* We are rarely able to study the impact of one variable by itself. Other "nuisance" or "intervening" variables often get in the way. The most obvious way to control for a nuisance variable is to remove it from the experimental setting. For instance, researchers often control extraneous variables such as temperature and illumination problems by collecting data in classroom "laboratory" settings where these sources of distraction may be eliminated completely.

- ◆ *Holding constant.* Technically, all control methods involve taking nuisance variables and holding them constant. When we eliminate variables, the nuisance variables are held constant at "zero presence." Sometimes researchers control for other variables by limiting the range of intervening variables so that they are equal across conditions. There are three major ways to hold variables constant in experiments. First, limiting the population may control a nuisance variable (for instance, in very early self-disclosure research, results showed wild variation when men and women were paired with each other—to control for the sex composition of pairs, researchers soon learned to limit their studies only to populations of people of the same sex self-disclosing to each other). Second, using subjects as their own controls may control for the impact of nuisance variables (people may be sampled before and after some experimental treatment to identify their average amount of improvement despite any differences they may have had at the outset). Third, **counterbalancing** may be used. With this method, such effects as cumulative learning effects or fatigue effects do not go away, but the variation produced is distributed across the experiment equally—hence, the term "counterbalanced."

- ◆ *Matching.* The method of **matching** involves attempting to compare similar participants on some key variables. Researchers sometimes use this method to control for initial differences people bring to a study. For instance, people might be matched because they share the same age, sex, job classification, intelligence level, or the like. In a study of attention to content of commercials by children, it might be important to control for sex of the child since girls tend to develop verbal abilities earlier than boys. Thus, a researcher might identify the number of boys and girls in a sample and then assign half of the girls to one experimental condition and

Control in research design, methods researchers use to remove or hold constant the effects of nuisance variables.

Counterbalancing rotating the sequence in which experimental treatments are introduced to subjects in an effort to control for extraneous variables.

Matching pairing events or participants on some variable on which they share equal levels and then assigning them to experimental or control conditions.

matching individuals or groups

---

[1]The third hypothesis was supported, and the first two were not.

half to a control group. Similarly, half the boys might be assigned to each group in the experiment. Researchers can match individuals or groups of people (the most frequent use of matching). Even so, you should know that some researchers consider many applications of matching doubtful since they can introduce distortions. You can "overmatch" subjects so that they no longer represent the population. Furthermore, when matching on several nuisance variables, you may begin to lose subjects. As Fred Kerlinger explained: "If one decides to match intelligence, sex, and social class, one may be fairly successful in matching the first two variables but not in finding pairs that are fairly equal on all three variables. Add a fourth variable and the problem becomes difficult, often impossible to solve" (1986, p. 289).

limits on matching

♦ *Blocking.* **Blocking** includes levels of variables into a study.[2] In a study of the impact of a female source's physical attractiveness on the persuasiveness of a message, the sex of the respondents might make a big difference in the results obtained. Thus, one might include the sex of the respondents into the study as another variable. Blocking permits one to draw conclusions about the impact of each independent variable separately or as part of an interaction. Of course, adding variables into a study requires that researchers have fairly sizable samples to permit the subdivisions. If such samples are available, however, this method may be among the most desirable options for control.

Blocking including a nuisance variable into the design as another independent variable of interest.

♦ *Randomization.* **Randomization** is a basic requirement for sound experimental control and subsequent inferential statistical analyses. In short, randomization involves using the rules of chance to balance groups of subjects. Respondents may be selected at random from the population, and they also may be assigned at random to experimental or control conditions. The ways in which groups of people can differ from each other are almost infinite. Yet, randomization increases the likelihood that groups of people in different conditions will be comparable in ways that researchers might otherwise never imagine. Fred Kerlinger explained the importance of randomization:

Randomization assigning subjects so that each event is equally likely to belong to any experimental or control condition (contrasted with random sampling, which is selection of data such that each event in the population has an equal chance of being selected).

> The *principle of randomization* may be stated thus: Since, in random procedures every member of a population has an equal chance of being selected, members with certain distinguishing characteristics—male or female, high or low intelligence, conservative or liberal, and so on and on—will, if selected, probably be offset in the long run by the selection of other members of the population with counterbalancing quantities or qualities of the characteristics. (1986, p. 115)
>
> Another way to phrase it is: if randomization has been accomplished, then the experimental groups can be considered statistically equal in all possible ways. This does not mean, of course, that the groups are equal in all the possible variables. We already know that by chance the groups can

---

[2]Some writers prefer to reserve the term "blocking" for situations in which the additional variable factor is on a nominal scale, such as the sex of respondents (Campbell & Stanley, 1963). When the additional variable is on a ranking scale, they suggest using the term "stratifying" rather than "blocking." If the additional variable is measured on an interval or ratio scale (such as dividing groups into high, moderate, and low self-esteem groups), they recommend using the term "leveling."

be unequal, but the probability of their being equal is greater, with proper randomization, than the probability of their not being equal. For this reason control of the extraneous variance by randomization is a powerful method of control. All other methods leave many possibilities of inequality. . . . A precept that springs from this equalizing power of randomization, then, is: Whenever it is possible to do so, randomly assign subjects to experimental groups and conditions, and randomly assign conditions and other factors to experimental groups. (1986, p. 288)

It should be noted that individual differences do not go away when randomization is used. Instead, these sources of variation appear as random variation or background noise across conditions.[3] Thus, randomization controls a host of sources of variation so that they do not influence one experimental condition more than any other.

◆ *Statistical control.* If you can measure a nuisance variable, it is possible to use statistical tools to hold it constant. "Analysis of covariance" and "partial correlation" are two common methods of statistical control. They compute the variation associated with each nuisance variable and then separate it from the remaining total variation in the experiment. Analysis of covariance is used when the independent variables are broken down into nominal categories (such as experimental group versus control group). The nuisance variable is called a *covariate* and is used as the basis for adjusting output variable scores. When studies investigate correlations among variables, partial correlations are used to explore the relationship between two variables while holding a third one constant. Though all methods of control are related to some statistical model (blocking and analysis of covariance methods are equivalent, for instance), the major tactical differences described here should help you understand the options available to researchers.

analysis of covariance and partial correlation as methods of statistical control

EXPERIMENTAL VALIDITY AND INVALIDITY

Experiments can blow up in a researcher's face. When experiments fall apart, they have fallen prey to sources of invalidity. Sources of **experimental invalidity** prevent researchers from drawing unequivocal conclusions. There are two families of invalidity in experiments.

Experimental invalidity errors that prevent researchers from drawing unequivocal conclusions.

Internal Invalidity

Internal invalidity consists of matters that may jeopardize an experiment. Table 10.1 lists the major sources of internal invalidity in experiments. To argue for cause-and-effect

Internal invalidity the presence of contamination that prevents the experimenter from concluding that a study's experimental variable is responsible for the observed effects.

---

[3]Actually, randomization causes assignable variation from nuisance variables to be confounded (or confused) with random variation.

TABLE 10.1   SOURCES OF INTERNAL INVALIDITY

History: Events not controlled by the researcher that occur during the experiment between any pretest and posttest.

Selection: Sampling biases in selecting or assigning subjects to experimental or control conditions (in essence, rigging the study by taking samples capriciously).

Maturation: Changes that naturally occur over time (including fatigue or suspicion), even if subjects are left alone.

Testing: Alterations that occur when subjects are tested and made testwise or anxious in ways that affect them when they are given a second test.

Instrumentation: Changes in the use of measuring instruments from the pretest to the posttest, including changes in raters or interviewers who collect the data in different conditions.

Statistical regression: Shift produced when subjects are selected due to some very high or very low scores on some test (such as selecting a group of people who score high in communication apprehension for participation in some experimental treatment) and then changes on that measurement are tracked in the experiment; statistical regression holds that people will "regress toward the mean" even if they simply are left alone.

Experimental mortality: Biases introduced when subjects differentially (nonrandomly) drop out of the experiment (for instance, subjects may drop out of a weight reduction program if they receive disappointing results; thus, the remaining subjects will show inflated levels of improvement).

Interaction of elements: Effects created by the interaction of selection biases with differential levels of maturation, history, or any other source of variation.

---

relationships, these sources of invalidity must be controlled or removed. If a researcher completes an experiment that controls for seven out of the eight sources of internal invalidity, the experiment still cannot lead to an unequivocal statement of experimental effect. That is, if all sources of internal invalidity are not controlled, it is not possible to claim that any observed effects were caused by the independent variable in the experiment. Instead, researchers have to add equivocating terms (if's and maybe's) as they draw their conclusions.

External Invalidity

External invalidity the degree to which experimental results may not be generalized to other similar circumstances.

External invalidity affects generalizability of results. In a strict sense, study findings can be generalized only to the sample groups from which they were drawn. Yet, researchers often carefully sample so that some generalization of results may be possible. Regrettably, experiments are sometimes completed in ways that make it difficult, if not impossible, to generalize results to larger populations without severe limitations. These sources of external validity do not mean that the experimental variable did not produce the alleged effects—internal validity assesses *that* issue. Instead, external invalidity sets *limits* on the sorts of populations to which results may be generalized. The major sources of external invalidity are found on Table 10.2.

> **TABLE 10.2   SOURCES OF EXTERNAL INVALIDITY**
>
> *Interaction of testing and the experimental variable:* Often called pretest sensitization, this defect is created when the pretesting makes subjects either more or less sensitive to the experimental variable.
>
> *Interaction of selection and the experimental variable:* Effects created by sampling groups in such a way that they are not representative of the population since they are more or less sensitive to the experimental variable than other subsamples from the same population (such as sampling college students in communication studies even though they may be more or less sensitive to the independent variable than the general population of people).
>
> *Reactive arrangements:* Elements in the experimental setting that make subjects react differentially to the experimental arrangements rather than to the experimental variable alone (such matters as awareness of participation in an experiment may alter normal reactions of people).
>
> *Multiple treatment interference:* Depending on the design, if subjects are exposed to repeated additional experimental treatments, they may react in ways that are not generalizable to subjects that are uncontaminated by such additional independent variables.

Ideally, an experiment should have both internal and external validity. But researchers actually give greatest attention to internal validity issues. The concern is natural. If a study does not have internal validity, its findings cannot be generalized. Even so, researchers often comment about external invalidity when reporting their work. Research articles usually include some statements that limit research findings and call for replications to test generalizability of results to other population groups.

SPECIFIC EXPERIMENTAL DESIGNS

Experimental designs tend to follow a protocol of notation, methods, and applications. Terms tend to be mentioned without explanation in research articles. This section will help you decipher these terms.

Notation for Experimental Designs

To show what goes on in a research design, a notation system has been developed, much like notation used to sketch out a football play. Three terms are prominent. The first of these terms is

notation

O

O is an abbreviation for an *observation* a researcher makes of the study's dependent variable. If several observations are made, researchers sometimes add subscript numbers to keep things straight, such as

observation

O_1 O_2 O_3 O_4

SPECIAL DISCUSSION 10-2

ADDITIONAL CONTROL ISSUES

Experiments require control over all sources of variation. The major sources of invalidity deal with failures to exhibit such strong control. Some other common sources of error in experiments are the following (after Isaac & Michael, 1981, pp. 85–89).

The halo effect. Sometimes strong positive or negative impressions of a source of communication may affect all ratings that follow. Researchers may find that their credibility creates pressure in the minds of subjects to respond positively or negatively, regardless of experimental treatments used.

The placebo effect. In medical research, a placebo is a stimulus containing no medicine or no experimental treatment at all. In nonmedical work, subjects may show changes even in the absence of treatments, in reaction to the mental suggestion that they may have been given some stimulus. Thus, researchers attempt to use control groups and to exercise control over methods of providing treatments to groups.

The John Henry effect. Named after the folklore hero who died trying to outwork a machine, this effect describes the actions of people who try to perform extra hard when they participate in an experiment. Thus, their behavior may not be consistent with their normal activity.

The pitfall of "do nothing" control groups. "Control groups ordinarily should experience *all things* in common with the treatment group *except* the critical factor, per se. Control groups that 'do nothing' are apt to differ from the treatment groups in more ways than just the isolated treatment variable" (Isaac & Michael, 1981, p. 88).

These are translated as "observation one," "observation two," "observation three," and "observation four."[4] Regardless of the ways in which measurement of observations is handled, the observations are made to help the researcher identify the effects that are found in a study.

A second term in experimental design is

X

experimental variable

This abbreviation stands for the *experimental variable* used by researchers. When there is more than one experimental variable, some researchers add subscript numbers to help keep exact conditions clear. For our introductory treatment, however, we will not clutter up our notation with such subscripts.

A final term is

R

randomization

This letter stands for *randomization*. Those experiments that include randomization (either random assignment or random sampling) include this notation prominently.

---

[4]Some might read these terms as "O sub-one," "O sub-two," and so forth. But we consider the technical affectation a barrier to understanding and advise that you use plain language whenever you can.

For control of systematic biases, randomization is the most effective means that may be used. Thus, it plays a strong role in sound experimentation.

Preexperimental Designs

Some designs have good intentions but do not really exercise the sort of control necessary for a solid experiment. They are considered here because they reflect the thinking that leads to full experiments and because they often are used by researchers who feel the need to make compromises.

- ◆ **One-shot case study.** In these studies, an experimental treatment is introduced and researchers look at effects on some output (dependent) variable. Unfortunately, as Figure 10.1 shows, this design does not really control for any source of experimental invalidity. You may have seen case studies used as teaching aids in classes you have taken. Often researchers complete case studies so that they can develop hypotheses for formal testing at a later time.

- ◆ **One-group pretest–posttest.** As an improvement, researchers sometimes have added a pretest. Thus, subjects in an experiment can serve as their own controls. This method is a step in the right direction—and the method frequently has been used in evaluation studies—but the design does not really control for enough sources of invalidity to permit drawing clear conclusions of experimental effects.

- ◆ **Static-group comparisons.** This design attempts to use a control group, but the two groups are not known to be comparable. A researcher may sample students in a sophomore class at 10 a.m. and expose them to an experimental message. The researcher might also sample students in a graduate class at 7 p.m. for a control group. These groups are "intact" and cannot be presumed to be comparable at the outset. These differences can throw a monkey wrench into the entire design. Sometimes researchers will complete random sampling of a smaller subgroup from each intact group. Yet, to ensure comparability, researchers should also randomly assign subjects to experimental or control conditions.

One-shot case study a preexperimental design in which an experimental treatment is introduced and researchers look at effects on some output (dependent) variable.

One-group pretest–posttest a preexperimental design in which a pretest is added to a one-shot case study.

Static-group comparisons a preexperimental design in which a control group is used, but the groups are not known to be comparable in other respects (typically because the experimental and control groups are separate "intact" groups.

True Experimental Designs

The three true experimental designs below serve as the basis for increasingly complicated factorial designs used in formal experiments.

Pretest–Posttest Control Group Design

Surely the most popular design for communication experiments, the **pretest–posttest control group design** is composed of an experimental group and a control group. Subjects in the experimental group are pretested. They are then exposed to the experimental variable and posttested. Subjects in the control group are treated the same way except, of course, they are not presented with the experimental variable.

Pretest–posttest control group design a true experimental design that includes randomly selected experimental and control groups, each of which is given a pretest and a posttest.

Sources of Invalidity

	Internal								External			
	History	Maturation	Testing	Instrumentation	Regression	Selection	Mortality	Interaction of Selection and Maturation, etc.	Interaction of Testing and X	Interaction of Selection and X	Reactive Arrangements	Multiple-X Interference
Pre-Experimental Designs:												
1. One-Shot Case Study X O	−	−				−	−			−		
2. One-Group Pretest–Posttest Design O X O	−	−	−	−	?	+	+	−	−	−	?	
3. Static-Group Comparison X O / O	+	?	+	+	+	−	−	−		−		
True Experimental Designs:												
4. Pretest–Posttest Control Group Design R O X O / R O O	+	+	+	+	+	+	+	+	−	?	?	
5. Solomon Four-Group Design R O X O / R O O / R X O / R O	+	+	+	+	+	+	+	+	+	?	?	
6. Posttest-Only Control Group Design R X O / R O	+	+	+	+	+	+	+	+	+	?	?	

Note: In the table, a minus indicates a definite weakness, a plus indicates that the factor is controlled, a question mark indicates a possible source of concern, and a blank indicates that the factor is not relevant.

It is with extreme reluctance that these summary tables are presented because they are apt to be "too helpful," and to be depended upon in place of the more complex and qualified presentation in the text. No + or − indicator should be respected unless the reader comprehends why it is placed there. In particular it is against the spirit of this presentation to create uncomprehended fears of, or confidence in, specific designs.

O: Observation of the Dependent Variable
X: Experimental Variable
R: Randomization

FIGURE 10.1 EXPERIMENTAL DESIGN VALIDITY FACTORS

Source: Campbell, Donald T., and Julian C. Stanley. *Experimental and Quasi-Experimental Designs for Research.* Copyright © 1963 by Houghton Mifflin Company. Used with permission.

You might suppose that researchers simply subtract pretests from posttests to see the amount of change observed. Despite the common sense that may be involved, there are statistical problems with analyzing "change scores." First, change scores may not have distributions that make them easy to interpret with standard statistical tools. Second, by definition, change scores have lower reliability than the original measures (Allen & Yen, 1979). Thus, prudent researchers usually try to use alternatives to change scores. Most often, researchers use a method of statistical control in which the posttest scores of experimental and control groups are compared with the pretest scores used as a covariate.

change scores are not advised

As you can see on Figure 10.1, the pretest–posttest control group design controls for all sources of internal invalidity. But the story is different when we consider external validity. Sometimes pretesting people can affect the way they respond to experimental variables. Rather than responding freshly to experimental variables, people may try to recall what they did on the pretest and respond in the same way (perhaps to avoid being "wishy washy"). Thus, the pretest may "sensitize" people and cause them to respond in somewhat inhibited ways. The internal validity of the experiment is just fine, of course, since the experimental variable is the cause of observed effects. But the results of the experiment can only be generalized directly to populations of people who have also been sensitized by a pretest. To overcome the problems with pretest sensitization, two other designs have been suggested (these designs will be mentioned next).

pretest sensitization described

Solomon Four-Group Design

You can add control groups to examine pretesting effects directly. The **Solomon four-group design** design actually uses three control groups. To check for pretest sensitization, you may compare the groups that have received a pretest with the groups that have not. If pretesting inhibited responses, the design will reveal it.[5] The problem with this design, however, is that it requires doubling the sample. Thus, it may be expensive.

> **Solomon four-group design** a true experimental design that assesses the impact of pretesting by adding control groups.

Posttest-Only Control Group Design

Another way to avoid pretest sensitization is to delete the pretest entirely. If the researcher does not need to pretest subjects, this design is preferred. Take a look at the static-group comparison design. Do you see the difference between it and the posttest-only control group design? The difference is randomization. With this extra step, the experimental and control groups are made comparable. The result is dramatic. Rather than facing the limitations of the static-group comparison, the **posttest-only control group design** introduces control over the major sources of experimental invalidity found on Table 10.1.

> **Posttest-only control group design** a true experimental design that avoids pretest sensitization by deleting the pretest entirely.

---

[5]If pretest sensitization is found, all is not lost. If the experimental variable produced a significant effect, pretest sensitization was not enough to prevent experimental effects. In such cases, the impact of pretest sensitization is minor when compared with the experimental variable.

SPECIAL DISCUSSION 10-3

SINGLE SUBJECT EXPERIMENTS

Much research in speech and hearing science has involved the *single subject* design (Herson & Barlow, 1976; Kratochwill, 1978), though the design long has been used in manufacturing under the rubric of the "component search" or "comparative experiments." Therapists attempting to find the best treatment for a patient often use the single subject design. The researcher starts by getting baseline information as a control. These observations often are abbreviated with the letter "A." Then the new treatment—perhaps a drug or a particular type of therapy—is introduced and effects measured. The new treatment may be identified as a "B" condition (standing for a "better" option, perhaps). Then researchers withdraw the treatment and see what happens. If a new treatment is effective, one would expect to see improvements with its presence and worsening with its withdrawal. To control for potential cyclical effects that have nothing to do with treatments, researcher may alter the order of interventions as in the design:

A B A B B A

To see if differences exist, researchers compare all of the "A" conditions with all of the "B" conditions. The formula for combinations can be used to assess how often such improvement patterns could be expected to occur by chance alone.

The approach can—and has been—extended to studies involving two, three, or more treatment options. Though of great value in therapeutic and medical settings, the use of single subject designs has limitations including the following: (1) it is most applicable to questions of individual difference, rather than patterns across people; (2) its limited generalizability prevents examining hypotheses of social significance to most communication researchers; and (3) it limits the sorts of statistical tools that might be used to help analyze results.

Factorial Designs

Factorial designs experimental designs in which more than one independent variable is used.

So far we have dealt with situations in which single experimental groups are compared with control groups. Yet, these days, you will not see as many single-variable experiments as once filled our journals. Instead, **factorial designs** with multiple independent variables are most frequent.

Uses of Factorial Designs in Research

Factors (also called "variable factors") variables broken down into levels.

When variables are broken down into levels (such as high self-esteem versus low self-esteem, high readability versus low readability, or high dysfluency versus low dysfluency), they are called variable factors, or just **factors.** These **levels** of variables are used in factorial designs to introduce independent variables. It is important not to confuse levels of a factor with a factor itself. If a researcher compares men's and women's interest in headline news stories, "men" and "women" are not two variables. Instead, "men" and "women" are simply the levels of the variable factor "sex of respondent." When factor levels are used, researchers are actually creating nominal

Levels the categories of variable factors.

categories for the independent variables involved.[6] As an abbreviation of sorts, researchers often list the number of levels of their variables when describing the designs. Thus, if a study involves two independent variables, each of which has two levels, the design may be called a "two-by-two factorial design." If the second independent variable has three levels, it may be called a "two-by-three factorial design," and so forth.

abbreviation for design structure by levels

Researchers employ factorial designs when they have multiple independent variables. But such a statement does not tell the full story. One could complete a series of single-variable designs with different input variables. Yet, factorial designs allow researchers to put input variables together to see if there are special combinations of variables that produce unique effects. Thus, these designs examine *interactions* among independent variables that might be missed if researchers did a bunch of single-variable designs.

factorial designs reveal interaction effects

Factorial designs really are extensions of experimental designs that we have previously described. An experiment with a single independent variable may be illustrated simply as Figure 10.2A shows. In a factorial design, researchers adapt this design to fit their needs. Suppose that a researcher wishes to complete a study with two independent variables in a factorial design. Each variable might be broken down into two levels—a high level and a low level, for instance (though the levels could refer to types of independent variable treatments, rather than degree). If the researcher wishes to use a posttest-only method, then each cell of the factorial design contains a little posttest-only control group design as shown in Figure 10.2B. In each case, the X is actually a combination of levels of each independent variable. After a time a researcher might notice that all of the control groups are treated pretty much the same. Thus, he or she might try to economize on data collection by gathering one control group sample rather than four. When this method is followed, the common control group may be placed outside the design for later comparisons. This technique is known as a factorial design with an offset control group and is illustrated in Figure 10.2C. Yet another variation builds the control group directly into the design. If both independent variables are true experimental variables, it may be possible to have a condition in the design in which the independent variables are absent. Figure 10.2D shows this adaptation. As you can see, a factorial model is not really a different method from the designs previously described, but an extension of them.

factorial designs allow analysis of more than one independent variable

specific designs may be placed in cells of the factorial design

use of offset control groups

Interpreting Factorial Results

Experimenters use factorial designs to find evidence of the impact of independent variables together and separately.

Main effects stem from independent variables one at a time. In factorial designs these main effects are identified by looking at differences between levels of each independent variable across levels of the other variables in the study. Sometimes

Main effects dependent variable effects that result from independent variables separately.

---

[6]An experiment typically involves a categorical independent variable and a continuous dependent variable. As you can identify (by recalling the discussion of measurement levels in Chapter 4), the levels of the experimental variable actually are nominal categories. Of course, the dependent variable could be measured on any scale that is appropriate.

A. Posttest-Only Control Group Design with a Single Independent Variable

R   X   O

R   O

B. Factorial Design with Two Independent Variables Using a Posttest-Only Control Group Design

Independent Variable 1

	Low			High		
Independent Variable 2 Low	R	X	O	R	X	O
	R		O	R		O
High	R	X	O	R	X	O
	R		O	R		O

C. Factorial Design with Two Independent Variables Using a Posttest-Only Control Group Design with Offset Control Groups

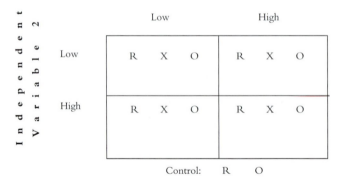

Independent Variable 1

	Low			High		
Independent Variable 2 Low	R	X	O	R	X	O
High	R	X	O	R	X	O

Control: R   O

D. Factorial Design with Two Independent Variables Using a Posttest-Only Control Group Design with Inclusive Control Groups

Independent Variable 1

	Without X			With X		
Independent Variable 2 Without X	R		O	R	X	O
With X	R	X	O	R	X	O

FIGURE 10.2   DESIGNS IN FACTORIAL MODES

A. Example of a Main Effect with a Single Independent Variable

Low   High

| 5 | 15 |

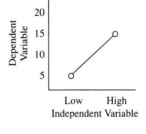

Numbers in cells are averages
of scores on the dependent variable.

B. Example of Main Effects with Two Independent Variables

X_1: Independent Variable 1

X_2: Independent Variable 2

FIGURE 10.3   MAIN EFFECTS

diagrams can help identify these effects. In Figure 10.3A we can see the impact
of one independent variable on a dependent variable. The main effect is indicated by the presence of a sloping line (upward in our example). The levels of
the independent variable are indicated in the horizontal axis of the diagram. If
there were no main effect, you would see a line that ran exactly parallel to the
horizontal axis. Since the line shows clear slope, the presence of a main effect is
evident.

When a second independent variable is added, it is necessary to draw two lines to
represent each level of the second independent variable. Figure 10.3B shows how
this process works. The lines are some distance apart from each other, indicating a
main effect for the second independent variable. If there were no main effect, we
would not see any distance between the lines at all.

Interaction effects stem from combinations of independent variables. These interaction effects involve variation arising from special combinations of levels of independent variables. Factorial designs allow researchers to identify them directly.
Figure 10.4 shows two major types of interactions that might occur in research. It is
important to distinguish between the types of interactions that exist because they affect the kinds of conclusions you can draw.

When drawing pictures of effects, interactions are indicated by lines that are
not parallel to each other. In Figure 10.4A the lines drawn are not parallel, but

Interaction effects
dependent variable effects
that result from indepen-
dent variables taken to-
gether and involving
variation arising from special combinations of levels
of independent variables.

A. Example of an Ordinal Interaction Effect

X_1: Independent Variable 1
X_2: Independent Variable 2

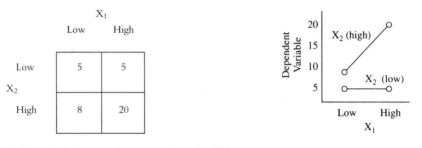

B. Example of a Disordinal or Crossed Interaction Effect

FIGURE 10.4   INTERACTION EFFECTS

distinguishing interactions:

Ordinal interaction
dependent variable interaction effects in the same direction as the main effects of the variables involved.

Disordinal interaction
(also called a "crossed interaction") dependent variable interaction effects that are not in the same direction as the main effects of the variables involved and that are diagrammatically revealed when lines drawn for each independent variable cross each other.

not permitted to interpret main effects for variables in disordinal interactions

they do not cross each other. This sort of pattern is called an **ordinal interaction.** Across the board, the high level for each independent variable produced higher scores on the dependent measure than the low levels did. Two main effects seemed to emerge. But put together, the high levels of each independent variable produced the same effect—but more so! Thus, the interaction is in the same direction as the main effects, but with a bonus effect thrown in. In our particular example, when variable 2 is at its low level, changing the level of variable 1 produces no appreciable effect. But when variable 2 is at its high level, changing the level of variable 1 results in great increases in the dependent variable. Thus, if the researchers wanted to produce high scores on the dependent variables, they would recommend setting both independent variables at their high levels: any other combination would not be quite so good. When researchers find an ordinal interaction, it is permissible to interpret main effects for the variables involved in the interaction without fear of misrepresenting the facts. But the interaction means that the real story lies in the special combinations of both variables, even though the interaction is in the same direction as the main effects.

A second sort of interaction effect has different lessons for researchers. A **disordinal interaction** occurs when the lines drawn for each independent variable cross each other. Because of this pattern, the effect is sometimes called a "crossed

RESEARCHERS IN THE FIELD: RANDY HIROKAWA

In the area of theorizing and researching group communication, Randy Hirokawa is a key figure. His "functional perspective" theory of group communication and decision-making effectiveness is essential reading in communication theory. At least four separate sources have identified his theory as one of the three most influential in small group communication. Not surprisingly, he has completed extensive research related to this work. He has published three edited books including the influential *Communication and Group Decision Making* coedited with Marshall Scott Poole. He has also published 36 refereed journal articles and 24 book chapters. Now dean of the College of Arts and Sciences at the University of Hawaii at Hilo, he is a native of Kaua'i and earned his bachelor's degree from the University of Hawaii at Manoa. From there he completed his M.A. and Ph.D. degrees at the University of Washington. He taught at Pennsylvania State University and at the University of Iowa, where he served as departmental executive officer. He edited the journal *Communication Studies* and regularly is part of the editorial boards of the field's top journals. Though he enjoys fishing, weight training, golf, tennis, and softball, he finds time to work on a full schedule of community service work, including serving on the board of directors and as the director of personnel of the Boys and Girls Club of the Big Island.

♦ *How did you get involved in our field?*
Like many people in our field, I was drawn to it because of my interest in debate back in high school. I continued to debate at the University of Hawaii and eventually became a speech major because one of the people who used to run debate workshops in high school (Dr. Donald Klopf) was the chair of the Speech Department at the University of Hawaii. It was Dr. Klopf who encouraged me to go to graduate school, and even helped get me a teaching assistantship at his *alma mater*, the University of Washington. At Washington, I met a lot of wonderful, caring professors like Tom Scheidel, Mae Bell, Steve Stephenson, Barnet Baskerville, and others who encouraged me to continue on for a Ph.D.

♦ *You have a reputation for being a generous researcher. You have often coauthored research, sometimes with established scholars and sometimes with emerging scholars and students. Has this effort to be collaborative been a specific choice you planned for your career?*
(Laughing) Well, I guess one interpretation is that I am a generous researcher. Another interpretation is that I had so many irons in the fire that I needed people to help me complete those projects. Since I spent most of my career in outstanding communication departments (Penn State University and the University of Iowa), there were always lots of talented, eager students who were willing to work with me on projects. So that's why I have quite a few coauthored studies with students. I have also been very fortunate to have worked with generous senior scholars like Dennis Gouran and Marshall Scott Poole, who not only coauthored with me, but more important, were highly instrumental in shaping my thinking.

♦ *Your work shows great balance between hypothesis testing and the development of theory, such as the functional perspective of group decision making. What kind of balance have you tried to maintain between theory and research? Is the distinction even helpful?*

To be honest, the balance between theory and research was not something that I consciously pursued. I think it was more of a natural consequence of my way of thinking. For me, everything begins with ideas and concepts—to summarize it in a word, theory. But I have always had a strong desire to see if my ideas actually worked out in "real life." So whenever I had an idea, I would design a study to test it out. If the data supported the idea, I would move on to testing another notion. If the data did not support the idea (as often was the case), I'd go back to the drawing board and try to figure out what went wrong and then revise the notion and test it again. The functional perspective is a perfect case in point of how my mind works. The functional perspective was never created as a visionary grand theory. It started off with some basic ideas—e.g., not all communication behaviors in groups are worth studying—only those that serve important functions should be examined. It was from that basic idea that Dennis Gouran and I eventually identified specific functions of communication relevant to group decision making and problem solving.

♦ *Though your work in group decision making is very well known, you also have been active in investigating questions involving such wide-ranging topics as relational dialectics and flawed decision making in the Challenger space shuttle disaster. Methodologically, you have moved easily from case studies, to experimental designs, to meta-analysis. Has this diversity in your work reflected a personal philosophy related to scholarship? Would you advise students to follow the same sort of approach to research?*

Again, I wish I could say that the diversity of my work was part of a grand plan. But truth be known, my wide-ranging topics of research are more a product of my ability to recognize the limitations of my current research and willingness to try new things that might better allow me to gather the kinds of data I needed to answer the questions I was interested in. For example, the laboratory experiments I conducted usually involved contrived group tasks that had little "real world" application. So to find out if the findings I obtained in the laboratory held up in the "real world," I actually sought cases of faulty group decision making and studied them to see if I could find evidence in those cases to support my laboratory findings.

♦ *What one or two things do you think students should know to deal successfully with communication research either as a consumer or as a researcher?*

As a consumer, I would advise students to always question the findings of researchers, rather than taking what they say as the gospel truth. So much of what we take today as God's truth (even in fields like medicine) has very little *solid* empirical support. In many cases, the data we use to justify policies and practices are based on anecdotal evidence or, at best, N $=$ 1 case studies. As a researcher, my best advice to students is to follow your interest—no matter how daunting the path to finding answers for those questions may be. When I was in graduate school, some of my professors advised me *not* to study group communication because studying groups (as compared to dyads) was perceived to have many more methodological and procedural complications. Also, operationalizing what a "good decision" is was so fraught with problems that my professors said I'd never get published. But I was so interested in understanding why groups make bad decisions that I pursued my interest anyway. Truth be known, it wasn't easy—and I had *many* more rejection letters than I did publications. But if I had it to do over again, I'd still pursue the same questions regarding group decision-making efficacy.

◆ *That's quite a lot to think about. What kind of advice would you give students who might be interested in becoming communication researchers, despite the challenges?*
The best advice I can give students is to go to a *good* graduate program. The fact is that not all graduate programs in communication are created equal. Some are much better than others. Students need to do a good job of researching graduate programs. Look at the faculty—what are their research interests? Are their interests similar to yours? Look at the curriculum—what is the emphasis of the program? Are they quantitatively oriented? Qualitatively oriented? Look at their graduate students—are they the kind of people you would like to have as colleagues? Are they getting the best jobs? Your entire career begins with the education and training you receive in graduate school. So, choose wisely.

◆ *What do you think is the most exciting future direction for the field's research?*
I hope future communication research will focus more on improving the human condition—whether it be on a macro scale like resolving international conflicts, or a micro scale like providing social support for people with terminal illnesses. We have some of the best minds in the country in our field and I'd love to see them apply their thinking to solving real-life social and political problems.

interaction" for short.[7] Figure 10.4B shows such a crossed interaction. Unlike ordinal interactions, when crossed interactions are found, researchers are forbidden from interpreting the main effects for the variables involved since such interpretations would be misleading. Furthermore, if researchers plan to make recommendations or take action based on the experiment, they know that they must respond by looking at two variables at once. Thus, the type of interaction sets limits on the sorts of conclusions that researchers can draw.

We have limited this introductory discussion to situations in which one or two independent variables are involved. But the number of variables in an interaction can include three, four, five, or potentially any number of independent variables. In such cases, separate diagrams are drawn for each level of the additional independent variables added. The number of diagrams can grow quite large. The problem is not really so troublesome, however. Experienced researchers know that whereas main effects and two-variable interaction effects are quite common, three-variable interactions are not as common, four-variable interactions seldom occur, and higher-order interactions are quite rare (they can occur once in a while, however, and researchers carefully examine them).

---

[7]Researchers sometimes just eyeball the averages of groups to determine what types of interactions occur. When drawing graphs to illustrate the relationships, researchers usually draw two graphs to switch the independent variable that is represented by lines and the independent variable that is indicated on the horizontal axis. The fact is that many times lines will cross under one set of circumstances but not with the other. Nevertheless, if either graph produces a crossing, a disordinal interaction is concluded.

SOME ELEMENTS FOUND IN GOOD EXPERIMENTS

Sound experiments tend to include additional features that distinguish them. Some of these considerations will be mentioned next.

Securing Informed Consent and Debriefing

Procedures for introducing participants to experiments and helping them to understand their rights are features of both solid and ethically acceptable experiments. This process involves both giving individuals instructions about experimental materials and providing explanations afterward.

details required for informed consent

As described in Chapter 9, information introducing any research study must make sure to inform participants about

♦ research purposes, "expected durations, and procedures";

♦ their "rights to decline to participate and to withdraw from the research";

♦ "the foreseeable consequences of decline or withdrawing";

♦ "potential risks, discomfort, or adverse effects";

♦ "any prospective research benefits";

♦ "limits of confidentiality [if any]";

♦ "incentives for participation [if any]"; and

♦ "whom to contact for questions about the research and research participants' rights" (Ethical Principles of Psychologists and Code of Conduct, 2002, section 8.02).

In an effort to show that such standards are met, researchers completing experiments are expected to explain such materials and methods to study participants prior to the study.

In addition, in experimental research, participants are extended additional protection. In particular, researchers using experimental methods are expected to inform participants of

(1) the experimental nature of the treatment;

(2) the services that will or will not be available to the control group(s) if appropriate;

(3) the means by which assignment to treatment and control groups will be made;

(4) available treatment alternatives if an individual does not wish to participate in the research or wishes to withdraw once a study has begun; and

(5) compensation for or monetary costs of participating including, if appropriate, whether reimbursement from the participant or a third-party payor will be sought. (8.02b)

Though many parts of such concerns appear to deal more with therapy and medical concerns, it is noteworthy how much attention to these matters exists in communication research. Table 10.3 shows such an informed consent form used in a study of

TABLE 10.3   INFORMED CONSENT FORM

I have been invited to take part in a research study being conducted to learn more about the views people have about themselves, childhood relationships, and religion. This research study is being conducted by Paul Wright, under the supervision of Dr. Robert Gass, Human Communication Studies Department, School of Communications, California State University Fullerton (CSUF). The responses that I give will contribute to our overall knowledge of peoples' perceptions of themselves, others, and religious beliefs and practices.

If I agree to be in this research study, I will read and react to a message from a Christian church describing what members like about the church, answer questions about different aspects of my life and personal beliefs, and reflect on my childhood relationship with my primary caregiver. The questionnaire will take approximately 15–20 minutes to complete.

I understand that participation in this survey is <u>voluntary</u> and <u>anonymous.</u> I will write my name on the authorization page only. I may refuse to participate, skip any question, or withdraw at any time without penalty. Non-participation will not affect my grades or academic standing.

If I do decide to participate, I will sign and detach <u>both</u> consent forms, keep one form for my records, and hand the other form to the person administering the survey when I hand my survey in. If I do participate in the study, it is possible that I may experience discomfort reading about religious views different than the ones I currently hold. If this occurs, I may contact the CSUF Psychological Counseling Department at (xxx) xxx-xxxx.

Through this written consent document and the oral introduction, the researcher has explained this study to me and answered my questions. For questions about my right as a research participant, I may contact the CSUF Regulatory Compliance Coordinator at (xxx) xxx-xxxx.

If I have any questions, concerns, or wish to report a research-related problem, I should not hesitate to contact:

Paul Wright	Robert Gass
Graduate Student	CSUF Faculty
Human Communication Studies	Human Communication Studies
CP xxx-xx	CP xxx-x
(xxx) xxx-xxxx	(xxx) xxx-xxxx
e-mail: xxxx	e-mail: xxxx

Please read and sign the following:

In consideration of my participation in this research and on behalf of myself, my heirs and assigns, I release and hold harmless the State of California, the California State University Trustees, Cal State Fullerton, and their officers, agents, volunteers and employees from liability and responsibility for any claims against any of them by reason of any injury to person or property, or death, in connection with my participation in this study.

(Continued)

TABLE 10.3   (Continued)

I have carefully read, and have had this study and the terms used in this Consent Form and their significance explained to me. I am fully competent to sign this Consent Form. I understand that I am to keep one of these consent forms for my files and hand the other one to the survey proctor.

AGREEMENT TO PARTICIPATE

_____   _____
Participant's Signature   Date

_____
Participant's Name (please print)

Used through courtesy of Paul Wright and Robert Gass, redacted.

response of individuals to a religious message (Wright, 2006). In this experiment it was possible that participants might hear information that could challenge some of their religious convictions. Each potential participant was given two copies of the informed consent form. After reading detailed information including instructions introducing the experience as a research project and describing services that were available, those participants who agreed to be involved in the study signed an

securing agreement to participate "Agreement to Participate" statement and returned one copy of the form to the researcher. If individuals chose not to participate, they were permitted to do so without any negative consequences directed toward them.

Since the study design did not permit research participants to know all the study procedures, further details about the assignment to treatment or control conditions was not included. In fact, the only experimental treatment was a common message that all participants read. Other material about resources available for participants was featured prominently.

The use of a study design that involved a certain amount of "deception" was required by Wright's purposes and methods. To deal with religious conversion messages, Wright had to represent a clerical source with the name of a religious organization. Both were inventions that were viewed as less invasive into student-participants' lives than recommending their involvement in an actual religious com-

limits on the use of deception munity. This matter was part of the acceptable use of deception found in the APA Code's section 8.07, which permits such methods if they are "justified by the study's significant prospective scientific, educational, or applied value and . . . effective non-deceptive alternative procedures are not feasible" and provided that the research is not "reasonably expected to cause physical pain or severe emotional distress." Table 10.4 shows the introductoy oral message that was given aloud to those agreeing to participate in the study.

importance of debriefing Debriefing is a significant matter, especially for studies in which deception is involved. The APA Code of Professional Conduct explains that—subject to only a few exceptions—researchers must "provide a prompt opportunity for participants to obtain appropriate information about the nature, results, and conclusions of the research, and . . . take reasonable steps to correct any misconceptions that participants may have. . . . " (§8.08).

TABLE 10.4 INTRODUCTORY ORAL MESSAGE

A. ORAL INTRODUCTORY SCRIPT

Good morning/afternoon/evening,

Researchers in the Department of Human Communication Studies are interested in peoples' perceptions of themselves, their relationships, and religion. I am here today to pass out an **anonymous** survey designed to gather information in these areas. Your participation in this study would be greatly appreciated; however, participation is **entirely** voluntary.

If you decide to participate, you will be asked to read and react to a religious message and answer questions about your opinions and beliefs regarding a variety of issues. The survey should take between 15 and 20 minutes to complete.

If, after reading the Consent Form you decide **not to** participate, please return the blank questionnaire to me. If, after reading the Consent Form you **do** decide to participate, please sign and date both consent forms, remove them from the survey, keep one for your own records, and hand the other one to me when you are finished with the questionnaire.

I will pass out the surveys now.

B. DEBRIEFING SCRIPT

Thank you very much for participating in this research.

It is important that you know that **both** Pastor Michael Davis and The Rock Church **do not exist.** You were led to believe that they existed to ensure that your answers to the survey would be as valid and true to real life as possible.

If you were interested in the church and are disappointed to find out that it does not exist, please use the information on your consent form to contact Paul Wright and he will give you the name of a website you can use to locate a similar church in your area.

Do you have any questions about why you were not told upfront that the message you were reading was from a fictional person and church?

Do you have any other questions about the study?

If you are interested in learning the results of this study, please e-mail or call Paul Wright using the contact information on the Consent Form.

Thank you, again, for your cooperation.

In the case of the study reviewed here, a set of introductory oral comments emphasized the rights of study participants and explained the use of the informed consent forms. Afterward, a debriefing message also was presented orally (see Table 10.4).

The Pilot Test

Sometimes what seems to be a beautiful experiment can blow up in a researcher's face. Many prudent experimenters complete dry runs or pilot studies to find existing problems. Though not all experiments are complicated enough to require a pilot

usefulness of pilot studies in experiments

study, in general, the more experienced researchers are, the more likely they are to complete one prior to full-scale experimentation. These **pilot studies** usually involve small samples of people (sometimes as small as 10 or 20) who take part in an experiment. They are interviewed, often as part of a focus group, to find out if they had difficulty with experimental materials or responding to measures. In addition, researchers often discover additional variables that—if left uncontrolled—may jeopardize the quality of study conclusions. After the pilot study, some modifications in the experiment may be made and additional controls may be added. Researchers cannot know in advance everything that might interfere with a successful experiment. Thus, pilot studies reveal valuable information that helps guide worthwhile experiments.

Pilot studies (also called "pilot tests") studies usually involving small samples of people who take part in a "dry run" of an experiment as an aid in developing materials, procedures, and protocols.

Manipulation Checks

It is one thing to introduce an independent variable, but quite another to make sure that it actually "took" in an experiment. To make sure that independent variables actually operated in a study, researchers often include manipulation checks. A **manipulation check** is placed on the independent variable's operational definitions. For instance, if people in an experiment were asked to read a message with prominent use of previews, the researcher might wish to check that people really paid attention to the message. Thus, a researcher might add a brief true-false test asking subjects about information in the message. Depending on the needs of the researcher, the degree to which people perceived the message to have contained previews also might be tested. Solid experiments rarely ask readers to assume that all variables in the study actually were operating. Instead, good experiments often include manipulation checks to ensure the presence of independent variables.

Manipulation check a researcher's measurement of a secondary variable to determine that an experimental variable actually was operating in a study.

Care in Interpretation

Experimental research can be exciting, and researchers sometimes get carried away when interpreting their results. Yet, solid experiments avoid misstatements. Three principles guide the interpretations of careful experimenters.

1. *Resist the tendency to infer long-term effects from short-term experiments.* Occasionally an experiment will be completed over an extended time period, but most experiments are short-term affairs. Nevertheless, researchers can get carried away and draw conclusions about long-term effects even though they collected only short-term data. For instance, many researchers have examined the persuasive effects of evidence. Early on it was found that evidence presented by a highly credible speaker did not seem as persuasive as evidence presented by a moderately or lowly credible speaker. But this result was based on short-term findings. When long-term effects (at least two weeks) were examined, however, evidence proved to be persuasive for all speakers (McCroskey, 1967; Reynolds & Burgoon, 1983, p. 93). Thus, researchers must be very careful when drawing conclusions, because short-term and long-term results can differ greatly.

SPECIAL DISCUSSION 10-4

QUASI EXPERIMENTS

Sometimes it is not possible for researchers to conduct experiments in which they have full control over all the variables in the design. Under such circumstances, they can employ an alternative called "quasi-experimental research" (Campbell & Stanley, 1963, pp. 34–63). In essence, quasi-experimental studies involve completion of experimental work where random assignment and control are not possible. Obviously, the sorts of conclusions that can be drawn are limited since no cause-and-effect statements can be demonstrated. But the method may be useful especially if the researcher is exploring a research field for potential hypotheses for subsequent study, or if the researcher is not particularly interested in generalizing to larger populations than the sample group.

Three major forms of quasi-experimental designs are shown below (after Campbell & Stanley, 1963, p. 40).

Time Series Designs

A time series design measures subjects across different times. In the simplest form of this design, several observations are made before an experimental intervention and several are made afterward. The design may be represented as follows:

$$O_1 \quad O_2 \quad O_3 \quad X \quad O_4 \quad O_5 \quad O_6$$

This design is often used in research that tries to find cyclical trends or the decay of information retention. It controls for all sources of internal invalidity, with the possible exception of instrumentation depending on the procedures used by the researcher. Sometimes the researcher tries to add control to this design, but doing so requires the addition of another group that may not be equivalent to the first.

Separate Sample Posttest Designs

Subjects might be sampled as part of another group of subjects who are close to, but not assured to be equivalent to, the experimental group. For instance, a group of employees who complete a communication skills training seminar might be compared with a group of employees who are from the same pool, but who have not had their training. One group would receive the experimental treatment (X), and the other would not. The basic form of these designs is illustrated as follows:

$$\frac{O \times O}{O \quad\quad O}$$

This design resembles the static-group comparison design, except that it includes a pretest. Yet, in this design the researcher tries to make groups comparable—or at least as comparable as possible without randomization. This design controls for all sources of internal invalidity except for interaction of selection with other sources of internal invalidity and (possibly, depending on the design) the regression effect.

(Continued)

> ### SPECIAL DISCUSSION 10-4 (Continued)
>
> **Counterbalanced Designs**
>
> Counterbalanced designs introduce several different experimental treatments to the subjects in different orders or sequences. Though not restricted to quasi experimentation as a method of control, the formal counterbalanced design allows for control of all sources of internal invalidity except for interaction of selection with other sources of internal invalidity.

Prudent researchers are careful to avoid the tendency to draw general or long-term conclusions based on short-term experiments.

2. *Search for nonlinear relationships.* Many experiments compare two levels of a variable, often a "high" and a "low" level, and draw conclusions that sound very certain. Yet, many relationships between independent and dependent variables are not simple straight-line relationships, but curved. That is, sometimes a low level of an experimental variable produces a low effect, a moderate level produces a high effect, and a high level produces a slightly lower effect. Unfortunately, if experimenters compare only two conditions, they will miss any curved relationships (since you cannot draw anything but a straight line between two plotted points). Prudent researchers do two things to avoid this difficulty. First, they carefully qualify their conclusions by noting that curved relationships have not been studied. Second, they follow initial experiments with other studies that include more than two levels of independent variables.

3. *Use multiple dependent variables.* Experimental variables rarely produce effects on only one output variable. Yet, some studies limit themselves to only one dependent measure. The experienced researcher knows how important it is to check for effects on additional related output measures. Hence, in studies on the impact of physical attractiveness of sources, researchers tend to look at a collection of influence variables, such as interpersonal attraction, source credibility, and liking for the source. The underlying patterns behind research findings may be explored. Inexperienced researchers may look only at effects on one pet output variable, whereas experienced researchers tend to employ a collection of relevant dependent measures so that interpretations of results can be increasingly sophisticated.

CHECKLIST TO EVALUATE EXPERIMENTAL DESIGNS

_____ Was the experimental design appropriate to the research equation, which asked about cause-and-effect relationships?

_____ Did the design eliminate confounding of the experimental variable with other variables?

_____ Were all nuisance variables controlled in the experiment (by what method—elimination or removal, holding constant, matching, blocking, statistical control)?

_____ Was randomization successful (by what methods)?

_____ Were designs used to control for all sources of internal invalidity (history, selection, maturation, testing, instrumentation, statistical regression, experimental mortality, interaction of elements)?

_____ Were all sources of external invalidity (interaction of testing and the experimental variable, interaction of selection and the experimental variable, reactive arrangements, multiple-treatment interference) controlled?

_____ If any were uncontrolled, were the study conclusions limited accordingly?

In factorial designs:

_____ Were main effects properly interpreted?

_____ Were types of interaction effects (ordinal or disordinal) correctly identified (sometimes requiring drawing charts repeatedly with different independent variables on the horizontal axis)?

_____ If disordinal interaction effects were found, did researchers make sure not to interpret main effects from the variables involved in the interaction?

_____ Did the authors complete a pilot test before completing the full experiment?

_____ Were manipulation checks of the operation of the independent variables included? Did researchers show care to

_____ resist the tendency to infer long-term effects from short-term experiments?

_____ search for possible nonlinear relationships?

_____ use multiple dependent variables?

_____ Was informed consent obtained from study participants?

_____ Were instructions introducing the experiment and debriefing materials complete and suitable to the research?

SUMMARY

An experiment is the study of the effects of variables manipulated by the researcher in a situation where all other influences are controlled, completed for the purpose of establishing causal relationships. Experiments are designed to answer research questions that deal with cause-and-effect relationships. But independent variables must be capable of manipulation. Confounding occurs when variation from one source is mixed (or confused) with variation from another source so that it is impossible to know whether effects are due to the impact of either variable separately or some combination of the two. Control refers to methods researchers use to remove or hold constant the effects of nuisance variables. Several major control approaches include (1) elimination and removal, in which a nuisance variable is removed from the experimental setting; (2) holding constant (by the methods of limiting the population, using subjects as their own controls, or counterbalancing, which rotates the sequence in which experimental treatments are introduced to subjects); (3) matching (pairing events or participants on some variable on which they share equal levels and then assigning them to experimental or control conditions); (4) blocking (adding a nuisance variable into the design as another independent variable of interest); (5) randomization (assigning subjects so that each event is equally likely to belong to any experimental or control condition); and (6) statistical control, in which statistical tools are used to hold nuisance variables constant.

Experimental invalidity prevents researchers from drawing alleged conclusions from the premises advanced in the experiment. Internal invalidity is the presence of contamination that prevents the experimenter from concluding that a study's experimental variable is responsible for the observed effects. External invalidity refers to the degree to which experimental results cannot be generalized to other similar circumstances.

Experimental designs follow strict protocols. A notation system has been developed that includes O (an observation made by a researcher), X (the experimental variable), and R (randomization). Preexperimental designs do not really exercise the sort of control necessary for a solid experiment. In the one-shot case study, an experimental treatment is introduced and researchers look at effects on some output (dependent) variable. The one-group pretest–posttest design adds a pretest. Static-group comparisons attempt to use a control group as a baseline to compare with an experimental group. Yet, these designs do not meet the requirements of internal validity. True experimental designs control sources of internal invalidity. The pretest–posttest control group design involves a pretest of experimental and control subjects. Though change scores may be considered, there are difficulties with the distribution and reliability of change scores that make them inferior to other measures. This design fails to control for the potential of pretest sensitization (an aspect of external invalidity). To control for pretest sensitization, one may use the Solomon four-group design (which tests for the impact of pretesting) or the posttest-only control group design (which omits the pretest). When more than one independent variable is used in an experiment, it is called a factorial design. When a variable is broken down into levels, the levels are called variable factors. The categories of each factor are called levels. Main effects are dependent-variable effects that result from independent variables separately. Interaction effects are dependent-variable effects that result from independent variables taken together (indicated by graphs of effects that show nonparallel lines). An ordinal interaction is an interaction in the same direction as the main effects. A disordinal interaction is an interaction that is not in the same direction as the main effects (indicated by graphs of effects that show nonparallel lines that cross).

Sound experiments tend to include additional features. First, they often include pilot studies to verify procedures and identify areas for improvements in experiments. Second, they often include manipulation checks (a researcher's measurement of a secondary variable to determine that an experimental variable actually was operating in a study). Third, they show care in interpretation, including resisting the tendency to infer long-term effects from short-term experiments, searching for nonlinear relationships, and recognizing the desirability of examining multiple dependent variables.

TERMS FOR REVIEW

experiment	blocking
confounding	randomization
control	experimental invalidity
counterbalancing	internal invalidity
matching	external invalidity

one-shot case study

one-group pretest–posttest

static-group comparisons

pretest–posttest control group design

Solomon four-group design

posttest-only control group design

factorial designs

factors

levels

main effects

interaction effects

ordinal interaction

disordinal interaction

pilot studies

manipulation check

JUST FOR THE SAKE OF ARGUMENT: A REVIEW

Look at the following questions and prepare your own answers to them. Look for the assumptions that underlie them.

1. What is the difference between an experiment and a very carefully conducted and controlled study? How may experiments be contrasted with carefully designed descriptive empirical studies?

2. If one observes main effects from two variables and then finds an interaction between those two variables, is it permissible to interpret the main effects?

3. How can randomization control for extraneous sources of variation? Aren't there so many possible variables that claims of such control are really phony?

4. The notation for factorial designs creates a grid. What are placed inside the cells—the independent or dependent variables? What is meant by the "low" and "high" levels when the levels are actually categorical rather than continuous variables?

5. What is the difference between the posttest-only control group design and the static-group comparison? How would a researcher transform one into another? Why would a researcher want to?

6. What impact does the regression effect have on the sorts of interpretations researchers should draw? What kinds of studies in communication are plagued by it most? What can be done about it?

ACTIVITIES TO PROBE FURTHER

Go to the website for this book, and look for the Student Study Materials for Chapter 10.

1. Take the study quiz and print out your answers. (Word of caution: Avoid giving answers that are your first impressions only.)

2. Look at the activity titled "Experimental Effects Identification." This Web page includes data that can be diagrammed to isolate main and interaction effects in experimental research. Graph the data and print out your results. Answer these questions about each example:
   a. Are there any main effects (if so, for which variables)? How do you know from the graph?
   b. Are there any interaction effects? How do you know from the graph?

    c. If there are interaction effects, what type are they? How do you know from the graph?

    d. Is it permissible to interpret any main effects?

    e. Suppose you wanted to maximize output (produce the highest scores on the dependent variable). What settings of independent variable(s) would you employ?

3. Compose an experimental hypothesis regarding the effects of your sitting in the front of the classroom (as opposed to sitting at the back of the classroom) in your communication research methods class. Suppose you were interested in the effects of this variable on some grades in the class.

    a. Phrase the hypothesis so that it invites an experiment.

    b. Outline the design for such an experiment. Make sure to include the following:

        (1) Your procedures to manipulate the experimental variables

        (2) Your procedures to measure the dependent variable

        (3) How you might get a sample

        (4) The experimental design you would use

        (5) Any additional problems with control that you would have to face

4. Complete a Web search for experimental issues including the following:

    The placebo effect

    The halo effect

    The John Henry effect

    The Hawthorne effect

    What warnings about these matters did you find? What suggestions to deal with these matters did you find?

5. Find out what experiments are under way by visiting the main office for the department in which you are taking this class. Interview the principal researcher for one of these experiments, and find out what steps tend to be the easiest and the most difficult parts of experiments. Find out what he or she believes is the most enjoyable part of such research.

CHAPTER 11

Sampling

You don't have to eat the whole cow to know the steak is tough.

—SAMUEL JOHNSON

CHAPTER OUTLINE

BEFORE WE GET STARTED . . .

Whether we complete descriptive empirical studies or experiments, we must collect data. Indeed, collecting data in empirical research means sampling populations of events. This chapter introduces you to the terms and methods used for sampling. In addition, it addresses some special issues that must be faced in selecting sample sizes and constructing so-called confidence intervals. By the end of this chapter you will have some guidelines to use when making your own inquiries and reading those of others.

THE ROLE OF SAMPLING IN QUANTITATIVE RESEARCH

You do not have to gather data on every single event in a population to draw reasonable conclusions. Careful **sampling** can often accurately identify population characteristics even with very small numbers of events. To understand the role of sampling in empirical research you need to understand how it fits with other concepts, its relationship to populations, and its purposes.

Sampling selecting events from a population.

Relating Sampling to Other Concepts

Researchers rarely sample all possible events, but they rely on a sample of all data to draw conclusions. Since a study's conclusions can be only as good as the data on which they are based, the sample must be gathered thoughtfully and with some solid reasoning behind choices. Anything less amounts to *non sequitur* thinking that threatens a study. It is helpful to define our terms to avoid this error.

A **population** is the universe of events from which the sample is drawn. Figure 11.1 shows the relationship between a sample and population. As you can see, a sample is simply a selection of events from the population (the term "events" is used to permit including samples of people, messages, behavior, or things). Researchers can sample toward the center of the population, or they might accidentally sample at the periphery of the population. These events are called pieces of **data.**

Population the universe of events from which the sample is drawn.

Data the actual individual events in a sample.

Numbers computed from a sample are called **statistics,** sometimes also called "sample statistics" or "test statistics." Grammatically, a single number computed from a sample is called a statistic and more than one number is called a group of statistics. You may have seen the term "statistics" used to refer to the study of quantitative information. In this latter sense, "statistics" is a singular term even though it ends with an *s*. Thus, you have to be careful when reading studies. If researchers refer to computed "test statistics," then you know that conclusions based on samples (and many events in the population) were omitted. If researchers talk about selecting statistics to analyze data, they mean the specific formulae they used in their studies. Almost always, communication researchers compute statistics because they gather samples to help answer questions.

Statistics (also called "test statistics") numbers computed from a sample.

"statistics" also refers to study of quantitative information

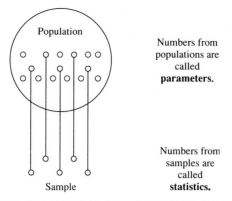

Numbers from
populations are
called
parameters.

Numbers from
samples are
called
statistics.

**FIGURE 11.1   THE RELATIONSHIP BETWEEN A SAMPLE AND
POPULATION**

Suppose you were able to sample every single event in the population—leaving out none. These numbers would be called **parameters,** not statistics. In practice, researchers rarely compute parameters. Instead, they often inherit parameters from some other source. For instance, the federal government has told automobile manufacturers the maximum emissions that may be permitted for cars sold in the United States. Similarly, customers often tell manufacturers what specifications must be satisfied for a product to be accepted. In each case these parameters are defined in advance as descriptions of the population.

> **Parameters** numbers computed from populations.

parameters rarely computed by researchers

Defining the Population

To draw samples from populations, researchers must first define the population. Suppose that you were interested in studying the degree to which senior citizens in the United States rely on televised news in preference to newspaper accounts. All senior citizens in the United States would be the population, and you would want to make sure that any samples carefully represented them. Though the population may be defined quite broadly—including all people or all television programs in the world, for instance—it may also be defined quite narrowly, such as including only students at large Western universities or only prime-time television programs from the three leading networks. The point is that populations are *defined* by the researcher as having certain characteristics.

populations defined by researchers

populations may be defined narrowly

Eliminating Bias

Sampling **bias** prevents the sample from accurately representing the population. Obviously, researchers work to eliminate or minimize bias. You may be mystified when you hear of the accuracy of some political polls or television rating services. They usually are able to give highly accurate reflections of the population based on

> **Bias** in sampling the tendency for the sample to err so that it fails to represent the population.

what seem to be very small samples, often as few as 1,200 people. Such accuracy does not happen by accident. Controlling bias is critical and is handled by the direct action discussed below.

ESSENTIALS OF SAMPLING

The basic concepts discussed here provide a framework for understanding sampling. This section also introduces ways to draw representative samples with appropriate sample sizes.

Representative Sampling: The Goal of Effective Sampling

A good sample must represent the population and be big enough to permit reasonable analysis of data. These matters are related, of course. Yet, for researchers, the fundamental test of whether a sample is good is the degree to which it is representative. A **representative sample** has characteristics that reflect the population from which it is drawn. Of course, unless researchers have the knowledge of gods, they will never know if samples are really representative. So, researchers take steps to prevent knowingly biasing samples. That way, they may presume that a sample is representative unless contrary evidence emerges.

> **Representative sample** sampling that accurately reflects characteristics of the population from which it was drawn.

Sample Size

Collecting a representative sample involves having one large enough to make reasonable interpretations. Still, a large sample size is not enough to prove that a sample is representative of the population. Gathering a reasonably sized sample is just one step in collecting a representative sample. Research students often ask, "How big should a sample be?" To answer this question, they must decide on the amount of sampling error they are willing to accept and to consider the demands created by research tools employed.

Sampling Error

You probably have heard news reports that describe political polls. They often tell what percentage of the voters favor each candidate. They also often report a certain "margin of error" for the poll. This "margin of error" is the amount of sampling error associated with the sample. The term **sampling error** involves this difference between sample and population characteristics. In general, as the sample size gets to be a larger and larger proportion of the population, the amount of sampling error is reduced. If you sample the entire population, there is no sampling error at all! Thus, a general piece of advice is to collect as big a sample as you can afford. But you often have to make some practical choices.

> **Sampling error** the degree to which a sample differs from the population on some measure.

RESEARCHERS IN THE FIELD: FELIPE KORZENNY

Felipe Korzenny is a very busy person. On one hand, he is a professor of advertising and integrated marketing communication, director of graduate studies of the Department of Communication, and director of the Center for Hispanic Marketing Communication at Florida State University. On the other hand, he is a founder of Cheskin Corporation, where he also serves as senior consultant to its program of services in marketing issues affecting Latinos. He received a bachelor's degree in advertising with a minor in television production from the Universidad Iberoamericana in Mexico City. He subsequently earned an M.A. and a Ph.D. from Michigan State University with emphases in mass communication and communication of innnovations across cultures. Following earning his doctorate, he held professorships at Michigan State University and San Francisco State University before joining the faculty of Florida State University. A specialist in multicultural marketing communication, he has coauthored a major book in the field, and coedited a book on *Mexican Americans and the Mass Media* and four volumes of the *International and Intercultural Communication Annual*. He has written nearly 70 book chapters, and articles in professional and trade publications in both English and Spanish language.

♦ *What drew you into our field?*

I wanted to be an actor when I was a teenager. My family, however, felt that I would not be able to make a living as an actor, particularly in Mexico. I guess that my interest in advertising and television production was a sublimation of my acting vocation. I studied "Sciences and Techniques of Information" at the Universidad Iberoamericana in Mexico City. That was the precursor of what is now known as "Communication." Public performance and the art of persuading others were my main interests then. The field of communication satisfied those inclinations. Later on I became more of a communication researcher than a practitioner, and that approach allowed me to improve my understanding of human motivation and the reasons that people do what they do. All related to my original interests.

♦ *You had a very successful career in Mexico before coming to the United States to complete graduate studies. Between 1970 and 1973 you held substantial positions in three advertising agencies in Mexico City and also were a professor of advertising and photography at the Universidad Iberoamericana. It must have taken more than a little courage to move from an established career and pursue doctoral studies in the United States. How did you manage that transition?*

It was interesting to me to be accepted in a Ph.D. program in the United States. In Mexico we used to look up to U.S. universities, and Michigan State University had the reputation of having one of the best communication programs in the world. I think that not knowing the degree of difficulty of going to MSU was a blessing. If I had known that I had to compete with 30 others who were accepted into the Ph.D. program at MSU in communication that year I might have not done it. I was somewhat arrogant and self-assured and determined not to be defeated. My motto was that I preferred to die rather than fail. It was certainly a status shock to move to being a graduate student from having been an executive in Mexico. I got used to it and I was one of the ten people out of the thirty who started the Ph.D. program that year who finished the degree and have a relatively successful career.

♦ *You have focused much of your communication research and scholarship on marketing to Latino groups. Your latest book coauthored with Betty Ann Korzenny is* Hispanic Marketing: A Cultural Perspective, *and you also are the director of the Center for Hispanic Marketing Communication at Florida State University. At the same time, you are senior consultant and cofounder of Cheskin, a company that has a specialization in issues of marketing to Latino audiences. How do you balance the applied work of business operations and scholarship? In particular, how does research in one area enrich the other?*

I enjoy pioneering efforts. My company Hispanic & Asian Marketing Communication Research was one of the first and largest companies specializing in niche ethnic markets in the United States. We merged with Cheskin in 1999 and stayed there until 2003. I have remained as a consultant to Cheskin and other companies for many reasons. One of the main reasons is the challenge to continue to be relevant to industry and bringing that relevancy to academia. I believe that students I teach and the research that I do these days benefit from my consulting work. My mission is to provide students with professional opportunities in the growing Hispanic marketing area and, at the same time, provide industry with trained professionals that understand the U.S. Hispanic market. For me, the partnership between academia and business is fundamental in bringing value to society.

♦ *What one or two things do you think students should know to deal successfully with communication research either as a consumer or as a researcher?*

Doing communication research requires a passion for understanding why people behave the way they do. A successful communication researcher must enjoy people watching, conversing with people, and then abstracting trends from those observations and conversations. Being able to write down what one learns is almost more important than one's passion. Both qualitative and quantitative approaches are crucial for anyone pursuing communication research. It is false that you can be good at only one of these two modalities because they complement each other. I am convinced that both approaches are needed to answer almost any communication question.

A good consumer of communication research needs to understand methodology. Most managers consume communication and other types of research. They need to understand the value and limitations of the research. Much of the value of the research is determined by its methodology.

♦ *What do you think is the most exciting future direction for the field's research?*

There is more than one direction that invites exciting work. Each of these matters needs attention. First, the study of consumer decision making based on interpersonal interaction is very important. Second, it is fascinating to study brand identity as the result of communication inputs. Third, the form and shape of a multicultural society as "minorities" become the majority in the United States requires serious research.

♦ *Is there any advice you would give students who might be interested in becoming communication researchers?*

A good communication researcher needs to be a combination of a lot of things. I think that to be a solid communication researcher you should be a scientist, a people-oriented person, a good moderator of group processes, a great writer, and someone who understands the workings of culture. Even so, research is fun when you do it to understand a problem that is interesting to you!

Sampling Guidelines

Sample sizes should be suitable to the research questions and study designs. Thus, in pilot studies, small samples may be used. In speech and hearing science, samples of 8 to 15 subjects may be used in experiments in which physiological reactions are involved (and where few additional variables may need to be randomized). For studies attempting to validate new measurement instruments, researchers may be told to use quite a large sample, at least 200 events. To use some statistical tools, such as multiple correlation or factor analysis, researchers need a minimum number of events for every variable to be studied. Table 11.1 shows some of the popular guidelines suggested by students of research methods.

sizes should be suitable to research questions and design

Guidelines Based on Sampling Error

If samples have been drawn at random, it is possible for researchers to report **confidence intervals** that indicate a range of values or "margins of error" of sample statistics within which a relevant population parameter is likely to fall. This section will explain how these margins of error are used and calculated by researchers.

For instance, take the case of a poll you might complete with a sample of 100 people selected at random. Suppose you found that 60% reported anxiety about taking a communication course, and 40% did not. You might wonder how far from the true population proportions your sample data are: after all, a sample of 100 does not sound all that big. To plug numbers into the formula in Table 11.2, you need only remember that proportions are numbers expressed with decimal points included (in other words, the proportion of anxious people is .6, not 60%). Then, you can fill in the blanks. As Table 11.2 shows, the formula reveals a "margin of error" in estimating how far from the true proportion of high-anxiety people in the population our sample may be 95% of the time. Put another way, this formula states that we are 95%

Confidence intervals
"a range of values of a sample statistic that is likely (at a given level of probability, called a confidence level) to contain a population parameter" (Vogt, 2005, p. 55).

confidence intervals for proportional data

TABLE 11.1   SAMPLE SIZE REQUIREMENTS FOR DIFFERENT RESEARCH TRADITIONS

Condition	Sample Size Requirements
Pilot studies	At least 10 events in a study (Isaac & Michael, 1981, p. 93).
Studies of physiological measures	At least 8 events randomly selected (if individual response ratings are involved, the sample must be increased to ordinary sample sizes for experiments).
Validation or cross validation studies	At least 200 events if standard methods of validation are used (such as multiple correlation or factor analysis); with other tools, "N should be at least about 60, and preferably 100 or more, for this purpose" (Tatsuoka, 1969, p. 27).
Studies that use multiple correlation methods	15 subjects for every predictor or independent variable (Stevens, 1986, p. 58).
Studies that use factor analysis	At least 10 events for each variable item to be included in the factor analysis (Nunnally, 1978, p. 421).

TABLE 11.2	CONFIDENCE INTERVALS FOR PROPORTIONS AND MEANS
Type of Measure	**Formulas and Examples**

A. For proportions (decimal point data) organized into two groups (such as yes or no):

90% C.I. $\;=$ observed proportion $\pm 1.645 \quad \star \quad \sqrt{\dfrac{p*(1-p)}{\text{sample size}}}$

95% C.I. $\;=$ observed proportion $\pm 1.96 \quad \star \quad \sqrt{\dfrac{p*(1-p)}{\text{sample size}}}$

99% C.I. $\;=$ observed proportion $\pm 2.58 \quad \star \quad \sqrt{\dfrac{p*(1-p)}{\text{sample size}}}$

where p $\;=$ proportion of responses for one category

Example: With a sample of 100 people selected at random, if 60% were anxious about taking a communication class, how far from the population proportion would the sample proportion be 95% of the time?

95% C.I $\;=$ observed proportion $\pm 1.96 \quad \star \quad \sqrt{\dfrac{p*(1-p)}{\text{sample size}}}$

$\quad\quad\quad = \quad\quad .60 \quad\quad \pm 1.96 \quad \star \quad \sqrt{\dfrac{.6*(1-.6)}{100}}$

$\quad\quad\quad = \quad\quad .60 \quad\quad \pm 1.96 \quad \star \quad \sqrt{\dfrac{.24}{100}}$

$\quad\quad\quad = \quad\quad .60 \quad\quad \pm 1.96 \quad \star \quad \sqrt{.0024}$

$\quad\quad\quad = \quad\quad .60 \quad\quad \pm 1.96 \quad \star \quad .049$

95% C.I. $\;= \quad\quad .60 \quad\quad \pm 0.96$

B. For means:

90% C.I. $\;=$ observed mean $\quad \pm 1.645 \quad \star \quad (s / \sqrt{\text{sample size}}\,)$
95% C.I. $\;=$ observed mean $\quad \pm 1.96 \quad \star \quad (s / \sqrt{\text{sample size}}\,)$
99% C.I. $\;=$ observed mean $\quad \pm 2.58 \quad \star \quad (s / \sqrt{\text{sample size}}\,)$

where s $\;=$ an estimate of variability in the population called the "standard deviation"(see Chapter 12 for computation of s)

Example: With a sample of 100 people selected at random, if the average number of hours of TV watched per week were 23 hours with a standard deviation observed (trust us!) of 8 hours, how far would the population mean be from the sample proportion 95% of the time?

95% C.I. $\;=$ observed mean $\quad \pm 1.96 \quad \star \quad (s / \sqrt{\text{sample size}}\,)$
$\quad\quad\quad = 23$ hours $\quad \pm 1.96 \quad \star \quad (8 / \sqrt{100}\,)$
$\quad\quad\quad = 23$ hours $\quad \pm 1.96 \quad \star \quad (8 / 10)$
$\quad\quad\quad = 23$ hours $\quad \pm 1.96 \quad \star \quad .8$
95% C.I. $\;= 23$ hours $\quad \pm 1.57$ hours

confident that the sample proportion is equal to the population proportion, plus or minus 9.6%. We could also say that we are 95% confident that the true population proportion of people anxious about taking a communication class is somewhere between 50.4% and 69.6%. Of course, in our example, there is a 5% chance that our sample is *way off*—not even close to the range we have reported. At least people know the odds and can make sensible choices about interpreting study results.

Not all data deal with proportions or percentages, of course. For studies that deal with means and averages, confidence intervals can also be constructed. To estimate these intervals you need to have some measure of the amount of variation that exists in the population.[1] The standard deviation is a statistic that is most often used. Though it will be explained in Chapter 12, for now let us just state that the **standard deviation** attempts to indicate how far from the average the data are (on the average). The standard deviation is often abbreviated by the lowercase letter s. Suppose you want to know the margin of error you would have if you surveyed 100 people and found that the average number of hours they watched TV per week was 23. Table 11.2B shows this example. With a computed standard deviation of 8 hours, you can construct a 95% confidence interval around the average. As the formula reveals, with such a sample size you can be 95% confident that the sample average is equal to the population average, plus or minus 1.57 hours. You can also say you are 95% confident that the true population average number of hours people watch TV per week is between 21.43 hours and 24.57 hours.

confidence intervals for means

Standard deviation though computed differently, a measure that attempts to summarize the average deviation of scores from the mean, by estimating such a value from the square root of the variance s^2; symbolized for the sample standard deviation as s.

With a little transposing of terms, you can use the formulas to help you choose the sample size for a study with different confidence intervals and margins for error. Table 11.3A shows what sample sizes might be required for different situations involving the use of proportional data. On occasion, researchers do not have measures (or even estimates) of variability but have to make some choices anyway. Fortunately, there are some guidelines. Table 11.3B shows such samples required for a 95% confidence interval and a margin of error expressed as a 5% range of variation, provided you know the size of the population. In national polling additional adaptations must be made. Assuming large variability in the population, increased sample sizes have been suggested to control for the additional background variation that usually exists (Yamane, 1967). Such tables indicate that a national poll would require only 100 respondents for a 10% margin of error. To reduce error to 5% you would need a sample of 400. To reduce error to 3% (typical among national polls) a sample of 1,111 would be needed. To trim the margin of error to 1% would require a sample of 10,000! As you can see, reducing margins of error or increasing confidence requires increasing sample sizes.

Statistical Effects of Small Samples

In general, small samples increase sampling error. Yet, another aspect of small samples may not have occurred to you. Because of the ways statistics are computed and

---

[1]This measure should be the variation known to exist in the population. But if the researcher does not have this information, the amount of variation in the sample may be substituted since the major measures of sample variability (standard deviation and variance) are unbiased estimators of population variability.

TABLE 11.3   SAMPLE SIZES REQUIRED FOR PROPORTIONAL DATA

A. For Proportional Data and an Estimate of Variability

Situation: This table presumes a single (dichotomous) stratification variable, conservative proportions of .5 and .5 (for maximum heterogeneity and to assume maximum internal sampling error), an unlimited population size, and truly random sampling.

		With Margin for Error of:			
		.10	*.05*	*.025*	*.01*
Confidence Interval:	90%	68	272	1089	6806
	95%	96	384	1537	9604
	99%	166	666	2663	16641

B. For Proportional Data from a Population of Known Size and No Estimate of Population Variability

Situation: This table presumes random samples of proportions drawn from populations of a known size so as to be within 5% of the population proportion at a 95% confidence interval (after Krejcie & Morgan, 1970).

Population Size	*Sample Size*
under 10	N A
10	10
15	14
20	19
30	28
40	36
50	44
75	63
100	80
250	152
500	217
1000	278
5000	357
10000	370
50000	381
100000	384

distributions entered, it is difficult for researchers to find evidence of relationships when sample sizes are small. It is easiest to spot differences when large samples are used because the relationships tend to stand out from the background noise and variability. When small samples are used, only very big effects stand out. Thus, the impact of small samples creates a double whammy for the researcher. Not only may the sample be thrown off, but a small sample may inhibit the chances of relationships being identified by most statistical tools.

small samples increase sampling error and make it difficult to find relationships

But isn't there a point at which a small sample turns into a large one? In reality, most statisticians have observed that samples of 30 or more events tend to produce nearly identical distributions. Without getting into the detailed background of this statement, we will mention that different distributions used in statistical analysis tend to diverge from each other when the samples drop below 30 events. In fact, Leonard Kazmier (1988, p. 132) recommended that any actual sample size should be

sample sizes of 30 or more invite reasonable use of statistical tools

SPECIAL DISCUSSION 11-1

THE USE OF VOLUNTEERS

All participants in modern studies are volunteers. This fact is part of the justification for calling them "participants" rather than "subjects" (as they once were called in the "old days" of research). You probably have been in classes in which you participated in a study by completing a questionnaire or interview. In a technical sense, then, you were volunteering your participation. But you were asked to participate. You did not ask the researcher to permit you to be a part of the sample group. Yet some research actually relies on subjects who are volunteers. Sometimes researchers place ads in newspapers asking people to participate, and they get a fair number of volunteers—especially if they offer to pay subjects. A question that faces researchers, however, is whether the volunteers give reactions that are typical of the population.

Many people are greatly concerned that volunteers differ from other members of the population. After all, people volunteer for a reason. If their reasons are not shared by the entire population, there is little reason to believe that the results from the volunteers are representative. Some scholars have noticed that volunteers tend to differ from the rest of the general population because they typically have increased needs for social approval, increased socioeconomic status, increased intelligence, and reduced conformity to authority figures (Rosenthal & Rosnow, 1969). The *Journal of Volunteerism* is dedicated to identifying ways in which volunteers behave, both in and out of research settings. Though the reasons volunteers choose to engage in research may be randomly distributed (Kruglanski, 1973)—and hence not a systematic source of variation in research—in many research settings there is no doubt that some types of volunteers can introduce great bias in studies. Thus, prudent researchers tend to be careful about providing full descriptions of the sample groups they have included. Typical descriptions for samples of college students include accounts of the ages, sexes, ethnic backgrounds, class standings, and academic majors. These pieces of information may be used to compare samples to known population characteristics. If there are noticeable differences, the researchers will know that they need to include additional limitation statements in their discussions of study results.

at least 30 events when estimating averages since the standard formulae for data analysis presume normal distributions. When sample sizes grow above 30, the distributions used by researchers and statisticians to help make decisions become fairly comparable to each other. So, big samples start somewhere near 30 events—but there is a catch. The events themselves in the sample must be drawn at random. To balance out other sampling concerns, researchers may need increased sample sizes.

FORMS OF SAMPLING

When sampling events from a population, researchers make critical choices. To give you an idea of those choices, we will consider categories of sampling that presume randomization and those that do not involve randomization.

Random Sampling

Probability sampling techniques that use randomization to identify samples.

Sometimes called **probability sampling** techniques, the use of randomization plays an important part in research. To understand random sampling, it is helpful to grasp key terms and its key role.

Random sampling selection of data such that each event in the population has an equal chance of being selected.

Random sampling involves drawing samples to maximize the chance that each event in the population has an equal chance of being included.[2] Random sampling (or, at least, random assignment) is presumed for nearly all statistical tools that may be applied to data. You can use distributions of randomly occurring events to figure the odds that a sample reflects what goes on in the population. When students hear of random sampling, they often mistakenly imagine that it is a hit-or-miss activity ("random" sounds a lot like "accidental"). The truth is that randomization is time-consuming, and many researchers try to take shortcuts. But the shortcuts throw off the whole sample and make it impossible to enter distributions accurately to decide whether research findings represent anything other than sampling error.

randomness not accidental

Obtaining a random draw of events is not a haphazard matter. One might imagine sampling a bunch of people at a nearby shopping mall. These places frequently are the stomping grounds for researchers who wish to find out people's reactions to commercials, promotional campaigns, and marketing strategies (you may have been approached at a mall by a person carrying a clipboard who asked you to answer questions or participate in a focus group meeting). Yet, sampling people at a mall is usually not random. People conducting surveys are usually told to gather data from the first set of people they can find who fall into a target population (sometimes limited to women under 30, people with children, or senior citizens). People arriving at the mall at a later time do not have the same chance to be sampled as those in the first grouping. Though researchers may claim to have

---

[2]In a mathematical sense, randomization means that the probability of any event following any other is equal to zero. But the mathematical definition presumes an infinite population. Thus, for practical purposes, a quasi-random method might be involved. To say that the chance for sampling is equal is close enough for us.

been relatively unbiased in selecting individuals, they cannot claim that the study was truly random.

To improve their studies, some researchers attempt to sample according to a schedule. They might select the first five people to enter the main entrance of the shopping mall each hour. Or, they might approach every tenth person entering the mall. Though this action is a step in the right direction, the sample is still not random since there is bias in favor of those who arrive promptly at the beginning of the hour. Thus, this method cannot claim all the advantages of random sampling. It is best identified as **systematic** or **periodic sampling.** You should be warned that some researchers actually use some form of systematic sampling and call it "random sampling" in passing.

systematic or periodic sampling distinguished from random sampling

Systematic or periodic sampling a method by which researchers select respondents according to a predetermined schedule rather than a random sequence.

Random sampling methods attempt to remove the human element from biasing the study. In the simplest sense, obtaining a random draw of events can be accomplished by taking care to ensure that each event has an equal chance of selection. For instance, if you wished to expose a random sample of students to speech from a severe stutterer, you might write class members' names on pieces of paper and put them in a hat. After tossing the pieces of paper around for a while, you might sample by pulling names from the hat. If you are successful, you might gather a fairly random sample. But if the population is fairly large, it may not be practical to draw names from your hat.

There is a superior way. Suppose you wanted to sample the population of voters in your city. No problem. Voters must register, and their names and addresses are matters of public record. You might assign each voter a number and then turn to a table of random numbers to select voters whose numbers have "randomly" come up. These tools of randomization help you effectively eliminate your own biases in data collection. Random sampling permits you to feel confident that the sample is as representative of the population—as free of bias—as possible. Randomization increases the chances that differences from one person to another in a sample will be random rather than systematic. Thus, random sampling allows you to control a host of background differences in sample groups that otherwise might foul up a study's meaningfulness.

using random numbers

There is more than one way to use random sampling. Since researchers often abbreviate their descriptions of methods, it is valuable to understand the labels used for these random sampling tools. There are three major random sampling varieties: simple random sampling, stratified random sampling, and cluster sampling.

methods of random sampling:

Simple Random Sampling

Selecting simple random samples involves identifying every event in the population and then drawing a sample by such methods as pulling names out of a hat or fishbowl. Most commonly, a method involving use of a table of random numbers is employed. **Simple random sampling** is useful in experiments in which assignment of subjects to experimental and control conditions can be done at random. This method is also useful when research problems do not require that samples be divided into subgroups (such as male-female, Republican-Democrat, stutterer-nonstutterer). This method has several advantages. First, sampling error can be computed for statistics

Simple random sampling a method by which researchers select participants or events such that each event in the population has an equal chance of being selected.

advantages

SPECIAL DISCUSSION 11-2

HOW TO USE A TABLE OF RANDOM NUMBERS

Random number tables are often used to help researchers draw random samples and to assign subjects to various conditions at random. Table 11.A contains a list of two-digit random numbers, but you should know that they actually came out of a computer as single digits (the publisher arranged them into two-digit numbers for convenience; thus, a good-sized table can be used by researchers for nearly any number of digits desired). Though there are several options, here is a way to use a random number table to select a sample:

1. Give every event in the population a number. To keep it simple, suppose we wanted to draw a sample of 30 college debaters from three universities with a total of 90 debaters. The possible range of numbers would be 01 through 90; thus, a two-digit table would do nicely (if we had to deal with three-digit numbers, we might add a third column of numbers).

2. Enter the number table at random. Don't just close your eyes and point your finger somewhere on the page (right-handed people tend to let their hands drop toward the right side the page, and lefties tend to drop their hands toward the left side of the page; the corners might as well not be on the page, given their chances of selection!). As an alternative, you could cut cards (let aces equal 1 and face cards equal 0) or throw dice to find the column number and the row number to start with, but who carries around playing cards or dice? Instead, you can use one of the following techniques (adapted from Leedy, 1989, pp. 154–155).

   ♦ Check the daily stock quotations to find the last two digits for the Dow Jones Industrial Average high and low (to represent the starting column and row).
   ♦ Pull a dollar bill from your pocket, and check the serial number. Suppose yours is L 38 7321 14 G. The first two-digit number is 38 and the final two-digit number is 14. To decide which number is the row and which one is the column reference, we might flip a coin. If the coin is heads, the first number will be the column. If the toss is tails, the last number will be the column. Say the coin came up tails. You would turn to the random number table and find the point where column 14 and row 38 intersect. On our table, the number at this intersection is 42 (find it for yourself!). If the row or column numbers are greater than the number of rows or columns on your table, just add the numbers together and use the sum as your new starting number.

3. Now, we need to know whether you will read the numbers by going across the page to the right, to the left, up, or down (don't mess with diagonals; it's too confusing). Take out a coin and flip it twice:

   ♦ Two heads mean you read to the right.
   ♦ Two tails mean you read to the left.
   ♦ Heads followed by tails means you read up the column.
   ♦ Tails followed by heads means you read down the column.

Say your flips give you two heads. So, you read to the right.

4. Since you want to sample 30 debaters, you simply take the individuals whose numbers "come up." In your case, you select person 42, person 84, person 05, person 04, person 98 (ignore it since it does not exist in this population), person 07, and so forth, until you have your sample. If the same number is repeated, you simply ignore it the second time.

There is another way to obtain random numbers, of course. These days, many inexpensive hand calculators have random number keys on them. If you purchase such a calculator, you need only press a button to generate random numbers.

TABLE 11.A   A Random Number Table

60 36 59 46 53	35 07 53 39 49	42 61 42 92 97	01 91 82 83 16
83 79 94 24 02	56 62 33 44 42	34 99 44 13 74	70 07 11 47 36
32 96 00 74 05	36 40 98 32 32	99 38 54 16 00	11 13 30 75 86
19 32 25 38 45	57 62 05 26 06	66 49 76 86 46	78 13 86 65 59
11 22 09 47 47	07 39 93 74 08	48 50 92 39 29	27 48 24 54 76
31 75 15 72 60	68 98 00 53 39	15 47 04 83 55	88 65 12 25 96
88 49 29 93 82	14 45 40 45 04	20 09 49 89 77	74 84 39 34 13
30 93 44 77 44	07 48 18 38 28	73 78 80 65 33	28 59 72 04 05
22 88 84 88 93	27 49 99 87 48	60 53 04 51 28	74 02 28 46 17
78 21 21 69 93	35 90 29 13 86	44 37 21 54 86	65 74 11 40 14
41 84 98 45 47	46 85 05 23 26	34 67 75 83 00	74 91 06 43 45
46 35 23 30 49	69 24 89 34 60	45 30 50 75 21	61 31 83 18 55
11 08 79 62 94	14 01 33 17 92	59 74 76 72 77	76 50 33 45 13
52 70 10 83 37	56 30 38 73 15	16 52 06 96 76	11 65 49 98 93
57 27 53 68 98	81 30 44 85 85	68 65 22 73 76	92 85 25 58 66
20 85 77 31 56	70 28 42 43 26	79 37 59 52 20	01 15 96 32 67
15 63 38 49 24	90 41 59 36 14	33 52 12 66 65	55 82 34 76 41
92 69 44 82 97	39 90 40 21 15	59 58 94 90 67	66 82 14 15 75
77 61 31 90 19	88 15 20 00 80	20 55 49 14 09	96 27 74 82 57
38 68 83 24 86	45 13 46 35 45	59 40 48 20 59	43 94 75 16 80
25 16 30 18 89	70 01 41 50 21	41 29 06 73 12	71 85 71 59 57
65 25 10 76 29	37 23 93 32 95	05 87 00 11 19	92 78 42 63 40
36 81 54 36 25	18 63 73 75 09	82 44 49 90 05	04 92 17 37 01
64 39 71 16 92	05 32 78 21 62	20 24 78 17 59	45 19 72 53 32
04 51 52 56 24	95 09 66 79 46	48 46 08 55 58	15 19 11 87 82
83 76 16 08 73	43 25 38 41 45	60 83 32 59 83	01 29 14 13 49
10 38 70 63 45	80 85 40 92 79	43 52 90 63 18	38 38 47 47 61
51 32 19 22 46	80 08 87 70 74	88 72 25 67 36	66 16 44 94 31
72 47 20 00 08	80 89 01 80 02	94 81 33 19 00	54 15 58 34 36
05 46 65 53 06	93 12 81 84 64	74 45 79 05 61	72 84 81 18 34
39 52 87 24 84	82 47 42 55 93	48 54 53 52 47	18 61 91 36 74
81 61 61 87 11	53 34 24 42 76	75 12 21 17 24	74 62 77 37 07
07 58 61 61 20	82 64 12 28 20	92 90 41 31 41	32 39 21 97 63
90 76 70 42 35	13 57 41 72 00	69 90 26 37 42	78 46 42 25 01

(Continued)

computed from such a sample. Second, simple randomization can be used by researchers as a means to control for individual differences among subjects in the sample. Third, the representativeness of the sample is virtually ensured since random sampling means that any differences between population and sample characteristics are at random. On the other hand, simple random sampling is difficult to use in many field settings because a list of all the events in the population may not exist. Furthermore, this sampling method may be time-consuming since the steps involved in identifying and choosing events can be somewhat complicated.

disadvantages

Stratified Random Sampling

Stratified random sampling a method by which researchers select participants or events to represent known proportions of characteristics in the population. After population characteristics are identified (such as the number of men and women in the population), a random sample of a given size is drawn from each population stratification variable consistent with the population proportions.

This variation of random sampling defines samples based on the known proportions within the population and follows them with random sampling within each group. In this **stratified random sampling,** population characteristics (called stratification variables) are identified, such as whether a sample of students is composed of national students or international students. For instance, you might know that the group of students studying intercultural communication in your major department is composed of 75% national students and 25% international students (mostly from Japan). Figure 11.2 might illustrate this population of students at your school. If you wanted to make sure to represent both types of students in your sampling, you would want to include 75% national students and 25% of the international students from Japan. In this case, if you wanted to complete a pilot study dealing with communication competence of intercultural communication students, you might wish to sample 12 students at random (though, of course, you often would include many, many more than 12). So, you could assign a number to every person in the sample, turn to a table of random numbers (as indicated in Special Discussion 11-2), and randomly select 9 national students and 3 international students, as shown on Figure 11.3. This method is used by most political polling companies and popularly reported surveys. Stratified random sampling is invited where dividing the sample according to some stratification variable is an important part of the study. In addition to the weaknesses of any form of random sampling, this method involves some unique costs. Since studies using this method tend to have fairly large sample sizes, stratified random sampling often involves increased expense for the researcher. Furthermore, many times the weights that should be associated with each stratification variable are not known. Thus, the method may not be practical to explore many research questions.

advantages

disadvantages

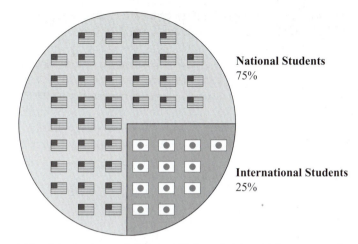

**FIGURE 11.2   A POPULATION OF NATIONAL AND
INTERNATIONAL STUDENTS**

Cluster Sampling

Though one must know a great deal about a population before doing stratified random sampling, cluster sampling requires much less initial knowledge. **Cluster sampling** involves selecting events "in two or more stages. It is typically used when researchers cannot get a complete list of the members of the population they wish to study, but can get a complete list of groups or clusters in the population" (Vogt, 2005, p. 46). One might decide to identify a group of neighborhoods, businesses, organizations, or cities, for instance (they may be much easier to identify than individuals). Then the researcher takes a random sample from within

Cluster sampling a method of sampling "in which elements are selected in two or more stages, with the first stage being the random selection of naturally occurring clusters and the last stage being the random selection of elements within clusters" (Schutt, 2006, pp. 1–5).

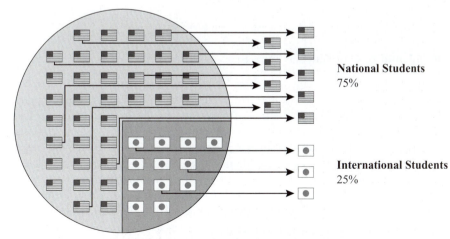

**FIGURE 11.3   A STRATIFIED RANDOM SAMPLE OF NATIONAL AND
INTERNATIONAL STUDENTS**

each cluster. Sometimes clusters are subdivided further before random samples are drawn (in which case, the sampling is called "multistage cluster sampling"). For instance, researchers might identify large groupings such as newspapers, and then lists of large city and small town newspapers might be prepared. Then random samples might be taken of newspapers in each category. Many large-scale status surveys use this method where it is easiest to find clusters of organizations rather than individuals. The method has been particularly useful when geographically based samples have been involved. This method carries the disadvantages found in any form of random sampling. In addition, the method requires larger samples than simple random sampling.

advantages of cluster sampling

disadvantages of cluster sampling

Nonrandom Sampling

randomization is not always possible

Despite its advantages, sometimes random sampling simply is not possible. It would not be possible for you to do an experiment in which you randomly assign a group of people to have cleft palates and another group of people not to have cleft palates. In this situation you pretty much have to take people as they are available to you. It would be unthinkable to create people with cleft palates for the purpose of maintaining the purity of a random sample. Yet, people with cleft palates may also have some other sorts of individual characteristics that are not shared to the same degree by the general population. They tend to show slightly higher levels of communication apprehension than others. They may also tend to experience lower levels of self-esteem than members of the general population. So, a researcher has a choice: give up, or go with the available data but qualify your conclusions carefully. The second option is obviously superior. You may remember John Paul Jones's famous advice: "Do the best you can with the means available to you." Sometimes random sampling is not feasible. So, you must do the best you can with the available methods of nonrandom sampling.

forms of nonrandom sampling

There are several different forms of nonrandom sampling. The four most prominent forms are accidental or convenience sampling, quota sampling, purposive or known group sampling, and snowball sampling.

Accidental or Convenience Sampling

Accidental or convenience sampling
selection of events that are most readily available.

Sometimes called "availability sampling," **accidental or convenience sampling** involves gathering data from groups that are immediately available to the researcher. For instance, researchers often sample college students in their experiments. They often persuade their colleagues to make their classes available to them. One class may receive an experimental treatment, and the other class may receive the control treatment. No attempt is made to randomize the groups. Thus, no steps are taken to ensure that they really are comparable groups. This method is often used for TV "call in" polls that invite viewers to participate. Such polls are usually identified as "nonscientific surveys" of opinion, and rightfully so. Though this sampling technique may be found in many studies, these samples are most useful in case studies and in pilot studies that are designed to help the researcher identify problems and get feedback about research materials.

SPECIAL DISCUSSION 11-3

A QUESTION OF ETHICS: ETHICAL ISSUES IN SAMPLING

Researchers can virtually guarantee any set of results by knowing what a sponsor wants and deliberately selecting an unrepresentative sample. Because these choices have been known to make a difference in more than one study, the selection of a sample is often recognized as an ethical issue. Section 12.1, d, v of the *Handbook of Research Ethics* prepared by the Australian government's National Health and Medical Research Council states that ethical research must have "a sample size adequate to demonstrate clinically and statistically significant effects." To explain what is meant by such a statement, they described what should be included in any research proposal:

A justification of the proposed sample size, based on the primary endpoint of the study, should be provided. Details should be given about expected clinically important differences between the test and control therapies and the expected variability of the outcome variables. Calculations of the required sample size based on such information are referred to as "power calculations." The sample size required for the conduct of any comparative study is directly proportional to the "power" of the study and the natural variation in the outcome of interest in the population, and inversely proportional to the size of the difference the researcher wishes to detect.

An ethics committee should be satisfied, usually on the basis of expert opinion, that a clinical trial design indicates that the trial can reliably show a reasonable comparative benefit in relation to the new drug or device simply because sufficient participants are to be studied.

Though such comments directly concern matters of medical and biological research, a lesson exists for communication researchers as well. If you wish to practice ethical research, you should make sure that the sample you use is large enough to detect meaningful effects, but not so large that substantively meaningless statements are advanced as meaningful, when they are not.

Another family of difficulty deals with selecting a sample that is deliberately misleading because of its size. Both too big and too small a sample can be misleading. The problem has to do with the power of a statistical test. This concept is covered in Chapter 13, but for the moment it is safe to say that with very large sample sizes, relationships that are trivial in magnitude are likely to be identified as beyond what would be expected to occur by chance alone. Such results are called "statistically significant." If a researcher wants to claim support for a hypothesis, the researcher can rig a study by using a large sample size. For instance, there is controversy regarding whether statistical or reporting evidence is most persuasive. In a meta-analysis (which combines samples from many studies, as covered in Chapter 15) of statistical versus "narrative" evidence (which is defined very differently across studies), two researchers (Allen & Preiss, 1997) computed a test of statistical significance on a total sample size of 1,836 [despite general recommendations against such an approach]). They observed that the correlation favoring statistical evidence had a "statistically significant" difference from zero. In fact, with such a sample size, any correlation accounting for .21% (that's .21 of one percent) of the variance would be reported as statistically significant. The observed average correlation accounted for 1% of the variance (a correlation of .101). Since it is difficult to get excited

(Continued)

SPECIAL DISCUSSION 11-3 (Continued)

about a relationship that accounts for 1% of the variance, it really seems that the reported test of statistical significance actually reveals only that with very large sample sizes even trivial differences can be interpreted as "statistically significant."

Contrariwise, a sample that is too small may be chosen to help prove a point. For instance, in this day and age, there is little doubt that cigarette smoking is hazardous to your health. Even packages of cigarettes include a statement of this fact. Nevertheless, under financial support of tobacco companies, H. J. Eysenck and L. J. Eaves (1980) completed a study of smoking behavior of identical and nonidentical twins. As part of this work, the researchers explored whether there really were differences in rates of illness (particularly lung cancer and heart disease) between pairs of identical twins, one of whom smoked and one of whom did not. They concluded that there was no statistically significant difference—results that must have made the tobacco company sponsors pleased. The problem is that it was difficult to find identical twins, one of whom smoked and one of whom did not. The sample size included fewer than 20 identical twins with different smoking habits. So, Eysenck and Eaves were unable to reject the null hypothesis of "no statistically significant difference" between the health of the two groups. Of course with such a small sample size, it would take an effect size accounting for at least 19.2% of the total variance to produce a "statistically significant" effect. Even during the worst plagues and health epidemics, effect sizes are usually below 15%. Even so, when Heath (1990) returned to the Eysenck and Eaves twin data, they could not even find support for the conclusions that "nicotine dependence is a major determinant of smoking persistence" because the "sample sizes in the London twin study were small" (Heath, 1990, p. 447).

To select a logical and ethically sound sample size, Kirby, Gebski, and Keech (2002) recommend that researchers make sure that samples are "large enough to detect reliably the smallest possible differences in the primary outcome" (p. 256) that is considered worthwhile. On the other hand, these authors suggest that it may be unethical to recruit participants into a study so that nearly any null hypothesis may be rejected.

Quota Sampling

Quota sampling samples are defined based on the known proportions within the population, and nonrandom sampling is completed within each group.

Except for the absence of randomization, **quota sampling** is very similar to stratified random sampling. In each form, population characteristics are identified, such as the number of men and women in the population. After deciding on the sample size to be drawn, a "quota" for each category is identified. Then, an accidental or convenience sample is taken from each level of the population stratification variable. This approach often is used in studies where researchers want to make sure that important parts of the population are not omitted in the sampling. Of course, many times quotas are filled by researchers' sampling friends and family members. Other individuals may be excluded because sampling them is inconvenient.

Purposive or Known Group Sampling

This sampling method begins by identifying groups that are known to possess a particular characteristic under investigation. If you wanted to study the persuasive strategies used by union organizers, it would make sense to sample the behavior only of union organizers. If you wanted to study the ways people with high intelligence communicate in their families, you might decide to sample members in the local chapter of Mensa (the organization for people with high IQ scores). In each case, random sampling would not be appropriate since you may not be interested in securing a cross section of the population. Thus, **purposive or known group sampling** is particularly useful for experiments or surveys where a criterion for admission to the sample clearly exists. Sometimes studies that try to validate new measurement tools use purposive sampling. In Chapter 4 you learned about the predictive validity method for determining the validity of a measure. This validation approach employs known group sampling. In addition, many intensive case studies of organizational leaders, communities, or associations make productive use of purposive or known group sampling. Purposive or known group sampling is convenient and economical when key population characteristics can be identified clearly. But sometimes the key characteristic is difficult to see in a group. Sometimes the key element is subjective, as with such variables as source attractiveness or communicator competence. In these cases, the results of known group sampling may not be trustworthy. In addition, since groups of people are identified, the observations may not be independent of each other (e.g., the local Mensa chapter would consist of people with high IQ scores who also like each other's company, probably because they share some other interests in common).

> **Purposive or known group sampling**
> selection of events from groups that are known to possess a particular characteristic under investigation.

Snowball Sampling

In **snowball sampling,** a population is defined, usually composed of people who engage in deviant or illegal behavior, such as street gang members, prostitutes, or criminals. Then, contact is made with a person in this grouping and an interview may be conducted. After trust is built with this person, the researcher asks for referrals to other individuals in the population group. These people are also asked for referrals, and the sample "snowballs" in size. This method is highly useful for studies of behavior that involve deviant or illegal activities. For instance, Yang (2000) used this sampling approach to study the ways that the Internet was used by homosexuals in Taiwan. Given the general fear of public disclosure of their sexual preferences, it was not possible to gather a random sample. Yet, based on referrals from one gay or lesbian person to another, a sample of over 700 eventually was collected. Sometimes this method is employed when the study group is a subculture and where random sampling is not an option. Snowball sampling is useful when it is not really possible to identify all members of the population at the outset. Yet, when researchers use snowball sampling, they do not really know whether enough referrals exist to penetrate into the group under investigation. The referrals might be to people who are on the periphery of the group, rather than at its heart. Unfortunately, the researcher may never know. Furthermore, since referrals are based on the acquaintances of initial contacts, the people in the sample cannot be considered independent. Even so, snowball sampling permits research in areas that might never be investigated otherwise.

> **Snowball sampling**
> selection of events based on referrals from initial informants.

Advantages and Disadvantages of Nonrandom Sampling

Naturally, strengths and weaknesses are associated with all methods of nonrandom sampling. Some of each have probably occurred to you. A first strength of such

strengths of nonrandom sampling

methods is that they are often invited by field and quasi-experimental research. Researchers may want to sample naturally occurring events—such as nonverbal displays of affection people show when saying good-bye at airports. In such settings, simple random sampling is simply not possible.[3] A second strength is that nonrandom sampling methods often allow the researcher to get samples that would otherwise be unavailable. If you wanted to study the communication strategies employed by drug dealers to sell their products, you could not really put an ad in the newspaper asking drug dealers to call you for an interview. You probably would hear only from police officers and narcotics agents. If the activity involves issues that are intimate, private, or deviant, nonrandom sampling may be the only way to gather information.

general disadvantages of nonrandom samples

Despite any advantages involved in nonrandom samples, they have severe limitations. Most of these matters are technical issues and involve the rigor that can be claimed for a study. First, nonrandom samples tend to show great biases. Respondents cannot be presumed to be a random draw from the population because they are not selected in ways that provide each event in the population with an equal chance of selection. Thus, without randomization, the sample may have clear biases. Sometimes researchers can take steps to describe these biases, but there are so many potential sources of bias that this strategy can be only partially successful. Second, since there is no distribution for nonprobability samples, no sampling error computation is possible. Hence, it is not possible to compute a confidence interval and estimate how closely our data probably are to population parameters. This limitation means that the researcher cannot use standard tools to determine the accuracy with which the sample captures population parameters. Third, the use of nonrandom samples severely limits conclusions that researchers can draw. The impact of experimental variables can be very different from one selected subgroup to another. Though nonrandom sampling provides analyses that apply to the single subgroup sampled, other subgroups cannot be generalized at all. In fact, the use of nonrandom sampling means that the conclusions a researcher can draw are limited to those suggesting relationships, but they exclude conclusions based on convincing evidence.

DEALING WITH SAMPLING PROBLEMS

Research books often describe sampling as though problems are rarities. The dismal truth is that the research craft is riddled with choices and compromises. Some of these matters should be addressed by us here.

---

[3]Of course, some efforts to include randomization might be added to this example. One might sample randomly selected months and randomly selected airports, during randomly selected time periods. Then a smaller random sample might be selected from this large grouping by numbering all the people saying good-bye and randomly selecting a group of people to serve as the final sample.

Participant Refusal to Participate

It will come as no surprise to you that people often do not want to participate in surveys. But if too many people refuse to be part of a sample, then randomization is jeopardized. People have reasons for refusing. If these reasons are systematically shared by the portion of the population that declines to become involved, then the remaining sample may not be truly random. Thus, researchers must report such information in their studies and qualify their results accordingly.

Respondents may refuse to participate in two ways. They can decline initially to accept a questionnaire, answer any questions, or return a survey. Or they can provide incomplete responses. In each case, the researcher is expected to describe how many subjects refused to participate and any differences they may have had from others who agreed to participate. A little refusal here and there may not be a big deal, but large-scale refusal suggests that something may be terribly wrong with the study research question or its procedures. David J. Fox explained:

> When attrition reaches 25 percent or higher, even assuming that there are no statistically significant differences between accepting and data-producing samples, the researcher and reader must be concerned with the phenomena of nonparticipation. There is extensive evidence in the literature that . . . those who answer initially hold different opinions from those who do not. As we analyze data for any one study this means that we must continually evaluate the data, particularly any data of particular significance, to determine if the nonresponders could have affected the response pattern. For example, assume we find that 70 percent of the selected sample of 100 actually produced data. In studying data for a particular question, we find that of the 70 respondents, 52 answered "yes" and 18 answered "no." We can have good confidence in these data, for even if the 30 nonrespondents had the same opinion, and it was "no," the majority would still be on the "yes" opinion. However, if the 70 respondents split 39 to 31 on another question, we could have little confidence in these data, for if a majority of the nonrespondents held to either point of view they could alter the result. (1969, pp. 345–346)

Researchers need to examine potential sources of nonresponse to limit conclusions and to discover additional variables for future study.

Evidence of Randomization in Research Articles

Researchers who use randomization tend to describe it in great detail. Research articles usually either explain how randomization was handled or make some reference to a table of random numbers. If researchers do not rely on either method, then we cannot—and probably should not—assume that randomization was used. Randomization is a pain in the neck, and researchers who do it properly often complain about it.

To some extent, the credibility of the research project may be tested by looking at the degree to which the researcher offers evidence of randomization. Highly skilled researchers spell out their methods in enough detail for the study to be replicated.

systematic reasons for refusal to participate as sampling error

1. initial refusal

2. incomplete responding

systematic attrition is meaningful to the researcher

researchers show randomization by either describing methods or referencing random number tables

CHECKLIST TO EVALUATE SAMPLING

_____ Is the population clearly identified?

_____ Is the sample size appropriate for the statistical tools the researchers plan to use?

_____ Are confidence intervals computed around key dependent measures?

_____ Are probability sampling methods used? If not, are study conclusions limited accordingly?

_____ Do the researchers clearly identify the types of sampling used?

_____ Do researchers claiming to use random sampling methods explain how the randomization was accomplished?

_____ Do researchers using nonrandom or nonprobability sampling justify their choices?

_____ Is information about the rates of refusal to participate included and are study conclusions limited accordingly?

SUMMARY

Sampling involves selecting events from a population. A population is the universe of events from which the sample is drawn. The actual individual events are called pieces of data. A number computed from a sample is called a statistic, sometimes also called "sample statistics" or "test statistics." A parameter is the label for a number computed from a population. To draw samples from populations, researchers must first define the population. Bias in sampling is a tendency for the sample to err so that it fails to represent the population. Obviously, researchers work to eliminate or minimize bias.

A good sample must be representative of the population and big enough to permit reasonable analysis of data. A representative sample is one that accurately reflects characteristics of the population from which it was drawn. Part of a representative sample involves having a large enough sample to make reasonable interpretations. Sampling error refers to the degree to which a sample differs from population characteristics on some measure. In general, as the sample size gets to be an increased proportion of the population, the amount of sampling error is reduced. Sample sizes should be suitable to the research questions and study designs. If samples have been drawn at random, it is possible to report confidence intervals indicating the probability that sample statistics "capture" population parameters, within certain margins of error. Small samples often invite sampling bias. In addition, because of the ways statistics are computed and distributions entered, it is very difficult for researchers to find evidence of relationships when sample sizes get small. Yet, statisticians have observed that random samples of 30 or more events tend to produce nearly identical distributions.

Sometimes called "probability sampling" techniques, randomization plays an important part in research. Random sampling is selection of data such that each event in the population has an equal chance of selection. Obtaining a random draw of events is not a haphazard matter. Systematic or periodic sampling is not true random sampling because it selects respondents according to a predetermined schedule rather than a random sequence. To select a sample, events may be assigned numbers and chosen by reference to a table of random numbers. Random sampling permits you to feel confident that the sample is representative of the population and that differences from one person to another in a sample will be random rather than systematic. Thus, random sampling allows control of a host of background differences in sample groups. In addition to simple random sampling, other random sampling methods may be used. Stratified random sampling defines samples based on the known proportions within the population and follows them with random sampling within each group. Stratified random sampling is invited where dividing the sample according to some stratification variable is an important part of the study. This method tends to require increased sample sizes that involve increased expenses for the researcher. Furthermore, the method may not be practical to explore many research questions because the weights associated with each stratification variable may not be known. Cluster sampling involves selecting events in two or more stages, with the first stage being the random selection of naturally occurring clusters, and the last stage being the random selection of elements within clusters. The method has been particularly useful when geographically based samples have been involved. Yet, cluster sampling typically requires larger samples than simple random sampling.

Sometimes random sampling is not possible. There are four general categories of nonrandom sampling. First, accidental or convenience sampling involves selecting events that are most readily available. These samples are most useful in case studies and in pilot studies that are designed to help the researcher identify problems and get feedback about research materials. Second, quota sampling defines samples based on the known proportions within the population, followed by nonrandom sampling completed in each group. This approach is often used in studies where researchers want to make sure that important parts of the population are not omitted in the sampling. Yet, quotas filled by researchers' sampling friends and family members are not representative. Third, purposive or known group sampling selects events from groups that are known to possess a particular characteristic under investigation. Purposive or known group sampling is useful for experiments or surveys where a criterion for admission to the sample clearly exists, or when new measures are validated by use of predictive validity methods. Though this method is convenient and economical when key population characteristics can be identified clearly, sometimes the key characteristic is difficult to see in a group or the key characteristic may be subjective. In addition, since groups of people are identified, the observations may not be independent. Fourth, snowball sampling selects events based on referrals from initial informants. This method is highly useful for studies of behavior that involve deviant or illegal activities. Yet, researchers using snowball sampling do not really know whether enough referrals exist to penetrate into the group under investigation. Furthermore, the people in the sample cannot be considered independent. These nonrandom methods often allow the researcher to get samples that might otherwise be unavailable and are often invited by field and quasi-experimental research. They have severe limitations, however: (1) they tend to show great biases; (2) since there is no distribution for nonprobability samples, no sampling error computation is possible; and (3) their use severely limits conclusions that may be drawn by researchers.

Researchers must often face problems of sampling and sampling error. First, participants may refuse to participate (either because they initially decline or because they provide incomplete responses). Second, researchers must provide evidence of randomization (either by explaining how they handled randomization or by referencing a table of random numbers).

TERMS FOR REVIEW

sampling	probability sampling
population	random sampling
data	systematic or periodic sampling
statistics	simple random sampling
parameters	stratified random sampling
bias	cluster sampling
representative sample	accidental or convenience sampling
sampling error	quota sampling
confidence intervals	purposive or known group sampling
standard deviation	snowball sampling

JUST FOR THE SAKE OF ARGUMENT: A REVIEW

Look at the following questions and prepare your own answers to them. Look for the underlying assumptions.

1. Why do researchers want to sample in ways that reduce bias? What is the fundamental notion of bias anyway?

2. Does sampling error mean that researchers have made mistakes in gathering data? What are sampling error terms that contemporary students should know?

3. What does it mean when a person says that the 95% confidence interval around a mean is equal to 4? What happened to the other 5%?

4. If you stopped every tenth person who walked into the main cafeteria of your school, would you have completed a random sample of people at the school? What is required of random sampling? What could be done to ensure random sampling of people at a school cafeteria?

5. How can you tell if researchers really used randomization in their research articles? What does all this detective work tell you about researchers?

6. Though random sampling methods allow probability methods to be used to explain the adequacy of samples, there are times when nonrandom samples are preferred. What are some times when you would prefer to use nonrandom sampling methods (give examples not found in the chapter)?

ACTIVITIES TO PROBE FURTHER

Go to the website for this book and look for the Student Study Materials for Chapter 11.

1. Take the study quiz and print out your answers. (Make sure to review these text materials before you answer the questions so that you avoid giving answers that are your first impressions.)

2. Draw a random sample from a set of names in the telephone directory.

Follow these steps:
  a. Get access to a telephone directory and select a page from it.
  b. Suppose you wished to sample 10 people at random from this page. Following instructions for using a table of random digits covered in this chapter, select a starting point.

Complete the rest of this work on a separate sheet of paper.

PART I: Taking a Simple Random Sample

  c. What was the starting point you used for the random number table, and which way did you decide to move in the table?
  d. Write down the random numbers that you used to select the 10 people (include all, including numbers not used to select sample events).
  e. List names of people finally selected.

PART II: Taking a Stratified Random Sample

Suppose you wanted to represent men and women equally in this sample. Draw a new sample from the telephone directory page.
  f. Using the names of individuals as identifiers, draw a random sample of five men and five women. Exclude those names for which it was not possible to determine their sex.
  g. Write the random numbers you used.
  h. Write the names of the men and women in this sample.

PART III: Evaluation

  i. How would you judge the representativeness of this sampling method?
  j. What shortcuts were you tempted to take? What shortcuts do you suspect some researchers might take?

3. Go to the website for this class, and follow the hyperlink to "Adequacy of a Sample: The Basketball Season." Complete the exercise listed on this page and report the following:
  a. What were the mean points found in your random sample of 16 games?
  b. What was the 95% confidence interval around your computed mean?
  c. Did this confidence interval really capture the population mean points for each game in the season?

4. Go to the website for this book. Use the hyperlink to go to "NCA: How America Communicates." Use the hyperlink to the NCA website, and download the NCA.SAV file.
  a. Go to the Web page for Chapter 11, and click on the hyperlink to "Random Sampling with SPSS." Follow these instructions to prepare you for drawing a random sample of 200 from the original NCA sample of 1,001. There is no comparable tool in Excel.
  b. Start SPSS and load NCA.SAV. Following the instructions given in the website, draw a random sample of 200 (20% of all cases).
  c. To see if this sample is representative of the larger sample, run a descriptive output for the variable identified as "sex." This item identified a person as male (coded as 1) or female (coded as 2). In the total sample, 52% of the sample was female.
  d. To complete this descriptive output, click on the "Analyze" menu; on subsequent menus that appear, click on "Descriptive Statistics" and then "Frequencies." In the dialog box titled "Frequencies" place sex on the variable list. Click the "Statistics" button. In the "Frequencies: Statistics" dialog box click on "Mean," "Std. deviation," and "S.E. mean." Click "Continue," and then click "OK" in the "Frequencies" dialog box.
  e. Print out your results and answer this question: How well does this sample of 200 capture the proportions in the larger sample? What are the reasons you might wish to use a reduced sample size?

PART 4

Statistical Analysis of Data

Descriptive Statistics

To understand God's thoughts, we must study statistics, for these are the measure of his purpose.

—FLORENCE NIGHTINGALE

CHAPTER OUTLINE

BEFORE WE GET STARTED . . .

Many students think that "research methods" is another term for statistics. But as you have seen, statistics are just tools used by scholars to understand information. In this chapter you will learn the language of descriptive statistics and the basic methods used to help characterize quantitative data. You will find that statistical analyses involve a lot of common sense. You do not have to remember your high school math to understand statistics. Instead, this chapter does not presume that you have any background in the subject.

STATISTICS IN COMMUNICATION RESEARCH

These days you cannot read the literature of the field without some basic knowledge of statistical tools. Thus, you must understand how to use different families of statistics because they are all around you. Furthermore, a knowledge of statistical tools allows you to think critically about research and to assess the worth of different studies.

importance of statistical understanding

There are two general types of statistics. **Descriptive statistics** are used to characterize data. Averages, variability, and correlations are examples of descriptions. **Inferential statistics** use probabilities to make inferences about related populations. This chapter discusses descriptive statistics, and the next two chapters cover major inferential statistical tools.

Descriptive statistics numbers that are designed to characterize some information in a data set.

It is helpful to realize that statisticians use the Greek alphabet to represent population parameters (remember that parameters are numbers that characterize populations) and when they discuss conceptual formulae. To balance things out, statisticians use the Roman alphabet (the one used in English) to symbolize sample statistics. This distinction will help you keep things straight.

Inferential statistics tools that help researchers draw conclusions about the probable populations to which samples did or did not belong.

Measures of Central Tendency

Measures of **central tendency** tell what is going on within sample groups or populations *on the average.* You may hear people talk about the "average" rainfall, "average" levels of communication apprehension, or "average" numbers of hours people watch TV. But researchers tend to use specific terms to describe averages. Let's take an example. Suppose that you gave a sample of eight classmates a 10-point rating scale to find out how much they liked the instruction of the research methods class they were taking (10 would be the most exciting course ever, and 1 would be the worst course ever). Suppose you received the following data:

Central tendency measures that report averages of different varieties.

$$3 \quad 4 \quad 5 \quad 6 \quad 6 \quad 7 \quad 8 \quad 9$$

There are several ways to describe the central tendency of these data. The **arithmetic mean** is the number most people call "the average." It adds a set of scores (represented as Xs in formulae) and divides by the number of scores. Other types of means are used in different situations,[1] but if you hear someone refer to

Arithmetic mean a measure of central tendency computed by adding a set of scores and dividing by the number of scores.

---

[1]For instance, the "geometric mean" is used to average ratios or proportions. If money deposited in a savings account grew from $100 to $300 in five years, the average percentage increase would *not* be computed by dividing the 200% increase by 5 (because of the presence of compounded interest). The *geometric mean* would be used. To find average miles per gallon for a car that was driven for 10 miles at 35 miles per hour, 5 miles at 20 miles per hour, and 8 miles at 40 miles per hour, use the *harmonic mean*.

"the mean," the word "the" is a definite article indicating the arithmetic mean. The population mean is computed by using this formula:

$$\mu = \frac{\Sigma X}{N}$$

The symbol μ is the Greek letter mu ("mew") and represents the population mean. The capital N stands for the number of events in the population. The Σ is called "sigma" and is a math symbol instructing us to "sum" or add up everything that follows. For the sample mean, the formula is

$$\overline{X} = \frac{\Sigma X}{n}$$

The sample mean is represented by $\overline{X}$, which is read "X bar." The lowercase n is used to indicate the number of events in the sample. If we plug in the numbers from our sample into the formula, we find that the mean is 6. The formulae for sample and population means are very similar. In fact, the sample mean is said to be an **unbiased estimator** of the population mean. This statement asserts that a representative sample mean is likely to approximate the population mean. Certainly, it is *more likely* to equal the population mean than any other measure we can find. Hence, if researchers do not have the population mean for a formula that requires it, the sample mean may be substituted. Though the mean is a very useful number, it can be thrown off by a small number of extreme scores. So, other methods of central tendency may be examined.

The **median** is a score that appears in the middle of an ordered list of scores. As such, the median separates one-half of the data from the other half. For our data, we have eight scores that have been listed from lowest to highest. So, there is no score in the "middle." What are we supposed to do? To identify the median, we "split the difference" between the two scores surrounding the middle. In our case, the two scores that surround the middle are 6 and 6. Hence, splitting the difference between these two numbers yields a score of, well, 6.

The **mode** is the most commonly occurring score. In this example, the score 6 appears most often. Sometimes data have more than one mode. When data have two modes, they are called **bimodal.** But if data have many modes, the mode may not be a meaningful way to depict central tendency.

Unbiased estimator a sample statistic that is most likely to approximate the corresponding population parameter.

Median a score in an ordered set of data that separates one-half of the data from the other.

Mode the most frequent score in a data set.

Bimodal a distribution that has two modes.

Measures of Variability or Dispersion

In addition to characterizing the averages of scores, researchers may want to determine how close the data are to the mean. This matter can be important. Suppose you were on a bowling team and one of your players got ill and you needed a substitute. If you had a choice between Pat (whose last three games were 155, 175, and 210) and Merle (whose last three games were 172, 180, and 188), which substitute bowler would you ask first? Each bowler has exactly the same average! Yet, most people would ask Merle first. Consistency with the average matters. Measures of dispersion or variability tell how far from the average the data tend to be.

SPECIAL DISCUSSION 12-1

HOW TO READ A STATISTICAL FORMULA

It often is helpful to read statistical formulae by using shorthand symbols. By learning a few details, the summary formulae can be very useful. Let's look at the formula for sample variance:

$$s^2 = \frac{\Sigma(X - \overline{X})^2}{n - 1}$$

To read such a formula, we start with items inside the parentheses. In this case, we are told to take an X score, subtract the sample mean $(\overline{X})$ from it, and square the difference. Because of the presence of the sigma sign, we know that we are going to continue this process for all the other X scores as well.

The sigma sign (Σ) tells us to sum—or add up—the values we have computed. This sigma sign is shown here in its abbreviated form, but you should know that it actually has subscripts and superscripts that may be used. For instance, the following form is fairly standard:

$$\sum_{i=1}^{n, 1} X_i$$

This statement still means that we sum the X scores that follow, but there is additional detail. The "$i = 1$" statement below the sigma sign means that we are to start our summation with the first instance. The "n, 1" above the sigma means that we are to continue through the total number of events in the data set by intervals of 1. Suppose we wanted to add up the even-numbered events out of our first 20 events. The sigma would indicate:

$$\sum_{i=2}^{20, 2} X_i$$

You will notice that the X score has an "i" to indicate that it represents instances of X scores that are to be included in the summation. If you see a sigma sign without the additional symbols, it is a shorthand for summing up scores starting with the first instance and moving through all of them by intervals of 1.

Other symbols frequently used in statistical discussions include the following:

★ *multiplied by*

/ *divided by*

> *greater than*

< *less or fewer than*

≥ *equal to or greater than*

≤ *equal to or less (or fewer) than*

≠ *not equal to*

In each case, these symbols can help summarize a great deal of information to be followed in making statistical calculations.

Range

Range the difference between the highest and lowest scores.

The **range** is the interval from the highest to the lowest scores. In our example, Pat has a range of 55 pins, and Merle's range is only 16 pins. Sometimes researchers further divide the range into quartiles to describe additional divisions. The range is often used to summarize data, but since the range does not deal with the spread of scores around a measure of central tendency, researchers may not be able to compare ranges very usefully. Furthermore, the range is greatly affected by extreme scores.

Variance

Variance a measure of the average of squared differences of scores from the mean, symbolized for the sample variance as s^2 and for the population variance as σ^2.

The **variance** is a measure of the typical squared difference score deviation from the mean. As a matter of notation, the symbol s^2 represents the variance of a sample. The symbol σ^2 (sigma squared; that's lowercase sigma) represents the variance of the population. But these definitions do not give you much of a feeling for these highly useful measures of variability.

Let's use some common sense. You really want to find a number that tells the average distance of data from the mean. Consider the following three pieces of data:

$$1$$
$$5$$
$$9$$

The mean for these data is 5. To assess dispersion, one might ask, How far from the mean of 5 are the remaining data points? If you said 4, you have just computed the sample standard deviation in your head. Congratulations! You may verify this matter by using the formula for sample standard deviation presented on the pages that follow. All measures of standard deviation are just that simple, even though it becomes handy to use an established formula to compute matters for larger and larger sample sizes. For now, pretend you have a data set that includes the entire population of events. If you want to tell people how far from the mean your data happen to be, you should find out how far each data point is from the mean; then you can average the distances. Do it one step at a time; it is important to understand the common sense of this statistic.

You could start by subtracting the mean (μ) from each score (X). If you used the data discussed earlier in the chapter, it would appear as:

X	μ	$(X - \mu)$
3	-6	-3
4	-6	-2
5	-6	-1
6	-6	0
6	-6	0
7	-6	1
8	-6	2
9	-6	3

SPECIAL DISCUSSION 12-2

A QUESTION OF ETHICS: DESCRIPTIVE STATISTICS TO AVOID MISUNDERSTANDINGS AND CONFUSION

The clarity of descriptive statistics is often viewed as a matter of professional conduct. But such a fact carries ethical implications. Professional codes of conduct and ethical guidelines regularly demand that researchers use sound statistical analysis tools to prevent any misinterpretations. But, ethically, these concerns are only the start. Clear presentations of descriptive statistics naturally might help consumers of research avoid misunderstandings. Hence, it is not surprising that the American Psychological Association Task Force on Statistical Inference dedicated a section of its final report to the suggestion that descriptive statistics should be reported in full to avoid creating erroneous impressions by researchers (Task Force on Statistical Inference, 1996):

> [W]e recommend that more extensive descriptions of the data be provided to reviewers and readers. This should include means, standard deviations, sample sizes, five-point summaries, box-and-whisker plots, other graphics, and descriptions related to missing data as appropriate. (¶ 6)
>
> [T]he use of techniques to assure that the reported results are not produced by anomalies in the data (e.g., outliers, points of high influence, non-random missing data, selection, attrition problems) should be a standard component of all analyses. (¶ 8)

Hence, not only does a spirit of professionalism require that researchers present full descriptive accounts of the data, but the proper interpretation of these pieces of descriptive information demands that researchers interpret the meaning of basic descriptive statistics.

What happens if the researcher knowingly fails to include all such relevant descriptive statistics and interpretations? Answer: Without such material included, the chances for misunderstanding are increased—and the researcher is to blame. Clearly, such descriptive statistics and interpretations must be included.

Without interpretations of relevant descriptive statistics, misinterpretations can—and have—been frequent. Lori Alden collected a set of examples of improperly interpreted statistics on her website, *Statistics Can Be Misleading* (2005). Here are a few examples.

- One report submitted that "Fluoride consumption by human beings increases the general cancer death rate. . . . People in fluoridated areas have a higher cancer death rate than those in non-fluoridated areas." (¶ 27)

  The example assumes causality from correlations—which is not founded unless the experimental research design permitted such conclusions. Most important, other characteristics of the sample were not reported and interpreted. For instance, Alden explains, *"Affluent areas are more likely to have fluoridation and they're also more likely to have older populations who are more likely to get cancer"* (¶ 28). Failure to include such interpretations of descriptive statistical information may be considered an ethical breach since it leads to a predictable misunderstanding.

- In February 2001, *U.S. News and World Report* magazine listed the airlines with the greatest and fewest numbers of customer complaints. The greatest complaints went to United (252 complaints), American (162 complaints), and Delta (119

(Continued)

SPECIAL DISCUSSION 12-2 (Continued)

complaints). The fewest complaints went to Alaska (13 complaints), Southwest (22 complaints), and Continental (60 complaints). Should people conclude that United, American, and Delta are the worst airlines? (¶ 13)

> The problem is that the number of flights and customers served is not provided. Thus, the raw numbers of complaints were misleading statistics. When the researcher reported the complaints as a proportion of the number of customers, the lowest proportion of complaints went to Southwest, followed by Alaska, followed by Delta.

♦ The observation was made that cities that had the greatest number of guns in homes also had the greatest number of murders. So, does gun ownership enhance chances of being murdered?

> *"Perhaps, but correlation does not imply causation"* (¶ 24). It just as well could be that people who live in an area that has a high murder rate respond by buying guns out of a desire to protect themselves.

In each case, the failure to include all the relevant descriptive statistics or to express alternative interpretations in the report could lead to complete misinterpretations of results—and failure to include these possibilities may be taken as an ethical problem in the use of descriptive statistics.

Now, we just need to average these differences, right? Try it!

It doesn't work, does it? When you add up all the "difference scores," the plus and minus signs cancel out the differences. When you add up the positive and negative numbers, you get 0. It happens every time you subtract a mean from the data points you used to compute that mean. So, you need to get rid of the negative numbers on a temporary basis. You could accomplish this objective by squaring the differences (multiplying each difference score by itself). Then you could average these "squared differences" and finish up by "unsquaring" the average so that you get back to the kinds of cardinal numbers you started with. Try it.

X	μ	$(X - \mu)$	$(X - \mu)^2$
3	−6	−3	9
4	−6	−2	4
5	−6	−1	1
6	−6	0	0
6	−6	0	0
7	−6	1	1
8	−6	2	4
9	−6	3	9

sum = 28

Sometimes this sum is called the "sum of squares" (short for the "sum of squared differences of scores from their mean"). Now, you take the average of this sum.

Twenty-eight divided by 8 is 3.5. This number is called the variance. Thus, the variance really is just the average of squared differences of scores from the mean. It is all common sense, but the plus and minus signs caused you to take an additional step or two.

When the pieces are put together, the formula for variance may be symbolized as follows:

$$\sigma^2 = \frac{\Sigma(X - \mu)^2}{N}$$

This formula reads, "sigma squared (the population variance) equals the sum of the squared differences of the population mean subtracted from each of the scores, and divided by the number of scores in the population."

You have been pretending to have the entire population of events. Suppose you had only a sample from the population. Then things change a little. You see, the mean of the sample $(\overline{X})$ is an unbiased estimator of the population mean (μ). But it is only an estimator. It is probably close, but it is not exact. Thus, if you acted as if the sample mean perfectly identified the population mean, not only would you fool yourself, but you would "low ball" the amount of variation that truly exists in the population. Furthermore, your sample variance (s^2) would become a biased estimator of the population variance (σ^2). That won't do.

Permit an explanation (see also Aczel, 1989, pp. 171–175). You could have computed variation many ways. You might have subtracted each score from every other score. But you did not. You used a fixed point—the sample mean—around which to make comparisons. Selecting that starting point meant that the range of variability of the individual scores was artificially restricted to average out to the sample mean. The degrees of freedom of the first data points in the sample to take on any values were unrestricted. But by the time the last data point was reached, the only way the mean could be reported is if the last data point could have only one value and had no degree of freedom in taking a value. Think of it this way. Suppose you offered to three friends their choice of candy bars: Milky Way, Three Musketeers, and Snickers. The first friend you ask has a choice (she chooses Snickers). The second person also has a choice (he chooses Milky Way). But by the time you get to your third friend, there is no choice left at all. Similarly, when you have an arbitrary point around which to make comparisons of events in a sample, the freedom of the events to take on values is restricted by the time you get to the last data point. If you had the entire population, you could live with it, since there would be no error in estimating the population mean. But every time you compute a *sample* variance, you "lose a degree of freedom" equal to the number of means you computed to make comparisons. Thus, statisticians say that every time one "estimates a parameter from a sample" (a sample mean is an unbiased estimator of the population mean, remember?), a degree of freedom is lost. It always works that way: every time you estimate a population mean, you lose a degree of freedom.[2]

losing a degree of freedom every time you estimate a parameter from samples

To estimate a population mean legitimately from a sample mean, you have to "pay the kitty" for the privilege. To use the sample mean in the formula for the variance,

---

[2]It works with all parameters estimated from samples. For instance, in multiple correlation, a degree of freedom is lost each time a beta weight is computed.

you must "ante up" by altering the way you compute the variance: divide the sum of squared differences of scores from the sample mean by the number of events *minus one for the mean you estimated from the sample.* Thus, the formula for sample variance is

$$s^2 = \frac{\Sigma(X - \overline{X})^2}{n - 1}$$

The sample variance in this case would be a little different since the divisor of this formula is $n - 1$ ($8 - 1$). Thus, if we divided 28 by 7, we would get a variance (s^2) of 4.

The variance is—with some adjusting for using sample means—the average squared difference of scores from the mean. But these numbers are difficult to interpret. To return to cardinal numbers, researchers need to remove the effect of squared differences on averaging. This step leads to the last part of our commonsense way of measuring variability.

Standard Deviation

Standard deviation though computed differently, a measure that attempts to summarize the average deviation of scores from the mean, by estimating such a value from the square root of the variance s^2; symbolized for the sample standard deviation as *s*.

The **standard deviation** is a measure of the deviation of scores from the mean. Since the variance is the average of squared deviations of differences of scores from the mean, if we want to get to "unsquared" differences (the cardinal numbers with which we started), we simply take the square root of the variance, using these formulae:[3]

Sample Standard Deviation	*Population Standard Deviation*
$$s = \sqrt{\frac{\Sigma(X - \overline{X})^2}{n - 1}}$$	$$\sigma = \sqrt{\frac{\Sigma(X - \mu)^2}{N}}$$

The standard deviation is, in essence, an average of "unsquared" deviations of scores from their own mean. It attempts to tell the average difference of scores from the mean. In the example, the variance (s^2) was 4. Thus, the sample standard deviation would be the square root of 4. Hence, in the previous example, the sample standard deviation (s) is 2. Since the population variance (σ^2) is 3.5, the population standard deviation (σ) is 1.87.

standard deviations permit using the standard normal curve

Another quality makes standard deviations so valuable to researchers. These numbers make it possible for researchers to use the standard normal curve to help make decisions. To grasp this matter, you must understand the notion of distributions.

DISTRIBUTIONS

Data tend to form distributions that have different appearances. A knowledge of the patterns they form can help researchers understand what the data are really saying. This section looks at two types of distributions: data distributions and the standard normal curve.

---

[3]These formulae are the correct ones for standard deviation of samples and populations. Without naming names, it is the case that for nearly a quarter of a century some books in communication research methods have gotten the formulae for sigma and *s* confused with each other.

Nonnormal and Skewed Distributions

The location of the median, mean, and mode can indicate quite a bit about the nature of underlying data patterns. Several different patterns might be found in the data. In each, the data are "talking" to the researcher; he or she just has to know how to listen.

Types of Skew

An off-center distribution is skewed. Contrary to popular belief, **skewness** does not tell where data are. Instead, it indicates where the long tail away from the "hump" of the data is located. There are formulae to compute skewness, but for this discussion it is most important just to understand the basic ideas. If the distribution is perfectly centered and symmetrical, there is no skew at all (and formulae report skewness coefficients of 0). The tails on each side of the mean would start at the same location and be equally as long. If skewness is negative, the long tail is "below" the mean (our "ground zero"). Then you could say that the distribution is "skewed to the left" or has "negative skew." Figure 12.1A shows such a pattern. If the skewness is positive, then the long tail is "above" the "ground zero" mean. As Figure 12.1B shows, positive skew means that the distribution is "skewed to the right." In the sample of class ratings, the distribution is not skewed one way any more than the other. A bimodal distribution, such as that found in Figure 12.1C, exaggerates skew because the hump in data is found at two different locations.

Peakedness of Distributions

In addition to measuring "centeredness," there are ways to find out how peaked a distribution is. The measure of peakedness is called **kurtosis.** Since the formula is a bit cumbersome, we will not present it here. But here is the basic idea. In a perfect normal distribution, the distribution is as high as 3 standard deviations is wide. If the peak is higher than 3 standard deviations is wide, then the kurtosis is greater than 3. If the peak is shorter than 3 standard deviations is wide, then the kurtosis is lower than 3. This explanation does not give credit to the computation methods for kurtosis. Furthermore, you should know that many popular computer programs now subtract 3 from the kurtosis formula. So, you must be careful when looking at kurtosis numbers to make sure you do not misinterpret them.

Figure 12.1D shows a distribution that has a kurtosis lower than 3. It is very flat, and its profile looks almost as though someone turned over a plate onto the baseline. This distribution is called, by coincidence, **platykurtic.** Figure 12.1E shows a distribution that has a peak that is neither very high nor very low (kurtosis of 3). This distribution is called **mesokurtic.** The last figure (12.1F) shows an extremely peaked distribution, which seems to leap upward. This pattern is called **leptokurtic.** By looking at both skewness and kurtosis, the researcher can get a good picture of the data.

Standard Normal Distribution

One of the basic tools used by researchers is called the **standard normal curve.** Because this distribution is the basis for many other distributions and statistics, we should understand something about it.

Skewness a measure of the centeredness of distributions.

negative or leftward skew

rightward or positive skew

Kurtosis a measure of the peakedness of a distribution.

distributions

Platykurtic a flat distribution with kurtosis under 3.

Mesokurtic a distribution that is neither very high nor very low, with a kurtosis close to 3.

Leptokurtic a distribution that is tall, with a kurtosis above 3.

Standard normal curve a probability distribution that tells the expected value that would be obtained by sampling at random.

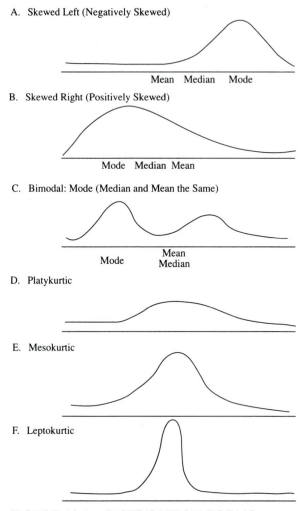

A. Skewed Left (Negatively Skewed)

Mean   Median   Mode

B. Skewed Right (Positively Skewed)

Mode   Median   Mean

C. Bimodal: Mode (Median and Mean the Same)

Mode

Mean
Median

D. Platykurtic

E. Mesokurtic

F. Leptokurtic

FIGURE 12.1   DISTRIBUTION FORMS

Probability distribution
the theoretical pattern of
expected "values of a
random variable and of
the probabilities of
occurrences of these
values" (Upton & Cook,
2002, p. 294).

Data distribution a
distribution of values in a
data set.

The Gaussian Curve

The standard normal curve is a mathematic ideal. It is a **probability distribution** that tells the expected value that would be obtained by sampling at random. Data you collect (**data distributions**) can form normal curves, but they cannot be the standard normal curve unless they meet the exact definitions for this kind of distribution. In the early part of the nineteenth century, mathematician Karl Friedrich Gauss (1777–1855) and the Marquis de Laplace (1749–1827) developed the language of the standard normal curve (Pearson, 1924). Though at the time, Gauss was trying to find clues to the normal deviations in orbits and polar "wobbles" of planets, he also found that many types of ordinary data tended to cluster around their averages with fewer and fewer pieces of data at the extremes. As you can see on Figure 12.2, the standard normal curve is perfectly centered and peaked. The median, mean, and mode are all at the same place on the distribution. The skewness is 0 since the distribution is completely centered. The kurtosis of the standard normal curve is 3. You can also see that the tails of the standard normal curve never really touch bottom: they go out forever.

Starting at the top of the curve, Gauss observed the point where the slope changed direction. To identify this location on the curve, he dropped a line down to the baseline. Then he noticed that there was a second point where the slope changed direction again. He dropped another line to mark the spot, and soon he observed that the intervals between his lines were identical whether he followed the curve above the mean or below the mean. He called these points deviations of slope on the standard normal curve, or "standard deviations" for short.

naming the standard deviation on the standard normal curve

The mean, median, and mode are symbolized by the letter mu (μ). The standard deviation is symbolized by the Greek lowercase letter sigma (σ). Figuring that numbers might be needed, statisticians defined the center of the distribution as ground zero, or just 0. Each standard deviation is set to be 1 unit wide. Hence σ is defined to be equal to 1. A standard deviation below ground zero has a negative sign in front of it, and a standard deviation above ground zero has a positive number. Researchers often collect data that have normal distributions. But if they do not have a mean of 0, a standard deviation of 1, a skewness of 0, a kurtosis of 3, and tails that stretch to infinity, they cannot be standard normal curves. Yet, we can compare

requirements of a standard normal curve

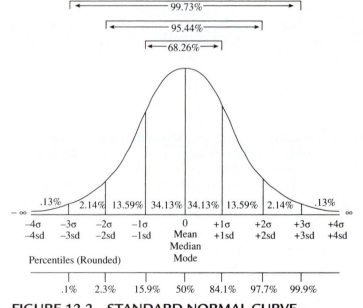

FIGURE 12.2 STANDARD NORMAL CURVE

John C. Reinard. *Foundations of Argument: Effective Communication for Critical Thinking.* Copyright © 1991. Dubuque, IA: Wm. C. Brown Communications Inc. Used with permission.

actual data to a standard normal curve to help identify long-range expectations and to make sound decisions. The section below shows how researchers use this curve.

Interpreting Areas under the Normal Curve

Gauss reported the density function for the standard normal curve, which indicates what percentage of the total area under the standard normal curve extends *from ground zero out* to a point of interest. As you can see, approximately two-thirds of the distribution exists from 1σ below the mean to 1σ above the mean (though the amount actually is 68.26%). Over 95% (actually 95.44%) of the curve extends from -2σ to $+2\sigma$. All but .27% (that's "point 27 percent," not "27 percent") exists from -3σ to $+3\sigma$. The density function has been summarized on tables that are widely available (see Appendix A). These tables have many uses. For instance, suppose you had an instructor who wished to "grade on the curve." Though few instructors really use a strict curve, the method submits that if you assume that grades have a generally normal distribution (and experience shows that grades generally do), then you should be able to slice off the top 10% of students to receive As and the bottom 10% to receive Fs. The next 20% in from each extreme would receive Bs and Ds, and the remaining 40% would receive Cs. Figure 12.3 shows how normally distributed scores are arranged when a teacher grades on the curve. The C range is in the middle of the distribution, and approximately 40% of the curve extends from ground zero up to $.53\sigma$ and down to $-.53\sigma$.

using the table for the standard normal curve

You may wish to look at Appendix A to see what is going on here. We have reproduced a portion of it in Figure 12.3. Here is how to use this table. The term z identifies the number of sigmas or standard deviations of interest. Read the column marked z until you find 0.5. That step brings you to the first decimal point. Now read across the top row to find the column identified .03. This column picks up the second decimal point: 0.53. Where this column and row intersect, you see the number .2019. This number means that 20.19% of the total area under the standard normal curve exists from ground zero out to .53 sigmas. The shaded area in the picture at the top of the table illustrates this relationship. This distribution is symmetrical. So, to figure out how much area exists from .53 sigmas below the mean up to .53 sigmas above the mean, simply double the area ($.2019 \star 2 = .4038$). Thus, the amount of area from $-.53\sigma$ to $+.53\sigma$ is approximately 40%. To pick up an additional 20% of the grades around C, you would have to go out to 1.29σ in each direction. The 10% of the total area left over on each side of the distribution would be identified as A and F ranges.

using the standard normal curve to identify unusual occurrences

As you can see, the standard normal curve can help identify long-run expectations you might have for samples you draw. These distributions are used as probability distributions to help you understand when unusual patterns exist in the data—so that you can make appropriate decisions.

z scores scores that transform values from other distributions into equivalent units under the standard normal curve with means of 0 and standard deviations and variances of 1.

Using z Scores

Researchers are usually not lucky enough to collect data that have a mean of zero and a standard deviation of 1. Yet, they can still use the standard normal curve to make decisions by changing data into "z scores." Because *z scores* allow us to use the "standard normal" curve to help make decisions, these scores are sometimes

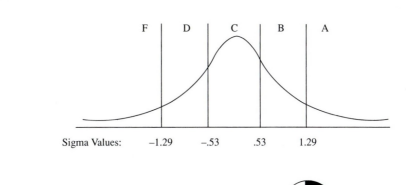

(A)

(B)

z	.00	.01	.02	.03	.04	.045	.05	.06	.07	.08	.09
0.0	.0000	.0040	.0080	.0120	.0160	.0179	.0199	.0239	.0279	.0319	.0359
0.1	.0398	.0438	.0478	.0517	.0557	.0576	.0596	.0636	.0675	.0714	.0753
0.2	.0793	.0832	.0871	.0910	.0948	.0968	.0987	.1026	.1065	.1103	.1141
0.3	.1179	.1217	.1255	.1293	.1331	.1350	.1368	.1406	.1443	.1480	.1517
0.4	.1554	.1591	.1628	.1664	.1700	.1718	.1736	.1772	.1808	.1844	.1879
0.5	.1915	.1950	.1985	.2019	.2054	.2071	.2088	.2123	.2157	.2190	.2224
0.6	.2257	.2291	.2324	.2357	.2389	.2405	.2422	.2454	.2486	.2517	.2549
0.7	.2580	.2611	.2652	.2673	.2704	.2719	.2734	.2764	.2794	.2823	.2852
0.8	.2881	.2910	.2939	.2967	.2995	.3009	.3023	.3051	.3078	.3106	.3133
0.9	.3159	.3186	.3212	.3238	.3264	.3277	.3289	.3315	.3340	.3365	.3389
1.0	.3413	.3438	.3461	.3485	.3508	.3520	.3531	.3554	.3577	.3599	.3621
1.1	.3643	.3665	.3686	.3708	.3729	.3739	.3749	.3770	.3790	.3810	.3830
1.2	.3849	.3869	.3888	.3907	.3925	.3934	.3944	.3962	.3980	.3997	.4015
1.3	.4032	.4049	.4066	.4082	.4099	.4107	.4115	.4131	.4147	.4162	.4177
1.4	.4192	.4207	.4222	.4236	.4251	.4258	.4265	.4279	.4292	.4306	.4319
1.5	.4332	.4345	.4357	.4370	.4382	.4388	.4394	.4406	.4418	.4429	.4441

**FIGURE 12.3   STANDARD NORMAL CURVE USED IN GRADING
ON THE CURVE**

called "standard scores." Z scores permit us to represent data scores as units under *z scores identified* the standard normal curve. Thus, we can use z scores to compare general patterns of scores to others. The formula for z is

$$z = \frac{X - \mu}{\sigma}$$

The X is a score of interest to the researcher. For example, much communication research examines the role of receiver intelligence on reactions to messages. Scores on the popular Stanford–Binet IQ test are normally distributed with a population mean (μ) of 100 and a population standard deviation (σ) of 15.[4] Suppose you scored 115 on an IQ test. Assuming for the sake of argument that IQ tests measure something, how many scores would your score exceed? We might insert numbers as follows:

$$z = \frac{X - \mu}{\sigma}$$

$$= \frac{115 - 100}{15}$$

$$= \frac{15}{15}$$

$$= 1.00$$

So, how many scores would yours exceed? You need only look at the table. On Figure 12.3 find the column for z and identify the row corresponding to 1.0. To find the second decimal point value, continue across the top of the table to the column marked ".00." The intersection of this column and this row reveals the number .3413, indicating that 34.13% of the area lies between the mean and a z value of 1.00.

How do you find out how many scores are below yours? You might suppose that you just double the value of .3413. *Don't do it!* The 115 score is above average, right? So, you have a higher score than all the people who were "below average." Since 50% of the area is below the mean (and 50% above the mean), you know that your score is automatically better than the 50% of the below-average scores. In addition, the z table shows that your score is greater than 34.13 of the scores that were average and above. Thus, your IQ score is greater than 50% + 34.13%, for a total of 84.13%. Your score is greater than approximately 84% of other IQ scores.

Suppose you do not have the population mean (μ) or the population standard deviation (σ)? No problem. The sample mean ($\overline{X}$) is an "unbiased estimator" of the population mean (μ). The sample standard deviation (s) is an "unbiased estimator" (provided the right formula was used for the sample standard deviation) of the population standard deviation (σ). So, you can substitute the sample means and standard deviations for population means and standard deviations to compute your answers. Let's return to the example of a teacher grading on the curve. Suppose the mean on the test is 50, your test score is 61, and the standard deviation is 10. What grade would you get, given the dividing points used in the example? We complete the following formula:

z scores when population mean and standard deviation are estimated from samples

$$z = \frac{X - \overline{X}}{s}$$

$$= \frac{61 - 50}{10}$$

---

[4]Though for many years versions of the Stanford-Binet IQ test had standard deviations of 16, starting with the fifth edition in 2004, the scale adopted a standard deviation of 15. See *Stanford-Binet Intelligence Scales, Fifth Edition: Features* (2004).

$$= \frac{11}{10}$$

$$= 1.10$$

Look up this value on Figure 12.3, and notice that you would get a B on this exam. If you wanted to know how many people got lower scores than you did, you could look at the z table. As the area under the normal curve shows, 36.43% of the scores on the normal distribution exist between the mean and 1.10 z scores. Thus, your test score is higher than the 50% of students who were below average, plus another 36.43%, for a total of 86.43%.

You might wonder why so much fuss is made about the standard normal curve. After all, it is just a distribution with random variation around the mean. Researchers often use the standard normal curve to describe the presumed way variables occur. They may gather samples and use the normal curve to learn how likely it is that such samples could be found at random from an underlying distribution in which only ordinary and random occurrences of variables exist. Suppose, for instance, that you gather some sample data whose typical z score is 2.6 or greater. By looking at the standard normal curve, you know that such data could be found very rarely if the distribution is normal and centered at its assumed mean. What would you do? You *could* conclude that you sampled data that just happened to come from the upper end of the underlying distribution. *Or,* you might conclude that the underlying distribution from which the sample was drawn is not really as ordinary as assumed. You might conclude—by looking at the odds of getting samples such as yours at random—that your data have been systematically influenced to make them different from the assumed "ordinary" distribution. By using the standard normal curve (and its variations) you can "play the odds" to

uses of the standard normal curve

RESEARCHERS IN THE FIELD: WILLIAM L. BENOIT

Bill Benoit is a professor in the Department of Communication at the University of Missouri in Columbia. He is one of the field's most productive researchers and regularly appears in the top ten of lists of the most published researchers in communication studies. He has published eight books since 1992, including the highly regarded volume *Seeing Spots: A Functional Analysis of Presidential Television Advertisements from 1952–1996.* He is a nationally known expert in the areas of political campaign communication, political debates, and crisis communication (particularly in issues of repair of public images). He has been the editor of the *Journal of Communication* and has received the Gerald Phillips Mentoring Award from the American Communication Association.

♦ *What drew you into our field?*
I was first introduced to communication through debate—a year in high school, and I debated in college. I liked researching the topics, preparing for debates, and I particularly enjoyed arguing against competitors.

♦ *In general, what have you hoped that your research would accomplish?*
Initially, I wanted to answer questions about communication. Later, I also hoped that I could share my research with a wider audience, and so I began writing press releases for the [University of Missouri] News Bureau to send out to reporters. I was quoted in the news many times during the 2004 presidential campaign, for example. I also created a webpage about my political campaign research which was accessed over 10,000 times during the 2004 campaign, hopefully reaching some voters, teachers, and students as well as some journalists/reporters.

♦ *That desire to reach large audiences for your research has been a strong theme in your work. What part of your research undertakings has made you most proud?*
The programmatic quality of my work.

♦ *You are one of the field's most prolific scholars. What personal qualities do you have that you think have contributed to your achievements as a communication scholar?*
The ability to make reasoned arguments has been helpful. Perseverance is very important. A thick skin against inevitable rejection and the ability to make use of constructive criticism also have been useful.

♦ *What one or two things do you think students should know to deal successfully with communication research either as a consumer or as a researcher?*
They need a strong understanding of the method or methods they will use or read about. I think the ability to argue from data/evidence/research findings to conclusions—including implications for theory and practice—is important.

♦ *What do you think is the most exciting future direction for the field's research?*
Structural equation modeling. Much of communication concerns process, and structural equation modeling helps understand process. I also think meta-analysis is an important relatively new development.

♦ *Aside from learning about structural equation modeling and meta-analysis, what advice would you give students who might be interested in becoming communication researchers?*
One must care enough to devote significant time and effort to communication; but if one is willing to do so, important and useful things can be accomplished.

♦ *If you had anything to do over in your communication scholarship, what would it be?*
I would have taken more instruction in statistics when I was in graduate school.

see how likely it is that new sample results could have occurred at random. This thinking is the basis for significance testing, which is described in the next chapter.

MEASURES OF ASSOCIATION

Correlation measure of the association or coincidence of variables.

One major way to describe data statistically uses measures of association or correlation.[5] A **correlation** is just a measure of the coincidence of variables. Most people use the word "coincidence" to mean an "accidental" or "bogus" relationship. But in reality, a

---

[5]Some writers reserve the term "association" for measures on the nominal or ordinal levels of measurement.

coincidence means simply that two variables "coincide" with each other. Correlations show the degree to which variables "coincide" with each other by use of formulae that show the amount of coincidence.

For correlations, you must have data on two measures (though some correlations allow the use of more than two variables) from each event in the sample. For instance, your income and the number of magazines to which you subscribe can be correlated. You could check the association between the severity of articulation disorders among children and their school grades. Each situation requires that events in the sample include scores that can be plotted and analyzed to reveal associations. This section considers the ways that correlations are interpreted and two major methods used to determine correlations.

Interpreting Correlations

Correlation coefficients can have a range of values from −1.00 to 1.00, but you probably will not see many 1.00 correlations in research. Instead, you will see numbers behind decimal points. Furthermore, the reliability of the measures set limits on the highest correlation that may be observed. The closer the number is to 1 (regardless of the sign before it), the stronger the correlation. Two types of relationships can be revealed. The first is called a **direct relationship,** which indicates that as one variable increases, the other variable also increases. Similarly, as one variable decreases, so does the other. Figure 12.4A shows the general patterns (called scatterplots) that indicate direct relationships. As an aid to interpretation, researchers often add a line of "best fit" through the data. This line is sometimes called a "line of regression," because Karl Pearson, who refined correlation formulae, used data that investigated the "regression effect" when he drew the first line—and the name stuck. Both diagrams reveal high direct correlations since the line of best fit shows that as the variable on the horizontal axis increases, so does the variable on the vertical axis. The second illustration shows a perfect 1.00 correlation since all the data are exactly on the line. Though often misunderstood, the correlation is not the steepness of the line's slope. Instead, correlation size is shown by the closeness of the data to the line of best fit. If you look at Figure 12.4C, you will see scatterplots showing no relationship. If one of the variables is held constant (and not a variable at all), a correlation of zero will also be found. As you can tell, if a chart is drawn according to standard protocols, zero correlations are reflected in plots that form perfect circles (or lines that are perfectly horizontal or perfectly vertical, in the case of situations in which one "variable" has only one value in the data).

An **inverse relationship** is one in which an increase in one variable corresponds to a decrease in the other. These correlations are identified by the use of negative signs, but you should not interpret negative signs as subtractions or "take away." A correlation of −.82 is a strong one. The negative sign does not mean that this correlation is "less than" a positive correlation of .15. The minus sign indicates only that as one variable increases, the other declines (see Figure 12.4B). There are many such examples in communication research. As the amount of conflict within a group increases, the amount of ambiguity the members feel about the issues declines. The higher one's intelligence, the fewer hours of television one might watch. Such patterns occur frequently in communication

Direct relationship a correlation with a positive slope indicating that the two variables move in the same direction.

line of best fit or regression noted

Inverse relationship a correlation with a negative slope indicating that the two variables move in different directions.

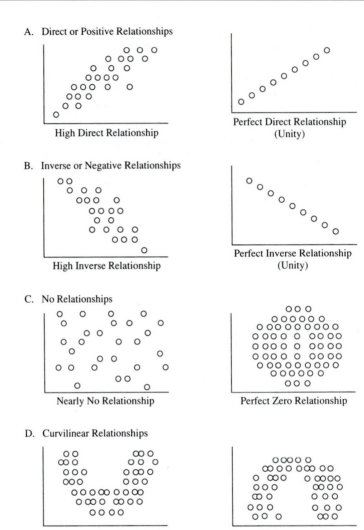

FIGURE 12.4   FORMS OF CORRELATIONS

guidelines to interpret correlations   research and can be very interesting. To understand how to judge the size of different correlations, statistician Robert Koenker developed this general guide (1961, p. 52):

.80 to 1.00   highly dependable relationship

.60 to .79   moderate to marked relationship

.40 to .59   fair degree of relationship

.20 to .39   slight relationship

.00 to .19   negligible or chance relationship

There are some commonsense exceptions to this guideline, of course. If you examine questions searching for the last few contributors to effects, you might interpret a small coefficient more favorably than you would otherwise.

Let's see how the method works. Many communication students eventually pursue careers in law, and they usually take the Law School Aptitude Test (LSAT). This test seems bothersome to most students, but the test scores correlate .50 with first-year grades in law school. When a student's undergraduate grades are added to the mix, the combination correlates .70 with first-year law school grades (Anastasi, 1968, pp. 431–432). Thus, it seems that the test alone is a "fair" predictor of first-year law school grades, and when undergraduate grades are included, the combination becomes a "marked" predictor of success in law school.

Some students look at correlation coefficients as percentages. They think that a .80 correlation explains 80% of the effect. *Not true!* A correlation uses its own metric to identify correspondence between scores. To find out the percentage relationship one variable has with another, you can simply square the correlation coefficient. This number is called a **coefficient of determination.** Hence a correlation of .80 means that 64% ($.80^2 = .64$) of the variation in one variable can be explained by the other one alone. In the example of LSAT scores, the combination of first-year test scores and undergraduate grades explains 49% of total variability—slightly under half. This relation surely is superior to intuition alone, but the coefficient of determination also reveals that there is plenty of room for improvement.

not confusing correlations for percentages

Coefficient of determination a number that shows the percentage of variation in one variable that can be explained by a knowledge of the other variable alone; the square of a correlation coefficient.

Sometimes the data show different patterns, as indicated on Figure 12.4D. These relationships are curvilinear since the best fit of a line to the data is not a straight line. These curves invite the use of special correlations that can identify the magnitude of the curved effect (such as the correlation ratio, eta [η]). Furthermore, they tell the researcher that there is an optimal low point or high point that will be missed if the researcher is not careful.

curvilinear relationships

Using Graphs to Understand Correlations

Though it is a good idea (and an ethical guideline) to examine graphs that present descriptive statistics, when interpreting correlations it is vital. The correlation coefficient can be thrown off by a few characteristics that only charts may reveal.

Outliers

Sometimes a piece of data comes from an event that is part of a different population than the rest of the sample group. For instance, one person taking a survey of communicator competence and communication apprehension might also be a person with bipolar disorder. If this person is in a manic state during the survey, the data would reflect an abnormal response that is outside the range of scores from other study participants who are not sufferers of bipolar disorder. The effect of even one **outlier** can be noteworthy. For instance, for the data found in Example A of Figure 12.4, the diagram of a "high direct relationship" actually produces a correlation coefficient of .86. But look what would happen if one extreme score were added to the data set at the bottom right of the chart:

Outlier a piece of data from a different population than others in the data set and that introduces extreme scores on one or more variables.

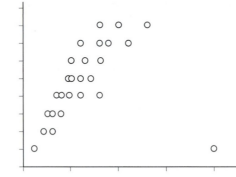

Now, the correlation is only .33. Thus, researchers should look for outliers and, if they can be explained as coming from events of a different population, they may be removed.

Unequal Spread

Homoscedasticity the
assumption in correlational
analyses of approximately
equal spread around the
line of best fit.

Sometimes called **homoscedasticity,** the spread of data about the line of best fit is assumed to be approximately equal across the range. If the spread is not approximately equal, as shown in this diagram, the correlation only applies to some data and not to others.

When this unequal scatter occurs, it tells the researcher that the reported correlation does not apply equally to all the data. This problem may emerge because of the difficulties in the distribution of one of the variables, as a result of a transformation that was made to the data, or because there are indirect relationships among variables. At any rate, the study conclusions must be limited accordingly.

As you can see, it is highly desirable for researchers to take the time to examine plots of correlations. Then, and only then, can conclusions be drawn with some comfort. To omit such reports of difficulties may be considered both sloppy writing and perhaps unethical activity.

Major Forms of Correlations

forms of correlations

There are many correlation formulae that have been developed for different sorts of data. Table 12.1 lists these major forms. As you can see, they differ most in the sorts

TABLE 12.1	FORMS OF ASSOCIATION AND CORRELATION	

MEASURES DESIGNED FOR TWO VARIABLES

Levels of Measurement for:

One Variable	Other Variable	Correlation Method
	Nominal	Tetrachoric Correlation (for two false dichotomies)
	Nominal	Yule's Q (for use if both variables have only two categories)
	Nominal	Phi Coefficient (computed from chi square based on two variables with only two categories)
N O M I N A L	Nominal	Asymmetric lambda (computed from number of events in mode category and distinction made between independent and dependent variable)
	Nominal	Symmetric lambda (computed from number of events in mode category)
	Nominal	Contingency Coefficient (for two or more categories in each variable; coefficient upper limit affected by category numbers)
	Nominal	Cramer's V (for two or more categories in each variable)
	Interval or Ratio	Biserial r (for false dichotomy in nominal variable)
	Interval or Ratio	Point Biserial r (for true dichotomy in nominal variable)
	Ordinal	Spearman Rank Order Correlation
	Ordinal	Goodman and Kruskal's gamma (for use with any sized tables)
O R D I N A L	Ordinal	Kendall's tau a, tau b, Kim's d (for use when many tied ranks are present)
	Ordinal	Kendall's tau c (for use when variables have different numbers of categories)
	Ordinal	Somers' d (for use when distinction made between independent and dependent variable)
	Interval or Ratio	Jaspen's coefficient of multiserial correlation (used when assuming that the ordinal variable is derived from a normally distributed interval variable)
	Interval or Ratio	Mayer and Robinson's M_{yu} (for assumption that the ordinal variable is composed of ordered levels of an underlying variable)
I N T E R V A L or R A T I O	Interval or Ratio	Pearson Product Moment Correlation (for linear relationships) Eta (a.k.a. correlation ratio) (for nonlinear relationships)

(Continued)

TABLE 12.1 (Continued)	
MEASURES DESIGNED FOR MORE THAN TWO VARIABLES	
Correlation Method	**Application**
Kendall's Coefficient of Concordance	Correlation of more than two sets of rankings
Partial Correlation	Correlation of an interval level dependent variable with one predictor variable while holding a third variable constant (the proportion of variance that is not associated with a third controlled variable)
Part Correlation (semipartial correlation)	Correlation equaling the unique contribution made by a predictor variable (the variation between the predictor variable and other potential predictors is eliminated)
Multiple Linear Correlation (Multiple Regression Analysis)	Correlation of a single interval level criterion variable with multiple predictor variables
Canonical Correlation	Correlation of a set of multiple predictor variables with a set of criterion variables
Multiple Discriminant Analysis	Correlational method used to predict group membership categories (measured on the nominal level) from a set of interval level variables
Multivariate Multiple Regression Analysis	An extension of multiple linear correlation for situations in which more than one criterion variable is treated as a common set

of data they allow researchers to examine. Thus, the levels of measurement for the independent and dependent variables are listed. If you need to use any of these tools, you can find them explained in many comprehensive statistics books (e.g., Aczel, 1989; Frankfort-Nachmias & Leon-Guerrero, 2000; Glass & Hopkins, 1984; Reinard, 2006). For the purposes of this book, only the two most commonly used tools will be described.

Pearson Product Moment Correlation

Pearson product moment correlation a correlation method suitable for situations in which the independent and dependent variables (identified as X and Y, respectively, in most notation) are interval or ratio level measures.

Developed by Karl Pearson, the **Pearson product moment correlation** method is suitable for situations in which the independent and dependent variables (identified as X and Y, respectively, in most notation) are *interval* or *ratio* level measures. Table 12.2 shows how to use the Pearson product moment formula. We compute the covariance and divide it by the product of the standard deviations of each variable. The "covariance" is often abbreviated s_{xy}.

Spearman Rank Order Correlation

Sometimes researchers have measures on the ordinal level. For instance, a manager might decide to explore whether there is a relationship between the number of successful salespeople and the number of hours they have spent in

CORRELATION AND CAUSALITY

Though causal relationships should produce high correlations, a correlation cannot show causation by itself. To show cause-and-effect relationships directly, researchers must use the experimental method (or use the method of history, if they can wait long enough). Researchers who think correlations show cause-and-effect relationships can make some silly mistakes. Li (1975) reported a study of factors predicting birthrates among Taiwanese. The researchers observed that birthrate decreased as the number of small appliances one owned increased. Thus, it seemed that one could control population growth by sending toasters, hair dryers, and the like to Taiwan. Of course, owning small appliances does not cause one to have a small family. But it might work the other way around: if you don't have children, you have more money to purchase small appliances. Thus, the researchers made a double error. Not only did they assume a causal relationship, but they claimed a mistaken direction for the difference.

Glass and Hopkins explained the reasons that it is unwise to assume a causal relationship based on correlational information (1984, p. 104):

> First, even when one can presume that a causal relationship does exist between two variables being correlated, r_{xy} can tell nothing by itself about whether X causes Y or Y causes X. Second, often variables other than the two under consideration could be responsible for the observed association. Third, the relationships that exist among variables in behavioral and social science are almost always too complex to be explained in terms of a single cause.

Experienced researchers resist the temptation to view correlations as identical with causal relationships.

---

communication skills training classes. The scores on each variable might be expressed by ranks. For instance, the manager might rank nine salespeople from best (number "1") to worst (number "9"). Then, they might be ranked according to the amount of communication skills training they have received. Though the Pearson product moment correlation method may be adapted if there are no ties among the rankings, the **Spearman rank order correlation** formula is suitable across settings. Table 12.3 shows how this formula can be used with both untied and tied ranks.

This method is usually abbreviated as r_s, though other notation is often used (some statistics books use rho [ρ] as the abbreviation for the Spearman rank order correlation). The Spearman rank order correlation coefficient is often used even when original data were measured on an interval scale but the researcher suspects that the underlying distributions are not normal. It may be interpreted as any other correlation, including computation of coefficients of determination.

Spearman rank order correlation a correlation method suitable for situations in which both the independent and dependent variables are ordinal level measures.

TABLE 12.2   COMPUTING THE PEARSON PRODUCT MOMENT CORRELATION

Consider a study relating the average amount of time spent watching sporting events on TV each week and the average number of bags of potato chips purchased per month.

One simply computes the differences between each score and its own mean. The result is multiplied by the difference of the other score subtracted from its mean. Then, the sum of these products is divided by the number of samples minus one.

$$\frac{\Sigma[(X - \overline{X}) \star (Y - \overline{Y})]}{n - 1}$$

This term is called the covariance.

To compute the Pearson product moment correlation for raw scores, the following formula may be used:

$$r = \frac{\text{covariance } (X, Y) \text{ or } s_{xy}}{s_x \star s_y}$$

For our example, we could compute these matters as follows:

Family	Hours Watching Sports on TV X	$(X - \overline{X})$	Bags of Potato Chips Purchased Monthly Y	$(Y - \overline{Y})$	$(X - \overline{X}) \star (Y - \overline{Y})$
Jones	3	-3	2	-4	12
Smith	4	-2	5	-1	2
Chan	6	0	6	0	0
King	9	3	4	-2	-6
Manson	5	-1	8	2	-2
Addams	7	1	7	1	1
Simpson	8	2	7	1	2
Mann	6	0	9	3	0
	$\overline{X} = 6$		$\overline{X} = 6$		sum = 9
	s = 2		s = 2.27		

The covariance is the sum of these differences multiplied by each other, divided by the number of scores minus one:

$$\text{covariance } (X, Y) = \frac{\Sigma(X - \overline{X}) \star (Y - \overline{Y})}{n - 1}$$

In our instance, this formula becomes:

$$\text{covariance } (X, Y) = \frac{9}{8 - 1} = 1.29$$

The overall correlation becomes:

$$r = \frac{\text{covariance } (X, Y) \text{ or } s_{xy}}{s_x \star s_y}$$

$$= \frac{1.29}{2 \star 2.27}$$

$$= .28, \text{ indicating a "slight" relationship}$$

TABLE 12.3 COMPUTING THE SPEARMAN RANK ORDER CORRELATION

Example without Tied Ranks

Here are data for a study relating the rankings of salespeople and rankings of the amount of communication skills training received.

Person	Ranking of Salesperson Ability X	Ranking of Amount of Communication Training Y
Manny	1	1
Moe	2	4
Jack	3	3
Larry	4	7
Curly	5	2
Patty	6	5
Maxine	7	6
Laverne	8	8
Gallagher	9	9

Differences between ranks are computed, and these differences are squared, creating a term abbreviated as D^2. Then these squared difference scores are added up. Here is how it works in our example.

Person	Ranking of Salesperson Ability X	Ranking of Amount of Communication Training Y	Differences D	D^2
Manny	1	1	$(1 - 1) = 0$	0
Moe	2	4	$(2 - 4) = -2$	4
Jack	3	3	$(3 - 3) = 0$	0
Larry	4	7	$(4 - 7) = -3$	9
Curly	5	2	$(5 - 2) = 3$	9
Patty	6	5	$(6 - 5) = 1$	1
Maxine	7	6	$(7 - 6) = 1$	1
Laverne	8	8	$(8 - 8) = 0$	0
Gallagher	9	9	$(9 - 9) = 0$	0
			sum of differences =	24

The formula for the Spearman rank order correlation is

$$r_s = 1 - \frac{6 \star \Sigma D^2}{n \star (n^2 - 1)}$$

In this formula, n is the number of events for which there are paired ranks. Employing our data, we may substitute the following numbers:

$$= 1 - \frac{6 \star 24}{9 \star (81 - 1)}$$

$$= 1 - \frac{144}{9 \star (80)}$$

$$= 1 - \frac{144}{720}$$

$$= 1 - .20$$

$$= .80, \text{ which is a "highly dependable" relationship}$$

(Continued)

TABLE 12.3 (Continued)

Example with Tied Ranks

Here are data for a study relating the rankings of salespeople and rankings of the amount of communication skills training received in which some people had the same number of hours of training.

Person	Ranking of Salesperson Ability X	Ranking of Amount of Communication Training Y
Manny	1	tied
Moe	2	for
Jack	3	first
Larry	4	7
Curly	5	5
Patty	6	6
Maxine	7	4
Laverne	8	tied for
Gallagher	9	eighth

To deal with tied ranks, one simply splits the difference among the tied ranks and assigns those values to all the tied ranks. Since three people are tied for first place (though they normally would receive ranks 1, 2, and 3), we give them the average of the three ranks (2 is the average of ranks 1, 2, and 3). The tie between ranks 8 and 9 is settled by giving each person an average rank of 8.5. Thus, we complete the computations as follows:

Person	Ranking of Salesperson Ability X	Ranking of Amount of Communication Training Y	Differences D	D^2
Manny	1	2	$(1 - 2) = -1$	1
Moe	2	2	$(2 - 2) = 0$	0
Jack	3	2	$(3 - 2) = 1$	1
Larry	4	7	$(4 - 7) = -3$	9
Curly	5	5	$(5 - 5) = 0$	0
Patty	6	6	$(6 - 6) = 0$	0
Maxine	7	4	$(7 - 4) = 3$	9
Laverne	8	8.5	$(8 - 8.5) = -.5$	.25
Gallagher	9	8.5	$(9 - 8.5) = .5$	.25
			sum of differences =	20.5

Thus,

$$r_s = 1 - \frac{6 \star \Sigma D^2}{n \star (n^2 - 1)}$$

$$= 1 - \frac{6 \star 20.5}{9 \star (81 - 1)}$$

$$= 1 - \frac{123}{9 \star (80)}$$

$$= 1 - \frac{123}{720}$$

$$= 1 - .17$$

$$= .83, \text{ which is a "highly dependable" relationship}$$

SUMMARY

Descriptive statistics are numbers that characterize information. Inferential statistics are tools that help researchers draw conclusions about the probable populations from which samples did or did not belong. Statisticians use the Greek alphabet to represent population parameters and the Roman alphabet when describing samples.

Measures of central tendency tell what is going on within sample groups or populations on the average. The arithmetic mean adds a set of scores and divides by the number of scores. The sample mean is an unbiased estimator of the population mean. The median is a score that appears in the middle of an ordered list of scores and separates one-half of the data from the other half. The mode is the most commonly occurring score. When data have two modes, they are called "bimodal." But if data have many modes, the mode may not meaningfully depict central tendency.

Measures of variability or dispersion tell how close to the mean the data are. The range is the difference between the highest and lowest scores in a data set. The variance is a measure of the average of squared differences of scores from the mean (we use the symbol s^2 to represent the variance of a sample and σ^2 to represent the variance of the population). The formulae for sample variance and standard deviation are different from population formulae so that unbiased estimators of population variance and standard deviation may be created. The standard deviation shows how far the average score deviates from the mean (s represents sample and σ population standard deviation).

Distributions of data often tend to be symmetrical around their averages, but sometimes it does not work that way. A distribution that is off-center is skewed. The measure of peakedness is called kurtosis. A very flat distribution is called platykurtic. A distribution with a peak that is neither very high nor very low is called mesokurtic. An extremely peaked distribution is called leptokurtic. The standard normal curve is a bell-shaped probability distribution that tells the expected value that would be obtained by sampling at random. Data distributions can form normal curves, but they cannot be "the standard normal curve" unless they meet the exact requirements for this special distribution (perfect centeredness and peakedness; median, mean, and mode equal to 0; standard deviation of 1). The areas under the standard normal curve are identified to reveal probabilities of drawing samples from one location on the distribution to another. Z scores permit representing scores from data as units under the standard normal curve. By looking at the standard normal curve, we can estimate whether such data could be found at random very frequently or very rarely if the distribution is normal and centered at its assumed mean.

A correlation is a measure of the coincidence of variables. Direct relationships mean that as one variable increases, the other variable also increases. An inverse relationship indicates that an increase in one variable corresponds to a decrease in the other (identified by negative signs). Correlation coefficients are not percentages. To know the percentage impact one variable has on another, the squared correlation coefficient (called a coefficient of determination) may be used. Sometimes relationships show curvilinear patterns since the best fit of a line to the data is not a straight line. The Pearson product moment correlation is suitable for situations in which *both* the independent and dependent variables (identified as X and Y, respectively, in most notation) are *interval* or *ratio* level measures. The Spearman rank order correlation is suitable when variables are measured on the ordinal level.

TERMS FOR REVIEW

descriptive statistics	mesokurtic
inferential statistics	leptokurtic
central tendency	standard normal curve
arithmetic mean	probability distribution
unbiased estimator	data distributions
median	z scores
mode	correlation
bimodal	direct relationship
range	inverse relationship
variance	coefficient of determination
standard deviation	outlier homoscedasticity
skewness	Pearson product moment
kurtosis	correlation
platykurtic	Spearman rank order correlation

JUST FOR THE SAKE OF ARGUMENT: A REVIEW

Look at the following questions and prepare your own answers to them. Look for the underlying assumptions.

1. What are the differences between descriptive and inferential statistics?

2. What is meant by an unbiased estimator? What use are unbiased estimators? What is an unbiased estimator of the population mean? What is an unbiased estimator of the population standard deviation?

3. How can you tell if you are presented with a population parameter or a sample statistic? What statistical notion seems most confusing?

4. What is the difference between the average and measures of central tendency?

5. If a friend asked you to explain what a standard deviation is, what would you say?

6. Is the standard normal curve a distribution of data? What type of distribution is it? What kinds of elements are represented in it? What features would a data distribution have to possess to be called a "standard normal distribution"?

ACTIVITIES TO PROBE FURTHER

Go to the website for this book and look for the Student Study Materials for Chapter 12.

1. Take the study quiz and print out your answers. (Make sure to review text materials before answering questions.)

2. Look at these data from a *sample:*

Person	Research Methods Final Grade (Measured as GPA Ranging from 0 to 4)	Reported Time Spent Studying for Final Exam (Hours Reported by Students)
1	4	20
2	3	20
3	0	8
4	2	9
5	2	15
6	2	15
7	3	16
8	0	3
9	1	5
10	3	10
11	1	8
12	2	6
13	2	7
14	0	8
15	0	3
16	3	11
17	4	17
18	1	8
19	2	9
20	3	12
21	3	14
22	3	7
23	1	6
24	2	5
25	3	8

	Final Grade	Time Spent Studying

a. For each variable in this *sample:*
   (1) What is the arithmetic mean? _____ _____
   (2) What is the mode? _____ _____
   (3) What is the median? _____ _____
   (4) What is the standard deviation? _____ _____
b. Compute the Pearson product moment correlation between the two variables.
   (1) What is the observed correlation between the final grade and time spent studying for the final exam? _____
   (2) What type of relationship is this one? _____
   (3) How may this correlation be interpreted verbally? _____

3. Watch television news for a week. How often were statistical pieces of information presented in numbers, in graphs, in both? Using a school grade (A through F), how would you rate the quality of interpretation you saw and heard?

4. Go to the website for this class, and follow the hyperlink to "Data Distributions Made Easy." Complete the exercise listed on this page and report the following:
   a. What effect was produced in the shape of the distribution when the mean was increased?
   b. What effect was produced in the shape of the distribution when the mean was decreased?

5. Go to the website for this book. Use the hyperlink to go to "NCA: How America Communicates." Use the hyperlink to the NCA website, and download the NCA.SAV file.

a. Go to the Web page for Chapter 12, and click on the hyperlink to "Computer Analysis with SPSS" or "Computer Analysis with Excel." There are two variables of interest to us: amount of education and comfort giving a public speech. The amount of education question is "Q18" and involved asking the respondents "What was the last level of education you have completed?" (responses range from 1 = less than high school graduate to 7 = Ph.D. or equivalent). The comfort giving a public speech question is "Q6speech" and asks "How comfortable do you feel giving a presentation or speech?" (responses range from 1 = not at all comfortable to 4 = very comfortable).

b. *If you wish to analyze data using SPSS,* follow these instructions.

(1) Start SPSS and load NCA.SAV. Following the instructions given in the Web page, complete a descriptive analysis of the data and a correlation.

(2) Some data definition will be required.

(a) Click on the "Variable View" tab at the bottom of the SPSS page and scroll down to variable "q6speech." Click on the cell in the "Type" column. We wish to treat this string variable as a numeric variable for data analysis. Click on the " . . . " button in this cell to produce the "Variable Type" dialog box. Select "Numeric" and click, "OK." Then go to the column for "Missing" and click on the " . . . " button to bring up the "Missing Values" dialog box. Select "Discrete missing values," enter 0 (zero) in the first cell, and click "OK" (the zero will have changed to .00, but the impact is the same).

(b) Scroll down to variable "q18," go to the column for "Missing," and click on the " . . . " button in this cell to bring up the "Missing Values" dialog box. Select "Discrete missing values," enter 8 in the first cell, and click "OK."

(3) To complete this descriptive output, click on the "Analyze" menu, and on subsequent menus that appear, click on "Descriptive Statistics" and then "Frequencies." In the dialog box titled "Frequencies," place "Q18" and "Q6speech" on the variable list. Click the "Statistics" button. In the "Frequencies: Statistics" dialog box, click on "Mean," "Std. deviation," and "S.E. mean." Click "Continue," and then click "OK" in the "Frequencies" dialog box.

(4) To complete the correlation, click on the "Analyze" menu, and on subsequent menus that appear, click on "Correlate" and then "Bivariate." In the dialog box titled "Bivariate Correlations," place "Q18" and "Q6speech" on the variable list. Click the "Statistics" button. In the "Frequencies: Statistics" dialog box, click on "Mean," "Std. deviation," and "S.E. mean." Click "Continue," and then click "OK" in the "Frequencies" dialog box.

(5) To complete this correlation, click on the "Analyze" menu, and on subsequent menus that appear, click on "Correlate" and then "Bivariate." In the dialog box titled "Bivariate Correlations," place "Q18" and "Q6speech" on the variable list and then click "OK."

c. *If you wish to analyze data using Excel,* follow these instructions.

(1) Start Excel and load NCA12.XLS. Following the instructions given in the Web page, complete a descriptive analysis of the data and a correlation.

(2) Some data definition will be required.

(a) Go to variable "Q6speech," find all cells that contain "###," and enter Delete from keyboard to replace these items with a blank.

(b) Go to variable "Q18," find all cells that contain "###", and enter Delete from keyboard to replace these items with a blank.

(3) To begin this descriptive output, click on the column label for "Q6speech." Click "Tools" menu, and on the subsequent menu that appears, click on "Data Analysis." In the dialog box titled "Data Analysis" select "Descriptive Statistics" and click "OK." In the dialog box for "Input Range," enter "$AW$2:" (AW is the column in which Q6speech appears, and row 2 is the first row of data) and AW1002 (the last row of data is row 1002). Check the box to indicate "Labels in First Row." Under "Output Options," click "Output Range" and enter "$AW$1005" (to indicate the location where output should be placed on the spreadsheet). Click "Summary Statistics" and "OK."

(4) To end this descriptive output, click on the column label for "Q18." Click "Tools" menu, and on the subsequent menu that appears, click on "Data Analysis." In the dialog box titled "Data Analysis," select "Descriptive Statistics" and click "OK." In the dialog box for "Descriptive Statistics," in the "Input Range" enter "$CP$2:" (CP is the column in which Q18 appears, and row 2 is the first row of data) and $CP$1002 (the last row of data is row 1002). Check the box to indicate "Labels in First Row." Under "Output Options," click "Output Range" and enter "$CP$1005" (to indicate the location where output should be placed on the spreadsheet). Click "Summary Statistics" and "OK."

(5) With Excel the two variables correlated must be in adjacent columns. (*Note:* this condition is not true if you use the "Insert . . . Functions" menu commands instead of the data analysis options under the "Tools" menu.)

   (a) Thus, we will have to move one variable. Click on the column label at AX (to the right of the "Q6speech" variable). Click on the "Insert" menu, and then click on "Column." Next, go to variable Q18 (now at column CQ). Click on the column label to highlight the column. Click on the "Edit" menu, and click on "Cut." Go to the new blank column at AX, and click on the column label to highlight the column. Click on the "Edit" menu, and click on "Paste."

   (b) Click on the "Tools" menu and then click on "Data Analysis." In the dialog box titled "Data Analysis," select "Correlation" and click "OK." In the dialog box for "Correlation," in the "Input Range" enter "$AW$2:" (AW is the column in which Q6speech appears, and row 2 is the first row of data) and $AX$1002 (the variable to be correlated is in column AX, and the last piece of data in it is found in row 1002). Check the box to indicate "Labels in First Row." Under "Output Options," click "Output Range" and enter "$AW$1005" (to indicate the location where output should be placed on the spreadsheet). Click on "OK."

(6) Print out your results and answer this question: What is the correlation between these variables? *Note:* Results were different for Excel because there are no separate ways to exclude missing values except manually (which was not done in this undertaking).

CHAPTER 13

Introductory Inferential Statistics I: Hypothesis Testing with Two Means

Statistics is a language that, through its own special symbols and grammar, takes the intangible facts of life and translates them into comprehensible meaning.

—PAUL D. LEEDY

CHAPTER OUTLINE

BEFORE WE GET STARTED . . .

Inferential statistics help researchers figure out how likely it is that their sample results may occur by chance. They play the odds by entering a distribution, such as the standard normal curve, to make comparisons. This chapter introduces some major tools researchers use with inferential statistics. This introduction stresses the logic behind using statistics to test hypotheses, with emphasis on making comparisons between means. The next chapter carries this notion further by looking at applications other than contrasting two means.

USING PROBABILITY DISTRIBUTIONS TO PLAY THE ODDS

To understand the process of statistical inference, we need to cover some basic ideas about ways that people can play the odds to figure out what to expect under normal circumstances. The section below examines what a probability distribution is and the ways in which it can be used.

Using the Statistics of Probability and Inference

The so-called law of averages implies to many of us that anything that can happen will (the Chicago Cubs may win the World Series, for instance—it could happen). But in the ordinary course of events, some things happen more often than others. So, it would be wise to figure the odds before concluding that you have found something striking or unusual in your research. Suppose you had a coin and tossed heads five times in a row. You might think that this pattern is very unusual among fair coins. So, is it a fair coin? If you want a certain answer, you are out of luck. But if you want to see how *probable* such a pattern is, you can get some answers. **Probability** concerns the frequency with which some events occur. You could figure the odds of getting five heads when tossing a fair coin five times. Here's how. The chance of getting heads on a single toss of a fair coin is fifty-fifty (excluding any chance of the coin landing on its edge).[1] Thus, the probability of getting heads is .5 (point five). What is the probability of getting heads if you toss a coin once, *and* heads again on the second toss, *and* heads again on the third toss, *and* heads again on the fourth toss, *and* heads again on the fifth toss? Compute it as

$$.5 \star .5 \star .5 \star .5 \star .5$$

> **Probability** the tendency or likelihood with which an event occurs in a population.

The probability of getting all heads in five tosses of a fair coin is .03125. Hence, the odds are only about three chances out of a hundred that you could get your observed pattern from a fair coin. So, what do we decide? It is always *possible* that the tosses reflect something that *can happen* approximately three times out of a hundred among fair coins—in which case, the run of heads would mean that only dumb luck or random occurrence is at work. But the odds of getting your run of heads by dumb luck from

---

[1]Do not use the word "percent" when you speak about probability: it drives statisticians nuts. In probability, we keep the decimal point. So, the probability of throwing heads is "point five," not "fifty percent."

random tosses of a fair coin are so *improbable* that the smart money would bet the coin probably is *not* fair. You could decide that your coin is *unlikely* to be fair since your sample findings could be observed very, very rarely among fair coins.

This example illustrates the basic idea behind playing the odds to see if observed relationships are unlikely to occur by chance. Statisticians have investigated probability theory in some detail and have found ways to identify the odds of getting different sorts of results for various sorts of data (see Chung, 1975; Feller, 1968, 1971). Without getting into the fine details, this chapter will discuss how to use probability distributions, the root of all statistical inference methods.

Using Probability Distributions

Distributions such as the standard normal curve can be useful to determine the probability of underlying patterns. They can describe what you might expect to see ordinarily. These distributions serve as **probability distributions** since they represent the theoretical patterns of expected sample data. This standard normal curve is very much like most data we have in much research. Despite limitations, we can often use the standard normal curve to help us figure the odds of different outcomes.

For instance, suppose that you were interested in studying communication apprehension of different sorts of students taking public speaking courses at your school. This variable typically is measured by the PRCA-24, which was presented in Chapter 4. This variable has been studied extensively, across a sample of more than 25,000 students from 52 different universities. The measure has a mean of 65.6 and a standard deviation of 15.3 (McCroskey, Beatty, Kearney, & Plax, 1985). These numbers may be taken as population values.

The department teaching the public speaking classes might have special materials to help students deal with extreme communication apprehension. Some programs have tapes to guide students through "systematic desensitization" sessions. Some programs refer students with debilitating communication apprehension to the university counseling center. If variation in communication apprehension is only random, however, the teachers may provide brief instruction on the subject and then rely on class speeches as ways to help students control their communication apprehension problems. You might notice that a class containing a large number of engineering students seems to be having particular difficulty making effective presentations. But how could you figure out if there is a need for setting aside time to use the special modules on communication apprehension? After all, just at random some students of public speaking might have high communication apprehension anyway. You could start by looking at the standard normal curve. You could say that if the communication apprehension levels of a class regularly fall in the top 5% of the area under the normal distribution of communication apprehension scores, you would decide that the class distribution of communication apprehension scores is not what is likely to be found in the population by chance—and you would help students get special training to deal with their fears.

You need to look at the standard normal curve table (Appendix A) to find the z value that covers 45% of the area from ground zero and leaves out the last 5% of the area. Figure 13.1 includes a portion of the z table. The z value of 1.645 corresponds

Probability distributions the theoretical patterns of expected "values of a random variable and of the probabilities of occurrence of these values" (Upton & Cook, 2002, p. 294).

using the standard normal curve to identify areas of unusual activity

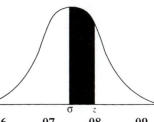

z	.00	.01	.02	.03	.04	.045	.05	.06	.07	.08	.09
1.6	.4452	.4463	.4474	.4484	.4495	.4500	.4505	.4515	.4525	.4535	.4545
1.7	.4554	.4564	.4573	.4582	.4591	.4695	.4599	.4608	.4616	.4625	.4633
1.8	.4641	.4649	.4656	.4664	.4671	.4675	.4678	.4686	.4693	.4699	.4706
1.9	.4713	.4719	.4726	.4732	.4738	.4741	.4744	.4750	.4756	.4761	.4767
2.0	.4772	.4778	.4783	.4788	.4793	.4796	.4798	.4803	.4808	.4812	.4817
2.1	.4821	.4826	.4830	.4834	.4834	.4840	.4842	.4646	.4850	.4854	.4857
2.2	.4861	.4864	.4868	.4871	.4875	.4876	.4878	.4881	.4884	.4887	.4890
2.3	.4893	.4896	.4898	.4901	.4904	.4905	.4906	.4909	.4911	.4913	.4916

FIGURE 13.1 SECTION FROM THE *Z* TABLE

to the location on the curve that includes 45% of the area from ground zero. Hence, only 5% of the area remains above that location.

using z scores

To figure out the minimum communication apprehension score that separates the top 5% of communication apprehension sufferers from the others, use the z score formula:

$$z = \frac{X - \mu}{\sigma}$$

To identify the minimum communication apprehension score that demands attention, we can solve the formula for X as follows:

$$X = \mu + (z \star \sigma)$$

The z value may be positive or negative. In our example, we suspect that the engineering students have *higher* communication apprehension than would be expected at random. Thus, our z value has a positive value. Putting the data into the formula, you have

$$X = 65.6 + (1.645 \star 15.3)$$
$$X = 65.6 + (25.1685)$$
$$X = 90.7685 \approx 91$$

Thus, any score of 91 or greater falls into the top 5% of communication apprehension scores. If the class of engineers regularly finds communication apprehension scores of 91 or above, there would be reason to ask for a special intervention because it appears that at random the assumed population could yield students with such communication apprehension levels among students no more than 5% of the time. Suppose you look at four engineering students from this class. The first has a score of 100, the second has a score of 95, the third has a score of 105, and the fourth scores 85. It appears that the first three students have communication apprehension levels that are very unlikely to be found if the class communication apprehension scores truly reflect no more than random variation around a population mean of 65.6. The first three students might feel justified in asking for the special materials on controlling communication apprehension. Indeed, if the instructor notes that a large portion of the class shares this difficulty, changes might be made in the course schedule to provide time for the special training materials. As you can see, the use of probability notions and disributions can help us play the odds very effectively.

REASONING IN STATISTICAL HYPOTHESIS TESTING

To test a statistical hypothesis, researchers need to have a formula and a distribution of the odds of finding different sorts of results.

Determining Statistical Hypotheses

statistical hypotheses test the improbability that research hypotheses are untrue

When you use tests of statistical significance, you *do not* find evidence that proves that your research hypothesis is true. Instead, you gather evidence that tests how improbable it would be to assume that your research hypothesis is untrue. This statement seems strange at first, but it is the way we handle such matters.

> **Hypothesis** "an expectation about events based on generalizations of the assumed relationship between variables" (Tuckman, 1999, p. 74).

To understand this idea, you need to recall the difference between the sorts of hypotheses used in research. A research **hypothesis** (H_1) is the prediction that researchers hope to examine. Arguing for this hypothesis requires the use of a null hypothesis that is capable of being judged improbable by use of statistical methods. A **null hypothesis** (H_0) states that there is no relationship between variables. This null hypothesis actually is tested directly by statistical tools:

null hypothesis used in testing: application to conclusions drawn

- ♦ If the null hypothesis is rejected, then the research hypothesis may be tenable and researchers conclude that a relationship exists among variables.

> **Null hypothesis** a statistical hypothesis that states that there is no relationship between variables.

- ♦ If the null hypothesis is not rejected (logically you cannot claim to "accept" a null hypothesis), then researchers make no claim that a relationship exists among variables.

Suppose we found a sample in which people who watch lots of television report being more fearful of violence than people who watch little TV. Does this sample prove that the amount of TV viewed is positively related to levels of fearfulness? The data are consistent with such a view, but how do you know for sure? Maybe you just got a weird sample: it happens sometimes even with randomization. Perhaps you have proof, or perhaps you don't. The fact is that when you look for positive proof, there is little way to find out if you are right, unless you are willing to wait a very long time for history to decide the matter.

So instead, for the sake of argument, you assume that there are no relationships among variables—and that the sample reflects only differences due to the vagaries of random sampling. In short, you temporarily assume the null hypothesis (H_0) is true. *Then,* you look at the data and ask, "How likely is it that we could find results such as we observed in our samples if no relationships existed?"

using probabilities to decide to reject the null hypothesis

- ♦ If finding results such as yours is *quite probable* when sampling from a population in which no relationships exist, you agree to continue assuming that any differences are just random.

- ♦ If it is very *improbable* that you could find results such as yours by sampling from a population in which no relationships exist, you reject the assumption that any differences are just random.

This reasoning is a clever way to help us decide whether to reject null hypotheses.[2] In short, we assume that nothing much is going on, and then we gather data that make continuing that assumption unreasonable or improbable. Put another way, researchers collect data that show that "nothing" probably "is *not*" what's going on.

Decisions in Testing Statistical Hypotheses

To make decisions based on probability, rather than intuition, researchers rely on probability distributions that presume no relationships. Then, researchers make decisions about their samples based on comparisons with those distributions.

Finding Unusual Occurrences

Researchers often look at distributions and isolate unusual patterns, or unlikely events. In communication research it is typical to state that a pattern or event is unusual or improbable if it could be found at random only 5% of the time. This statement corresponds to a probability of .05 for finding such results by random sampling error alone. Finding such results will lead us to conclude that our sample probably *does not* come from a population of events in which no relationships exist among variables (this fact is the reason for calling these tools "inferential statistics").

unusual events usually identified if probability of occurrence by chance is .05 or lower

Returning to the example involving the communication apprehension levels of a group of engineering students in public speaking, suppose you want to do a serious study by random-sampling 36 engineering students enrolled in sections of the public

---

[2]This reasoning method was not invented by statisticians. Thomas Aquinas used this method to argue for the existence of God. In *He Who Is,* Aquinas asked, "What would the world look like if God did not exist?" Then he concluded that the world was inconsistent with those explanations, leading to support for his claims that God exists. The application to scientific inquiry predates Aquinas. Aristotle explained how researchers reject chance as an explanation: "If then, it is agreed that things are either the result of coincidence or for an end, and these cannot be the result of coincidence or spontaneity, it follows that they must be for an end" (*Physics*).

SPECIAL DISCUSSION 13-1

DETERMINISM VERSUS PROBABILITY

There is a philosophical glitch that researchers often have to face. If they believe that predictable patterns of human behavior can be identified, doesn't this fact mean that they are presuming that human behavior is not the result of free will but the product of some predetermined pattern? Though this concept can neither be proved nor disproved, the notion of determinism means that "the general course of events is determined by structures deemed to be fundamental" (Bothamley, 1993, p. 144), and thus, "any event whatsoever is an instance of some law of nature" (Urmson & Ree, 1989, p. 78). The good news is that this approach implies that research can be very productive since if every event has a cause, the determined patterns can be unearthed by serious inquiry. The bad news is that it implies that none of us really has free will or responsibility (a position none of us really accepts). Yet, if we reject determinism, we seem to be rejecting a presupposition of science.

How do we deal with this philosophical problem? We could embrace notions developed from the concept of probability. First, determinism does not mean that we must accept the prediction of any single event from any starting point with absolutely no margin for error. Relationships are found with high degrees of probability. Of course, nobody claims to predict individual acts, but groups of acts begin to form predictable patterns. What is determined is that such probabilities exist (along with certain indeterminacies), but the degrees of probability are matters we can find through our research. Second, we may recognize that relationships between causes and effects are very complicated. Thus, we should not expect to find that one single cause can be tapped to predict any complicated or interesting effects. Thus, for practical purposes, even if determinism holds, you will seem to find enough "exceptions to the rules" to keep things interesting in your own research. It should be noted, however, that these approaches are a response to determinism, but they are not—and cannot be—a refutation of it.

Another view of the matter attempts to respond to determinism by viewing communication as a series of voluntary choices. Since determinism does not apply to volition, it might be said that studying volitional choices people make (such as communication behaviors) means that determinism is not an issue. But how can we expect to discover relationships if only volition is at work? We may say that people *choose to behave* in ways that are *capable of prediction* from significant antecedent variables (at least, more often than not). Thus, communication patterns may be found. Before we begin to think the issue is settled, however, we might ask another question: *Why* do people choose to communicate in ways that are capable of prediction from significant antecedent variables? Could the answer be that such apparent choices actually are predetermined?

speaking class. You suspect that engineering students have higher mean communication apprehension scores than found in the population. You could use the standard normal curve by slicing off a point of the distribution that separates the top 5% of communication apprehension scores from the rest. So, you could divide up the normal curve as shown by Figure 13.2. The last 5% shaded in Figure 13.2 is called the

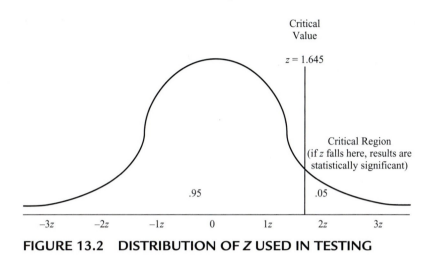

FIGURE 13.2   DISTRIBUTION OF *Z* USED IN TESTING

critical region since if your test statistic falls in that zone, you can claim to have found a "statistically significant difference." A **statistically significant difference or relationship** is one that is beyond what might be expected to occur by chance alone. Results that place you in the critical region will cause you to reject the null hypothesis. If our results do not place us in the critical region, we will not reject the null hypothesis. The line that divides the critical region from the rest of the distribution is called the **critical value.** Here is the key: researchers want to find statistics that are equal to or beyond the critical value on the distribution. Test statistics that do not reach this point lead the researcher *not* to reject the null hypothesis. On Figure 13.2, the critical region is shaded. The critical value is 1.645.

You might compute a communication apprehension mean of 75 from the 36 engineering students. You could enter the *z* distribution to compare the means of your two groups using the *z* formula:

$$z = \frac{\overline{X} - \mu}{\sigma}$$

But there is a slight problem. The new formula compares a couple of *means,* but divides these differences by a σ based on *raw scores.* That's like playing basketball on a football field. You have to put the measures on the same playing field if you want to divide like terms. The difference between *means* should be divided by a standard deviation *of means.* You could go out and complete a big study to find out the size of the standard deviation of a bunch of means—but who's got time? There is another way around it. The central limit theorem (see Special Discussion 13-2) shows that the standard deviation of a sampling distribution of means can be found by dividing the standard deviation of raw scores by the square root of the number of events to compute the standard deviation. By the way, you should know that the standard deviation of a distribution of means is often called the **standard error of the mean.** Yet, you *should not* think "standard error" refers to mistakes. Whenever a standard

Critical region in statistical significance testing, the portion of the probability distribution that would cause rejection of the null hypothesis if it were the area in which the test statistic fell.

Statistically significant difference or relationship as a result of a test of statistical significance, finding a relationship or effect size that is unlikely to have been found from random sampling error if the null hypothesis were true.

adaptations to standard deviation required to use z when comparing means

Critical value in statistical significance testing, the line that divides the critical region from the rest of the probability distribution.

Standard error of the mean the standard deviation of a distribution of means.

Standard error the standard deviation of a distribution of elements other than raw scores.

deviation is based on measures other than raw scores, it is called the **standard error** of something—for example, standard error of the variance (for distributions of variances), standard error of the range (for distributions of ranges), and standard error of estimate (for distributions of predicted values). When you apply the standard deviation of the means as the key term, the resulting z formula takes this form:

$$z = \frac{\overline{X} - \mu}{\sigma_{\bar{x}}} \quad \text{or} \quad z = \frac{\overline{X} - \mu}{\sigma/\sqrt{n}}$$

Now, you can compute the z value to see if the resulting test statistic places us in the top 5% of the area under that standard normal curve. If so, you can conclude that the sample of 36 engineering students probably is *not* from the historical population defined as having a mean of 65.6 and a standard deviation of 15.3.

Run the numbers and you will find:

$$z = \frac{\overline{X} - \mu}{\sigma/\sqrt{n}}$$
$$= \frac{75 - 65.6}{15.3/\sqrt{36}}$$
$$= \frac{9.4}{15.3/6}$$
$$= \frac{9.4}{2.55}$$
$$= 3.6863$$

This z value places the test statistic in the top 5% of all differences between population and sample means. Hence, a difference such as that observed between the communication apprehension mean of the engineering students and the population communication apprehension mean could be found no more than 5% of the time if there really were no difference between the sample and population mean. Hence, you would conclude that the engineering students have higher communication apprehension than the general population.

Choice and Errors in Testing Statistical Hypotheses

using the decision table to identify errors and risks in hypothesis testing

Researchers look at test statistics—such as z in our examples so far—and decide whether to reject the null hypothesis. This fact creates some interesting possibilities for the researcher, which are illustrated on Table 13.1. Each row indicates the decision the researcher makes based on available sample statistics—either to reject or not to reject the null hypothesis. The columns show the reality of the matter. Of course, if you knew this reality, you would not have to complete a study. But at the time the research is completed, the researcher has only the sample data to go on.

Suppose that you gather data that lead you to reject the null hypothesis (the first row). If the null hypothesis truly is false, you have made a correct decision. It is also possible for researchers to reject the null hypothesis when, in reality, the null hypothesis is true.

TABLE 13.1   DECISION TABLE

Decision Based on Statistical Results	Actual Situation (Unknown)	
	H_0 **is false**	H_0 **is true**
Reject H_0	Correct decision	Type I error
Do not reject H_0	Type II error	Correct decision

A **Type I error** occurs when sampling error gives the researcher samples that represent unusual (but randomly occurring) events—and the researcher incorrectly rejects the null hypothesis. At the time a study is completed, you do not know whether this mistake has been made, but you can tell the *chances* that this error might be made. The probability of incorrectly rejecting the null hypothesis is called **alpha risk** (α risk). Alpha risk is announced by the researcher at the beginning of a study for all the world to see. The alpha level determines how much area under a distribution is in the critical region. For alpha risk of .05, 5% of the distribution is in the critical region. For alpha risk of .01, only 1% of the distribution is established as the critical region.

It is also possible that you could fail to reject the null hypothesis (fail to claim that a nonrandom relationship exists). As the second row in Table 13.1 shows, a researcher who fails to reject the null hypothesis when, in fact, there is a relationship in the population commits a **Type II error,**[3] which means that researchers have failed to detect a relationship that is present. Though we cannot tell in advance if a Type II error has been made, the chances of such an error can be identified. This probability is called **beta risk** (β risk) and is usually associated with a study's use of samples that may not be large enough to permit existent relationships to cast a shadow. **Power** of a statistical test is the probability of rejecting the null hypothesis correctly.

Type I error incorrectly rejecting the null hypothesis.

Alpha (α) risk the probability of committing Type I error by incorrectly rejecting the null hypothesis.

Type II error incorrectly failing to reject the null hypothesis and failing to detect a relationship that is present.

Beta (β) risk the probability of committing Type II error by incorrectly failing to reject the null hypothesis.

The Process of Examining Statistical Hypotheses

There are four major steps in testing statistical hypotheses. These steps will be considered in the order that researchers are supposed to follow them.

steps in testing statistical hypotheses

1. Determining a Decision Rule for Rejecting Null Hypotheses

Before researchers collect data, they must decide the levels of alpha risk and beta risk. As a matter of convention—and *only* as a matter of convention—researchers

Power a statistical test's probability of rejecting the null hypothesis correctly.

---

[3]The reason for these Type I and Type II labels stems from Aristotle's remark: "To say about that which is true, that it is false, is false. To say about that which is untrue, that it is true, is false. The first is an error of the first type. The second is an error of the second type."

RESEARCHERS IN THE FIELD: ANITA VANGELISTI

Anita Vangelisti is an international authority in the area of family and interpersonal communication. She is a professor of communication studies at the University of Texas at Austin, the same university where she received a Ph.D., following earning a bachelor's and master's degree at the University of Washington. She teaches courses in the areas of communication, cognition, and emotion; family communication; interaction analysis; quantitative research methods; and communication in personal relationships. She has authored or coauthored five books in interpersonal and family communication, edited or coedited five more, and authored or coauthored over 60 articles and chapters in scholarly books. She has received the Bernard J. Brommel Award for Outstanding Scholarship or Distinguished Service in Family Communication and the Franklin H. Knower Article Award, both sponsored by divisions of the National Communication Association. Those who work with her know her as a rigorous scholar and a warm and supportive teacher.

♦ *What drew you into our field?*
In high school and college, I was very interested in psychology and human development. I was lucky enough to take a course on interpersonal communication from Lee Buxton and then another one from John Stewart (both of whom were at the University of Washington at the time). What I learned from those two professors convinced me that communication in personal relationships is central to individuals' well-being and I wanted to learn more about that.

♦ *When you were honored by the National Communication Association by receiving its 2004 Bernard J. Brommel Award for Outstanding Scholarship or Distinguished Service in Family Communication, one of the nominators wrote, "I cannot envision any graduate-level course in family communication . . . that wouldn't include an extensive number of her research articles or chapters. And I can't imagine any textbook on family communication that isn't filled with citations to her research." That kind of influence must be gratifying, but what have you hoped that your research would accomplish?*
I hope that my research helps people to understand some of the communication problems and challenges that they experience and that this increased understanding will equip them to deal with those problems and challenges more effectively.

♦ *What was it about family communication that influenced you to focus so much of your energy in this area?*
I believe that the way family members interact profoundly influences people's lives. The first relationships that most of us form are with family members, and these relationships often are the most long-lasting ones that we will have. Our family members show us how to communicate—they teach us how to get our needs met, how and when to express our emotions, and how to approach and interact with others. Both the foundational nature of family relationships and their duration make their impact particularly strong.

♦ *What do you think is the most exciting future direction for the field's research?*
A lot of good research is being conducted on a number of different topics. I think the most exciting development in the field over the past few years is the

integration of solid theoretical arguments and sophisticated methods to tackle practical communication problems.

♦ *What one or two things do you think students should know to deal successfully with communication research either as a consumer or as a researcher?*

They should know that the research they see presented in the media often is oversimplified. People in the media have limited time and space to describe research findings and, as a consequence, they often leave out details that affect the way studies should be interpreted. Becoming a careful consumer of research is important. Students need to consider the methods used in research, the limitations of those methods, and the claims that actually are made by researchers before making any conclusions about findings that they hear or read about.

Students also should understand that building a body of research is a process and that any given study represents only a small part of that larger process. Research is conducted by people who often have great passion for what they study—they are seeking answers to questions that they believe are important. Even though the questions they ask in any particular study represent a small part of a larger process, every study they conduct and each question they ask has the potential to increase our understanding.

♦ *What advice would you give students who might be considering becoming communication researchers?*

I would suggest that students interested in becoming communication researchers begin their careers by finding a general topic or issue that inspires them—something that makes them want to get up in the morning—and then that they find professors and other mentors who can guide them in the process of refining their interests. Some mentors may help them deal directly with the topic or issues they plan to study, others may help them learn how to think in theoretical terms, others may give them the methodological tools they need to conduct their research, and still others may help them understand the practical aspects of academic life. There are a lot of people out there who are willing to work with students who are excited about and dedicated to their studies—take advantage of what those people have to offer.

---

usually set alpha risk at .05, often just announcing "alpha was set at .05" in their description of the statistical analyses. This statement sets a decision rule:

♦ If observed results could have been found by chance no more than 5 times out of 100, researchers will claim to have found real (nonrandom) differences.

♦ If observed results could have been found by chance *more* than 5 times out of 100, researchers will *not* claim to have found real (nonrandom) relationships.

Applying these decision rules, when differences are claimed, researchers report finding "statistically significant" differences. The term "statistical significance" does not mean that an important relationship has been found, but just that such results are unlikely to be due to chance alone.

statistical significance does not mean importance

There are implications for selecting risk levels. By choosing an alpha risk of .05 researchers are telling others that 5 times out of 100, they *will* claim differences

controlling alpha risk and beta risk

SPECIAL DISCUSSION 13-2

THE CENTRAL LIMIT THEOREM

Data distributions in communication studies sometimes show abnormalities. Curiously though, a distribution of means does not work that way. This surprising finding is called the *central limit theorem* and states that a sampling distribution of means tends toward normal distribution with increased sample size regardless of the shape of the parent population. If you reached into a population and got a sample of 2 events and computed a mean for it, and then did it again, and again, and again (say 30 or 40 times), you could construct a histogram of these means. The distribution would tend to look pretty much like the underlying data—flaws and all. Suppose, instead, you reached into a population and repeatedly sampled 20 events and computed means. The distribution would tend toward a normal distribution. The bigger the sample gets, the more normal the distribution of means gets. This pattern is beyond common sense, but it is a regular characteristic of distributions of means.

Because of the central limit theorem, studies comparing means can safely presume underlying normal distributions. Furthermore, the average of a distribution of means ought to come closer to identifying the population mean than any other estimation. As such, the central limit theorem is the backbone of the so-called "law of large numbers." A useful application of the central limit theorem is its expression of the relationship between the standard deviations of means and of raw scores (see proof for this statement in Glass & Hopkins, 1984, pp. 188–191):

$$\sigma_{\bar{x}} \; = \; \frac{\sigma}{\sqrt{n}}$$

This statement is used in formulae employed in tests that compare means.

---

when it really is just sampling error playing a joke on them. This ratio works out to 1 test out of every 20 turning out to be "significant" by sampling error alone. Thus, researchers may replicate their studies to see if a pattern of results is stable. Beta risk is addressed by researchers' attempts to reduce background variation and by drawing sufficiently large samples.

2. Computing the Test Statistic

Test statistic in statistical hypothesis testing, a number computed from a statistical formula, "which is a function of the observations in a random sample" (Upton & Cook, 2002, p. 165).

A **test statistic** is a number computed from a statistical formula to test the statistical hypothesis. So far, we have used the z statistic, but other formulae are also used.

3. Finding the Critical Value

To find the critical region, the researcher must find the portion of the distribution corresponding to alpha risk. For most distributions, tables are available showing the critical value at which this critical region begins. When using a directional hypothesis, we are interested in only one side of the distribution. Any other location on the distribution (even the extreme opposite tail) would not support the research hypothesis. Figure 13.3 shows how this critical region is distinguished in one-tailed and

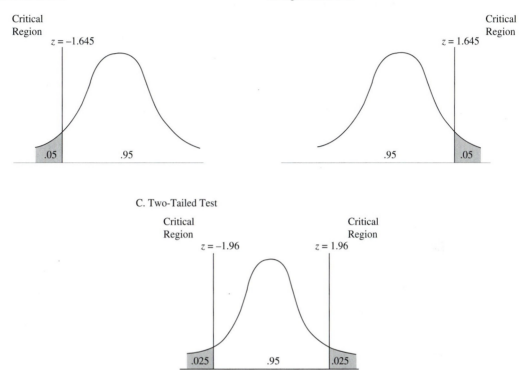

FIGURE 13.3   USING DISTRIBUTIONS FOR ONE-TAILED VERSUS TWO-TAILED TESTS

two-tailed tests when using the standard normal curve. Figure 13.3A shows a left-tailed test, and Figure 13.3B shows a right-tailed test. These tests are called **one-tailed tests** since the critical region lies on only one side of a two-tailed distribution. The relevant side of the distribution is determined by the way the research hypothesis is stated. A directional hypothesis might state:

> H_1: The current average amount of time children watch television is greater than the average amount of time children watched television in 2005.

Expressed symbolically, this hypothesis states:

$$H_1: \mu_{current} > \mu_{amount\ in\ 2005}$$

The direction sign lets us know that we have a right-tailed test. To support this hypothesis, the difference must be significant *and* in the predicted direction.

A nondirectional hypothesis predicts *some* difference regardless of the direction. As Figure 13.3C shows, the alpha risk must be divided equally for both sides of the distribution. For this reason, these tests are called **two-tailed tests** since the last 2.5% on the left tail *and* the last 2.5% on the right tail of the distribution are isolated as the critical

One-tailed test a test of a one-tailed or directional material hypothesis that states the form of predicted differences and requires using a critical range on one side of a probability distribution.

Two-tailed test a test of a two-tailed or nondirectional material hypothesis that does not state the form of predicted differences and requires using a critical range on both sides of a probability distribution.

regions that add up to the total alpha risk of .05. As you can see, for the directional hypothesis, the critical region begins closer to the center of the distribution than it does for nondirectional hypotheses. Thus, it should be easiest to find statistically significant differences if researchers know enough to make directional predictions.

4. Rejecting or Failing to Reject the Null Hypothesis

If a test statistic falls in the critical region, the null hypothesis is rejected. Sometimes researchers try to get fancy about this rather simple and mechanical step. For instance, after setting alpha risk at .05, they might observe that their test statistic placed them in the last 1% of the distribution, and they will report a statistically significant difference at the .01 level. This step—though common—is unnecessary since the null hypothesis died as soon as the critical region was entered. It cannot be killed again after it has been rejected.

COMPARISONS OF TWO MEANS: THE *t* TEST

Parametric tests
statistical significance tests that make assumptions about populations from which the data were drawn.

development of the t *test*

Among the tools to examine how often observed results could have been found by chance alone are **parametric tests,** which make assumptions about populations from which the data were drawn. This section considers a family of parametric tests called the *t* test.

   The *t* test is used to compare observed means with those normally expected from a distribution of means. In short, the *t* test compares means to each other to check for statistical significance. This test was developed by William S. Gosset, who was a chemist for Guinness Stout Malt Liquor (the same people who publish the famous book of world records). He had to control the quality of the production, but he was not permitted to take large samples. So, he designed a distribution to describe what happens to distributions of means as sample sizes get smaller and smaller. Gosset also developed a formula to permit researchers to compare one mean with another. Because he was concerned with comparing *two* means, he called this test the *t* test, and the distribution of means the *t* distribution. It is easy to remember: it is called the *t* test because it means "*t* for two and two for *t*."[4] When Gosset made his discovery in 1908, Guinness had a policy forbidding employees to publish under their own names. So, he used the pen name "Student"—and to this day, the method is often called the "Student's *t* test" (Student, 1908).

Forms of the t Test

Four major applications of the *t* test are illustrated here with a formula for each and an example of its use in a little communication study.

---

[4]The song "Tea for Two" had nothing to do with Gosset's labeling. The song was written for a 1926 musical called *No, No, Nanette*.

SPECIAL DISCUSSION 13-3

ASSUMPTIONS UNDERLYING PARAMETRIC TESTS

To use parametric statistical significance tests, researchers assume four things about the populations from which the samples were drawn:

1. Randomization in selecting events and/or assigning events drawn from populations.
2. Measurement of the dependent variable on an interval or ratio level.
3. Underlying normal distribution of events in a population.
4. Homogeneous variances of the groups compared (this homogeneity requirement means that any differences in variances should be within the limits of sampling error).

What happens if we do not meet these assumptions? The first two assumptions are fairly firm. The remaining assumptions are the ones that you may wonder about.

Research indicates that the impact of nonnormal distributions is rarely significant. Studies (Boneau, 1960; Hsu & Feldt, 1969) show that if sample sizes are 5 or below, the combination of a normal and skewed distribution and a rectangular and a skewed distribution can result in studies rejecting more null hypotheses than the announced alpha. Yet, when sample sizes are at least 15 events in each group, statisticians have found that the actual proportion of Type I errors is within 1% of the announced alpha risk—close enough to make this assumption relatively unimportant for significance testing.

If the variances are not homogenous, effects on Type I errors are insignificant if researchers keep sample sizes equal—or at least within a 4 to 5 ratio of each other (Glass, Peckham, & Sanders, 1972). If sample sizes are not equal, the true Type I error will be *less* than the announced alpha risk if the large variance comes from the large sample. If the large variance comes from the small sample, the true Type I error will be *greater* than the announced alpha risk. The bottom line is that the last two assumptions of parametric tests are not practical concerns in studies with roughly equal sample sizes.

The effects of unequal variances may reveal other interesting things for researchers. Unequal variances can stem from two families of causes: *ceiling or floor effects* in the data or *subjects by treatments interactions*. Ceiling or floor effects occur when scores are so high (or so low) in samples that the data are "crunched up" (or down) near the end of the measurement range. Thus, variances for these samples are artificially reduced since they do not have the full room to spread. If ceiling or floor effects exist (measured by correlating cell means and variances with each other), the amount of explained variation made by the researcher is understated. Thus, these effects understate the size of relationships observed. The second family of unequal variances is caused by subjects by treatments interaction, which means that at least one additional variable uncontrolled by the researcher introduced systematic variation influencing subjects in some conditions more than others. Thus, subjects by treatments interactions mean that researchers' studies have blown up in their faces. The researchers must reconsider their designs to find the additional variables that should be included in the study. Obviously, researchers who find unequal variances would prefer ceiling or floor effects as the explanation—otherwise, they know that they have missed including at least one other significant moderating variable.

One-sample t Test

This "classic" form of the *t* test involves examining when a new sample mean differs from a known population mean (μ) under conditions when the population standard deviation is unavailable. This application uses the following formula:

$$t = \frac{\overline{X} - \mu}{s / \sqrt{n}}$$

You may notice that this formula looks somewhat familiar. It is. In our example dealing with communication apprehension, we used the standard normal curve (z) to help compare a mean with a standard. Aside from the use of a different distribution, the only difference between that formula and this one is that we use the sample standard deviation (s) instead of sigma (σ). Thus, *t* really is a logical extension of the standard normal curve.

computing degrees of freedom (number of events minus number of new parameters estimated from samples)

On the *t* table (Appendix B) there are many rows, corresponding to different "degrees of freedom" (found in the first column). Degrees of freedom are the number of events in a study minus the number of population parameters estimated from samples. Thus, for all *t* tests, one need only look at the formula to determine degrees of freedom. For the **one-sample t test,** you can see that only *one* new sample mean is computed. Thus, degrees of freedom here are the number of events in the study minus one.

One-sample *t* test an application of the *t* test that examines when a new sample mean differs from a known population mean under conditions when the population standard deviation is unavailable.

Table 13.2 shows an example in which the null hypothesis is rejected after using the one-sample *t* test. This method is useful to learn if samples adequately identify the population means. In addition, if researchers find differences between population and sample means, they may conclude that the new sample probably does not come from the same population—or that the population is no longer described accurately by the presumed parameters. In short, the population may have changed from its previous form, perhaps inviting corrective action.

t Test for Independent Samples

Independent samples *t* test an application of the *t* test that compares the means of two sample groups.

The **independent samples t test** is probably the most frequently used *t* test in communication research. We often wish to compare two sample groups to each other (one of which is often a control or current condition). These samples are independent because the events are not matched in advance, and there is no sort of before-and-after scoring of the samples.

The conceptual test statistic for this *t* test is

$$t = \frac{\overline{X} - \overline{X}}{s_{\text{diff}}}$$

differences from one-sample t test

The formula still looks like the previous formula, doesn't it? The population mean has been replaced by another sample (often a control group mean). Otherwise, the only difference is that the standard deviation of means has been replaced by the standard deviation of the differences between means (s_{diff}). The term s_{diff} is sometimes called the "standard error of the difference," although, as you know, it has nothing whatsoever to do with making mistakes. To compute the standard deviation of the differences between means, a couple of steps should be explained.

standard error of the difference

TABLE 13.2   THE ONE-SAMPLE t TEST

EXAMPLE

Twenty-five people are sampled from a Communication Research Methods class to find their level of "math anxiety" on a standardized measure, which has a known population mean of 50 for college students. The communication students produced a mean of 58 and a standard deviation of 20. Do the communication students have a higher level of math anxiety than the known population of college students? With alpha risk set at .05, test the null hypothesis that the mean of the new sample is not different from the population mean of 50:

H_0: μ indicated by new sample $= 50$

The degrees of freedom for this test are $n - 1$; 24 in this case.
Critical t value (for a one-tailed test) $= 1.71$.

COMPUTING THE TEST STATISTIC

$$t = \frac{\overline{X} - \mu}{s/\sqrt{n}}$$

$$t = \frac{58 - 50}{20 / \sqrt{25}}$$

$$t = \frac{8}{20/5}$$

$$t = \frac{8}{4}$$

$$t = 2$$

Since the t statistic ($t = 2$) was greater than the critical value (1.71), the null hypothesis was rejected. Thus, communication students were found to have higher levels of math anxiety than the general population of students.

Effect size computation:

$$r = \sqrt{\frac{t^2}{t^2 + \text{degrees of freedom}}}$$

$$r = \sqrt{\frac{4}{4 + 24}}$$

$$r = \sqrt{.14}$$

$$r = .37, \text{ a slight relationship}$$

SPECIAL DISCUSSION 13-4

A QUESTION OF ETHICS:
A CODE OF STATISTICAL REPORTING

Statistics are often treated the same way as a surgeon's scalpel: as a tool that is neither moral nor immoral. Yet, researchers who use statistical tools know that the respect statistics hold in society creates a need for individuals to practice ethical use of statistical analyses. The American Statistical Association adopted its Ethical Guidelines for Statistical Practice on August 7, 1999, to help encourage "ethical and effective statistical work in morally conducive working environments [and also] . . . to assist students in learning to perform statistical work responsibly" (American Statistical Association, 1999, ¶ 1). Since statistics are used in so many scientific, governmental, economic, and social applications, researchers were encouraged to use their statistics as they would expect such things to be practiced by good professional citizens.

In reporting results, among other things, researchers are required to do the following:

2. Report statistical and substantive assumptions made in the study. . . .

5. Account for all data considered in a study and explain the sample(s) actually used.

6. Report the sources and assessed adequacy of the data.

7. Report the data cleaning and screening procedures used, including any imputation.

8. Clearly and fully report the steps taken to guard validity. Address the suitability of the analytic methods and their inherent assumptions relative to the circumstances of the specific study. Identify the computer routines used to implement the analytic methods.

9. Where appropriate, address potential confounding variables not included in the study.

10. In publications or testimony, identify the ultimate financial sponsor of the study, the stated purpose, and the intended use of the study results.

11. When reporting analyses of volunteer data or other data not representative of a defined population, include appropriate disclaimers.

12. Report the limits of statistical inference of the study and possible sources of error. For example, disclose any significant failure to follow through fully on an agreed sampling or analytic plan and explain any resulting adverse consequences.

13. Share data used in published studies to aid peer review and replication, but exercise due caution to protect proprietary and confidential data, including all data which might inappropriately reveal respondent identities.

14. As appropriate, promptly and publicly correct any errors discovered after publication.

15. Write with consideration of the intended audience. (For the general public, convey the scope, relevance, and conclusions of a study without technical distractions. For the professional literature, strive to answer the questions likely to occur to your peers.)

These guidelines suggest that researchers reporting statistical analyses are obligated to make full reports and to make sure that reasonable qualifications, limitations, and contrary interpretations are not ignored. Rather than assuming that what the reader does not know cannot hurt, the researcher is obligated to communicate those limitations as part of a complete report. If such matters are omitted from the final report, the problem is not just sloppy research writing; the problem is an ethical breach.

You will remember that a standard deviation of means can be computed by taking the standard deviation of raw scores used to compute a mean and dividing it by the square root of the number of events, such as

$$s_{\bar{x}} = \frac{s}{\sqrt{n}}$$

But when you have two samples, you have more than one standard deviation and more than one sample size. What can you do? You could start by averaging together the standard deviations from each group to get a **pooled standard deviation** (abbreviated s_p). Yet, mathematically, you cannot average the standard deviations, since that arrangement would presume an ordered effect that does not apply here: instead, we must average the variances (s^2) and then take the square root of that average:

Pooled standard deviation (s_p) the square root of the average of variances in subgroups involved in comparisons.

$$s_p = \sqrt{\text{average of variances}} = \left[(s^2 + s^2)/2 \right]$$

This formula can be used if sample sizes are equal in both groups. If the sample sizes are not the same, a slightly longer formula is used:

$$s_p = \sqrt{\frac{(n-1)\,s^2 + (n-1)\,s^2}{(n-1) + (n-1)}}$$

Regardless of computation, the logic is the same. We have a pooled standard deviation created from both samples.

According to the original formula, you might expect to divide this pooled standard deviation by the number of events in the sample. But since you have two samples, you must make an adjustment. Instead of *dividing* the pooled standard deviation of the sample groups by $\sqrt{n}$, we could accomplish the same thing by *multiplying* by the pooled standard deviation as follows:

$$s_p \star \sqrt{\frac{1}{n} + \frac{1}{n}}$$

This pattern yields a test statistic formula, found on Table 13.3. This example illustrates the case with unequal sample sizes—you may use the described shortcut if you have equal sample sizes in the compared groups.

For the *t* test for independent samples, degrees of freedom are the number of events in the total of the samples minus two (the number of new means that have been computed to estimate population parameters).

degrees of freedom for t *test for independent samples*

t Test for Dependent Samples

Sometimes also called the "*t* test for correlated groups," the **dependent samples *t* test** may be used in situations where subjects are matched or sampled twice. For instance, to find the impact of coupon advertising on grocery purchases, you could ask a sample of people to report the average amount spent on certain groceries during a month. Then, after exposing those same people to a newspaper advertising campaign using discount

Dependent samples *t* test an application of the *t* test that compares the means of two sample groups in which subjects are matched or sampled twice.

TABLE 13.3 *t* TEST FOR INDEPENDENT SAMPLES

EXAMPLE

A random sample of 7 students read a message that featured colored printing of the headline title. A sample of 9 students in a control condition read the same message with a standard black headline. Comprehension of the information was rated on a 10-item true-false test. The mean comprehension score for the experimental condition was 8 (standard deviation of 1; variance = 1). The mean comprehension score for the control group was 6 (standard deviation of 2; variance = 4).

With alpha risk set at .05, test the null hypothesis that the mean of the color headline group is significantly different from the mean of the noncolor headline group:

$H_0: \mu_{color\ headline} = \mu_{standard\ headline}$

The degrees of freedom for this test are $n - 2$ or 14.
Critical *t* value (for a one-tailed test) = 1.76.

COMPUTING THE TEST STATISTIC

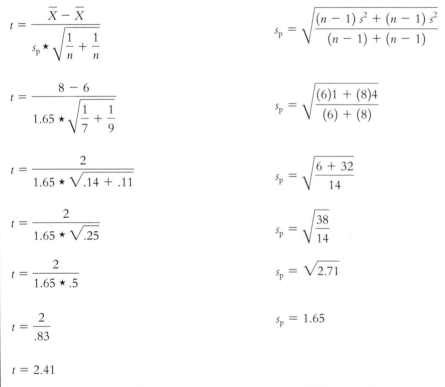

$$t = \frac{\overline{X} - \overline{X}}{s_p \star \sqrt{\dfrac{1}{n} + \dfrac{1}{n}}}$$

$$s_p = \sqrt{\frac{(n-1)\,s^2 + (n-1)\,s^2}{(n-1) + (n-1)}}$$

$$t = \frac{8 - 6}{1.65 \star \sqrt{\dfrac{1}{7} + \dfrac{1}{9}}}$$

$$s_p = \sqrt{\frac{(6)1 + (8)4}{(6) + (8)}}$$

$$t = \frac{2}{1.65 \star \sqrt{.14 + .11}}$$

$$s_p = \sqrt{\frac{6 + 32}{14}}$$

$$t = \frac{2}{1.65 \star \sqrt{.25}}$$

$$s_p = \sqrt{\frac{38}{14}}$$

$$t = \frac{2}{1.65 \star .5}$$

$$s_p = \sqrt{2.71}$$

$$t = \frac{2}{.83}$$

$$s_p = 1.65$$

$t = 2.41$

Since the *t* statistic (*t* = 2.41) was greater than the critical value (1.76), the null hypothesis was rejected.

(Continued)

TABLE 13.3 (Continued)
Effect size computation:

$$r = \sqrt{\frac{t^2}{t^2 + \text{degrees of freedom}}}$$

$$r = \sqrt{\frac{5.81}{5.81 + 14}}$$

$$r = \sqrt{.29}$$

$$r = .54, \text{ a fair relationship}$$

coupons for targeted products, you could ask those people to report the amount spent on the targeted groceries they purchased in the *following* month. You could look at the differences in the amount spent on coupon-advertised items in the months before and after the newspaper ads appeared. To employ this form, you use the following t test statistic:

$$t = \frac{\overline{X}_{\text{diff}}}{s_D / \sqrt{n}}$$

In this formula, $\overline{X}_{\text{diff}}$ is the mean difference between two measures of the same individuals. The standard deviation in the denominator of this formula (s_D) is the simple standard deviation of the difference scores.

Degrees of freedom for this form of the t test are found by taking the total number of events in the sample (*not* the total number of scores) and subtracting one for the new mean that is computed in the formula ($\overline{X}_{\text{diff}}$). The standard deviation in the denominator of this formula (s_D) is the simple standard deviation of the difference scores. As Table 13.4 shows, this method is a simple way to look at "before and after" changes, and it is also sensitive to differences that might get lost if data were clumped into groupings as in the t test for independent samples.

degrees of freedom for the dependent samples t text

t Test for the Difference between Zero and an Observed Correlation

Though the t test has been described for comparisons among means, it can also be used to test whether a correlation is significantly different from zero (no correlation at all). This application allows you to discover if a correlation is greater than one would expect to occur by chance alone. For instance, consider the correlation that was computed on Table 12.2. This sample of 8 families revealed a correlation of .28 between hours of sports watched on TV and the number of bags of potato chips

testing a correlation's statistical significance

TABLE 13.4   *t* TEST FOR DEPENDENT SAMPLES

EXAMPLE

A sample of 10 employees was tested for listening ability before and after attending a seminar in effective listening. Did the employees show significant improvements (increases in scores)? With alpha risk set at .05, test the null hypothesis that there was no statistically significant improvement:

H_0: μ difference $= 0$

The degrees of freedom for this test are $n - 1$; 9 in this case.
Critical *t* value (for a one-tailed test) $=1.83$.

COMPUTING THE TEST STATISTIC

The data are as follows:

Person	*Posttest Score*	*Pretest Score*	*Difference*
Larry	5	4	1
Moe	5	5	0
Curly	4	4	0
Manny	7	5	2
Moe	5	6	−1
Patty	6	4	2
Maxine	7	6	1
Laverne	8	6	2
Jerry	9	7	2
Dino	8	7	1
			$\overline{X}_{\text{diff}} = 1$
			$s_{\text{diff}} = 1.05$

Test Statistic

$$t = \frac{\overline{X}_{\text{diff}}}{s_{\text{diff}} / \sqrt{n}}$$

$$t = \frac{1}{1.05 / \sqrt{10}}$$

$$t = \frac{1}{1.05 / 3.16}$$

$$t = \frac{1}{.32}$$

$$t = 3.13$$

Effect Size Computation

$$r = \sqrt{\frac{t^2}{t^2 + \text{degrees of freedom}}}$$

$$r = \sqrt{\frac{3.13^2}{3.13^2 + 9}}$$

$$r = \sqrt{\frac{9.8}{9.8 + 9}}$$

$$r = \sqrt{.52}$$

$$r = .72, \text{ a marked relationship}$$

Since the *t* statistic ($t = 3.13$) was greater than the critical value (1.83), the null hypothesis was rejected. Thus, there was a statistically significant difference between the pretest and posttest scores.

purchased by each family. To see if this correlation is significantly different from zero, you would use the following t test:

$$t = \frac{r\sqrt{n-2}}{\sqrt{1-r^2}}$$

For our example, you could test this correlation with alpha risk at .05 for a one-tailed test. If you substitute the observed correlation (r) and the sample size (8) into the formula (and round to the second decimal place at each step), the t test is

$$t = \frac{.28\sqrt{8-2}}{\sqrt{1-.08}} = .72$$

Degrees of freedom for this test are the number of events minus two (one degree of freedom is lost for each of the two variables being correlated). In this case, the critical t value was 1.953. Since the t statistic did not meet or exceed the critical value, you cannot reject the null hypothesis. Thus, you conclude that the correlation is not significantly different from zero.

degrees of freedom for t tests of correlations

Determining Effect Sizes

Tests of statistical significance allow the researcher to rule out chance as the probable explanation of results. But significance testing does not reveal how big or small the nonchance relationships are. So, a researcher is also expected (and required in professional journals) to report the magnitude of effects. One useful way to do so involves taking information from a t test and determining what kind of correlation is indicated between the variables. Then, a large effect can be identified and distinguished from a small effect.

other formulae required for effect size computation

For the t test, the following formula will reveal this effect size:

$$r = \sqrt{\frac{t^2}{t^2 + \text{degrees of freedom}}}$$

This tool allows researchers to take the observed t value from the test statistic and to compute a number that can be interpreted as any other correlation.

SUMMARY

Probability refers to the tendency or likelihood that an event occurs in a population. This notion is a foundation of statistical inference in which we attempt to see if observed relationships are unlikely to occur by chance. Distributions such as the standard normal curve can be useful. These distributions serve as probability distributions since they represent the theoretical patterns of expected sample data. The z distribution can be used to make such statistical inferences.

When researchers use tests of statistical significance, they *do not* find evidence that proves that their research hypotheses are so. Instead, they gather evidence that tests how improbable it would be to assume that their research hypotheses are untrue. The null hypothesis, which states that there is no relationship between variables, is the one actually tested statistically. If the null hypothesis is rejected, then the research hypothesis may be tenable and researchers conclude that a relationship exists among variables; if the null hypothesis is not rejected (logically we cannot claim to "accept" a null hypothesis), then researchers make no claim that a relationship exists among variables.

Researchers look at distributions and isolate unusual patterns or events. In communication research it is typical to state that a pattern or event is unusual or improbable if it could be found at random no more than 5% of the time. One location on distributions is called the critical region since if the test statistic falls in that zone, you can claim to have found a "significant difference." A statistically significant difference or relationship is one that is beyond what might be expected to occur by chance alone. The line that divides the critical region from the rest of the distribution is called the critical value. The standard deviation of a distribution of means is often called the standard error of the mean and is used in formulae that compare means.

The ability of a statistical test to reject the null hypothesis correctly is called statistical power. Type I error involves incorrectly rejecting the null hypothesis (the probability of committing a Type I error is called alpha risk). Type II error means that researchers have failed to detect a relationship that is present (the probability of committing a Type II error is called beta risk).

There are four major steps in testing statistical hypotheses: (1) determining a decision rule for rejecting the null hypothesis (researchers usually set alpha risk at .05; the term *statistical significance* does not mean that an important relationship has been found, but that such results are not likely to be due to chance alone); (2) computing the test statistic (a test statistic is a number computed from a statistical formula to test the statistical hypothesis); (3) finding the critical value (when using a directional hypothesis only one side of the distribution is involved; one-tailed tests are identified as those in which the critical region lies on only one side of a two-tailed distribution; nondirectional hypotheses predict some difference regardless of the direction, requiring that critical regions be divided equally for both sides of the distribution); (4) rejecting or failing to reject the null hypothesis (if a test statistic falls in the critical region, the null hypothesis is rejected).

Parametric tests make assumptions about populations from which the data were drawn. In addition to the z distribution, this chapter considers another parametric test called the t test, which is primarily designed to compare two means. The one-sample t test involves examining when a new sample mean differs from a known population mean under conditions when the population standard deviation is unavailable. For all t tests, degrees of freedom are the number of events in a study minus the number of population parameters estimated from samples. The t test for independent samples compares two sample groups to each other (which are independent because the events are not matched in advance, and there is no before-and-after scoring of the samples). The t test for dependent samples is used when subjects are matched or sampled twice. The t test of correlations examines whether an observed correlation is significantly different from zero. After finding a significant difference, researchers may determine effect sizes by use of equivalent methods to compute correlations.

TERMS FOR REVIEW

probability	**critical region**
probability distributions	**statistically significant difference or**
hypothesis	**relationship**
null hypothesis	**critical value**

standard error of the mean	**one-tailed test**
standard error	**two-tailed test**
Type I error	**parametric tests**
alpha (α) risk	**ceiling or floor effects**
Type II error	**subjects by treatments**
beta (β) risk	**interactions**
power	**one-sample t test**
test statistic	**independent samples t test**

JUST FOR THE SAKE OF ARGUMENT: A REVIEW

Look at the following questions and prepare answers to them. Look for the underlying assumptions.

1. Why do we need null hypotheses? What meaningful role can they play in helping researchers make decisions?

2. If the data show no significant differences, is the null hypothesis accepted? Where does the burden of proof lie in accepting or rejecting hypotheses?

3. What is the difference between the standard deviation and the standard error of the mean? What sorts of measures have standard errors?

4. What is the relationship between changing the level of alpha risk and statistical power? What are the ways that you could increase power?

5. What are the circumstances under which you would set alpha risk at .01 or .001? What is an acceptable level of beta risk?

6. Does the central limit theorem state that distributions become increasingly normal with increased sample sizes? What are its limitations (and implicit guarantees)?

7. Which assumptions of parametric tests are critical and which are not so substantial in practical applications to sample data? When would your plans as a researcher be affected by them? What would you do about a violation of any of them?

8. When is the t test for dependent samples used? How is it contrasted with a one-sample t test: after all, don't these forms involve sampling one new group of people?

ACTIVITIES TO PROBE FURTHER

Go to the website for this book and look for the Student Study Materials for Chapter 13.

1. Take the study quiz and print out your answers. (Make sure to review text materials before answering questions.)

2. A communication specialist developed a new way to teach statistical methods. One class was given the new method, and their scores for the semester were tallied. The other method was retained for another class. Samples of students were taken from each class. The two sets of data are found below:

Current Method	New Method
85	92
89	81
90	93
81	87
78	83
79	81

The total number of points possible for the course was 100.

Answer these questions:

a. What is the null hypothesis?

b. How many degrees of freedom are there in the study?

c. What is the critical t value for a two-tailed t test with an alpha risk of .05?

d. What was the observed t statistic?

e. At alpha risk of .05, is there a statistically significant difference between the means of the two groups?

3. A speech therapist gave patients a measure of articulation defects before and after the period of therapy. It was hoped that posttest scores would be lower than pretest scores. The two scores for each person are shown below:

	Posttest Method	Pretest Method
Manny	96	90
Moe	72	77
Jack	98	100
Larry	74	80
Moe	57	59
Curly	75	74
Maxine	92	93
Laverne	85	91
Patty	82	85
Elvis	87	89

Answer these questions:

a. What is the null hypothesis?

b. How many degrees of freedom are there in the study?

c. What is the critical t value for a one-tailed t test with an alpha risk of .05?

d. What was the observed t statistic?

e. Was there a statistically significant difference between the means of the two groups?

4. In this exercise you will compute the t using SPSS or Excel.

a. Go to the website for this book. Click on the "Data Sets" hyperlink. If you have not already downloaded the parent file to complete the exercise at the end of Chapter 4, you will need to download these files now.

  ◆ If you wish to complete this data analysis using SPSS, download the file ATTITUD1.SAV.

  ◆ If you wish to complete this data analysis using Excel, download the file ATTITUD1.XLS.

b. The dependent variable is attitude toward the topic (as created in Chapter 4), which is the sum of the scores of the scales "wise-foolish," "good-bad," "positive-negative," and "beneficial-harmful."

c. For this assignment, follow the instructions that are found in the Web page for Chapter 13, and click on hyperlink to "*t* Tests with SPSS" or "*t* Tests with Excel." Determine if there is a significant difference between the two conditions in this experiment. The first group received a message with a *non sequitur* fallacy argument in it. The second group received the same message with the fallacy deleted. These two conditions are the levels of the independent variable. The variable that identified this fact is "falexper" (1 = with the fallacy presented to subjects; 2 = without the fallacy presented to subjects).

d. *If you wish to analyze data using SPSS,* follow these instructions.

   (1) Start SPSS and load ATTITUD1.SAV (if you have not already done so). Following the instructions given in the Web page, complete a *t* test with alpha risk at .05, one-tailed.

   (2) To compute this *t* test, click on the "Analyze" menu, and on subsequent menus that appear, click on "Compare Means" and "Independent-Samples T-Test." In the dialog box titled "Independent-Samples T-Test," place "Attitude" in the "Test Variable(s)" list. In this same dialog box, place "falexper" in the "Grouping Variable" list. Click the "Define Groups" button. Click on "Use Specified Values" button, and enter 1 in the "Group 1" field and 2 in the "Group 2" field. Click "Continue" and then "OK" buttons.

e. *If you wish to analyze data using Excel,* follow these instructions.

   (1) Start Excel and load ATTITUD1.XLS (if you have not already done so). Following the instructions given in the Web page, complete a *t* test with alpha risk of .05, one-tailed.

   (2) With Excel, the dependent score conditions must be in separate columns.

      (a) Thus, we will have to separate the attitude data into two columns, one for each group. In column Y row 1 enter "fallwith." In column Z row 1 enter "fallnone."

         ♦ Click on cell Y2 (column Y, row 2) to make it active. Click on "Insert" menu and then "Function." In the "Paste Function" dialog box, click on "Logical" in the "Function Category" field. Click on "If" in the "Function Name" field, and then click "OK." In the "Logical Test" field of the dialog box, enter "D2=1" (D is the column in which the "falexper" variable is located, 2 is the second row number, and "=1" specifies the condition to be satisfied). In the "value if true" field, enter X2 (to indicate that we wish the value in cell X2 to be placed in our new cell), and in the "value if false" field, enter zero (Excel cannot handle missing values with the *t* test function; zeros must be inserted). Click on cell Y2 to make it active. On the "Edit" menu, click on "Copy." Go to cell Y2 and hold down the left mouse button while moving down column Y until the end of the data is reached. Press "Return."

         ♦ Repeat the process for column Z. Click on cell Z2 (column Z, row 2) to make it active. Click on "Insert" menu and then "Function." In the "Paste Function" dialog box, click on "Logical" in the "Function Category" field. Click on "If" in the "Function Name" field, and then click "OK." In the "Logical Test" field of the dialog box, enter "D2=2" (D is the column in which the "falexper" variable is located, 2 is the second row number, and "=2" specifies the condition to be satisfied). In the "value if true" field, enter Z2 (to indicate that we wish the value in cell Z2 to be placed in our new cell), and in the "value if false" field, enter zero. Click on cell Z2 to make it active. On the "Edit" menu, click on "Copy." Go to cell Z2 and hold down the left mouse button while moving down column Y until the end of the data is reached. Press "Return." (Excel cannot handle missing values in the t test function. Thus, we must sort the columns to create columns with all the data at the top for falexper and fallnone. From the "Data" menu, click "Sort." In the "Sort" dialog box, click the "Sort by" field and enter "falexper." In the "followed by" field, enter "fallnone." Click "descending" sorting for each of the variables. For "My list has . . . ," click "header row." This sort will create one column with zeros above scores. For this column, highlight all the zeros and click on the "Edit" menu and click on "Delete." On the "Delete" dialog box, click on "shift cells up" and click "OK." Now, you have all the data at the top of each column.

(b) To compute t, locate a place to put the output. Go to row 56 column Y, and click on the cell to make it active. Click on the "Tools" menu, and then click on "Data Analysis." In the dialog box titled "Data Analysis," select "t-Test: Two-Sample Assuming Equal Variances" and click "OK." In the dialog box "t-Test: Two-Sample Assuming Equal Variances," go to the "Input," "Variable 1 Range" field and enter the starting cell and ending cell for the "fall-with" variable (in this case, $Y$2:$Y$24). For the "Variable 2 Range" field, enter the starting cell and ending cell for the "fallnone" variable (in this case, $Z$2:$Z$30). Click on the "Output Range" button, and enter the target cell in the field ($Y$56). Click "OK."

Inferential Statistics II: Beyond Two Means

Statistics are numbers used as arguments.

—LEONARD LOUIS LEVINSON

CHAPTER OUTLINE

BEFORE WE GET STARTED . . .

This chapter extends consideration of hypothesis testing to two of the most frequently used tools found in research: analysis of variance, and the nonparametric statistic called chi-square. Since the logic of other tools is consistent with those covered here, you should have little difficulty understanding other advanced applications you might encounter in your own work.

SELECTING AN APPROPRIATE STATISTICAL TEST

To explore statistical significance, researchers need a test statistic or formula to help them enter a distribution and play the odds. Table 14.1 presents the major tests to be used to see whether significant differences exist between groups. The statistics

TABLE 14.1   SELECTING A STATISTIC TO TEST FOR DIFFERENCES

	MEASUREMENT LEVEL OF DEPENDENT VARIABLE		
	Nominal Level	**Ordinal Level**	**Interval or Ratio**
Number of Sample Groups Compared			
1 (sample compared to a theoretically presumed population value)	One-sample chi-square (goodness of fit test) Binomial z test (for data that have only two possible values)	Kolmogorov-Smirnov one-sample test One-sample runs test	z test (if $n \geq 30$ and σ known) One-sample t test
2 independent samples	Chi-square test of independence z test (difference between proportions) Fisher exact test (for expected frequencies <5)	Wilcoxon rank sum test Mann-Whitney U test (good for large samples) Kolmogorov-Smirnov two-sample test (for small samples) Wald-Wolfowitz runs test (detects any differences in central tendency or skew; assumes initially continuous output measures) Median test	t test for independent groups
2 dependent samples	McNemar test for significance of changes (for dependent sample pairs)	Sign test (for matched sample pairs; does not show magnitude of differences) Wilcoxon matched pairs signed ranks test (for matched sample pairs)	Randomization test for matched pairs (for small n) t test for matched dependent sample pairs t test for paired samples
More than 2	Chi-square test of independence Cochran's Q test (for matched or paired samples) Log-linear analysis	Kruskal-Wallis H test Friedman two-way analysis of variance	Analysis of variance Factorial analysis of variance (for two or more independent variables) Analysis of covariance

are listed by the type of data used for the dependent variable and the number of groups in the independent variable. To select a tool to test for differences between groups, you start by finding the *column* that identifies the level of measurement for the dependent variable. Next, you identify how many new sample groups are to be compared in the study and find the appropriate *row*. If the subjects in the study are pairs of sample data (such as pretests and posttests of the same subjects), or if subjects have been matched on some variable into pairs for comparison, special sets of tools are available. For ordinary independent samples, the appropriate tools are also listed. Though many test statistics are listed, you will find that only one test really will be suitable for your particular needs in a given study.

using the table to select tests of statistical significance

Because covering the details of all these tests and their computation are beyond the scope of this introductory book, you are encouraged to check specific statistics books to find details about many of the formulas listed (some of the most readable of these books are Aczel, 1989; Champion, 1970; Frankfort-Nachmias & Leon-Guerrero, 2000; Glass & Hopkins, 1984; Ott & Hildebrand, 1983; Reinard, 2006; and Wagner, 1992). The rest of our discussion will illustrate some *most commonly used* tests found in communication research.

COMPARISONS OF MORE THAN TWO MEANS: ANALYSIS OF VARIANCE

When you have more than two groups, the *t* test is inappropriate. Thus, the statistic called **analysis of variance** (ANOVA) is invited.[1] Analysis of variance involves use of the *F* distribution to compare results with those normally expected from a distribution of variances. In essence, the *F* distribution—named in honor of Sir Ronald Fisher—is a distribution of variances that have been divided into each other. We can use this distribution to test for differences among sample means. To compare means, researchers may compute a variance (s^2) using sample means as the data—just as if they were ordinary scores. Then, this variance may be compared to the kind of background variation that already exists within each group. This idea is the backbone of the conceptual formula:

Analysis of variance a test of statistical significance that compares the means of two or more groups.

the notion of the F *statistic*

$$F = \frac{\text{between groups variance}}{\text{within groups variance}}$$

This formula is not a computational guide. But the idea is simple enough. The "between groups" variance is computed using sample group means as the scores of interest (a variance of means $s_{\bar{x}}^2$). This difference is divided by a measure of background variation called "within groups" variance. Within groups variance is

if the variances of means are real, they will be greater than background noise

---

[1]You might wonder what would happen if we used both *F* tests and *t* tests to compare two means. The answer is that under these circumstances $F = t^2$.

pooled variance ($s_p{}^2$)
the mean of the variances of subgroups involved in comparisons using analysis of variance (weighted for sample sizes in the case of unequal sample sizes).

the logic of the F statistic: variances of means get big if the means differ from each other

degrees of freedom for ANOVA

simply the average of the variances within each of the sample groups in the study. This measure is known to us as the **pooled variance** ($s_p{}^2$). The pooled variance is nothing more than the squared *pooled standard deviation* that we computed for the *t* test for independent samples (Chapter 13).

The idea behind analysis of variance is simple. If there are no differences among group means, then the variance computed from them will be very small. In fact, if the means are all the same, a variance computed from them will be zero. But if there *are* differences among means, then the variance computed from the means will get bigger and bigger. If the differences are beyond chance, then this variance of means will be greater than the average amount of background noise within groups. That's what the *F* statistic does—divides a variance of means by background noise.

When using analysis of variance there are two sets of degrees of freedom, a set for the numerator of the fraction and a set for the denominator of the fraction. Indeed, if you look at the *F* table in Appendix C, you will notice that the upper left corner of the table shows the fraction from our conceptual formula. Thus, to find the degrees of freedom for the numerator, you move *left to right* to the appropriate column. In general, the degrees of freedom for the numerator are the number of means compared minus 1 (1 lost for the new mean parameter that must be computed to arrive at a variance from the sample means). To find the denominator degrees of freedom, you move *down* the table to the appropriate row. The degrees of freedom for the numerator are the number of events in the study minus 1 for each of the means computed within each of the sample groups (to compute an estimate of within groups variance).

One-Way Analysis of Variance

one-way analysis of variance analysis of variance in which the groups are levels for the independent variable.

description of one-way ANOVA

To compare several means for one independent variable you use **one-way analysis of variance**. The number of levels for the independent variable is often included in labeling of such studies. For instance, a researcher may describe a "one-by-three analysis of variance." The term is shorthand for a one-way analysis of variance with three levels for the independent variable. This section describes what goes on with one-way analysis of variance, use of follow-up tests to find relationships, and how researchers may use the method to look for nonlinear relationships.

Let's suppose that 3 groups of 10 people each were exposed to a message from a lowly, a moderately, and a highly credible source. Their attitudes might be illustrated on a 1 to 20 attitude scale. Results might be as follows:

Lowly Credible	Moderately Credible	Highly Credible
$\overline{X} = 5$	$\overline{X} = 10$	$\overline{X} = 15$
$s^2 = 15$	$s^2 = 25$	$s^2 = 35$

The null hypothesis to be tested directly is

$$H_0: \mu_1 = \mu_2 = \mu_3$$

You can compute a variance of the three means by entering the means as data into the formula for s^2 (see Chapter 13). If you do so, the answer is 25. Since the groups have equal sample sizes, to obtain the pooled variance s_p^2, you can just average the variances within groups. In this case—as you can see—the average of background variances is 25.

To compute F for these data, you actually use a formula that allows you to compare variances of means with averages of background variance. This appropriate adjustment leads to the following formula:

$$F = \frac{n \star s_{\bar{x}}^2}{s_p^2}$$

$$= \frac{10 \star 25}{25}$$

$$= \frac{250}{25}$$

$$= 10$$

To figure out what this test statistic means, we check how likely these results are to occur by chance alone. The degrees of freedom for this test are as follows:

using the F *table to interpret results*

- 2 for the numerator (number of group means minus one; $3 - 1 = 2$). Thus, we find ourselves on column 2 of the chart.
- 27 for the denominator (the number of events in the sample groups minus the number of means that were computed within each group to compute the variance; $10 + 10 + 10 - 1 - 1 - 1$). Thus, we would go to row 27 on the F table.

To test for statistical significance with alpha risk at .05, we would use the portion of the F table found in Figure 14.1. The intersection of column 2 and row 27 gives a critical F value of 3.35 for alpha risk at .05. Since variances are always positive numbers, only one side of the F distribution is used to test hypotheses. As Figure 14.1 also shows, the critical value at which the critical region begins is 3.35. To reject the null hypothesis, the test statistic must fall somewhere in the critical region: the test statistic must be equal to or greater than 3.35. Since the test statistic is 10, you can reject the null hypothesis.

In the example, we had equal sample sizes. If there were *unequal* sample sizes, then you would compute the numerator of these fractions differently. The contribution to the total between groups variance must be weighted by the different sample sizes. The grand mean of all group means also must be computed from the total sample, rather than as a simple average of cell means. Otherwise, the process is pretty much the same (using the long formula for the pooled variance). The example shown on Table 14.2 indicates how to compute and summarize ANOVA with unequal sample sizes. Of course, these formulae can be used for equal sample sizes as well, though the extra steps involved are unnecessary.

adjustments for unequal sample sizes

What to Do after Finding Statistical Significance

Analysis of variance is not the end of the road. Additional follow-up work must be completed after finding a significant F ratio.

Portion of the F Table

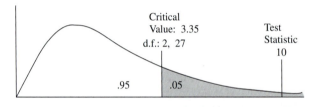

.95th Percentile Values
for the F Distribution
($d.f._1$ degrees of freedom in numerator)
($d.f._2$ degrees of freedom in denominator)

$$\frac{\text{Between Groups Degrees of Freedom}}{\text{Within Groups Degrees of Freedom}}$$

	1	2	3	4	5	6	7	8	9	10
1	161.40	199.50	215.70	224.60	230.20	234.00	236.80	238.90	240.50	241.90
2	18.51	19.00	19.16	19.25	19.30	19.33	19.36	19.37	19.38	19.39
3	10.13	9.55	9.28	9.12	9.01	8.94	8.89	8.85	8.81	8.79
27	4.21	3.35	2.96	2.73	2.57	2.46	2.37	2.31	2.25	2.20

F Distribution and Example Test Statistic

Critical
Value: 3.35
d.f.: 2, 27

Test
Statistic
10

.95   .05

**FIGURE 14.1   EXAMINING THE F DISTRIBUTION FOR A ONE-
WAY ANALYSIS OF VARIANCE EXAMPLE**

**Multiple comparison
tests** tests completed after
finding a statistically significant analysis of variance
effect; completed for the
purpose of determining
the location of differences
among group means.

Tukey's HSD (John
Tukey's Honestly Signifi-
cant Difference test) a
multiple comparison test
designed to contrast all
possible comparisons of
means, when the means
are taken two at a time.

Scheffe's critical S a
multiple comparison test
designed to contrast all
possible comparisons of
means, when the means
are taken as part of com-
plex comparisons.

Multiple Comparison Tests

Our simple example produced evidence showing a statistically significant difference
among the group means. But *where* were the differences? Was one group different
from the other two? Were all three significantly different from each other? To tease
out these differences you can use some follow-up methods called **multiple comparison tests.** These methods are generally computed so that alpha risk is stretched
out across comparisons.

Table 14.3 on page 525 shows several major forms of multiple comparison tests
and their uses. For the most part, in communication studies, researchers tend to
use two tools: Tukey's HSD and Scheffe's S. Though they can be applied to the
same data, the methods actually have different functions. The **Tukey's HSD** (abbreviation for John Tukey's Honestly Significant Difference test) is used to make
all possible comparisons of means, when the means are taken two at a time. For
complex comparisons, such as comparing two cells against four others, **Scheffe's
critical S** method is a powerful tool. Each of these methods has its own method
of computation, and researchers should report the test statistics in their results. As
Table 14.3 shows, however, there are other tools that are suitable for different
sorts of situations.

TABLE 14.2   ONE-WAY ANALYSIS OF VARIANCE INCLUDING UNEQUAL SAMPLE SIZES

EXAMPLE

Researchers wanted to test whether the groups of children, adults, or senior citizens were most persuaded by "negative campaign" ads. So, they contacted three groups of people and showed them a typical negative political ad. Their reactions were assessed on an attitude scale ranging from 3 (negative attitude) to 21 (positive attitude). The following list shows the cell means, variances, and sample sizes:

Children	Adults	Senior Citizens
$\overline{X} = 14$	$\overline{X} = 9$	$\overline{X} = 12$
$s^2 = 18$	$s^2 = 15$	$s^2 = 15$
$n = 15$	$n = 10$	$n = 20$

The first thing to do is compute the grand mean from *all* the data (you cannot just average the means since there are unequal cell sizes). You compute it by multiplying each cell group mean by the number of events in each cell. Then you add up all these numbers and divide by the total number of events in the study. In this case, the computation of the grand mean is

$$\overline{X} = \frac{(n \star \overline{X}_1) + (n \star \overline{X}_2) + (n \star \overline{X}_3)}{n_1 + n_2 + n_3}$$

In this example the following numbers may be substituted:

$$\overline{X} = \frac{(15 \star 14) + (10 \star 9) + (20 \star 12)}{15 + 10 + 20}$$

$$\overline{X} = \frac{540}{45}$$

$$\overline{X} = 12$$

To compute between groups variance, subtract each cell mean from this grand mean, square the difference, and multiply by the number of events in the cell. After completing this process for each cell, add up the totals. Then, divide this number by the degrees of freedom (number of groups minus one). Complete this process as follows:

$$\text{Between groups variance} = \frac{\Sigma\, n_i(\overline{X}_i - \overline{\overline{X}})^2}{\text{degrees of freedom} = \text{groups} - 1}$$

$$= \frac{[15 \star (14 - 12)^2] + [10 \star (9 - 12)^2] + [20 \star (12 - 12)^2]}{3 - 1}$$

$$= \frac{150}{2}$$

$$= 75$$

To compute within groups variance, use the long form of the formula for the pooled variance estimate:

$$s_p^{\,2} = \frac{(n - 1)\, s^2 + (n - 1)\, s^2 \ldots x}{(n - 1) + (n - 1) \ldots x}$$

(Continued)

TABLE 14.2   (Continued)

This pooled variance simply averages background variation after giving weights for different sample sizes. With these data, the numbers become

$$s_p^2 = \frac{(14 \star 18) + (9 \star 15) + (19 \star 15)}{14 + 9 + 19}$$

$$= \frac{672}{42}$$

$$= 16$$

The degrees of freedom for this within groups variance (the pooled variance) are 42. To find out if there is a difference among the means of these groups, the between groups variance is divided by the within groups variance as summarized on the ANOVA table below.

ANOVA TABLE

Source	d.f.	Mean Square	F
Between groups	2	75	4.69
Within groups	42	16	

Since the critical value for 2 and 42 degrees of freedom is 3.22, the observed F value falls into the critical region with alpha risk of .05. Thus, researchers would reject the null hypothesis and claim significance differences between the groups.

Of course, if only two levels are used in the analysis of variance, the F test is a direct comparison of the two conditions. Thus, no additional multiple comparison test is necessary to examine differences.

Determining Effect Sizes

Eta (η) also known as the "correlation ratio," eta is directly interpreted as any correlation and is used to determine the size of effects following finding a significant F. Eta may also be used to identify nonlinear as well as linear effects.

Eta squared (η^2) a coefficient of determination computed form eta.

Though analysis of variance permits researchers to identify nonchance differences, the size of those differences is not directly observed. Thus, differences could be big ones, little ones, or somewhere in between. The researcher needs to supplement statistical significance testing with a measure of effect size. Though more than one tool is available,[2] perhaps the most readily interpretable are **eta (η)** and **eta squared (η^2).** Eta, known as the "correlation ratio," is directly interpreted as you would interpret any correlation. An added advantage of the correlation ratio is that it can identify the size of nonlinear as well as linear effects. Thus, the overall correlation can be identified, regardless of its form.

---

[2]Two other methods are the intraclass correlation $\hat{\rho}_I$, which applies to the "random effects" model of analysis of variance) and omega squared ($\hat{\omega}^2$, which is suitable to the "fixed effects" model of analysis of variance). These methods adjust for expected within groups sums of squares and mean squares, respectively (Kirk, 1982, pp. 161–163). To keep it simple, we describe eta here.

TABLE 14.3	MAJOR MULTIPLE COMPARISON METHODS	
METHOD	**APPLICATION**	**COMMENT**
Dunn's	Used when making comparisons that have been planned or hypothesized in advance; the number is restricted to a small number of comparisons by the number of hypotheses.	Most powerful multiple comparison test (aside from running t's or F's).
Dunnett's d'	Used to compare a control group against multiple treatment groups in the study.	Pairwise comparisons only.
Newman-Keuls	Used when it is desired to have a different critical value for comparisons of individual means with each other (in descending order).	First comparisons very powerful, others less so; the method does not control for experimentwise alpha risk; requires equal sample sizes.
Duncan Multiple Range Test	Used when desired to have a different critical value for comparisons of mean arranged in descending order.	Controversial since predicated on debatable notion that as number of conditions increases, the probability of finding differences increases; first comparisons very powerful, others less so; the method does not control for experimentwise alpha risk; requires equal sample sizes.
Tukey's HSD	For pairwise comparisons; thus used as a follow-up test only.	Spreads out alpha risk for all possible comparisons; requires the use of equal sample sizes (for unequal sample sizes, use Spjøtvoll and Stoline's modification of HSD).
Scheffe's S	Most useful for compound comparisons (e.g., two cells versus four cells).	Most powerful for compound comparisons; but least powerful when applied to pairwise comparisons.

The formula for eta is

effect size computation by eta or eta squared

$$\eta = \sqrt{\frac{\text{between groups variance} \star \text{degrees of freedom}}{\text{total of all mean squares multiplied by their degrees of freedom}}}$$

In our example using equal sample sizes, the numbers work out as follows:

$$\eta = \sqrt{\frac{(10 \star 25)}{25 \star 27}}$$

$$= \sqrt{\frac{250}{675}}$$

$$= \sqrt{.37}$$

$$= .61$$

Thus, a correlation of .61—a "moderate to marked relationship"—appears to exist between the independent and dependent variables in this study. To report

SPECIAL DISCUSSION 14-1

A QUESTION OF ETHICS: STATISTICAL REPORTING

The General Assembly of the International Statistical Institute passed a *Declaration of Professional Ethics* in which ethical conduct for statistical analyses were identified. The Declaration "is designed to be applicable as far as possible to different areas of statistical methodology and application" (International Statistical Institute, 1985, ¶ 11). In addition to dealing with issues of sponsorship, and treatment of colleagues, section 1 of the Declaration focused attention on "obligations to society." Statistical analysts share a belief that great access to statistical information is to be promoted. Even so, they warn that statisticians must be careful since "statistical information can be misconstrued and misused, or that its impact can be different on different groups" (International Statistical Institute, 1985, ¶ 15). Furthermore, statistical analysts "should also not engage or collude in selecting methods designed to produce misleading results, or in misrepresenting statistical findings by commission or omission" (§ 1.3). "Science can never be entirely objective, and statistics is no exception" (§ 1.3, ¶ 2), thus researchers conducting statistical analyses are required "to resist approaches to data collection, analysis, interpretation and publication that are likely (explicitly or implicitly) to misinform or to mislead rather than to advance knowledge" (§ 1.3, ¶ 2).

This concern for reporting misleading statistics, unfortunately, causes a great deal of difficulty. In addition to the fact that reports of "statistically significant effects" often are misunderstood by ordinary people (who think that it means that an important or sizable relationship has been found), researchers also may find that statistical tools can mislead them. Authors for Math Talk, sponsored by the American Association of Variable Star Observers (operating, in part, under a grant from the National Science Foundation), explained the problem. Writing for a general audience, they noted that when a null hypothesis is rejected at alpha risk of .05, this

> means that if we do a scientific experiment, and get a result that's only 5% likely to happen by accident, we have evidence that it is not an accident. We can write our results in a scientific paper, and every statistician will agree that our evidence is significant. (Math Talk, 2006, ¶ 18) . . .
>
> Suppose a university employs 100 scientists, and each one does a different scientific experiment. From probability theory, we *expect* 5% of them to get a result that's only 5% likely, *by accident!* So *just by accident,* about 5 of the 100 scientists will get evidence that they can call "statistically significant" and publish in a scientific paper.
>
> And they *do* have evidence, strong enough that their claim deserves further study. But they do not have proof. That is one of the reasons scientific experiments have to be *repeated*. If you get a "significant result" once, you have evidence. If two people get the same result, there is very strong evidence. If a dozen people do the same experiment, and they all get a significant result, then we can start to believe it. (Math Talk, 2006, ¶¶ 19–20)

When one recognizes that publications have a strong bias in favor of presenting statistically significant results, the chance to feature misleading results may be particularly pronounced. Certainly, there is no intentional effort to mislead anyone. But reporting statistics can sometimes lead to inadvertent confusion when researchers fail to explain the actual meaning of "statistical significance" claims. Since statistics can confuse or mislead people, it makes sense for researchers to take extra care when sharing reports.

the percentage impact of one variable based on a knowledge of the other alone, eta squared (η^2) may be employed. In this example, η^2 is .37.

Looking for Nonlinear Relationships

So far, you have learned how to look for simple differences among the means of several groups. Yet, sometimes the underlying independent variable has levels that are arranged in some sort of continuum. This arrangement allows researchers to identify trends in the dependent variable.[3] For instance, suppose the independent variable involved low, moderate, and high amounts of information possessed by employees. The amount of employee satisfaction is the dependent measure. Given that you have three groups, you can use analysis of variance to detect any differences. You can also adapt analysis of variance to help reveal the exact contour of the relationship.

After identifying a significant difference, researchers can use a method called **trend analysis.** Trend analysis isolates the nature of linear and nonlinear trends in effects identified as significant by analysis of variance. Without getting into computational details, it is useful to show you what a set of results might look like for hypothetical data from the example. Suppose that the means, variances, and sample sizes for the three levels are as follows:

> **Trend analysis** a method that isolates the nature of linear and nonlinear trends in effects identified as statistically significant by analysis of variance.

AMOUNTS OF COMMUNICATION

Low	Moderate	High
$\overline{X} = 5$	$\overline{X} = 15$	$\overline{X} = 10$
$s^2 = 15$	$s^2 = 25$	$s^2 = 35$
$n = 10$	$n = 10$	$n = 10$

Obviously, these data look a great deal like our previous example, but the three means now seem to rise and fall as we move from low to high amounts of communication received by employees. If you drew a line to connect the means, it would show a curve. To identify this trend in the data, you can use trend analysis. The overall observed F value remains 10 (with 2 and 27 degrees of freedom), since the means are the same as our previous example. Thus, there appear to be differences in satisfaction stemming from the three amounts of communication received by employees.

the method of trend analysis

Trend analysis multiplies the means by weights (called "orthogonal polynomials") to reflect linear and nonlinear trends. After weighting the means, simple analysis of variance is computed again. Thus, we can tell if the significant differences reflect a linear or nonlinear trend. The result of this analysis is a set of results as follows:[4]

---

[3]Statisticians prefer that the spacing between the levels of the independent variable be equal. Provided that the levels are rationally chosen to cover the range of interest to the researcher, there is little difficulty created by this requirement.

[4]Though discussing these computation methods is beyond the scope of this book, they may be found in the discussion by Kirk (1982, pp. 150–161). In this case the linear effect orthogonal polynomial weights were -1, 0, and 1; the nonlinear weights were 1, -2, and 1. The formula used to compute the effect was

$$MS = \frac{n \star \left[\Sigma(\text{weights} \star \overline{X}) \right]^2}{\dfrac{\Sigma \text{ weights}^2}{\text{degrees of freedom}}}$$

BETWEEN GROUPS VARIANCE

Source of Variation	d.f.	Mean Square	F
Amount of communication	2	250	10
Linear trend	1	125	5
Nonlinear trend	1	375	15
Within groups	27	25	

"mean square" is a synonym for the variance

The term "mean square" is a synonym for the variance (shorthand for "the mean of the squared differences of scores from their mean"). The linear (straight line) and nonlinear (curved) effects are tested directly. These trends are indented on our listing to indicate that they are not new independent variables but just the main effect examined for trends. If you look at Appendix C, you will find that for alpha risk at .05, the critical value is 4.21 for 1 and 27 degrees of freedom (the degrees of freedom we use for examining the trends). As you can see, both the linear and nonlinear trends are significant. This finding means that although the linear effect exists, the nonlinear or curved trend really tells the tale. Thus, the best fit of a trend to the data is a curved one.

Obviously, trend analysis can help identify whether curved or linear effects exist in the data. This example had three groups—so only a simple nonlinear effect could be found. If we had more than three groups, we could examine additional types of trends in the data as well (such as cubic, quartic, or quintic trends). Thus, this method can help researchers identify fairly subtle patterns in the data.

Variable factor (also called factor) a variable that has been divided into levels or groups.

Factorial analysis of variance analysis of variance applied to multiple independent variables that have been divided into levels or groups.

Main effects dependent variable effects that result from independent variables separately.

language of factorial analysis of variance

Interaction effects dependent variable effects that result from independent variables taken together and involving variation arising from special combinations of levels of independent variables.

Factorial Analysis of Variance

We often ask questions that involve more than one independent variable of interest, each one with two or more levels. Factorial analysis of variance is invited for these sorts of situations. The term **variable factor** is used to identify a variable that has been broken down into levels or groups. Thus, "factorial analysis of variance" is analysis of variance applied to multiple independent variables that have been broken down into levels or groups.

Specifically, **factorial analysis of variance** is a test of statistical significance that identifies main and interaction effects between independent variables. **Main effects** are effects produced by predictor variables taken one at a time. In factorial designs, these main effects are identified by looking at differences between levels of each independent variable across levels of any other independent variables in the study. **Interaction effects** stem from predictor variables taken together.

Rather than complete a bunch of studies on each independent variable separately, researchers may economize by sampling once and getting as much information as possible from the data. The language of factorial analysis of variance often describes the layout of a design. Figure 14.2 shows two designs. The first design is a single-factor design, and the second is a two-factor design. Since the first has only one independent variable with three levels, it is often called a "one-by-three" design. This sort of design can identify only a main effect since only one variable is included. Furthermore, the design invites use of a one-way analysis of variance as its statistical test.

SPECIAL DISCUSSION 14-2

INTERVAL ESTIMATION METHODS

The tools of statistical significance testing we have been describing are called *point estimation* methods. This term derives from the estimating of a single value or point for a population based on the samples. When testing for statistical significance, we hope (and have reason to do so) that our sample mean will lie very close to the population mean. Despite the usefulness of this method, it is not the only way to view things.

Another group of statisticians prefers to rely on interval estimates; that is, they like to report a range of values that they believe will capture population parameters. Though it may seem that both these methods are valuable, some writers have used the logic of interval estimation as a basis for attacking standard methods of significance testing, such as are described in this book's introductory treatment.

Those who prefer to use interval estimation methods suggest that instead of computing whether there are differences between means of samples (point estimates), we should construct confidence intervals around means and contrast them. Thus, the probable range of population values could be identified. The most extreme members of this camp also have been known to write disapproving essays about what they view as faults with significance testing statistics.

There is no reason that researchers could not do *both,* of course, but they rarely do. Mathematically, the methods of interval estimation and point estimate tests of statistical significance are equivalent. Thus, the interval estimation method also permits one to identify the presence of significant differences among groups. For instance, if a researcher found three means such as those in the following example, a sampling confidence interval could be constructed around each mean. In this case, the circles in the centers of the distributions are the means and the lines extending up and down reflect 95% confidence intervals:

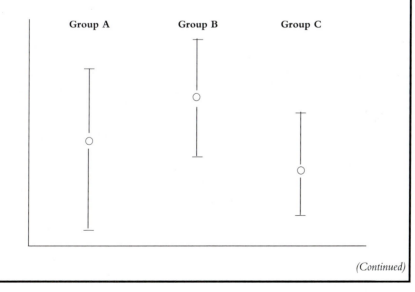

(Continued)

SPECIAL DISCUSSION 14-2 (Continued)

If the width of the confidence interval around one mean is large enough to include the mean of another group, then there is no difference (in this case no difference at alpha risk = .05, two-tailed). If the mean of a group is outside the confidence interval of another group, then there is a significant difference (p = .05). In our example, there is a significant difference between Group B and Group C, indicated by the fact that the means are outside the other's confidence interval (the confidence intervals may overlap, but that fact does not matter). But there is no difference between Group A and the other groups since the confidence interval of Group A is so large that it includes the means of Group B and Group C. Thus, the use of interval estimation methods has been advanced as a subtle way to identify the location and form of differences, just as point estimation methods attempt to reveal them directly.

---

layout of design

The second design features two independent variables, each of which has two levels. Depending on the preferences of the researcher, analysis of variance for this design is called a "two factor ANOVA," a "two-way ANOVA," a "two-by-two ANOVA," or a "two variable factorial ANOVA." The specific combinations of con-

cells identified

ditions are called "cells" of the design because they are framed by levels of independent variables. Though the figure shows only two independent variables, there is no limit to the number of independent variables that could be examined. Thus, one could have a "two-by-two-by-two design," a "three-by-six-by-two-by-four design," or any other combination of variable factors with different levels.

Computing Factorial ANOVA

Once the design of the factorial analysis of variance is decided, researchers may col-

two factor ANOVA preferred if sample sizes equal

lect dependent measure data for each condition. ANOVA is computed to determine where the differences in dependent measures are found in the design. Though designs can be extended for three or more factors, a two factor design for equal sample sizes will be illustrated here (though, of course, the method can also be applied to unequal sample sizes). If a design has *radically* unequal sample sizes across cells, the researcher cannot really claim to have a balanced design and the statistics may not be robust to violations of the assumptions of normal distribution and homogeneous variances.

Computing factorial analysis of variance is very much like one-way analysis of variance. An example may help. Let's look at a study to examine whether men and women who take a seminar on communication skills differ in their scores of communication competence. The competence test has a possible range of scores from 1

notation

to 50 (high scores indicate increased competence). Consider a study in which half of randomly selected groups of 42 men and 42 women at a large company are randomly assigned to take a standard training course in "Improving Interpersonal Communication," while the other half are not assigned to take it. Thus, the design has 21 subjects in each cell. Scores on the communication competence measure could be secured for each person. Table 14.4 shows the means $(\overline{X})$ and variances (s^2) for each cell. We also have provided information about the column and row

SINGLE-FACTOR DESIGN

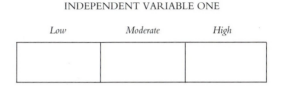

TWO-FACTOR DESIGN

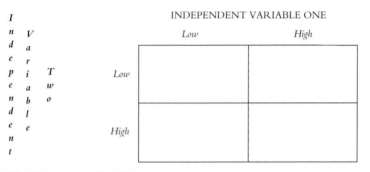

FIGURE 14.2   DESIGNS

means ($\bar{\bar{X}}$—pronounced "X bar bar"). Furthermore, the **grand mean** or average of the averages is provided ($\bar{\bar{\bar{X}}}$—pronounced "X bar bar bar").

As Table 14.4 shows, formulae produce answers that are placed in a summary table. Start by computing the **within groups variance** (sometimes this line is called "error" for **"error variance,"** or "residual" for "residual variance"). Names notwithstanding, the within groups variance is simply the pooled variance (s_p^2). When we have equal sample sizes, the pooled variance is just the average of the variances within each cell. In our case, this number is 40. Degrees of freedom are the number of events in the study minus the number of cells (the number of mean parameters computed within each cell to obtain a variance). For this example, there is a total sample of 84 minus 4 cells, for a total of 80 degrees of freedom.

Thus, the row for within groups variance may be filled in as follows:

ANOVA TABLE

Source	d.f.	Mean Square	F
Within groups	80	40	

Now, you can look at the two main effects and the one interaction effect between the two variables. To find the effect for the sex of the individuals who went through training:

Grand mean in factorial analysis of variance, the average of the mean conditions from predictor variables.

Within groups variance in analysis of variance, the pooled variance (s_p^2) residual.

Error variance another name for "within groups variance" or "residual variance."

constructing the ANOVA summary table

computing between groups variance for sex variable

TABLE 14.4   DATA FOR THE COMMUNICATION COMPETENCE STUDY

COMPLETION OF COMMUNICATION CLASS

		Completed Class	Did Not Take Class	
S E X	**Men**	$\overline{X} = 30$ $s^2 = 40$ (cell 1)	$\overline{X} = 24$ $s^2 = 34$ (cell 2)	$\overline{\overline{X}} = 27$
	Women	$\overline{X} = 36$ $s^2 = 50$ (cell 3)	$\overline{X} = 26$ $s^2 = 36$ (cell 4)	$\overline{\overline{X}} = 31$
		$\overline{\overline{X}} = 33$	$\overline{\overline{X}} = 25$	$\overline{\overline{\overline{X}}} = 29$

TABLE OF ANALYSIS OF VARIANCE WITH COMPUTATIONS

Source	d.f.	Mean Square	F
Main effects: Training	(columns − 1)	$\dfrac{n \text{ in column} \star s_{\overline{x}}^{2} \text{ column means}}{\text{degrees of freedom}}$	$\dfrac{\text{Mean square}}{\text{Within groups mean square}}$
Sex *Interaction effects:*	(rows − 1)	$\dfrac{n \text{ in row} \star s_{\overline{x}}^{2} \text{ row means}}{\text{degrees of freedom}}$	$\dfrac{\text{Mean square}}{\text{Within groups mean square}}$
Sex × training	(rows − 1) × (columns − 1)	$\dfrac{n \text{ in each cell} \star (\text{each cell} - \text{row mean} - \text{column mean} + \text{grand mean})^2}{\text{degrees of freedom}}$	$\dfrac{\text{Mean square}}{\text{Within groups mean square}}$
Within groups variance	(total sample − number of cells)	s_{P}^{2}	

♦ Compute a variance using the two row means $(\overline{\overline{X}})$ for men and for women as our two pieces of data. The variance is 8.

♦ Multiply this variance by the number of events in each row grouping. Multiply 8 by 42 (there were 42 men and 42 women—42 events in each row). The result of this step is 336, which is placed in the "mean square" column.

Degrees of freedom are the number of conditions (rows), minus 1. Here 2 rows minus 1 equals 1. This number is placed in the column marked d.f. To compute an F ratio:

♦ Divide between groups variance (mean square) by within groups variance (mean square). In this case, divide 336 by 40. The result is 8.4. This number is placed in the column marked *F*, as follows:

F ratio for the sex variable

Source	d.f.	Mean Square	F
Sex	1	336	8.4
Within groups	80	40	

To learn whether this difference is beyond chance alone, you need only look at the *F* table in Appendix C. For 1 degree of freedom in the numerator (column 1 on the table) and 80 degrees of freedom in the denominator (row 80), the critical *F* value for alpha risk at .05 is 3.96, as Figure 14.3 shows. Since the calculated *F* exceeds this critical value, our observed *F* statistic falls in the *F* distribution's critical region. Thus, you can reject the null hypothesis and conclude that there is a statistically significant difference between the competence scores of men and women. Women in our sample score higher in communication competence than men.

Portion of the *F* Table

95th Percentile Values
for the *F* Distribution
(d.f.$_1$ degrees of freedom in numerator)
(*d.f.*$_2$ degrees of freedom in denominator)

Between Groups Degrees of Freedom
Within Groups Degrees of Freedom

	1	2	3	4	5	6	7	8	9	10
1	161.40	199.50	215.70	224.60	230.20	234.00	236.80	238.90	240.50	241.90
2	18.51	19.00	19.16	19.25	19.30	19.33	19.36	19.37	19.38	19.39
3	10.13	9.55	9.28	9.12	9.01	8.94	8.89	8.85	8.81	8.79
80	3.96	3.11	2.72	2.48	2.33	2.21	2.12	2.05	1.99	1.95

F Distribution and Example Test Statistic

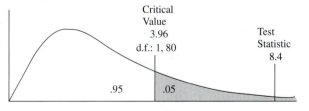

FIGURE 14.3   EXAMINING THE *F* DISTRIBUTION FOR FACTORIAL ANALYSIS OF VARIANCE EXAMPLE

To identify any main effects from training, you can follow the same general process. Start by:

♦ Computing a variance from the 2-column means (across levels of the sex independent variable). With this step, you obtain 32.

♦ Multiplying by the number of events in each column (42). This action reveals the mean square for this source of variation: 1,344.

♦ Identifying degrees of freedom as the number of columns minus 1, yielding 1 degree of freedom in this example (2 − 1).

The F ratio is computed by dividing the treatment mean square by the within groups mean square, which produces a value of 33.6. When you enter it into the summary table, you get the following:

Source	d.f.	Mean Square	F
Sex	1	336	8.4
Training	1	1344	33.6
Within groups	80	40	

This F value is also statistically significant with 1 and 80 degrees of freedom (column 1 and row 80 on the F table). By looking at the means, you can observe that people who take the communication skills training score higher in competence than those who do not take the training.

The computation of the interaction is accomplished by:

♦ Taking each cell mean, subtracting the corresponding row mean, subtracting the corresponding column mean, and then adding grand mean into the mix.[5] For our example, we get the following numbers: cell one = −1; cell two = 1; cell three = 1; cell four = −1.

♦ Squaring the answer for each cell.

♦ Adding up these squared answers from all the cells (4 in this example).

♦ Multiplying this sum by the number of events in each cell. Multiplying 4 by 21 (the number of events in each cell) produces 84, which is placed in the mean square column.

♦ Computing degrees of freedom by multiplying the degrees of freedom for each of the main effects of the variables in the interaction. Since each variable in the interaction had 1 degree of freedom, the total degrees of freedom are $1 \times 1 = 1$.

♦ Compute the F ratio by dividing this mean square by the within groups variance and placing the answer in the column indicated as F:

---

[5]If we had three independent variables, the three-variable interaction would be computed by taking the cell mean and subtracting the row mean, subtracting the column mean, subtracting the slice (that's what they call the third variable division) mean, and adding in the grand mean twice (to keep the numbers sensible).

Source	d.f.	Mean Square	F
Sex	1	336	8.4
Training	1	1344	33.6
Sex × Training interaction	1	84	2.1
Within groups	80	40	

As you can see, the interaction F ratio is smaller than the critical F ratio. Thus, no statistically significant interaction effect can be claimed. Hence, it appears that women score higher in communication competence than men, and that those who attend the communication skills training score higher than those who do not take such training. Moreover, these effects are additive since there is no significant interaction between the two.

Examining Effect Patterns

As you recall from Chapter 10, main effects indicate the impact of one variable across levels of others in the design. As such, main effects can be interpreted as if a simple one-way analysis of variance had been completed. But there is a catch. If there are significant interactions, the researcher may or may not be permitted to interpret main effects for involved independent variables. If the interaction effect is shown to be a crossed interaction (disordinal), then the researcher should not interpret main effects for variables involved, since such information would be misleading. Yet, if the interaction effect is uncrossed (ordinal), main effects may be interpreted without fear of misleading the reader. Thus, the interactions must be teased out, often using multiple comparison tests and even formal diagrams.

main effects not interpreted if disordinal interactions present

As in one-way ANOVA, it is important for researchers to identify the size of the relationships observed. You can use the same eta statistic discussed previously. Thus, the comparative importance of each significant source of variation may be evaluated by the researcher.

BASIC NONPARAMETRIC TESTING

So far, this chapter has emphasized ways to compare the means of interval or ratio level dependent variables. But sometimes the data are simple frequency counts in categories and require different tools.

The Nature of Nonparametric Tests: The Randomization Assumption

Nonparametric tests are sometimes called "distribution-free" statistics. But this statement does not mean that there are no assumptions made at all. On the contrary, there is one assumption made when using nonparametric tests: randomization. If you wish to examine how often a given set of categorical data or rankings could be found by chance, you must use randomization to begin figuring the odds of finding

Nonparametric tests statistical methods that do not make assumptions about population distributions or population parameters.

required for nominal or ordinal dependent measures

a set of results at random. Thus, as with parametric tests, randomization is a consistent requirement of statistical testing.

Nonparametric tests are required when researchers examine dependent measures on ordinal or nominal levels of measurement. Of course, the dependent variable data originally may have been measured on the interval level, but researchers can reduce the level of measurement to lower-level data. For instance, a researcher might be interested in examining the impact of watching presidential debates on the credibility of candidates. People could fill out credibility scales before and after the debates. Instead of examining the degree of differences, researchers simply could count the number of people who rated the candidates more credible, less credible, or unchanged after the debate. Of course, when you move to a lower level of measurement, you lose sensitivity contained in the original data. Thus, researchers tend to make such a choice only when practical matters of design and control demand it.

Tests for Nominal Level Dependent Variables

Chi-square test a family of nonparametric tests that permit examining observed frequencies of events with expected frequencies.

use of the chi-square statistic: count data

Nonparametric tests apply to situations in which the dependent measures are on the ordinal or nominal level. Though there are many formulae in these categories, the most popular ones in communication research are variations of chi-square tests. Thus, we will focus on them for this introductory treatment. The **chi-square test** is designed to deal with "count" data. That is, chi-square allows us to use categories and determine if there are differences between the number of data that fall into each category. The "count" of the number of events in each category is analyzed by using the applications of chi-square that we describe here: the one-sample test and the test for independence of samples.

RESEARCHERS IN THE FIELD: JAMES B. STIFF

James Stiff is a professional trial consultant who is president of Trial Analysts Inc., a nationally known firm specializing in training lawyers in communication skills, conducting pretrial research, assisting in jury selection, running shadow juries, and guiding trial teams through the trial process. Jim also has impressive academic credentials. He received a bachelor's degree at Arizona State University and earned his M.A. and Ph.D. degrees at Michigan State University. He held professorships at Michigan State University, Arizona State University, and the University of Kansas. He also compiled an enviable record of research and scholarship. He has authored or coauthored more than 20 articles in academic journals and two scholarly books, one on *Persuasive Communication* (now in its second edition) and another on *Deceptive Communication*.

♦ *What drew you into our field?*
   I was initially interested in organizational behavior and communication, and as a freshman at Arizona State University I transferred from the Business College to the Department of Communication. Once I arrived in the Department of

Communication, I quickly became interested in persuasive communication and group decision making.

♦ *The corporation you lead seems actively involved in research. A major part of your corporate mission statement includes, "Trial Analysts conduct research using the standards of the scientific method. . . . " You also regularly conduct research using focus groups, applying your sampling expertise, and using community surveys. How important is a mastery of communication research methods in your work and that of your company?*
Skills in research are very important to us. When we conduct mock trial and focus group research, we combine scientific research methods with qualitative methods to provide lawyers with a comprehensive analysis of how jurors are likely to perceive their case. Our interviewing methods are helpful in developing community attitude surveys, conducting post-trial juror interviews, developing questions for *voir dire* [the process of questioning potential jurors to select a trial jury], and preparing cross-examination questions for witnesses at trial.

♦ *In general, what do you try to achieve for your clients through your research?*
We try to provide an objective and accurate assessment of how jurors are likely to perceive their cases, develop strategies for improving the comprehension and persuasiveness of case presentations, and in some cases provide estimates of likely damage awards in the event of an adverse verdict. We work with attorneys and witnesses to improve their communication skills and enhance the credibility of their presentations.

♦ *What one or two things do you think students should know to deal successfully with practical communication research either as a consumer or as a researcher?*
I believe students need a thorough understanding of research methods and analysis. They also need to understand how to synthesize key research findings and present them in a clear fashion to clients and consumers. (Although we may use sophisticated statistical analyses in our analyses, we rarely present more than basic descriptive statistics to our clients.) Clients and consumers want to be assured that the research findings are valid and then they want to understand the key implications or findings.

♦ *What do you think is the most exciting future direction for communication research in applied settings such as those you face with your clients?*
Trial lawyers are becoming more focused on understanding their cases from the perspective of the jury. They are becoming more sophisticated consumers of research in communication and are always looking for practical applications of communication theory. Testing the effectiveness of practical applications from communication theory is very exciting.

♦ *What is the most satisfying thing about being involved in applied communication research?*
We receive definitive feedback in the form of jury verdicts on our effectiveness as communicators and our ability to predict jury verdicts as researchers. When it is favorable, definitive feedback is quite rewarding.

♦ *Is there any advice you would give students who might be interested in becoming applied communication researchers?*
I would recommend three things right away. First, learn as much as you can about research methods and analysis. Second, learn to communicate effectively, in both written and oral presentations. Third, focus on application of communication theory to practical, everyday communication problems.

SPECIAL DISCUSSION 14-3

BELLS AND WHISTLES: A READER'S GUIDE TO ADVANCED STATISTICAL METHODS

Many statistical methods go far beyond an initial understanding of statistical tools. This guide defines some advanced techniques for you and identifies some things to look for when you read reports of them.

Multiple Regression Correlation (a.k.a. multiple correlation): produces a correlation of multiple predictors with a single output variable. **Beta weights** tell the contribution made by each predictor to the overall correlation. Predictors are supposed to be uncorrelated with each other (called absence of **multicollinearity**).

Multiple Discriminant Analysis: membership in particular groups from a knowledge of a number of predictor variables (measured on the interval or ratio level). Researchers report discriminant functions composed of linear combinations of variables, which, in turn, are tested for significance. Prediction is also evaluated by using **canonical correlation** and hit ratio success.

Log-Linear Analysis: an extension of chi-square testing for analysis of more than two variables measured on the nominal level. The technique uses applications of maximizing methods (e.g., maximum likelihood estimation) to identify explanatory models and patterns.

Multivariate Analyses

Canonical Correlation: an extension of multiple regression correlating two sets of variables. Scholars interpret roots of canonical correlations (tested for significance using chi-square) and identify components for each root (interpreted as meaningful the farther they are from zero). The redundancy index tells whether sets of variables should be interpreted differentially for additional canonical component roots (look for a redundancy index greater than .05).

MANOVA (Multivariate Analysis of Variance): an extension of analysis of variance for multiple dependent variables. The method represents interrelated dependent variables (checked by a test of "sphericity") as a weighted linear combination. The method tests to determine if effects are on some dependent variables more than others (such as Wilks' lambda) or whether effects are shared across dependent variables (such as Pillai's trace).

Multivariate Multiple Correlation: an extension of multiple regression for many interrelated dependent measures—combined with canonical correlation, omnibus (Wilks'), and trace (e.g., Pillai's) statistics to interpret results.

Multivariate Analysis of Covariance: an extension of MANOVA to adapt analysis of covariance for multiple interrelated dependent variables (see MANOVA guides).

Hotelling's T^2: t test for intercorrelated dependent variables.

Modeling Methods

Path Models: use correlational tools to interpret relationships to identify causal models with exogenous (input variable) sources, endogenous (mediating) variables, and dependent (output or criterion) variables. Tests of fit are often expected in acceptable models.

AMOS: a computer program to isolate relationships by examining covariances among variables. The method develops simultaneous equations (usually employing a method such as maximum likelihood estimation to maximize the degree of relationship found) to represent relations among variables. Tests of fit using residual mean square and chi-square tests are usually included; also may be used for confirmatory factor analysis and path modeling.

The One-Sample Chi-Square Test

Sometimes inelegantly called the "goodness of fit" test, the **one-sample chi-square test** allows a researcher to take a single independent variable that is broken down into nominal categories and identify whether the arrangement among categories is beyond what would have been expected by chance alone.

The **chi-square (χ^2) distribution** is enlisted to help play the odds. This distribution may be thought of as a probability distribution of squared differences of scores. Hence, it may be used to help assess differences among proportions and to identify when actual counts of data differ from counts that could have been expected by chance. As Figure 14.4 shows, this chi-square distribution is not symmetrical, though it does tend to become more and more normal as degrees of freedom increase. This distribution's properties permit us to identify unusual differences by isolating the critical region, as we have with other distributions.

The one-sample chi-square test is often used when researchers gather data that they believe can be contrasted with theoretically expected patterns. For instance, it is known that the proportion of children with speech handicaps is about 7% of the population. Suppose a teacher noticed that a surprising number of her pupils seemed to have speech defects. She might randomly sample a group of 100 children and find this pattern:

One-sample chi-square test (also called "goodness of fit" test) a test of statistical significance for nominal level variables for which frequency data are obtained.

Chi-square (χ^2) distribution a probability distribution of squared differences of scores.

one-sample test used when contrasts with theoretically expected frequencies exist

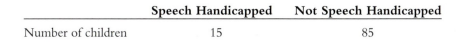

	Speech Handicapped	Not Speech Handicapped
Number of children	15	85

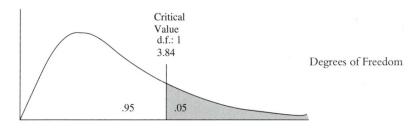

Chi-Square Distribution

Critical
Value
d.f.: 1
3.84

.95   .05

Portion of the Chi-Square Table

Alpha Risk Levels
(indicating the proportion of the chi-square distribution that lies to the right of the critical value)

Degrees of Freedom	.95	.10	.05	.025	.01
1	.004	2.71	3.84	5.02	6.64
2	.10	4.61	5.99	7.38	9.21
3	.35	6.25	7.81	9.35	11.34
4	.71	7.78	9.49	11.14	13.28
5	1.15	9.24	11.07	12.83	15.09

FIGURE 14.4   USING THE CHI-SQUARE DISTRIBUTION

To test whether this pattern is statistically significant, you may use the chi-square test with alpha risk set at .05. Using the symbol p for the probabilities or proportions of occurrence of events, the null hypothesis is

$$H_0: p_1 = p_2$$

Since theory guides the teacher, those expectations can be compared against the actual observations. Since 7% percent of children in the population have speech defects, we could expect that 7 out of 100 children would have such defects, and 93 would not. This expectation would contrast with the observed frequencies:

	Speech Handicapped	Not Speech Handicapped
Number of children	15	85
Theoretic expectation	7	93

The test statistic for this case is shown by the following formula:

$$\chi^2 = \sum \frac{(f_{observed} - f_{expected})^2}{f_{expected}}$$

computation of chi-square

The f stands for the frequency or count. To use the formula, you subtract the expected frequency from each observed frequency, square the difference (to get rid of minus signs since chi-square has no negative numbers), and divide by the expected frequency. Then you repeat the process for all other groups. Finally you total the numbers and obtain a chi-square test statistic. In this case, you get the following numbers:

$$\chi^2 = \frac{(15 - 7)^2}{7} + \frac{(85 - 93)^2}{93}$$
$$\chi^2 = 9.14 + .69$$
$$\chi^2 = 9.83$$

degrees of freedom for chi-square

Degrees of freedom are computed by looking at the number of groups minus 1. Thus, in this example, degrees of freedom are $2 - 1$, or 1. As Figure 14.4 and Appendix D show, the critical chi-square value for alpha risk at .05 and 1 degree of freedom is 3.84. Since our computed chi-square of 9.83 is greater than 3.84, we enter the critical region—and the null hypothesis is rejected. It seems that the teacher's children have a higher rate of speech handicaps than found in the general population.

Sometimes researchers do not have theory to go on. Thus, they make use of the **equal probability hypothesis** to form expected frequencies. For instance, suppose that you sampled 300 people to find out if there were differences among their preference for reading weekly newsmagazines: *Time, Newsweek, U.S. News and World Report.* You might find the following:

Equal probability hypothesis a method of determining expected frequencies for the one-sample chi-square test assuming an equal proportion of events in each category.

	Time	Newsweek	U.S. News and World Report
Number of people preferring	130	110	60

To find out if the observed pattern differs from what might be expected at random, you could hypothesize that if there were no preferences, each magazine would have an equal chance of selection. If each magazine were equally preferred, you would expect one-third of the sample to prefer each magazine. Thus, the equal probability hypothesis would lead you to the following comparisons:

	Time	Newsweek	U.S. News and World Report
Number of people preferring	130	110	60
Expected frequencies	100	100	100

The test statistic for this case is

$$\chi^2 = \sum \frac{(f_{observed} - f_{expected})^2}{f_{expected}}$$

$$\chi^2 = \frac{(130 - 100)^2}{100} + \frac{(110 - 100)^2}{100} + \frac{(60 - 100)^2}{100}$$

$$\chi^2 = 9 + 1 + 16$$

$$\chi^2 = 26$$

Degrees of freedom are computed by looking at the number of groups minus 1. Hence, the degrees of freedom are $3 - 1$, or 2 degrees of freedom. Since at alpha risk of .05 the critical region of chi-square begins at 5.99, the null hypothesis is rejected. Consequently, researchers would conclude that there is a difference in newsmagazine preferences.

degrees of freedom for the one-sample chi-square

The Chi-Square Test of Independence

If researchers have two or more ways to classify variables, they may create what are called "contingency tables" and see if there is a relationship between the variables that compose the framework of the table. For instance, suppose you wanted to find out whether teams of male or female college debaters won more or fewer debates than each other. You could find a sample of debate teams composed of men and a sample of debate teams composed of women. Then during the preliminary rounds of a tournament, you could count the number of debates each team won or lost. The null hypothesis in this case would be that the two classification variables are independent (unrelated to each other). After finding 150 debates by males and 150 debates by female debate teams (none involving the same pairs of debate teams debating against each other), the data might be found as follows:

using contingency tables with two classification variables

test of independence

	Number of Debates Won	Number of Debates Lost	
Debates by males	90	60	150 (50%)
Debates by females	80	70	150 (50%)
Total	170	130	

The formula for the **chi-square test of independence** is the same as the "goodness of fit" test. The only difference lies in the source of the expected frequencies. If the two

Chi-square test of independence adaptation of chi-square test to the analysis of contingency tables.

computing expected frequencies for the chi-square test of independence

classification variables are independent of and unrelated to each other, then you expect to see a roughly equal distribution of counts across conditions. In this case, look at the row percentages and the column totals. As you can see, each row includes 50% of the data. Thus, if there were no relationship between classification variables (sex of team and win–loss record), you would expect to see 50% of each column total composed of male debate teams and 50% composed of female debate teams. Thus, researchers compute the row percentages and use those percentages to identify the expected frequencies

---

SPECIAL DISCUSSION 14-4

THE USE OF FACTOR ANALYSIS IN MEASUREMENT

Factor analysis is a commonly used statistical method that helps "the researcher discover and identify the unities or dimensions, called factors, behind many measures" (Kerlinger, 1986, p. 138). Largely because convenient computer programs are widespread, researchers routinely report results of factor analyses for scales as part of the report of reliability of measures. In fact, in communication research, this statistical tool is most often used as part of the reliability assessment of measures. Since reliability is computed for measures that deal with the same dimension, factor analysis is a useful way to learn which items really measure things on the same dimension. This discussion deals with factor analysis applied primarily to measurement reliability concerns.

Though factor analysis has some complicated applications, when it is used in measurement, researchers follow a rather consistent pattern. Factor analysis begins with a researcher giving the measure of interest to a group of subjects. Then, all the items on the measure are correlated with each other (sometimes using alternatives to correlations). Items that tend to be highly interrelated are identified as measuring common dimensions.

As a second step, factor analyses mathematically extract chief factors underlying the larger number of measures. Though there are other options, the most common method, though not *strictly* a form of "factor analysis," is the "Principal Components Solution," which attempts to identify the number of common centers of variation that underlie the variables. If one factor emerges as the center of variation for a set of test items, then the test items appear to measure only that one dimension. If two factors are found, the test items would appear to measure two different things. If three factors emerge, three dimensions would appear to underlie the test items. For each emerging factor, the association of each test item to the common factor is identified by a set of "item loadings" that reveal how closely the items are related to each factor.

As a third step, the factors are interpreted. To aid interpretation of factor loadings, the factors are "rotated" (contrary to popular confusion about the matter, "rotation" does not affect the factor analysis solution, but is only an aid in understanding factors). Rotations are usually made orthogonally so that the nature of factor loadings can be identified with greatest separation (i.e., a 90-degree rotation system is used). Next, we try to decide what each factor really measures. The item loadings are checked to see which ones "load" or "define" each factor. As a protocol of sorts, researchers usually consider rotated item scores loaded on a factor if the item has a score of at least .60 and

---

no loading on another factor of .40 or greater. The following example shows a typical loading pattern:

	Factor I	Factor II
Test item 1	.80	.18
Test item 2	.77	.22
Test item 3	.45	.45
Test item 4	.31	.66
Test item 5	.28	.71
Test item 6	.44	.62

As you can see, items 1 and 2 measure factor I, and items 4 and 5 measure factor II. These two dimensions would then be scored as separate measures for which reliability is assessed. By examining available theory and the properties shared by items on each factor, the researcher identifies an appropriate label to use to refer to the scores produced on each factor.

---

for each row.[6] Let's apply this logic to our example. The column for number of debates won was 170. Thus, we would expect to see 50% of this 170 on the row for women and 50% on the row for men. Similarly, the column indicating the number of debates lost was 130. Thus, we would expect to see 50% of this 130 on the row for women and 50% on the row for men. The result is shown on this revised table:

	Number of Debates Won	Number of Debates Lost	
Debates by males	90	60	150
Expected frequency:	(85)	(65)	(50%)
Debates by females	80	70	150
Expected frequency:	(85)	(65)	(50%)
Total	170	130	

The test statistic uses the standard formula for chi-square:

$$x^2 = \sum \frac{(f_{observed} - f_{expected})^2}{f_{expected}}$$

$$x^2 = \frac{(90 - 85)^2}{85} + \frac{(60 - 65)^2}{65} + \frac{(80 - 85)^2}{85} + \frac{(70 - 65)^2}{65}$$

$$x^2 = .29 + .38 + .29 + .38$$

$$x^2 = 1.34$$

Degrees of freedom are equal to the number of columns minus 1 multiplied by the number of rows minus 1. In this case, you have $(2 - 1)$ times $(2 - 1)$, which yields

---

[6]There are other ways to get the expected frequency. For instance, to find it for a given cell you can multiply the column frequency by the row frequency and divide by the total frequencies in the study table.

degrees of freedom for the chi-square test of independence
1 degree of freedom. Since the critical chi square value is 3.84, it is clear that the test statistic does not fall into the critical region of the chi-square distribution. Thus, the researcher fails to reject the null hypothesis and concludes that there is no difference indicated by the data. Hence, there did not appear to be a relationship between the sex of the debaters and the win–loss record.

Determining Effect Sizes

The chi-square test permits you to identify whether chance can be eliminated to explain research findings. But the test does not identify how big the effects are. Thus, it is useful to assess effect size. Several measures are available, but among the most frequently employed is the **contingency coefficient.** This method involves taking the observed chi-square value and computing the following formula:

Contingency coefficient a method to determine effect sizes following a significant chi-square test.

$$C = \sqrt{\frac{\chi^2}{N + \chi^2}}$$

This formula permits individuals to identify the size of relationships between variables equivalent to a correlation. Thus, the contingency coefficient is an important counterpart to significance testing.

SUMMARY

Analysis of variance involves the use of the F distribution to compare more than two means. Researchers may compute a variance using sample means as the data (between groups variance) and compare this variance to the kind of background variation that already exists within each group (within groups variance). This latter term is represented by the "pooled variance" (the squared pooled standard deviation used for the t test). To compare several means for one independent variable, we use one-way analysis of variance. Additional follow-up work must be completed after finding a significant F ratio. To identify the location of differences, multiple comparison tests may be used (these methods are generally computed so that alpha risk is stretched out across comparisons). Tukey's HSD is used to make all possible comparisons of means, when the means are taken two at a time. For complex comparisons, Scheffe's critical S method is recommended. The researcher needs to supplement the measure of statistical significance with measures of effect size, such as eta (η) and eta squared (η^2) (also called the "correlation ratio"). To identify nonlinear relationships, researchers may follow up by using trend analysis, a method that isolates the nature of linear and nonlinear effects by considering weighted means.

A variable factor is a variable that has been broken down into levels or groups. Factorial analysis of variance is analysis of variance applied to multiple independent variables that have been broken down into levels or groups. This test of significance identifies main and interaction effects between independent variables. Main effects are dependent variable effects from independent variables separately. Interaction effects are dependent variable effects from independent variables taken together. If there is a crossed interaction (disordinal), then the researcher should not interpret main effects for variables involved, since such information would be misleading.

Nonparametric tests are statistical methods that do not make assumptions about population distributions or population parameters. Yet, these methods make one assumption for use of these tests: randomization. The family of nonparametric tests applies to situations in which the dependent measures are on the ordinal or nominal level. The most popular ones in communication research are applications of chi-square tests. The chi-square test is designed to deal with "count" data. The one-sample chi-square test allows a researcher to take a single variable that is broken down into nominal categories and identify whether the arrangement among categories is beyond what would have been expected by chance alone. It is often used when researchers gather data that they believe can be contrasted with theoretically expected patterns. At other times when researchers do not have theory to go on, they make use of the "equal probability hypothesis" to form expected frequencies. The chi-square test of independence is used when there are two or more ways to classify variables that can be classed into "contingency tables." After finding a significant chi-square, researchers follow up by using a measure of effect size, such as the contingency coefficient.

TERMS FOR REVIEW

analysis of variance	within groups variance
one-way analysis of variance	error variance
pooled variance	nonparametric tests
multiple comparison tests	chi-square test
Tukey's HSD	beta weights
Scheffe's critical S	multicollinearity
eta	canonical correlation
eta squared	chi-square distribution
trend analysis	one-sample chi-square test
variable factor	equal probability hypothesis
factorial analysis of variance	chi-square test of independence
main effects	factor analysis
interaction effects	contingency coefficient
grand mean	

JUST FOR THE SAKE OF ARGUMENT: A REVIEW

Look at the following questions and prepare your own answers to them. Look for the underlying assumptions.

1. If the t test compares the difference between two means, does the analysis of variance compare the differences among sample variances?

2. Does analysis of variance reveal the location of differences among several means? Does it reveal the location of differences if there are two groups compared? When are the different multiple comparison tests used?

3. How does one determine whether a significant effect is large or small? What evidence is provided by looking at significance levels?

4. When one wishes to test the significance of the difference between the frequency of dependent variables measured on the nominal level, what options are available?

5. What is the difference between analysis of variance and factorial analysis of variance? Why would one want to bother with completing factorial analyses of variance?

6. What tools are used when researchers wish to correlate multiple independent variables with one or more than one dependent variable? What kind of research purpose would be satisfied by using such a method?

ACTIVITIES TO PROBE FURTHER

Go to the website for this book and look for the Student Study Materials for Chapter 14.

1. Take the study quiz and print out your answers. (Make sure to review text materials before answering questions.)

2. Look at the data below and conduct a one-way ANOVA. A researcher completed a study to find out the number of "uhs" and "ums" spoken by local television news broadcasters from three local stations. The table below shows the samples from each of the networks during a period of five days. The number of "uhs" and "ums" counted in each time period is listed in each column.

	Network A	Network B	Network C
Monday	22	20	24
Tuesday	12	18	9
Wednesday	14	11	17
Thursday	12	12	13
Friday	12	13	9

Answer these questions:
   a. What is the null hypothesis?
   b. What was the critical F value?
   c. What degrees of freedom were used for this test?
   d. What was the observed F statistic?
   e. At alpha risk of .05, was there a statistically significant difference among the means of the three groups?

3. Go to the website for this chapter, and examine the exercise "Determining If Variances Are Equal." Using Hartley's H and the data in the previous exercise, answer these questions:
   a. What is the critical H value for these data?
   b. What is the observed H statistic?
   c. Are the variances among these groups equal or unequal?
   d. If the variances were unequal, what would be the implications for your research?

4. In this exercise we will compute two-way analysis of variance on SPSS or Excel.
   a. Go to the website for this book. Click on the "Data Sets" hyperlink. If you have not already downloaded the parent file to complete the exercise at the end of Chapter 4, you will need to download these files now.

♦ If you wish to complete this data analysis using SPSS, download the file ATTTUD1. SAV.

♦ If you wish to complete this data analysis using Excel, download the file FALANOVA.XLS.

b. The dependent variable is attitude toward the topic (as created in Chapter 4).

c. For this assignment, follow the instructions that are found in the Web page for Chapter 14, and click on hyperlink to "ANOVA with SPSS" or "ANOVA with Excel." Determine if there are significant main and interaction effects produced by the use or nonuse of the *non sequitur* fallacy in a persuasive message as moderated by the sex of the respondent. Thus, each independent variable has two levels. The experimental variable dealing with the use of the *non sequitur* fallacy is identified as "falexper" (1 = with the fallacy presented to subjects; 2 = without the fallacy presented to subjects). The remaining independent variable is "sex" and is identified with 1 equal to males and 2 equal to females.

d. *If you wish to analyze data using SPSS,* follow these instructions.

(1) Start SPSS and load ATTITUD1.SAV (if you have not already done so). Following the instructions given in the Web page, complete ANOVA with alpha risk at .05.

(2) To compute this test, click on the "Analyze" menu, and on subsequent menus that appear, click on "General Linear Model" and "Univariate." In the dialog box titled "Univariate," place "Attitude" in the "Dependent Variable" list. Place "sex" and "falexper" in the "Fixed Factor(s)" list. Click on the "Options" button. On the "Univariate: Options" dialog box, check the "Descriptive Statistics" and "Homogeneity of Variance" boxes. Click "Continue" and then "OK" buttons.

e. *If you wish to analyze data using Excel,* follow these instructions. *Note:* Excel places considerable limitations on format for inputting data for two-factor analysis of variance. In the first place, you must have equal numbers of events in the cells of the factorial design. In the second place, the levels of one independent variable must be placed in separate columns of the spreadsheet. In the third place, the cell entries must be placed in the cells created by this arrangement: they cannot be placed in a separate column.

(1) Start Excel and load FALANOVA.XLS. Following the instructions given in the Web page, complete analysis of variance with alpha risk of .05.

(2) Locate a place to put the output. Go to row 2 column E, and click on the cell to make it active. Click on the "Tools" menu, and then click on "Data Analysis." In the dialog box titled "Data Analysis," select "ANOVA: Two-Factor with Replication" and click "OK." In the dialog box "ANOVA: Two-Factor with Replication," go to the "Input Range" field and enter the starting cell and ending cell for the entire matrix (in this case, $A$1:$C$17). For the "Rows per sample" field, enter the number of events in each condition (8 in this case). Click on the "Output Range" button, and enter the target cell in the field ($E$2). Click "OK."

Meta-Analysis

Our knowledge is the amassed thought and experience of innumerable minds.

—Ralph Waldo Emerson

CHAPTER OUTLINE

BEFORE WE GET STARTED . . .

To understand the meaning of a field's research, we have to look at the literature and attempt to summarize it from time to time. As an alternative to critical essays alone, meta-analysis brings together the results from past quantitative studies and statistically analyzes them collectively. In such a way, the actual results—not the interpretations of researchers—are combined for statistical examination. The purpose of a meta-analysis is to provide a summary of the existence and sizes of overall relationships among variables across a number of studies. Though this method once was rare in communication studies, it has become a common staple of researchers and now is a tool that is used widely. This chapter explains what meta-analysis can do, its assumptions, and the steps involved in the typical meta-analysis study. At the end of the chapter some of the advantages and disadvantages of the method also are given attention.

META-ANALYSIS AS A METHOD OF SUMMARIZING QUANTITATIVE RESEARCH LITERATURE

There is more than one way to review literature to make a research-based argument. Most of the time, students use the traditional methods of literature reviewing described in Chapter 5 and do quite well by it. But sometimes literature may be difficult to evaluate.

Sometimes the research literature seems to be contradictory. For instance, research into the persuasive effects of fear appeals, the strength of the reciprocity effect of self-disclosure, and the impact of computer-mediated instruction on student learning has sometimes been alleged to be in conflict. **Meta-analysis** is an effort to provide a way to summarize research findings by going "right to the horse's mouth" and looking at the actual statistical effects found in quantitative research studies. Meta-analysis is another way to review quantitative research literature. It is also another form of research for itself.

> **Meta-analysis** a tool by which quantitative results from previous studies are combined and analyzed statistically

Contrasting Standard Literature Review Argument with Meta-Analysis Evidence

Literature reviews take many different forms, and meta-analysis is just another way to help organize the high-quality evidence. It would be a mistake to say that there is only one way to complete a high-quality literature review. But it is true enough to

> *ways to draw conclusions about research literature*

say that we often need some help to organize information and past research. It makes sense to consider alternative ways of doing such research:

Primary analysis "the original analysis of data in a research study" (Glass, 1976, p. 3).

♦ **Primary analysis** is what we get by completing a single research study. Unfortunately, this approach rarely yields clear answers to research questions in isolation. Furthermore, some methods, such as one-shot studies, usually do not provide conclusive research findings

Secondary analysis "the re-analysis of data for the purpose of answering the original research question with better statistical techniques, or answering new questions with old data" (Glass, 1976, p. 3).

♦ **Secondary analysis** involves returning to past studies and reanalyzing their data. One example of such work was completed by James Webster (2005), who examined "peoplemeter" data collected by the A. C. Nielsen Company. He found the degree of fragmentation of United States audiences over 62 available networks was greater than generally believed. Furthermore, growing numbers of small audiences were both loyal network viewers and strongly disloyal to some specialized channels. It is not always useful to review past data sets with different statistical tools. Furthermore, in many cases, original data may not be available for analysis at some later time.

Narrative reviews reviews of literature in which published material (typically) is examined and nonquantitative assessments are made about the state of research.

♦ **Narrative reviews** are the most typical forms of literature reviews published in the field. They provide nonquantitative analyses of past research. Such work is the most typical literature review form in publication. The reasons for such prominence are easy to understand. Narrative reviews rely on strong inductive arguments that reason from past research to general conclusions, and that suggest theoretic directions for future research. Though most narrative reviews emphasize quantitative studies, qualitative studies also may be considered. Unfortunately, narrative reviews completed by researchers with strong biases or poor reasoning skills may not draw sound conclusions. Furthermore, researchers using narrative reviews sometimes reach conclusions that differ from each other. In contrast, meta-analyses examine many quantitative studies to arrive at conclusions about a body of research.

The Problem Statement in the Modern Meta-Analysis Study

suitable when

1. research questions ask about strength of relationships

Problem statements that involve questions about the strength of relationships often invite the use of meta-analysis. Researchers may ask about the size of relationships or the sizes of effects stemming from different kinds of studies. Such problem questions as the following typically invite the use of meta-analysis:

What is the size of the relationship between communication apprehension and communicator competence?

What is the size of the relationship between source credibility and persuasiveness of fear appeals?

Do studies sampling college students show greater relationships between the use of internal organizers in messages and the retention of information than studies that sample adults?

Do experimental studies show greater relationships between the use of statistical evidence in messages and the amount of attitude change than field studies?

The first two of these problem questions ask about simple relationships between variables. In meta-analysis—though the *existence* or *nonexistence* of relationships may be explored—the most useful information deals with the *size* of relationships. The second two research problem questions deal with whether different sorts of studies using different designs and methods produce differences in the effect sizes of relationships.

2. making comparisons of results from studies of different designs

Meta-analysis may also be used to explore research questions that involve the impact of different moderator variables. In fact, these different sources of variability typically are the most interesting parts of these sorts of studies. Such problem questions as the following examine the sources of different effect sizes:

3. studying the impact of moderator variables

> Is there a difference between the size of the relationship between value-based appeals in messages and perceptions of interpersonal attraction among same-sex or opposite-sex friends?

> What is the relationship between perceived similarity and depth of self-disclosure among friends and among coworkers?

Such research problem questions involve issues that ask whether different settings or different variables explain the different findings produced in studies.

Sometimes meta-analyses are used to test how well different theories explain phenomena. For instance, in an examination of the Elaboration Likelihood Model, the influence of messages involving strong evidence use, predictions based on an alternative theory proved to be most potent (Stiff, 1986). Thus, looking at meta-analyses may make researchers conclude that one theory offers superior explanations over another.

4. testing different theories

ASSUMPTIONS FOR A META-ANALYSIS STUDY

Meta-analyses make several assumptions. First, meta-analyses can only look at empirical studies (descriptive empirical studies and experiments). Furthermore, the studies must be reported in enough detail to permit the researcher to compute effect sizes. To complete a meta-analysis, you need to know such things as sample sizes[1] and actual effect sizes—or you must have access to all the coefficients necessary to compute the effect sizes. You will also want to know the reliability for measured variables. Incomplete reports of statistical output cause studies to be excluded from the eventual sample. Since only quantitative studies, rather than qualitative studies, are included for meta-analyses, reasonably complete reports of statistical results may be expected.

assumptions:

1. empirical studies only — must be completely reported

A second assumption of meta-analysis is that the empirical studies are **independent.** This assumption is not always easy to satisfy. "Since the same researchers at the same institutions tend to complete studies that repeatedly dip into the same populations, it may be difficult to find studies where samples really are

Independence the statistical assumption that groups, samples, or (in meta-analysis) studies are unaffected by each other.

---

[1]This sample size refers to the samples used for the actual statistical analyses, rather than the sample size that the researchers initially collected before deleting events.

2. *independent studies*

independent" (Reinard, 2006, p. 319). Furthermore, when researchers find methods, procedures, and messages that work, they tend to rely on the same materials for many studies. This replication may be strong, but the studies can only be called "independent" in some ways.

3. *comparability of studies*

Third, the studies must be comparable in meaningful ways. If studies follow similar designs and procedures, it makes sense to combine their results. Yet, if the studies are too different, it may not be sensible to put them together. Fortunately, there are some ways that seem to get around this problem. "One approach would be to quantify how similar the different studies are to each other (Draper et al., 1993) or how similar they are to the target circumstances, and exclude or discount in ad hoc ways those studies regarded as too dissimilar" (Wolpert & Mengersen, 2004, p. 2). Furthermore, researchers may use a method called "diffuse comparison testing" to see if there really are differences in effect sizes among the studies included in the samples. If there are no differences, the researcher may continue assuming that differences in study methods are not important enough influences on study effects to alter the size of relationships between the primary variables under study. You might wonder how we can balance the need for independence of studies with the need for comparability. The answer is that "comparable" studies are not the same as "identical" studies that use the same populations, sample groups, or materials. We can ask for studies to be both comparable and independent.

STEPS IN META-ANALYSIS RESEARCH

To illustrate the steps of meta-analysis, it would make sense to examine a hypothetical meta-analysis example. Let us suppose that you wanted to answer the following research question:

> What is the size of the relationship between teachers' levels of nonverbal immediacy and students' recall of information?

effects may be examined by using r, d, *or probabilities*

A teacher's nonverbal immediacy is his or her use of behaviors that "enhance closeness to and nonverbal interaction with another" (Mehrabian, 1969, p. 213). Following the research question, the researcher deciding on meta-analysis should look ahead a bit and decide some matters before advancing hypotheses. In particular, the researcher needs to know what effect size measures will be used. For studies dealing with continuous variables—such as those in the problem question above—using the effect size of a correlation r usually is preferred. When studies deal with categorical independent variables, the d statistic that looks at differences in means often (but not always) is recommended. In addition, based on research and theory, the direction of the relationship needs to be identified. These matters affect the phrasing of the research hypotheses (leading to either hypotheses of relationships or hypotheses of mean differences). In the case of looking at teacher nonverbal immediacy and student recall of information, past research (e.g., Kelley & Gorham, 1988) may indicate to you that there is a direct relationship between the two. Hence, you might offer the following hypothesis:

> H: Studies reveal a positive relationship between teachers' levels of nonverbal immediacy and students' recall of information.

Though such a meta-analysis hypothesis is typical, it sometimes invites researchers to make a simple mistake. Some researchers test such a hypothesis simply by examining the statistical significance of the difference between correlation of zero and the mean effect size $\bar{r}$ of a collection of studies. Nevertheless, there are many objections to this approach. One of the most obvious problems is that combining samples from different studies tends to increase sample size so much that it is almost impossible *not* to reject the null hypothesis—even when any difference really is trivial. In fact, two critics of meta-analysis (Kotiaho & Tomkins, 2002) noted that meta-analyses *cannot* really fail to claim that an observed average relationship size is beyond what would be expected due to random sampling error.[2] But it is silly to assert that *all* variables *always* are related. So, sophisticated meta-analysis hypotheses often deal with minimum effect sizes that deserve attention. For instance, in the example shown here, you might have used the interpretation guide for correlations found in Chapter 12 (Koenker, 1961, p. 52). Then, the hypothesis could be stated as "Studies reveal slight or greater positive relationship between teachers' levels of nonverbal immediacy and students' recall of information." Since a minimum correlation of .20 (equal to explaining at least 4% of the shared variance among variables) was identified as "slight" in Chapter 12, you would claim support for the hypothesis only if this minimum were reached.[3] Some researchers avoid this whole situation by not stating hypotheses at all. Instead, they rely on research questions to guide them through exploratory research using meta-analysis.

testing significance of difference between average r and zero misleading

The remaining steps in meta-analysis are similar to the steps for most other empirical studies. Of course, the raw data are from previous studies, rather than new samples from individual participants.

Sampling Quantitative Studies

Collecting the actual studies takes some work. Researchers try to complete exhaustive searches for research studies. Just as any sample needs to be "representative" of

step 1: sampling studies

---

[2]"Procedures that combine significance tests have been criticized for several reasons. First, the focus is on an overall probability instead of on distributions. In meta-analysis, however, it is necessary to examine the variation of results because both positive and negative outcomes could cancel each other out, and because conflicting results should represent a challenge to identify substantial sources of variation. Second, a *p* value just indicates the probability of an error in rejecting the null hypothesis if it were true (Type I error). It does not provide, however, an estimate of the magnitude of treatment effects. In the present example, there is evidence that the drug is beneficial, but to what degree?" (Schwarzer, 1998, ¶ 31).

[3]Of course, not everyone who completes meta-analyses is concerned about these matters. In fact, the majority of studies feature simple tests of whether the observed mean effect size is different from a zero effect size.

the population in descriptive empirical studies and experiments, the studies included in a meta-analysis must be representative of the actual scope of research that has been completed in the past.

Deciding whether to include a study sometimes depends on considering the assumptions underlying the use of meta-analysis. First, the number of studies drawn from a single article or research report should not be too great. Studies completed with the same basic materials and samples cannot be assumed to be independent. As a matter of common practice, you probably want to limit yourself to sampling no more than two or three studies from the same research article or report. Second, studies should not be included if they are radically different from others. For instance, you might wish to omit a study that involves samples of preschool students when all other studies are drawn from college and high school samples, or if measurement involves eccentric methods that defy comparison with other studies. But you must have a *reason* to delete a study. There must be an argument to show that the excluded studies were from a different population than the included studies. You cannot omit studies because you do not like their results or because they contain large effect sizes in the "wrong" direction.

other criteria:

1. limit number of studies from single sources

2. omit radically different studies

Finding Published and Unpublished Studies

methods of searching for research:

Obtaining a collection of studies that represents all relevant research requires you to exercise some solid "library" skills. There is minor controversy over whether unpublished studies should be included, but the tendency for **publication bias** (the preference for research journals to favor studies with statistically significant results [see Ashenfelter, Harmon, & Oosterbeek, 1999; DeLong & Lang, 1992; Fagley & McKinney, 1983; Givens, Smith, & Tweedie, 1997]) has led most meta-analysts to resist this bias by including as diverse a sample of studies as possible. Thus, the basic tools identified in Appendix G can be helpful. Several sources are particularly worth checking:

Publication bias the tendency for research publications to favor empirical studies reporting statistically significant effects and to deny publication to studies finding no statistically significant relationship between variables.

finding published research

♦ For published work in communication, the standard search tools of *ComAbstracts* (www.cios.org), *Communication & Mass Media Complete,* and *PsychINFO* may be used. For speech and hearing science, the indexing systems known as *PubMed* and *Linguistics and Language Behavior Abstracts* are useful. These sources are conveniently available electronically. In addition, the *Social Science Citation Index* (SSCI) can be very helpful to track down major articles, especially the most influential studies in an area. This index tracks the references that cite a particular study. It has become popular for many scholars to place copies of their research reports on their own websites. Hence, many researchers make a general search of the World Wide Web as their first option. Unfortunately, this broad search strategy also tends to produce distracting lists of commercial operations and consultants trying to sell something.

finding unpublished research

♦ For unpublished work, such as convention papers, researchers have a couple of options. *ERIC* (short for Education Resource Information Clearinghouse and also published in abstracts called *Resources in Education*) regularly indexes copies of research reports presented at professional meetings, working papers, and materials not always available in hardcopy publication. Searching *Dissertation Abstracts International* and *Masters Abstracts International* can permit researchers to identify worthy research that was completed, but may not have made the transition to formal publication. The International Communication Association provides access to full texts of papers presented at their annual convention. The archives of the National Communication Association also contain special reports not published elsewhere. In addition, the Communication Institute for Online Scholarship hosts *ComWeb MegaSearch*, which indexes nearly 90,000 Web resources in communication and mass communication studies. Furthermore, on the website for this book is *COMFile!*, which lists communication-based websites organized according to the categories of the National Communication Association. The combination of these sources, along with a search of individual websites where unpublished research papers may be posted (using the name of the author as the object of the keyword search), can help researchers find a great deal of unpublished research.

Accounting for the Possibility of Unavailable Contrary Studies

Sometimes researchers wonder if they have identified enough studies so that any undetected studies would not make any difference. This problem often is called the **file drawer effect** and assumes that a researcher who completes a study and finds no relationships usually tosses the study into a file drawer, since there is little chance that it can be published. Logically, there really is no way to be *sure* that a body of unavailable studies does *not* exist. Yet, there have been some attempts to deal with this problem. One of the most popular approaches has been computation of the so-called **fail-safe number.**

A fail-safe point is a location where jet bombers carrying nuclear weapons must receive further authorization for attack or turn back. Stretching the analogy a bit, a fail-safe number is the number of studies showing no relationship that would have to exist for the researchers to turn back and conclude that there is, in fact, no relationship between variables (see Gleser & Olkin, 1996). The larger this number is, one may reason, the less likely it is that such a body of undetected studies actually exists. But, of course, one cannot really know for sure.

To compute the fail-safe number for meta-analyses dealing with effect sizes, the following formula may be used:

> **File drawer effect** the tendency for studies that fail to find significant relationships to remain unpublished and become abandoned in hypothetical "file drawers."

> **Fail-safe number** the number of additional studies showing a zero effect that would have to exist to reverse the reported relationship size pattern.

computing the fail-safe number

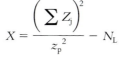

$$X = \frac{\left(\sum Z_j \right)^2}{z_p{}^2} - N_L$$

In this formula,

- Z_j is ($Z_{rj} \star \sqrt{n_j - 3}$) (the Fisher's Z transformation of correlations (r) for each (j) study included in the meta-analysis multiplied by $\sqrt{n_j - 3}$, where n_j is the sample size of each (j) study). Fisher's Z transformation is used to take correlations, which tend to have truncated distributions, and represent them as units under the standard normal curve. This Fisher's Z transformation for correlations is computed as

$$Z_r = \frac{1}{2}\ln\left(\frac{1 + r}{1 - r}\right)$$

The term "ln" instructs the researcher to take the natural logarithm of the values that follow in the parentheses.

♦ z_p^2 is the square of the z value that corresponds to the one-tailed probability level of the significance tests. Since p is commonly .05, the one-tailed z score including all but the last 5% of the area under the standard normal curve is 1.645 (see Appendix A).

♦ N_L is the number of studies located for use in the meta-analysis.

To provide an illustration, we may return to the example previously introduced. You wished to explore the question "What is the size of the relationship between teachers' levels of nonverbal immediacy and students' recall of information?" As shown on Table 15.1, you may have found studies with sample sizes ranging from 80 to 200 participants, and showing positive effect sizes expressed as correlations from .25 to .45. The table includes a column in which the correlations have been converted to Fisher's Z transformations.

Using the formula for the fail-safe number:

TABLE 15.1   META-ANALYSIS OF STUDIES ON TEACHER NONVERBAL IMMEDIACY AND RECALL OF INFORMATION

Study and Date	Sample size (n)	Direction of Relationship	r	Z_r	Number of Variables in Studies	Quality Ratings	Ranking of Studies for Soundness of Measurement	Control for Receiver Interest in the Subject	Type of Sample: 1 = college 2 = high school
1990	200	+	.33	.34	4	8	7	1	1
1995	80	+	.45	.48	2	5	3	2	2
1996	90	+	.38	.40	3	6	8	1	1
1997	100	+	.40	.42	3	7	1	2	1
1998	120	+	.25	.26	4	4	6	1	2
1999	144	+	.37	.39	2	5	4	1	1
2001	130	+	.43	.46	3	6	5	2	1
2004	110	+	.39	.41	2	8	2	1	1

RESEARCHERS IN THE FIELD: FRANKLIN J. BOSTER

Franklin J. Boster is a professor of communication at Michigan State University, the same school where he received his Ph.D. in 1978. Coming from a varied background, Frank has been a steelworker, at one time studied for the ministry and served as an evangelist, and has tirelessly promoted the use of meta-analysis in communication research. As a student at Southern Illinois University (where he earned a B.A. and an M.A.), he completed extensive study in physics and philosophy, eventually settling on psychology for graduate work. Before joining the Michigan State University faculty, he taught at Arizona State University. He has served as the editor of *Communication Monographs,* published over 60 articles, and made over 80 research presentations at professional conventions. His teaching specialties are in the areas of data analysis, research methods, social influence, and group dynamics.

♦ *You started your academic career in fields other than communication. What drew you into our field?*

As an undergraduate student I was influenced by a philosophy professor, Tom Solon. He was an excellent teacher of logic and the philosophy of science. Although I majored in psychology, Tom was my mentor. He encouraged me, and pushed me to develop and clarify arguments, regardless of the subject to which they were applied.

Because I was interested in several of the social and behavioral sciences, I applied for, and was accepted into, a master's program in behavioral science. There I was fortunate to work for an exceptional social statistician, Betty Crowther. Under her tutelage I received an excellent background in statistics and research methods. I also studied with Warren Handel, an ethnomethodologist, who explained the social world in a very different way than that to which I had been exposed. Finally, Robert O. Engbretson directed my thesis. He was teaching in a department of psychology, but his Ph.D. was in communication. In fact, Bob was Gerald Miller's first Ph.D., and it was Bob who encouraged me to go to Michigan State University to work on my Ph.D. in communication (despite my having taken only one course that could be described as a communication course). Indeed, as Gerry Miller later explained to me, it was Bob who was responsible for getting me accepted into that program. It seems that Bob had written letters recommending other students to the MSU program, and those letters were uniformly negative. Gerry said that his letter for me said something to the effect that I was OK and that I might be able to cut it, and in contrast to his other letters Gerry figured that I must be exceptional.

♦ *I know you were inspired by a number of highly respected professors with whom you became very close friends. How important were those friendships in motivating you in your career in the communication field?*

At Michigan State University I was fortunate to have a number of outstanding professors. Two in particular stand out. Gerald R. Miller was an intellectual leader in the field of communication for many years. He published more than 100 articles, many of which shaped the field as many of us know it today, and approximately a dozen books. He taught communication to me, was an incisive critic, and was one of my best friends. John E. Hunter was a psychologist whose psychometrics and mathematical modeling courses shaped the thinking of several generations of MSU Ph.D. students. He also had encyclopedic knowledge about human behavior, and he shared it freely with those who were interested. Years later I still marvel at, and am thankful for, the time these busy and productive scholars were willing to share with me.

♦ *What drew you to specialize in influence and group communication?*
As an undergraduate in my junior year I took a course in social psychology. I was intrigued by it in general and in particular by two topics, group dynamics and social influence. When I began examining these topics from the standpoint of communication—how message exchanges affect these processes—my fascination with them increased dramatically. I still am fascinated by these phenomena. I cannot explain it. Nothing preceding it or anything that I have examined later in life has interested me as much.

♦ *What do you think is the most exciting future direction for the field's research?*
The manner in which technology shapes messages, and the ways in which people interact with others using technology, raises a host of exciting questions. More generally, the development of a theory or theories that would explain many of the fragmented results that we generate would be most exciting.

♦ *Your own research on compliance-gaining message strategies has been recognized as a seminal body of work that has stimulated a lot of scholarship by others. When you prepare a research project, how much do you consider the heuristic potential of the project as you design it?*
Not too much. I do not decide to start projects by calculating how much of an impact they will have on the field or on society. I pursue matters that interest me. It may be, however, that what piques my interest is a topic that has heuristic potential.

♦ *What one or two lessons have you learned along the way that could help the novice research student have a successful career in the field's research?*
The main lesson is not to think of what you do as a profession. Think of it as a vocation or craft. Consider the process one of moving from apprentice to journeyman to master craftsman. Keep your tools in good repair and keep up with the new tools that promote your craft. Read something new each day, write something original each day, and work daily to improve your methodological and analytic skills. As you move up, remember that your craft only improves if those who come after you are better than you are. Give them big shoulders on which to stand and spend part of your day helping them develop.

$$X = \frac{\left(\sum z_j \right)^2}{z_p^{\,2}} - N_L$$

$$X = \frac{\left(\begin{array}{c} \left[.34 \star \sqrt{200 - 3} \right] + \left[.48 \star \sqrt{80 - 3} \right] + \\[4pt] \left[.40 \star \sqrt{90 - 3} \right] + \left[.42 \star \sqrt{100 - 3} \right] + \\[4pt] \left[.26 \star \sqrt{120 - 3} \right] + \left[.39 \star \sqrt{144 - 3} \right] + \\[4pt] \left[.46 \star \sqrt{130 - 3} \right] + \left[.41 \star \sqrt{110 - 3} \right] \end{array} \right)^2}{1.645^2} - 8$$

$$X = \frac{(4.78 + 4.24 + 3.75 + 4.16 + 2.82 + 4.65 + 5.20 + 4.26)^2}{2.71} - 8$$

$$X = \frac{33.86^2}{2.71} - 8$$

$$X = \frac{1146.5}{2.71} - 8$$

$$X = 423.06 - 8 = 415.06 \sim 416$$

Rosenthal (1979, 1991) suggested that a researcher should feel confident if the fail-safe number is at least $5N_L + 10$. In this case, $5N_L + 10 = 5 * 8 + 10 = 50$. Since the fail-safe number is much greater than this number, you probably would continue presuming that the effect sizes reported in this study are not likely to be overwhelmed by the discovery of a bunch of previously unknown studies that show no statistically significant effect sizes.

Not everyone is impressed by the use of fail-safe numbers. One of the biggest problems is that there is more than one way to compute a fail-safe number (such as the alternative method by Iyengar & Greenhouse, 1988), and the approaches produce different numbers. Even so, an increasingly problematic matter is that omitted studies may not show only "no differences," but they may show differences in the opposite direction. Yet, fail-safe numbers are based on the assumption that unpublished studies are unbiased and show "no effect" (a correlation coefficient of zero). If unreported studies are in the opposite direction from the average reported effect size, the actual fail-safe number could be lower than reported (Møller & Jennions, 2001, p. 584). If the unreported studies are large and in the opposite direction, the actual fail-safe number could be much lower than previously believed. Furthermore, it seems that even a small amount of publication bias

criticism of the fail-safe number:

1. more than one way to compute

2. unreported studies may not show only "no effect"

in favor of studies showing statistically significant effects can lead to spurious results (Scargle, 2000).

Computing Relationship Sizes

step 2: compute relationship sizes

After a satisfactory sample of quantitative studies, meta-analysts combine effect sizes from the different studies. There are many choices to be made. Researchers need to decide what effect size measures will be used and how to combine them.

Choosing a Measure of Effects

Meta-analyses can combine different sorts of effect sizes. Though there is a strong preference for one approach in meta-analyses, there remains more than one useful approach. As will be seen, however, collecting effect sizes has to be completed very carefully. Though researchers may combine probability levels, the author is not

---

SPECIAL DISCUSSION 15-1

HOW DO WE TEST WHETHER PUBLICATION BIAS EXISTS?

The idea that published research is biased toward research that reports statistically significant findings remains a serious question. The matter has become an area of research as well as a problem for research.

♦ *Direct Computation of Publication Bias.* Given that bias is assumed to favor research that finds statistically significant relationships, "studies showing a negligible or negative effect" (Wolpert & Mengersen, 2004, p. 33) should be published much less often than studies that show positive effects—even if they had small samples and statistically insignificant results. If researchers correlate effect sizes and sample sizes of published articles, they would expect to find an inverse relationship. Two researchers actually developed a test statistic to explore this effect (Begg & Mazumdar, 1994).

♦ *Studying the Size of Statistical Coefficients.* Since studies that use t tests tend to have large t values when sample sizes also are large, this fact can be used to measure the presence of publication bias. The researcher could take the square root of the degrees of freedom (in essence, sample size adjusted for the number of population parameters estimated from samples) and compute a simple regression coefficient with the logarithm of the absolute e of the t value (Card & Kruger, 1995). Then a statistically significant regression coefficient would be evidence of publication bias (Görg & Stobl, 2001).

♦ *Assessing the Probability of Publication Bias.* By using Bayesian statistics to contrast the probabilities for or against tendencies for publication bias, Givens, Smith, and Tweedie (1997) developed a method to compute the odds that publication bias is present.

familiar with any meta-analyses in communication studies that combine these tests alone. Instead, meta-analysis studies usually examine standardized difference scores or effects expressed as correlations.

Examining mean difference statistics is common in meta-analysis studies. At one time, meta-analysts computed the difference between experimental and control group means and standardized these differences by dividing by the standard deviation. Though many scholars still use this approach, it tends to create a biased estimator of the population difference in means. Fortunately, there is a solution to this problem. This alternative approach is called Hedges' *d* and is easily computed by the formulae found in Table 15.2. Hedges' *d* still may be interpreted as units under the standard normal curve. For instance, a Hedges' *d* of +1.5 indicates that the difference between the experimental and control group means was equal to one and a half standard deviation units in the positive direction. A *d* of −.5 indicates that the difference between the experimental and control group means was equal to a shift of one-half of a standard deviation unit in the negative direction.

examining mean standardized differences

Hedges' d preferred

It sounds simple, but some studies may make this process complicated. Many studies include more than two experimental groups. Under such circumstances, researchers need to decide which experimental condition is the most important one to compare with the control group. Then a contrast may be computed with this key comparison.[4]

differences must be computed between actual experimental and control groups

Examining effects in correlation form is most common in communication meta-analyses. One of the reasons is that effect sizes expressed as correlations are often included as standard parts of computerized output.[5] For instance, SPSS regularly provides effect sizes for analysis of variance output. Editorial boards now routinely demand researchers to report effect sizes when they find statistically significant relationships. But not all pieces of research are so completely reported. At minimum, you must be able to find the sample sizes used for the analyses and the actual test statistics. Meta-analysts often must recompute these numbers to make sure that they have coefficients that are equivalent to correlations, rather than percentages of shared variance. Even so, the convenience of getting such information from summary tables makes looking at correlations an attractive option. The formulae to obtain correlations from other statistics are found on Table 15.3.

examining effect sizes expressed as correlations

---

[4]With more than two means, the use of contrasts is recommended to tease out the differences in means that should be contrasted (DeCoster, 2005, p. 16) using the formula $L = \sum c_j \overline{X}_j$. The pooled standard error $s_p = \sqrt{\dfrac{\sum s_j^2 c_j^2 (n_j - 1)}{\sum c_j^2 (n_j - 1)}}$. To calculate the effect size as g, the formula is $g = \dfrac{L}{s_p}$. Since computing effects for within groups and mixed effects models (not covered in this book) require somewhat different approaches, interested students may check other sources (see Reinard, 2006, pp. 326–328).

[5]You have to be cautious about trusting such output. As Levine and Hullett (2002) observed, as part of its output for one-way analysis of variance, SPSS actually reports "partial eta squared," rather than eta squared itself. This measure shows a larger effect size than eta squared, and researchers must compute actual eta squared by hand.

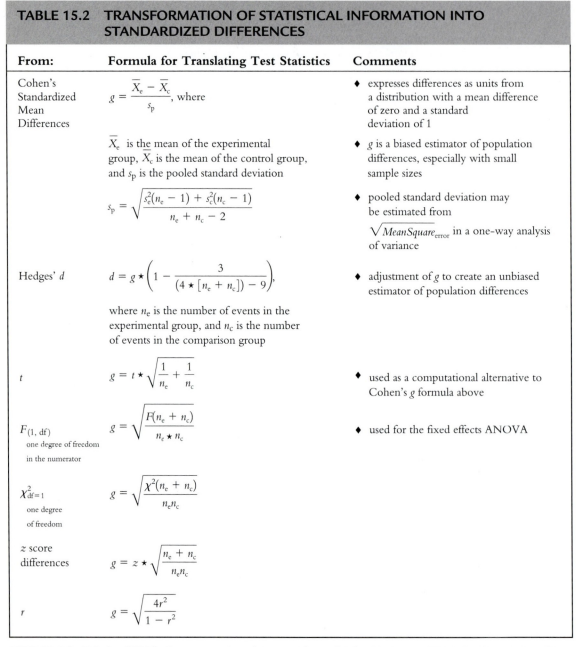

TABLE 15.2   TRANSFORMATION OF STATISTICAL INFORMATION INTO STANDARDIZED DIFFERENCES

From:	Formula for Translating Test Statistics	Comments
Cohen's Standardized Mean Differences	$g = \dfrac{\overline{X}_e - \overline{X}_c}{s_p}$, where	♦ expresses differences as units from a distribution with a mean difference of zero and a standard deviation of 1
	$\overline{X}_e$ is the mean of the experimental group, $\overline{X}_c$ is the mean of the control group, and s_p is the pooled standard deviation	♦ g is a biased estimator of population differences, especially with small sample sizes
	$s_p = \sqrt{\dfrac{s_e^2(n_e - 1) + s_c^2(n_c - 1)}{n_e + n_c - 2}}$	♦ pooled standard deviation may be estimated from $\sqrt{MeanSquare_{error}}$ in a one-way analysis of variance
Hedges' d	$d = g \star \left(1 - \dfrac{3}{(4 \star [n_e + n_c]) - 9}\right)$,	♦ adjustment of g to create an unbiased estimator of population differences
	where n_e is the number of events in the experimental group, and n_c is the number of events in the comparison group	
t	$g = t \star \sqrt{\dfrac{1}{n_e} + \dfrac{1}{n_c}}$	♦ used as a computational alternative to Cohen's g formula above
$F_{(1, df)}$ one degree of freedom in the numerator	$g = \sqrt{\dfrac{F(n_e + n_c)}{n_e \star n_c}}$	♦ used for the fixed effects ANOVA
$\chi^2_{df=1}$ one degree of freedom	$g = \sqrt{\dfrac{\chi^2(n_e + n_c)}{n_e n_c}}$	
z score differences	$g = z \star \sqrt{\dfrac{n_e + n_c}{n_e n_c}}$	
r	$g = \sqrt{\dfrac{4r^2}{1 - r^2}}$	

SOURCE: John C. Reinard (2006). *Communication Research Statistics*. Thousand Oaks, CA: Sage, p. 327. Used with permission of Sage Publications.

correcting correlations for sampling bias

Sometimes researchers look for ways to correct these correlations for imperfections prior to using them in meta-analysis computations. For instance, sample correlations (r) tend to be somewhat higher than population correlations (ρ). To correct for this bias, the transformation found on the first row of Table 15.3 may be used.

From:	Formula for Translating Test Statistics

TABLE 15.3   TRANSFORMATION OF STATISTICAL INFORMATION INTO CORRELATIONS

From:	Formula for Translating Test Statistics
Adjustment for bias in sample correlations	$G_{(r)} = r + \dfrac{r(1 - r^2)}{2(n - 3)}$, where n is the number of events in the sample, and r is the sample correlation
t	$r = \sqrt{\dfrac{t^2}{t^2 + n_e + n_c - 2}}$, where n_e is the number of events in the experimental group, and n_c is the number of events in the comparison group
$F_{(1, df)}$ one degree of freedom in the numerator	$r = \sqrt{\dfrac{F}{F + n_e + n_c - 2}}$, where F is the F ratio from the chief independent variable of interest; n_e is the number of events in the experimental group; and n_c is the number of events in the comparison group
Two-way analysis of variance (compare with η [eta]) (see Chapter 14)	$r = \sqrt{\dfrac{F_a \star d.f._a}{(F_a \star d.f._a) + (F_b \star d.f._b) + (F_{ab} \star d.f._{ab}) + d.f._e}}$, where F_a is the main effect F ratio from the chief independent variable, $d.f._a$ is the number of degrees of freedom from the chief independent variable, F_b is the F ratio from the second independent variable in the study, $d.f._b$ is the number of degrees of freedom from the second independent variable in the study, F_{ab} is the F ratio from the interaction of the independent variables in the study, $d.f._{ab}$ is the number of degrees of freedom from the interaction of the independent variables in the study, and $d.f._e$ is the number of degrees of freedom from the error term in the two-way analysis of variance
$\chi^2_{df=1}$ one degree of freedom	$r = \sqrt{\dfrac{\chi^2}{n}}$, where n is the number of events in the study
z	$r = \sqrt{\dfrac{z^2}{n}}$, where n is the number of events in the study
d (when sample sizes are unequal)	$r = \sqrt{\dfrac{d^2}{d^2 + \dfrac{1}{pq}}}$, where $p = \dfrac{n_e}{n_e + n_c}$ and $q = 1 - p$; n_e is the number of events in the experimental group; and n_c is the number of events in the comparison group
d (when sample sizes are equal)	$r = \sqrt{\dfrac{d^2}{d^2 + 4}}$
g	$r = \sqrt{\dfrac{g^2 n_e n_c}{g^2 n_e n_c + ([n_e + n_c] \star [n_e + n_c - 2])}}$

SOURCE: John C. Reinard (2006). *Communication Research Statistics*. Thousand Oaks, CA: Sage, p. 329. Used with permission of Sage Publications.

This $G_{(r)}$ value provides an estimate of the population correlation. Researchers use $G_{(r)}$ in their meta-analyses when they want to base their calculations on unbiased estimators of population correlations.

Another correction researchers often employ is the **correction for attenuation in reliability.** Failure to have perfect reliability of 1.0 reduces the size of the correlation that may be observed. For instance, if a researcher measured the relationship between assertiveness and source attractiveness, with measures that had reliability coefficients of .80 each, the highest observable correlations between these variables would be .80.

Correction for attenuation in reliability a method of adjusting observed correlation coefficients for imperfections in reliability of the measurement of variables.

But the blame is not the relationships between the variables; it's the imperfections in measurement. The correction of attenuation adjusts the observed correlations to show what extent of association would have been possible if measurement reliability were perfect. The correction for attenuation is computed by

$$\hat{r}_{xy} = \frac{r_{xy}}{\sqrt{r_x}\sqrt{r_y}},$$

where

$\hat{r}_{xy}$ is the correlation between variables x and y after correction for attenuation;

r_{xy} is the observed correlation between variables x and y;

r_x is the reliability coefficient for variable x; and

r_y is the reliability coefficient for variable y.

To find reliability of measures, researchers examine the coefficients presented by such tools as Cronbach's coefficient alpha covered in Chapter 4. It might be mentioned that this matter of reliability coefficients really only applies to measured variables. When it comes to experimental variables, it is not possible to compute such reliability coefficients.

experimental variables usually assumed to have reliability coefficients of 1.0

Hence, as a matter of convenience, researchers simply assign experimental variables reliability coefficients of 1.0. Though test-retest measures can be taken for demographic variables such as age, sex, and academic class, most researchers correcting for attenuation also assume that these matters have reliability coefficients of 1.0. Though researchers find a lot of common sense in using a correction for attenuation before conducting a meta-analysis,

correction for attenuation sometimes critcized

not everyone encourages researchers to use this method. The other side of the argument holds that since the correction for attenuation causes measures with low reliability to jump greatly, it seems to reward researchers who use poor measurement. In addition, it should be admitted that researchers who correct for attenuation often include analyses based on uncorrected correlations. So, they find that the correction for attenuation is not always treated as a full substitution for the use of raw correlations treated as effect sizes.

Identifying Essential Differences in Studies: Separating the Apples from the Oranges

step 3: separate the "apples and oranges"

Sometimes researchers using meta-analysis are accused of combining studies that are so different that the analyses are not reasonable. The issue is sometimes called the confusion of "apples and oranges" in research studies. If researchers did *not* take some action to deal with the differences among studies, there would be great justification for this position. This concern, however, involves a matter that can be tested by contrasting different characteristics of research studies. Since research rarely involves simple replication of past work, meta-analysts are wise to code different characteristics of research studies and to use methods called "focused comparisons" to test whether there are any differences produced in research effects. These comparisons can be some of the most interesting findings reported in meta-analyses. Researchers may wonder if different settings, different sample groups, or different moderating variables produce changes in effect sizes.

To deal with different sorts of studies, researchers must decide on potential differences among studies and then code these differences in basic categories. Among the most interesting results of such work is finding ways that these coded differences produce different sorts of effects. As a matter of tradition, researchers typically code characteristics of different studies:

coding moderator variables

- ◆ *Years Studies Were Completed.* Meta-analysts usually identify the year that each study was published to check whether findings from old studies are fundamentally different from findings from recent studies. Recent studies might be the most sophisticated in an area. So, researchers usually try to find out if they reflect the mainstream of research more than early studies.

- ◆ *Laboratory or Field Studies.* As previously has been observed in this book, field research and laboratory research differ in many ways. Some researchers believe that variables in field studies are often believed to be stronger than in many laboratory settings. Others take the opposite point of view. Even so, control of extraneous variables tends to be stronger in laboratory studies than in field studies. Measurement adequacy also tends to be a special strength in laboratory studies. Not surprisingly, researchers might imagine that study effect sizes might also vary from laboratory to field studies.

- ◆ *Numbers of Independent Variables.* You can only have 100% of anything, including shared variance between variables. Since studies tend to add variables to the previous studies, the number of predictor variables easily may increase from one study to the next. Thus, the effect sizes for individual variables may be artificially reduced because there are so many among which total variance must be divided. The researcher may check for this possibility by comparing study effect sizes with the number of independent variables.

- ◆ *Soundness of Measurement.* If chief variables are measured with different reliabilities, effect sizes might be expected to vary as well. Studies with low reliability generally would be expected to reveal lower effect sizes than studies with high reliability. Though the correction for attenuation may adjust for this problem, sometimes researchers wish to study the matter as a direct influence on the effect sizes of different studies.

- ◆ *Other Moderator Variables.* Sometimes researchers find that the presence or absence of some other moderator variables can make a change in the effect sizes that are observed. The moderators change from study to study. Thus researchers often find it useful to examine studies to see if there were collections in which some critical variables were present or absent. These collections of moderator variables can play an important role in explaining seemingly different patterns of results. A careful review of studies similar to those made in thoughtful narrative reviews of literature can help researchers develop lists of important moderators. Researchers often look at differences in samples (often comparing results from student and from adult samples), the presence or absence of controls, the type of research design (often comparing results from surveys and from experiments), and the use of variables reflecting different theoretic explanations.

coding possible from:

1. theoretical indices

2. archival and historical sources

The search for variables to code may be completed by direct coding, such as described above. Yet, there are two other ways researchers may identify study characteristics. First, researchers may use theoretic differences. "Sometimes, for some research paradigms, there is some numerical facet of the study's procedure, which when subjected to some theory-driven transformation gives rise to a new variable, which can then be used to predict and explain variation in study outcomes" (Mullen & Miller, 1991, p. 439). Second, researchers might rely on archival and historical sources. "Sometimes we are able to locate information about the sample, setting, or historical context of each study, which helps to explain why some studies obtained larger and more significant effects than other studies" (Mullen & Miller, 1991, p. 439). Combined with direct coding methods, these additional options can help researchers discover reasons that different studies produced very different effect sizes.

coding for study quality

A criticism sometimes made is that meta-analyses often combine effect sizes from studies of radically different quality. Preference should be given to the studies that have the highest quality, rather than treating all studies the same way. There is a way to avoid this difficulty. Study quality could be rated by a group of five or six experts.[6] These experts could rate the quality of studies on simple 10-point scales, or they could be given complex check sheets and trained to evaluate details of research inquiries. Following assessment of reliability of the measure (by use of such tools as measures of intercoder reliability), differences such as the mean ratings for the quality of each study could be calculated and used to contrast with the effect sizes (such as assigning 0 to evaluations considering no quality for the work and 10 indicating quality of the highest possible level). This method is a way to develop an operational definition of quality. Though these quality ratings are not objective, they are **intersubjective,** which means that individuals may share common agreement despite any differences in their individual perceptions. Developing rating scales and completing assessments can be time-consuming, but the effort often pays great dividends to careful researchers. Concern for study quality also goes a long way in responding to critics who believe that meta-analyses do not consider the quality of studies.

though experts' ratings of study quality are not objective, they are intersubjective

Intersubjectivity the degree to which different researchers with essentially different beliefs draw essentially the same interpretations of the meaning of observations.

---

[6]Researchers should not be the ones to complete such quality ratings. There are examples where different meta-analysts have concluded different patterns of effects from the same initial studies because they have rated the quality of studies very differently, though according to their own biases.

Assessing Mean Relationship Sizes

One might think that determining effect sizes would involve a simple process of averaging effect sizes, but it can get a little complicated. The first step involves computing the effects using standardized differences or correlations. But there is a minor problem.

step 4: compute mean relationship size

A sampling distribution of standardized differences and correlations—the latter being most often used—may be skewed. Hence, meta-analysts often make an attempt to normalize the distribution so that statistical analyses may be completed with a certain amount of confidence. Researchers typically transform the observed correlations (using the population correlation estimate and/or correction for attenuation in reliability—or not, depending on the decision of the researcher) into Fisher's Z values using the formula

$$z_r = \frac{1}{2} \ln\left(\frac{1 + r}{1 - r}\right)$$

With these new values, the researchers may use one of the formulae found on Table 15.4 to compute the mean effects. After examining these averages, researchers may work back from their computations to find the corresponding raw correlation or standardized effect sizes. Table 15.4 also shows how such computations might be made for meta-analysts who wish to examine probability assessments from statistical significance testing in past studies.

Before computing mean effect sizes, there is an additional decision to be made, whether or not to "weight" studies. Most researchers believe that studies with large sample sizes probably have more stable effect sizes than studies with small sample sizes. The reason stems from the fact that random sampling error decreases as sample sizes increase. So, the reasoning goes, studies with large sample sizes should get more weight than other studies with small sample sizes. Yet, not everyone agrees. The contrary argument is that large samples may be featured in studies that are part of a well-supported research tradition. So, weighting effects by sample sizes may give an unfair advantage to some research approaches over others (Mullen & Miller, 1991, p. 442). Another argument against weighting goes to the heart of meta-analysis. Since the "data" in meta-analyses are studies, the studies (the reasoning goes) should be used as the individual data points representing single observation units. Hence, not weighting studies may seem wise. In reality, weighted and unweighted effect sizes tend to yield different sorts of information. On one hand, analyzing weighted studies tends to reveal the nature of relationships among participants in studies. On the other hand, analyzing unweighted studies tends to reveal the nature of relationships among research studies (see DeCoster, 2005, p. 37). In most cases, communication researchers are interested in examining effect sizes associated with variables in people. So, the weighted approach remains most common.

deciding whether to weight studies, advantages and disadvantages

weighted results show relationships among study participants; unweighted results relate research studies

If weighting is to be completed, however, researchers may wonder how it should be done. Simply multiplying each Z_r by the study sample size has been common enough. Yet, modern use of meta-analysis has featured a preference for using the "inverse variance weight" (Sánchez-Meca & Marín-Martínez, 1998). This weight gives an advantage to studies that have reliably measured effect sizes. The inverse

preference for the inverse variance weight

TABLE 15.4 COMPUTATION OF MEAN EFFECTS

Combined Measures	Weighted Means	Unweighted Means
Probabilities from significance levels:	$$\overline{Z} = \frac{\sum w_j Z_j}{\sqrt{\sum w_j^2}}$$	$$\overline{Z} = \frac{\sum Z_j}{J}$$

where:

$\overline{Z}$ is the mean of the Z values of one-tailed significance tests (e.g., $p = .05$ has a corresponding Z value of 1.645); w_j is the sample size weight for study j; and J is the number of studies

Standardized differences or correlations:	$$\overline{Z}_{Fisher} = \frac{\sum w_j Z_{Fisher\,j}}{\sum w_j}$$	$$\overline{Z}_{Fisher} = \frac{\sum Z_{Fisher\,j}}{J}$$

where:

$\overline{Z}_{Fisher}$ is the mean of the Z_{Fisher} transformations of the difference values (d or g if standardized differences; r or $G_{(r)}$ if expressed as correlations); w_j is the sample size weight for study j; Z_{Fisher} is the Z transformation of the difference values transformations (d or g if standardized differences; r or $G_{(r)}$ if expressed as correlations) from study j; and J is the number of studies

NOTE: For these analyses, standardized differences are expressed as correlations using the appropriate formula from Table 15.3.

SOURCE: John C. Reinard (2006). *Communication Research Statistics*. Thousand Oaks, CA: Sage, p. 331. Used with permission of Sage Publications.

variance weight is computed by $w = \frac{1}{se^2}$. The term se^2 is the standard error of the correlation that has been transformed into Fisher's Z. Because of this transformation, the inverse variance weight turns out to be the number of events in the sample minus 3 ($n - 3$).[7] To apply the inverse variance weight to compute the mean effect size, the researcher multiplies each Fisher's Z transformed effect size by $n - 3$ for that study. After summing these values, the total is divided by the sum of all the $n - 3$ values for

---

[7]The last statement may not be immediately obvious. Here is how it occurs. The weight is $w = \frac{1}{se^2}$, but the term se^2 for a correlation subjected to Fisher's Z is $se = \sqrt{\frac{1}{n-3}}$, which means that se^2 is $\frac{1}{n-3}$. Hence, the formula for the inverse variance weight is the same as $w = \frac{1}{\left(\frac{1}{n-3}\right)}$. Working through the arithmetic, the term $1 \div \frac{1}{n-3}$ is the same as $1 \star \frac{n-3}{1}$, which becomes $w = n - 3$.

all studies. Of course, Fisher's Z values are not correlations. To transform the effect size back to its original metric, the researcher uses the following formula:

$$r = \frac{e^{2^{Z_{Fisher}}} - 1}{e^{2^{Z_{Fisher}}} + 1}$$

where e is the natural logarithm. Of course, researchers also could report the mean of raw effect sizes, but such means would show a bias when estimating population effect sizes. To identify the mean effect size for the data found on Table 15.1, you would make the following computation using the inverse variance weight:

$$\overline{Z}_{Fisher} = \frac{\sum w_j Z_{Fisher\,j}}{\sum w_j}$$

$$= \frac{\begin{array}{c}([200 - 3] \star .34) + ([80 - 3] \star .48) + ([90 - 3] \star .40) \\ + ([100 - 3] \star .42) + \\ ([120 - 3] \star .26) + ([144 - 3] \star .39) + ([130 - 3] \star .46) \\ + ([110 - 3] \star .41)\end{array}}{\begin{array}{c}(200 - 3) + (80 - 3) + (90 - 3) + (100 - 3) + (120 - 3) \\ + (144 - 3) + (130 - 3) + (110 - 3)\end{array}}$$

$$= \frac{\begin{array}{c}66.98 + 36.96 + 34.8 + 40.74 + \\ 30.42 + 54.99 + 58.42 + 43.87\end{array}}{950} = \frac{367.18}{950}$$

$$= .3865 \approx .39$$

In contrast, the unweighted Z_r was .395, which rounds to .40. To transform this $\overline{Z}_r$ value back to an equivalent correlation, you would use the formula

$$r = \frac{e^{2^{Z_{Fisher}}} - 1}{e^{2^{Z_{Fisher}}} + 1}, \text{ where } e^2 \text{ is the square of the base of the natural logarithm}$$

$$r = \frac{7.389056^{.39} - 1}{7.389056^{.39} + 1} = \frac{2.18 - 1}{2.18 + 1} = \frac{1.18}{3.18} = .3711 \approx .37$$

The equivalent transformation back to correlations for the unweighted mean effect would be a correlation of .3799, which rounds to an average correlation of .38.

Interpreting the meaning of the mean effect size begins by using standard guidelines, such as those for correlations found in Chapter 12. Using such a standard, the weighted and unweighted mean correlations would be taken as evidence of a "slight" relationship. When researchers look for standardized mean differences, a popular guideline is to consider differences of at least .2 as "small," a minimum of .5 as "medium," and any standardized difference of at least .8 as "large" (Cohen, 1992). Many researchers test whether this mean effect size has a statistically significant difference from zero. But, as we have previously explained in this chapter, this approach is misguided. Given the sample sizes involved across meta-analyses, this step rarely reveals much of interest. The test is nearly always "statistically significant" as an artifact of large sample sizes, even though the actual effect sizes

interpreting mean effect sizes

inadvisability of testing the mean effect size for statistical significance

may be trivial at best. Furthermore, there is some doubt as to whether samples of statistics based on samples of studies, rather than on raw data, meet many of the assumptions underlying most tests of statistical significance of effect sizes (Strube & Hartmann, 1983).

Making Diffuse Comparisons

step 5: making diffuse comparisons

One of the most important parts of a meta-analysis is checking to see if the collection of effect sizes shows consistency or inconsistency. If the effect sizes are inconsistent, the researcher has reason to believe that there is at least another variable that is making a contribution to the variance associated with different study outcomes. On the other hand, if the effect sizes are fairly consistent, the researcher may be comfortable assuming that the studies in the meta-analysis come from the same population.

using the diffuse comparisons of effect sizes test

To test for the consistency of study effects, researchers complete a **diffuse comparisons of effect sizes** test of the observed effect sizes. The null hypothesis tested is that the collected effect sizes are homogenous and differ only at random. Finding a statistically significant (usually with alpha risk set at .05) diffuse comparison test indicates that this assumption is not tenable.[8] The formula for the diffuse comparison test for effect size is

Diffuse comparisons of effect sizes measures of the homogeneity of effect sizes in meta-analyses.

$$\chi^2_{k-1} = \sum ([n_j - 3] \star [Z_{Fisher\,j} - \overline{Z}_{Fisher}]^2),$$

where

n is the number of events in study j,

$Z_{Fisher\,j}$ is the Fisher Z for the effect from study j,

$\overline{Z}_{Fisher}$ is the mean Fisher Z score, and

k is the number of effects analyzed.

The critical value of chi-square (Appendix D) is found with degrees of freedom equal to the number of study effects minus 1. For the data found in Table 15.1, you would compute the diffuse comparisons of effect sizes test as

$$\chi^2_{k-1} = \sum ([n_j - 3] \star [Z_{Fisher\,j} - \overline{Z}_{Fisher}]^2),$$

$$= ([200 - 3] \star [.34 - .39]^2) \star ([80 - 3] \star [.48 - .39]^2) +$$
$$([90 - 3] \star [.40 - .39]^2) +$$
$$([100 - 3] \star [.42 - .39]^2) + ([120 - 3] \star [.26 - .39]^2) +$$
$$([144 - 3] \star [.39 - .39]^2) +$$
$$([130 - 3] \star [.46 - .39]^2) + ([110 - 3] \star [.41 - .39]^2)$$

$$= .49 + .62 + .01 + .09 + 1.98 + 0 + .62 + .04 = 3.85$$

At alpha risk of .05 and 7 degrees of freedom (number of effects analyzed minus $1 = 8 - 1$), the critical value of chi-square was 14.07. Since the test statistic does not fall in the critical region, you would not reject the null hypothesis of homogenous effect sizes.

---

[8]This test tends to be powerful unless studies with small samples are included in collections of large numbers of studies (Harwell, 1995).

SPECIAL DISCUSSION 15-2

WHEN ARE "SMALL" EFFECTS NOT SO SMALL?

Researchers often complete studies only to find that the effect sizes they observe are disappointingly small. Such minor effects may appear in meta-analyses when seemingly small average effect size results show limited magnitudes of effects. Many meta-analyses may be dismissed if the mean effect sizes seem small. But there is an interpretation of correlations that sometimes is ignored in introductory research and statistics books. Called the "binomial effect size display," it reveals the potential importance of even small effect sizes.

The *binomial effect size display* (often abbreviated B.E.S.D.) looks at correlations to examine their potential use to aid interpreting the actual importance of results (Rosenthal, 1983; Rosenthal, Rosnow, & Rubin, 2000; Rosenthal & Rubin, 1982a, 1982b). Correlations may inform situations where there are two options (hence the name "binomial," which is Latin for "two names"), such as "persuaded" or "not persuaded;" "win" or "lose;" "guilty" or "not guilty." A meta-analyst might look at debate teams composed of same- or opposite-sex members and find that the effect size reveals a mean correlation of .16 favoring opposite-sex debate team members. The results might be disappointing on the surface. But suppose that there were a .50-.50 chance of a debate team winning or losing a debate. This ratio would be the same as randomly guessing win-and-loss records. If the mean correlation were divided in half as .16/2, the result would be .08. This value may be interpreted as the amount that may be added or subtracted to the .50-.50 split. In other words, if there were initially a .50-.50 split in the chances of winning a debate, the research findings would reveal that—all other things being equal—the presence of same-sex debate team members would lead to a probability of winning of only .42 (42% of the time). On the other hand, including opposite-sex debate team members would lead to a probability of winning of .58 (58%). Expressing this matter differently, when starting with a .50-.50 split in probability of winning the debate, one could say that the amount of time that debate teams composed of opposite-sex members would win debates would be 58% in comparison with the 42% probability for debate teams composed of same-sex teams. Thus, in this case, the change from 42% to 58% probability shows an increase of 38%, depending on whether the debate coach pairs opposite-sex or same-sex team members. Taking care not to overstate the matter, this example shows that under some circumstances, even an effect size that seems modest can be meaningful.

In our example, the diffuse comparison of effect sizes indicated that study effect sizes showed only random variation around the mean effect size. But researchers often find that this test *is* statistically significant and they conclude that the effect sizes are not homogenous. What do they do then? By definition, the researchers know that at least two different populations of effect sizes have been mixed in the sample of studies. In short, they know their samples do, in fact, contain a mix of "apples and oranges." So, researchers must look for other variables that may explain the sources of different effect sizes. They complete a series of focused comparisons.

follow up a statistically significant diffuse comparisons effect size test with focused comparisons

Making Focused Comparisons

A statistically significant diffuse comparison of effect sizes tells us that there must be at least one moderator variable at work and operating in a nonrandom fashion.

step 6: focused comparisons

Focused comparisons
assessments in meta-
analyses to determine
whether differences in
other variables are related
to differences in the sizes
of study effects on primary
variables.

*focused comparisons for
continuous moderator variables*

*correlations may help inform
the researcher of the possible
role of some moderator variables*

Focused comparisons permit the researchers to explore the relationships between study effect sizes on one hand, and any moderator variables that may have been operating, on the other hand. Thus, the list of potential moderator variables researchers prepared and coded may be examined for possible explanations for the different effect sizes. As such, focused comparisons help researchers explain differences in effect sizes in the observed studies. It should be mentioned that meta-analysts that have specific hypotheses about differences in effects that they suspect stem from different subgroups of studies should complete focused comparisons regardless of any diffuse comparison test results.

Continuous Moderator Variables

Potential moderator variables measured as interval, ratio, or as rank ordered variables may be examined. In the example of the data found on Table 15.1, continuous measures included the year of the study (ratio level measurement), the number of independent variables in the studies (ratio level measurement), experts' *ratings* of the quality of the studies (interval or quasi-interval level measurement), and experts' *rankings* of the quality of measurement of variables (ordinal level measurement). Of course, there is more than one way to examine the association of continuous variables with effect sizes.

You could correlate effect sizes (expressed as Fisher's Z) with each of the continuous measures. In this case, the Pearson product moment correlation between the effect sizes and the date of publication was .21, a small relationship no more than "slight" using the interpretation guide found in Chapter 12. The Pearson product moment correlation between the effect sizes and the number of independent variables in a study was $-.70$, a "moderate to marked" relationship. Thus, this relationship indicates that as the number of independent variables increased in a study, the effect sizes from the primary variables was reduced. Hence, adding independent variables tended to divide contributions to total variance that somewhat reduced the reported effect sizes of interest to the researcher. The Pearson product moment correlation between the effect sizes and the experts' ratings of study quality was .19, "negligible" relationship. Thus, it seemed that the effect sizes were robust to differences in study quality. Though testing correlation coefficients for such data is highly controversial, "the correlation between study outcomes and predictors is an illuminating and informative index of the extent to which study outcomes might be accounted for by the predictor under consideration" (Mullen & Miller, 1991, p. 445).

*focused comparisons may be
used to test influences from
moderator variables*

Focused comparisons using a form of trend analysis may be applied to the experts' rankings of the soundness of measurement in the studies to be analyzed. Table 15.1 shows what happened when a group of experts ranked studies from 1 best through 9 worst. Here is a portion of the data from that table:

Rankings of Studies for Soundness of Measurement	7	3	8	1	6	4	5	2
Z_r Effect Sizes	.34	.48	.40	.42	.26	.39	.46	.41
n_j	200	80	90	100	120	144	130	110

To complete a focused comparison with these rank order variables, you would enter the *Z* distribution to help decide if there are differences stemming from levels of moderator variables. After choosing an alpha risk of .05, you might test the null hypothesis that there is no difference in effect sizes stemming from contrast levels of the moderator variable. In this case, you may be expected to use an alpha risk of .05. The test statistic is

focused comparisons with a rank order moderator variable

$$Z = \frac{\sum \lambda_j Z_{Fisher\,j}}{\sqrt{\sum \dfrac{\lambda_j^2}{n_j - 3}}},$$

formula for focused comparisons using Fisher's Z

where

λ_j (lambda) is the contrast weight for the comparison involving study j;

$Z_{Fisher\,j}$ is the Fisher's Z transformation of the effect size of study j;

n_j is the sample size for study j.

The contrast weights are orthogonal polynomials used to complete the linear effects trend analysis (as described briefly in Chapter 14). Table 15.5 shows the orthogonal polynomials for linear trends that may be applied to assessments involving 3 to 13 groups. The table's linear contrasts, however, may be continued for any number of studies in the meta-analysis.

For the data on Table 15.1, you would examine effect sizes from eight studies. Hence, the contrast weights for eight groups $(-7, -5, -3, -1, 1, 3, 5, 7)$ are arranged next to the experts' rankings of measurement quality (starting with the lowest ranking and continuing through the highest), as shown at the top of the next page.

TABLE 15.5 LINEAR ORTHOGONAL POLYNOMIALS

Number of Group Effects j	CONTRAST WEIGHT (δ_j) FOR CODING EFFECT												
	1	2	3	4	5	6	7	8	9	10	11	12	13
3	−1	0	1										
4	−3	−1	1	3									
5	−2	−1	0	1	2								
6	−5	−3	−1	1	3	5							
7	−3	−2	−1	0	1	2	3						
8	−7	−5	−3	−1	1	3	5	7					
9	−4	−3	−2	−1	0	1	2	3	4				
10	−9	−7	−5	−3	−1	1	3	5	7	9			
11	−5	−4	−3	−2	−1	0	1	2	3	4	5		
12	−11	−9	−7	−5	−3	−1	1	3	5	7	9	11	
13	−6	−5	−4	−3	−2	−1	0	1	2	3	4	5	6

Rankings of Studies for Soundness of Measurement	7	3	8	1	6	4	5	2
Contrast Weight λ_j for the Comparison Involving Study j	-5	3	-7	7	-3	1	-1	5
Z_r Effect Sizes	.34	.48	.40	.42	.26	.39	.46	.41
n_j	200	80	90	100	120	144	130	110

Carrying out the computations becomes

$$Z = \frac{\sum \lambda_j Z_{Fisher\,j}}{\sqrt{\sum \dfrac{\lambda_j^2}{n_j - 3}}}$$

$$= \frac{\begin{array}{c}(-5 \star .34) + (3 \star .48) + (-7 \star .40) + (7 \star .42) + \\ (-3 \star .26) + (1 \star .39) + (-1 \star .46) + (5 \star .41)\end{array}}{\sqrt{\begin{array}{c}\left(\dfrac{-5^2}{200 - 3}\right) + \left(\dfrac{3^2}{80 - 3}\right) + \left(\dfrac{-7^2}{90 - 3}\right) + \left(\dfrac{7^2}{100 - 3}\right) + \\ \left(\dfrac{-3^2}{120 - 3}\right) + \left(\dfrac{1^2}{144 - 3}\right) + \left(\dfrac{-1^2}{130 - 3}\right) + \left(\dfrac{5^2}{110 - 3}\right)\end{array}}}$$

$$= \frac{\begin{array}{c}(-1.7) + (1.44) + (-2.8) + (2.94) + \\ (-.78) + (.39) + (-.46) + (2.05)\end{array}}{\sqrt{\begin{array}{c}\left(\dfrac{25}{197}\right) + \left(\dfrac{9}{77}\right) + \left(\dfrac{49}{87}\right) + \left(\dfrac{49}{97}\right) + \\ \left(\dfrac{9}{117}\right) + \left(\dfrac{1}{141}\right) + \left(\dfrac{1}{127}\right) + \left(\dfrac{25}{107}\right)\end{array}}}$$

$$= \frac{1.08}{\sqrt{.13 + .12 + .56 + .51 + .08 + .01 + .01 + .23}} = \frac{1.08}{\sqrt{1.65}}$$

$$= \frac{1.08}{1.28} = .84$$

Checking the probability of the focused comparison of effect sizes is completed by looking at Appendix A and examining what portion of the area under the standard normal curve lies above this location. The value on the z table corresponding to a z value of .84 is .2995, which means that the area above that location is .3005 (.50 − .2995). Since this effect is not .05 or lower, you would not reject the null hypothesis for the focused comparison.

focused comparison example
with interval level moderator
variable

dealing with ties

In addition to examining moderators measured on the ordinal level, focused comparisons also may be applied to continuous variables measured on the interval level, if the researcher wishes. As an illustration, you might wish to complete a focused comparison (at alpha risk of .05) stemming from the number of independent variables included in the studies analyzed in the meta-analysis. You might suspect that as the number of independent variables in a study increases, smaller and smaller proportions of variance might remain among the chief independent and dependent variables. In this case, you might notice a minor difficulty since several studies feature the same number of variables. Hence, you would have to deal with ties. Here is the arrangement of data and the ties among the orthogonal polynomials:

Number of Independent Variables	Orthogonal Polynomials	Using Tied Orthogonal Polynomials
2	−7	
2	−5	−5
2	−3	
3	−1	
3	1	1
3	3	
4	5	6
4	7	

Because there are 3 studies with two independent variables, 3 with three independent variables, and 2 with four independent variables, the studies tied with the same number of independent variables must share the mean orthogonal polynomial values in that category. As can be seen below, the observed Z statistic for this focused comparison was

$$Z = \frac{\sum \lambda_j Z_{Fisher\,j}}{\sqrt{\sum \dfrac{\lambda_j^2}{n_j - 3}}}$$

$$= \frac{\begin{matrix}(6\star.34) + (-5\star.48) + (1\star.40) + (1\star.42) + \\ (6\star.26) + (-5\star.39) + (1\star.46) + (-5\star.41)\end{matrix}}{\sqrt{\begin{matrix}\left(\dfrac{6^2}{200-3}\right) + \left(\dfrac{-5^2}{80-3}\right) + \left(\dfrac{1^2}{90-3}\right) + \left(\dfrac{1^2}{100-3}\right) + \\ \left(\dfrac{6^2}{120-3}\right) + \left(\dfrac{-5^2}{144-3}\right) + \left(\dfrac{1^2}{130-3}\right) + \left(\dfrac{-5^2}{110-3}\right)\end{matrix}}}$$

$$= \frac{\begin{matrix}(2.04) + (-2.4) + (.4) + (.42) + \\ (1.56) + (-1.95) + (.46) + (-2.05)\end{matrix}}{\sqrt{\begin{matrix}\left(\dfrac{25}{197}\right) + \left(\dfrac{9}{77}\right) + \left(\dfrac{49}{87}\right) + \left(\dfrac{49}{97}\right) + \\ \left(\dfrac{9}{117}\right) + \left(\dfrac{1}{141}\right) + \left(\dfrac{1}{127}\right) + \left(\dfrac{25}{107}\right)\end{matrix}}}$$

$$= \frac{-1.52}{\sqrt{.18 + .32 + .01 + .01 + .31 + .18 + .01 + .23}} = \frac{-1.52}{\sqrt{1.25}}$$

$$= \frac{-1.52}{1.12} = -1.36$$

The negative coefficient indicates that as the number of independent variables in the study increased, the size of the relationship between the primary variables of interest decreased. To determine if this finding would be statistically significant with alpha risk of .05, you would use the left side of the standard normal curve. The question for testing is what portion of the area of the standard normal distribution lies to the left of the z value identified in this test. Appendix A reveals that the area from the mean to a z value of -1.36 includes .4131 of the area under that standard normal curve. Thus, .0869 of the distribution is below this location $(.50 - .4131)$. Since this value is greater than .05, you would not conclude the focused comparison showed a statistically significant influence from the moderator variable of number of studies.[9]

Categorical Moderator Variables

using focused comparisons for categorical variables

Many moderator variables are categorical (such as whether studies involved samples of college or high school students; whether or not a study controlled for participant interest levels in the message topic). Focused comparisons may be computed for such matters. For example, Table 15.1 identified the types of samples. College student samples were coded as "1" and high school student samples were coded as "2." Of the 8 studies examined, 6 involved samples of college students. Since the 8 orthogonal polynomials range from -7 to $+7$, some ties must be involved.[10] In this case, the orthogonal polynomials typically are tied and all the

categorical moderators often create tied weights

---

[9]Though direct examination of correlations may have been "instructive," focused comparisons showed that other continuous moderators produced no statistically significant differences (consistent with a statistically insignificant overall diffuse test). Quality rating assessments with the following data would lead to a z value of .06.

Quality Ratings	8	5	6	7	4	5	6	8
Contrast Weight λ_j for the Comparison Involving Study j using Tied Ranks	6	-4	0	3	-7	-4	0	6
Z_r Effect Sizes	.34	.48	.40	.42	.26	.39	.46	.41
n_j	200	80	90	100	120	144	130	110

Similarly, focused comparisons completed by the years of presentation with the following data produced a Z value of .17.

Years of Presentation of Studies	1990	1995	1996	1997	1998	1999	2001	2004
Contrast Weight λ_j for the Comparison Involving Study j	-7	-5	-3	-1	1	3	5	7
Z_r Effect Sizes	.34	.48	.40	.42	.26	.39	.46	.41
n_j	200	80	90	100	120	144	130	110

[10]For categorical variables taking on two values, it is arbitrary which level is given the "low" ranking polynomial coefficient.

studies in each category with ties are given the same score. This pattern is shown in the table below:

Type of Sample	Orthogonal Polynomials	Using Tied Orthogonal Polynomials
1	−7	
1	−5	
1	−3	
1	−1	−2
1	1	
1	3	
2	5	6
2	7	

Hence, in this case, you would give a polynomial weight of −2 to all the studies involving college student samples, which is the mean of all the orthogonal polynomials. Similarly, in this case, you would give a weight of 6 to the studies dealing with samples of high school students. Inserting these weights is illustrated as follows:

Sample of students:
1 = college;
2 = high school

	1	2	1	1	2	1	1	1
Contrast Weight λ_j for the Comparison Involving Study j using tied ranks	−2	6	−2	−2	6	−2	−2	−2
Z_j Effect Sizes	.34	.48	.40	.42	.26	.39	.46	.41
n_j	200	80	90	100	120	144	130	110

To complete this focused comparison for this categorical variable, you would compute

$$Z = \frac{\sum \lambda_j Z_{Fisher\,j}}{\sqrt{\sum \dfrac{\lambda_j^2}{n_j - 3}}}$$

$$= \frac{(-2\star.34) + (6\star.48) + (-2\star.40) + (-2\star.42) + (6\star.26) + (-2\star.39) + (-2\star.46) + (-2\star.41)}{\sqrt{\left(\dfrac{-2^2}{200-3}\right) + \left(\dfrac{6^2}{80-3}\right) + \left(\dfrac{-2^2}{90-3}\right) + \left(\dfrac{-2^2}{100-3}\right) + \left(\dfrac{6^2}{120-3}\right) + \left(\dfrac{-2^2}{144-3}\right) + \left(\dfrac{-2^2}{130-3}\right) + \left(\dfrac{-2^2}{110-3}\right)}}$$

$$= \frac{-.40}{\sqrt{.02 + .47 + .05 + .04 + .31 + .03 + .03 + .04}} = \frac{-.40}{\sqrt{.99}}$$

$$= \frac{-.40}{.99} = .40$$

SPECIAL DISCUSSION 15-3

A QUESTION OF ETHICS: THE MISUSE OF META-ANALYSIS

Since meta-analyses do not rely on gathering new data from research participants, they usually are welcomed by institutional research boards. Because it is a form of secondary analysis, such problems as security for original data and reducing risks to study participants do not seem to enter into the research. Yet, ethical problems can still emerge in meta-analytic studies.

One problem occurs when researchers include studies that they know are fundamentally flawed. By definition such studies are not from the same population as other legitimate studies. For instance, Susan Blackmore of the Department of Psychology at the University of the West of England, Bristol, unsuccessfully attempted to replicate research of psychic phenomena using the "Gansfeld experiment" method (in which a "psychic" attempts to identify an image that a person in another room is viewing). When she visited the Cambridge laboratory where Carl Sargent and his associates had claimed to find consistent support for this psychic phenomenon (Blackmore, 1987), she found both signs of fraud and widespread failures to follow the experimental procedures that had been claimed in publications. After the criticism was made public, the lead researcher there left the field. Despite knowing this information, two scholars (Bem & Honorton, 1994) published a widely quoted meta-analysis including 9 of these discredited studies in a final review of 28 studies. While claiming support for the so-called psi effect, these researchers concealed the fact that they had included a large proportion of supportive studies they knew to be flawed. They admitted that "one of the laboratories contributed nine of the studies but they do not say which one. Not a word of doubt is expressed, no references to my investigation are given, and no casual reader could guess there was such controversy over a third of the studies in the database" (Blackmore, 2001, p. 24). Ray Hyman (1985) noted that his meta-analyses did not support the psi effect when studies were excluded if they failed to randomize, allowed increases in Type I error beyond announced alpha risk, and failed to use duplicate copies of targets of identification. Since a meta-analysis can only be as good as the studies analyzed, it is not surprising that when fatally flawed studies were removed, meta-analyses showed that alleged effects were unfounded on such topics as the effects of phases of the moon on human behavior (Kelly, Rotton, & Culver, 1986) and the legitimacy of graphology (handwriting analysis) (Dean, 1992).

In the use of meta-analysis, an issue on the ethical borderline involves the use of statistical significance testing methods with research studies that have enormous collective sample sizes. Sometimes researchers who have no actual effects worth noting will use tests of statistical significance to claim spurious statistical effects. Yet, tests of "statistical significance" do not mean "substantive importance." Such tests only reveal how rarely observed relationships could have been found by random sampling error. With enormous sample sizes, random sampling error is reduced so much that relationships that substantively may mean nothing still are identified as "statistically significant." Many who promote meta-analysis view it as an alternative to statistical significance testing and advise against making omnibus tests of statistical significance. In some areas where there is no real support from credible individual studies, researchers might wish to misuse meta-analysis to gain this sort of illusory advantage.

Attempts to validate pseudoscience have been particularly prone to misapply meta-analyses. As an example, Dean Radin published a defense of psychic phenomena called

The Conscious Universe: The Scientific Truth of Psychic Phenomena (1997). As part of this work, he cited meta-analysis he completed with a colleague (Radin & Nelson, 1989) on the ability of psychics to use their minds to influence the sequence of numbers produced by electronic random number generators. The authors included 832 experiments, of which 235 were "controlled" studies in which psychics were not asked to influence the sequence of numbers. The sample size was the set of individual trials, which numbered in the millions. The mean effect size in the direct experimental studies was very, very small, .00032. But given the sample sizes involved (my computations suggest over 35 million trials), the researchers claimed "statistically significant" effect sizes. In a study examining "precognition," Honorton and Ferrari (1989) combined 309 studies involving nearly 2 million trials with over 50,000 participants. They found a mean effect size of only .02, but exalted that tie as "statistically significant." Derek Briggs of the University of Colorado (2005) was particularly troubled by this strategy. He warned that although typical meta-analysis studies report confidence intervals and probability levels, readers should not think that it is appropriate to report tests of statistical significance for average effects computed from combined studies. He alerted researchers and students that such practices could lead meta-analyses to be used as often to confuse as to enlighten.

As Appendix A reveals, the area under the standard normal curve that is located above a z value of .40 is .3446 (.5 − .1554). Thus, this focused comparison also was not statistically significant. Differences in effect sizes could not really be explained by the types of sample groups. The remaining categorical moderator variable—whether or not the study controlled for student interest in the topics presented by the teachers—also did not produce a statistically significant focused comparison.[11]

What happens if the researcher finds a statistically significant focused comparison? The researcher completes new diffuse tests of the groups of effect sizes created by each category level of the moderator variable. If the diffuse tests reveal that the effect sizes in each category still are not homogeneous, the researcher concludes that the critical moderator variable has not yet been found. The process continues with other moderator variables in the search for category groups with homogeneous effect sizes.

follow-up to a statistically significant focused comparison: complete diffuse comparisons

A final comment should be made about this examination of moderator variables. Moderator variables can sometimes be intercorrelated with each other. For instance, though it was not the case in the study examined here, the quality of studies might be highly correlated with their year of presentation. The presence of controls might be

check for intercorrelated moderators

---

[11]Control for student interest produced a Z of 1.31 using the following comparisons:

Control for Student Interest in the Subject								
1 = no control								
2 = control	1	2	1	2	1	1	2	1
Contrast Weight λ_j for the Comparison Involving Study j	−3	5	−3	5	−3	−3	5	−3
Z_r Effect Sizes	.34	.48	.40	.42	.26	.39	.46	.41
n_j	200	80	90	100	120	144	130	110

highly correlated with ratings of study quality. So, the researcher should look for such intercorrelations and report them (see DeCoster, 2005, p. 46). If moderators are highly correlated, then the contributions that each one actually makes to explaining differences in effect sizes will not be clear.

ASSESSING META-ANALYSIS IN COMMUNICATION RESEARCH

Meta-analysis is an established tool in communication and social science research. When applied to research questions that invite it, meta-analysis can be a highly versatile way to address research questions. Even so, when misapplied or misunderstood—as with any other research method—meta-analyses may not be helpful to gather useful information. It is wise to consider the advantages and disadvantages of using this method.

Advantages of Meta-Analysis

advantages:

1. distance from personal biases

Many elements of meta-analysis recommend it to researchers. First, by attempting to structure the examination of study findings for statistical analyses, researchers get some distance from their own biases. Researchers often find that their pet theories and explanations are exploded by one or two focused comparisons of effect sizes. In contrast, in many (but not all) narrative reviews, writers may be stimulated to see what they expect to see, rather than testing those expectations against actual findings based on research data. Though narrative reviews also rely on sound reasoning, it is possible for clever writers to interpret study findings in partial or unique ways that support an argument, rather than finding a general pattern that actually underlies research. Second, a sound meta-analysis is capable of being replicated statistically by other researchers. When meta-analyses fail to replicate each other, the differences usually turn out to be different coding choices of moderator variables or selective sampling of studies. These biases are immediately revealed by conflicts in meta-analyses. Then any differences may be corrected or conclusions may be qualified accordingly. Third, the statistics of meta-analysis allow studies with large sample sizes and accompanying reduced sampling error—those whose findings are most likely to show stable results—to be represented according to their degree of reduced sampling error. In contrast, narrative literature reviews do not have mechanisms to weight studies in a similar way. A careful writer might include such concerns in a narrative review, of course, but it is difficult to identify any narrative analysis that deliberately gives preference to past studies based on increased stability produced by large sample sizes that accompany reduced sampling error.

2. capable of replication statistically

3. allow greatest representation of studies with the least sampling error

Disadvantages of Meta-Analysis

disadvantages:

1. cannot study moderator variables unless past researchers studied them

Meta-analyses, as with all research methods, can promote only partial understandings of the richness of communication phenomena. Hence, one disadvantage of the method is that it cannot study the influences of moderator variables unless researchers have already decided to make them repeated objects of research. One study that includes a critical moderator variable rarely is enough for the focused comparisons to detect the influence of a major explanatory variable. If other researchers have not been interested in studying critical moderators, the meta-analyst is stuck. This matter gives rise to a second disadvantage: meta-analyses may not be as valuable as primary research efforts. Though some writers might disagree, the advantage of research is the discovery and development of new knowledge. In this regard, to paraphrase Wil Durant, meta-analysis is not in the front line of the siege for truth; it is captured territory. Though meta-analyses are serious research efforts, they remain a tool of secondary, rather than primary, research. A third disadvantage of meta-analysis is that it does not promote assessing conceptual issues underlying the concepts of inquiry. Though the impact of different theoretic explanations for phenomena can be coded and explored, meta-analysis is not equipped to deal with some of the important issues of research—defining the concepts under inquiry. In fact, many conflicts in research literature can be traced to researchers' using incompatible definitions and conceptualizations of their basic concepts. Finally, even though qualitative research can inform most important questions in communication, meta-analysis is restricted to analyses of quantitative research studies alone. This criticism is not a devastating one, but it means that meta-analysts sometimes limit the sources of insights that could help a serious thinker draw comprehensive conclusions about relationships among communication phenomena.

2. limited to secondary analyses only

3. no assessment of conceptual issues

4. limited to insights from quantitative research

So, where does this discussion leave us? Meta-analysis is a rich tool in the set of modern research methods. Furthermore, it helps provide researchers with high-quality evidence about research findings so that they can make reasoned arguments about important relationships among variables. Though admiring meta-analyses, researchers should expect this method to "enhance rather than replace an intelligent discussion of the critical issues" (Slavin, 1983, p. 14). Solid thinking rooted in narrative and in meta-analyses will remain welcome in the field.

meta-analysis gives high quality evidence to enhance, not replace, narrative reviews

In passing, it might be observed that some of the things sometimes alleged to be disadvantages to meta-analysis often are illusions. Though poor use of meta-analysis by some researchers certainly exists, some of the alleged disadvantages seem to be mistaken, including the reservations that

many alleged disadvantages of meta-analysis are mistaken

- ♦ meta-analyses combine studies that are so fundamentally different that they really are trying to equate "apples" with "oranges" (Response: in fact, meta-analysts code differences in study methods to avoid mixing "apples" and "oranges");

- ♦ meta-analyses typically combine studies of dubious quality (Response: many meta-analysts screen research to include only the best studies; the vast majority of meta-analysts usually code message quality and use focused comparisons of effect sizes to assess whether studies of different quality produce different effect sizes);

- ♦ meta-analyses are biased in favor of published research that shows statistical significance (Response: not only do researchers typically attempt to find unpublished studies, but they regularly test for the potential number of conflicting studies that would be required to reject the meta-analytic conclusions they draw); and

- ♦ meta-analyses emphasize single-variable influences and "main effects" (Response: coding moderator variables and conducting focused comparisons helps researchers discover important sources of interactions).

On the other hand, without attempting to denigrate narrative reviews, it should be mentioned that writers completing narrative reviews can also be plagued by each of the problems that must be faced by meta-analysts.

CHECKLIST FOR EVALUATING META-ANALYSES

_____ Was there a need for the meta-analysis indicated by uncertainty about the strength of relationships or conflicts in past research?

_____ Was the research problem question suitable for meta-analysis? Did it deal with

♦ the strength of relationships?

♦ whether different sorts of studies with different designs and methods produce differences in the effect sizes?

♦ whether different moderator variables were associated with different relationship effects?

♦ whether different theories explain different effect sizes?

_____ Were only quantitative studies included?

_____ Were the included studies reported in enough detail to permit computing effect sizes? (What information is provided about the excluded studies?)

_____ Are the included studies independent? If not, were limits placed on the number of studies (typically no more than two) reported from the same publication?

_____ Were the studies comparable in meaningful ways?

_____ What evidence is there to show that a complete search was made to find published and unpublished studies?

_____ Was the "file drawer effect" handled with a tool such as a "fail-safe" number? If so, was the fail-safe number properly interpreted (such as the standard requiring a minimum fail-safe number of $5N_L + 10$)?

_____ Was there evidence that effect sizes were correctly computed? For instance,

♦ were effect sizes computed by comparing comparable control and experimental groups?

♦ for differences, was Hedges' d used or a justification for an alternative choice?

♦ were standardized differences and correlations normalized by Fisher's Z transformation (if not, is there a justification for the alternative choice made)?

♦ for correlations, was there evidence that r was computed from appropriate information and such required computations made (such as re-computation of eta—not to be confused with partial eta reported in SPSS)?

_____ Were methods of weighting studies described (if not weighting by the inverse variance weight)?

♦ Was a rationale provided if the researcher used no weighting or an alternative to inverse variance weighting?

♦ Did the researcher avoid the mistake of testing the statistical significance of the mean effect size?

_____ Were all major moderator variables coded in the assessment of studies?

♦ How was study quality coded and what was the result of the related focused comparison?

♦ Was the rating of study quality completed by experts other than the researcher?

♦ What was the reliability of the ratings completed by the experts?

♦ Were standard elements coded, such as whether the studies were laboratory or field studies; numbers of independent variables; soundness of measurement; the presence of other moderator variables?

♦ Were moderator variables uncorrelated with each other (if any were highly correlated, what steps were made to avoid mixing influences)?

_____ If the diffuse comparison is statistically significant, were different characteristics of studies coded and made the object of focused comparisons?

♦ Were all hypothesis-based focused comparisons completed?

♦ Were all other potential moderator variables the object of focused comparisons?

_____ In the case of statistically significant focused comparisons,

♦ were follow-up diffuse tests of effect sizes computed for the levels of the critically identified moderator variables?

♦ if the diffuse test is statistically significant, what steps were taken to find other moderator variables as explanations in future meta-analyses?

SUMMARY

Meta-analysis is a tool by which quantitative results from previous studies are combined and analyzed statistically. There are several other ways to draw conclusions about research. Primary analysis is "the original analysis of data in a research study" (Glass, 1976, p. 3). Secondary analysis is "the re-analysis of data for the purpose of answering the original research question with better statistical techniques, or answering new questions with old data" (Glass, 1976, p. 3). In narrative reviews, published material (typically) is examined and nonquantitative assessments are made about the state of research. Since these latter methods sometimes reach conclusions that differ from each other, meta-analyses may be examined to arrive at conclusions about a body of research.

Problem statements that involve questions about the strength of relationships often invite the use of meta-analysis. Researchers may ask about the size of relationships, whether different sorts of studies using different designs and methods produce differences in the effect sizes of relationships, whether different moderator variables are associated with different relationship effects (whether different settings or different variables explain the different findings produced by studies), or occasionally even whether different theories explain different effects.

Meta-analyses make several assumptions. First, meta-analyses can only look at empirical studies (descriptive empirical studies and experiments) in enough detail to permit computing effect sizes. Second, the included empirical studies are assumed to be independent (the assumption that groups, samples, or [in meta-analysis] studies are unaffected by each other). Third, the studies must be comparable in meaningful ways.

After deciding that meta-analysis is the appropriate way to answer the research questions at hand, the meta-analysis may be guided by a hypothesis about effect sizes expressed as differences or as correlations. Yet researchers will not test this hypothesis for statistical significance, but typically rely on identifying minimum effect sizes. The first step after this process is to sample quantitative studies. Limits should be set on the number of studies drawn from a single article or research report (often no more than two permitted). Studies should not be included if they are radically different from others. Researchers typically are advised to look for both published and unpublished studies. The tendency for publication bias (the tendency for research publications to favor empirical studies reporting statistically significant effects and to deny publication to studies finding no statistically significant relationship between variables) encourages researchers to search for both published and unpublished material that is representative of the universe of all research related to a subject. The "file drawer effect" is the tendency for studies that fail to find significant relationships to remain unpublished and become abandoned in hypothetical "file drawers." To deal with the problem, researchers may report a "fail-safe number," which is the number of additional studies showing a zero effect that would have to exist to reverse the reported relationship size pattern. Efforts to compute fail-safe numbers have been criticized because different formulae for fail-safe numbers give different results, and for the fact that fail-safe numbers are based on the assumption that unpublished studies are unbiased (even though they could be biased in the opposite direction and, as such, the true fail-safe number could be lower than reported).

A second step in meta-analysis is computing relationship sizes. Meta-analyses usually examine standardized difference scores or effects expressed as correlations. Standardized difference (computing the difference between experimental and control group means and standardizing these differences by dividing by the standard deviation) creates a biased estimator of the population difference in means. A preferred alternative is the use of Hedges' d. Examining effects in correlation form are most common in communication meta-analyses. These study correlations may be corrected for bias in estimating population correlations by use of the $G_{(r)}$ value. Correlations may also be subjected to the correction for attenuation, which is a method of adjusting observed correlation coefficients for imperfections in reliability of the measurement of variables (in such corrections, manipulated experimental variables are assumed to have reliability coefficients of 1.0). The correction for attenuation has been criticized for seeming to reward researchers who use poor measurement.

A third step in meta-analysis is identifying essential differences in studies or separating the "apples" from the "oranges." Meta-analysts are wise to code different characteristics of research studies and to use methods called "focused comparisons" to test whether there are any differences produced in research effects. Researchers typically code the years studies were completed; whether the studies were laboratory or field studies; the numbers of independent variables; the soundness of measurement; and the presence of other moderator variables. Direct coding may be guided by use of theoretical indices, or archival and historical sources. Study quality is often handled by including studies that have the highest quality. A frequent method is to have study quality rated by a group of experts and then include these ratings (or rankings) as a variable to be coded. Though these quality ratings are not objective, they may be intersubjective (the degree to which different researchers with different beliefs draw essentially the same interpretations of the meaning of observations).

A fourth step in meta-analysis involves assessing mean relationship sizes. Since a distribution of standardized differences and correlations may be skewed, normalization is usually completed by the Fisher's Z transformation. Most researchers weight studies according to some indication of sample size, since most researchers believe that studies with large sample sizes probably have more stable effect sizes than studies with small sample sizes. The contrary argument is that weighting effects by sample sizes may give an unfair advantage to some research approaches over others, since large samples may be featured in studies that are part of well-supported research traditions. Some also believe that since the "data" in meta-analyses are studies, the studies should be used as the individual data points representing single observation units. On one hand, analyzing weighted studies tends to reveal the nature of relationships among participants in studies. On the other hand, analyzing unweighted studies tends to reveal the nature of relationships among research studies. Though simple weighting by sample sizes has been common enough, modern use of meta-analysis has featured a preference for using the "inverse variance weight," which is believed to give an advantage to studies that have reliably measured effect sizes. Though some researchers have routinely tested whether this mean effect size has a statistically significant difference from zero, this approach is misguided. Such tests rarely reveal much of interest since it is nearly always "statistically significant" (as an artifact of large sample sizes across studies), and the underlying "data" may not meet many of the assumptions underlying most tests of statistical significance of effect sizes.

A fifth step is making diffuse comparisons, which are tests of the homogeneity of effect sizes. If the effect sizes are inconsistent, the researcher has reason to believe that there is at least another variable that is making a contribution to the variance associated with different study outcomes. A statistically significant diffuse comparisons test invites the use of focused comparisons to explain the sources of different effect sizes.

A sixth step involves making focused comparisons, which are assessments to determine whether differences in other variables are related to differences in the sizes of study effects on primary variables. Potential moderator variables measured as interval, ratio, or as rank ordered variables may be examined by examining correlations with study effect sizes (though it is not advised to test these correlations for statistical significance). Focused comparisons using linear orthogonal polynomials may be applied to the analysis of such continuous variables. A statistically significant focused comparison test is taken as evidence that the moderator variable used in the analysis is associated with nonrandom variation in sizes of study effect sizes. Categorical moderator variables may also be the object of focused comparisons, though an increase in the number of inevitably tied orthogonal polynomials may create an extra computational step for the researcher. After a statistically significant focused comparison test, the researcher completes new diffuse tests of the groups of effect sizes created by each category level of the moderator variable. If the diffuse tests reveal that the effect sizes in each category still are not homogeneous, the researcher concludes that the critical moderator variable has not yet been found and the search continues with other moderator variables to explain the heterogeneous effect sizes. Researchers should look for intercorrelations among moderators and report them because if moderators are highly correlated, the contributions that each one actually makes to explaining differences in effect sizes will not be clear.

Meta-analysis has several advantages: (1) by attempting to structure the examination of study findings for statistical analyses, re searchers get some distance from their own biases; (2) sound meta-analyses are capable of being replicated statistically by other researchers; and (3) the statistics of meta-analysis allow studies with large samples to be represented according to their degree of reduced sampling error. Meta-analyses have several disadvantages including that (1) they cannot study the influences of moderator variables unless researchers have already decided to make them repeated objects of research; (2) they may not be as valuable as primary research efforts in the discovery and development of new knowledge; (3) they do not promote assessing conceptual issues underlying the concepts of inquiry; and (4) they are restricted to analyses of quantitative research studies alone. Though admiring meta-analyses, most researchers realize that the method is not likely to replace narrative reviews, but to enhance reasoned discussions that flow from them. Some things sometimes alleged to be disadvantages often are illusions, including charges that meta-analyses combine studies that are so fundamentally different that they really are trying to equate "apples" with "oranges"; combine studies of dubious quality; are biased in favor of published research that shows statistical significance; and emphasize single-variable influences and "main effects." In each case, meta-analysis methods feature procedures to test these alternative possibilities.

TERMS FOR REVIEW

meta-analysis	fail-safe number
primary analysis	correction for attenuation
secondary analysis	intersubjectivity
narrative reviews	binomial effect size display
independence	diffuse comparisons of effect sizes
publication bias	focused comparisons of effect sizes
file drawer effect	

JUST FOR THE SAKE OF ARGUMENT: A REVIEW

Look at the following questions and prepare your own answers to them. As you address the questions, consider the underlying questions.

1. Some writers argue that narrative literature reviews should be replaced with meta-analyses of research literature. They think that meta-analyses give objective information and narrative reviews are filled with personal opinion and biases. To what extent is such a position justified and to what extent is such a position unjustified?

2. One body of research on the Elaboration Likelihood Model of persuasion has been completed mostly by a group of Ohio State University psychology professors and their students. If you wanted to complete a meta-analysis of research on this theory, how would you assure the assumption of independence of studies?

3. A diffuse comparison of effect sizes test can reveal whether the effect sizes from different studies are inconsistent with each other. But how can a researcher tell what may cause the differences that are observed?

4. If a researcher completes a meta-analysis that reveals a statistically significant diffuse comparison of effect sizes test followed by no statistically significant focused comparison tests, what should be concluded?

5. Suppose you completed a meta-analysis that revealed a statistically significant diffuse comparison of effect sizes test. Then you examined the focused comparison test stemming

from the difference between field and laboratory studies. As a follow-up activity, you might complete a diffuse comparison of effect sizes test for the set of field studies and another diffuse comparison of effect sizes test for the set of laboratory studies. Yet, neither of these diffuse comparison of effect sizes tests was statistically significant. What should you conclude?

6. What can be revealed by the use of moderator variables that are highly correlated with each other? What should researchers do if they face this problem?

ACTIVITIES TO PROBE FURTHER

Go to the website for this book and look for the Student Study Materials for Chapter 15.

1. Take the study quiz and print out your answers. (Make sure to review text materials before answering questions.)

2. Here are some data for a meta-analysis of surveys of the relationship between the amount of self-disclosure and the degree of liking reported between recent acquaintances. In addition to effect sizes, researchers had a group of raters assess study quality on a scale ranging from 0 (lowest possible quality) to 10 (highest possible quality). Other moderator variables include the date of publication of the study, the number of independent variables in the study, whether the relational partners were same-sex or opposite-sex partners, and whether the samples were college students or adult populations.

Study and Date	Sample size (n)	Direction of Relationship	r	Number of Variables in Studies	Quality Ratings	Sex Composition of the Relationship Pairs 1 = same sex 2 = opposite sex	Type of Sample: 1 = college 2 = adult
1975	100	+	.33	3	8	1	2
1980	120	−	−.15	2	6	1	1
1990	290	+	.28	5	8	2	1
1990	80	+	.40	3	9	2	2
1992	150	+	.22	4	4	1	1
1997	140	−	−.20	4	5	2	1
1999	170	+	.30	5	7	1	2
2002	300	+	.33	2	6	1	2
2002	175	+	.25	2	8	1	2

Based on these data, complete a meta-analysis of these nine studies. In particular, answer the following questions:

a. If a researcher wants to identify relationships that are at least a "slight" relationship (as identified in Chapter 13), what would be his research hypothesis?

b. What would be the Fisher's Z transformed correlation for each of the studies?

c. What would be the mean effect size for these data? What would be the mean effect size if transformed back into raw scores? *Hint:* To transform a Z_{Fisher} correlation back to an untransformed correlation, the following formula is used: $r = \dfrac{e^{2Z_{Fisher}} - 1}{e^{2Z_{Fisher}} + 1}$.

d. What is the result of the diffuse comparison test?

3. Complete a diffuse comparison test for each of the moderator variables.

   a. For the number of independent or predictor variables moderator variable:
      (1) What is the z value for the focused comparison test of the "number of variables" moderator variable?
      (2) Is this effect statistically significant with an alpha risk of .05?

   b. For the sex composition of the relationship pairs moderator variable:
      (1) What are the orthogonal polynomials for each of the studies in the following arrangement?

Study Date	1975	1980	1990	1990	1992	1997	1999	2002	2002
Sex Composition	1	2	2	2	1	2	1	1	1
Polynomial with Ties									

   (2) Is this effect statistically significant with an alpha risk of .05?

   c. For the type of sample moderator variable:
      (1) What are the orthogonal polynomials for each of the studies in the following arrangement?

Study Date	1975	1980	1990	1990	1992	1997	1999	2002	2002
Type of Sample	2	1	1	2	1	1	2	2	1
Polynomial with Ties									

4. There are three continuous variables in the study: the study date for publication, the number of variables, and experts' quality ratings. What are the intercorrelations for the continuous moderator variables in the study? What interpretations must be made about the influences on moderator variables?

5. What is the "fail-safe" number for these data? Given Rosenthal's guidelines for the interpretations of the fail-safe number, what is the interpretation for these data?

6. Neither SPSS nor Excel includes a built-in subroutine to complete meta-analyses. Yet, it is possible to design a spreadsheet in Excel that includes macros and formulae that deal with the major computations involved in meta-analysis. To do so, go to the website for this book. Click on the "Chapter 15" hyperlink. Click on the link identified as "Excel File for Meta-analysis."[*]

   ◆ You will need to have Microsoft Excel installed on your computer to open this file.
   ◆ You may replace the data on this spreadsheet with your own data. In particular for the first four columns, insert your own data for those in the grid.
   ◆ What is the mean effect size?
   ◆ What is the fail-safe number?
   ◆ What is the diffuse comparison test for these studies?

---

[*]Microsoft Excel is a registered trademark of Microsoft Corporation.

APPENDIX A

Areas under the Standard Normal Curve

$$z = \frac{X - mean}{standard\ deviation}$$

z	.00	.01	.02	.03	.04	.045	.05	.06	.07	.08	.09
0.0	.0000	.0040	.0080	.0120	.0160	.0179	.0199	.0239	.0279	.0319	.0359
0.1	.0398	.0438	.0478	.0517	.0557	.0576	.0596	.0636	.0675	.0714	.0753
0.2	.0793	.0832	.0871	.0910	.0948	.0968	.0987	.1026	.1064	.1103	.1141
0.3	.1179	.1217	.1255	.1293	.1331	.1350	.1368	.1406	.1443	.1480	.1517
0.4	.1554	.1591	.1628	.1664	.1700	.1718	.1736	.1772	.1808	.1844	.1879
0.5	.1915	.1950	.1985	.2019	.2054	.2071	.2088	.2123	.2157	.2190	.2224
0.6	.2257	.2291	.2324	.2357	.2389	.2405	.2422	.2454	.2486	.2517	.2549
0.7	.2580	.2611	.2642	.2673	.2704	.2719	.2734	.2764	.2794	.2823	.2852
0.8	.2881	.2910	.2939	.2967	.2995	.3009	.3023	.3051	.3078	.3106	.3133
0.9	.3159	.3186	.3212	.3238	.3264	.3277	.3289	.3315	.3340	.3365	.3389
1.0	.3413	.3438	.3461	.3485	.3508	.3520	.3531	.3554	.3577	.3599	.3621
1.1	.3643	.3665	.3686	.3708	.3729	.3739	.3749	.3770	.3790	.3810	.3830
1.2	.3849	.3869	.3888	.3907	.3925	.3934	.3944	.3962	.3980	.3997	.4015
1.3	.4032	.4049	.4066	.4082	.4099	.4107	.4115	.4131	.4147	.4162	.4177
1.4	.4192	.4207	.4222	.4236	.4251	.4258	.4265	.4279	.4292	.4306	.4319
1.5	.4332	.4345	.4357	.4370	.4382	.4388	.4394	.4406	.4418	.4429	.4441
1.6	.4452	.4463	.4474	.4484	.4495	.4500	.4505	.4515	.4525	.4535	.4545
1.7	.4554	.4564	.4573	.4582	.4591	.4595	.4599	.4608	.4616	.4625	.4633
1.8	.4641	.4649	.4656	.4664	.4671	.4675	.4678	.4686	.4693	.4699	.4706
1.9	.4713	.4719	.4726	.4732	.4738	.4741	.4744	.4750	.4756	.4761	.4767
2.0	.4772	.4778	.4783	.4788	.4793	.4796	.4798	.4803	.4808	.4812	.4817
2.1	.4821	.4826	.4830	.4834	.4838	.4840	.4842	.4846	.4850	.4854	.4857
2.2	.4861	.4864	.4868	.4871	.4875	.4876	.4878	.4881	.4884	.4887	.4890
2.3	.4893	.4896	.4898	.4901	.4904	.4905	.4906	.4909	.4911	.4913	.4916
2.4	.4918	.4920	.4922	.4925	.4927	.4928	.2929	.4931	.4932	.4934	.4936
2.5	.4938	.4940	.4941	.4943	.4945	.4945	.4946	.4948	.4949	.4951	.4952
2.6	.4953	.4955	.4956	.4957	.4959	.4959	.4960	.4961	.4962	.4963	.4964
2.7	.4965	.4966	.4967	.4968	.4969	.4970	.4970	.4971	.4972	.4973	.4974
2.8	.4974	.4975	.4976	.4977	.4977	.4978	.4978	.4979	.4979	.4980	.4981
2.9	.4981	.4982	.4982	.4983	.4984	.4984	.4984	.4985	.4985	.4986	.4986
3.0	.4987	.4987	.4987	.4988	.4988	.4988	.4989	.4989	.4989	.4990	.4990
3.1	.4990	.4991	.4991	.4991	.4992	.4992	.4992	.4992	.4992	.4993	.4993
3.2	.4993	.4993	.4994	.4994	.4994	.4994	.4994	.4994	.4995	.4995	.4995
3.5	.4998										
4.0	.49997										
4.5	.499997										
5.0	.4999997										
6.0	.499999997										

APPENDIX B

Critical Values of t

Degrees of freedom:	.05 .10	.025 .05	.01 .02	.005 .01

Alpha risk for one-tailed tests

Alpha risk for two-tailed tests

Degrees of freedom:	.05 / .10	.025 / .05	.01 / .02	.005 / .01
1	6.314	12.706	31.821	63.657
2	2.920	4.303	6.965	9.925
3	2.353	3.182	4.541	5.841
4	2.132	2.776	3.747	4.604
5	2.015	2.571	3.365	4.032
6	1.943	2.447	3.143	3.707
7	1.895	2.365	2.998	3.500
8	1.860	2.306	2.896	3.355
9	1.833	2.262	2.821	3.250
10	1.812	2.228	2.764	3.169
11	1.796	2.201	2.718	3.106
12	1.782	2.179	2.681	3.054
13	1.771	2.160	2.650	3.012
14	1.761	2.145	2.624	2.977
15	1.753	2.132	2.602	2.947
16	1.746	2.120	2.584	2.921
17	1.740	2.110	2.567	2.898
18	1.734	2.101	2.552	2.878
19	1.729	2.093	2.540	2.861
20	1.725	2.086	2.528	2.845
21	1.721	2.080	2.518	2.831
22	1.717	2.074	2.508	2.819
23	1.714	2.069	2.500	2.807
24	1.711	2.064	2.492	2.797
25	1.708	2.060	2.485	2.787
26	1.706	2.056	2.479	2.779
27	1.706	2.052	2.473	2.771
28	1.701	2.048	2.467	2.763
29	1.699	2.045	2.462	2.756
30	1.697	2.042	2.457	2.750
35	1.690	2.030	2.438	2.724
40	1.684	2.021	2.423	2.704
50	1.676	2.009	2.403	2.678
75	1.666	1.993	2.378	2.644
100	1.660	1.984	2.364	2.626
150	1.655	1.976	2.352	2.609
200	1.652	1.972	2.345	2.601
500	1.648	1.965	2.334	2.586
∞	1.645	1.960	2.326	2.576

(Number of events minus the number of new means computed in the numerator of the *t* statistic formula)

Example:

$$t = \frac{\overline{X} - \overline{X}}{s_{\text{diff}}}$$

d.f. $= n - 2$

APPENDIX C

Critical Values of F *with Alpha Risk = .05*

between groups degrees of freedom
within groups degrees of freedom

	1	2	3	4	5	6	7	8	9	10	11	12	15	20	25
1	161.4	199.5	215.7	224.6	230.2	234	236.8	238.9	240.5	241.9	242.5	243.9	245.9	248.0	249.3
2	18.51	19.00	19.16	19.25	19.30	19.33	19.36	19.37	19.38	19.39	19.40	19.41	19.43	19.44	19.46
3	10.13	9.55	9.28	9.12	9.01	8.94	8.89	8.85	8.81	8.79	8.76	8.74	8.70	8.66	8.63
4	7.71	6.94	6.59	6.39	6.26	6.16	6.09	6.04	6.00	5.96	5.93	5.91	5.86	5.80	5.77
5	6.61	5.79	5.41	5.19	5.05	4.95	4.88	4.82	4.77	4.74	4.70	4.68	4.62	4.56	4.52
6	5.99	5.14	4.76	4.53	4.39	4.28	4.21	4.15	4.10	4.06	4.03	4.00	3.94	3.87	3.83
7	5.59	4.74	4.35	4.12	3.97	3.87	3.79	3.73	3.68	3.64	3.60	3.57	3.51	3.44	3.40
8	5.32	4.46	4.07	3.84	3.69	3.58	3.50	3.44	3.39	3.34	3.31	3.28	3.22	3.15	3.11
9	5.12	4.26	3.86	3.63	3.48	3.37	3.29	3.23	3.18	3.13	3.10	3.07	3.01	2.94	2.89
10	4.96	4.10	3.71	3.48	3.33	3.22	3.14	3.07	3.02	2.97	2.94	2.91	2.85	2.77	2.73
11	4.84	3.98	3.59	3.36	3.20	3.09	3.01	2.95	2.90	2.86	2.82	2.79	2.72	2.65	2.60
12	4.75	3.88	3.49	3.26	3.11	3.00	2.92	2.85	2.80	2.76	2.72	2.69	2.62	2.54	2.50
13	4.67	3.81	3.41	3.18	3.03	2.92	2.84	2.77	2.72	2.67	2.63	2.60	2.53	2.46	2.41
14	4.60	3.74	3.34	3.11	2.96	2.85	2.77	2.70	2.65	2.60	2.56	2.53	2.46	2.39	2.34
15	4.54	3.68	3.29	3.06	2.90	2.79	2.71	2.64	2.59	2.55	2.51	2.48	2.40	2.33	2.28
16	4.49	3.63	3.24	3.01	2.85	2.74	2.66	2.59	2.54	2.49	2.45	2.42	2.35	2.28	2.23
17	4.45	3.59	3.20	2.96	2.81	2.70	2.62	2.55	2.50	2.45	2.41	2.38	2.31	2.23	2.18
18	4.41	3.55	3.16	2.93	2.77	2.66	2.58	2.51	2.46	2.41	2.37	2.34	2.27	2.19	2.14
19	4.38	3.52	3.13	2.90	2.74	2.63	2.55	2.48	2.43	2.38	2.34	2.31	2.23	2.16	2.11
20	4.35	3.49	3.10	2.87	2.71	2.60	2.52	2.45	2.40	2.35	2.31	2.28	2.20	2.12	2.07
21	4.32	3.47	3.07	2.84	2.68	2.57	2.49	2.42	2.37	2.32	2.28	2.25	2.18	2.10	2.05
22	4.30	3.44	3.05	2.82	2.66	2.55	2.47	2.40	2.35	2.30	2.26	2.23	2.15	2.07	2.02
23	4.28	3.42	3.03	2.80	2.64	2.53	2.45	2.38	2.32	2.28	2.24	2.20	2.143	2.05	2.00
24	4.26	3.40	3.01	2.78	2.62	2.51	2.43	2.36	2.30	2.26	2.22	2.18	2.11	2.03	1.97
25	4.24	3.39	2.99	2.76	2.60	2.49	2.41	2.34	2.28	2.24	2.20	2.16	2.09	2.01	1.96
26	4.23	3.37	2.98	2.74	2.59	2.47	2.39	2.32	2.27	2.22	2.18	2.15	2.07	1.99	1.94
27	4.21	3.35	2.96	2.73	2.57	2.46	2.37	2.31	2.25	2.20	2.16	2.13	2.06	1.97	1.92
28	4.20	3.34	2.95	2.71	2.56	2.45	2.36	2.29	2.24	2.19	2.15	2.12	2.04	1.96	1.91
29	4.18	3.33	2.93	2.70	2.55	2.43	2.35	2.28	2.22	2.18	2.14	2.10	2.03	1.94	1.89
30	4.17	3.32	2.92	2.69	2.53	2.42	2.34	2.27	2.21	2.16	2.12	2.09	2.01	1.93	1.88
40	4.08	3.23	3.84	2.61	2.45	2.34	2.25	2.18	2.12	2.08	2.04	2.00	1.92	1.84	1.78
80	3.96	3.11	2.72	2.48	2.33	2.21	2.12	2.05	1.99	1.95	1.91	1.88	1.80	1.70	1.64
120	3.92	3.07	2.68	2.45	2.29	2.18	2.09	2.02	1.96	1.91	1.87	1.83	1.75	1.66	1.60
200	3.89	3.04	2.65	2.41	2.26	2.14	2.05	1.98	1.92	1.87	1.83	1.80	1.72	1.62	1.56
∞	3.84	3.00	2.61	2.37	2.21	2.10	2.01	1.94	1.88	1.83	1.79	1.75	1.67	1.57	1.51

APPENDIX D
Critical Values of Chi-Square

	Alpha Risk Levels indicating the proportion of the chi-square distribution that lies to the right of the critical value				
Degrees of freedom:	.95	.10	.05	.025	.01
1	.004	2.71	3.84	5.02	6.64
2	.10	4.61	5.99	7.38	9.21
3	.35	6.25	7.81	9.35	11.34
4	.71	7.78	9.49	11.14	13.28
5	1.15	9.24	11.07	12.83	15.09
6	1.64	10.64	12.59	14.45	16.81
7	2.17	12.02	14.07	16.01	18.48
8	2.73	13.36	15.51	17.53	20.09
9	3.33	14.68	16.92	19.02	21.67
10	3.94	15.99	18.31	20.48	23.21
11	4.57	17.28	19.68	21.92	24.72
12	5.23	18.55	21.03	23.34	26.22
13	5.89	19.81	22.36	24.74	27.69
14	6.57	21.06	23.68	26.12	29.14
15	7.26	22.31	24.99	27.49	30.58
16	7.96	23.54	26.30	28.85	32.00
17	8.67	24.77	27.59	30.19	33.41
18	9.39	25.99	28.87	31.53	34.81
19	10.12	27.20	30.14	32.85	36.19
20	10.85	28.41	31.41	34.17	37.57
21	11.59	29.62	32.67	35.48	38.93
22	12.34	30.81	33.92	36.78	40.29
23	13.09	32.01	35.17	38.08	41.64
24	13.85	33.20	36.42	39.26	42.98
25	14.61	34.38	37.65	40.65	44.31
26	15.38	35.56	38.89	41.92	45.61
27	16.15	36.74	40.11	43.19	46.96
28	16.93	37.92	41.34	44.46	48.28
29	17.71	39.09	42.56	45.72	49.59
30	18.49	40.26	43.77	46.98	50.89
40	26.51	51.81	55.76	59.34	63.69
50	34.76	63.17	67.50	71.42	76.15
75	56.07	91.06	96.21	100.83	103.60
100	77.93	118.50	124.34	129.56	135.81

APPENDIX D

APPENDIX E
*Using Computers to Analyze Data: SPSS**

SPSS is a set of statistical programs that permits you to analyze data with a minimum of fuss and bother. But that statement requires some qualification: after all, we are talking about a computer program here. When it was originally developed in the late 1960s, SPSS stood for "Statistical Package for the Social Sciences." But by the time the 1990s had arrived, the program had switched from a package supported on mainframe computers for social scientists to one made widely available on PCs to students and researchers in a whole host of fields. The SPSS Corporation now uses the name without bothering to translate it. This guide will introduce you to the basics of using the SPSS **Data Editor** so that you can use data supplied to you through this book's website and so that you can make progress on your own. This guide is not meant to be a substitute for detailed training or reading of SPSS manuals. Nevertheless, as a brief aid to help get you up and running, it contains most of the "survival skills" you need to know immediately.

This appendix is based on SPSS version 14.0 for PCs (sometimes called SPSS XP) but the same basic instructions for data analysis should work for other versions as well. Rather than take users through a labyrinth of dialog boxes to define characteristics of data, SPSS now keeps **Data View** and **Variable View** tabs available to you at all times while you are in the **Data Editor.** Aside from this major format change, you should not have difficulty modifying information provided in this guide from previous versions of SPSS for Windows.†

This appendix deals with SPSS and assumes that you have some familiarity with a computer (that you know how to turn on the computer and you know that a mouse does not refer to a rodent). If these matters are not familiar to you, you should run the Windows,† brief tutorial: "Tour: Ten Minutes to Using Windows." (To run this program, select **Help** from the **Start** menu. Select the **Contents** tab on the "Help Topics: Windows Help" dialog box. Select "Tour: Ten Minutes to Using Windows," and click the **Display** button.) Second, it is assumed that you know how to navigate to find files on disks of interest to you. Third, in this discussion, when a statement instructs you to click, the reference is to a left mouse button click.

---

*SPSS is a registered trademark of the SPSS Corporation.

†Windows, Excel, and Visual Basic Script are registered trademarks of the Microsoft Corporation.

The Basic Elements of SPSS

SPSS has three windows of interest to us. The first window is the **Data Editor,** in which files of data are opened, recorded, and managed. This window is divided into two tabs to permit you to move from the data in the **Data View** to the variable definition information in the **Variable View.** The second window is the **SPSS for Windows Viewer,** usually known as the **Output** window (and we will often refer to it that way here since SPSS uses that label when the window is minimized on the screen), which displays the results of data analyses. You can also enter the **Viewer** window and edit it (since it has nearly all the tools of a modest word processing program), and eventually save it, copy it, or print out the output for insertion into papers and projects. The **Syntax Editor** allows you to enter SPSS commands using a set of program commands that resemble much of the old command language of the mainframe and DOS versions of SPSS. Though the syntax language can be valuable, especially for experienced SPSS users, our emphasis will be on the **Data Editor** and **Output** windows since these are the places where new users spend most of their time.

SPSS will usually begin by presenting you with a dialog box that invites you to take some shortcuts to organize your data analysis efforts. These options cover most of the initial steps you might wish to take. One element of great interest to novices is the tutorial. This tutorial is very clear and has colorful presentation of concepts that can help you develop your skills rapidly. The "existing data source" refers to a data file, and "another type of file" concerns such things as syntax and output files.

After this start-up dialog box, when you first start the program, **Data Editor** emerges:

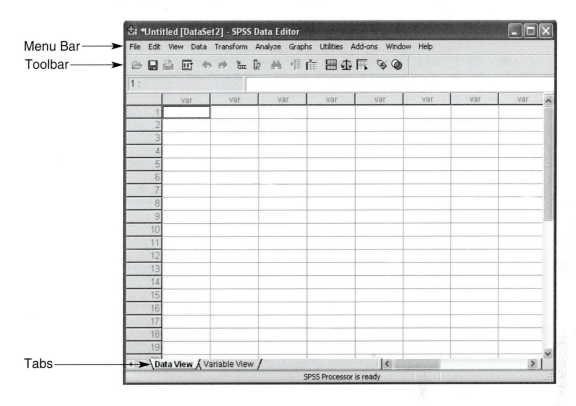

Some language should be identified. A *cell* is a rectangle that contains a piece of data in the **Data Editor.** The **Data Editor** has two parts, a tab for the **Data View** and a tab for the **Variable View.** A *menu* is a list of commands that are introduced on a succeeding list of submenus and dialog boxes. A *toolbar* is located under the main *menu bar* that provides quick access to features of SPSS. Many of the menus and the items on the toolbar are just extensions of standard Windows commands and you already may be familiar with many of them.

Menu Bar Items on the Data Editor

The menu bar on the **Data Editor** contains 10 words. Each word has its own menu. You may click on the menu bar to open a menu, or you may type "Alt" and the first letter of the menu bar. Once a menu is opened, if a word has an underlined letter, you may type this letter and the menu or window will be opened.

| File | Edit | View | Data | Transform | Analyze | Graphs | Utilities | Add-ons | Window | Help |

The **File** menu is listed first and has several functions:

♦ The **New** category creates and displays a *new* **Data, Syntax, Output, Draft Output,** and **Script** window. In addition to the simple file identifications, this menu permits you to create a new **Draft** output in the **Draft Output Viewer** and use procedures that issue special commands using OLE automation and the SPSS script language similar to Visual Basic Script.

♦ When **Open** is used, you have the ability to open a file that has already been created and saved. Files may be **Data** (data files include those written for SYSTAT, Excel, Lotus, SYLK files, dBase files, SAS, STATA, *dat, and text files), **Syntax, Output, Output Script,** or **Other** (including files in **SPSS Script** or **Viewer Document**).

♦ **Open Database** activates the *Database Wizard* to permit you to join data sets and read many different databases into SPSS.

♦ **Open Dimensions Data** imports data created and managed by the Dimensions Data Model products that create and manage survey data.

♦ **Read Text Data** permits you to import data stored as text files.

♦ **Close** when more than one data file is open, this command closes the data file in the active window.

♦ **Save** will save the current displayed file.

♦ **Save As** displays a save as window that permits you to save the currently displayed file with a different file name or file format.

♦ **Save All Data** saves all data files when more than one data file is open.

♦ **Mark File Read Only/Write** toggles back and forth to protect a file as a "read only" file or to turn off the "read only" restriction to permit writing over the file.

♦ **Rename Dataset** permits the researcher to rename a dataset file to replace the automatically assigned file name DataSet1 (or DataSet2, etc.) so that a conveniently descriptive name may be used to open the file in command syntax.

♦ **Display Data Info** permits you to display dictionary information about the selected data files (names, formats, value labels).

♦ **Apply Data Dictionary** permits you to associate a data dictionary with a data set.

♦ **Cache Data** creates a data cache during the next specified pass through the data.

♦ **Stop Processor** halts processing of data.

♦ **Switch Server** changes or adds a server as a network location.

♦ **Print Preview** displays pages that would appear in printed form.

♦ **Print** opens the print dialog to print pages or a selection on an output device.

♦ **Recently Used Data** provides a list of data sets previously used.

♦ **Recently Used Files** provides a list of previously used files, such as syntax files.

♦ Click **Exit** to close SPSS.

File **Edit** View Data Transform Analyze Graphs Utilities Add-ons Window Help

The **_Edit_** menu has several functions that allow you to manipulate your data:

♦ **_Undo_** reverses the last action taken. The same thing can be done by using the little reverse arrow key   . This process can be completed through several steps back.

♦ **_Redo_** reverses **_Undo_** and renews an erased change. The reverse arrow on the toolbar   also performs this function.

♦ **_Cut_** removes an item from the spreadsheet and places a copy on the clipboard so that the selection can be pasted at a later time.

♦ **_Copy_** places a copy of the current selection on the clipboard for pasting at a later time while also retaining the original item.

♦ Use **_Paste_** to place the contents of the clipboard at an active location.

♦ **_Paste Variables_** from the "variable view" folder, this command opens a dialog box to paste a previously copied variable with a new variable name.

♦ Use **_Clear_** to delete the contents of a cell or a range of cells.

♦ **_Insert Variable_** permits you to place a new variable in the middle of a grid of data.

♦ **_Insert Case_** permits a new data point to be inserted into a data set.

♦ **_Find_** helps you locate specific phrases, words, or values within a worksheet.

♦ **_Go to Case_** moves the active cell to a particular case event.

♦ **_Options_** are characteristics that can be adjusted by the user.

File Edit **View** Data Transform Analyze Graphs Utilities Add-ons Window Help

The **_View_** menu gives you different looks for your worksheet's toolbars and format:

♦ The **_Status Bar_** turns the status bar at the bottom of the frame on or off.

♦ **_Toolbars_** displays a submenu with all the toolbars on each window.

♦ **_Fonts_** opens a dialog box to control the SPSS font, size and style.

♦ Checking **_Grid Lines_** turns the grid lines on or off.

♦ Use **_Value Labels_** to turn on or off the display of variable value labels.

♦ **_Variables/Data_** toggles between the "Data View" folder and the "Variable View" folder.

File Edit View **Data** Transform Analyze Graphs Utilities Add-ons Window Help

The **_Data_** menu controls aspects of data definition and treatment.

♦ **_Define Variable Properties_** opens dialog boxes to aid in screening and identifying variables that may need "cleaning." In particular, it scans data and lists all variable values, reports all unlabeled values, and permits copying value labels from other variables.

- *Copy Data Properties* opens a "Copying Data Properties Wizard" to permit detailed copying of variable and data set properties from another data set or SPSS file. The actual data are not copied, but their method of treatment and their details are defined.
- *Define Dates* produces a dialog box that creates dates as variables for such things as time series analyses.
- *Define Multiple Response Sets* opens a dialog box to aid in coding data in multiple response sets of variables that underlie a common measure. The variables involve items for which persons are permitted to provide more than one answer. Each response item is treated as a separate categorical variable.
- *Identify Duplicate Cases* opens a dialog box to aid in identifying multiple responses of the same type (duplicated elements may be entire cases, variables, or sets of variables).
- *Sort cases* is a command that sorts a column of data either numerically or alphabetically.
- *Transpose* creates a new data file in which the rows and columns in the original data file are transposed so that cases (rows) become variables and variables (columns) become cases.
- *Restructure* opens the "Restructure Data" wizard to permit saving data in files with restructured form (restructuring selected variables into cases, cases into variables, and reversing all rows and column elements of data).
- *Merge Files* changes files by adding data to them from another file, updating from another file, or adding variables from another file.
- *Aggregate* produces a dialog box to permit combining groups of cases into single summary cases in a new data file in which cases are aggregated based on the value of variables identified as grouping variables.
- *Orthogonal Design* produces dialog boxes that either create or display orthogonal main effect designs of several factors without testing every combination of variable levels.
- *Copy Dataset* automatically duplicates the current data set in a new window under the names DataSet1, DataSet2, and so forth.
- *Split File* permits splitting the data file according to some cutoff criterion variable or matrix characteristic.
- *Select Cases* selects random samples to represent a set percentage of the total data set.
- *Weight Cases* is a command that gives cases different weights as a form of simulated replication.

File   Edit   View   Data   Transform   Analyze   Graphs   Utilities   Add-ons   Window   Help

Transform is a category that involves creating composite scales, scoring data, and recoding elements.

- ◆ *Compute* creates a new variable by adding (or subtracting, or multiplying, etc.) scores from other variables.

- ◆ *Recode* permits the researcher to change scores (such as reversing values for negative phrased scale items) prior to other data analysis (dialog boxes permit changes of values into the same or different variables).

- ◆ *Visual Bander* produces a dialog box to permit researchers to create new variables from continuous measures into categorical data (such as "high" and "low" levels of a variable).

- ◆ *Count* produces a dialog box that creates a variable counting how often values occur in a list of variables.

- ◆ *Rank Cases* provides for rankings produced for numeric variables only.

- ◆ *Automatic Recode* is a procedure that converts string and numeric values into consecutive integers.

- ◆ *Date/Time* opens a "Date and Time" wizard that creates new variables that are dates and times, and that also control the format to establish periods for use in other analyses.

- ◆ *Create Time Series* creates new variables that are functions (including differences, moving averages, running medians, lag, and lead functions) of existing continuous time series variables.

- ◆ *Replace Missing Values* replaces missing values with means, interpolation, or other estimating functions.

- ◆ *Random Number Generators* opens a dialog box with two random number generator options (including the Mersenne Twister generator particularly recommended for simulation studies) along with a "Set Starting Point" option that controls the random number sequence for the SPSS 12 format generator.

- ◆ *Run Pending Transforms* causes transforms to be executed.

File   Edit   View   Data   Transform   (Analyze)   Graphs   Utilities   Add-ons   Window   Help

Analyze is the actual collection of statistics. SPSS features over 100 different tools (more than you will ever use), but they are grouped into these categories:

- ◆ *Reports* include descriptions of cases, data in rows, columns, and OLAP cubes.

- ◆ *Descriptive* statistics include frequency counts and descriptive characteristics of data, including histograms, quantitative descriptive output, initial data exploration, and crosstabs (which include chi-square tests of independence and measures of association).

- ◆ *Tables* provides analysis with selected statistics of data that are presented in tabular format.

- ◆ *Compare Means* provides all forms of *t* tests and one-way analysis of variance, trend analysis, and multiple comparison tests.

- *General Linear Model* presents factorial analysis of variance and other ANOVA forms, including univariate, analysis of covariance, multivariate, repeated measures designs, and *a posteriori* tests (called *post hoc* tests here).

- *Mixed Models* opens a "Linear Mixed Models" dialog box for mixed effects models including repeated measures.

- *Correlate* computes bivariate, partial, and proximity analyses.

- *Regression* includes all forms of multiple correlation, including *Linear Multiple Regression Correlation, Curve Estimation, Binary Logistic Correlation, Multinomial Logistic Regression, Ordinal Regression, Probit Analysis, Nonlinear Regression, Weight Estimation, 2-stage Least Squares,* and *Regression with Optimal Scaling.*

- *Loglinear* includes all major forms of log linear analysis, including general, logit, and saturated forms.

- *Classify* supports two forms of cluster analysis and multiple discriminant analysis.

- *Data Reduction* includes comprehensive programs for all major methods of factor analysis, as well as correspondence analysis, and optimal scaling by alternative least squares.

- *Scale* includes both reliability assessments such as coefficient alpha and multidimensional scaling.

- *Nonparametric Tests* features most major "distribution free" statistics, including binomial z, chi-square, runs tests, and measures for multiple dependent and independent samples.

- *Time Series* packages feature methods for sequential and time series studies, including *Exponential Smoothing, Autogression, ARIMA,* and *Seasonal Decomposition.*

- *Survival* measures include *Life Tables, Kaplan-Meier Test,* and *Cox Regression.*

- *Multiple Response* tools include methods for defining sets and dealing with multiple response data from the same subjects.

- *Missing Value Analysis* analyzes patterns to detect nonrandom patterns in omitted data. Estimates (using pairwise and listwise deletion, along with expectation-maximization and regression methods) are made for descriptive statistics. For this subroutine to operate, the Missing Value Analysis option must have been chosen at the time of installation of the program.

- Depending on whether you loaded the auxiliary program or not, another set of analytic tools called *AMOS* may appear on this menu. *AMOS* is a tool that develops and analyzes path models.

File   Edit   View   Data   Transform   Analyze   Graphs   Utilities   Add-ons   Window   Help

This section includes a potpourri of 18 categories of graph applications ranging from varieties of bar charts, Pareto diagrams, and error bars, to scatterplots and examinations of autocorrelation.

File   Edit   View   Data   Transform   Analyze   Graphs   (Utilities)   Add-ons   Window   Help

Utilities permit examination of data sets and management of the analytic environment.

♦ *Variables* produces a menu that displays information about specific variables.

♦ *OMS Control Panel* opens a dialog box that permits writing selected output to different files and types, including SPSS data file format (.sav), XML format (for tables, text, and some charts), HTML (standard charts, tree models, and image files), and simple text files (with tab-delimitation or space-separation).

♦ *OMS Identifiers* opens a dialog box that helps compose OMS command syntax (including command names and subtype identifiers for production of pivot tables).

♦ *Data File Comments* permits comments to be inserted and stored with the data file.

♦ *Define Sets* identifies common sets subject to further analysis.

♦ *Use Sets* employs sets previously defined.

♦ *Run Script* calls up the use of an SPSS program script (such as VBS) or subroutine written outside the SPSS programming language environment.

♦ *Menu Editor* controls the display, order, and use of menus and submenus in SPSS.

File   Edit   View   Data   Transform   Analyze   Graphs   Utilities   (Add-ons)   Window   Help

SPSS markets a host of supplemental programs that may be used in combination with the SPSS base system. This list of *Add-ons* takes the user to SPSS Web pages that contain information about these programs and their purchase. These programs include *SPSS Maps, SPSS Exact Tests, SPSS Complex Samples, SPSS Classification Trees, SPSS Data Validation, Applications* (listing 16 programs including AMOS, Answer Tree, Clementine, Decision Time, Sample Power, SmartViewer WebServer, SPSS Data Entry, SPSS Server, WebApp, Visualization Toolkit, Text Analysis, mrInterview, mrPaper/mrScan, mrTranslate, mrTables, and mrStudio), *Services* (SPSS Consulting and SPSS Training), and *Statistics Guides* (listing three books published by SPSS on statistical analysis with SPSS).

File   Edit   View   Data   Transform   Analyze   Graphs   Utilities   Add-ons   (Window)   Help

Windows actually involves movement from one SPSS window to another. One set of windows simply lists those that are available to the user. The *Minimize All Windows* command causes all open windows to be minimized and listed at the bottom of the SPSS window.

| File | Edit | View | Data | Transform | Analyze | Graphs | Utilities | Add-ons | Window | Help |

Help menu is extensive—and very helpful—in SPSS. It includes a ***Statistics Coach*** that attempts to guide you through selection of tools. The online tutorial is really quite good. The help available includes ***Topics*** (including contents, index, find, and "ask me"); ***Tutorial; Case Studies*** (an eight-chapter tutorial that guides the user through examples illustrating the use of SPSS data analysis); ***Statistics Coach***; ***Command Syntax Reference*** (references for commands in the SPSS command language); ***Algorithms*** (an extensive set of files describing and explaining all statistics used in SPSS computations); ***SPSS Home Page*** (with many useful aids and discussion papers); ***About. . .*** (reminding you what program version you are using, your license name, and the like); ***License Authorization Wizard*** (which guides the user through the process of activating a user license); ***Register Product*** (an online registration system); and ***Check for Updates*** (selecting this item takes the user to the SPSS Web pages containing updates and upgrades). To get help at any time, press the F1 key to produce the ***Topics*** materials.

Data Editor Toolbars

Toolbars are shortcuts that let you get to commands in the SPSS system. But you do not have to show any if you choose. Display of toolbars is controlled through the ***View*** menu followed by ***Toolbars. . . .*** The toolbar icons will become fairly understandable once you have had a little experience with them, but if you forget what one means, you should not have any trouble. Just place the mouse indicator over the icon, and a written message will appear to describe what it means.

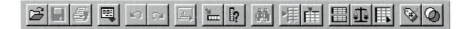

On the ***Data Editor*** the major icons across the toolbar are *"Open File," "Save File," "Print," "Dialog Recall," "Undo," "Redo," "Go To Chart," "Go To Case," "Variables," "Find," "Insert Case," "Insert Variable," "Split File," "Weight Cases," "Select Cases," "Value Labels,"* and *"Use Sets."*

Analyzing Data

The immediate step in the process of data analysis with SPSS is securing data to analyze. If you have a data set already in the works, you may use it. To enter such data, you need to begin from the location of the ***Data Editor.*** Click on ***File, Open,*** and then on ***Data*** to open the data file. A dialog box will emerge, and if you have a data set ready, you may open it, as in this example of a study dealing with the persuasive effects of a form of *non sequitur* fallacy.

If you look at these data, you will notice that variables already have been defined for them. To look at these variable definition issues, click on the **Variable View** tab at the bottom of the page.

fallacy.sav [DataSet1] - SPSS Data Editor

File Edit View Data Transform Analyze Graphs Utilities Add-ons Window Help

1 : sex   1

	sex	age	gpa	falexper	wise	good	positive	benefici	honest
1	1.00	18.00	4.00	1.00	7.00	7.00	7.00	7.00	7.00
2	2.00	19.00	3.00	2.00	6.00	6.00	7.00	6.00	3.00
3	2.00	19.00	3.00	2.00	7.00	7.00	7.00	7.00	6.00
4	2.00	19.00	3.00	2.00	4.00	5.00	5.00	5.00	4.00
5	1.00	19.00	2.70	2.00	5.00	5.00	5.00	6.00	5.00
6	1.00	19.00	2.00	1.00	4.00	3.00	4.00	4.00	2.00
7	2.00	20.00	2.80	1.00	7.00	7.00	7.00	7.00	4.00
8	2.00	19.00	3.30	1.00	4.00	4.00	4.00	4.00	6.00
9	2.00	19.00	3.50	1.00	6.00	4.00	4.00	4.00	4.00
10	2.00	28.00	3.70	1.00	1.00	1.00	1.00	1.00	4.00
11	2.00	28.00	2.70	1.00	7.00	7.00	7.00	7.00	7.00
12	2.00	22.00	3.10	2.00	5.00	5.00	5.00	5.00	6.00
13	2.00	20.00	3.00	2.00	6.00	6.00	6.00	2.00	4.00
14	2.00	18.00	3.00	2.00	6.00	6.00	7.00	7.00	6.00
15	2.00	23.00	2.80	1.00	6.00	4.00	5.00	4.00	4.00
16	2.00	25.00	2.50	1.00	4.00	4.00	4.00	4.00	4.00
17	2.00	19.00	3.20	2.00	5.00	5.00	5.00	5.00	5.00
18	1.00	18.00	2.00	2.00	5.00	5.00	5.00	5.00	4.00
19	1.00	18.00	3.90	2.00	5.00	5.00	6.00	5.00	4.00
20	1.00	18.00	3.00	1.00	5.00	5.00	5.00	5.00	4.00
21	1.00	18.00	3.80	2.00	6.00	7.00	7.00	6.00	5.00
22	1.00	20.00	1.70	2.00	4.00	5.00	7.00	6.00	5.00

◄ ► \ **Data View** ⁄ Variable View ⁄

SPSS Processor is ready

This page emerges:

fallacy.sav [DataSet1] - SPSS Data Editor

File Edit View Data Transform Analyze Graphs Utilities Add-ons Window Help

	Name	Type	Width	Decimals	Label	Values	Missing	Columns	Align	Measure
1	sex	Numeric	8	2		None	None	8	Right	Ordinal
2	age	Numeric	8	2		None	None	8	Right	Ordinal
3	gpa	Numeric	8	2		None	None	8	Right	Ordinal
4	falexper	Numeric	8	2		None	None	8	Right	Scale
5	wise	Numeric	8	2		None	None	8	Right	Ordinal
6	good	Numeric	8	2		None	None	8	Right	Ordinal
7	positive	Numeric	8	2		None	None	8	Right	Ordinal
8	benefici	Numeric	8	2		None	None	8	Right	Ordinal
9	honest	Numeric	8	2		None	None	8	Right	Ordinal
10	nice	Numeric	8	2		None	None	8	Right	Ordinal
11	virtuous	Numeric	8	2		None	None	8	Right	Ordinal
12	friendly	Numeric	8	2		None	None	8	Right	Ordinal
13	competen	Numeric	8	2		None	None	8	Right	Ordinal
14	intellig	Numeric	8	2		None	None	8	Right	Ordinal
15	trained	Numeric	8	2		None	None	8	Right	Ordinal
16	logical	Numeric	8	2		None	None	8	Right	Ordinal
17	rational	Numeric	8	2		None	None	8	Right	Ordinal
18	reason	Numeric	8	2		None	None	8	Right	Ordinal
19	support	Numeric	8	2		None	None	8	Right	Ordinal
20	clear	Numeric	8	2		None	None	8	Right	Ordinal
21	specific	Numeric	8	2		None	None	8	Right	Ordinal
22	underst	Numeric	8	2		None	None	8	Right	Ordinal
23	fallacy	Numeric	8	2		None	None	8	Right	Scale

◄ ► \ Data View \ **Variable View** ⁄

SPSS Processor is ready

The data in this sample are fairly simple. So, there is little need to change or recode scores.

How to Enter Your Own Data

A second way to deal with data is to enter your own. To do so, you need to begin with a fresh grid. From the *File* menu, click on *New* and then click on *Data.* Now, with a blank spreadsheet in front of you, you can begin entering data. But you cannot just start placing numbers on the grid. First, you must define the variables. To do so, click on the *Variable View* tab and go to the cell at the top left corner. At this location, you are in a column marked *Name.* Click or double-click it (whatever it takes) to make it active. In this cell (row 1 column 1), type the name of the first variable of interest to you. Suppose you have a little study in which you have men and women rating their attitudes toward a male and a female speaker. The first variable might be the receiver sex. Because of a convention left over from the old days, variable names must not be longer than eight characters (and must begin with a letter, may not end with a period, and may not include blanks and special characters). Thus, we will call the first variable *Receiver,* and we will enter it into the active cell.

	Name	Type	Width	Decimals	Label	Values	Missing	Columns	Align	Measure
1	receiver	Numeric	8	2		None	None	8	Right	Scale
2										
3										

To make sure that the type of variable is what we desire, we need to move to the next column to the right to make it active. When we click on the little menu bar, we get this *Variable Type* dialog box.

Since the sex of the receiver variable is an integer, we do not need any decimal places (though it wouldn't kill us to keep them). So, change the "Decimal Places" field from 2 to zero. The other options are to use a comma to delimit every three fields of data, a dot to delimit every three fields (with a comma as the decimal delimiter), scientific notation in which values include an embedded E and a signed power-of-ten exponent, the date, currency formats, and string values that are not numbers. After you have made the desired changes, click on **OK.** The field now says "Numeric" so that you know that your desired change has been made.

Clicking on the next column to the right activates a column to set **Widths.** By using the up and down arrows, you can increase or reduce the width of the data display. Clicking in the column marked **Decimals** permits you to add or subtract the number of decimal places in the data. Of course, you can also assign decimal places as part of general data definition, but this location permits a rapid change.

When you want to use a variable name that is longer than the eight characters you have been allowed, the **Label** column is permitted to accept extended variable labels. Just click on the column to make it active, and type in the full label you want up to 120 characters (though SPSS will not really print out that many characters in the output). This label is the one that will actually appear in your output and in many dialog boxes you use when analyzing data. In our example, we may want to remind ourselves that **Receiver** refers to the "receivers' sex." So, we could enter that phrase in the cell in the **Label** column.

Clicking on the **Values** column brings up a dialog box that permits you to assign a descriptive label for each value of a variable. For instance, in our data set, men were assigned to category 1 and women were assigned to category 2. The **Value Labels** dialog box lets you define how each value is to be identified. You place a value in the field next to the term **Value** and then place the label for this value in the field called, logically enough, **Value Label.** Then, by pressing the **Add** button, this change is placed in the main field. You repeat the process for the second value (as is being done in our example here) so that the word "female" will be associated with the value of 2. When done, you need only click **OK** to store this set of value labels. Value labels can be used liberally and are very useful for categorical data, but they cannot be more than 60 characters.

Researchers often find that respondents do not—or will not—give responses to some questions asked of them. SPSS permits you to place a missing value code in the place of actual data (for instance, researchers using 7-point scales may use the number zero or 9 to represent missing responses). When SPSS encounters these values for a variable, it treats them as missing, rather than actual numbers. In our example, the researchers have decided to use a zero to identify missing values. To let the computer know what is going on, missing values may be defined by clicking on the **Missing** column (sounds funny, but that's what it's called) to make it active for the variable in question. Then, a **Missing Values** dialog box appears when the selection is made. You select the **Discrete Missing**

Missing Values   [?] [X]

  ○ <u>N</u>o missing values   [OK]

  ◉ <u>D</u>iscrete missing values   [Cancel]

    [0] [   ] [   ]   [Help]

  ○ <u>R</u>ange plus one optional discrete missing value

    Low: [   ] High: [   ]

    Discrete value: [   ]

Values option and list the missing value(s) that will be used for the variable. As you can see, more than one missing value can be used (as in the case of "no response," "don't know," or "not applicable" responses to the same item). There are other options available. You could select *No Missing Values* (the default condition). Or you could select *Range Plus One Optional Discrete Missing Value* to define missing values from a range extending from a low to a high score, along with another optional missing value as well.

Clicking in the column marked *Columns* permits you to add or subtract the number of spaces wide the variable will be in the *Data Editor.* By using the up and down arrows, you can increase or reduce the width of the display. Of course, you can accomplish the same thing by clicking and dragging the column borders. By the way, column width only changes the display of values, not the actual numbers in the cells. Clicking on *Align* lets you determine if the data you enter should be right-justified, left-justified, or centered in the column in the *Data Editor.* Unless you have special reasons for making changes, you probably will want to use the defaults for these two columns.

The last column is called *Measure* and identifies the level of measurement for the variable. When you click on the variable cell in this column, a menu appears in which you specify if this variable is measured on the *Nominal, Ordinal,* or *Scale* (i.e., interval or ratio) level.

Suppose you want to have some variables follow a set pattern for such things as *Missing Values* or *Measurement* levels. You are in luck. You can copy one or more attributes and apply them to one or more other variables. All you have to do is know how to do basic *Copy* and *Paste* operations. You find the attribute you wish to apply elsewhere and *Copy* it (you may use the *Control-C* keyboard command if you want to save time). Then, you *Paste* it to the same column for a different variable row. There really is no limit. You may *Copy* a single characteristic and *Paste* it to the corresponding characteristic for another variable(s). Or, you can *Copy* all the data definition elements of one variable and apply them to another by *Paste*-ing them in complete form.

After you have defined the variables in your study, click on the *Data View* tab and you will see that all your variables are listed in columns, and you may enter data a row at a time for each event in your sample. You will notice that SPSS almost expects you to add variables. Instead of a blank column at the end of the data, another column is presented that is labeled VAR00001. If you look at the *Variable View* tab, you will notice that variable attributes have already been defined for them, resembling the adjacent variables.

Recoding and Computing

Before data can be analyzed, some effort has to be made to ensure that the variables make sense and are scored properly. One of the most common experiences is a researcher's use of scales in which some items are phrased positively and some are phrased negatively. As a result, the negatively phrased items need to be "recoded" so that they may be added with other scales to produce a reliable index. Suppose a researcher had three 1 to 7 scales (foolish-wise, good-bad, negative-positive), but the second scale item had been phrased negatively. That is, it appeared as "good-bad"— a score of 1 corresponded to a positive rating (and the other scales had it just the opposite). The researchers might wish to recode the negative scale so that they could add these items to create a common scale.

To recode the negative item, you go to the **Transform** menu, select **Recode,** and then click on one of two options: **Into Same Variables** or **Into Different Variables.** It takes some nerve to code them into the same variables (if you make a mistake, it is a hassle trying to get things right again). So, we will choose the second option, **Into Different Variables.** When we click this option, the following screen emerges and we can enter our choices in the fields provided. In the far left field, we click on the variable to recode, *good.* This variable is placed in the *"Numeric Variable ->Output Variable."*

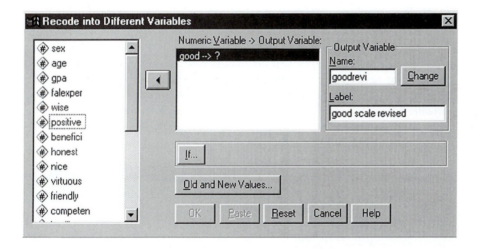

In the **Output Variable Name** field, we are asked to enter a name for the new variable (maximum of eight characters). We enter *goodrevi* and run out of space before we could complete *goodrevised.* The variable **Labels** field lets us add a full name, *good scale revised.* Click on the **Change** button to complete your changes in labels so far. If you wish to recode scores only if certain conditions are met, then click on the **If. . .** button to be taken to a dialog box that guides you through those conditions one condition at a time. Since we wish to make no exceptions, we can click on the **Old and New Values. . .** button. When we do so, this dialog box appears. The current value is placed in the field next to **Old Value,** and the new value is located in the field next to **New Value.** After each number is recoded, the **Add** button is clicked and the changes are recorded in the **Old->New** field. Missing values may be identified at this point. When the process is over, you need only press **Continue** and then **OK** to complete the recoding. The new variable appears in the last column in the data set. Then, the properly coded variables may be combined, analyzed, or examined appropriately.

To compute a new variable, we may click on the **Transform** menu and click on **Compute.** To create a composite attitude scale, we might use the compute function on a dialog box such as the one that follows. As you can see, we must first announce a label for the new variable we wish to create. In this case, we have chosen the label "Attitude" (a label with no more than eight characters) in the field marked **Target Variable.** Then, we create a little formula in the **Numeric Expression** field. The formula simply adds the three scales of interest, including the one that we have recoded. After the formula is complete, we click on **OK.**

There are options available with the ***Compute Variable*** dialog box that make it possible to compute a new variable ***If. . .*** it meets specific circumstances. Hence, ***Compute*** and ***Recode*** are very powerful tools that are favorites among researchers (though some researchers seem partial to one approach and other researchers are fond of the other). By the way, you may have noticed that it is possible to do many ***Recode*** functions with ***Compute.*** For instance, you could have recoded the negatively phrased "good-bad" scale by subtracting that 7-point scale from 8 as part of a ***Compute*** formula (i.e., wise + (8 − good) + positive).

Analysis of Data

The hardest part of SPSS is getting the data set up and ready to run. The actual process of data crunching is quite simple. Assuming that you know what statistics you wish to use, or that you know how to use the ***Statistics Coach,*** it does not take much to get meaningful output from SPSS. The assignments in this book guide you through some of the major methods of interest and need not be reviewed again here, but three tools will be illustrated since the methods to use them resemble so many others that you might be using. The three tools are ***Frequencies, Correlation,*** and ***Factorial Analysis of Variance.***

Frequencies

Sometimes researchers need some information about their data sets before they can deal with application of advanced tools. To get a description of the data set, the ***Frequencies*** subroutine is often used. By doing so, researchers can find out if their data have only the data values that they should possess and what kind of distribution of scores is available. To begin the program, you go to the ***Analyze*** menu, select ***Descriptive Statistics. . . ,*** and then click on ***Frequencies. . . .*** For our example, let us suppose that we are most interested in examining "age" as a variable. The *Frequencies* dialog box emerges. We highlight the "age" variable in the field on the left and use the arrow key to move it to the field marked *Variable(s)*. You may repeat this process as many times as you wish, but we will stop with the age variable for our example.

Since we may wish to apply specific statistical tests, we should click the *Statistics. . .* button to produce the *Frequencies: Statistics* dialog box. As the example shows, we might select statistics to provide us with the mean, median, mode, standard deviation, minimum score, maximum score, kurtosis, and skewness. When we are done, we can click on *Continue* to return to the *Frequencies* dialog box.

You could select options by clicking the *Charts. . .* button, but there is little need for us to do so given the initial level of data snooping involved here (the *Charts* option provides for bar, pie, and histograms). The *Format. . .* button takes us to a dialog box that allows us to change the nature of the output by reporting data values in ascending and descending order, lists by frequencies of occurrence, and lists comparing variables. Again, there is no need to use these options here. To run the subroutine, we need only click *OK*. The following *Output Viewer* is revealed.

The elements in the screen include the *outline field* on the left (that reports, not surprisingly, an outline of all the elements in the content field) and a *content field* on the right. You may edit the content field by clicking on the elements (most of which have been saved as objects) and adding your own content for moving, cutting, and pasting elements as you wish. In addition to the initial

```
Output1 - SPSS Viewer
File  Edit  View  Data  Transform  Insert  Format  Analyze  Graphs  Utilities  Add-ons  Window  Help
```

Frequencies

[DataSet1] C:\mm\3resbook\datafiles\fallacy.sav

Statistics

age

N	Valid	52
	Missing	0
Mean		20.0000
Median		19.0000
Mode		19.00
Std. Deviation		2.95057
Skewness		.152
Std. Error of Skewness		.330
Kurtosis		4.397
Std. Error of Kurtosis		.650
Minimum		9.00
Maximum		28.00

SPSS Processor is ready

table in the output shown above, the elements in the *content field* include this item:

AGE

	Frequency	Percent	Valid Percent	Cumulative Percent
Valid 9.00	1	1.9	1.9	1.9
18.00	12	23.1	23.1	25.0
19.00	14	26.9	26.9	51.9
20.00	13	25.0	25.0	76.9
21.00	1	1.9	1.9	78.8
22.00	3	5.8	5.8	84.6
23.00	2	3.8	3.8	88.5
24.00	1	1.9	1.9	90.4
25.00	2	3.8	3.8	94.2
26.00	1	1.9	1.9	96.2
28.00	2	3.8	3.8	100.0
Total	52	100.0	100.0	

As is obvious, these elements give you a good reason to develop a sense of understanding for your data. Furthermore, if there are key stroke errors or "impossible" data scores included, you can spot them. For instance, in these data, there is a score of 9 for the data. This response is really a missing value, and it should be defined as such before proceeding with other analyses. Indeed, this step was taken after examination of this output.

Correlation

Researchers often wish to correlate one variable with another. SPSS makes this process simple by use of a set of handy subroutines. For our analyses, let's test that old hypothesis that young people are most persuasible by correlating "age" with "attitude." To run the correlation, select the *Analyze* menu, followed by *Correlate. . . .* Then, click on *Bivariate* to see the *Bivariate Correlations* dialog box.

The box on the left includes all the variables in the data set. To include a variable in the correlation, click on it to highlight it and then use the arrow key to move it to the field marked *Variable(s).* After you have both age and attitude included, make sure that you have checked boxes to indicate which *Correlation Coefficient(s)* you wish to use. In this case, we will use the *Pearson* product moment correlation since both our variables are on the interval or ratio levels of measurement. The *Options* button is not of interest to us since we do not really need to change the output to include means, standard deviations, cross products, and covariances. Similarly, since the options for missing values are to exclude missing values pairwise or listwise (from all comparisons), we do not really need to make any changes (the default is to exclude missing values pairwise). To run the program, we click *OK.* This effort produces the output on the next page.

In this case, the correlation is inverse (it has a negative sign). Hence, the older one gets, the less positive will be one's attitude toward a new message. Of course, the oldest people in our sample were 28. So, it really wasn't much of a test. Moreover, the correlation is not significantly different from zero (as revealed by a test of significance that shows that this sized correlation based on this sample size could have been found by chance alone more often than 5 times out of 100 (67.7 times to be exact). Thus, we do not claim that these data support the hypothesis.

Output2 - SPSS Viewer

File   Edit   View   Data   Transform   Insert   Format   Analyze   Graphs   Utilities   Add-ons   Window   Help

- Output
  - Correlations
    - Title
    - Notes
    - Active Dataset
    - Correlations

Correlations

[DataSet1] C:\mm\3resbook\datafiles\fallacy.sav

Correlations

		age	fallacy
age	Pearson Correlation	1	-.059
	Sig. (2-tailed)		.677
	N	52	52
fallacy	Pearson Correlation	-.059	1
	Sig. (2-tailed)	.677	
	N	52	52

SPSS Processor is ready

Factorial Analysis of Variance

To examine the main and interaction effects of independent variables on the dependent variables, factorial analysis of variance is often completed. This method involves testing at least two independent variables to see if they produce effects on dependent variables alone or separately. In our case, we have an experiment in which arguments with (and without) fallacious non sequitur appeals were presented to men and women. We have two levels of "fallacy use" called "falexper" in this study (1 = with, 2 = without), and two levels of "receiver sex" (1 = male, 2 = female). Thus, we could treat each of these variables as an independent variable with two levels each. The dependent variable could be "attitude" toward the topic advocated in the message. To run the program, select **Analyze** from the main menu bar and then select **General Linear Model. . . .** Click on **Univariate. . .** and the dialog box on the next page will appear.

The **Dependent Variable** field is the place where we identify our study's dependent variable. Find that variable—"attitude" in our example—in the list of variables appearing in the field on the left and click to highlight it. Click on the arrow button next to the **Dependent Variable** field to transfer the attitude variable. The **Fixed Factors** are the independent variables. In this case we highlight "receiver sex" and "falexper" and use the arrow button to transfer them into the **Fixed Factor(s)** field. We have no **Random Factor(s)** or **Covariates** in this study. So, we can leave those fields empty. Similarly, since we are not using "weighted least squares," we leave blank the field for **WLS Weight.** Since we are using a standard fixed effects analysis of variance model, we do not need to click on the **Model** button to bring up the **Univariate: Model** dialog box to customize designs

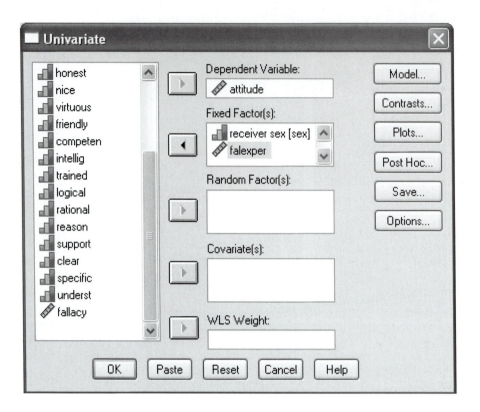

or select other ANOVA models. We also have no special contrasts of some conditions with others. Hence, we need not click on the **Contrasts** button to bring up the **Univariate: Contrasts** dialog box. Given that we do not want any output plots, we will not click the **Plots** button to open with the **Univariate: Profile Plots** dialog box. If we had more than two levels for each of our independent variables, it would make sense to have some *a posteriori* tests run among the conditions. Under those circumstances, we would click on the **Post Hoc** button and select from among 18 different multiple comparison tests on the **Univariate: Post Hoc Multiple Comparisons for Observed Means** dialog box. Unfortunately, the only reason to use multiple comparison tests is to tease out the effect sources for interaction effects. To do so, we must create a new variable with each level corresponding to a cell condition (1 through 4) and complete a 1 × 4 ANOVA using these *a posteriori* tests. Since, as results showed, there was no significant interaction effect, this step is not described here.

Clicking on the **Options** button takes us to a menu that controls output and selection of statistics. To take advantage of these options, you must provide information. First, if you want to find information about row, column, and interaction means, click on the terms in the field identified as **Estimated Marginal Means Factor(s)** and **Factor Interactions** to highlight them. Then transfer them (you might as

Univariate: Options   ☒

Estimated Marginal Means

Factor(s) and Factor Interactions: Display Means for:

(OVERALL)   (OVERALL)
sex   sex
falexper   ▶   falexper
sex*falexper   sex*falexper

                                            ☑ Compare main effects

                                            Confidence interval adjustment:

                                            LSD (none)   ▼

Display
☑ Descriptive statistics   ☑ Homogeneity tests
☑ Estimates of effect size   ☐ Spread vs. level plot
☐ Observed power   ☐ Residual plot
☐ Parameter estimates   ☐ Lack of fit
☐ Contrast coefficient matrix   ☐ General estimable function

Significance level: .05   Confidence intervals are 95%

                        Continue   Cancel   Help

well get all the effects reported) to the **Display Means For** field by using the arrow button. The other options are found in the **Display** check boxes. In this case we would like a full set of **Descriptive Statistics, Estimates of Effect Size** (at least for significant effects), and tests of homogeneity of variance called simply **Homogeneity Tests.** When done, we may click **Continue.**

At the bottom of the **Univariate** dialog box is another button identified as **Paste.** This button allows you to copy command syntax that has been created for you by the actions taken in the dialog boxes and paste in additional commands. If you choose this button, you will see a **Syntax Editor** dialog box. After you have copied and pasted what you choose, you will be returned to the **Data Editor.** So, you probably should avoid this button unless you wish to switch to a command syntax basis for running SPSS.

When you are done with the **Univariate** dialog box, click **OK.** The **Output Viewer** will produce the following result.

After expanding the **Content Area** these additional elements of the output may be found:

DESCRIPTIVE STATISTICS

Dependent Variable: ATTITUDE

Receiver Sex	FALEXPER	Mean	Std. Deviation	N
male	with fallacy	14.7500	4.1662	8
	without fallacy	16.3846	2.6938	13
	Total	15.7619	3.3302	21
female	with fallacy	15.2667	4.7879	15
	without fallacy	17.3125	3.1138	16
	Total	16.3226	4.0775	31
Total	with fallacy	15.0870	4.4915	23
	without fallacy	16.8966	2.9197	29
	Total	16.0962	3.7691	52

LEVENE'S TEST OF EQUALITY OF ERROR VARIANCES

Dependent Variable: ATTITUDE

F	df1	df2	Sig.
1.021	3	48	.392

Tests the null hypothesis that the error variance of the dependent variable is equal across groups.

TESTS OF BETWEEN-SUBJECTS EFFECTS

Dependent Variable: ATTITUDE

Source	Type III Sum of Squares	df	Mean Square	F	Sig.	Eta Squared
Corrected Model	49.571[a]	3	16.524	1.175	.329	.068
Intercept	12260.863	1	12260.863	871.951	.000	.948
SEX	6.303	1	6.303	.448	.506	.009
FALEXPER	40.912	1	40.912	2.910	.095	.057
SEX ★ FALEXPER	.511	1	.511	.036	.850	.001
Error	674.948	48	14.061			
Total	14197.000	52				
Corrected Total	724.519	51				

[a]R Squared = .068 (Adjusted R Squared = .010)

Estimated Marginal Means

1. Grand Mean

Dependent Variable: ATTITUDE

Mean	Std. Error	95% CONFIDENCE INTERVAL	
		Lower Bound	Upper Bound
15.928	.539	14.844	17.013

2. Receiver Sex

ESTIMATES

Dependent Variable: ATTITUDE

Receiver Sex	Mean	Std. Error	95% CONFIDENCE INTERVAL	
			Lower Bound	Upper Bound
male	15.567	.843	13.873	17.261
female	16.290	.674	14.935	17.644

PAIRWISE COMPARISONS

Dependent Variable: ATTITUDE

(I) receiver sex	(J) receiver sex	Mean Difference (I–J)	Std. Error	Sig.[a]	95% CONFIDENCE INTERVAL FOR DIFFERENCE[a]	
					Lower Bound	Upper Bound
male	female	−.722	1.079	.506	−2.891	1.447
female	male	.722	1.079	.506	−1.447	2.891

Based on estimated marginal means

[a]Adjustment for multiple comparisons: Least Significant Difference (equivalent to no adjustments).

UNIVARIATE TESTS

Dependent Variable: ATTITUDE

	Sum of Squares	df	Mean Square	F	Sig.	Eta Squared
Contrast	6.303	1	6.303	.448	.506	.009
Error	674.948	48	14.061			

The F tests the effect of receiver sex. This test is based on the linearly independent pairwise comparisons among the estimated marginal means.

3. FALEXPER

ESTIMATES

Dependent Variable: ATTITUDE

FALEXPER	Mean	Std. Error	95% CONFIDENCE INTERVAL	
			Lower Bound	Upper Bound
with fallacy	15.008	.821	13.358	16.659
without fallacy	16.849	.700	15.441	18.256

PAIRWISE COMPARISONS

Dependent Variable: ATTITUDE

(I) FALEXPER	(J) FALEXPER	Mean Difference (I–J)	Std. Error	Sig.[a]	95% CONFIDENCE INTERVAL FOR DIFFERENCE[a]	
					Lower Bound	Upper Bound
with fallacy	without fallacy	−1.840	1.079	.095	−4.009	.329
without fallacy	with fallacy	1.840	1.079	.095	−.329	4.009

Based on estimated marginal means

[a]Adjustment for multiple comparisons: Least Significant Difference (equivalent to no adjustments).

UNIVARIATE TESTS

Dependent Variable: ATTITUDE

	Sum of Squares	df	Mean Square	F	Sig.	Eta Squared
Contrast	40.912	1	40.912	2.910	.095	.057
Error	674.948	48	14.061			

The F tests the effect of FALEXPER. This test is based on the linearly independent pairwise comparisons among the estimated marginal means.

4. *Receiver Sex * FALEXPER*

Dependent Variable: ATTITUDE

Receiver Sex	FALEXPER	Mean	Std. Error	95% CONFIDENCE INTERVAL	
				Lower Bound	Upper Bound
male	with fallacy	14.750	1.326	12.084	17.416
	without fallacy	16.385	1.040	14.294	18.476
female	with fallacy	15.267	.968	13.320	17.213
	without fallacy	17.313	.937	15.428	19.197

Thus, it seems that with this small a sample size, there were few if any differences worth noting. It might be noted that SPSS subroutines follow most of the same sets of protocols through other tools. Thus, with just these few examples you should have an idea of the major tools that are available to you with this powerful program.

Using the Output View Editor

Since the **Output View Editor** has adopted many characteristics of word processing programs, you will find that many of the tools it provides make it fairly easy to prepare a report—or, at least, part of one—from within the SPSS environment. To understand your options, therefore, we present a review of the unique elements in the **Output View Editor** that are not shared by the rest of the SPSS program.

Menu Bar Items on the Output View Editor

The **Output View Editor** contains some different items in four of the menus. This condition stems from the fact that over the years, the **View Editor** has grown in importance as a useful tool for researchers. There are two areas in the **Output View Editor.**

The location on the left is the **Information Area,** but most often it is called the **Outline Area** since it keeps a full outline of the elements in the output. The location on the right is the **Content Area** and provides the actual output of interest. Selecting an item in the **Outline** pane selects and displays the corresponding item in the **Content** pane. Thus, moving an item in the **Outline Area** moves the corresponding item in the **Content Area.** This **Content Area** is the part that you may wish to edit and prepare to export in other programs (though you could just save it as an output file and edit what you wish later).

Because the output can be edited in ways that would be inappropriate for the **Data Editor,** four menus contain different commands in the **Output Viewer.** These four menus with different content are **Edit, View, Insert,** and **Format.**

Output1 - SPSS Viewer

File   Edit   View   Data   Transform   Insert   Format   Analyze   Graphs   Utilities   Add-ons   Window   Help

The *File* menu for the output window includes some different items than the same menu in the variable view windows.

♦ The *New* category creates and displays a *new* **Data**, **Syntax**, **Output**, **Draft Output, Script** window.

♦ The *Open* menu item opens previously saved files.

♦ *Open Database* activates the *Database Capture Wizard* to read and to join data sets from different databases.

♦ *Read Text Data* imports data stored as text files.

♦ *Close* when two or more files are open, this item closes the file in the active window.

♦ *Save* will save the current displayed file that previously has been saved.

♦ *Save As* displays a save-as window control that permits saving the viewer (.spo) file.

♦ *Save With Password* allows password-protecting of viewer files.

♦ *Export Output* saves selected text and pivot tables in various formats (Excel files, HTML, Microsoft Word files, Microsoft Powerpoint, and as text files).

♦ *Display Data Info* permits you to display dictionary information about selected data files (names, measurement level, formats).

♦ *Display Data File Information* produces a report of the characteristics of working or external data files (file characteristics and variable characteristics including value labels).

♦ *Stop Processor* halts processing of data.

♦ *Switch Server* changes or adds a server as a network location.

♦ *Page Setup* controls the paper size and orientation (landscape or portrait) of images on paper.

♦ *Print Preview* shows the layout of the pages for which printing will be ordered.

♦ When you select *Print* the print window opens so that you can print the currently displayed window.

♦ *Send Mail* opens the Profile Wizard required to create a profile for sending e-mail.

♦ *Recently Used Data* provides a list of data sets previously used.

♦ *Recently Used Files* provides a list of previously used files, such as syntax files.

♦ Click *Exit* to close SPSS.

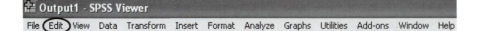

The **_Edit_** menu has several functions that allow you to manipulate your output and handle text:

♦ **_Undo_** reverses the last action taken. The same thing can be done by using the little reverse arrow key.

♦ **_Cut_** removes an item from the spreadsheet and places a copy on the clipboard so that the selection can be pasted at a later time.

♦ **_Copy_** places a copy of the current selection on the clipboard for pasting at a later time while also retaining the original item.

♦ **_Copy Objects_** places a copy of a selected object on the clipboard for pasting at a later time while also retaining the original item.

♦ **_Paste After_** places the contents of the clipboard following a point at an active location.

♦ **_Paste Special_** gives you the opportunity to paste a specific part of output as a Word document or a picture.

♦ **_Delete_** removes only the current selection's contents.

♦ **_Select_** produces a menu that causes only some types of elements in the output box to be selected and highlighted.

♦ **_Go to Case_** opens a dialog box to select a case of data in the "Data View" window of the data editor.

♦ **_Outline_** produces a menu that permits elements of an outline to be promoted to a higher level or demoted to a lower level.

♦ **_Options_** are characteristics that can be adjusted by the user.

♦ **_Links_** creates or modifies links to the active file and others.

♦ **_Objects_** produces a menu that lets you edit objects of different forms.

Output1 - SPSS Viewer
File   Edit (View) Data   Transform   Insert   Format   Analyze   Graphs   Utilities   Add-ons   Window   Help

The **_View_** menu gives you different looks for your **_Output Window_**'s toolbars and format:

♦ **_Status Bar_** turns on or off the status bar at the bottom of the screen to indicate if the processor is on or what operations are under way in the output areas.

After a collection of output elements has been selected, the next four commands may be used:

♦ **_Expand_** is used to take output items that have been *collapsed* in part of an outline (as shown on the **_information Area_**) and expand the category by showing the details within the outline category as part of the **Content Area.**

♦ **Collapse** causes a group of items on the substructure of the outline in the information field to have their output hidden in the **Content Area** as only the parent category is revealed.

♦ **Show** takes individual output items that have been hidden and makes them visible again.

♦ **Hide** takes selected output items and hides them (does not make them visible) in the **Content Area.**

The final two items, **Outline Size** and **Outline Font,** determine appearance for elements in the outline in the information area.

Output1 - SPSS Viewer

File   Edit   View   Data   Transform   (Insert)   Format   Analyze   Graphs   Utilities   Add-ons   Window   Help

The **Insert** menu permits you to add elements to your output:

♦ Use **Page Break** to identify the end of a page at the location where you would like the printing to cease and a new page to begin.

♦ Use **Clear Page Break** to remove a page break previously inserted.

♦ **New Heading** will add another section to the outline (and in its place in the **Content Window**) or will add another subheading or subpoint.

♦ **New Title** adds a title at the beginning of the **Content Window.**

♦ **New Page Title** adds a title at the beginning of a page in the **Content Window.**

♦ **New Text** adds a text box in the **Content Window.**

♦ **Interactive 2-D Graph** enters a subprogram for producing two-dimensional graphs.

♦ **Interactive 3-D Graph** enters a subprogram for producing three-dimensional or "exploded" graphs.

♦ **New Map** enables insertions of graphic summary of data by geographic regions.

♦ **Text File** permits insertion of text file into output.

♦ **Object** inserts user-created objects from a menu of object types.

Output1 - SPSS Viewer

File   Edit   View   Data   Transform   Insert   (Format)   Analyze   Graphs   Utilities   Add-ons   Window   Help

This set of categories permits alignment of text and objects to the right, the center, or the left of the **Content Area.**

Output Viewer Toolbars

For the **Output Viewer** a different set of toolbars is available. Either may be selected or deselected by clicking on the **View** and **Toolbars. . . .** You may select full, partial, or no toolbars. The **Viewer Standard** toolbar is:

These icons represent "*Open File,*" "*Save File,*" "*Print,*" "*Print Preview,*" "*Export,*" "*Dialog Recall,*" "*Undo,*" "*Go To Data,*" "*Go To Case,*" "*Variables,*" "*Use Sets,*" "*Select Last Output,*" and "*Designate Window.*"

The **Viewer Outlining** toolbar is:

These icons represent "*Promote,*" "*Demote,*" "*Expand,*" "*Collapse,*" "*Show,*" "*Hide,*" "*Insert Heading,*" "*Insert Title,*" and "*Insert Text.*"

A Final Thought

There are entire books dedicated to SPSS and its various versions. You might wish to purchase one or more of them so that you can fine-tune your answers to relevant questions about SPSS use. This brief guide has only introduced some high points to you. Fortunately, if you run into trouble, SPSS has a terrific online help system. The help system is only a click away (F1 will get you there), and the **Statistics Coach** is ready to help you make the best statistical choices. Though you could spend a lot of time getting ready to use SPSS, the best way to learn it is still by using it. The combination of this guide and the exercises on the website for this book should help get you moving in the right direction.

APPENDIX F
*Using Computers to Analyze Data: Excel XP**

Excel is a spreadsheet program that allows you to examine rows and columns of data and perform computations. Though Excel is not a dedicated statistical analysis program, it has many functions that permit data analysis. Each version of Excel becomes increasingly powerful, but this power has come with a certain cost. In many respects, Excel is daunting and not as flexible as one might wish for full-scale data analysis. Even so, many researchers find this tool to be a convenient way to analyze data and draw conclusions. This brief report is designed to give you some of the survival skills that you may need to be successful in completing preliminary data analysis with this powerful tool.

This discussion describes data analysis on Excel XP. Yet, those familiar with Excel 6.0 through Excel 2000 will find that the explanations also apply to those versions with little adjustment. The adaptations of this version involve mostly enhanced Internet integration and improved *Help* support.

A few assumptions are made here. First, it is presumed that you have some working knowledge of the Windows operating system and the basic operation of personal computers (how to turn them on, how to start a program, etc.). If you need to review these matters, you should run the Windows brief tutorial, "Tour: Ten Minutes to Using Windows." (To run this program, select **Help** from the **Start** menu. Select the **Contents** tab on the "Help Topics: Windows Help" dialog box. Select "Tour: Ten Minutes to Using Windows," and click the **Display** button.) Second, it is assumed that you understand the operation of a mouse (and understand that we are not talking about furry creatures) and can complete simple operations with one. Third, it is assumed that you know how to navigate to find files on disks of interest to you.

In this discussion, when a statement instructs you to make a click, the reference is to a left mouse button click.

The Basic Elements of Excel

When you start Excel, you are presented with the Excel Main Window as shown on page A–42.

---

*Excel and Windows are registered trademarks of the Microsoft Corporation.

Some nomenclature is in order. A *cell* is a rectangle that is contained within a workbook or worksheet that can contain values or formulae that return a value. A *formula* is an equation that performs various operations within a worksheet. A *hyperlink* is a word or phrase that, when clicked, displays another Microsoft Office file or an Internet website. A *toolbar* is a bar located under the main *menu bar* that provides quick access to features of Excel XP. A *worksheet* is a page of cells contained within a workbook. A *workbook* is an Excel XP file that contains a series of worksheets.

Menu Bar ———►
Toolbar ———►

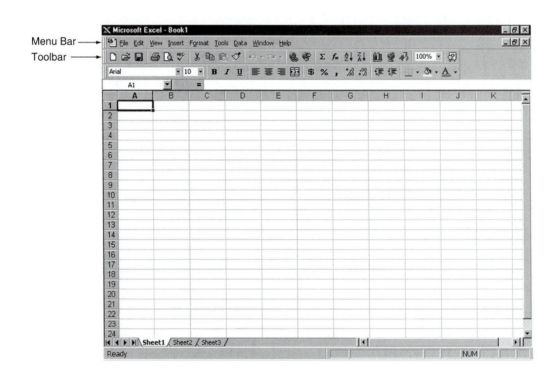

The menu bar has nine different words. Each word has its own menu. You may click on the menu bar to open a menu, or you may type "Alt" and the first letter of the menu bar. Once a menu is opened, if a word has an underlined letter, you may type this letter and the menu or window will be opened.

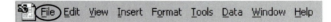

The **File** menu is listed first and has several functions:

♦ The **New** category creates and displays a new workbook file.

♦ When **Open** is used, you have the ability to open a workbook file that has already been created and saved.

♦ *Close* will close the open workbook file you are working on (a prompt will be displayed if you have not saved your changes).

♦ *Save* will save the current displayed file.

♦ *Save As* displays a "save as" window that provides you with the ability to save the currently displayed file with a different file name or file format.

♦ *Save As Web Page* saves the current file in HTML (Hypertext Markup Language) format used on the Internet.

♦ *Save Workspace* lets you save multiple workbooks as a Workspace; all workbooks contained within the Workspace will be opened when the Workspace is opened.

♦ *Search* identifies other files according to certain words or pieces of information about file types.

♦ *Web Page Preview* provides you the ability to preview an Excel XP file, as it will appear when saved as a Web page and viewed on the Internet.

♦ *Page Setup* is the window that provides access to the printing features that are available in Excel XP.

♦ The option *Print Area* prints only selected cells. To select a cell range, hold down the left mouse button and drag until all the desired cells are included in the highlighted area and then select this option.

♦ *Print Preview* displays a screen representation of a workbook or worksheet as it will appear when it is printed.

♦ When you select *Print,* the print window opens so that you can print the current displayed workbook. The print window gives you the opportunity to choose the Print range: All pages or Pages listed From-To; Number of copies; and Print what: Selection, Active sheets, or Entire workbook.

♦ *Send To* sends a workbook or worksheet to an e-mail recipient.

♦ The *Properties* window permits you to store information about the file (subcategories that contain information are General, Summary, Statistics, Contents, and Custom).

♦ A list of workbooks, recently opened, appears in *Recent Documents,* and you can reopen a desired file when you click on the file name.

♦ Click *Exit* to close Excel XP.

File (Edit) View Insert Format Tools Data Window Help

The *Edit* menu has several functions that allow you to manipulate your data:

♦ *Undo* reverses the last action taken. The same thing can be done by using the little reverse arrow key. ⤺ If the last task cannot be reversed, *Can't Undo* appears.

♦ Click *Repeat* so that the last action will be repeated.

- ◆ **Cut** removes an item from the spreadsheet and places a copy on the clipboard so that the selection can be pasted at a later time.

- ◆ **Copy** places a copy of the current selection on the clipboard for pasting at a later time while also retaining the original item.

- ◆ **Office Clipboard** has a window that lists all items on the clipboard.

- ◆ Use **Paste** to place the contents of the clipboard at an active location.

- ◆ **Paste Special** gives you the opportunity to paste a specific part of a cell's contents into the currently displayed document (this option is helpful when you wish to copy only the formula of a cell into a new cell).

- ◆ **Paste As Hyperlink** lets you paste a hyperlink into a document (hyperlinks can be Internet website addresses or other files, which have been created in other Microsoft Office applications).

- ◆ **Fill** allows you to fill rows or columns with data from the clipboard.

- ◆ Use **Clear** to delete the contents of a cell or a range of cells.

- ◆ **Delete** removes only the current selection's contents.

- ◆ **Delete Sheet** deletes the currently displayed worksheet from the workbook.

- ◆ **Move or Copy Sheet** permits you to move or copy a worksheet in a different location either within itself or to a different workbook.

- ◆ **Find** helps you locate specific phrases, words, or values within a worksheet.

- ◆ **Replace** lets you find and replace the contents with different phrases, words, or values.

- ◆ **Go To** permits you to display a worksheet within a workbook by entering the worksheet name or number.

- ◆ A window is displayed when you use **Links,** allowing you to update or change links in a workbook.

- ◆ **Object** permits you to edit objects in a workbook.

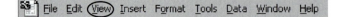

The **View** menu gives you different looks for your worksheet's toolbars and format:

- ◆ The **Normal** option displays the sheet in the standard (default) view.

- ◆ **Page Break Preview** shows the current page breaks (page breaks show where pages end).

- ◆ **Task Pane** displays a window on the right side of the screen giving you the choice to open a workbook, create a new workbook from a blank form, create a new workbook from an existing workbook, or create a new workbook from a template; also tracks clipboard materials, searches, and access to websites, and Microsoft.com.

- ◆ **Toolbars** displays a submenu with 21 different toolbars available in Excel XP for easy access. To choose a toolbar, click on its box.

- Checking **Formula Bar** and/or **Status Bar** will display these toolbars (or hide them) as you work on your document.
- Use **Header and Footer** to place headers or footers on each page (these items are labels and page numbers placed at the top or bottom of the page).
- **Comments** gives you the ability to see comments located within the cells.
- **Custom Views** allows you to identify custom view options and hidden fields.
- **Full Screen** makes the current document fill the monitor screen.
- By using **Zoom** you can magnify the display of the document.

File Edit View (Insert) Format Tools Data Window Help

The **Insert** menu permits you to add elements to your worksheet:

- Use **Cells** to insert cells, **Rows** to insert rows, and **Columns** to insert addition columns into the worksheet.
- The **Worksheet** option inserts another worksheet into a workbook.
- Use **Chart** to create and insert a chart or graph.
- Selecting **Symbol** lists symbols in 31 subsets such as Greek, Hebrew, or Arabic alphabets, as well as a full set of math symbols. There are 20 choices under the special characters such as copyright, registered, trademark, and proofreading symbols.
- To insert a page break, click **Page Break** at the location needed (this step forces the page to end at a certain line).
- The **Function** option opens a window, providing different categories of functions (including statistical analysis functions) and types of formulae.
- **Name** has a submenu that permits you to label cell ranges.
- **Comment** permits you to insert a comment into a cell.
- The **Picture** option permits the insertion of graphic files, clip art, or pictures into a worksheet.
- **Diagram** reveals the *Diagram Gallery* with six chart formats: hierarchical organizational, cyclical, radial, pyramid, Venn, and target diagrams.
- **Object** lets you insert an object created in another application.
- **Hyperlink** lets you insert an Internet hyperlink into your worksheet.

File Edit View Insert (Format) Tools Data Window Help

The fifth menu is the **Format** menu that deals with matters of displaying the worksheet:

- The **Cells** option produces a collection of matters of display, including the ways each *number* may be entered (as currency, dates, time, etc.); the alignment of numbers in cells; the character *font;* the type of border surrounding the cells; and *patterns* of colors and designs to fill cells.

- In the **Row** submenu, you can choose the height for the rows or whether the rows will be hidden or unhidden.
- The **Column** submenu is the same as the row submenu except as applied to columns.
- **Sheet** permits you to hide, unhide, rename, or change the background color of the worksheet.
- **AutoFormat** displays a window with the options to change the table to certain automatic designs such as an accounting table.
- **Conditional Formatting** permits you to highlight certain cells so that you can monitor data for comparisons.
- The **Style** window records the cell style settings for application elsewhere.

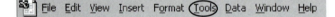

The **Tools** menu includes many options that are essential in statistical analysis of data:

- **Spelling** provides a spell check for the worksheet.
- **Error Checking** performs checks of the worksheet for logic and computational errors.
- **Speech** activates drop-down menus that use Microsoft Office voice recognition (*Speech Recognition* permits you to use a microphone and establish a personal vocabulary with your spoken voice. *Show Text to Speech Toolbar* places the *Language Toolbar* on the top of the spreadsheet permitting your own control dictation, voice commands, handwriting, and drawing pad).
- **Share Workbook** lets you share a workbook over an area network.
- **Track Changes** permits changes in the worksheet to be highlighted, accepted, or rejected as an aid in keeping track of the changes.
- **Compare and Merge Workbooks** collects information from separate workbooks and cross references the differences; also merges workbooks into a single workbook file.
- The **Protection** option keeps a worksheet or workbook exclusive by locking cells or hiding formulae (if you label a file as read-only, no one can make corrections on your document).
- **Online Collaboration** provides you the ability to track and schedule online meetings and other Web discussions.
- **Goal Seek** identifies an input value required for a formula to become operational.
- The **Scenarios** option manages a set of values in other workbooks as an aid in forecasting.

- *Formula Auditing* on the toolbar lets you trace precedent and dependent cells with arrows to show their connection to each other (you may also audit the worksheet with a new comment, or you may circle invalid data).

- *Tools on the Web* interfaces to the Internet by sending you to Microsoft Office Online. Updates, assistance, and training to name a few can be found at this site.

- *Macro* permits you to examine macros, which are instructions for routine tasks to be completed in the worksheet; also includes commands to open Visual Basic Editor and Microsoft Script Editor to compose or modify macros.

- *Add-Ins* are additional sets of programs and functions for special tasks (although stored with the program, they are not operational until installed in this submenu).

- *AutoCorrect* provides you the ability to have misspelled words corrected automatically.

- *Customize* involves making changes in icons and elements of toolbars.

- *Options* are workbook characteristics that can be adjusted by the user.

- Depending on the *Add-Ins,* additional tools might be included, such as *Wizard. . .* (for installed Wizards) and *Data Analysis. . .* (for data Analysis ToolPack).

File   Edit   View   Insert   Format   Tools   Data   Window   Help

The *Data* menu permits you to deal with and to record data.

- *Sort* is a command that sorts a column or row of data either numerically or alphabetically. (When using this command watch out: [1] blanks are not interpreted as numeric data but as text data; [2] although you will receive a warning, only highlighted columns or rows will be sorted—the rows that correspond with the sort will not automatically be sorted along with the row—thus, under ordinary circumstances, highlight the whole spreadsheet before sorting.)

- *Filter* is a command that permits you to specify data only if they meet certain criteria of importance to you, such as a minimum value.

- *Form* provides you with a way to automate or simplify data entry into particular cells of the spreadsheet.

- *Subtotals* permits you to identify a target cell as containing a subtotal.

- *Validation* is a command that permits you to validate whether data entered into a cell is acceptable or outside the range of acceptable data.

- *Table* permits you to define a collection of cells as a table, which can then be sorted, extracted, or inserted elsewhere as any ordinary table.

- *Text to Columns* permits you to format data (the ones that might appear in a cell defining experimental and control conditions) into columns for use in other analysis programs or routines.

- ◆ **Co̲nsolidate** produces a window that permits you to combine data from different sources or merge them into one set for use.
- ◆ **G̲roup and Outline** permit you to highlight elements on the worksheet, to group or ungroup them (for easy movement and manipulation), and to create automatic outlines of several features of the common set.
- ◆ **P̲ivotTable and PivotChart Report** call up another set of tools to create charts and to produce displays for comparisons of data.
- ◆ **Import External D̲ata** allows you to import data from different locations, such as data for different databases and Web sources.
- ◆ **R̲efresh Data** is a command that lets you update existing data files in light of importing new data.

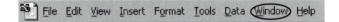

W̲indow menu provides simple navigation, definition, and use of portions of the spreadsheet.

- ◆ **N̲ew Window** is yet another way to display a new blank worksheet.
- ◆ **A̲rrange** permits you to control the order in which Windows are opened and displayed.
- ◆ **H̲ide** is a command that makes invisible any content in the highlighted cell.
- ◆ **U̲nhide** is a command that reverses the **Hide** command.
- ◆ The **S̲plit** command divides the selected window into "subwindows" called panes.
- ◆ **Un/F̲reeze Pane** is a command that releases panes from a frozen or "uneditable" form.

This section also displays the names of all open worksheets so that you can navigate from one to another.

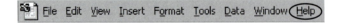

H̲elp menu is extensive in advanced versions of Excel. It includes an "Office Assistant" that attempts to coach you through difficult issues and provides an actual tutorial of sorts. The help available includes **Microsoft Excel Help; Show/Hide O̲ffice Assistant** (to help you control the appearance of the pesky Office Assistant); **What's T̲his?** (in which you may ask questions to solve your Excel problems); **Office on the W̲eb** (which connects you to the Excel website); **Lotus 1-2-3Help** (for those who want help with Lotus 1-2-3 conversions); **Detect and R̲epair** (which makes corrections to the program and attempts to take action on corrupted files); and **A̲bout Microsoft Excel** (reminding you what program version you are using, your license name, and the like).

Many of the commands require that you first highlight columns to make them active. When you do so, the columns change color, are shaded, or take on a different looking border. Do not worry if you forget; the commands will prompt you.

Toolbars

Toolbars are shortcuts that let you get to commands in the Excel system. There are many different toolbars that you may introduce depending on your interests—and you do not have to show any if you choose. Display of toolbars is controlled through the *View* menu followed by *Toolbars. . . .* This menu shows 13 different toolbars you could place on the worksheet, plus an additional menu for customizing your output.

If you forget the meaning of the toolbar icons, you can always go through the menus on the menu bar. But if you wish, you may hold the mouse pointer over the icon and a short label will occur, reminding you what the icons indicate. For instance, in the first row of the example provided above, the icons produce messages corresponding to *"New," "Open," "Save," "Print," "Print Preview," "Spelling," "Cut," "Copy," "Paste," "Format Painter," "Undo"* (not highlighted here because there is no previous command in memory), *"Redo," "Insert Hyperlink," "Web Toolbar," "Autosum," "Functions," "Sort Ascending," "Sort Descending," "Chart Wizard," "Map," "Drawing," "Zoom,"* and *"Office Assistant."*

Using Excel

When you start Excel, you will have a blank worksheet with rows numbered 1, 2, 3, and columns labeled A, B, C. Each combination of these numbers and letters permits you to identify a cell. Hence, A1 corresponds to the empty cell in the upper left corner. To enter data or a formula, you simply click on a cell to make it active and start typing. What you type appears in the *formula bar* at the top of the page. When you push **Return,** your entry goes in the cell. If you've entered a formula, you can have either the result or the formula placed in the cell.

To use statistical analysis of data, we need to check on some setup issues. To run statistical analyses conveniently, you have to make sure that your Excel program has the appropriate subprograms loaded. Go to the *menu row* and place your mouse cursor on **Tools.** On the drop-down menu, look for **Data Analysis.** Click on it. A menu should appear that lists a host of statistical options. If the drop-down menu does not say **Data Analysis** or if the statistical options are missing, you need to activate the **Add-In** program that contains the statistics. Here is how to do it: On the

Tools menu, click on *Add-Ins.* Click on the *Analysis ToolPack* check box, and click on the *OK* button. Now, you've got it installed. On the *Tools* menu there is now a line that says *Data Analysis,* which, if clicked, will produce a dialog box with a series of options for statistical analysis. To run statistics, you can check to see if your statistic of interest is supported by one of the functions, or you can look at the combination of functions in the *ToolPack* by clicking *Tools* and *Data Analysis* and examining the list of options. One way or another, you should be set.

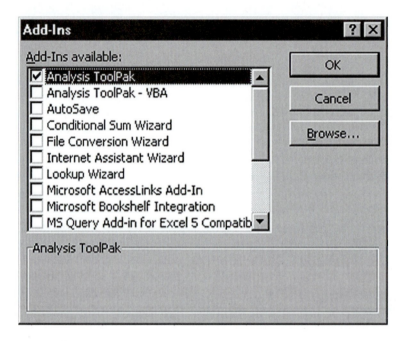

The most immediate step for the analysis of data, of course, is to *have* some for study. You begin by entering data or opening a data file.

♦ To enter data, list the variables by name in the first row of each column. Then insert data one row at a time to represent data from each event in the sample. Excel determines if you are entering a value or text based on what you type. Typing a number is interpreted as a number, and it is justified on the right side of the cell when you press *Return.* Typing a letter is interpreted as text and is justified on the left side of the cell when you press *Return.*

♦ In the case of the exercises in this book and on our website, we already have data sets that can be opened for analysis. In the rest of this guide, we will rely on examples from these formats. Yet, if you need to import data sets from different formats, you should be prepared to do a little work in redefining your variables and "cleaning" the data. Excel does not handle "missing values" very graciously. Though the spreadsheet often includes blanks as missing data (and often excludes such data in computing its preset functions), there is no guarantee that it will do so with the *Data Analysis* routines from the *Analysis ToolBox.* You may have to sort data or rearrange things to remove missing data from active fields (where blanks often are interpreted as text characters). It should be noted that it is very easy to import data that was composed in SPSS since data may be saved in Excel format.

Using Variables

The Excel program allows for the creation of new variables and the coding of variables to create a scale index that may be useful. To create a new variable that is the sum of a series of scores, we need only move to an empty column, enter a name for it on the first row, and click on the column to make it active. In our example, suppose we wish to create a new variable called "ATTITUDE" that is the sum of four 7-point scales: positive(negative), wise(foolish), good(bad), and beneficial(harmful). We might proceed to a new column, click on the first row, and enter a heading, "ATTITUDE." Then we would click on the second row in the column to make it active. Finally, we would enter a formula to add the scales that appear in columns E through H. To do so, we would enter an equal sign in the cell followed by "E2 + F2 + G2 + H2" as in this example (cell addresses are not case sensitive).

Courier					B	I	U					$	%	,							
IF			X √	=	=E2+F2+G2+H2																
?		Formula result = 28					OK		Cancel			**V** UNDERST		**W** FALLACY		**X** ATTITUDE				**Y**	
2	1.00	1.00	1.00	1.00	1.00		1.00		1.00		1.00	2+F2+G2+H2									
3	3.00	2.00	2.00	2.00	2.00		2.00		4.00		3.00										
4	4.00	4.00	4.00	4.00	4.00		4.00		4.00		4.00										
5	4.00	4.00	4.00	4.00	3.00		3.00		3.00		4.00										
6	5.00	4.00	6.00	5.00	4.00		6.00		4.00		4.00										
7	6.00	2.00	4.00	4.00	4.00		4.00		2.00		1.00										
8	4.00	4.00	4.00	4.00	4.00		4.00		4.00		1.00										

After entering **Return,** the actual number appears in the cell X2. If you had wanted the formula to appear, you could have omitted the equal sign in the cell and in the formula field above. To copy this formula for all the cells in the row (so that each row of data adds up the same columns of data), highlight cell X2 to make it active. Go to the **Edit** menu and click **Copy.** This action changes the border of cell X2. Go to cell X2, and while holding down the left mouse button, move down the column through all the data rows. The column will be highlighted as you do. Press **Return,** and the highlighted cells will all have the new sum for that column.

Courier				B	I	U					$	%	,							
X2				=	=E2+F2+G2+H2															
	P	**Q**	**R**	**S**	**T**	**U**	**V**	**W**	**X**	**Y**										
1	LOGICAL	RATIONAL	REASON	SUPPORT	CLEAR	SPECIFIC	UNDERST	FALLACY	ATTITUDE											
2	1.00	1.00	1.00	1.00	1.00	1.00	1.00	1.00	28.00											
3	3.00	2.00	2.00	2.00	2.00	2.00	4.00	3.00												
4	4.00	4.00	4.00	4.00	4.00	4.00	4.00	4.00												
5	4.00	4.00	4.00	4.00	3.00	3.00	3.00	4.00												
6	5.00	4.00	6.00	5.00	4.00	6.00	4.00	4.00												
7	6.00	2.00	4.00	4.00	4.00	4.00	2.00	1.00												
8	4.00	4.00	4.00	4.00	4.00	4.00	4.00	1.00												

The symbols used in the formula field are fairly standard. Excel uses keystroke operators, which tell Excel what kind of calculations you want to perform. The four categories of operators are arithmetic, comparison, text, and reference.

♦ The arithmetic operators are + (addition), − (subtraction), × (multiplication), / (division), % (percent), and ∧ (exponents).

♦ The comparison operators are = (equal to), > (greater than), < (less than), ≥ (greater than or equal to), ≤ (less than or equal to), and <> (not equal to).

♦ The text operator is **&** (adjoins text): for example, Ian & Aaron produce IanAaron.

♦ The first reference operator symbol is a ":"(colon), which means all cells included; that is, A4:A15 includes all cells in column A between rows 4 and 15. The second reference operator, "," (comma) combines multiple cells into one reference; that is, A4,A15 means only the cells A4 and A15.

When forming complicated formulae or formulae with more than one operator, you have to use the operators in a certain order. Be liberal with the parentheses because the order makes a difference. Percents are done first, exponents second, multiplication and division third, and finally addition and subtraction.

Formulae can also use any of a large collection of preset functions. This list is only the starting point (though it covers what you would be looking at 80% of the time). Excel now has more than 450 mathematical calculations already created.

When you press the function icon on the toolbar (_fx_), a dialog box appears as follows.

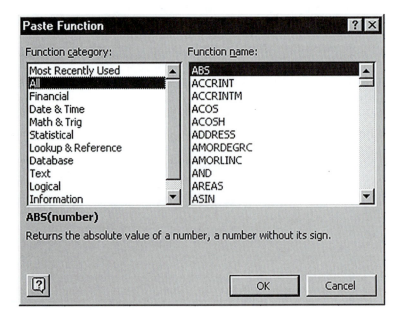

Here are some of the functions available which can be called up by pressing the function button ƒx (function names are not case sensitive).

Function	Example	Result
SUM	=SUM(B1:D1)	Values in row 1 from B to D are added.
COUNT	=COUNT(C2:C15)	The number of cells containing values in column C from row 2 to row 15 is counted.
MAX	=MAX(C2:F5)	Finds the maximum value extending in the range from column C row 2 to column F row 5.
MIN	=MIN(C2:F5)	Finds the minimum value extending in the range from column C row 2 to column F row 5.
ABS	=ABS(A2)	Gives the absolute value of the contents of cell A2.
SQRT	=SQRT(A1)	Finds the square root of value in cell A1.

Calling the Statistics

There are two ways to get data analysis tools. The first method is to use the **Data Analysis** options. The second method is to examine the functions (ƒx) and then paste the answers into empty cell locations. We will mention each.

Using Data Analysis Options:

Go to **Tools** menu, and click on the **Data Analysis** command.

This dialog box allows you to select any of the following statistical collections.

Data Analysis Tool	Action
ANOVA: Single Factor	One-way analysis of variance to analyze the differences among the means of two or more samples.
ANOVA: Two-Factor With Replication	Two-way analysis of variance to analyze differences from two independent variables with at least two levels. This model requires equal sample sizes.
ANOVA: Two-Factor Without Replication	Two-way analysis of variance that does not include more than one sampling per group.
Correlation	Measurement of the relationship between two data sets that are scaled to be independent of the unit of measurement.
Covariance	The average of the product of deviations of data points from their respective means (covariance is a measure of the slope of the relationship between two variables).
Descriptive Statistics	A set of tools, including the means, standard error, median, mode, standard deviation, variance, kurtosis, skewness, range, minimum, maximum, sum, count, and confidence intervals.
Exponential Smoothing	An analysis tool that predicts a value based on the forecast for the prior period, adjusted for the error in that prior forecast (the smoothing constant determines how strongly forecasts respond to errors in the prior forecast).
F-Test Two-Sample Variance	A test of homogeneity of variance.
Fourier Analysis	Tool for problem solving in linear systems by use of the *Fast Fourier Transform* (also includes inverse transformations).
Histogram	Production of a bar chart with variables representing units along a continuum.
Moving Average	A moving average provides a smoothing trend line that is an average of a set number of succeeding periods.
Random Number Generation	A function that produces a range of independent random numbers drawn from a selection of distribution types.
Rank and Percentile	Produces a table that contains the ordinal and percentile ranks of each value in the data.

Regression	Multiple linear correlation in which one dependent variable (identified as Input Variable X) is correlated with a number of predictor variables (identified as Input Variable Y).
Sampling	Selection of a sample from a population by treating the input range as a population.
t-Test: Paired Two-Sample for Means	Analysis of the difference between two groups with pairs of scores from the same individuals.
t-Test: Two-Sample Assuming Equal Variances	Analysis of the difference between the means of two independent groups using the pooled standard deviation.
t-Test: Two-Sample Assuming Unequal Variances	Analysis of the difference between the means of two independent groups using the separate variance estimate.
z-Test: Two-Sample for Means	Analysis of the difference between the means of groups with known population variances.

As an example, we will show how the dialog boxes work for one analysis: *t-Test: Two-Sample Assuming Equal Variances.* Other relevant examples are found on the Web pages for the book in the sections corresponding to Chapters 12 through 14. To run this test, go to *Tools,* click on *Data Analysis,* and in the dialog box click on *t-Test: Two-Sample Assuming Equal Variances.* The dialog box below will appear. The field for *Variable 1 Range* is the place to indicate the column or row where the data for the first group are located, and the field for *Variable 2 Range* is the column or row where the data for the second group are located.

To enter this range, you may write the numbers of the cells (e.g., B1:B10) or you may click on the symbol at the right of the field. This step brings up a small dialog box such as:

Simply move the mouse pointer to the starting point for the first group of data and hold down the left mouse button while highlighting the data from the first group that will be involved in the comparison. This step would create a result such as this screen:

Q	R	S	T	U	V	W
IONAL	REASON	SUPPORT	CLEAR	SPECIFIC	UNDERST	FALLACY AT
1.00	1.00	1.00	1.00	1.00	1.00	1.00
2.00						
4.00						
4.00						
4.00	6.00	5.00	4.00	6.00	4.00	4.00
2.00	4.00	4.00	4.00	4.00	2.00	1.00
4.00	4.00	4.00	4.00	4.00	4.00	1.00
4.00	4.00	4.00	4.00	4.00	4.00	2.00
2.00	2.00	1.00	4.00	5.00	3.00	2.00
7.00	7.00	1.00	7.00	7.00	7.00	2.00
7.00	7.00	4.00	4.00	7.00	7.00	2.00

Within the screen, overlaid dialog box:

t-Test: Two-Sample Assuming Equal Variances   ? X

$U$1:$U$53

The letters in the small box reflect the cell where the data start for the first group (U1) through the cell where the data stop (U53). You may wonder why the cell address has those dollar signs. The reason is that this formula setup uses what is called an *absolute* address—one that does not change when copied. The **$** sign locks the label for the particular row or column. Thus, cell $U$1 will always be cell $U$1, no matter where the cell is copied in the worksheet. Addresses such as U1 are called *relative* addresses since, for instance, U1 will change to U2 if the formula is copied down to the next row; the A1 will change to A2. After you have entered the cell addresses in this little dialog box, enter **Return.**

To continue with the independent *t* test, click on the icon at the right of the field marked **Variable 2 Range** to go to a little dialog box so that you may enter the data location for the second group of data. For this example, let us include data starting with cell V1 and extending through cell V54. Press **Return** to enter this decision. The **t-Test: Two-Sample Assuming Equal Variance** dialog box will appear. Check the box marked **Labels** because we have included the row that contains the variable labels. We will specify an output range to identify a place where the presentation of results will be placed on this worksheet. When we are finished, we may click **OK.**

t-Test: Two-Sample Assuming Equal Variances ? ☒

Input
Variable 1 Range: $U$1:$U$53
Variable 2 Range: $V$1:$V$53

Hypothesized Mean Difference:

☑ Labels

Alpha: 0.05

Output options
⦿ Output Range: $Y$3
◯ New Worksheet Ply:
◯ New Workbook

OK
Cancel
Help

The output for this *t* test may be found on column y, row 3 (though some resizing of column width may be required to help make all the labels readable):

t-Test: Two-Sample Assuming Equal Variances		
	SPECIFIC	UNDERST
Mean	4.403846154	4.711538462
Variance	2.088612368	2.091628959
Observations	52	52
Pooled Variance	2.090120664	
Hypothesized Mean	0	
df	102	
t Stat	−1.08521961	
P(T<=t) one-tail	0.140191324	
t Critical one-tail	1.659930149	
P(T<=t) two-tail	0.280382649	
t Critical two-tail	1.983494258	

This treatment is just one example, although most other applications of Excel to statistical analysis are variations. To read a discussion of all the commands and requirements for each tool of data analyses, click on the **Help** menu and then click on **Microsoft Excel Help.** In the dialog box, type the name of the formula of interest. Then click on one of the buttons to provide a full description for you. You should know that Excel often makes data analysis difficult since it has some major limitations (especially difficulties in dealing with missing data) and has difficulty dealing with complicated data. To respond to these issues, some other companies have provided supplemental programs to advance Excel's abilities to complete comprehensive statistical analyses (see **www.unistat.com** and **http://www.analyse-it.com**).

Using Functions

Many statistical tools are simply included as functions. For most of these functions, you first must click on an available cell (one that is not in use) and then either insert a function from the *Insert* menu or press the functions toolbar (*fx*) to call forth the following dialog box.

Remember, when you are using simple functions, you must be located in an active cell that you have highlighted. Otherwise, the output value you generate will have no place to be located.

Here is a list of *some* of the functions you might find useful, though many others actually are available:

Function	Example	Result
AVERAGE	=AVERAGE(c3:c8)	Nonempty cells in column C, rows 3 through 8 are averaged.
AVERAGE1	=AVERAGE1(c3:c8)	All cells in column C, rows 3 through 8 are averaged.
CHITEST	=CHITEST(c3:D4:c7:D8)	Computes a chi-square test of independence where the first set of cells is the actual range of data, and the second set of cells is the expected range (the ratio of the product of row totals and column totals to the grand total) of the data for the cells, respectively.

CONFIDENCE	CONFIDENCE(.05,2,10)	Computes a two-sided confidence interval for a population mean with an alpha risk of .05, a known population standard deviation of 2, and a sample size of 10.
CORREL	CORREL(a2:a9,b2:b9)	Computes a correlation coefficient for data from cells A2 through A9 with data from cells B2 through B9 (treats empty cells as missing data, but will not return a correlation for unequal numbers of data points); can also enter raw scores, such as CORREL ({1,2,3},{4,5,6}).
FTEST	FTEST(a2:a9,b2:b9)	Computes heterogeneous variances for two samples extending from column A rows 2 through 9, and from column B rows 2 through 9 (can be used by substituting actual scores for cell arrays; can also enter raw scores, such as FTEST({1,2,3},{4,5,6}).
GEOMEAN	GEOMEAN(A2:A9)	Computes geometric mean from a single data array (may also receive raw data instead of cell references).
HARMEAN	HARMEAN (A2:A9)	Computes harmonic mean from a single data array (or raw data as arguments).
KURT	KURT(A2:A9)	Computes kurtosis from a single data array (or raw data as arguments).
MEDIAN	MEDIAN(A2:A9)	Computes median from a single data array (or raw data as arguments).
MODE	MODE(A2:A9)	Computes mode from a single data array (or raw data as arguments).
PEARSON	PEARSON(a2:a9,b2:b9)	Computes Pearson product moment correlation coefficient for data from cells A2 through A9 with data from cells B2 through B9 (treats empty cells as missing data, but will not return a correlation for unequal numbers of data points); can also enter raw scores, such as CORREL ({1,2,3},{4,5,6}).
RSQ	RSQ(a2:a9,b2:b9)	Computes square of Pearson product moment correlation in following similar conventions as PEARSON.
STDEV	STDEV(A2:A9)	Standard deviation of sample in cells A2 through A9 (with logical values ignored).
TTEST	TTEST (A2:A9,B2:B9,2,2)	Computes value of t for two variables (the first extending from cells A2 to A9 and the second extending from B2 to B9) for a two-tailed test, for a two-sample equal variance test (1 = paired t test; 2 = two-sample equal variance test; 3 = two-sample unequal variance test).

APPENDIX G
Using Communication Research Sources

Approaching Research Materials

The "Why?" Research Uses Past Work to Develop Arguments

The "What?" Purposeful Library Research—Information to Get

The "When?" Guiding Yourself with a Research Outline

The "How?" Managing Research Materials

Techniques for Bibliographic Research

The Library Research Strategies

The "Where?" The Key Library Tools

Hierarchical Systems for Books and Collections

Keyword-Based Systems

Troubleshooting in the Library

When the Source Is Unavailable

When There Is "No Information on My Topic"

When the Journals Are Missing

When the Material Is Technical and Complex

Using the Internet

Approaching Research Materials

Research involves sifting through materials to make cases. This section will answer some questions about these research dimensions: why? what? when?

The "Why?" Research Uses Past Work to Develop Arguments

Looking at past work helps us build research arguments. In this sense, an **argument** is a process of advancing conclusions based on reasons and evidence. *argument defined* Research argues to conclusions from the raw materials of information. In turn, the reasons may be tested with established standards of sound argument. Past inquiry guides us in several ways.

1. finding premises for arguments

♦ *Past research gives premises for argument.* A **premise** is a statement in a logical argument that is the foundation for others drawn from it. Students, therefore, can use past research as a premise for new research arguments. The reasoning does not prove the conclusion is true, of course. Yet, we can justify advancing some ~~possibilities~~ ⟨highlighted⟩ future research.

2. finding evidence for arguments

♦ ~~*Past research gives evidence f*~~*or argument.* Many issues—even in a field as wide ~~as communication⟩—~~munication—have been studied successfully in the past. You can look at both the results and the theories that have guided research. Past research also helps you learn when a theory's limits have been found. Such information and criticism can be recorded for later use in your own arguments.

3. balancing scholarly opinions against data

♦ *Past research helps balance reliance on authority and empirical data.* When reviewing literature you will encounter many different opinions. When an authority's interpretations stay close to the facts, we may feel comfortable accepting them. But when an authority ignores the facts or refuses to stick to them, you can feel justifiably suspicious. Since research is an argument, the papers you write also are arguments. Some inexperienced researchers believe they can ignore past work and use entirely new ideas and methods. Keith Stanovich calls this misguided ap-

"Einstein syndrome" defined

proach the "**Einstein syndrome**" (1986, chap. 8) since researchers who suffer from it fail to connect their "sudden breakthroughs" with lessons from others. By discarding previous lessons as irrelevant (hardly ever wise), they fail to learn from the successes of others. So, it is useful to spend time looking at ways writers and scholars have conceptualized, justified, studied, and interpreted a research area.

The "What?" Purposeful Library Research— Information to Get

research should be conducted with a goal or purpose

Though you must take the time getting to know the specialized language of a subject, your library research—traditional library or electronic library—will be most productive if you know what things you want to find. Do not interview experts, search libraries, or surf the Internet unless you have first decided what you are looking for. Do not worry about closing your mind to new information. You will find unexpected material along the way, and you will want to take advantage of it. But do not just look for "background information." What is background anyway? When do you know when you have enough background? Experienced researchers know that back-

topics to look for in library research

ground materials flow naturally from a search for specifics. Yet, regardless of your problem statement, some of the most obvious things to seek at the library are

♦ definitions of key concepts and variables;

♦ ways concepts and variables have been measured and studied;

♦ summary statements that people (especially textbook writers) seem to make about the subject;

- classic research studies on a subject (the studies that all the textbooks seem to reference);

- research that shows what methods to use; and

- research that shows what mistakes to avoid.

Sometimes you may find surprisingly little on your subject. That absence is very useful information. It suggests that the subject cries out for research. It also may indicate that most people have found the subject uninteresting (so what? most people may not have thought about the subject the way you have). Get used to finding that past research has not answered your particular research question. The field is wide open, and you may find valuable things to investigate for yourself.

absence of information is important to know

Where do you find information to answer these questions? Table G.1 shows source categories that can help to answer many questions (along with a rating of the usefulness of each source). Sometimes you do not find what you wish in these sources. For instance, we usually expect textbook writers to define their terms, but there are exceptions. Wayne C. Booth wrote an entire book called *The Rhetoric of Fiction* (1964) without ever defining the term "rhetoric." Similarly, Briankle G. Chang wrote a chapter on "Communication as Communicability" (2006) without directly defining either term in that title. Research articles rarely state definitions. Instead, they may refer to sources with acceptable definitions. Thus, you should consider the resources indicated in Table G.1 when you seriously explore libraries. Aside from looking at textbooks and articles (for which guidance will be given later in this appendix), there are three forms you should examine:

- *Encyclopedias.* You may find useful context, reviews of general issues, and definitions from encyclopedias. In mass communication, for instance, encyclopedias can be useful sources *early* in the search effort, since many provide annual updates that describe new technologies and changes in communication law. You also may wish to check specialized encyclopedias available for each field.

encyclopedias

- *Handbooks and annual reviews.* Though you may think of a handbook as the same thing as an employee manual, the term has been enlisted by scholars to refer to books containing summaries of literature and brief reviews of common topics. Most handbooks offer both summaries and criticisms of controversial issues.

handbooks, yearbooks, and annual reviews

- *Specialized dictionaries.* Dictionaries of English usage (such as Webster's) are poor sources for technical definitions because they rarely are written by people in the applied field you investigate. On the other hand, dictionaries of psychology, communication, mass media, and speech and hearing science attempt to provide correct technical definitions.

specialized dictionaries

As you read, you will see references to other sources that you can track down later. Students sometimes read a literature review from a book and accept it as sufficient. Unfortunately, literature reviews tend to be dated by over a year by the time a book is published. Furthermore, some authors may summarize literature inaccurately or with a biased point of view. By checking original sources, you can find out what the research really discovered. Furthermore, by browsing through journals published shortly after the original articles, you can tell if serious objections and reactions were raised to them.

dangers of relying on secondary reviews of literature

TABLE G.1   SOURCES USEFUL TO OBTAIN INFORMATION IN LIBRARY SEARCHES

RATINGS OF SOURCES*

MATTERS TO INVESTIGATE	CATEGORIES OF SOURCES			
	Textbooks	Handbooks, Yearbooks, and Annual Reviews	Specialized Encyclopedias Dictionaries	Articles
Definitions of key concepts and variables	A	B	A	C
Ways concepts and variables have been measured and studied	C	B	D	A
General summary statements about the subject	A	A	F	C
Classic research studies in the field	A	A	F	B
Research that shows what methods to use	C	B	F	A
Research that shows what mistakes to avoid	C	B	F	A

SOURCES FOR INFORMATION

Source	Comment
Encyclopedias	
Hudson, R. V. (1987). *Mass media: A chronological encyclopedia of television, motion pictures, magazines, newspapers, and books in the United States.* New York: Garland. P 92.U5 H77 1987[†]	Covers mass media history from 1638 through 1987 in the United States
International encyclopedia of communications. (1989). New York: Oxford University Press. (4 vols.). P 87.5.I5 1989	Precis of over 500 topics of interest to communication
Schement, J. R. (Ed.). (2002). *Encyclopedia of communication and information.* New York: Macmillan Reference. (3 vols.). P 87.5.E53 2002	Reviews of communication issues with volume 3 specializing in recent developments in applied areas of communication studies

*These subjective ratings indicate A: excellent source

B: often useful source

C: occasionally useful source

D: rarely useful

F: forget it

[†]For these sources the Library of Congress call numbers are provided so that you may conveniently find these periodicals in your local library. Our checking across a host of research libraries reveals that some minor variation in call numbers occurs as local operations face their own clerical difficulties and as new volumes of multivolume series are acquired.

TABLE G.1   (Continued)

Sills, D. L. (Ed.). (1991). *International encyclopedia of the social sciences*. New York: Macmillan. (18 vols.) H 40.A2 I5

Useful background with emphasis on classic work in the social sciences

Dictionaries

General

Bothamley, J. (1993). *Dictionary of theories*. London: Gale Research International. R 118.H26 2003

Over 5,000 theories, metatheories, hypotheses, and systems of principles from the natural sciences, linguistics, philosophy, psychology, and the broad realms of the social sciences

Cardwell, M. (1999). *Dictionary of psychology*. Chicago: Fitzroy Dearborn. BF 31.C33 1999

Terms in psychology including social psychology and behavioral sciences

Chaplin, J. P. (1985). *Dictionary of psychology* (2nd rev. ed.). New York: A Laurel Book, Dell. BF 31.C45 1985

Particularly useful for presenting definitions relatively free of jargon

Colman, A. M. (2003). *Oxford dictionary of psychology*. Oxford, UK: Oxford University Press. BF 31.C65 2003

Terms in psychology, education, social work, sociology, and nursing

Corsini, R. J. (2002). *The dictionary of psychology*. New York: Brunner/Routledge. BF 31.C72 2002

Listing of terms in clinical and social psychology

Danesi, M. (2000). *Encyclopedic dictionary of semiotics, media, and communications*. Toronto, Canada: University of Toronto Press. P 87.5.D36 2000

Terms emphasizing mass communication and the study of meaning

Davey, H. (Ed.). (2005). *The encyclopaedic dictionary of psychology*. London: Hodder Arnold. BF 31.E493 2005

Dictionary organized in eight sections dealing with developmental, social, cognitive, biological, personality, abnormal, clinical, and health psychology

DeVito, J. A. (1986). *The communication handbook: A dictionary*. New York: Harper and Row. P 87.5.D46 1986

Definitions of terms and essays on broad communication topics

The encyclopedic dictionary of psychology (4th ed.). (1991). Guilford, CT: Dushkin Publishing Group. BF 31.E564 1991

Definitions and commentary on terms in psychology and social sciences

English, H. B., & English, A. C. (1958). *A comprehensive dictionary of psychological and psychoanalytical terms*. New York: McKay. BF 31.E58 1958

An oldie but a goodie; contains clear explanations and criticisms of different schools of thought

Givens, D. B. (2005). *The nonverbal dictionary of gestures, signs & body language cues*. Spokane, WA: Center for Nonverbal Studies Press. Available: http://members. aol.com/nonverbal2/diction1.htm#The%20NONVERBAL%20DICTIONARY

Extensive list of terms used to identify forms of nonverbal cues

Harré, R., & Lamb, R. (Eds.). (1986). *The dictionary of personality and social psychology*. Cambridge, MA: MIT Press. BF 698 D527 1986

Terms in social psychology and personality concepts

(Continued)

TABLE G.1   (Continued)

Hayes, N., & Stratton, P. (2003). *A student's dictionary of psychology* (4th ed.). London: Hodder Arnold. BF 31.S69 2003	Comprehensive list of terms in psychology and social sciences
Longman dictionary of psychology and psychiatry. (1984). New York: Longman. BF 31.L66 1984	Definitions of over 21,000 terms; among the largest of such dictionaries
Marriot, F. H., & Kendall, M. G. (1990). *A dictionary of statistical terms* (5th ed.). New York: Longman. HA 17.K4 1990	Definitions of concepts and formulae in statistical analysis of data
Nowlan, R. A., & Nowlan, G. L. (Eds.). (2000). *A dictionary of quotations about communication.* Jefferson, NC: McFarland. PN 6081.D535 2000	Entertaining set of statements about communication organized in dictionary format
Reber, A. S., & Reber, E. S. (2001). *The Penguin dictionary of psychology* (3rd ed.). London: Penguin. BF 31.R43 2001	Comprehensive listing of terms in the field of psychology and social sciences
Roekelein, J. E. (1998). *Dictionary of theories, laws, and concepts in psychology.* Westport, CT: Greenwood Press. BF 31 Internet	An electronic reproduction available on the Web through licensed library outlets; composed of 548 pages of summaries of theories and metatheories in psychology and the social sciences
Schwandt, T. A. (1997). *Qualitative inquiry: A dictionary of terms.* Thousand Oaks, CA: Sage. H 61.S4435 1997	Terms and concepts in qualitative research methods and philosophies
Statt, D. A. (1998). *The concise dictionary of psychology* (3rd ed.). London: Routledge. BF 31.S62 1998	Brief treatment of definitions of terms in psychology and social sciences
Statt, D. A. (2003). *A student's dictionary of psychology.* Hove, UK: Psychology Press. BF 31.S64 2003	List of terms and concepts that play a central role in the study of psychology and the social sciences
Stempel, G. H., & Gifford, J. N. (Eds.). (1999). *Historical dictionary of political communication in the United States.* Westport, CT: Greenwood Press. JA 85.2.U6 H57 1999	Terms emphasizing mass communication and the study of meaning
Sutherland, S. (1996). *The international dictionary of psychology* (2nd ed.). New York: Crossroad. BF 31.S83 1996	Descriptions of terms in clinical, social, and comparative psychology
Vogt, W. Paul. (2005). *Dictionary of statistics and methodology: A nontechnical guide for the social sciences* (3rd ed.). Thousand Oaks, CA: Sage. HA 17.V64 2005	Descriptions of terms in research design, methods, and statistical analysis; frequent examples given
Wolman, B. B. (Ed.). (1989). *Dictionary of behavioral science* (2nd ed.). San Diego: Academic Press. BF 31.D48 1989	Broad review of terms in the social and behavioral sciences

Mass Communication

Abercrombie, N., & Longhurst, B. (2007). *The Penguin dictionary of media studies.* Baltimore, MD: Penguin. P 87.5.A1 2007	Reviews definitions focusing primarily on mass media, journalism, broadcasting, and cultural studies

(Continued)

TABLE G.1 (Continued)

Demers, D. P. (2005). *Dictionary of mass communication & media research: A guide for students, scholars, and professionals.* Spokane, WA: Marquette Books. P 87.5.D449 2005	Terms related to journalism, broadcasting, and mass media, along with methods of mass media inquiry
Diamant, L. (Ed.). (1992). *The broadcast communications dictionary* (3rd ed., rev. & exp.). New York: Greenwood Press. PN 1990.4.D5 1992	Listings limited to broadcast terms, definitions on mass media operations, and technology
Dictionary of media studies. (2006). London: A & C Black. P 87.5.B4 2006	A. C. Black dictionary of terms in the field of mass communication
Ellmore, R. T. (1991). *NTC's mass media dictionary.* Lincolnwood, IL: National Textbook. P 87.5.E45 1991	Terms in journalism and telecommunications
Fletcher, J. (1988). *Broadcast research definitions.* Washington, DC: National Association of Broadcasters. PN 1990.4.B76 1988	Definitions of terms related to television and radio broadcasting
Hartley, J. (2002). *Communication, cultural and media studies: The key concepts* (3rd ed.). London: Routledge. P 90.H33463 2002	Terms related to the cultural studies approach to inquiry mass media communication
Longman dictionary of mass media and communication. (1983). New York: Longman. P 87.5.I66 1983	Definitions of terms used across mass media specialties
Orlebar, J. (2003). *The practical media dictionary.* London: Arnold. P 87.5.O7 2003	Terms in mass communication emphasizing terms in applied rather than theoretic applications of mass communication
Watson, J., & Hill, A. (2003). *A dictionary of communication and media studies* (6th ed.). London: Edward Arnold. P 87.5.W38 2003	Definitions of concepts in the broad realm of mass communication studies
Weik, M. H. (1996). *Communications standard dictionary* (3rd ed.). New York: Van Nostrand Reinhold. TK 5102.W437 1996	Definitions of concepts and terms involving mass mediated communication and technology
Weiner, R. (1996). *Webster's New World dictionary of media and communications* (rev. ed.). New York: Webster's New World. P 87.5.W45 1996	Coverage of technical terms in journalism and telecommunications
Wiechmann, J. G., & Urdang, L. (Ed.). (1993). *NTC's dictionary of advertising* (rev. ed.). Lincolnwood, IL: National Textbook. HF 5803.W54 1993	Emphasis on layout, public relations, and advertising

Speech and Hearing Science

Morris, D. W. H. (1997). *A dictionary of speech therapy.* (3rd ed.). London: Taylor and Francis. RC 423.M597 1997	Terms related to treatment and measurement in speech correction
Nicolosi, L., Harryman, E., & Kresheck, J. (Eds.). (2004). *Terminology of communication disorders: Speech, language, and hearing* (5th ed.). Philadelphia: Lippincott, Williams and Wilkins. RC 423.N52 2004	Terms emphasizing speech, hearing, and language diagnostic items for the therapist and clinician

(Continued)

TABLE G.1   (Continued)

Advertising, Public Relations, and Marketing Communication

Bennett, P. D. (Ed.). (1995). *Dictionary of marketing terms* (2nd ed.). Lincolnwood, IL: NTC Business Books. HF 5415.D4874 1995	Terms in mass communication emphasizing mass communication and the study of meaning
Govoni, N. A. (2004). *Dictionary of marketing communications.* Thousand Oaks, CA: Sage. HF 5412.G68 2004	Comprehensive listing of terms in marketing and advertising communication
Imber, J., & Toffler, B. (2000). *Dictionary of marketing terms* (3rd ed). Hauppauge, NY: Barron's. HF 5803.T56 2000	Revision of the popular dictionary treatment of concepts in marketing and advertising communication
Urdang, L. (Ed.). (1992). *The dictionary of advertising.* Lincolnwood, IL: NTC Business Books. HF 5803.D5 1992	Emphasis on layout, public relations, art design, and advertising jargon

Handbooks, Yearbooks, and Annual Reviews

General

Arnold, C. C., & Bowers, J. W. (Eds.). (1984). *Handbook of rhetorical and communication theory.* Boston: Allyn and Bacon. P 90.H296 1984	14 topics covered of interest to general communication theory and rhetorical studies
Berger, C. R., & Chaffee, S. H. (Eds.). (1987). *Handbook of communication science.* Newbury Park, CA: Sage. P 90.H294 1987	28 chapters with essays covering major aspects of social science communication research
Brown, R., & Gaertner, S. L. (Eds.). (2001). *Blackwell handbook of social psychology: Intergroup processes.* Malden, MA: Blackwell. HM 1086.B53 2001	25 chapters on topics including assessments of research and theory on cognition, motivation, emotion, communication and social influence, and intergroup relations
Communication yearbook. (1977–). Newbury Park, CA: Sage. P 87.C5974	Essays and top papers of each division of the International Communication Association
Delamater, J. (Ed.). (2003). *Handbook of social psychology.* New York: Kluwer Academic/Plenum. HM 1033.H36 2003	Coverage of theory and research in social psychology including sections on influence, interpersonal relations, and group interaction
Dillard, J. P., & Pfau, M. (Eds). (2002). *The persuasion handbook: Developments in theory and practice.* Thousand Oaks, CA: Sage. HM 1196.P47 2002	Chapters dedicated to research and theory persuasive functions, theoretic orientations, chief variables of influence, and persuasive communication in applied settings
First amendment law handbook. New York: Boardman. KF 4770.A15 F57 1998–99 (published annually with changing dates)	Emphasis on legal issues in freedom of speech
Gilbert, D. T., Fiske, S. T., & Lindzey, G. (Eds.). (1998). *The handbook of social psychology* (4th ed.). Boston: McGraw-Hill (2 vols.) HM 251.H224 1998	Syntheses of theory and research on areas in social psychology, often communication related
Greene, J. O., & Burleson, B. R. (Eds.). (2003). *Handbook of communication and social interaction skills.* Mahwah, NJ: Erlbaum. HM 1111.H36 2003	23 summary essays organized according to general theoretical and methodological issues, fundamental interaction skills, communication functions, communication skills in close personal relationships, and skills in public and cultural settings

(Continued)

TABLE G.1 (Continued)

Higgins, E. T., & Kruglanski, A. W. (Eds.). (1996). *Social psychology: Handbook of basic principles.* New York: Guilford Press. HM 251.S6743 1996	Chapters reviewing research and theory on biological, cognitive, motivational, interpersonal, and group/cultural forces in social psychology
Hogg, M. A. (Ed.). (2001). *Blackwell handbook of social psychology: Group processes.* Malden, MA: Blackwell. HM 1033.B5935 2001	26 chapters dealing with the broad realm of group applications including group decision making, jury behavior, leadership, negotiation and bargaining, and computer-mediated communication
Hogg, M. A., & Cooper, J. (Eds). (2003). *Sage handbook of social psychology.* Thousand Oaks, CA: Sage. HM 1033.S24 2003	23 chapters including topics dealing with individual, intergroup, interpersonal, and persuasive communication
Isaac, S., & Michael, W. B. (Eds.). (1995). *Handbook in research and evaluation* (3rd ed.). San Diego: EdITS. BF 76.5.I8 1995	Designs and critical standards for evaluating research
Jensen, K. B. (Ed) (2002). *A handbook of media and communications research: Qualitative and quantitative methodologies.* London: Routledge. P 91.3.H34 2002	15 essays dealing with history of media and communication research, mass media systems, and applications of qualitative and quantitative research processes in communication studies
Mann, C., & Stewart, F. (2000). *Internet communication and qualitative research: A handbook for researching online.* London: Sage. HA 33.5.M36 2000	Methods of qualitative research with specific applications to the Internet (includes both discussion of methods and treatments in applied studies)
Robinson, W. P., & Giles, H. (Eds.). (2001). *The new handbook of language and social psychology.* Chichester, UK: Wiley. P 106.N447 2001	32 chapters with sections dedicated to foundations of the subject of language (including nonverbal communication), face-to-face communication, social categories, social relations, and studies in applied settings
Rubin, R. B., Palmgreen, P., & Sypher, H. E. (Eds.). (1994). *Communication research measures: A sourcebook.* New York: Guilford. P 91.3.C62 1994	62 measurement tools related to communication described, their validity discussed, and critiqued
Smith, K., Moriarty, S., Barbatsis, G., & Kenney, K. (Eds.). (2005). *Handbook of visual communication: Theory, methods, and media.* Mahwah, NJ: Erlbaum. P 93.5.H363 2005	Chapters dedicated to reviewing major theories in visual communication followed by exemplar studies illustrating various methodological options in visual communication
Tardy, C. H. (Ed.). (1988). *A handbook for the study of human communication: Methods and instruments for observing, measuring and assessing communication processes.* Norwood, NJ: Ablex. P 91.H36 1988	15 measurement tools in communication described and their validity discussed
Tesser, A., & Schwarz, N. (Eds.). (2001). *Blackwell handbook of social psychology: Intraindividual processes.* Malden, MA: Blackwell. BF 311.B54 2001	28 essays dealing with research and theory in social cognition and social motivation

Mass Communication

Dowling, J. D. H. (Ed.). (2004). *The Sage handbook of media studies.* Thousand Oaks, CA: Sage. P 90.S18 2004	Essays on theoretic approaches to studying media, global and comparative perspectives, media and economic power, and media users

(Continued)

TABLE G.1 (Continued)

Gerbner, G., & Siefert, M. (Eds.). (1984). *World communications: A handbook*. New York: Longman. P 96.I5 W67 1984	Reviews of communication technology globally, emphasizing international development
Mass communication review yearbook (1980 through 1987). Newbury Park, CA: Sage. P 87.M28	Studies on mass communication and applied areas (no longer published)
Rosen, P. T. (Ed.). (1988). *International handbook of broadcasting systems*. New York: Greenwood Press. HE 8689.6 I54 1988	Mass media publications and associations for each nation with emphasis on those hosting UN Centres
Singer, D. G., & Singer, J. L. (Eds.). (2001). *Handbook of children and the media*. Thousand Oaks, CA: Sage. HQ 784.T4 S533 2001	Essays organized to deal with issues including popular media as educators and socializers of growing children, forging the media environment for the future, the media industry and its technology, and policy issues and advocacy
World media handbook. (1990). New York: United Nations. P 88.8.W66 1990	Descriptions of global systems of radio and TV broadcasting
World radio TV handbook: A complete directory of international radio and television. (Annual). New York: Billboard Publications. TK 6540.W67	Global listing of radio and TV broadcasting organizations including much technical detail

Speech and Hearing Science

Glennen, S. L., & DeCoste, D. C. (Eds.). (1997). *The handbook of augmentative and alternative communication*. San Diego: Singular Publishing Group. RC 423.H325 1997	16 essays dealing with augmentative communication devices, their uses, and availability
Travis, L. (Ed.). (1971). *The handbook of speech pathology and audiology*. New York: Appleton-Century-Crofts. RC 423.T67 1971	A classic work detailing contributions in speech and hearing science

Special Topics

Intercultural Communication

Gudykunst, W. B., & Mody, B. (Eds.). (2002). *Handbook of international and intercultural communication* (2nd ed). Thousand Oaks, CA: Sage. P 94.6 H36 2002	Collected essays on intercultural, international, and interethnic communication variables
Gudykunst, W. B., Newmark, E., & Assante, M. K. (Eds.). (1994). *Handbook of international and intercultural communication* (2nd ed). Newbury Park, CA: Sage. P 96.I5 H37 1994	Follow-up to 1989 handbook includes essays on the status of the field and intercultural communication research issues
International and intercultural communication annual. (1974–). Newbury Park, CA: Sage. various call numbers (1998 edition: GN 345.6C66 1998)	Articles, research summary essays, and book reviews
Matsumoto, D. (Ed.). (2001). *The handbook of culture and psychology*. New York: Oxford University Press. GN 502 H362 2001	Independent chapters are dedicated to sections on conceptual foundations of culture in psychology, personality, and social behavior

(Continued)

TABLE G.1   (Continued)

Interpersonal and Group Communication

Andersen, P. A., & Guerrero, L. K. (1998). *Handbook of communication and emotion: Research, theory, applications, and contexts.* San Diego: Academic Press. BF 637.C45 H283 1998	Issues of emotion and affective responses and expressions in verbal and nonverbal communication
Duck, S. (Ed.). (1997). *Handbook of personal relationships: Theory, research and interventions* (2nd ed.). New York: Wiley. HM 132.H3325 1997	Concern with interpersonal relationships from psychological, sociological, and communication views
Frey, L. R. (Ed.). (1999). *The handbook of group communication theory and research.* Thousand Oaks, CA: Sage. HM 133.H354 1999	Essays on all aspects of small-group communication and theory
Hare, A. P., Blumberg, H. H., Davies, M. F., & Kent, M. V. (1994). *Small group research: A handbook.* Norwood, NJ: Ablex. HM 133.S646 1994	Small-group behavior organized into topics that have focused research; emphasis on literature summation
Hargie, O. (1997). *A handbook of communication skills* (2nd ed.). London: Routledge. BF 637.C45 H284 1997	Practical emphasis on communication skills training
Knapp, M. L., & Daley, J. A. (Eds.). (2002). *Handbook of interpersonal communication* (3rd ed.). Thousand Oaks, CA: Sage. BF 637.C45 H287 2002	Emphasis on reviews of interpersonal communication since the 1960s
Spitzberg, B. H., & Cupach, W. R. (1989). *Handbook of interpersonal competence research.* New York: Springer-Verlag. BF 637.C45 S67 1989	Conceptualization, research, and measurement concerns regarding communicator competence

Organizational Communication

Goldhaber, G., & Barnett, G. A. (Eds.). (1988). *Handbook of organizational communication.* Norwood, NJ: Ablex Publishing Corp. HD 30.3.H357 1988	Reviews of methods and application areas in organizational communication
Jablin, F. M., & Putnam, L. L. (Eds.). (2001). *The new handbook of organizational communication.* Newbury Park, CA: Sage. HD 30.3.N3575 2001	Follow-up to the 1987 handbook, covering 21 chapters on issues in organizational communication from different perspectives
Jablin, F. M., Putnam, L. L., Karlene, H. R., & Porter, L. W. (Eds.). (1987). *Handbook of organizational communication: An interdisciplinary perspective.* Newbury Park, CA: Sage. HD 30.3.H3575 1987	Chapters on organizational communication contexts, structures, issues, and processes across academic fields
Ruch, W. (1989). *International handbook of corporate communication.* Jefferson, NC: McFarland. HD 30.3.R823 1989	Essays on business communication applications to international public relations and communication in multinational corporations

Political Communication

Nimmo, D. D., & Sanders, K. R. (Eds.). (1981). *Handbook of political communication.* Beverly Hills, CA: Sage. JA 74.H34 1981	First handbook on subject with primary emphasis on U.S. politics

(Continued)

TABLE G.1　(Continued)

Swanson, D. L., & Nimmo, D. (Eds.). (1990). *New directions on political communication*. Newbury Park, CA: Sage. JA 74.N49 1990	Companion to 1981 handbook; includes bibliography of post-1981 materials

Public Relations

Caywood, C. L. (Ed.). (1997). *The handbook of strategic public relations and integrated communications*. New York: McGraw-Hill. HM 263.H317 1997	39 essays dealing with public relations research and applications to various organizations and industries
Dilenschneider, R. L., & Forestal, D. J. (1987). *Dartnell public relations handbook* (3rd ed., rev.). Chicago: Dartnell. HD 59.D28 1987	Review pieces on applications of internal and external public relations including many case studies
Lesly, P. (Ed.). (1991). *Lesly's handbook of public relations and communications* (2nd ed.). Chicago: Probus. HM 263.L46 1991	Reviews of applied issues in public relations and related mass media applications
Public relations research annual. (1989–). Hillsdale, NJ: Erlbaum.	Original research in public relations and publicity

Other

Deutsch, M., & Coleman, P. T. (Eds.). (2000). *The handbook of conflict resolution: Theory and practice*. San Francisco: Jossey-Bass. HM 1126.H35 2000	Essays dedicated to the study of conflict with particular emphasis on methods of managing productive competitive conflict
Free speech yearbook. (1960–). Carbondale: Southern Illinois University Press. P 87.F853	Reviews of free press/free speech issues and case studies
Nussbaum, J. F., & Coupland, J. (Eds.). (2004). *The handbook of communication and aging research* (2nd ed.). Mahwah, NJ: Erlbaum. HQ 1061.H3365 2004	Essays on issues in communication and the aging process, needs of senior citizens, and challenges of aging
Thompson, T. L., Dorsey, A., Miller, K., & Parrott, R. (Eds.). (2003). *Handbook of health communication*. Mahwah, NJ: Erlbaum. R 118.H26 2003	39 essays dealing with public relations research and applications to various organizations and industries
Vangelisti, A. L. (Ed.). (2004). *The handbook of family communication*. Mahwah, NJ: Erlbaum. HQ 519 H36 2004	Focus on family communication with an emphasis on theory and research that deals with interpersonal and intergenerational issues

The "When?" Guiding Yourself with a Research Outline

use of a planning outline

Sometimes new students overhear horror stories from other students about long hours spent in the library. The stories tell more about the inefficiency of some students than the use of resource materials. The easiest way to use time effectively is to create a research planning outline. At the library, start at the top of your outline and work your way through. Instead of spending hours looking for random information, you can find materials in an orderly fashion without getting sidetracked into interesting but irrelevant areas. It may seem obvious to plan your time efficiently by making some notes, but next time you visit a library watch the other students. You won't see many people who have organized their time. Some of them may look very frustrated. They will spend more time than you in the library—but they will have less to show for it. Plan your time and you will have all you need.

managing time with research planning outlines will enhance your efficiency

Setting limits on the scope of your research is critical before you look for resources. If you have an exhaustive literature review for which a month's preparation time is provided, you may set limits very broadly. If you have only a week to complete a review of chief definitions, you may need to limit your examination to key books, specialized dictionaries, and "think piece" articles.

setting limits on scope

The "How?" Managing Research Materials

Learning from experience is an effective way to develop research skills, but it is very inefficient. Thus, it would be a good idea to develop some survival skills to *prepare* for your first literature searches.

Techniques for Bibliographic Research

Searching for source material is dominated by assembling bibliographic materials of one sort or another. You must remain flexible to find and record information as it comes your way.

Mastering the Library

A "library" used to mean a building with a lot of books, journals, magazines, and special collections. Though such libraries are wonderful places for researchers, these days "electronic libraries" may be searched at a distance. In fact, many universities founded in recent years feature libraries that rely on electronically available materials even more than traditional hard copy materials. We might refer to the physical library as a "local library" and extended sets of resources as "electronic libraries." Each local library has its own unique qualities. Thus, it is a good idea to tour your local library and find out its approaches. You will find that the person at the reference desk is ready and willing to help you. But do not ask that librarian how to read an index or to tell you how to do a project you have been assigned. This book and your instructor are supposed to teach you those skills. Remember, you will want the library people to help you if you run into a special problem: do not burn them out with questions you can get answered in class or by reading this book. You soon will grow comfortable with the layout of things and will be able to make library searches with ease.

learning local library qualities

Tactical Skills in Bibliographic Research

To be effective, bibliographic research requires observing some basic skills:

- ◆ *Take notes in brief form.* Your working notes or cards (containing quotations and summary information) should be selective and to the point. Long quotations or

importance of brevity

lists of statistics often can be summarized since you rarely will report such specifics in your projects.

importance of good note-taking skills

♦ *Practice good note-taking skills.* Since examining information requires you to summarize materials, it is vital to take notes accurately. Most people take either too many notes or too few. Instead, you should get the main ideas first. Then you may add appropriate details or explanations.

proper quotation and reference form

♦ *Follow proper reference form.* In different branches of communication, the proper citations follow the current editions of the *MLA Handbook for Writers of Research Papers* or the *Publication Manual of the American Psychological Association.* By the late 1980s nearly all communication journals accepted the latter style sheet (hence, this book uses it). All materials should be quoted fully and in context. You may wish to photocopy key pages just to be safe. If other sources are referenced in quoted material, you must obtain full citations for them. Though you should avoid editing others' words, if a portion of a quotation must be omitted, ellipses (. . .) should be put in their place. If words or phrases must be added to make a statement clear, the additions should be placed within brackets [ ]. If you notice a grammatical or spelling error, leave the words as in the original statement and follow the offending passage with the word *sic* within brackets (*sic* means "thus" or "so" in Latin).

The Library Research Strategies

selecting a library search strategy

Getting started in the library can be invigorating. Plunge in with your research planning outline, note cards, laptop computer (if you have one), and plenty of writing materials. But plunge in with a strategy to guide you. Use your research outline sheet. Then, go wherever you need to trace down information. Two major library research strategies can help give you a starting place.

General to Specific

general-to-specific strategy

Starting with general sources and then finding leads to specific sources is useful when you do not have much background on the subject. At the beginning of your research career, that condition will occur most often. Furthermore, if the topic is fairly broad, you may wish to start with the general-to-specific method, just to make sure that you do not omit important theoretical foundations of the work. If you do not know enough to be sure about which strategy to use, this one is for you.

Start your research with general textbooks, handbooks, yearbooks, and specialized encyclopedias. Sometimes students do not know what textbooks to grab. There is a simple method. Look at your problem and ask yourself the title of the class in which people usually study such a subject. Textbook publishers prefer using textbook titles that reflect names of courses for which they are intended. Write down keywords from the course title. Then, look up the books whose titles include those keywords.

keywords defined

Keywords are terms under which information about the topic may be found. Hence, if you are interested in looking at communication styles of leaders in business, you may rightly think that this topic usually is covered in courses on organizational communication, business and professional communication, and management communication.

SPECIAL DISCUSSION G-1
Ten Commandments of Library Use

Librarians can be very helpful, but many students do not know how to work with them. "The most common complaint heard among reference librarians about their work is that few people know how to ask reference questions" (Katz, 1982, p. 16). Two librarians (Gardner & Zelevansky, 1975) suggested these ten commandments:

I. Thou shalt be prepared with a valid, logical and/or reasonable query and not an inchoate question, without form and void.

II. Thou shalt request all information in the beginning.

III. Thou shalt be honest and true with thy librarian in revelation of what thou seekest, much as thou wouldst not hold back symptoms from thy physician.

IV. Thou shalt exhibit the patience of Job in waiting at the librarian's desk (or at the other end of the telephone) so that when the answer to thy query is divined, the search shall not have been in vain.

V. Thou shalt express thine appreciation of labor well done by thy librarian through written testimony to his/her supervisor.

VI. Thou shalt not designate the "Source," but rather utter clearly that which is sought.

VII. Thou shalt not require thy librarian to be accountable for that which is not yet published.

VIII. Thou shalt not require thy librarian to interpret data in chapter and verse.

IX. Thou shalt not scorn a wise referral, for surely a sage counsel cannot lead thee far astray and may indeed bear fruit.

X. Thou shalt not steal.

SOURCE: Reprinted from *Special Libraries*, v. 66, no. 7 (July 1975), p. 326. © by Special Libraries Association.

Look up a few books to find their location in the library. Then, browse through them (starting at the index sections) to select the most useful sources.

Though general sources may not answer your research questions directly, start with them and copy down relevant statements. Most important, write down references the authors used in *their* general surveys. After looking at a handful of textbooks, you probably will have enough specific references to know where to go for further detailed information. Try to choose sources that have the most promising sounding titles. It is fairly easy to tell whether an article is worth reading since most scholarly articles have boring yet descriptive titles. Though there are exceptions, standard phrases used in titles (or subtitles) can tell much about the article. For instance, the following phrases often reveal what to expect:

- ◆ "A Case Study of . . . " (translation: a situation examined in detail)

- ◆ "An Experimental Study of . . . " (translation: a quantitative study—in the field or laboratory—in which variables were manipulated under controlled settings)

- ◆ "A Survey of . . . " (translation: a quantitative study in which an area is characterized but no variables are manipulated)

- "Theories of . . . " (translation: a review and critique of theories or orientations)

- "Measurement of . . . " (translation: a review/critique; or suggestions for a new method to measure a construct)

- "On the Meaning of . . . " (translation: a review/critique of major approaches to define a concept)

- "A Content Analysis of . . . " (translation: a quantitative analysis of some examples of communication)

- "A (Burkean, Aristotelian, Fantasy Theme, etc.) Analysis of . . . " (translation: a rhetorical critique of a piece of communication, a movement, or a source of communication)

- *Foundations of* . . . (translation: usually books covering the broad domain of a subject)

- *Handbook of* . . . (translation: a book containing essays and brief guides to literature and methods in an area of study)

- *A Theory of* . . . (translation: a book or an article—advancing a theory or fundamental orientation).

interpreting study articles

Most historical studies do not identify the method of inquiry in their titles. Instead, they just announce the object of the historical inquiry. Look at references you find in your searches to tell what articles may be most relevant. Do not just read citations. Try to consider what they are about.

Specific to General

specific-to-general strategy

Sometimes you may read an article or essay that grabs your interest. Perhaps you have asked your instructors about specific topics. You may have received a reference to help you get started. You can begin with these specific sources and write down the citations to related research and theory identified in them. Then, you may repeat the process with the new sources. Soon, information snowballs as one reference leads to others.

uses of the specific-to-general pattern

You will find that different articles often reference the same "classic" research or theories. You will want to take the time to note such patterns across studies. You also can extend the search by using other abstracts and citation indices. This search method is effective when you have a specific starting piece or author name and are interested primarily in unearthing other general findings. Furthermore, the method can be helpful when you are uncertain about the most common keywords used to index the research.

The "Where?" The Key Library Tools

Entire books have been written about library resources (e.g., Beasley, 1988; Paradis, 1966; Rubin, Rubin, & Piele, 2005), and you probably already know how to find general materials. But the best training to find scholarly research materials is brief direction, followed by library experience. Rather than cover such matters exhaustively, we will guide you to *some* of the most helpful tools for communication studies. Library tools really boil down to two forms: hierarchical systems and keyword systems.

Hierarchical Systems for Books and Collections

Hierarchical systems of filing tell you where common material is found—in the same location in the library. Such things as catalogs of books and special collections files are examples of these hierarchical guides. These guides help you locate where you can find books, handbooks, and other collections.

hierarchical systems

You might remember large wooden card files listing the books possessed by libraries. They are only a memory now. Nearly every college library uses an electronic catalog of books and periodicals. The speed at which books can be identified is enhanced by using such systems. Of the many computerized library systems, the Colorado Alliance of Research Libraries (CARL) and Online Public Access Catalog (OPAC) have been adopted in most college libraries. Listings are available on book titles, names of authors, or subjects. A typical listing for such an item appears in Figure G.2 on page A–80. You may wish to read all the listings in a given subject heading to select the most recent books available, just to make sure that you do not miss recent contributions. You will also want to notice any **subject tracings** or keywords that list other subject headings under which the book is also listed. These headings can be used if you reach a dead end with your current keywords.

systems of book catalogs

subject tracings identified

These systems are more useful than they once were. In addition to books, they list journals held by the library and often permit you to use some online search systems. For instance, IngentaConnect (www.ingentaconnect.com) permits you to search nearly 30,000 publications including many journals in communication as well as in the *National Newspaper Index,* the *Newspaper & Periodical Index,* and the *Transcript* systems. This simplifying of search systems is progressing in leaps and bounds. So, it would be a good idea to make friends with reference librarians at your school so that you can keep up with the latest time-saving tools.

catalog systems often permit access to other search tools

To identify the call numbers of the works relevant to your topic, you will rely on one of the two major systems in use. The Dewey Decimal System was invented by Melvil Dewey in 1873 to help organize the Amherst College library, when he was an undergraduate student (see Paradis, 1966, p. 4; Best, 1981, pp. 313–315). The method became dominant in public libraries and some college libraries use it today. Yet, it became difficult to add new specialized topics gracefully. Over time, many libraries adopted the Library of Congress method first developed by Herbert Putnam pursuant to an 1880 act of Congress. Today, most college libraries and government depositories (libraries that regularly receive copies of federal government documents) employ this system (see Table G.2 on page A–81).

the Dewey Decimal System

the Library of Congress method

Most libraries also subscribe to electronic systems that list what books, journals, recordings, films, and nonprint media are available at other libraries. For instance, the Online Computer Library Center (OCLC) sponsors *WorldCat,* which catalogs holdings

systems to identify holdings at other libraries

SPECIAL DISCUSSION G-2
Bibliographic Research Records: Elements of a Bibliographic Card

It is helpful to record key information on note cards. Figure G.1 shows such a card. In fact, you should have some blank 4 × 6 or 5 × 8 cards before you enter a local library (do not use 3 × 5 cards—they are just too small to use flexibly). As you go through resource materials, keep track of your work by completing full bibliographic cards. If you have a laptop computer, you may have software to record note cards on disk for electronic sorting later. Regardless of the tools you use, some things that should be on all bibliographic cards are the following:

Bibliographic Card

Verbal Aggression Hurts Most from Friends Unless Teasing
Martin, M.M., Anderson, C.M., & Horvath, C.L. (1996). Feelings about verbal aggression: Justifications for sending and hurt from receiving verbally aggressive messages. *Communication Research Reports, 13,* 19–26.

"Clearly, receiving verbally aggressive messages from friends is considered more hurtful than messages from acquaintances. An exception was that no difference was found when the verbally aggressive message was in the form of teasing." (p. 23)

Study was a survey of the degree to which college students perceived justification and hurt from verbally aggressive messages in the abstract.

Figure G.1   Bibliographic Card

- *Title.* A newspaper-type headline title that summarizes information on the card and helps with filing material. Record only one thought on each card—to continue material, simply start another card.

- *Citation.* Use full citations in proper bibliographic form. Do not abbreviate this part since detecting errors may prove very time-consuming (you may have multiple works from the same authors, or from authors who share the same last name).

- *Quotation or abstract: The two types of bibliographic cards.* If direct quotations are used, such material is placed within quotation marks. If materials refer to other sources, include those original citations on your note card (you will want to check on exact wording by going to the original source later). Using abstracts (summaries in your own words) of methods, findings, and conclusions will help you keep track of all sources you examine so that you do not visit the same sources repeatedly. Additionally, using cards allows you to compare recent work on a subject with previous thinking.

- *Commentary.* Add brief comments of your own about the work (placed within brackets to emphasize that they are not claims of the author of the original work). Such comments are also called "**annotations**" and offer additional explanations, comments, evaluations, or criticisms, to help understand the material.

> After collecting information on cards, you may sort them by key topics. Start with the general questions listed in this chapter:
>
> ♦ Definitions of key concepts and variables
>
> ♦ Ways concepts and variables have been measured and studied
>
> ♦ General summary statements about the subject
>
> ♦ The classic research studies in the field
>
> ♦ Problems that researchers have struggled to solve
>
> ♦ Research that shows what methods to use
>
> ♦ Research that shows what mistakes to avoid.
>
> If you notice a void in any category, let that category be the object of a brief, intensive visit to the library. You may wish to use insert dividers between sections (do not buy dividers that have printed letters on them—you are filing information by topics, not by the alphabet). If you do an exhaustive literature search, you may wish to compile a master "key" of any subdivisions. Of course, you should review your bibliography cards frequently to keep current on the status of your inquiry. Curiously, students who "do not have time" to put together bibliography cards nearly always need *more* time to complete projects than students who rely on the use of this valuable tool.

at hundreds of U.S. libraries. If your library does not have a book, the system tells you the other libraries that do. The Research Libraries Information Network (RLIN) performs virtually the same function for more than a score of America's largest libraries. Similar systems are also available regionally. So you should check your local library to see which systems are available to you (for free, that is).

Services are available that index critiques of new books. For trade publications— *indices and guides to books* books that are likely to be sold at the major commercial bookstores—some guides may be worth checking, depending on your topic. *Book Review Digest* presents summaries and critiques, and the *Book Review Index* lists the places where book reviews have been published. For speech and hearing scientists, the *Technical Book Review Index* can be particularly valuable. For rhetorical studies and film and mass media criticism, the *Index to Book Reviews in the Humanities* provides a guide to 685 related publications. In mass communication, the guides tend to be narrow and somewhat dated. Among the most popular has been *Mass Media Bibliography: An Annotated Guide to Books and Journals for Research and Reference,* edited by Eleanor Blum and Frances Wilhoit and covering selected books through the late 1980s.

Keyword-Based Systems

Keyword-based systems, such as the *Psychological Abstracts* and *Communication Abstracts,* *use of index and abstract* send you to different locations in libraries to find articles and papers. The major guides *sources* to these materials are known as indices and abstracts. There are two major categories of such keyword guides to books and articles: computerized systems and hard copy systems. They are not different—they just list the same materials in different form.

| Change Search Term | Request | Save Records | MARC Display | Try Link+ | Another Search |

(Search History)

| TITLE | the persuasion handbook | All collections |

System Sorted   Search

☐ Limit results to available items

Record: Prev Next

1 ——

| Title | **The persuasion handbook : developments in theory and practice / James Price Dillard, Michael Pfau, [editors]** |
| Imprint | Thousand Oaks, CA : Sage Publications, c2002 |

2 ——

LOCATION	CALL NO.	STATUS
5th FL SOUTH	HM1196 .P47 2002	CHECK SHELVES

3 ——
4 ——

Descript	xx, 874 p. ; 26 cm
Subject	Persuasion (Psychology) -- Social aspects
	Persuasion (Rhetoric)
Alt author	Dillard, James Price
	Pfau, Michael

5 ——
6 ——

| Note | Includes bibliographical references and indexes |
| ISBN/ISSN | 0761920064 (c) |

Note: This item was taken from the OPAC listing at the California State University, Fullerton Main Library.

1. The imprint contains information necessary for a citation, including the city of publication, the publisher, and the date.

2. The location, call number, and current status are listed. In this case, the book is located along with the other books on the fifth floor, The call number uses the Library of Congress classification system. The book is located on the shelves and is not checked out.

3. The book is described as 874 pages long with a length of 26 centimeters.

4. Since the subject matter was persuasion, the keywords listed here were used to identify it. These keywords and phrases may be used to find other books with similar content.

5. Features of the book are listed to help readers use it.

6. The ISBN (International Standard Book Number) serial number is assigned by book-numbering agencies such as R. R. Bowker Company, in the United States.

Figure G.2   Sample Catalog Listing

TABLE G.2 DEWEY DECIMAL SYSTEM AND LIBRARY OF CONGRESS CLASSIFICATIONS WITH EMPHASIS ON CATEGORIES FOR THE COMMUNICATION FIELD

Dewey Decimal System		Library of Congress		
000	General Works:	A		General Works
		B		Philosophy, Psychology, Religion
070	Journalism	B	Philosophy (General)	
		BC	Logic	
100	Philosophy and Related Fields	BF	Psychology (for social psychology, see HM) including communication theory	
120	Epistemology, Causation, Humankind	BH	Aesthetics	
		BJ	Ethics	
140	Specific Philosophic Systems	C		History
150	Psychology	D		World History
160	Logic	E, F		American History
170	Ethics	G		Geography, Anthropology
		H		Social Science
200	Religion	H	Social Science (General)	
		HA	Statistics	
300	Social Sciences	HE	Transportation and Communication (telecommunication, 7601–8688; radio and television, 8689–8700)	
310	Statistics			
340	Law			
350	Public Administration	HF	Commerce (business administration and personnel management, 5001–5549; advertising, 5801–6191)	
370	Education			
400	Language	HM	Sociology (social psychology, 251–291)	
		HQ	Social Groups (family and marriage, 503–1064)	
410	Linguistics			
420	English Languages	HS	Societies	
		HT	Communities, Classes, Races	
500	Pure Sciences	K		Law
		L		Education
600	Technology (Applied Sciences)	M		Music
610	Medical Sciences (including speech and hearing disorders 616.85)	N		Fine Arts
		P		Language and Literature
		P	Philology and Linguistics (General)	
620	Engineering	PE	English	
650	Management and Auxiliary Services	PN	Literature (drama, 1600–3299; oratory, speech communication, debating, recitations, 4001–4355; journalism, communication law, practical journalism, amateur journalism, by region or country, 4699–5650)	
700	Arts and Recreation			
800	Literature	Q		Science
		R		Medicine

(Continued)

TABLE G.2 (Continued)			
900	History	RC	Internal Medicine (stuttering, speech correction, and therapies, 423–430)
		RF	Otorhinolaryngology
		S	Agriculture
		T	Technology
		U	Military Science
		V	Naval Science
		Z	Library Science-Bibliography

Computer Searches

Communication databases have made quick work of literature searches. Two forms of delivering computerized materials are available, although additional forms are constantly in development.

Online Databases

use of online databases

Online database systems connect the researcher with a central computer and can be used to search for books, articles, and reports on key topics. The online search usually results in listing large numbers of entries in bibliographic format with many accompanying abstracts. Since online searches have been around for some time, there are many systems for completing them. Some require that you work through your local library, but others require only that you have access to a computer so that you can go online. Table G.3 lists some of the major database search systems relevant to our field. If one does not help you find what you are looking for, another might. Though many database systems charge for their services, subscriptions to these same organizations often are maintained by local libraries located at colleges.

Although many tools to find past research are available, and although they all have their advantages, there are some that stand out for their usefulness. The author finds that these two sources are most valuable. As such, they remain the sources that are checked first.

- ◆ *ComAbstracts* is a service of the CIOS (the Communication Institute for Online Scholarship) and is one of the most versatile. Using an option called "Com-Search," it is possible to review all the journals in the field, with the exception of those dedicated to speech and hearing science. This source provides abstracts and tables of contents and, for many recent titles, includes full texts of articles. CIOS sponsors the *Electronic Journal of Communication,* which appears in both French and English. It also has begun a collection of special reports as part of the CIOS Electronic Encyclopedia of Communication. This source may be accessed through subscribing libraries, though for individuals, membership can be purchased directly (www.cios.org) or with a reduced fee as an option of membership in the International Communication Association (www.icahdq.org).

TABLE G.3   ONLINE COMPUTER SEARCH SYSTEMS

SYSTEM	CONTENT AND COMMENTARY	USEFUL FOR
I. Search Systems with Dedication to Communication Studies Resources		
Academic Search Elite (EBSCO)	Comprehensive view of articles from publications across academic fields including communication, the social sciences, education, language and linguistics, arts and literature, medical sciences, ethnic studies, and other fields (often including full texts of scholarly publications)	All major fields of communication studies
ComAbstracts (CIOS)	Abstracts of international articles, reports, papers, and books from both publishers and research institutions, including work in general communication, mass communication, advertising, marketing, broadcasting, and communication theory	All major fields of communication studies, except speech and hearing science
Communication & Mass Media Complete Publications (EBSCO)	Abstracts and many full-texts of articles in such areas as mass communication, human communication, rhetoric, new media, journalism, and communication theory	Communication studies—emphasizing mass communication studies—except speech and hearing science
Linguistics & Language Behavior Abstracts (CSA)	Attention to issues in speech and hearing science, language, and linguistic activity	All major fields of communication studies including speech and hearing science
II. Text Listings or Abstracts		
CQ Researchers	Full-text in-depth reports on social, economic, political, educational, health, environmental, and current affairs	Rhetoric, political communication, environmental, and health communication background issues
CQ Historic Documents Series Online Edition	Over 2,500 full-text primary sources covering world history from 1972	Background materials in rhetoric and political communication
Education: A Sage Full-Text Collection (CSA)	Full-text presentation of 23 peer-reviewed journals published by Sage and participating societies dealing with issues of educational research	Communication education
Emerald Fulltext (Emerald)	Over 40,000 articles from more than 100 journals in management, library and information science, and science and technology (allows browsing journals by title)	Organizational communication, information systems, communication technology
Ethnic NewsWatch	English- and Spanish-language text collection of 275 newspapers and periodicals from ethnic, minority, and native press	Intercultural communication and mass media communication
Factiva (Dow Jones)	Full-text news and journal articles dealing with business and management, psychology, entertainment, and education	Organizational communication, social science treatments in popular media, entertainment communication

(Continued)

TABLE G.3   (Continued)

SYSTEM	CONTENT AND COMMENTARY	USEFUL FOR
FactSearch (OCLC)	Full-text statistical statements on current social, economic, political, health, and environmental issues with information derived from over 1,100 newspapers	Rhetoric, political communication, environmental, and health communication background issues
HRAF Collection of Ethnography	Partial (to the paragraph level) textbooks, articles, dissertations, and field reports related to issues of culture broadly defined to include over 150 ethnic, religious, and national groups	Intercultural communication
JSTOR	Partial and full texts of journals in anthropology, Asian studies, African American studies, ecology, economics, education, finance, general science, history, literature, mathematics, philosophy, political science, sociology, and statistics	Intercultural communication, communication education, and social science background in communication theory
LexisNexis Academic	Permits printing of full-text articles from over 5,000 newspapers, law reviews, and government sources, on most subjects, but with an emphasis in business news, law, and medicine; breaking news updated several times daily	Rhetorical criticism and public address, legal communication, communication law and policy
Magazine ASAP	Information from popular magazines indexed in *Magazine Index*	Mass communication and historical background
National Newspaper Index	Abstracts and index of items appearing in the *New York Times, Los Angeles Times, Wall Street Journal,* and *Christian Science Monitor*	Mass media, public relations, and historical background
Opposing Viewpoints (Gale)	Newspaper and magazine materials organized according to public controversies in the social, educational, political, religious, medical, and health fields	Argumentation and debate, rhetorical criticism, political communication, health communication, mass media studies
Project MUSE Premium	Articles from journals in African studies, American studies, anthropology, art, Asian studies, classics, culture and society, demography, economics, education, film, theater and performance, folklore, French studies, gay and lesbian studies, history, Judaic studies	Intercultural communication, rhetorical theory and criticism
PsycArticles (EBSCO)	Full-text versions of peer-reviewed scholarly and scientific articles in psychology from 53 journals	Communication theory and processes, social sciences, and psychology in applied areas
ScienceDirect	Articles (many full-text) in the natural sciences, business and management, biological sciences, and medicine	Speech and hearing science, organizational communication
Wiley InterScience	Scholarship published in business, management, education, law, psychology,	Organizational communication, communication education, communication

(Continued)

TABLE G.3   (Continued)

	medicine, science, and math	theory and processes, communication and the law
Women's Studies International (NISC)	Publications (since 1972) in newspapers, newsletters, books, and reports dealing with women's studies and feminist research	Women and communication, intercultural communication

III. Other Computerized Systems of Existing Hard Copy Index Services

Art and Humanities Search (OCLC)	Articles from 1,300 journals in the humanities and 5,800 social science journals	Communication theory, rhetoric, argumentation, and qualitative research inquiries
Book Review Digest (OCLC)	Reviews of non-textbook sources from over 144 magazines and journals	Rhetoric, oral interpretation, and work involving humanistic methods
CIS/Index	Same as hard copy version of *CIS/Index* (index and abstracts of congressional publications) (from 1970 forward)	Rhetoric and public address, mass communication
Dissertation Abstracts Online	Same as hard copy version of *Dissertation Abstracts* (from 1861 forward)	All fields
Education Full-Text (Wilson)	Same as hard copy version of *Education Abstracts* including nearly 400 publications broadly related to education (from 1983 forward; full text from 1996)	Rhetoric, communication education, communication theory and processes
ERIC and *ERIC FirstSearch*	Same as hard copy version of *Resources in Education* and *Current Index to Journals in Education* (from 1966 forward)	Most social science subfields in education and communication; particularly valuable for listings of unpublished sources, such as convention papers
Legal Resources Index	Index and some abstracts of articles from 800 law journals and over 3,000 ancillary publications (from 1980 forward)	Communication and the law and mass communications law
Management Contents	Indices and abstracts from over 130 international publications in management and public administration (from 1974 forward)	Organizational communication
Newspaper & Periodical Indexes	Indices and abstracts from over 25 newspapers, 1,600 periodicals, and 70 television news and information broadcasts (periodicals from 1986 forward; newspapers from 1989 forward; broadcasts vary)	Mass communication, journalism, criticism
Newsearch	Most recent two to six weeks of information in guides published by Information Access Inc. (includes *Academic Index, Legal Resource Index, Management Contents, National Newspaper Index, PR Newswire*)	Communication theory, communication and the law, mass communication law, organizational communication, journalism, mass communication, and public relations
PAIS International (OCLC)	International index of books, articles, government publications, and Internet resources dealing with political and social issues, law, human rights, international relations, and military affairs	Political communication, mass communication law, communication law and policy

(Continued)

TABLE G.3   (Continued)

SYSTEM	CONTENT AND COMMENTARY	USEFUL FOR
PsychINFO (EBSCO)	Comprehensive view of over 1.7 million books, journals, research reports, book chapters, and dissertations	Support for research in communication theory and relevant background
PsychINFO	Same as hard copy version of *Psychological Abstracts;* index and abstracts of journal articles, books, and book chapters in psychology and other social sciences (from 1974 forward)	Social sciences, communication theory and processes, and psychology in applied areas
PubMed (www.ncbi.nlm. nih.gov/entrez/query. fcgi?DB=pubmed)	A service provided by the National Library of Medicine; features links to over 15 million articles including many full-text articles dating back to the 1950s	Speech and hearing science
SciSearch	Same as hard copy version of *Science Citation Index;* index of citations used in over 600 journals in the natural sciences (from 1975 forward)	Speech and hearing science; useful to find who is quoting whom and to find commentaries on published articles
Social Sciences Abstracts	Same as hard copy version of *Social Sciences Abstracts;* index of over 400 journals and magazines related to the social sciences (from 1983 forward)	Social sciences, communication theory and processes
Social SciSearch	Same as hard copy version of *Social Sciences Citation Index;* index of references used in articles from over 1,400 social science journals (from 1981 forward)	Social sciences; useful to find who is quoting whom and to find commentaries on published articles
Sociological Abstracts	Same as hard copy version of *Sociological Abstracts;* index and abstracts of articles from journals and related publications throughout the social sciences including some communication journals (from 1963 forward)	Social sciences, communication theory and processes, mass communication
Transcript (Journal Graphics)	A catalog of the *Transcript/Video Index;* listings and abstracts of transcripts of over 20,000 news and information television broadcasts for sale by Journal Graphics	Mass communication, political communication, and public relations
Web of Science (ISI)	Access back and forth to the *Science Citation Expanded* (including over 164 scientific fields), and *Social Sciences Citation Index* (including over 50 fields)	Social sciences, communication theory and processes
H. W. Wilson guides *Wilson:*	Largely duplications of:	
Business Abstracts;	*Business Periodical Index* (from 1982 forward including abstracts from June 1990)	Organizational communication and public relations
Humanities Abstracts	*Humanities Index* (from 1984 forward including abstracts from 1994)	Rhetoric, criticism, communication theory

♦ *Linguistics & Language Behavior Abstracts* (CSA) is a database that may be one of the first stops for researchers in speech and hearing science. This comprehensive database presents article abstracts, and occasionally convention papers, books, and doctoral dissertations. These journals include the range of speech and language activity, hearing, speech, phonology, and other aspects of second-language acquisition, psycholinguistics, and nonverbal communication.

Using Keywords

The following steps can make learning to use keywords fairly simple.

electronic search steps

1. Select keywords from the problem statement. Pause before you look at electronic indices to jot down the keywords that describe topics you are investigating. Some common sense is required. If you look for information about the impact of televising a speech on the speaker's credibility, you may list such words as "television," "speeches," and "credibility." The online database *Dialog* includes automatic prompts, so that you can use the precise vocabulary of the system. In online searches, using very broad terms might produce long lists of irrelevant materials—a waste of time for you and potentially costly as well.

1. find keywords

2. Develop alternative lists of descriptor terms. Unless you have a lot of experience researching a topic, your initial keywords may not be the same ones used by the index service staffs. You may need to think creatively. For instance, for many years the *Education Index* listed studies of "communication apprehension" under the subject heading "bashfulness." You need to prepare synonyms in case the first keywords do not work for you. Fortunately, many indexing services have guides for selecting keywords and computer systems have automatic prompts to help you.

2. find alternative keywords

3. Combine keywords. In an online search you need to see if keywords (tested individually by you to make sure they are meaningful in the system) can be combined. That is, instead of asking for one topic at a time, you might combine keywords. For instance, you might use the three keywords "television," "speeches," and "source credibility" (the latter actually is two keywords, but it serves as one for us). The search system would start by looking for all the listings on "television." Then, the system would subdivide the list to identify citations that also have the keyword "speeches." Finally, a pass would be made for listings that also have the term "source credibility." Eventually, the system would produce a very focused list.

3. combine keywords

4. Undertake online activity. During the search, the system will prompt you with questions and will respond to your input. The systems listed on Table G.3 are a bit different from each other, but you will find that the prompting systems are very extensive and are easy to use. You may wish to change databases and search different materials. Though it is admittedly a bother, it is vital to record (preferably on your research outline) things you have searched and keywords you have used. Without such a record, you may find yourself

4. undertake online activity

examining the same materials more than once. In many cases you may wish to have the list of abstracts, citations, and references printed out or down-loaded to a disk of your own. Make sure that facilities are set up for you when you request these services. It is frustrating to log off and then find that no hard copy system was attached. Take the time to consult with your local librarian to understand the options that are available to you.

Indices and Abstracts

use of index and abstract sources

Though computerized systems have collected indices and abstracts, you may have to rely on hard copy volumes to find some sources. An index lists locations of resource materials and articles. On the other hand, an abstract also provides a brief summary of the work. Since indices and abstracts often are found in companion reference works, we can describe them together. Regrettably, no single hard copy index covers the breadth of our field. So, you may wish to check different sources to find citations to the most valuable articles.

Sometimes you may wish to look at popular press treatments, such as when you need to find reactions to speakers or communication trends. The indices to non-scholarly literature have been omitted from the tables in this chapter. Surely the most popular of these sources is the *Reader's Guide to Periodical Literature,* an index that includes more than 130 general public interest magazines. For magazines published a very long time ago, you can check *Poole's Index to Periodical Literature, 1802–1906* and the *Nineteenth Century Reader's Guide to Periodical Literature 1890–1899.* For popular sources outside the United States, one might wish to review the *Canadian Index* or the *Subject Index to Periodicals* (for British periodicals). Major newspapers also index their publications. A very useful newspaper indexing source is *Proquest Newspapers* (ProQuest), available in most libraries. This service includes full text of over 300 newspapers in the United States and around the world. Similar guides can be found to government documents, regulations, and reports.

Suppose you wonder if there is any commentary or critcism of a scholarly work. The *Social Science Citation Index* and the *Science Citation Index* list articles that have cited a particular reference. These sources are available using the *Web of Science* guide. Sometimes the references are in passing, but sometimes the citations indicate extended critiques.

Special bibliographies can also help you find useful materials. Surely the most useful guide is the *Bibliographic Index,* which lists publications containing at least 50 references on a subject (useful to find reviews of literature). Sometimes entire books are published that are little more than annotated bibliographies. Thus, you should inspect book listings in detail before moving on to research articles.

Troubleshooting in the Library

For all the fascination libraries hold—the collected wisdom of ages is just waiting for us—inexperienced people can become frustrated. We will consider some student complaints, along with some suggested solutions.

> ## SPECIAL DISCUSSION G-3
> ### Using Legal Resource Materials
>
> Materials in the law must often be examined to study mass communication law, legal communication, and freedom of speech. Though you may not be at a school with extensive collections in the law, you still are not far from a county law library, which you can use. It is helpful to understand legal citations. For instance, a law in the *United States Code* may be cited as 12 U.S.C. § 724. The citation is read, "Title 12 of the *United States Code*, Section 724." The *U.S. Code Annotated* summarizes major laws, and the *U.S. Code Service* lists related court decisions and legislative history, and provides additional references in each category.
>
> Supreme Court decisions are identified as, for example, *Roe v. Wade*, 410 U.S. 113 (1973). The case title lists the plaintiff and the defendant. The number following the title is the volume number of *U.S. Reports* in which the decision is located. The page number on which the decision begins is listed next. The date is placed in parentheses after the rest of the citation. The *Supreme Court Reporter* indexes cases with abstracts of legal issues raised in the case. *Lawyer's Edition of the U.S. Supreme Court Reports* provides a legal analysis and includes statements from the briefs and arguments actually made by the lawyers. As general collections, West's Digests are popular, including the *General Digest* that summarizes cases and the *Federal Practice Digest* organized by topic areas.
>
> Many guides can help you find articles in the law. The *Index to Legal Periodicals* is the major guide to U.S. law journals, just as the *Index to Foreign Legal Periodicals and Collections of Essays* is the counterpart for law journals in foreign countries. The *Law Review Digest* provides bimonthly summaries of law journal articles, and the *Index to Periodical Articles Related to Law* covers sources other than law journals.

When the Source Is Unavailable

Sometimes a key source is not available at your library. The sources may have been checked out, the library may not own the resource, or the materials have been lost or vandalized. There are two general ways around this problem. First, you may use interlibrary loan programs. Every library has such a cooperative venture. At the interlibrary loan desk, you can request other libraries to lend you the missing work. If an article is involved, other libraries often will send you a photocopy. Interlibrary loans are not as slow as often believed, but if you require instant information, you may need to seek another option. Another way around the problem involves reading other articles that offer some descriptions about the key source. By triangulating information from different sources, you may get an idea of what was done in the original piece. This method is dangerous, however, since writers are selective in describing others' work, and because secondary summaries may contain flaws. Furthermore, the method of triangulation is very time-consuming for the amount of benefit it might produce.

when sources are unavailable:

interlibrary loan

triangulating reports of research

When There Is "No Information on My Topic"

A word to the wise: Do not say to your instructor, "There is no information on my topic." Your instructor knows that somewhere, someone has said *something* relevant to your topic. Your *specific* research question may not have been answered yet (much to your credit, since you are an original thinker), but there is always something out there related to your topic. To find materials you should try the "known to unknown" search pattern. With this strategy, you take your research issue, such as the impact of teleconferencing on interpersonal attraction of group members, and then look at research into each concept separately. You might investigate the things that affect interpersonal attraction generally. Such material is *known*. But you may observe that there is little information about attraction in teleconferencing settings. This material remains *unknown*. You might decide to reason from what is known generally to develop arguments about possible relationships that might exist between teleconferencing methods and attraction. By looking at the issue broadly, it is possible to unearth much valuable information.

use the "known to unknown" search strategy

When the Journals Are Missing

missing journals: use microforms and

Sometimes journals may not be on the shelves. Before panicking, find out if the library has microform copies. Sometimes journals are available, but the names have been changed. For instance, if you chase down a citation (from another source) to a journal called *Communication Studies* for 1983, you may grow nervous when you find that the library has this journal only from 1989 forward. In reality, this journal was called the *Central States Speech Journal* until volume 40 in 1989. Titles change often enough that you should not give up at first. Yet, if you find that journals truly are not available, you will need to contact interlibrary loan services for help.

check for changed journal names

When the Material Is Technical and Complex

dealing with very technical material: use specialized dictionaries

Research articles sometimes seem complicated and bewilderingly technical. Rather than get bogged down, you may wish to rely on some of the specialized dictionaries listed on Table G.1. Sometimes books and critiques are available to help you put some perspective on the matter. Most journal essays and articles place abstracts at the beginning of articles. These guides are good starting points with technical and complex materials. Begin by asking, What was the purpose of the research? By doing so, you often can grasp extended background discussions. Then ask, What method or reasoning was used to draw conclusions? Sometimes you may wish to outline these methods (briefly) in your own notes. Finally ask, What did the work find and conclude? Many times the conclusion is an afterthought, but sometimes it is the lion's share of the materials.

ask key questions

Using the Internet

growth in the Internet

The Internet has its roots in the efforts of the U.S. Department of Defense to link military bases, the Pentagon, universities, and defense contractors in a system that could not be destroyed by a single nuclear attack. But it was not until the end of the cold war that the Internet became an information system that developed into the commercial tool we see today. There is a lot of talk about the Internet as some sort of "information superhighway." Forget it. The Internet is much more like a disorganized attic than a well-constructed superhighway. Thus, researchers use comprehensive browsers to help get information they want.

   One nice thing about the Internet is that it makes available the resources of major libraries. For instance, suppose you wish to hear what presidents Grover Cleveland

and Theodore Roosevelt really sounded like. If you have a sound card in your computer, you can surf to the Vincent Voice Library (see the figure below) and click on "Select a President." After you identify a president, you will have to wait for a moment for the file to be transferred to you. Then you will actually hear a voice that you might never otherwise hear.[1] You might wish to search ERIC without going to the library. No problem. Just contact the AskERIC website. You might wish to search CARL for materials held in that interlibrary system. No problem. Just contact the CARL website. You may wish to see what is being done in psychology related to your topic. No problem. Just contact PsychREF. These sources actually are just ways to use the Internet to connect with many sources identified on Table G.3.

availability of standard library sources through Internet

---

[1]A word to the wise. Listening to this collection can be both surprising and a little depressing. For instance, Theodore Roosevelt doesn't sound a bit like the actors who played him in the movies. Instead, he sounds like Maxwell Smart on the old *Get Smart* TV show.

GLOSSARY

A

absolute zero   A score that indicates that the property measured is completely absent.

abstract bibliographic card   Bibliographic cards featuring summaries of materials.

abstract calculus   The logical structure of relationships in a theory.

accidental or convenience sampling   Selection of events that are most readily available.

accretions   Deposits of material left by some action.

act   In Burke's dramatistic pentad, the symbolic action (the speech, for instance).

acts   In Hymes' (1974) "ethnography of communication" approach, message elements including message form ("how something is said by members in a given speech community and according to [its] . . . descriptive characteristics") and message content ("topic and change of topic").

***ad hoc* rescue**   A fallacy of research in which support for a theory is claimed despite failed predictions.

adjacency pair   In conversational analysis, a pair of utterances in which the latter element is supposed to be related to the previous element.

advertising   The study of mass media methods of influence to promote a product, service, or cause.

agency   In Burke's dramatistic pentad, the symbolic and linguistic strategies used to secure identification.

agent   In Burke's dramatistic pentad, the actor or rhetor who performs the act.

alpha   *See* Cronbach's coefficient alpha.

alpha (α) risk   The probability of committing Type I error by incorrectly rejecting the null hypothesis.

alternate forms reliability   Constructing different forms of the same test from a common pool of measurement items, giving them to a group of people, and determining the degree of consistency between them.

analogy   *See* argument from analogy.

analysis of covariance   A method of statistical control that determines the variation associated with each nuisance variable and then separates it from the remaining total variation in the experiment by use of analysis of variance methods.

analysis of variance   A test of statistical significance that compares the means of two or more groups.

analytic induction   "An approach in qualitative research that develops theory by examining a small number of cases. Theory then leads to formulation of a [very tentative] hypothesis, which is tested through the study of more cases. This usually leads to refinement or reformulation of the hypothesis, which is then tested with further cases until the researcher judges that the inquiry can be concluded" (Vogt, 2005, p. 10).

annotations   Additional explanations, comments, evaluations, or criticisms that clarify the material.

anonymity   Protection of research participants by separating specific identities from the information given.

applied research   Study completed to develop a product or solve an immediately practical problem.

a priori   Literally, "from the earlier part." A "way of knowing" that claims knowledge before having any experience with events.

argument from analogy   A method of reasoning that compares "two things known to be alike in one or more features and . . . suggests that they will be alike in other features as well" (McDonald, 1980, p. 164).

argument from definition   A method of reasoning in which people submit that things do or do not belong in a certain class.

argument from example and generalization   A method of reasoning taking some particular cases and arguing that what is true of instances is generally true in the population of events.

arguments   Claims advanced on the basis of reasoning from evidence.

arithmetic mean   A measure of central tendency computed by adding a set of scores and dividing by the number of scores.

arrangement   The canon of rhetoric concerning the organization of ideas.

association   *See* correlation.

attenuation   A reduction of the size of observed effects because of measurement imperfections.

authority   A way of knowing in which a claim is accepted because authority figures have accepted it.

autoethnography   Combination of "autobiography, the story of one's own life, with ethnography, the study of a particular social group" (Dyer, 2006b, ¶ 1).

B

basic research   Research completed to learn about relationships among variables, regardless of any immediate commercial product or service.

beta (β) risk   The probability of committing Type II error by incorrectly failing to reject the null hypothesis.

beta weights   In multiple correlation, the contribution made by each predictor to the overall correlation.

bias   In sampling, the tendency for the sample to err so that it fails to represent the population.

bimodal   A distribution that has two modes.

blocking   Including a nuisance variable into the design as another independent variable of interest.

C

canonical correlation   An extension of multiple regression correlating two sets of variables.

canons of rhetoric   Five established major categories that help explain communication.

case studies and interpretive studies   Intensive inquiries about single events, people, or social units (interpretive studies attempt to look for themes or stories that are helpful to *interpret* or understand the case).

categorical data   Data taking the form of identification of attributes or levels of a variable.

categorical syllogism   A syllogism composed of categorical or "allness" statements.

causal argument   Reasoning that "a given factor is responsible for producing certain other results" (Reinard, 1991, p. 197).

central limit theorem   The statement that a sampling distribution of means tends toward normal distribution with increased sample size regardless of the shape of the parent population.

central tendency   Measures that report averages of different varieties.

check question   A check on test-taking behavior that involves asking the same question twice at different locations in the questionnaire or interview, usually once positively worded and once negatively worded.

chi-square distribution   A probability distribution of squared differences of scores.

chi-square test   A family of nonparametric tests that permit examining observed frequencies of events with expected frequencies.

chi-square test of independence   Adaptation of chi-square test to the analysis of contingency tables.

chronological summary   A summary strategy that reviews literature by considering studies in their order of publication from the oldest study through the most recent one.

circularity   Definitions that simply repeat things.

climate questions   Follow-up interview questioning that asks respondents to explain how they feel about the interview.

closed-ended questions   Questions to which people respond in fixed categories of answers.

cluster sampling   1. In content analysis, sampling in which groups of messages exist in a cluster (such as the cluster of articles that appears in a single newspaper). 2. A method of sampling "in which elements are selected in two or more stages, with the first stage being the random selection of naturally occurring clusters and the last stage being the random selection of elements within clusters" (Schutt, 2006, p. I–5).

code systems   The study of the uses of verbal and nonverbal symbols and signs in human communication.

coding   In grounded theory, "the process of deciding how to conceptually divide up raw qualitative data" (Lacey & Luff, 2001, p. 34).

coding units In content analysis, categories used to count the communication forms in the examples chosen.

coefficient alpha *See* Cronbach's coefficient alpha.

coefficient of determination A number that shows the percentage of variation in one variable that can be explained by a knowledge of the other variable alone; the square of a correlation coefficient.

coefficient of reproducibility In Guttman scales, a measure of reliability.

Cohen's *kappa* A measure of intercoder reliability that compensates for the number of times rating categories are used.

communication "The field of communication focuses on how people use messages to generate meanings within and across various contexts, cultures, channels and media. The field promotes the effective and ethical practice of human communication" (Daley et al., 1995).

communication disorders *See* speech and hearing science.

communication education The study of communication in pedagogical contexts (including communication development, oral communicaion skills, and instructional communication).

communication policy The study of public policy and regulation of mass media communication and freedom of speech.

communication technology The study of the mechanisms and technologies of mass media.

communicative act "The minimal term of the speech event (Hymes) utterances considered in terms of what they do and how we use them in conversation" (Malcolm, 2001, ¶ 70).

communicative style "Linguistic difference according to the formality of the interaction (which depends on such factors as the social occasion, the social, age and other differences of the participants, the emotional involvement, etc.)" (Malcolm, 2001, ¶ 30).

complete observer Inquiry that observes individuals in settings in which there is no contact between the observed and the observer.

complex questions Questionnaire items that include extra qualifying words or phrases that render simple yes or no answers misleading.

complex statements A research fallacy in which loaded or complicated statements are made that assume facts not in evidence.

concepts *See* hypothetical constructs.

conceptual (or constitutive) definition A definition that relies on other concepts to describe a term.

concurrent validity A method of test validity that involves correlating a new measure with a previously validated measure of the same construct.

conditional syllogism A form of syllogism whose major premise makes an conditional or "if-then" statement.

confidence intervals "A range of values of a sample statistic that is likely (at a given level of probability, called a confidence level) to contain a population parameter" (Vogt, 2005, p. 55).

confidentiality The requirement that all information gathered from individual subjects is secret; the protection of the identity of research participants.

confounding Mixing (or confusing) variation from one source with variation from another source so that it is impossible to know whether effects are due to the impact of either variable separately or some combination of them.

conjectural emendation When attempting to assess textual authenticity, a method in which researchers with different available versions of texts make arguments to explain which of the competing textual alternatives is most reasonable and, thus, should be accepted.

consent *See* informed consent.

constant A characteristic to which only one number may be assigned.

constant comparative method In grounded theory, "concepts or categories emerging from one stage of the data analysis are compared with concepts emerging from the next. The researcher looks for relationships between these concepts and categories, by constantly comparing them, to form the basis of the emerging theory" (Lacey & Luff, 2001, p. 7).

constitutive definition *See* conceptual definition.

constructs "Generalizations about observables according to some common property" (Deutsch & Krauss, 1964, p. 7).

construct validity A method of test validity that involves correlating the new measure with at least two other measures, one of which is a valid measure of a construct that is known conceptually to be directly related to the new measure, and another one of which should be a valid measure of a construct that is known conceptually to be inversely related to the construct of interest.

content analysis "Any of several research techniques used to describe and systematically analyze the content of written, spoken, or pictorial communication—such as books, newspapers, television programs, or interview transcripts" (Vogt, 2005. p. 59).

contingency coefficient A method to determine effect sizes following a significant chi-square test.

contingency questions (also called "filter questions") Questions, the answers to which, direct respondents to other items.

continuous variables Data taking the form of numbers indicating matters of degree on some variable.

control 1. As a function of theory, the power to direct things. 2. In research design, methods researchers use to remove or hold constant the effects of nuisance variables. 3. The power to direct things.

convenience sampling *See* accidental or convenience sampling.

conversational analysis Textual analysis that attempts to identify "turns" taken by people during exchanges.

conversational and discourse analyses Forms of content analysis in which the categories are suggested from naturally occurring conversations and their settings. Yet, these approaches do not produce numerical information. The structure or organization of conversations is examined along with functions that conversations perform for communicators. A distinction is often drawn between conversational analysis (which tends to analyze macroscopic message characteristics such as themes and stories and the rules they suggest) and discourse analysis (which tends to analyze microscopic message components in a pattern much like traditional linguistic analysis or translation).

correction for attenuation in reliability A method of adjusting observed correlation coefficients for imperfections in reliability of the measurement of variables.

correlation Measure of the association or coincidence of variables.

counterbalanced designs Quasi experiments that introduce several different experimental treatments presented to the subjects in different orders or sequences.

counterbalancing Rotating the sequence in which experimental treatments are introduced to subjects in an effort to control for extraneous variables, such as fatigue or cumulative learning effects.

creative studies Use of the method of performance or demonstration to explore an aesthetic or creative experience.

criterion validity Methods including concurrent and predictive validity that assess a measure's worth by examining its relation to some outside criterion.

critical realism A view that although an objective reality exists, understanding it involves recognizing that there are two faces of reality. First, there is an *intransitive* dimension that is the actual structure of events. Second, there is a *transitive* dimension that consists of our understanding of reality. Discussions about the intransitive dimension involve questions of ontology, or the study of being. On the other hand, discussions of the transitive dimension involve questions of epistemology or the issues we face in claiming to know things about reality.

critical region In statistical significance testing, the portion of the probability distribution that would cause rejection of the null hypothesis if it were the area in which the test statistic fell.

critical value In statistical significance testing, the line that divides the critical region from the rest of the probability distribution.

criticism Message evaluation in which standards of excellence are announced and the degree of conformity of the message to the standards determines the evaluation made.

Cronbach's coefficient alpha A formula for reliability, used when researchers want to determine the reliability of a measure that has no "correct" answer.

crossed interaction *See* disordinal interaction.

curvilinear relationship In correlations, relationships in which the best fit of a line to the data is not a straight line.

D

daily definitions Statements of definition generally adopted by members of a society.

data The actual individual events in a sample.

data distribution A distribution of values in a data set.

data first inquiry Sometimes called the inductive approach to research, a method of inquiry that starts with gathering information and follows by developing theoretic explanations.

deductive reasoning A form of reasoning in which a valid conclusion necessarily follows from premises.

deductive summary A summary strategy that reviews literature by considering what is known in general categories, followed by increasingly specific categories that are related to the topic.

definitions   Statements asserting that one term may be substituted for another.

degrees of freedom   The number of events in a study minus the number of population parameters estimated from samples; used to enter probability distributions.

delivery   The canon of rhetoric concerning the use of voice and gesture.

Delphi fallacy   A special fallacy of research involving the use of vague predictions as research claims.

dependability   In qualitative research, the counterpart of measurement reliability in which efforts are made to assure stability in identifications and interpretations.

dependability audits   In qualitative research, an approach to assure dependability by having experts evaluate procedures and interpretations.

dependent samples *t* test   An application of the *t* test that compares the means of two sample groups in which subjects are matched or sampled twice.

dependent variables   Variables whose values or activities are presumed to be conditioned on the independent variable in the hypothesis.

description   The lowest level of theorizing in which behavior is characterized into different forms.

descriptive or observational surveys   A method of research that gathers data to survey a matter in nonexperimental settings in which no variables are manipulated by the researcher.

descriptive empirical research   Survey research in which contemporaneous data are gathered to answer research questions dealing with ascertaining norms, establishing goals, or developing methods.

descriptive statistics   Numbers that are designed to characterize some information in a data set.

determination   *See* coefficient of determination.

determinism   The philosophic notion that the general course of events is an instance of some law of nature.

diffuse comparisons of effect sizes   Measures of the homogeneity of effect sizes in meta-analyses.

direct classification variables   Operational definitions that rely on simple identification or classification of observable characteristics of information.

directional material hypotheses   Hypotheses that state the form of predicted differences.

direct questions   Questionnaire items that ask for obvious reports.

direct relationship   A correlation with a positive slope indicating that the two variables move in the same direction.

discourse analysis   Considerations of naturally occurring messages to examine "sequential and hierarchical organization, system and structure" using methods that are fairly "standard in phonology and linguistics" (Stubbs, 1981, p. 107).

discourse/conversational analyses   Methods of examining utterances people exchange for the purpose of discovering the rules and strategies people use to structure, sequence, and take turns in speaking to learn how people manage their interactions with others.

disjunctive syllogism   A form of syllogism whose major premise makes an "either-or" statement.

disordinal interaction   Dependent variable interaction effects that are not in the same direction as the main effects of the variables involved and that are diagrammatically revealed when lines drawn from each independent variable cross each other.

dispreferred response   In conversational analysis, a response not consistent with the first part of a common adjacency pair.

distributions   Arrangements of scores along a continuum.

double-barreled questions   Questionnaire items that include multiple objects of evaluation.

double interacts   The combination of one person's conversation, a reaction by another, and the first person's response to the other's reaction.

E

Einstein syndrome   A malady in which researchers fail to connect their "sudden breakthroughs" with lessons from others.

elaboration   In grounded theory, "elaboration involves developing and examining its variation systematically" (Punch, 2005, p. 214).

elimination and removal   A method of control that removes a nuisance variable from the experimental setting.

emic approach   "Culturally relative approaches . . . that stress participants' understanding of their own culture. Derived, by an indirect route, from the linguistic term phon*emic*" (Vogt, 2005, p. 105).

empirical   Refers to those things that are observable.

ends   In Hymes' (1974) "ethnography of communication" approach, the purposes including outcomes ("the expected outcome of a speech event as recognized by the speech community") and goals ("the intentions of participants and the strategies they define").

epistemic fallacy In critical realism, the error of thinking that "ontological questions can always be reparsed in epistemological form: that is, that statements about being can always be analysed in terms of statements about our knowledge (of being), that is sufficient for philosophy to 'treat only the network and not what the network describes'" (Bhaskar, 1989, p. 13).

equal probability hypothesis A method of determining expected frequencies for the one-sample chi-square test assuming an equal proportion of events in each category.

erosions Observations of evidence of the wear or use of objects.

error variance Another name for "within groups variance" or "residual variance."

eta (η) Also known as the "correlation ratio," eta is directly interpreted as any correlation and is used to determine the size of effects following finding a significant F. Eta may also be used to identify nonlinear as well as linear effects.

eta squared (η²) A coefficient of determination computed from eta.

ethical and rhetorical theories Principles that describe good and effective communication, respectively.

ethnography Research in which the investigator participates, overtly or covertly, in people's lives for an extended period of time, collecting whatever data are available to describe behavior.

ethnomethodology (also called the "new ethnography," originally developed by anthropologists to study societies of humans) An approach (rather than a rigorous method) in which researchers find an ethnic group, live within it, and attempt to develop insight into the culture; emphasis is placed on the mundane and ordinary activities of everyday life, concentrating on the methods used by people to report their commonsense, practical actions to others in acceptable rational terms.

ethos Sometimes called "ethical appeal," an element of the canon of invention (artistic proofs) referring to the speaker's credibility.

etic approach "Methods of study . . . stressing material—rather than cultural—explanations for social and cultural phenomena. Derived, by an indirect route, from the linguistic term phon*etic*" (Vogt, 2005, p. 109).

evidence Information used to support claims.

example *See* argument from example and generalization.

exemplary literature reviews Surveys of only the most important contributions to the literature.

exhaustive literature reviews Research surveys that include all material related to the subject.

experiment A type of study using experimental methods in which researchers examine the effects of variables manipulated by the researcher in situations where all other influences are held constant. Variables are manipulated or introduced by experimenters for the purpose of establishing causal relationships.

experimental invalidity Errors that prevent researchers from drawing unequivocal conclusions (*see also* internal invalidity; external invalidity).

experimental methods A method of studying the effects of variables in situations where all other influences are held constant. Variables are manipulated or introduced by experimenters to see what effect they may have.

experimental mortality A source of internal invalidity involving biases introduced when subjects differentially (non-randomly) drop out of the experiment.

experimental variable An independent variable manipulated in an experiment.

expert jury validity A method of test validity that involves having a group of experts in the subject matter examine the measurement device and judge its merit.

expert opinions Opinions from people who have special knowledge or training in the field of inquiry.

explanation Taking an event and treating it as an instance of a larger system of things (after Homans, 1961, p. 10).

explication A literature review that makes an issue clear and comprehensible.

external invalidity The degree to which experimental results may not be generalized to other similar circumstances.

extrinsic criticism In rhetorical criticism, evaluation of aspects beyond the text of a message, focusing predominately on assessing textual authenticity, authorship, settings, and message effects.

F

face validity A method of test validity that involves researchers' looking at the content of the measurement items and advancing an argument that, on its face, the measure seems to identify what it claims.

factor   *See* variable factor.

factor analysis   A statistical method that helps "the researcher discover and identify the unities or dimensions, called factors, behind many measures" (Kerlinger, 1986, p. 138).

factorial analysis of variance   Analysis of variance applied to multiple independent variables that have been divided into levels or groups.

factorial designs   Experimental designs in which more than one independent variable is used.

factors   Variables broken down into levels.

factual evidence   Descriptions and characterizations of things used to support arguments.

fail-safe number   In meta-analysis, the number of additional studies showing a zero effect that would have to exist to reverse the reported relationship size pattern.

fallacy of misplaced precision   Attempts by researchers to claim precision that goes beyond the data.

false precision   *See* fallacy of misplaced precision.

falsification   The requirement that any theory must deal with statements that could be falsified by data and information if the theory were untrue.

fantasy   "A story about people, real or fictitious, in a dramatic situation, in a setting other than the here-and-now communication of the group" (Bormann, 1993, p. 365).

fantasy theme analysis   A method of analyzing collections of communication to determine underlying "world views" that people hold, judging by the messages that they use.

F distribution   In essence, a distribution of variances that have been divided into each other.

fieldwork   "The study of people acting in the natural course of their daily lives" (Emerson, 1983, p. 1).

figurative analogy   An analogy that compares something to a hypothetical situation.

file drawer effect   The tendency for studies that fail to find significant relationships to remain unpublished and become abandoned in hypothetical "file drawers."

focused comparisons   Assessments in meta-analyses to determine whether differences in the sizes of study effects may be explained by particular independent variables.

focus group   An interview style designed for small groups. Focus group interviews are either guided or unguided discussions addressing a particular topic of interest or relevance to the group and the researcher.

forced choice format   A question system in which researchers give subjects two statements, one of which must be chosen.

full participant observation   A role in ethnography or participant observation research characterized by the investigator's gathering data while taking part in the activities of a group—and while concealing his or her research identity.

functional utterance   In functional group theory, "an uninterrupted utterance of a single group member which appears to perform a specific function within the group interaction process" (Hirokawa, 1982, p. 139).

funnel questions   A questioning strategy that starts with an open-ended question and follows up with increasingly narrow questions.

G

generalization   *See* argument from example and generalization.

general to specific   A library search strategy in which one starts with general sources that lead to specific sources.

genres   In Hymes' (1974) "ethnography of communication" approach, the "categories of speech (e.g. poem, myth, tale, proverb, riddle, curse, prayer, oration, lecture, etc.); though often coincidental with speech event, genres must be treated as analytically independent."

goodness of fit test   *See* one-sample chi-square test.

grand mean   In factorial analysis of variance, the average of the mean conditions from predictor variables.

grounded theory   A set of explanations that has immediate relevance to a specific field setting under investigation. Participant observers attempt to discover categories to describe their observations after they have entered the field. Then, researchers make additional observations to refine and modify these categories and potentially develop theory.

Guttman scalogram   A scale involving a series of statements dealing with one topic and arranged according to their level of intensity.

H

halo effect   A special source of experimental invalidity in which strong positive or negative impressions of a source of communication may affect all other ratings that follow.

hermeneutics   "Literally, the study of interpretation[,] the term was originally associated with biblical studies, but a philosophical tendency has been developed" emphasizing the importance of understanding "beyond mere external description. . . . Gadamer has emphasized the way interpretation develops gradually by an interplay between the interpreter and the subject-matter, denying both that there is a single objectively correct interpretation and that we can never get beyond our own initial interpretation" (Bothamley, 1993, p. 281).

heuristic merit   The ability of a theory or research effort to stimulate scholars to discover new inventions, ideas, applications, or research directions.

historical-critical methods   Research designed to describe a period, person, or phenomenon for the purpose of interpreting or evaluating communication and its effects.

history   A source of internal invalidity in which events not controlled by the researcher occur during the experiment between any pretest and posttest.

holding constant   Controlling for other variables by limiting the range of intervening variables so that they are equal across studies (technically, all control methods involve taking nuisance variables and holding them constant).

homogeneous variances   The parametric test assumption that any differences in variances should be within the limits of sampling error.

homoscedasticity   The assumption in correlational analyses of approximately equal spread around the line of best fit.

Hotelling's T t test for intercorrelated dependent variables.

hypothesis   "An expectation about events based on generalizations of the assumed relationship between variables" (Tuckman, 1999, p. 74).

hypothetical constructs   Also known as concepts; constructs for which direct observations cannot be made.

I

identification   The uniting of people by the use of ideas, images, and attitudes.

idiographic research   Scholarship designed to develop a full understanding of "a particular event or individual" (English & English, 1958, p. 347).

impressionistic criticism   Statements of opinion (or personal impression) made by reviewers.

independence   The statistical assumption that groups, samples, or (in meta-analysis) studies are unaffected by each other.

independent samples t test   An application of the t test that compares the means of two sample groups (*see also t test for independent samples*).

independent variables   Variables that predict outcomes (dependent variables) posited in hypotheses.

inductive reasoning   A process of reasoning "by which we infer that what we know to be true in a particular case or cases, will be true in all cases which resemble the former in certain assignable respects. In other words, Induction is the process by which we conclude that what is true of certain individuals is true of the whole class, or that what is true at certain times will be true in similar circumstances at all times" (Mill, 1872/1959, p. 188).

inductive summary   A summary strategy that reviews literature by producing general propositions (laws or rules) that are demonstrated by each subcollection (studies are grouped largely by their findings, rather than their input variables).

inferential statistics   Tools that help researchers draw conclusions about the probable populations to which samples were or were not derived.

informed consent   The "procedure in which individuals choose whether to participate in an investigation after being informed of the facts that would be likely to influence their decision" (Diener & Crandall, 1978, p. 34).

infrequency index   A measure of the inconsistency of response, indicative of a person giving random responses.

instrumentality   In Hymes' (1974) "ethnography of communication" approach, the channels ("the medium of speech transmission [e.g. oral, written, visual, etc.]") and forms of speech ("the different languages, dialects, varieties, and registers used in a speech event/act; may be joined with channels as means or agencies of speaking").

instrumentation   A source of internal invalidity involving changes in the use of measuring instruments from the pretest to the posttest, including changes in raters or interviewers who collect the data in different conditions.

interactional and relational analyses   Forms of content analysis designed to describe the continuing oral communication between people.

interaction analysis   Studies that focus on ways of tracking individual acts of communicators.

interaction effects   Dependent variable effects that result from independent variables taken together and involving variation arising from special combinations of levels of independent variables.

interaction of elements   A source of internal invalidity involving effects created by the interaction of selection biases with differential levels of maturation, history, or any other source of variation.

interaction of selection and the experimental variable   Effects created by sampling groups in such a way that they are not representative of the population since they are more or less sensitive to the experimental variable than other subsamples from the same population (such as sampling college students in communication studies even though they may be more or less sensitive to the independent variable than the general population of people).

interaction of testing and the experimental variable   Also called "pretest sensitization," this source of experimental external invalidity is created when pretesting alters participants' sensitivity to the experimental variable.

interacts   The combination of one person's conversation and the reaction of another.

intercoder reliability   Determining the consistency of different raters who respond to the same events by using some sort of check sheet.

internal invalidity   The presence of contamination that prevents the experimenter from concluding that a study's experimental variable is responsible for the observed effects.

internal organizers   Phrases that preview, summarize, and provide transitions between main points.

interpretive analysis of data   A naturalistic approach that identifies communicators' interactions, uses of themes, and uses of stories to determine such things as the situations in which people find themselves, the structures within which they work, and the practical features of their world. (*See also* case studies and interpretive studies.)

intersubjectivity   The degree to which different researchers with essentially different beliefs draw essentially the same interpretations of the meaning of observations.

interval level measurement   Assignment of numbers to items as a matter of degree such that "the intervals between the numbers are *equal* in size" (Cozby, 1989, p. 149).

interval sampling   Sampling by selecting instances of communication at specific units (such as coding every third commercial during prime time for a month).

interview surveys   The use of personal contacts between a questioner and respondent in which the questions and answers are exchanged orally.

invention   The canon of rhetoric concerning the types and sources of ideas.

inventory questions   Closed-ended questions that ask respondents to list all responses that apply to them.

inverse relationship   A correlation with a negative slope indicating that the two variables move in different directions.

inverted funnel questions   A questioning strategy that starts with a very specific question and expands by asking increasingly general questions.

isolate   In network analysis, an individual who is not actively involved in any established communication network.

item-to-total reliability   Computing measurement reliability by correlation of items with the total test.

J

Jeanne Dixon fallacy   A special fallacy of research that involves making multiple predictions and claiming partial support.

John Henry effect   A special source of experimental invalidity in which respondents try to perform extra hard when they participate in an experiment.

K

kappa   *See* Cohen's *kappa*.

key   In Hymes' (1974) "ethnography of communication" approach, "tone, manner, or spirit of a speech act (e.g. seriousness, sarcasm, etc.)."

keywords   Terms under which information about a topic may be found.

known group validity   (also called "predictive" validity) A method of test validity that examines the degree to which scores on a measure predict membership in a known group in which the construct must exist.

known-to-unknown summary   A summary strategy that reviews literature by considering what (little) is known separately about each variable in the research review question and then announces what remains to be learned.

K-R 20   Kuder-Richardson formula 20 for reliability, used when researchers want to determine the reliability of a measure that has items that are scored as "correct" or "incorrect" answers.

kurtosis   A measure of the peakedness of a distribution.

L

law "A verbal statement, supported by such ample evidence as not to be open to doubt unless much further evidence is obtained, of the way events of a certain class consistently and uniformly occur" (English & English, 1958, p. 288).

law of large numbers A rule that holds that the assumptions of statistical methods are best satisfied by large samples.

leading questions Questions that imply their answer.

leptokurtic A distribution that is tall, with a kurtosis above the ordinary range.

levels The categories of variable factors.

liaison In network analysis, a person linking together people of different networks.

lie scale *See* MMPI lie (L) scale.

life history or life story research Naturalistic study that involves "the autobiography of a person which has been obtained through interview and guided conversation" (McNeill, 1990, p. 85).

Likert scales Scales composed of statements that reflect clear positions on an issue, for which subjects indicate their agreement on (typically) 5-point scales.

line of regression In correlations, a line of "best fit" through the data.

LISREL (Linear Structural Relations) A computer program that isolates relationships by examining covariances among variables.

literal analogy An analogy that compares something to an event or object that really exists.

literature reviews *See* exhaustive literature reviews; exemplary literature reviews.

loaded language Questionnaire items worded to imply an evaluation.

logical atomism A form of positivism in which statements beyond what can be observed are acceptable if they can be shown to be composed of other statements that deal with matters that can be observed (*see also* objectivist view, positivism, logical positivism, and logical empiricism).

logical empiricism A form of positivism that takes the view that concepts that cannot be observed directly are acceptable matters for theorizing if they stimulate other statements that can be tested by looking at observable phenomena (*see also* objectivist view, positivism, logical positivism, and logical atomism).

logical positivism A form of positivism in which concepts that cannot be observed are dismissed as metaphysical (things beyond the world of experience) statements (*see also* positivism, objectivist view, logical atomism, and logical empiricism).

log-linear analysis Extension of chi-square testing for analysis of more than two variables measured on the nominal level.

logos In rhetoric, part of the artistic proofs in the canon of invention dealing with the use of rational appeals.

M

μ The Greek letter mu, representing the population mean.

macroaggregation To avoid breaching confidentiality, the process of constructing "average persons" from the data.

main effects Dependent variable effects that result from independent variables separately.

manipulated independent variables Sometimes called "stimulus variables" because researchers introduce and control them in experiments.

manipulation check A researcher's measurement of a secondary variable to determine that an experimental variable actually was operating in a study.

MANOVA (multivariate analysis of variance) Extension of analysis of variance for multiple dependent variables.

matching Pairing events or participants on some variable on which they share equal levels and then assigning them to experimental or control conditions.

material hypothesis *See* hypothesis.

matrix questions Closed-ended questions that ask respondents to use the same categories to supply information.

maturation A source of internal invalidity involving changes that naturally occur over time (including fatigue or suspicion), even if subjects are left alone.

mean *See* arithmetic mean.

measured/assigned variables Variables not introduced or controlled by the researcher, but carefully observed and/or measured.

measurement Assigning numbers to variables according to some system.

median A score in an ordered set of data that separates one-half of the data from the other.

memo In grounded theory, a note the researcher makes about the meaning of a category or property, or about possible relationships among categories.

memory The canon of rhetoric concerning the ability to recall passages and examples for utterance.

mesokurtic A distribution that is neither very high nor very low, with a kurtosis within the ordinary range.

message The set of verbal and nonverbal cues communicators exchange.

meta-analysis A tool by which quantitative results from previous studies are combined and analyzed statistically.

metatheories Ways to think about theories (called "metatheory" to indicate notions "beyond the theories" themselves).

methodological studies Inquiries that deal with the development and validation of new tools, measuring instruments, or research approaches.

mirror questions A strategy of follow-up interview questioning that repeats previous responses to gain additional information.

misplaced precision *See* fallacy of misplaced precision.

MMPI lie (L) scale A scale to identify respondents who are attempting to avoid being candid and honest in their responses (not a general personality disposition toward dishonesty).

mode The most frequent score in a data set.

model An expression that not only states relationships but exhibits them.

moderator variables Variables that mediate the independent variable's prediction of the dependent variable.

mortality *See* experimental mortality.

multicollinearity In multiple correlation, the quality of predictors' being correlated with each other.

multimodal A condition in which a distribution possesses many modes.

multiple-choice questions Closed-ended questions that ask respondents to select a category response from a range of possible responses.

multiple comparison tests Tests completed after finding a statistically significant analysis of variance effect; completed for the purpose of determining the location of differences among group means.

multiple discriminant analysis A method that predicts membership in particular groups from a knowledge of a number of predictor variables (measured on the interval or ratio level).

multiple regression correlation (a.k.a. multiple correlation) A method that produces a correlation of multiple predictors with a single output variable.

multiple treatment interference A source of experimental external invalidity, in which participants exposed to repeated additional experimental treatments react in ways that are not generalizable to participants that are uncontaminated by such additional independent variables.

multistage sampling Sampling in which instances are selected sequentially (such as selecting commercials from one month, selecting one week from that month, selecting three hours from the days of the week, etc.).

multivariate analyses Statistical analyses in which multiple dependent variables are treated as a common set.

multivariate analysis of covariance Extension of MANOVA to adapt analysis of covariance for multiple interrelated dependent variables.

multivariate multiple correlation Extension of multiple regression for many interrelated dependent measures.

mythic perspective An approach to criticism that attempts to identify the underlying stories to which speakers appeal (a myth is defined as "a story about a particular incident which is put forward as containing or suggesting some general truth" [Sykes, 1970, p. 17]).

N

narrative In Fisher's narrative paradigm, "symbolic actions—words and/or deed—that have significance and meaning for those who live, create, or interpret them" (Fisher, 1987, p. 58).

narrative fidelity In Fisher's narrative paradigm, the consistency of new accounts with other stories people have heard.

narrative paradigm An approach to criticism that analyzes messages by looking at them as stories.

narrative reviews Reviews of literature in which published material (typically) is examined and nonquantitative assessments are made about the state of research.

naturalistic studies Nonexperimental inquiries completed as subjects are involved in the natural course of their lives.

negative case analysis In qualitative research, an approach to assure trustworthiness by accounting for negative or contrary cases that seem to disagree or disprove the researcher's interpretations.

negative skew Skewness in which the longest tail of the distribution lies to the left of the mean.

neo-Aristotelian criticism Criticism using Aristotelian standards and involving the canons of rhetoric.

network analysis   1. Traditionally, a method that obtains individuals' reports of their communication activities with others for the purpose of observing and describing the flow of information in a particular organizational system. 2. In its most general sense, "a set of research procedures for identifying structures in social systems based on the relations among the system's components rather than the attributes of individual cases" (Barnett, 1998, p. 154).

nodes   In network analysis, the members of the network that report data.

nominal level measurement   Use of numbers as simple identifications of variables.

nomothetic research   Scholarship designed to find general laws that apply to many instances.

nondirectional material hypotheses   Hypotheses that state simply that there will be some kind of relationship between variables (sometimes called "two-tailed" hypotheses because of the way statistics are used to test them).

nonlinear relationships   Relationships between independent and dependent variables that are not simple straight line relationships, but curved.

nonparametric tests   Statistical methods that do not make assumptions about population distributions or population parameters.

non sequitur   A fallacy of reasoning in which a conclusion does not follow from premises because the necessary steps in between are omitted.

normative and prescriptive theories   Theories whose principles involve defining the qualities that make communication meaningful or desirable.

normative science   "A discipline that systematically studies man's attempts to determine what is correct, valuable, good, or beautiful" (English & English, 1958, p. 349), which has given rise to normative and prescriptive theories.

norms   In Hymes' (1974) "ethnography of communication" approach, the norms of interaction ("rules governing speaking") and norms of interpretation ("the belief system of a community and how that interacts with the frame of references for understanding utterances").

null hypothesis   A statistical hypothesis that states that there is no relationship between variables.

O

O   An abbreviation for an observation a researcher makes of the study's dependent variable.

objectivist view   The notation that considers reality something that can be revealed by attempting to use methods that try to separate the researcher from the actual data (*see also* positivism).

observational surveys   *See* descriptive or observational surveys.

"one-across" statement   In relational control analysis, a statement in which one extends the discussion without increasing assertions or accepting others' statements.

"one-down" statement   In relational control analysis, a statement in which one person submits to the opinions or definitional rights of another.

one-group pretest–posttest   A preexperimental design in which a pretest is added to a one-shot case study.

one-sample chi-square test   A test of statistical significance for nominal level variables for which frequency data are obtained.

one-sample *t* test   An application of the *t* test that examines when a new sample mean differs from a known population mean under conditions when the population standard deviation is unavailable.

one-shot case study   A preexperimental design in which an experimental treatment is introduced and researchers look at effects on some output (dependent) variable.

one-tailed hypotheses   *See* directional material hypotheses.

one-tailed test   A test of a one-tailed or directional material hypothesis that states the form of predicted differences and requires using a critical range on one side of a probability distribution.

"one-up" statement   In relational control analysis, a statement in which one person is dominant over another because he or she asserts one's "definitional rights."

one-way analysis of variance   Analysis of variance in which the groups are levels for the independent variable.

open coding   In grounded theory, "initial familiarisation with the data" (Lacey & Luff, 2001, p. 7) with no initial categories.

open-ended questions   Questions to which people respond in their own words.

operational definition   Isolating a concept by specifying the steps researchers follow to make observations of the variables.

opinions   Interpretations of the meaning of collections of facts.

opinion surveys   Assessments of reports from individuals about topics of interest.

ordinal interaction Dependent variable interaction effects in the same direction as the main effects of the variables involved.

ordinal level measurement Measurement involving rank order on some variable.

organizational communication The study of interrelated behaviors, technologies, and systems functioning within an organization.

organized skepticism The norm of researchers, holding that "researchers are responsible for verifying the results on which they base their work" (Kerlinger, 1986, p. 9). Researchers do not accept claims blindly. They question research claims and offer criticism for each other.

outlier A piece of data from a different population than others in the data set and that introduces extreme scores on one or more variables.

overlap methods In qualitative research, an approach to assure dependability by use of multiple methods to triangulate a dependable set of interpretations of communication phenomena.

P

paired-comparison questions Questions that ask respondents to make a judgment between alternatives taken two at a time.

parameters Numbers computed from populations.

parametric tests Statistical significance tests that make assumptions about populations from which the data were drawn.

paraphrasing In interviews, summarizing the interviewee's message in one's own words, usually to check understanding.

partial correlation A method of statistical control that determines the variation associated with each nuisance variable and then separates it from the remaining total variation in the correlation.

participant as observer A role in ethnography or participant observation research characterized by the investigator's gathering data while taking part in the activities of a group—and after making his or her research identity known to the group.

participant observation Fieldwork in which researchers study groups by gaining membership or close relationships with them (see Wax, 1968, p. 238).

participants In Hymes' (1974) "ethnography of communication" approach, typically including "speaker or sender; addressor; hearer, or receiver, or audience; addressee."

patchwork quilt fallacy A special fallacy of research in which no predictions are made, but explanations are offered after the fact.

path models Use of correlational tools to interpret relationships to identify causal models with exogenous (input variable) sources, endogenous (mediating) variables, and dependent (output or criterion) variables.

pathos Sometimes called "pathetic appeals," an element of the canon of invention (artistic proofs) referring to the use of emotional or motivational appeals.

Pearson product moment correlation A correlation method suitable for situations in which the independent and dependent variables (identified as X and Y, respectively, in most notation) are interval or ratio level measures.

periodic sampling A method by which researchers select respondents according to a predetermined schedule rather than a random sequence.

pi *See* Scott's *pi*.

pilot studies Studies usually involving small samples of people who take part in a "dry run" of an experiment as an aid in developing materials, procedures, and protocols.

placebo effect A placebo is a stimulus containing no medicine or no experimental treatment at all; hence, a special source of experimental invalidity in which participants show changes even in the absence of any treatments at all, in reaction to the mental suggestion that they may have been given some stimulus.

plagiarism Using "another person's ideas or expressions in your writing without acknowledging the source" (Gibaldi, 1999, p. 30).

platykurtic A flat distribution with kurtosis lower than the ordinary range.

poetic definitions Statements that involve figurative interpretations of objects.

polarity rotation A check on test-taking behavior that avoids response set by (1) avoiding phrasing all items positively and (2) avoiding placing all positive adjectives on the same side of the measurement items.

polymodal *See* multimodal.

pooled standard deviation (s_p) The square root of the average of variances in subgroups involved in comparisons.

pooled variance (s_p^2) The mean of the variances of subgroups involved in comparisons using analysis of variance (weighted for sample sizes in the case of unequal sample sizes).

population The universe of events from which the sample is drawn.

positive skew   Skewness in which the longest tail of the distribution lies to the right of the mean.

positivism   A form of objectivist view in which researchers are advised to use the methods similar to those of the natural sciences to develop statements that depict an observable reality (see logical positivism, logical atomism, and logical empiricism).

postcritical ethnography   A research position in which researchers include a critique of the ways in which their own experiences studying groups of people in an ethnographic project may contribute to domination of the groups under study.

posttest-only control group design   A true experimental design that avoids pretest sensitization by deleting the pretest entirely.

power   A statistical test's probability of rejecting the null hypothesis correctly.

prediction   Descriptions of what can be expected in subsequent tests to be made.

predictive validity   (also called "known group" validity) A method of test validity that examines the degree to which scores on a measure predict membership in a known group in which the construct must exist.

premise   A statement in a logical argument that is the foundation for others drawn from it.

presumptive questions   Questions that assume information (e.g., "Have you stopped beating your spouse?").

pretest–posttest control group design   A true experimental design that includes randomly selected experimental and control groups, each of which is given a pretest and a posttest.

primary analysis: "The original analysis of data in a research study" (Glass, 1976, p. 3).

primary sources   Reports provided by individuals who have firsthand experience with the events reported.

principal components solution   In factor analysis, a method to identify the number of common centers of variation that underlie the manifest variables.

probability   The tendency or likelihood with which an event occurs in a population.

probability distribution   The theoretical pattern of expected "values of a random variable and of the probabilities of occurrences of these values" (Upton & Cook, 2002, p. 294).

probability sampling   Techniques that use randomization to identify samples.

probe   In interviews, the use of scripted or spontaneous follow-up questions designed to help interviewers secure additional detail, elaboration, or clarification.

probing questions   A strategy of follow-up interview questioning that directly asks for elaboration and explanation.

problems   (also known as research problem questions) Questions we expect to answer through research.

problem-solution summary   A summary strategy that reviews literature by considering a problem and its cause, followed by a research suggestion that might solve the problem.

professional responsibility   The requirement that researchers follow accepted rules of conduct with thoroughness and attention to concerns of subjects.

pseudoscience   "Fake science" in which the self-correcting nature of science is absent and scientific claims are made without serious regard for competent use of the scientific method (Carey, 1998, pp. 125–130).

publication bias   The tendency for research publications to favor empirical studies reporting statistically significant effects and to deny publication to studies finding no statistically significant relationship between variables.

purpose   In Burke's dramatistic pentad, the intention of the rhetor.

purposive or known group sampling   Selection of events from groups that are known to possess a particular characteristic under investigation.

Q

qualitative interview   An unstructured interview method aimed toward discussing topics in depth.

qualitative observational studies   Methods designed to use predominantly attribute-type data to interpret contemporaneous communication interactions.

qualitative research   Inquiry involving "in-depth, case-oriented study of a relatively small number of cases, including the single-case study. Qualitative research seeks detailed knowledge of specific cases, often with the goal of finding out 'how' things happen (or happened). Qualitative researchers' primary goal is to 'make the facts understandable,' and often place less emphasis on deriving inferences or predictions from cross-case patterns" (Ragin, Nagel, & White, 2004, p. 10).

quantitative research   Inquiries in which observations are expressed predominantly in numerical terms.

quasi experiments Studies involving completion of experimental work where random assignment and control are not possible.

quasi-interval measures Though perhaps not strictly measured on the interval or ratio level, data that share enough qualities of interval data to permit the use of interval level statistical tools.

questionnaires Survey forms in which individuals respond to items they have read.

quota sampling Samples are defined based on the known proportions within the population, and nonrandom sampling is completed within each group.

R

R 1. In experimental design, an abbreviation for randomization. 2. In statistics, an abbreviation for the coefficient of multiple correlation.

random assignment *See* randomization.

randomization Assignment so that each event is equally likely to belong to any experimental or control condition.

random sampling Selection of data such that each event in the population has an equal chance of being selected.

range The difference between the highest and lowest scores.

ranking questions Closed-ended questions that ask respondents to rank a set of options.

ratio level measurement Assignment of numbers to items such that "any adjoining values are the same distance apart and in which there is a true zero point" (Vogt, 2005, p. 264).

reactive arrangements A source of experimental external invalidity, consisting of elements in the experimental setting that make participants react differentially to the experimental arrangements rather than to the experimental variable alone (such matters as awareness of participation in an experiment may alter normal reactions of people).

reciprocal pattern In network analysis, a condition in which individuals share nearly an identical network pattern.

redundancy index In canonical correlation, a coefficient that tells whether sets of variables should be interpreted differentially for additional canonical component roots.

referential adequacy In qualitative research, an approach to assure trustworthiness by maintaining referential materials such as recordings and documentary materials to ground the credibility of research interpretations.

regression 1. Statistical regression. 2. Line of regression. 3. Multiple regression correlation.

relational control analysis Studies that track message sequences to determine the relative patterns of position and control in the relationship.

reliability The internal consistency of a measure.

reliability coefficient A correlation of the internal consistency of a measure.

repeatability The ability of operational definitions and methods to be used by different researchers.

replication The ability of other scholars to reproduce research.

reports Accounts of what took place whether by participants or by outside observers.

representative sample Sampling that accurately reflects characteristics of the population from which it was drawn.

research (1) "A process of asking a question (or related series of questions) and then initiating a systematic process to obtain valid answers to that question" (Meltzoff, 1998, p. 13). (2) A way of knowing that makes claims by using the tools of scholarship and science.

research hypothesis *See* hypothesis.

research positions The stances that researchers take regarding the objectives for research (ventriloquizing others' interests, giving voice to silenced groups, engaging direct activism).

research prospectus A complete proposal for a research activity to be completed at a future date.

response set A tendency for participants to follow predictable patterns when responding to test items.

rhetoric According to Aristotle, "the faculty of discovering in the particular case what are the available means of persuasion."

rhetorical criticism The use of standards of excellence to interpret and evaluate communication.

rhetorical visions "A representation of the collective consciousness of the participants in the interaction and is a product of the community's fantasies" (Alemán, 2005, p. 9).

rotation In factor analysis, an aid in interpretation that helps reveal the items that are used to understand a factor.

rule "A theory that explains a pattern of effects by referring to human intentions, reasons, or goals" (M. J. Smith, 1988, p. 354).

rules of correspondence   The degree to which a theory's constructs and abstract calculus can be applied to actual experience.

S

s   A symbol that represents the standard deviation of a sample.

s^2 A symbol that represents the variance of a sample.

sacrifice groups   A method to check the accuracy of respondent reports by interrupting groups during the interview or questionnaire process to see if they really understand what is meant by specific questions. Since these respondents have been distracted somewhat, they are "sacrificed" and their responses are used only to validate the survey question content.

sampling   Selecting events from a population.

sampling error   The degree to which a sample differs from the population on some measure.

scene   In Burke's dramatistic pentad, the setting in which the act takes place.

Scheffe's critical S   A multiple comparison test designed to contrast all possible comparisons of means, when the means are taken as part of complex comparisons.

scholarly definitions   Highly specific statements that have technical meanings for a group of scholars.

science   A way of testing statements by systematic application of the scientific method.

scientific method   A method that involves collecting data and establishing "a functional relationship among these data" (Bachrach, 1981, p. 4); generally a method involving four steps: observation of facts, development of a working hypothesis or theoretical solution to guide the research, test of expectations against information, establishing a conclusion or functional relationship based on deciding whether the working hypothesis or theoretic solution is supported.

Scott's *pi*   A measure of intercoder reliability, which also compensates for the rates of agreement that would be expected by chance alone.

scripts   In interview studies, the instructions given to the interviewers regarding what they will say to respondents and how they will answer questions and probe for further information.

secondary analysis   "The re-analysis of data for the purpose of answering the original research question with better statistical techniques, or answering new questions with old data" (Glass, 1976, p. 3).

secondary sources   Reports provided by individuals who do not have firsthand experience with the events reported.

selection   A source of internal invalidity involving sampling biases in selecting or assigning participants to experimental or control conditions (in essence, rigging the study by taking samples capriciously).

semantic differential-type scales   Scales (often seven-point intervals) bounded by pairs of bipolar adjectives.

semantic network   An application of network analysis to examine the relationships among words in a message.

sequence   In conversational analysis, "a sequence is a unit of conversation that consists of two or more adjacent and functionally related turns" (LingualLinks Library, 2005, ¶ 1).

serendipity   Finding something valuable while looking for something else.

significance   *See* statistically significant difference or relationship.

simple random sampling   A method by which researchers select participants or events such that each event in the population has an equal chance of being selected.

single subject designs   Also called "component search studies," experimental designs that determine the effect of treatments by strategically repeated exposures for a single subject.

situation   In Hymes' (1974) "ethnography of communication" approach, the setting ("the time and place of a speech act and, in general, the physical circumstances") and the scene ("the cultural definition of an occasion; the 'psychological setting'") of the communication being researched.

skewness   A measure of the centeredness of distributions.

snowball sampling   Selection of events based on referrals from initial informants.

social desirability   A measure of the degree to which people attempt to describe themselves in ways that they think are acceptable, desirable, or approved by others.

Solomon four-group design   A true experimental design that assesses the impact of pretesting by adding control groups.

sophists   Teachers in ancient times who traveled around instructing people wherever there was a market.

Spearman rank order correlation   A correlation method suitable for situations in which both the independent and dependent variables are ordinal level measures.

specific questions Questions that focus on individual activities.

specific to general A library search strategy in which one starts with a reference and writes down the citations to related research and theory identified in them. Then, the process is completed with the new sources until the information "snowballs" as one reference leads to others.

speech and hearing science The study of the physiology and acoustical aspects of speech and hearing (including biological, phonological, and physiological aspects of speech and hearing).

speech community "A set of people with a common language, or who share a repertoire of varieties (accents, styles, even languages in multilingualism); people who live together and interact through language; people with shared social attributes (young people, lawyers, women); people in the same social system. The term is most relevant to small well-defined, stable communities" (Bothamley, 1993, p. 499).

speech event "The basic unit for the analysis of verbal interaction in speech communities; it covers stretches of utterances and focuses on the exchange between speakers; . . . speech events are cognitive phenomena that play an essential part in managing and interpreting everyday communications (Gumperz)" (Malcolm, 2001, ¶ 67).

speech pathology *See* speech and hearing science.

speech situation "Situations associated with (or marked by the absence of) speech (Hymes)" (Malcolm, 2001, ¶ 71).

split-half reliability Computing measurement reliability by dividing a test into two parts, scoring them separately, and checking consistency between the two scores.

standard deviation Though computed differently, a measure that attempts to summarize the average deviation of scores from the mean, by estimating such a value from the square root of the variance s^2; symbolized for the sample standard deviation as s.

standard error The standard deviation of a distribution of elements other than raw scores.

standard error of the mean The standard deviation of a distribution of means.

standard normal curve A probability distribution that tells the expected value that would be obtained by sampling at random.

standard scores *See* z scores.

static-group comparisons A preexperimental design in which a control group is used, but the groups are not known to be comparable in other respects (typically because the experimental and control groups are separate "intact" groups).

statistical control Taking measures of nuisance variables and using statistical tools to hold them constant.

statistical regression A source of internal invalidity involving shifts produced when subjects are selected due to very high or very low scores on a test; statistical regression holds that people will "regress toward the mean" even if they simply are left alone.

statistically significant difference or relationship As a result of a test of statistical significance, finding a relationship or effect size that is unlikely to have been found from random sampling error if the null hypothesis were true.

statistics (1) Quantitative reports based on observations in a sample. (2) The study of quantitative information.

stepwise replication In qualitative research, an approach to assure dependability by involving at least two researchers in comparisons of fieldwork experiences at different times.

stimulus variables *See* manipulated independent variables.

stratification Sampling in which strata are identified (such as geographic region, type of radio station format, type of ad) and a random sample within each strata is proportionately selected.

stratified random sampling A method by which researchers select participants or events to represent known proportions of characteristics in the population. After population characteristics are identified (such as the number of men and women in the population), a random sample of a given size is drawn from each population stratification variable consistent with the population proportions.

straw man fallacy Attacking of a person for a position that was not actually taken by the person.

structured interviews Interviews that use specific lists of questions.

studies of behavior, facts, and opinions Studies designed to determine the current status of conditions or attitudes by using questionnaires, interviews, or direct observations of communicators.

studies of status and development Intensive detailed studies of individual cases over time.

style The choice and use of words; the canon of rhetoric concerning the use of language.

subjectivist view An approach taking the perspective that research and the researcher cannot be separated and that (in the extreme statement) the reality of research data does not exist apart from the influences brought to bear upon it by the researcher. As a result, these researchers take the view that all research is value laden, a fact that researchers should admit and embrace, rather than trying to control its influences. In the extreme form, some take the view that reality does not exist at all, but is a "social construction." In its most extreme form, this viewpoint is a "solipsism" in which people believe that there is no reality except that which they personally encounter.

subject tracings   Keywords that list other subject headings under which a book is also listed.

survey   A study that uses questionnaires or interviews to discover descriptive characteristics of phenomena.

syllogism   A formal logical system in which the premises lead to a conclusion.

systematic sampling   *See* periodic sampling.

T

telefocus sessions   Forms of focus groups in which discussion sessions are completed by teleconferencing methods typically involving telephones or linked computers with visual transmission capabilities.

tenacity   A way of knowing in which we claim to know something because we have always believed it.

tentativeness   The requirement that scholars recognize that a theory's answers are provisional.

testing   A source of internal invalidity involving alterations that occur when subjects are tested and made testwise or anxious in ways that affect them when they are given a second test.

test-retest reliability   Giving the measure twice and reporting consistency between scores.

test statistic   In statistical hypothesis testing, a number computed from a statistical formula, "which is a function of the observations in a random sample" (Upton & Cook, 2002, p. 165).

texts   What are believed to be the actual messages or words of a communicator.

theoretical saturation   In grounded theory, the point at which "no new significant categories or concepts are emerging" (Lacey & Luff, 2001, p. 7) from the process of constant comparison despite a reasonable search.

theoretical sensitivity   The ability "to see the research situation and its associated data in new ways, and to explore the data's potential for developing theory" (Strauss & Corbin, 1990, p. 44).

theoretic constructs   Terms that are substituted into the abstract calculus of a theory (*see* constructs).

theory   "A body of interrelated principles that explain or predict" (*Longman Dictionary of Psychology,* 1984, p. 744).

theory first inquiry   Sometimes called the deductive approach to research, a method of inquiry that develops theory and then gathers data to test it (particularly its limits).

Thurstone equal appearing interval scales   Scales composed of statements for which agreement with any individual item is assigned a predetermined point value.

time-budgeting studies   Inquiries in which "the researcher asks the subjects of the research to keep a detailed diary over a given period" (McNeill, 1990, p. 88).

time series design   A type of quasi experiment that measures subjects at different times.

topical summary   A summary strategy that reviews literature by reference to content categories into which the studies fall.

trend analysis   A method that isolates the nature of linear and nonlinear trends in effects identified as statistically significant by analysis of variance.

trial and error   A "way of knowing" that claims knowledge by making repeated trials to eliminate unacceptable answers.

***t* test**   A test of statistical significance designed to assess the difference between the means of two groups.

***t* test for dependent samples**   An application of the test that compares the means of two sample groups in which subjects are matched or sampled twice.

***t* test for independent samples**   An application of the test that compares the means of two sample groups.

trustworthiness   In qualitative research, the counterpart of measurement validity in which efforts are made to persuade audiences that study findings are credible and deserving of attention.

Tukey's HSD   (John Tukey's Honestly Significant Difference test) A multiple comparison test designed to contrast all possible comparisons of means, when the means are taken two at a time.

two-tailed hypotheses   *See* nondirectional material hypotheses.

two-tailed test   A test of a two-tailed or nondirectional material hypothesis that does not state the form of predicted differences and requires using a critical range on both sides of a probability distribution.

Type I error   Incorrectly rejecting the null hypothesis.

Type II error   Incorrectly failing to reject the null hypothesis and failing to detect a relationship that is present.

U

unbiased estimator   A sample statistic that is most likely to approximate the corresponding population parameter.

universalism   The view that "scientific laws are the same everywhere. A scientific law states a relation between phenomena that is invariable under the same conditions" (Kerlinger, 1986, p. 9).

unobtrusive measurement   Use of artifacts that do not hold the potential to influence the behavior being studied, including the use of accretions and erosions.

unstructured interviews   Interviews that permit respondents to indicate their reactions to general issues without guidance from highly detailed questions.

urban archaeology   Examination of modern artifacts of urban life (such as searching trash cans in a neighborhood to find evidence of alcoholism rates).

utterance   In conversational analysis, what a person actually says in conversation.

V

validity   1. Test validity is the consistency of a measure with a criterion; the degree to which a measure actually measures what is claimed. 2. Experimental validity refers to the absence of errors that prevent researchers from drawing unequivocal conclusions.

variable   A characteristic to which numbers may be assigned.

variable factor   (also called "factor") A variable that has been divided into levels or groups.

variance   Though computed differently, a measure that attempts to summarize the average of squared differences of scores from the mean, symbolized for the sample variance as s^2 and for the population variance as σ^2.

verbal cues   Words people use in communication.

W

ways of speaking   "Rule-governed patterns of communicative behaviour within a speech community (Hymes)" (Malcolm, 2001, ¶ 72).

within groups variance   In analysis of variance, the pooled variance (s_p^2) residual.

working hypothesis   A tentative hypothesis assumed for the purposes of initiating research and subject to change as research progresses.

X

X An abbreviation for (1) a score from a continuous distribution or (2) the experimental variable used by researchers.

$\overline{X}$ "X bar," representing the sample mean.

Z

z scores   Scores that transform values from other distributions into equivalent units under the standard normal curve with means of 0 and standard deviations and variances of 1.

References

Aczel, A. D. (1989). *Complete business statistics*. Homewood, IL: Irwin.

Adair, J. G., Dushenko, T. W., & Lindsay, R. C. L. (1985). Ethical regulations and their impact on research practice. *American Psychologist, 40,* 59–72.

Adair, J. G., & Spinner, B. (1981). Subjects' access to cognitive processes: Demand characteristics and verbal report. *Journal for the Theory of Social Behavior, 11,* 31–52.

Adler, M. J., & Van Doren, C. (1977). *Treasury of Western thought: A compendium of important statements on man and his institutions by the great thinkers in Western history*. New York: R. R. Bowker.

Afifi, T. D., & Keith, S. (2004). A risk and resiliency model of ambiguous loss in postdivorce stepfamilies. *Journal of Family Communication 4(2),* 65–98.

Agar, M. H. (1988). *Speaking of ethnography*. Newbury Park, CA: Sage.

Alcock, J. E. (1981). *Parapsychology, science or magic? A psychological perspective*. Oxford, England: Pergamon Press.

Alden, L. (2005). *Statistics can be misleading*. Retrieved March 5, 2006, from www.econoclass.com/misleadingstats.html

Alemán, M. W. (2005). Embracing and resisting romantic fantasies as the rhetorical vision on a SeniorNet discussion board. *Journal of Communication, 55,* 5–21.

Alexander, M., & Danowski, J. (1990). Analysis of an ancient network. *Social Networks, 12,* 313–335.

Alfred, R. (1976). The church of Satan. In C. Glock & R. Bellah (Eds.), *The new religious consciousness* (pp. 180–202). Berkeley: University of California Press.

Allen, M., & Preiss, R. W. (1997). Comparing the persuasiveness of narrative and statistical evidence using meta-analysis. *Communication Research Reports, 14,* 125–131.

Allen, M. J., & Yen, W. M. (1979). *Introduction to measurement theory*. Monterey, CA: Brooks-Cole.

Altheide, D., & Johnson, J. M. C. (1998). Criteria for assessing interpretive validity in qualitative research. In N. K. Denzin & Y. S. Lincoln (Eds.), *Collecting and interpreting qualitative materials* (pp. 283–312). Thousand Oaks, CA: Sage.

American Association for Public Opinion Research. (1954–1955). Propaganda analysis. *Proceedings,* pp. 445–446.

American Psychological Association. (2002). *Ethical Principles of Psychologists and Code of Conduct*. Retrieved October 10, 2005, from American Psychological Association website: www.apa.org/ethics/code2002.pdf

American Psychological Association Council of Representatives. (1994, August). Council Policy Manual: M. Scientific Affairs. *APA Online*. Retrieved August 15, 2005, from www.apa.org/about/division/cpmscientific.html

American Statistical Association. (1999, August 7). *Ethical guidelines for statistical practice*. Retrieved October 10, 2005, from www.amstat.org/profession/index.cfm?fuseaction=ethicalstatistics

Amidon, E. J., & Hough, J. B. (1967). *Interaction analysis: Theory, research, and application*. Reading, MA: Addison-Wesley.

Anastasi, A. (1968). *Psychological testing* (3rd ed.). New York: Macmillan.

Anderson, J. P., Anderson, P. A., & Jenson, A. D. (1979). *The measurement of nonverbal immediacy*. Paper presented at the Annual Meeting of the Eastern Communication Association, Philadelphia. (ERIC Document Reproduction Service No. ED203409)

Angelelli, C. (2000) Interpretation as a communicative event: A look through Hymes' lenses. *Meta, 45,* 580–592.

Anker, E. (2005). Villains, victims and heroes: Melodrama, media, and September 11. *Journal of Communication, 55,* 22–38.

Antaki, C. (2002). *Basic transcription notation conventions.*
Retrieved March 14, 2006, from Loughborough
University website: www-staff.lboro.ac.uk/~sscal/
notation.htm

Antaki, C. (2004a). *Conversation analysis I—the roots in
sociology.* Retrieved March 14, 2006, from Loughborough University website: www-student.lut.ac.
uk/~sscal/ttlecture03CAroots.htm

Antaki, C. (2004b). *Conversation analysis II—conversational structures.* Retrieved March 14, 2006, from
Loughborough University website: www-staff.lboro
.ac.uk/~ssca1/ttlecture04CAbasics.htm

Archer, M. S. (2000). For structure: Its reality, properties and powers: A reply to Anthony King, *The Sociological Review, 48*(3), 464–472.

Archer, M. S., Bhaskar, R., Collier, A., Lawson, T., &
Norrie, A. (Eds.). (1998). *Critical realism: Essential
readings.* London: Routledge.

Armstrong, R. L. (1987). The midpoint on a five-point
Likert-type scale. *Perceptual and Motor Skills, 64,*
359–362.

Ashenfelter, O., Harmon, C., & Oosterbeek, H. (1999).
A review of estimates of the schooling/earnings relationship, with tests for publication bias. *Labour Economics, 6,* 453–470.

Auer, J. J. (1959). *An introduction to research in speech.*
New York: Harper and Row.

Babbie, E. (1999). *The basics of social research.* Belmont,
CA: Wadsworth.

Babbie, E. (2003). *The practice of social research* (10th ed.).
Belmont, CA: Wadsworth.

Bachrach, A. J. (1981). *Psychological research: An introduction* (4th ed.). New York: Random House.

Baker, B. O., Hardyck, C. D., & Petrinovich, L. F.
(1966). Weak measurements vs. strong statistics: An
empirical critique of S. S. Stevens' proscriptions on
statistics. *Educational and Psychological Measurement,
26,* 291–309.

Bales, R. F. (1948). A set of categories for the analysis
of small group interactions. *American Sociological Review, 15,* 257–263.

Bales, R. F. (1950). *Interaction process analysis.* Cambridge,
MA: Addison-Wesley.

Bales, R. F., & Cohen, S. P. (1979). *SYMLOG: A system for the multilevel observation of groups.* New York:
Free Press.

Bandler, R., & Grinder, J. (1979). *Frogs into princes:
Neuro linguistic programming,* Moab, UT: Real People
Press.

Barnett, G. A. (1998). Social structure of international
telecommunications. In H. Sawhney & G. A.
Barnett (Eds.), *Progress in communication science, volume
XV* (pp. 151–186). Stamford, CT: Ablex.

Barnett, G. A., & Choi, Y. (1995). Physical distance
and language as determinants of the international
telecommunication network. *International Political
Science Review, 16,* 249–265.

Barnett, G. A., & Danowski, J. (1992). The structure of
communication: A network analysis of the International Communication Association. *Human Communication Research, 19,* 264–285.

Barnett, G. A., Hamlin, D. M., & Danowski, J. A.
(1981). The use of fractionation scales for communication audits. In M. Burgoon (Ed.), *Communication
yearbook, 5* (pp. 455–471). New Brunswick, NJ:
Transaction.

Barnett, G. A., Jacobson, T., Choi, Y., & Sun-Miller,
S. (1996). An examination of the international
telecommunication network. *The Journal of International Communication, 3,* 19–43.

Barnett, G., & Kim, J. H. (2005, May). *A structural
analysis of international conflict from a communication perspective.* Paper presented at the International Communication Association Convention, New York.

Barnett, G. A., & Salisbury, J. G. T. (1996). Communication and globalization: A longitudinal analysis of
the international telecommunication network.
Journal of World System Research, 2(16), 1–17.

Barnette, J. J. (1999). *Likert response alternative direction:
SA to SD or SD to SA: Does it make a difference?*
Paper presented at the Annual Meeting of the
American Educational Research Association, Mon-
treal, Canada. (ERIC Document Reproduction Ser-
vice No. ED429125)

Barnette, J. J. (2000). Effects of stem and Likert response
option reversals on survey internal consistency: If you

feel the need, there is a better alternative to using those negatively worded stems. *Educational and Psychological Measurement, 60,* 361–370.

Baron, R. A. (1981). The "costs of deception" revisited: An openly optimistic rejoinder. *IRB: A Review of Human Subjects Research, 3*(1), 8–10.

Barsalou, L. W. (1983). Ad hoc categories. *Memory and Cognition, 11,* 211–227.

Bashi, V. (2004). Improving qualitative research proposal evaluation. In C. C. Ragin, J. Nagel, & P. White, *Workshop on scientific foundations of qualitative research* (pp. 39–43). Washington, DC: National Science Foundation. Available: www.nsf.gov/pubs/2004/nsf04219/start.htm

Bassett, E. H., & O'Riordan, K. (2001, December). *Ethics of Internet research: Contesting the human subjects research model.* Paper presented at the Computer Ethics: Philosophical Enquiries (CEPE) Conference, Lancaster University, United Kingdom. Retrieved April 18, 2006, from New York University website: www.nyu.edu/projects/nissenbaum/ethics_bas_full.html

Beasley, D. (1988). *How to use a research library.* New York: Oxford University Press.

Beebe, S. A., Beebe, S. J., & Ivy, D. K. (2004). *Communication: Principles for a lifetime* (2nd ed.). Boston: Pearson/Allyn and Bacon.

Begg, C. B., & Mazumdar, M. (1994). Operating characteristics of a rank correlation test for publication bias. *Biometrics, 50,* 1088–1101.

Bell, J. (2002). Narrative inquiry: More than just telling stories. *TESOL Quarterly, 36*(2), 207–212.

Bell, L., & Nutt, L. (2002). Divided loyalties, divided expectations: Research ethics, professional and occupational responsibilities. In M. Mauthner, M. Birch, J. Jessop, & T. Miller (Eds.), *Ethics in qualitative research* (pp. 70–90). London: Sage.

Bello, R. (1996). A Burkean analysis of the "political correctness" confrontation in higher education. *Southern Communication Journal, 61,* 243–252.

Bem, D. J., & Honorton, C. (1994). Does psi exist? Replicable evidence for an anomalous process of information transfer. *Psychological Bulletin, 115,* 4–18.

Benoit, W. L. (1991). Two tests of the mechanism of inoculation theory. *Southern Speech Communication Journal, 56,* 219–229.

Benson, J., & Hocevar, D. (1985). The impact of item phrasing on the validity of attitude scales for elementary school children. *Journal of Educational Measurement, 22,* 231–240.

Berelson, B. (1952). *Content analysis of communication research.* New York: Free Press.

Berg, B. L. (1989). *Qualitative research methods for the social sciences.* Boston: Allyn and Bacon.

Berg, B. L. (2007). *Qualitative research methods for the social sciences* (6th ed.). Boston: Allyn and Bacon.

Berg, B. L., Ksander, M., Loughlin, J., & Johnson, B. (1983, August). *Cliques and groups: Adolescent affective ties and criminal activities.* Paper presented at the Society for the Study of Social Problems Convention, Detroit.

Berger, C. R. (2005). Interpersonal communication: Theoretical perspectives, future prospects. *Journal of Communication, 55,* 415–447.

Berger, C., & Calabrese, R. J. (1975). Some explorations in initial interaction and beyond: Toward a developmental theory of interpersonal communication. *Human Communication Research, 1,* 99–112.

Bergstrom, B. A., & Lunz, M. E. (1998). *Rating scale analysis: Gauging the impact of positively and negatively worded items.* Paper presented at the Annual Meeting of the American Educational Research Association, San Diego, CA. (ERIC Document Reproduction Service No. ED423289)

Berlo, D. K. (1960). *The process of communication: An introduction to theory and practice.* San Francisco: Rinehart Press.

Bernard, H. R., & Killworth, P. D. (1977). Informant accuracy in social-network data II. *Human Communication Research, 4,* 3–18.

Bernard, H. R., Killworth, P. D., & Sailer, L. (1982). Informant accuracy in social-network data V: An experimental attempt to predict actual communication from recall data. *Social Science Research, 11,* 30–66.

Best, J. W. (1981). *Research in education* (4th ed.). Englewood Cliffs, NJ: Prentice-Hall.

Beyerstein, B. L. (1996, October). *Distinguishing science from pseudoscience.* Centre for Curriculum and Professional

Development. Victoria, British Columbia, Canada. Available: www.sfu.ca/~beyerste/research/articles/02SciencevsPseudoscience.pdf

Bhaskar, R. (1978). *A realist theory of science.* Sussex, England: Harvester Press.

Bhaskar, R. (1986). *Scientific realism and human emancipation.* London: Verso.

Bhaskar, R. (1989). *Reclaiming reality: A critical introduction to contemporary philosophy.* London: Verso.

Bhaskar, R. (1998). *The possibility of naturalism* (3rd ed.). London: Routledge.

Billig, M. (2006). A psychoanalytic discursive psychology: From consciousness to unconsciousness. *Discourse Studies, 8,* 17–24.

Black, E. (2000). On objectivity and politics in criticism. *American Communication Journal,* 4(1). Retrieved March 3, 2006, from http://acjournal.org/holdings/vol4/iss1/special/black.htm

Black, J. (2001). Semantics and ethics of propaganda. *Journal of Mass Media Ethics, 16*(2–3), 121–137.

Blackmore, S. J. (1987). A report of a visit to Carl Sargent's laboratory. *Journal of the Society for Psychical Research, 54,* 186–198.

Blackmore, S. J. (2001, March/April). What can the paranormal teach us about consciousness? *Skeptical Inquirer, 25*(2), 22–27.

Blommaert, J., Bock, M., & McCormick, K. (2006). Narrative inequality in the TRC hearings: On the hearability of hidden transcripts. *Journal of Language & Politics, 5,* 37–70.

Bock, M. (2004). Family snaps: Life-worlds and information *habitus. Visual Communication, 3,* 281–293.

Bogardus, E. S. (1933). A social distance scale. *Sociology and Social Research, 17,* 265–271.

Bok, S. (1974, November). The ethics of giving placebos. *Scientific American,* pp. 17–23.

Bokeno, R. M. (1987). The rhetorical understanding of science: An explication and critical commentary. *Southern Speech Communication Journal, 52,* 285–311.

Boller, P. F., & George, J. (1989). *They never said it.* New York: Oxford University Press.

Boneau, C. A. (1960). The effects of violations of assumption underlying the t-test. *Psychological Bulletin, 57,* 49–64.

Booth, W. C. (1964). *The rhetoric of fiction.* Chicago: University of Chicago Press.

Borg, W. R. (1963). *Educational research: An introduction.* New York: McKay.

Borgatti, S. P., Everett, M. G., & Freeman, L. C. (2002). *UCInet for Windows: Software for social network analysis.* Harvard, MA: Analytic Technologies.

Bormann, E. G. (1972). Fantasy and rhetorical vision: The rhetorical criticism of reality. *Quarterly Journal of Speech, 58,* 396–407.

Bormann, E. G. (1993). Fantasy theme analysis and rhetorical theory. In J. L. Golden, G. F. Berquist, & W. F. Coleman (Eds.), *The rhetoric of Western thought* (pp. 365–384). Dubuque, IA: Kendall/Hunt.

Bormann, E. G., Cragan, J. F., & Shields, D. C. (2001). Three decades of developing, grounding, and using symbolic convergence theory (SDCT). *Communication Yearbook, 25,* 271–313.

Bormann, E. G., Knutson, R. I., & Musolf, K. (1997). Why do people share fantasies? An empirical investigation of the symbolic convergence communication theory. *Communication Studies, 48,* 254–276.

Bothamley, J. (1993). *Dictionary of theories.* London: Gale Research International.

Bower, B. (1990). Subliminal deceptions. *Science News, 138*(8), 124.

Bowers, K. S. (1967). The effect of demands for honesty on reports of visual and auditory hallucinations. *International Journal of Clinical and Experimental Hypnosis, 15,* 31–36.

Boyle, M. P., Schmierbach, M., Armstrong, C. L., Cho, J., McCluskey, M., McLeod, D. M., & Shah, D. V. (2006). Expressive responses to news stories about extremist groups: A framing experiment. *Journal of Communication, 56,* 271–288.

Briggs, D. C. (2005). Meta-analysis: A case study. *Evaluation Review, 29,* 87–127.

Brinson, S. L. (1995). The myth of white superiority in *Mississippi Burning. Southern Communication Journal, 60,* 211–221.

Brooks, P. (1995). *The melodramatic imagination: Balzac, Henry James, melodrama, and the mode of excess.* New Haven, CT: Yale University Press.

Brown, L. M. (1961). A content analysis of anti-Catholic documents circulated through the mails during the 1960 presidential election campaign. Unpublished master's thesis, University of Iowa, Iowa City.

Budd, R. W., Thorp, R. K., & Donohew, L. (1967). *Content analysis of communications.* New York: Macmillan.

Bullock, A., & Stallybrass, O. (Eds.). (1977). *The Harper dictionary of modern thought.* New York: Harper and Row.

Burgoon, M., Hall, J., & Pfau, M. (1991). A test of the "messages-as-fixed-effect fallacy" argument: Empirical and theoretical implications of design choices. *Communication Quarterly, 39,* 18–34.

Burke, J. A., Earley, M., Dixon, L. D., Wilke, A., & Puczynski, S. (2006). Patients with diabetes speak: Exploring the implications of patients' perspectives for their diabetes appointments. *Health Communication, 19,* 103–114.

Burke, K. (1969a). *A grammar of motives.* Reprint. Berkeley: University of California Press. (Original work published 1945)

Burke, K. (1969b). *A rhetoric of motives.* Reprint. Berkeley: University of California Press. (Original work published 1950)

Burkholder, T. R. (1989). Kansas populism, woman suffrage, and the agrarian myth: A case study in the limits of mythic transcendence. *Communication Studies, 40,* 292–307.

Burleson, B. R. (1980). The place of nondiscursive symbolism, formal characterizations, and hermeneutics in argument analysis and criticism. *Journal of the American Forensic Association, 16,* 222–231.

Burleson, B. R., Holmstrom, A. J., & Gilstrap, C. M. (2005). Guys can't say that to guys: Four experiments assessing the normative motivation account for deficiencies in the emotional support provided by men. *Communication Monographs, 72,* 468–501.

Burnham, T. (1975). *The dictionary of misinformation.* New York: Ballantine.

Burrell, G., & Morgan, G. (1979). *Sociological paradigms and organizational analysis.* London: Heinemann.

Burton, L. M. (2004). Ethnographic protocol for welfare, children, and families: A three city study. In C. C. Ragin, J. Nagel, & P. White, *Workshop on scientific foundations of qualitative research* (pp. 59–69). Washington, DC: National Science Foundation. Available: www.nsf.gov/pubs/2004/nsf04219/start.htm

Bush, A., & Bush, V. D. (1994). The narrative paradigm as a perspective for improving ethical evaluations of advertisements. *Journal of Advertising, 23*(3), 31–41.

Byrne, D., Ervin, C. R., & Lamberth, J. (1970). Continuity between the experimental study of attraction and real-life computer dating. *Journal of Personality and Social Psychology, 16,* 157–165.

Camic, P. M., Rhodes, J. E., & Yardley, L. (2003). Naming the stars: Integrating qualitative methods into psychological research. In P. M. Camic, J. E. Rhodes, L. Yardley (Eds.), *Qualitative research in psychology: Expanding perspective in methodology and design* (pp. 3–29). Washington, DC: American Psychological Association.

Campbell, D. T., & Stanley, J. C. (1963). *Experimental and quasi-experimental designs for research.* Chicago: Rand McNally.

Campbell, N. J., & Grisson, S. (1979). *Influence of item direction on student responses in attitude assessment.* Paper presented at the Annual Meeting of the American Educational Research Association, San Francisco. (ERIC Document Reproduction Service No. ED170366)

Cappella, J. N. (1990). The method of proof by example in interaction analysis. *Communication Monographs, 57,* 236–240.

Cappella, J. N., Lerman, C., Romantan, A. & Baruh, L. (2005). News about genetics and smoking: Priming, family smoking history, and news story believability on inferences of genetic susceptibility to tobacco addiction. *Communication Research, 32,* 478–502.

Capurro, R., & Pingel, C. (2001, December). *Ethical issues of online communication research.* Paper presented at the Computer Ethics: Philosophical Enquiries (CEPE) Conference, Lancaster University, United Kingdom. Retrieved April 18, 2006, from New York University website: www.nyu.edu/projects/nissenbaum/ethics_cap_full.html

Card, D., & Krueger, A. B. (1995). Time series minimum-wage studies: A meta-analysis. *American Economic Review, 85,* 238–243.

Carey, S. S. (1998). *A beginner's guide to scientific method* (2nd ed.). Belmont, CA: Wadsworth.

Carlson, A. C., & Hocking, J. E. (1988). Strategies of redemption at the Vietnam Veterans' Memorial. *Western Journal of Speech Communication, 52,* 203–215.

Carragee, K., & Roefs, W. (2004). The neglect of power in recent framing research. *Journal of Communication, 54,* 214–233.

Carroll, R. T. (2003). *The skeptic's dictionary: A collection of strange beliefs, amusing deceptions, and dangerous delusions.* Hoboken, NJ: Wiley.

Carter, E. S., & Fife, I. (1961). The critical approach. In C. W. Dow (Ed.), *An introduction to graduate study in speech and theatre* (pp. 81–103). East Lansing: Michigan State University Press.

Ceccarelli, L. (1998). Polysemy: Multiple meanings in rhetorical criticism. *Quarterly Journal of Speech, 84,* 395–415.

Cegala, D. J., Wall, V. D., & Rippey, G. (1987). An investigation of interaction involvement and the dimensions of SYMLOG: Perceived communication behaviors of persons in task-oriented groups. *Central States Speech Journal, 38,* 81–93.

Champion, D. J. (1970). *Basic statistics for social research.* Scranton, PA: Chandler.

Chang, B. G. (2006). Communication as communicability. In G. J. Shepherd, J. St. John, & T. Striphas (Eds.), *Communication as . . . : Perspectives on theory* (pp. 242–248). Thousand Oaks, CA: Sage.

Chang, L. (1995). Connotatively consistent and reversed connotatively inconsistent items are not fully equivalent: Generalizability study. *Educational and Psychological Measurement, 55,* 991–997.

Chaplin, J. P. (1985). *Dictionary of psychology* (2nd ed.). New York: Laurel Books, Dell.

Charmaz, K., & Mitchell, R. (1997). The myth of silent authorship: Self, substance, and style in ethnographic writing. In R. Hertz (Ed.), *Reflexivity and voice* (pp. 193–215). London: Sage.

Chase, S. (1954). *The power of words.* New York: Harcourt Brace.

Chiseri-Strater, E., & Sunstein, B. S. (1997). *Fieldworking: Reading and writing research.* Upper Saddle River, NJ: Blair Press.

Chon, B. S., Choi, J. H., Barnett, G. A., Danowski, J. A., & Joo, S. J. (2003). A structural analysis of media convergence: Cross-industry mergers and acquisitions in the information industries. *Journal of Media Economics, 16,* 141–157.

Christenson, P. (1992). The effects of parental advisory labels on adolescent music preferences. *Journal of Communication, 42,* 106–113.

Chung, K. L. (1975). *Probability theory with stochastic processes.* New York: Springer-Verlag.

Claffe, G. A. (1996, May). *Customer feedback: Using content analysis to reduce uncertainty in a changing environment.* Paper presented at the International Communication Association Convention, Chicago.

Clark, R. D., & Word, L. E. (1974). Where is the apathetic bystander? Situational characteristics of the emergency. *Journal of Personality and Social Psychology, 29,* 279–287.

Cloud, D. (2001). The affirmative masquerade. *American Communication Journal,* 4(1). Retrieved March 3, 2006, from http://acjournal.org/holdings/vol4/iss1/special/cloud.htm

Coe, K., & Domke, D. (2006). Petitioners or prophets? Presidential discourse, God, and the ascendancy of the religious conservatives. *Journal of Communication, 56,* 308–330.

Coelho, C. A. (1990). Acquisition and generalization of simple manual sign grammars by aphasic subjects. *Journal of Communication Disorders, 23,* 383–400.

Coffey, P. (1999). *The ethnographic self.* London: Sage.

Cohen, J. (1960). A coefficient of agreement for nominal scales. *Educational and Psychological Measurements, 20,* 37–46.

Cohen, J. (1992). A power primer. *Psychological Bulletin, 112,* 155–159.

Coke-Pepsi slugfest. (1976, July 26). *Time.* pp. 64–65.

Coker, D. A., & Burgoon, J. K. (1987). The nature of conversational involvement and nonverbal encoding patterns. *Human Communication Research, 13,* 463–494.

Collier, A. (1994). *Critical realism: An introduction to Roy Bhaskar's philosophy.* London: Verso.

Collier, D., Seawright, J., & Brady, H. E. (2004). Qualitative versus quantitative: What might this distinction mean? In C. C. Ragin, J. Nagel, & P. White, *Workshop on scientific foundations of qualitative research* (pp. 70–76). Washington, DC: National Science Foundation. Available: www.nsf.gov/pubs/2004/nsf04219/start.htm

Cooper, J., & Cooper, G. (2002). Subliminal motivation: A story revisited. *Journal of Applied Social Psychology, 32,* 2211–2227.

Copi, I. M. (1968). *Introduction to logic* (3rd ed.). New York: Macmillan.

Copi, I. M. (1986). *Introduction to logic* (7th ed.). New York: Macmillan.

Courtenay, B. C., & Weidemann, C. (1985). The effects of a don't know response on Palmore's Facts on Aging quizzes. *The Gerontologist, 25,* 177–181.

Cousins, N. (1957, October 5). Smudging the subconscious. *Saturday Review,* p. 20.

Cozby, P. C. (1989). *Methods in behavioral research* (4th ed.). Mountain View, CA: Mayfield.

Cragan, J. F., & Shields, D. C. (1981). *Applied communication research: A dramatistic approach.* Prospect Heights, IL: Waveland Press.

Craig, H. (1952). Woodrow Wilson as an orator. *Quarterly Journal of Speech, 38,* 145–148.

Cronbach, L. J. (1970). *Essentials of psychological testing* (3rd ed.). New York: Harper and Row.

Crowne, D. P., & Marlowe, D. (1960). A new scale of social desirability independent of psychopathology. *Journal of Consulting Psychology, 24,* 349–354.

Czaja, R., & Blair, J. (1996). *Designing surveys: A guide to decisions and procedures.* Thousand Oaks, CA: Pine Forge Press.

Dahlstrom, W. G., Welsh, G. S., & Dahlstrom, L. E. (Eds.). (1972). *An MMPI handbook* (Vol. 1). Minneapolis: University of Minnesota Press.

Daly, J., Chesebro, J., Duncan, R., Hayes, J., Levin, S., Long, L., Palmerton, P., & White-Newman, J. B. (1995, August). *Final definition: Defining the field of communication.* Summer conference on defining the field of communication. Annandale, VA: Association for Communication Administration. Available: National Communication Association (2005, February 10), *1995 definition of communication studies.* Retrieved February 10, 2005, from www.natcom.org/nca/Template2.asp?bid=408

Danowski, J. A. (1982). A network-based content analysis methodology for computer mediated communication: An illustration with a computer bulletin board. In M. Burgoon (Ed.), *Communication yearbook, 6* (pp. 904–925). New Brunswick, NJ: Transaction.

Danowski, J., Barnett, G. A., & Friedland, M. (1986). Interorganizational network position, media coverage, and public's images. In M. L. McLaughlin (Ed.), *Communication yearbook, 10* (pp. 808–830). Newbury Park, CA: Sage.

Danowski, J. A., & Choi, J. (1998). Convergence in the information industries: Telecommunications,

broadcasting, and data processing—1981–1996. In H. Sawhney & G. A. Barnett (Eds.), *Progress in communication science, volume XV* (pp. 125–150). Stamford, CT: Ablex.

Danzig, F. (1962, September 17). Subliminal advertising: Today it's just historic flashback for researcher Vicary. *Advertising Age,* pp. 72–73.

Darroch, R. K., & Steiner, I. D. (1970). Role playing: An alternative to laboratory research? *Journal of Personality, 38,* 302–311.

David, M., Edwards, R., & Alldred, P. (2001). Children and school-based research: "Informed consent" or "educated consent"? *British Educational Research Journal, 27,* 347–365.

Dean, G. (1992). The bottom line: Effect size. In B. L. Beyerstein & D. F. Beyerstein (Eds.), *The write stuff: Evaluations of graphology—the study of handwriting analysis* (pp. 269–341). Amherst, NY: Prometheus Books.

DeCoster, J. (2005, June 29). *Meta-analysis notes.* Amsterdam: Department of Social Psychology, Free University Amsterdam, the Netherlands. Retrieved November 28, 2005, from http://artemis.austincollege.edu/acad/psych/lbrown/meta.pdf

Deemer, S. A., & Minke, K. M. (1999). An investigation of the factor structure of the teacher efficacy scale. *Journal of Educational Research, 93,* 3–10.

de Finetti, B. (1981). Funzione caratteristica di un fenomeno aleatorio. In *Scritti [1926–1930].* Padova, Italy: Cedam. (Reprinted from *Memorie della Reale Accademia dei Lincei, 6,* 86–133, 1930)

DeGroot, T., & Motowidlo, S. J. (1999). Why visual and vocal interview cues can affect interviewers' judgments and predict job performance. *Journal of Applied Psychology, 84,* 986–993.

Delia, J. G., & Grossberg, L. (1977). Interpretation and evidence. *Western Journal of Speech Communication, 41,* 32–42.

DeLong, B., & Lang, K. (1992). Are all economic hypotheses false? *Journal of Political Economy, 100,* 1257–1272.

Denzin, N. K. (1983). Interpretive interactionism. In G. Morgan (Ed.), *Beyond method: Strategies for social research.* Newbury Park, CA: Sage.

Denzin, N. (1997). *Interpretive ethnography: Ethnographic practices for the 21st century.* London: Sage.

Denzin, N. K., & Lincoln, Y. S. (2000). The policies and practices of interpretation. In N. K. Denzin &

Y. S. Lincoln (Eds.), *Handbook of qualitative research* (2nd ed., pp. 897–992). Thousand Oaks, CA: Sage.

DeStephen, R. S. (1983). Group interaction differences between high and low consensus groups. *Western Journal of Speech Communication, 47,* 340–363.

Deutsch, M., & Krauss, R. (1965). *Theories in social psychology.* New York: Basic Books.

DeVito, J. A. (1986). *The communication handbook: A dictionary.* New York: Harper and Row.

DeVito, J. A. (2007). *The interpersonal communication book* (11th ed.). Boston: Pearson/Allyn and Bacon.

Dewey, J. (1910). Science as subject-matter as a method. *Science, 31,* 121–127.

Dey, I. (1999). *Grounding grounded theory: Guidelines for qualitative inquiry.* San Diego, CA: Academic Press.

Dickinson, G. (2005). Selling democracy: Consumer culture and citizenship in the wake of September 11. *Southern Communication Journal, 70,* 271–284.

Dickson, P., & Goulden, J. C. (1983). *There are alligators in our sewers and other American credos.* New York: Delacorte Press.

Diener, E., & Crandall, R. (1978). *Ethics in social and behavioral research.* Chicago: University of Chicago Press.

Dingley, K. (2002, November). *Using conversational analysis to ascertain whether commercially available synchronous messengers can support real world ad hoc interactions.* Paper presented at the Conference on Computer Supported Cooperative Work, New Orleans, LA. Retrieved March 12, 2006, from University of Oregon website: www.cs.uoregon.edu/research/wearables/cscw2002ws/papers/Dingley.pdf

Dingwall, R., Murphy, E., Watson, P., Greatbatch, D., & Parker, S. (1998). Catching gold-fish: Quality in qualitative research. *Journal of Health Services Research & Policy, 3,* 167–172.

Doerfel, M. L., & Barnett, G. A. (1999). A semantic network analysis of the international communication association. *Human Communication Research, 25,* 589–603.

Doerfel, M. L., & Connaughton, S. L. (2005, May). *The semantic structure of competition: Election year winners and losers in U.S. televised presidential debates, 1960–2004.*

Paper presented at the International Communication Association Convention, New York.

Doerfel, M. L., & Taylor, M. (2004). Network dynamics of inter organizational cooperation: The Croatian Civil Society movement. *Communication Monographs, 71,* 373–394.

Dolin, D. (1995). An alternate form of teacher affinity-seeking measurement. *Communication Research Reports, 12,* 220–226.

Dominick, J. R., & Rauch, G. (1972). The image of women in network TV commercials. *Journal of Broadcasting, 16,* 259–265.

Dorsey, L. K. (2003). African American female small group communication: An application of group-as-a-whole theory. *Electronic Journal of Communication, 13*(2–3). Retrieved March 10, 2006, from www.cios.org/getfile/01325_EJC

Dougherty, D. S., & Smythe, M. J. (2004). Sensemaking, organization culture, and sexual harassment. *Journal of Applied Communication Research, 32,* 293–317.

Dowling, R. E., & Ginder, G. A. (1995). An ethical appraisal of Ronald Reagan's justification for the invasion of Grenada. In E. Schiappa (Ed.), *Warranting assent: Case studies in argument evaluation* (pp. 103–124). Albany, NY: SUNY Press.

Doxtader, E. (2003). Reconciliation—a rhetorical concept/ion. *Quarterly Journal of Speech, 89,* 267–292.

Draper, D., Hodges, J. S., Mallows, C. L., & Pregibon, D. (1993). Exchangeability and data analysis. *Journal of the Royal Statistical Society* (Series A), *156,* 9–37.

Drenth, J. D. (2003). Growing anti-intellectualism in Europe; a menace to science. *Studia Psychologica, 45,* 5–13.

Druckman, D., & Swets, J. A. (Eds.). (1988). *Enhancing human performance: Issues, theories, and techniques* (pp. 138–149). Washington DC: National Academy Press.

Drumheller, K. (2005). Millennial dogma: A fantasy theme analysis of the millennial generation's uses and gratifications of religious content media. *Journal of Communication & Religion, 28,* 47–70.

Drummond, H. C. (1951, September 2). Spoils system. *New York Times,* sec. 6, p. 4.

Duffy, M. E. (2003). Web of hate: A fantasy theme analysis of the rhetorical vision of hate groups online. *Journal of Communication Inquiry, 27,* 291–312.

Duncan, O. D., & Lieberson, S. (1959). Ethnic segregation and assimilation. *American Journal of Sociology, 64,* 364–374.

Duncombe, J., & Jessop, J. (2002). "Doing rapport" and the ethics of "faking friendship." In M. Mauthner, M. Birch, J. Jessop, & T. Miller (Eds.), *Ethics in qualitative research* (pp. 107–122). London: Sage.

Dyer, K. (2006a). *Making use of autoethnography in the classroom.* Retrieved June 5, 2006, from Humboldt State University website: www.humboldt.edu/~kd3/Makinguse.htm

Dyer, K. (2006b). *Toward a definition.* Retrieved June 5, 2006, from Humboldt State University website: www.humboldt.edu/~kd3/Toward.htm.

Edwards, R., & Mauthner, M. (2002). Ethics and feminist research: Theory and practice. In M. Mauthner, M. Birch, J. Jessop, & T. Miller (Eds.), *Ethics in qualitative research* (pp. 14–31). London: Sage.

Eggers, S. J. (2000). Spirituality in mid-life and late adulthood. Doctoral dissertation, The University of Memphis. *Dissertation Abstracts International,* 61 (3A), 878.

Eisenberg, E. M., & Goodall, H. L. (2004). *Organizational communication: Balancing creativity and restraint* (4th ed.). Boston: Bedford/St. Martin's.

Ellingson, L. L. (2003). Interdisciplinary health care teamwork in the clinic backstage. *Journal of Applied Communication Research, 31,* 93–117.

Ellis, C., & Bochner, A. (2000). Autoethnography, personal narrative, reflexivity: Researcher as subject. In N. K. Denzin & Y. S. Lincoln (Eds.), *Handbook of qualitative research* (2nd ed., pp. 733–768). Thousand Oaks, CA: Sage.

Ellis, D. G. (1979). Relational control in two group systems. *Communication Monographs, 46,* 153–166.

Elms, A. C., & Janis, I. L. (1965). Counter-norm attitudes induced by consonant vs. dissonant conditions of role-playing. *Journal of Experimental Research in Personality, 1,* 50–60.

Elsaesser, T. (1972). Tales of sound and fury: Observations on the family melodrama. *Monogram, 4,* 1–15.

Emerson, R., Ed. (1983). *Contemporary field research.* Boston: Little, Brown.

Emerson, S., & Furman, J. (1991, November 18). The conspiracy that wasn't. *The New Republic,* pp. 12–15.

Emmert, P. (1989). Philosophy of measurement. In P. Emmert & L. L. Barker (Eds.), *Measurement of communication behavior* (pp. 87–116). New York: Longman.

Emmert, P., & Barker, L. L. (Eds.). (1989). *Measurement of communication behavior.* New York: Longman.

English, H. B., & English, A. C. (1958). *A comprehensive dictionary of psychological and psychoanalytical terms.* New York: McKay.

Erickson, B. H., & Nosanchuck, T. A. (1977). *Understanding data.* Toronto: McGraw-Hill Ryerson.

Errata note. (1995). *Western Journal of Communication, 59,* 355–356.

Eysenck, H. J., & Eaves, L. J. (1980). *The causes and effects of smoking.* London: Maurice Temple Smith.

Fagley, N. S., & McKinney, I. J. (1983). Reviewer bias for statistically significant results: A reexamination. *Journal of Counseling Psychology, 30,* 298–300.

Fearless predictions: The content world, 2005. (1999, July/August). *Brill's Content.*

Feigl, H. (1945). Operationism and scientific method. *Psychological Review, 52,* 250–259.

Feller, W. (1968). *An introduction to probability theory and its applications* (2nd ed., Vol. 1). New York: Wiley.

Feller, W. (1971). *An introduction to probability theory and its applications* (3rd ed., Vol. 2). New York: Wiley.

Ferguson, M. (1983). *Forever feminine: Women's magazines and the cult of femininity.* London: Heinemann.

Fern, E. F. (1983). Focus groups: A review of some contradictory evidence, implications, and suggestions for future researchers. *Advances in Consumer Research, 10,* 121–126.

Festinger, L., & Carlsmith, J. M. (1959). Cognitive consequences of forced compliance. *Journal of Abnormal and Social Psychology, 58,* 203–210.

Festinger, L., Rieken, H. W., & Schachter, S. (1956). *When prophecy fails.* New York: Harper and Row.

Fine, M. (1994). Dis-tance and other stances: Negotiations of power inside feminist research. In A. Gitlin

(Ed.), *Power and methods* (pp. 13–55). London: Routledge.

Fisher, B. A. (1970). Decision emergence: Phases in group decision-making. *Speech Monographs, 37,* 53–66.

Fisher, B. A., & Drexel, G. L. (1983). A cyclical model of developing relationships: A study of relational control interaction. *Communication Monographs, 50,* 66–78.

Fisher, B. A., Glover, T. W., & Ellis, D. G. (1977). The nature of complex communication systems. *Communication Monographs, 44,* 231–240.

Fisher, B. A., & Hawes, L. C. (1971). An interact system model: Generating a grounded theory of small groups. *Quarterly Journal of Speech, 57,* 444–453.

Fisher, C. B. (2003). *Decoding the ethics code: A practical guide for psychologists.* Thousand Oaks, CA: Sage.

Fisher, W. R. (1984). Narration as a human communication paradigm: The case of public moral argument. *Communication Monographs, 51,* 1–22.

Fisher, W. R. (1987). *Human communication as narration: Toward a philosophy of reason, value, and action.* Columbia: University of South Carolina Press.

Fleiss, J. L. (1971). Measuring nominal scale agreement among many raters. *Psychological Bulletin, 76,* 378–382.

Fleiss, J. L. (1981). *Statistical methods for rates and proportions.* New York: Wiley.

Flewelling, R. I., Praschell, M. J., & Ringwalt, C. (2004). The epidemiology of underage drinking in the United States: An overview. In R. J. Bonnie & M. E. O'Connell (Eds.), *Reducing underage drinking: A collective responsibility* (pp. 319–350). Washington, DC: National Academy Press.

Folger, J. P., & Poole, M. S. (1982). Relational coding schemes: The question of validity. In M. Burgoon (Ed.), *Communication yearbook 5.* New Brunswick, NJ: Transaction.

Follman, F., Lucoff, M., Small, L., & Power, F. (1974). *Kinds of keys of student rating of faculty effectiveness.* Paper presented at the Annual Meeting of the American Educational Research Association, Chicago. (ERIC Document Reproduction Service No. ED093985).

Foss, S. K., & Griffin, C. L. (1995). Beyond persuasion: A proposal for an invitational rhetoric. *Communication Monographs, 62,* 2–18

Fox, D. J. (1969). *The research process in education.* New York: Holt, Rinehart and Winston.

Franck, A. L., Jackson, R. A., Pimentel, J. T., & Greenwood, G. S. (2003). School-age children's perceptions of a person who stutters. *Journal of Fluency Disorders, 28,* 1–15.

Frankfort-Nachmias, C., & Leon-Guerrero, A. (2000). *Social statistics for a diverse society* (2nd ed.). Thousand Oaks, CA: Pine Forge Press.

Frankfort-Nachmias, C., & Nachmias, D. (1996). *Research methods in the social sciences* (5th ed.). New York: St. Martin's Press.

Freedman, J. L. (1969). Role playing: Psychology by consensus. *Journal of Personality and Social Psychology, 13,* 107–114.

Freeman, C. A., & Barnett, G. A. (1994). An alternative approach to using interpretative [*sic*] theory to examine corporate messages and organizational culture. In L. Thayer & G. A. Barnett (Eds.), *Organization communication: Emerging perspectives IV* (pp. 60–73). Norwood, NJ: Ablex.

Freeman, D. (1983). *Margaret Mead and Samoa: The making and unmaking of an anthropological myth.* Cambridge, MA: Harvard University Press.

Freeman, D. (1999). *The fateful hoaxing of Margaret Mead: A historical analysis of her Samoan research.* Cambridge, MA: Westview Press.

Frey, L. R., Botan, C. H., & Kreps, G. L. (2000). *Investigating communication: An introduction to research methods* (2nd ed.). Needham Heights, MA: Allyn and Bacon.

Friedman, H. (1968). Magnitude of experimental effect and a table for its rapid estimation. *Psychological Bulletin, 70,* 245–251.

Frith, K., Shaw, P., & Cheng, H. (2005). The construction of beauty: A cross-cultural analysis of women's magazine advertising. *Journal of Communication, 55,* 56–70.

Frobish, T. S. (2000). Altar rhetoric and online performance: Scientology, ethos, and the World Wide Web. *American Communication Journal, 4*(1). Retrieved April 5, 2006, from http://acjournal.org/holdings/vol4/iss1/articles/frobish.htm

Frymier, A. B., & Wanzer, M. B. (2003). Examining differences in perceptions of students' communication with professors: A comparison of students with and without disabilities. *Communication Quarterly, 51,* 174–191.

Funk & Wagnalls standard desk dictionary. (1983). 2 vols. New York: Funk & Wagnalls.

Gallup, G., & Rae, S. F. (1940). *The pulse of democracy.* New York: Simon and Schuster.

Gannon, K. M., & Ostrom, T. M. (1996). How meaning is given to rating scales: The effects of response language on category activation. *Journal of Experimental Social Psychology, 32,* 337–360.

Gardner, R. J., & Zelevansky, L. (1975). The ten commandments for library customers. *Special Libraries, 66,* 326.

Garrett, D., & Hodkinson, P. (1999). Can there be criteria for selecting research criteria? A hermeneutical analysis of an inescapable dilemma. *Qualitative Inquiry, 4,* 515–539.

Geiger, W., Bruning, J., & Harwood, J. (2001). Talk about TV: Television viewers' interpersonal communication about programming. *Communication Reports, 14,* 49–57.

Gerbner, G. (1971). Violence in television drama: Trends and symbolic functions. In G. A. Comstock and E. A. Rubinstein (Eds.), *Television and social behavior: Vol. I, Media content and control.* Washington, DC: G.P.O.

Gerbner, G., Gross, L., Morgan, M., & Signorielli, N. (1980). The "mainstreaming" of America: Violence profile no. 11. *Journal of Communication, 30*(3), 10–29.

German, K. M. (1995). Invoking the glorious war: Framing the Persian Gulf conflict through directive language. *Southern Communication Journal, 60,* 292–302.

Germond, J., & Witcover, J. (1989). *Whose broad stripes and bright stars?* New York: Time-Warner Books.

Gibaldi, J. (1999). *MLA handbook for writers of research papers* (5th ed.) New York: Modern Language Association of America.

Giere, R. N. (1979). *Understanding scientific reasoning.* New York: Holt, Rinehart and Winston.

Gilbert, K. R. (1988). Interactive grief and coping in the marital dyad following the fetal or infant death of their child. (Doctoral dissertation, Purdue University, West Lafayette, IN, 1987). *Dissertation Abstracts International, 49*(04A), 962.

Gilbert, K. R. (2001). Collateral damage? Indirect exposure of staff members to the emotions of qualitative research. In K. R. Gilbert (Ed.), *The emotional nature of qualitative research* (pp. 147–161). Boca Raton, FL: CRC Press.

Gilbert, K. R., & Smart, L. S. (1992). *Coping with infant or fetal loss: The couple's healing process.* New York: Brunner/Mazel.

Gilljam, M., & Granberg, D. (1993). Should we take don't know for an answer? *Public Opinion Quarterly, 57,* 348–357.

Ginsburg, G. P. (1979). The effective use of role-playing in social psychological research. In G. P. Ginsburg (Ed.), *Emerging strategies in social psychological research* (pp. 4–16). London: Wiley.

Givens, G. H., Smith, D. D., & Tweedie, R. L. (1997). Publication bias in meta-analysis: A Bayesian data-augmentation approach to account for issues exemplified in the passive smoking debate. *Statistical Science, 12,* 221–250.

Glaser, B. G. (1992). *Basics of grounded theory analysis: Emergence vs forcing.* Mill Valley, CA: Sociology Press.

Glaser, B. G., & Strauss, A. L. (1967). *The discovery of grounded theory.* Chicago: Aldine.

Glass, G. V (1976). Primary, secondary, and meta-analysis of research. *Educational Researcher, 5,* 3–8.

Glass, G. V, & Hopkins, K. D. (1984). *Statistical methods in education and psychology* (2nd ed.). Englewood Cliffs, NJ: Prentice-Hall.

Glass, G. V, Peckham, P. D., & Sanders, J. R. (1972). Consequence of failure to meet assumption underlying the fixed effects analysis of variance and covariance. *Review of Educational Research, 42,* 237–288.

Gleser, L. J., & Olkin, I. (1996). Models for estimating the number of unpublished studies. *Statistical Medicine, 15,* 2493–2507.

Glesne, C., & Pleshkin, A. (1992). *Becoming qualitative researchers: An introduction.* New York: Longman.

Goldschmidt, M. M. (2004). Good person stories: The favor narrative as a self-presentation strategy. *Qualitative Research Reports in Communication, 5,* 28–33.

Goldstein, R. (1981). On deceptive rejoinders about deceptive research: A reply to Baron. *IRB: A Review of Human Subjects Research, 3*(8), 5–6.

Gonzales, A., Houston, M., & Chen, V. (2004). Introduction. In A. Gonzales, M., Houston, & V. Chen (Eds.), *Our voices: Essays on culture, ethnicity, and communication* (pp. 1–13). Los Angeles: Roxbury.

Gordon, W. I., & Infante, D. A. (1991). Test of a communication model of organizational commitment. *Communication Quarterly, 39,* 144–155.

Görg, H., & Strobl, E. (2001). Multinational companies and productivity spillovers: A meta-analysis with a test for publication bias. *Economic Journal, 111,* 723–739.

Gouran, D. S., Hirokawa, R. Y., Julian, K. M., & Leatham, G. B. (1993). The evolution and current status of the functional perspective on communication in decision-making and problem-solving groups. *Communication Yearbook, 16* (pp. 573–600). Newbury Park, CA: Sage.

Graham, W. K., & Dillon, P. C. (1974). Creative supergroups: Group performance as a function of individual performance on brainstorming tasks. *Journal of Social Psychology, 93,* 101–105.

Gravlee, G. J. (1981). Reporting proceedings and debates in the British Commons. *Central States Speech Journal, 32,* 85–99.

Greenberg, J., & Folger, R. (1988). *Controversial issues in social research methods.* New York: Springer-Verlag.

Greenwald, A. G. (1992). New look 3: Unconscious cognition reclaimed. *American Psychologist, 47,* 766–779.

Greenwald, A. G., Spangenberg, E. R., Pratkanis, A. R., & Eskenazi, J. (1991). Double-blind tests of subliminal self-help audio tapes. *Psychological Science, 2,* 119–122.

Greitemeyer, T. (2005). Receptivity to sexual offers as a function of sex, socioeconomic status, physical attractiveness, and intimacy of the offer. *Personal Relationships, 12,* 373–386.

Griffin, E. (2000). *A first look at communication theory* (4th ed.). Boston: McGraw-Hill.

Gubrium, J. F., & Holstein, J. A. (2000). Analyzing interpretive practice. In N. K. Denzin & Y. S. Lincoln (Eds.), *Handbook of qualitative research* (pp. 487–508). Thousand Oaks, CA: Sage.

Gudykunst, W. B., & Nishida, T. (1989). Theoretical perspectives for studying intercultural communication. In M. K. Asante & W. B. Gudykunst (Eds.), *Handbook of international and intercultural communication* (pp. 17–46). Newbury Park, CA: Sage.

Guttman, L. (1944). A basis for scaling quantitative data. *American Sociological Review, 9,* 139–150.

Hadaway, C. K., Marler, P. L., & Chaves, M. (1993). What the polls don't show: A closer look at U.S. church attendance. *American Sociological Review, 55,* 243–254.

Haiman, F. (1949). An experimental study of the effects of ethos in public speaking. *Speech Monographs, 16,* 190–202.

Hale, J. L., Boster, F. J., & Mongeau, P. A. (1991). The validity of choice dilemma response scales. *Communication Reports, 4,* 30–34.

Hall, B. (2005). *Methods: Fieldnotes.* Retrieved November 5, 2005, from University of Pennsylvania website: www.sas.upenn.edu/anthro/CPIA/METHODS/ Fieldnotes.html

Hall, S., & Jefferson, T. (1975). *Resistance through rituals: Youth subcultures in post-war Berlin.* London: Hutchinson.

Halualani, R. T., Chitgopekar, A. S., Morrison, J. H. T. A., & Dodge, P. S-W. (2004). Diverse in name only? Intercultural interaction at a multicultural university. *Journal of Communication, 54,* 270–286.

Hancock, B. (2002). *Trent Focus for research and development in primary health care: An introduction to qualitative research* (Updated ed.). Nottingham, England: Trent Focus. Available: www.trentfocus.org.uk/Resources/ Qualitative%20Data%20Analysis.pdf

Hansen, C. H., & Hansen, R. D. (1990). The influence of sex and violence on the appeal of rock music videos. *Communication Research, 17,* 212–234.

Harrington, N. G., Lane, D. R., Donohew, L., Zimmerman, R. S., Norling, G. R., An, J-H., Cheah, W. H., McCLure, L., Buckinghan, T., Garofalo, E., & Bevins, C. C. (2003). Persuasive strategies for effective anti-drug messages. *Communication Monographs, 70,* 16–38.

Hart, R. P. (1977). *The political pulpit.* West Lafayette, IN: Purdue University Press.

Harter, J. K. (1997). The psychometric utility of the midpoint on a Likert scale. Doctoral dissertation, University of Nebraska, Lincoln. *Dissertation Abstracts International, 58* (4-A), 1198.

Harwell, M. (1995). An empirical study of the Hedges (1982) homogenity test. *Resources in Education.* (ERIC Document Reproduction Service No. ED392822)

Hawes, L. (1972). Development and application of an interview coding system. *Central States Speech Journal, 23,* 92–99.

Hayes, J. J., & Tathum, C. B. (1989). *Focus group interviews: A reader* (2nd ed.). Chicago: American Marketing Association.

Heap, M. (1989). Neurolinguistic programming: What is the evidence? In D. Waxman, D. Pederson, I. Wilkie, & P. Mellett (Eds.), *Hypnosis: The fourth European congress at Oxford* (pp. 118–124). London: Whurr.

Heath, A. C. (1990). Persist or quit? Testing for a genetic contribution to smoking persistence. *ACTA Geneticae Medicae et Gemellologiae (Roma), 39,* 447–458.

Helmer, J. (1993). Storytelling in the creation and maintenance of organizational tension and stratification. *Southern Communication Journal, 59,* 34–44.

Hensley, C. W. (1975). Rhetorical vision and the persuasion of a historical movement: The Disciples of Christ in nineteenth century American culture. *Quarterly Journal of Speech, 61,* 250–264.

Herring, S. C. (1996). Linguistic and critical analysis of computer-mediated communication: Some ethical and scholarly considerations. *The Information Society, 12,* 153–168.

Herson, M., & Barlow, D. H. (1976). *Single case experimental designs: Strategies for studying behavior change.* New York: Pergamon.

Hill, Forbes I. (1972). Conventional wisdom—traditional form: The President's message of November 3, 1969. *Quarterly Journal of Speech, 58,* 373–386.

Hines, T. (1990). *Pseudoscience and the paranormal.* Buffalo, NY: Prometheus Books.

Hirokawa, R. Y. (1982). Group communication and problem-solving effectiveness I: A critical review of inconsistent findings. *Communication Quarterly, 30*(2), 134–141.

Hocking, J. E., Stacks, D. W., & McDermott, S. T. (2003). *Communication research* (3rd ed.). Boston: Allyn and Bacon.

Hogan, J. (2006). Letters to the editor in the "war on terror": A cross-national study. *Journal of Mass Communication & Society, 9,* 63–83.

Holt, N. L. (2003). Representation, legitimation, and autoethnography: An autoethnographic writing story. *International Journal of Qualitative Methods, 2*(1). Retrieved May 6, 2006, from www.ualberta.ca/~iiqm/backissues/2_1final/html/holt.html

Homans, G. C. (1961). *Social behavior: Its elementary forms.* New York: Harcourt, Brace and World.

Honorton, C., & Ferrari, D. C. (1989). "Future telling": A meta-analysis of forced-choice precognition experiments, 1935–1987. *Journal of Parapsychology, 53,* 281–308.

Hoogestraat, W. E. (1960). Memory: The lost canon? *Quarterly Journal of Speech, 46,* 141–147.

Hoover, K. (1979). *The elements of social scientific thinking* (2nd ed.). New York: St. Martin's Press.

Hopkins, K. D., & Glass, G. V (1978). *Basic statistics for the behavioral sciences.* Englewood Cliffs, NJ: Prentice-Hall.

Hornsby-Smith, M. (1993). Gaining access. In N. Gilbert (Ed.), *Researching social life.* London: Sage.

How to ask the questions you want. (1995–2006). *Survey tool kit.* Pearson Education, Inc. Retrieved April 10, 2006, from http://survey.pearsonncs.com/planning/wording.htm

Hsu, T. C., & Feldt, L. S. (1969). The effect of limitations on the number of criterion score values on the significance of the F test. *American Educational Research Journal, 6,* 515–527.

Huesmann, L. (1982). Violence and aggression. In D. Pearl, L. Bouthilet, & J. Lazar (Eds.), *Television and behavior: Ten years of scientific progress and implications for the eighties.* Washington, DC: G.P.O.

Huff, D. (1954). *How to lie with statistics.* New York: Norton.

Humphreys, L. (1970). *Tearoom trade: Impersonal sex in public places* (Enlarged ed.). Chicago: Aldine.

Hyman, R. (1985). The ganzfeld psi experiment: A critical appraisal. *Journal of Parapsychology, 49,* 3–49.

Hymes, D. (1972). Models of the interaction of language and social life. In J. Gumperz & D. Hymes (Eds.), *Directions in sociolinguistics: The ethnography of communication* (pp. 35–71). New York: Holt, Rinehart and Winston.

Hymes, D. (1974). *Foundations in sociolinguistics: An ethnographic approach.* Philadelphia: University of Pennsylvania Press.

Illinois State Board of Education. (2005, October 10). *Illinois Learning Standards for Science.* Retrieved October 10, 2005, from www.isbe.net/ils/science/standards.htm

International Statistical Institute. (1985, August). *Declaration of professional ethics.* Retrieved January 10, 2006, from http://isi.cbs.nl/ethics.htm

Irizarry, C. A. (2004). Face and the female professional: A thematic analysis of face-threatening communication in the workplace. *Qualitative Research Reports in Communication, 5,* 15–21.

Isaac, S., & Michael, W. B. (Eds.). (1981). *Handbook in research and evaluation: For education and the behavioral sciences* (2nd ed.). San Diego, CA: EdITS.

Iyengar, S., & Greenhouse, J. (1988). Selection models and the file drawer problem (with discussion). *Statistical Science, 3,* 109–135.

Jablin, F. M., Seibold, D. R., & Sorenson, R. (1977). Potential inhibitory effects of group participation on brainstorming performance. *Central States Speech Journal, 28,* 113–121.

Jackson, D. N. (1973). *The IPA.* San Francisco, CA: Psychological Research Organization.

Jacobs, S., & Jackson, S. (1979a, November). *Collaborative aspects of natural argument.* Paper presented at the Speech Communication Association Convention, San Antonio, TX.

Jacobs, S., & Jackson, S. (1979b, November). *Routes for the expansion of influence attempts in conversation.* Paper presented at the Speech Communication Association Convention, San Antonio, TX.

Jang, H., & Barnett, G. A. (1995). Cultural differences in organizational communication: A semantic network analysis. *Bulletin de Methodologie Sociologique, 44,* 31–59.

Johanson, G. A., & Osborn, C. J. (2000). *Acquiescence as differential person functioning.* Paper presented at the Annual Meeting of the American Education Research Association, New Orleans, LA. (ERIC Document Reproduction Service No. ED441022).

Johnson, I. D., O'Malley, P. M., & Bachman, J. G. (2002). *National survey results on drug use from the Monitoring the Future study.* Rockville, MD: U.S. Department of Health and Human Services, National Institute on Drug Abuse.

Jones, R. (1973). The nature of research. In R. H. Jones (Ed.), *Methods and techniques of educational research.* Danville, IL: Interstate.

Judd, C. M., Smith, E. R., & Kidder, L. H. (1991). *Research methods in social relations* (6th ed.). Fort Worth, TX: Holt, Rinehart and Winston.

Kaplan, A. (1964). *The conduct of inquiry: Methodology for behavioral science.* Scranton, PA: Chandler.

Kaplan, K. J. (1972). On the ambivalence-indifference problem in attitude theory and measurement: A suggested modification of the semantic differential technique. *Psychological Bulletin, 77,* 361–372.

Katz, J. (1997). Ethnography's warrants. *Sociological Methods & Research, 25,* 391–423.

Katz, W. A. (1982). *Introduction to reference work* (Vol. 1). New York: McGraw-Hill.

Katzmarek, J. M. (2001). Teachers learning collaboratively about student-centered discussions of literature: A discourse analysis. Doctoral dissertation, University of Wisconsin, Madison. *Dissertation Abstracts International, 62* (07A), 2364.

Kazmier, L. J. (1988). *Business statistics* (2nd ed.). New York: McGraw-Hill.

Kelman, H. C. (1967). The human use of human subjects: The problem of deception in social psychological experiments. *Psychological Bulletin, 67,* 1–11.

Kerlinger, F. N. (1986). *Foundations of behavioral research* (3rd ed.). New York: Holt, Rinehart and Winston.

Kerlinger, F. N., & Lee, H. B. (2000). *Foundations of behavioral research* (4th ed.). Fort Worth, TX: Harcourt College Publishers.

Kidwell, M., & Zimmerman, D. (2006). "Observability" in the interactions of very young children. *Communication Monographs, 73,* 1–28.

Killworth, P. D., & Bernard, H. R. (1979a). Informant accuracy in social network data. *Human Organization, 35,* 269–286.

Killworth, P. D., & Bernard, H. R. (1979b). Informant accuracy in social network data III: A comparison of triadic structure in behavioral and cognitive data. *Social Networks, 2,* 19–46.

King, A. (1999a). Against structure: A critique of morphogenetic social theory. *Sociological Review, 47,* 199–227.

King, A. (1999b). The impossibility of naturalism: The antimonies of Bhaskar's realism. *Journal for the Theory of Social Behaviour, 29,* 267–288.

Kinsella, W. J. (2004). Nuclear discourse and nuclear institutions: A theoretical framework and two empirical examples. *Qualitative Research Reports in Communication, 5,* 8–14.

Kiousis, S. (2004). Explicating media salience: A factor analysis of *New York Times* issues coverage during the 2000 U.S. presidential election. *Journal of Communication, 54,* 71–87.

Kirby, A., Gebski, V., & Keech, A. C. (2002). Determining the sample size in a clinical trial. *Medical Journal of Australia, 177,* 256–257.

Kirk, R. E. (1982). *Experimental design: Procedures for the behavioral sciences* (2nd ed.). Belmont, CA: Brooks/Cole.

Klein, J. F., & Hood, S. B. (2004). The impact of stuttering on employment opportunities and job performance. *Journal of Fluency Disorders, 29,* 255–273.

Kline, S. L., & Stafford, L. (2004). A comparison of interaction rules and interaction frequency in relationship to marital quality. *Communication Reports, 17,* 11–26.

Klofas, J. M., & Cutshall, C. R. (1985). The social archeology of a juvenile facility: Unobtrusive methods in the study of institutional culture. *Qualitative Sociology, 8,* 368–382.

Koenker, R. (1961). *Simplified statistics.* Bloomington, IL: McKnight & McKnight.

Kotiaho, J. S., & Tomkins, J. L. (2002). Meta-analysis, can it ever fail? *Oikos, 96,* 551–553.

Kovach, B. (1999, September). Report from the ombudsman. *Brill's Content,* pp. 20–21.

Kramer, M. W. (2004). Toward a communication theory of group dialectics: An ethnographic study of a community theatre group. *Communication Monographs, 71,* 311–332.

Kramer, M. W. (2005). Communication in a fund-raising marathon group. *Journal of Communication, 55,* 257–276.

Krantz, D. C. (1979). Naturalistic study of social influence on meal size among moderately obese and nonobese subjects. *Psychosomatic Medicine, 41,* 19–27.

Kratochwill, T. R. (Ed.). (1978). *Single subject research: Strategies for evaluative change.* New York: Academic Press.

Kraut, R. E., & Johnston, R. E. (1979). Social and emotional messages of smiling: An ethological approach. *Journal of Personality and Social Psychology, 37,* 1539–1553.

Krejcie, R. V., & Morgan, D. W. (1970). Determining sample size for research activities. *Educational and Psychological Measurement, 30,* 607–610.

Krippendorff, K. (1980). *Content analysis: An introduction to its methodology.* Beverly Hills, CA: Sage.

Krone, K. (2005). Trends in organizational communication research: Sustaining the discipline, sustaining ourselves. *Communication Studies, 56,* 95–105.

Kruglanski, A. W. (1973). Much ado about the "volunteer artifacts." *Journal of Personality and Social Psychology, 28,* 350.

Kuypers, J. A. (2000). Must we all be political activists? *American Communication Journal, 4*(1). Retrieved March 3, 2006, from http://acjournal.org/holdings/vol4/iss1/special/kuypers.htm

Kuzel, A., & Engel, J. (2001). Some pragmatic thought on evaluating qualitative health research. In J. Morse, J. Swanson, & A. Kuzel (Eds.), *The nature of qualitative evidence* (pp. 114–138). Thousand Oaks, CA: Sage.

Labov, W., & Fanshel, D. (1977). *Therapeutic discourse: Psychotherapy as conversation.* New York: Academic Press.

Lacey, A., & Luff, D. (2001). *Trent Focus for research and development in primary health care: An introduction to qualitative analysis.* Trent, UK: Trent Focus.

Lacy, S., Fico, F., & Simon, T. F. (1991). Fairness and balance in the prestige press. *Journalism Quarterly, 68,* 363–370.

Lafferty, B. A., & Goldsmith, R. E. (2004). How influential are corporate credibility and endorser attractiveness when innovators react to advertisements for a new high-technology product? *Corporate Reputation Review, 7*(1), 24–36.

LaFrance, M., & Ickes, W. (1981). Posture mirroring and interactional involvement: Sex and sex typing effects. *Journal of Nonverbal Behavior, 5,* 139–154.

Lambe, J. L., Kaplan, S. E., Cai, X., & Signorielli, N. (2004). Public perceptions of media performance at the beginning of the war on terrorism. *Communication Research Reports, 21,* 299–309.

Lamm, H., & Trommsdorf, G. (1973). Group versus individual performance on tasks requiring ideational proficiency (brainstorming): A review. *European Journal of Social Psychology, 3,* 361–388.

Lane, D. C. (2001). *Rerum cognoscere causas*: Part I— How do the ideas of system dynamics relate to traditional social theories and the voluntarism/determinism debate? *System Dynamics Review, 17*(2), 97–118.

La Pastina, A. C. (2004). Telenovela reception in rural Brazil: Gendered readings and sexual mores. *Critical Studies in Media Communication, 21,* 162–181.

Lauf, E. (2005). National diversity of major international journals in the field of communication. *Journal of Communication, 55,* 139–151.

Lawton, M. P., Moss, M., Hoffman, C., Kleban, M. H., Ruckdeschel, K., & Winter, L. (2001). Valuation of life: A concept and a scale. *Journal of Aging and Health, 13,* 3–31.

Lee, R. M. (1993). *Doing research on sensitive topics.* London: Sage.

Leedy, P. D. (1989). *Practical research: Planning and design* (4th ed.). New York: Macmillan.

Lemert, E. M. (1953). Some Indians who stutter. *Journal of Speech and Hearing Disorders, 18,* 168–174.

Lengua, L. J., Roosa, M. W., Schupak-Neuberg, E., Michaeles, M. L., Berg, C. N., & Weschler, L. F. (1992). Using focus groups to guide the development of a parenting program for difficult-to-reach, high risk families. *Family Relations, 41,* 163–168.

Leno, J. (1991). *Headlines III: Not the movie, still the book.* New York: Warner Books.

Levine, M. (1988). *Effective problem solving.* Englewood Cliffs, NJ: Prentice-Hall.

Levine, T. R., & Hullett, C. R. (2002). Eta squared, partial eta squared, and misreporting of effect size in communication research. *Human Communication Research, 28,* 612–625.

Levinson, S. C. (1983). *Pragmatics.* Cambridge, UK: Cambridge University Press.

Lewicki, P., Hill, T., & Czyzewska, M. (1992). Nonconscious acquisition of information. *American Psychologist, 47,* 796–801.

Li, C. (1975). *Path analysis: A primer.* Pacific Grove, CA: Boxwood Press.

Liang, X. (2006). Identity and language functions: High school Chinese immigrant students' code-switching dilemmas in ESL classes. *Journal of Language, Identity & Education, 5,* 143–167.

Libresco, J. D. (1983, August/September). Focus groups: Madison Avenue meets public policy. *Public Opinion,* pp. 51–53.

Lilienfeld, S. O., Lynn, S. J., & Lohr, J. M. (Eds.). (2003). *Science and pseudoscience in clinical psychology.* New York: Guilford Press.

Lincoln, Y. S., & Guba, E. G. (1985). *Naturalistic inquiry.* Beverly Hills, CA: Sage.

Lindey, A. (1952). *Plagiarism and originality.* New York: Harper.

LinguaLinks Library. (2004, January 5). *What is a sequence?* Retrieved March 10, 2006, from www.sil.org/linguistics/glossaryoflinguisticterms/WhatIsASequence.htm

Lippert, L. R., Titsworth, B. S., & Hunt, S. K. (2005). The ecology of academic risk: Relationships between communication apprehension, verbal aggression, supportive communication, and students' academic risk status. *Communication Studies, 56,* 1–21.

Lofland, J., & Lofland, L. H. (1984). *Analyzing social settings: A guide to qualitative observation and analysis* (2nd ed.). Belmont, CA: Wadsworth.

Lofland, J., & Lofland, L. H. (1995). *Analyzing social settings* (3rd ed.). Belmont, CA: Wadsworth.

Long, M., Slater, M. D., Bolarsky, G., Stapel, L., & Keefe, T. (2005). Obtaining nationally representative samples of local news media outlets. *Mass Communication and Society, 8,* 299–322.

Longman dictionary of psychology and psychiatry: A Walter D. Glanze book. (1984). New York: Longman.

Lopes, S. (1987). *The wall: Images and offerings of the Vietnam Veterans' Memorial.* New York: Collins.

Louisiana Department of Education. (1997, May 22). *Louisiana science framework.* Baton Rouge, LA. Available: www.doe.state.la.us/lde/uploads/2911.pdf

Luff, D. (1999). Dialog across the divides: "Moments of rapport" and power in feminist research with antifeminist women. *Sociology, 33,* 687–703.

MacCoun, R. J. (1990). The emergence of extralegal bias during jury deliberation. *Criminal Justice and Behavior, 17,* 303–314.

Madden, T. M., & Klopfer, F. J. (1978). The "cannot decide" option in Thurstone-type attitude scales. *Educational and Psychological Measurement, 38,* 259–264.

Magazine, S. L., Williams, L. J., & Williams, M. L. (1996). A confirmatory factor analysis examination of reverse coding effects in Meyer and Allen's affective and continuance commitment scales. *Educational and Psychological Measurement, 56,* 241–250.

Malcolm, I. (2001). *Sociolinguistic foundations: A review of terminology.* Retrieved April 10, 2006, from Edith Cowan University (Australia) website: www.ecu.edu.au/ses/research/CALLR/sociowww/definitions.htm

Mallory, L. A. (1943). Patrick Henry. In W. N. Brigance (Ed.), *A history and criticism of American public address* (Vol. II). New York: McGraw-Hill.

Mann, C., & Steward, S. (2000). *Internet communication and qualitative research: A handbook for researching online.* London: Sage.

Manusov, V. (1992). Mimicry of synchrony: The effects of intentionality attributions for nonverbal mirroring behavior. *Communication Quarterly, 40,* 69–83.

Mark, R. A. (1970). *Parameters of normal family communication in the dyad.* Unpublished doctoral dissertation, Department of Communication, Michigan State University, East Lansing.

Mark, R. A. (1971). Coding communication at the relationship level. *Journal of Communication, 21*(3), 221–232.

Markham, A. (1998). *Life online: Researching real experience in virtual space.* London: Altamira Press.

Markham, C., & Dean, T. (2006). Parents' and professionals' perceptions of quality of life in children with speech and language difficulty. *International Journal of Language & Communication Disorders, 41,* 89–212.

Marks, D., & Kammann, R. (1981). The nonpsychic powers of Uri Geller. In K. Frazier (Ed.), *Paranormal borderlands of science* (pp. 113–121). Buffalo, NY: Prometheus Books.

Marsh, H. W. (1984). *The bias of negatively-worded items in ratings scales for preadolescent children: A cognitive-developmental phenomenon.* (ERIC Document Reproduction Service No. ED242772)

Martin, J. N., & Butler, R. L. W. (2001). Towards an ethic of intercultural communication research. In V. H. Milhouse, M. K. Asante, & P. O. Nwosu (Eds.), *Transcultural realities: Interdisciplinary perspectives on cross-cultural relations* (pp. 283–298). Thousand Oaks, CA: Sage.

Mason, E. J., & Bramble, W. J. (1989). *Understanding and conducting research: Application in education and the behavioral sciences* (2nd ed.). New York: McGraw-Hill.

Matelski, M. J. (2001). A critical analysis of breast cancer sites: Searching the Web for answers. *Electronic Journal of Communication, 11,* 3–4. Available: www.cios.org/www/ejc/v11n3.htm#analyse

Math Talk. (2006). *The (un)truth about statistics.* Retrieved February 18, 2006, from the American Association of Variable Star Observers website: http://hoa.aavso.org/mathtalk.htm

Matveev, A. V. (2004). Describing intercultural communication competence: In-depth interviews with American and Russian managers. *Qualitative Research Reports in Communication, 5,* 55–62.

May, T. (1993). Social research: Issues, methods and process. Buckingham, England: Open University Press.

Mays, N., & Pope, C. (2000). Qualitative research in health care: Assessing quality in qualitative research. *British Medical Journal, 320,* 50–52.

Mazur, M. A., & Hubbard, A. S. E. (2004). "Is there something I should know?" Topic avoidant responses in parent-adolescent communication. *Communication Reports, 17,* 27–37.

McAnulla, S. (2005a, December). *Challenging the new interpretivist approach: Towards a critical realist alternative.*

POLIS Working Paper No. 22, School of Politics and International Studies, University of Leeds.

McAnulla, S. (2005b). Making hay with actualism? The need for a realist concept of structure. *Politics, 25,* 31–38.

McCann, R. M., Dailey, R. M., Giles, H., & Ota, H. (2005). Beliefs about intergenerational communication across the lifespan: Middle age and the roles of age stereotyping and respect norms. *Communication Studies, 56,* 293–311.

McCroskey, J. C. (1966). Scales for the measurement of ethos. *Speech Monographs, 33,* 65–72.

McCroskey, J. C. (1967). *Studies of the effects of evidence in persuasive communication.* East Lansing: Michigan State University, Speech Communication Research Laboratory, SCRL 4–67.

McCroskey, J. C. (1972). *An introduction to rhetorical communication* (2nd ed.). Englewood Cliffs, NJ: Prentice-Hall.

McCroskey, J. C. (1977). Oral communication apprehension: A summary of recent theory and research. *Human Communication Research, 4,* 78–96.

McCroskey, J. C. (1978). Validity of the PRCA as an index of oral communication apprehension. *Communication Monographs, 45,* 192–203.

McCroskey, J. C. (1982). *An introduction to rhetorical communication* (4th ed.). Englewood Cliffs, NJ: Prentice-Hall.

McCroskey, J. C., Beatty, M. J., Kearney, P., & Plax, T. G. (1985). The content validity of the PRCA-24 as a measure of communication apprehension across communication contexts. *Communication Quarterly, 33*(3), 165–173.

McCroskey, J. C., & Young, T. J. (1981). Ethos and credibility: The construct and its measurement after three decades. *Central States Speech Journal, 32,* 24–34.

McDonald, D. (1980). *The language of argument* (3rd ed.). New York: Harper and Row.

McDonald, J. L. (2004). The optimal number of categories for numerical rating scales. Doctoral dissertation, University of Denver. *Dissertation Abstracts International, 65*(5-A), 1664.

McGee, M. C. (2001). On objectivity and politics in rhetoric. *American Communication Journal, 4*(3). Retrieved March 3, 2006, from http://acjournal.org/holdings/vol4/iss3/special/mcgee.htm

McGuire, M. (1977). Mythic rhetoric in *Mein Kampf:* A structuralist critique. *Quarterly Journal of Speech, 63,* 1–13.

McInerney, V., McInerney, D., & Roche, L. (1994). *Definitely not just another computer anxiety instrument: The development and validation of CALM: computer anxiety and learning measure.* Paper presented at the Annual Stress and Anxiety Research Conference, Madrid, Spain. (ERIC Document Reproduction Service No. ED386161)

McNeill, P. (1990). *Research methods* (2nd ed.). London: Routledge.

Mechling, E. W. (1979). Patricia Hearst: MYTH AMERICA 1974, 1975, 1976. *Western Journal of Speech Communication, 43,* 168–179.

Meehl, P. E., & Hathaway, S. R. (1946). The K factor as a suppressor variable in the Minnesota Multiphasic Personality Inventory. *Journal of Applied Psychology, 30,* 525–564.

Mehrabian, A. (1969). Some referents and measures of nonverbal behavior. *Behavioral Research Methods and Instrumentation, 1,* 213–217.

Meltzoff, J. (1998). *Critical thinking about research: Psychology and related fields.* Washington, DC: American Psychological Association.

Merton, R. K. (1987). The focused interview and focus groups. *Public Opinion Quarterly, 51,* 550–566.

Milavsky, J. R., Kessler, R. C., Stipp, H. H., & Rubens, W. S. (1982). *Television and aggression: A panel study.* New York: Academic Press.

Milburn, T. (2000). Enacting "Puerto Rican time" in the United States. In M. J. Collier (Ed.), *Constituting cultural difference through discourse: The International and Intercultural Communication Annual, 23.* Thousand Oaks, CA: Sage.

Milburn, T. (2006a). Ethnography of communication: Conducting your own study. *Electronic encyclopedia of communication.* Retrieved May 23, 2006, from the Communication Institute for Online Scholarship website: www.cios.org/encyclopedia/ethnography/7-2-1conducting_study_findings.htm

Milburn, T. (2006b). Ethnography of communication: Ethnography of communication defined. *Electronic encyclopedia of communication.* Retrieved May 23, 2006, from the Communication Institute for Online Scholarship website: www.cios.org/encyclopedia/ethnography/2eoc_defined.htm

Milburn, T. (2006c). Ethnography of communication: S.P.E.A.K.I.N.G.: A research tool. *Electronic encyclopedia of communication.* Retrieved May 23, 2006, from the Communication Institute for Online Scholarship website: www.cios.org/encyclopedia/ethnography/4speaking.htm

Milburn, T. (2006d). Ethnography of communication: Theoretical overview. *Electronic encyclopedia of communication.* Retrieved May 23, 2006, from the Communication Institute for Online Scholarship website: www.cios.org/encyclopedia/ethnography/3theoretical_background.htm

Mill, J. S. (1872). *A system of logic: Ratiocinative and inductive* (8th ed.). New impression, 1959. London: Longmans.

Millar, F. E., & Rogers, L. E. (1976). A relational approach to interpersonal communication. In G. R. Miller (Ed.), *Explorations in interpersonal communication* (pp. 87–103). Beverly Hills, CA: Sage.

Millar, F. E., & Rogers, L. E. (1987). Relational dimensions of interpersonal dynamics. In M. E. Roloff & G. R. Miller (Eds.), *Interpersonal processes: New directions in communication research* (pp. 117–139). Beverly Hills, CA: Sage.

Miller, H., & Arnold, J. (2001). Breaking away from grounded identity? Women academics on the Web. *CyberPsychology & Behavior, 4,* 95–108.

Miller, K. (2002). The experience of emotion in the workplace: Professing in the midst of tragedy. *Management Communication Quarterly, 15,* 571–600.

Miller, K. (2005). *Communication theories: Perspectives, processes, and contexts* (2nd ed.). Boston: McGraw-Hill.

Millham, J., & Jacobson, L. I. (1978). The need for approval. In H. London & J. E. Exner (Eds.), *Dimensions of personality* (pp. 365–390). New York: Wiley.

A million random digits with 100,000 normal deviates. (1955). New York: Free Press.

Minnesota Academic Standards Committee, Minnesota Department of Education. (2003, December 19). *Minnesota Academic Standards: Science K–12.* St. Paul, MN. Available: http://education.state.mn.us/mde/static/078664.doc

Mohrmann, G. P., & Leff, M. C. (1974). Lincoln at Cooper Union: A rationale for neo-classical criticism. *Quarterly Journal of Speech, 60,* 459–467.

Møller, A. P., & Jennions, M. D. (2001). Testing and adjusting for publication bias. *TRENDS in Ecology & Evolution, 16,* 580–586.

Monge, P. R. (1987). The network level of analysis. In C. R. Berger & S. H. Chaffee (Eds.), *Handbook of communication science* (pp. 239–270). Newbury Park, CA: Sage.

Monge, P. R., & Miller, G. R. (1985). Communication networks. In A. Kuper & J. Kuper (Eds.), *The social science encyclopedia* (pp. 130–131). London: Routledge & Kegan.

Mongeau, P. A. (1993, February). *The brainstorming myth.* Paper presented at the Western States Communication Association, Albuquerque, NM.

Montana Office of Public Instruction. (2002, January 4). *Montana standards for science.* Helena, MT. Available: www.opi.state.mt.us/pdf/Standards/ContStds-Science.pdf

Moore, T. E. (1982). Subliminal advertising: What you see is what you get. *Journal of Marketing, 46,* 38–47.

Moore, T. E. (1988). The case against subliminal manipulation. *Psychology & Marketing, 5,* 297–316.

Morales-Lopez, E., Prego-Vazquez, G., & Dominguez-Seco, L. (2005). Interviews between employees and customers during a company restructuring process. *Discourse and Society, 16,* 225–268.

Morgan, D. L. (1998). *Planning focus groups.* Thousand Oaks, CA: Sage.

Morgan, S. E., & Miller, J. K. (2002). Communication about gifts of life: The effect of knowledge, attitudes, and altruism on behavior and behavioral intentions regarding organ donation. *Journal of Applied Communication Research, 30,* 163–178.

Morrow, V., & Richards, M. (1996). The ethics of social research with children: An overview. *Children & Society, 10,* 90–105.

Morse, J. M., Barrett, M., Mayan, M., Olson, K., & Spiers, J. (2002). Verification strategies for establishing reliability and validity in qualitative research. *International Journal of Qualitative Methods, 1*(2). Retrieved July 4, 2002, from www.ualberta.ca/~ijqm/

Mortensen, C. D. (1972). *Communication.* New York: McGraw-Hill.

Motley, M. T. (1990). On whether one can(not) communicate: An examination via traditional communication postulates. *Western Journal of Speech Communication, 54,* 1–20.

Motley, M. T., & Reeder, H. M. (1995). Unwanted escalation of sexual intimacy: Male and female perceptions of connotations and relational consequences of resistance messages. *Communication Monographs, 62,* 355–382.

Mullen, B., & Miller, N. (1991). Meta-analysis. In C. M. Judd, E. R. Smith, & L. H. Kidder, *Research methods in social relations* (6th ed., pp. 425–449). Fort Worth, TX: Holt, Rinehart and Winston.

Mullen, L. J., & Fisher, J. D. (2004). A visual analysis of prescription drug advertising imagery: Elaborating Foss's rhetorical techniques. *Communication Studies, 55,* 185–196.

Myers, S. A., & Bryant, L. E. (2004). College students' perceptions of how instructors convey credibility. *Qualitative Research Reports in Communication, 5,* 22–27.

Nabi, R. L. (2002). Anger, fear, uncertainty and attitudes: A test of the cognitive function model. *Communication Monographs, 69,* 204–216.

Nachmias, D., & Nachmias, C. (1996). *Research methods in the social sciences* (5th ed.). New York: St. Martin's Press.

Naisbitt, J., & Aburdene, P. (1990). *Megatrends 2000.* New York: William Morrow.

Nance, J. (1975). *The gentle Tasaday: A stone age people in the Philippine rain forest.* New York: Harcourt Brace Jovanovich.

Natale, J. A. (1988, September). Are you open to suggestion? *Psychology Today,* pp. 28–30.

National Center for Education Statistics. (2002a). *Communication, journalism, and related programs. Classification of instructional programs (CIP 2000).* U.S. Department of Education. Available: http://nces.ed.gov/pubs2002/cip2000/ciplist.asp?CIP2=09

National Center for Education Statistics. (2002b). *English language and literature/letters. Classification of instructional programs (CIP 2000).* U.S. Department of Education. Available: http://nces.ed.gov/pubs2002/cip2000/ciplist.asp?CIP2=23

National Center for Education Statistics. (2002c). *Foreign languages, literatures, and linguistics. Classification of instructional programs (CIP 2000).* U.S. Department of Education. Available: http://nces.ed.gov/pubs2002/cip2000/ciplist.asp?CIP2=16

National Center for Education Statistics. (2002d). *Health professions and related clinical sciences. Classification of instructional programs (CIP 2000).* U.S. Department of Education. Available: http://nces.ed.gov/pubs2002/cip2000/ciplist.asp?CIP2=51

National Health and Medical Research Council. (2005, June). *Human research ethics handbook.* Retrieved March 10, 2006, from Australian Government website: www.nhmrc.gov.au/publications/hrecbook/01_commentary/12.htm

Nelson, J., & Flannery, M. A. (1990). The sanctuary movement: A story of religious confrontation. *Southern Communication Journal, 55,* 372–387.

Neuage, T. (2004). Conversational analysis of chatroom talk. Doctoral dissertation, University of South Australia. Retrieved May 10, 2006, from http://neuage.org/All.htm#_Toc134054304

Neuro-linguistic programming. (2005, October 3). *Wikipedia.* Retrieved October 3, 2005, from http://en.wikipedia.org/wiki/Neuro-linguistic_programming

Nevins, A. (1938). *The gateway to history.* Boston: D. C. Heath.

Newhagen, J. E., Cordes, J. W., & Levy, M. R. (1995). Nightly@nbc.com: Audience scope and the perception of interactivity in viewer mail on the Internet. *Journal of Communication, 45*(3), 164–175.

New Jersey Department of Education. (2004, July). *The New Jersey core curriculum content standards for science.* Trenton, NJ. Available: www.state.nj.us/njded/cccs/s5_science.pdf

New Mexico Public Education Department. (2005, November 10). *Science—glossary, literacy and technology standards.* Retrieved November 10 from www.nmlites.org/standards/science/glossary_5.htm

Newsweek. (2006, June 5). p. cover.

Nicotera, A. M., & Rancer, A. S. (1994). The influence of sex on self-perception and social stereotyping of aggressive communication predispositions. *Western Journal of Communication, 58,* 283–307.

Nisbett, R. E., & Wilson, T. D. (1977a). Telling more than we can know. Verbal reports on mental processes. *Psychological Review, 84,* 231–259.

Nisbett, R. E., & Wilson, T. D. (1977b). The halo effect: Evidence for unconscious alteration of judgments. *Journal of Personality and Social Psychology, 35,* 250–256.

Noblit, G. W., Flores, S. Y., & Murillo, E. G. (Eds.). (2004). *Postcritical ethnography: An introduction.* Cresskill, NJ: Hampton Press.

North Dakota Department of Public Instruction. (2002, November). *North Dakota Standards and Benchmarks Content Standards: Science.* Bismarck, ND. Available: www.dpi.state.nd.us/standard/content/science.pdf

Nunnally, J. (1978). *Psychometric theory* (2nd ed.). New York: McGraw-Hill.

Olson, L. N. (2004). The role of voice in the (re)construction of a battered woman's identity: An autoethnography of one woman's experiences of abuse. *Women's Studies in Communication, 27,* 1–33.

Orbe, M. P., & Groscurth, C. R. (2004). A co-cultural theoretical analysis of communication on campus and at home: Exploring the negotiation strategies of first-generation college (FGC) students. *Qualitative Research Reports in Communication, 5,* 41–47.

Orlikowski, W. J., & Baroudi, J. J. (1991). Studying information technology in organizations: Research approaches and assumptions. *Information Systems Research, 2*(1), 1–28.

Orne, M. T. (1970). Hypnosis, motivation, and the ecological validity of the psychological experiment. *Nebraska Symposium on Motivation, 18,* 187–265.

Ory, J. C. (1982). Item placement and wording effects on overall ratings. *Educational and Psychological Measurement, 42,* 767–775.

Osgood, C. E., Suci, G. J., & Tannenbaum, P. H. (1957). *The measurement of meaning.* Urbana: University of Illinois Press.

Ott, L., & Hildebrand, D. K. (1983). *Statistical thinking for managers.* Boston: PWS.

Paradis, A. A. (1966). *The research handbook: A guide to reference sources.* New York: Funk and Wagnalls.

Park, J. H., Gabbadon, N. G., & Chernin, A. R. (2006). Naturalizing racial differences through comedy: Asian, Black, and White views on racial stereotypes in *Rush Hour 2. Journal of Communication, 56,* 157–177.

Patten, M. L. (1997). *Understanding research methods: An overview of the essentials.* Los Angeles: Pryczak.

Patton, M. Q. (1990). *Qualitative evaluation and research methods* (2nd ed.). Newbury Park, CA: Sage.

Patton, T. O. (2004). In the guise of civility: The complicitous maintenance of inferential forms of sexism and racism in higher education. *Women's Studies in Communication, 27,* 60–87.

Paugh, A. L. (2005). Learning about work at dinnertime: Language socialization in dual-earner American families. *Discourse and Society, 15,* 55–78.

Pavitt, C. (1990). The ideal communicator as the basis for competence judgments of self and friend. *Communication Reports, 3,* 9–14.

Pavitt, C., & Johnson, K. K. (2001). The association between group procedural MOPS and group discussion procedure. *Small Group Research, 32,* 591–620.

Pavitt, C., & Johnson, K. K. (2002). Scheidel and Crowell revisited: A descriptive study of group proposal sequencing. *Communication Monographs, 69,* 19–32.

Pavitt, C., Philipp, M., & Johnson, K. K. (2004). Who owns a group's proposals: The initiator or the group as a whole? *Communication Research Reports, 21,* 221–230.

Pearson, K. (1924). Historical note on the origin of the normal curve of errors. *Biometrika, 16,* 402–404.

Peirce, C. (1955). *Philosophical writings of Peirce,* J. Buchler (Ed.). New York: Dover.

Pepper, G. L., & Larson, G. S. (2006). Cultural identity tensions in a post-acquisition organization. *Journal of Applied Communication Research, 34,* 49–71.

Perry, S. D., & Roesch, A. L. (2004). He's in a new neighborhood now: Religious fantasy themes about Mister Rogers' neighborhood. *Journal of Media & Religion, 3,* 199–218.

Pfau, M., & Burgoon, M. (1988). Inoculation in political campaign communication. *Human Communication Research, 15,* 91–111.

Polk, D. M. (2005). Communication and family caregiving for Alzheimer's dementia: Linking attributions and problematic integration. *Health Communication, 18,* 257–273.

Pomerantz, A. (1990). Conversation analytic claims. *Communication Monographs, 57,* 231–235.

Popper, K. R. (1968a). *Conjectures and refutations: The growth of scientific knowledge* (2nd ed.). New York: Harper Torchbooks.

Popper, K. R. (1968b). *The logic of scientific discovery* (2nd ed.). New York: Harper Torchbooks.

Popper, K. R. (1972). *Objective knowledge.* Oxford, England: Oxford University Press.

Pornpitakpan, C. (2003). The effect of celebrity endorsers' perceived credibility on product purchase intention: The case of Singaporeans. *Journal of International Consumer Marketing, 16*(2), 55–74.

Potter, J. (2003). Discourse analysis and discursive psychology. In P. M. Camic, J. E. Rhodes, & L. Yardley (Eds.), *Qualitative research in psychology: Expanding perspectives in methodology and design* (pp. 73–94). Washington, DC: American Psychological Association.

Pratkanis, A. R. (1992). The cargo-cult science of subliminal persuasion. *Skeptical Inquirer, 16,* 260–272. Available: www.csicop.org/si/9204/subliminal-persuasion.html

Pratkanis, A. R., & Greenwald, A. G. (1988). Recent perspectives on unconscious processing: Still no marketing applications. *Psychology & Marketing, 5,* 339–355.

Pratschke, J. (2003). Realistic models? Critical realism and statistical models in the social sciences. *Philosophica, 71,* 13–38.

Publication manual of the American Psychological Association (5th ed.). (2001). Washington, DC: American Psychological Association.

Punch, K. F. (2005) *Introduction to social research: Quantitative and qualitative approaches* (2nd ed.). London: Sage.

Quine, W. (1946). Truth by convention. In O. H. Lee (Ed.), *Philosophical essays for Alfred North Whitehead.* New York: Longmans Greens.

Raaijmakers, Q., vanHoof, A., Hart, H., Varbogt, T., & Vollebergh, W. A. (2000). Adolescents' midpoint responses on Likert-type scale items: Neutral or missing values? *International Journal of Public Opinion Research, 12,* 208–216.

Radin, D. I. (1997). *The conscious universe: The scientific truth of psychic phenomena.* New York: HarperEdge.

Radin, D. I., & Nelson, R. D. (1989). Evidence for consciousness-related anomalies in random physical systems. *Foundations of Physics, 19,* 1499–1514.

Ragin, C. C., Nagel, J., & White, P. (2004). *Workshop on scientific foundations of qualitative research.* Washington, DC: National Science Foundation. Available: www.nsf.gov/pubs/2004/nsf04219/start.htm

Randi, J. (1981). New evidence in the Uri Geller matter. In K. Frazier (Ed.), *Paranormal borderlands of science* (pp. 122–127). Buffalo, NY: Prometheus Books.

Ransford, H. E. (1968). Isolation, powerlessness, and violence: A study of attitudes and participants in the Watts riots. *American Journal of Sociology, 73,* 581–591.

Ray, J., & Zavos, H. (1966). Reasoning and argument: Some special problems and types. In G. R. Miller & T. R. Nilsen (Eds.), *Perspectives on argumentation* (pp. 80–109). Chicago: Scott, Foresman.

Ray, W. J., & Ravizza, R. R. (1988). *Methods: Toward a science of behavior and experience* (3rd ed.). Belmont, CA: Wadsworth.

Reed-Danahay, D. E. (1997). Introduction. In D. E. Reed-Danahay (Ed.), *Auto/ethnography: Rewriting the self and the social* (pp. 1–17). Oxford, England: Berg.

Reinard, J. C. (1986, February). *Nonverbal communication research in legal settings: Considerations of limits and effects.* Paper presented at the Western Speech Communication Association Convention, Tucson, AZ.

Reinard, J. C. (1991). *Foundations of argument: Effective communication for critical thinking.* Dubuque, IA: W. C. Brown.

Reinard, J. C. (2006). *Communication research statistics.* Thousand Oaks, CA: Sage.

Reinard, J. C., & Boster, F. J. (1978, May). *Information processing under stress: Developments on a theory of stress coping to communication.* Paper presented at the Speech Communication Association Convention, Minneapolis, MN.

Reinard, J. C., Fu, P-W., Hoover, G., Barr, D., Bybee, K., Corralejo, E. A., Dela, K. A., Le, N., Levengood, M., Oropeza, M. R., Santos, C. F., Shi, W., Tuason, C., & Wagner, A. D. (2002, February). *Speed versus accuracy: A content analysis of media report accuracy and the alacrity hypothesis.* Paper presented at the Western States Communication Association Convention, Long Beach, CA.

Reynolds, P. D. (1971). *A primer in theory construction.* Indianapolis: Bobbs-Merrill.

Reynolds, P. D. (1975). Ethics and status: Value dilemmas in professional conduct of social science. *International Social Science Journal, 27,* 563–611.

Reynolds, R. A., & Burgoon, M. (1983). Belief processing, reasoning, and evidence. In R. Bostrom (Ed.), *Communication yearbook 7* (pp. 83–104). Beverly Hills, CA: Sage.

Richardson, D. (1945, January 7). They didn't say it. *New York Times Magazine,* p. 39.

Richardson, L. (2000). New writing practices in qualitative research. *Sociology of Sport Journal, 17,* 5–20.

Richardson, L. S. (1970). Stokely Carmichael: Jazz artist. *Western Speech, 34,* 212–218.

Rieke, R. D., & Stutman, R. K. (1990). *Communication in legal advocacy.* Columbia: University of South Carolina Press.

Riecken, H. W., & Boruch, R. F. (1979). *Social experimentation.* Orlando, FL: Academic Press.

Riffe, D., & Freitag, A. (1997). A content analysis of content analyses: Twenty-five years of *Journalism Quarterly. Journalism and Mass Communication Quarterly, 75,* 515–524.

Ring, K., Wallston, K., & Corey, M. (1970). Mode of debriefing as a factor affecting subjective reaction to a Milgram-type obedience experiment: An ethical inquiry. *Representative Research in Social Psychology, 1,* 67–88.

Ritchie, L. D., & Fitzpatrick, M. A. (1990). Family communication patterns: Measuring intrapersonal perceptions of interpersonal relationships. *Communication Research, 17,* 523–544.

Ritter, K., & Henry, D. (1992). *Ronald Reagan: The great communicator.* Westport, CT: Greenwood Press.

Robinson, J. P., Shaver, P. R., & Wrightsman, L. S. (Eds.). (1991). *Measures of personality and social psychological attitudes* (Vol. 1). San Diego: Academic Press.

Rogers, E. M., & Kincaid, D. L. (1981). *Communication networks: Toward a new paradigm for research.* New York: Free Press.

Rogers, L. E., & Farace, R. V. (1975). Analysis of relational communication in dyads: New measurement procedures. *Human Communication Research, 1,* 222–239.

Rogers, L. E., & Millar, F. E. (1988). Relational communication. In S. Duck (Ed.), *Handbook of personal relationships* (pp. 289–306). New York: Wiley.

Rogers-Millar, L. E., & Millar, F. E. (1979). Domineeringness and dominance: A transactional view. *Human Communication Research, 5,* 238–245.

Rosenthal, P. (2001, September 13). Cruelest images go unseen. *Chicago Sun-Times,* p. C1.

Rosenthal, R. (1979). The "file drawer problem" and tolerance for null results. *Psychological Bulletin, 86,* 638–641.

Rosenthal, R. (1983). Assessing the statistical and social importance of the effects of psychotherapy. *Journal of Consulting and Clinical Psychology, 51,* 4–13.

Rosenthal, R. (1991). *Meta-analytic procedures for social research* (Rev. ed.). Newbury Park, CA: Sage.

Rosenthal, R., & Rosnow, R. L. (1969). The volunteer subject. In R. Rosenthal & R. L. Rosnow (Eds.), *Artifact in behavioral research* (pp. 59–118). New York: McGraw-Hill.

Rosenthal, R., Rosnow, R. L., & Rubin, D. B. (2000). *Contrast and effect sizes in behavioral research: A correlational approach.* New York: Cambridge University Press.

Rosenthal, R., & Rubin, D. B. (1982a). Comparing effect sizes of independent studies. *Psychological Bulletin, 99,* 400–406.

Rosenthal, R., & Rubin, D. B. (1982b). A simple, general purpose display of magnitude of experimental effect. *Journal of Educational Psychology, 74,* 166–169.

Rouveyrol, L., Maury-Rouan, C., Vion, R., & Noël-Jorand, M-C. (2005). A linguistic toolbox for discourse analysis: Towards a multidimensional handling of verbal interactions. *Discourse Studies, 7,* 289–313.

Rowland, R. C. (1987). Narrative: Mode of discourse or paradigm? *Communication Monographs, 54,* 264–275.

Rowland, R. C. (1989). On limiting the narrative paradigm: Three case studies. *Communication Monographs, 56,* 39–54.

Rubin, R. B., Palmgreen, P., & Sypher, H. E. (Eds.). (2004). *Communication research measures: A sourcebook.* Mahwah, NJ: Erlbaum.

Rubin, R. B., Rubin, A. M., & Piele, L. J. (2005). *Communication research: Strategies and sources* (6th ed.). Belmont, CA: Wadsworth.

Rubin, Z., & Shenker, S. S. (1978). Friendship, proximity, and self-disclosure. *Journal of Personality, 46,* 1–22.

Ruggicro, T. E. (2000). Uses and gratifications theory in the 21st century. *Mass Communication & Society, 3,* 3–37.

Rushing, J. H. (1986). Mythic evolution of "the new frontier" in mass mediated rhetoric. *Critical Studies in Mass Communication, 3,* 265–296.

Russo, T. C. & Koester, J. (2005). Brief report: Prestige, centrality, and learning: A social network analysis of an online class. *Communication Education, 54,* 254–261.

Rutherford, F. J., & Ahlgren, A. (1994). *Science for all Americans: AAAS project 2061* (Rev. ed.). New York: Oxford University Press.

Ryan M. (1980). The Likert scale's midpoint in communications research. *Journalism Quarterly, 57,* 305–313.

Sacks, H. (1992). *Lectures on conversation* (2 vols.). G. Jefferson (Ed.). Oxford, UK: Blackwell.

Sanbonmatsu, A. (1971). Darrow and Rorke's use of Burkean identification strategies in *New York v. Gitlow* (1920). *Speech Monographs, 37,* 36–48.

Sánchez-Meca, J., & Marín-Martínez, F. (1998). Weighting by inverse-variance or by sample size in meta-analysis: A simulation study. *Educational and Psychological Measurement, 58,* 211–220.

Sandberg, C. (1954). *Abraham Lincoln: The prairie years and the war years, One-volume edition.* New York: Galahad Books.

Sandoval, J., & Lambert, N. M. (1978). *Reliability and validity of teacher rating procedures in the assessment of hyperactivity as a function of rating scale format.* Paper presented at the Annual Meeting of the American Educational Research Association, Toronto, Canada. (ERIC Document Reproduction Service No. ED160614)

Scantlin, R. M., & Jordan, A. B. (2006). Families' experiences with the v-chip: An exploratory study. *Journal of Family Communication, 6,* 139–159.

Scargle, J. D. (2000). Publication bias: The "file-drawer" problem in scientific inference. *Journal of Scientific Exploration, 14,* 91–106.

Scheidel, T. M., & Crowell, L. (1964). Idea development in small group communication. *Quarterly Journal of Speech, 50,* 140–145.

Schmid, J., & Fiedler, K. (1996). Language and implicit attributions in the Nuremberg trials. *Human Communication Research, 22,* 371–398.

Schmierbach, M., Boyle, M. P., & McLeod, D. M. (2005). Civic attachment in the aftermath of September 11. *Mass Communication and Society, 8,* 323–346.

Schriesheim, C. A., & Hill, K. D. (1981). Controlling acquiescence response bias by item reversals: The effect on questionnaire validity. *Educational and Psychological Measurement, 41,* 1101–1114.

Schutt, R. K. (2006). *Investigating the social world: The process and practice of research* (5th ed.). Thousand Oaks, CA: Pine Forge Press.

Schwarzer, R. (1998, September). *Meta-analysis: Manual and programs.* Retrieved August 7, 2005, from www.euronet.nl/users/warnar/demostatistiek/meth/metaanalyse.htm

Scott, W. (1955). Reliability of content analysis: The case of nominal scale coding. *Public Opinion Quarterly, 17,* 321–325.

Selby, G. S. (2005). Scoffing at the enemy: The burlesque frame in the rhetoric of Ralph David Abernathy. *Southern Communication Journal, 70,* 134–145.

Senft, T. M. (2002). *Homecame heroines: Gender, celebrity and performance on the World Wide Web.* New York: Peter Lang.

Sieber, J. E. (2000). Planning research: Basic ethical decision-making. In B. D. Sales & S. Folkman (Eds.), *Ethics in research with human participants* (pp. 13–26). Washington, DC: American Psychological Association.

Signorielli, N. (2005). Age-based ratings, content designations, and television content: Is there a problem? *Mass Communication and Society, 8,* 277–298.

Silbey, S. S. (2004). Designing qualitative research projects. In C. C. Ragin, J. Nagel, & P. White (Eds.), *Workshop on scientific foundations of qualitative research* (pp. 121–125). Washington, DC: National Science Foundation. Available: www.nsf.gov/pubs/2004/nsf04219/start.htm

Simpson, C. (1994). *Science of coercion: Communication research and psychological warfare 1945–1960.* New York: Oxford University Press.

Singer, B. (2001). *Melodrama and modernity.* New York: Cambridge University Press.

Singer, E. (1983). Informed consent procedures in surveys: Some reasons for minimal effects on response. In R. F. Boruch & J. S. Cecil (Eds.), *Solutions to ethical and legal problems in social research* (pp. 183–211). Orlando, FL: Academic Press.

Singer, M. T., & Lalich, J. (1996). *Crazy therapies: What they are? Do they work?* New York: Jossey-Bass.

Slavin, R. E. (1983). *Cooperative learning.* New York: Longman.

Sluzki, G. E., & Beavin, J. (1965). Simetriay complementaridid: Una definición operacional y una tipologia de parejas. *Acta Psiquiátrica y Psicológica de América Latina, 11,* 321–330.

Smith, C. R. (2000). Criticism of political rhetoric and disciplinary integrity. *American Commun ication Journal, 4*(1). Retrieved March 3, 2006, from http://acjournal.org/holdings/vol4/iss1/special/smith.htm

Smith, E. V., Wakely, M. B., De Kruif, R. E. L., & Swartz, C. W. (2003). Optimizing rating scales for self-efficacy (and other) research. *Educational and Psychological Measurement, 63,* 369–391.

Smith, H. W. (1991). *Strategies of social research* (3rd ed.). Orlando, FL: Holt, Rinehart and Winston.

Smith, M. B. (2000). Moral foundations in research with human participants. In B. D. Sales & S. Folkman (Eds.), *Ethics in research with human participants* (pp. 3–10). Washington, DC: American Psychological Association.

Smith, M. J. (1988). *Contemporary communication research methods.* Belmont, CA: Wadsworth.

Snow, M. (1985). Martin Luther King's "letter from Birmingham jail" as Pauline epistle. *Quarterly Journal of Speech, 71,* 318–334.

Sobal, J. (1984). The content of survey introductions and the provisions of informed consent. *Public Opinion Quarterly, 48,* 788–793.

Sohn, D., & Jee, J. (2005). Network structures of commercial portal sites: Implications for web advertising planning. *International Journal of Advertising, 24,* 425–440.

Sparkes, A. C. (2000). Autoethnography and narratives of self: Reflections on criteria in action. *Sociology of Sport Journal, 17,* 21–41.

Spitzberg, B. H. (1988). Communication competence: Measures of perceived effectiveness. In H. Tardy (Ed.), *A handbook for the study of human communication* (pp. 67–106). Norwood, NJ: Ablex.

Spradley, J. P. (1979). *The ethnographic interview.* New York: Holt, Rinehart and Winston.

Squires, S. (1988, April 17) The pentagon's twilight zone. *Washington Post,* p. A1.

Stanford-Binet Intelligence Scales, Fifth Edition: Features. (2004). Retrieved September 20, 2005, from the Riverside Publishing Company website: www.riverpub.com/products/clinical/sbis5/features.html

Stanovich, K. E. (1986). *How to think straight about psychology.* Glenview, IL: Scott, Foresman.

Starr, V. H. (1979). *The effective use of nonverbal communication in jury selection* [audiocassette]. Washington, DC: Association of Trial Lawyers of America.

Stevens, J. (1986). *Applied multivariate statistics for the social sciences.* Hillsdale, NJ: Erlbaum.

Stevens, S. S. (1951). Scales of measurement. In S. S. Stevens (Ed.), *Handbook of experimental psychology* (pp. 23–30). New York: Wiley.

Stewart, C. J., & Cash, W. B. (1988). *Interviewing: Principles and practices.* Dubuque, IA: W. C. Brown.

Stewart, D. W., & Shamdasani, P. M. (1990). *Focus groups: Theory and practice.* Newbury Park, CA: Sage.

Stiff, J. B. (1986). Cognitive processing of persuasive message cues: A meta-analytic review of the effects of supporting information on attitudes. *Communication Monographs, 53,* 75–89.

Stinchcombe, A. L. (1968). *Constructing social theories.* New York: Harcourt, Brace and World.

Stivers, T. (2004). "No no no" and other types of multiple sayings in social interaction. *Human Communication Research, 30,* 260–293.

Stohl, C. (1993). European managers' interpretation of participation: A semantic network analysis. *Human Communication Research, 20,* 97–117.

Strauss, A. (1987). *Qualitative analysis for social scientists.* New York: Cambridge University Press.

Strauss, A., & Corbin, J. (1990). *Basics of qualitative research: Grounded theory procedures and techniques.* London: Sage.

Strickland, B. R. (1977). Approval motivation. In T. Blass (Ed.), *Personality variables in social behavior* (pp. 315–356). Hillsdale, NJ: Erlbaum.

Stroud, S. R. (2005). Ontological orientation and the practice of rhetoric: A perspective from the *Bhagavad Gita. Southern Communication Journal, 70,* 146–160.

Strube, M. J., & Hartmann, D. P. (1983). Meta-analysis: Techniques, applications, and functions. *Journal of Consulting and Clinical Psychology, 51,* 14–27.

Strunk, W., Jr., & White, E. B. (1979). *The elements of style* (3rd ed.). New York: Macmillan.

Stubbs, M. (1981). Motivating analyses of exchange structure. In M. Coulthard & M. Montgomery (Eds.), *Studies in discourse analysis.* London: Routledge and Kegan Paul.

Stuckey, M. E., & Antczak, F. J. (1994). The battle of issues and images: Establishing interpreting dominance. *Communication Quarterly, 42,* 120–132.

Student. (1908). On the probable error of the mean. *Biometrika, 6,* 1–25.

Subliminal ad is transmitted in test but scores no popcorn sales. (1958, January 20). *Advertising Age,* p. 20.

Sun, S., & Barnett, G. A. (1994). An analysis of the international telephone network and democratization. *Journal of the American Society for Information Science, 45,* 411–421.

Susskind, A. M., Schwartz, D. F., Richards, W. D., & Johnson, J. D. (2005). Evolution and diffusion of the Michigan State University tradition of organizational communication network research. *Communication Studies, 56,* 397–418.

Sussman, S., Burton, D., Dent, C. W., Stacy, A. W., & Flay, B. R. (1991). Use of focus groups in developing an adolescent tobacco use cessation program: Collection norm effects. *Journal of Applied Social Psychology, 21,* 1772–1782.

Swenson, W. M., Pearson, J. S., & Osbourne, D. (1973). *An MMPI sourcebook: Basic item, scale, and pattern data on 50,000 medical patients.* Minneapolis: University of Minnesota Press.

Sykes, A. J. M. (1970). Myth in communication. *Journal of Communication, 20,* 17–31.

Sypher, H. E. (1980). Illusory correlation in communication research. *Human Communication Research, 7,* 83–87.

Taft-Kaufman, J. (2000). Critical claims, critical functions: Autoethnography and postscholarship. *American Journal of Communication, 4*(1). Retrieved November 5, 2005, from http://acjournal.org/holdings/vol4/iss1/special/taft.htm

Tanaka-Matsumi, J., & Kameoka, V. A. (1986). Reliabilities and concurrent validities of popular self-report measures of depression, anxiety, and social desirability. *Journal of Consulting and Clinical Psychology, 54,* 328–333.

Tardy, Charles H. (Ed.). (1988a). *A handbook for the study of human communication: Methods and instruments for observing, measuring and assessing communication processes.* Norwood, NJ: Ablex.

Tardy, Charles H. (1988b). Interpersonal interaction coding systems. In C. H. Tardy (Ed.), *A handbook for the study of human communication: Methods and instruments for observing, measuring and assessing communication processes.* Norwood, NJ: Ablex.

Task Force on Statistical Inference. (1996, December 14–15). Task Force on Statistical Inference initial report, Board of Scientific Affairs. *APA Online.* Retrieved February 17, 2003, from the American Psychological Association website: www.apa.org/science/tfsi.html

Tatsuoka, M. (1969). *Validation studies: The use of multiple regression equations.* Champaign, IL: Institute for Personality and Ability Testing.

ten Have, P. (1990, June). Methodological issues in conversation analysis. *Bulletin de Méthodologie Sociologique,* No. 27, pp. 23–51. Retrieved February 5, 2006, from www.ai.univ-paris8.fr/corpus/papers/tenHave/mica.htm

ten Have, P. (2002). Reflections on transcription. *Cahiers de praxématique, 39,* 21–43.

ten Have, P. (2004a). Ethnomethodology. In C. Seale, D. Silverman, J, Gubrium, & G. Gobo (Eds.), *Qualitative research practice* (pp. 151–164), London: Sage.

ten Have, P. (2004b). *Understanding qualitative research and ethnomethodology.* London: Sage.

Tey, J. (1951). *The daughter of time.* New York: Macmillan.

Thergerge, L. J. (Ed.). (1981). *Crooks, conmen and clowns: Businessmen in TV entertainment.* Washington, DC: The Media Institute.

Thill, J. V., & Bovee, C. L. (1991). *Excellence in business communication.* New York: McGraw-Hill.

Thomas, S., & LeShay, S. V. (1992). Bad business? A reexamination of television's portrayal of businesspersons. *Journal of Communication, 42,* 95–105.

Tierney, W. G. (1998). Life history's history: Subjects foretold. *Qualitative Inquiry, 4,* 49–70.

Tilley, E. (2005). Responding to terrorism using ethical means: The propaganda index. *Communication Research Reports, 22,* 69–77.

Transcript notation. (1999). *Aphasiology, 13,* 243–249.

Trapp, R., & Hoff, N. (1985). A model of serial argument in interpersonal relationships. *Journal of American Forensic Association, 22,* 1–11.

Tuckman, B. W. (1999). *Conducting educational research* (5th ed.). Fort Worth, TX: Harcourt Brace.

Tuttle, L. P., Terry, D., & Shinedling, M. M. (1977). Note on increase of social interacting of mental patients during a camping trip. *Psychological Reports, 33,* 72–74.

Twain, M. (1959 ed.). *The autobiography of Mark Twain,* C. Neider (Ed.). New York: Harper and Brothers.

2001 National household survey on drug abuse: Field interviewer manual. (2000, October). Substance Abuse and Mental Health Services Administration, United States Public Health Service, Department of Health and Human Services (Contract No. 283-98-9008, prepared by Research Triangle Institute). Retrieved April 19, 2006, from www.oas.samhsa.gov/NHSDA/2k1FI/toc.htm

Typing and improved academic performance. (1976, July). Brochure. Smith-Corona.

United States General Accounting Office. (1996). *Content analysis: A methodology for structuring and analyzing written material.* GAO/PEMD-10.3.1. Washington, DC.

Upton, G., & Cook, I. (2002). *Oxford dictionary of statistics.* Oxford, UK: Oxford University Press.

Urmson, J. O., & Ree, J. (Eds.). (1989). *The concise encyclopedia of Western philosophy and philosophers* (New ed.). London: Unwin Hyman.

Vancil, D. L., & Pendell, S. D. (1987). The myth of viewer-listener disagreement in the first Kennedy-Nixon debate. *Central States Speech Journal, 38,* 16–27.

Vanlear, C. A., Jr., & Zeitlow, P. H. (1990). Toward a contingency approach to marital interaction: An empirical integration of three approaches. *Communication Monographs, 57,* 202–218.

Van Maanen, J. (1983). The moral fix: On the ethics of fieldwork. In R. Emerson (Ed.), *Contemporary field research: A collection of essays* (pp. 269–287). Prospect Heights, IL: Waveland.

van Zoonen, L. (2004). Imagining the fan democracy. *European Journal of Communication, 19,* 39–52.

Vaughan, B. L. (1986a). *Courtroom psychology and jury selection.* Sacramento, CA: Interstate College of Personology.

Vaughan, B. L. (1986b, February). *Jury selection and nonverbal cues.* Western States Communication Association Convention, Tucson, AZ.

Verser, R., & Wicks, R. H. (2006). Managing voter impressions: The use of images on presidential candidate web sites during the 2000 campaign. *Journal of Communication, 56,* 178–197.

Vogt, W. P. (2005). *Dictionary of statistics & methodology* (3rd ed.). Thousand Oaks, CA: Sage.

Wadensjo, C. (1998). *Interpreting as interaction.* New York: Addison Wesley Longman.

Wagner, S. F. (1992). *Introduction to statistics.* New York: HarperCollins.

Wallas, G. (1926). *The art of thought.* New York: Harcourt, Brace.

Walther, J. B. (1992). Interpersonal effects in computer-mediated interaction: A relational perspective. *Communication Research, 19,* 52–90.

Warland, R. H., & Sample, J. (1973). Response certainty as a moderator variable in attitude measurement. *Rural Sociology, 38,* 174–186.

Warren, C. A. B., & Karner, T. X. (2005). *Discovering qualitative methods: Field research, interviews, and analysis.* Los Angeles: Roxbury.

Wartella, E., Heintz, K. E., Aidman, A. J., & Mazzarella, S. R. (1990). Television and beyond: Children's video media in one community. *Communication Research, 17,* 45–64.

Warwick, D. (1975, October). Deceptive research: Social scientists ought to stop lying. *Psychology Today,* pp. 38–40.

Wasserstrom, J. N. (2002). Using history to think about the Beijing Olympics: The use and abuse of the Seoul 1988 analogy. *Harvard International Journal of Press Politics, 7,* 126–129.

Watzlawick, P., Beavin, J. H., & Jackson, D. D. (1967). *Pragmatics of human communication*. New York: Norton.

Wax, R. H. (1968). Participant observation. *International encyclopedia of social sciences* (p. 238). New York: Macmillan.

Webb, E., Campbell, D. T., Schwartz, R. D., Sechrest, L., & Grove, J. B. (1981). *Nonreactive measures in the social sciences*. Boston: Houghton Mifflin.

Weber, K. D., & Patterson, B. R. (1996). Construction and validation of a communication based emotional support scale. *Communication Research Reports, 13,* 68–76.

Webster, J. G. (2005). Beneath the veneer of fragmentation: Television audience polarization in a multichannel world. *Journal of Comunication, 55,* 366–382.

Weems, G. H. (2004). Impact of the number of response categories on frequency scales. *Research in the Schools, 11*(1), 41–49.

Weems, G. H., & Onwuegbuzie, A. J. (2001). The impact of midpoint responses and reverse coding on survey data. *Measurement and Evaluation in Counseling and Development, 34,* 166–176.

Weems, G. H., Onwuegbuzie, A. J., Schreiber, J. B., & Eggers, S. J. (2003). Characteristics of respondents who respond differently to positively and negatively worded items on rating scales. *Assessment & Evaluation in Higher Education, 28,* 587–607.

Weick, K. E. (1969). *The social psychology of organizing*. Reading, MA: Addison-Wesley.

Weinberg, M. S. (1965). Sexual modesty, social meanings, and the nudist camp. *Social Problems, 12,* 311–318.

Weir, W. (1984, October 15). Another look at subliminal "facts." *Advertising Age,* p. 46.

West, M., & Gastil, J. (2004). Deliberation at the margins: Participant accounts of face-to-face public deliberation at the 1999–2000 World Trade protests in Seattle and Prague. *Qualitative Research Reports in Communication, 5,* 1–7.

West, R., & Turner, L. H. (2007). *Introducing communication theory: Analysis and application* (3rd ed.). Boston: McGraw-Hill.

Whately, R. A. (1844). *Elements of logic*. London: B. Fellows.

Wheeler, M. (1977). *Lies, damn lies, and statistics: The manipulation of public opinion in America*. New York: Laurel Edition, Dell.

Wheeless, L. R., Frymier, A. B., & Thompson, C. A. (1992). A comparison of verbal output and receptivity in relation to attraction and communication satisfaction in interpersonal relationships. *Communication Quarterly, 40,* 102–115.

White, P. (1980). Limitations on verbal reports of internal events: A refutation of Nisbett and Wilson and of Bem. *Psychological Review, 87,* 105–112.

White, S. E. (1995). A content analytic technique for measuring the sexiness of women's business attire in media presentations. *Communication Research Reports, 12,* 178–185.

Whitney, F. L. (1950). *The elements of research* (3rd ed.). New York: Prentice-Hall.

Wiemann, J. M. (1977). Explication and test of a model of communicative competence. *Human Communication Research, 3,* 195–213.

Willard, C. A. (1981). The status of the non-discursiveness thesis. *Journal of the American Forensic Association, 17,* 190–214.

Williams, R. L., Bush, V. J., Park, S. H., Malone, Y., & Jessup, K. (2001). *Work ethic scale for middle school students*. (ERIC Document Reproduction Service No. ED452257)

Wilson, B. J., Kunkel, D., Linz, D., Potter, J., Donnerstein, E., Smith, S. L., Blumenthal, E., & Gray, T. (1997). Violence in television programming overall: University of California, Santa Barbara study. In M. Seawall (Ed.), *National television violence study* (Vol. 1, pp. 3–184). Thousand Oaks, CA: Sage.

Wilson, B. J., Kunkel, D., Linz, D., Potter, J., Donnerstein, E., Smith, S. L., Blumenthal, E., & Berry, M. (1998). Violence in television programming overall: University of California, Santa Barbara study. In M. Seawall (Ed.), *National television violence study* (Vol. 2, pp. 3–204). Thousand Oaks, CA: Sage.

Wilson, T. D., & Nisbett, R. E. (1978). The accuracy of verbal reports about the effects of stimuli on evaluation and behavior. *Social Psychology, 41,* 118–131.

Wimmer, R. D., & Dominick, J. R. (1983). *Mass media research: An introduction*. Belmont, CA: Wadsworth.

Wimmer, R. D., & Dominick, J. R. (1997). *Mass media research: An introduction* (5th ed.). Belmont, CA: Wadsworth.

Wincup, E. (2001). Feminist research with women awaiting trial: The effects on participants in the qualitative research process. In K. R. Gilbert (Ed.), *The emotional nature of qualitative research* (pp. 17–35). Boca Raton, FL: CRC Press.

Wise, S. (1987). A framework for discussing ethical issues in feminist research: A review of the literature. In V. Griffith, M. Humm, R. O'Rourke, J. Batsleer, F. Poland, & S. Wise (Eds.), *Writing feminist biography 2: Using life histories*. Studies in Sexual Politics No. 19, University of Manchester, England.

Woal, M. (1987). Listening to monotony: All-news radio. *Central States Speech Journal, 38,* 28–34.

Wolpert, R. L., & Mengersen, K. L. (2004). Adjusted likelihoods for synthesizing empirical evidence from studies that differ in quality and design: Effects of environmental tobacco smoke. *Statistical Science, 19*(3), 1–42.

Woo, A. (2000). Investigating the effects of item wording on rating responses. Doctoral dissertation, Michigan State University. *Dissertation Abstracts International, 61* (2A), 586.

Wood, J. T. (2004). Monsters and victims: Male felons' accounts of intimate partner violence. *Journal of Social and Personal Relationships, 21,* 555–576.

Wrench, J. S., & Punyanunt, N. M. (2004). Advisee-advisor communication: An exploratory study examining interpersonal communication variables in the graduate advisee-advisor relationship. *Communication Quarterly, 52,* 224–236.

Wrench, J. S., & Richmond, V. P. (2004). Understanding the psychometric properties of the humor assessment instrument through an analysis of the relationships between teacher humor assessment and instructional communication variables in the college classroom. *Communication Research Reports, 21,* 92–102.

Wright, M. H. (1994). Burkean and Freudian theories of identification. *Communication Quarterly, 42,* 301–310.

Wright, P. J. (2006, April). *Predicting reaction to a message of ministry: An audience analysis.* Unpublished master's thesis, California State University, Fullerton.

Yamane, T. (1967). *Elementary sampling theory.* Englewood Cliffs, NJ: Prentice-Hall.

Yang, Ch-C. (2000). The use of the Internet among academic gay communities in Taiwan: An exploratory study. *Information Communication & Society, 3,* 153–172.

Youngblood, J. D., & Winn, J. E. (2004). Shout glory: Competing communication codes experienced by the members of the African American Pentecostal Genuine Deliverance Holiness Church. *Journal of Communication, 54,* 355–370.

Zeldes, G. A., & Fico, F. (2005). Race and gender: An analysis of sources and reporters in the networks' coverage of the 2000 presidential campaign. *Mass communication and society, 8,* 373–385.

Zhang, Q., & Oetzel, J. G. (2006). Constructing and validating a teacher immediacy scale: A Chinese perspective. *Communication Education, 55,* 218–241.

Zhang, Y. B., & Harwood, J. (2004). Modernization and tradition in an age of globalization: Cultural values in Chinese television commercials. *Journal of Communication, 54,* 156–172.

Zwarun, L. (2005). Doing what they say, saying what they mean: Self-regulatory compliance and depictions of drinking in alcohol commercials in televised sports. *Mass communication and society, 8,* 347–371.

NAME INDEX

SUBJECT INDEX